21ST CENTURY SYNONYM AND ANTONYM FINDER

*Because your brightest ideas deserve the
right words . . .*

The convenient dictionary format makes the *21st
Century Synonym and Antonym Finder* easy to use,
and the 10,000 main entries make it the biggest
bargain in paperback word finders. Plus, it's all new
and up-to-date, created for today's writers by the
prestigious Princeton Language Institute, a leading
expert in the English language.

You'll find the perfect choice of words to get your
ideas across with impact and accuracy. Unlike other
paperback word finders, this comprehensive reference
includes essential definitions, and unlike a classic
thesaurus, it avoids outmoded, useless entries. This is
a word finder specially created for contemporary
writers and speakers, in a handy size to put in your
backpack, briefcase, or purse.

—21ST—
CENTURY
SYNONYM AND
ANTONYM FINDER

EDITED BY

PRINCETON LANGUAGE INSTITUTE

BARBARA ANN KIPFER, PH.D.,
Head Lexicographer

Produced by The Philip Lief Group, Inc.

A LAUREL BOOK

Published by Dell Publishing
a division of
Bantam Doubleday Dell Publishing Group, Inc.
1540 Broadway
New York, New York 10036

Published by arrangement with
The Philip Lief Group, Inc.
6 West 20 Street
New York, NY 10011

ISBN: 0-440-21323-1

Printed in the United States of America

Published simultaneously in Canada

May 1993

10 9 8 7 6 5 4 3 2

INTRODUCTION

The *21st Century Synonym and Antonym Finder* is designed to provide you with the most accurate, useful lists of synonyms and antonyms available in one volume. The compilation is entirely new, representing an up-to-the minute overview of English vocabulary, meaning, and use as we move toward the 21st century. It contains thousands of word entries, and over 200,000 synonyms and antonyms. The dictionary format and word selection have been chosen to most accurately reflect how writers use a word finder, eliminating the difficulties of other finders and word references by providing a varied list of synonyms and antonyms for each headword.

Successful writers strive to find the most precise words to describe their thoughts. Two marks of a strong piece of writing are the clarity with which ideas and images are expressed and the ability to hold a reader's interest. To achieve these goals, a writer must develop a vocabulary flexible and expansive enough to express fine shades and subtle nuances of meaning.

Using a reference work of synonyms and antonyms provides the opportunity to hone and refine your ideas, and to add color and variety to your vocabulary. Even experienced writers turn to a synonym and antonym finder when the word they have in mind is *not* the one they want to use—the instance may call for a word that is either broader or more specific, conveys a positive tone, or contrasts directly with the original idea. By exposing yourself to the thousands of word alternatives contained within the *21st Century Synonym and Antonym Finder*, you will be able to breathe new life into your writing.

To begin your hunt for a synonym or antonym to a specific

word, simply look up that word within the A to Z arrangement of entries. You will find entries listed in boldface type, followed by the part of speech in brackets, and a concise, italicized definition. Beginning on an entry's next line, look for the extensive alphabetical listing of synonyms, followed by an accompanying list of antonyms. The selection of synonyms and antonyms is diverse, providing you with ample opportunity to decide which word will best suit your needs.

While the *21st Century Synonym and Antonym Finder* provides definitions for every headword, it is not the purpose of this work to define synonyms and antonyms; a dictionary is the appropriate tool for learning a word's etymology and meanings. Lack of familiarity with some of the alternatives listed in this book will prove that your research is broadening your vocabulary. Complete the process by turning to a dictionary for definitions of the many interesting and challenging words you discover.

Meanings and connotations are often dependent upon the context within which they are used. Writers fare best when they choose words that most clearly and explicitly signify the image or idea they desire to express. Every time you look up a word, you will find a list of words characterized by a varying degree of connotative similarity or opposition to the boldface entry. Some words within these lists will be exact synonyms and antonyms, while others will be related words which stray slightly from that direct parallel. When turning to the *21st Century Synonym and Antonym Finder* to locate an alternative to a specific word, always exercise care and discrimination in arriving at your final decision, making sure your new word will adequately carry the precise nuance you wish to convey.

The very process of browsing through this 21st century selection of compelling word choices will help clarify writers' thoughts providing them with an exciting springboard to new ideas and modes of expression.

SPECIAL FEATURES

Special features distinguish the *21st Century Synonym and Antonym Finder* from all previous references, making it the clearcut choice for all writers:

- *Part of speech*
  The part of speech—noun, verb, adjective, adverb, or preposition—is listed for every headword. This feature prevents confusion over the proper use of a word.

  intrepid [*adj*]
  haggle [*v*]

- *Headword definitions*
  Unlike other finders, the *21st Century Synonym and Antonym Finder* gives a concise definition (**cryptic** [*adj*] *secret; obscure in meaning*) for every main entry, insuring that you understand the word's meaning and use. For a more detailed definition, or a definition of any synonym or antonym, consult a dictionary.

- *Multiple entries for different uses*
  Separate entries are presented for each of a headword's common uses. Words taking on several parts of speech (**elaborate** [*adj*] *intricate; involved* and **elaborate** [*v*] *make detailed; expand*) and those with several distinct uses of the same form (**glaring** [*adj2*] *bright, dazzling; flashy*) all have their own synonym and antonym lists.

- *First-time compilation containing new words*
  The words you will find in the *21st Century Synonym and Antonym Finder* have been collected solely for the purpose of creating an entirely new reference, one that

accurately reflects the way we write and speak American English today. This book includes many new words and uses that have only recently entered the language through a variety of venues and academic disciplines, including:

> **hermeneutical** [adj] *interpretive*
> **pastiche** *[n] work of art formed from disparate sources*
> **downsize** *[v] to decrease in size, especially workforce*

- *Nondiscriminatory word choices*
  The *21st Century Synonym and Antonym Finder* will help you rid your writing and speech of biased words and phrases. In particular, all headwords, definitions, synonyms, and antonyms use gender-neutral language, freeing offensive words from their sex-linked connotations.

> **executive** [n] *person who manages organization*
> ▪ *Syn* administrator, boss, businessperson, chief, commander, director, entrepreneur, government, governor, head, hierarchy, industrialist, leader, leadership, management, official, supervisor, tycoon; ▪ *Ant* flunky, hired hand, laborer, menial, subordinate, underling, worker.

Whether you're composing a report, paper, letter, speech, or otory, the *21st Century Synonym and Antonym Finder* will add variety to your writing and help you express yourself more clearly. Utilizing the most advanced linguistic theories, the *21st Century Synonym and Antonym Finder* is the perfect reference for students, teachers, businesspeople, professional writers, and people writing simply for pleasure. It puts writers and speakers in touch with the right word choices for all occasions.

A

abandon [n] *careless disregard for consequences* ▪ **Syn** freedom, impetuosity, recklessness, spontaneity, thoughtlessness, wantonness, wildness; ▪ **Ant** caution, control, deliberation, inhibition, moderation, prudence, repression, restraint, self-restraint, suppression.

abandon [v] *leave behind, relinquish* ▪ **Syn** abdicate, back out, cast aside, desert, discard, discontinue, ditch, drop, drop out, duck, dump, leave, let go, opt out, pull out, quit, run out on, ship out, stop, surrender, vacate, walk out on, withdraw, yield; ▪ **Ant** adopt, cherish, claim, defend, keep, maintain, possess, pursue, retain, support.

abandoned [adj] *free from moral restraint; uninhibited* ▪ **Syn** depraved, dissolute, immoral, incontinent, licentious, profligate, shameless, sinful, unrestrained, wanton, wicked, wild; ▪ **Ant** chaste, controlled, innocent, moral, principled, pure, restrained, upright, virtuous.

abase [v] *deprive of self-esteem, confidence* ▪ **Syn** belittle, debase, degrade, demean, diminish, disgrace, dishonor, humble, humiliate, lower, mortify, reduce, shame; ▪ **Ant** cherish, dignify, elevate, exalt, extol, honor, raise, respect, uplift.

abashed [adj] *exhibiting mental discomfort, ill at ease* ▪ **Syn** ashamed, bewildered, bugged, chagrined, confounded, confused, crushed, daunted, disconcerted, embarrassed, fazed, fuddled, humbled, humiliated, mortified, rattled, shamed, taken aback; ▪ **Ant** at ease, composed, confident, emboldened, heartened, pleased, proud, reassured, undaunted.

abate [v] *lessen, grow or cause to grow less* ▪ **Syn** allay, cool, decline, decrease, diminish, dull, dwindle, ebb, let go, let up, moderate, quell, recede, reduce, slacken, slow, subdue, subside, taper, taper off, wane; ▪ **Ant** amplify, enhance, enlarge, extend, heat up, increase, intensify, magnify, prolong, quicken, revive, rise.

abbreviate [v] *shorten*
▪ **Syn** abridge, abstract, clip, compress, condense, contract, curtail, cut, cut back, cut off, digest, pare, prune, reduce, shorten, summarize, take out, trim; ▪ **Ant** amplify, elongate, enlarge, expand, extend, increase, inflate, lengthen.

abdicate [v] *give up a right, position, or power* ▪ **Syn** abandon, abjure, abnegate, cede, demit, drop, forgo, give up, leave, quit, quitclaim, relinquish, renounce, resign, retire, surrender, vacate, waive, withdraw, yield; ▪ **Ant** appropriate, arrogate, assert, assume, challenge, claim, defend, defy, hold, maintain, remain, retain, treasure, usurp.

abduct [v] *take by force and without permission* ▪ **Syn** carry off, grab, kidnap, make off with, remove, seize, snatch; ▪ **Ant** free, give up, let go, release, restore, return.

aberrant [adj] *not normal; varying from the usual* ▪ **Syn** abnormal, atypical, deviant, different, nonstandard, odd, off-base, off-color, peculiar, strange, unusual, weird; ▪ **Ant** natural, normal, regular, same, standard, true, typical, usual.

aberration [n] *different from that expected* ▪ **Syn** departure, deviation, difference, distortion, divergence, diversion, irregularity, lapse, straying, wandering; ▪ **Ant** conformity, sameness.

abet [v] *assist, help in wrongdoing*
▪ **Syn** advocate, back, condone, egg on, encourage, endorse, goad, incite, promote, provoke, sanction, spur, support, urge; ▪ **Ant** counter, denounce, deter, discourage, dissuade, frustrate, hinder, impede, obstruct, resist, thwart, undermine.

abeyance [n] *being inactive or suspended temporarily* ▪ **Syn** deferral, discontinuation, dormancy, inactivity, intermission, latency, pending, postponement, quiescence, recess, remission, suspension, waiting; ▪ **Ant** action, activity, continuance, continuation, operation, renewal, revival.

abhor [v] *regard with contempt or disgust* ▪ **Syn** abominate, despise, detest, disdain, hate, loathe, scorn; ▪ **Ant** admire, adore, approve, cherish, delight in, desire, enjoy, like, love, relish, treasure, value.

abide [v1] *live in a certain place*
• **Syn** bide, dwell, inhabit, lodge, nest, perch, reside, room, roost, settle, squat, stay; • **Ant** depart, go, journey, leave, migrate, move.

abide [v2] *remain or continue in a state*
• **Syn** continue, endure, keep on, last, persevere, persist, remain, survive; • **Ant** leave, quit, refuse, stop.

abiding [adj] *continuing or existing for an indefinite time* • **Syn** constant, continuing, enduring, eternal, everlasting, fast, indissoluble, lasting, permanent, perpetual, persistent, steadfast; • **Ant** ephemeral, fleeting, impermanent, passing, temporary, transient.

ability [n1] *power to act, perform*
• **Syn** aptitude, capability, competence, comprehension, dexterity, endowment, faculty, intelligence, might, potentiality, qualification, resourcefulness, skill, strength, talent, understanding; • **Ant** impotence, inability, limitation, paralysis.

ability [n2] *natural or acquired power in a particular activity* • **Syn** adeptness, adroitness, bent, capability, command, deftness, expertise, genius, handiness, ingenuity, knack, mastery, proficiency, savvy, skill, strength, talent; • **Ant** clumsiness, ignorance, inability, inadequacy, inanity, incapability, incapacity, incompetence, ineptness, stupidity, weakness.

abject [adj] *hopeless and downtrodden*
• **Syn** base, contemptible, dejected, forlorn, groveling, hangdog, low, miserable, outcast, pitiable, submissive, wretched; • **Ant** commendable, dignified, esteemed, exalted, excellent, honorable, hopeful, magnificent, noble, proud, worthy.

ablaze [adj1] *very excited*
• **Syn** afire, ardent, enthusiastic, fervent, fuming, furious, heated, impassioned, on fire, passionate, raging, stimulated, vehement; • **Ant** dispassionate, dull, unenthusiastic, unexcited.

ablaze [adj2] *brightly illuminated*
• **Syn** aflame, aglow, brilliant, flashing, gleaming, glowing, luminous, radiant, refulgent, sparkling; • **Ant** dark, dim.

able [adj1] *capable of performing; having an innate capacity* • **Syn** adept, adroit, agile, bright, capable, dexterous, effortless, endowed, equipped, facile, good, intelligent, knowing, powerful, ready, smart, strong, worthy; • **Ant** incom-

petent, ineffective, inept, infirm, powerless, unable, useless.

able [adj2] *able to perform well; having a proven capacity* • **Syn** accomplished, agile, brilliant, capable, clever, deft, dexterous, effective, efficient, experienced, facile, gifted, ingenious, intelligent, keen, learned, masterful, practiced, proficient, qualified, responsible, savvy, sharp, skillful, talented, trained; • **Ant** delicate, feeble, inept, stupid, unqualified, untrained, weak.

abnegation [n] *denial, renouncement of something* • **Syn** abandonment, abstinence, continence, eschewal, forbearance, giving up, rejection, relinquishment, renouncement, renunciation, sacrifice, self-denial, temperance; • **Ant** abandonment, acquiescence, admittance, concession, indulgence, surrender, yielding.

abnormal [adj] *different from standard or norm* • **Syn** aberrant, anomalous, atypical, bizarre, curious, deviant, divergent, eccentric, exceptional, extraordinary, heteroclite, heteromorphic, irregular, odd, peculiar, preternatural, queer, strange, uncommon, unusual, weird; • **Ant** common, conventional, customary, natural, normal, regular, standard, straight, typical, unexceptional, usual.

aboard [adj] *on or in a transportation object* • **Syn** boarded, consigned, embarked, en route, in transit, loaded, on, on board, traveling; • **Ant** not on, off.

abolish [v] *do away with or put an end to* • **Syn** abate, abrogate, annihilate, annul, cancel, destroy, disestablish, dissolve, eradicate, expunge, extinguish, extirpate, finish, invalidate, kill, negate, nix, nullify, obliterate, overturn, prohibit, put an end to, quash, repeal, rescind, revoke, squelch, stamp out, subvert, supersede, terminate, undo, vitiate, void, wipe out; • **Ant** build, confirm, continue, create, enact, establish, found, institute, legalize, promote, ratify, support, uphold.

abominable [adj] *awful, detestable*
• **Syn** abhorrent, atrocious, awful, base, beastly, contemptible, cursed, despicable, disgusting, foul, grim, hateful, heinous, hellish, horrible, horrid, loathsome, nauseating, odious, offensive, repellent, reprehensible, repugnant, repulsive, revolting, rotten, stinking, terrible, vile, wretched; • **Ant** admirable, alluring, ap-

pealing, commendable, delightful, desirable, enjoyable, laudable, likable, lovable, pleasant, respectable, wonderful.

aboriginal [adj] *belonging to a place, existing in a place since prehistory* ▪ Syn ancient, birth native, earliest, endemic, first, indigenous, native, original, primary, primeval, primitive, primordial; ▪ Ant alien, foreign, immigrant, newcomer.

abort [v] *stop or cancel something* ▪ Syn arrest, break off, call it quits, call off, check, cut off, drop, end, fail, halt, interrupt, miscarry, nullify, scrap, scratch, terminate; ▪ Ant carry through, conclude, continue, execute, finish, follow through, keep.

abortive [adj] *failing to achieve a goal* ▪ Syn failed, fruitless, futile, ineffective, ineffectual, miscarried, unproductive, unsuccessful, useless, vain, worthless; ▪ Ant complete, consummated, effectual, efficient, fruitful, productive, successful.

abound [v] *overflow; exist in abundance* ▪ Syn be plentiful, crowd, flourish, infest, luxuriate, proliferate, run wild, swarm, swell, teem, thrive; ▪ Ant be deficient, fail, be lacking, be needed, be short, be wanting.

above [prep1] *higher in position* ▪ Syn atop, beyond, on top of, over, superior to, upon; ▪ Ant below, beneath, under, underneath.

above [prep2] *more, higher in amount, degree* ▪ Syn beyond, exceeding, greater than, larger than, more than, over; ▪ Ant below, deficient, fewer than, less than.

above [prep3] *superior to* ▪ Syn beyond, exceeding, higher than, surpassing, transcending; ▪ Ant inferior to, lower than, under.

aboveboard [adj] *candid* ▪ Syn forthright, frank, honest, open, overt, square, straight, straightforward, true, trustworthy, truthful, veracious; ▪ Ant deceitful, devious, evasive, lying, shady, underhanded.

abrasive [adj1] *irritating in manner* ▪ Syn annoying, biting, caustic, cutting, galling, hateful, hurtful, nasty, rough, sharp, unpleasant; ▪ Ant gentle, healing, likable, mild, pleasant, pleasing, soothing.

abrasive [adj2] *scraping or wearing* ▪ Syn chafing, cutting, erosive, grinding, polishing, rough, scratching, scuffing,

sharpening, smoothing; ▪ Ant smooth, softening.

abreast [adj/adv] *up-to-date* ▪ Syn acquainted, au courant, au fait, contemporary, familiar, informed, in touch, knowledgeable, up, versed; ▪ Ant lost, out of touch, unaware, uninformed.

abridge [v] *shorten* ▪ Syn abbreviate, abstract, clip, compress, condense, contract, curtail, cut, decrease, diminish, lessen, narrow, reduce, restrict, slash, summarize, trim, truncate; ▪ Ant add, amplify, augment, enlarge, expand, extend, increase, lengthen, pad, supplement.

abroad [adj] *in a foreign country* ▪ Syn away, elsewhere, in foreign lands, in foreign parts, out of the country, overseas, touring, traveling; ▪ Ant at home, here, nearby, remaining.

abrogate [v] *formally put an end to* ▪ Syn abate, abolish, annul, cancel, dissolve, invalidate, negate, nix, nullify, quash, reject, renege, repeal, retract, revoke, vitiate, void; ▪ Ant approve, establish, fix, institute, legalize, ratify, sanction, support.

abrupt [adj1] *rude or brief in manner* ▪ Syn blunt, brusque, crusty, curt, direct, discourteous, gruff, impetuous, impolite, rough, rude, short, snappy, snippy; ▪ Ant at ease, calm, civil, courteous, gracious, kind, polite.

abrupt [adj2] *happening suddenly and unexpectedly* ▪ Syn hasty, hurried, jerky, precipitate, precipitous, quick, rushing, sudden, surprising, unanticipated, unceremonious, unexpected, unforeseen; ▪ Ant anticipated, deliberate, expansive, expected, gradual, leisurely.

abscond [v] *run away, depart secretly* ▪ Syn break, decamp, disappear, duck out, escape, fade, flee, get out, leave, make off, pull out, run off, slip, sneak away, steal away, vanish; ▪ Ant abide, continue, endure, give up, remain, stay, stop, yield.

absent [adj] *not present* ▪ Syn astray, away, elsewhere, ghost, gone, missing, no-show, removed, truant, vanished; ▪ Ant attendant, attending, existing, present.

absent-minded [adj] *unaware of events, surroundings* ▪ Syn absorbed, bemused, distracted, dreamy, engrossed, faraway, heedless, inattentive, lost, oblivious, preoccupied, remote, unconscious, unheeding, unmindful, unobservant, withdrawn; ▪ *Ant* alert, attentive, aware, conscious, heedful, observant, wary, watchful.

absolute [*adj1*] *without limit*
▪ *Syn* complete, consummate, downright, entire, free, full, infinite, plenary, pure, sheer, supreme, thorough, total, unabridged, unadulterated, unconditional, unlimited, unrestricted, utter; ▪ *Ant* accountable, circumscribed, limited, restricted.

absolute [*adj2*] *in control or complete authority* ▪ *Syn* arbitrary, authoritarian, autocratic, autonomous, despotic, dictatorial, monocratic, preeminent, sovereign, supreme, totalitarian, tyrannical; ▪ *Ant* accountable, complaisant, compliant, restricted, submissive, tractable, yielding.

absolute [*adj3*] *certain*
▪ *Syn* actual, categorical, conclusive, consummate, decisive, definite, exact, factual, fixed, genuine, infallible, positive, precise, sure; ▪ *Ant* ambiguous, conditional, dependent, equivocal, indecisive, indefinite, limited, partial, questionable.

absolute [*adj4*] *excellent, perfect*
▪ *Syn* categorical, complete, faultless, flawless, ideal, impeccable, thorough, ultimate, untarnished; ▪ *Ant* blemished, flawed, imperfect, tarnished.

absolutely [*adv1*] *certainly, without question* ▪ *Syn* actually, categorically, decidedly, definitely, doubtless, exactly, positively, precisely, really, surely, truly; ▪ *Ant* conditionally, doubtfully, indefinitely, not certainly, not surely, probably, questionably.

absolutely [*adv2*] *in a complete manner, degree* ▪ *Syn* completely, consummately, entirely, fully, thoroughly, utterly, wholly; ▪ *Ant* fairly, incompletely, partially, partly, somewhat.

absolve [*v*] *free from responsibility, duty* ▪ *Syn* acquit, bleach, clear, discharge, exculpate, exempt, exonerate, free, go easy on, liberate, pardon, release, relieve, set free, spare, vindicate, whitewash; ▪ *Ant* accuse, bind, blame, charge, condemn, convict, hold, impeach, incriminate, obligate, punish, sentence.

absorb [*v1*] *physically take in a liquid* ▪ *Syn* blot, consume, devour, drink in, imbibe, ingest, ingurgitate, osmose, soak up, swallow, take in; ▪ *Ant* disperse, dissipate, eject, emit, exude, spew, vomit.

absorb [*v2*] *mentally take in information* ▪ *Syn* apprehend, assimilate, comprehend, digest, follow, get, grasp, incorporate, learn, sense, soak up, take in, understand; ▪ *Ant* misapprehend, miss the point, misunderstand, not get.

absorb [*v3*] *occupy complete attention* ▪ *Syn* captivate, concern, consume, employ, engage, engross, fascinate, fill, hold, immerse, involve, monopolize, obsess, preoccupy, rivet; ▪ *Ant* distract, divert, draw away, sidetrack.

absorbed [*adj*] *being completely occupied mentally* ▪ *Syn* captivated, consumed, deep in thought, engrossed, fascinated, fixed, held, immersed, intent, lost, preoccupied, rapt; ▪ *Ant* bored, disinterested, distracted, indifferent, uninterested.

absorbent [*adj*] *capable of physically taking in a liquid* ▪ *Syn* absorptive, bibulous, dry, imbibing, penetrable, permeable, porous, pregnable, retentive, spongy, thirsty; ▪ *Ant* impermeable, impregnable, moistureproof, waterproof, water-repellent, watertight.

abstain [*v*] *hold back from doing* ▪ *Syn* abjure, abnegate, avoid, cease, constrain, decline, deny oneself, eschew, fast, forbear, forgo, give up, keep from, pass up, quit, refrain, shun, sit out, spurn, starve, withhold; ▪ *Ant* give in, indulge, partake, surrender, use, yield.

abstemious [*adj*] *restraining behavior or appetite* ▪ *Syn* abstinent, ascetic, austere, continent, frugal, moderate, restraining, self-denying, sober, sparing, temperate; ▪ *Ant* abandoned, gluttonous, greedy, hedonistic, hungry, immoderate, profligate, self-indulgent.

abstinence [*n*] *restraint from desires, especially physical desires* ▪ *Syn* abnegation, abstemiousness, asceticism, avoidance, chastity, fasting, forbearance, frugality, moderation, renunciation, self-denial, self-restraint, sobriety, teetotalism, temperance; ▪ *Ant* dissipation, drunkenness, excess, indulgence, intemperance, intoxication, revelry, self-indulgence, wantonness.

abstract [*adj*] *conceptual, theoretical* ▪ *Syn* abstruse, complex, deep, hypothetical, ideal, indefinite, intellectual, philosophical, recondite, transcendental; ▪ *Ant* actual, concrete, factual, material, objective, physical, real.

abstract [v] *prepare short document from longer one* ▪ *Syn* abbreviate, abridge, condense, digest, outline, review, shorten, summarize; ▪ *Ant* complete, expand, insert, lengthen, strengthen.

abstruse [adj] *difficult to understand* ▪ *Syn* abstract, complex, deep, enigmatic, esoteric, intricate, involved, muddy, obscure, perplexing, profound, puzzling, recondite, subtle, unfathomable, vague; ▪ *Ant* clear, comprehensible, concrete, direct, easy, lucid, obvious, plain, simple.

absurd [adj] *ridiculous, senseless* ▪ *Syn* batty, crazy, daffy, foolish, freaky, illogical, incongruous, irrational, jokey, loony, ludicrous, nonsensical, nutty, off the wall, preposterous, silly, unreasonable, wacky; ▪ *Ant* certain, logical, rational, reasonable, sensible, sound, wise.

abundant [adj] *plentiful, large in number* ▪ *Syn* abounding, ample, bountiful, copious, exuberant, full, generous, heavy, lavish, luxuriant, overflowing, plenteous, profuse, rich, sufficient, teeming; ▪ *Ant* lacking, meager, rare, scarce, skimpy, sparse.

abuse [v1] *physically hurt or injure* ▪ *Syn* corrupt, damage, defile, desecrate, harm, ill-treat, impair, manhandle, mar, mishandle, misuse, molest, oppress, persecute, roughhouse, ruin, spoil, taint, victimize, violate; ▪ *Ant* cherish, defend, help, preserve, protect, respect.

abuse [v2] *use wrongly* ▪ *Syn* dissipate, exhaust, misemploy, mishandle, misuse, oppress, overburden, overtax, overwork, prostitute, spoil, squander, taint, waste; ▪ *Ant* benefit, care for, esteem, prize, respect, revere.

abuse [v3] *attack with words* ▪ *Syn* backbite, bad-mouth, bash, berate, castigate, defame, derogate, insult, offend, persecute, pick on, put down, reproach, revile, scold, upbraid, vituperate; ▪ *Ant* acclaim, adulate, approve, commend, compliment, extol, laud, praise.

abuse [v4] *take advantage of* ▪ *Syn* do an injustice to, exploit, impose on, use, wrong; ▪ *Ant* cherish, esteem, honor, respect, revere, treasure.

abusive [adj] *exhibiting unkind behavior or words* ▪ *Syn* calumniating, castigating, contumelious, defamatory, derisive, insolent, invective, libelous, maligning, offensive, opprobrious, reproachful, reviling, rude, scathing, scurrilous, sharp-tongued, slanderous, traducing, upbraiding, vilifying, vituperative; ▪ *Ant* complimentary, just, kind, respectful.

abysmal [adj] *having great extent; immeasurable* ▪ *Syn* bottomless, boundless, complete, deep, endless, extreme, illimitable, incalculable, infinite, profound, thorough, unending, unfathomable, vast; ▪ *Ant* fathomable, finite, limited, measurable.

academic [adj1] *relating to schooling, learning* ▪ *Syn* bookish, book-learned, college, collegiate, erudite, intellectual, learned, pedantic, scholarly, scholastic, studious, university; ▪ *Ant* ignorant, nonstudious, unschooled, untaught, untutored.

academic [adj2] *relating to theories, philosophy* ▪ *Syn* abstract, conjectural, formalistic, hypothetical, notional, speculative, theoretical; ▪ *Ant* commonsense, functional, ordinary, plain, practical, realistic, simple.

accede [v] *agree or consent* ▪ *Syn* accept, acquiesce, admit, comply, concede, cooperate, endorse, fold, go along with, grant, let, permit, subscribe, yield; ▪ *Ant* condemn, demur, denounce, denounce, deny, disallow, oppose, protest, refuse, veto.

accelerate [v] *increase speed, timing* ▪ *Syn* advance, drive, expedite, further, hasten, hurry, impel, precipitate, quicken, rev up, spur, stimulate; ▪ *Ant* brake, decelerate, defer, delay, hinder, impede, postpone, retard, slacken, slow down.

accent [v] *place emphasis, importance on* ▪ *Syn* accentuate, draw attention to, emphasize, highlight, intensify, punctuate, stress; ▪ *Ant* attenuate, de-emphasize, downplay, lessen, minimize, slight.

accept [v1] *receive something given physically* ▪ *Syn* acquire, gain, get, obtain, secure, take, welcome; ▪ *Ant* decline, deny, discard, refuse, reject.

accept [v2] *allow into group* ▪ *Syn* admit, receive, welcome; ▪ *Ant* blackball, decline, deny, reject.

accept [v3] *believe* ▪ *Syn* accede to, acknowledge, affirm, approbate, approve, fancy, favor, hold,

hold with, recognize, relish, trust; ▪ *Ant* disagree, dispute, reject, renounce, repudiate.

accept [*v4*] *put up with*
▪ *Syn* acknowledge, acquiesce, assent, bear, capitulate, defer to, endure, fit in, go along with, live with, recognize, stand, stomach, submit to, swallow, take, tolerate, yield to; ▪ *Ant* demur, disallow, reject.

acceptable [*adj*] *satisfactory, agreeable*
▪ *Syn* adequate, admissible, common, decent, fair, okay, passable, pleasing, respectable, sufficient, tolerable, unobjectionable, welcome; ▪ *Ant* disagreeable, disturbing, inadequate, inadmissible, unacceptable, unsatisfactory, unwelcome.

accepted [*adj*] *generally agreed upon*
▪ *Syn* acknowledged, approved, authorized, confirmed, conventional, customary, established, normal, orthodox, popular, preferred, recognized, regular, standard, time-honored, universal, unopposed, usual; ▪ *Ant* irregular, questionable, unconventional, unorthodox.

accessible [*adj*] *approachable; ready for use* ▪ *Syn* attainable, available, employable, handy, near, obtainable, open, operative, practicable, public, reachable, unrestricted, usable; ▪ *Ant* inaccessible, limited, restricted.

accession [*n*] *coming to power*
▪ *Syn* assumption, attainment, inauguration, induction, investment, succession, taking on, taking over; ▪ *Ant* abdication, decline, deposition, fall, impeachment, renunciation, resignation, withdrawal.

accidental [*adj*] *happening unexpectedly*
▪ *Syn* adventitious, chance, contingent, fortuitous, inadvertent, incidental, random, unexpected, unintentional, unplanned; ▪ *Ant* decided, designed, essential, intended, intentional, planned, premeditated.

acclaim [*v*] *give approval*
▪ *Syn* applaud, approve, boost, brag, celebrate, cheer, commend, eulogize, exalt, hail, honor, laud, praise, rave, recommend, salute; ▪ *Ant* berate, censure, damn, denounce, disapprove, dishonor, vituperate.

accommodate [*v1*] *make room, lodging available* ▪ *Syn* board, contain, domicile, entertain, furnish, harbor, hold, house, quarter, receive, rent, shelter, take in, welcome; ▪ *Ant* turn away, turn out.

accommodate [*v2*] *perform service*
▪ *Syn* afford, aid, assist, benefit, comfort, convenience, defer, favor, furnish, gratify, help, humor, indulge, oblige, pamper, please, provide, suit, supply, support, yield; ▪ *Ant* bar, block, frustrate, hinder, impede, limit, obstruct, prevent, stop.

accommodating [*adj*] *willing to help*
▪ *Syn* considerate, cooperative, friendly, handy, helpful, hospitable, kind, neighborly, obliging, polite; ▪ *Ant* alienating, disobliging, estranged.

accompany [*v*] *go or be with something*
▪ *Syn* attend, chaperon, consort, convoy, date, escort, follow, guide, keep company with, look after, squire, take out, usher; ▪ *Ant* abandon, desert, forsake, leave, quit, withdraw.

accomplice [*n*] *helper, especially in committing a crime* ▪ *Syn* abettor, accessory, aid, ally, assistant, associate, collaborator, colleague, confederate, conspirator, insider, partner; ▪ *Ant* adversary, enemy, opponent.

accomplish [*v*] *succeed in doing*
▪ *Syn* achieve, arrive, attain, bring about, carry out, consummate, effect, finish, fulfill, gain, manage, perform, produce, reach, realize, win; ▪ *Ant* abandon, fail, give up, not finish, nullify, relinquish.

accomplished [*adj*] *skilled in activity*
▪ *Syn* able, adept, consummate, cultivated, expert, gifted, masterly, polished, practiced, proficient, sharp, skillful, talented; ▪ *Ant* inept, inexpert, unable.

accord [*v*] *give approval, grant*
▪ *Syn* accede, acquiesce, admit, allow, award, bestow, concede, confer, endow, give, present, render, tender, vouchsafe; ▪ *Ant* argue, challenge, deny, disallow, disapprove, oppose, question, refuse, withhold.

accordingly [*adv*] *in an appropriate, suitable way* ▪ *Syn* appropriately, correspondingly, duly, ergo, hence, in respect to, in that event, properly, proportionately, respectively, subsequently, suitably, therefore, thus, under the circumstances; ▪ *Ant* inappropriately, unsuitably.

accost [*v*] *approach for conversation or solicitation* ▪ *Syn* address, annoy, bother, call, challenge, confront, cross, dare, entice, face, flag, greet, hail, proposition, salute, welcome; ▪ *Ant* avoid, dodge, evade, ignore, scorn, shun.

accountable [*adj*] *responsible for having done* ▪ *Syn* answerable, charged with, culpable, liable, obligated, obliged; ▪ *Ant* blameless, innocent, irresponsible, unaccountable, unreliable, untrustworthy.

accredit [*v*] *give authorization or control* ▪ *Syn* appoint, approve, authorize, certify, commission, empower, enable, endorse, entrust, guarantee, license, recognize, sanction, vouch for; ▪ *Ant* deny, disapprove, reject.

accrue [*v*] *increase by addition or growth, often financial* ▪ *Syn* accumulate, amass, build up, collect, enlarge, flow, gather, grow, increase; ▪ *Ant* decrease, lose.

accumulate [*v*] *gather or amass something* ▪ *Syn* accrue, acquire, aggregate, amalgamate, bring together, cache, collect, compile, cumulate, expand, gain, grow, hoard, increase, mass, procure, profit, stockpile, store up, swell, unite; ▪ *Ant* disperse, dissipate, dwindle, lessen, lose, spend, squander, waste.

accurate [*adj1*] *precise* ▪ *Syn* concrete, correct, definite, distinct, exact, explicit, factual, matter-of-fact, meticulous, particular, proper, punctilious, punctual, right, rigid, rigorous, scientific, scrupulous, sharp, specific, strict, systematic, true, veracious; ▪ *Ant* careless, faulty, inaccurate, lax, vague.

accurate [*adj2*] *correct, without error* ▪ *Syn* absolute, authentic, authoritative, certain, conclusive, definitive, exact, final, flawless, genuine, infallible, irrefutable, official, perfect, right, straight, strict, true, truthful, valid, veracious; ▪ *Ant* doubtful, erroneous, false, inaccurate, misleading, mistaken, questionable, untruthful, wrong.

accuse [*v*] *place blame for wrongdoing, fault* ▪ *Syn* allege, apprehend, arraign, attribute, blame, censure, charge, denounce, file claim, hold accountable, implicate, incriminate, inculpate, indict, libel, litigate, name, prosecute, slander, sue, summon; ▪ *Ant* absolve, exculpate, exonerate, praise, vindicate.

accustomed [*adj1*] *being prepared for, used to* ▪ *Syn* acclimatized, acquainted, adapted, addicted, confirmed, disciplined, familiar, given to, in the habit,

inured, seasoned, settled in, trained; ▪ *Ant* unaccustomed.

accustomed [*adj2*] *normal, usual* ▪ *Syn* accepted, chronic, conventional, customary, established, everyday, expected, general, habitual, ordinary, regular, routine, set, traditional; ▪ *Ant* abnormal, unaccustomed, unusual.

ace [*adj*] *exhibiting expertise in some activity* ▪ *Syn* brilliant, champion, distinguished, excellent, expert, first-rate, great, master, outstanding, superb, virtuoso; ▪ *Ant* inept, unskilled.

acerbity [*n1*] *bitterness of taste* ▪ *Syn* acidity, astringency, sourness, tartness; ▪ *Ant* mellowness, mildness, sweetness.

acerbity [*n2*] *harsh speech, behavior* ▪ *Syn* acrimony, asperity, causticity, ill temper, irritability, mordancy, rancor, rudeness, sarcasm, vitriol; ▪ *Ant* kindness, mildness, sweetness.

ache [*n*] *sore feeling; dull pain* ▪ *Syn* anguish, hurt, misery, pang, pounding, smarting, soreness, spasm, suffering, throb, throbbing, throe, twinge; ▪ *Ant* comfort, ease, health, relief.

achieve [*v*] *bring to successful conclusion; reach a goal* ▪ *Syn* accomplish, actualize, attain, bring about, complete, consummate, do, end, execute, finish, follow through, fulfill, gain, manage, negotiate, obtain, perform, procure, produce, reach, realize, score, win, work out; ▪ *Ant* fail, fall short, lose, miss.

acid [*adj1*] *bitter, sour in taste* ▪ *Syn* acerbic, acidulous, biting, piquant, pungent, sharp, tart, vinegary; ▪ *Ant* bland, sweet.

acid [*adj2*] *having acidic, corrosive properties* ▪ *Syn* acerbic, acrid, anti-alkaline, biting, bleaching, corroding, disintegrative, eating away, eroding, erosive, oxidizing, rusting; ▪ *Ant* alkaline, basic.

acid [*adj3*] *bitter in words or behavior* ▪ *Syn* acerbic, biting, caustic, cutting, dry, harsh, hateful, mordant, nasty, offensive, sarcastic, sharp, stinging, trenchant, vitriolic; ▪ *Ant* kind, nice.

acidulous [*adj1*] *bitter, sour* ▪ *Syn* acerb, acerbic, acetous, dry, piquant, sharp, tart; ▪ *Ant* sugary, sweet.

acidulous [*adj2*] *bitter in speech* ▪ *Syn* biting, cutting, ironical, mocking, sarcastic; ▪ *Ant* kind, nice, sweet.

acknowledge [v1] *verbally recognize authority* ▪ *Syn* accede, accept, acquiesce, approve, certify, defend, defer to, endorse, grant, own, ratify, support, uphold, yield; ▪ *Ant* ignore, refuse, renounce, repudiate.

acknowledge [v2] *admit truth or reality of something* ▪ *Syn* accede, accept, acquiesce, allow, attest to, avow, concede, confess, declare, grant, own, profess, recognize, yield; ▪ *Ant* abjure, contradict, disavow, forswear, renounce.

acknowledge [v3] *take notice of, recognize receipt of something* ▪ *Syn* address, answer, get back to, greet, hail, notice, react, remark, reply, respond, return, salute, thank; ▪ *Ant* disregard, ignore.

acme [n] *pinnacle of achievement or physical object* ▪ *Syn* apogee, capstone, climax, culmination, height, highest point, high point, meridian, optimum, peak, summit, top, ultimate, vertex, zenith; ▪ *Ant* nadir.

acquaint [v] *inform oneself or another about something new* ▪ *Syn* accustom, advise, apprise, clue, disclose, divulge, enlighten, familiarize, habituate, inform, introduce, make familiar, notify, present, reveal, tell, warn; ▪ *Ant* conceal, deceive, falsify, hide, hold back, mislead, misrepresent, withhold.

acquiesce [v] *agree with some reluctance* ▪ *Syn* accede, accommodate, adapt, adjust, allow, bow to, come around, comply, consent, give in, go along, pass, reconcile, set, submit, subscribe, yes, yield; ▪ *Ant* disagree, dissent, object, protest.

acquiescence [n] *reluctant agreement* ▪ *Syn* acceptance, accession, approval, compliance, concurrence, consent, obedience, permission, resignation, submission, yielding; ▪ *Ant* disagreement, insubordination, rebellion.

acquire [v] *obtain or receive* ▪ *Syn* access, achieve, amass, annex, attain, buy, catch, collect, earn, gain, gather, get, latch onto, pick up, procure, promote, secure, take, take possession, win; ▪ *Ant* fail, forfeit, forgo, lose, relinquish, surrender, yield.

acquisitive [adj] *eager to obtain knowledge or things* ▪ *Syn* avaricious, covetous, demanding, desirous, grasping, greedy, predatory, prehensile, rapacious; ▪ *Ant* abnegating, abstemious, altruistic,

generous, giving, nonpossessive, self-denying, spartan.

acquit [v] *announce removal of blame* ▪ *Syn* absolve, clear, deliver, discharge, exculpate, excuse, exonerate, free, let go, let off, liberate, release, relieve, vindicate; ▪ *Ant* blame, censure, condemn, convict, damn, denounce, doom, sentence.

acrid [adj1] *bitter, sour to taste* ▪ *Syn* acid, amaroidal, astringent, biting, burning, caustic, harsh, irritating, pungent, sharp, stinging; ▪ *Ant* delicious, palatable, savory, sweet.

acrid [adj2] *nasty in behavior or words* ▪ *Syn* acrimonious, austere, biting, bitter, caustic, cutting, harsh, mordant, sarcastic, sharp, trenchant, vitriolic; ▪ *Ant* amicable, benign, complimentary, kind, nice.

acrimonious [adj] *nasty in behavior or speech* ▪ *Syn* acerbic, astringent, biting, bitter, caustic, churlish, indignant, irascible, irate, mordant, peevish, petulant, rancorous, sharp, splenetic, tart, trenchant, wrathful; ▪ *Ant* kind, kindly, peaceable.

act [v] *do something* ▪ *Syn* accomplish, achieve, begin, carry out, create, develop, enforce, execute, function, labor, maneuver, move, officiate, operate, perpetrate, practice, pursue, respond, serve, take part, take up, undertake; ▪ *Ant* abstain, cease, discontinue, give up, halt, hesitate, idle, refrain, stop.

acting [adj] *substituting in a role* ▪ *Syn* ad interim, adjutant, alternate, assistant, delegated, deputy, interim, pro tem, pro tempore, provisional, surrogate, temporary; ▪ *Ant* permanent.

activate [v] *initiate something; start a function* ▪ *Syn* actuate, arouse, call up, energize, impel, mobilize, motivate, move, prompt, propel, rouse, set in motion, start, stimulate, stir, switch on, trigger, turn on; ▪ *Ant* arrest, stop.

active [adj1] *having movement* ▪ *Syn* alive, astir, bustling, efficacious, functioning, impelling, in process, mobile, moving, operative, progressive, rolling, running, rushing, shifting, traveling, turning, working; ▪ *Ant* abeyant, dormant, immobile, inactive, inert, lazy, sluggish.

active [adj2] *very involved in activity* ▪ *Syn* aggressive, animated, assiduous, bustling, busy, dashing, dynamic, energetic, engaged, enlivened, enterprising, forceful, hard-working, industrious, intense, keen, lively, nimble, on the move, persevering, pushing, quick, rapid, ready, resolute, sharp, spry, zealous; ▪ *Ant* disinterested, idle, indifferent, lazy, quiescent, quiet.

actor [*n*] *person who performs, entertains by role-playing* ▪ *Syn* artist, bit player, character, entertainer, extra, foil, headliner, impersonator, ingenue, lead, leading man/woman, mime, performer, playactor, player, soubrette, stand-in, star, thespian, trouper, understudy, walk-on; ▪ *Ant* audience, fan.

actual [*adj1*] *truly existing, real* ▪ *Syn* absolute, authentic, categorical, concrete, definite, factual, genuine, hard, indisputable, indubitable, physical, positive, realistic, substantial, tangible, true, undeniable, unquestionable, verified; ▪ *Ant* counterfeit, false, fictitious, imaginary, legendary, pretended, unreal.

actual [*adj2*] *existing at the present time* ▪ *Syn* current, exact, existent, extant, live, living, original, prevailing; ▪ *Ant* hypothetical, imaginary, nominal, past, reputed, theoretical, unreal.

actuality [*n*] *something that truly exists, is real* ▪ *Syn* achievement, actualization, attainment, fact, materiality, materialization, reality, substance, truth; ▪ *Ant* falseness, illusion, make-believe, pretense.

actuate [*v*] *start a function or action, motivate* ▪ *Syn* activate, animate, arouse, cause, drive, energize, excite, impel, incite, inspire, instigate, mobilize, move, prompt, propel, quicken, rouse, spur, stimulate; ▪ *Ant* impede, stop.

acumen [*n*] *ability to understand and reason* ▪ *Syn* astuteness, awareness, brilliance, comprehension, cunning, discernment, discrimination, farsightedness, grasp, guile, ingenuity, insight, intellect, intuition, judgment, keenness, perception, perspicacity, sagacity, sharpness, shrewdness, smartness, understanding, vision, wisdom, wit; ▪ *Ant* denseness, ignorance, inability, ineptness, obtuseness, stupidity.

acute [*adj1*] *deeply perceptive* ▪ *Syn* astute, clever, discerning, discriminating, incisive, ingenious, intense, intuitive, judicious, keen, observant,

perspicacious, piercing, sensitive, sharp, smart; ▪ *Ant* dense, imperceptive, insensitive, obtuse, slow, stupid.

acute [*adj2*] *very important* ▪ *Syn* afflictive, critical, crucial, dangerous, decisive, desperate, dire, essential, grave, serious, severe, sudden, urgent, vital; ▪ *Ant* not serious, unimportant.

acute [*adj3*] *severe, intense* ▪ *Syn* cutting, distressing, excruciating, fierce, keen, overwhelming, piercing, poignant, racking, severe, sharp, shooting, stabbing, violent; ▪ *Ant* mild, moderate.

adamant [*adj1*] *unyielding* ▪ *Syn* determined, firm, fixed, immovable, inflexible, obdurate, relentless, resolute, rigid, stiff, stubborn, unbending, uncompromising, unrelenting; ▪ *Ant* flexible, pliant, submissive, swayable, yielding.

adamant [*adj2*] *hard like rock* ▪ *Syn* adamantine, flinty, impenetrable, indestructible, rock-hard, tough, unbreakable; ▪ *Ant* flexible, soft, supple.

adapt [*v*] *adjust to a different situation or condition* ▪ *Syn* acclimate, accustom, alter, change, conform, familiarize, get used to, harmonize, match, modify, prepare, qualify, readjust, remodel, revise, shape, square, suit, tailor; ▪ *Ant* disarrange, dislocate, disorder, disturb, unfit.

adaptable [*adj*] *able and usually willing to change* ▪ *Syn* adjustable, alterable, compliant, convertible, ductile, easygoing, flexible, malleable, plastic, pliant, resilient, supple, tractable, variable, versatile; ▪ *Ant* inflexible, intractable, nonconforming, unadaptable.

add [*v1*] *simple arithmetical process of increase; accumulation* ▪ *Syn* calculate, cast, compute, count up, enumerate, figure, reckon, reckon up, sum, summate, tally, total; ▪ *Ant* deduct, subtract.

add [*v2*] *adjoin, increase; make further comment* ▪ *Syn* annex, append, augment, boost, build up, charge up, continue, figure in, hike, include, join together, parlay, reply, say further, speed up, spike, supplement, tag; ▪ *Ant* decrease, deduct, diminish, lessen, reduce, remove, withdraw.

addicted [*adj*] *dependent on something, compulsive* ▪ *Syn* attached, dependent, devoted, disposed, fanatic, fond, given to, habituated, hooked, inclined, obsessed, predisposed, prone, under the influence; ▪ **Ant** disinclined, independent, opposed, unaccustomed.

address [*vl*] *devote effort to something*
  ▪ **Syn** apply, attend to, concentrate on, devote oneself to, direct, engage in, focus on, give, take care of, take up, throw, try, turn, turn to, undertake; ▪ **Ant** avoid, cut, disregard, ignore, overlook, pass, shun, slight.

adept [*adj*] *very able*
  ▪ **Syn** accomplished, adroit, capable, deft, dexterous, expert, masterful, proficient, quick, savvy, sharp, skillful, smooth, versed; ▪ **Ant** awkward, clumsy, incompetent, inept, unskilled.

adequate [*adj*] *enough, able*
  ▪ **Syn** acceptable, all right, capable, commensurate, competent, fair, passable, requisite, satisfactory, sufficient, suitable, tolerable, unexceptional, unobjectionable; ▪ **Ant** inadequate, inferior, insufficient, unequal, unfit, unqualified, unsuitable, useless.

adequately [*adv*] *sufficiently*
  ▪ **Syn** acceptably, appropriately, competently, copiously, decently, fairly well, fittingly, modestly, satisfactorily, sufficiently, suitably, on an acceptable degree, tolerably, well enough; ▪ **Ant** inadequately, insufficiently, unequally, unsatisfactorily, unsuitably.

adhere [*vl*] *conform to or follow rules exactly* ▪ **Syn** abide by, be devoted to, be faithful, be loyal, be true, cleave to, cling, comply, fulfill, heed, keep, maintain, mind, obey, observe, practice, respect, stand by, support; ▪ **Ant** disjoin, not conform.

adhere [*v2*] *stick or become stuck to, either physically or mentally* ▪ **Syn** attach, cement, cleave, cling, cohere, fasten, fix, glue, hold fast, lodge, stay, put, unite; ▪ **Ant** loose, loosen, separate, unfasten.

adhesive [*adj*] *sticking*
  ▪ **Syn** adherent, agglutinant, attaching, clinging, glutinous, gummed, holding, hugging, mucilaginous, pasty, resinous, sticky, tenacious, viscid, viscous, waxy; ▪ **Ant** inadhesive, loose, open, separated, slippery.

adieu [*n*] *parting remark or action*
  ▪ **Syn** adios, congé, farewell, goodbye, leave-taking, parting, so long, valediction; ▪ **Ant** greeting, hello.

adjacent [*adj*] *next to, abutting*
  ▪ **Syn** adjoining, beside, bordering, close, contiguous, near, neighboring, next door, touching; ▪ **Ant** apart, away, detached, disconnected, distant, far, faraway, nonadjacent, remote, separate.

adjoin [*v*] *attach*
  ▪ **Syn** add, affix, annex, append, combine, connect, couple, interconnect, join, link, unite; ▪ **Ant** detach.

adjoining [*adj*] *being next to*
  ▪ **Syn** abutting, adjacent, approximal, bordering on, connecting, conterminous, contiguous, interconnecting, joined, juxtaposed, near, neighboring, touching, verging; ▪ **Ant** detached, divided, separate.

adjourn [*v*] *stop a proceeding*
  ▪ **Syn** curb, defer, delay, discontinue, hold off, hold over, hold up, postpone, prorogue, put off, recess, restrain, shelve, stay, suspend; ▪ **Ant** begin, convene, convoke, encourage, further, keep on, open.

adjudicate [*v*] *formally judge*
  ▪ **Syn** adjudge, arbitrate, decide, determine, mediate, referee, settle; ▪ **Ant** defer, ignore, not judge.

adjunct [*n*] *addition; help*
  ▪ **Syn** accessory, addendum, appendage, appendix, appurtenance, associate, auxiliary, complement, detail, partner, subordinate, supplement; ▪ **Ant** detriment, lessening, subtraction.

adjust [*vl*] *become or make prepared, adapted* ▪ **Syn** acclimatize, accommodate, accustom, adapt, compose, conform, dispose, fine-tune, fix, habituate, harmonize, modify, order, reconcile, rectify, remodel, suit, tailor, tune; ▪ **Ant** confuse, derange, disarrange, disorder, disorganize, upset.

adjust [*v2*] *mechanically alter, especially to improve* ▪ **Syn** align, balance, calibrate, connect, correct, fine-tune, fit, fix, focus, grind, improve, mend, overhaul, polish, put in working order, rectify, regulate, renovate, repair, service, set, sharpen, square, tighten, tune up; ▪ **Ant** derange, disarrange, unsuit.

adjust [*v3*] *bring into agreement or to a standard* ▪ **Syn** accord, allocate, arrange, clarify, conclude, conform, coordinate, fine-tune, fix up, grade, methodize, modify, organize, reconcile, regulate, settle, sort, standardize, straighten, systematize, tally; ▪ **Ant** confuse, derange, unfit, unsuit.

ad-lib [adj] improvised
▪ **Syn** extemporaneous, extempore, impromptu, off-the-cuff, spontaneous, unprepared, unrehearsed; ▪ **Ant** deliberate, planned, prepared, rehearsed, written.

ad-lib [v] improvise speech
▪ **Syn** extemporize, invent, make up, speak extemporaneously, speak off the cuff; ▪ **Ant** plan, prepare, rehearse, write.

administer [v1] manage an organization or effort ▪ **Syn** administrate, carry out, conduct, control, direct, execute, govern, head, oversee, render, run, superintend, supervise; ▪ **Ant** mismanage, neglect.

administer [v2] dispense something needed ▪ **Syn** apply, apportion, authorize, contribute, deal, deliver, disburse, distribute, dole, extend, furnish, issue, measure out, mete out, offer, perform, portion, proffer, provide, regulate, serve, supply, tender; ▪ **Ant** deny, frustrate, refuse, withhold.

administrator [n] person who manages organization ▪ **Syn** ambassador, authority, boss, bureaucrat, captain, CEO, chairperson, chief, consul, controller, dean, director, executive, governor, head, inspector, judge, leader, manager, officer, official, organizer, president, producer, superintendent, supervisor; ▪ **Ant** employee, worker.

admirable [adj] deserving of great respect ▪ **Syn** attractive, choice, commendable, deserving, estimable, excellent, exquisite, fine, good, great, laudable, meritable, meritorious, praiseworthy, rare, solid, superior, valuable, wonderful, worthy; ▪ **Ant** contemptible, despicable, detestable, hateful, loathsome, repugnant, repulsive, shameful, unworthy.

admire [v] hold in high regard
▪ **Syn** adore, applaud, appreciate, cherish, commend, delight in, esteem, extol, glorify, hail, honor, idolize, laud, look up to, marvel at, pay homage to, praise, respect, revere, think highly of, venerate, worship; ▪ **Ant** abhor, condemn, despise, detest, dislike, execrate, hate, scorn.

admissible [adj] able or deserving of consideration; allowable ▪ **Syn** acceptable, applicable, appropriate, fair, fitting, justifiable, lawful, legitimate, passable, permissible, possible, proper, rational, reasonable, relevant, right, suitable, tolerable, warranted, worthy; ▪ **Ant** illegitimate, inadmissible, inapplicable, irrelevant, unfair, unjust, unsuitable, wrong.

admit [v1] allow entry
▪ **Syn** accept, bless, buy, concede, enter, entertain, give access, grant, harbor, house, initiate, introduce, lodge, permit, receive, shelter, suffer, take in; ▪ **Ant** debar, deny, dismiss, eject, exclude, expel, oust, refuse, reject, repel, shut out.

admit [v2] confess, acknowledge
▪ **Syn** accept, acquiesce, affirm, agree, avow, bare, concede, confide, confirm, consent, declare, disclose, divulge, expose, grant, indicate, make known, narrate, open up, own, permit, profess, recognize, reveal, tell, uncover, unveil, yield; ▪ **Ant** confute, deny, dispute, dissent, gainsay, refuse.

admonish [v] warn, strongly criticize
▪ **Syn** advise, berate, censure, chide, counsel, enjoin, exhort, forewarn, rebuke, reprimand, reprove, scold, upbraid, warn; ▪ **Ant** applaud, approve, commend, compliment, extol, flatter, laud, praise.

adolescent [adj] preadult or immature
▪ **Syn** boyish, girlish, growing, juvenile, pubescent, puerile, teen, teenage, young, youthful; ▪ **Ant** adult, grown-up, infant, mature.

adopt [v1] choose or take something as one's own ▪ **Syn** accept, adapt, affirm, appropriate, assent, assume, borrow, choose, embrace, endorse, follow, imitate, maintain, mimic, pick, ratify, seize, select, support, use; ▪ **Ant** disown, leave alone, pass over, reject, repudiate, repulse.

adopt [v2] legally care for another's child ▪ **Syn** foster, raise, take in; ▪ **Ant** disinherit, give up for adoption, place.

adorable [adj] cute, lovable
▪ **Syn** appealing, attractive, captivating, charming, darling, dear, delectable, delightful, fetching, heavenly, luscious, pleasing, precious; ▪ **Ant** cursed, despicable, detestable, hateable, hateful.

adore [v] love intensely
▪ **Syn** admire, cherish, delight in, dote on, esteem, exalt, fall for, glorify, honor, idolize, prize, revere, treasure, venerate, worship; ▪ **Ant** abhor, condemn, despise, detest, hate.

adorn [v] decorate
▪ **Syn** array, beautify, bedeck, deck, dress up, embellish, enhance, furbish, garnish,

grace, ornament, spruce up, trim; ▪ *Ant* damage, deform, hurt, leave plain, mar.

adrift [*adv1*] *floating out of control*
▪ *Syn* afloat, drifting, loose, unanchored; ▪ *Ant* anchored, moored, stable, tied down.

adrift [*adv2*] *without purpose*
▪ *Syn* aimless, directionless, goalless, purposeless; ▪ *Ant* determined, purposeful.

adrift [*adv3*] *off course*
▪ *Syn* amiss, astray, erring, wrong; ▪ *Ant* on course, on target.

adroit [*adj*] *very able or skilled*
▪ *Syn* adept, clever, cunning, deft, dexterous, expert, handy, ingenious, masterful, nimble, proficient, quick-witted, savvy, sharp, skillful, wizard; ▪ *Ant* awkward, clumsy, dense, inept, stupid, unskilled.

adulation [*n*] *overenthusiastic praise*
▪ *Syn* applause, blandishment, commendation, fawning, flattery, sycophancy, worship; ▪ *Ant* abuse, criticism.

adult [*adj*] *being mature, fully grown*
▪ *Syn* developed, grown, grown-up, of age, ripe, ripened; ▪ *Ant* adolescent, infant.

adulterate [*v*] *alter or debase, often for profit* ▪ *Syn* alloy, attenuate, blend, cheapen, contaminate, corrupt, defile, degrade, depreciate, falsify, impair, infiltrate, make impure, mingle, mix, pollute, taint, transfuse, vitiate, weaken; ▪ *Ant* clarify, clean, cleanse, distill, filter, free, purify, refine.

adulterated [*adj*] *debased or dirty*
▪ *Syn* attenuated, blended, contaminated, corrupt, defiled, degraded, devalued, impaired, mixed, polluted, tainted, vitiated, weakened; ▪ *Ant* clean, moral, virtuous.

adulterous [*adj*] *unfaithful*
▪ *Syn* cheating, illicit, immoral, unchaste; ▪ *Ant* chaste, clean, pure.

advance [*n1*] *money given beforehand*
▪ *Syn* accommodation, allowance, credit, deposit, down payment, hike, increase, loan, prepayment, retainer, score, stake; ▪ *Ant* deferred payment, payment on account.

advance(s) [*n2*] *desirous pursuit of someone* ▪ *Syn* approach, move, overture, proposal, proposition, suggestion; ▪ *Ant* disinterest, ignorance.

advance [*adj*] *ahead in position or time*
▪ *Syn* beforehand, earlier, early, first,

foremost, forward, in front, in the forefront, in the lead, leading, previous, prior; ▪ *Ant* after, behind.

advance [*v1*] *move something forward, often quickly* ▪ *Syn* accelerate, achieve, conquer, dispatch, drive, elevate, forge ahead, gain ground, get ahead, go forward, hasten, launch, make headway, march, press on, progress, propel, push ahead, speed, storm; ▪ *Ant* back down, halt, hesitate, recede, retreat, retrogress, stop, turn, withdraw, yield.

advance [*v2*] *promote or propose an idea* ▪ *Syn* adduce, allege, ballyhoo, benefit, boost, cite, encourage, foster, further, introduce, offer, present, proffer, push, put forward, serve, set forth, submit, suggest, urge; ▪ *Ant* hesitate, stop, withdraw.

advance [*v3*] *give money beforehand*
▪ *Syn* furnish, lend, loan, pay, provide; ▪ *Ant* defer payment, withhold payment.

advance [*v4*] *increase in amount, number, or position* ▪ *Syn* boost, develop, elevate, enlarge, grow, improve, magnify, multiply, prosper, raise, thrive, up, upgrade, uplift; ▪ *Ant* decrease, take back, withdraw.

advanced [*adj*] *ahead in position, time, manner* ▪ *Syn* avant-garde, breakthrough, cutting-edge, exceptional, extreme, first, foremost, forward, higher, late, leading-edge, precocious, progressive, radical, state-of-the-art, unconventional; ▪ *Ant* after, behind.

advantage [*n*] *benefit, favored position or circumstance* ▪ *Syn* asset, avail, blessing, boon, break, choice, comfort, dominance, edge, eminence, favor, gain, help, influence, lead, leverage, luck, position, power, preference, prevalence, protection, resources, sanction, superiority, supremacy, utility; ▪ *Ant* disadvantage, drawback, handicap, hindrance, loss, obstacle, restriction.

advent [*n*] *beginning or arrival of something anticipated* ▪ *Syn* appearance, approach, arrival, coming, entrance, occurrence, onset, rearing, visitation; ▪ *Ant* departure, end.

adventure [*n*] *risky or unexpected undertaking* ▪ *Syn* chance, contingency, enterprise, experience, exploit, feat, happening, hazard, incident, jeopardy, occurrence, peril, scene, speculation, trip, undertaking, venture; ▪ *Ant* avoidance, inaction, inactivity, inertia, latency, passiveness, stillness.

adventurous [adj] *daring, risk-taking*
▪ **Syn** audacious, bold, brave, courageous, dangerous, daredevil, enterprising, foolhardy, hazardous, headstrong, intrepid, rash, reckless, risky, temerarious, venturesome, venturous; ▪ **Ant** careful, cautious, prudent, unadventurous.

adversary [n] *opponent*
▪ **Syn** antagonist, attacker, competitor, contestant, enemy, foe, match, opposer, oppugner, rival; ▪ **Ant** ally, assistant, backer, friend, helper, helpmate, supporter.

adverse [adj] *unfavorable, antagonistic*
▪ **Syn** conflicting, contrary, detrimental, disadvantageous, inimical, injurious, inopportune, negative, opposed, opposing, opposite, oppugning, reluctant, repugnant; ▪ **Ant** advantageous, aiding, auspicious, favorable, fortunate, helpful, lucky, propitious.

adversity [n] *bad luck, situation*
▪ **Syn** affliction, calamity, catastrophe, disaster, distress, hardship, hurting, ill fortune, jam, jinx, misfortune, reverse, sorrow, suffering, trial, trouble; ▪ **Ant** aid, encouragement, favor, fortune, good luck, help, prosperity.

advertise [v] *publicize for the purpose of selling or causing one to want* ▪ **Syn** acquaint, announce, apprise, bill, blazon, build up, circularize, communicate, display, endorse, exhibit, expose, flaunt, herald, hype, inform, make known, notify, pitch, promote, push, sponsor, tout; ▪ **Ant** hide, keep secret.

advice [n] *recommendation*
▪ **Syn** admonition, advocacy, consultation, counsel, directions, exhortation, guidance, help, information, injunction, input, instruction, judgment, opinion, persuasion, proposition, recommendation, suggestion, teaching, tidings, view, word; ▪ **Ant** betrayal, deceit, deception, falsehood, lie, misinformation, misrepresentation.

advisable [adj] *recommended, wise*
▪ **Syn** appropriate, apt, commendable, desirable, expedient, fit, fitting, judicious, politic, prudent, seemly, sensible, sound, suggested, suitable, tactical; ▪ **Ant** improper, imprudent, inadvisable, inappropriate, incorrect, injudicious, unwise.

advise [v1] *offer recommendation*
▪ **Syn** advocate, caution, counsel, direct, enjoin, exhort, guide, instruct, move, opine, point out, prescribe, prompt, recommend, steer, suggest, tout, urge, warn; ▪ **Ant** betray, deceive, delude, fool, lie, pretend, trick.

advise [v2] *offer information*
▪ **Syn** acquaint, apprise, fill in, inform, make known, notify, report, show, tell, update, warn; ▪ **Ant** keep mum, keep quiet, keep secret.

advocate [v] *support idea or cause publicly* ▪ **Syn** argue for, back, bless, campaign for, champion, countenance, defend, encourage, favor, further, justify, press for, promote, propose, push, recommend, side with, speak for, support, tout, uphold, urge, vindicate; ▪ **Ant** assail, attack, criticize, impugn, oppose, protest.

aesthetic/esthetic [adj] *beautiful or artful* ▪ **Syn** artistic, creative, gorgeous, inventive; ▪ **Ant** displeasing, ugly.

afar [adv] *a great distance away*
▪ **Syn** distant, far away, far off, remote; ▪ **Ant** close, near.

affable [adj] *friendly*
▪ **Syn** amiable, benevolent, congenial, cordial, courteous, genial, good-humored, gracious, kindly, obliging, pleasant, polite, sociable, urbane, warm; ▪ **Ant** complaining, disdainful, grouchy, grumbling, impolite, miserable, reserved, surly, unfriendly.

affect [v] *influence, affect emotionally*
▪ **Syn** act on, alter, change, disturb, impinge, impress, influence, modify, move, overcome, perturb, prevail, relate, stir, sway, touch, transform, upset; ▪ **Ant** bore, leave cold, leave unmoved.

affected [adj1] *deeply moved or hurt emotionally* ▪ **Syn** afflicted, altered, concerned, distressed, excited, grieved, influenced, injured, overwhelmed, overwrought, stimulated, stirred, sympathetic, touched, troubled, upset; ▪ **Ant** calm, unmoved, unperturbed, unswayed, untroubled.

affected [adj2] *changed in a bad or artificial way* ▪ **Syn** artificial, assumed, awkward, contrived, false, feigned, hollow, imitated, melodramatic, ostentatious, overdone, pedantic, pompous, pretentious, self-conscious, shallow, simulated, spurious, stiff, studied, superficial, theatrical, unnatural; ▪ *Ant* unchanged, unhurt, unimpaired, uninjured.

affectionate [*adj*] *having or showing fondness* ▪ *Syn* attached, caring, devoted, doting, fond, friendly, kind, loving, sympathetic, tender, warm; ▪ *Ant* antagonistic, cold, cool, disliking, undemonstrative.

affective [*adj*] *concerning feelings and intuition* ▪ *Syn* emotional, emotive, feeling, intuitive, noncognitive, perceptual, visceral; ▪ *Ant* cerebral, cognitive, intellectual, objective, rational.

affiliate [*v*] *associate or be associated with a larger organization* ▪ *Syn* ally, amalgamate, annex, band together, combine, confederate, connect, incorporate, join, team up, tie up, unite; ▪ *Ant* disassociate, disjoin, leave, quit, separate, stay away

affinity [*n1*] *liking or inclination toward something* ▪ *Syn* affection, attraction, closeness, compatibility, fondness, leaning, partiality, rapport, sympathy; ▪ *Ant* dislike, hatred.

affinity [*n2*] *similarity* ▪ *Syn* alliance, analogy, association, closeness, connection, correspondence, kinship, likeness, relation, relationship, resemblance, similitude; ▪ *Ant* difference, dissimilarity; distinction.

affirm [*v*] *declare the truth of something* ▪ *Syn* assert, asseverate, attest, certify, confirm, declare, guarantee, insist, maintain, predicate, pronounce, ratify, repeat, state, swear, testify, vouch, witness; ▪ *Ant* deny, negate, nullify, veto.

affirmative [*adj*] *being agreeable or assenting* ▪ *Syn* acknowledging, acquiescent, approving, concurring, confirmatory, consenting, corroborative, endorsing, favorable, positive, ratifying, supporting; ▪ *Ant* dissenting, negative.

affix [*v*] *attach or install* ▪ *Syn* add, annex, append, bind, fasten, glue, join, paste, put on, rivet, subjoin, tack, tag; ▪ *Ant* detach, let go, loosen.

afflict [*v*] *to cause suffering* ▪ *Syn* annoy, bother, burden, crucify, distress, grieve, harass, harrow, irk, lacerate, martyr, oppress, plague, press, rack, smite, torment, trouble, try, vex, worry; ▪ *Ant* aid, comfort, help, solace, stay away from, take care of.

affluent [*adj1*] *wealthy* ▪ *Syn* opulent, prosperous, rich, upper class, upscale, well-off, well-to-do; ▪ *Ant* destitute, impoverished, needy, penniless, poor.

affluent [*adj2*] *plentiful* ▪ *Syn* abundant, bountiful, copious, full, plenteous; ▪ *Ant* insufficient, lacking, needy, suffering, wanting.

afford [*v*] *give, produce* ▪ *Syn* bestow, furnish, grant, impart, offer, provide, render, supply, yield; ▪ *Ant* take away.

affront [*n*] *an insult* ▪ *Syn* abuse, indignity, injury, offense, outrage, provocation, slight, slur, vexation, wrong; ▪ *Ant* appeasement, compliment, pleasantry.

affront [*v*] *insult or offend* ▪ *Syn* abuse, anger, annoy, confront, dispraise, encounter, face, outrage, pique, provoke, slander, slight, taunt, vex; ▪ *Ant* appease, assuage, compliment, gratify, mollify, placate, please, satisfy, soothe.

afraid [*adj1*] *fearful* ▪ *Syn* aghast, anxious, apprehensive, blanched, cowed, daunted, distressed, disturbed, faint-hearted, frightened, frozen, horrified, intimidated, nervous, petrified, rattled, scared, terrified, terror-stricken, trembling, upset, worried; ▪ *Ant* bold, brave, composed, confident, cool, courageous, fearless, intrepid, undaunted, valiant.

afraid [*adj2*] *reluctant, regretful* ▪ *Syn* averse, backward, disinclined, hesitant, indisposed, loath, reluctant, sorry, unwilling; ▪ *Ant* confident, eager, happy, undismayed, venturesome.

after [*adj*] *following in position or time* ▪ *Syn* afterwards, back, back of, behind, below, ensuing, hind, hindmost, in the rear, later, next, posterior, postliminary, rear, subsequential, subsequently, succeeding, thereafter; ▪ *Ant* before, previous.

afternoon [*n*] *period after 12 noon and before sunset* ▪ *Syn* cocktail hour, P.M., post meridiem, siesta, teatime; ▪ *Ant* A.M., dawn, morning.

afterthought [*n*] *idea that occurs after it is timely* ▪ *Syn* reconsideration, review, second thought; ▪ *Ant* forethought, presupposition.

afterward/afterwards [*adv*] *following a time, event* ▪ *Syn* another time, at a later time, behind, by and by, eventually, in a while, later, next, on the next day, soon, subsequently, then, thereafter, ultimately; ▪ *Ant* beforehand, previously.

aged [adj] old
- **Syn** age-old, ancient, antediluvian, antiquated, antique, elderly, gray, senescent, timeworn, venerable; **Ant** new, unripe, young, youthful.

aggrandize [v] cause something to seem or be greater, bigger **Syn** acclaim, augment, boost, commend, dignify, enlarge, ennoble, glorify, heighten, hype, increase, intensify, magnify, multiply, parlay, praise; **Ant** belittle, debase, degrade, depress, disgrace, humble, lower.

aggravate [v1] annoy
- **Syn** bother, bug, dog, exasperate, gall, grate, hack, irk, irritate, nag, needle, peeve, pester, provoke, tease, vex; **Ant** appease, gladden, make happy, mollify, soften.

aggravate [v2] cause to become worse
- **Syn** complicate, deepen, exacerbate, exaggerate, heighten, increase, inflame, intensify, magnify, mount, rise, worsen; **Ant** alleviate, help, improve, relieve, soothe.

aggregate [adj] forming a collection from separate parts **Syn** accumulated, added, amassed, assembled, collected, collective, combined, composite, corporate, cumulative, heaped, mixed, piled, total; **Ant** individual, part, particular.

aggregate [v] combine into a collection
- **Syn** accumulate, add up, amass, amount, assemble, collect, combine, come to, heap, mix, number, pile, sum, total; **Ant** break up, disperse, divide.

aggressive [adj1] belligerent, hostile
- **Syn** antipathetic, assailing, attacking, barbaric, bellicose, combative, destructive, disruptive, intrusive, invading, martial, offensive, pugnacious, quarrelsome, rapacious, threatening, warlike; **Ant** calm, easygoing, laid-back.

aggressive [adj2] assertive
- **Syn** bold, domineering, dynamic, energetic, enterprising, forceful, imperious, militant, pushy, strenuous, tough, vigorous, zealous; **Ant** complaisant, laid-back.

aggrieved [adj] very distressed
- **Syn** afflicted, depressed, disturbed, grieving, harmed, hurt, injured, oppressed, pained, persecuted, saddened, unhappy, woeful, wronged; **Ant** happy, pleased.

aghast [adj] horrified; very surprised
- **Syn** agape, agog, alarmed, appalled,

astonished, astounded, awestruck, confounded, dismayed, dumbfounded, frightened, horror-struck, overwhelmed, shocked, startled, stunned, terrified, thunderstruck; **Ant** unsurprised.

agile [adj] physically or mentally nimble, deft **Syn** active, acute, alert, athletic, brisk, buoyant, bustling, clever, dexterous, energetic, fleet, limber, lithe, mercurial, prompt, quick, ready, sharp, sportive, spry, supple, swift, vivacious, winged; **Ant** brittle, clumsy, stiff.

agitate [v1] shake physically
- **Syn** beat, churn, concuss, convulse, disturb, rock, rouse, stir, toss; **Ant** calm, lull, quiet, soothe, tranquilize.

agitate [v2] disturb, trouble someone
- **Syn** alarm, confuse, debate, disconcert, disquiet, distract, excite, ferment, incite, perturb, rouse, stimulate, stir, trouble, upset, worry; **Ant** calm, not bother, placate, quiet, soothe.

agnostic [n] person unsure that God exists **Syn** doubter, freethinker, materialist, skeptic, unbeliever; **Ant** believer.

agonizing [adj] difficult and painful, suffering **Syn** excruciating, extreme, fierce, harrowing, intense, racking, struggling, tormenting, torturing, vehement, violent; **Ant** easy, enjoyable, restful.

agrarian [adj] concerning land, farming
- **Syn** agricultural, natural, peasant, rural, rustic, uncultivated, undomesticated; **Ant** industrial, manufacturing, suburban, urban.

agree [v1] be in unison, assent with another **Syn** accede, acknowledge, acquiesce, admit, allow, come to terms, comply, concede, concur, consent, engage, go along with, grant, permit, settle, side with, subscribe; **Ant** contend, contradict, decline, disagree, dispute, dissent, oppose, protest, refuse.

agree [v2] be similar or consistent
- **Syn** accord, answer, attune, be in harmony, blend, coincide, concur, correspond, equal, fit, go together, harmonize, jibe, match, parallel, square, synchronize; **Ant** differ.

agreeable [adj1] pleasing
- **Syn** acceptable, delightful, enjoyable, fine, gratifying, mild, nice, pleasant, ready, satisfying, to one's liking, welcome; **Ant** disagreeable, discordant, distasteful, harsh, hateful, mean, nasty, offensive, unpleasant.

agreeable [adj2] appropriate, in keeping ▪ **Syn** befitting, compatible, congruous, consistent, consonant, fitting, proper; ▪ **Ant** disagreeable, discordant, incompatible, incongruous, unsuitable.

agreeable [adj3] willing to be in unison, assent ▪ **Syn** acquiescent, amenable, approving, complying, concurring, congenial, consenting, in accord, responsive, sympathetic, well-disposed, willing; ▪ **Ant** disagreeable, incongruous, repugnant, unwilling.

aground [adv] on the bottom or shore of a body of water ▪ **Syn** ashore, beached, disabled, foundered, grounded, marooned, reefed, shipwrecked, stranded, stuck, swamped, wrecked; ▪ **Ant** afloat.

ahead [adj/adv] in front or advance of ▪ **Syn** advancing, at an advantage, before, beforehand, earlier, first, foremost, forward, in the foreground, in the lead, leading, onward, progressing, to the fore; ▪ **Ant** after, behind, following, in the rear, subsequently.

aid/aide [n] person who helps ▪ **Syn** abettor, adjutant, aide-de-camp, assistant, attendant, coadjutant, coadjutor, crew, deputy, helper, lieutenant, second, supporter; ▪ **Ant** boss, leader, superior.

aid [v] help, support ▪ **Syn** abet, alleviate, assist, befriend, encourage, mitigate, promote, relieve, subsidize, sustain; ▪ **Ant** block, hinder, hurt, impede, injure, obstruct.

ailing [adj] not feeling well ▪ **Syn** below par, debilitated, diseased, down, down with, enfeebled, feeble, feeling awful, ill, indisposed, sick, sickly, unwell, wasting, weak; ▪ **Ant** healthy.

aim [n] goal ▪ **Syn** ambition, aspiration, course, desideratum, direction, end, intention, mark, objective, plan, purpose, scheme, target, wish; ▪ **Ant** aimlessness, avoidance, neglect, purposelessness, thoughtlessness.

aimless [adj] having no goal ▪ **Syn** accidental, blind, capricious, careless, desultory, directionless, drifting, erratic, haphazard, heedless, indiscriminate, pointless, random, stray, thoughtless, unavailing, vagrant, wandering, wanton, wayward; ▪ **Ant** determined, directed, goal-oriented, guided, motivated, planned, pointed, purposeful, resolute.

air [v1] put into the atmosphere; freshen ▪ **Syn** aerate, circulate, cool, eject, expel, expose, fan, open, oxygenate, purify, refresh, ventilate; ▪ **Ant** close up, smother, stifle.

air [v2] express opinion publicly ▪ **Syn** broadcast, circulate, communicate, declare, display, divulge, exhibit, make known, proclaim, publicize, reveal, state, utter, ventilate, voice; ▪ **Ant** be quiet, conceal, hide, repress, silence, suppress.

airs [n] affectation; pretended behavior ▪ **Syn** arrogance, front, haughtiness, hauteur, mannerism, ostentation, pomposity, pretense, pretension, show, superciliousness; ▪ **Ant** personality, realness, truthfulness.

airtight [adj1] sealed ▪ **Syn** closed, impenetrable, impermeable, shut; ▪ **Ant** loose, open, penetrable, permeable, unclosed, unsealed.

airtight [adj2] certain ▪ **Syn** incontestable, indisputable, invulnerable, irrefutable, unassailable; ▪ **Ant** possible, questionable, uncertain.

airy [adj1] open to the atmosphere ▪ **Syn** aerial, breezy, drafty, exposed, fresh, gusty, light, lofty, out-of-doors, vaporous, ventilated, windy; ▪ **Ant** close, closed, oppressive, stuffy.

airy [adj2] delicate or ethereal ▪ **Syn** diaphanous, flimsy, frail, illusory, immaterial, intangible, light, rarefied, tenuous, vaporous, visionary, weightless, wispy; ▪ **Ant** burdensome, dense, heavy, massive, ponderous, weighty.

airy [adj3] buoyant, light, or lively in nature ▪ **Syn** animated, blithe, cheery, effervescent, fanciful, flippant, gay, high-spirited, jaunty, light-hearted, merry, nonchalant, resilient, sprightly, volatile, whimsical; ▪ **Ant** burdened, heavy, lumbering, sluggish.

ajar [adj/adv] slightly open ▪ **Syn** open, unclosed, unlatched, unshut; ▪ **Ant** closed.

akin [adj] related or connected ▪ **Syn** affiliated, agnate, allied, analogous, cognate, comparable, consonant, corresponding, incident, kindred, like, parallel, similar; ▪ **Ant** alien, disconnected, unconnected, unrelated.

alacrity [n] liveliness; promptness ▪ **Syn** alertness, briskness, dispatch, eagerness, enthusiasm, fervor, gaiety, promptitude, quickness, readiness, speed, willingness, zeal; ■ *Ant* apathy, aversion, disinclination, dullness, indifference, reluctance, slowness.

alarm [v] *upset*
■ *Syn* amaze, astonish, chill, daunt, dismay, distress, frighten, panic, scare, startle, surprise, terrify; ■ *Ant* assure, calm, gladden, reassure, repose, soothe.

alcoholic [adj] *intoxicating*
■ *Syn* brewed, distilled, fermented, hard, inebriant, inebriating, spirituous, vinous; ■ *Ant* non-alcoholic, nonintoxicating, soft.

alert [adj] *attentive, lively*
■ *Syn* active, bright, careful, circumspect, clever, heedful, intelligent, observant, perceptive, quick, ready, sharp, spirited, vigilant, wary, watchful, wide-awake, wired, wise; ■ *Ant* asleep, drowsy, inattentive, lethargic, sluggish, unobservant, weary.

alien [adj] *foreign*
■ *Syn* estranged, exotic, extraneous, extrinsic, inappropriate, incompatible, incongruous, opposed, remote, separate; ■ *Ant* akin, appropriate, native, proper.

alienate [v] *cause unfriendliness, hostility* ■ *Syn* break off, come between, disunite, divorce, estrange, make indifferent, part, separate, set against, turn away, wean; ■ *Ant* be friendly, disarm, endear.

align [v1] *line up, arrange next to*
■ *Syn* adjust, coordinate, even, fix, make parallel, order, range, regulate, straighten; ■ *Ant* divide, mess up, separate.

align [v2] *join; bring to agreement*
■ *Syn* affiliate, agree, ally, associate, cooperate, enlist, follow, join sides, sympathize; ■ *Ant* disjoin.

alike [adj] *similar*
■ *Syn* akin, analogous, cognate, comparable, duplicate, equivalent, even, identical, kindred, matched, parallel, proportionate, resembling, same, undifferentiated, uniform; ■ *Ant* different, dissimilar, distinct, diverse, opposite, unlike.

alive [adj1] *being animately existent*
■ *Syn* animate, awake, breathing, cognizant, conscious, dynamic, existing, extant, functioning, living, subsisting, viable, vital, zoetic; ■ *Ant* dead, deceased, inanimate, lifeless.

alive [adj2] *being active, full of life*
■ *Syn* abounding, alert, animated, awake, brisk, bustling, cheerful, dynamic, energetic, lively, quick, replete, rife, spirited,

swarming, teeming, vital, vivacious, zestful; ■ *Ant* dispirited, dull, lifeless, morose, sluggish, spiritless.

all [n] *whole; totality*
■ *Syn* accumulation, aggregate, collection, ensemble, entirety, gross, mass, quantity, sum, sum total, total; ■ *Ant* none, zero, zilch, zip.

all [adj] *exclusive*
■ *Syn* alone, nothing but, only, solely; ■ *Ant* incomplete, partial.

all [adv] *completely, without exception*
■ *Syn* across the board, all in all, altogether, entirely, exactly, fully, just, purely, quite, totally, utterly, wholly; ■ *Ant* incompletely.

allay [v] *reduce something, usually a pain or a problem* ■ *Syn* abate, alleviate, assuage, calm, compose, decrease, ease, lessen, lighten, mitigate, moderate, mollify, pacify, quiet, square; ■ *Ant* intensify, provoke, stir, worsen.

allege [v] *assert; claim*
■ *Syn* adduce, asseverate, avow, charge, cite, declare, lay, maintain, offer, present, profess, put forward, recite, recount, state, testify; ■ *Ant* contradict, deny, disagree, dissent, object, protest, repudiate.

alleged [adj] *asserted, often dubiously*
■ *Syn* averred, declared, described, dubious, ostensible, pretended, professed, purported, questionable, so-called, stated, supposed, suspect, suspicious; ■ *Ant* certain, definite, sure.

allegiance [n] *loyalty*
■ *Syn* adherence, ardor, consecration, dedication, devotion, faithfulness, fidelity, homage, honor, obedience, obligation, piety; ■ *Ant* disloyalty, enmity, sedition, treachery, treason.

alleviate [v] *relieve; lessen*
■ *Syn* allay, assuage, ease, lighten, mitigate, mollify, pacify; ■ *Ant* aggravate, heighten, increase, intensify, magnify.

allied [adj] *friendly; united*
■ *Syn* affiliated, amalgamated, associated, bound, cognate, confederate, connected, incident, in league, joined, linked, unified, wed; ■ *Ant* disunited, estranged, unfriendly.

allocate [v] *assign; divide among*
■ *Syn* admeasure, allot, apportion, appropriate, budget, cut, designate, divvy, earmark, give, mete, set aside, share, slice; ■ *Ant* keep, keep together.

allot [v] *assign; give portion*
- *Syn* allocate, appoint, assign, budget, designate, distribute, dole, earmark, mete, share, slice, split up; *Ant* disallow, keep, retain, withhold.

all-out [adj] *complete*
- *Syn* absolute, determined, entire, exhaustive, full, full-blown, full-fledged, maximum, optimum, resolute, supreme, thorough, total, undivided, unlimited, utmost; *Ant* halfhearted, halfway.

allow [v1] *admit; acknowledge*
- *Syn* acquiesce, avow, concede, confess, grant, let on, own; *Ant* deny, refuse, reject.

allow [v2] *permit an action*
- *Syn* approve, authorize, brook, certify, consent, endorse, favor, grant, hear of, indulge, license, oblige, pass, permit, recognize, stand, tolerate, warrant; *Ant* deny, disallow, disapprove, forbid, prohibit, protest, refuse, reject, resist, withstand.

allow [v3] *set aside*
- *Syn* admeasure, allocate, allot, apportion, assign, deduct, grant, lot, mete, provide, remit, spare; *Ant* hold, keep.

alloy [v1] *mix metals*
- *Syn* admix, amalgamate, blend, combine, compound, fuse, intermix, mix; *Ant* clear, not mix, purify.

alloy [v2] *adulterate*
- *Syn* debase, denature, devalue, diminish, impair, reduce; *Ant* clean, clear, purify.

all right [adj1] *satisfactory*
- *Syn* acceptable, adequate, appropriate, decent, fair, fitting, good, okay, passable, sufficient, swell, tolerable; *Ant* unsatisfactory.

all right [adj2] *in good condition or health* *Syn* hale, healthy, safe, sound, unharmed, unhurt, unimpaired, well, whole; *Ant* sick, unhealthy.

all right [adj3] *correct; excellent*
- *Syn* accurate, exact, good, great, precise, right; *Ant* wrong.

all right [adv1] *satisfactorily*
- *Syn* acceptably, adequately, okay, passably, tolerably, unobjectionably, well enough; *Ant* unsatisfactorily.

all right [adv2] *yes*
- *Syn* agreed, certainly, definitely, of course, okay, positively, surely, very well, without a doubt; *Ant* no.

allude [v] *hint at* *Syn* advert, bring up, imply, insinuate, intimate, point, refer,

suggest; *Ant* advertise, keep quiet, keep secret, trumpet.

allure [v] *entice*
- *Syn* attract, beguile, captivate, charm, draw, enchant, fascinate, inveigle, lure, pull, seduce, tempt, win over; *Ant* deter, discourage, dissuade, prevent, repel, threaten, turn off, warn.

ally [n] *individual or group united with another, especially by treaty* *Syn* accessory, accomplice, associate, coadjutor, collaborator, colleague, confederate, co-worker, friend, helper, partner; *Ant* antagonist, enemy.

almighty [adj1] *having complete power, control* *Syn* absolute, all-powerful, invincible, mighty, omnipotent, puissant, supreme, unlimited; *Ant* insignificant, powerless, weak.

almighty [adj2] *godlike*
- *Syn* all-knowing, boundless, celestial, deific, divine, enduring, everlasting, godly, heavenly, immortal, infinite, omnipotent, pervading; *Ant* lay, lowly.

almost [adv] *nearly, very nearly*
- *Syn* about, approximately, around, bordering on, close to, essentially, just about, most, near to, nigh, practically, relatively, roughly, substantially, virtually; *Ant* certainly, definitely, exactly, surely.

alone [adj1] *separate; apart*
- *Syn* abandoned, by itself/oneself, companionless, forsaken, hermit, individual, isolated, lonesome, only, on one's own, single, sole, solitary, solo; *Ant* accompanied, attended, together.

alone [adj2] *to the exclusion of; unique*
- *Syn* incomparable, matchless, peerless, singular, solely, unequalled, unique, unsurpassed; *Ant* among others, equaled, equally, overshadowed, surpassed.

along [adv1] *together with*
- *Syn* accompanying, additionally, also, as companion, as well, besides, coupled with, furthermore, in addition to, likewise, moreover, side by side, simultaneously, too, with; *Ant* apart, separate.

along [adv2] *near*
- *Syn* adjacent, at, by; *Ant* far.

aloof [adj] *remote*
- *Syn* apart, cold, cool, detached, distant, forbidding, hard-hearted, indifferent, reserved, supercilious, withdrawn; *Ant* approachable, concerned, friendly, sociable.

aloud [adv] *in a spoken voice, usually not softly* ▪ **Syn** audibly, clearly, distinctly, intelligibly, loudly, lustily, noisily, out loud, plainly, vociferously; ▪ **Ant** inaudibly, silently.

alter [v] *change* ▪ **Syn** adjust, amend, convert, diversify, metamorphose, modify, recast, refashion, renovate, revise, shift, transform, vary; ▪ **Ant** continue, fix, keep, let stand, maintain, preserve, remain, retain, sustain.

altercation [n] *fight, often verbal* ▪ **Syn** argument, combat, contest, controversy, dispute, embroilment, hassle, quarrel, row, wrangle; ▪ **Ant** agreement, concord, harmony, peace, union, unity.

alternate [adj] *substitute* ▪ **Syn** alternative, another, backup, different, interchangeable, makeshift, second, surrogate, temporary; ▪ **Ant** essential, necessary, original, required, requisite.

alternative [n] *possible choice* ▪ **Syn** back-up, option, other, pick, preference, recourse, redundancy, selection, substitute; ▪ **Ant** compulsion, constraint, necessity, obligation, restraint.

altitude [n] *height in the sky* ▪ **Syn** apex, distance, elevation, eminence, loftiness, peak, summit; ▪ **Ant** abyss, depth, pit.

altogether [adv1] *as a whole* ▪ **Syn** all, all things considered, bodily, collectively, conjointly, en masse, in all, in sum, in toto, on the whole; ▪ **Ant** partly.

altogether [adv2] *completely* ▪ **Syn** absolutely, fully, perfectly, quite, thoroughly, totally, utterly, well, wholly; ▪ **Ant** incompletely.

altruistic [adj] *unselfish* ▪ **Syn** benevolent, charitable, generous, humanitarian, kind, magnanimous, openhanded, philanthropic, self-sacrificing; ▪ **Ant** selfish, unsacrificing.

always [adv] *forever; continually* ▪ **Syn** constantly, eternally, ever, everlastingly, evermore, forevermore, in perpetuum, invariably, perpetually, unceasingly; ▪ **Ant** at no time, never.

amalgamate [v] *blend* ▪ **Syn** alloy, coalesce, combine, compound, consolidate, fuse, incorporate, join together, meld, merge, network, pool, tie in, unite; ▪ **Ant** divide, separate.

amass [v] *gather, accumulate* ▪ **Syn** aggregate, assemble, collect, compile, garner, hoard, pile, stockpile, store; ▪ **Ant** disburse, disperse, dissipate, divide, dole, scatter, spend.

amateur [n] *casual participant* ▪ **Syn** abecedarian, apprentice, aspirant, beginner, dabbler, dilettante, greenhorn, hopeful, learner, neophyte, novice, probationer, recruit; ▪ **Ant** professional.

amatory [adj] *affectionate, desirous* ▪ **Syn** admiring, ardent, attracted, devoted, doting, erotic, fervent, fond, languishing, loving, passionate, rapturous, tender, yearning; ▪ **Ant** hateful, unfriendly.

amazement [n] *state of surprise* ▪ **Syn** astonishment, awe, bewilderment, confoundment, marvel, perplexity, shock, stupefaction, wonder; ▪ **Ant** calmness, composure, cool, coolness, indifference, preparation.

ambiguous [adj] *having more than one meaning* ▪ **Syn** cryptic, dubious, enigmatic, equivocal, indeterminate, obscure, puzzling, questionable, tenebrous, unclear, unintelligible, vague; ▪ **Ant** clear, definite, explicit, lucid.

ambitious [adj1] *desiring success* ▪ **Syn** aggressive, aspiring, avid, determined, eager, energetic, enterprising, enthusiastic, high-reaching, hungry, industrious, intent, purposeful, resourceful, sharp, thirsty, vaulting, zealous; ▪ **Ant** content, fulfilled, satisfied, unassuming.

ambitious [adj2] *requiring great effort, ability* ▪ **Syn** arduous, bold, challenging, demanding, difficult, elaborate, formidable, grandiose, hard, impressive, lofty, pretentious, strenuous, visionary; ▪ **Ant** easy, facile.

ambivalent [adj] *conflicting* ▪ **Syn** clashing, contradictory, debatable, doubtful, equivocal, fluctuating, hesitant, inconclusive, irresolute, mixed, opposed, uncertain, undecided, unresolved, unsure, vacillating, warring, wavering; ▪ **Ant** certain, definite, resolved, settled, sure, unequivocal

amble [v] *walk casually* ▪ **Syn** dawdle, drift, gander, loiter, meander, ramble, saunter, stroll, wander; ▪ **Ant** hurry, race, run, rush.

ambulatory [adj] *changing position; able to move under own power* ▪ **Syn** itinerant, nomadic, perambulant, perambulatory, peripatetic, roving, vagabond, vagrant; ▪ **Ant** steady, stiff, unchanging.

ameliorate [v] *make, become better*
▪ *Syn* alleviate, amend, help, improve, lighten, meliorate, mitigate, relieve, step up, upgrade; ▪ *Ant* decline, deteriorate, weaken, worsen.

amenable [adj1] *willing, cooperative*
▪ *Syn* acquiescent, agreeable, biddable, docile, influenceable, manageable, obedient, open, persuadable, pliable, responsive, susceptible, tractable; ▪ *Ant* intractable, nonconforming, uncooperative, unwilling.

amenable [adj2] *able to be judged; responsible* ▪ *Syn* accountable, answerable, chargeable, liable, subject; ▪ *Ant* irresponsible, not responsible, unaccountable, unanswerable.

amend [v] *improve, correct*
▪ *Syn* alter, ameliorate, change, enhance, mend, modify, rectify, remedy, repair, revise, right; ▪ *Ant* blemish, corrupt, debase, depress, harm, impair, injure, mar, reduce, subtract, worsen.

amiable [adj] *friendly, agreeable*
▪ *Syn* affable, amicable, benign, charming, complaisant, cordial, friendly, genial, good-humored, kind, obliging, pleasant, responsive, sociable, warm, winning; ▪ *Ant* crabby, disagreeable, gloomy, hateful, irritable, mean, quarrelsome, rude, surly, testy, unfriendly.

amicable [adj] *friendly, especially regarding an agreement* ▪ *Syn* accordant, amiable, concordant, courteous, empathic, good-humored, harmonious, kind, like-minded, mellow, neighborly, pacific, peaceable, sympathetic, understanding; ▪ *Ant* hostile, unfriendly.

amid/amidst [prep] *in the middle of; among* ▪ *Syn* amongst, between, during, in the thick of, mid, surrounded by, throughout; ▪ *Ant* away from, outside, separate.

amiss [adj] *wrong; imperfect*
▪ *Syn* awry, bad, confused, erroneous, fallacious, flawed, haywire, imperfect, improper, inaccurate, incorrect, mistaken; ▪ *Ant* good, right, suitable.

among [prep] *in the middle of; between* ▪ *Syn* amid, amidst, betwixt, in the midst of, in the thick of, mid, surrounded by, with; ▪ *Ant* away from, outside, separate.

amorous [adj] *loving, affectionate*
▪ *Syn* amatory, ardent, doting, enamored, erotic, fond, infatuated, lovesick, lustful, passionate, romantic; ▪ *Ant* cold, cool, frigid, hateful, indifferent, unfriendly.

amorphous [adj] *without definite shape, character*
▪ *Syn* characterless, formless, inchoate indeterminate, nebulous, nondescript, shapeless, vague; ▪ *Ant* definite, distinct, distinctive, shaped, shapely.

ample [adj] *more than necessary, sufficient* ▪ *Syn* abundant, bountiful, broad, capacious, commodious, extensive, full, generous, great, heavy, large, liberal, plentiful, profuse, rich, roomy, spacious, spare, substantial, unrestricted, voluminous, wide; ▪ *Ant* insufficient, meager, not enough.

amplify [v] *increase in size or effect*
▪ *Syn* add, augment, boost, build up, deepen, develop, elaborate, exaggerate, expand, extend, heighten, inflate, intensify, lengthen, magnify, pad, pyramid, raise, strengthen, stretch, supplement, swell, widen; ▪ *Ant* abridge, compress, condense, contract, curtail, decrease, lessen, reduce, shorten, summarize.

amply [adv] *fully, sufficiently*
▪ *Syn* abundantly, adequately, bountifully, capaciously, copiously, enough, extensively, fittingly, generously, lavishly, liberally, plentifully, profusely, properly, richly, satisfactorily, substantially, thoroughly, well; ▪ *Ant* illiberal, inadequately, insufficiently.

amuse [v] *entertain; make laugh*
▪ *Syn* charm, cheer, delight, divert, gladden, gratify, interest, occupy, please, regale, tickle; ▪ *Ant* anger, annoy, bore, dull, tire, upset.

amusing [adj] *entertaining, funny*
▪ *Syn* agreeable, charming, cheerful, cheering, comical, delightful, diverting, droll, enchanting, engaging, enjoyable, entertaining, fun, gladdening, gratifying, humorous, interesting, jocular, laughable, lively, merry, pleasant, pleasing, priceless, witty; ▪ *Ant* annoying, boring, tiring, unfunny.

analogous [adj] *agreeing, similar*
▪ *Syn* akin, alike, comparable, consonant, correspondent, equivalent, homologous, interchangeable, kindred, like, parallel, related, resembling, uniform; ▪ *Ant* disagreeing, disparate, dissimilar, unalike, unlike, unrelated.

analytic/analytical [adj] *examining and determining* ▪ *Syn* cogent, diagnostic, dissecting, expository, inquiring, interpretive, investigative, judicious, logical, organized, penetrating, perceptive, perspicuous, questioning, rational, scientific, searching, systematic, testing; ▪ **Ant** chaotic, disorganized, illogical, unsystematic.

analyze [v1] *examine and determine* ▪ **Syn** assay, consider, estimate, evaluate, figure, interpret, judge, resolve, scrutinize, sort out, study, test, think through; ▪ **Ant** ignore, neglect, overlook, pass over, pay no heed to.

analyze [v2] *break down to components* ▪ **Syn** anatomize, break up, cut up, decompose, decompound, determine, disintegrate, dissect, dissolve, divide, electrolyze, hydrolyze, lay bare, parse, part, resolve, separate, x-ray; ▪ **Ant** assemble, combine, compose, compound, construct, integrate, synthesize, unite.

anarchy [n] *lawlessness; absence of government* ▪ **Syn** chaos, confusion, disorder, disorganization, misrule, mob rule, nihilism, nongovernment, rebellion, reign of terror, revolution, riot, turmoil, unrest; ▪ **Ant** lawfulness, order, rule.

anathema [n1] *something hated* ▪ **Syn** abomination, bane, bugbear, detestation, enemy, hate, pariah; ▪ **Ant** beloved, love, welcomed.

anathema [n2] *denouncement* ▪ **Syn** ban, censure, commination, condemnation, curse, damnation, denunciation, excommunication, execration, imprecation, malediction, proscription, reprehension, reprobation, reproof; ▪ **Ant** benediction, blessing.

ancestry [n] *family predecessors; family history* ▪ **Syn** ancestor, antecedent, blood, breed, derivation, extraction, forebear, foregoer, forerunner, genealogy, heritage, kindred, line, lineage, origin, parentage, pedigree, precursor, progenitor, race, source, stock; ▪ **Ant** descendants, posterity, progeny issue.

anchor [v] *hold, be held securely* ▪ **Syn** attach, berth, catch, dock, drop, fasten, fix, imbed, make port, moor, plant, secure, stay, tie; ▪ **Ant** break free, detach, let go, lift anchor, loosen, unfasten, weigh anchor.

ancient [adj] *old, often very old* ▪ **Syn** aged, age-old, antiquated, antique, archaic, bygone, elderly, obsolete, older, old-fashioned, outmoded, out-of-date, primal, primeval, primordial, remote, rusty, timeworn, venerable; ▪ **Ant** modern, new, young.

ancillary [adj] *extra; supplementary* ▪ **Syn** accessory, accompanying, additional, adjuvant, attendant, attending, coincident, collateral, concomitant, contributory, incident, satellite, secondary, subordinate, subsidiary; ▪ **Ant** necessary, needed.

anemic [adj] *weak and pale* ▪ **Syn** bloodless, feeble, frail, infirm, pallid, sickly, wan, watery; ▪ **Ant** flushed, strong.

anesthetic/anaesthetic [n] *sleep-inducing or numbing drug* ▪ **Syn** analgesic, anodyne, gas, hypnotic, inhalant, opiate, pain-killer, shot, soporific, spinal; ▪ **Ant** analeptic, stimulant.

anew [adj/adv] *fresh; again* ▪ **Syn** afresh, another time, come again, de novo, from scratch, from the beginning, in a different way, in a new way, lately, new, newly, once again, once more, one more time, over, over again, recently; ▪ **Ant** never again, nevermore.

angelic [adj] *sweet, kind, and usually beautiful* ▪ **Syn** adorable, beatific, beneficent, celestial, cherubic, devout, divine, entrancing, ethereal, godly, good, heavenly, holy, humble, innocent, lovely, otherworldly, pure, radiant, rapturous, righteous, saintly, self-sacrificing, seraphic, virtuous; ▪ **Ant** demonic, devilish, fiendish, unkind.

anger [v] *make someone mad; become mad* ▪ **Syn** acerbate, aggravate, agitate, annoy, antagonize, arouse, bait, bristle, chafe, cross, displease, embitter, enrage, fret, gall, goad, incense, inflame, infuriate, irritate, madden, nettle, offend, pique, provoke, rankle, ruffle, seethe, stew, vex; ▪ **Ant** calm, forbear, make happy, quiet, soothe.

angry [adj] *being mad, often extremely mad* ▪ **Syn** annoyed, antagonized, bitter, chafed, choleric, displeased, enraged, exasperated, ferocious, fierce, fuming, furious, galled, hateful, heated, ill-tempered, incensed, inflamed, infuriated, irate, maddened, nettled, offended, outraged, piqued, provoked, resentful, riled, sore, splenetic, tumultuous/tumultuous, turbulent, uptight, vexed, wrathful; ▪ **Ant** calm, collected, content, happy, joyful, joyous.

anguish [n] *severe upset or pain* ▪ **Syn** affliction, agony, dolor, grief, heartache, heartbreak, hurting, misery, pang, rue, sorrow, suffering, throe, torment, torture, woe, wretchedness; ▪ *Ant* comfort, contentment, happiness, joy, joyfulness, solace.

angular [*adj1*] *bent*
▪ *Syn* akimbo, bifurcate, cornered, crooked, crossing, crotched, divaricate, forked, intersecting, jagged, oblique, sharp-cornered, skewed, slanted, staggered, V-shaped, Y-shaped, zigzag; ▪ *Ant* straight.

angular [*adj2*] *thin, especially referring to people* ▪ *Syn* awkward, bony, gaunt, lank, lanky, lean, rangy, rawboned, scrawny, sharp, skinny, spare; ▪ *Ant* fat, heavy, thick, weighted.

animal [*adj*] *beastlike; carnal*
▪ *Syn* beastly, bestial, bodily, brute, brutish, corporeal, earthly, feral, fleshy, mammalian, muscular, natural, physical, sensual, wild, zoological; ▪ *Ant* delicate, genteel, intellectual, reasoning, refined, spiritual.

animate [*adj1*] *alive*
▪ *Syn* breathing, live, living, mortal, moving, viable, vital, zoetic; ▪ *Ant* dead.

animate [*adj2*] *lively*
▪ *Syn* activated, active, alert, animated, dynamic, energized, gay, happy, spirited, vivacious; ▪ *Ant* discouraged, dull, quiet, shy, spiritless.

animate [*v*] *bring to life*
▪ *Syn* activate, arouse, cheer, energize, enliven, exalt, fire, hearten, impel, incite, instigate, invigorate, kindle, liven, move, quicken, revive, rouse, spark, spur, stimulate, urge, vitalize, vivify; ▪ *Ant* deaden, discourage, kill.

animated [*adj*] *lively*
▪ *Syn* activated, alert, animate, ardent, brisk, buoyant, dynamic, ebullient, energized, enthusiastic, excited, fervent, gay, happy, passionate, peppy, quick, sprightly, vibrant, vigorous, vitalized, vivacious, zealous, zestful; ▪ *Ant* apathetic, boring, depressed, devitalized, disheartened, dull, inert, lethargic, lifeless, listless, monotonous, sluggish, spiritless, stolid.

animosity [*n*] *extreme dislike, hatred*
▪ *Syn* acrimony, antagonism, antipathy, bad blood, bitterness, displeasure, enmity, hostility, malevolence, malice, rancor, resentment, virulence; ▪ *Ant* affection, friendship, good will, harmony, love.

annex [*v*] *join or add*
▪ *Syn* adjoin, affix, append, appropriate,

associate, attach, connect, fasten, join, link, subjoin, tag, take on, take over, unite; ▪ *Ant* detach, disconnect, leave off, leave out, separate, truncate.

annihilate [*v*] *destroy completely*
▪ *Syn* abolish, annul, decimate, demolish, eradicate, expunge, exterminate, extinguish, extirpate, invalidate, liquidate, murder, nullify, obliterate, quash, quell, ruin, slaughter, vitiate, wreck; ▪ *Ant* help, preserve, revive, save.

announce [*v1*] *make a proclamation*
▪ *Syn* advertise, blazon, broadcast, communicate, declare, divulge, impart, intimate, issue, make known, make public, proclaim, promulgate, publicize, publish, release, reveal, state, tell, trumpet; ▪ *Ant* bottle up, conceal, keep secret, refrain, repress, suppress, withhold.

announce [*v2*] *declare arrival*
▪ *Syn* augur, forebode, forecast, forerun, foreshadow, foretell, herald, indicate, portend, predict, presage, signal, signify; ▪ *Ant* be quiet, hide, withhold.

annoy [*v*] *irritate, upset*
▪ *Syn* abrade, agitate, badger, bedevil, beleaguer, chafe, displease, disturb, exasperate, gall, harry, irk, madden, needle, peeve, perturb, pester, ride, ruffle, tease, vex, worry; ▪ *Ant* aid, gratify, make happy, please, soothe.

annul [*v*] *void an agreement*
▪ *Syn* abate, abolish, abrogate, annihilate, cancel, countermand, declare, dissolve, expunge, invalidate, kill, negate, neutralize, nullify, obliterate, quash, recall, retract, revoke, vacate, vitiate; ▪ *Ant* keep, restore, retain, revalidate, validate.

anomalous [*adj*] *deviating from normal, usual* ▪ *Syn* aberrant, abnormal, atypical, bizarre, divergent, eccentric, exceptional, foreign, heteroclite, incongruous, inconsistent, irregular, odd, peculiar, preternatural, rare, strange; ▪ *Ant* conforming, natural, normal, regular, standard, typical, usual.

anonymous [*adj*] *unknown, usually by choice* ▪ *Syn* incognito, innominate, nameless, pseudonymous, secret, unacknowledged, unattested, unavowed, unclaimed, uncredited, undisclosed, unsigned, unspecified; ▪ *Ant* designated, identified, known, named.

answer [*v1*] *reply, react*
▪ *Syn* acknowledge, answer back, argue, claim, contest, counterclaim, defend, deny, disprove, dispute, echo, explain,

feedback, parry, plead, rebut, refute, re-join, remark, resolve, respond, retaliate, retort, return, say, settle, solve, squelch; ▪ *Ant* ask, question.

answer [v2] *solve; fulfill*
▪ *Syn* clarify, conform, correlate, corre-spond, dope, elucidate, fill, measure up, meet, pass, qualify, satisfy, serve, suf-fice, suit, work, work through; ▪ *Ant* differ, fail.

answerable [adj] *responsible*
▪ *Syn* accountable, amenable, bound, chargeable, compelled, constrained, lia-ble, obligated, obliged, subject; ▪ *Ant* irrefutable, unaccountable, unprovable.

antagonize [v] *cause problem; oppose*
▪ *Syn* alienate, anger, annoy, counteract, estrange, insult, irritate, offend, repel, struggle, work against; ▪ *Ant* agree, aid, help.

antecedent [adj] *prior*
▪ *Syn* anterior, earlier, foregoing, former, past, precedent, preceding, precursory, preliminary, previous; ▪ *Ant* after, fol-lowing.

antedate [v] *occur or cause to occur earlier* ▪ *Syn* antecede, backdate, fore-run, misdate, pace, precede, predate; ▪ *Ant* predate.

antediluvian [adj] *out-of-date; prehis-toric* ▪ *Syn* age-old, ancient, antiquated, antique, archaic, hoary, obsolete, old, old-fashioned, pass, primeval, primitive, primordial, timeworn, venerable; ▪ *Ant* modern, new, up-to-date, young.

anterior [adj] *beginning, prior*
▪ *Syn* antecedent, foregoing, former, past, precedent, preceding, previous; ▪ *Ant* ending, posterior, subsequent.

anticipate [v1] *expect; predict*
▪ *Syn* assume, await, conjecture, divine, forecast, foretell, hope for, look forward to, plan on, prepare for, prognosticate, prophesy, see, suppose, visualize, wait; ▪ *Ant* be amazed, be surprised, doubt.

anticipate [v2] *act in advance of*
▪ *Syn* apprehend, block, delay, forestall, hinder, intercept, precede, preclude, pre-pare for, prevent, provide against; ▪ *Ant* be unready.

anticlimax [n] *ineffective conclusion*
▪ *Syn* bathos, comedown, decline, de-scent, disappointment, drop, letdown, slump; ▪ *Ant* climax.

antidote [n] *counteracting agent*
▪ *Syn* antitoxin, corrective, counteragent, countermeasure, cure, medicine, negator,

neutralizer, nullifier, preventive, remedy; ▪ *Ant* poison, venom.

antipathy [n] *strong dislike, disgust*
▪ *Syn* abhorrence, allergy, animus, antag-onism, aversion, contrariety, distaste, dyspathy, enmity, hatred, hostility, ill will, loathing, opposition, rancor, repug-nance, repulsion; ▪ *Ant* admiration, ap-preciation, approval, esteem, honor, like, liking, love, rapport, regard, respect, sympathy.

antiquated [adj] *obsolete, old*
▪ *Syn* aged, ancient, antediluvian, an-tique, archaic, dated, elderly, hoary, moldy, obsolescent, old, old-fashioned, outmoded, out-of-date, outworn, super-annuated; ▪ *Ant* forward-looking, mod-ern, new, recent.

antique [adj1] *old*
▪ *Syn* aged, ancient, obsolescent, obso-lete, outdated, prehistoric, superannu-ated; ▪ *Ant* modern, new, recent, up-to-date.

antique [adj2] *old-fashioned*
▪ *Syn* antiquarian, archaic, classic, obso-lete, olden, outdated, vintage; ▪ *Ant* current, fresh, modern.

antiseptic [adj] *completely clean, un-contaminated; decontaminating* ▪ *Syn* antibacterial, antibiotic, aseptic, bacteri-cidal, clean, disinfectant, germicidal, hygienic, medicated, prophylactic, puri-fying, sanitary, sterile; ▪ *Ant* con-taminated, polluted, unclean, unsanitary, unsterile.

antisocial [adj] *nonparticipating; avoid-ing company* ▪ *Syn* alienated, austere, cold, eremitic, introverted, misanthropic, reclusive, reserved, solitary, standoffish, withdrawn; ▪ *Ant* friendly, fun-loving, participating, sociable.

antithesis [n] *contrast, opposition*
▪ *Syn* antagonism, contradiction, contra-distinction, contraposition, contrariety, inversion, opposure, reversal; ▪ *Ant* same.

antonym [n] *word with opposite meaning to another word* ▪ *Syn* opposite, reverse; ▪ *Ant* synonym.

anxious [adj1] *worried, tense*
▪ *Syn* afraid, apprehensive, careful, con-cerned, disquieted, distressed, dreading, fearful, jumpy, nervous, overwrought, restless, scared, solicitous, taut, troubled, watchful; ▪ *Ant* assured, calm, content, content, cool, happy, indifferent, peace-ful, tranquil, unconcerned, unworried.

anxious [adj2] *eager*
▪ **Syn** agog, ardent, avid, breathless, desirous, enthusiastic, expectant, fervent, impatient, intent, keen, thirsty, yearning, zealous; ▪ **Ant** dreading, unwilling.

apart [adv] *separate*
▪ **Syn** afar, alone, aloof, disassociated, disconnected, distant, divorced, excluded, freely, independent, independently, isolated, separated, separately, singly, special; ▪ **Ant** adjoining, near, surrounded, together.

apathetic [adj] *uncaring, disinterested*
▪ **Syn** callous, cold, emotionless, flat, impassive, indifferent, languid, passive, stoic, stolid, unresponsive; ▪ **Ant** caring, concerned, interested, responsive.

apex [n] *top, high point*
▪ **Syn** acme, apogee, climax, crest, crown, culmination, cusp, greatest, height, maximum, meridian, ne plus ultra, peak, pinnacle, point, roof, spire, sublimity, summit, tip, tops, vertex, zenith; ▪ **Ant** abyss, nadir, perigee, rock bottom.

apiece [adv] *each*
▪ **Syn** all, aside, for each, from each, individually, one by one, per, respectively, separately, severally, singly, successively, to each; ▪ **Ant** all together, as a group, collectively, en masse, overall, together.

apocryphal [adj] *questionable; fake*
▪ **Syn** counterfeit, doubtful, dubious, equivocal, false, fictitious, inaccurate, mythical, spurious, wrong; ▪ **Ant** authentic, doubtless, real, true.

apologetic [adj] *expressing remorse, regret* ▪ **Syn** attritional, conciliatory, contrite, expiatory, penitential, propitiatory, regretful, remorseful, repentant, self-effacing, self-incriminating, sorry, supplicating; ▪ **Ant** defiant, defying, recalcitrant, recusant, resistant, unyielding.

apologize [v] *express remorse, regret*
▪ **Syn** admit guilt, ask forgiveness, ask pardon, atone, beg pardon, confess, excuse oneself, make amends, offer compensation, offer excuse, purge, retract, withdraw; ▪ **Ant** defy.

apostate [n] *traitor*
▪ **Syn** backslider, defector, deserter, dissenter, heretic, nonconformist, recreant, renegade; ▪ **Ant** adherent, faithful, loyalist.

apostle [n] *preacher; supporter*
▪ **Syn** advocate, champion, companion, converter, evangelist, follower, herald, messenger, missionary, pioneer, propagandist, proponent, proselytizer, witness; ▪ **Ant** detractor, opponent.

appall/appal [v] *horrify*
▪ **Syn** alarm, amaze, astound, awe, consternate, daunt, disconcert, faze, frighten, insult, outrage, petrify, scare, terrify, throw, unnerve; ▪ **Ant** comfort, encourage, reassure, satisfy.

appalling [adj] *horrifying*
▪ **Syn** alarming, astounding, awful, daunting, dire, dismaying, dreadful, fearful, formidable, frightful, ghastly, grim, harrowing, hideous, horrific, intimidating, terrible; ▪ **Ant** comforting, encouraging, reassuring, satisfying.

apparent [adj1] *seeming, not proven real*
▪ **Syn** credible, illusive, illusory, likely, ostensible, outward, plausible, possible, probable, semblant, specious, superficial, supposed, supposititious; ▪ **Ant** doubtful, dubious, equivocal, hidden, improbable, obscure, questionable, uncertain, unclear, unlikely.

apparent [adj2] *obvious*
▪ **Syn** barefaced, clear, conspicuous, discernible, distinct, evident, glaring, indubitable, manifest, marked, noticeable, observable, overt, palpable, patent, perceivable, self-evident, transparent, understandable, visible; ▪ **Ant** ambiguous, disguised, doubtful, equivocal, indistinct, uncertain, unclear, veiled.

apparently [adv1] *seemingly*
▪ **Syn** allegedly, as though, most likely, ostensibly, outwardly, plausibly, possibly, professedly, reasonably, reputably, speciously, superficially, supposedly, tangibly, to all appearances; ▪ **Ant** dubiously, equivocally, improbably, questionably, uncertainly, unlikely.

appeal [v1] *request*
▪ **Syn** address, adjure, advance, apply, ask, beg, beseech, bid, call upon, claim, contest, crave, demand, entreat, implore, importune, petition, plead, pray, propose, proposition, question, refer, require, solicit, strike, submit, sue, supplicate, urge; ▪ **Ant** deny, disclaim, recall, refuse, renounce, retract, revoke.

appeal [v2] *attract, interest*
▪ **Syn** allure, beguile, captivate, catch the eye, charm, enchant, engage, entice, fascinate, intrigue, invite, please, tantalize,

tempt; ▪ *Ant* disgust, repel, turn away, turn off.

appear [v1] *come into sight*
▪ *Syn* arise, arrive, attend, be within view, break through, come forth, come into view, develop, emerge, expose, issue, loom, materialize, occur, present, recur, rise, show, spring, surface; ▪ *Ant* disappear, hide, recede, vanish.

appear [v2] *be obvious, clear*
▪ *Syn* be apparent, be evident, be manifest, be patent, be plain; ▪ *Ant* be doubtful, be uncertain, be unclear, be unknown.

appease [v] *satisfy, pacify*
▪ *Syn* allay, alleviate, assuage, blunt, calm, conciliate, content, diminish, ease, gratify, lessen, lull, meet halfway, mitigate, mollify, placate, propitiate, quell, quiet, soften, soothe, subdue, tranquilize; ▪ *Ant* aggravate, annoy, incite, irritate, provoke, tease.

append [v] *add, join*
▪ *Syn* adjoin, affix, annex, attach, conjoin, fasten, fix, subjoin, supplement; ▪ *Ant* disjoin, subtract, take away.

appendix [n] *added material at end of document* ▪ *Syn* addendum, addition, adjunct, appendage, appurtenance, attachment, codicil, excursus, index, notes, postscript, rider, sample, supplement, table, verification; ▪ *Ant* front matter, introduction, introductory material, main body.

appertain [v] *belong, be connected*
▪ *Syn* apply, bear, be part of, be pertinent, be proper, be relevant, have to do with, pertain, refer, relate, touch upon, vest; ▪ *Ant* be irrelevant, be unrelated to, have no bearing upon.

appetizing [adj] *tasting very good*
▪ *Syn* aperitive, appealing, delectable, delicious, flavorsome, heavenly, inviting, luscious, mouthwatering, palatable, saporous, savory, scrumptious, succulent, tantalizing, tasty, tempting, toothsome; ▪ *Ant* disgusting, distasteful, unappetizing, unsavory.

applaud [v] *clap for; express approval*
▪ *Syn* acclaim, approve, boost, cheer, commend, compliment, encourage, eulogize, extol, give ovation, glorify, hail, laud, magnify, praise, rave, recommend; ▪ *Ant* boo, censure, criticize, deride, disparage, keep silent.

applicable [adj] *appropriate*
▪ *Syn* applicative, apposite, apropos, apt,

befitting, felicitous, fit, fitting, germane, kosher, material, pertinent, relevant, suitable, to the point, useful; ▪ *Ant* inapplicable, inappropriate, unsuitable.

apply [v] *work hard*
▪ *Syn* address, bear down, be diligent, be industrious, bend, commit, concentrate, dedicate, devote, dig, direct, give, grind, make effort, persevere, scratch, study, throw, try, turn; ▪ *Ant* let slide, neglect, pass over, slight.

appoint [v] *assign responsibility; decide*
▪ *Syn* accredit, allot, assign, choose, commission, delegate, designate, determine, elect, enjoin, establish, fix, install, name, nominate, ordain, select; ▪ *Ant* discharge, dismiss, fire, refuse, reject.

apportion [v] *divide into shares*
▪ *Syn* accord, admeasure, administer, allocate, allot, assign, bestow, deal, dispense, distribute, dole out, lot, measure, mete, parcel, part, partition, prorate, quota, ration, slice; ▪ *Ant* hold, keep, monopolize, withhold.

appreciable [adj] *easily noticed; considerable* ▪ *Syn* apparent, ascertainable, discernible, estimable, evident, healthy, large, manifest, marked, material, measurable, observable, obvious, perceptible, plain, recognizable, sizable, substantial, tangible, visible; ▪ *Ant* imperceptible, inconsiderable, negligible, unappreciable, unnoticed.

appreciate [v1] *be grateful, thankful*
▪ *Syn* acknowledge, be indebted, be obliged, enjoy, give thanks, welcome; ▪ *Ant* be critical, criticize, disparage, disregard, neglect, overlook.

appreciate [v2] *increase in worth*
▪ *Syn* enhance, gain, grow, improve, inflate, raise the value of, rise; ▪ *Ant* decrease, depreciate, lose value.

appreciate [v3] *recognize worth*
▪ *Syn* acknowledge, be aware of, be conscious of, comprehend, fathom, grasp, know, perceive, read, realize, savvy, take account of, understand; ▪ *Ant* be insensitive to, be unaware of, ignore, misconceive, misjudge, misunderstand, neglect.

appreciate [v4] *value highly*
▪ *Syn* admire, adore, applaud, apprise, cherish, enjoy, esteem, extol, honor, like, look up to, love, praise, prize, rate highly, regard, respect, savor, treasure; ▪ *Ant* underestimate, underrate, undervalue.

appreciative [*adj*] *thankful*
▪ *Syn* beholden, grateful, indebted, obliged, responsive; ▪ *Ant* unappreciative, ungrateful.

apprehend [*v1*] *catch and arrest*
▪ *Syn* capture, collar, grab, nab, place under arrest, seize, take in, take into custody; ▪ *Ant* discharge, free, liberate, lose, not catch, release.

apprehend [*v2*] *understand*
▪ *Syn* absorb, appreciate, believe, catch, comprehend, conceive, digest, fathom, grasp, imagine, know, perceive, read, realize, recognize, sense, think; ▪ *Ant* misunderstand.

apprehensive [*adj*] *anxious, fearful*
▪ *Syn* afraid, alarmed, concerned, disquieted, doubtful, foreboding, mistrustful, stiff, suspicious, troubled, uncertain, uneasy, uptight, worried; ▪ *Ant* at ease, calm, quiet, unafraid, undoubting, unsuspicious, unworried.

apprentice [*n*] *novice/learner of a trade*
▪ *Syn* amateur, beginner, neophyte, newcomer, novitiate, probationer, pupil, starter, student, tyro; ▪ *Ant* expert, mentor, teacher.

approach [*n*] *way, means of arriving*
▪ *Syn* access, advance, advent, avenue, coming, drawing near, entrance, gate, landing, nearing, passage, path, reaching, road, way; ▪ *Ant* departure, distancing, leaving.

approach [*v1*] *come nearer*
▪ *Syn* advance, approximate, bear, border, come close, contact, converge, correspond to, draw near, equal, gain on, impend, loom, match, meet, progress, resemble, surround, take after, threaten, verge upon; ▪ *Ant* depart, distance, go away, leave.

approach [*v2*] *begin*
▪ *Syn* commence, embark, set about, start, undertake; ▪ *Ant* draw away, end, finish, leave.

approachable [*adj1*] *accessible*
▪ *Syn* attainable, convenient, obtainable, reachable; ▪ *Ant* formal, inaccessible, unapproachable, unreachable.

approachable [*adj2*] *friendly*
▪ *Syn* affable, agreeable, congenial, cordial, open, receptive, sociable; ▪ *Ant* uncongenial, unfriendly, unsociable.

approbation [*n*] *praise*
▪ *Syn* admiration, approval, consent, endorsement, esteem, favor, high regard, okay, permission, recognition, sanction, support; ▪ *Ant* criticism, disapprobation.

appropriate [*adj*] *suitable*
▪ *Syn* adapted, appurtenant, apropos, apt, befitting, congruous, correct, desired, due, felicitous, fitting, germane, just, opportune, pertinent, proper, relevant, right, useful, well-suited, well-timed; ▪ *Ant* improper, unbecoming, unfitting, unseemly, unsuitable, unsuited.

appropriate [*v1*] *set aside; allocate*
▪ *Syn* allot, allow, appoint, apportion, assign, budget, devote, disburse, earmark, reserve, set apart; ▪ *Ant* keep, refuse, reject.

appropriate [*v2*] *steal*
▪ *Syn* annex, confiscate, embezzle, hijack, liberate, misappropriate, pilfer, pocket, secure, snatch, usurp; ▪ *Ant* bequeath, bestow, give, return.

appropriation [*n1*] *allocation, setting aside* ▪ *Syn* allotment, allowance, apportionment, assignment, concession, donation, grant, provision, stipend, stipulation, subsidy; ▪ *Ant* keeping, refusal, rejection.

approve [*v1*] *agree something is good*
▪ *Syn* accept, acclaim, admire, applaud, appreciate, approbate, commend, countenance, esteem, favor, go along with, like, praise, regard highly, respect, think highly of; ▪ *Ant* disagree, disapprove.

approve [*v2*] *allow, authorize*
▪ *Syn* accede, advocate, affirm, assent, authorize, certify, concur, confirm, consent, empower, encourage, endorse, license, mandate, permit, pronounce, ratify, recommend, sanction, second, support, uphold, validate; ▪ *Ant* disallow, disapprove, invalidate, oppose, refuse, reject.

approximate [*adj1*] *almost accurate, or act* ▪ *Syn* almost, close, comparative, near, proximate, relative, rough; ▪ *Ant* accurate, certain, clear, definite, exact, precise.

approximate [*adj2*] *similar*
▪ *Syn* alike, analogous, close, comparable, like, matching, near, relative, resembling, verging on; ▪ *Ant* different, dissimilar, exact, same.

approximate [*adj3*] *near*
▪ *Syn* adjacent, bordering, close together, contiguous, nearby, neighboring; ▪ *Ant* away, far.

approximately [adv] nearly
▪ *Syn* about, almost, around, bordering on, circa, closely, comparatively, generally, in the neighborhood of, in the vicinity of, loosely, not far from, not quite, relatively, roughly; ▪ *Ant* accurately, clearly, definitely, exactly, precisely.

apropos [adj] relevant, suitable
▪ *Syn* apposite, appropriate, apt, belonging, correct, fitting, germane, material, opportune, pertinent, proper, right, seemly; ▪ *Ant* inappropriate, irrelevant, unsuitable.

apt [adj1] suitable
▪ *Syn* applicable, apposite, appropriate, apropos, befitting, correct, felicitous, fitting, germane, just, pertinent, proper, relevant, seemly, suitable, timely; ▪ *Ant* incorrect, unsuitable.

apt [adj2] tending, inclined
▪ *Syn* disposed, given, liable, likely, of a mind, prone, ready; ▪ *Ant* disinclined, inapt.

apt [adj3] quick to learn
▪ *Syn* able, astute, bright, clever, expert, gifted, ingenious, intelligent, prompt, ready, savvy, sharp, smart, talented, teachable; ▪ *Ant* incapable, stupid, unskilled.

aptitude [n1] inclination
▪ *Syn* bent, disposition, drift, leaning, predilection, proclivity, proneness, propensity, tendency; ▪ *Ant* disinclination, inaptitude, skillessness.

aptitude [n2] quickness at learning
▪ *Syn* ability, capacity, cleverness, competence, faculty, flair, gift, intelligence, proficiency, talent; ▪ *Ant* incapacity, stupidity.

arbitrary [adj1] whimsical, chance
▪ *Syn* capricious, discretionary, erratic, frivolous, inconsistent, injudicious, irrational, offhand, random, supercilious, superficial, wayward, willful; ▪ *Ant* circumspect, rational, reasonable, reasoned, supported.

arbitrary [adj2] dictatorial
▪ *Syn* absolute, autocratic, bossy, despotic, dogmatic, domineering, downright, flat out, high-handed, imperious, magisterial, monocratic, overbearing, peremptory, straight out, summary, tyrannical, tyrannous; ▪ *Ant* democratic, impersonal, objective.

arcane [adj] hidden, secret
▪ *Syn* cabalistic, esoteric, impenetrable,

mysterious, mystic, occult, recondite, unknowable; ▪ *Ant* common, commonplace, known, normal, outward.

arch [adj1] principal, superior
▪ *Syn* accomplished, champion, chief, consummate, expert, first, foremost, greatest, head, leading, main, major, master, preeminent, premier, primary, top; ▪ *Ant* inferior, lesser, minor, petty.

arch [adj2] knowing, coy
▪ *Syn* artful, frolicsome, mischievous, pert, playful, roguish, saucy, sly, waggish, wily; ▪ *Ant* forthright, frank, modest, open.

archaic [adj] very old
▪ *Syn* ancient, antiquated, antique, bygone, obsolete, olden, old-fashioned, outmoded, out of date, pass, primitive, superannuated; ▪ *Ant* current, modern, new, present, young.

archetype [n] typical example
▪ *Syn* classic, exemplar, form, ideal, model, original, paradigm, pattern, perfect specimen, prime example, prototype, standard; ▪ *Ant* anomaly, atypical.

arctic [adj] very cold
▪ *Syn* chill, chilly, cool, freezing, frigid, frosty, frozen, gelid, glacial, icy, nippy, polar; ▪ *Ant* hot, sultry, torrid, tropic, warm.

ardent [adj1] very enthusiastic
▪ *Syn* agog, avid, blazing, burning, desirous, eager, fervent, fierce, fiery, hungry, intense, keen, lusty, passionate, spirited, thirsty, vehement, zealous; ▪ *Ant* cold, cold-blooded, cool, dispassionate, frigid, indifferent, lukewarm, unenthusiastic.

ardent [adj2] loyal
▪ *Syn* allegiant, constant, devoted, faithful, resolute, steadfast, true; ▪ *Ant* disloyal, false, traitorous.

arduous [adj] difficult, hard to endure
▪ *Syn* backbreaking, burdensome, exhausting, grueling, harsh, laborious, onerous, painful, rigorous, severe, strenuous, taxing, tiring, troublesome, trying; ▪ *Ant* easy, facile, motivating.

area [n1] extent, scope of a surface
▪ *Syn* breadth, compass, distance, expanse, field, range, size, space, sphere, stretch, width; ▪ *Ant* circumference, outline.

argue [v1] verbally fight
▪ *Syn* altercate, bicker, contend, cross swords, disagree, dispute, feud, pettifog, put up a struggle, quibble, row, squabble,

talk back, wrangle; ▪ *Ant* agree, harmonize, ignore, overlook.

argue [*v2*] *try to convince; present support* ▪ *Syn* appeal, assert, claim, contend, controvert, defend, denote, display, elucidate, evince, exhibit, explain, hold, imply, indicate, justify, maintain, persuade, plead, present, prevail upon, reason, show, suggest, testify, vindicate, witness; ▪ *Ant* agree, comply, contradict, deny, gainsay.

argue [*v3*] *discuss*
▪ *Syn* agitate, canvass, clarify, debate, dispute, expostulate, hold, maintain, question, reason, remonstrate; ▪ *Ant* abstain, keep quiet, keep silent.

argumentative [*adj*] *wanting to quarrel*
▪ *Syn* belligerent, combative, contentious, contrary, controversial, disputatious, factious, litigious, opinionated, pugnacious, quarrelsome; ▪ *Ant* agreeable, complaisant, friendly.

arid [*adj1*] *dry*
▪ *Syn* barren, bone-dry, desert, dry as a bone, dry as dust, dusty, parched, thirsty; ▪ *Ant* damp, humid, moist, watered, wet.

arid [*adj2*] *uninterested, spiritless*
▪ *Syn* boring, colorless, drab, dreary, dry, dull, flat, insipid, lackluster, lifeless, tedious, uninspired, vapid, wearisome; ▪ *Ant* animated, interested, lively, spirited

arise [*v1*] *come into being; proceed*
▪ *Syn* appear, begin, come to light, commence, emanate, emerge, flow, follow, happen, issue, occur, originate, result, rise, spring, start, stem; ▪ *Ant* cease, die, disappear, end, fade, go away, stop.

arise [*v2*] *get, stand, or go up*
▪ *Syn* ascend, climb, jump, mount, move upward, rise, soar, stand, tower, turn out, wake up; ▪ *Ant* lie, recline, retire, sit.

aristocratic [*adj*] *privileged, elegant*
▪ *Syn* aloof, blue-blooded, dignified, elegant, elite, fine, haughty, noble, patrician, polished, refined, snobbish, upperclass; ▪ *Ant* bourgeois, common, humble, modest, uncouth, unrefined, vernacular, vulgar.

arm [*v*] *equip with weapon or power*
▪ *Syn* appoint, array, deck, equalize, fortify, furnish, gear, gird, guard, heel, issue, mobilize, outfit, prepare, prime, protect, rig, strengthen, supply; ▪ *Ant* disarm, dismantle, divest, relieve of, strip, take away.

armistice [*n*] *peace-establishing agreement* ▪ *Syn* ceasefire, suspension, treaty, truce; ▪ *Ant* dispute, fight, war.

aromatic [*adj*] *distinctive smelling*
▪ *Syn* ambrosial, balmy, fragrant, odoriferous, perfumed, pungent, redolent, savory, scented, spicy, sweet, sweet-smelling; ▪ *Ant* acrid, bland, unsavory.

arouse [*v*] *excite, entice*
▪ *Syn* agitate, alert, awaken, challenge, electrify, enliven, foment, foster, goad, incite, inflame, instigate, kindle, move, provoke, rally, rouse, send, spark, spur, stimulate, stir, thrill, waken, wake up, warm, whet; ▪ *Ant* bore, calm, lull, quiet.

arraign [*v*] *accuse*
▪ *Syn* blame, charge, criminate, hang on, incriminate, inculpate, indict, summon; ▪ *Ant* discharge, exonerate, free, let go.

arrange [*v1*] *put in an order*
▪ *Syn* align, array, classify, dispose, file, form, group, line up, methodize, organize, position, range, rank, regulate, sort, systematize, tidy; ▪ *Ant* confuse, derange, disarrange, disorder, disorganize, disperse, disturb, mix up, scatter.

arrange [*v2*] *make plans, often involving agreement* ▪ *Syn* adapt, adjust, chart, compromise, concert, contrive, design, determine, devise, draft, establish, harmonize, manage, map out, negotiate, organize, prepare, project, promote, provide, resolve, schedule, scheme, settle; ▪ *Ant* disorganize, not plan.

array [*v*] *arrange in collection or order*
▪ *Syn* align, display, exhibit, form, group, line up, methodize, organize, parade, range, set, show, systematize; ▪ *Ant* disarrange, mess up, mix up.

arrest [*v1*] *take into authorized custody*
▪ *Syn* apprehend, book, capture, catch, collar, detain, imprison, incarcerate, jail, take in; ▪ *Ant* let go, release, set free.

arrest [*v2*] *stop or slow*
▪ *Syn* block, can, check, delay, drop, end, freeze, halt, hinder, hold, inhibit, interrupt, obstruct, prevent, restrain, restrict, retard, scrub, shut down, stall, stay, suppress; ▪ *Ant* activate, encourage, let go, release.

arrive [*v1*] *come to a destination*
▪ *Syn* access, alight, appear, attain, disembark, dismount, enter, reach, show, visit; ▪ *Ant* depart, disappear, go, leave.

arrive [v2] *achieve recognition*
▪ **Syn** accomplish, become famous, flourish, make it, prosper, reach the top, score, succeed, thrive; ▪ **Ant** fail, fall.

arrogant [adj] *having exaggerated self-opinion* ▪ **Syn** aloof, assuming, audacious, autocratic, bossy, cavalier, conceited, contemptuous, disdainful, egotistic, haughty, high-handed, imperious, insolent, overbearing, peremptory, pompous, presumptuous, pretentious, proud, scornful, self-important, smug, supercilious, superior, vain; ▪ **Ant** humble, meek, servile, unconceited.

arrogate [v] *claim without justification*
▪ **Syn** accroach, appropriate, assume, commandeer, confiscate, demand, expropriate, preempt, presume, seize, take, usurp; ▪ **Ant** appropriate, give, hand over.

artful [adj] *skillful; cunning*
▪ **Syn** adept, adroit, clever, crafty, designing, dexterous, ingenious, masterly, politic, proficient, resourceful, scheming, sharp, shrewd, sly, tricky, wily; ▪ **Ant** artless, ingenuous, naive, unskillful.

articulate [adj] *clearly, coherently spoken* ▪ **Syn** clear, coherent, comprehensible, definite, distinct, eloquent, fluent, intelligible, lucid, meaningful, understandable, well-spoken; ▪ **Ant** misrepresented, unclear, unintelligible.

articulate [v1] *say clearly, coherently*
▪ **Syn** enunciate, express, pronounce, say, speak, state, talk, utter, verbalize, vocalize, voice; ▪ **Ant** bumble, misrepresent, misspeak.

articulate [v2] *connect*
▪ **Syn** concatenate, couple, fit together, hinge, integrate, join, link; ▪ **Ant** disconnect.

artifice [n1] *hoax; clever act*
▪ **Syn** contrivance, device, dodge, expedient, gambit, machination, maneuver, play, ploy, ruse, stratagem, subterfuge, tactic, wile; ▪ **Ant** candor, frankness, honesty, honor, ingenuousness, innocence, openness, reality, sincerity, truthfulness.

artifice [n2] *cunning; deception*
▪ **Syn** artfulness, chicanery, craftiness, dishonesty, duplicity, guile, scheming, slyness, trickery, wiliness; ▪ **Ant** candor, frankness, honesty, honor, ingenuousness, innocence, openness, reality, sincerity, truthfulness.

artifice [n3] *skill, cleverness*
▪ **Syn** ability, adroitness, deftness, facility, finesse, ingenuity, invention, inventiveness, skill; ▪ **Ant** artlessness, inability, incapacity, simplicity.

artificial [adj1] *fake; imitation*
▪ **Syn** counterfeit, ersatz, fabricated, factitious, false, manufactured, mock, plastic, sham, simulated, spurious, substitute, synthetic; ▪ **Ant** genuine, natural, real.

artificial [adj2] *pretended; affected*
▪ **Syn** assumed, contrived, false, feigned, forced, hollow, insincere, labored, mannered, meretricious, spurious, theatrical; ▪ **Ant** genuine, natural, unaffected, unpretentious.

artistic [adj1] *beautiful, satisfying to senses* ▪ **Syn** aesthetic, creative, cultivated, decorative, dramatic, elegant, exquisite, fine, grand, harmonious, ideal, imaginative, ornamental, picturesque, pleasing, poetic, refined, rhythmical, stimulating, stylish, sublime, tasteful; ▪ **Ant** distasteful, horrible, inelegant, ugly.

artistic [adj2] *being skilled in creative activity* ▪ **Syn** accomplished, artful, arty, discriminating, gifted, imaginative, inventive, skillful, talented; ▪ **Ant** scientific.

artless [adj] *simple*
▪ **Syn** direct, genuine, guileless, honest, ingenuous, innocent, naive, natural, open, plain, pure, sincere, straightforward, true, unaffected; ▪ **Ant** artful, complicated, contrived, pretentious, sophisticated.

ascend [v] *go up*
▪ **Syn** arise, climb, escalate, float, fly, lift off, mount, rise, scale, soar, sprout, take off, tower; ▪ **Ant** decline, descend, go down, lower.

ashamed [adj] *regretting, remorseful*
▪ **Syn** abashed, apologetic, chagrined, compunctious, conscience-stricken, contrite, crestfallen, debased, demeaned, disconcerted, embarrassed, flustered, guilty, humiliated, meek, mortified, penitent, regretful, repentant, shamefaced, sheepish, sorry; ▪ **Ant** bold, defiant, immodest, not sorry, shameless, unremorseful, unselfconscious.

ask [v1] *question*
▪ **Syn** canvass, catechize, challenge, cross-examine, demand, direct, enjoin, examine, go over, inquire, institute, in-

terrogate, investigate, pry into, pump, query, quiz, request, strike; • *Ant* answer, claim, command, insist, reply, repudiate, tell.

ask [v2] *request*
• *Syn* angle, appeal, apply, beg, beseech, call for, charge, claim, command, contend for, crave, demand, entreat, file for, implore, impose, levy, order, petition, plead, pray, request, requisition, seek, solicit, sue, supplicate, urge; • *Ant* answer, claim, command, insist, tell.

ask [v3] *invite*
• *Syn* bid, call upon, propose, suggest, summon, urge; • *Ant* disinvite, ignore.

askew [adj] *crooked*
• *Syn* askance, askant, aslant, awry, bent, buckled, crookedly, curved, knotted, lopsided, oblique, off-center, slanted, slanting, to one side, turned, twisted; • *Ant* aligned, centered, even, in line, plumb, right, straight, true.

asleep [adj] *unconscious*
• *Syn* dormant, dreaming, hibernating, inactive, inert, in repose, resting, slumbering, somnolent; • *Ant* attentive, awake, conscious.

aspect [n] *element to consider*
• *Syn* angle, direction, facet, feature, outlook, perspective, phase, point of view, position, prospect, regard, scene, side, situation, slant, view, vista; • *Ant* whole.

aspersion [n] *verbal exhibition of bad temper* • *Syn* abuse, backbiting, calumny, defamation, detraction, invective, libel, obloquy, slander, vituperation; • *Ant* compliment, kindness, praise.

asphyxiate [v] *cut off air*
• *Syn* choke, drown, smother, stifle, strangle, suffocate; • *Ant* breathe, loosen.

ass [n] *stupid person*
• *Syn* dolt, dope, dunce, fool, idiot, imbecile; • *Ant* brain, genius, sage.

assail [v] *attack, usually with words*
• *Syn* abuse, assault, berate, beset, blast, blister, charge, criticize, encounter, impugn, invade, lambaste, malign, maltreat, revile, vilify, work over; • *Ant* champion, defend, retreat, support, withdraw.

assault [v] *attack*
• *Syn* abuse, advance, assail, bash, beset, blitz, bushwhack, charge, invade, jump, rape, ruin, set upon, slam, storm, strike, trash, violate, work over; • *Ant* defend,

protect, resist, retreat, withdraw, withstand.

assemblage [v] *gathering of people*
• *Syn* aggregation, association, collection, company, congregation, convergence, crowd, group, throng; • *Ant* dispersal, scattering.

assemble [v1] *congregate*
• *Syn* accumulate, agglomerate, amass, call together, collect, come together, convene, flock, gather, group, huddle, meet, muster, rally, reunite, round up, summon, unite; • *Ant* disperse, scatter.

assemble [v2] *put together*
• *Syn* compile, connect, construct, contrive, erect, fabricate, fashion, fit, form, join, make, manufacture, model, mold, piece together, produce, set up, shape, unite, weld; • *Ant* divide, separate, take apart.

assent [v] *agree*
• *Syn* accede, accept, accord, acquiesce, adopt, allow, approve, buy, comply, concur, conform, consent, defer, embrace, espouse, give in, go along with, grant, permit, recognize, sanction, subscribe; • *Ant* disagree, disallow, disapprove, dissent, reject.

assert [v] *insist, declare, maintain*
• *Syn* advance, affirm, allege, argue, asservate, attest, aver, avouch, avow, cite, claim, contend, defend, justify, predicate, proclaim, profess, pronounce, protest, put forward, say, state, stress, swear, uphold, vindicate, warrant; • *Ant* deny, reject.

assertive [adj] *aggressive*
• *Syn* certain, confident, decisive, demanding, dogmatic, domineering, emphatic, firm, forward, insistent, positive, self-assured, self-confident, strongwilled, sure; • *Ant* diffident, quiet, shy, unconfident.

asset [n] *advantage*
• *Syn* aid, benefit, blessing, boon, credit, distinction, help, resource, service, treasure; • *Ant* disadvantage, liability.

assiduous [adj] *hard-working*
• *Syn* active, attentive, busy, constant, diligent, exacting, industrious, laborious, persevering, scrupulous, sedulous, studious; • *Ant* lazy, neglectful, negligent.

assign [v] *select and give a responsibility*
• *Syn* accredit, appoint, ascribe, attach, cast, charge, commission, commit, credit, delegate, designate, draft, elect,

empower, entrust, hire, hold responsible, impute, name, nominate, ordain, refer, select; ▪ *Ant* discharge, discredit, dismiss, divest, relieve.

assimilate [*v1*] *absorb mentally*
▪ *Syn* comprehend, digest, grasp, incorporate, ingest, learn, osmose, sense, understand; ▪ *Ant* misunderstand, reject, unlearn.

assimilate [*v2*] *become adjusted; adjust*
▪ *Syn* acclimatize, accommodate, acculturate, accustom, adapt, blend in, conform, fit, homogenize, homologize, intermix, match, mingle, standardize; ▪ *Ant* not adapt.

assist [*v*] *help*
▪ *Syn* abet, aid, back, benefit, boost, collaborate, cooperate, expedite, facilitate, further, reinforce, relieve, serve, stand up for, support, sustain, work for, work with; ▪ *Ant* hinder, hurt, stop, thwart.

associate [*v1*] *connect in the mind*
▪ *Syn* affiliate, blend, bracket, combine, conjoin, correlate, couple, group, identify, join, league, link, lump together, mix, pair, relate, unite, yoke; ▪ *Ant* disconnect, disjoin, dissociate, disunite, divide, part, separate, sever.

associate [*v2*] *befriend*
▪ *Syn* accompany, amalgamate, confederate, consort, fraternize, hobnob, join, mingle, mix, pool, take up with, team up, throw in together, tie up, work with; ▪ *Ant* avoid, disassociate, disjoin, disunite, divorce.

assorted [*adj*] *various*
▪ *Syn* different, diverse, diversified, heterogeneous, hybrid, indiscriminate, miscellaneous, mixed, motley, sundry, varied, variegated; ▪ *Ant* homogeneous, identical, same, uniform.

assuage [*v*] *soothe, relieve*
▪ *Syn* allay, alleviate, appease, calm, conciliate, ease, lessen, lighten, mitigate, moderate, mollify, pacify, palliate, placate, propitiate, quench, quiet, sate, satisfy, still, sweeten, temper, tranquilize; ▪ *Ant* exacerbate, upset.

assume [*v1*] *believe, take for granted*
▪ *Syn* accept, ascertain, conjecture, consider, count upon, deduce, deem, divine, estimate, expect, fancy, find, gather, guess, hypothesize, imagine, judge, posit, postulate, predicate, presume, speculate, suppose, surmise, suspect, the-

orize, think, understand; ▪ *Ant* doubt, not believe.

assume [*v2*] *take, undertake*
▪ *Syn* accept, acquire, appropriate, arrogate, attend to, begin, confiscate, don, embark upon, embrace, enter upon, seize; ▪ *Ant* abandon, relinquish, renounce.

assumed [*adj*] *pretended*
▪ *Syn* affected, artificial, counterfeit, fake, false, feigned, fictitious, imitation, make-believe, pretended, sham, simulated, spurious; ▪ *Ant* genuine, natural, real.

assure [*v*] *promise*
▪ *Syn* affirm, attest, aver, brace up, certify, confirm, guarantee, pledge, swear, vouch for, vow; ▪ *Ant* deny, disavow, disbelieve, disclaim, doubt, lie.

assured [*adj1*] *absolutely certain*
▪ *Syn* beyond doubt, confirmed, decided, definite, dependable, ensured, fixed, guaranteed, indubitable, insured, irrefutable, pronounced, sealed, secure, set, settled, sure; ▪ *Ant* doubted, doubtful, feared, questionable, uncertain.

assured [*adj2*] *confident*
▪ *Syn* assertive, audacious, bold, brazen, certain, collected, complacent, composed, confident, imperturbable, poised, positive, sanguine, secure, self-confident, self-possessed, sure; ▪ *Ant* confused, dismayed, distrustful, doubtful, doubting, fearful, hesitant, nervous.

astern [*adv*] *backward*
▪ *Syn* abaft, aft, rear, rearward; ▪ *Ant* forward.

astonish [*v*] *surprise*
▪ *Syn* amaze, astound, bewilder, confound, daze, dumbfound, overwhelm, shock, stagger, startle, stun, stupefy; ▪ *Ant* bore, calm, expect.

astonishing [*adj*] *surprising*
▪ *Syn* amazing, astounding, bewildering, breathtaking, extraordinary, impressive, marvelous, miraculous, spectacular, staggering, startling, stunning, stupefying, wonderful, wondrous; ▪ *Ant* boring, dull, expected.

astound [*v*] *amaze*
▪ *Syn* astonish, bewilder, confound, daze, dumbfound, flabbergast, overwhelm, shock, startle, stun, stupefy, surprise, take aback; ▪ *Ant* bore, dull.

astray [*adj*] *off the path or right direction*
▪ *Syn* adrift, afield, amiss, awry, lost, off course, wandering, wrong; ▪ *Ant* on course, right, straight.

astringent [adj] harsh
- **Syn** acetic, acrid, biting, bitter, cutting, sharp, tonic; - **Ant** bland, mild.

astute [adj] perceptive
- **Syn** adroit, bright, calculating, clever, discerning, intelligent, keen, knowing, perspicacious, sagacious, sharp, shrewd; - **Ant** asinine, idiotic, ignorant, imbecile, obtuse, shallow, stupid, thick, unintelligent.

atheism [n] belief that no god exists
- **Syn** disbelief, doubt, freethinking, godlessness, heresy, iconoclasm, impiety, infidelity, irreverence, nihilism, skepticism; - **Ant** belief, godliness, piety, religion.

athletic [adj] agile; prepared to participate in sports - **Syn** able-bodied, active, energetic, fit, lusty, muscular, powerful, robust, strong, sturdy, vigorous; - **Ant** frail, sedentary, unathletic, unfit, weak.

atrocious [adj1] outrageous; widely condemned - **Syn** awful, beastly, diabolical, fiendish, flagrant, heinous, monstrous, nefarious, rotten, scandalous, shocking, villainous; - **Ant** admirable, elegant, fine, good, high-class, tasteful.

atrocious [adj2] offensive
- **Syn** appalling, bad, beastly, detestable, disgusting, dreadful, execrable, foul, horrid, loathsome, noisome, obscene, repulsive, sickening, terrible; - **Ant** benevolent, humane, inoffensive, kind, virtuous.

atrophy [n] wasting away, disintegration
- **Syn** decline, degeneracy, degeneration, deterioration, diminution, downfall, downgrade; - **Ant** development, exercise, growth, strength, use.

attach [v1] join, fasten
- **Syn** add, adhere, affix, annex, append, bind, connect, couple, fix, link, make fast, rivet, secure, tie, unite; - **Ant** detach, disconnect, disjoin, remove, separate, sever, unfasten.

attach [v2] attribute, ascribe
- **Syn** allocate, allot, appoint, assign, associate, connect, consign, designate, detail, earmark, impute, lay, name, place, put, send; - **Ant** disunite, take away.

attack [v1] assault physically
- **Syn** advance, ambush, assail, assault, beat, besiege, bombard, charge, club, combat, harm, hit, hurt, invade, jump, lay siege to, molest, mug, overwhelm, punch, rush, set upon, stab, storm, strike, turn on; - **Ant** aid, defend, protect, resist,

retreat, shelter, shield, submit, support, surrender, sustain.

attack [v2] assault verbally
- **Syn** abuse, berate, blame, censure, criticize, impugn, lay into, malign, refute, reprove, revile, stretch, vilify; - **Ant** defend, resist, submit, withstand.

attack [v3] set to work
- **Syn** deal with, dive into, plunge into, set to, start in on, tackle, take up; - **Ant** be lazy, slough off.

attain [v] achieve, accomplish
- **Syn** accede to, acquire, arrive, arrive at, complete, effect, fulfill, gain, hit, obtain, procure, promote, reach, realize, reap, score, secure, succeed, win; - **Ant** abandon, desert, fail, forfeit, give in, give up, lose, miss, surrender.

attempt [n] try, effort
- **Syn** attack, endeavor, experiment, pursuit, struggle, trial, try, tryout, undertaking, venture; - **Ant** certainty, laziness, success.

attend [v1] be present at
- **Syn** appear, be a guest, be present, frequent, haunt, make an appearance, show, show up, sit in on, turn up, visit; - **Ant** be absent, miss.

attend [v2] care for
- **Syn** be in the service of, doctor, look after, mind, minister to, nurse, serve, take care of, tend, wait upon, watch, work for; - **Ant** ignore, neglect.

attend [v3] pay attention; apply oneself
- **Syn** catch, concentrate on, devote oneself, follow, hearken, heed, listen, mark, mind, note, observe, pick up, regard, see to, watch; - **Ant** be lazy, disregard, ignore, neglect.

attendant [adj] being present or related
- **Syn** accessory, accompanying, ancillary, associated, attending, coincident, concomitant, consequent, incident; - **Ant** absent, detached.

attentive [adj1] concentrating
- **Syn** alert, awake, aware, conscientious, enthralled, fascinated, heedful, immersed, intent, interested, mindful, observant, preoccupied, rapt, studious, vigilant, watchful; - **Ant** disregarding, heedless, ignorant, inattentive, inconsiderate, neglectful, neglecting.

attentive [adj2] considerate
- **Syn** accommodating, civil, courteous, devoted, gallant, gracious, kind, obliging, polite, respectful, solicitous,

thoughtful; ▪ *Ant* heedless, ignorant, inattentive, inconsiderate, neglectful.

attenuate [v] *weaken*
▪ *Syn* abate, constrict, cripple, debilitate, deflate, disable, enfeeble, extenuate, lessen, mitigate, sap, shrink, thin, undermine, vitiate; ▪ *Ant* expand, increase, intensify, strengthen.

attest [v] *affirm, vouch for*
▪ *Syn* adjure, announce, argue, assert, authenticate, aver, bear witness, certify, confirm, corroborate, declare, demonstrate, display, exhibit, indicate, prove, ratify, seal, show, substantiate, support, swear, testify, uphold, verify, warrant, witness; ▪ *Ant* deny.

attire [v] *clothe*
▪ *Syn* accoutre, array, clad, costume, deck, drape, dress, equip, fit out, outfit, suit up, tog, turn out; ▪ *Ant* bare, denude, disrobe, strip, unclothe, undress.

attract [v] *draw attention*
▪ *Syn* allure, appeal to, beckon, beguile, bewitch, captivate, charm, draw, enchant, enthrall, entice, entrance, fascinate, induce, intrigue, inveigle, invite, lure, magnetize, pull, seduce, solicit, spellbind, steer, tempt, wile; ▪ *Ant* repel, repulse, revulse.

attractive [adj] *appealing, drawing attention* ▪ *Syn* adorable, beautiful, charming, comely, fair, fetching, good-looking, gorgeous, handsome, inviting, lovely, magnetic, mesmeric, pretty, provocative, seductive, stunning, tantalizing, winning, winsome; ▪ *Ant* repellent, repulsive, ugly, unappealing, unattractive.

attrition [n1] *wearing down or away*
▪ *Syn* abrasion, attenuation, debilitation, depreciation, disintegration, erosion, grinding, rubbing, thinning, weakening, wear; ▪ *Ant* building, strengthening.

attrition [n2] *regret*
▪ *Syn* contriteness, penance, penitence, remorse, remorsefulness, repentance; ▪ *Ant* happiness.

atypical [adj] *nonconforming*
▪ *Syn* aberrant, abnormal, anomalous, deviant, different, divergent, exceptional, heteroclite, irregular, odd, peculiar, preternatural, strange; ▪ *Ant* conforming, normal, ordinary, standard, typical, usual.

audacious [adj1] *reckless, daring*
▪ *Syn* adventurous, bold, brave, coura-geous, daredevil, dauntless, foolhardy, intrepid, rash, resolute, risky, valiant, venturesome; ▪ *Ant* cautious, gentle, humble, meek, mild, modest, modest, reserved, timid, yielding.

audacious [adj2] *arrogant, presumptuous* ▪ *Syn* assuming, bold, brash, brassy, brazen, defiant, disrespectful, forward, impudent, insolent, nervy, rude, saucy, shameless; ▪ *Ant* humble, modest, reserved, shy, timid.

audible [adj] *able to be heard*
▪ *Syn* aural, auricular, clear, deafening, detectable, discernible, distinct, loud, perceptible, plain, resounding, roaring, sounding, within earshot; ▪ *Ant* faint, inaudible, muffed.

augment [v] *make greater; improve*
▪ *Syn* aggrandize, amplify, boost, build up, compound, develop, enhance, enlarge, expand, extend, grow, heighten, increase, inflate, intensify, magnify, mount, multiply, progress, raise, reinforce, strengthen, swell; ▪ *Ant* decrease, degrade.

august [adj] *dignified, noble*
▪ *Syn* baronial, brilliant, eminent, exalted, glorious, grand, grandiose, high-minded, high-ranking, honorable, imposing, impressive, lofty, lordly, magnificent, majestic, monumental, pompous, regal, resplendent, stately, superb, venerable; ▪ *Ant* common, ignoble, ridiculous, undignified.

auspicious [adj] *encouraging; favorable*
▪ *Syn* advantageous, bright, favorable, felicitous, fortunate, golden, halcyon, happy, hopeful, lucky, opportune, promising, propitious, prosperous, rosy, timely, well-timed; ▪ *Ant* inauspicious, inopportune, ominous, unfortunate, unhappy, unlucky.

austere [adj1] *severe in manner*
▪ *Syn* astringent, cold, exacting, forbidding, grave, grim, hard, harsh, inexorable, inflexible, obdurate, rigid, rigorous, serious, sober, solemn, stern, strict, stringent; ▪ *Ant* bland, calm, gentle, meek, mild.

austere [adj2] *refraining; abstinent*
▪ *Syn* abstemious, ascetic, chaste, continent, economical, puritanical, self-denying, self-disciplined, sober, straight-laced, strict, subdued; ▪ *Ant* elaborate, encouraging, extravagant, indulgent, spending.

austere [adj3] *grim, barren*
▪ *Syn* bald, bare, bleak, clean, dour, plain, primitive, rustic, severe, simple, spare, spartan, stark, subdued; ▪ *Ant* extravagant, luxurious.

authentic [adj] *real, genuine*
▪ *Syn* accurate, actual, authoritative, bona fide, certain, convincing, credible, dependable, factual, legitimate, official, original, pure, reliable, sure, trustworthy, valid, veritable; ▪ *Ant* counterfeit, fake, false, falsified, unauthorized, unreal.

authenticate [v] *establish as real, genuine* ▪ *Syn* accredit, attest, authorize, bear out, certify, confirm, corroborate, endorse, guarantee, justify, prove, substantiate, validate, verify, vouch, warrant; ▪ *Ant* contravene, deny, discredit, disprove, gainsay, impugn, invalidate, negate, refute, reject, repudiate, spurn.

authoritarian [adj] *domineering*
▪ *Syn* authoritative, autocratic, despotic, dictatorial, disciplinarian, doctrinaire, dogmatic, harsh, imperious, magisterial, rigid, severe, strict, totalitarian, tyrannical; ▪ *Ant* democratic, indulgent, lenient, liberal, yielding.

authoritative [adj1] *recognized as true, valid* ▪ *Syn* accurate, attested, authentic, authenticated, confirmed, definitive, documented, factual, faithful, learned, proven, reliable, scholarly, sound, supported, trustworthy, validated, verified, veritable; ▪ *Ant* doubtable, spurious, unofficial, unverified.

authoritative [adj2] *being domineering*
▪ *Syn* assertive, commanding, confident, decisive, dictatorial, doctrinaire, dogmatic, dominating, imperative, imperious, imposing, officious, peremptory, self-assured; ▪ *Ant* democratic.

authoritative [adj3] *official, authorized*
▪ *Syn* approved, canonical, ex cathedra, executive, ex officio, imperial, lawful, legitimate, magisterial, mandatory, ruling, sanctioned, sovereign, supreme; ▪ *Ant* illegitimate, illicit, unofficial.

authorize [v1] *give power or control*
▪ *Syn* accredit, bless, commission, empower, enable, entitle, invest, license, vest; ▪ *Ant* deny, reject.

authorize [v2] *permit, allow*
▪ *Syn* affirm, approve, confirm, countenance, endorse, give leave, let, license, qualify, ratify, sanction, suffer, tolerate, warrant; ▪ *Ant* deny, disallow, reject.

autocratic [adj] *holding power exclusively* ▪ *Syn* absolute, all-powerful, arbitrary, despotic, dictatorial, domineering, imperious, monocratic, tyrannical, tyrannous; ▪ *Ant* democratic, lenient, tolerant.

automated [adj] *made or done by a machine* ▪ *Syn* automatic, computerized, electrical, electronic, mechanical, mechanized, motorized, programmed, robotic; ▪ *Ant* by hand, manual.

automatic [adj1] *done by habit*
▪ *Syn* autogenetic, habitual, impulsive, instinctual, involuntary, mechanical, natural, perfunctory, reflex, routine, spontaneous, unmeditated, unwilling; ▪ *Ant* conscious, deliberate, thought-out, voluntary.

automatic [adj2] *occurring as a natural consequence* ▪ *Syn* assured, certain, inescapable, inevitable, necessary, routine, unavoidable; ▪ *Ant* stilted, unnatural.

autonomous [adj] *independent*
▪ *Syn* free, self-determining, self-governing, self-ruling, sovereign, uncontrolled; ▪ *Ant* dependent, subject.

autumn [n] *season between summer and winter* ▪ *Syn* autumnal equinox, fall, harvest, Indian summer; ▪ *Ant* spring.

auxiliary [adj] *supplementary*
▪ *Syn* adjuvant, ancillary, appurtenant, backup, complementary, contributory, extra, reserve, secondary, spare, subordinate, subservient, subsidiary, supporting; ▪ *Ant* body, main.

avail [v] *be of use; use*
▪ *Syn* account, advantage, answer, be adequate, benefit, fill, fulfill, meet, profit, satisfy, serve, suffice, work; ▪ *Ant* be useless, harm, hinder, hurt.

available [adj] *ready for use*
▪ *Syn* accessible, applicable, at hand, attainable, convenient, feasible, free, obtainable, procurable, purchasable, reachable, realizable, securable, serviceable, usable, vacant; ▪ *Ant* unavailable, unhandy, unobtainable.

avalanche [n] *falling large mass; sudden rush of large quantity* ▪ *Syn* barrage, deluge, flood, inundation, landslide, landslip, snowslide, torrent; ▪ *Ant* dearth, deficiency, drought, famine, insufficiency, lack, paucity, scantiness, shortage.

avant-garde [adj] *unconventional, forward-looking* ▪ *Syn* experimental, innovative, liberal, new wave, pioneering, progressive, radical, state-of-the-art, vanguard; ▪ *Ant* conservative, conventional, mainstream.

avarice [n] *extreme greed*
▪ *Syn* avidity, covetousness, cupidity, frugality, greediness, miserliness, parsimony, penuriousness, rapacity, stinginess, thrift; ▪ *Ant* generosity, philanthropy.

avenge [v] *retaliate*
▪ *Syn* chasten, chastise, even the score, get even, pay back, punish, redress, requite, revenge, take vengeance, vindicate; ▪ *Ant* accept, be resigned to, excuse, forgive, overlook, pardon, tolerate.

average [adj] *normal, typical*
▪ *Syn* common, commonplace, everyday, familiar, general, intermediate, mainstream, mediocre, medium, moderate, ordinary, passable, regular, standard, tolerable, undistinguished, unexceptional, usual; ▪ *Ant* abnormal, atypical, exceptional, extraordinary, extreme, outstanding, unusual.

averse [adj] *opposing*
▪ *Syn* afraid, allergic, antagonistic, antipathetic, contrary, disinclined, hesitant, hostile, ill-disposed, indisposed, inimical, loath, perverse, reluctant, unfriendly, unwilling; ▪ *Ant* caring, eager, liking, loving, sympathetic.

avert [v] *thwart; ward off*
▪ *Syn* avoid, deflect, deter, fend off, foil, forestall, frustrate, halt, preclude, prevent, rule out, shunt, stave off, turn, turn aside, turn away; ▪ *Ant* aid, help.

avid [adj] *enthusiastic*
▪ *Syn* ardent, avaricious, breathless, covetous, desirous, devoted, eager, fanatical, fervent, greedy, hungry, impatient, insatiable, intense, keen, passionate, rapacious, thirsty, voracious, zealous; ▪ *Ant* dispassionate, indifferent, unenthusiastic.

avocation [n] *hobby*
▪ *Syn* amusement, diversion, occupation, pastime, recreation, side interest, sideline; ▪ *Ant* profession, vocation, work.

avoid [v] *refrain or stay away from; prevent* ▪ *Syn* abstain, avert, bypass, circumvent, divert, dodge, elude, eschew, evade, flee, hide, hold off, jump, keep clear, obviate, recoil, shake off, shrink from, shun, shy, sidestep, step aside, turn aside, ward off, weave, withdraw; ▪ *Ant* face, meet, seek, want.

avow [v] *state; profess*
▪ *Syn* acknowledge, admit, affirm, allow, assert, aver, avouch, concede, confess, declare, grant, maintain, proclaim, swear; ▪ *Ant* censure, condemn, deny, disclaim, disown, dispute, renounce, repudiate.

awake [adj] *conscious; alert*
▪ *Syn* aroused, attentive, awakened, aware, cognizant, excited, heedful, knowing, observant, on guard, roused, vigilant, wakeful, watchful; ▪ *Ant* asleep, unconscious.

awake [v1] *become alert or cause to rise from sleep* ▪ *Syn* arise, awaken, call, gain consciousness, get up, roll out, rouse, stir, wake, wake up; ▪ *Ant* go to sleep, sleep.

awake [v2] *become or make aware*
▪ *Syn* activate, alert, animate, arouse, awaken, call forth, enliven, excite, incite, kindle, provoke, revive, stimulate, stir up, vivify; ▪ *Ant* deaden, lull.

awaken [v] *make conscious or alert*
▪ *Syn* activate, animate, arouse, awake, call, enliven, excite, fan, incite, kindle, provoke, rally, revive, rouse, stimulate, stir up, vivify, wake; ▪ *Ant* deaden, go to sleep, hypnotize.

award [v] *give prize or reward*
▪ *Syn* accord, allocate, allot, apportion, assign, bestow, concede, decree, distribute, donate, endow, gift, grant, hand out, present, render, reward, shell out; ▪ *Ant* deny, disallow, refuse, withhold.

aware [adj] *knowledgeable*
▪ *Syn* acquainted, alert, appraised, appreciative, apprehensive, apprised, attentive, au courant, awake, cognizant, conscious, enlightened, familiar, heedful, informed, knowing, mindful, perceptive, receptive, sentient, sharp; ▪ *Ant* ignorant, insensitive, unaware, unconscious.

awe [v] *amaze*
▪ *Syn* alarm, appall, astonish, daunt, dazzle, flabbergast, frighten, grandstand, horrify, impress, intimidate, overawe, scare, startle, strike, stun, stupefy, terrify; ▪ *Ant* expect.

awesome [adj] *amazing*
▪ *Syn* astonishing, breathtaking, daunting, exalted, fearsome, formidable, frightening, grand, impressive, intimidating, magnificent, majestic, moving, overwhelming, shocking, striking, stunning, stupefying, terrifying, wondrous; ▪ *Ant*

blah, commonplace, dull, ordinary, unexciting, unimpressive.

awful [adj] very bad; terrible
▪ *Syn* abominable, appalling, atrocious, deplorable, depressing, dire, distressing, dreadful, frightful, ghastly, gruesome, harrowing, hideous, horrendous, horrific, offensive, repulsive, shocking; ▪ *Ant* beautiful, good, pleasing.

awhile [adv] for a short period
▪ *Syn* briefly, for a bit, for a little while, for a moment, for a spell, for a while, for the moment, momentarily, not for long, temporarily, transiently; ▪ *Ant* permanently.

awkward [adj1] clumsy, inelegant
▪ *Syn* amateurish, artless, blundering, bumbling, coarse, floundering, graceless, incompetent, inept, lumbering, maladroit, oafish, stiff, stumbling; ▪ *Ant* adroit, artful, dexterous, elegant, graceful, handy, skillful.

awkward [adj2] difficult to handle
▪ *Syn* annoying, bulky, cramped, cumbersome, disagreeable, hazardous, incommodious, inconvenient, perilous, risky, troublesome; ▪ *Ant* convenient, easy, straightforward.

awkward [adj3] embarrassing
▪ *Syn* compromising, delicate, difficult, embarrassed, ill at ease, inopportune, painful, perplexing, troublesome, trying; ▪ *Ant* clever.

awry [adj] off course; amiss
▪ *Syn* afield, askance, askew, aslant, astray, badly, bent, cockeyed, crooked, curved, slanting, turned, wrong, zigzag; ▪ *Ant* aligned, on course, right, straight.

ax/axe [v] dismiss from service
▪ *Syn* cancel, discharge, dispense with, eliminate, fire, lay off, remove, terminate, throw out; ▪ *Ant* engage, hire, take on.

axiom [n] principle
▪ *Syn* adage, aphorism, apothegm, device, dictum, fundamental, law, maxim, moral, postulate, proposition, proverb, saying, theorem, truism, truth; ▪ *Ant* absurdity, ambiguity, foolishness, nonsense, paradox.

axiomatic [adj] understood; aphoristic
▪ *Syn* absolute, accepted, aphoristic, assumed, certain, fundamental, given, indubitable, manifest, obvious, presupposed, proverbial, self-evident; ▪ *Ant* misunderstood, questionable, uncertain.

B

baby [n] infant
▪ *Syn* babe, bairn, bambino, bundle, cherub, chick, child, crawler, kid, newborn, nursling, papoose, suckling, toddler, tot; ▪ *Ant* adolescent, adult, grown-up, parent.

baby [adj] miniature
▪ *Syn* babyish, diminutive, little, midget, mini, minute, petite, small, tiny, wee; ▪ *Ant* big, giant, large.

babyish [adj] acting like an infant
▪ *Syn* childish, foolish, immature, infantile, juvenile, puerile, silly; ▪ *Ant* adult, grown-up, mature.

back [adj1] end
▪ *Syn* aback, abaft, aft, after, astern, back of, backward, behind, final, following, hind, hindmost, in the wake of, posterior, rear, rearmost, rearward, tail; ▪ *Ant* ahead, anterior, before, front.

back [adj2] from earlier time
▪ *Syn* delayed, elapsed, former, overdue, past, previous; ▪ *Ant* future, subsequent.

back [v1] support
▪ *Syn* abet, abide by, advocate, ally, assist, bankroll, boost, champion, countenance, encourage, endorse, favor, finance, sanction, second, sponsor, stand behind, subsidize, sustain, underwrite, uphold; ▪ *Ant* discourage, dissuade, oppose.

back [v2] put in reverse direction
▪ *Syn* backtrack, drive back, fall back, recede, regress, repel, repulse, retire, retract, retreat, reverse, turn tail, withdraw; ▪ *Ant* advance, go forward.

backbiting [n] hateful talk
▪ *Syn* abuse, aspersion, calumny, defamation, denigration, depreciation, gossip, invective, lie, malice, obloquy, slander, spite, spitefulness, traducement, vilification; ▪ *Ant* approval, encouragement, praise.

backbone [n] strength of character
▪ *Syn* courage, determination, firmness, fortitude, grit, heart, mettle, moral fiber, nerve, pluck, resolution, resolve, stamina, steadfastness, tenacity, toughness, willpower; ▪ *Ant* ineptness, powerlessness, spinelessness, weakness.

back down [v] withdraw from agreement or statement ▪ *Syn* abandon, accede, admit, balk, cancel, defeat, demur, give in, give up, recant, recoil, resign, retreat,

surrender, withdraw, yield; ▪ *Ant* continue, go forward, persist, proceed.

backer [n] *supporter*
▪ *Syn* advocate, ally, benefactor, champion, endorser, follower, patron, promoter, protagonist, sponsor, underwriter, well-wisher; ▪ *Ant* antagonist, opponent, opposer.

backside [n] *rear end*
▪ *Syn* behind, bottom, buttocks, derriere, posterior, rear; ▪ *Ant* front.

backward [adj1] *toward the rear*
▪ *Syn* astern, behind, inverted, rearward, regressive, retrograde; ▪ *Ant* ahead, forward, to the front.

backward [adj2] *slow in growth*
▪ *Syn* arrested, behind, checked, delayed, dense, late, subnormal, undeveloped; ▪ *Ant* advanced, ahead, developing, fast.

backward [adv] *toward the rear*
▪ *Syn* aback, abaft, about, astern, back, behind, in reverse, inverted, rearward; ▪ *Ant* ahead, forward.

backwoods [n/adj] *forests; land distant from settled area* ▪ *Syn* backcountry, boondocks, frontier, hinterland, interior, isolation, outback, rural area, timberland, woodland; ▪ *Ant* city, inner city, metropolis, suburbia.

bad [adj1] *poor quality*
▪ *Syn* abominable, atrocious, awful, beastly, cheap, defective, erroneous, fallacious, faulty, imperfect, inadequate, inferior, off, poor, rough, slipshod, substandard; ▪ *Ant* good, honest, reputable, right, upright, virtuous, worthy.

bad [adj2] *harmful*
▪ *Syn* damaging, dangerous, deleterious, detrimental, hurtful, injurious, ruinous; ▪ *Ant* advantageous, beneficial, benevolent, good, honest, profitable, virtuous.

bad [adj3] *immoral*
▪ *Syn* base, corrupt, criminal, delinquent, evil, iniquitous, mean, reprobate, sinful, vile, villainous, wicked, wrong; ▪ *Ant* good, honest, just, reputable, right, true, virtuous.

badly [adv1] *inadequately*
▪ *Syn* awkwardly, clumsily, crudely, defectively, erroneously, faultily, feebly, haphazardly, incompetently, ineptly, maladroitly, negligently, poorly, shoddily, weakly, wrongly; ▪ *Ant* adequately, satisfactorily.

badly [adv2] *very much; desperately*
▪ *Syn* acutely, deeply, exceedingly, ex-
tremely, gravely, greatly, hard, intensely, painfully, roughly, seriously, severely; ▪ *Ant* calmly, little, mildly.

baffle [v1] *perplex*
▪ *Syn* amaze, astound, befuddle, bewilder, confound, confuse, disconcert, dumbfound, embarrass, faze, muddle, mystify, nonplus, puzzle, rattle, stun, throw; ▪ *Ant* clear up, enlighten, explain.

baffle [v2] *hinder*
▪ *Syn* block, check, circumvent, defeat, foil, frustrate, impede, obstruct, prevent, ruin, thwart, upset; ▪ *Ant* abet, aid, assist, encourage, help, relieve, support.

bag [v] *catch*
▪ *Syn* acquire, apprehend, capture, collar, gain, get, hook, land, nab, nail, net, seize, shoot, take, trap; ▪ *Ant* free, lose, release, surrender.

baggy [adj] *drooping*
▪ *Syn* billowing, bulging, droopy, flabby, ill-fitting, loose, oversize, roomy, sagging, slack; ▪ *Ant* firm, fitting, tight.

balance [v] *make equal; cause to have equilibrium* ▪ *Syn* accord, adjust, attune, cancel, collate, compensate, correspond, counteract, equate, even, harmonize, level, match, neutralize, nullify, offset, parallel, poise, readjust, redeem, set, square, stabilize, steady, tie, weigh; ▪ *Ant* disproportion, overbalance, unbalance.

balanced [adj] *equalized*
▪ *Syn* counterbalanced, equitable, equivalent, evened, fair, just, offset, proportional, stabilized, symmetrical; ▪ *Ant* disproportionate, imbalanced, unequal, unsymmetrical.

bald [adj1] *having no covering*
▪ *Syn* bare, barren, depilated, exposed, glabrous, hairless, naked, shaven, skin head, smooth, stark; ▪ *Ant* hairy, hirsute.

bald [adj2] *simple, unadorned*
▪ *Syn* austere, bare, direct, forthright, outright, plain, severe, straight; ▪ *Ant* adorned, decorated, embellished.

baleful [adj] *menacing*
▪ *Syn* deadly, dire, foreboding, malevolent, noxious, ominous, pernicious, ruinous, sinister, threatening, venomous, woeful; ▪ *Ant* advantageous, auspicious, favorable, good, helping, promising.

balk [v] *thwart*
▪ *Syn* baffle, bar, beat, check, circumvent, cramp, dash, defeat, disappoint, disconcert, foil, frustrate, hinder, ob-

struct, prevent, ruin, stall, stop; ▪ *Ant* aid, help, make easier.

balky [*adj*] *uncooperative*
▪ *Syn* averse, contrary, hesitant, immovable, inflexible, intractable, loath, negative, obstinate, ornery, perverse, reluctant, stubborn; ▪ *Ant* accommodating, compliant, cooperative, docile.

balloon [*v*] *billow out; bloat*
▪ *Syn* belly, blow up, bulge, dilate, distend, enlarge, expand, inflate, puff out, swell; ▪ *Ant* collapse, deflate, flatten, shrink.

balmy [*adj*] *comfortable with respect to weather* ▪ *Syn* mild, moderate, pleasant, refreshing, summery, temperate, tropical; ▪ *Ant* cool, foul, harsh, inclement, wintery.

ban [*v*] *officially forbid*
▪ *Syn* banish, bar, disallow, enjoin, exclude, halt, illegalize, inhibit, interdict, outlaw, prevent, prohibit, proscribe, restrict, suppress; ▪ *Ant* allow, permit.

banal [*adj*] *commonplace*
▪ *Syn* bland, bromidic, cliched, conventional, flat, hackneyed, insipid, mundane, ordinary, pedestrian, platitudinous, stale, stereotyped, stock, tired, tripe, trite, vapid, watery; ▪ *Ant* fresh, new, original.

band [*v*] *group or join group*
▪ *Syn* affiliate, ally, amalgamate, belt, combine, conjoin, consolidate, federate, gather, league, merge, team, unite; ▪ *Ant* disband, disperse, divide, scatter, split up.

baneful [*adj*] *ruinous, injurious*
▪ *Syn* baleful, calamitous, deadly, deleterious, destructive, disastrous, evil, fatal, harmful, hurtful, malefic, noxious, pernicious, pestilent, pestilential, poisonous, venomous, wicked; ▪ *Ant* advantageous, beneficent, beneficial, fortunate, helpful, lucky.

banish [*v*] *expel from place or situation*
▪ *Syn* cast out, deport, discharge, dispel, eject, eradicate, evict, excommunicate, exile, expel, extradict, isolate, ostracize, oust, outlaw, proscribe, relegate, remove, sequester; ▪ *Ant* allow, keep, welcome.

bank [*v1*] *collect money or advantage*
▪ *Syn* amass, deposit, hoard, invest, lay aside, lay away, mass, mound, save, squirrel, stash; ▪ *Ant* disburse, spend.

bank [*v2*] *lean or tilt*
▪ *Syn* bend, camber, cant, incline, pitch, slant, slope; ▪ *Ant* align, plumb, straighten.

bankrupt [*adj*] *unable to pay debts*
▪ *Syn* broke, depleted, destitute, exhausted, failed, impoverished, insolvent, lost, ruined, spent; ▪ *Ant* rich, solvent, wealthy.

bantam [*adj*] *small*
▪ *Syn* diminutive, little, petite, tiny; ▪ *Ant* big, huge, large.

bar [*v1*] *secure, usually with a length of material* ▪ *Syn* barricade, block, close, dam, deadbolt, dike, fasten, fence, jam, latch, lock, plug, seal, secure, trammel, wall; ▪ *Ant* loosen, open, unfasten.

bar [*v2*] *prohibit*
▪ *Syn* ban, boycott, circumvent, condemn, deny, disallow, discourage, eliminate, enjoin, exclude, exile, forbid, frustrate, hinder, interdict, interfere, limit, obstruct, ostracize, preclude, prevent, refuse, restrain, rule out, segregate, suspend; ▪ *Ant* advocate, allow, open, permit.

barb [*n*] *pointed comment*
▪ *Syn* affront, criticism, cut, dig, gibe, insult, rebuff, sarcasm, scoff, sneer; ▪ *Ant* compliment, kindness, praise.

barbaric [*adj*] *crude, savage*
▪ *Syn* boorish, brutal, coarse, cruel, fierce, graceless, inhuman, lowbrow, primitive, rough, tasteless, vulgar, wild; ▪ *Ant* civilized, cultivated, gracious, highbrow, polite, refined.

barbarous [*adj*] *crude, savage*
▪ *Syn* atrocious, barbaric, brutal, coarse, cruel, ferocious, heartless, inhumane, monstrous, primitive, rough, rude, ruthless, sadistic, truculent, vicious, vulgar, wicked, wild; ▪ *Ant* civilized, cultured, educated, kind, nice, polite, refined, sophisticated.

bare [*adj1*] *without clothing*
▪ *Syn* bald, bareskinned, denuded, disrobed, divested, exposed, naked, nude, peeled, shorn, stripped, unclad, uncovered; ▪ *Ant* clothed, dressed, outfitted, robed.

bare [*adj2*] *without covering or content*
▪ *Syn* arid, barren, blank, bleak, clear, desert, desolate, empty, lacking, mean, scanty, scarce, stark, vacant, vacuous, void; ▪ *Ant* covered, filled, full.

bare [*adj3*] *simple, unadorned*
▪ *Syn* austere, bald, basic, cold, essential, hard, literal, meager, modest, scant, severe, sheer, simple, spare, stark; ▪ *Ant* adorned, decorated, embellished.

bare [v] *reveal*
- *Syn* disclose, divulge, exhibit, expose, publish, show, unroll; ▪ *Ant* cloak, cover, hide, secret, veil.

barefaced [adj] *shameless; open*
- *Syn* audacious, blatant, brash, candid, flagrant, frank, glaring, impudent, insolent, manifest, obvious, palpable, transparent; ▪ *Ant* careful, quiet, shamed.

barefoot [adj] *wearing no shoes*
- *Syn* discalceate, discalced, shoeless, unshod; ▪ *Ant* booted, shod.

barely [adv] *not quite*
- *Syn* almost, hardly, just, only just, scantily, scarcely; ▪ *Ant* abundantly, amply, copiously, enough, profusely, sufficiently.

bark [v] *shout*
- *Syn* bawl, bellow, berate, clamor, cry, growl, roar, snap, snarl, yell; ▪ *Ant* murmer, mutter, whisper.

baroque [adj] *decorative, especially architecture* ▪ *Syn* elaborate, embellished, extravagant, flamboyant, florid, gilt, grotesque, ornamented, ornate, overdecorated, rich, rococo; ▪ *Ant* plain, unadorned, undecorated.

barren [adj1] *unable to support growth*
- *Syn* arid, depleted, desolate, dry, effete, empty, fallow, fruitless, impotent, impoverished, parched, sterile, waste; ▪ *Ant* developing, fecund, fertile, filled, full, growing, productive, useful.

barren [adj2] *unprofitable*
- *Syn* dull, flat, fruitless, futile, uninspiring, unproductive, unrewarding, useless, vain; ▪ *Ant* developing, growing, productive, profitable.

barricade [v] *block, usually to protect*
- *Syn* bar, blockade, defend, fortify, obstruct, shut in; ▪ *Ant* allow, open.

barrier [n] *obstruction*
- *Syn* barricade, blockade, boundary, confines, enclosure, fence, fortification, hurdle, impediment, moat, obstacle, pale, railing, roadblock, stop, trench, wall; ▪ *Ant* opening, passage.

base [adj] *vulgar, low*
- *Syn* abject, abominable, contemptible, corrupt, depraved, despicable, disgraceful, foul, humble, ignoble, immoral, loathsome, menial, offensive, pitiful, plebeian, poor, scandalous, shameful, sordid, squalid, vile, worthless, wretched; ▪ *Ant* good, honest, moral, noble.

baseless [adj] *without substantiation*
- *Syn* flimsy, gratuitous, groundless, unconfirmed, uncorroborated, unjustifiable, unjustified, untenable, unwarranted; ▪ *Ant* based, founded, reasoned, substantial, well-founded.

basement [n] *room on lower floor of building* ▪ *Syn* bottom, cellar, crypt, excavation, furnace room, storage, substructure, vault; ▪ *Ant* attic, garrett, loft.

bashful [adj] *shy*
- *Syn* blushing, chary, constrained, diffident, embarrassed, humble, modest, nervous, reticent, retiring, self-conscious, self-effacing, shamefaced, sheepish, timid, timorous; ▪ *Ant* confident, unabashed, unshy.

bashing [n] *physical or verbal abuse against a group or individual based on identity or ideological beliefs* ▪ *Syn* assault, attack, beating, beating up, bias crime, censure, charge, condemnation, criticism, denigration, harassment, hate crime, hounding, jumping, offensive, persecution, strike, torment; ▪ *Ant* acceptance, affirmation, approval, embrace, protection, support, tolerance.

basic [adj] *elementary, fundamental*
- *Syn* basal, central, elemental, essential, inherent, intrinsic, key, main, necessary, primary, principal, underlying, vital; ▪ *Ant* additional, extra, inessential, nonessential, outside, peripheral, secondary.

basically [adv] *fundamentally*
- *Syn* at heart, essentially, firstly, in essence, inherently, in substance, intrinsically, primarily; ▪ *Ant* additionally, extra.

bastion [n] *support; fortified place*
- *Syn* breastwork, bulwark, citadel, defense, fortification, fortress, mainstay, parapet, prop, protection, rock, stronghold, support; ▪ *Ant* weakness, weak spot.

batch [n] *group of same objects*
- *Syn* accumulation, amount, array, assemblage, assortment, bunch, bundle, clump, cluster, group, lot, pack, parcel, quantity, set, shipment, volume; ▪ *Ant* individual, single.

bathe [v] *wash with water and, usually, soap* ▪ *Syn* clean, cleanse, douse, flood, immerse, moisten, rinse, scrub, shower, soap, sponge, steep, suffuse; ▪ *Ant* dirty, smudge, stain.

batten [v] *fasten securely*
- *Syn* board up, clamp down, fix, nail down, secure, tie, tighten; ▪ *Ant* loosen, unfasten, unfix.

battle [v] *fight, struggle*
- **Syn** agitate, argue, clamor, combat, contend, dispute, feud, oppugn, skirmish, strive, war, wrestle; **Ant** make peace.

bawdy [adj] *vulgar, dirty*
- **Syn** blue, cheap, coarse, dirty, erotic, gross, indecent, indecorous, indelicate, lascivious, lecherous, lewd, licentious, obscene, prurient, ribald, risque, rude, salacious, suggestive; **Ant** chaste, clean, decent, ethical, modest, proper.

bawl [v] *yell*
- **Syn** bellow, call, cheer, clamor, howl, roar, scream, screech, shout, shriek, vociferate; **Ant** murmur, mutter, whisper.

beam [v] *smile broadly*
- **Syn** gleam, glow, grin, laugh, radiate, shine, smirk; **Ant** frown, scowl.

beaming [adj1] *radiant; beautiful*
- **Syn** bright, effulgent, flashing, gleaming, glowing, incandescent, lucent, luminous, refulgent, sparkling; **Ant** dark, dusky, gloomy, tenebrous.

beaming [adj2] *very happy*
- **Syn** animated, cheerful, genial, grinning, joyful, radiant, shining, smiling, sparkling, sunny; **Ant** frowning, sad, sullen, unhappy.

bear [v1] *bring*
- **Syn** carry, convey, deliver, ferry, fetch, move, pack, take, tote, transfer, transport; **Ant** refuse, take, throw away.

bear [v2] *endure*
- **Syn** abide, admit, allow, brook, experience, permit, stomach, suffer, tolerate, undergo; **Ant** avoid, dodge, evade, shun.

bearded [adj] *having facial hair*
- **Syn** barbate, bewhiskered, bristly, bushy, goateed, hairy, hirsute, shaggy, stubbled, stubbly, whiskered; **Ant** clean-shaven, unbearded, unhirsute.

beastly [adj1] *savage; vulgar*
- **Syn** abominable, animal, barbarous, base, bestial, brutal, brute, carnal, coarse, cruel, degraded, depraved, disgusting, feral, ferine, foul, inhuman, loathsome, low, monstrous, obscene, prurient, repulsive, sadistic, unclean, vile; **Ant** good, kind, nice, superior.

beastly [adj2] *offensive*
- **Syn** awful, disagreeable, disgusting, foul, mean, revolting, rotten, terrible, unpleasant, vile; **Ant** good, inoffensive, kind, nice.

beat [adj] *very tired*
- **Syn** exhausted, fatigued, wearied, weary, worn out; **Ant** invigorated, replenished, rested.

beat [v1] *injure by striking*
- **Syn** bash, batter, belt, bruise, clout, crush, cudgel, drub, flail, flog, hammer, hit, knock, lambaste, lash, maul, punch, punish, rap, slug, smack, strike, thrash, trounce, wallop, whip; **Ant** aid, assist, guard, help, protect.

beat [v2] *defeat, surpass*
- **Syn** best, better, be victorious, conquer, exceed, excel, outdo, outshine, overcome, overwhelm, subdue, top, transcend, triumph, vanquish, whip; **Ant** cede, lose, relinquish, retreat, surrender.

beaten [adj] *defeated*
- **Syn** baffled, bested, conquered, cowed, crushed, disheartened, humbled, overcome, overwhelmed, routed, subjugated, thwarted, trounced, vanquished; **Ant** triumphant, uplifted, victorious.

beautiful [adj] *physically attractive*
- **Syn** alluring, appealing, beauteous, charming, comely, dazzling, delicate, divine, elegant, enticing, excellent, exquisite, fair, fine, good-looking, gorgeous, handsome, ideal, lovely, magnificent, pretty, pulchritudinous, radiant, ravishing, resplendent, sightly, stunning, sublime, superb, wonderful; **Ant** disgusting, grotesque, hideous, homely, offensive, plain, repulsive, ugly, unattractive.

beautify [v] *make more physically attractive* **Syn** adorn, array, bedeck, deck, decorate, embellish, enhance, garnish, gild, glamorize, grace, improve, make up, ornament, set off, trim; **Ant** disfigure, harm, injure, mar, spoil.

beckon [v] *call, signal, or lure*
- **Syn** bid, coax, command, demand, draw, entice, gesticulate, gesture, invite, motion, nod, sign, summon, tempt, wave; **Ant** drive away, repel, repulse, ward off.

becoming [adj1] *flattering*
- **Syn** agreeable, attractive, beautiful, comely, cute, enhancing, excellent, fair, graceful, handsome, neat, nice, presentable, pretty, seemly, tasteful, welcome, well-chosen; **Ant** indecorous, tasteless, ugly, unattractive, unbecoming, unfitting, unsuitable.

becoming [adj2] *suitable; appropriate*
▪ *Syn* befitting, comme il faut, compatible, conforming, congruous, correct, decent, decorous, fit, fitting, in keeping, nice, proper, right, seemly, worthy; ▪ *Ant* improper, inappropriate, unbecoming, unfitting, unseemly, unsuitable.

bedlam [n] *chaotic situation*
▪ *Syn* chaos, clamor, commotion, confusion, din, disquiet, furor, madhouse, maelstrom, noise, pandemonium, racket, tumult, turmoil, uproar; ▪ *Ant* calm, peace, quiet.

bedraggled [adj] *unkempt*
▪ *Syn* decrepit, dirty, disheveled, dowdy, faded, muddied, run-down, seedy, slovenly, sodden, soiled, stained, sullied, tacky, tattered, threadbare; ▪ *Ant* clean, neat, ordered, tidy.

befitting [adj] *appropriate*
▪ *Syn* apt, becoming, beseeming, comme il faut, correct, decent, decorous, felicitous, just, nice, proper, seemly, suitable; ▪ *Ant* improper, inappropriate, incorrect, unbecoming, unfitting, unsuitable.

before [adv] *earlier*
▪ *Syn* afore, antecedently, anteriorly, back, ere, fore, formerly, heretofore, in advance, in days of yore, past, precendently, previously, since, sooner, up to now, vanward; ▪ *Ant* after, afterward, behind, later.

before [prep] *earlier than*
▪ *Syn* ahead of, ante, antecedent to, anterior to, ere, preceding, previous to, prior to, since; ▪ *Ant* after, afterward, behind, later.

befriend [v] *make social acquaintance; support* ▪ *Syn* advise, aid, assist, benefit, encourage, favor, help, patronize, side with, stand by, sustain, uphold, welcome; ▪ *Ant* ignore, neglect.

befuddle [v] *confuse*
▪ *Syn* addle, baffle, bewilder, daze, disorient, dumbfound, fluster, muddle, puzzle, shake, stupefy; ▪ *Ant* clear up, explain.

beg [v1] *request*
▪ *Syn* abjure, advocate, ask, beseech, besiege, canvass, entreat, implore, importune, invoke, obsecrate, obtest, petition, plead, press, requisition, solicit, sue, urge, worry; ▪ *Ant* answer, reply, respond.

beg [v2] *seek charity*
▪ *Syn* ask alms, benefit, brace, call on, call upon, clamor for, hustle, knock, mendicate, panhandle, scrounge, solicit charity, tap, touch, want; ▪ *Ant* donate, give, offer.

begin [v1] *start*
▪ *Syn* activate, bring about, cause, commence, create, do, drive, effect, embark on, establish, eventuate, found, generate, impel, inaugurate, induce, initiate, instigate, institute, introduce, launch, lay foundation for, lead, make, motivate, mount, occasion, open, originate, prepare, produce, set about, set in motion, trigger, undertake; ▪ *Ant* complete, conclude, consummate, end, finish.

begin [v2] *come into being; become functional* ▪ *Syn* appear, arise, be born, come into existence, commence, dawn, emanate, emerge, enter, germinate, issue forth, originate, proceed from, result from, rise, set, spring, sprout, start; ▪ *Ant* die, end.

begrudge [v] *wish that someone did not have* ▪ *Syn* be jealous, be reluctant, be stingy, covet, eat one's heart out, envy, grudge, resent; ▪ *Ant* be happy for, congratulate, wish well.

behave [v] *act reasonably, properly*
▪ *Syn* act with decorum, be civil, be good, be orderly, comport oneself, conduct oneself properly, control, demean oneself, direct, discipline oneself, manage, manage oneself; ▪ *Ant* act up, misbehave.

behind [adv/prep] *position farther back; following* ▪ *Syn* after, at the rear of, back of, in the background, in the wake, later than, next, off the pace, subsequently, trailing; ▪ *Ant* ahead of, in advance, in front, out front.

behold [v] *regard; look at*
▪ *Syn* catch, consider, descry, discern, eye, note, notice, observe, perceive, regard, see, survey, view, watch, witness; ▪ *Ant* disregard, ignore, miss, overlook.

beholden [adj] *indebted*
▪ *Syn* bound, grateful, obligated, obliged, owing, responsible, under obligation; ▪ *Ant* thankless, ungrateful.

being [n1] *existence*
▪ *Syn* actuality, animation, journey, life, living, presence, reality, subsistence, vitality, world; ▪ *Ant* deadness, nonexistence, nothingness, nullity.

being [n2] *animate object*
▪ *Syn* animal, beast, body, creature, en-

tity, human, human being, individual, living thing, mortal, organism, person, personage, soul; ▪ *Ant* abstract, inanimate, thing.

belated [*adj*] *late, slow*
▪ *Syn* behindhand, behind time, delayed, overdue, remiss, tardy; ▪ *Ant* early, on time, punctual, timely.

belie [*v1*] *disprove*
▪ *Syn* confute, contradict, contravene, controvert, deny, disagree, explode, gainsay, negate, oppose, repudiate; ▪ *Ant* affirm, attest, prove.

belie [*v2*] *deceive*
▪ *Syn* color, conceal, disguise, distort, falsify, gloss over, hide, mislead, misrepresent, misstate, pervert, twist, warp; ▪ *Ant* be honest, indicate, reveal, verify.

believable [*adj*] *trustworthy*
▪ *Syn* acceptable, authentic, conceivable, convincing, credible, fiduciary, imaginable, impressive, likely, persuasive, plausible, presumable, probable, rational, reasonable, reliable, straight, supposable, tenable, tried, unquestionable; ▪ *Ant* doubtful, dubious, fabulous, implausible, incredible, questionable, suspect, unacceptable, unbelievable, unconvincing, unreliable.

believe [*v*] *trust, rely on*
▪ *Syn* accept, accredit, admit, affirm, be of the opinion, conceive, conclude, consider, count on, credit, deem, give credence to, have faith in, hold, opine, posit, postulate, presume true, presuppose, regard, suppose, swear by, take for granted, think, trust, understand; ▪ *Ant* disbelieve, distrust, doubt, question, suspect.

belittle [*v*] *detract*
▪ *Syn* blister, criticize, decry, depreciate, derogate, diminish, discount, discredit, lower, minimize, pan, put down, scoff at, scorn, sneer at, write off; ▪ *Ant* build up, exaggerate, praise, value.

belligerent [*adj*] *nasty, argumentative*
▪ *Syn* aggressive, antagonistic, bellicose, combative, contentious, fierce, hostile, hot-tempered, mean, militant, pugnacious, quarrelsome, truculent, warlike; ▪ *Ant* cooperative, helping, kind, nice.

bellow [*v*] *holler*
▪ *Syn* bark, bawl, bay, blare, bluster, bray, clamor, howl, low, roar, scream, shout, shriek, wail, whoop, yell; ▪ *Ant* murmur, mutter, whisper.

belonging [*n*] *sense of security in friendship* ▪ *Syn* acceptance, affinity, association, attachment, inclusion, kinship, loyalty, rapport; ▪ *Ant* antipathy, insecurity.

beloved [*adj*] *adored*
▪ *Syn* admired, cared for, cherished, darling, esteemed, favorite, hallowed, highly regarded, highly valued, idolized, loved, precious, prized, revered, treasured, venerated, worshiped; ▪ *Ant* despised, disliked, hated.

below [*adv/prep1*] *lower*
▪ *Syn* beneath, down, down from, under, underneath; ▪ *Ant* above, over.

below [*prep2*] *less than; beneath*
▪ *Syn* inferior, lesser, lower, subject, subordinate, unworthy; ▪ *Ant* above, more, over.

bemoan [*v*] *express sorrow*
▪ *Syn* bewail, complain, deplore, grieve for, lament, moan over, mourn, regret, rue, weep for; ▪ *Ant* be happy, celebrate, exult, gloat, laugh.

bemuse [*v*] *confuse*
▪ *Syn* addle, amaze, bewilder, daze, moon, muddle, overwhelm, paralyze, perplex, puzzle, stun, stupefy; ▪ *Ant* clear up, enlighten, explain, illuminate, tell.

bend [*v*] *form or cause a curve*
▪ *Syn* angle, bow, buckle, careen, contort, curl, detour, double, flex, genuflect, hook, incline, lean, loop, pervert, round, spiral, turn, twist, verge, warp, waver, yaw, zigzag; ▪ *Ant* align, square, straighten.

beneath [*adv*] *in a lower place*
▪ *Syn* below, underneath; ▪ *Ant* above, higher, over.

beneath [*prep*] *inferior*
▪ *Syn* below, lesser, less than, lower than, subordinate, under, underneath, unworthy of; ▪ *Ant* above, higher, over, superior.

benediction [*n*] *approval; closing prayer* ▪ *Syn* amen, approbation, approval, beatitude, benedictus, blessing, consecration, favor, grace, gratitude, invocation, orison, praise, sanctification, thanks, thanksgiving; ▪ *Ant* anathema, curse, execration.

benefactor [*n*] *donor*
▪ *Syn* aid, altruist, assistant, backer, contributor, fan, good Samaritan, helper, humanitarian, mark, patron, philanthro-

pist, promoter, sponsor, subsidizer, supporter, well-wisher; ▪ **Ant** antagonist, opponent, opposer.

beneficial [*adj*] *advantageous*

▪ **Syn** benign, constructive, favorable, gainful, good, healthful, helpful, propitious, salubrious, salutary, useful, valuable, worthy; ▪ **Ant** disadvantageous, harmful, hurting, unfortunate, unhelpful, unrewarding.

beneficiary [*n*] *person who gains, benefits* ▪ **Syn** assignee, charity case, devisee, donee, grantee, heir, heiress, inheritor, legatee, payee, pensioner, possessor, receiver, recipient, stipendiary, successor; ▪ **Ant** donor, giver, payer.

benefit [*v*] *help, enhance*

▪ **Syn** advance, advantage, aid, ameliorate, assist, avail, better, build, contribute to, favor, further, improve, pay, profit, promote, relieve, serve, succor; ▪ **Ant** handicap, harm, hinder, hurt, injure.

benevolent [*adj*] *charitable, kind*

▪ **Syn** altruistic, beneficent, benign, bighearted, bounteous, caring, chivalrous, compassionate, considerate, generous, helpful, humanitarian, kindhearted, liberal, magnanimous, philanthropic, warmhearted, well-disposed; ▪ **Ant** greedy, malevolent, mean, selfish, spiteful, unkind.

benign [*adj1*] *kindly*

▪ **Syn** amiable, beneficent, benevolent, complaisant, congenial, favorable, friendly, good, goodhearted, gracious, kind, liberal, merciful, mild, obliging, sympathetic; ▪ **Ant** hateful, hostile, hurtful, injurious, malignant, unkind.

benign [*adj2*] *mild, especially describing weather* ▪ **Syn** auspicious, balmy, bright, favorable, fortunate, gentle, healthful, propitious, refreshing, temperate, warm; ▪ **Ant** bad, harsh, severe.

benign [*adj3*] *advantageous*

▪ **Syn** auspicious, benevolent, bright, charitable, encouraging, favorable, good, lucky, merciful, propitious, salutary, smiling; ▪ **Ant** disadvantageous, harmful, hurtful.

benign [*adj4*] *not cancerous*

▪ **Syn** curable, early stage, harmless, limited, remediable, slight, superficial; ▪ **Ant** cancerous, malignant.

bent [*adj1*] *curved*

▪ **Syn** angled, arched, bowed, contorted, crooked, curvilinear, hooked, inclined, looped, rounded, sinuous, slumped, twined, twisted, warped; ▪ **Ant** rigid, straight, straight as an arrow, unbent, unbowed, uncurved.

bent [*adj2*] *determined*

▪ **Syn** bound, decided, dedicated, disposed, firm, fixed, inclined, insistent, intent, predisposed, resolute, resolved, set, settled; ▪ **Ant** uncaring, undecided.

berate [*v*] *criticize hatefully*

▪ **Syn** blister, call down, castigate, censure, chide, rate, rebuke, reprimand, reproach, reprove, scold, scorch, tonguelash, upbraid, vituperate; ▪ **Ant** compliment, hail, praise.

bereft [*adj*] *lacking; missing*

▪ **Syn** bereaved, cut off, deprived, destitute, dispossessed, divested, minus, robbed, shorn, stripped, wanting, without; ▪ **Ant** endowed, full, happy, supplied.

beseech [*v*] *beg*

▪ **Syn** adjure, appeal, ask, entreat, implore, importune, petition, plead, pray, solicit, sue, supplicate; ▪ **Ant** give, offer.

best [*adj1*] *most excellent*

▪ **Syn** ace, capital, champion, choicest, culminating, finest, first-class, foremost, greatest, highest, incomparable, inimitable, leading, matchless, nonpareil, optimum, outstanding, paramount, peerless, pre-eminent, superlative, terrific, transcendent; ▪ **Ant** least, lowest, minimal, minimum, worst.

best [*adj2*] *correct, right*

▪ **Syn** advantageous, apt, desirable, golden, most desirable, most fitting, preferred, presentable; ▪ **Ant** incorrect, not right.

best [*adj3*] *most*

▪ **Syn** biggest, bulkiest, greatest, largest; ▪ **Ant** fewest, least.

best [*v*] *defeat; gain advantage*

▪ **Syn** better, conquer, exceed, excel, outdo, outstrip, overcome, prevail, surpass, top, triumph, trounce, wallop; ▪ **Ant** give up, lose, relent, surrender.

bestow [*v*] *give, allot*

▪ **Syn** accord, apportion, award, bequeath, commit, confer, devote, donate, entrust, favor, gift, grant, honor with, impart, lavish, offer, present, render to; ▪ **Ant** deprive, refuse, take.

betray [*v1*] *be disloyal*

▪ **Syn** abandon, be unfaithful, break promise, commit treason, cross, deceive, double-cross, forsake, seduce, trick, turn in; **Ant** be faithful, be loyal, defend, protect, support.

betray [v2] *divulge, expose information*
- **Syn** disclose, evince, give away, inform, lay bare, make known, manifest, reveal, show, spill, tattle, tell, turn in, unmask; **Ant** be quiet, cover up, hide, keep secret.

better [adj1] *excelling, more excellent*
- **Syn** choice, exceptional, finer, greater, improved, larger, preferable, prominent, sharpened, superior, surpassing, worthier; **Ant** inferior, lesser, poorer, worse.

better [adj2] *improved in health*
- **Syn** convalescent, cured, fitter, fully recovered, healthier, improving, mending, on the mend, progressing, recovering, stronger, well; **Ant** more ill, sicker, unhealthy, worse.

better [adj3] *larger*
- **Syn** bigger, greater, longer, more, preponderant, weightier; **Ant** littler, smaller, tinier.

better [v] *improve performance; outdo*
- **Syn** advance, amend, correct, enhance, exceed, further, help, meliorate, mend, outshine, promote, raise, refine, revamp, surpass, top, transcend; **Ant** deteriorate, get worse, worsen.

better [adv] *in a more excellent manner*
- **Syn** finer, greater, more, more advantageously, more competently, more completely, preferably, to a greater degree; **Ant** worse.

between [adv/prep] *middle from two points* **Syn** amid, among, betwixt, bounded by, enclosed by, halfway, in, intervening, in the midst of, medially, midway, separating, surrounded by, within; **Ant** around, away, away from, outside, separate.

beverage [n] *liquid refreshment*
- **Syn** cooler, draft, drink, drinkable, libation, liquor, potable, potation; **Ant** food, victuals.

bevy [n] *swarm*
- **Syn** assembly, band, bunch, cluster, collection, covey, crew, crowd, flight, flock, gathering, group, pack, party, troupe; **Ant** individual, one.

bewail [v] *cry over, lament*
- **Syn** bemoan, deplore, grieve, moan, mourn, regret, rue, take on, wail, weep over; **Ant** be happy, be joyous, exalt, gloat, praise, vaunt.

beware [v] *be careful*
- **Syn** attend, avoid, be cautious, be wary, guard against, heed, look out, mind, notice, refrain from, shun, take heed, watch out; **Ant** court, invite, risk, take on.

bewilder [v] *confuse*
- **Syn** addle, baffle, bemuse, confound, daze, disconcert, distract, mystify, perplex, puzzle, rattle, stupefy, throw, upset; **Ant** clear up, explain, orient.

bewildered [adj] *confused*
- **Syn** agape, agog, astonished, astounded, awed, baffled, befuddled, dazed, disconcerted, dumbstruck, flustered, lost, muddled, reeling, shocked, startled, stunned, stupefied, surprised, taken aback, thrown; **Ant** clear, oriented, understanding.

bewitch [v] *charm*
- **Syn** allure, attract, bedevil, beguile, captivate, control, dazzle, enchant, enrapture, entrance, fascinate, hex, hypnotize, spellbind, trick, vamp, wile; **Ant** disenchant, disgust, turn off.

bewitched [adj] *charmed*
- **Syn** captivated, enamored, enchanted, enraptured, ensorcelled, entranced, fascinated, mesmerized, possessed, spellbound, transformed; **Ant** disenchanted, disgusted, turned off.

beyond [adv/prep] *further; outside limits*
- **Syn** above, after, ahead, at a distance, away from, before, besides, clear of, farther, in addition to, in advance of, moreover, on the other side, out of range, out of reach, outside, over, past, remote, superior to, without, yonder; **Ant** close, inside.

bias [v] *cause to favor*
- **Syn** distort, incline, influence, make partial, prejudice, prepossess, slant, sway, twist, warp, weight; **Ant** be fair, be impartial, be just.

bicker [v] *nastily argue*
- **Syn** altercate, brawl, caterwaul, cavil, dig, disagree, dispute, fall out, fight, hassle, quarrel, quibble, row, spar, squabble, wrangle; **Ant** agree, concede, discuss.

bidding [n] *command*
- **Syn** behest, call, charge, demand, dictate, direction, injunction, instruction, invitation, mandate, order, request, summons, word; **Ant** answer.

bide [v] *wait*
- **Syn** attend, await, continue, dwell, hang

around, linger, live, remain, reside, stay, tarry; ▪ *Ant* go, hurry, move.

big [*adj1*] *large, great*
▪ *Syn* ample, bulky, colossal, copious, enormous, extensive, fat, full, gigantic, hefty, huge, hulking, immense, jumbo, king-sized, mammoth, massive, packed, ponderous, roomy, sizable, strapping, substantial, thundering, tremendous, vast, voluminous; ▪ *Ant* little, small, tiny.

big [*adj2*] *important*
▪ *Syn* considerable, eminent, influential, leading, main, meaningful, momentous, paramount, prime, prominent, serious, significant, substantial, valuable, weighty; ▪ *Ant* blah, bland, dull, unimportant.

big [*adj3*] *grown*
▪ *Syn* adult, elder, full-grown, grown-up, mature, tall; ▪ *Ant* adolescent, baby, babyish, infant, infantile, juvenile.

big [*adj4*] *generous*
▪ *Syn* altruistic, benevolent, bighearted, chivalrous, considerate, free, gracious, heroic, liberal, lofty, magnanimous, noble, unselfish; ▪ *Ant* selfish, ungenerous, ungiving.

big [*adj5*] *arrogant*
▪ *Syn* boastful, bragging, conceited, flamboyant, haughty, imperious, inflated, overblown, pompous, presumptuous, pretentious, proud; ▪ *Ant* humble, shy, unconfident.

bigoted [*adj*] *intolerant, prejudiced*
▪ *Syn* biased, dogmatic, illiberal, narrow-minded, obstinate, opinionated, partial, sectarian, small-minded, twisted, unfair, warped; ▪ *Ant* broad-minded, fair, humanitarian, just, liberal, open-minded, tolerant, unprejudiced.

bilateral [*adj*] *having two sides*
▪ *Syn* mutual, reciprocal, respective, two-sided; ▪ *Ant* multilateral, unilateral.

bilk [*v*] *cheat*
▪ *Syn* beat, circumvent, con, deceive, defraud, foil, frustrate, ruin, swindle, thwart, trick; ▪ *Ant* give, give away.

billow [*v*] *surge*
▪ *Syn* balloon, bounce, bulge, heave, pitch, puff up, ripple, rise up, roll, swell, toss, undulate, wave; ▪ *Ant* cave in, collapse, deflate, give way, shrivel.

bind [*v1*] *fasten, secure*
▪ *Syn* adhere, attach, bandage, chain, cinch, clamp, connect, dress, edge, en-

case, fetter, fold, furl, glue, hamper, handcuff, hem, lace, lash, leash, manacle, muzzle, paste, pin, pinion, restrain, restrict, rope, shackle, strap, swathe, tether, tie, trammel, unite, wrap, yoke; ▪ *Ant* free, loose, loosen, release, set free, unbind, unfasten, untie.

bind [*v2*] *obligate; restrict*
▪ *Syn* compel, confine, constrain, detain, enslave, force, hinder, indenture, lock up, necessitate, oblige, prescribe, require, restrain, restrict, yoke; ▪ *Ant* allow, free, let, permit, set free.

binding [*adj*] *confining*
▪ *Syn* attached, enslaved, fastened, indentured, limiting, restraining, tied, tying; ▪ *Ant* alterable, breakable, revocable, unbinding, unconfining, unnecessary.

birth [*n1*] *becoming alive*
▪ *Syn* bearing, beginning, childbearing, creation, delivery, labor, nascency, natality, nativity, parturition, producing; ▪ *Ant* death, decease, demise, passing.

birth [*n2*] *beginning*
▪ *Syn* commencement, dawn, emergence, fountainhead, genesis, onset, opening, origin, rise, source, start; ▪ *Ant* conclusion, death, end, ending, finale, finish.

bisect [*v*] *divide in two*
▪ *Syn* bifurcate, cleave, cross, cut in half, dichotomize, dimidiate, divaricate, fork, furcate, halve, hemisect, intersect, separate, split; ▪ *Ant* combine, join.

bit [*n*] *tiny piece*
▪ *Syn* atom, chip, crumb, division, dose, dot, driblet, droplet, end, excerpt, flake, fraction, fragment, grain, iota, lump, mite, modicum, molecule, morsel, parcel, particle, pinch, sample, scintilla, scrap, section, segment, shard, shaving, shred, slice, sliver, snippet, speck, splinter, sprinkling, taste, trace, trickle; ▪ *Ant* complete, entire, total, whole.

biting [*adj1*] *piercing, sharp*
▪ *Syn* bitter, bleak, blighting, cold, crisp, cutting, freezing, harsh, nipping, penetrating, raw; ▪ *Ant* bland, calm, mild.

biting [*adj2*] *sarcastic*
▪ *Syn* acerbic, acrimonious, bitter, caustic, cutting, incisive, mordant, scathing, severe, sharp, trenchant, withering; ▪ *Ant* kind, nice, sweet.

bitter [*adj1*] *pungent, sharp*
▪ *Syn* acerbic, acid, acrid, amaroidal, astringent, harsh, sour, tart, unsweetened,

vinegary; ▪ *Ant* bland, mild, pleasant, sweet.

bitter [*adj2*] *hostile, nasty*
▪ *Syn* acrimonious, antagonistic, begrudging, biting, caustic, embittered, estranged, fierce, freezing, hateful, intense, irreconcilable, morose, rancorous, resentful, sardonic, severe, sore, sour, sullen, virulent, vitriolic; ▪ *Ant* agreeable, content, genial, kind, nice, pleasant, sweet.

bitter [*adj3*] *painful, distressing*
▪ *Syn* afflictive, brutal, calamitous, cruel, dire, distasteful, galling, grievous, hard, harsh, heartbreaking, inclement, intense, merciless, offensive, poignant, provoking, rigorous, ruthless, savage, sharp, stinging, vexatious, woeful; ▪ *Ant* good, helping, wonderful.

bizarre [*adj*] *strange, wild*
▪ *Syn* comical, curious, eccentric, extraordinary, fantastic, freakish, grotesque, ludicrous, offbeat, outlandish, peculiar, queer, ridiculous, singular, unusual, weird; ▪ *Ant* normal, reasonable, usual.

black [*adj1*] *dark-colored, inky*
▪ *Syn* atramentous, charcoal, clouded, dusky, ebon, ebony, jet, obsidian, onyx, piceous, pitch, raven, sable, shadowy, slate, sloe, sooty, stygian; ▪ *Ant* ashen, chalky, ivory, light, pale, pearly, white.

black [*adj2*] *hopeless*
▪ *Syn* bleak, depressing, dismal, dispiriting, distressing, doleful, dreary, foreboding, funereal, gloomy, lugubrious, mournful, ominous, oppressive, sad, sinister, somber, threatening; ▪ *Ant* hopeful, optimistic.

black [*adj3*] *dirty*
▪ *Syn* dingy, filthy, foul, grimy, impure, nasty, soiled, sooty, spotted, squalid, stained; ▪ *Ant* clean, immaculate, snowy, spotless.

black [*adj4*] *angry*
▪ *Syn* enraged, fierce, furious, hostile, menacing, resentful, sour, sullen, threatening; ▪ *Ant* bright, cheerful, happy, lively, merry.

blacken [*v1*] *darken*
▪ *Syn* befoul, begrime, blot, cloud, deepen, ebonize, grow dim, ink, shade, soil; ▪ *Ant* bleach, lighten, whiten.

blacken [*v2*] *malign; smear*
▪ *Syn* asperse, attack, calumniate, decry, defame, defile, denigrate, libel, malign, slander, slur, stain, sully, tarnish, traduce, vilify; ▪ *Ant* compliment, enhance, praise.

blacklist [*v*] *ban*
▪ *Syn* banish, bar, blackball, boycott, debar, exclude, expel, ostracize, proscribe, reject, repudiate; ▪ *Ant* accept, allow, ask in, permit, welcome.

black out [*v1*] *delete; cover*
▪ *Syn* batten, conceal, cover up, cross out, cut off, darken, eclipse, eradicate, erase, obfuscate, rub out, shade; ▪ *Ant* add, pencil in, uncover.

black out [*v2*] *faint*
▪ *Syn* collapse, lose consciousness, slip into coma; ▪ *Ant* resuscitate, revive.

blame [*v*] *accuse; place responsibility*
▪ *Syn* ascribe, attribute, censure, charge, chide, condemn, criticize, denounce, disapprove, frame, indict, rebuke, reprehend, reproach, reprove, saddle, upbraid; ▪ *Ant* absolve, acquit, applaud, clear, commend, exalt, exculpate, exonerate, praise, thank.

blameless [*adj*] *not responsible*
▪ *Syn* above suspicion, clean, clear, exemplary, faultless, guiltless, immaculate, inculpable, innocent, irreprehensible, perfect, righteous, stainless, upright, virtuous; ▪ *Ant* at fault, culpable, guilty, impeachable, reproachable, responsible.

bland [*adj1*] *tasteless; undistinctive*
▪ *Syn* banal, boring, dull, flat, flavorless, insipid, monotonous, tame, tedious, vapid, watery, weak; ▪ *Ant* delicious, distinctive, sharp, tasty.

bland [*adj2*] *friendly, gracious*
▪ *Syn* affable, amiable, civilized, congenial, courteous, gentle, good-natured, ingratiating, pleasant, smooth, suave, unctuous, urbane; ▪ *Ant* blase, dull, unfriendly, ungracious.

bland [*adj3*] *mild, temperate*
▪ *Syn* balmy, calm, clear, lenient, mollifying, nonirritating, smooth, soft, soothing; ▪ *Ant* bitter, caustic, severe, sharp.

blank [*adj1*] *clear*
▪ *Syn* bare, clean, empty, fresh, new, plain, vacant, vacuous, void; ▪ *Ant* filled, full, habited, occupied, packed, replete.

blank [*adj2*] *expressionless*
▪ *Syn* deadpan, dull, empty, hollow, immobile, impassive, inane, lifeless, masklike, meaningless, noncommittal, stiff, stupid, vacant, vacuous, vague; ▪ *Ant* animated, expressive, lively.

blank [adj3] *dumbfounded*
- **Syn** awestruck, bewildered, confounded, confused, dazed, disconcerted, muddled, nonplussed, stupefied; **Ant** aware, excited, understanding.

blanket [adj] *comprehensive*
- **Syn** absolute, all-inclusive, overall, sweeping, unconditional; **Ant** incomplete, uncomprehensive.

blanket [v] *cover*
- **Syn** bury, cloak, cloud, coat, conceal, eclipse, envelop, hide, mask, obscure, overlay, overspread, suppress, surround; **Ant** lay bare, uncover.

blasé [adj] *nonchalant*
- **Syn** apathetic, bored, disenchanted, indifferent, jaded, knowing, mellow, mondaine, unconcerned, uninterested, unmoved, weary, worldly; **Ant** enthusiastic, excited.

blasphemous [adj] *irreverent*
- **Syn** disrespectful, godless, impious, insulting, irreligious, profane, sacrilegious; **Ant** godly, pious, religious, respectful, reverent.

blatant [adj1] *obvious; brazen*
- **Syn** arrant, barefaced, clear, conspicuous, flagrant, garish, impudent, loud, naked, obtrusive, ostentatious, overt, plain, prominent, pronounced, protrusive, shameless, unabashed, unmitigated; **Ant** inconspicuous, quiet, subtle, unpronounced.

blatant [adj2] *deafening*
- **Syn** boisterous, clamorous, harsh, loud, noisy, obstreperous, obtrusive, piercing, strident, vociferous; **Ant** quiet, silent, subtle.

bleach [v] *whiten*
- **Syn** achromatize, blanch, blench, decolorize, etiolate, fade, lighten, pale, peroxide; **Ant** blacken, darken, yellow.

bleak [adj1] *barren*
- **Syn** austere, bare, blank, blighted, burned, cleared, cold, deforested, deserted, desolate, dreary, exposed, grim, open, raw, scorched, stripped, wild, windswept; **Ant** appealing, bright, comfortable, nice, pleasant, populated, sunny.

bleak [adj2] *depressing*
- **Syn** black, cheerless, dark, discouraging, disheartening, dismal, dreary, funereal, gloomy, hopeless, joyless, lonely, melancholy, mournful, oppressive, somber; **Ant** cheerful, comforting, congenial, encouraging, nice, pleasant.

blemish [v] *flaw, disfigure*
- **Syn** blot, blotch, damage, deface, distort, harm, impair, injure, maim, mangle, mar, mark, mutilate, scar, smudge, spoil, spot, stain, sully, taint, tarnish, twist, vitiate; **Ant** adorn, beautify, decorate, embellish, ornament.

blend [v1] *mix*
- **Syn** amalgamate, cement, coalesce, combine, commingle, commix, compound, fuse, integrate, interblend, intermix, meld, merge, mingle, synthesize, unite, weld; **Ant** disperse, divide, separate, unmix.

blend [v2] *harmonize*
- **Syn** arrange, complement, integrate, orchestrate, suit, symphonize, synthesize, unify; **Ant** disharmonize, unmix.

bless [v1] *sanctify*
- **Syn** absolve, anoint, baptize, beatify, canonize, commend, confirm, consecrate, dedicate, enshrine, eulogize, exalt, extol, glorify, hallow, honor, laud, magnify, ordain, panegyrize, praise, pray for, pronounce holy, sacrifice, thank; **Ant** condemn, curse, damn.

bless [v2] *grant, bestow*
- **Syn** celebrate, endow, favor, give, glorify, grace, laud, magnify, praise, provide; **Ant** deny, disallow, disapprove, refuse, veto.

blessed [adj1] *sanctified*
- **Syn** adored, beatified, consecrated, divine, exalted, glorified, hallowed, holy, inviolable, redeemed, revered, sacred, sacrosanct, spiritual; **Ant** condemned, cursed, damned, disapproved, profane.

blessed [adj2] *happy*
- **Syn** blissful, content, favored, fortunate, glad, joyful, joyous, lucky; **Ant** condemned, cursed, damned, unhappy, unlucky.

blight [v] *ruin, destroy*
- **Syn** annihilate, crush, damage, dash, decay, disappoint, frustrate, injure, mar, nullify, spoil, taint, wither, wreck; **Ant** aid, bless, guard, help, prosper, protect.

blind [adj1] *sightless*
- **Syn** amaurotic, dark, eyeless, groping, purblind, typhlotic, visionless; **Ant** seeing, sighted.

blind [adj2] *indifferent*
- **Syn** careless, heedless, ignorant, imperceptive, inattentive, insensitive, myopic, neglectful, oblivious, unconscious, undiscerning, unmindful, unobservant;

• *Ant* aware, cunning, perceptive, quick, quick, sharp, understanding.

blind [*adj3*] *uncontrolled*
• *Syn* hasty, heedless, impetuous, mindless, rash, reckless, senseless, thoughtless, unthinking, violent, wild; • *Ant* cautious, controlled, rational.

blind [*adj4*] *hidden or covered*
• *Syn* blocked, closed, concealed, dead-end, dim, disguised, impassable, obscured, obstructed, secluded, unmarked; • *Ant* open, revealed, uncovered.

blindly [*adv1*] *without direction, purpose*
• *Syn* aimlessly, at random, confusedly, indiscriminately, instinctively, madly, wildly; • *Ant* carefully, cautiously, purposely, reasonably, sensibly.

blindly [*adv2*] *carelessly*
• *Syn* foolishly, heedlessly, impulsively, inconsiderately, obtusely, passionately, purblindly, recklessly, senselessly, thoughtlessly, tumultuously, unreasonably, willfully, without rhyme or reason; • *Ant* carefully, cautiously, considerately, sensibly.

blink [*v*] *ignore*
• *Syn* condone, connive, discount, disregard, fail, forget, neglect, omit, overlook, pass by, slight, turn a blind eye; • *Ant* attend, be aware, pay attention.

blissful [*adj*] *happy*
• *Syn* beatific, delighted, dreamy, ecstatic, elated, enraptured, euphoric, heavenly, joyful, joyous, rapturous; • *Ant* grieving, miserable, sorrowful, unhappy, upset, wretched.

blithe [*adj*] *happy*
• *Syn* animated, buoyant, cheerful, gay, gladsome, gleeful, jaunty, jocund, jovial, joyful, lighthearted, merry, mirthful, sprightly, sunny, vivacious; • *Ant* heavyhearted, morose, sad, sorrowful, unhappy.

bloat [*v*] *blow up like a balloon*
• *Syn* belly, billow, dilate, distend, enlarge, expand, inflate, puff up, swell; • *Ant* deflate, shrink, shrivel, tighten.

block [*v*] *obstruct*
• *Syn* arrest, barricade, catch, clog, close, congest, cut off, dam, deter, halt, hinder, impede, intercept, occlude, plug, prevent, stall, stop, thwart; • *Ant* clear, let go, let up, open, unblock.

blockade [*n*] *barrier*
• *Syn* blank wall, closure, encirclement, hindrance, impediment, infarction,

obstruction, restriction, roadblock, wall; • *Ant* breach, break, opening, space.

blond/blonde [*adj*] *having light-colored hair* • *Syn* albino, auricomous, bleached, champagne, fair-haired, flaxen, golden-haired, light, pale, platinum, sallow, sandy-haired, straw, washed-out, yellow-haired; • *Ant* brunet, brunette, dark, swarthy.

bloodless [*adj1*] *unfeeling*
• *Syn* cold, coldhearted, dull, indolent, insensitive, languid, lifeless, listless, passionless, sluggish, torpid; • *Ant* caring, feeling, lively, sensitive.

bloodless [*adj2*] *pale*
• *Syn* anemic, ashen, cadaverous, chalky, colorless, ghostly, pallid, pasty, sallow, sickly, wan; • *Ant* blushing, flushed, rosy, ruddy, sanguine.

bloom [*v*] *flower; flourish*
• *Syn* blossom, bud, burgeon, burst, develop, effloresce, fructify, germinate, grow, open, prosper, sprout, succeed, thrive, wax; • *Ant* shrink, shrivel, wane, wither.

blossom [*v1*] *flower*
• *Syn* bloom, blow, burgeon, burst, effloresce, leaf, open, shoot, unfold; • *Ant* fade, shrink, shrivel, wither.

blossom [*v2*] *flourish*
• *Syn* batten, bloom, develop, grow, mature, progress, prosper, succeed, thrive; • *Ant* deteriorate, die, diminish, fade, shrink.

blot [*v1*] *disgrace, disfigure*
• *Syn* blemish, dirty, discolor, mark, smudge, soil, spoil, spot, stain, sully, tarnish; • *Ant* beautify, grace, prettify.

blot [*v2*] *soak up*
• *Syn* absorb, dry, take up; • *Ant* dampen, moisten, soak, wet.

blotch [*n*] *smudge*
• *Syn* acne, blemish, blot, breakout, eruption, mark, mottling, patch, splash, spot, stain, stigma; • *Ant* blank, clarity, cleanness.

blow [*n*] *catastrophe*
• *Syn* affliction, balk, calamity, chagrin, debacle, disappointment, disaster, frustration, jolt, misfortune, reverse, shock, tragedy, upset; • *Ant* comfort, good fortune, luck.

blow [*v1*] *leave suddenly*
• *Syn* depart, go, split; • *Ant* arrive, come, come in.

blow [v2] *ruin a chance*
- *Syn* fail, flounder, miscarry, miss;
- *Ant* do well, succeed.

blow up [v1] *inflate*
- *Syn* billow, bloat, distend, enlarge, expand, fill, inflate, puff up, pump up, swell; *Ant* deflate, let out, shrink, shrivel.

blow up [v2] *magnify importance*
- *Syn* enlarge, exaggerate, heighten, overstate; *Ant* ignore, let go, play down.

blow up [v3] *burst with anger*
- *Syn* become angry, become enraged, erupt, lose control, lose one's temper, rage, rave; *Ant* be calm.

blue [adj] *sad*
- *Syn* dejected, depressed, disconsolate, dispirited, downcast, gloomy, glum, low, melancholy, moody, woebegone; *Ant* gay, happy, joyful, joyous, lighthearted, upbeat.

bluff [n] *boast; deceit*
- *Syn* bluster, braggadocio, bravado, deception, facade, fake, feint, fraud, front, lie, pretense, pretext, ruse, sham, subterfuge, trick; *Ant* honesty, reality, truth.

bluff [v] *deceive*
- *Syn* affect, beguile, betray, con, defraud, delude, feign, fool, lie, mislead, pretend, simulate, trick; *Ant* come clean, reveal, tell truth.

blunder [v] *make a mistake*
- *Syn* blow, botch, bungle, confuse, err, flounder, foul up, fumble, mess up, misjudge, stumble; *Ant* correct, fix, restore.

blunt [adj1] *not sharp*
- *Syn* dull, dulled, edgeless, insensitive, obtuse, pointless, round, rounded, unsharpened; *Ant* honed, needled, pointed, sharp.

blunt [adj2] *straightforward*
- *Syn* abrupt, brief, brusque, curt, explicit, forthright, frank, gruff, impolite, matter-of-fact, plain-spoken, rude, short, tactless, trenchant, unceremonious; *Ant* courteous, diplomatic, polite, subtle, tactful.

blunt [v] *make dull*
- *Syn* attenuate, cripple, deaden, debilitate, desensitize, enfeeble, numb, obtund, sap, soften, take the edge off, undermine, weaken; *Ant* hone, needle, point, sharpen.

blur [v1] *cloud, fog*
- *Syn* bedim, blear, blind, darken, daze, dim, make indistinct, mask, muddy, obscure, shade, soften; *Ant* clear, uncloud, unsmudge.

blur [v2] *make dirty*
- *Syn* besmear, blemish, blot, discolor, smear, smudge, spot, stain, taint, tarnish; *Ant* clarify, clean, cleanse, purify.

blush [v] *become colored, pink*
- *Syn* color, crimson, flush, glow, mantle, pink, redden, rouge, turn scarlet; *Ant* blanch, pale.

board [v1] *embark on vehicle*
- *Syn* catch, climb on, embus, emplane, enter, entrain, get on, hop on, mount; *Ant* disembark, get off, leave.

board [v2] *provide food and sleeping quarters* *Syn* accommodate, bed, canton, feed, harbor, house, lodge, put up, quarter, room; *Ant* dislodge, evict, turn out.

boast [v] *brag*
- *Syn* advertise, aggrandize, blow, bluster, con, crow, exaggerate, exult, flatter oneself, flaunt, flourish, gloat, glory, prate, preen, strut, swagger, triumph; *Ant* be modest, deprecate.

boastful [adj] *bragging*
- *Syn* arrogant, bombastic, cocky, conceited, egotistic, egotistical, exultant, loudmouth, pompous, self-aggrandizing, self-applauding, vainglorious, vaunting; *Ant* deprecating, modest.

bodily [adj] *concerning animate structure* *Syn* actual, animal, carnal, corporeal, fleshly, human, material, natural, normal, organic, physical, sensual, somatic, substantial, tangible; *Ant* mental, soulful, spiritual.

boil [v1] *heat to bubbling*
- *Syn* agitate, coddle, cook, decoct, effervesce, evaporate, foam, froth, poach, seethe, simmer, smolder, steam, steep, stew; *Ant* chill, cool, freeze, ice.

boil [v2] *be angry*
- *Syn* be indignant, blow up, bristle, burn, flare, fulminate, fume, rage, rave, sputter, storm; *Ant* appease, assuage, be happy, calm, simmer down, subside.

boisterous [adj] *noisy and mischievous*
- *Syn* clamorous, disorderly, effervescent, impetuous, loud, obstreperous, raucous, rollicking, rowdy, strident, tumultous/tumultuous, uproarious, vocif-

erous, wild; ▪ *Ant* calm, quiet, restrained, silent.

bold [*adj1*] *brave*
▪ *Syn* adventurous, audacious, courageous, daring, dauntless, fearless, forward, heroic, intrepid, resolute, undaunted, valiant, valorous; ▪ *Ant* afraid, cowardly, fearful, meek, shy, timid, weak.

bold [*adj2*] *brazen, insolent*
▪ *Syn* audacious, barefaced, brash, confident, forward, fresh, impudent, insolent, presumptuous, rude, saucy, shameless, smart; ▪ *Ant* meek, quiet, reticent, retiring, shy, timid, timorous.

bold [*adj3*] *bright, striking*
▪ *Syn* clear, colorful, conspicuous, definite, evident, eye-catching, flashy, forceful, lively, loud, manifest, prominent, pronounced, spirited, strong, vivid; ▪ *Ant* faint, fair, light.

bolster [*v*] *help*
▪ *Syn* aid, assist, bear up, boost, brace, bulwark, buoy, buttress, carry, cushion, help, maintain, pillow, prop, reinforce, shore up, stay, strengthen, support, sustain, uphold; ▪ *Ant* hinder, not support, obstruct, prevent, undermine.

bolt [*v1*] *run quickly away*
▪ *Syn* abscond, bound, dart, dash, escape, flee, flight, fly, hurtle, rush, scamper, sprint, take flight; ▪ *Ant* amble, saunter, stay, stroll, wait.

bolt [*v2*] *fasten securely*
▪ *Syn* bar, deadbolt, latch, lock, secure; ▪ *Ant* loosen, open, unbolt, unfasten, unlock.

bombastic [*adj*] *pompous, grandiloquent* ▪ *Syn* declamatory, euphuistic, flowery, fustian, grandiose, highflown, histrionic, inflated, loudmouthed, magniloquent, ostentatious, rhapsodic, rhetorical, sonorous, turgid, verbose, wordy; ▪ *Ant* humble, quiet, reserved, restrained.

bond [*v*] *fasten; stick*
▪ *Syn* bind, connect, fix, fuse, glue, gum, paste; ▪ *Ant* let go, loosen, open, unfasten, unstick.

bonus [*n*] *unexpected extra*
▪ *Syn* benefit, bounty, commission, dividend, fringe benefit, gift, gratuity, honorarium, premium, prize, reward, tip; ▪ *Ant* fine, penalty, withholding.

book [*v1*] *register, arrange for*
▪ *Syn* bill, charter, engage, enroll, enter, hire, make reservation, order, organize, procure, program, reserve, schedule, set up; ▪ *Ant* bow out, cancel, disengage.

book [*v2*] *arrest*
▪ *Syn* accuse, charge, take into custody; ▪ *Ant* exonerate, free, let go.

boom [*n*] *prosperity*
▪ *Syn* advance, boost, development, expansion, gain, growth, improvement, increase, inflation, upsurge, upswing, upturn; ▪ *Ant* collapse, failure, loss.

boom [*v*] *prosper*
▪ *Syn* appreciate, bloom, develop, expand, flourish, flower, grow, increase, intensify, strengthen, succeed, swell, thrive; ▪ *Ant* collapse, fail, falter, lose.

boon [*n*] *advantage*
▪ *Syn* benefaction, benefit, benevolence, blessing, donation, favor, gift, godsend, gratuity, help, largess, present, windfall; ▪ *Ant* disadvantage, drawback, inconvenience, privation.

boorish [*adj*] *crude, awkward*
▪ *Syn* bad-mannered, barbaric, churlish, coarse, ill-mannered, impolite, lowbred, oafish, provincial, rough, rustic, tasteless, vulgar; ▪ *Ant* charming, cultured, exciting, gracious, polite, refined, sophisticated.

boost [*v1*] *further, improve*
▪ *Syn* advance, assist, encourage, foster, inspire, praise, promote, push, support, sustain; ▪ *Ant* discourage, halt, hinder, hurt, prevent, undermine.

boost [*v2*] *push, usually up*
▪ *Syn* advance, elevate, heave, heighten, hoist, lift, raise, shove, thrust, upraise, uprear; ▪ *Ant* drop, let down, lower, plunge, push down, sink.

boost [*v3*] *increase*
▪ *Syn* aggrandize, amplify, augment, enlarge, expand, extend, heighten, hike, jump, magnify, multiply, raise; ▪ *Ant* blow, decrease, hinder, set back.

border [*v*] *bound on; be on the edge*
▪ *Syn* abut, adjoin, be adjacent to, circumscribe, contour, define, delineate, edge, encircle, enclose, flank, frame, fringe, hem, line, outline, rim, surround, trim, verge; ▪ *Ant* be inside, center.

borderline [*adj*] *inexact*
▪ *Syn* ambiguous, ambivalent, doubtful, equivocal, indeterminate, marginal, undecided, unsettled; ▪ *Ant* certain, decisive, definite, exact, sure.

bore [n] *nuisance*
- **Syn** bother, bromide, headache, nag, pest, soporific; **Ant** charmer, exciter, pleasure.

bore [v] *cause weariness, disinterest*
- **Syn** annoy, bother, discomfort, exhaust, fatigue, irk, irritate, jade, pall, pester, tire, trouble, vex, wear, weary; **Ant** amuse, charm, excite, interest, please.

boring [adj] *uninteresting*
- **Syn** arid, bromidic, colorless, dull, insipid, irksome, lifeless, mundane, platitudinous, plebeian, prosaic, repetitious, routine, stale, tame, tedious, tiresome, trite, vapid; **Ant** exciting, fascinating, interesting.

borrow [v1] *take for temporary use*
- **Syn** acquire, beg, hire, lift, obtain, pawn, pledge, rent, soak; **Ant** give, lend, pay, return.

borrow [v2] *adopt from another source; appropriate* - **Syn** acquire, adopt, assume, copy, imitate, obtain, pilfer, pirate, plagiarize, simulate, steal, take, use, usurp; **Ant** give, return.

bosom [n] *heart; core*
- **Syn** affections, center, circle, conscience, inside, interior, sentiments, soul, spirit; **Ant** exteriority, outside.

boss [v] *control; command*
- **Syn** administrate, chaperon, direct, employ, manage, oversee, run, superintend, supervise; **Ant** behave, follow.

botch [v] *blunder*
- **Syn** bumble, bungle, distort, err, flounder, fumble, mar, mess, miscalculate, misconjecture, misconstrue, mismanage, muddle, mutilate, ruin, spoil, wreck; **Ant** accomplish, achieve, do well, succeed, triumph.

bother [v] *harass, annoy; give trouble*
- **Syn** afflict, aggravate, agitate, badger, bedevil, browbeat, cross, discommode, disconcert, distress, disturb, exacerbate, exasperate, goad, harry, hinder, impede, irk, irritate, molest, needle, perturb, plague, ride, spite, tantalize, taunt, tease, torment, upset, vex, worry; **Ant** aid, help, please.

bothersome [adj] *troubling*
- **Syn** aggravating, annoying, distressing, disturbing, exasperating, incommodious, inconvenient, irritating, tiresome, troublesome, vexatious, vexing; **Ant** convenient, helpful, untroubling.

bottle up [v] *to confine (used of feelings)*
- **Syn** check, collar, contain, corner, cramp, curb, restrain, restrict, shut in, suppress, trap; **Ant** confide, reveal, tell.

bottom [adj] *lowest; fundamental*
- **Syn** basal, base, basic, foundational, ground, last, lowest, nethermost, primary, rock-bottom, underlying; **Ant** highest, top, unnecessary.

bounce [n] *spring*
- **Syn** animation, dynamism, elasticity, energy, liveliness, rebound, resilience, vigor, vitality, vivacity; **Ant** calmness, composure, staidness, tiredness, tranquility, weariness.

bound [adj] *obligated; destined*
- **Syn** articled, coerced, compelled, constrained, contracted, driven, enslaved, forced, impelled, indentured, necessitated, obligated, pledged, required, restrained, sure, under compulsion; **Ant** allowed, free, permitted, unbounded, unobliged, unrestricted.

bound [v1] *jump, bounce*
- **Syn** caper, frisk, gambol, hop, hurdle, leap, pounce, prance, recoil, ricochet, skip, spring, vault; **Ant** amble, crawl, creep, hop, limp.

bound [v2] *restrict*
- **Syn** circumscribe, confine, define, delimit, demarcate, determine, encircle, enclose, hem in, limit, measure, restrain, restrict, surround, terminate; **Ant** allow, let go, permit, unbind, unrestrict.

bounded [adj] *limited, confined*
- **Syn** circumscribed, compassed, defined, determinate, encircled, encompassed, enveloped, fenced, fringed, girdled, hedged, restricted, rimmed, surrounded, walled; **Ant** free, loose, unbounded, unconfined, unlimited.

boundless [adj] *endless, without limit*
- **Syn** great, illimitable, immense, indefinite, infinite, limitless, measureless, tremendous, vast, wide open; **Ant** confined, limited, restricted.

bountiful [adj] *abundant*
- **Syn** ample, bounteous, copious, free, generous, lavish, liberal, magnanimous, munificent, plenteous, plentiful, plenty, prolific; **Ant** insufficient, lacking, meagre, sparse, wanting.

bourgeois [adj] *commonplace*
- **Syn** common, conventional, hidebound, materialistic, middle-class, traditional;

- *Ant* adventurous, imaginative, inspired, nonconforming, original, untraditional.

bow [n] *front of boat*
- *Syn* beak, bowsprit, fore, forepart, head, nose, prow, stem; *Ant* rear, stern.

bow [v1] *bend over*
- *Syn* arch, crook, curtsy, curve, debase, do obeisance, genuflect, hunch, incline, nod, round, stoop; *Ant* stand up, straighten.

bow [v2] *submit, concede*
- *Syn* accept, acquiesce, bend, capitulate, cave, comply, defer, relent, succumb, surrender, yield; *Ant* defend, fight, overpower.

boycott [v] *ban; refrain from using*
- *Syn* avoid, bar, blacklist, embargo, exclude, ostracize, prohibit, refuse, reject, spurn, strike; *Ant* buy, encourage, patronize, support, use.

brace [v] *support*
- *Syn* bandage, bind, bolster, buttress, fasten, fortify, gird, hold up, prepare, prop, ready, reinforce, shove, steady, strap, strengthen, support, tie, tighten, uphold; *Ant* let go, loosen, unfasten.

bracing [adj] *brisk; exhilarating*
- *Syn* animating, chilly, crisp, energizing, exhilarative, fortifying, fresh, invigorating, quickening, refreshing, restorative, rousing, stimulating, tonic, vigorous; *Ant* debilitating, exhausting, tiring.

brag [v] *talk boastingly*
- *Syn* boast, exult, gasconade, gloat, grandstand, prate, rodomontade, swagger, vaunt; *Ant* be modest, be quiet, deprecate.

brain [n] *mind, intelligence*
- *Syn* cerebellum, cerebrum, encephalon, head, intellect, medulla oblongata, mentality, wit; *Ant* body, physicality.

brake [v] *check; stop*
- *Syn* bar, block, dam, decelerate, halt, hinder, impede, moderate, obstruct, slacken, slow; *Ant* accelerate, speed, spur.

branch [n] *department*
- *Syn* annex, arm, bureau, category, chapter, derivative, division, extension, local, member, office, part, section, subdivision, subsection, subsidiary, tributary, wing; *Ant* company, complex, composite, mass.

brandish [v] *flaunt, swing around*
- *Syn* display, disport, exhibit, expose,

flash, gesture, parade, raise, sport, swing, threaten, wield; *Ant* lower, not show, put away, put down, sheathe.

brash [adj] *impulsive, brazen*
- *Syn* bold, foolhardy, forward, hasty, heedless, ill-advised, impetuous, impolitic, impudent, insolent, maladroit, precipitate, rash, reckless, rude, tactless, thoughtless; *Ant* afraid, careful, cautious, discreet, fearful, reserved.

brassy [adj] *vulgar, loud to the senses*
- *Syn* arrant, blatant, bold, flashy, forward, garish, gaudy, grating, harsh, jarring, loudmouthed, noisy, obtrusive, pert, piercing, rude, saucy, shameless, showy, shrill, strident, unabashed, unblushing; *Ant* careful, cautious, circumspect, humble, prudent.

bravado [n] *boastfulness*
- *Syn* bluster, bombast, bravura, grandiosity, pomposity, pretension, self-glorification, talk; *Ant* cowardice, fear, fearfulness, humility, modesty, restraint.

brave [adj] *bold*
- *Syn* adventurous, chivalrous, daring, dauntless, fearless, forward, gallant, hardy, heroic, intrepid, plucky, resolute, spirited, stalwart, stouthearted, valiant, venturesome; *Ant* afraid, cautious, fearful, frightened, humble, meek, reticent, retiring, shy, timid.

brave [v] *endure bad situation*
- *Syn* bear, beard, challenge, confront, defy, face, risk, suffer, venture, withstand; *Ant* break down, capitulate, complain, dodge, fear, give up, hide, run away, skip.

brawny [adj] *muscular, strong*
- *Syn* able-bodied, athletic, burly, fleshy, hardy, hefty, husky, powerful, robust, stalwart, sturdy, tough, vigorous, vital; *Ant* frail, skinny, slight, thin, weak.

breach [n1] *gap*
- *Syn* aperture, break, chasm, cleft, crack, discontinuity, fissure, hole, opening, rift, rupture, slit, split; *Ant* bridge, connection.

breach [n2] *violation of a law*
- *Syn* contravention, delinquency, dereliction, infraction, infringement, neglect, noncompliance, offense, transgression, trespass, violation; *Ant* adherence, observance, upholding.

break [v1] *destroy; make whole into pieces* *Syn* annihilate, burst, crack, crush, damage, disintegrate, eradicate, fracture, fragment, part, rend, separate, sever, shatter, smash, snap, splinter, tear; ▪ *Ant* attach, fasten, fix, join, mend, put together, secure.

break [v2] *violate law*
▪ *Syn* breach, contravene, disobey, disregard, infract, infringe, offend, renege on, transgress, violate; ▪ *Ant* agree, obey.

break [v3] *weaken, cause instability*
▪ *Syn* bankrupt, bust, controvert, cow, cripple, degrade, demoralize, enfeeble, humiliate, impair, impoverish, pauperize, refute, ruin, subdue; ▪ *Ant* stabilize, strengthen.

break [v4] *stop an action*
▪ *Syn* abandon, cut, discontinue, give up, interrupt, pause, rest, suspend; ▪ *Ant* allow, cause.

break [v5] *tell news*
▪ *Syn* announce, communicate, convey, disclose, divulge, impart, inform, let out, make public, proclaim, reveal, tell, transmit; ▪ *Ant* hide, keep quiet, secret.

break [v6] *emerge, happen*
▪ *Syn* appear, befall, burst out, come forth, come off, come to pass, develop, erupt, go, occur, transpire; ▪ *Ant* cease, die away, die down, diminish, end, halt, stop.

break [v7] *run away*
▪ *Syn* abscond, dash, decamp, escape, flee, fly; ▪ *Ant* stay, wait.

breakable [adj] *easily hurt or destroyed*
▪ *Syn* brittle, crisp, delicate, flimsy, fragile, frail, friable, splintery, vitreous, weak; ▪ *Ant* durable, sturdy, unbreakable.

break off [v1] *snap off something*
▪ *Syn* detach, disassemble, divide, part, pull off, separate, sever, splinter, take apart; ▪ *Ant* combine, join, mend.

break off [v2] *end activity*
▪ *Syn* cease, desist, discontinue, end, finish, halt, pause, stop, suspend, terminate; ▪ *Ant* begin, continue, start.

breakthrough [n] *advance, progress*
▪ *Syn* boost, development, discovery, find, gain, hike, improvement, increase, invention, leap, progress, rise; ▪ *Ant* step back, step backward.

break up [v] *end relationship, activity*
▪ *Syn* adjourn, disband, dismantle, dissolve, divide, divorce, end, halt, part, put an end to, separate, sever, split, sunder, take apart, terminate; ▪ *Ant* reconcile, resolve, settle.

breathe [v] *tell information*
▪ *Syn* articulate, confide, express, murmur, say, sigh, utter, voice, whisper; ▪ *Ant* hide, secret.

breathless [adj] *unable to respire normally* ▪ *Syn* asthmatic, blown, choking, emphysematous, exhausted, gasping, panting, short of breath, short-winded, stertorous, wheezing, winded; ▪ *Ant* breathy, calm.

breathtaking [adj] *beautiful, awesome*
▪ *Syn* amazing, astonishing, awe-inspiring, exciting, heart-stopping, impressive, magnificent, moving, overwhelming, spine-tingling, stunning, thrilling; ▪ *Ant* banal, disgusting, hideous, ordinary, repulsive, ugly.

breed [v] *generate, bring into being*
▪ *Syn* bear, bring forth, create, deliver, engender, father, hatch, impregnate, mother, multiply, originate, procreate, produce, propagate, reproduce, sire; ▪ *Ant* block, demolish, destroy, eradicate, erase, extinguish, harm, hinder, injure, kill, obstruct, stifle, stop, wipe out.

breezy [adj1] *windy*
▪ *Syn* airy, blowing, blowy, blusterous, blustery, drafty, fresh, gusty, stormy; ▪ *Ant* calm, peaceful, quiet, still.

breezy [adj2] *easy, lighthearted*
▪ *Syn* airy, animated, blithe, buoyant, carefree, casual, debonair, easy-going, gay, jaunty, light, relaxed, sparkling, spirited, sprightly, sunny, vivacious; ▪ *Ant* careworn, depressed, difficult, dull, heavy, heavyhearted, lifeless, morose, mournful, sad, serious, unspirited.

bridge [n] *structure or something that makes connection* ▪ *Syn* arch, branch, catwalk, connection, extension, gangplank, link, overpass, platform, pontoon, scaffold, span, trestle, viaduct, wing; ▪ *Ant* break, chasm, division, schism, separation, split.

bridge [v] *connect, extend*
▪ *Syn* attach, bind, branch, couple, cross, cross over, join, link, reach, span, subtend, traverse, unite; ▪ *Ant* detach, disconnect, disjoin, disunite, unlink.

bridle [v] *check, hold back*
▪ *Syn* constrain, control, curb, govern, inhibit, moderate, repress, restrain, rule, subdue, suppress, withhold; ▪ *Ant* let go, release, set free, unbridle, unharness.

brief [adj1] *short, compressed*
▪ *Syn* abrupt, blunt, breviloquent, com-

pendious, concise, crisp, curt, hasty, laconic, pithy, small, succinct, terse, to the point;   ▪ *Ant* extended, lengthy, long, prolonged.

brief [*adj2*] *short in time*
▪ *Syn* concise, ephemeral, fast, fleeting, hasty, instantaneous, momentary, passing, quick, short-lived, swift, temporary, transient, transitory;   ▪ *Ant* enduring, lasting, lengthy, long, long-lived.

brief [*v*] *inform of facts*
▪ *Syn* advise, apprise, edify, enlighten, explain, fill in, inform, initiate, instruct, orient, prepare, prime, recapitulate, summarize, update;   ▪ *Ant* hide, secrete.

brigade [*n*] *fleet of trained people*
▪ *Syn* army, band, body, company, contingent, corps, crew, detachment, force, group, organization, outfit, party, posse, squad, team, troop, unit;   ▪ *Ant* individual, one.

bright [*adj1*] *shining, glowing in appearance* ▪ *Syn* ablaze, aglow, auroral, brilliant, coruscating, effulgent, fulgent, gleaming, illuminated, incandescent, lambent, luminous, lustrous, moonlit, phosphorescent, polished, radiant, scintillating, sparkling, sunlit, vivid;   ▪ *Ant* dark, dreary, dull, obscure, somber.

bright [*adj2*] *sunny, clear (weather)*
▪ *Syn* clement, cloudless, fair, favorable, limpid, lucid, mild, pellucid, pleasant;   ▪ *Ant* black, cloudy, dark, dreary, dusky, gloomy, murky.

bright [*adj3*] *intelligent*
▪ *Syn* alert, astute, aware, brilliant, clear-headed, clever, discerning, ingenious, keen, knowing, precocious, quick-witted, sharp, smart;   ▪ *Ant* dull, stupid, unaware, unintelligent.

bright [*adj4*] *hopeful, promising*
▪ *Syn* airy, auspicious, benign, encouraging, excellent, favorable, golden, optimistic, propitious, rosy;   ▪ *Ant* depressing, horrible, threatening, unpromising.

bright [*adj5*] *cheerful*
▪ *Syn* alert, animated, gay, glad, happy, joyful, joyous, lighthearted, lively, merry, optimistic, sanguine;   ▪ *Ant* depressed, depressing, doleful, dreary, gloomy, unhappy.

bright [*adj6*] *vivid in color*
▪ *Syn* brilliant, clear, colored, colorful, deep, flashy, hued, intense, psychedelic, rich, sharp;   ▪ *Ant* light, pale, pastel.

brighten [*v1*] *make shine or glow*
▪ *Syn* burnish, enliven, gleam, illuminate, illumine, intensify, kindle, lighten, light up, polish;   ▪ *Ant* darken, deepen, dull, fade.

brighten [*v2*] *make happy, feel better*
▪ *Syn* buck up, buoy up, cheer, encourage, enliven, gladden, hearten, improve, look up, perk up;   ▪ *Ant* depress, upset.

brilliant [*adj1*] *shining, glowing in appearance* ▪ *Syn* bright, dazzling, flashy, glittering, glossy, intense, lucent, lustrous, radiant, scintillating, showy, sparkling, vivid;   ▪ *Ant* dark, dull, dulled, subdued.

brilliant [*adj2*] *famous, outstanding*
▪ *Syn* celebrated, distinguished, eminent, excellent, exceptional, illustrious, magnificent, prominent, superb;   ▪ *Ant* normal, typical.

brilliant [*adj3*] *very intelligent*
▪ *Syn* accomplished, astute, bright, clever, discerning, expert, gifted, ingenious, intellectual, knowledgeable, profound, quick-witted, sharp, smart, talented;   ▪ *Ant* stupid, unaware, unintelligent.

brimming/brimful [*adj*] *overflowing; up to the top* ▪ *Syn* awash, crowded, filled, flush, full, jammed, level with, loaded, overfull, packed, running over;   ▪ *Ant* empty, unfilled.

bring [*v1*] *transport or accompany*
▪ *Syn* attend, bear, chaperon, companion, consort, convey, deliver, escort, guide, import, lead, pack, pick up, ride, shoulder, tote, transfer, transport, truck, usher;   ▪ *Ant* drop, leave, quit, refuse, shun, take.

bring [*v2*] *cause; influence*
▪ *Syn* begin, compel, create, dispose, engender, force, induce, make, occasion, persuade, prevail upon, produce, result in;   ▪ *Ant* avoid, back out, desist, give up, hold back, pass up.

bring about [*v*] *cause success*
▪ *Syn* accomplish, achieve, beget, bring to pass, create, draw on, generate, give rise to, manage, occasion, produce, realize, secure, succeed;   ▪ *Ant* halt, kill, stop.

bring down [*v*] *reduce or hurt*
▪ *Syn* abase, damage, drop, fell, floor, injure, level, lower, overthrow, prostrate, undermine, upset, wound;   ▪ *Ant* aid, encourage, help, raise.

brink [*n*] *edge of an object or area*
 ▪ *Syn* boundary, brim, fringe, frontier, limit, lip, perimeter, periphery, point, rim, threshold, verge; ▪ *Ant* center, interior, middle.

brisk [*adj1*] *fast-moving; active*
 ▪ *Syn* adroit, agile, animated, busy, energetic, lively, nimble, quick, sprightly, spry, vigorous, vivacious; ▪ *Ant* inactive, slow, sluggish, unenergetic.

brisk [*adj2*] *chilly, refreshing (weather)*
 ▪ *Syn* biting, bracing, crisp, exhilarating, fresh, invigorating, keen, nippy, sharp, stimulating; ▪ *Ant* temperate, warm.

brittle [*adj1*] *fragile*
 ▪ *Syn* breakable, crisp, delicate, fragile, frail, frangible, friable, vitreous, weak; ▪ *Ant* durable, elastic, flexible, lithe, moveable, resilient, supple.

brittle [*adj2*] *tense*
 ▪ *Syn* curt, edgy, irritable, nervous, prim, short, stiff, stilted; ▪ *Ant* relaxed, resilient.

broach [*v1*] *bring up a topic*
 ▪ *Syn* advance, approach, hint at, interject, introduce, mention, offer, propose, submit, suggest, ventilate; ▪ *Ant* not mention, suppress.

broach [*v2*] *open, pierce*
 ▪ *Syn* begin, crack, decant, draw off, puncture, start, tap, uncork; ▪ *Ant* close, close up.

broad [*adj1*] *wide physically*
 ▪ *Syn* ample, capacious, deep, expansive, generous, immense, large, latitudinous, outstretched, roomy, spacious, squat, thick, vast, voluminous; ▪ *Ant* confined, constricted, narrow, small.

broad [*adj2*] *extensive*
 ▪ *Syn* all-inclusive, comprehensive, copious, encyclopedic, far-reaching, general, inclusive, sweeping, ubiquitous, universal, wide, widespread; ▪ *Ant* detailed, exclusive, limited, narrow, small, specific.

broad [*adj3*] *liberal-minded*
 ▪ *Syn* advanced, open, open-minded, permissive, progressive, tolerant, wide; ▪ *Ant* close-minded, dogmatic, rigid, small-minded, strict.

broadcast [*v*] *make public*
 ▪ *Syn* advertise, announce, blare, circulate, declare, distribute, proclaim, promulgate, report; ▪ *Ant* hide, keep quiet, secrete.

broaden [*v*] *extend, supplement*
 ▪ *Syn* augment, develop, enlarge, expand, grow, increase, ream, spread, stretch, widen; ▪ *Ant* decrease, narrow, restrict.

broad-minded [*adj*] *liberal*
 ▪ *Syn* catholic, cosmopolitan, flexible, indulgent, liberal, open-minded, permissive, receptive, responsive, tolerant; ▪ *Ant* biased, bigoted, close-minded, prejudiced, small-minded.

broil [*v*] *cook under direct heat*
 ▪ *Syn* burn, melt, roast, scorch, sear, swelter; ▪ *Ant* chill, freeze, refrigerate.

broiling [*adj*] *very hot*
 ▪ *Syn* baking, burning, fiery, red-hot, roasting, scalding, scorching, sizzling, sweltering, torrid; ▪ *Ant* chilly, cold, freezing, frigid.

broke [*adj*] *without money*
 ▪ *Syn* bankrupt, destitute, impoverished, indigent, insolvent, needy, penniless, penurious, poor, ruined; ▪ *Ant* affluent, rich, solvent, wealthy.

broken [*adj1*] *destroyed; made into pieces from a whole* ▪ *Syn* cracked, disintegrated, fractured, fragmentary, hurt, injured, mutilated, pulverized, riven, ruptured, severed, shattered, shredded, slivered, split; ▪ *Ant* complete, connected, fixed, unbroken, whole.

broken [*adj2*] *discontinuous*
 ▪ *Syn* disconnected, erratic, fragmentary, incomplete, intermittent, interrupted, irregular, spasmodic; ▪ *Ant* complete, connected, continuous, unbroken.

broken [*adj3*] *mentally defeated*
 ▪ *Syn* beaten, browbeaten, crushed, demoralized, depressed, discouraged, disheartened, heartsick, humbled, oppressed, overpowered, subdued, vanquished; ▪ *Ant* happy, satisfied, uplifted.

broken [*adj4*] *not working*
 ▪ *Syn* defective, disabled, down, faulty, in disrepair, inoperable, out of order, ruined, run-down; ▪ *Ant* fixed, functioning, unbroken, working.

broken [*adj5*] *forgotten, ignored (promise)* ▪ *Syn* abandoned, disregarded, ignored, infringed, retracted, traduced, transgressed, violated; ▪ *Ant* honored, kept.

brokenhearted [*adj*] *devastated*
 ▪ *Syn* crestfallen, desolate, despairing, disconsolate, grieved, inconsolable, mournful, prostrated, sorrowful, wretched; ▪ *Ant* happy, lighthearted, pleased.

brook [v] *endure, accept*
▪ *Syn* bear, countenance, stomach, suffer, support, swallow, take, tolerate, withstand; ▪ *Ant* decline, disallow, dismiss, forbear, forbid, prohibiit, rebuff, refuse, reject, renounce, repudiate, resist, shun, spurn.

browbeat [v] *castigate, nag*
▪ *Syn* badger, bully, cow, despotize, dragoon, frighten, harass, intimidate, oppress, threaten, tyrannize; ▪ *Ant* boost, coax, compliment, praise.

brunette/brunet [adj] *dark hair and/or skin* ▪ *Syn* brown, dusky, pigmented, swart, swarthy, tanned, tawny; ▪ *Ant* blond/blonde, fair, flaxen.

brush aside/brush off [v] *ignore; refuse* ▪ *Syn* contradict, cut, deny, disclaim, disregard, ostracize, rebuff, repudiate, scorn, slight, snub; ▪ *Ant* attend, pay attention, see.

brusque [adj] *curt, surly*
▪ *Syn* abrupt, blunt, brief, discourteous, hasty, impolite, sharp, short, tart, terse; ▪ *Ant* courteous, kind, polite, tactful.

brutal [adj1] *cruel, remorseless*
▪ *Syn* callous, ferocious, harsh, heartless, inhuman, merciless, pitiless, remorseless, ruthless, savage, severe, vicious; ▪ *Ant* generous, humane, kind, nice.

brutal [adj2] *crude, rough*
▪ *Syn* animal, beastly, bestial, brute, carnal, coarse, feral, inhumane, rude, savage; ▪ *Ant* gentle, kind, nice.

brutally [adv] *cruelly, without remorse*
▪ *Syn* barbarously, callously, diabolically, ferociously, heartlessly, inexorably, mercilessly, murderously, relentlessly, savagely, viciously; ▪ *Ant* gently, humanely, kindly, nicely.

brute [adj] *very strong; animallike*
▪ *Syn* animal, bestial, bodily, carnal, feral, instinctive, mindless, physical, senseless; ▪ *Ant* gentle, mild, weak.

buckle [v] *contort, warp*
▪ *Syn* bend, bulge, cave in, collapse, crumple, distort, fold, twist, yield; ▪ *Ant* flatten, smooth.

buckle down [v] *concentrate on*
▪ *Syn* address, apply oneself, bend, devote oneself to, exert oneself, keep one's mind on, occupy oneself with, pitch in, set to, throw, turn; ▪ *Ant* be lazy, ignore, relax.

bud [v] *sprout*
▪ *Syn* burgeon, burst forth, develop, grow, pullulate, shoot; ▪ *Ant* die, shrink, waste, wither.

budding [adj] *developing, flowering*
▪ *Syn* blossoming, embryonic, fledgling, fresh, germinating, growing, incipient, maturing, nascent, opening, potential, promising, pubescent, young; ▪ *Ant* dying, shrinking, withering.

buddy [n] *friend*
▪ *Syn* associate, co-mate, companion, comrade, confidant, co-worker, intimate, mate, pal, peer, sidekick; ▪ *Ant* adversary, enemy, foe, opponent, rival.

buff [n] *enthusiast*
▪ *Syn* addict, admirer, aficionado, connoisseur, devotee, expert, fan, fiend, freak, habitué, hound; ▪ *Ant* detractor, opponent.

build [v1] *construct structure*
▪ *Syn* assemble, carpenter, cast, compose, contrive, engineer, erect, fabricate, fashion, forge, form, frame, manufacture, model, produce, raise, reconstruct, sculpture, set up, synthesize; ▪ *Ant* demolish, destroy, dismantle, knock down, raze, ruin, take down.

build [v2] *initiate, found*
▪ *Syn* base, begin, constitute, establish, formulate, inaugurate, institute, originate, set up, start; ▪ *Ant* destroy, overthrow, overturn, ruin.

build [v3] *increase, accelerate*
▪ *Syn* amplify, augment, boost, compound, develop, enlarge, expand, extend, heighten, intensify, magnify, strengthen, swell, wax; ▪ *Ant* decelerate, decrease, destroy, ruin.

build up [v] *amplify, advertise*
▪ *Syn* boost, develop, enhance, expand, fortify, heighten, promote, publicize, reinforce, spotlight, strengthen; ▪ *Ant* lessen, let down, play down, weaken.

built-in [adj] *included*
▪ *Syn* congenital, constitutional, deep-seated, essential, implicit, inborn, incorporated, ingrained, inherent, innate, integral; ▪ *Ant* added, extra, extraneous, not included.

bulge [v] *project outward*
▪ *Syn* bag, balloon, billow, bloat, dilate, distend, enlarge, expand, jut, overhang, pouch, protrude, sag, stick out, swell; ▪ *Ant* cave in, depress.

bulky [adj] *huge*
▪ *Syn* awkward, big, colossal, cumbersome, enormous, gross, heavy, immense,

large, mammoth, massive, ponderous, substantial, voluminous, weighty; ▪ *Ant* insubstantial, miniature, small, thin, tiny.

bulldoze [*v*] *demolish*
▪ *Syn* drive, elbow, flatten, force, jostle, level, press, propel, push, raze, shove, thrust; ▪ *Ant* build, construct.

bully [*v*] *intimidate, push around*
▪ *Syn* browbeat, coerce, cow, domineer, dragoon, harass, lean on, menace, oppress, persecute, terrorize, threaten, tyrannize; ▪ *Ant* allow, leave alone.

bunch [*v*] *gather in group*
▪ *Syn* assemble, bundle, cluster, collect, congregate, cram, crowd, flock, group, herd, huddle, mass, pack; ▪ *Ant* disperse, divide, let go, scatter, separate, spread.

bundle [*v*] *accumulate, package*
▪ *Syn* bale, bind, clothe, fasten, pack, tie, truss, wrap; ▪ *Ant* disperse, divide, let go, scatter, separate, spread.

bungle [*v*] *blunder, mess up*
▪ *Syn* boggle, botch, err, flub, fumble, make a mess of, mar, mess up, miscalculate, mishandle, mismanage, ruin, spoil; ▪ *Ant* do well, fix, manage, succeed.

buoy (up) [*v*] *make light, encourage*
▪ *Syn* bolster, boost, buck up, cheer, encourage, hearten, keep afloat, lift, prop, raise, support, sustain, uphold; ▪ *Ant* discourage, dishearten.

buoyant [*adj1*] *light in weight*
▪ *Syn* afloat, airy, bouncy, floatable, floating, resilient, supernatant, unsinkable, weightless; ▪ *Ant* heavy, weighted.

buoyant [*adj2*] *light in spirit*
▪ *Syn* animated, blithe, breezy, carefree, cheerful, debonair, effervescent, expansive, gay, happy, jaunty, joyful, lighthearted, resilient, sunny, vivacious; ▪ *Ant* depressed, down, heavy, heavyhearted.

burden [*v*] *encumber, strain*
▪ *Syn* afflict, bear down on, crush, depress, encumber, hamper, hinder, impede, load, make heavy, oppress, overload, overwhelm, press, saddle with, strain, tax, try, vex, weigh down; ▪ *Ant* aid, help, relieve.

burdensome [*adj*] *troublesome*
▪ *Syn* carking, demanding, difficult, disturbing, exacting, exigent, irksome, onerous, oppressive, taxing, tough, trying, wearing, wearying, weighty; ▪ *Ant* aiding, helpful, helping, relieving, unburdensome.

burly [*adj*] *husky*
▪ *Syn* able-bodied, athletic, big, brawny, bruising, bulky, hefty, hulking, muscular, portly, powerful, stocky, stout, strapping, strong, sturdy, thickset, well-built; ▪ *Ant* light, slim, small, thin.

burn [*v1*] *be on fire; set on fire*
▪ *Syn* be ablaze, blaze, brand, broil, cauterize, char, combust, cook, cremate, enkindle, flame, flare, glow, heat, ignite, incinerate, kindle, light, melt, parch, roast, scorch, sear, smolder, torch, wither; ▪ *Ant* cool, extinguish, put out, quench, smother, wet.

burn [*v2*] *be excited about; yearn for*
▪ *Syn* blaze, boil, bristle, desire, fume, lust, rage, seethe, simmer, tingle, yearn; ▪ *Ant* stifle, subdue.

burning [*adj1*] *blazing, flashing*
▪ *Syn* afire, blistering, conflagrant, enkindled, fiery, flaming, flaring, glowing, heated, hot, ignited, illuminated, incandescent, kindled, on fire, oxidizing, scorching, searing, sizzling, smoking, smouldering, torrid; ▪ *Ant* chilled, cold, cool, freezing.

burning [*adj2*] *fervent, excited*
▪ *Syn* all-consuming, ardent, blazing, eager, fervid, frenzied, heated, intense, passionate, vehement, zealous; ▪ *Ant* apathetic, cold, cool, numbed, unexcited, unimportant.

burnish [*v*] *polish, brighten*
▪ *Syn* buff, furbish, glance, glaze, gloss, luster, patina, put on a finish, rub, sheen, shine, smooth, wax; ▪ *Ant* dull, tarnish.

burrow [*v*] *dig a hole*
▪ *Syn* delve, excavate, hollow out, scoop out, tunnel, undermine; ▪ *Ant* cover, fill.

burst [*v*] *blow up, break out*
▪ *Syn* break, crack, detonate, disintegrate, erupt, explode, fly open, fragment, gush forth, perforate, puncture, rupture, shatter, split, tear apart; ▪ *Ant* attach, connect, fasten, hold together, join, put together, secure, unite.

bury [*v1*] *lay to rest after death*
▪ *Syn* coffin, cover up, deposit, embalm, ensepulcher, enshrine, entomb, hold services for, inearth, inhume, inter, inurn, lay out, mummify, sepulcher, tomb; ▪ *Ant* dig out, disinter, exhume, uncover.

bury [*v2*] *conceal, cover*
▪ *Syn* cache, cover up, ensconce, enshroud, hide, plant, screen, secrete,

shroud, stash, stow away; ▪ *Ant* dig out, reveal, uncover.

bury [*v3*] *plant in ground*
▪ *Syn* drive in, embed, engulf, implant, sink, submerge; ▪ *Ant* dig out.

bushy [*adj*] *shaggy, unkempt*
▪ *Syn* bristly, disordered, fluffy, fringed, furry, hairy, hirsute, leafy, luxuriant, prickly, rough, rumpled, thick, tufted, unruly, wiry, woolly; ▪ *Ant* bald, neat, well-kept.

businesslike [*adj*] *efficient, professional*
▪ *Syn* accomplished, concentrated, diligent, direct, disciplined, earnest, effective, hardworking, industrious, matter-of-fact, methodical, orderly, organized, painstaking, practical, purposeful, routine, sedulous, systematic, thorough; ▪ *Ant* amateur, disorganized, inefficient, unbusinesslike, unprofessional.

bust [*v1*] *ruin, impoverish*
▪ *Syn* become insolvent, break, crash, fail, fold up, go bankrupt, pauperize; ▪ *Ant* aid, help.

bust [*v2*] *arrest for illegal action*
▪ *Syn* apprehend, catch, collar, cop, detain, nab, pick up, pinch, pull in, raid, run in, search; ▪ *Ant* exonerate, let go.

bustle [*n*] *quick and busy activity*
▪ *Syn* ado, agitation, clamor, commotion, excitement, flurry, haste, hubbub, pother, rumpus, tumult, uproar, whirl, whirlwind; ▪ *Ant* laziness, relaxation.

busy [*adj1*] *engaged, at work*
▪ *Syn* active, assiduous, buried, diligent, employed, engrossed, hustling, industrious, occupied, overloaded, persevering, slaving, tied up; ▪ *Ant* idle, quiet, unbusy, unemployed, unengaged.

busy [*adj2*] *active, on the go*
▪ *Syn* bustling, energetic, full, hustling, lively, restless, strenuous, tireless, tiring; ▪ *Ant* idle, inactive, lazy.

buttress [*v*] *support, bolster*
▪ *Syn* back up, brace, build up, bulwark, carry, prop, reinforce, shore, strengthen, sustain, uphold; ▪ *Ant* let down, weaken.

buy [*v*] *purchase*
▪ *Syn* acquire, bargain for, barter for, contract for, invest in, market, obtain, pay for, procure, purchase, redeem, score, secure, shop for, sign for, take; ▪ *Ant* market, peddle, sell, vend.

buyer [*n*] *someone who purchases*
▪ *Syn* client, consumer, customer, emptor, patron, prospect, purchaser, representative, shopper, user, vendee; ▪ *Ant* marketer, seller, vendor.

bygone [*adj*] *in the past*
▪ *Syn* antiquated, archaic, belated, defunct, departed, erstwhile, extinct, forgotten, of old, of yore, old-fashioned, out-of-date, previous, sometime, vanished; ▪ *Ant* coming, future, modern, new, prospective, recent, subsequent, succeeding.

bystander [*n*] *person who watches*
▪ *Syn* eyewitness, looker-on, observer, onlooker, passerby, spectator, viewer, watcher, witness; ▪ *Ant* participant.

C

cabin [*n*] *tiny house; lodging*
▪ *Syn* box, bungalow, camp, chalet, cottage, deckhouse, home, hovel, hut, lodge, log house, quarters, room, shack, shanty, shed, shelter; ▪ *Ant* castle, chateau, mansion, palace.

cache [*v*] *hide a supply of something*
▪ *Syn* accumulate, bury, conceal, cover, ditch, ensconce, lay away, maintain, screen, secrete, stash, store; ▪ *Ant* array, display, exhibit, show.

cacophonous [*adj*] *harsh sounding*
▪ *Syn* discordant, dissonant, grating, ill-sounding, jarring, noisy, raucous, sour, strident; ▪ *Ant* euphonious, harmonic, mellifluous, quiet.

cadaverous [*adj*] *pale, corpselike*
▪ *Syn* ashen, blanched, bloodless, deathly, emaciated, gaunt, haggard, pallid, peaked, sick, skeletal, thin, wasted; ▪ *Ant* flushed, lifelike, lively.

cage [*v*] *hold in enclosure*
▪ *Syn* close in, confine, coop up, enclose, envelop, fence in, hem, immure, impound, imprison, incarcerate, jail, lock up, mew, pen, restrain, shut in, shut up; ▪ *Ant* free, let go, let out, release.

cajole [*v*] *attempt to coax; flatter*
▪ *Syn* beguile, blandish, con, deceive, delude, entice, influence, inveigle, jolly, lure, maneuver, massage, push, seduce, stroke, tantalize, tempt, urge, wheedle; ▪ *Ant* bully, force, repel.

calamitous [*adj*] *disastrous; tragic*
▪ *Syn* adverse, cataclysmic, catastrophic, devastating, dire, fatal, grievous, harmful, lamentable, pernicious, regrettable, ruinous, woeful; ▪ *Ant* blessed, comfort-

ing, favorable, fortunate, happy, joyous, wonderful.

calculable [*adj*] *able to be computed or estimated* ▪ *Syn* accountable, ascertainable, countable, discoverable, estimable, foreseeable, measurable, predictable, reckonable; ▪ *Ant* incalculable, inestimable, uncomputable.

calculating [*adj*] *scheming to manipulate* ▪ *Syn* artful, canny, crafty, cunning, designing, devious, guileful, intelligent, Machiavellian, politic, premeditating, shrewd, sly, wily; ▪ *Ant* artless, naive, unassuming, uncalculating.

call [*v1*] *yell declaration* ▪ *Syn* announce, arouse, awaken, bawl, bellow, cry out, exclaim, hail, holler, hoot, howl, proclaim, roar, rouse, scream, screech, shout, shriek, vociferate, waken, whoop, yawp, yowl; ▪ *Ant* be quiet, conceal, listen, murmur, mutter, whisper.

call [*v2*] *arrange meeting* ▪ *Syn* ask, assemble, bid, collect, contact, convene, convoke, gather, invite, rally, request, subpoena, summon; ▪ *Ant* cancel, stop.

call [*v3*] *demand or announce action* ▪ *Syn* appeal to, appoint, ask, challenge, charge, claim, command, declare, decree, elect, entreat, exact, ordain, order, postulate, proclaim, require, requisition, set apart, solicit, summon; ▪ *Ant* dismiss, stop.

callous [*adj*] *cruel, insensitive* ▪ *Syn* case-hardened, cold, cold-blooded, hard-boiled, hardened, heartless, impassive, impenitent, indurated, inflexible, insensitive, inured, obdurate, spiritless, stony, thick-skinned, torpid, tough, unfeeling; ▪ *Ant* compassionate, feeling, kind, nice, sensitive, sympathetic, tender.

callow [*adj*] *immature* ▪ *Syn* crude, green, guileless, inexperienced, infant, jejune, juvenile, kid, naive, puerile, raw, sophomore, tenderfoot, untrained, untried, young; ▪ *Ant* experienced, initiated, mature, sophisticated.

calm [*adj1*] *peaceful, quiet (inanimate)* ▪ *Syn* at a standstill, bland, cool, halcyon, harmonious, hushed, motionless, pacific, placid, quiescent, restful, serene, soothing, still, stormless, tranquil, waveless, windless; ▪ *Ant* excited, fierce, frenzied, rough, stormy, turbulent, violent, wild.

calm [*adj2*] *composed, cool (animate)* ▪ *Syn* aloof, amicable, collected, detached, dispassionate, equable, gentle, impassive, imperturbable, levelheaded, moderate, neutral, patient, placid, relaxed, restful, satisfied, sedate, serene, temperate; ▪ *Ant* agitated, angry, excitable, excited, furious, mad, passionate, roused, ruffled, wild, worried.

calm [*v*] *make composed, quiet* ▪ *Syn* allay, alleviate, assuage, balm, becalm, compose, lull, mitigate, mollify, pacify, placate, quiet, relax, sedate, soothe, steady, still, tranquilize; ▪ *Ant* agitate, anger, disquiet, distract, excite, inflame, irritate, outrage, rouse, ruffle, worry.

camaraderie [*n*] *friendship* ▪ *Syn* companionability, companionship, comradeship, conviviality, esprit de corps, intimacy, sociability, togetherness; ▪ *Ant* bad blood, dislike, hate, hostility.

camouflage [*v*] *disguise, cover* ▪ *Syn* becloud, befog, cloak, conceal, cover up, deceive, dim, hide, mask, obfuscate, obscure, screen, veil; ▪ *Ant* reveal, show, uncover.

can [*v*] *fire from job* ▪ *Syn* cashier, discharge, dismiss, expel, let go, terminate; ▪ *Ant* employ, hire.

cancel [*v1*] *call off; erase* ▪ *Syn* abolish, abort, abrogate, annul, break, countermand, cross out, cut, deface, destroy, efface, eliminate, eradicate, expunge, kill, obliterate, omit, remove, render invalid, repeal, repudiate, rescind, revoke, rub out, strike out, undo; ▪ *Ant* allow, approve, arrange, establish, permit, uphold.

cancel [*v2*] *equal out* ▪ *Syn* balance out, compensate for, counteract, counterbalance, discard, discharge, make up for, negate, neutralize, nullify, offset, recant, redress, render null and void, repeal, rule out; ▪ *Ant* imbalance, tip.

candid [*adj*] *honest* ▪ *Syn* aboveboard, blunt, equitable, forthright, frank, genuine, guileless, impartial, just, open, plain, scrupulous, sincere, straightforward, truthful, upright; ▪ *Ant* artful, deceitful, devious, lying, tricky.

canny [*adj*] *clever, artful* ▪ *Syn* acute, astute, cagey, cautious, circumspect, cunning, discreet, ingenious, intelligent, judicious, knowing, perspicacious, prudent, quick, sagacious, shrewd, wary; ▪ *Ant* foolish, inept, silly.

canonical [*adj*] *accepted, recognized*
▪ *Syn* approved, authoritative, authorized, official, orthodox, received, sanctioned, statutory; ▪ *Ant* unacceptable, unauthorized, uncanonical, unorthodox, unrecognized, unsanctioned.

cantankerous [*adj*] *difficult, crabby*
▪ *Syn* bad-tempered, choleric, contrary, cross, disagreeable, dour, ill-humored, irascible, morose, obstinate, perverse, petulant, quarrelsome, sour, testy; ▪ *Ant* easy, good-natured, happy, nice, pleasant.

canyon [*n*] *gulf in mountain area*
▪ *Syn* coulee, glen, gorge, gulch, gully, ravine, valley; ▪ *Ant* mountain, peak, pinnacle, summit.

capable [*adj*] *able to perform*
▪ *Syn* able, accomplished, adept, adequate, apt, au fait, competent, efficient, experienced, gifted, intelligent, proficient, qualified, skillful, suited, talented; ▪ *Ant* impotent, incapable, incompetent, inept, unable, unskilled, unskillful.

capacious [*adj*] *ample, extensive*
▪ *Syn* broad, commodious, comprehensive, expandable, expansive, extended, generous, liberal, plentiful, roomy, sizable, spacious, substantial, vast, voluminous, wide; ▪ *Ant* confined, cramped, restricted, small, squeezed, tiny.

capital [*n*] *upper case written symbol*
▪ *Syn* cap, initial, majuscule, small cap, uncial; ▪ *Ant* lower case letter, minuscule, small letter.

capital [*adj1*] *main, essential*
▪ *Syn* basic, cardinal, central, chief, dominant, first, fundamental, important, leading, major, paramount, preeminent, primary, principal, vital; ▪ *Ant* extra, minor, nonessential, secondary, unimportant.

capital [*adj2*] *superior*
▪ *Syn* best, champion, choice, excellent, famous, fine, first, great, prime, splendid, superb, top; ▪ *Ant* inferior, low-class, minor, poor, unimportant.

capitalism [*n*] *economic system of private ownership* ▪ *Syn* commercialism, competition, free enterprise, free market, industrialism, laissez-faire economics, mercantilism, private enterprise; ▪ *Ant* collectivism, communism, socialism.

capitulate [*v*] *give in*
▪ *Syn* accede, bow, buckle, cave in, cede, concede, defer, fold, relent, submit, succumb, surrender, yield; ▪ *Ant* defend, fight.

capricious [*adj*] *given to sudden behavior change* ▪ *Syn* arbitrary, contrary, erratic, fanciful, fickle, impulsive, lubricious, mercurial, moody, mutable, queer, quirky, temperamental, variable, volatile, wayward, whimsical; ▪ *Ant* constant, dependable, sensible, stable, staid, steadfast, steady.

capsize [*v*] *overturn*
▪ *Syn* invert, keel over, roll, tip over, turn over, upset; ▪ *Ant* right, upright.

captious [*adj*] *very critical*
▪ *Syn* acrimonious, caviling, censorious, contrary, cross, demanding, deprecating, disparaging, exacting, fault-finding, irritable, peevish, petulant, sarcastic; ▪ *Ant* commendatory, complimentary, encouraging, flattering, laudatory, praising.

captivate [*v*] *attract, enchant*
▪ *Syn* allure, beguile, bewitch, charm, dazzle, draw, enrapture, ensnare, enthrall, entrance, fascinate, gratify, hold, hook, hypnotize, intrigue, lure, magnetize, mesmerize, seduce, spellbind, take, wile, win; ▪ *Ant* disgust, disillusion, offend, repel, repulse.

captive [*adj1*] *physically held by force*
▪ *Syn* bound, caged, confined, enslaved, ensnared, imprisoned, incarcerated, incommunicado, in custody, jailed, restricted, subjugated; ▪ *Ant* at liberty, emancipated, free, independent, liberated, loose, unconfined.

captive [*adj2*] *mentally enchanted, held*
▪ *Syn* beguiled, charmed, delighted, enraptured, enthralled, fascinated, hypnotized, infatuated; ▪ *Ant* disillusioned, uninterested.

capture [*v*] *catch and forcefully hold*
▪ *Syn* abduct, apprehend, arrest, catch, conquer, land, net, occupy, overwhelm, seize, snare, take captive, take prisoner; ▪ *Ant* free, let go, liberate, lose, release.

caravan [*n*] *group traveling together*
▪ *Syn* band, campers, cavalcade, expedition, procession, safari, train, troop; ▪ *Ant* individual.

cardinal [*adj*] *important, key*
▪ *Syn* basal, basic, central, chief, essential, foremost, fundamental, highest, indispensable, leading, main, overriding,

overruling, paramount, pivotal, preeminent, primary, principal, ruling, vital; ▪ *Ant* inessential, insignificant, minor, negligible, secondary, unimportant.

care [*v1*] *tend to*
▪ *Syn* attend, baby sit, consider, foster, look after, mind, minister, nurse, nurture, protect, provide for, sit, tend, wait on, watch, watch over; ▪ *Ant* disregard, ignore, neglect.

care [*v2*] *regard highly*
▪ *Syn* cherish, desire, enjoy, hold dear, like, love, prize, respect, take to, want; ▪ *Ant* abhor, detest, dislike, hate, loathe.

career [*n*] *occupation*
▪ *Syn* calling, course, employment, field, job, lifework, livelihood, profession, pursuit, specialty, vocation, work; ▪ *Ant* amusement, avocation, entertainment, recreation, sideline.

carefree [*adj*] *lighthearted, untroubled*
▪ *Syn* airy, at ease, blithe, calm, cheerful, cheery, cool, easy, easy-going, insouciant, jaunty, jovial, radiant, secure, sunny; ▪ *Ant* anxious, heavyhearted, troubled, worried.

careful [*adj*] *cautious; painstaking*
▪ *Syn* accurate, alert, assiduous, attentive, chary, circumspect, concerned, conscientious, deliberate, discreet, exacting, fastidious, guarded, judicious, meticulous, mindful, observant, particular, precise, protective, provident, prudent, punctilious, regardful, rigorous, scrupulous, self-disciplined, solicitous, solid, thorough, thoughtful, vigilant, wary; ▪ *Ant* careless, inattentive, incautious, thoughtless, uncareful, unconcerned, unscrupulous.

carefully [*adv*] *cautiously; painstakingly*
▪ *Syn* attentively, correctly, deliberately, faithfully, fastidiously, guardedly, in detail, laboriously, meticulously, precisely, prudently, rigorously, scrupulously, thoroughly, thoughtfully, warily, watchfully; ▪ *Ant* carelessly, incautiously, thoughtlessly, uncarefully.

careless [*adj1*] *without sufficient attention* ▪ *Syn* absent-minded, casual, forgetful, heedless, improvident, imprudent, incautious, injudicious, irresponsible, loose, negligent, nonchalant, oblivious, offhand, perfunctory, reckless, remiss, slipshod, thoughtless, wasteful; ▪ *Ant* accurate, attentive, careful, cautious, concerned, mindful, painstaking, prudent, ready, thoughtful.

careless [*adj2*] *artless*
▪ *Syn* casual, modest, naive, natural, nonchalant, simple, unstudied; ▪ *Ant* cautious, guarded, kind, mindful, scrupulous.

carnal [*adj*] *erotic, sensual*
▪ *Syn* animal, bodily, corporal, corporeal, earthly, fleshly, impure, lascivious, lewd, libidinous, lustful, physical, salacious, sensuous, temporal, venereal, voluptuous, vulgar, wanton, worldly; ▪ *Ant* chaste, intellectual, pure, spiritual.

carnivorous [*adj*] *eating animal flesh*
▪ *Syn* cannibal, flesh-eating, omnivorous, predatory, rapacious; ▪ *Ant* herbivorous, vegetarian.

carouse [*v*] *make merry, often with liquor* ▪ *Syn* booze, drink, frolic, imbibe, play, quaff, revel, riot, roister, wassail; ▪ *Ant* be sad, grieve, lament.

carry [*v*] *win; accomplish*
▪ *Syn* be victorious, capture, gain, impress, influence, inspire, move, prevail, secure, strike, sway, touch, urge; ▪ *Ant* fail, lose.

carry on [*v1*] *continue activity*
▪ *Syn* achieve, endure, last, maintain, perpetuate, persevere, persist, proceed; ▪ *Ant* discontinue, stop.

carry on [*v2*] *lose control emotionally*
▪ *Syn* act up, be indecorous, misbehave, rage; ▪ *Ant* be calm.

carry out [*v*] *complete activity*
▪ *Syn* accomplish, achieve, consummate, discharge, effect, execute, fulfill, implement, meet, perform, realize; ▪ *Ant* leave, not finish, stop.

cascade [*v*] *fall in a rush*
▪ *Syn* descend, disgorge, flood, gush, overflow, plunge, spew, spill, surge, tumble; ▪ *Ant* dribble, drip, drop, seep, trickle.

cast [*v1*] *throw aside*
▪ *Syn* drop, fling, heave, hurl, impel, launch, peg, pitch, shed, thrust, toss; ▪ *Ant* catch, gather, keep, retain.

cast [*v2*] *emit, give*
▪ *Syn* aim, bestow, diffuse, direct, distribute, point, radiate, scatter, shed, spatter, spray, sprinkle, strew, train; ▪ *Ant* receive, take.

castigate [*v*] *criticize severely*
▪ *Syn* berate, cane, censure, chasten, chastise, correct, criticize, discipline, drub, excoriate, lash, penalize, punish, rail, ream, rebuke, reprimand, scathe,

scold, upbraid; ▪ *Ant* compliment, laud, praise.

casual [*adj1*] *chance, random*
▪ *Syn* accidental, adventitious, contingent, erratic, extemporaneous, fortuitous, impromptu, improvised, impulsive, incidental, infrequent, irregular, occasional, serendipitous, spontaneous, unforeseen; ▪ *Ant* deliberate, painstaking, planned, premeditated.

casual [*adj2*] *nonchalant, relaxed in manner* ▪ *Syn* aloof, apathetic, blas, cursory, detached, easygoing, incurious, indifferent, informal, insouciant, mellow, offhand, perfunctory, pococurante, purposeless, remote; ▪ *Ant* formal, serious.

cataclysm [*n*] *disaster*
▪ *Syn* calamity, cataract, catastrophe, debacle, flood, inundation, misadventure, ruin, torrent, tragedy, upheaval, woe; ▪ *Ant* boon, good fortune, happiness, miracle, wonder.

catalyst [*n*] *something which incites activity* ▪ *Syn* adjuvant, agitator, enzyme, goad, impetus, incendiary, incentive, motivation, reactionary, spur, stimulant, synergist; ▪ *Ant* block, blockage, preventer, prevention.

catastrophe [*n*] *calamity; unhappy conclusion* ▪ *Syn* adversity, affliction, blow, casualty, cataclysm, debacle, denouement, devastation, disaster, end, fiasco, hardship, havoc, ill, infliction, misadventure, misery, misfortune, reverse, stroke, tragedy, trial, trouble, upshot, wreck; ▪ *Ant* benefit, blessing, favor, good fortune, good luck, happiness, miracle, success, wonder.

catch [*v1*] *ensnare, apprehend*
▪ *Syn* arrest, capture, clutch, entangle, entrap, grab, grasp, grip, hook, lasso, pluck, pounce on, secure, seize, snare, snatch, trap; ▪ *Ant* free, let go, let off, lose, misplace, miss, release.

catch [*v2*] *find out, discover*
▪ *Syn* descry, detect, encounter, expose, spot, surprise, take unawares, unmask; ▪ *Ant* miss, misunderstand.

catch [*v3*] *contract an illness*
▪ *Syn* become infected with, break out with, come down with, develop, fall ill with, fall victim to, incur, succumb to, suffer from, take; ▪ *Ant* be immune, be resistant to.

catching [*adj*] *contagious (disease)*
▪ *Syn* communicable, endemic, epidemic, infectious, miasmatic, pandemic, pestiferous, pestilential, taking, transferable, transmittable; ▪ *Ant* noninfectious, uncontagious.

catechize [*v*] *instruct and question*
▪ *Syn* ask, cross-examine, drill, educate, examine, inquire, interrogate, query, quiz, teach, train; ▪ *Ant* answer, listen.

categorical [*adj*] *explicit, unconditional*
▪ *Syn* absolute, certain, clear-cut, definitive, emphatic, express, forthright, positive, specific; ▪ *Ant* ambiguous, conditional, equivocal, implied, qualified, questionable, tentative, vague.

catharsis [*n*] *purging, purification*
▪ *Syn* ablution, abreaction, cleansing, expurgation, lustration, purgation, release; ▪ *Ant* contamination, defilement, dirtying.

catholic [*adj*] *all-embracing, general*
▪ *Syn* all-inclusive, broad, comprehensive, diffuse, eclectic, extensive, global, inclusive, liberal, open-minded, planetary, receptive, tolerant, universal, whole, world-wide; ▪ *Ant* limited, narrow, parochial, provincial, specific.

catty [*adj*] *nasty, malicious*
▪ *Syn* evil, hateful, ill-natured, malevolent, mean, rancorous, spiteful, venomous, vicious, wicked; ▪ *Ant* kind, nice, pleasant.

cause [*v*] *bring into being; bring about*
▪ *Syn* begin, breed, compel, create, effect, engender, evoke, generate, incite, induce, kindle, motivate, originate, precipitate, provoke, result in, revert, secure; ▪ *Ant* deter, foil, forestall, inhibit, prevent, stop, ward off.

caustic [*adj1*] *burning, corrosive*
▪ *Syn* abrasive, acerbic, acid, acrid, alkaline, astringent, biting, erosive, keen, mordant, pungent; ▪ *Ant* calm, mild, soothing.

caustic [*adj2*] *sarcastic*
▪ *Syn* acerb, acrimonious, bitter, cutting, harsh, incisive, pithy, pungent, rough, satiric, scathing, severe, sharp, stinging, trenchant, virulent; ▪ *Ant* kind, nice, unsarcastic.

cautious [*adj*] *careful, guarded*
▪ *Syn* alert, cagey, chary, discreet, heedful, judicious, leery, politic, provident, safe, shrewd, tentative, vigilant, wary, watchful; ▪ *Ant* careless, hasty, heedless, imprudent, incautious, rash, thoughtless, unguarded, unobservant.

cavalier [adj] arrogant
• **Syn** condescending, curt, disdainful, haughty, insolent, lofty, offhand, overbearing, proud, scornful, snooty, supercilious; • **Ant** humble, reticent, shy.

cavernous [adj] hollow and large
• **Syn** broad, chambered, concave, deepset, echoing, gaping, huge, resonant, reverberant, sepulchral, spacious, vast, wide, yawning; • **Ant** confined, cramped, crowded, filled, restricted, small.

cease [v] stop, conclude
• **Syn** break off, bring to an end, close, culminate, die, end, fail, finish, halt, intermit, quit, refrain, shut down, terminate; • **Ant** begin, commence, continue, go, initiate, keep on, start.

ceaseless [adj] never-ending
• **Syn** amaranthine, constant, continual, endless, eternal, incessant, perennial, perpetual; • **Ant** ceasing, completed, concluded, ending, finished, infrequent, irregular, occasional.

cede [v] abandon, surrender
• **Syn** abdicate, alienate, capitulate, communicate, concede, convey, deed, grant, leave, part with, relinquish, remise, renounce, resign, sign over, transfer, vouchsafe, waive, yield; • **Ant** defend, fight, gain, guard, retain, take over, win, withhold.

ceiling [n] maximum
• **Syn** legal price, record, superiority, top; • **Ant** floor, minimum.

celebrate [v] commemorate occasion, achievement • **Syn** ceremonialize, commend, consecrate, dedicate, eulogize, feast, fete, glorify, hallow, honor, keep, laud, memorialize, observe, rejoice, revel, revere, ritualize, solemnize; • **Ant** disregard, forget, ignore, neglect, overlook.

celebrated [adj] distinguished, famous
• **Syn** acclaimed, eminent, famed, glorious, illustrious, important, laureate, notable, outstanding, popular, preeminent, prominent, renowned, revered, wellknown; • **Ant** inglorious, obscure, plain, unexalted, unknown.

celerity [n] swiftness
• **Syn** alacrity, dispatch, expeditiousness, fleetness, haste, hurry, legerity, promptness, quickness, rapidity, speed, velocity, vivacity; • **Ant** slowness, sluggishness.

celestial [adj] heavenly
• **Syn** angelic, astral, divine, elysian, empyral, eternal, ethereal, godlike, hallowed, holy, immortal, Olympian, otherworldly, seraphic, spiritual, sublime, supernatural, transcendental; • **Ant** earthly, hellish, infernal, mortal, mundane.

celibate [adj] abstaining from sexual activity • **Syn** chaste, continent, pure, virgin, virginal, virtuous; • **Ant** active, promiscuous.

cellar [n] underground story of building
• **Syn** apartment, basement, subbasement, subterrane, underground room, vault; • **Ant** attic, garret, upstairs.

cement [v] attach securely, often with sticky material • **Syn** bind, blend, bond, cohere, combine, connect, fasten, fuse, glue, gum, join, merge, mortar, paste, plaster, seal, solder, unite, weld; • **Ant** divide, separate, unfix.

censor [v] forbid; ban; selectively remove • **Syn** abridge, blacklist, bowdlerize, control, decontaminate, delete, edit, excise, expurgate, inspect, narrow, purge, purify, restrain, restrict, review, revile, sanitize, sterilize, suppress, withhold; • **Ant** allow, approve, endorse, permit, sanction.

censorious [adj] very critical
• **Syn** accusatory, captious, caviling, chiding, complaining, condemnatory, condemning, critical, culpatory, denouncing, disparaging, reprehending, reproaching, severe; • **Ant** complimentary, encouraging, flattering, laudatory, praising.

censure [v] condemn; criticize severely
• **Syn** asperse, attack, berate, blame, castigate, chastise, contemn, denigrate, denounce, deprecate, exprobate, impugn, judge, knock, lecture, ostracize, rebuke, remonstrate, reproach, scold, upbraid; • **Ant** allow, approve, compliment, endorse, laud, permit, sanction.

center [n] middle
• **Syn** axis, core, focus, halfway point, inside, interior, mean, middle, midpoint; • **Ant** border, edge, exterior, margin, outside, periphery.

center [v] concentrate, draw together
• **Syn** attract, bring together, centralize, collect, consolidate, converge upon, focalize, focus, gather, intensify, join, medialize, meet, unify; • **Ant** disperse, dissipate, scatter.

central [adj] main, principal; in the middle ▪ **Syn** axial, basic, cardinal, chief, dominant, essential, focal, important, intermediate, key, leading, median, nuclear, paramount, pivotal, prime, ruling, salient, significant; ▪ **Ant** exterior, minor, outside, peripheral, secondary.

centrifugal [adj] radiating from a central point ▪ **Syn** deviating, diffusive, diverging, eccentric, efferent, outward, radial, spiral, spreading; ▪ **Ant** centralizing, centripetal, consolidating.

ceremonial [adj] ritual, formal ▪ **Syn** august, conventional, liturgical, mannered, ritualistic, solemn, stately, studied, stylized; ▪ **Ant** casual, informal, unceremonial.

ceremonious [adj] ritual, formal ▪ **Syn** civil, courteous, courtly, decorous, deferential, dignified, grandiose, impressive, majestic, precise, proper, punctilious, seemly, solemn, stately; ▪ **Ant** casual, informal, relaxed, simple, unceremonious, unobserved.

certain [adj1] confident ▪ **Syn** assertive, assured, calm, convinced, positive, sanguine, satisfied, secure, self-confident, sure; ▪ **Ant** doubtful, doubting, hesitant, uncertain, unconfident, unsure.

certain [adj2] undoubtable, valid ▪ **Syn** ascertained, authoritative, clear, conclusive, definite, determined, evident, fixed, genuine, guaranteed, incontrovertible, infallible, irrefutable, known, plain, positive, provable, real, reliable, sound, trustworthy, verifiable; ▪ **Ant** doubtful, dubious, faltering, questionable, uncertain, unreliable, unsure.

certain [adj3] fixed ▪ **Syn** assured, bound, certified, concluded, decided, definite, determined, ensured, established, insured, set, settled, stated, stipulated, sure; ▪ **Ant** uncertain, undecided, unfixed, unpredictable.

certainly [adv] without doubt ▪ **Syn** absolutely, assuredly, exactly, of course, positively, surely, unquestionably, without fail; ▪ **Ant** doubtfully, dubiously, equivocally, questionably.

certify [v] declare as true ▪ **Syn** accredit, approve, ascertain, assure, attest, authenticate, authorize, aver, avow, confirm, corroborate, endorse, guarantee, license, notify, profess, reassure, sanction, show, state, swear, testify, validate, verify, vouch, witness; ▪ **Ant** contradict, counteract, deny, disavow, discredit, invalidate, reject, repudiate.

cessation [n] ending ▪ **Syn** abeyance, arrest, break, cease, close, conclusion, discontinuance, end, finish, hiatus, intermission, interval, pause, recess, remission, respite, rest, standstill, stay, stop, stoppage, suspension, termination; ▪ **Ant** beginning, commencement, start.

chafe [v1] rub, grind against ▪ **Syn** abrade, corrode, erode, excoriate, grate, graze, hurt, inflame, irritate, peel, ruffle, scrape, scratch, skin, wear; ▪ **Ant** cool, protect, soothe.

chafe [v2] annoy ▪ **Syn** anger, annoy, bother, exasperate, exercise, fret, fume, gall, grate, harass, incense, inflame, irk, irritate, offend, provoke, rasp, rub, vex, worry; ▪ **Ant** calm, make happy, pacify.

chagrin [v] cause displeasure ▪ **Syn** abash, annoy, confuse, crush, discomfit, discompose, disconcert, disgrace, dismay, displease, disquiet, dissatisfy, embarrass, humiliate, irk, irritate, mortify, perturb, shame, upset, vex; ▪ **Ant** delight, make happy, please.

challenge [v] dispute, question ▪ **Syn** accost, assert, beard, brave, call out, claim, confront, cross, dare, defy, denounce, impeach, impose, impugn, inquire, insist upon, investigate, invite competition, provoke, query, reclaim, require, stimulate, summon, tax, test, try, vindicate; ▪ **Ant** agreement, answer, decision, victory.

champion [adj] best, excellent ▪ **Syn** blue-ribbon, capital, chief, choice, distinguished, first, greatest, head, illustrious, outstanding, premier, prime, principal, prize-winning, splendid, super, superior, unbeaten, undefeated; ▪ **Ant** poorest, worst.

champion [v] advocate, support ▪ **Syn** back, battle, contend, defend, espouse, fight for, patronize, plead for, promote, stand behind, stand up for, support, uphold; ▪ **Ant** be against, oppose.

chance [adj] accidental, unforeseeable ▪ **Syn** adventitious, at random, casual, contingent, fortuitous, fortunate, happy, inadvertent, incidental, lucky, odd, unforeseen, unintentional, unlooked for, unplanned; ▪ *Ant* designed, foreseeable, planned, understood.

chance [v] *risk, endanger*
▪ *Syn* attempt, draw lots, gamble, hazard, jeopardize, plunge, speculate, stake, try, venture, wager; ▪ *Ant* aim, design, plan, scheme, understand.

chancy [adj] *dangerous, risky*
▪ *Syn* capricious, contingent, erratic, fluctuant, hazardous, incalculable, precarious, problematic, rocky, speculative, ticklish, tricky, uncertain, unpredictable, unsound; ▪ *Ant* certain, not dangerous, safe, secure, sure, tried.

change [v] *make or become different*
▪ *Syn* accommodate, adapt, adjust, alter, commute, convert, diminish, diverge, diversify, evolve, fluctuate, merge, metamorphose, modify, modulate, mutate, naturalize, recondition, reduce, reform, regenerate, remake, remodel, renovate, reorganize, replace, resolve, restyle, revolutionize, shape, shift, substitute, temper, transfigure, transform, translate, transmute, transpose, turn, vacillate, vary, veer, warp; ▪ *Ant* continue, hold, keep, persist, remain, stay.

changeable [adj] *erratic*
▪ *Syn* capricious, commutative, convertible, fickle, fitful, fluctuating, fluid, impulsive, inconstant, indecisive, irregular, irresolute, irresponsible, kaleidoscopic, mercurial, mobile, mutable, permutable, protean, restless, reversible, revocable, spasmodic, transformable, transitional, vacillating, vagrant, variable, variant, varying, versatile, volatile, wavering, whimsical; ▪ *Ant* certain, changeless, constant, fixed, lasting, predictable, reliable, stable, steady, sure, unchangeable, undeviating.

chaotic [adj] *utterly confused*
▪ *Syn* anarchic, deranged, lawless, purposeless, rampageous, riotous, tumultuous, turbid, turbulent; ▪ *Ant* calm, harmonized, normal, ordered, organized, quiet, systematic.

characteristic [adj] *typical; distinguishing* ▪ *Syn* appropriate, distinctive, emblematic, essential, idiosyncratic, indicative, inherent, innate, marked, normal, original, particular, peculiar, personal, regular, representative, singular, specific, symbolic, symptomatic, unique; ▪ *Ant* abnormal, rare, uncharacteristic, untypical, uunusual.

charge [v1] *accuse*
▪ *Syn* arraign, blame, censure, criminate, finger, impeach, impugn, impute, incriminate, inculpate, indict, involve, reprehend, reproach; ▪ *Ant* absolve, exculpate, exonerate, free.

charge [v2] *attack*
▪ *Syn* assail, assault, chase, dash, invade, lunge, rush, stampede, storm; ▪ *Ant* flee, recoil, retreat.

charge [v3] *ask a price*
▪ *Syn* demand, impose, levy, price, require, sell for; ▪ *Ant* compensate, pay.

charge [v4] *pay with credit card*
▪ *Syn* buy on credit, chalk up, debit, encumber, incur debt, nick, paste, put on account, put on one's card, put on the tab, receive credit, run up; ▪ *Ant* pay by check, pay cash.

charitable [adj1] *giving, generous*
▪ *Syn* accommodating, altruistic, beneficent, benevolent, benign, bountiful, eleemosynary, humane, humanitarian, kindly, lavish, liberal, obliging, philanthropic, sympathetic; ▪ *Ant* inhumane, malevolent, mean, uncharitable, unkind, unsympathetic.

charitable [adj2] *kind, lenient*
▪ *Syn* benevolent, broad-minded, clement, considerate, forbearing, forgiving, gracious, humane, magnanimous, merciful, sympathetic, thoughtful, tolerant, understanding; ▪ *Ant* cruel, hard, harsh, inhumane, mean, rough, severe, tough.

charm [v] *enchant*
▪ *Syn* allure, beguile, bewitch, cajole, captivate, delight, draw, enamor, enrapture, ensorcell, enthrall, entrance, fascinate, hypnotize, inveigle, magnetize, mesmerize, please, possess, tickle, transport, win; ▪ *Ant* displease, irritate, offend, repel, repulse, turn off.

charming [adj] *captivating*
▪ *Syn* alluring, appealing, attractive, charismatic, desirable, engaging, enthralling, entrancing, fetching, inviting, irresistible, likable, pleasing, provocative, rapturous, seductive, sweet, tantalizing, tempting; ▪ *Ant* frightening, irritating, offensive, repellent, repulsive, terrifying.

charter [v] *reserve, commission*
▪ *Syn* allow, authorize, contract, employ, engage, hire, lease, let, license, permit, rent, sanction; ▪ *Ant* cancel.

chary [adj] *careful, cautious*
▪ *Syn* cagey, calculating, circumspect, constrained, discreet, economical, fastid-

ious, frugal, guarded, heedful, hesitant, inhibited, leery, loath, miserly, prudent, reluctant, restrained, scrupulous, suspicious, thrifty, wary, watchful; ▪ *Ant* careless, hasty, heedless, incautious, rash, uncareful, willing.

chase [v] *run after, pursue*
▪ *Syn* charge, chivy, course, drive, expel, follow, hound, hunt, run down, seek, shag, track, track down, trail; ▪ *Ant* escape, retreat, run away.

chasm [n] *gap, abyss*
▪ *Syn* abysm, arroyo, breach, cavity, cleft, crater, crevasse, fissure, flume, gorge, gulch, hiatus, hollow, opening, preterition, ravine, rift, schism, split, void, yawn; ▪ *Ant* closure, junction, juncture.

chaste [adj] *pure, incorrupt*
▪ *Syn* austere, celibate, clean, continent, decent, decorous, elegant, immaculate, innocent, modest, monogamous, moral, neat, platonic, proper, prudish, quiet, refined, restrained, simple, spotless, stainless, vestal, virtuous, wholesome; ▪ *Ant* contaminated, corrupt, corrupt, defiled, dirty, lewd, unchaste, wanton.

chasten [v] *correct, humiliate*
▪ *Syn* abase, admonish, berate, chastise, chide, cow, discipline, exprobate, humble, objurgate, penalize, punish, rebuke, reprehend, reprimand, reproach, reprove, restrain, scold, scourge, soften, subdue, tame, upbraid; ▪ *Ant* aid, animate, assist, boost, cheer, comfort, embolden, encourage, help, honor, uplift.

chastise [v] *scold, discipline*
▪ *Syn* beat, berate, castigate, censure, chasten, correct, punish, scourge; ▪ *Ant* cheer, comfort, compliment, encourage, forgive, inspirit, promote.

chatter [v] *speak fast and non-stop*
▪ *Syn* babble, blather, chitchat, clack, gabble, gibber, gossip, jaw, natter, palaver, prate, tattle; ▪ *Ant* drawl.

chatty [adj] *talkative*
▪ *Syn* colloquial, communicative, conversational, familiar, friendly, garrulous, informal, intimate, loose-lipped, loquacious, spontaneous; ▪ *Ant* laconic, quiet, silent, terse, untalkative.

chauvinism [n] *extreme devotion to a belief or nation* ▪ *Syn* fanatical patriotism, fanaticism, jingoism, nationalism; ▪ *Ant* impartiality, neutrality, objectivity.

cheap [adj1] *inexpensive*
▪ *Syn* bargain, budget, competitive, depreciated, economical, half-priced, irregular, low-priced, marked down, moderate, nominal, on sale, reasonable, reduced, sale; ▪ *Ant* costly, dear, expensive.

cheap [adj2] *inferior, low in quality*
▪ *Syn* bad, base, catchpenny, common, garbage, mean, meretricious, ordinary, paltry, poor, rotten, shoddy, tawdry, trashy, two-bit, valueless, worthless; ▪ *Ant* excellent, noble, precious, priceless, superior, valuable, worthy.

cheap [adj3] *low, vulgar*
▪ *Syn* abject, base, beggarly, contemptible, despicable, dirty, dishonest, mean, pitiable, sordid, tawdry, vile; ▪ *Ant* sophisticated, superior, upper.

cheap [adj4] *concerned with saving money* ▪ *Syn* mean, mingy, miserly, stingy, thrifty; ▪ *Ant* charitable, generous, open-handed.

cheapen [v] *diminish worth*
▪ *Syn* abase, belittle, corrupt, damage, debase, decline, decry, degrade, demean, denigrate, depreciate, derogate, devalue, disparage, lower, mar, minimize, reduce, ruin, spoil, undervalue; ▪ *Ant* appreciate, enhance, increase, raise, upgrade.

check [v1] *inspect, examine*
▪ *Syn* analyze, ascertain, audit, balance account, compare, confirm, count, investigate, keep account, monitor, note, probe, review, scrutinize, study, take stock, verify; ▪ *Ant* disregard, ignore, overlook.

check [v2] *hinder, restrain*
▪ *Syn* arrest, baffle, bar, bridle, checkmate, circumvent, constrain, control, counteract, curb, delay, discourage, foil, frustrate, halt, harness, impede, inhibit, limit, moderate, neutralize, obstruct, obviate, pause, preclude, prevent, rebuff, reduce, rein in, repress, retard, stay, stop, suppress, tame, terminate, thwart, withhold; ▪ *Ant* aid, allow, assist, expedite, help, hurry, indulge, liberate, permit.

cheek [n] *audacity, boldness*
▪ *Syn* brashness, confidence, disrespect, effrontery, gall, impertinence, impudence, insolence, presumption, rudeness, temerity; ▪ *Ant* humbleness, meekness, timidity.

cheer [v1] *make someone feel happier*
▪ *Syn* animate, brace up, brighten, buoy,

comfort, console, elate, elevate, encourage, enliven, exhilarate, gladden, hearten, help, incite, inspirit, solace, strengthen, uplift; ▪ **Ant** bring down, depress, dishearten, make unhappy.

cheer [v2] *encourage in activity*
▪ **Syn** acclaim, applaud, clap, hail, hurrah, rise to, root, salute, support; ▪ **Ant** discourage, dishearten, dissuade.

cheerful [adj] *happy*
▪ **Syn** airy, animated, blithe, bright, chipper, contented, effervescent, enthusiastic, gay, glad, good-humored, hearty, hilarious, hopeful, jaunty, jocund, jolly, joyful, lighthearted, lively, merry, optimistic, pleasant, roseate, sanguine, sparkling, sprightly, upbeat, vivacious, winsome; ▪ **Ant** cheerless, depressed, gloomy, grave, heavy, melancholy, sad, serious, unhappy.

cheering [adj] *encouraging*
▪ **Syn** auspicious, bright, comforting, heartening, hopeful, promising, propitious; ▪ **Ant** dejecting, depressing, discouraging, disheartening.

cheerless [adj] *depressing, unhappy*
▪ **Syn** austere, bleak, despondent, disconsolate, dolorous, forlorn, funereal, gloomy, joyless, miserable, mournful, oppressive, sad, somber, sullen, tenebrific, wintry, woebegone; ▪ **Ant** bright, cheerful, comforting, happy, uplifting.

cherish [v] *care about deeply*
▪ **Syn** adore, apprize, cleave to, coddle, cosset, cultivate, defend, dote on, embrace, enshrine, fancy, guard, harbor, hold dear, idolize, love, nourish, nurture, pet, prize, revere, shelter, shield, treasure, value, venerate, worship; ▪ **Ant** abandon, denounce, forsake, not care, renounce.

chic [adj] *fashionable*
▪ **Syn** chichi, clean, current, dapper, dashing, elegant, exclusive, faddish, modern, modish, natty, sharp, smart, stylish, swank, trendy, voguish; ▪ **Ant** dull, old-fashioned, outmoded, unfashionable.

chicanery [n] *deception, trickery*
▪ **Syn** artifice, cheating, dishonesty, dodge, double-crossing, duplicity, feint, fourberie, fraud, gambit, intrigue, machination, maneuver, plot, ploy, ruse, skullduggery, sophistry, stratagem, subterfuge; ▪ **Ant** forthrightness, honesty, truthfulness.

chide [v] *criticize, lecture*
▪ **Syn** admonish, berate, blame, castigate, censure, check, condemn, exprobate, find fault, flay, rate, rebuke, reprehend, reprimand, reproach, reprove, scold, tell off, upbraid; ▪ **Ant** compliment, laud, praise.

chief [adj] *most important, essential*
▪ **Syn** arch, capital, cardinal, central, consequential, crucial, first, foremost, grand, head, highest, key, leading, main, major, outstanding, paramount, predominant, preeminent, primary, prime, principal, ruling, significant, star, stellar, superior, supreme, telling, uppermost, vital; ▪ **Ant** inessential, minor, secondary, subordinate, unimportant, unnecessary.

chiefly [adv] *most important*
▪ **Syn** above all, especially, essentially, in general, in the first place, in the main, largely, mainly, mostly, on the whole, overall, predominantly, primarily, principally, usually; ▪ **Ant** last, least, least of all, unimportantly.

childish [adj] *immature, silly*
▪ **Syn** babyish, childlike, foolish, green, infantile, juvenile, naive, puerile, young, youthful; ▪ **Ant** adult, mature, sensible, serious, wise.

childlike [adj] *innocent, naive*
▪ **Syn** artless, credulous, guileless, immature, ingenuous, natural, simple, spontaneous, trustful, trusting, unaffected, unfeigned; ▪ **Ant** complicated, experienced, sophisticated, untrusting.

chill/chilly [adj1] *cold, raw*
▪ **Syn** arctic, biting, brisk, cool, freezing, frigid, frosty, glacial, icy, nippy, sharp, wintry; ▪ **Ant** hot, tropical, warm.

chill/chilly [adj2] *unfriendly, aloof*
▪ **Syn** cool, dismal, dispiriting, distant, emotionless, formal, frigid, glacial, hostile, icy, indifferent, reserved, stony, unemotional, ungenial, unwelcoming, withdrawn; ▪ **Ant** friendly, responsive, sympathetic, warm.

chill [v1] *make cold*
▪ **Syn** air-condition, congeal, cool, freeze, frost, ice, refrigerate; ▪ **Ant** heat, warm.

chill [v2] *discourage*
▪ **Syn** cloud, dampen, dash, deject, demoralize, depress, dishearten, dismay, disparage, dispirit; ▪ **Ant** encourage, hearten, incite, inspirit.

chimera [n] *dream, fantasy*
▪ **Syn** delusion, fabrication, fancy, fig-

ment, hallucination, ignis fatuus, illusion, monster, specter; ▪ *Ant* reality, truth.

choice [*adj*] *best, superior*
▪ *Syn* elect, elite, excellent, exceptional, exclusive, exquisite, fine, hand-picked, popular, precious, preferential, preferred, prime, prize, rare, select, special, uncommon, unusual, valuable, winner; ▪ *Ant* inferior, poor, sad, worst.

choke [*v*] *smother, block*
▪ *Syn* asphyxiate, bar, check, clog, congest, constrict, dam, die, drown, fill, gag, garrote, gasp, gibbet, kill, noose, obstruct, occlude, overpower, retard, stifle, stop, stopper, strangle, stuff, stunt, suffocate, suppress, throttle, wring; ▪ *Ant* release, unblock, unconstrict.

choose [*v*] *pick, select*
▪ *Syn* accept, adopt, appoint, cast, co-opt, crave, cull, designate, desire, determine, elect, embrace, espouse, excerpt, extract, fancy, favor, glean, judge, name, opt for, predestine, prefer, separate, set aside, settle upon, single out, sort, tab, tap, want, weigh, winnow; ▪ *Ant* cast away, decline, disclaim, dismmiss, eschew, forbbear, forgo, refuse, reject, repudiate, spurn, throw aside.

choosy [*adj*] *fussy, discriminating*
▪ *Syn* exacting, fastidious, finical, finicky, nice, particular, select, selective; ▪ *Ant* undemanding, unfastidious, unfussy.

choppy [*adj*] *wavy*
▪ *Syn* inclement, ripply, rough, uneven, violent, wild; ▪ *Ant* calm, smooth.

chorus [*n*] *agreement*
▪ *Syn* accord, concert, concord, consonance, harmony, tune, unison; ▪ *Ant* disagreement, discord.

chosen [*adj*] *preferred*
▪ *Syn* called, conscript, elect, exclusive, named, popular, preferential, select; ▪ *Ant* ignored, inferior.

chronic [*adj*] *incessant, never-ending*
▪ *Syn* abiding, ceaseless, continual, enduring, fixed, habitual, incurable, ineradicable, lasting, perennial, persistent, protracted, recurrent, rooted, settled, stubborn, tenacious, usual; ▪ *Ant* curable, eradicable, intermittent, occasional, temporary.

chronicle [*v*] *report, recount*
▪ *Syn* enter, narrate, record, register, relate, set down, tell; ▪ *Ant* hide, secret.

chubby [*adj*] *slightly fat*
▪ *Syn* ample, big, flabby, fleshy, full-figured, hefty, husky, plump, portly, pudgy, rotund, round, stout; ▪ *Ant* skinny, slim, thin.

chuck [*v*] *throw aside, throw away, throw out* ▪ *Syn* abandon, cast, desert, discard, ditch, eject, fire, forsake, heave, hurl, jettison, launch, pitch, quit, reject, renounce, scrap, shed, sling, toss; ▪ *Ant* continue, endure, keep, maintain, persevere.

chum [*n*] *friend*
▪ *Syn* associate, buddy, comate, companion, comrade, crony, mate, pal, playmate; ▪ *Ant* acquaintance, enemy, stranger.

chummy [*adj*] *friendly*
▪ *Syn* affectionate, close, confidential, constant, cozy, familiar, intimate; ▪ *Ant* aloof, cool, distant, unfriendly, unsociable.

chunky [*adj*] *fat, plump*
▪ *Syn* chubby, dumpy, heavyset, husky, rotund, squat, stocky, stout, thick-bodied, thickset; ▪ *Ant* skinny, slender, slim, thin.

churlish [*adj*] *crude,*
▪ *Syn* base, crude, discourteous, dour, grouchy, gruff, grumpy, harsh, ill-tempered, impolite, loutish, lowbred, miserly, morose, oafish, rude, sullen, surly, ugly, unmannerly, unpolished, unsociable, vulgar; ▪ *Ant* agreeable, amiable, civil, gentle, pleasant, polite.

circuitous [*adj*] *going around, indirect*
▪ *Syn* by way of, circular, complicated, devious, labyrinthine, meandering, oblique, rambling, roundabout, tortuous, winding around; ▪ *Ant* direct, in line, straight.

circular [*adj*] *going around*
▪ *Syn* annular, circling, indirect, oblique, orbicular, round, rounded, spheroid; ▪ *Ant* linear, rectangular, square, straight.

circulate [*v1*] *make known*
▪ *Syn* bring out, broadcast, disperse, disseminate, distribute, exchange, interview, issue, propagate, publicize, radiate, report, spread, troll; ▪ *Ant* conceal, hide, hush up, keep secret, suppress.

circulate [*v2*] *flow*
▪ *Syn* actuate, circle, get around, gyrate, mill around, mobilize, radiate, revolve, rotate; ▪ *Ant* block, hold back.

circumference [*n*] *edge, perimeter*
▪ *Syn* ambit, border, boundary, circuit,

confines, extremity, fringe, girth, limits, lip, margin, outline, periphery, rim, verge; ▪ *Ant* inside, interior, middle.

circumlocution [*n*] *indirect speech*
▪ *Syn* diffuseness, discursiveness, euphemism, indirectness, periphrasis, prolixity, tautology, verbal evasion, verbiage, wordiness; ▪ *Ant* conciseness, directness, straightforwardness, terseness.

circumscribe [*v*] *mark off, delimit*
▪ *Syn* bar, bound, confine, define, delineate, encircle, enclose, encompass, girdle, hamper, limit, outline, restrain, restrict, surround, trammel; ▪ *Ant* free, loose, open.

circumspect [*adj*] *cautious, discreet*
▪ *Syn* careful, discriminating, guarded, heedful, judicious, politic, prudent, punctilious, safe, sagacious, scrupulous, vigilant, wary, watchful; ▪ *Ant* audacious, bold, careless, incautious, indiscreet, rash.

circumvent [*v*] *fool, mislead; go around*
▪ *Syn* avoid, beat, bypass, circumnavigate, deceive, dodge, elude, escape, evade, foil, frustrate, hoodwink, prevent, sidestep, trick; ▪ *Ant* aid, assist, conform, face, follow, help.

citation [*n*] *award*
▪ *Syn* charge, commendation, encomium, mention, panegyric, reward, salutation, summons, tribute; ▪ *Ant* demerit.

citizen [*n*] *inhabitant of a country*
▪ *Syn* aborigine, civilian, denizen, dweller, member of community, national, naturalized person, occupant, resident, taxpayer, urbanite, voter; ▪ *Ant* alien, foreigner, immigrant, tourist, transient, visitor.

city [*adj*] *metropolitan*
▪ *Syn* civic, civil, interurban, intraurban, megalopolitan, municipal, oppidan, urban; ▪ *Ant* rural, suburban.

civil [*adj*] *obliging, kind*
▪ *Syn* accommodating, affable, complaisant, cordial, courteous, courtly, diplomatic, genteel, gracious, mannerly, polished, polite, politic, refined, suave, urbane, well-bred, well-mannered; ▪ *Ant* ill-mannered, impolite, rude, unkind.

civilian [*adj*] *nonmilitary*
▪ *Syn* noncombatant, nonmilitant, pacificist, private, unhostile; ▪ *Ant* combative, martial, military.

claim [*v*] *demand, maintain property or right* ▪ *Syn* adduce, allege, assert, believe, challenge, declare, exact, hold, insist, justify, postulate, pretend, profess, pronounce, require, requisition, solicit, take, uphold, vindicate; ▪ *Ant* deny, disclaim, question.

clammy [*adj*] *damp*
▪ *Syn* close, dank, moist, mucous, pasty, slimy, soggy, sticky, sweaty, wet; ▪ *Ant* cool, dry.

clamor [*v*] *cry out, make commotion*
▪ *Syn* agitate, bawl, bellow, bluster, claim, debate, demand, dispute, holler, roar, rout, shout; ▪ *Ant* be quiet, be silent, mutter, whisper.

clamp [*v*] *fasten*
▪ *Syn* brace, clench, clinch, fix, impose, make fast, secure; ▪ *Ant* loosen, open, unbuckle, unclamp, unfasten, unlock.

clandestine [*adj*] *secret, sly*
▪ *Syn* artful, cloak-and-dagger, concealed, covert, furtive, hidden, illegitimate, illicit, private, stealthy, surreptitious, undercover; ▪ *Ant* aboveboard, forthright, open, truthful.

clannish [*adj*] *exclusive, select*
▪ *Syn* cliquish, close, insular, like, narrow, reserved, restricting, sectarian; ▪ *Ant* friendly, open, welcoming.

clap [*v*] *applaud; slap with approbation*
▪ *Syn* acclaim, approve, cheer, pat, praise, slap; ▪ *Ant* boo, hiss, jeer.

clarify [*v1*] *explain, make clear*
▪ *Syn* analyze, define, delineate, elucidate, formulate, illuminate, interpret, make plain, resolve, settle, simplify; ▪ *Ant* cloud, confuse, muddle.

clarify [*v2*] *purify*
▪ *Syn* clean, cleanse, depurate, distill, filter, rarefy, refine; ▪ *Ant* dirty, muddle, muddy.

clarion [*adj*] *clear, stirring sound*
▪ *Syn* blaring, definite, inspiring, loud, ringing, sharp, shrill, strident; ▪ *Ant* dull, low, muffled, muted, soft.

clash [*v*] *fight about, often verbally*
▪ *Syn* argue, battle, brawl, buck, combat, conflict, contend, cross swords, differ, disagree, encounter, feud, fret, gall, grapple, grate, quarrel, row, try, war, wrangle; ▪ *Ant* agree, concur, make up.

clasp [*v*] *grab tightly*
▪ *Syn* clamp, clinch, clutch, coll, connect, embrace, enfold, fasten, grasp, grip, hold, hug, pin, press, seize, snatch, squeeze; ▪ *Ant* let go, loose, release.

class [adj] stylish; with panache
▪ **Syn** chic, classy, dashing, fashionable, fine, sharp; ▪ **Ant** plain, unstylish.

classic/classical [adj1] best, model
▪ **Syn** archetypal, consummate, definitive, distinguished, esthetic, excellent, exemplary, famous, fine, first-rate, flawless, ideal, paradigmatic, paramount, perfect, prime, quintessential, ranking, standard, superior, vintage; ▪ **Ant** atypical, inferior, poor, worst

classic [adj2] characteristic, regular
▪ **Syn** prototypal, prototypical, representative, standard, time-honored, typical, usual, vintage; ▪ **Ant** abnormal, irregular, uncharacteristic.

classical [adj] concerning ancient culture ▪ **Syn** academic, Attic, Augustan, belletristic, bookish, canonic, canonical, classic, classicistic, Doric, Grecian, Greek, Hellenic, Homeric, humanistic, Ionic, Latin, Roman, scholastic, Virgilian; ▪ **Ant** modern, unclassical.

classy [adj] stylish, having panache
▪ **Syn** chic, dashing, elegant, exclusive, fashionable, high-class, in vogue, mod, select, sharp, superior, swanky, uptown; ▪ **Ant** inelegant, inferior, plain, unstylish.

clean [adj1] not dirty; uncluttered
▪ **Syn** blank, bright, cleansed, clear, flawless, fresh, hygienic, immaculate, laundered, neat, orderly, pure, sanitary, sparkling, spotless, stainless, taintless, tidy, trim, washed, well-kept; ▪ **Ant** cluttered, dirty, filthy, foul, polluted, stained, tarnished.

clean [adj2] sterile
▪ **Syn** antiseptic, aseptic, decontaminated, disinfected, hygienic, pure, purified, sanitary, sterilized, wholesome; ▪ **Ant** adulterated, contaminated, dirty, impure, unsterile.

clean [adj3] chaste, virtuous
▪ **Syn** blameless, crimeless, decent, exemplary, faultless, guiltless, honorable, inculpable, innocent, moral, respectable, sinless, upright, wholesome; ▪ **Ant** besmirched, defiled, impure, unchaste, unvirtuous.

clean [adj4] precise, sharp
▪ **Syn** clear, correct, definite, distinct, legible, neat, plain, readable, simple, trim; ▪ **Ant** cluttered, imprecise, indefinite, muddled.

clean [adj5] complete, thorough
▪ **Syn** absolute, conclusive, decisive, entire, final, perfect, total, whole; ▪ **Ant** fragmentary, incomplete, partial.

clean [v] make undirty, uncluttered
▪ **Syn** absterge, bathe, cauterize, clarify, cleanse, deterge, disinfect, expunge, expurgate, flush, launder, lave, mop, neaten, polish, purge, purify, rinse, sanitize, scald, scour, scrape, scrub, shampoo, soak, soap, sponge, spruce up, sterilize, sweep, vacuum, wash; ▪ **Ant** adulterate, defile, dirty, foul, soil, stain.

clean-cut [adj] neat, clearly outlined
▪ **Syn** categorical, chiseled, definite, definitive, etched, explicit, sharp, specific, well-defined; ▪ **Ant** ambiguous, hazy, ruffled.

cleanse [v] make undirty; wash
▪ **Syn** absolve, clarify, clean, clear, depurate, disinfect, expurgate, launder, lustrate, purge, purify, refine, restore, rinse, sanitize, scour, scrub, sterilize; ▪ **Ant** dirty, soil, spot.

clear [adj1] cloudless, bright
▪ **Syn** clarion, crystal, fair, fine, halcyon, light, luminous, pleasant, shining, sunny, sunshiny; ▪ **Ant** cloudy, dark, dim, dull, fuzzy, gloomy, shadowy, unclear.

clear [adj2] understandable, apparent
▪ **Syn** apprehensible, coherent, conspicuous, distinct, evident, explicit, express, incontrovertible, knowable, lucid, manifest, obvious, palpable, patent, perceptible, pronounced, recognizable, simple, straightforward; ▪ **Ant** ambiguous, complicated, indistinct, mysterious, obscure, unintelligible, vague.

clear [adj3] open, unhindered
▪ **Syn** bare, empty, free, smooth, stark, unhampered, unlimited, unobstructed, vacant, vacuous; ▪ **Ant** blocked, clogged, closed, congested, hindered.

clear [adj4] transparent
▪ **Syn** crystal, crystal clear, crystalline, glassy, limpid, pellucid, pure, thin, translucent, translucid; ▪ **Ant** clouded, foggy, obscured, smudged.

clear [adj5] free of guilt
▪ **Syn** absolved, blameless, clean, discharged, dismissed, exculpated, exonerated, guiltless, immaculate, innocent, pure, sinless, stainless; ▪ **Ant** culpable, guilty, responsible.

clear [adj6] certain in one's mind
▪ **Syn** absolute, confirmed, convinced, de-

cided, definite, positive, resolved, satisfied, sure; ▪ *Ant* uncertain, unclear, unintelligible.

clear [*v1*] *clean, clear away*
▪ *Syn* ameliorate, brighten, clarify, cleanse, disencumber, disentangle, eliminate, empty, erase, extricate, free, lighten, lose, meliorate, open, purify, rid, sweep, vacate, void, wipe; ▪ *Ant* clutter, deteriorate, pile up.

clear [*v2*] *liberate; free from uncertainty*
▪ *Syn* absolve, acquit, clarify, discharge, disculpate, emancipate, exculpate, exonerate, explain, find innocent, let go, release, relieve, set free, vindicate; ▪ *Ant* condemn, find guilty, sentence.

clear [*v3*] *pass over, often by jumping*
▪ *Syn* hurdle, leap, miss, negotiate, overleap, surmount, vault; ▪ *Ant* hit, run into.

clear-cut [*adj*] *definite*
▪ *Syn* categorical, crystalline, decided, definitive, distinct, evident, explicit, express, indubitable, lucent, lucid, obvious, plain, precise, pronounced, specific, straightforward, well-defined; ▪ *Ant* ambiguous, fuzzy, indefinite, vague.

clearly [*adv*] *without any doubt*
▪ *Syn* apparently, certainly, conspicuously, decidedly, definitely, discernibly, evidently, incontestably, incontrovertibly, indubitably, manifestly, markedly, noticeably, obviously, openly, overtly, perceptibly, plainly, prominently, purely, recognizably, sharply, sonorously, surely, translucently; ▪ *Ant* indefinitely, indistinctly, mysteriously, vaguely.

clear out [*v1*] *empty something*
▪ *Syn* clean out, dispose of, eliminate, exhaust, get rid of, remove, sort, tidy up; ▪ *Ant* fill, fill up, put.

clear out [*v2*] *leave, often quickly*
▪ *Syn* begone, decamp, depart, go, retire, take off, withdraw; ▪ *Ant* arrive, rush in.

clear up [*v1*] *explain; resolve*
▪ *Syn* answer, clarify, decipher, dissolve, elucidate, figure out, illuminate, illustrate, resolve, solve; ▪ *Ant* complicate, question.

clear up [*v2*] *become improved*
▪ *Syn* become fair, become sunny, blow over, brighten, die away, die down, lapse, lift, pick up; ▪ *Ant* decline, worsen.

cleave [*v1*] *divide, split*
▪ *Syn* carve, chop, cut, dissect, dissever,

divorce, hack, open, part, pierce, rend, rip, separate, sever, stab, tear asunder; ▪ *Ant* join, meld, unite.

cleave [*v2*] *stand by, stick together*
▪ *Syn* abide by, adhere, agree, associate, attach, be devoted to, cling, cohere, combine, hold, join, link, remain, unite; ▪ *Ant* abandon, forsake, release, relinquish, separate

cleft [*adj*] *separated, split*
▪ *Syn* broken, cloven, cracked, crannied, crenelated, parted, perforated, pierced, rent, riven, ruptured, separated, sundered, torn; ▪ *Ant* joined, joint, united.

clemency [*n*] *forgiveness*
▪ *Syn* caritas, compassion, endurance, equitableness, forbearance, grace, humanity, indulgence, justness, kindness, lenience, mercifulness, mercy, moderation, sufferance, tenderness, tolerance; ▪ *Ant* cruelty, harshness, mercilessness, severity.

clement [*adj1*] *calm, mild (weather)*
▪ *Syn* balmy, clear, fair, fine, moderate, peaceful, temperate, warm; ▪ *Ant* harsh, severe, violent.

clement [*adj2*] *forgiving*
▪ *Syn* benevolent, charitable, compassionate, easy, forbearing, gentle, humane, indulgent, kind-hearted, lenient, merciful, mild, soft-hearted, sympathetic, tender, tolerant; ▪ *Ant* hard, hardhearted, harsh, mean, unforgiving.

clench [*v*] *grasp*
▪ *Syn* clamp, clasp, clinch, clutch, constrict, contract, double up, grip, hold; ▪ *Ant* let go, loose, loosen, release.

clerical [*adj*] *concerning clergy*
▪ *Syn* apostolic, canonical, churchly, ecclesiastic, ecclesiastical, episcopal, holy, ministerial, monastic, papal, parsonical, pastoral, pontifical, priestly, rabbinical, sacerdotal, sacred, theocratical; ▪ *Ant* lay, secular.

clever [*adj*] *bright, ingenious*
▪ *Syn* able, adept, apt, astute, brilliant, cagey, canny, cunning, deep, discerning, expert, gifted, intelligent, inventive, keen, knowledgeable, qualified, quick-witted, resourceful, sagacious, savvy, sensible, sharp, shrewd, skilled, skillful, sly, smart, talented, versatile, wise, witty; ▪ *Ant* awkward, foolish, idiotic, ignorant, naive, senseless, stupid.

cliché [*n*] *overused, hackneyed phrase*
▪ *Syn* adage, banality, bromide, buzz-

word, commonplace, motto, platitude, prosaism, proverb, saying, shibboleth, slogan, triviality, truism; ▪ *Ant* coinage, nuance, profundity.

client [*n*] *customer*
 ▪ *Syn* applicant, buyer, consumer, dependent, follower, habitué, patient, patron, protégé, purchaser, shopper, walk-in, ward; ▪ *Ant* manager, owner.

clientele [*n*] *customers of a business*
 ▪ *Syn* audience, business, clients, constituency, cortege, dependents, following, market, patronage, public, regulars, trade; ▪ *Ant* management, ownership.

climactic/climacteric [*adj*] *decisive*
 ▪ *Syn* acute, climactical, critical, crucial, desperate, dire, paramount, peak; ▪ *Ant* anticlimactic, anticlimactical, bathetic, indecisive, trivial, undecided.

climax [*n*] *peak, culmination*
 ▪ *Syn* acme, apex, apogee, ascendancy, climacteric, crest, extremity, head, height, limit, maximum, meridian, ne plus ultra, orgasm, pinnacle, pitch, summit, top, utmost, zenith; ▪ *Ant* anticlimax, cliffhanger.

climax [*v*] *come to the top; culminate*
 ▪ *Syn* accomplish, achieve, cap, conclude, content, crown, end, finish, fulfill, orgasm, peak, satisfy, succeed, terminate, top, tower; ▪ *Ant* delve, dip, drop, fall off.

climb [*v*] *crawl, move up*
 ▪ *Syn* ascend, clamber, escalade, escalate, go up, mount, rise, scale, soar, top; ▪ *Ant* descend, dismount, go down, retreat.

cling [*v*] *attach to*
 ▪ *Syn* adhere, cherish, clasp, cleave to, clutch, cohere, continue, embrace, endure, fasten, freeze to, grasp, grip, hang onto, hold fast, hug, linger; ▪ *Ant* detach, let go, unfasten.

clinical [*adj*] *dispassionate*
 ▪ *Syn* analytic, antiseptic, cold, detached, disinterested, impersonal, objective, scientific; ▪ *Ant* emotional, feeling, passionate, subjective.

clip [*v*] *cut short*
 ▪ *Syn* bob, crop, curtail, decrease, dock, lower, mow, pare, prune, reduce, shave, shear, shorten, trim, truncate; ▪ *Ant* elongate, extend, lengthen.

cloak [*v*] *disguise*
 ▪ *Syn* blanket, camouflage, conceal, cover, curtain, dissemble, dissimulate, hide, mask, obscure, shroud, veil; ▪ *Ant* reveal, uncloak, uncover.

clog [*v*] *block, hinder*
 ▪ *Syn* burden, choke, close, congest, encumber, fetter, glut, hamper, impede, jam, leash, obstruct, plug, seal, stopper, stuff, tie, trammel; ▪ *Ant* clear, free, open, unblock, unclog, unencumber, unstop.

cloistered [*adj*] *secluded*
 ▪ *Syn* confined, hermitic, hidden, insulated, recluse, reclusive, restricted, seclusive, sequestered, sheltered, shielded, shut off, withdrawn; ▪ *Ant* free, open, unsecluded.

close [*adj1*] *near, nearby*
 ▪ *Syn* abutting, adjacent, at hand, contiguous, convenient, handy, hard by, immediate, impending, nearest, neighboring, nigh, proximate; ▪ *Ant* away, beyond, detached, distant, far, faraway.

close [*adj2*] *dense, cramped*
 ▪ *Syn* circumscribed, compact, confined, congested, consolidated, cropped, crowded, impenetrable, impermeable, narrow, packed, restricted, solid, thick, tight; ▪ *Ant* loose, open, uncramped.

close [*adj3*] *accurate, precise*
 ▪ *Syn* conscientious, exact, faithful, lifelike, literal, resembling, similar, strict; ▪ *Ant* far, imprecise, inaccurate.

close [*adj4*] *intimate*
 ▪ *Syn* attached, confidential, dear, devoted, familiar, inseparable, loving, private, related; ▪ *Ant* alienated, estranged, unfriendly.

close [*adj5*] *oppressive, humid*
 ▪ *Syn* airless, breathless, confined, fusty, heavy, moldy, motionless, muggy, stagnant, stifling, stuffy, suffocating, sultry, sweltering, thick, tight, unventilated; ▪ *Ant* cool, dry.

close [*adj6*] *secret, reserved*
 ▪ *Syn* close-lipped, closemouthed, hidden, private, reticent, retired, secluded, secretive, silent, taciturn, uncommunicative; ▪ *Ant* open, unreserved.

close [*v1*] *obstruct, seal*
 ▪ *Syn* bar, block, caulk, choke, clog, confine, congest, cork, dam, exclude, fasten, fill, lock, occlude, plug, secure, shut off, stopper, stuff, turn off; ▪ *Ant* open, release, unclose, unplug, unseal, unstop.

close [*v2*] *complete, finish, stop*
 ▪ *Syn* call off, cease, clinch, con-

clude, consummate, culminate, cut loose, discontinue, end, fold, fold up, halt, shut down, terminate, ultimate; ▪ *Ant* begin, continue, not finish, open, start.

close [*v3*] *join, unite*
▪ *Syn* agree, bind, chain, coalesce, connect, couple, encounter, fuse, grapple, inclose, meet, tie, tie up; ▪ *Ant* disjoin, disunite, open.

closed [*adj1*] *shut, out of service*
▪ *Syn* bankrupt, dark, fastened, folded, locked, padlocked, sealed, shut down; ▪ *Ant* in business, open, running, working.

closed [*adj2*] *finished, terminated*
▪ *Syn* concluded, decided, ended, final, over, resolved, settled; ▪ *Ant* beginning, continuing, open, started, starting, unsettled.

losed [*adj3*] *exclusive, independent*
▪ *Syn* restricted, self-contained, self-sufficient, self-supporting, self-sustained; ▪ *Ant* open, welcoming.

closemouthed [*adj*] *silent, reserved*
▪ *Syn* close, quiet, reticent, sedate, taciturn, tight-lipped, uncommunicative; ▪ *Ant* chatty, open, talkative.

clot [*v*] *coagulate*
▪ *Syn* coalesce, congeal, curdle, gel, gelatinize, jell, lump, set, solidify, thicken; ▪ *Ant* loose, thin.

clothe [*v*] *cover with apparel*
▪ *Syn* apparel, attire, bedizen, bedrape, bundle up, cloak, costume, deck, dress, dress up, endow, equip, fit out, garb, habit, invest, jacket, livery, mantle, outfit, rig, robe, spruce, suit up, swathe, tog, turn out, vest; ▪ *Ant* reveal, take off, unclothe, uncover.

cloud [*v1*] *become foggy or obscured*
▪ *Syn* adumbrate, becloud, blur, darken, eclipse, envelop, fog, gloom, mist, overcast, overshadow, shade, shadow, veil; ▪ *Ant* clear, unfog, unveil.

cloud [*v2*] *confuse*
▪ *Syn* addle, befuddle, disorient, distort, distract, impair, muddle, muddy, obscure, perplex, puzzle; ▪ *Ant* clear up, explain, explicate.

cloudy [*adj*] *hazy; darkened*
▪ *Syn* blurred, confused, dim, dull, emulsified, foggy, gloomy, heavy, indistinct, leaden, misty, muddy, nebulous, obscure, opaque, overcast, somber, sunless, vaporous; ▪ *Ant* clear, cloudless.

clue [*v*] *give information*
▪ *Syn* acquaint, advise, apprise, fill in, hint, indicate, inform, intimate, lead to, leave evidence, leave trace, notify, point to, post, suggest, tell, warn, wise up; ▪ *Ant* hide, keep secret.

clumsy [*adj*] *not agile; awkward*
▪ *Syn* blundering, bungling, clownish, elephantine, gauche, graceless, heavy-handed, incompetent, inelegant, inept, inexperienced, lumbering, maladroit, oafish, ponderous, splay, stumbling, uncouth; ▪ *Ant* adroit, agile, athletic, clever, coordinated, couth, dexterous, expert, graceful.

cluster [*v*] *assemble, group*
▪ *Syn* accumulate, aggregate, associate, bunch, bunch up, bundle, collect, cumulate, flock, gather, package, parcel, round up; ▪ *Ant* disperse, dissemble, let go, scatter.

clutch [*v*] *grab, snatch*
▪ *Syn* catch, clasp, clench, clinch, cling to, embrace, fasten, grasp, grip, hold, hook, keep, nab, seize, snatch; ▪ *Ant* let go, unfasten.

clutter [*n*] *disarray, mess*
▪ *Syn* ataxia, chaos, confusion, derangement, disorder, hodgepodge, jumble, litter, melange, muddle, rummage, scramble, tumble; ▪ *Ant* neatness, order, tidiness.

clutter [*v*] *cause mess, disarray*
▪ *Syn* dirty, jumble, litter, muddle, scatter, snarl, strew; ▪ *Ant* array, clean up, neaten, order, tidy.

coach [*n*] *instructor, usually in recreation* ▪ *Syn* educator, mentor, physical education instructor, teacher, trainer, tutor; ▪ *Ant* player, pupil, student.

coach [*v*] *instruct, usually in recreation*
▪ *Syn* drill, educate, hone, prepare, ready, school, teach, train, tutor; ▪ *Ant* accept, learn, listen.

coagulate [*v*] *clot*
▪ *Syn* coalesce, compact, concentrate, condense, congeal, consolidate, curdle, dry, gel, harden, inspissate, jell, set, solidify, thicken; ▪ *Ant* dilute, dissolve, melt, open, thin, unclot.

coalesce [*v*] *blend, come together*
▪ *Syn* amalgamate, associate, bracket, cleave, cling, commingle, conjoin, consolidate, fuse, incorporate, join up with, link, merge, relate, stick, unite, wed; ▪ *Ant* divide, separate.

coarse [adj1] *not fine, rude*
- **Syn** base, boorish, cheap, common, crass, dirty, earthy, filthy, foul, gross, impolite, improper, impure, loutish, mean, nasty, obscene, offensive, raw, ribald, rough, rude, vulgar; **Ant** civil, gentle, nice, polite, refined, sophisticated.

coarse [adj2] *rough, unrefined*
- **Syn** chapped, crude, grainy, harsh, homespun, inferior, loose, lumpy, poor-quality, rough-hewn; **Ant** delicate, refined, smooth, soft.

coat [v] *cover with layer of material*
- **Syn** apply, enamel, foil, glaze, incrust, laminate, paint, plaster, plate, smear, spread, stain, surface, varnish; **Ant** reveal, uncover.

coax [v] *persuade*
- **Syn** allure, beguile, blandish, cajole, con, entice, flatter, influence, inveigle, lure, pester, plague, prevail upon, sweet-talk, tease, tempt, urge, wangle, wheedle, work on, worm; **Ant** allow, compel, dissuade, force.

cockeyed [adj] *crooked, askew*
- **Syn** askance, askant, asymmetrical, awry, canted, crazy, crooked, cross-eyed, lopsided; **Ant** level, straight.

cocky/cocksure [adj] *self-assured, full of oneself* • **Syn** arrogant, conceited, egotistical, hubristic, nervy, overconfident, positive, presumptuous, self-confident, swaggering, vain; **Ant** humble, modest, uncertain, unselfconfident, unsure.

cocoon [v] *spend leisure time at home*
- **Syn** be a homebody, escape, hide, insulate, nest, rest, retreat, stay at home; **Ant** explore, roam, step out, travel, venture, voyage.

coddle [v] *indulge, pamper*
- **Syn** baby, caress, cater to, cosset, favor, humor, mollycoddle, nurse, pet, spoil; **Ant** ignore, neglect, turn away.

co-dependent [adj] *psychologically reliant upon another in an unhealthy manner* • **Syn** addicted, attached, hooked, interdependent, interconnected, mutually dependent, slavishly trusting; **Ant** disjunctive, free, healthy, healthful, independent, separate, unrelated.

codify [v] *systematize*
- **Syn** arrange, catalogue, classify, code, condense, digest, order, organize, summarize, tabulate; **Ant** disorganize, unsystematize.

coerce [v] *compel, press*
- **Syn** beset, browbeat, bully, constrain, cow, drive, force, impel, intimidate, menace, oblige, push, repress, restrict, strong-arm, suppress, terrorize, threaten; **Ant** allow, leave alone, permit.

cogent [adj] *effective or relevant*
- **Syn** apposite, apt, compelling, conclusive, consequential, convincing, fitting, forceful, influential, justified, meaningful, momentous, persuasive, pertinent, potent, puissant, significant, solid, sound, telling, urgent, valid, weighty, well-grounded; **Ant** impotent, ineffective, invalid, weak.

cogitate [v] *think deeply about*
- **Syn** brainstorm, cerebrate, conceive, consider, contemplate, deliberate, envision, figure, imagine, meditate, mull over, muse, ponder, reason, reflect, ruminate, speculate; **Ant** forget, ignore.

cognate [adj] *alike, associated*
- **Syn** affiliated, agnate, akin, allied, analogous, comparable, connate, connatural, connected, general, generic, incident, kindred, like, related, same, similar, universal; **Ant** disassociated, dissimilar, unalike, unallied, unconnected, unlike.

cognitive [adj] *concerning knowledge and judgment* • **Syn** conceptual, ideative, intellectual, logical, noetic, ratiocinative, rational, prehensile; **Ant** affective, emotional, emotive, irrational, noncognitive.

cognizant [adj] *aware*
- **Syn** acquainted, apprehensive, au courant, awake, conscious, conversant, familiar, grounded, informed, knowing, observant, perceptive, savvy, sensible, sentient, versed; **Ant** ignorant, unaware, unfamiliar, uninformed, unknowledgeable, unwitting.

cohere [v1] *stick to, cling*
- **Syn** adhere, bind, blend, cleave, coalesce, combine, consolidate, fuse, glue, join, merge; **Ant** divide, fall off, separate.

cohere [v2] *agree, conform*
- **Syn** accord, be consistent, check, comport, conform, correspond, dovetail, harmonize, hold, relate, square; **Ant** disagree, dispute, not conform.

coherent [adj] *understandable*
- **Syn** articulate, comprehensible, intelligible, logical, lucid, meaningful, orga-

nized, rational, reasoned, systematic;
▪ *Ant* disorganized, incomprehensible, irrational, unintelligible, unsystematic.

cohort [n] *partner in activity*
▪ *Syn* accomplice, aide, associate, companion, comrade, disciple, friend, hand,
legion, mate, partisan, regiment, satellite,
sidekick, supporter; ▪ *Ant* enemy, opponent.

coincide [v] *go along with; coexist*
▪ *Syn* accompany, accord, acquiesce,
agree, concert, concur, correspond, eventuate, harmonize, identify, jibe, match,
quadrate, square, synchronize, tally;
▪ *Ant* clash, deviate, differ, disagree, diverge, mismatch.

coincidental [adj] *accidental*
▪ *Syn* casual, chance, circumstantial,
fluky, fortuitous, incidental, unintentional; ▪ *Ant* decided, deliberate, designed, planned.

cold [n] *frigid conditions*
▪ *Syn* algidity, chill, congelation, draft,
freeze, frostbite, frostiness, gelidity,
gelidness, glaciation, goose flesh, ici-
ness, inclemency, rawness, refriger-
ation, snow, wintertime; ▪ *Ant* heat,
warmth.

cold [adj1] *chilly, freezing*
▪ *Syn* algid, arctic, benumbed, biting,
bitter, boreal, brisk, brumal, cool, crisp,
cutting, frigid, frosty, frozen, gelid, glacial, hawkish, icy, inclement, keen,
nippy, numbing, penetrating, piercing,
polar, raw, rimy, severe, sharp, Siberian,
sleety, snowy, wintry; ▪ *Ant* hot, lukewarm, tepid, warm.

cold [adj2] *aloof, unresponsive*
▪ *Syn* apathetic, cool, distant, emotionless, frigid, icy, impersonal, indifferent,
inhibited, joyless, matter-of-fact, passionless, reserved, reticent, spiritless,
stony; ▪ *Ant* animated, ardent, eager,
enthusiastic, excited, fervid, friendly, interested, warm, zealous.

cold-blooded [adj] *cruel, heartless*
▪ *Syn* barbarous, brutal, callous, cold,
dispassionate, hardened, inhuman, merciless, obdurate, pitiless, ruthless, savage,
steely; ▪ *Ant* compassionate, demonstrative, feeling, friendly, merciful, sympathetic.

collaborate [v] *work together*
▪ *Syn* coact, cofunction, collude, concert,
concur, conspire, cooperate, coproduce,
fraternize, join forces, participate, team

up, work with; ▪ *Ant* disagree, divorce,
part.

collapse [v] *fall apart, break down*
▪ *Syn* break, cave in, crumple, disintegrate, exhaust, fail, fold, founder, give
way, languish, shatter, subside, succumb,
topple, weaken, wilt, yield; ▪ *Ant* build,
increase, rise, withstand.

collar [v] *apprehend*
▪ *Syn* abduct, appropriate, arrest, capture,
catch, corner, grab, hook, nab, nail, secure, seize, take; ▪ *Ant* let go, lose,
release.

collateral [adj] *indirect, secondary*
▪ *Syn* accessory, accompanying, added,
adjuvant, ancillary, attendant, auxiliary, coincident, complementary, concomitant, concurrent, corresponding, dependent, incident, lateral, parallel,
related, satellite, subordinate, subsidiary,
tributary, under; ▪ *Ant* chief, direct, fundamental, main, primary, principal, superior.

colleague [n] *associate, fellow worker*
▪ *Syn* aide, ally, assistant, auxiliary, coadjutor, cohort, collaborator, companion,
compatriot, compeer, comrade, confederate, co-worker, crony, friend, helper,
partner, teammate, workmate; ▪ *Ant*
antagonist, detractor, enemy, opponent,
opposer.

collect [v1] *accumulate, come together*
▪ *Syn* aggregate, amass, array, assemble,
cluster, compile, congregate, congress,
converge, convoke, corral, flock, gather,
group, hoard, rally, rendezvous, stockpile; ▪ *Ant* dispense, disperse, disseminate, distribute, divide, scatter, share.

collect [v2] *obtain (money)*
▪ *Syn* acquire, dig up, muster, raise, requisition, secure, solicit; ▪ *Ant* compensate, give, meed.

collected [adj] *composed, calm*
▪ *Syn* composed, confident, cool, easy,
levelheaded, nonchalant, placid, poised,
quiet, sanguine, serene, still, sure, temperate, together, tranquil; ▪ *Ant* agitated,
disorganized, excited, mixed up, upset,
worried.

collective [adj] *composite*
▪ *Syn* aggregate, assembled, collated,
combined, common, compiled, concentrated, consolidated, cooperative, cumulative, gathered, heaped, joint, massed,
piled, shared, united; ▪ *Ant* divided, separate.

colloquial [adj] *particular, familiar to an area, informal* ▪ *Syn* chatty, common, conversational, demotic, dialectal, everyday, idiomatic, popular, vernacular; ▪ *Ant* correct, formal, standard, stilted.

color [v1] *make pigmented; shade* ▪ *Syn* chalk, darken, daub, dye, emblazon, fresco, glaze, gloss, illuminate, imbue, infuse, lacquer, paint, pigment, rouge, stain, stipple, suffuse, tinge, tint, tone, variegate, wash; ▪ *Ant* discolor, pale, whiten.

color [v2] *distort, exaggerate* ▪ *Syn* belie, disguise, fake, falsify, garble, magnify, misrepresent, misstate, pervert, prejudice, taint; ▪ *Ant* be truthful, represent.

colored [adj] *distorted* ▪ *Syn* angled, biased, false, falsified, jaundiced, one-sided, partial, partisan, perverted, prejudiced, tendentious, warped; ▪ *Ant* genuine, honest, real, truthful.

colorful [adj1] *brilliant, intensely hued* ▪ *Syn* bright, chromatic, flashy, gay, intense, kaleidoscopic, loud, multicolored, prismatic, psychedelic, rich, showy, variegated, vibrant, vivid; ▪ *Ant* colorless, drab, dreary, faded, plain, uncolored, uncolorful.

colorful [adj2] *full of life, interesting* ▪ *Syn* distinctive, gay, glamorous, graphic, jazzy, lively, picturesque, rich, stimulating, unusual, vivid; ▪ *Ant* boring, dull, lifeless, plain, uninteresting.

colorless [adj1] *without hue* ▪ *Syn* achromatic, anemic, ashy, blanched, bleached, cadaverous, doughy, dull, faded, flat, ghastly, livid, neutral, pale, sickly, wan, washed out; ▪ *Ant* brilliant, colored, colorful, motley, rich, stimulating, vibrant, vivid.

colorless [adj2] *unlively, uninteresting* ▪ *Syn* characterless, dreary, dull, insipid, lackluster, lifeless, prosaic, tame, vacuous, vapid; ▪ *Ant* brilliant, distinctive, intense, interesting, lively, stimulating, vibrant.

colossal [adj] *very large* ▪ *Syn* behemothic, cyclopean, elephantine, gargantuan, gigantic, huge, immense, jumbo, mammoth, monstrous, mountainous, super, titanic, vast; ▪ *Ant* minute, small, tiny.

comatose [adj] *unconscious* ▪ *Syn* cold, dead, drowsy, drugged, insensible, lethargic, out, senseless, sleepy, sluggish, slumberous, somnolent, stupid, stuporous, torpid; ▪ *Ant* alert, awake, conscious.

combat [v] *fight* ▪ *Syn* battle, buck, clash, contend, contest, defy, dispute, do battle with, duel, engage, fight, oppose, repel, resist, strive, struggle, traverse, war, withstand; ▪ *Ant* agree, compromise, retreat, run, surrender.

combative [adj] *aggressive* ▪ *Syn* antagonistic, bellicose, belligerent, contentious, hawkish, militant, pugnacious, quarrelsome, truculent, warlike, warring; ▪ *Ant* agreeable, compromising, peaceful, peaceloving.

combine [v] *connect, integrate* ▪ *Syn* amalgamate, associate, band, bond, bracket, coalesce, compound, fuse, incorporate, interface, join, league, link, marry, merge, network, pool, relate, synthesize, unify; ▪ *Ant* detach, disconnect, dissolve, divide, separate.

combustible [adj] *able to be exploded* ▪ *Syn* burnable, comburent, explosive, fiery, flammable, ignitable, incendiary, inflammable, kindling, volatile; ▪ *Ant* noncombustible, nonexplosive.

come [v] *advance, approach* ▪ *Syn* appear, arrive, attain, become, close in, draw near, enter, fall in, happen, materialize, move, near, occur, originate, reach, show, turn out; ▪ *Ant* depart, go, leave, recede, retreat.

comeback [n] *recovery, triumph* ▪ *Syn* improvement, rally, rebound, resurgence, return, revival, victory, winning; ▪ *Ant* decline, degeneration, failure, regression.

come back [v] *return* ▪ *Syn* come again, reappear, recover, recur, re-enter, resume; ▪ *Ant* depart, go, leave.

come between [v] *alienate* ▪ *Syn* divide, estrange, interfere, interpose, interrupt, intervene, meddle, part, put at odds, separate; ▪ *Ant* bring together, join, unite.

come by [v] *acquire* ▪ *Syn* get, lay hold of, obtain, procure, secure, take possession of, win; ▪ *Ant* give, lose, miss.

come clean [v] *acknowledge information* ▪ *Syn* admit, confess, explain, own up, reveal; ▪ *Ant* hide, hold, secrete.

comedown [n] *letdown, blow*
- *Syn* anticlimax, blow, comeuppance, decline, defeat, deflation, disappointment, downfall, fall, humiliation, ruin, setback; *Ant* ascent, boon, boost, fortune, promotion.

come down [v] *worsen*
- *Syn* decline, decrease, degenerate, descend, deteriorate, fail, fall, go downhill, reduce, suffer; *Ant* boost, improve.

come down on [v] *criticize strongly*
- *Syn* attack, dress down, jump on, rebuke, reprimand, scold; *Ant* compliment, laud, praise.

come down with [v] *contract illness*
- *Syn* be stricken with, catch, contract, fall ill, fall victim to, sicken; *Ant* be immune.

comedy [n] *funny entertainment*
- *Syn* burlesque, camp, drollery, facetiousness, farce, fun, hilarity, humor, interlude, jesting, joking, laughs, satire, sitcom, slapstick, takeoff, travesty, witticism; *Ant* melodrama, seriousness, tragedy.

come in [v] *enter place*
- *Syn* alight, arrive, cross threshold, disembark, intrude, land, pass in, reach, set foot in, show up; *Ant* depart, exit, go, leave.

comely [adj] *beautiful*
- *Syn* attractive, beauteous, blooming, fair, fine, good-looking, handsome, nice, pleasing, pretty, pulchritudinous, stunning, winsome; *Ant* bad-looking, despicable, disagreeable, offensive, repellent, repulsive, revolting, ugly, unattractive.

come on [v] *advance, progress*
- *Syn* decline, deteriorate, develop, fall, gain, improve, increase, make headway, proceed Ant. retreat, reduce, worsen.

come out with [v] *disclose information*
- *Syn* acknowledge, bring out, come clean, declare, deliver, divulge, lay open, own, own up, say, state, tell, utter; *Ant* cover up, hide, secrete.

come through [v1] *accomplish goal*
- *Syn* achieve, be successful, be victorious, carry out, contribute, prevail, score, succeed, triumph, win; *Ant* fail, flounder.

come through [v2] *survive bad situation*
- *Syn* endure, live through, persist, pull through, ride, ride out, survive, withstand; *Ant* collapse, decline, fail, languish.

comfort [v] *make to feel better*
- *Syn* aid, ameliorate, assuage, bolster, calm, cheer, commiserate with, console, divert, ease, encourage, hearten, help, inspirit, invigorate, mitigate, nourish, reassure, relieve, remedy, salve, solace, soothe, succor, support, sympathize, upraise; *Ant* aggravate, annoy, bother, distress, exasperate, hurt, irritate, provoke, torment, torture, trouble, vex.

comfortable [adj1] *providing or enjoying physical ease* *Syn* agreeable, appropriate, cheerful, complacent, contented, cozy, delightful, easy, enjoyable, gratified, happy, healthy, loose-fitting, pleasant, pleased, protected, relaxed, relieved, restful, restored, satisfactory, satisfying, serene, sheltered, soft, soothed, strengthened, warm, well-off; *Ant* discontented, hopeless, miserable, neglected, uncomfortable, unhappy, upset.

comfortable [adj2] *affluent, wealthy*
- *Syn* easy, prosperous, substantial, sufficient, suitable, well-heeled, well-off, well-to-do; *Ant* destitute, hopeless, needy, pitiable, poor, uncomfortable, wretched.

comic/comical [adj] *amusing*
- *Syn* absurd, crazy, diverting, droll, entertaining, facetious, farcical, funny, gelastic, humorous, ironic, jocular, joking, laughable, light, ridiculous, risible, side-splitting, silly, waggish, whimsical, witty; *Ant* grave, sad, serious, sober, solemn, tragic, unfunny.

coming [n] *arrival*
- *Syn* accession, advent, approach, landing, reception; *Ant* departing, departure, exit, going, leaving.

command [v1] *demand*
- *Syn* adjure, appoint, authorize, ban, bar, beckon, bid, charge, cite, compel, debar, dictate, direct, enact, enjoin, exact, forbid, give orders, grant, impose, inflict, instruct, interdict, oblige, ordain, order, proclaim, prohibit, require, requisition, restrain, subpoena, summon, take charge, take lead, task, tell, warn; *Ant* contradict, countermand, oppose, recall, reverse, revoke.

command [v2] *rule, have power*
- *Syn* administer, conquer, control, dictate, dominate, exercise power, force, govern, guide, have authority, hinder, influence, lead, manage, officiate, predominate, preside over, prevail, regulate,

reign, run, subdue, superintend, supervise, sway, tyrannize, wield; ■ *Ant* follow, give allegience to, obey.

commanding [*adj*] *superior, authoritative* ■ *Syn* advantageous, arresting, assertive, autocratic, compelling, controlling, decisive, dictatorial, dominant, forceful, imperious, imposing, impressive, lofty, peremptory, striking; ■ *Ant* indecisive, inferior, unassertive, uncontrolling.

commemorate [*v*] *honor, observe occasion* ■ *Syn* celebrate, immortalize, keep, memorialize, observe, pay tribute to, perpetuate, remember, salute; ■ *Ant* dishonor, forget, neglect.

commence [*v*] *start action* ■ *Syn* arise, begin, embark on, enter upon, inaugurate, initiate, launch, lead off, open, originate; ■ *Ant* cease, complete, end, finish, stop.

commend [*v1*] *recommend, praise* ■ *Syn* acclaim, applaud, compliment, countenance, endorse, extol, hail, laud, sanction, speak highly of, support; ■ *Ant* censure, criticize, disapprove, rebuke, reprimand.

commend [*v2*] *hand over with confidence* ■ *Syn* assign, commit, confer, confide, consign, deliver, entrust, relegate, resign, trust; ■ *Ant* deny, keep, refuse.

commendable [*adj*] *praiseworthy* ■ *Syn* admirable, creditable, deserving, estimable, excellent, exemplary, laudable, meritorious; ■ *Ant* blameworthy, poor, unworthy.

commensurate [*adj*] *adequate, corresponding* ■ *Syn* appropriate, coextensive, comparable, compatible, consistent, due, equal, equivalent, in accord, proportionate, sufficient; ■ *Ant* inadequate, inappropriate, incommensurate, unacceptable, unfitting.

comment [*v*] *make statement of opinion, explanation* ■ *Syn* affirm, annotate, clarify, conclude, disclose, explicate, express, gloss, illustrate, interject, mention, note, observe, pronounce, reflect, remark, say, state; ■ *Ant* keep quiet, refrain.

commercial [*adj*] *intended for financial gain* ■ *Syn* exploited, investment, materialistic, mercenary, monetary, money-making, pecuniary, venal; ■ *Ant* charitable, noncommercial, not-for-profit.

commingle [*v*] *blend* ■ *Syn* amalgamate, combine, compound, integrate, intermingle, intermix, join, merge, unite; ■ *Ant* divide, separate.

commiserate [*v*] *listen to woes of another* ■ *Syn* condole, console, feel, feel for, have mercy, pity, share sorrow, sympathize; ■ *Ant* be indifferent, turn away.

commission [*v*] *authorize or delegate task* ■ *Syn* appoint, assign, bespeak, charge, command, constitute, contract, deputize, dispatch, employ, empower, enable, engage, enlist, hire, inaugurate, instruct, license, name, ordain, order, select, send; ■ *Ant* retract, unauthorize.

commit [*v1*] *perform an action* ■ *Syn* accomplish, achieve, act, carry out, complete, do, enact, execute, perpetrate; ■ *Ant* cease, desist, end, idle, loaf, omit, rest, stop, wait.

commit [*v2*] *deliver, entrust* ■ *Syn* allocate, apportion, authorize, charge, commission, consign, convey, delegate, dispatch, empower, engage, grant authority, imprison, institutionalize, invest, ordain, promise, put away, relegate, rely upon, remove, send, submit, transfer, vest; ■ *Ant* keep, keep from, withhold.

commodious [*adj*] *ample, spacious* ■ *Syn* big, capacious, comfortable, convenient, expansive, extensive, large, loose, roomy, wide; ■ *Ant* confined, cramped, inconvenient, small, squeezed, uncomfortable.

common [*adj1*] *average, ordinary* ■ *Syn* accepted, banal, bourgeois, colloquial, colorless, commonplace, conventional, current, customary, daily, familiar, frequent, general, habitual, hackneyed, informal, mediocre, monotonous, obscure, plain, prevalent, prosaic, prosy, regular, routine, simple, stale, standard, stereotyped, stock, trite, trivial, typical, universal, unvaried, usual, wearisome; ■ *Ant* abnormal, extraordinary, infrequent, noteworthy, rare, scarce, uncommon, unusual, valuable.

common [*adj2*] *low, coarse* ■ *Syn* cheap, crass, déclassé, impure, inferior, low-grade, mean, middling, Philistine, plebeian, poor, raffish, second-class, vulgar; ■ *Ant* aristocratic, cultured, excellent, high, noble, refined, sophisticated, superior.

commonly [*adv*] *usually* ■ *Syn* as a rule, frequently, generally, ordinarily, regularly; ■ *Ant* uncommonly, unusually.

commonplace [adj] *usual, everyday*
▪ **Syn** customary, familiar, hackneyed, mainstream, matter-of-course, mediocre, middling, mundane, natural, normal, obvious, ordinary, pedestrian, prosaic, stale, stereotyped, threadbare, trite, typical, widespread, worn-out; ▪ **Ant** exceptional, infrequent, peculiar, rare, uncommon, unusual.

commonsense [adj] *reasonable*
▪ **Syn** astute, cool, down-to-earth, judicious, levelheaded, matter-of-fact, practical, rational, realistic, sane, sensible, shrewd, sound; ▪ **Ant** foolish, impractical, insane, unreasonable, unsensible, unsound.

communal [adj] *collective; shared*
▪ **Syn** common, community, conjoint, conjunct, cooperative, general, intermutual, joint, mutual, neighborhood, public; ▪ **Ant** individual, personal, private, unshared.

communicable [adj] *able to be contracted* ▪ **Syn** catching, communicative, contagious, infectious, pandemic, transferable, transmittable; ▪ **Ant** incontractable, noncommunicable, noncontagious.

communicate [v] *give or exchange information, ideas* ▪ **Syn** advertise, advise, announce, break, broadcast, carry, connect, contact, convey, correspond, declare, disclose, discover, divulge, enlighten, hint, impart, imply, inform, interact, interface, make known, network, pass on, phone, proclaim, publicize, publish, raise, relate, report, reveal, signify, spread, state, suggest, tell, touch base, transfer, transmit, unfold, write; ▪ **Ant** bottle up, conceal, cover, keep quiet, suppress, withhold.

communicative [adj] *informative*
▪ **Syn** candid, chatty, conversational, demonstrative, effusive, enlightening, expansive, forthcoming, frank, garrulous, loquacious, open, outgoing, talkative, voluble; ▪ **Ant** close-mouthed, reserved, reticent, unfriendly, uninformative, unsociable.

communion [n] *affinity, agreement*
▪ **Syn** accord, association, closeness, concord, contact, converse, harmony, intercommunication, intercourse, intimacy, participation, rapport, sympathy, togetherness, unity; ▪ **Ant** antagonism, contention, disagreement, discord, disunity, division, hostility, variance.

communism [n] *socialist government*
▪ **Syn** Bolshevism, collectivism, Leninism, Marxism, rule of the proletariat, socialism, state ownership, totalitarianism; ▪ **Ant** capitalism, democracy.

community [n] *agreement, similarity*
▪ **Syn** affinity, identity, kinship, likeness, sameness, semblance; ▪ **Ant** disagreement, dissimilarity.

commute [v1] *reduce punishment*
▪ **Syn** alleviate, curtail, decrease, mitigate, modify, remit, shorten, soften; ▪ **Ant** increase, lengthen.

commute [v2] *exchange, alter*
▪ **Syn** barter, change, convert, interchange, metamorphose, substitute, switch, trade, transfer, transform, translate, transmogrify, transmute, transpose; ▪ **Ant** keep, remain.

compact [adj1] *condensed*
▪ **Syn** bunched, close, compressed, crowded, dense, firm, hard, impenetrable, impermeable, packed, solid, thick, tight; ▪ **Ant** loose, slack, uncondensed.

compact [adj2] *short, brief*
▪ **Syn** compendious, concise, epigrammatic, laconic, meaty, pithy, pointed, succinct, terse, to the point; ▪ **Ant** big, large, lengthy, long, unabridged.

compact [v] *make condensed*
▪ **Syn** combine, compress, concentrate, condense, consolidate, contract, integrate, pack, solidify, unify, unite; ▪ **Ant** enlarge, loosen, slacken, thin, uncondense.

companionable [adj] *friendly*
▪ **Syn** affable, amicable, complacent, congenial, conversable, convivial, cordial, familiar, genial, good-natured, gregarious, intimate, neighborly, outgoing, sociable, social; ▪ **Ant** antagonistic, foreign, opposing, unfriendly.

comparable [adj1] *worthy of comparison* ▪ **Syn** commensurable, commensurate, equal, equipollent, equivalent, proportionate, tantamount; ▪ **Ant** incomparable, unequal, unworthy.

comparable [adj2] *corresponding, similar* ▪ **Syn** agnate, akin, alike, analogous, cognate, consonant, like, parallel, related, relative, similar, undifferenced, uniform; ▪ **Ant** dissimilar, unalike, unlike.

comparative [adj] *approximate, close to*
▪ **Syn** allusive, analogous, conditional, connected, contingent, contrastive, correlative, corresponding, equivalent, in

proportion, like, matching, metaphorical, near, parallel, provisional, qualified, related, relative, restricted, similar; **Ant** far, unequal, unlike.

compass [v] *achieve, get*
▪ **Syn** accomplish, attain, effect, execute, fulfill, gain, obtain, perform, procure, realize, secure, win; ▪ **Ant** fail, lose.

compassionate [adj] *having tender feelings* ▪ **Syn** all heart, benevolent, charitable, commiserative, humanitarian, indulgent, kindhearted, lenient, merciful, pitying, responsive, softhearted, sparing, sympathetic, tender, tenderhearted, understanding, warm, warmhearted; ▪ **Ant** cruel, hard, harsh, hateful, indifferent, mean, merciless, tyrannous.

compatible [adj] *agreeable, in harmony* ▪ **Syn** accordant, adaptable, appropriate, congenial, congruous, consistent, consonant, cooperative, harmonious, likeminded, meet, proper, reconcilable, suitable, sympathetic, together; ▪ **Ant** antagonistic, antipathetic, disagreeable, incompatible, inharmonious, unsuitable, unsuited.

compel [v] *force to act*
▪ **Syn** coerce, concuss, constrain, dragoon, drive, enforce, exact, impel, make, necessitate, oblige, restrain, urge; ▪ **Ant** block, check, delay, deter, hinder, impede, obstruct, stop.

compendious [adj] *abridged*
▪ **Syn** abbreviated, breviloquent, brief, close, compact, comprehensive, concise, condensed, contracted, curt, laconic, short, succinct, summarized, summary, synoptic; ▪ **Ant** enlarged, lengthened, unabridged.

compensate [v1] *make restitution*
▪ **Syn** atone, commit, indemnify, pay, recompense, recoup, refund, reimburse, remunerate, repay, requite, reward, satisfy; ▪ **Ant** deprive, fine, forfeit, lose.

compensate [v2] *offset, make up for*
▪ **Syn** abrogate, annul, balance, cancel out, counteract, counterbalance, counterpoise, fix, invalidate, negate, neutralize, nullify, outweigh, repair, set off; ▪ **Ant** damage, deprive, penalize.

competent [adj] *able*
▪ **Syn** adapted, adequate, appropriate, au fait, capable, clever, efficient, endowed, enough, equal, fit, proficient, qualified, satisfactory, skilled, sufficient, suitable;

▪ **Ant** inadequate, incapable, incompetent, inefficient, inept, unable.

competitive [adj] *willing to oppose*
▪ **Syn** aggressive, ambitious, antagonistic, at odds, combative, cutthroat, emulous, rival, vying; ▪ **Ant** collaborative, cooperative, noncompetitive, unambitious.

compile [v] *assemble, accumulate*
▪ **Syn** amass, anthologize, arrange, assemble, collate, collect, colligate, collocate, compose, concentrate, congregate, consolidate, cull, garner, gather, glean, group, marshal, muster, organize, recapitulate, unite; ▪ **Ant** disperse, dissemble, scatter, separate.

complacent [adj] *contented*
▪ **Syn** conceited, confident, egoistic, egotistic, gratified, happy, obsequious, pleased, satisfied, self-assured, self-contented, self-satisfied, serene, smug; ▪ **Ant** concerned, discontent, discontented, dissatisfied.

complain [v] *grumble about*
▪ **Syn** ascribe, attack, bemoan, bewail, carp, cavil, demur, denounce, deplore, deprecate, dissent, gainsay, grieve, impute, lament, moan, object, oppose, protest, refute, reproach, snivel, wail, whimper, whine; ▪ **Ant** applaud, approve, be content, be happy, commend, praise, recommend, sanction.

complaisant [adj] *agreeable*
▪ **Syn** accommodating, amiable, conciliatory, deferential, easy-going, friendly, generous, good-humored, good-natured, indulgent, lenient, mild, obliging, polite, solicitous, submissive; ▪ **Ant** antagonistic, disagreeable, discontented, dissatisfied, obstinate.

complement [v] *complete*
▪ **Syn** accomplish, achieve, cap, conclude, consummate, crown, finish, fulfill, perfect, top off; ▪ **Ant** diminish, reduce, subtract, take away.

complementary [adj] *filling, completing* ▪ **Syn** conclusive, correlative, correspondent, corresponding, equivalent, integral, integrative, interconnected, interdependent, interrelated, matched, parallel, reciprocal; ▪ **Ant** independent, unrelated.

complete [adj1] *total, not lacking*
▪ **Syn** all, entire, exhaustive, full, intact, integral, organic, outright, plenary, replete, thorough, unabridged, unitary,

whole; ▪ *Ant* condensed, defective, deficient, expurgated, imperfect, incomplete, lacking, missing, needy, short, wanting.

complete [*adj2*] *finished*
▪ *Syn* all-embracing, all-inclusive, concluded, consummate, done, effected, ended, entire, executed, full-fledged, perfect, plenary, realized, terminated, through; ▪ *Ant* imperfect, incomplete, unfinished.

complete [*adj3*] *utter, absolute*
▪ *Syn* blank, blanket, categorical, consummate, downright, flawless, impeccable, outright, perfect, positive, sheer, thorough, total, unblemished, unconditional, unmitigated, unqualified; ▪ *Ant* incomplete, inconclusive, partial.

complete [*v*] *carry out an action*
▪ *Syn* accomplish, carry off, close, conclude, consummate, crown, determine, develop, discharge, end, execute, finalize, finish, fulfill, perfect, perform, realize, refine, settle, supplement, terminate; ▪ *Ant* forget, give up, halt, ignore, neglect, stop.

complex [*adj1*] *involved, intricate*
▪ *Syn* circuitous, complicated, composite, compound, confused, conglomerate, convoluted, elaborate, entangled, heterogeneous, labyrinthine, manifold, miscellaneous, mosaic, motley, multifarious, multiform, multiple, variegated; ▪ *Ant* clear, easy, evident, homogeneous, obvious, plain, simple, uniform.

complex [*adj2*] *difficult to understand*
▪ *Syn* abstruse, bewildering, Byzantine, convoluted, cryptic, Daedalean, discursive, disordered, enigmatic, excursive, Gordian, impenetrable, involved, labyrinthine, meandering, obscure, paradoxical, perplexing, puzzling, recondite, sinuous, sophisticated, tangled; ▪ *Ant* apparent, clear, direct, discernible, easy, evident, obvious, plain.

compliance [*n*] *agreement*
▪ *Syn* acquiescence, assent, complaisance, concession, concurrence, conformity, consent, deference, docility, obedience, observance, passivity, submission, yielding; ▪ *Ant* defiance, denial, disagreement, disobedience, dissent, fight, nonconformity, refusal, veto.

complicate [*v*] *confuse, make difficult*
▪ *Syn* bedevil, clog, combine, confound, convolute, derange, disarrange, elaborate, embroil, entangle, impede, inter-

fuse, interweave, involve, jumble, muddle, obscure, perplex, tangle, twist, upset; ▪ *Ant* disentangle, ease, explain, facilitate, make simple, untangle.

complicated [*adj*] *difficult, complex*
▪ *Syn* abstruse, arduous, Byzantine, convoluted, Daedalean, difficult, elaborate, entangled, Gordian, hard, intricate, involved, labyrinthine, perplexing, problematic, puzzling, recondite, sophisticated, troublesome, various; ▪ *Ant* easy, facile, simple.

compliment [*n*] *praise, flattery*
▪ *Syn* acclaim, admiration, adulation, applause, appreciation, approval, blessing, cajolery, commendation, confirmation, congratulations, courtesy, eulogy, favor, felicitation, homage, honor, laud, ovation, panegyric, regard, tribute, veneration; ▪ *Ant* blame, censure, complaint, criticism, denunciation, insult, libel, slander.

compliment [*v*] *praise, flatter*
▪ *Syn* acclaim, adulate, applaud, cajole, commend, congratulate, endorse, eulogize, exalt, fawn upon, glorify, hail, honor, magnify, pay tribute to, recommend, salute, speak highly of, toast; ▪ *Ant* blame, censure, complain, criticize, denounce, insult, libel, slander.

complimentary [*adj*] *flattering*
▪ *Syn* appreciative, approbative, commendatory, congratulatory, encomiastic, eulogistic, fawning, honeyed, plauditory, polite, respectful, sycophantic, unctuous, well-wishing; ▪ *Ant* blaming, censuring, critical, denouncing, disparaging, insulting, reproachful, unflattering.

comply [*v*] *abide by, follow agreement or instructions* ▪ *Syn* accede, accord, acquiesce, consent to, defer, discharge, fulfill, keep, mind, obey, observe, perform, respect, submit, yield; ▪ *Ant* decline, deny, disobey, oppose, rebuff, refuse, reject, resist.

compose [*v1*] *be part of construction*
▪ *Syn* be an adjunct, be an element of, belong to, build, compound, comprise, consist of, constitute, construct, form, make; ▪ *Ant* destroy, disarrange, disperse, ruin, scatter.

compose [*v2*] *calm, bring under control*
▪ *Syn* adjust, allay, appease, assuage, check, collect, comfort, console, contain, control, cool, ease, mitigate, placate, quell, relax, restrain, settle, simmer

down, soften, solace, soothe, still, suppress, temper, tranquilize; ▪ *Ant* agitate, anger, arouse, distress, excite, upset.

composed [*adj*] *calm, collected*
▪ *Syn* at ease, clearheaded, confident, cool, easygoing, imperturbable, levelheaded, nonchalant, poised, possessed, quieted, relaxed, repressed, sedate, self-possessed, serene, soothed, staid, temperate, tranquil, unflappable; ▪ *Ant* agitated, angered, annoyed, aroused, distressed, excited, perturbed, upset, worried.

composite [*adj*] *combined, mixed*
▪ *Syn* blended, complex, compound, conglomerate, melded, synthesized; ▪ *Ant* homogeneous, simple, unblended, uncombined, uniform, unmixed.

compound [*v1*] *mix, combine*
▪ *Syn* admix, amalgamate, associate, blend, coalesce, commingle, commix, concoct, connect, couple, fuse, intermingle, join, link, meld, mingle, synthesize, unite; ▪ *Ant* divide, separate, unmix.

compound [*v2*] *make difficult; complicate* ▪ *Syn* add to, aggravate, augment, confound, confuse, exacerbate, extend, heighten, intensify, magnify, multiply, worsen; ▪ *Ant* better, make easy, simplify, uncomplicate.

comprehend [*v1*] *understand*
▪ *Syn* appreciate, apprehend, assimilate, cognize, conceive, discern, envisage, envision, fathom, grasp, know, perceive, read, see, take in; ▪ *Ant* misapprehend, misconceive, misinterpret, mistake, misunderstand.

comprehend [*v2*] *include*
▪ *Syn* comprise, contain, embody, embrace, enclose, encompass, involve, subsume; ▪ *Ant* exclude, not include.

comprehensible [*adj*] *understandable*
▪ *Syn* apprehensible, clear, coherent, comprehendible, conceivable, explicit, fathomable, intelligible, lucid, luminous, plain; ▪ *Ant* exclusive, incomplete, nonunderstandable, unintelligible.

comprehensive [*adj*] *inclusive*
▪ *Syn* absolute, all-embracing, blanket, broad, catholic, compendious, complete, encyclopedic, exhaustive, expansive, extensive, full, global, in depth, infinite, overall, synoptic, thorough, umbrella, whole, wide, widespread; ▪ *Ant* exclusive, incomprehensive, particular, selective, specific.

compress [*v*] *compact, condense*
▪ *Syn* abbreviate, abridge, bind, concentrate, constrict, crush, decrease, dehydrate, epitomize, narrow, pack, ram, restrict, shorten, shrink, squash, squeeze, summarize, syncopate, tighten, wedge; ▪ *Ant* blow up, expand, extend, fill, increase, loosen, spread, stretch.

comprise [*v*] *make up, consist of*
▪ *Syn* add up to, amount to, be composed of, compass, compose, constitute, contain, cover, embody, encircle, enclose, encompass, form, hold, include, incorporate, involve, span, sum up; ▪ *Ant* except, exclude, fail, fall short, lack, need, want.

compromise [*v1*] *give and take*
▪ *Syn* adjust, agree, arbitrate, compose, concede, conciliate, make concession, meet halfway, negotiate, settle, strike balance, trade off; ▪ *Ant* contest, differ, disagree, dispute, dissent, quarrel.

compromise [*v2*] *put in jeopardy or discredit* ▪ *Syn* blight, discredit, endanger, expose, hazard, imperil, jeopardize, menace, peril, prejudice, put under suspicion, risk; ▪ *Ant* enhance, guard, protect, save, support.

compulsive [*adj*] *driving, obsessive*
▪ *Syn* compelling, enthusiastic, irresistible, overwhelming, passionate, uncontrollable, urgent; ▪ *Ant* controlled, easygoing, free, independent.

compulsory [*adj*] *binding*
▪ *Syn* de rigueur, forced, imperative, mandatory, necessary, obligatory, required, requisite; ▪ *Ant* free, liberalized, liberated, optional, unstipulated, voluntary.

compunction [*n*] *regret, sorrow*
▪ *Syn* attrition, conscience, contrition, misgiving, penitence, pity, qualm, reluctance, remorse, repentance, ruth, shame, sympathy; ▪ *Ant* defiance, meanness, remorselessness; shamelessness.

computation [*n*] *performing arithmetic*
▪ *Syn* calculation, ciphering, computing, counting, figuring, gauging, reckoning, summing, totaling; ▪ *Ant* conjecture, guessing, guesswork.

compute [*v*] *calculate, estimate*
▪ *Syn* add up, cipher, count, enumerate, figure, gauge, measure, rate, reckon, sum, take account of, tally, total; ▪ *Ant* conjecture, guess, guesstimate, suppose, surmise.

comrade [n] *ally*
- *Syn* associate, bosom buddy, chum, colleague, comate, companion, confederate, confidante, coworker, crony, friend, intimate, mate, pal, partner, sidekick;
- *Ant* enemy, foe, opponent.

con [v] *deceive, defraud*
- *Syn* bilk, cajole, cheat, chicane, coax, double-cross, dupe, fool, hoax, hoodwink, inveigle, mislead, rook, swindle, trick; *Ant* be forthright, be honest, enlighten, inform, wise up.

concatenation [n] *connection, sequence*
- *Syn* chain, continuity, integration, interlocking, link, nexus, series, succession;
- *Ant* disintegration, dispersion, interruption.

concave [adj] *curved, depressed*
- *Syn* cupped, dented, dimpled, dipped, excavated, hollowed, indented, rounded, sagging, scooped, sinking, sunken; *Ant* convex, distended.

conceal [v] *hide, disguise*
- *Syn* bury, cache, camouflage, cloak, cover, enshroud, harbor, mask, obscure, screen, shelter, skulk, stash, stow, tuck away, veil, wrap; *Ant* disclose, divulge, expose, lay bare, let out, open, reveal, show, tell, uncover.

concealed [adj] *hidden, secret*
- *Syn* buried, camouflaged, covert, enshrouded, guarded, holed up, incognito, inconspicuous, masked, obscured, perdu, privy, recondite, screened, shrouded, stashed, tucked away, ulterior, veiled;
- *Ant* bare, clear, disclosed, exposed, obvious, open, plain, revealed, shown, told, uncovered.

concede [v] *acknowledge, give in*
- *Syn* accept, admit, allow, avow, capitulate, confess, grant, hand over, knuckle under, quit, relinquish, surrender, waive, yield; *Ant* contradict, disacknowledge, disagree, dispute, dissent, fight, refuse, reject, repudiate.

conceited [adj] *egotistical*
- *Syn* arrogant, cocky, immodest, narcissistic, overweening, phony, self-important, vain, vainglorious; *Ant* diffident, humble, meek, modest, self-conscious, self-effacing, shy, timid.

conceivable [adj] *reasonable, easy to understand* *Syn* believable, convincing, credible, earthly, imaginable, likely, possible, probable; *Ant* difficult, inconceivable, unbelievable, unimaginable, unreasonable, unthinkable.

conceive [v] *understand*
- *Syn* accept, appreciate, believe, catch, comprehend, deem, envisage, fancy, follow, gather, get, imagine, judge, perceive, realize, reckon, suppose, suspect;
- *Ant* doubt, misunderstand, not believe, question.

concentrate [v] *gather, collect*
- *Syn* accumulate, agglomerate, aggregate, assemble, center, cluster, coalesce, combine, conglomerate, congregate, consolidate, constrict, contract, converge, draw together, focus, garner, hoard, integrate, localize, mass, muster, strengthen, swarm, unify; *Ant* disperse, scatter.

concentrated [adj1] *condensed, reduced* *Syn* boiled down, evaporated, fixed, full-bodied, potent, rich, robust, straight, strong, thick, thickened, total, whole; *Ant* diffuse, loose, thin.

concentrated [adj2] *intense*
- *Syn* all-out, deep, desperate, exquisite, fierce, furious, hard, intensive, terrible, vehement, vicious; *Ant* diffuse, diluted, free, loose.

concept [n] *idea*
- *Syn* abstraction, approach, conceit, conception, hypothesis, image, impression, notion, perception, slant, supposition, theory, thought, twist, view; *Ant* being, concrete, percept, sensation.

conception [n1] *understanding; idea*
- *Syn* apperception, apprehension, cognition, comprehension, conceit, consideration, exposition, fancy, image, impression, inkling, interpretation, notion, perception, picture, realization, representation, speculation, thought, version; *Ant* being, concrete.

conception [n2] *beginning, birth*
- *Syn* fertilization, formation, germination, impregnation, inception, initiation, insemination, invention, launching, origin, outset, start; *Ant* abortion, completion, death, ending, finish, outcome, result, termination.

concern [v] *relate to, have reference to*
- *Syn* appertain to, apply to, be applicable to, bear on, depend upon, involve, pertain to, refer to, regard; *Ant* be immaterial, be irrelevant, be of no consequence.

concerned [adj1] *worried*
- *Syn* anxious, bothered, distressed, disturbed, perturbed, troubled, uneasy, up-

set, uptight; ▪ *Ant* calm, happy, undisturbed, unperturbed, untroubled, unworried.

concerned [*adj2*] *engaged, involved*
▪ *Syn* active, affected, attentive, caring, implicated, interested, mixed up, privy to, solicitous; ▪ *Ant* disinterested, inattentive, uncaring, unconcerned, uninvolved, uninvolved.

concert [*n*] *agreement, harmony*
▪ *Syn* accord, chorus, collaboration, concord, consonance, league, unanimity, union, unison; ▪ *Ant* disagreement, disharmony, disunity.

concerted [*adj*] *coordinated*
▪ *Syn* agreed upon, collaborative, combined, joint, mutual, planned, prearranged, united; ▪ *Ant* disarranged, disordered, disorganized, separate, uncoordinated.

concession [*n*] *yielding, adjustment*
▪ *Syn* acknowledgment, admission, assent, authorization, compromise, deal, grant, indulgence, permission, privilege, rollback, sellout, surrender, trade-off, warrant; ▪ *Ant* denial, difference, disagreement, disputation, fighting, protest, refusal, repudiation.

conciliatory [*adj*] *placid, yielding*
▪ *Syn* appeasing, assuaging, calm, civil, disarming, mollifying, pacific, peaceable, propitiative, quiet, willing; ▪ *Ant* antagonistic, fighting, refusing, stubborn.

concise [*adj*] *short, to the point*
▪ *Syn* abridged, breviloquent, brief, compact, compendiary, condensed, curt, epigrammatic, laconic, lean, pithy, succinct, summary, synoptic, terse; ▪ *Ant* discursive, expansive, lengthy, long, longwinded, redundant, repetitive, wordy.

conclude [*v1*] *finish, come to an end*
▪ *Syn* achieve, cease, close, complete, consummate, crown, desist, draw to close, end, halt, stop, terminate, top off, wind up, wrap up; ▪ *Ant* begin, commence, introduce, preface, start.

conclude [*v2*] *settle, resolve*
▪ *Syn* accomplish, achieve, bring about, carry out, clinch, confirm, decide, determine, effect, establish, fix; ▪ *Ant* prolong, unsettle.

conclusive [*adj*] *definite, final*
▪ *Syn* absolute, clear, cogent, compelling, convincing, decisive, demonstrative, determinant, incontrovertible, indisputable, irrefutable, irrevocable, precise, telling,

ultimate; ▪ *Ant* ambiguous, inconclusive, indefinite.

concomitant [*adj*] *contributing, accompanying* ▪ *Syn* accessory, adjuvant, attendant, coexistent, coincident, collateral, complementary, concordant, concurrent, conjoined, contemporaneous, coordinate, corollary, coterminous, fellow, incident, isochronal, joint, satellite, synchronous, synergetic; ▪ *Ant* accidental, chance, unrelated.

concord [*n1*] *unity, harmony*
▪ *Syn* accord, agreement, amity, concert, concordance, consensus, consonance, friendship, goodwill, peace, rapport, serenity, tranquility, unanimity, understanding; ▪ *Ant* discord, disunity.

concord [*n2*] *an agreement, treaty*
▪ *Syn* compact, concordat, contract, convention, entente, pact, protocol; ▪ *Ant* disagreement, discord.

concrete [*adj1*] *actual, factual*
▪ *Syn* accurate, corporeal, definite, detailed, explicit, material, objective, particular, precise, real, sensible, solid, specific, substantial, tangible; ▪ *Ant* abstract, ideal, immaterial, intangible.

concrete [*adj2*] *hardened*
▪ *Syn* caked, calcified, cemented, congealed, conglomerated, consolidated, dried, firm, indurate, monolithic, petrified, poured, set, solidified, strong, unyielding; ▪ *Ant* bending, flexible, pliable.

concur [*v*] *agree, approve*
▪ *Syn* accede, accord, acquiesce, assent, coadjute, coincide, collaborate, combine, consent, cooperate, equal, harmonize, join, meet, unite; ▪ *Ant* argue, differ, disagree, disapprove, dispute, object, oppose, reject.

concurrent [*adj*] *agreeing, converging*
▪ *Syn* allied, centrolineal, coinciding, compatible, concerted, confluent, consentient, consistent, convergent, cooperating, coterminous, harmonious, in rapport, joined, like-minded, mutual, unified; ▪ *Ant* different, disagreeing, divergent, incompatible, nonconcurrent.

condemn [*v*] *blame, convict*
▪ *Syn* adjudge, belittle, castigate, censure, criticize, damn, denounce, deprecate, judge, knock, pronounce, punish, reprobate, reprove, sentence, skin, upbraid; ▪ *Ant* absolve, acquit, approve,

clear, discharge, exonerate, free, pardon, release, set free.

condense [v] *abridge*
- **Syn** abbreviate, boil down, coagulate, compact, concentrate, contract, curtail, digest, edit, encapsulate, epitomize, precipitate, reduce, shorten, solidify, summarize, synopsize, telescope, thicken, trim; **Ant** enlarge, expand, lengthen.

condescend [v] *stoop, humble oneself*
- **Syn** accommodate, accord, acquiesce, bend, comply, concede, degrade oneself, deign, demean oneself, grant, lower oneself, oblige, submit, vouchsafe, yield; **Ant** respect, rise above.

condescending [adj] *snobby, disdainful* **Syn** arrogant, egotistic, lofty, patronizing, supercilious, superior, uppity; **Ant** approachable, congenial, friendly, humble.

condition [v] *adapt, prepare*
- **Syn** accustom, build up, equip, habituate, inure, make ready, modify, practice, program, ready, sharpen, tone up, toughen up, train, warm up; **Ant** disqualify, incapacitate, unaccustom.

conditional [adj] *dependent*
- **Syn** codicillary, contingent, guarded, incidental, limited, modified, provisional, qualified, relative, restricted, subject to, tentative, with reservations; **Ant** absolute, categorical, independent, unconditional, unrestricted.

condominium [n] *tenant-owned apartment building* **Syn** apartment, condo, co-op, time-share, townhouse; **Ant** hotel, motel, rental.

condone [v] *make allowance for*
- **Syn** disregard, excuse, forget, forgive, ignore, overlook, pardon, pass over, remit; **Ant** censure, condemn, denounce, forbid, prevent.

conducive [adj] *favorable for*
- **Syn** accessory, contributive, contributory, helpful, leading, productive of, promotive, tending, useful; **Ant** adverse, discouraging, hindering, unconducive, unfavorable.

conduct [v] *transport*
- **Syn** accompany, attend, bring, carry, chaperon, companion, convoy, escort, guide, lead, move, pilot, route, send, shepherd, show, steer, transfer; **Ant** leave.

confederate [n] *abettor*
- **Syn** accessory, accomplice, ally, associate, coconspirator, collaborator, colleague, conspirator, partner; **Ant** enemy, foe, opponent, rival.

confer [v] *give honor, award*
- **Syn** accord, allot, award, bestow, donate, give, grant, lay on, present, provide, vouchsafe; **Ant** deny, dishonor, take away, withdraw, withhold.

confess [v] *admit, confirm*
- **Syn** acknowledge, affirm, attest, avow, concede, confide, declare, divulge, evince, grant, manifest, narrate, own up, profess, recognize, reveal, vent; **Ant** conceal, deny, disavow, disown, hide, mask, repudiate, secrete.

confidant [n] *close friend*
- **Syn** acquaintance, adherent, adviser, alter ego, bosom buddy, companion, crony, familiar, intimate, mate, pal; **Ant** adversary, enemy, foe.

confide [v1] *divulge information*
- **Syn** admit, breathe, confess, disclose, hint, impart, insinuate, intimate, reveal, suggest, tell, whisper; **Ant** conceal, hide, secrete, suppress.

confide [v2] *entrust*
- **Syn** bestow, charge, commend, commit, consign, delegate, hand over, present, relegate, trust; **Ant** hold back, keep, retain.

confident [adj] *certain, assured*
- **Syn** bold, brave, convinced, courageous, dauntless, expectant, fearless, hopeful, intrepid, positive, presumptuous, sanguine, satisfied, secure, trusting, valiant; **Ant** uncertain, unsure.

confidential [adj] *secret*
- **Syn** arcane, classified, closet, hushed, inside, intimate, private, privy; **Ant** common, familiar, known, public, wellknown.

confidentially [adv] *in secret*
- **Syn** between us, covertly, in confidence, personally, privately, sub rosa; **Ant** commonly, familiarly, openly, publicly.

confine [v] *enclose, limit*
- **Syn** bar, bind, circumscribe, constrain, cramp, delimit, detain, enslave, fix, hem in, immure, imprison, incarcerate, jail, restrain, restrict, shorten, shut up; **Ant** free, let go, liberate, release.

confined [adj] *limited, enclosed*
- **Syn** bedridden, bound, circumscribed, cooped up, cramped, detained, grounded, hampered, held, immured, imprisoned,

incarcerated, indisposed, jailed, locked up, pent, restricted, sealed up, shut in; ■ *Ant* free, liberated, unlimited.

confirm [*v1*] *ratify, validate, prove*
■ *Syn* affirm, approve, attest, authenticate, back, bear out, certify, circumstantiate, corroborate, double-check, endorse, establish, explain, justify, sanction, settle, subscribe, substantiate, support, uphold, verify, vouch, warrant, witness; ■ *Ant* annul, cancel, contradict, deny, destroy, disprove, invalidate, oppose, veto, void.

confirm [*v2*] *reinforce*
■ *Syn* assure, buttress, clinch, establish, fix, fortify, invigorate, settle, strengthen; ■ *Ant* contradict, deny, destroy, oppose, repudiate, void.

confirmed [*adj*] *habitual; rooted*
■ *Syn* accustomed, chronic, deep-rooted, entrenched, fixed, habituated, hardened, ingrained, inured, inveterate, proved, rooted, seasoned, settled, staid, valid, worn; ■ *Ant* indefinite, infrequent, sporadic, uncommitted, unconfirmed, undecided.

confiscate [*v*] *steal; seize*
■ *Syn* accroach, annex, appropriate, assume, commandeer, confisticate, expropriate, hijack, impound, liberate, preempt, sequester, take over, usurp; ■ *Ant* give, offer, release, return.

conflict [*v*] *be at odds*
■ *Syn* clash, collide, combat, contend, contest, contrast, cross swords with, differ, disagree, discord, disturb, fight, interfere, jar, mismatch, oppose, square off with, struggle, tangle, vary; ■ *Ant* agree, be calm, harmonize.

conflicting [*adj*] *contradictory*
■ *Syn* antagonistic, antipathetic, contrary, discordant, discrepant, dissonant, incompatible, incongruous, inconsistent, inconsonant, opposed, paradoxical; ■ *Ant* agreeable, harmonious, nonconflicting, peaceful.

confluence [*n*] *coming together*
■ *Syn* assembly, concourse, concurrence, conflux, convergence, crowd, gathering, host, junction, meeting, union; ■ *Ant* divergence, split.

conform [*v1*] *adjust, adapt*
■ *Syn* accommodate, comply, coordinate, fit, follow, harmonize, integrate, mind, obey, proportion, quadrate, reconcile, square, suit, tailor, tune, yield; ■ *Ant* differ, disobey, fight, oppose, rebel, refuse.

conform [*v2*] *correspond, match*
■ *Syn* accord, agree, assimilate, be regular, dovetail, fit in, harmonize, jibe, square, suit, tally; ■ *Ant* mismatch, not correspond.

conformable [*adj*] *appropriate; matching* ■ *Syn* agreeable, amenable, compliant, consistent, docile, fitting, harmonious, like, obedient, proper, regular, similar, submissive, suitable, suited, tractable; ■ *Ant* inappropriate, mismatched, nonconforming.

confound [*v*] *confuse*
■ *Syn* abash, astonish, astound, baffle, bewilder, confute, discomfit, discountenance, embarrass, faze, mystify, nonplus, perplex, puzzle, rattle, startle, surprise; ■ *Ant* clarify, clear up, enlighten, explain, make clear, relate.

confront [*v*] *challenge*
■ *Syn* accost, affront, beard, brave, dare, defy, encounter, flout, meet, oppose, repel, resist, scorn, withstand; ■ *Ant* avoid, back down, evade, flee.

confuse [*v1*] *bewilder someone*
■ *Syn* addle, astonish, baffle, bedevil, bemuse, confound, daze, discompose, disconcert, discountenance, disorient, faze, fluster, fog, frustrate, mislead, mystify, obscure, perplex, puzzle, stump, throw off; ■ *Ant* clarify, clear up, enlighten, explain.

confuse [*v2*] *mix up; involve*
■ *Syn* blend, clutter, disarrange, disarray, disorder, disorganize, embroil, encumber, entangle, intermingle, involve, jumble, litter, mingle, mistake, muddle, snarl up, tangle; ■ *Ant* order, organize, separate.

confused [*adj1*] *disoriented mentally*
■ *Syn* abashed, addled, baffled, befuddled, bewildered, dazed, disconcerted, disorganized, distracted, flustered, misled, nonplussed, perplexed, perturbed, puzzled, stumped, taken aback, thrown; ■ *Ant* clear, organized, oriented, understanding.

confused [*adj2*] *mixed up, disordered*
■ *Syn* anarchic, blurred, chaotic, disarranged, disorderly, disorganized, haywire, involved, jumbled, messy, miscellaneous, misunderstood, obscured, snarled, unsettled, untidy; ■ *Ant* methodical, ordered, organized, separated, systematic.

confute [v] *disprove, refute*
- **Syn** break, contradict, controvert, defeat, demolish, dismay, disprove, expose, invalidate, negate, oppugn, overthrow, overturn, overwhelm, parry, rebut, silence, subvert, upset, vanquish; **Ant** affirm, attest, confirm, endorse, prove, verify.

congeal [v] *coagulate*
- **Syn** cake, clabber, clot, concrete, condense, curdle, dry, freeze, gelatinize, harden, indurate, jell, refrigerate, set, solidify, stiffen, thicken; **Ant** dissolve, liquify, melt, separate, thin.

congenial [adj] *friendly, compatible*
- **Syn** affable, agreeable, companionable, compatible, complaisant, cordial, delightful, favorable, genial, good-humored, happy, harmonious, jovial, kindly, mellow, pleasant, sociable, sympathetic, well-suited; **Ant** disagreeable, ill-suited, incompatible, uncongenial, unfriendly, unsympathetic.

congenital [adj] *inborn*
- **Syn** connate, connatural, constitutional, inbred, indigenous, indwelling, ingrained, inherent, inherited, innate, intrinsic, inveterate, latent, native, natural; **Ant** acquired, contracted, extrinsic, learned.

congested [adj] *blocked, clogged*
- **Syn** choked, closed, crowded, filled, glutted, gorged, gridlocked, jammed, massed, mobbed, obstructed, occluded, overflowing, packed, plugged, stopped, stuffed, teeming; **Ant** clear, empty, free, open, unblocked, unclogged, uncongested, uncrowded.

conglomerate [adj] *composite*
- **Syn** amassed, assorted, blended, clustered, heterogeneous, massed, melded, miscellaneous, motley, multifarious, promiscuous, varied, variegated; **Ant** individual, separate, single.

congratulate [v] *compliment on achievement, luck* **Syn** applaud, bless, laud, praise, rejoice with, salute, toast, wish joy to, wish one well; **Ant** commiserate, criticize, harp.

congregate [v] *assemble, come together*
- **Syn** besiege, collect, congress, convene, converge, corral, gather, mass, meet, muster, pack, raise, rally, rendezvous, swarm, teem, throng; **Ant** divide, scatter, separate.

congruent [adj] *agreeable, harmonious*
- **Syn** coinciding, compatible, concurring, conforming, consistent, corresponding, in agreement; **Ant** disagreeable, incongruent, unharmonious.

congruous [adj] *corresponding, suitable* **Syn** accordant, appropriate, apt, becoming, compatible, concordant, consonant, correspondent, harmonious, meet, proper, seemly, sympathetic; **Ant** disagreeing, incongruous, unfitting, unharmonious, unsuitable.

conjectural [adj] *speculative*
- **Syn** academic, assumed, doubtful, figured, guessing, hypothetical, putative, reputed, supposed, surmised, tentative, theoretical; **Ant** certain, factual, proven, real, truthful.

conjecture [v] *speculate*
- **Syn** assume, believe, conceive, conclude, deem, estimate, expect, fancy, figure, glean, guess, hypothesize, imagine, infer, judge, presume, suppose, surmise, suspect, theorize, think; **Ant** know, prove.

conjunction [n] *combination*
- **Syn** affiliation, agreement, alliance, coincidence, concomitance, concurrence, congruency, juxtaposition, parallelism, partnership, union; **Ant** detachment, disconnection, division, separation.

conjure up [v] *bring to mind*
- **Syn** call, contrive, create, evoke, materialize, recall, recollect, remember, review, summon, urge; **Ant** forget, ignore, neglect.

connect [v] *combine, link*
- **Syn** affix, ally, associate, attach, bridge, cohere, conjoin, consociate, correlate, equate, fasten, hook up, interface, join, marry, meld with, plug into, relate, span, tie in, unite, wed, yoke; **Ant** detach, disconnect, divide, separate, sunder.

connected [adj] *related, affiliated*
- **Syn** allied, associated, bracketed, coherent, combined, coupled, joined, linked, pertinent, united; **Ant** disconnected, disjoined, unaffiliated, uncombined, unconnected, unrelated.

connection [n] *something that connects, links* **Syn** affiliation, alliance, association, attachment, bond, combination, conjointment, conjunction, coupling, fastening, joint, junction, link, network, seam, tie, union; **Ant** breach, disconnection.

connoisseur [n] *authority*
- **Syn** adept, aesthete, aficionado, appre-

ciator, arbiter, bon vivant, cognoscente, critic, devotee, epicure, expert, fan, gourmet, judge, maven, savant, specialist; ▪ *Ant* amateur, dabbler, dilettante.

connote [*v*] *imply*
▪ *Syn* add up to, betoken, express, hint at, import, indicate, insinuate, intend, intimate, involve, mean, signify, spell, suggest; ▪ *Ant* denote, designate, evidence.

conquer [*v1*] *defeat, overcome*
▪ *Syn* beat, control, drub, foil, frustrate, humble, outwit, overpower, overthrow, prevail, quell, rout, subdue, subjugate, succeed, surmount, throw, thwart, triumph, vanquish, whip; ▪ *Ant* capitulate, fail, give up, lose, retreat, succumb, surrender, yield.

conquer [*v2*] *win; obtain*
▪ *Syn* achieve, acquire, annex, best, occupy, overcome, overrun, prevail, seize, succeed, triumph; ▪ *Ant* forfeit, lose, surrender.

conscientious [*adj1*] *thorough, careful*
▪ *Syn* complete, diligent, exact, exacting, faithful, fastidious, meticulous, painstaking, particular, punctilious, punctual, reliable, tough; ▪ *Ant* careless, inexact, inscrupulous, irresponsible, uncareful, unconscientious.

conscientious [*adj2*] *moral, upright*
▪ *Syn* conscionable, high-minded, high-principled, honest, honorable, just, pious, principled, responsible, right, scrupulous, strict, true; ▪ *Ant* corrupt, dishonest, immoral, unjust, vulgar.

conscious [*adj1*] *alert, awake*
▪ *Syn* attentive, au courant, aware, cognizant, discerning, informed, keen, mindful, percipient, responsive, sentient, vigilant, watchful, witting; ▪ *Ant* ignorant, impassive, indifferent, oblivious, senseless, unaware, unconscious.

conscious [*adj2*] *intentional*
▪ *Syn* affected, calculated, deliberate, knowing, mannered, premeditated, rational, reflective, self-conscious, studied, willful; ▪ *Ant* indifferent, not deliberate, unconscious, unfeeling, unintentional, unstudied.

consecrate [*v*] *declare sacred, devote to religion* ▪ *Syn* anoint, beatify, bless, dedicate, devote, exalt, hallow, honor, ordain, sanctify, venerate; ▪ *Ant* defile, deprecate, profane.

consecutive [*adj*] *in sequence*
▪ *Syn* chronological, continuous, ensu-

ing, following, increasing, later, logical, numerical, one after another, progressive, running, sequential, serial, succedent, succeeding, successive; ▪ *Ant* broken, discontinuous, infrequent, intermittent, interrupted, unconsecutive.

consensus [*n*] *general agreement*
▪ *Syn* accord, concord, concurrence, consent, harmony, unanimity, unison, unity; ▪ *Ant* disagreement, discord.

consent [*v*] *agree*
▪ *Syn* accede, acquiesce, approve, bless, concede, concur, fold, give in, permit, sanction, subscribe, yield; ▪ *Ant* differ, disagree, disapprove, dissent, object, oppose, protest, refuse.

consequent [*adj*] *resultant*
▪ *Syn* consistent, ensuing, following, logical, rational, resulting, sequential, sound, subsequent, successive; ▪ *Ant* beginning, causal, commencing, originating, preparatory, starting.

consequential [*adj*] *significant*
▪ *Syn* considerable, far-reaching, grave, important, material, momentous, serious, substantial, weighty; ▪ *Ant* inconsequential, insignificant, uneventful, unimportant.

conservation [*n*] *preservation*
▪ *Syn* conservancy, conserving, control, custody, economy, governing, maintenance, management, protection, safeguarding, salvation, saving, storage, supervision, upkeep; ▪ *Ant* destruction, neglect, spending, squandering, waste.

conservative [*adj*] *cautious, moderate, tending to preserve the status quo*
▪ *Syn* bourgeois, constant, conventional, guarded, inflexible, orthodox, quiet, reactionary, right-wing, sober, stable, steady, traditional; ▪ *Ant* avant-garde, exaggerated, imaginative, incautious, left-wing, liberal, progressive, radical, revolutionary.

conserve [*v*] *save, protect*
▪ *Syn* cut back, hoard, keep, maintain, nurse, preserve, safeguard, store up, support, sustain, use sparingly; ▪ *Ant* destroy, neglect, spend, squander, use, waste.

consider [*v1*] *turn over in one's mind*
▪ *Syn* acknowledge, concede, contemplate, deliberate, envisage, examine, inspect, meditate, mull over, muse, ponder, reason, reflect, regard, ruminate, scrutinize, speculate, think over; ▪ *Ant*

discard, dismiss, forget, ignore, neglect, reject.

consider [v2] *regard a certain way*
▪ *Syn* believe, count, credit, deem, estimate, feel, hold, hold an opinion, judge, look upon, respect, sense, suppose, view; ▪ *Ant* abandon, dismiss, disregard, ignore, leave, reject.

considerable [adj1] *abundant, large*
▪ *Syn* ample, appreciable, big, bountiful, extensive, great, hefty, large-scale, major, marked, noticeable, plentiful, reasonable, respectable, substantial, tolerable; ▪ *Ant* inconsiderable, insignificant, little, slight, small, undistinguished, unnoticeable.

considerable [adj2] *important*
▪ *Syn* consequential, distinguished, essential, influential, material, meaningful, momentous, noteworthy, renowned, significant, substantial, venerable, weighty; ▪ *Ant* insignificant, unimportant, unnoteworthy, unnoticeable.

considerably [adv] *significantly*
▪ *Syn* appreciably, far, greatly, markedly, noticeably, quite, rather, remarkably, substantially, very much, well; ▪ *Ant* insignificantly, little, slightly, unappreciably, unremarkably.

considerate [adj] *respectful of others*
▪ *Syn* accommodating, amiable, benevolent, compassionate, complaisant, discreet, forbearing, generous, kindly, magnanimous, mellow, mindful, obliging, polite, solicitous, sympathetic, thoughtful, warmhearted; ▪ *Ant* disrespectful, impatient, inattentive, inconsiderate, mean, scornful, selfish, thoughtless, unfeeling, unmindful.

considered [adj] *deliberate, thought-out*
▪ *Syn* advised, contemplated, designed, examined, express, intentional, investigated, mediated, premeditated, studied, studious, treated, voluntary, weighed, willful; ▪ *Ant* disregarded, forgotten, neglected, unplanned, unstudied.

consign [v] *entrust, hand over for care*
▪ *Syn* appoint, assign, authorize, commend to, commission, commit, confide, convey, delegate, deliver, dispatch, forward, issue, relegate, remit, send, ship, transfer, transmit, turn over; ▪ *Ant* hold, keep, receive, retain.

consistent [adj1] *constant, regular*
▪ *Syn* dependable, even, expected, homogeneous, invariable, logical, persistent, rational, same, steady, true, uniform; ▪ *Ant* erratic, inconsistent, inconstant, irregular, varying.

consistent [adj2] *agreeing, compatible*
▪ *Syn* accordant, agreeable, all of a piece, coherent, compatible, congenial, congruous, consonant, harmonious, like, logical, matching, sympathetic; ▪ *Ant* disagreeing, incompatible, incongruous, inconsistent, unfitting, unsuitable.

console [v] *relieve, comfort*
▪ *Syn* assuage, calm, cheer, encourage, gladden, inspirit, lift spirits, solace, soothe, tranquilize, upraise spirits; ▪ *Ant* agitate, annoy, antagonize, depress, discourage, dispirit, disturb, hurt, sadden, trouble, upset.

consolidate [v] *combine; make firm*
▪ *Syn* amalgamate, amass, bind, blend, cement, compound, concentrate, condense, develop, federate, fortify, fuse, harden, incorporate, join, league, mass, meld, mix, pool, reinforce, secure, solidify, stabilize, strengthen, thicken, unify; ▪ *Ant* disjoin, disperse, divide, part, separate, separate, sever.

consonant [adj] *agreeing, consistent*
▪ *Syn* accordant, agnate, akin, alike, analogous, coincident, comparable, compatible, concordant, congenial, congruous, correspondent, harmonious, in rapport, like, parallel, similar, suitable, uniform; ▪ *Ant* disagreeing, dissonant, incompatible, incongruent, incongruous, inconsistent, inconsonant.

consort [n] *associate, partner*
▪ *Syn* companion, concomitant, fellow, friend, husband, mate, spouse, wife; ▪ *Ant* antagonist, enemy, foe.

consort [v1] *be friendly with*
▪ *Syn* accompany, associate, attend, befriend, bring, chaperon, company, conduct, convoy, join, mingle, mix, pal; ▪ *Ant* dissociate, estrange, part, separate.

consort [v2] *agree*
▪ *Syn* accord, coincide, concur, conform, correspond, dovetail, harmonize, march, square; ▪ *Ant* differ, disagree, jar.

conspicuous [adj1] *obvious, easily seen*
▪ *Syn* apparent, clear, discernible, distinct, evident, manifest, noticeable, patent, perceptible, plain, visible; ▪ *Ant* concealed, hidden, imperceptible, inconspicuous, obscure, secret, unnoticeable, unremarkable, unseen.

conspicuous [adj2] *important, prominent* ▪ *Syn* arresting, blatant, commanding, distinguished, eminent, flagrant, glaring, loud, marked, notable, notorious, outstanding, pointed, remarkable, renowned, salient, signal, striking, well-known; ▪ *Ant* inconspicuous, obscure, unimportant, unknown, unremarkable.

constant [adj1] *fixed* ▪ *Syn* consistent, continual, equable, even, firm, habitual, homogeneous, immutable, invariable, monotonous, nonstop, permanent, perpetual, regular, stabile, stable, standardized, steadfast, steady, uniform; ▪ *Ant* changeable, fickle, fluctuating, inconstant, irregular, unstable, unsteady, varying, wavering.

constant [adj2] *never-ending* ▪ *Syn* abiding, ceaseless, chronic, continuous, endless, enduring, eternal, incessant, interminable, lasting, nonstop, perpetual, persistent, relentless, sustained; ▪ *Ant* concluding, ending, interrupted, stopping, terminable, terminating.

constant [adj3] *loyal, determined* ▪ *Syn* allegiant, attached, dependable, devoted, dogged, faithful, fast, persevering, resolute, staunch, tried-and-true, trustworthy, trusty; ▪ *Ant* disloyal, fickle, flagging, inconstant, undecided, undetermined, untrue, untrustworthy.

consternation [n] *dismay, distress* ▪ *Syn* alarm, anxiety, confusion, dread, fear, fright, panic, shock, trepidation, wonder; ▪ *Ant* calm, composure, happiness, peacefulness, tranquility.

constituent [n] *element* ▪ *Syn* board, component, division, essential, factor, fraction, ingredient, makings, part, portion, principle, unit; ▪ *Ant* aggregate, composite, whole.

constituent [adj] *component, part* ▪ *Syn* basic, composing, elemental, essential, factor, fundamental, ingredient, integral; ▪ *Ant* compound, whole.

constitute [v] *authorize* ▪ *Syn* appoint, commission, decree, delegate, designate, draft, empower, enact, establish, legislate, name, nominate, ordain, order; ▪ *Ant* abolish, deny, refuse, repeal.

constitutional [adj] *inherent* ▪ *Syn* built-in, congenital, deep-seated, essential, inborn, inbred, ingrained, innate, intrinsic, natural, organic, vital; ▪ *Ant* acquired, contracted, learned.

constrain [v] *force; restrain* ▪ *Syn* ban, bar, bridle, chain, compel, confine, constrict, cork, curb, deny, hold back, immure, imprison, incarcerate, inhibit, jail, oblige, pressure, stifle, urge, withhold; ▪ *Ant* free, let go, liberate, release.

constrict [v] *inhibit* ▪ *Syn* astringe, choke, circumscribe, compress, concentrate, condense, confine, contract, cramp, curb, limit, narrow, pinch, restrain, restrict, shrink, squeeze, strangle, tauten, tense, tighten; ▪ *Ant* expand, free, let go, loosen, open, release.

construct [v] *assemble, build* ▪ *Syn* compose, compound, constitute, create, design, elevate, engineer, erect, establish, fabricate, fashion, forge, form, found, frame, invent, make, manufacture, organize, produce, raise, set up, shape; ▪ *Ant* annihilate, break, demolish, destroy, dismantle, raze, ruin.

constructive [adj] *helpful* ▪ *Syn* effective, positive, practical, productive, useful, valuable; ▪ *Ant* destructive, hurting, injurious, negative, unhelpful.

consult [v] *ask, confer* ▪ *Syn* argue, brainstorm, commune, confabulate, consider, debate, deliberate, discuss, examine, interview, negotiate, parlay, question, refer to, regard, respect, review, seek advice, seek opinion of, take counsel; ▪ *Ant* bypass, disregard, ignore.

consume [v1] *use up* ▪ *Syn* absorb, deplete, devour, dissipate, drain, eat up, exhaust, expend, finish, go through, spend, squander, throw away, trifle, waste, wear out; ▪ *Ant* accumulate, collect, gather, neglect, not use, store.

consume [v2] *eat, drink* ▪ *Syn* absorb, bolt, devour, down, eat up, feed, gorge, gulp, guzzle, ingest, ingurgitate, inhale, partake, snack, swallow, swill, take; ▪ *Ant* fast, starve.

consume [v3] *destroy* ▪ *Syn* annihilate, crush, demolish, devastate, exhaust, expend, extinguish, lay waste, overwhelm, ravage, raze, ruin, suppress, waste, wreck; ▪ *Ant* build, construct.

consumer [n] *person who buys merchandise, services* ▪ *Syn* buyer, customer, end user, enjoyer, purchaser, shopper, user; ▪ *Ant* marketer, merchandiser.

consummate [*adj*] *ultimate, best*
- *Syn* absolute, accomplished, complete, downright, finished, flawless, gifted, ideal, impeccable, matchless, peerless, perfect, polished, practiced, ripe, skilled, superb, superlative, talented, trained, utter, virtuosic; *Ant* deficient, inadequate, incomplete, raw, unfinished, worst.

consummate [*v*] *achieve, finish*
- *Syn* accomplish, carry out, clinch, close, complete, conclude, crown, effectuate, end, fold up, perfect, perform, sign, terminate, wind up, wrap up; *Ant* begin, initiate, start.

contact [*v*] *communicate with*
- *Syn* approach, call, connect, get in touch with, interact, interface, network, phone, reach, relate, speak to, talk, telephone, visit, write to; *Ant* avoid, evade.

contagious [*adj*] *communicable*
- *Syn* catching, deadly, endemic, epidemic, impartible, infectious, inoculable, pestilential, poisonous, spreading, transmittable; *Ant* noncommunicable, noninfectious.

contain [*v1*] *include, hold*
- *Syn* accommodate, comprehend, comprise, consist of, embody, embrace, encompass, hold, incorporate, seat, subsume, take in; *Ant* eliminate, except, exclude, omit.

contain [*v2*] *hold back, control*
- *Syn* check, collect, compose, control, curb, harness, rein, repress, restrain, restrict, smother, stifle, stop; *Ant* express, let go, release, vent.

contaminate [*v*] *pollute*
- *Syn* alloy, befoul, corrupt, debase, defile, desecrate, harm, infect, pervert, poison, stain, sully, taint, tarnish, vitiate; *Ant* clean, cure, heal, purify, sterilize.

contemplate [*v1*] *think about seriously; plan* *Syn* aim, brood over, consider, deliberate, design, envisage, excogitate, expect, foresee, intend, mull over, observe, ponder, propose, reflect upon, ruminate, speculate, study; *Ant* discard, disregard, forget, neglect, scorn, slight.

contemplate [*v2*] *gaze at*
- *Syn* audit, behold, consider, examine, inspect, notice, observe, peer, penetrate, pore over, regard, scan, scrutinize, see, stare at, study, view, witness; *Ant* disregard, look away, scorn.

contemplative [*adj*] *deep in thought*
- *Syn* attentive, cogitative, introspective, lost, meditative, musing, pensive, pondering, reflective, ruminative, speculative, thoughtful; *Ant* disdainful, disregarding, negligent, rejecting, scornful, shallow, unreflective.

contemporary [*adj1*] *modern*
- *Syn* abreast, au courant, current, extant, in fashion, instant, in vogue, latest, new, now, present, present-day, recent, state-of-the-art, up-to-date, up-to-the-minute, voguish; *Ant* archaic, obsolete, old, old-fashioned, past, preceding.

contemporary [*adj2*] *existing, occurring at same time* *Syn* accompanying, associated, attendant, coetaneous, coexistent, coincident, concomitant, concurrent, linked, related, simultaneous, synchronal, synchronous; *Ant* future, past, preceding, succeeding.

contemptible [*adj*] *despicable, shameful* *Syn* abhorrent, abject, abominable, base, cheap, crass, degenerate, despisable, detestable, dirty, disgusting, hateful, ignoble, ignominious, inferior, low, mean, odious, outcast, paltry, pitiable, poor, sad, shameful, sordid, unworthy, vile, worthless, wretched; *Ant* admirable, admired, good, honorable, loved, respectable, worthy.

contemptuous [*adj*] *arrogant, insolent*
- *Syn* audacious, bold, cavalier, cheeky, condescending, contumelious, cool, derisive, disdainful, disrespectful, haughty, insulting, opprobrious, sardonic, scornful, sneering, supercilious, temperamental, uppity; *Ant* humble, polite, respected, shy.

contend [*v1*] *compete, fight*
- *Syn* argue, battle, confront, contest, dispute, emulate, encounter, face, grapple, jostle, litigate, meet, oppose, oppugn, resist, rival, skirmish, stand, strive, struggle, tangle with, tug, vie; *Ant* abandon, desert, give up, leave, retreat.

contend [*v2*] *argue*
- *Syn* affirm, allege, avow, charge, claim, debate, defend, dispute, enjoin, hold, insist, jump on, justify, maintain, prescribe, report, tell, urge, vindicate, warrant; *Ant* cede, give in, give up, surrender.

content [*adj*] *happy, agreeable*
- *Syn* appeased, at ease, comfortable, complacent, contented, fulfilled, gratified, satisfied, smug, willing; *Ant* depressed, disagreeable, discontent, dis-

satisfied, disturbed, needy, unhappy, upset, wanting.

content [v] *please*
▪ *Syn* appease, charm, delight, enrapture, gladden, gratify, humor, indulge, mollify, placate, reconcile, satisfy, suffice, thrill, tickle; ▪ *Ant* anger, displease, disturb, upset.

contented [adj] *at ease; happy*
▪ *Syn* at peace, cheerful, comfortable, complacent, glad, gratified, pleased, satisfied, serene, thankful; ▪ *Ant* depress, discontent, discontented, dissatisfied, disturbed, unhappy, unsatisfied, upset.

contention [n] *competition or dispute*
▪ *Syn* altercation, battle, combat, controversy, discord, dispute, enmity, feuding, hostility, quarrel, rivalry, strife, struggle, variance, war; ▪ *Ant* affection, consideration, friendliness, friendship, good will, kindness, sympathy.

contentment [n] *comfort, happiness*
▪ *Syn* complacency, ease, equanimity, fulfillment, gladness, gratification, peace, pleasure, repletion, satisfaction, serenity; ▪ *Ant* discomfort, discontent, displeasure, dissatisfaction, misery, sadness, unhappiness.

contest [n] *fight, struggle*
▪ *Syn* altercation, battle, brawl, brush, combat, conflict, controversy, debate, discord, dispute, emulation, encounter, engagement, fray, hassle, rivalry, row, run-in, scrap, shock, skirmish, strife, tug-of-war; ▪ *Ant* agreement, calm, peace, quiet, stillness, tranquility.

contest [v1] *argue, challenge*
▪ *Syn* blast, call in question, debate, dispute, doubt, litigate, object to, oppose, push, question; ▪ *Ant* agree, allow, give up, resign.

contest [v2] *fight*
▪ *Syn* attack, battle, brawl, buck, compete, conflict, contend, cross, defend, duel, feud, quarrel, repel, rival, row, scuffle, square off, strike, struggle, tilt, traverse, vie, withstand, wrangle; ▪ *Ant* accede, agree, submit, surrender.

contiguous [adj] *adjacent, in contact*
▪ *Syn* abutting, adjoining, approximal, beside, bordering, close, conterminous, juxtaposed, meeting, near, nearby, neighboring, next, next to; ▪ *Ant* apart, divided, separated.

continent [adj] *chaste, pure*
▪ *Syn* abstemious, abstinent, ascetic, bridled, celibate, curbed, inhibited, modest, restrained, sober, temperate; ▪ *Ant* impure, incontinent, unchaste.

contingent [adj] *conditional; possible*
▪ *Syn* accidental, casual, chance, dependent, fortuitous, haphazard, incidental, likely, odd, probable, random, unexpected, unforeseeable, unforeseen, unpredictable; ▪ *Ant* certain, definite, real, sure, truthful, unconditional.

continual [adj] *constant, incessant*
▪ *Syn* aeonian, around-the-clock, ceaseless, consecutive, continuous, endless, enduring, eternal, everlasting, interminable, perpetual, persistent, persisting, recurrent, regular, relentless, running, steady, timeless; ▪ *Ant* broken, ceasing, checked, halting, inconstant, infrequent, intermittent, interrupted, occasional, temporary.

continue [v1] *persist, carry on*
▪ *Syn* abide, advance, carry forward, draw out, endure, extend, forge ahead, last, lengthen, linger, live on, loiter, maintain, outlast, outlive, perdure, persevere, progress, project, prolong, promote, pursue, reach, remain, rest, ride, stand, stay, stick to, survive, sustain, uphold; ▪ *Ant* cease, complete, desist, discontinue, end, finish, halt, stop.

continue [v2] *begin again; resume*
▪ *Syn* carry on, pick up, proceed, recapitulate, recommence, reestablish, reinstate, reinstitute, renew, reopen, restart, restore, return to, take up; ▪ *Ant* complete, desist, discontinue, end, finish.

continuity [n] *uninterrupted progression*
▪ *Syn* chain, cohesion, connection, constancy, continuance, continuum, duration, endurance, extension, flow, perpetuity, persistence, prolongation, protraction, sequence, stability, stamina, succession, survival, train, unity, vitality, whole; ▪ *Ant* break, discontinuity, intermittence, interruption, stoppage.

continuous [adj] *constant, unending*
▪ *Syn* connected, consecutive, continued, extended, interminable, perpetual, prolonged, regular, repeated, stable, steady, timeless; ▪ *Ant* ceasing, completed, discontinuous, ending, finished, halting, intermittent, interrupted, sporadic, stopping.

contort [v] *disfigure, distort*
▪ *Syn* bend, convolute, curve, deform, gnarl, knot, misshape, torture, twist,

warp, wrench, writhe; ▪ *Ant* beautify, smooth, straighten, unbend.

contraband [*adj*] *black-market; unlawful* ▪ *Syn* banned, bootleg, excluded, forbidden, illegal, illicit, interdicted, prohibited, proscribed, smuggled, taboo; ▪ *Ant* allowed, authorized, lawful, legal, permitted.

contract [*v1*] *condense* ▪ *Syn* abate, abbreviate, abridge, compress, confine, constrict, consume, curtail, decline, decrease, deflate, dwindle, ebb, edit, epitomize, evaporate, lessen, narrow, omit, purse, recede, reduce, shrink, shrivel, subside, syncopate, tighten, wane, waste, weaken, wither, wrinkle; ▪ *Ant* amplify, dilate, enlarge, expand, extend, increase, lengthen, spread, stretch.

contract [*v2*] *come to terms* ▪ *Syn* agree, arrange, assent, bargain, bound, buy, circumscribe, close, commit, consent, covenant, engage, give one's word, limit, make terms, negotiate, obligate, owe, pact, pledge, promise, set, settle, sign up, stipulate, swear to, undertake; ▪ *Ant* break off, disagree.

contract [*v3*] *catch disease* ▪ *Syn* acquire, afflict, be afflicted with, become infected with, be ill with, come down with, decline, develop, fall victim to, get, incur, indispose, induce, sicken, sink, succumb to, take, weaken; ▪ *Ant* give, transmit.

contradict [*v*] *be at variance with* ▪ *Syn* belie, challenge, confront, contravene, controvert, counter, cross, dare, deny, disclaim, disprove, dispute, gainsay, impugn, negate, oppose, repudiate, traverse; ▪ *Ant* accept, agree, approve, concede, confirm, corroborate, reconcile, sign, verify, vouch.

contradictory [*adj*] *conflicting* ▪ *Syn* adverse, against, antipodal, antipodean, antithetic, antithetical, contrary, converse, counter, counteractive, diametric, discrepant, incompatible, incongruous, inconsistent, irreconcilable, opposing, opposite, paradoxical, polar, repugnant, reverse; ▪ *Ant* agreeing, confirming, consistent, reconcilable, reconciled, vouching.

contrary [*adj*] *antagonistic; opposite* ▪ *Syn* adverse, anti, antipathetic, antithetical, contradictory, contrariant, contumacious, converse, counter, diametric,

discordant, dissident, froward, headstrong, hostile, inconsistent, inimical, insubordinate, intractable, negative, nonconformist, obstinate, opposed, paradoxical, perverse, rebellious, recalcitrant, recusant, refractory, stubborn, unruly, wayward, wrongheaded; ▪ *Ant* accommodating, agreeing, alike, concordant, correspondent, harmonious, homogeneous, like, obliging, similar.

contrast [*v*] *compare, differ* ▪ *Syn* balance, be contrary to, be diverse, be variable, bracket, collate, conflict, contradict, depart, deviate, disagree, distinguish, diverge, oppose, separate, set off, stand out, vary; ▪ *Ant* accord, agree, be alike, be equal, be similar, coincide, concur, conform.

contravene [*v*] *go against, contradict* ▪ *Syn* abjure, breach, break, combat, conflict with, counteract, cross, defy, encroach, exclude, fight, gainsay, hinder, impugn, infringe, interpose, intrude, negate, offend, oppose, overstep, refute, reject, repudiate, resist, spurn, thwart, transgress, traverse, trespass, violate; ▪ *Ant* agree, aid, allow, approve, assent, assist, concur, consent, endorse, help, permit, uphold.

contribute [*v1*] *donate, provide* ▪ *Syn* add, afford, ante up, assign, bequeath, bestow, chip in, commit, confer, devote, dispense, endow, enrich, furnish, give, grant, hand out, present, proffer, sacrifice, share, subscribe, subsidize, supply, tender, will; ▪ *Ant* harm, hurt, neglect, oppose, shun, subtract, take, take away, withdraw, withhold.

contribute [*v2*] *be partly responsible for* ▪ *Syn* add to, advance, aid, assist, augment, be instrumental, conduce, fortify, help, lead, redound, reinforce, strengthen, supplement, support, tend, uphold; ▪ *Ant* counteract, disapprove, neglect, shun, withhold.

contrite [*adj*] *regretful* ▪ *Syn* apologetic, attritional, chastened, compunctious, conscience-stricken, humble, penitent, remorseful, repentant, sorrowful, sorry; ▪ *Ant* hurtful, indifferent, mean, unrepentant.

contrive [*v*] *bring about, succeed with difficulty* ▪ *Syn* achieve, arrange, collude, compass, concoct, connive, develop, devise, effect, elaborate, engineer, execute, hatch, intrigue, machinate, maneuver, manipulate, negotiate, plan, project, scheme, swing, work out; ▪ *Ant* demolish, destroy, ruin, stop, waste, wreck.

control [*v1*] *have charge of*
▪ *Syn* administer, administrate, advise, boss, command, conduct, direct, discipline, dominate, domineer, govern, guide, handle, head, instruct, lead, manage, manipulate, overlook, oversee, pilot, predominate, regulate, rule, steer, subjugate, superintend, supervise; ▪ *Ant* abandon, forsake, give up, let go, relinquish, renounce, resign.

control [*v2*] *curb, hold back*
▪ *Syn* bridle, check, collect, compose, constrain, contain, cool, corner, cow, limit, quell, regulate, rein in, repress, restrain, subdue; ▪ *Ant* jump in, let go, risk, rush.

controversial [*adj*] *at issue*
▪ *Syn* arguable, contended, contentious, contestable, debatable, disputable, doubtable, doubtful, dubious, litigious, polemical, questionable, suspect; ▪ *Ant* agreeable, incontrovertible, peaceful, uncontroversial, undisputed, undoubted, unquestionable.

controvert [*v*] *oppose, argue*
▪ *Syn* challenge, confound, confute, contest, counter, debate, deny, disconfirm, discuss, disprove, dispute, oppugn, question, rebut, refute, wrangle; ▪ *Ant* agree, corroborate, forbear, harmonize, make peace, refrain from comment, verify.

contumacious [*adj*] *headstrong, obstinate* ▪ *Syn* contrary, disaffected, estranged, factious, froward, haughty, inflexible, insurgent, intractable, mutinous, obdurate, perverse, rebellious, recalcitrant, refractory, seditious, stubborn, unyielding; ▪ *Ant* following, obedient, subordinate, tractable, willing.

convalescent [*adj*] *improving, recuperating* ▪ *Syn* ambulatory, healing, mending, rallying, recovering, rejuvenated, restored, strengthening; ▪ *Ant* failing, faltering, regressing, sickly, weak, worsening.

convene [*v*] *bring together; meet*
▪ *Syn* assemble, call, collect, come together, congregate, convoke, gather, muster, open, rally, round up, sit, summon, unite; ▪ *Ant* adjourn, call off, cancel, disperse, dissemble.

convenient [*adj1*] *appropriate, useful*
▪ *Syn* acceptable, accommodating, adapt-

able, advantageous, agreeable, aiding, assisting, available, beneficial, comfortable, commodious, conducive, decent, favorable, handy, helpful, opportune, proper, ready, roomy, serviceable, suitable, time-saving, well-planned; ▪ *Ant* awkward, inappropriate, inconvenient, ineffectual, inopportune, unadaptable, unhandy, unsuited, unuseful.

convenient [*adj2*] *nearby*
▪ *Syn* accessible, adjacent, adjoining, at hand, available, central, close, close-by, contiguous, handy, immediate, next door, nigh, within reach; ▪ *Ant* distant, far, inconvenient, out-of-the-way, unavailable.

conventional [*adj1*] *common, normal*
▪ *Syn* accepted, commonplace, customary, decorous, expected, formal, general, habitual, ordinary, orthodox, popular, predominant, prevalent, proper, regular, ritual, routine, standard, traditional, typical, usual; ▪ *Ant* abnormal, exotic, foreign, irregular, strange, uncommon, unconventional, uncustomary, unusual.

conventional [*adj2*] *unoriginal*
▪ *Syn* conservative, doctrinal, dogmatic, hackneyed, moderate, narrow, obstinate, pedestrian, prosaic, routine, run-of-the-mill, stereotyped; ▪ *Ant* different, exotic, foreign, new, original, strange, unique.

converge [*v*] *gather*
▪ *Syn* assemble, coincide, combine, concenter, concentrate, concur, encounter, enter in, focalize, focus, join, meet, merge, mingle, rally, unite; ▪ *Ant* disperse, diverge, divide, scatter, separate, spread.

conversant [*adj*] *experienced, familiar with* ▪ *Syn* abreast, acquainted, apprehensive, au courant, au fait, aware, cognizant, conscious, informed, knowledgeable, learned, perceptive, percipient, practiced, proficient, sensible, sentient, skilled, up-to-date, versant, versed; ▪ *Ant* ignorant, inexperienced, quiet, silent.

converse [*n*] *opposite*
▪ *Syn* antipode, antipole, antithesis, contra, contrary, counter, counterpole, inverse, obverse, reverse; ▪ *Ant* equal, same, similarity.

converse [*adj*] *opposite*
▪ *Syn* antipodal, antipodean, antithetical, contradictory, contrary, counter, differ-

ent, reverse, transposed; ▪ *Ant* complementary, equal, same, similar.

converse [v] *talk*
▪ *Syn* chat, commune, confer, discourse, exchange, parley, speak; ▪ *Ant* be quiet, be silent.

convert [v1] *change; adapt*
▪ *Syn* alter, metamorphose, modify, remodel, revise, switch, transfigure, transform, translate, transmogrify, transpose, turn; ▪ *Ant* endure, hold, idle, keep, persist, remain, stay, wait.

convert [v2] *change belief, especially regarding religion* ▪ *Syn* actuate, assimilate to, baptize, bend, bias, brainwash, bring around, convince, incline, lead, make over, move, persuade, proselytize, redeem, reform, regenerate, save, sway, turn; ▪ *Ant* hold, remain.

convex [adj] *rounded, curving outward*
▪ *Syn* arched, bent, biconvex, bulged, bulging, gibbous, protuberant, raised; ▪ *Ant* concave, depressed, sunken.

convey [v1] *transport*
▪ *Syn* bear, bring, carry, channel, conduct, dispatch, fetch, forward, funnel, guide, lug, move, pack, ride, send, shoulder, siphon, support, tote, traject, transfer, transmit; ▪ *Ant* hold, keep, maintain, retain.

convey [v2] *express message*
▪ *Syn* break, carry, communicate, disclose, impart, pass on, project, relate, reveal, send, tell, transmit; ▪ *Ant* keep secret, refrain, withhold.

convict [v] *find guilty*
▪ *Syn* adjudge, attaint, bring to justice, condemn, declare guilty, doom, frame, imprison, pass sentence on, pronounce guilty, put away, sentence; ▪ *Ant* exonerate, free, liberate, release.

convincing [adj] *persuasive*
▪ *Syn* acceptable, believeable, cogent, credible, dependable, impressive, likely, moving, powerful, rational, reasonable, satisfactory, solid, sound, telling, valid; ▪ *Ant* doubtful, dubious, implausible, improbable, incredible, unconvincing, unlikely, unpersuasive.

convivial [adj] *fun-loving*
▪ *Syn* cheerful, companionable, entertaining, festive, friendly, gay, genial, happy, jocund, jolly, jovial, lively, merry, mirthful, pleasant, sociable, vivacious; ▪ *Ant* dull, grave, serious, solemn, staid.

convocation [n] *assembly*
▪ *Syn* conclave, concourse, conference, congregation, congress, convention, council, diet, meet, synod; ▪ *Ant* adjournment, disbanding.

convolution [n] *loop, spiral*
▪ *Syn* coil, complexity, contortion, curlicue, gyration, helix, intricacy, involution, serpentine, sinuosity, sinuousness, swirl, tortuousness, twist, undulation; ▪ *Ant* line, straightness.

convoy [v] *protect, escort*
▪ *Syn* accompany, attend, bear, bring, chaperon, companion, company, conduct, consort, defend, guard, pilot, safeguard, shepherd, shield, usher, watch; ▪ *Ant* ignore, neglect.

convulsion [n] *disturbance*
▪ *Syn* agitation, cataclysm, clamor, commotion, disaster, ferment, furor, outcry, seism, shock, tumult, turbulence, upheaval, upturn; ▪ *Ant* harmony, peace.

cool [adj1] *cold, nippy*
▪ *Syn* air-conditioned, algid, arctic, chill, chilly, frigid, frosty, gelid, refreshing, refrigerated, snappy, wintry; ▪ *Ant* hot, temperate, warm.

cool [adj2] *calm, collected*
▪ *Syn* assured, composed, detached, dispassionate, impassive, imperturbable, levelheaded, nonchalant, phlegmatic, placid, quiet, relaxed, self-controlled, serene, together, tranquil; ▪ *Ant* agitated, annoyed, excited, upset.

cool [adj3] *aloof, disapproving*
▪ *Syn* apathetic, distant, frigid, incurious, indifferent, lukewarm, offhand, offish, procacious, reserved, solitary, standoffish, withdrawn; ▪ *Ant* approving, friendly, kind, responsive, sociable, warm.

cool [v1] *chill*
▪ *Syn* abate, air-condition, calm, freeze, frost, infrigidate, lessen, mitigate, moderate, reduce, refrigerate, temper; ▪ *Ant* heat, warm.

cool [v2] *take a break; abate*
▪ *Syn* allay, assuage, calm, calm down, compose, control, dampen, lessen, mitigate, moderate, quiet, reduce, rein, repress, restrain, simmer down, suppress, temper; ▪ *Ant* continue, go on, increase, step up.

cooperate [v] *aid, assist*
▪ *Syn* abet, advance, agree, back up, band, befriend, coadjute, collaborate,

combine, comply with, concert, concur, conduce, conspire, contribute, coordinate, espouse, forward, further, help, join forces, participate, second, share in, side with, succor, unite, uphold, work together; ▪ *Ant* block, delay, disturb, encumber, handicap, hinder, impede, obstruct, prevent, stop.

cooperative [*adj1*] *joint, unified*
▪ *Syn* coactive, coefficient, collaborative, collective, collusive, concerted, coordinated, harmonious, in league, interdependent, reciprocal, shared, symbiotic, synergetic, team, united; ▪ *Ant* disjoint, disobliging, disunited, divided, separate, uncooperative, uncoordinated.

cooperative [*adj2*] *helpful*
▪ *Syn* accommodating, companionable, obliging, responsive, sociable, supportive, useful; ▪ *Ant* disobliging, encumbering, hindering, preventing, uncooperative, unhelpful, unsupportive.

co-opt [*v*] *assimilate in order to take over or appropriate* ▪ *Syn* absorb, accept, adopt, admit, bring in, bring into the fold, bring into line, connaturalize, convert, draw in, elect, embrace, encompass, enfold, homogenize, homologize, include, incorporate, make one's own, take over, take in; ▪ *Ant* dismiss, fight against, ignore, leave be, oppose, reject repel.

coordinate [*adj*] *equal in importance or rank* ▪ *Syn* alike, coequal, correlative, correspondent, counterpart, equal, like, parallel, tantamount; ▪ *Ant* different, dissimilar, unequal, unparallel.

coordinate [*v*] *match, relate*
▪ *Syn* agree, atune, combine, conduce, conform, correlate, harmonize, integrate, mesh, organize, pool, proportion, reconcile, reconcile, regulate, synchronize, systematize, team up; ▪ *Ant* disintegrate, mismatch, uncoordinate, unrelate.

copious [*adj*] *abundant*
▪ *Syn* ample, bountiful, extensive, full, generous, heavy, lavish, liberal, lush, overflowing, plentiful, profuse, prolix, replete, rich; ▪ *Ant* lacking, meager, needing, needy, poor, rare, scarce, wanting.

cop out [*v*] *abandon, quit*
▪ *Syn* back down, back off, back out, backpedal, desert, dodge, excuse, rationalize, renege, renounce, revoke, welsh, withdraw; ▪ *Ant* be ready, face, ready, take on.

copulate [*v*] *have sexual relations*
▪ *Syn* bed, breed, cohabit, conjugate, couple, fornicate, have coition, have sex, lay, lie with, make love, mate, sleep together, sleep with, unite; ▪ *Ant* abstain, refrain.

copy [*v*] *imitate*
▪ *Syn* ape, burlesque, echo, embody, emulate, epitomize, follow, illustrate, mimic, mirror, mock, model, parody, parrot, pirate, prefigure, repeat, sham, simulate, steal, travesty, typify; ▪ *Ant* create, originate.

cordial [*adj*] *friendly, sociable*
▪ *Syn* affable, affectionate, agreeable, amicable, cheerful, companionable, congenial, convivial, genial, gracious, happy, heartfelt, jovial, mellow, neighborly, polite, responsive, sincere, sympathetic, tender, warm, welcoming, wholehearted; ▪ *Ant* aloof, cool, disagreeable, hostile, indifferent, inhospitable, uncordial, unfriendly, unpleasant, unsociable.

core [*n*] *center, gist*
▪ *Syn* base, basis, body, bulk, corpus, crux, essence, focus, foundation, heart, importance, kernel, mass, middle, nub, nucleus, origin, pith, pivot, quick, root, significance, staple, substance, thrust, upshot; ▪ *Ant* covering, exterior, exteriority, outside, perimeter, surface.

corner [*v*] *trap*
▪ *Syn* bottle, bring to bay, capture, catch, fool, nab, put out, seize, tree, trick, trouble; ▪ *Ant* allow, let go, release.

corny [*adj*] *trite, clichéd*
▪ *Syn* banal, commonplace, feeble, hackneyed, mawkish, melodramatic, old-fashioned, sentimental, shopworn, stale, stereotyped, tired; ▪ *Ant* fresh, new, original, unique.

corporal [*adj*] *bodily, physical*
▪ *Syn* anatomical, carnal, corporeal, fleshy, gross, human, material, objective, phenomenal, somatic, substantial, tangible; ▪ *Ant* cerebral, immaterial, intangible, mental, spiritual.

corporeal [*adj*] *bodily, physical*
▪ *Syn* anatomical, carnal, corporal, fleshly, fleshy, human, material, mortal, objective, phenomenal, sensible, somatic, substantial, tangible; ▪ *Ant* cerebral, immaterial, intangible, mental, spiritual.

corpulent [*adj*] *fat, chubby*
▪ *Syn* bulky, burly, fat, fleshy, heavy,

husky, large, obese, overweight, plump, portly, rotund, stout, weighty; ▪ *Ant* skinny, slender, slight, thin.

correct [*adj1*] *accurate, exact*
▪ *Syn* actual, appropriate, equitable, factual, faithful, flawless, impeccable, just, legitimate, precise, regular, right, stone, strict, true, veracious; ▪ *Ant* flawed, imprecise, inaccurate, incorrect, inexact, wrong.

correct [*adj2*] *proper, appropriate*
▪ *Syn* acceptable, becoming, careful, comme il faut, conforming, conventional, decent, decorous, diplomatic, fitting, meticulous, punctilious, right, righteous, scrupulous, standard, suitable; ▪ *Ant* improper, inappropriate, incorrect, unfitting, unsuitable.

correct [*v1*] *fix, adjust*
▪ *Syn* alter, ameliorate, amend, change, edit, help, improve, mend, polish, put in order, reconstruct, rectify, reform, regulate, remedy, repair, review, revise, right, set straight; ▪ *Ant* blow, blunder, goof, mistake.

correct [*v2*] *discipline, chastise*
▪ *Syn* administer, admonish, castigate, chasten, chide, penalize, punish, reprimand, reprove; ▪ *Ant* be permissive, coddle, indulge, pamper, pet, spoil.

corrective [*adj*] *healing, curing*
▪ *Syn* antidotal, counteracting, curative, disciplinary, palliative, penal, punitive, reformatory, rehabilitative, remedial, restorative, therapeutic; ▪ *Ant* harmful, hurtful, hurting, injurious, paining.

correlate [*v*] *equate, compare*
▪ *Syn* associate, connect, coordinate, correspond, interact, parallel; ▪ *Ant* differ, disassociate, disconnect, imbalance.

correspond [*v*] *agree, complement*
▪ *Syn* accord, amount, approach, assimilate, be consistent, coincide, compare, conform, correlate, equal, fit, harmonize, match, reciprocate, resemble, rival, square; ▪ *Ant* differ, disagree, diverge.

corresponding [*adj*] *equivalent, matching* ▪ *Syn* agnate, akin, alike, analogous, comparable, complementary, consonant, correlative, correspondent, identical, interrelated, kindred, like, parallel, reciprocal, similar, synonymous; ▪ *Ant* differing, disparaging, dissimilar, mismatched, unlike.

corroborate [*v*] *back up information, story* ▪ *Syn* approve, authenticate, certify,

confirm, document, endorse, justify, prove, ratify, strengthen, substantiate, support, validate, verify; ▪ *Ant* contradict, deny, disallow, disclaim, refute, reject.

corrode [*v*] *wear away; eat away*
▪ *Syn* bite, consume, corrupt, destroy, deteriorate, erode, gnaw, impair, oxidize, rot, rust, scour, waste; ▪ *Ant* aid, build, fortify, help.

corrosive [*adj*] *consuming, wearing; bitter* ▪ *Syn* acerbic, acrid, biting, caustic, cutting, destructive, erosive, incisive, trenchant, virulent, wasting; ▪ *Ant* contributing, fortifying, supporting.

corrugated [*adj*] *ridged, grooved*
▪ *Syn* channeled, creased, crumpled, flexed, fluted, folded, furrowed, puckered, roughened, wrinkled; ▪ *Ant* flat, smooth.

corrupt [*adj1*] *dishonest*
▪ *Syn* base, bribable, crooked, debauched, double-dealing, foul, fraudulent, iniquitous, knavish, mercenary, nefarious, perfidious, reprobate, rotten, shady, snide, tainted, treacherous, two-faced, underhanded, venal; ▪ *Ant* decent, honest, honorable, principled, pure, trustworthy, truthful, uncorrupt, upright.

corrupt [*adj2*] *debased, vicious*
▪ *Syn* abandoned, baneful, degenerate, degraded, deleterious, depraved, dishonored, evil, flagitious, infamous, low, monstrous, nefarious, perverse, profligate, rotten, villainous; ▪ *Ant* clean, decent, helpful, high, kind, noble, sound, wholesome.

corrupt [*adj3*] *adulterated, rotten*
▪ *Syn* altered, contaminated, decayed, defiled, foul, infected, noxious, polluted, putrid, tainted; ▪ *Ant* clean, pure, purified, sound, wholesome.

corrupt [*v*] *pervert; pollute*
▪ *Syn* abuse, adulterate, bastardize, blemish, bribe, contaminate, damage, debase, debauch, deface, defile, deform, degrade, demean, demoralize, deprave, depreciate, disgrace, dishonor, harm, hurt, impair, infect, injure, lower, lure, maltreat, mar, mistreat, outrage, putrefy, ravage, reduce, rot, ruin, spoil, stain, subvert, taint, undermine, violate, vitiate, warp, waste; ▪ *Ant* better, chasten, cleanse, dignify, improve, purify.

cosmetic [*adj*] *beautifying; relating to appearance* ▪ *Syn* corrective, improving, nonessential, painted, remedial, restorative, superficial, surface; ▪ *Ant* damaging, disfiguring, marring.

cosmic [*adj*] *limitless; universal*
▪ *Syn* catholic, cosmogonal, cosmogonic, ecumenical, empyrean, global, grandiose, huge, immense, infinite, measureless, planetary, vast, worldwide; ▪ *Ant* bounded, limited, narrow.

cosmopolitan [*adj*] *worldly-wise*
▪ *Syn* catholic, cultivated, cultured, ecumenical, global, gregarious, metropolitan, polished, public, smooth, sophisticated, universal, urbane, well-travelled, worldly; ▪ *Ant* country, parochial, provincial, rural, rustic.

costly [*adj1*] *expensive*
▪ *Syn* excessive, exorbitant, extravagant, fancy, high, high-priced, inordinate, precious, premium, steep, top, valuable; ▪ *Ant* cheap, inexpensive, reasonable.

costly [*adj2*] *priceless*
▪ *Syn* inestimable, invaluable, lavish, luxurious, opulent, precious, rich, splendid, sumptuous, valuable; ▪ *Ant* cheap, not valuable, poor.

costly [*adj3*] *harmful, damaging*
▪ *Syn* catastrophic, deleterious, disastrous, ruinous, sacrificial; ▪ *Ant* aiding, helpful.

cottage [*n*] *tiny house; lodging*
▪ *Syn* box, bungalow, cabana, cabin, caboose, camp, carriage house, chalet, cot, home, hut, lean-to, lodge, ranch, shack, shanty; ▪ *Ant* chateau, manor house, mansion, palace, townhouse.

couch potato [*n*] *inactive person*
▪ *Syn* bystander, idler, laggard, lazy person, loafer, lounger, observer, slouch, sluggard, spectator, televiewer, TV viewer, viewer; ▪ *Ant* bustler, doer, eager beaver, overachiever, person of action, workaholic.

count [*v1*] *add, check in order*
▪ *Syn* add up, calculate, cast, cipher, compute, enumerate, estimate, figure, number, numerate, reckon, score, sum, take account of, tally, tell, tick off, total; ▪ *Ant* estimate, guess.

count [*v2*] *consider, deem*
▪ *Syn* await, esteem, expect, hope, impute, judge, look, rate, regard, think; ▪ *Ant* disregard, ignore.

count [*v3*] *include*
▪ *Syn* consider, number among, take into account, take into consideration; ▪ *Ant* except, exclude.

countenance [*v*] *approve, support*
▪ *Syn* abet, advocate, approbate, bear with, champion, commend, condone, endorse, help, invite, put up with, sanction, uphold; ▪ *Ant* deny, disagree, disapprove, discourage, fight, oppose, refuse.

counter [*adj*] *opposite, opposing*
▪ *Syn* adverse, against, antagonistic, antithetical, conflicting, contradictory, converse, diametric, hindering, impeding, obstructive, opposed, polar, reverse; ▪ *Ant* agreeing, concurring, corresponding, corroborating, equal, same, similar.

counter [*v*] *answer, respond in retaliation* ▪ *Syn* buck, circumvent, contravene, disappoint, foil, frustrate, hinder, match, offset, oppose, parry, pit, return, ruin, vie, ward off; ▪ *Ant* accept, give in, give up, surrender, take, yield.

counter [*adv*] *contrary, reverse*
▪ *Syn* against, at variance with, contrarily, contrariwise, conversely, opposite; ▪ *Ant* equally, same, similarly.

counteract [*v*] *do opposing action*
▪ *Syn* annul, buck, cancel, check, countercheck, cross, defeat, fix, foil, frustrate, go against, hinder, invalidate, negate, neutralize, offset, oppose, prevent, redress, thwart; ▪ *Ant* aid, approve, assist, help, promote, support.

counterfeit [*adj*] *fake, simulated*
▪ *Syn* assumed, brummagem, copied, crock, delusory, ersatz, faked, false, feigned, fictitious, forged, framed, fraudulent, imitation, mock, pirate, pretentious, pseudo, sham, spurious; ▪ *Ant* authentic, genuine, real, true.

counterfeit [*v*] *make deceitful imitation*
▪ *Syn* affect, ape, assume, bluff, carbon, cheat, clone, coin, copy, defraud, delude, ditto, dupe, fabricate, fake, feign, forge, imitate, impersonate, knock off, mimeo, mimic, pretend, sham, simulate; ▪ *Ant* be genuine, be honest.

countermand [*v*] *annul, cancel a command* ▪ *Syn* override, recall, repeal, rescind, retract, retreat, reverse, revoke; ▪ *Ant* allow, approve, permit, sanction.

counterpart [*n*] *match; identical part or thing* ▪ *Syn* analogue, copy, correlate, correspondent, doppelganger, duplicate, equivalent, like, mate, pendant, supplement, twin; ▪ *Ant* opposite.

countless [*adj*] *innumerable*
▪ *Syn* endless, immeasurable, incalculable, infinite, legion, limitless, many,

measureless, multitudinous, myriad, numberless; ▪ *Ant* calculable, countable, counted, limited, measurable, numbered, numerable.

count on/count upon [v] *depend on; rely* ▪ *Syn* bank on, bargain for, believe, bet on, expect, place confidence in, plan on, reckon on, take for granted, trust; ▪ *Ant* disbelieve, distrust, not expect.

count out [v] *disregard, exclude* ▪ *Syn* bar, debar, eliminate, except, leave out, mark off, pass over, rule out, suspend; ▪ *Ant* consider, figure on, include, regard.

country [adj] *rural, pastoral* ▪ *Syn* agrarian, Arcadian, bucolic, campestral, georgic, outland, provincial, rustic; ▪ *Ant* city, metropolitan, urban.

couple [v] *join two things* ▪ *Syn* bracket, bring together, buckle, clasp, coalesce, cohabit, conjoin, conjugate, connect, copulate, harness, hitch, link, marry, match, pair, unite, wed, yoke; ▪ *Ant* disconnect, disjoin, divide, separate, unbuckle, uncouple.

courageous [adj] *brave, bold* ▪ *Syn* adventurous, audacious, cool, dauntless, fearless, fiery, game, hardy, heroic, high-spirited, impavid, indomitable, intrepid, nervy, resolute, stalwart, stouthearted, strong, tenacious, tough, valiant, venturous; ▪ *Ant* cowardly, fainthearted, fearful, fearing, meek, shy, timid, weak.

courier [n] *messenger* ▪ *Syn* bearer, carrier, dispatcher, emissary, envoy, express, go-between, herald, internuncio, runner; ▪ *Ant* receiver, sender.

court [v] *fawn over, pay attention to* ▪ *Syn* beseech, charm, chase, cultivate, curry favor, date, entice, entreat, flatter, importune, invite, pander to, please, praise, propose to, pursue, seek, serenade, solicit, spark, sue, woo; ▪ *Ant* avoid, disregard, ignore, reject, shun, spurn.

courteous [adj] *gentle, mannerly* ▪ *Syn* affable, ceremonious, civil, complaisant, cultivated, gracious, polite, respectful, soft-spoken, thoughtful, urbane; ▪ *Ant* bad-mannered, discourteous, impolite, rude, uncivil, uncourteous, unmannerly, unrefined.

courtly [adj] *refined, mannerly or mannered* ▪ *Syn* affable, aristocratic, august,

ceremonious, chivalrous, cultured, decorous, dignified, elegant, flattering, gallant, gracious, high-bred, imposing, lofty, obliging, polished, refined, stately, studied, urbane; ▪ *Ant* impolite, indecorous, inelegant, low-bred, provincial, rough, uncivil, unpolished, unrefined.

covenant [v] *agree* ▪ *Syn* concur, contract, engage, pledge, plight, promise, stipulate, swear, undertake, vow; ▪ *Ant* break an agreement, disagree.

cover [v1] *wrap, hide* ▪ *Syn* blanket, bury, cache, camouflage, cloak, conceal, curtain, disguise, dress, eclipse, encase, enclose, enfold, enshroud, envelop, hood, invest, layer, mantle, mask, obscure, protect, screen, shield, shroud, veil; ▪ *Ant* expose, lay bare, lay out, reveal, uncover, unwrap.

cover [v2] *protect, guard* ▪ *Syn* bulwark, defend, fend, house, reinforce, safeguard, screen, secure, shelter, shield, watch over; ▪ *Ant* abandon, disregard, forget, ignore, leave alone.

cover [v3] *include, contain* ▪ *Syn* comprehend, comprise, consider, embody, embrace, encompass, examine, incorporate, involve, meet, provide for, suffice, survey; ▪ *Ant* exclude, leave out.

cover [v4] *describe in published writing* ▪ *Syn* broadcast, detail, investigate, narrate, recount, relate, report, tell of, write up; ▪ *Ant* disregard, exclude, forget, ignore, omit.

covert [adj] *clandestinely, underhanded* ▪ *Syn* camouflaged, concealed, disguised, furtive, hidden, incognito, masked, obscured, private, privy, secret, shrouded, stealthy, sub rosa, surreptitious, ulterior, undercover, veiled; ▪ *Ant* aboveboard, candid, frank, honest, open, overt, public, unconcealed.

covertly [adv] *clandestine, underhandedly* ▪ *Syn* clandestinely, furtively, on the sly, privately, secretly, stealthily, sub rosa, surreptitiously, undercover; ▪ *Ant* candidly, frankly, honestly, openly, overtly, publicly.

covet [v] *desire strongly* ▪ *Syn* aspire to, begrudge, choose, crave, envy, fancy, long for, lust after, spoil for, thirst for, want, wish for, yearn for; ▪ *Ant* abjure, be generous, forswear, give, not want, reject.

covetous [adj] greedy; very desirous
- **Syn** acquisitive, avaricious, avid, eager, envious, gluttonous, grasping, jealous, keen, mercenary, prehensile, rapacious, ravenous, selfish, voracious, yearning;
- **Ant** benevolent, generous, giving.

cow [v] browbeat, intimidate
- **Syn** abash, bludgeon, bulldoze, bully, daunt, dishearten, dismay, dragoon, embarrass, faze, frighten, hector, rattle, scare, subdue, terrorize; • **Ant** encourage, hearten, inspirit.

cowardly [adj] fearful
- **Syn** afraid, anxious, apprehensive, craven, dastardly, diffident, dismayed, fainthearted, frightened, nervous, panicky, pusillanimous, recreant, scared, shrinking, shy, timid, timorous, weak; • **Ant** bold, brave, courageous, daring, dauntless, unafraid, undaunted, unfearful.

cower [v] hide, hover in fear
- **Syn** blench, cringe, crouch, fawn, flinch, grovel, recoil, shrink, sneak, tremble, wince; • **Ant** come out, stand tall, swagger.

coy [adj] very modest
- **Syn** bashful, blushing, demure, evasive, flirtatious, overmodest, prudish, reserved, retiring, self-effacing, shy, skittish, timid; • **Ant** aggressive, assertive, forward, immodest, impudent.

cozy [adj] comforting, soft, warm
- **Syn** comfortable, cushy, easeful, in clover, restful, safe, secure, sheltered, snug; • **Ant** uncomfortable.

crabby/crabbed [adj] in a bad mood
- **Syn** acid, acrimonious, blunt, brusque, choleric, churlish, crotchety, dour, fretful, harsh, ill-humored, irascible, misanthropic, peevish, petulant, saturnine, snappish, sour, splenetic, surly, tart, testy; • **Ant** happy, sociable.

crack [v1] break, usually into parts
- **Syn** burst, chip, chop, cleave, crackle, crash, damage, detonate, explode, fracture, hurt, impair, injure, pop, ring, rive, sever, shiver, snap, splinter, split; • **Ant** fix, mend.

crack [v2] lose self-control
- **Syn** become deranged, become insane, blow up, break down, collapse, go crazy, succumb, yield; • **Ant** be calm, compose.

crack [v3] discover meaning, answer
- **Syn** break, decipher, decode, decrypt, fathom, figure out, get answer, solve, work out; • **Ant** misunderstand.

crafty [adj] clever, scheming
- **Syn** adroit, artful, astute, calculating, canny, cunning, deceitful, devious, disingenuous, fraudulent, guileful, insidious, keen, knowing, sharp, shrewd, sly, smart, subtle, tricky, vulpine, wily; • **Ant** guileless, honest, naive.

craggy [adj] jagged
- **Syn** asperous, broken, harsh, precipitous, rockbound, rocky, rough, rugged, scabrous, scraggy, stony; • **Ant** even, flat, level, smooth.

cram [v] fill to overflowing; compress
- **Syn** charge, chock, choke, compact, crowd, force, gorge, heap, ingurgitate, jam, load, overcrowd, overeat, overfill, pack, press, ram, satiate, shove, squash, squeeze, stive, stuff, thrust, wedge; • **Ant** deplete, empty, let out, open, release.

cramp [v] hinder, restrain
- **Syn** check, circumscribe, clog, confine, constrain, encumber, fasten, hamper, handicap, impede, inhibit, limit, object, obstruct, restrict, stymie, thwart; • **Ant** allow, forward, let go, release.

cramped [adj] congested, overcrowded
- **Syn** awkward, circumscribed, close, confined, crowded, incommodious, irregular, minute, narrow, packed, pent, restricted, small, tight; • **Ant** free, open, uncongested, uncramped, uncrowded, uninhibited, unobstructed.

cranky [adj] in bad mood
- **Syn** bad-humored, bearish, cantankerous, choleric, crabby, cross, crotchety, disagreeable, grouchy, grumpy, hot-tempered, irascible, irritable, mean, out of sorts, perverse, quick-tempered, ratty, snappish, ugly; • **Ant** amiable, cheerful, happy.

crass [adj] coarse, insensitive
- **Syn** blundering, boorish, churlish, doltish, gross, indelicate, inelegant, loutish, lowbrow, oafish, obtuse, raw, rough, rude, vulgar; • **Ant** careful, delicate, kind, nice, refined, sensitive, tactful.

crave [v] desire intensely
- **Syn** ache for, covet, dream, fancy, long for, lust after, need, require, suspire, want, yearn for; • **Ant** abjure, dislike, hate, not want, spurn.

craven [adj] weak, timid
- **Syn** cowardly, dastardly, fearful, gutless, mean-spirited, pusillanimous,

scared, timorous; ▪ *Ant* bold, brave, courageous, heroic, strong.

crawl [v] *move very slowly*
▪ *Syn* clamber, creep, drag, grovel, inch, lag, plod, poke, scrabble, slide, slither, squirm, worm, wriggle, writhe; ▪ *Ant* dart, dash, fly, hasten, hightail, hurry, race, rush.

crazy [adj1] *mentally strange*
▪ *Syn* barmy, batty, berserk, cracked, cuckoo, daft, delirious, demented, deranged, erratic, flaky, idiotic, insane, lunatic, mad, maniacal, nuts, of unsound mind, silly, wacky; ▪ *Ant* balanced, realistic, reasonable, responsible, sane, sensible, smart.

crazy [adj2] *unrealistic, fantastic*
▪ *Syn* absurd, bizarre, cockeyed, eccentric, fatuous, foolhardy, idiotic, imprudent, insane, ludicrous, odd, outrageous, peculiar, quixotic, ridiculous, senseless, strange, weird, wild; ▪ *Ant* believeable, realistic, reasonable, sensible.

cream [n] *the best*
▪ *Syn* choice, elite, fat, favorite, finest, pick, pride, prize, top; ▪ *Ant* dregs, scum, worst.

creamy [adj] *smooth, buttery*
▪ *Syn* feathery, fluffy, greasy, luscious, lush, milky, oily, rich, soft, velvety; ▪ *Ant* chunky, lumpy.

crease [v] *fold, rumple*
▪ *Syn* bend, cockle, corrugate, crimp, crumple, double up, plait, pleat, pucker, purse, ridge, wrinkle; ▪ *Ant* flatten, iron, smooth, straighten.

create [v] *develop in mind or physically*
▪ *Syn* author, beget, build, coin, compose, conceive, concoct, devise, discover, dream up, establish, fabricate, fashion, found, generate, give birth to, imagine, initiate, institute, make, originate, parent, procreate, produce, shape, spawn, start; ▪ *Ant* annihilate, demolish, destroy, ruin.

creative [adj] *artistic, imaginative*
▪ *Syn* clever, demiurgic, fertile, gifted, ingenious, innovative, inspired, inventive, original, originative, productive, prolific, stimulating, visionary; ▪ *Ant* uncreative, ungifted, unimaginative, uninspired, unproductive, untalented.

creator [n] *inventor; God*
▪ *Syn* architect, author, begetter, brain, deity, designer, founder, framer, generator, initiator, maker, originator, prime mover, producer; ▪ *Ant* destroyer, destructor.

credence [n] *trust, acceptance*
▪ *Syn* admission, assurance, belief, certainty, confidence, credit, dependence, faith, reliance, stock, store; ▪ *Ant* distrust, doubt, faithlessness, skepticism.

credible [adj] *believable*
▪ *Syn* conceivable, dependable, honest, imaginable, likely, plausible, possible, rational, reasonable, reliable, sincere, solid, sound, tenable, thinkable, trustworthy, trusty, valid; ▪ *Ant* implausible, impossible, improbable, inconceivable, incredible, unbelievable, unimaginable, unlikely, untenable.

credit [v1] *believe, depend on*
▪ *Syn* accept, bank on, consider, deem, feel, have faith in, hold, rely on, sense, think, trust; ▪ *Ant* disbelieve, mistrust, question.

credit [v2] *accredit, assign to*
▪ *Syn* ascribe to, attribute to, charge to, defer, impute, lay, refer; ▪ *Ant* discredit, renege.

creditable [adj] *praiseworthy*
▪ *Syn* admirable, commendable, decent, estimable, excellent, exemplary, honest, honorable, laudable, meritorious, palmary, reputable, respectable, satisfactory, suitable, worthy; ▪ *Ant* disrespected, unworthy.

credulous [adj] *gullible, naive*
▪ *Syn* accepting, believing, green, simple, trusting, unquestioning, unsuspecting, unwary; ▪ *Ant* skeptical, suspecting, suspicious, untrusting.

creep [v] *crawl along, usually on ground*
▪ *Syn* edge, glide, grovel, inch, insinuate, lurk, scrabble, scramble, skulk, slink, slither, sneak, squirm, steal, tiptoe, worm, wriggle, writhe; ▪ *Ant* blunder, bluster, hurry, race, rush, trample.

creepy [adj] *nasty, scary*
▪ *Syn* direful, disturbing, dreadful, eerie, frightening, ghoulish, gruesome, hairraising, horrible, macabre, menacing, nightmarish, ominous, sinister, terrifying, threatening, weird; ▪ *Ant* good, nice, normal, pleasant, pleasing.

crest [n] *highest point*
▪ *Syn* acme, apex, apogee, climax, crescendo, crown, culmination, fastigium, head, height, peak, pinnacle, ridge, summit, top, vertex; ▪ *Ant* base, bottom, nadir.

crestfallen [adj] *disappointed*
- *Syn* blue, chapfallen, dejected, despondent, disconsolate, discouraged, disheartened, downcast, inconsolable, low, sad;
- *Ant* cheered, elated, encouraged, excited, happy, hearted, inspirited.

crime [n] *offense against the law*
- *Syn* atrocity, breach, caper, corruption, delict, delinquency, dereliction, felony, illegality, infraction, infringement, malefaction, misconduct, misdemeanor, outrage, racket, scandal, tort, transgression, trespass, villainy, violation, wrong, wrongdoing; *Ant* good deed, kindness.

criminal [adj] *lawless, felonious*
- *Syn* corrupt, crooked, culpable, deplorable, illegal, illegitimate, illicit, indictable, iniquitous, nefarious, peccant, scandalous, vicious, villainous, wicked, wrong; *Ant* correct, lawful, legal, moral, right, righteous.

crimp [v] *fold or curl*
- *Syn* coil, crease, crinkle, crumple, frizz, pleat, rimple, ruck, scrunch, swirl, undulate, wave, wrinkle; *Ant* flatten, smooth, straighten.

cringe [v] *flinch, recoil from danger*
- *Syn* blench, cower, crawl, crouch, dodge, duck, grovel, kneel, quail, quiver, shrink, shy, start, stoop, tremble, wince; *Ant* come forward, flout, strut, swagger.

cripple [v1] *disable; make lame*
- *Syn* attenuate, blunt, debilitate, enfeeble, hurt, immobilize, incapacitate, injure, lame, maim, mangle, mutilate, palsy, paralyze, prostrate, sap, stifle, undermine, weaken; *Ant* aid, assist, enable, help, strengthen, support.

cripple [v2] *hinder action, progress*
- *Syn* bring to standstill, cramp, damage, destroy, halt, impair, ruin, spoil, stifle, vitiate; *Ant* aid, allow, assist, capacitate, encourage, help.

crippled [adj] *disabled*
- *Syn* broken, damaged, defective, deformed, enfeebled, handicapped, impaired, lame, maimed, marred, mutilated, paralyzed; *Ant* functioning, healthy.

crisis [n] *critical situation*
- *Syn* catastrophe, climax, contingency, crossroad, crux, culmination, deadlock, dilemma, disaster, emergency, entanglement, exigency, extremity, imbroglio, impasse, juncture, perplexity, plight, predicament, puzzle, quandary, situation, stew, strait, trauma, trial, trouble, turning point, urgency; *Ant* calm, peace.

crisp [adj1] *brittle, dry*
- *Syn* crumbly, crunchy, crusty, firm, fresh, friable, green, plump, ripe, short; *Ant* flexible, limp, soft, wilted.

crisp [adj2] *fresh, chilly*
- *Syn* bracing, brisk, clear, cloudless, invigorating, refreshing, stimulating; *Ant* balmy, temperate, warm.

crisp [adj3] *short, curt in presentation*
- *Syn* abrupt, biting, brief, brusque, clear, cutting, incisive, penetrating, pithy, succinct, tart, terse; *Ant* lengthy, long.

crisp [adj4] *smart, snappy in appearance*
- *Syn* clean-cut, neat, orderly, spruce, tidy, well-groomed, well-pressed; *Ant* ruffled, rumpled.

critical [adj1] *fault-finding, detracting*
- *Syn* analytical, belittling, calumniatory, carping, censorious, choleric, cynical, demeaning, derogatory, exacting, exceptive, particular, scolding, severe, sharp, trenchant, withering; *Ant* complimentary, laudatory, praising.

critical [adj2] *urgently important*
- *Syn* acute, climacteric, crucial, dangerous, determinative, dire, exceptive, grave, hazardous, integral, momentous, pivotal, pressing, serious, significant, urgent, vital; *Ant* trivial, uncritical, unimportant.

criticize [v1] *disapprove, judge as bad*
- *Syn* blame, blister, carp, castigate, censure, chastise, condemn, denounce, disparage, excoriate, fustigate, hit, lambaste, pan, reprehend, reprimand, reprobate, reprove, scathe; *Ant* approve, compliment, laud, praise.

criticize [v2] *analyze, interpret*
- *Syn* appraise, assess, comment upon, evaluate, examine, judge, probe, review, scrutinize, study; *Ant* estimate, guess, suppose.

critique [n] *analysis, essay*
- *Syn* appraisal, assessment, comment, commentary, criticism, editorial, examination, exposition, judgment, notice, review, study, write-up; *Ant* compliment, praise.

crony [n] *ally, companion*
- *Syn* accomplice, acquaintance, associate, buddy, chum, colleague, comate, comrade, confidant, friend, intimate, mate, pal, partner; *Ant* enemy, foe.

crooked [adj1] *bent, angled*
- *Syn* angular, asymmetric, awry, bowed, circuitous, contorted, curved, deviating, distorted, errant, gnarled, hooked, irreg-

ular, lopsided, meandering, oblique, rambling, serpentine, sinuous, skewed, slanted, spiral, tilted, tortuous, twisted, warped, winding, zigzag; ▪ *Ant* even, flat, straight.

crooked [*adj2*] *dishonest, corrupt*
▪ *Syn* crafty, criminal, devious, double-dealing, dubious, fraudulent, illegal, indirect, iniquitous, knavish, lying, nefarious, ruthless, shady, shifty, suborned, treacherous; ▪ *Ant* good, honest, law-abiding, lawful, moral, principled.

cross [*adj*] *very angry; in a bad mood*
▪ *Syn* annoyed, cantankerous, choleric, churlish, fractious, ill-tempered, irritable, peevish, petulant, querulous, quick-tempered, short, splenetic, surly, testy, touchy, vexed; ▪ *Ant* animated, cheerful, happy, pleasant.

cross [*v1*] *traverse an area*
▪ *Syn* bridge, cruise, cut across, ford, go across, navigate, overpass, pass over, ply, sail, span, transverse, voyage; ▪ *Ant* remain, stay.

cross [*v2*] *intersect, lie across*
▪ *Syn* bisect, crisscross, crosscut, decussate, intercross, intertwine, lie athwart of, rest across; ▪ *Ant* divide, part, separate.

cross [*v3*] *betray, hinder*
▪ *Syn* block, bollix, buck, deny, double-cross, flummox, foil, frustrate, impede, interfere, obstruct, oppose, resist, stump, thwart; ▪ *Ant* abet, aid, assist, help.

crosswise/crossways [*adj*] *across, at an angle* ▪ *Syn* athwart, awry, diagonally, horizontally, longways, on the bias, over, perpendicular, sideways, transverse, traverse, vertically; ▪ *Ant* head on, lengthwise, straight on.

crouch [*v*] *stoop low; cringe*
▪ *Syn* bend, bend down, bow, cower, dip, duck, grovel, huddle, hunch, hunker down, kneel, quail, squat, stoop; ▪ *Ant* stretch.

crowd [*v*] *cram, press into area*
▪ *Syn* bunch, bundle, cluster, congest, crush, deluge, elbow, flock, gather, huddle, jam, mass, pack, shove, squash, squeeze, surge, swamp, swarm, throng; ▪ *Ant* disperse, empty, retreat, scatter.

crowded [*adj*] *busy, congested*
▪ *Syn* awash, brimful, compact, crushed, dense, full, huddled, jammed, loaded, massed, mobbed, overflowing, packed, populous, stuffed, swarming, teeming, thronged, tight; ▪ *Ant* empty, uncongested, uncrowded, unfilled.

crown [*v*] *reward, dignify*
▪ *Syn* adorn, authorize, commission, coronate, delegate, determine, dignify, dower, endow, endue, ennoble, enthrone, erect, establish, exalt, festoon, fix, honor, inaugurate, induct, install, invest, raise, sanction; ▪ *Ant* depose, dethrone, dishonor, disregard, fine, punish.

crucial [*adj*] *critical, important*
▪ *Syn* acute, central, climactic, compelling, decisive, desperate, dire, essential, imperative, momentous, necessary, pivotal, pressing, urgent, vital; ▪ *Ant* inessential, trivial, uncritical, unimportant.

crucify [*v1*] *execute by nailing to a cross; torture* ▪ *Syn* excruciate, hang, harrow, kill, martyr, martyrize, nail to cross, persecute, rack, torment, torture; ▪ *Ant* console, exalt, solace.

crucify [*v2*] *browbeat, destroy with words* ▪ *Syn* afflict, agonize, bedevil, harrow, lampoon, pan, ridicule, smite, torment, torture, try; ▪ *Ant* compliment, exalt, laud, praise.

crude [*adj1*] *vulgar, unpolished in manner* ▪ *Syn* awkward, backward, boorish, cheap, clumsy, coarse, crass, filthy, foul, ill-bred, insensible, lewd, lowbred, oafish, obscene, raw, rough, rude, savage, tactless; ▪ *Ant* delicate, fine, gentle, polished, refined, tasteful.

crude [*adj2*] *unrefined, natural*
▪ *Syn* amateurish, callow, coarse, green, homemade, homespun, immature, impure, makeshift, prentice, primitive, raw, rough, rough-hewn, rude, rudimentary, rustic, simple, sketchy; ▪ *Ant* finished, formal, planned, refined, sophisticated, stilted.

cruel [*adj*] *vicious, pitiless; causing pain*
▪ *Syn* atrocious, barbarous, bloodthirsty, brutal, callous, cold-blooded, evil, ferocious, fierce, hard, harsh, hellish, implacable, inexorable, malevolent, merciless, pernicious, rancorous, relentless, ruthless, sadistic, spiteful, tyrannical, vengeful, vicious, virulent, wicked; ▪ *Ant* charitable, compassionate, considerate, feeling, gentle, kind, merciful, sympathetic, thoughtful.

crumble [*v*] *break or fall into pieces*
▪ *Syn* break up, collapse, crush, decay, decompose, degenerate, deteriorate, disintegrate, dissolve, fragment, granulate, grind, molder, perish, powder, pulverize, putrefy, triturate; ▪ *Ant* build, put together.

crush [v1] compress, smash
- *Syn* break, bruise, comminute, contuse, crease, crowd, crumble, crunch, enfold, hug, jam, mash, pound, powder, press, pulverize, push, squash, squeeze, trample; *Ant* expand, let go, release, spread, stretch, uncompress, unwrinkle.

crush [v2] humiliate
- *Syn* abash, browbeat, chagrin, dump, hurt, mortify, overwhelm, quash, quell, shame, suppress; *Ant* build up, compliment, encourage, inspirit, praise.

crusty [adj1] irritable, often because of old age *Syn* abrupt, blunt, brief, brusque, cantankerous, choleric, cranky, curt, dour, gruff, harsh, irascible, peevish, prickly, saturnine, short, splenetic, surly, testy, vinegary; *Ant* cheerful, happy, patient, placid, pleasant.

crusty [adj2] brittle on outside
- *Syn* crisp, crispy, crunchy, friable, hard, short, well-baked, well-done; *Ant* flexible, pliable, pliant, soft, soggy.

crux [n] most important part
- *Syn* body, core, decisive point, essence, gist, heart, kernel, matter, meat, nittygritty, nub, pith, purport, substance, thrust; *Ant* extra, minutia, trivia.

cry [v1] weep and make sad sounds
- *Syn* bawl, bemoan, bewail, break down, caterwaul, choke up, grieve, groan, howl, keen, lament, moan, mourn, regret, sob, sorrow, squall, wail, weep, whimper, whine; *Ant* giggle, laugh, rejoice, snicker, titter.

cry [v2] call out, yell
- *Syn* bark, bay, bellow, call, cheer, clamor, crow, ejaculate, exclaim, hail, holler, hoot, howl, pipe, roar, scream, shout, shriek, squawk, trill, vociferate, whistle, whoop, yell; *Ant* breathe, mumble, mutter, whisper.

cryptic [adj] secret; obscure in meaning
- *Syn* abstruse, ambiguous, cabbalistic, Delphic, enigmatic, esoteric, hidden, incomprehensible, inexplicable, mysterious, mystical, opaque, oracular, recondite, secretive, strange, tenebrous, vague, veiled; *Ant* clear, obvious, plain, seen, straightforward.

crystal [adj] clear, transparent
- *Syn* clear-cut, limpid, lucent, lucid, luminous, pellucid, translucent, transpicuous; *Ant* clouded, foggy.

cuddle [v] hold fondly, closely
- *Syn* bundle, burrow, caress, clasp, cos-

set, curl up, embrace, enfold, fondle, huddle, hug, kiss, love, nestle, nuzzle, pet, snuggle, touch; *Ant* flinch, push away, recoil, shrink.

culminate [v] come to a climax
- *Syn* cap, climax, close, conclude, crown, end, finish, round off, terminate; *Ant* begin, commence, open, start.

culpable [adj] responsible for an action
- *Syn* answerable, at fault, blameworthy, censurable, demeritorious, guilty, impeachable, indictable, liable, punishable, reprehensible, sinful, wrong; *Ant* blameless, inculpable, innocent, not guilty, right.

cultivate [v1] enrich situation; give special attention *Syn* advance, ameliorate, better, bolster, court, develop, discipline, elevate, encourage, foster, further, improve, nurse, nurture, promote, refine, train; *Ant* ignore, neglect, slight.

cultivate [v2] nurture, take care of
- *Syn* aid, cherish, devote oneself to, educate, encourage, forward, foster, further, help, improve, instruct, nurse, promote, raise, rear, refine, support, teach, train; *Ant* harm, ignore, neglect.

cultivation [n] culture, sophistication, education *Syn* advancement, aestheticism, breeding, civility, delicacy, discernment, discrimination, enlightenment, gentility, good taste, learning, manners, polish, progress, refinement, schooling, taste; *Ant* ignorance, unsophistication.

cultured [adj] experienced, educated
- *Syn* accomplished, au courant, civilized, courteous, cultivated, distingué, enlightened, erudite, genteel, informed, intellectual, lettered, literary, mannerly, polished, polite, refined, savant, scholarly, sophisticated, tasteful, traveled, urbane, versed, well-informed; *Ant* coarse, ignorant, inexperienced, uneducated, unsophisticated.

cumbersome [adj] clumsy, awkward
- *Syn* bulky, burdensome, clunky, heavy, hefty, inconvenient, leaden, massive, oppressive, ponderous, tiresome, wearisome, weighty; *Ant* commodious, graceful, manageable.

cumulative [adj] accruing; growing in size or effect *Syn* additive, aggregate, amassed, augmenting, chain, collective, heaped, heightening, increasing, increscent, magnifying, multiplying, summative; *Ant* decreasing, subtracting.

cunning [adj1] *devious*
▪ *Syn* astute, cagey, crafty, foxy, guile-ful, insidious, keen, Machiavellian, shifty, shrewd, slippery, smart, smooth, tricky, wily; ▪ *Ant* gullible, ingenuous, kind, naive, shy, sincere.

cunning [adj2] *imaginative*
▪ *Syn* able, adroit, canny, clever, deft, dexterous, ingenious, intelligent, skillful, sly, subtle, well-laid, well-planned; ▪ *Ant* clumsy, insipid, unimaginative, un-inspired, vapid.

cupidity [n] *greed, strong desire*
▪ *Syn* avarice, avidity, covetousness, craving, eagerness, greediness, hunger, infatuation, itching, longing, lust, pas-sion, rapacity, voracity, yearning; ▪ *Ant* dislike, distaste.

curable [adj] *able to be improved, fixed*
▪ *Syn* amenable, correctable, corrigible, healable, improvable, mendable, repara-tive, restorable; ▪ *Ant* hopeless, incur-able, irreparable.

curative [adj] *healing, health-giving*
▪ *Syn* alleviative, beneficial, corrective, healthful, helpful, invigorating, medica-tive, medicinal, remedial, restorative, sal-utary, therapeutic, tonic, vulnerary, wholesome; ▪ *Ant* harmful, hurting, in-jurious, painful.

curb [n] *restraining device; check*
▪ *Syn* barrier, border, brake, bridle, chain, control, deterrent, harness, hin-drance, limitation, rein, restraint, restric-tion, rim; ▪ *Ant* encouragement, opening.

curb [v] *repress, restrict*
▪ *Syn* abstain, bridle, check, constrain, control, entrammel, fetter, hamper, im-pede, inhibit, leash, moderate, refrain, rein in, restrain, retard, shackle, subdue, suppress, tame, tie, withhold; ▪ *Ant* aid, assist, encourage, foster, help.

cure [v] *heal, ease bad situation*
▪ *Syn* alleviate, ameliorate, correct, doc-tor, dress, help, improve, make healthy, make whole, medicate, mend, minister to, nurse, palliate, rectify, redress, reha-bilitate, relieve, remedy, repair, restore, right, treat; ▪ *Ant* depress, hurt, injure.

curious [adj1] *desiring knowledge, un-derstanding* ▪ *Syn* analytical, disquisi-tive, impertinent, inquisitive, interested, interfering, intrusive, investigative, med-dlesome, nosy, prurient, prying, ques-tioning, scrutinizing, searching,

tampering; ▪ *Ant* disinterested, incuri-ous, indifferent, uninterested.

curious [adj2] *very odd*
▪ *Syn* bizarre, exotic, extraordinary, mar-velous, mysterious, novel, oddball, pecu-liar, quaint, queer, rare, singular, strange, unique, unorthodox, unusual, weird, wonderful; ▪ *Ant* average, conventional, normal, ordinary, typical, usual.

curl [v] *bend, loop*
▪ *Syn* buckle, coil, contort, convolute, corkscrew, crimp, crook, curve, entwine, fold, frizz, indent, kink, lap, meander, ringlet, ripple, roll, scallop, snake, spiral, swirl, turn, twine, twirl, twist, undulate, wave, wind, wreathe, writhe, zigzag; ▪ *Ant* align, straighten, unwind.

current [adj] *contemporary; common*
▪ *Syn* accepted, accustomed, customary, existent, fashionable, general, in circula-tion, in progress, instant, in the news, in vogue, modern, ongoing, popular, present, present-day, prevailing, preva-lent, regnant, ruling, topical, trendy, up-to-date, widespread; ▪ *Ant* antiquated, old, old-fashioned, past, uncommon, un-contemporary.

cursed [adj1] *damned, doomed for bad ending* ▪ *Syn* accursed, blighted, cast out, confounded, excommunicate, execrable, fey, foredoomed, ill-fated, infernal, star-crossed, unholy; ▪ *Ant* blessed.

cursed [adj2] *detestable, hateful*
▪ *Syn* abominable, accursed, atrocious, damnable, detestable, disgusting, execra-ble, fiendish, flatitous, heinous, infa-mous, loathsome, odious, pernicious, pestilential, vile; ▪ *Ant* great, kind, nice, sweet.

cursory [adj] *casual, hasty*
▪ *Syn* brief, careless, desultory, fast, hap-hazard, offhand, passing, quick, random, shallow, sketchy, slapdash, slight, sum-mary, superficial, swift; ▪ *Ant* complete, meticulous, painstaking, perfect, thor-ough, unhurried.

curt [adj] *abrupt, rude*
▪ *Syn* blunt, breviloquent, brief, brusque, churlish, concise, gruff, laconic, offhand, peremptory, pithy, short, succinct, sum-mary, tart, terse; ▪ *Ant* ceremonious, civil, discursive, gracious, lengthy, po-lite.

curtail [v] *cut short; abridge*
▪ *Syn* abbreviate, boil down, chop, con-tract, decrease, diminish, dock, halt,-

lessen, lop, pare down, reduce, shorten, slash, trim, truncate; ▪ *Ant* extend, increase, lengthen, prolong.

curvaceous [*adj*] *voluptuous, full-figured* ▪ *Syn* buxom, rounded, shapely, statuesque, well-rounded, zaftig; ▪ *Ant* flat, skinny, spare.

curve [*v*] *bend in a shape or course* ▪ *Syn* arc, arch, bend, bow, buckle, bulge, coil, crook, curl, deviate, divert, gyrate, hook, incurve, inflect, loop, round, skew, snake, spiral, stoop, swerve, turn, twist, veer, wind, wreathe; ▪ *Ant* straighten.

custody [*n*] *confinement, jailing* ▪ *Syn* arrest, detention, duress, imprisonment, incarceration, jail, keeping; ▪ *Ant* freedom, liberation, liberty.

customarily [*adv*] *ordinarily; as a rule* ▪ *Syn* as a matter of course, as usual, commonly, consistently, conventionally, frequently, generally, habitually, naturally, normally, regularly, routinely, traditionally, usually; ▪ *Ant* differently, divergently, occasionally, rarely, sometimes.

customary [*adj*] *usual, established* ▪ *Syn* accepted, accustomed, acknowledged, common, conventional, established, everyday, familiar, fashionable, general, habitual, normal, ordinary, orthodox, popular, prescriptive, recognized, regular, regulation, routine, standard, stipulated, traditional, understood, wonted; ▪ *Ant* abnormal, different, irregular, occasional, rare, sometime, unusual.

cut [*v1*] *shorten, reduce* ▪ *Syn* abbreviate, abridge, bob, clip, condense, contract, crop, curtail, decrease, delete, dock, excise, lessen, lower, mow, pare, ration, reduce, shave, slash, slim, trim, truncate; ▪ *Ant* increase, lengthen.

cut [*v2*] *ignore, avoid* ▪ *Syn* disregard, duck, evade, insult, neglect, ostracize, pain, shirk, slight, snub, spurn, sting, turn aside; ▪ *Ant* confront, face, greet.

cut [*v3*] *dilute* ▪ *Syn* impair, thin, undermine, weaken; ▪ *Ant* add, enhance.

cutback [*n*] *reduction* ▪ *Syn* curtailment, cut, decrease, decrement, economy, lessening, retrenchment, shortening; ▪ *Ant* increase, raise.

cut back [*v*] *economize* ▪ *Syn* check, clip, curb, curtail, cut, cut down, decrease, lessen, lower, pare, prune, reduce, retrench, shave, shorten, slash, trim; ▪ *Ant* spend.

cute [*adj*] *perky, attractive* ▪ *Syn* adorable, beautiful, charming, dainty, delightful, pleasant, pretty; ▪ *Ant* homely, ugly, unattractive.

cut off [*v1*] *prevent; interrupt* ▪ *Syn* block, break in, catch, disconnect, halt, intercept, intersect, intervene, intrude, isolate, obstruct, renounce, segregate, separate, sequester; ▪ *Ant* allow, encourage, permit.

cut off [*v2*] *disinherit in will* ▪ *Syn* cut out of will, disown, renounce, ▪ *Ant* endow, give.

cut out [*v*] *excise, remove* ▪ *Syn* carve, delete, displace, eliminate, exclude, exsect, extirpate, extract, oust, pull out, refrain from, sever, stop, supersede, supplant, usurp; ▪ *Ant* add, include.

cut out for [*adj*] *adapted* ▪ *Syn* adequate, competent, designed, equipped, fit, fitted, good for, qualified, suitable, suited; ▪ *Ant* inadequate, incompetent, unfitted, unqualified, unsuitable, unsuited, wrong.

cut short [*v*] *bring to an end; leave unfinished* ▪ *Syn* abbreviate, abort, abridge, break off, check, diminish, end, finish, halt, hinder, interrupt, postpone, quit, shorten, stop, terminate; ▪ *Ant* continue, lengthen, prolong.

cutting [*adj*] *nasty, hateful* ▪ *Syn* acerbic, acid, acrimonious, barbed, bitter, caustic, hurtful, incisive, malicious, pointed, raw, sarcastic, sardonic, scathing, sharp, stinging, trenchant, wounding; ▪ *Ant* consoling, kind, mild, pleasant, soothing.

cut up [*v*] *be rowdy* ▪ *Syn* act up, caper, cavort, clown, fool around, horse, joke, misbehave, play, romp, roughhouse, show off; ▪ *Ant* behave, be serious, heed, mind, obey.

cynical [*adj*] *nonbelieving; doubtful* ▪ *Syn* contemptuous, derisive, ironic, pessimistic, sardonic, scoffing, skeptical, sneering, suspicious; ▪ *Ant* believing, hopeful, optimistic, trusting, undoubting.

D

dab [n] *small quantity*
▪ *Syn* bit, dollop, drop, fleck, flick, pat, peck, smidgen, smudge, speck, spot, touch; ▪ *Ant* glob, mass.

dabble [v] *play at; tinker*
▪ *Syn* amuse oneself with, dally, idle, play, toy with, trifle; ▪ *Ant* be into, be proficient, take seriously.

daft [adj] *stupid; crazy*
▪ *Syn* absurd, asinine, demented, deranged, flaky, giddy, idiotic, inane, lunatic, mad, nuts, ridiculous, silly, witless; ▪ *Ant* judicious, rational, sane, sensible, sound, wise.

daily [adj] *occurring every day; during the day* ▪ *Syn* circadian, common, commonplace, cyclic, diurnal, everyday, often, ordinary, per diem, periodic, quotidian, regular, routine; ▪ *Ant* at night, intermittent, nightly, nocturnal, periodic, sporadic.

dainty [adj1] *delicate, fragile, fine*
▪ *Syn* airy, diaphanous, elegant, exquisite, fragile, frail, graceful, light, lovely, neat, petite, precious, rare, recherché, subtle, tasteful; ▪ *Ant* clumsy, coarse, harsh, heavy, rough, vulgar.

dainty [adj2] *finicky, particular*
▪ *Syn* choosy, delicate, fastidious, fussy, mincing, nice, perceptive, refined, scrupulous, tasteful; ▪ *Ant* accepting, easy.

dally [v] *dawdle, delay*
▪ *Syn* drag, fritter away, idle, lag, procrastinate, put off, tarry, trail, trifle with, waste time, while away; ▪ *Ant* hasten, hurry, push, rush.

dam [v] *hold back; block*
▪ *Syn* bar, barricade, brake, check, choke, clog, close, confine, hinder, hold in, impede, obstruct, repress, restrain, restrict, retard, slow, stop up, suppress; ▪ *Ant* free, let go, liberate, release, unblock, unclog, unloose.

damage [v] *cause injury, loss*
▪ *Syn* abuse, batter, blight, break, contaminate, corrode, corrupt, deface, defile, disfigure, harm, hurt, impair, incapacitate, injure, lacerate, maim, mangle, mar, mutilate, pollute, ravage, rot, ruin, scathe, scorch, scratch, smash, split, spoil, stab, stain, tarnish, tear, undermine, wound, wreck, wrong; ▪ *Ant* benefit, bless, enhance, favor, fix, improve, mend, perfect, repair.

damaged [adj] *broken, not working*
▪ *Syn* beat-up, bent, blemished, down, flawed, hurt, impaired, imperfect, injured, in need of repair, in poor condition, marred, run-down, shot, spoiled, unsound; ▪ *Ant* fixed, mended, perfect, repaired, unbroken, undamaged, working.

damaging [adj] *harmful*
▪ *Syn* bad, deleterious, detrimental, disadvantageous, evil, injurious, nocuous, prejudicial, ruinous; ▪ *Ant* beneficial, favorable, helpful, innocuous.

damn [v] *condemn, denounce*
▪ *Syn* abuse, attack, blaspheme, castigate, censure, convict, curse, excoriate, execrate, imprecate, jinx, objurgate, proscribe, punish, revile, sentence, slam; ▪ *Ant* bless, cherish, commend, elevate, exalt, favor, glorify, laud, praise, promote.

damp [adj] *wet, humid*
▪ *Syn* clammy, cloudy, dank, dewy, dripping, drizzly, misty, moist, muggy, oozy, saturated, soaked, sodden, soggy, steamy, sticky, vaporous, waterlogged; ▪ *Ant* arid, desiccated, dried, dry, parched.

dampen [v1] *make wet*
▪ *Syn* bedew, besprinkle, humidify, moisten, rinse, spray, sprinkle, water, wet; ▪ *Ant* blot, drain, dry, towel, wipe.

dampen [v2] *spoil spirits*
▪ *Syn* chill, cloud, cool, curb, deject, depress, diminish, discourage, dismay, dispirit, dull, humble, inhibit, moderate, muffle, mute, restrain, stifle; ▪ *Ant* brighten, encourage, hearten, inspirit, uplift.

dandy [adj] *fine, excellent*
▪ *Syn* capital, exemplary, famous, first-class, first-rate, glorious, grand, great, keen, marvelous, model, neat, nifty, paragon, prime, splendid, superior, swell, terrific; ▪ *Ant* bad, inferior, not good, second-rate, unacceptable.

dangerous [adj] *hazardous, troubling*
▪ *Syn* alarming, bad, chancy, critical, deadly, exposed, fatal, formidable, impending, impregnable, jeopardous, malignant, perilous, precarious, risky, serious, shaky, terrible, threatening, treacherous, urgent, vulnerable, wicked; ▪ *Ant* careful, guarded, healthy, safe, secure, unhazardous, untroubled.

dangerously [*adv*] *precariously*
- *Syn* alarmingly, critically, desperately, gravely, harmfully, hazardously, perilously, precariously, recklessly, seriously, severely; - *Ant* carefully, on guard, safely, securely.

dank [*adj*] *clammy*
- *Syn* chilly, close, damp, dewy, humid, moist, muggy, slimy, soggy, steamy, sticky, wet; - *Ant* dry, parched.

dare [*v*] *take a risk; be courageous*
- *Syn* adventure, attempt, brave, endanger, endeavor, gamble, hazard, presume, risk, speculate, stake, try, undertake, venture; - *Ant* be careful, hold back, refrain.

daring [*adj*] *adventurous*
- *Syn* audacious, bold, brave, cheeky, courageous, fearless, foolhardy, forward, game, gritty, impudent, impulsive, intrepid, nervy, obtrusive, plucky, rash, reckless, temerarious, valiant, venturesome; - *Ant* afraid, bashful, chicken, cowardly, fearful, meek, shy, timid, unadventurous, unwilling.

dark [*adj1*] *lack of light*
- *Syn* aphotic, black, caliginous, cloudy, crepuscular, dim, dull, dusky, faint, ill-lighted, indistinct, inky, lurid, murky, nebulous, obscure, opaque, overcast, pitch-black, shadowy, shady, sooty, stygian, sunless, tenebrous, unlit, vague; - *Ant* bright, brilliant, illuminated, light, lucid, luminous, radiant, shining, visible, vivid.

dark [*adj2*] *hidden, secret*
- *Syn* abstruse, arcane, cabalistic, complicated, concealed, cryptic, deep, Delphian, enigmatic, esoteric, intricate, mysterious, mystic, mystical, mystifying, obscure, occult, puzzling, recondite; - *Ant* apparent, distinct, evident, manifest, plain, visible.

dark [*adj3*] *grim, hopeless*
- *Syn* bleak, cheerless, dismal, doleful, drab, foreboding, gloomy, joyless, morbid, morose, mournful, ominous, sinister, somber, unpropitious; - *Ant* bright, brilliant, encouraging, hopeful, shining.

dark [*adj4*] *evil, satanic*
- *Syn* bad, corrupt, damnable, foul, hellish, horrible, immoral, infamous, infernal, nefarious, sinful, sinister, vile, wicked; - *Ant* good, moral.

darken [*v*] *become shaded, unlit*
- *Syn* becloud, blacken, cloud over, deepen, dim, eclipse, fog, gray, haze, obscure, overcast, overshadow, shade, shadow; - *Ant* brighten, illuminate, illumine, lighten, whiten.

darling [*n*] *sweetheart, favorite person*
- *Syn* beloved, boyfriend, dear, dearest, dear one, flame, friend, girlfriend, love, lover, precious; - *Ant* enemy, foe.

dash [*v1*] *run very fast for short distance*
- *Syn* bolt, bound, career, charge, chase, course, dart, fly, gallop, hasten, hurry, lash, race, rush, scamper, scoot, scurry, shoot, speed, spring, sprint, tear; - *Ant* dally, languish, saunter.

dash [*v2*] *discourage, frustrate*
- *Syn* abash, beat, blast, chagrin, chill, circumvent, cloud, confound, dampen, disappoint, discomfort, dismay, dispirit, foil, ruin, spoil, thwart; - *Ant* aid, assist, encourage, help, inspirit.

dashing [*adj*] *bold, flamboyant*
- *Syn* adventurous, chic, dapper, debonair, exuberant, fashionable, fearless, gallant, gay, jaunty, keen, lively, modish, plucky, rousing, smart, spirited, sporty, stylish, vivacious; - *Ant* boring, calm, drab, dull, plain, unimpressive, unstylish.

daunt [*v*] *frighten, alarm*
- *Syn* appall, baffle, browbeat, bully, consternate, cow, deter, discourage, dismay, dispirit, foil, horrify, intimidate, overawe, scare, shake, terrify, thwart; - *Ant* aid, assist, embolden, encourage, hearten, help, incite, inspirit, stimulate, urge.

dauntless [*adj*] *bold, courageous*
- *Syn* brave, daring, doughty, fearless, gallant, game, heroic, intrepid, lionhearted, resolute, stouthearted, valiant, valorous; - *Ant* afraid, daunted, discouraged, disheartened, fearful, frightened, intimidated, scared, terrified.

dawdle [*v*] *delay; waste time*
- *Syn* amble, dally, drag, idle, lag, laze, loaf, loiter, loll, lounge, procrastinate, saunter, stroll, tarry, trifle, wait, waste; - *Ant* forward, hasten, hurry, push, rush, speed.

dawn [*v*] *start*
- *Syn* appear, begin, emerge, glimmer, initiate, lighten, loom, open, originate, rise, unfold; - *Ant* end, finish, set.

day [*n*] *light part of every 24 hours*
- *Syn* bright, daylight, daytime, diurnal course, light, light of day, mean solar day, nautical day, sidereal day, sunlight,

sunrise-to-sunset, sunshine, working day; ▪ *Ant* evening, night, nighttime.

daybreak [n] *beginning of light hours*
▪ *Syn* aurora, break of day, bright, cockcrow, dawn, daylight, early bright, first light, morn, morning, sunrise, sunup; ▪ *Ant* darkness, eventide, sundown, sunset.

dazed [adj] *confused, shocked*
▪ *Syn* addled, astounded, befogged, befuddled, bewildered, confounded, flabbergasted, fuddled, mystified, numbed, overwhelmed, perplexed, petrified, puzzled, staggered, startled, stunned, stupefied, surprised; ▪ *Ant* alert, aroused, awake, aware, expectant.

dazzle [v] *confuse, amaze*
▪ *Syn* astonish, awe, blind, blur, daze, excite, fascinate, hypnotize, impress, overpower, overwhelm, stupefy, surprise; ▪ *Ant* bore, jade, tax, weary.

dead [adj1] *no longer alive*
▪ *Syn* bereft of life, deceased, defunct, departed, erased, expired, extinct, gone, inanimate, late, lifeless, perished, spiritless, stiff; ▪ *Ant* alive, animate, animated, being, existent, existing, live, living, subsisting.

dead [adj2] *indifferent, cold*
▪ *Syn* anesthetized, apathetic, callous, deadened, dull, flat, frigid, glazed, inert, insensitive, insipid, numb, paralyzed, spiritless, stagnant, still, torpid, vapid, wooden; ▪ *Ant* active, animated, interested, live, living, responsive, spirited, warm.

dead [adj3] *not working*
▪ *Syn* defunct, inactive, inoperable, inoperative, lost, obsolete, spent, stagnant, still, tired, useless, worn, worn out; ▪ *Ant* active, alive, animated, live, operative, working.

deaden [v] *diminish, muffle, quiet*
▪ *Syn* abate, anesthetize, benumb, blunt, cushion, damp, depress, deprive, desensitize, dim, dull, frustrate, hush, impair, injure, lessen, mute, numb, paralyze, quieten, repress, retard, slow, smother, stifle, stun, stupefy, suppress, tire, tone down, weaken; ▪ *Ant* amplify, animate, build, enliven, heighten, increase, strengthen.

deadlock [n] *stalemate, impasse*
▪ *Syn* cessation, checkmate, corner, dead end, dilemma, draw, gridlock, halt, pause, plight, predicament, quandary,

standstill, tie; ▪ *Ant* agreement, breakthrough.

deadly [adj] *causing end of life*
▪ *Syn* carcinogenic, dangerous, deleterious, destructive, fatal, grim, injurious, killing, lethal, malignant, mortal, murderous, noxious, pernicious, poisonous, toxic, venomous, virulent; ▪ *Ant* animating, energizing, harmless, healthful, healthy, invigorating, wholesome.

deaf [adj] *unwilling to listen*
▪ *Syn* blind, headstrong, indifferent, intractable, oblivious, obstinate, pertinacious, perverse, self-willed, strongwilled, stubborn; ▪ *Ant* attentive, aware, conscious, listening, willing.

deal [n] *agreement, bargain*
▪ *Syn* accord, arrangement, compromise, contract, pact, pledge, prearrangement, transaction, understanding; ▪ *Ant* disagreement, misunderstanding.

deal [v1] *do business*
▪ *Syn* bargain, barter, bicker, buy and sell, handle, negotiate, sell, stock, swap, trade, traffic; ▪ *Ant* deny, refuse.

deal [v2] *distribute*
▪ *Syn* administer, allot, apportion, assign, bestow, deliver, disburse, dispense, disperse, disseminate, distribute, divide, hand out, impart, inflict, measure, mete out, partition, render, reward, share; ▪ *Ant* collect, gather, hold, keep, receive, take back.

dean [n] *leader of institution*
▪ *Syn* administrator, authority, dignitary, guide, lead, legislator, pilot, president, principal, professor, senior; ▪ *Ant* pupil, student.

dear [adj1] *beloved, favorite*
▪ *Syn* cherished, darling, endeared, esteemed, familiar, intimate, loved, pet, precious, prized, respected, treasured; ▪ *Ant* common, despised, hateful, unimportant, valueless, worthless.

dear [adj2] *very expensive*
▪ *Syn* costly, fancy, high, high-priced, overpriced, prized, steep, valuable; ▪ *Ant* cheap, inexpensive, low-priced, valueless, worthless.

dearth [n] *insufficiency, scarcity*
▪ *Syn* absence, deficiency, famine, inadequacy, lack, meagerness, need, poverty, privation, rareness, scantiness, shortage, sparsity, want; ▪ *Ant* abundance, excess, plentifulness, plenty, plethora, sufficiency.

death [n] *end of life*
▪ *Syn* annihilation, bereavement, casualty, decease, departure, end, exit, extermination, extinction, fatality, finish, grave, loss, mortality, necrosis, obliteration, oblivion, parting, passing, quietus, repose, termination; ▪ *Ant* being, birth, entity, existence, life, living.

deathly [adj1] *suggesting end of life*
▪ *Syn* appalling, cadaverous, deathlike, dreadful, gaunt, ghastly, grim, gruesome, haggard, horrible, macabre, pallid, wan, wasted; ▪ *Ant* animated, beginning, blooming, blossoming, lively.

deathly [adj2] *fatal*
▪ *Syn* deadly, extreme, lethal, mortal, noxious, pestilent, pestilential; ▪ *Ant* benign, harmless, healthful, healthy, lifegiving, strengthening.

debacle [n] *catastrophe*
▪ *Syn* breakdown, collapse, defeat, devastation, disaster, dissolution, downfall, drubbing, failure, fiasco, havoc, overthrow, rout, ruin, trouncing, wreck; ▪ *Ant* boon, miracle, success, triumph, victory, wonder.

debase [v1] *degrade, shame*
▪ *Syn* abase, cast down, cheapen, debauch, debilitate, demean, demoralize, deprave, devalue, disgrace, dishonor, enfeeble, humble, humiliate, lower, reduce, sap, sink, undermine, weaken; ▪ *Ant* elevate, honor, laud, praise, upgrade, value.

debase [v2] *adulterate*
▪ *Syn* abase, contaminate, corrupt, defile, depreciate, impair, load, pervert, pollute, spoil, taint, vitiate, worsen; ▪ *Ant* clean, clear, enhance, improve, purify.

debatable [adj] *controversial*
▪ *Syn* arguable, borderline, contestable, disputable, doubtful, dubious, moot, questionable, uncertain, undecided, unsettled; ▪ *Ant* certain, inarguable, incontrovertible, indubitable, sure, uncontestable, undoubted.

debate [v] *argue, discuss*
▪ *Syn* agitate, altercate, bicker, confute, contest, controvert, deliberate, dispute, oppose, pettifog, prove, question, reason, rebut, refute, set to, wrangle; ▪ *Ant* agree, concur, go along.

debauched [adj] *violated, corrupted*
▪ *Syn* abandoned, corrupt, debased, defiled, degraded, depraved, immoral, licentious, perverted, reprobate, wanton,

wicked; ▪ *Ant* clean, cleansed, improved, pure, purified, unpolluted, virtuous.

debilitate [v] *incapacitate*
▪ *Syn* attenuate, devitalize, disable, emasculate, enervate, enfeeble, eviscerate, extenuate, harm, injure, mar, prostrate, sap, undermine, weaken; ▪ *Ant* aid, assist, cure, energize, help, invigorate, mend, strengthen.

debonair [adj] *charming, elegant*
▪ *Syn* affable, buoyant, casual, cheerful, courteous, dashing, happy, jaunty, lighthearted, nonchalant, pleasant, refined, smooth, suave, urbane, well-bred; ▪ *Ant* awkward, clumsy, gauche, inelegant.

debt [n] *money owed to others*
▪ *Syn* arrears, bill, check, claim, credit, debit, deficit, dues, duty, encumbrance, indebtedness, invoice, liability, manifest, mortgage, note, obligation, promissory note, receipt, responsibility, score, tab, tally, voucher; ▪ *Ant* asset, cash, credit, excess, profit.

debunk [v] *disprove, ridicule*
▪ *Syn* deflate, demystify, discover, disparage, expose, mock, puncture, uncloak, unmask; ▪ *Ant* prove, support, uphold.

debut [n] *first public appearance*
▪ *Syn* admission, appearance, beginning, bow, entrance, entreé, graduation, inauguration, initiation, introduction, presentation; ▪ *Ant* closing, finale.

decadent [adj] *corrupt, self-indulgent*
▪ *Syn* debased, debauched, degenerate, degraded, depraved, dissolute, evil, lost, moribund, overripe, wanton, wicked; ▪ *Ant* abstemious, benevolent, good, humble, kind, moral.

decay [v] *deteriorate, crumble*
▪ *Syn* atrophy, blight, collapse, corrode, crumble, decline, decompose, depreciate, disintegrate, lessen, molder, mortify, putrefy, rot, sap, shrivel, sink, spoil, suppurate, turn, wane, waste away, weaken; ▪ *Ant* build, develop, flourish, germinate, grow, improve, ripen, strengthen.

decease [v] *pass away; expire*
▪ *Syn* cease, depart, die, go, pass, pass away, pass on, pass over, perish, succumb; ▪ *Ant* arrive, bear, be born.

deceitful [adj] *dishonest, insincere*
▪ *Syn* artful, crafty, cunning, delusive, disingenuous, duplicitous, fallacious, fraudulent, furtive, guileful, hypocritical,

illusory, indirect, insidious, insincere, lying, mendacious, misleading, stealthy, subtle, treacherous, tricky, underhanded; ▪ **Ant** faithful, frank, honest, ingenuous, loyal, open, sincere, trustworthy, truthful, upright.

deceive [v] *mislead; be dishonest*
▪ **Syn** beat, beat out of, beguile, betray, bilk, burn, cheat, circumvent, con, defraud, delude, disappoint, double-cross, dupe, ensnare, entrap, fake, falsify, fleece, fool, gouge, gull, hoax, hoodwink, outwit, rob, scam, sell, skin, swindle, take in, trick, victimize; ▪ **Ant** disabuse, enlighten, guide.

decent [adj1] *respectable, appropriate*
▪ **Syn** befitting, chaste, clean, comme il faut, continent, decorous, ethical, fit, fitting, good, honorable, immaculate, mannerly, moral, noble, polite, proper, prudent, reserved, right, seemly, spotless, stainless, standard, straight, suitable, thoughtful, trustworthy, upright, virtuous, worthy; ▪ **Ant** inappropriate, indecent, poor, unrespectable, unsuitable, unsuited.

decent [adj2] *kind, generous*
▪ **Syn** accommodating, courteous, friendly, gracious, helpful, obliging, virtuous; ▪ **Ant** disobliging, indecent, unaccommodating, ungenerous, unkind.

decent [adj3] *sufficient, tolerable*
▪ **Syn** adequate, ample, average, competent, enough, fair, good, mediocre, middling, passable, reasonable, satisfactory, tolerable; ▪ **Ant** insufficient, intolerable, unsuitable.

deceptive [adj] *dishonest*
▪ **Syn** ambiguous, deceitful, delusory, designing, disingenuous, fake, fraudulent, illusory, indirect, insidious, misleading, mock, oblique, phony, serpentine, slick, slippery, sly, sneaky, specious, spurious, subtle, treacherous, tricky, underhanded, wily; ▪ **Ant** forthright, frank, honest, open, truthful, upright.

decide [v] *make a determination; settle an issue* ▪ **Syn** adjudge, adjudicate, award, choose, conclude, conjecture, decree, determine, elect, end, establish, figure, gather, guess, judge, mediate, opt, pick, poll, purpose, resolve, rule, select, set, surmise, vote, will; ▪ **Ant** defer, delay, hesitate, postpone, procrastinate, put off, vacillate, wait.

decided [adj1] *certain, definite*
▪ **Syn** absolute, assured, categorical, clear, clear-cut, destined, determined, distinct, emphatic, explicit, express, fated, indisputable, positive, prearranged, predetermined, pronounced, resolved, settled, sure, unalterable, undeniable, undisputed; ▪ **Ant** ambiguous, indefinite, questionable, uncertain, undecided.

decided [adj2] *determined, strong-willed*
▪ **Syn** assertive, bent, certain, decisive, deliberate, earnest, emphatic, established, firm, fixed, inflexible, intent, positive, purposeful, resolute, serious, settled, sure; ▪ **Ant** deferential, delaying, hesitant, postponing, procrastinating, undecided.

deciding [adj] *determining*
▪ **Syn** conclusive, critical, crucial, important, influential, key, necessary, prime, principal, significant; ▪ **Ant** inconclusive, insignificant, secondary, trivial, uncritical, unimportant.

decipher [v] *figure out, understand*
▪ **Syn** analyze, break, break down, cipher, construe, crack, decode, deduce, disentangle, elucidate, explain, expound, interpret, read, render, reveal, solve, spell, translate, understand, unfold, unravel; ▪ **Ant** code, encode, scramble.

decisive [adj] *definite*
▪ **Syn** absolute, assured, certain, conclusive, definitive, fateful, final, firm, forceful, imperative, incisive, intent, momentous, peremptory, positive, resolute, resolved, set, settled, strong-minded, trenchant; ▪ **Ant** inconclusive, indecisive, indefinite, procrastinating.

deck [v] *dress up, decorate*
▪ **Syn** accouter, adorn, appoint, array, attire, beautify, bedeck, clothe, dress, embellish, festoon, garland, garnish, grace, ornament, primp; ▪ **Ant** denude, disrobe, strip, unclothe.

declare [v1] *make known clearly or officially* ▪ **Syn** acknowledge, advance, advocate, affirm, allege, announce, argue, assert, attest, aver, avow, certify, cite, claim, confess, confirm, contend, convey, demonstrate, disclose, enunciate, inform, insist, maintain, manifest, notify, pass, proclaim, profess, promulgate, pronounce, propound, publish, reaffirm, reassert, render, repeat, reveal, show, sound, state, stress, swear, tell, testify, validate, vouch; ▪ **Ant** deny, disavow, retract.

declare [v2] *claim as possession*
▪ *Syn* acknowledge, admit, avouch, avow, disclose, divulge, impart, indicate, manifest, notify, own, profess, represent, reveal, state, swear; ▪ *Ant* deny, disclaim.

decline [v1] *say no*
▪ *Syn* abjure, abstain, avoid, balk, bypass, demur, deny, desist, disapprove, dismiss, forbear, forgo, gainsay, pass on, refrain, refuse, reject, renounce, reprobate, repudiate, send regrets, spurn, turn down; ▪ *Ant* accept, agree, confirm, say yes.

decline [v2] *lessen, become less*
▪ *Syn* abate, backslide, decrease, degenerate, depreciate, deteriorate, diminish, disintegrate, ebb, fade, fail, flag, lapse, lower, pine, recede, relapse, retrograde, return, sag, settle, shrink, sink, slide, subside, wane, weaken, worsen; ▪ *Ant* burgeon, improve, increase, mount, rise.

decline [v3] *descend*
▪ *Syn* dip, droop, drop, fall, go down, lower, sag, set, settle, sink, slant, slope; ▪ *Ant* ascend, go up, rise.

decompose [v1] *rot, break up*
▪ *Syn* crumble, decay, disintegrate, dissolve, fester, molder, putrefy, putrefy, spoil, taint, turn; ▪ *Ant* combine, develop, grow, improve.

decompose [v2] *analyze by taking apart*
▪ *Syn* anatomize, atomize, break down, disintegrate, dissect, dissolve, distill, resolve, separate; ▪ *Ant* combine, join, put together, unite.

decorative [adj] *beautifying*
▪ *Syn* cosmetic, embellishing, enhancing, fancy, florid, ornamental, pretty; ▪ *Ant* detracting, ugly.

decorous [adj] *appropriate, suitable*
▪ *Syn* becoming, befitting, conventional, correct, decent, dignified, elegant, fitting, formal, polite, prim, proper, punctilious, refined, respectable, right, seemly, staid, well-behaved; ▪ *Ant* impolite, inappropriate, indecent, indecorous, unbecoming, unfit, unrefined, unseemly, unsuitable.

decorum [n] *appropriate behavior, good manners* ▪ *Syn* breeding, civility, conduct, convention, correctness, decency, demeanor, deportment, dignity, etiquette, form, gentility, habits, order, politeness, politesse, properness, propriety, protocol, punctilio, respectability, seemliness;

▪ *Ant* bad behavior, bad manners, impoliteness, indecency, rudeness.

decrease [v] *grow less or make less*
▪ *Syn* abate, check, contract, curb, curtail, decline, devaluate, diminish, drop, dry up, dwindle, ease, ebb, evaporate, fade, lighten, lower, modify, quell, reduce, restrain, settle, shrink, shrivel, sink, slacken, slump, soften, subside, wane; ▪ *Ant* add, develop, enlarge, expand, grow, increase, raise.

decrepit [adj] *deteriorated, debilitated, especially as a result of age* ▪ *Syn* aged, anile, antiquated, battered, bedraggled, broken-down, dilapidated, feeble, fragile, haggard, incapacitated, infirm, old, ramshackle, run-down, superannuated, threadbare, tired, wasted, weak; ▪ *Ant* fit, healthy, new, sound, young.

decry [v] *criticize, blame*
▪ *Syn* abuse, belittle, calumniate, censure, condemn, defame, denounce, depreciate, derogate, disparage, malign, opprobriate, reprehend, reprobate, traduce, vilify; ▪ *Ant* applaud, compliment, exalt, laud, praise.

dedicate [v1] *donate, set aside for special use* ▪ *Syn* address, allot, apply, apportion, appropriate, assign, commit, consign, devote, inscribe, offer, pledge, restrict, surrender; ▪ *Ant* misapply, misuse, steal, take.

dedicate [v2] *sanctify*
▪ *Syn* anoint, bless, consecrate, hallow, set apart; ▪ *Ant* alienate, desecrate, misuse.

dedicated [adj] *loyal, hard-working*
▪ *Syn* committed, devoted, enthusiastic, single-minded, sworn, wholehearted, zealous; ▪ *Ant* apathetic, lazy.

deduct [v] *take away or out; reduce*
▪ *Syn* abstract, allow, bate, diminish, discount, dock, lessen, rebate, reduce, remove, roll back, subtract, take, withdraw; ▪ *Ant* add, increase, raise.

deep [adj1] *extending very far, usually down* ▪ *Syn* abysmal, bottomless, broad, buried, distant, far, fathomless, inmost, low, profound, rooted, subaqueous, submarine, submerged, subterranean, sunk, wide, yawning; ▪ *Ant* flat, shallow.

deep [adj2] *abstract, complicated in meaning* ▪ *Syn* abstruse, arcane, complex, Delphic, esoteric, hermetic, intricate, mysterious, obscure, occult, Orphic, profound, recondite, sagacious, serious, Sibylline, wise; ▪ *Ant* frivolous, ignorant, shallow, superficial, trivial, unintelligent.

deep [adj3] *scheming, devious*
▪ *Syn* acute, astute, crafty, cunning, designing, guileful, insidious, intriguing, keen, plotting, sharp, shrewd, sly, tricky, wily; ▪ *Ant* aboveboard, artless, open.

deep [adj4] *absorbed, engrossed in activity* ▪ *Syn* abstracted, centered, engaged, fixed, focused, immersed, intent, into, lost, preoccupied, rapt, wrapped up; ▪ *Ant* flighty, inattentive, superficial, unfocussed.

deep [adj5] *intense in effect on senses*
▪ *Syn* bass, booming, dark, extreme, full-toned, grave, hard, low, low-pitched, profound, resonant, rich, sonorous, strong, vivid; ▪ *Ant* light, pale, quiet, soft.

deepen [v] *make more intense*
▪ *Syn* enhance, expand, extend, grow, heighten, increase, intensify, magnify, mount, redouble, reinforce, rise, rouse, strengthen; ▪ *Ant* lighten, pale, quieten, soften.

deface [v] *mar, mutilate*
▪ *Syn* blemish, contort, damage, deform, disfigure, distort, harm, impair, mangle, misshape, obliterate, ruin, sully, tarnish, vandalize, wreck; ▪ *Ant* adorn, beautify, decorate, embellish, fix, mend, ornament, repair.

defamatory [adj] *libelous, slanderous*
▪ *Syn* abusive, calumnious, contumelious, derogatory, injurious, insulting, opprobrious, vituperative; ▪ *Ant* approving, commending, complimentary, exalting, praising.

defame [v] *inflict libel or slander*
▪ *Syn* asperse, calumniate, denigrate, detract, discredit, disgrace, disparage, knock, malign, pan, roast, scandalize, smear, stigmatize, traduce, vilify; ▪ *Ant* approve, commend, compliment, exalt, praise.

default [n] *failure; want*
▪ *Syn* absence, blemish, dearth, defect, deficiency, delinquency, dereliction, disregard, error, fault, imperfection, inadequacy, lack, lapse, miss, neglect, offense, omission, oversight, privation, shortcoming, slight, transgression, vice, weakness, wrongdoing; ▪ *Ant* advantage, payment, perfection, satisfaction, success.

defeat [v1] *win; conquer*
▪ *Syn* ambush, annihilate, beat, best, crush, decimate, demolish, entrap, halt, impede, obliterate, outmaneuver, overpower, overthrow, parry, rout, sack, sink, slaughter, smash, subdue, subjugate, suppress, surmount, upset, vanquish; ▪ *Ant* capitulate, give up, lose, succumb, surrender.

defeat [v2] *conquer in athletic contest*
▪ *Syn* beat, edge, lambaste, lick, outhit, outplay, outrun, overpower, take, thrash, total, trounce, win; ▪ *Ant* give up, lose, surrender.

defeat [v3] *frustrate*
▪ *Syn* baffle, balk, block, checkmate, circumvent, confound, contravene, counterplot, cross, disconcert, disprove, foil, invalidate, neutralize, nullify, puzzle, quell, refute, ruin, scuttle, spoil, stump, subdue; ▪ *Ant* abet, aid, encourage, help, inspirit.

defect [v] *break from belief, faith*
▪ *Syn* abandon, abscond, apostatize, depart, desert, fall away from, forsake, lapse, leave, quit, rebel, reject, renounce, revolt, turn, withdraw; ▪ *Ant* associate, come in, enlist, join, participate.

defective [adj] *broken, not working*
▪ *Syn* abnormal, amiss, damaged, deficient, faulty, flawed, impaired, imperfect, incomplete, insufficient, lacking, out of order, poor, seconds, sick, subnormal; ▪ *Ant* excellent, faultless, flawless, perfect, unbroken.

defend [v1] *protect*
▪ *Syn* avert, battle, bulwark, conserve, contend, entrench, fend off, fight for, fortify, foster, garrison, guard, hedge, hold at bay, insure, maintain, oppose, preserve, prevent, protect, resist, retain, safeguard, save, screen, secure, shelter, shield, stave off, sustain, uphold, war, ward off, watch over, withstand; ▪ *Ant* abandon, attack, desert, leave, quit, relinquish, resign, surrender.

defend [v2] *show support for*
▪ *Syn* advocate, aid, apologize for, argue, assert, back up, befriend, champion, cover for, endorse, espouse, exculpate, exonerate, guarantee, justify, maintain, plead, rationalize, recommend, second, speak up for, support, sustain, uphold, vindicate, voice, warrant; ▪ *Ant* deny, forsake, renounce.

defenseless [adj] *powerless, vulnerable*
▪ *Syn* endangered, exposed, helpless, indefensible, open, unarmed, weak; ▪ *Ant* guarded, powerful, protected, strong.

defensible [adj] *justifiable*
▪ *Syn* condonable, excusable, logical, pardonable, permissible, plausible, tenable, valid, vindicable, warrantable; ▪ *Ant* indefensible, invalid, unjustifiable, vindicable.

defer [v1] *hold off, put off*
▪ *Syn* adjourn, delay, detain, extend, impede, intermit, lengthen, obstruct, postpone, procrastinate, prolong, prorogue, protract, remit, retard, shelve, slow, stay, suspend, table; ▪ *Ant* advance, expedite, forge, forward, hasten, hurry.

defer [v2] *yield*
▪ *Syn* accede, accommodate, acquiesce, adapt, adjust, admit, agree, assent, bow, buckle, capitulate, cave, comply, concede, obey, submit, succumb, waive; ▪ *Ant* advance, force, forge.

deferential [adj] *respectful, considerate*
▪ *Syn* civil, complaisant, courteous, dutiful, ingratiating, insinuating, obedient, obeisant, obsequious, polite, reverential, submissive; ▪ *Ant* arrogant, disobedient, disrespectful, forceful, immodest, impolite, inconsiderate, noncompliant.

deferred [adj] *put off till a later time*
▪ *Syn* adjourned, charged, delayed, postponed, prolonged, protracted, remanded, renegotiated, scrubbed, stalled, staved off, temporized; ▪ *Ant* advanced, forwarded, furthered, hastened, hurried.

defiant [adj] *disobedient, disregardful*
▪ *Syn* audacious, bold, brazen, contumacious, daring, insolent, insubordinate, mutinous, obstinate, provocative, rebellious, recalcitrant, reckless, refractory, resistant, truculent; ▪ *Ant* acquiescent, obedient, respectful, submissive, submitting, subordinating.

deficient [adj] *imperfect, inadequate*
▪ *Syn* amiss, damaged, defective, exiguous, faulty, flawed, impaired, incomplete, inferior, insufficient, lacking, marred, meager, rare, scant, short, shy, wanting, weak; ▪ *Ant* adequate, ample, enough, excessive, faultless, flawless, perfect, satisfactory, sufficient, superfluous.

deficit [n] *shortage of something needed, required* ▪ *Syn* arrears, defalcation, default, deficiency, dues, inadequacy, insufficiency, lack, loss, paucity,

shortcoming, shortfall; ▪ *Ant* enough, excess, plenty, superfluousness.

deficit spending [n] *paying out in excess of income* ▪ *Syn* debt, debt explosion, deficit financing, being in the red, megadebt, negative cash flow, overspending; ▪ *Ant.* balanced budget, being in the black.

defile [v] *corrupt, violate*
▪ *Syn* abuse, adulterate, besmirch, contaminate, debase, desecrate, dirty, hurt, molest, pollute, soil, stain, sully, taint, vitiate; ▪ *Ant* clean, cleanse, hallow, honor, purify, sanctify.

defiled [adj] *corrupted, violated*
▪ *Syn* besmirched, desecrated, exposed, impure, polluted, profaned, ravished, spoilt, tainted, vitiated; ▪ *Ant* clean, cleansed, hallowed, honorable, pure, purified, sanctified.

define [v] *give description*
▪ *Syn* ascertain, assign, characterize, construe, decide, delineate, denominate, denote, describe, designate, detail, determine, dub, elucidate, entitle, etch, exemplify, explain, expound, formalize, illustrate, interpret, label, name, prescribe, represent, specify, spell out, tag, translate; ▪ *Ant* confuse, distort, tangle, twist.

definite [adj1] *exact, clear*
▪ *Syn* audible, categorical, distinct, downright, explicit, express, forthright, full, graphic, incisive, marked, minute, obvious, palpable, particular, positive, pronounced, ringing, severe, sharp, specific, straightforward, tangible, visible, vivid, well-defined; ▪ *Ant* imprecise, indefinite, indistinct, inexact, obscure, uncertain, unclear, undefined, vague.

definite [adj2] *fixed, certain, positive*
▪ *Syn* assigned, assured, circumscribed, convinced, decided, determinate, determined, established, guaranteed, limited, narrow, precise, prescribed, restricted, set, sure; ▪ *Ant* indeterminate, inexact, uncertain, unfixed, unlimited, vague.

definitely [adv] *certainly*
▪ *Syn* absolutely, categorically, clearly, decidedly, doubtless, easily, explicitly, expressly, finally, indubitably, obviously, plainly, positively, specifically, surely, without fail, without question; ▪ *Ant* doubtfully, dubiously, indefinitely, maybe, perhaps, questionably.

definitive [adj] authoritative
▪ Syn absolute, actual, categorical, complete, conclusive, decisive, determining, exhaustive, express, final, last, perfect, plain, precise, real, reliable, specific, straight out, terminal, ultimate; ▪ Ant incomplete, inconclusive, inexact, interim, temporary, unreliable.

deflate [v1] reduce or cause to contract
▪ Syn collapse, contract, decrease, depreciate, depress, devalue, diminish, empty, exhaust, flatten, puncture, shrink, squash, void; ▪ Ant blow up, expand, inflate.

deflate [v2] humiliate
▪ Syn chasten, dash, debunk, disconcert, dispirit, humble, mortify; ▪ Ant boost, build up, inflate.

defraud [v] cheat, bilk
▪ Syn burn, chouse, circumvent, con, deceive, delude, embezzle, fleece, flimflam, foil, hoax, outwit, pilfer, rob, swindle, trick, victimize; ▪ Ant contribute, help, repay, support.

deft [adj] agile, clever
▪ Syn able, adept, adroit, apt, dexterous, expert, fleet, handy, ingenious, neat, nimble, proficient, prompt, quick, ready, skilled, skillful; ▪ Ant awkward, clumsy, inept, unhandy, unskillful.

defunct [adj] extinct, not functioning
▪ Syn bygone, cold, dead, deceased, expired, gone, invalid, nonexistent, obsolete, vanished; ▪ Ant alive, existent, existing, functioning, live, operating, operative, valid, working.

defy [v] challenge, frustrate
▪ Syn beard, brave, confront, dare, defeat, face, foil, front, oppose, provoke, resist, scorn, slight, spurn, thwart, violate, withstand; ▪ Ant give in, obey, surrender, surrender, yield.

degenerate [adj] corrupt, deteriorated
▪ Syn base, debased, debauched, degraded, dissolute, failing, fallen, immoral, infamous, low, mean, miscreant, nefarious, perverted, rotten, villainous, vitiated, wicked; ▪ Ant healthy, moral, upright, virtuous.

degenerate [v] decay, deteriorate
▪ Syn backslide, corrode, corrupt, decline, decrease, deprave, descend, disintegrate, lapse, regress, retrogress, return, revert, rot, sink, slip, vitiate, worsen; ▪ Ant develop, flourish, improve, revive.

degrade [v] shame, humiliate
▪ Syn abase, belittle, corrupt, debase,

debauch, decry, degenerate, demean, deprave, derogate, deteriorate, detract, discredit, dishonor, disparage, humble, impair, lessen, lower, pervert, reduce; ▪ Ant admire, approve, elevate, honor, promote, upgrade.

dehydrate [v] take moisture out of
▪ Syn desiccate, drain, dry, dry out, dry up, evaporate, exsiccate, parch, sear; ▪ Ant hydrate, moisten, wet.

deify [v] elevate, glorify
▪ Syn adore, apotheosize, consecrate, ennoble, enthrone, exalt, extol, idealize, idolize, immortalize, venerate, worship; ▪ Ant debase, degrade, dishonor, lower.

deign [v] lower oneself
▪ Syn condescend, consent, patronize, stoop, vouchsafe; ▪ Ant be proud, hold head high.

dejected [adj] depressed, blue
▪ Syn abject, black, bleak, cast down, crestfallen, dampened, despondent, disconsolate, discouraged, disheartened, dismal, dispirited, doleful, downcast, gloomy, glum, heavyhearted, lowspirited, melancholy, miserable, moody, morose, sad, spiritless, woebegone, wretched; ▪ Ant cheerful, encouraged, happy, joyous.

delay [v] cause stop in action
▪ Syn adjourn, arrest, bar, block, check, confine, curb, dawdle, detain, deter, discourage, encumber, filibuster, hamper, hold, impede, inhibit, interfere, intermit, lag, linger, loiter, obstruct, postpone, procrastinate, prolong, protract, put off, remand, repress, restrict, retard, slacken, stall, stave off, stay, stop, suspend, table, tarry, temporize, withhold; ▪ Ant advance, dispatch, expedite, further, hasten, hurry, rush, speed.

delectable [adj] delicious, enjoyable
▪ Syn ambrosial, appetizing, choice, delicate, delightful, divine, enticing, gratifying, heavenly, inviting, luscious, palatable, pleasurable, rare, sapid, satisfying, savory, scrumptious, tasty, toothsome; ▪ Ant bad, disagreeable, horrible, nauseating, offensive, repulsive, sickening, unpleasant, unsatisfying.

delegate [v] assign responsibility
▪ Syn authorize, consign, devolve, entrust, give, hand over, relegate, shunt, transfer; ▪ Ant keep, withhold.

delete [v] erase, remove
▪ Syn annul, blot out, cancel, clean, clean

up, cross out, cut, destroy, drop, edit, efface, eliminate, exclude, expunge, obliterate, omit, rub out, trim, wipe out; ▪ *Ant* add, insert, put in.

deleterious [*adj*] *harmful, damaging*
▪ *Syn* destructive, detrimental, hurtful, injurious, mischievous, nocent, nocuous, pernicious, prejudicial, prejudicious, ruinous; ▪ *Ant* aiding, assisting, beneficial, helpful.

deliberate [*adj*] *intentional*
▪ *Syn* advised, calculated, careful, considered, designed, express, fixed, intended, judged, meticulous, planned, premeditated, purposeful, reasoned, schemed, studied, thought out, voluntary, weighed, willful, witting; ▪ *Ant* chance, impetuous, impulsive, unintentional, unmethodical, unsystematic, unwitting.

delicate [*adj1*] *dainty, weak*
▪ *Syn* aerial, choice, delightful, elegant, ethereal, exquisite, faint, filmy, finespun, flimsy, fragile, frail, gauzy, gentle, gossamer, graceful, mild, pale, recherché, select, slight, subdued, subtle, superior, tender; ▪ *Ant* coarse, harsh, heavy, inelegant, robust, rough, strong.

delicate [*adj2*] *sickly*
▪ *Syn* ailing, debilitated, decrepit, feeble, fragile, frail, infirm, sick, slight, susceptible, tender, unhealthy, weak; ▪ *Ant* healthful, healthy, strong.

delicate [*adj3*] *careful, tactful*
▪ *Syn* accurate, adept, cautious, considerate, deft, detailed, diplomatic, discreet, expert, heedful, minute, politic, precise, proficient, prudent, sensitive, skilled, tactical, wary; ▪ *Ant* careless, indelicate, inelegant, insensitive, unscrupulous, vulgar.

delicious [*adj*] *pleasing, especially to the taste* ▪ *Syn* ambrosial, appetizing, choice, dainty, delectable, delightful, divine, enticing, exquisite, good, gratifying, heavenly, luscious, mellow, mouthwatering, nectarous, piquant, rare, rich, sapid, savory, scrumptious, tasty, tempting, toothsome; ▪ *Ant* disagreeable, distasteful, horrible, unpleasant, unsavory.

delight [*v*] *make happy; experience happiness* ▪ *Syn* allure, amuse, attract, charm, cheer, content, divert, enchant, enrapture, entertain, exult, fascinate, gladden, gratify, jubilate, please, ravish, rejoice, satisfy, send, thrill; ▪ *Ant* depress, disappoint, dismay, distress, irk, pain, trouble.

delighted [*adj*] *very happy*
▪ *Syn* captivated, charmed, ecstatic, elated, enchanted, fulfilled, gladdened, joyous, jubilant, overjoyed, pleased, thrilled; ▪ *Ant* depressed, disappointed, dismayed, melancholy, miserable, pained, sorrowful, troubled, unhappy.

delightful [*adj*] *pleasant, charming*
▪ *Syn* adorable, alluring, captivating, congenial, darling, enjoyable, gratifying, lovely, luscious, rapturous, refreshing, satisfying, thrilling; ▪ *Ant* bad, disappointing, horrible, irritating, repugnant, unhappy, unpleasant.

delight in [*v*] *take pleasure from*
▪ *Syn* admire, adore, appreciate, cherish, enjoy, feast on, glory in, indulge in, like, love, luxuriate in, relish, revel in, savor; ▪ *Ant* abhor, dislike, hate.

delinquent [*adj*] *irresponsible, defaulting* ▪ *Syn* behind, blameworthy, careless, censurable, criminal, culpable, derelict, faulty, guilty, lax, negligent, offending, overdue, remiss, reprehensible, slack, tardy; ▪ *Ant* behaving, careful, dutiful, mindful, responsible.

delirious [*adj1*] *mentally imbalanced*
▪ *Syn* aberrant, crazed, demented, deranged, disturbed, hallucinatory, incoherent, irrational, mad; ▪ *Ant* balanced, collected, normal, sane.

delirious [*adj2*] *excited; very happy*
▪ *Syn* corybantic, delighted, ecstatic, enthused, frantic, frenzied, hysterical, intoxicated, mad, overexcited, overwrought, rapturous, thrilled, transported, wild; ▪ *Ant* calm, unexcited, unhappy.

deliver [*v1*] *transfer, carry*
▪ *Syn* bear, bring, cart, convey, distribute, drop, give, hand over, pass, remit, transport, truck; ▪ *Ant* hold, keep, retain.

deliver [*v2*] *relinquish possession*
▪ *Syn* abandon, cede, commit, grant, hand over, resign, surrender, transfer, turn over, yield; ▪ *Ant* capture, limit, restrain, restrict.

deliver [*v3*] *free, liberate*
▪ *Syn* acquit, discharge, emancipate, loose, ransom, redeem, release, rescue, save, set free; ▪ *Ant* confine, detain, imprison, restrain, restrict.

deliver [*v4*] *announce, proclaim*
▪ *Syn* address, broach, communicate, de-

clare, express, impart, present, pronounce, publish, read, say, state, tell, utter, vent, voice; ▪ *Ant* be quiet, keep, withhold.

delude [v] *deceive, fool*
▪ *Syn* beguile, betray, cheat, cozen, illude, misguide, mislead, outfox, string along, take in, trick; ▪ *Ant* be truthful, elucidate, enlighten.

deluge [n] *downpour, flood of something*
▪ *Syn* avalanche, barrage, cataclysm, cataract, flux, inundation, niagara, pour, rush, spate, torrent; ▪ *Ant* abatement, dearth, drought, lack.

delusive [adj] *deceptive*
▪ *Syn* apparent, beguiling, chimerical, deceiving, fallacious, fanciful, fantastic, illusive, illusory, imaginary, ostensible, quixotic, seeming, specious, spurious, visionary; ▪ *Ant* actual, certain, factual, honest, real, truthful.

deluxe [adj] *superior, plush*
▪ *Syn* choice, elegant, exclusive, expensive, exquisite, first-class, grand, luscious, lush, luxurious, opulent, posh, rare, recherche, rich, ritzy, select, special, splendid, sumptuous, super; ▪ *Ant* inferior, ordinary, poor.

demand [v1] *ask strongly for something*
▪ *Syn* appeal, apply, arrogate, beseech, besiege, bid, clamor for, coerce, command, compel, enjoin, entreat, exact, expect, force, implore, importune, inquire, insist on, interrogate, necessitate, oblige, order, pester, petition, postulate, press, question, request, require, solicit, stipulate, sue for, summon, supplicate, tax, urge; ▪ *Ant* give, grant, offer, reply.

demand [v2] *require*
▪ *Syn* ask, call for, command, crave, involve, lack, necessitate, need, oblige, take, want; ▪ *Ant* give, present, supply.

demanding [adj] *challenging, urgent*
▪ *Syn* ambitious, bothersome, clamorous, critical, dictatorial, difficult, exacting, exhausting, exigent, fussy, grievous, hard, imperious, importunate, insistent, onerous, oppressive, querulous, strict, stringent, taxing, tough, troublesome, weighty; ▪ *Ant* easy, facile, trivial, unchallenging, undemanding.

demean [v] *humble, humiliate*
▪ *Syn* abase, belittle, contemn, debase, decry, degrade, derogate, descend, despise, detract, disparage, lower, scorn; ▪ *Ant* boost, enhance, improve, upgrade.

demented [adj] *crazy, insane*
▪ *Syn* daft, delirious, deranged, foolish, frenzied, hysterical, lunatic, mad, maniacal, non compos mentis, psychopathic, psychotic; ▪ *Ant* balanced, rational, reasonable, sane, sensible.

democratic [adj] *representative, self-governing* ▪ *Syn* autonomous, communal, constitutional, egalitarian, equal, free, individualistic, libertarian, orderly, populist, self-ruling; ▪ *Ant* authoritarian, autocratic, communistic, despotic, oligarchic, totalitarian.

demolish [v] *destroy; consume*
▪ *Syn* annihilate, bulldoze, crush, decimate, devastate, devour, dismantle, level, obliterate, overthrow, overturn, pulverize, raze, ruin, tear down, wrack, wreck; ▪ *Ant* build, construct, fix, produce, rebuild, repair, restore.

demonstrable [adj] *provable, evident*
▪ *Syn* ascertainable, attestable, axiomatic, conclusive, deducible, evident, incontrovertible, indubitable, irrefutable, obvious, palpable, positive, verifiable; ▪ *Ant* distorted, doubtful, obscure, undemonstrable, unverifiable, vague.

demonstrate [v1] *display, show*
▪ *Syn* authenticate, determine, establish, evidence, exhibit, expose, flaunt, indicate, make evident, manifest, prove, test, testify to, try, validate; ▪ *Ant* conceal, disguise, hide.

demonstrate [v2] *explain, illustrate*
▪ *Syn* confirm, debunk, describe, express, proclaim, set forth, show how, teach, testify to; ▪ *Ant* confuse, distort, falsify, misrepresent.

demonstrative [adj1] *expressive, communicative* ▪ *Syn* affectionate, candid, effusive, emotional, expansive, expository, frank, histrionic, illustrative, indicative, loving, open, outgoing, outspoken, plain, profuse, symptomatic, tender, warmhearted; ▪ *Ant* cold, cool, inexpressive, reserved, restrained, uncommunicative, undemonstrative, unemotional.

demonstrative [adj2] *conclusive*
▪ *Syn* authenticating, certain, convincing, decisive, definite, final, specific, validating; ▪ *Ant* anticlimactic, confusing, inconclusive, mysterious.

demoralize [v1] *depress, unnerve*
▪ *Syn* abash, chill, cripple, dampen, daunt, debilitate, deject, disarrange, disconcert, discountenance, discourage, dis-

order, disorganize, disparage, disturb, embarrass, enfeeble, nonplus, rattle, sap, shake, undermine, upset, weaken; ▪ *Ant* boost, comfort, encourage, uplift.

demoralize [v2] *corrupt, pervert*
▪ *Syn* bastardize, bestialize, brutalize, debase, debauch, deprave, lower, vitiate, warp; ▪ *Ant* make good, moralize, purify.

demote [v] *downgrade, lower in rank*
▪ *Syn* break, degrade, demean, demerit, dismiss, lower, reduce, relegate; ▪ *Ant* improve, promote, rate, upgrade.

demur [v] *disagree*
▪ *Syn* balk, cavil, challenge, combat, complain, disapprove, dispute, doubt, fight, hesitate, object, oppose, pause, protest, refuse, remonstrate, resist, shy, strain, vacillate, waver; ▪ *Ant* accept, agree, consent, go along.

demure [adj] *modest, affectedly reserved*
▪ *Syn* bashful, blushing, coy, decorous, diffident, humble, prim, proper, reticent, shy, sober, solemn, staid, straitlaced, timid; ▪ *Ant* aggressive, bold, extroverted, outgoing, shameless, strong.

denigrate [v] *belittle, malign*
▪ *Syn* asperse, besmirch, blacken, blister, calumniate, decry, defame, disparage, impugn, libel, revile, scandalize, slander, traduce, vilify; ▪ *Ant* boost, cherish, compliment, praise.

denizen [n] *resident*
▪ *Syn* citizen, dweller, habitant, inhabitant, national, native, occupant, resider; ▪ *Ant* alien, foreigner, immigrant.

denounce [v] *condemn, attack*
▪ *Syn* accuse, adjudicate, blacklist, blame, brand, castigate, censure, charge, criticize, damn, declaim, decry, excoriate, expose, implicate, impugn, ostracize, proscribe, prosecute, rebuke, reprehend, reproach, reprobate, revile, stigmatize, threaten, upbraid, vilify, vituperate; ▪ *Ant* approve, commend, compliment, praise.

dense [adj1] *compressed, thick*
▪ *Syn* close, compact, condensed, crowded, heaped, heavy, impenetrable, jammed, massed, opaque, packed, piled, solid, substantial, thickset; ▪ *Ant* meager, open, scant, scattered, sparse, thin.

dense [adj2] *slow to understand*
▪ *Syn* boorish, doltish, dull, half-witted,

ignorant, lethargic, oafish, obtuse, phlegmatic, simple, sluggish, stolid, thick, torpid; ▪ *Ant* alert, clever, intelligent, smart.

denunciation [n] *condemnation, criticism* ▪ *Syn* accusation, arraignment, blame, castigation, censure, derogation, fulmination, incrimination, indictment, obloquy, reprimand, reprobation, vilification; ▪ *Ant* appreciation, approval, commendation, compliment, praise.

deny [v] *disagree, renounce, decline*
▪ *Syn* abjure, abnegate, ban, contradict, disavow, disbelieve, discredit, disown, disprove, doubt, eschew, forgo, forsake, gainsay, negate, oppose, rebuff, rebut, recant, refute, reject, revoke, spurn, taboo, veto, withhold; ▪ *Ant* accede, acknowledge, admit, affirm, agree, allow, concede, confess, corroborate, go along, grant.

depart [v1] *leave, retreat*
▪ *Syn* abandon, abdicate, absent, decamp, desert, disappear, emigrate, escape, evacuate, exit, go, migrate, part, perish, quit, remove, retire, secede, take leave, tergiversate, vacate, vanish, withdraw; ▪ *Ant* arrive, come, enter.

depart [v2] *diverge from normal, expected* ▪ *Syn* desert, deviate, differ, digress, disagree, dissent, forsake, ramble, reject, repudiate, stray, swerve, vary, veer, wander; ▪ *Ant* abide by, continue, keep to, linger, stay, wait.

departure [n] *leaving*
▪ *Syn* abandonment, adieu, decampment, desertion, egress, embarkation, emigration, escape, evacuation, exit, exodus, expatriation, farewell, flight, hegira, migration, parting, passage, recession, removal, retirement, retreat, separation, stampede, takeoff, vacation, walkout, withdrawal; ▪ *Ant* arrival, coming, entrance.

dependable [adj] *reliable, responsible*
▪ *Syn* certain, constant, faithful, loyal, secure, stable, staunch, steadfast, steady, sturdy, tried-and-true, true, trustworthy, trusty, unfailing; ▪ *Ant* dishonest, irresponsible, uncertain, undependable, unreliable, unsteady, unsure.

dependence/dependency [n] *addiction, need* ▪ *Syn* attachment, habit, hook, security blanket, servility, subjection, subordination, subservience, vulnerability, weakness, yoke; ▪ *Ant* abstinence, independence.

dependent [*adj1*] *reliant upon*
▪ *Syn* abased, clinging, defenseless, humbled, minor, secondary, subordinate, under, vulnerable; ▪ *Ant* independent, mature, strong.

dependent [*adj2*] *contingent, determined by* ▪ *Syn* ancillary, appurtenant, conditional, depending, incidental to, liable to, provisory, regulated by, relative, subject to, subordinate, susceptible; ▪ *Ant* free, independent.

depict [*v*] *describe, render in drawing or writing* ▪ *Syn* characterize, delineate, design, detail, draw, illustrate, interpret, limn, narrate, outline, paint, picture, portray, relate, represent, reproduce, sculpt, sketch, state; ▪ *Ant* confuse, distort, mix up.

deplete [*v*] *consume, exhaust supply*
▪ *Syn* bankrupt, diminish, drain, dry up, empty, evacuate, expend, finish, impoverish, lessen, reduce, sap, spend, squander, undermine, waste, weaken; ▪ *Ant* add, augment, expand, fill, give, increase.

deplorable [*adj*] *unfortunate, shameful*
▪ *Syn* awful, calamitous, dire, disastrous, disgraceful, disreputable, distressing, dolorous, dreadful, execrable, grievous, grim, heartrending, intolerable, lamentable, miserable, opprobrious, pitiable, regrettable, reprehensible, scandalous, sickening, terrible, tragic, unbearable, woeful, wretched; ▪ *Ant* cheerful, delightful, excellent, good, happy, shameless.

deplore [*v*] *regret; condemn*
▪ *Syn* abhor, bemoan, bewail, censure, complain, cry, denounce, deprecate, hate, hurt, lament, moan, mourn, regret, repent, rue, weep; ▪ *Ant* approve, be happy, delight, praise, rejoice, revel.

deport [*v*] *banish*
▪ *Syn* cast out, dismiss, displace, exile, expatriate, expel, extradite, oust, relegate, transport; ▪ *Ant* allow, permit, stay.

deportation [*n*] *banishment*
▪ *Syn* displacement, eviction, exile, expatriation, expulsion, extradition, ostracism, relegation; ▪ *Ant* approval, permission, recall, restoration.

depose [*v*] *oust from position*
▪ *Syn* demote, dethrone, dismiss, displace, eject, impeach, overthrow, sub-

vert, unseat, upset; ▪ *Ant* empower, enthrone, install, invest.

deposit [*v*] *locate, put in place for safekeeping* ▪ *Syn* accumulate, amass, bank, collect, deliver, entrust, garner, hoard, install, invest, lay away, precipitate, put aside, repose, rest, save, settle, stash, stock up, store, stow, treasure; ▪ *Ant* disburse, draw out, spend, take away, take out, withdraw.

depraved [*adj*] *corrupt, immoral*
▪ *Syn* abandoned, base, debased, debauched, degenerate, degraded, dissolute, evil, lascivious, lewd, licentious, low, miscreant, nefarious, perverted, profligate, shameless, sinful, twisted, vicious, vile, wanton, warped, wicked; ▪ *Ant* good, honorable, just, moral, noble, pure, upright, virtuous.

depravity [*n*] *corruption, immorality*
▪ *Syn* baseness, contamination, criminality, debauchery, degradation, depravation, evil, iniquity, lewdness, perversion, sinfulness, vice, wickedness; ▪ *Ant* good, honor, justice, morality, nobility, purity, uprightness, virtue.

deprecate [*v*] *belittle, condemn*
▪ *Syn* depreciate, derogate, detract, discountenance, disfavor, disparage, expostulate, frown, object, take dim view of; ▪ *Ant* approve, build up, commend, compliment, endorse, laud, praise.

depreciate [*v*] *devalue, lose value*
▪ *Syn* abate, cheapen, decay, decrease, deflate, depress, deteriorate, diminish, downgrade, drop, dwindle, erode, fall, lessen, lower, mark down, reduce, underrate, undervalue, worsen; ▪ *Ant* gain value, increase, overrate, raise, rate.

depredation [*n*] *devastation, destruction*
▪ *Syn* burglary, crime, desecration, desolation, despoiling, marauding, pillage, plunder, rapine, robbery, sacking, spoliation, theft; ▪ *Ant* boon, construction, goodness, miracle, wonder.

depress [*v1*] *deject, make despondent; exhaust* ▪ *Syn* afflict, ail, bear down, beat, bother, cast down, damp, dampen, darken, daunt, debilitate, desolate, devitalize, discourage, dismay, dispirit, distress, drain, dull, enervate, faze, lower, mortify, oppress, perturb, press, reduce, sadden, scorn, slow, torment, trouble, try, upset, weaken, weary; ▪ *Ant* cheer, comfort, encourage, excite, hearten, lift, make happy, stimulate.

depress [v2] *devalue*
▪ *Syn* cheapen, debase, depreciate, devaluate, diminish, downgrade, impair, lessen, lower, reduce; ▪ *Ant* increase, raise.

depress [v3] *push down*
▪ *Syn* dip, droop, flatten, level, lower, settle, sink, squash; ▪ *Ant* pull up, push up, raise, uplift.

depressed [adj1] *discouraged*
▪ *Syn* crestfallen, dejected, despondent, disconsolate, dispirited, down, downcast, glum, grim, low, low-spirited, lugubrious, melancholy, moody, morose, pessimistic, sad, spiritless, woebegone; ▪ *Ant* cheerful, comforted, encouraged, happy, satisfied, unburdened.

depressed [adj2] *disadvantaged*
▪ *Syn* depreciated, deprived, destitute, devalued, distressed, impaired, needy, poor, poverty-stricken; ▪ *Ant* blessed, flourishing, prosperous, rich.

depressing [adj] *discouraging, upsetting* ▪ *Syn* black, bleak, disheartening, dismal, dispiriting, dreary, funereal, gloomy, hopeless, joyless, melancholic, melancholy, mournful, oppressive, sad, somber; ▪ *Ant* cheering, encouraging, happy.

depression [n1] *low spirits; despair*
▪ *Syn* abasement, abjection, bleakness, dejection, desolation, despondency, discouragement, distress, dolor, dreariness, dullness, ennui, gloom, gloominess, hopelessness, lowness, melancholy, misery, qualm, sadness, sorrow, trouble, worry; ▪ *Ant* cheerfulness, encouragement, happiness, hope, hopefulness.

depression [n2] *economic decline*
▪ *Syn* bankruptcy, bust, crash, crisis, deflation, downturn, drop, failure, inactivity, inflation, overproduction, panic, paralysis, recession, retrenchment, sag, slide, slump, stagnation, unemployment; ▪ *Ant* recovery, surge.

depression [n3] *concavity, cavity*
▪ *Syn* basin, bowl, crater, dent, dimple, dip, excavation, hole, hollow, impression, indentation, pit, pocket, sink, sinkhole, vacuity, vacuum, valley, void; ▪ *Ant* bulge, convexity, protuberance.

deprive [v] *keep or take away something wanted, needed* ▪ *Syn* bankrupt, bare, bereave, denude, despoil, disinherit, dismantle, dispossess, disrobe, divest, dock, expropriate, lose, oust, rob, seize, skim, stiff, strip, wrest; ▪ *Ant* appropriate, bestow, confer, endow, give, indulge, offer, present, supply.

depth [n] *distance down or across*
▪ *Syn* base, bottom, declination, drop, expanse, extent, intensity, lowness, measure, measurement, pit, pitch, profundity, remoteness, sounding; ▪ *Ant* height.

deranged [adj] *crazy, insane*
▪ *Syn* berserk, crazed, delirious, demented, distracted, frantic, frenzied, irrational, lunatic, mad, maniacal, unsettled, unsound; ▪ *Ant* balanced, calm, sane.

deregulate [v] *remove imposed controls on a system* ▪ *Syn* decontrol, denationalize, leave be, let alone, not interfere, not meddle, not tamper; ▪ *Ant* centralize, control, nationalize, regulate, rule, run, socialize.

derelict [adj1] *careless, negligent*
▪ *Syn* delinquent, disregardful, irresponsible, lax, remiss, slack; ▪ *Ant* careful, dependable, faithful, reliable, responsible.

derelict [adj2] *deserted, forsaken*
▪ *Syn* abandoned, castoff, desolate, dilapidated, faded, lorn, neglected, ownerless, ruined, run-down, seedy, shabby, solitary, threadbare; ▪ *Ant* attended, improved, maintained, populated.

deride [v] *make fun of; insult*
▪ *Syn* banter, chaff, disdain, disparage, flout, gibe, jeer, mock, ridicule, scoff, scorn, sneer, taunt; ▪ *Ant* commend, compliment, flatter, praise, revere.

de rigueur [adj] *proper, right*
▪ *Syn* au fait, comme il faut, conventional, correct, decent, decorous, done, fitting, necessary, required; ▪ *Ant* improper, unbecoming, unnecessary, wrong.

derisive [adj] *ridiculing*
▪ *Syn* cocky, contemptuous, derisory, disdainful, fresh, insulting, jeering, mocking, rude, sarcastic, scornful, taunting; ▪ *Ant* commend, complimentary, flattering, praising, respectful.

derivation [n] *root, source*
▪ *Syn* ancestry, basis, beginning, descent, etymology, foundation, genealogy, inception, origin, provenance, provenience, wellspring; ▪ *Ant* conclusion, consequence, effect, end, outgrowth, result.

derivative [n] *product, descendant*
▪ *Syn* by-product, offshoot, outgrowth, spin-off, wave; ▪ *Ant* invention, original, root, source.

derivative [adj] *borrowed, transmitted from source*
▪ *Syn* acquired, ancestral, cognate, connate, evolved, hereditary, inferred, obtained, plagiaristic, procured, secondary, secondhand, subordinate; ▪ *Ant* antecedent, inventive, original, primary, unborrowed, unique.

derive [v] *deduce a conclusion*
▪ *Syn* arrive at, conclude, determine, develop, draw, educe, elaborate, elicit, evolve, excogitate, extract, follow, formulate, gather, infer, judge, obtain, reach, trace; ▪ *Ant* create, intuit, invent.

derogatory [adj] *offensive, uncomplimentary* ▪ *Syn* belittling, critical, damaging, degrading, demeaning, deprecatory, disdainful, humiliating, malevolent, opprobrious, sarcastic, scornful, spiteful, vilifying; ▪ *Ant* appreciative, complimentary, favorable, flattering, praising.

descend [v] *move down, lower*
▪ *Syn* alight, cascade, cataract, decline, dip, dive, drop, fall, incline, light, lower, pitch, plummet, plunge, prolapse, set, settle, sink, slant, slide, slope, stoop, submerge, subside; ▪ *Ant* ascend, climb, go up, increase, rise.

descendant [n] *person in line of ancestry* ▪ *Syn* brood, child, children, heir, issue, kin, offspring, posterity, product, progeny, scion, seed; ▪ *Ant* ascendant, predecessor, progenitor.

descent [n1] *moving down; lowering*
▪ *Syn* crash, declension, decline, declivity, dip, downgrade, drop, drop-off, fall, grade, gradient, hill, incline, landslide, plunge, precipitation, sag, settlement, slant, slide, slip, slope; ▪ *Ant* ascension, ascent, elevation, increase, rise, upgrade.

descent [n2] *deterioration*
▪ *Syn* abasement, anticlimax, cadence, comedown, debasement, decline, degradation, downfall, lapse, slump; ▪ *Ant* improvement, upgrade.

describe [v] *explain in speech, writing*
▪ *Syn* characterize, chronicle, communicate, construe, define, delineate, depict, detail, distinguish, draw, elucidate, explicate, expound, express, illuminate, illustrate, interpret, narrate, outline, paint, particularize, picture, portray, recite, recount, relate, report, represent, sketch, specify, state, tell, term, trace, transmit; ▪ *Ant* confuse, misrepresent, mix up.

descriptive [adj] *explanatory*
▪ *Syn* anecdotal, characteristic, circumstantial, clear, definitive, delineative, depictive, detailed, eloquent, explicative, expository, expressive, extended, graphic, illuminative, illustrative, indicative, interpretive, lifelike, narrative, particularized, pictorial, picturesque, specific, vivid; ▪ *Ant* confusing, cursory, undescriptive, vague.

desecrate [v] *abuse, violate*
▪ *Syn* befoul, blaspheme, contaminate, defile, depredate, desolate, despoil, devastate, devour, dishonor, pervert, pillage, pollute, profane, prostitute, ravage, spoil, waste; ▪ *Ant* honor, praise, sanctify.

desecration [n] *violation, abuse*
▪ *Syn* blasphemy, debasement, defilement, impiety, irreverence, profanation, sacrilege; ▪ *Ant* honor, praise, sanctification.

desert [adj] *barren, uncultivated*
▪ *Syn* arid, bare, desolate, infertile, solitary, sterile, uninhabited, unproductive, untilled, waste, wild; ▪ *Ant* cultivated, fertile, productive.

desert [v] *abandon, defect*
▪ *Syn* abscond, apostatize, beach, betray, bolt, decamp, depart, escape, flee, fly, forsake, leave, light, maroon, quit, relinquish, renounce, resign, strand, tergiversate, throw over, vacate, walk; ▪ *Ant* aid, assist, come back, help, stay, support.

deserted [adj] *abandoned, unoccupied*
▪ *Syn* bare, barren, bereft, cast off, derelict, desolate, empty, forlorn, forsaken, isolated, lonely, lorn, neglected, solitary, uninhabited, vacant; ▪ *Ant* busy, crowded, populated, populous.

deserving [adj] *worthy, meritorious*
▪ *Syn* admirable, commendable, due, estimable, laudable, meritable, praiseworthy, righteous, rightful; ▪ *Ant* contemptible, undeserving, unworthy.

desiccate [v] *take moisture out of*
▪ *Syn* dehydrate, deplete, devitalize, divest, drain, dry, dry up, evaporate, exsiccate, parch, sear, shrivel, wither, wizen; ▪ *Ant* moisten, moisturize, wet.

designedly [adv] *intentionally*
▪ *Syn* by design, deliberately, knowingly, on purpose, prepensely, purposely, studi-

ously, willfully; ▪ *Ant* impulsively, innocently, unconsciously, unintentionally, unknowingly, unwittingly.

designing [*adj*] *plotting, crafty*
▪ *Syn* artful, astute, conniving, conspiring, devious, intriguing, Machiavellian, observant, scheming, shrewd, sly, treacherous, tricky, unscrupulous, wily; ▪ *Ant* aboveboard, artless, honest, not clever, unplanned.

desirable [*adj1*] *attractive, seductive*
▪ *Syn* adorable, alluring, charming, enticing, fascinating, fetching, sexy; ▪ *Ant* bad, disagreeable, disgusting, unattractive, undesirable.

desirable [*adj2*] *advantageous, good*
▪ *Syn* acceptable, advisable, agreeable, beneficial, enviable, expedient, helpful, preferable, profitable, useful, welcome, worthwhile; ▪ *Ant* bad, detrimental, disadvantageous, evil, harmful, hurtful, injurious, unprofitable.

desire [*n*] *want, longing*
▪ *Syn* ambition, appetite, aspiration, avidity, covetousness, craving, cupidity, devotion, eagerness, fancy, fervor, fondness, greed, hunger, inclination, love, lust, mania, need, passion, proclivity, propensity, rapture, salacity, thirst, urge, voracity, will, wish, yearning; ▪ *Ant* aversion, disgust, dislike, distaste, hate, hatred, repulsion.

desire [*v*] *want, long for*
▪ *Syn* aim, aspire to, covet, crave, fancy, hunger for, lust after, pine, spoil for, thirst, wish for, yearn for; ▪ *Ant* eschew, not want, reject, repudiate; ▪ spurn.

desirous [*adj*] *aspiring, hopeful*
▪ *Syn* acquisitive, ambitious, amorous, avid, covetous, eager, enthusiastic, grasping, greedy, keen, lustful, passionate, prehensile, wishful, yearning; ▪ *Ant* abstemious, generous, reluctant.

desist [*v*] *stop, refrain from*
▪ *Syn* abandon, abstain, cease, discontinue, end, forbear, give up, halt, leave off, pause, quit, relinquish, resign, surcease, suspend, yield; ▪ *Ant* carry on, continue, endure, go on, keep on, persevere, restart, resume.

desolate [*adj1*] *unused, barren*
▪ *Syn* abandoned, bare, bleak, derelict, desert, destroyed, dreary, empty, forsaken, isolated, lonely, lonesome, lorn, ruined, solitary, vacant, waste, wild; ▪ *Ant* cultivated, inhabited, populated, used.

desolate [*adj2*] *depressed, despondent*
▪ *Syn* bereft, black, bleak, dejected, disconsolate, dismal, dolorous, downcast, forlorn, funereal, gloomy, inconsolable, joyless, lonely, lonesome, melancholy, miserable, somber, tragic, wretched; ▪ *Ant* cheerful, comforted, happy, pleased.

desolation [*n*] *distress, unhappiness*
▪ *Syn* anguish, dejection, despair, gloom, loneliness, melancholy, misery, mourning, sadness, sorrow, woe, wretchedness; ▪ *Ant* cheer, comfort, happiness, joy.

despair [*n*] *depression, hopelessness*
▪ *Syn* anguish, dejection, desperation, despondency, discouragement, gloom, misery, pain, sorrow, trial, tribulation, wretchedness; ▪ *Ant* cheer, cheerfulness, confidence, faith, happiness, hopefulness, joy, joyfulness, trust.

despair [*v*] *give up hope*
▪ *Syn* abandon hope, despond, destroy, drop, flatten, lose faith, lose heart, relinquish, renounce, resign, surrender, yield; ▪ *Ant* anticipate, expect, have faith, hope, wish for.

despairing [*adj*] *upset, despondent*
▪ *Syn* anxious, broken-hearted, cynical, dejected, desperate, disconsolate, downcast, forlorn, frantic, grief-stricken, hopeless, inconsolable, melancholy, miserable, oppressed, pessimistic, sad, suicidal, wretched; ▪ *Ant* confident, encouraged, expectant, hopeful.

desperate [*adj1*] *reckless, outrageous*
▪ *Syn* audacious, bold, careless, dangerous, devil-may-care, foolhardy, frantic, hazardous, headlong, impetuous, madcap, monstrous, precipitate, rash, risky, scandalous, violent, wild; ▪ *Ant* careful, cautious, confident, content, satisfied, secure.

desperate [*adj2*] *extreme, intense*
▪ *Syn* acute, climacteric, critical, crucial, dire, drastic, exquisite, extreme, fierce, furious, great, terrible, urgent, vehement, vicious, violent; ▪ *Ant* calm, content, contented, satisfactory, satisfied.

desperate [*adj3*] *hopeless*
▪ *Syn* despairing, despondent, downcast, forlorn, futile, inconsolable, sad, useless, vain, wretched; ▪ *Ant* hopeful, promising.

desperately [*adv*] *severely*
▪ *Syn* badly, dramatically, fiercely, gravely, greatly, perilously, seriously; ▪ *Ant* calmly, easily, trivially.

desperation [n] *hopelessness*
 ▪ *Syn* agony, anguish, anxiety, dejection, depression, desolation, despair, despondency, fear, gloom, grief, heartache, misery, pain, pang, sorrow, torture, worry; ▪ *Ant* confidence, contentment, security.

despicable [adj] *hateful; beyond contempt* ▪ *Syn* abject, awful, base, beastly, contemptible, detestable, dirty, disreputable, ignominious, infamous, loathsome, low, mean, pitiful, reprehensible, shameful, sordid, vile, worthless, wretched; ▪ *Ant* desirous, honorable, likable, loveable, respectable, virtuous, worthy.

despise [v] *look down on*
 ▪ *Syn* abhor, abominate, contemn, deride, detest, disdain, execrate, flout, hate, loathe, misprize, neglect, reject, renounce, repudiate, revile, scorn, shun, slight, snub, spurn; ▪ *Ant* admire, appreciate, cherish, like, love.

despoil [v] *ravage, destroy*
 ▪ *Syn* denude, depopulate, depredate, desecrate, desolate, devastate, devour, dispossess, divest, loot, maraud, pillage, plunder, raid, rob, sack, spoil, spoliate, strip, vandalize, waste, wreck; ▪ *Ant* build, construct, improve.

despondent [adj] *depressed*
 ▪ *Syn* dejected, disconsolate, discouraged, disheartened, dispirited, doleful, downcast, downhearted, forlorn, griefstricken, hopeless, low, low-spirited, melancholy, miserable, morose, mourning, sad, sorrowful, woebegone, wretched; ▪ *Ant* cheerful, elated, happy, hopeful, spirited, up.

destination [n] *goal; place one wants to go* ▪ *Syn* aim, ambition, design, end, harbor, haven, intention, journey's end, landing-place, objective, purpose, station, stop, target, terminal, terminus; ▪ *Ant* beginning, source, start.

destined [adj] *bound for, fated*
 ▪ *Syn* at hand, certain, compelled, condemned, designed, directed, doomed, foreordained, forthcoming, impending, inevitable, inexorable, intended, looming, meant, near, ordained, predestined, predetermined, sealed, settled, stated; ▪ *Ant* avoidable, unscheduled.

destiny [n] *fate*
 ▪ *Syn* certainty, circumstance, conclusion, design, doom, expectation, finality, fortune, future, inevitability, intent, intention, karma, lot, luck, Moirai, portion, predestination, predetermination, pros-

pect; ▪ *Ant* accident, chance, choice, free will, volition.

destitute [adj] *down and out; wanting*
 ▪ *Syn* bankrupt, bereft, deficient, depleted, divested, drained, empty, exhausted, impecunious, impoverished, indigent, insolvent, lacking, necessitous, needy, penniless, pinched, poor, povertystricken; ▪ *Ant* lucky, prosperous, rich, secure, wealthy.

destroy [v] *demolish, devastate*
 ▪ *Syn* annihilate, annul, consume, deface, desolate, dismantle, dispatch, end, eradicate, erase, exterminate, extinguish, extirpate, kill, lay waste, level, liquidate, mutilate, quash, quell, ravage, ravish, raze, ruin, sabotage, shatter, slay, stamp out, suppress, total, vaporize, waste, wipe out, wreck; ▪ *Ant* build, construct, create, improve, repair, restore.

destruction [n] *demolition, devastation*
 ▪ *Syn* abolition, annihilation, carnage, demolishing, dissolving, downfall, elimination, end, eradication, extermination, extinction, extirpation, havoc, invalidation, liquidation, loss, massacre, murder, overthrow, ravaging, ruin, slaughter, subjugation, subversion, undoing, wreckage; ▪ *Ant* building, construction, creation, improvement, reparation, restoration.

destructive [adj] *injurious, devastating*
 ▪ *Syn* baleful, baneful, cataclysmic, catastrophic, damaging, deadly, detrimental, dire, disastrous, evil, fatal, hurtful, internecine, lethal, mortal, noisome, noxious, pernicious, pestilential, ruinous, toxic, venomous; ▪ *Ant* aiding, assisting, building, creative, helpful, productive.

detach [v] *disconnect, cut off*
 ▪ *Syn* abstract, disassociate, disengage, disentangle, disjoin, dissociate, divide, divorce, free, isolate, loose, loosen, part, remove, segregate, sever, sunder, withdraw; ▪ *Ant* attach, combine, connect, couple, fasten, link, merge, unite.

detached [adj1] *disconnected*
 ▪ *Syn* alone, apart, discrete, disjoined, divided, emancipated, free, isolated, loose, loosened, removed, separate, severed; ▪ *Ant* attached, combined, connected, coupled, linked, merged, united.

detached [adj2] *aloof, disinterested; neutral* ▪ *Syn* abstract, apathetic, casual, dispassionate, distant, impartial, impersonal, incurious, indifferent, objective, remote, removed, reserved, staid, stolid, unbiased, unconcerned, uninvolved, unprejudiced, withdrawn; ▪ *Ant* biased, compassionate, engaged, impassioned, interested, sympathetic.

detail [*n*] *feature, specific aspect*
▪ *Syn* accessory, article, component, element, fact, factor, fine point, fraction, item, minor point, minutia, part, particular, point, portion, singularity, specialty, specific, specification, technicality, trait, trivia, triviality; ▪ *Ant* aggregate, sum, total, whole.

detailed [*adj*] *itemized, particularized*
▪ *Syn* accurate, all-inclusive, amplified, circumstantial, complete, complicated, comprehensive, copious, definite, elaborate, exact, exhaustive, full, individual, individualized, intricate, meticulous, minute, narrow, nice, particular, point-by-point, precise, seriatim, specific, thorough; ▪ *Ant* brief, cursory, inexhaustive, nonspecific, sparing, uncomplicated, undetailed.

detain [*v*] *hold, keep back; arrest*
▪ *Syn* apprehend, check, confine, constrain, decelerate, delay, hinder, hold, impede, inhibit, intern, jail, keep, mire, pick up, reserve, restrain, withhold; ▪ *Ant* free, let go, liberate, release.

detect [*v*] *discover*
▪ *Syn* ascertain, catch, descry, disclose, distinguish, encounter, espy, expose, find, identify, note, notice, observe, recognize, reveal, scent, see, spot, turn up, uncover, unmask; ▪ *Ant* miss, not see, overlook, pass by.

deter [*v*] *check, inhibit from action*
▪ *Syn* avert, block, caution, damp, dampen, daunt, debar, discourage, dissuade, divert, forestall, forfend, frighten, hinder, impede, intimidate, obstruct, obviate, preclude, prevent, prohibit, restrain, scare, stave off, stop, warn; ▪ *Ant* encourage, instigate, persuade, promote, stimulate, support, urge.

deteriorate [*v*] *decay, degenerate*
▪ *Syn* adulterate, break, corrode, corrupt, crumble, debase, decompose, degrade, deprave, depreciate, disintegrate, ebb, fade, fail, flag, impair, injure, languish, lapse, lower, mar, pervert, regress, retrogress, rot, sink, spoil, undermine, vitiate, weaken, wear away, worsen; ▪ *Ant* build, construct, develop, get better, improve.

determination [*n*] *perseverance*
▪ *Syn* boldness, certainty, certitude, constancy, conviction, courage, dedication, dogmatism, drive, fortitude, intrepidity, obstinacy, persistence, purpose, resolve, single-mindedness, steadfastness, stubbornness, tenacity, willpower; ▪ *Ant* disinterest, doubt, hesitation, irresolution, vacillation.

determine [*v1*] *conclude, decide*
▪ *Syn* actuate, arbitrate, call the shots, cinch, clinch, complete, dispose, drive, end, figure, finish, fix upon, halt, impel, incline, induce, move, ordain, persuade, regulate, resolve, rule, settle, take a decision, tap, terminate; ▪ *Ant* balk, demur, falter, hesitate, vacillate.

determine [*v2*] *discover, find out*
▪ *Syn* ascertain, catch on, certify, check, demonstrate, detect, divine, establish, figure, figure out, hear, learn, make out, see, size up, tell, verify, work out; ▪ *Ant* disregard, ignore, miss, overlook.

determined [*adj*] *driven, persistent*
▪ *Syn* bent, constant, decided, decisive, dogged, earnest, firm, fixed, intent, obstinate, purposeful, resolute, serious, set, settled, single-minded, solid, steadfast, strong-minded, strong-willed, stubborn, tenacious; ▪ *Ant* flexible, hesitating, irresolute, vacillating, wavering, weak.

deterrent [*n*] *impediment, restraint*
▪ *Syn* bridle, check, curb, defense, discouragement, hindrance, leash, obstacle, preventative, preventive, rein, shackle; ▪ *Ant* catalyst, encouragement, incentive.

detest [*v*] *hate; feel disgust toward*
▪ *Syn* abhor, abominate, despise, execrate, feel aversion toward, feel hostility toward, loathe, recoil from, reject, repudiate; ▪ *Ant* adore, cherish, like, love, prize, respect.

detestable [*adj*] *loathsome, abominable*
▪ *Syn* abhorrent, atrocious, despicable, disgusting, execrable, hateful, heinous, horrid, low-down, monstrous, odious, offensive, outrageous, repugnant, repulsive, revolting, rotten, shocking, sorry, vile; ▪ *Ant* admirable, adorable, adored, cherished, likeable, loveable, prized, respectable, respected.

detour [*n*] *indirect course*
▪ *Syn* alternate route, back road, branch, bypath, byway, circuit, circuitous route, circumvention, deviation, divergence, diversion; ▪ *Ant* beeline, direct route.

detract [v] *take away a part; lessen*
• *Syn* cheapen, decrease, depreciate, diminish, discount, lower, minimize, misprize, reduce, subtract from, underrate, undervalue, vilipend, withdraw, write off; • *Ant* add to, increase, optimize.

detraction [n] *misrepresentation; slander* • *Syn* abuse, aspersion, calumny, damage, defamation, denigration, deprecation, disparagement, injury, injustice, insinuation, libel, lie, obloquy, pejorative, ridicule, scandal, scurrility, tale, traducement, vilification, vituperation; • *Ant* admiration, adulation, flattery, praise.

detriment [n] *disadvantage*
• *Syn* damage, disability, disservice, drawback, handicap, harm, hurt, impairment, injury, liability, loss, mischief, prejudice; • *Ant* advantage, assistance, benefit, gain, help, profit.

detrimental [adj] *damaging, disadvantageous* • *Syn* adverse, bad, baleful, deleterious, destructive, evil, harmful, hurtful, ill, inimical, injurious, negative, nocuous, pernicious, prejudicial, unfavorable; • *Ant* advantageous, assisting, beneficial, helpful, profitable.

devalue [v] *depreciate*
• *Syn* cheapen, decrease, lower, mark down, take down, underrate, undervalue, write down, write off; • *Ant* increase, overvalue, raise.

devastate [v] *demolish, destroy*
• *Syn* depredate, desecrate, desolate, despoil, devour, lay waste, level, ravage, raze, ruin, spoil, spoliate, waste, wreck; • *Ant* build, construct, enrich, help, improve.

devastation [n] *destruction*
• *Syn* defoliation, demolition, desolation, havoc, loss, pillage, plunder, ravages, ruin, ruination, spoliation, waste; • *Ant* building, construction, creation.

develop [v1] *cultivate, prosper*
• *Syn* advance, age, establish, evolve, expand, flourish, foster, grow, maturate, mature, mellow, progress, promote, ripen, thrive; • *Ant* decline, halt, repress.

develop [v2] *expand, work out*
• *Syn* actualize, amplify, augment, broaden, build up, cultivate, deepen, dilate, elaborate, enlarge, enrich, extend, finish, heighten, improve, intensify, lengthen, magnify, materialize, perfect, polish, promote, realize, refine, spread, strengthen, stretch, unfold, widen; • *Ant* circumscribe, compress, confine, decrease, lessen, narrow.

develop [v3] *begin; occur*
• *Syn* acquire, arise, befall, betide, break, break out, chance, come about, commence, contract, ensue, establish, follow, form, generate, happen, invest, originate, result, start, transpire; • *Ant* cease, discontinue, end, halt, stop.

development [n] *growth*
• *Syn* addition, advance, advancement, augmentation, boost, buildup, enlargement, evolution, expansion, hike, improvement, increase, maturation, maturity, progress, progression, ripening, spread; • *Ant* decline, decrease, fall, stoppage.

deviant [adj] *abnormal, different*
• *Syn* aberrant, anomalous, atypical, deviate, divergent, freaky, heretical, heteroclite, irregular, off-key, preternatural, variant, wayward, weird; • *Ant* normal, orthodox, regular, representative, standard, typical, usual.

deviate [v] *stray from normal path*
• *Syn* angle off, avert, bend, contrast, deflect, depart, depart from, differ, digress, diverge, drift, err, part, shy, swerve, turn, vary, veer, wander; • *Ant* conform, go straight, keep, stay.

deviation [n] *change, departure*
• *Syn* aberration, alteration, anomaly, breach, deflection, detour, difference, digression, discrepancy, disparity, divergence, diversion, fluctuation, modification, shift, transgression, turning, variance, variation; • *Ant* conformity, consistency, regularity, sameness, uniformity.

devilish [adj] *wicked*
• *Syn* accursed, atrocious, cursed, damnable, demonic, diabolical, evil, execrable, fiendish, hellish, infernal, iniquitous, Mephistophelian, nefarious, satanic; • *Ant* angelic, godlike, good, moral.

devious [adj1] *dishonest, crafty*
• *Syn* artful, calculating, crooked, deceitful, duplicitous, errant, evasive, fraudulent, guileful, insidious, insincere, roundabout, scheming, shady, shifty, shrewd, sly, treacherous, tricky, underhanded, wily; • *Ant* artless, frank, honest, open, straightforward, trustworthy, truthful.

devious [adj2] *crooked; indirect*
▪ *Syn* ambiguous, circuitous, confounding, confusing, curving, detouring, errant, erratic, excursive, flexuous, misleading, obscure, rambling, remote, removed, roundabout, serpentine, straying, tortuous, twisting, wandering; ▪ *Ant* direct, straight.

devoid [adj] *empty, wanting*
▪ *Syn* bare, barren, bereft, deficient, denuded, destitute, lacking, needed, sans, vacant, void, without; ▪ *Ant* complete, filled, full, replete.

devoted [adj] *committed, loyal*
▪ *Syn* adherent, ardent, caring, concerned, consecrated, constant, dedicated, devout, dutiful, faithful, fervid, fond, staunch, steadfast, thoughtful, zealous; ▪ *Ant* apathetic, disloyal, inconstant, neglectful, negligent, uncommitted, unfaithful, untrustworthy.

devotee [n] *ardent supporter; fan*
▪ *Syn* addict, adherent, admirer, aficionado, believer, booster, buff, disciple, enthusiast, fanatic, fancier, fiend, follower, groupie, habitue, junkie, lover, votary; ▪ *Ant* adversary, antagonist, enemy.

devotion [n] *commitment; loyalty*
▪ *Syn* adherence, adoration, affection, allegiance, attachment, dedication, deference, earnestness, enthusiasm, faithfulness, fealty, fervor, fidelity, observance, passion, piety, reverence, sincerity, worship, zeal; ▪ *Ant* apathy, carelessness, indifference, neglect, negligence.

devour [v] *swallow, consume*
▪ *Syn* absorb, bolt, drink in, eat, enjoy, feast on, feed on, go through, gulp, guzzle, imbibe, ingest, inhale, partake of, ravage, relish, revel in, take, take in; ▪ *Ant* abstain, disgorge, pass up, pick, refuse, regurgitate.

devout [adj] *sincerely believing; devoted*
▪ *Syn* adherent, ardent, earnest, faithful, fervent, fervid, genuine, heart-and-soul, heartfelt, intense, passionate, profound, religious, reverent, serious, sincere, zealous; ▪ *Ant* insincere, irreligious, unbelieving.

dexterity [n] *aptitude, ability*
▪ *Syn* address, adroitness, aptness, craft, deftness, expertise, facility, finesse, handiness, ingenuity, knack, know-how, proficiency, skill, skillfulness, smoothness, tact, touch; ▪ *Ant* awkwardness, clumsiness, inability, ineptness.

dexterous [adj] *ingenious, proficient*
▪ *Syn* able, active, adept, adroit, agile, apt, artful, canny, clever, deft, effortless, expert, facile, handy, neat, nimble, nimble-fingered, prompt, quick, savvy, skilled, skillful, slick, sly, smooth; ▪ *Ant* awkward, clumsy, inept, inexpert, unable, unhandy, unskilled.

diabolic [adj] *evil, fiendish*
▪ *Syn* atrocious, cruel, damnable, demonic, devilish, hellish, impious, infernal, Mephistophelian, nefarious, satanic, villainous, wicked; ▪ *Ant* gentle, kind, moral, saintly.

diagonal [adj] *angled*
▪ *Syn* askew, beveled, bias, biased, cross, crossways, crosswise, inclining, oblique, slanted, transversal, transverse; ▪ *Ant* horizontal, straight, vertical.

dialectical/dialectic [adj] *logical argumentation* ▪ *Syn* analytic, argumentative, controversial, polemical, rationalistic; ▪ *Ant* illogical, irrational.

diametric/diametrical [adj] *opposed, conflicting* ▪ *Syn* adverse, antipodal, antipodean, antithetical, contradictory, contrary, converse, counter, opposite, polar, reverse; ▪ *Ant* approving, coinciding, like, same, similar.

diaphanous [adj] *fine, see-through*
▪ *Syn* chiffon, clear, delicate, filmy, flimsy, gauzy, gossamer, light, pellucid, sheer, thin, translucent, transparent; ▪ *Ant* opaque, thick.

diaspora [n] *the spreading out of a group of people* ▪ *Syn* disbandment, dispersal, dispersion, dissolution, escape, exodus, mass exodus, refugee flow; ▪ *Ant* assembly, bringing together, centralization, collection, concentration, congregation, focus, gathering, stasis.

dicey [adj] *risky*
▪ *Syn* capricious, chancy, dangerous, difficult, erratic, fluctuant, incalculable, ticklish, tricky; ▪ *Ant* certain, predictable, safe, sure.

dictate [v] *command; give instructions*
▪ *Syn* bid, charge, decree, direct, enjoin, impose, instruct, lay down the law, lead, ordain, order, prescribe, pronounce, regiment, rule, set; ▪ *Ant* ask, follow, implore, obey, request.

dictatorial [adj] *tyrannical, authoritarian* ▪ *Syn* arbitrary, autocratic, bossy, despotic, doctrinaire, dogmatic, domineering, imperious, iron-handed, magisterial, overbearing, peremptory, stern, totalitarian; ▪ *Ant* democratic, docile, passive.

dictatorship [n] *absolute rule*
▪ *Syn* absolutism, authoritarianism, autocracy, despotism, totalitarianism, tyranny; ▪ *Ant* anarchy, democracy.

die [v1] *pass away; stop living*
▪ *Syn* be taken, decease, depart, drop off, drown, expire, finish, perish, relinquish life, succumb, suffocate; ▪ *Ant* be born, begin, live.

die [v2] *wither, dwindle*
▪ *Syn* abate, bate, crumble, decay, decline, degenerate, diminish, disappear, ebb, end, expire, lapse, moderate, pass, recede, retrograde, rot, sink, slacken, stop, subside, vanish, wane, weaken, wear away, wilt; ▪ *Ant* develop, flourish, grow, improve.

die-hard [adj] *uncompromising*
▪ *Syn* extremist, firm, immovable, inflexible, intransigent; ▪ *Ant* compromising, conceding, flexible.

diet [v] *abstain from food*
▪ *Syn* eat sparingly, fast, go without, lose weight, reduce, slim, slim down, starve; ▪ *Ant* gorge, indulge.

differ [v1] *be dissimilar, distinct*
▪ *Syn* alter, conflict with, contradict, contrast, deviate from, digress, disagree, diverge, modify, qualify, reverse, run counter to, vary; ▪ *Ant* agree, be the same, conform, match.

differ [v2] *clash; hold opposing views*
▪ *Syn* clash, contend, debate, demur, disagree, discord, dispute, dissent, divide, fight, object, oppose, quarrel, squabble, take issue, vary, war; ▪ *Ant* accord, agree, concur, consent, harmonize.

different [adj1] *dissimilar, unlike*
▪ *Syn* at odds, at variance, contrary, contrasting, discrepant, disparate, distant, distinct, divergent, divers, diverse, inconsistent, individual, opposed, particular, peculiar, single, variant, various; ▪ *Ant* alike, comparable, correspondent, equal, homogeneous, like, related, resembling, same, similar.

different [adj2] *separate, distinct*
▪ *Syn* atypical, bizarre, discrete, distinctive, especial, extraordinary, individual, novel, original, out of the ordinary, rare, several, singular, special, specific, uncommon, unique, unusual; ▪ *Ant* conventional, correspondent, harmoni-

ous, normal, same, standard, unified, united.

different [adj3] *miscellaneous, various*
▪ *Syn* assorted, collected, diverse, heterogeneous, manifold, many, multifarious, numerous, omnifarious, several, sundry, varied; ▪ *Ant* normal, same, similar, standard, uniform.

difficult [adj1] *hard on someone; hard to do* ▪ *Syn* arduous, burdensome, challenging, crucial, demanding, exacting, formidable, hard, heavy, immense, intricate, laborious, onerous, problematic, rigid, severe, strenuous, titanic, toilsome, tough, trying, unyielding, uphill, wearisome; ▪ *Ant* easy, free, manageable, plain, simple, uncomplicated.

difficult [adj2] *complicated; hard to comprehend* ▪ *Syn* abstract, abstruse, complex, deep, enigmatic, entangled, esoteric, formidable, hard, hidden, knotty, labyrinthine, mysterious, mystical, obscure, obstinate, paradoxical, profound, subtle, tangled, thorny, troublesome, unfathomable, unintelligible; ▪ *Ant* easy, simple, straightforward, uncomplicated.

difficult [adj3] *unmanageable socially*
▪ *Syn* argumentative, demanding, fastidious, impolite, intractable, irritable, oafish, obstreperous, perverse, picky, refractory, rude, troublesome, trying; ▪ *Ant* accommodating, amenable, calm, friendly, sociable.

diffident [adj] *hesitant; unconfident*
▪ *Syn* backward, bashful, chary, constrained, coy, demure, distrustful, doubtful, dubious, flinching, humble, insecure, meek, modest, reluctant, reserved, retiring, self-conscious, self-effacing, shrinking, shy, suspicious, timid, timorous, unsure, withdrawn; ▪ *Ant* assertive, bold, confident, forward.

diffuse [adj1] *spread out*
▪ *Syn* broadcast, catholic, circulated, diluted, dispersed, disseminated, distributed, extended, general, prevalent, propagated, radiated, scattered, separated, strewn, thin, universal, widespread; ▪ *Ant* compact, compressed, concentrated, confined, limited, restricted.

diffuse [adj2] *wordy*
▪ *Syn* circumlocutory, copious, digressive, discursive, dull, lengthy, long, long-winded, meandering, profuse, prolix, rambling, random, redundant, verbose;

• *Ant* abbreviated, abridged, brief, short, succinct.

dig [n] *insult*
• *Syn* crack, cut, cutting remark, gibe, innuendo, jeer, quip, slur, sneer, taunt, wisecrack; • *Ant* compliment, flattery, praise.

dig [v1] *delve into; hollow out*
• *Syn* bore, bulldoze, burrow, channel, depress, discover, dredge, drill, enter, excavate, exhume, gouge, hoe, investigate, mine, pierce, pit, probe, quarry, root out, rout, sap, scoop, search, shovel, sift, spade, till, tunnel, undermine, unearth; • *Ant* cover, cover up, fill, pile.

dig [v2] *enjoy, like*
• *Syn* appreciate, follow, love, mind, relish, understand; • *Ant* abhor, detest, dislike, loathe.

dig [v3] *understand*
• *Syn* accept, apprehend, catch, comprehend, follow, grasp, recognize, see, take in; • *Ant* misapprehend, misunderstand, not get.

digest [v1] *make shorter; abridge*
• *Syn* abbreviate, abstract, compress, condense, cut, decrease, epitomize, inventory, methodize, reduce, shorten, summarize, summate, survey, synopsize, tabulate; • *Ant* detail, enlarge, expand, lengthen.

digest [v2] *come to understand*
• *Syn* absorb, analyze, assimilate, consider, contemplate, deliberate, meditate, ponder, study, understand; • *Ant* misunderstand, reject.

dignified [adj] *honorable*
• *Syn* aristocratic, august, decorous, distinguished, eminent, formal, grand, great, imperial, imperious, lofty, noble, ornate, proud, refined, regal, respected, solemn, stately, superior, upright; • *Ant* crass, dishonorable, ignoble, indecorous, undignified, vulgar.

dignify [v] *make honorable; glorify*
• *Syn* adorn, advance, aggrandize, distinguish, elevate, ennoble, erect, exalt, grace, honor, magnify, promote, raise, sublime; • *Ant* belittle, condemn, degrade, demote, detract, disgrace, humiliate, insult, shame.

dignity [n] *excellence, nobility*
• *Syn* cachet, character, consequence, decency, decorum, distinction, eminence, etiquette, grace, grandeur, hauteur, honor, importance, merit, morality, poise, prestige, quality, respectability, self-respect, significance, solemnity, splendor, stature, virtue, worth, worthiness; • *Ant* inconsequence, lowliness.

digress [v] *stray, deviate*
• *Syn* be diffuse, depart, divagate, drift, meander, ramble, roam, stray, veer, wander; • *Ant* advance, be direct, proceed, stay.

dilapidated [adj] *falling apart; in ruins*
• *Syn* battered, broken-down, crumbling, decayed, decrepit, faded, impaired, injured, marred, neglected, old, ramshackle, rickety, ruined, seedy, shabby, threadbare, used-up, worn-out; • *Ant* in good repair, neat, rebuilt, spruce, tidy, trim, well-kept.

dilate [v] *stretch, widen*
• *Syn* amplify, augment, broaden, develop, distend, enlarge, expand, expatiate, expound, extend, increase, inflate, lengthen, prolong, protract, swell; • *Ant* compress, constrict, contract, lessen, reduce, shrink.

dilatory [adj] *procrastinating*
• *Syn* backward, delaying, deliberate, laggard, lax, lazy, leisurely, loitering, moratory, neglectful, negligent, remiss, slack, sluggish, tardy, tarrying; • *Ant* assiduous, diligent, eager, enthusiastic, hard-working, prompt, ready, zealous.

dilemma [n] *difficult choice or situation*
• *Syn* corner, crisis, difficulty, embarrassment, fix, impasse, jam, mess, perplexity, predicament, quandary, scrape, spot, strait; • *Ant* miracle, solution, wonder.

diligent [adj] *persevering, hard-working*
• *Syn* active, assiduous, attentive, careful, conscientious, earnest, indefatigable, industrious, laborious, operose, painstaking, persistent, pertinacious, sedulous, studious, tireless, unflagging, unrelenting; • *Ant* inactive, indifferent, languid, lazy, lethargic, negligent.

dilute [v] *make thinner; weaken*
• *Syn* alter, attenuate, cut, decrease, deliquesce, diffuse, diminish, irrigate, lace, lessen, liquefy, mitigate, mix, moderate, modify, qualify, reduce, spike, temper, water, water down; • *Ant* concentrate, strengthen, thicken.

diluted/dilute [adj] *thinned, weakened*
• *Syn* attenuated, cut, impaired, light, moderated, reduced, spiked, tempered, watery, weak; • *Ant* concentrated, strengthened, thickened.

dim [*adj*] *darkish*
▪ *Syn* bleary, blurred, caliginous, cloudy, dull, dusky, faded, faint, gloomy, ill-defined, indistinct, lackluster, monotone, obscured, opaque, shadowy, tenebrous, unclear, vague; ▪ *Ant* bright, brilliant, clear, distinct, illuminated.

dim [*v*] *darken; obscure*
▪ *Syn* becloud, blur, cloud, dull, eclipse, fade, fog, haze, muddy, obfuscate, pale, tarnish; ▪ *Ant* brighten, clarify, lighten.

diminish [*v1*] *become or cause to be less*
▪ *Syn* abate, attenuate, close, curtail, decrease, depreciate, dwindle, ebb, fade away, lessen, recede, reduce, shrink, taper, wane, weaken; ▪ *Ant* develop, enlarge, expand, extend, grow, increase, lengthen, prolong.

diminish [*v2*] *belittle*
▪ *Syn* abuse, cheapen, decry, demean, depreciate, derogate, devalue, disparage, minimize; ▪ *Ant* compliment, flatter, magnify, praise.

din [*n*] *loud, continuous noise*
▪ *Syn* babel, bedlam, clamor, clatter, commotion, disquiet, outcry, pandemonium, percussion, racket, tumult, uproar; ▪ *Ant* calm, harmony, quiet, silence, stillness.

dingy [*adj*] *soiled*
▪ *Syn* colorless, dark, dim, dirty, discolored, drab, dreary, dull, faded, grimy, muddy, shabby, tarnished; ▪ *Ant* bright, clean, immaculate, neat, pure, spotless.

dip [*v*] *lower, descend*
▪ *Syn* bend, decline, droop, fade, fall, incline, nose-dive, plummet, plunge, recede, slip, slope, slump, spiral, subside, tilt, tumble, veer, verge; ▪ *Ant* ascend, raise.

diplomatic [*adj*] *politic, tactful*
▪ *Syn* adept, cagey, conciliatory, courteous, crafty, dexterous, discreet, gracious, polite, prudent, savvy, sensitive, sharp, shrewd, strategic, suave, wily; ▪ *Ant* artless, impolite, rude, tactless.

dire [*adj1*] *urgent; crucial*
▪ *Syn* acute, burning, clamorous, critical, desperate, drastic, exigent, immoderate, importunate, pressing; ▪ *Ant* trivial, unimportant.

dire [*adj2*] *terrible, ominous*
▪ *Syn* afflictive, black, calamitous, cataclysmic, catastrophic, disastrous, dismal, fierce, frightful, grim, horrible, oppress-

ing, portentous, regrettable, ruinous, shocking, ugly, woeful; ▪ *Ant* fortunate, good, lucky, nice, propitious.

direct [*adj1*] *honest*
▪ *Syn* absolute, blunt, candid, downright, explicit, frank, matter-of-fact, open, plain, point-blank, sincere, straightforward; ▪ *Ant* ambiguous, devious, dishonest, indirect, wily.

direct [*adj2*] *undeviating; uninterrupted*
▪ *Syn* continuous, even, horizontal, linear, nonstop, right, shortest, straight, through, unswerving; ▪ *Ant* changing, deviating, indirect, intermittent, interrupted, varying.

direct [*v1*] *manage, oversee*
▪ *Syn* administer, advise, boss, conduct, dominate, govern, guide, handle, influence, keep, lead, ordain, preside over, regulate, run, supervise; ▪ *Ant* misguide, mismanage, neglect.

direct [*v2*] *give instructions; teach*
▪ *Syn* advise, bid, command, deliver, dictate, enjoin, inform, instruct, lecture, order, read, tell, warn; ▪ *Ant* misguide, mislead.

direct [*v3*] *point in a direction; guide*
▪ *Syn* aim, beam, cast, conduct, escort, fix, focus, head, incline, indicate, lay, lead, level, mean, pilot, point, present, route, see, set, show, sight, steer, target, train, turn, zero in; ▪ *Ant* diverge, misdirect.

directly [*adv1*] *by the shortest route*
▪ *Syn* dead, direct, due, exactly, precisely, right, straight, straightly, undeviatingly, unswervingly; ▪ *Ant* circuitously, deviously, indirectly.

directly [*adv2*] *as soon as possible*
▪ *Syn* at once, first off, forthwith, immediately, instantaneously, instantly, presently, promptly, quickly, right away, shortly, soon, speedily, straightaway, straight off; ▪ *Ant* afterward, eventually, later, subsequently.

directly [*adv3*] *straightforwardly*
▪ *Syn* candidly, face-to-face, honestly, in person, literally, openly, personally, plainly, point-blank, truthfully, verbatim, word for word; ▪ *Ant* ambiguously, discursively, equivocally, indirectly.

direful [*adj*] *fearful; horrible*
▪ *Syn* apocalyptic, appalling, baleful, baneful, calamitous, dreadful, fateful, ghastly, gloomy, horrid, ill-boding, ominous, shocking, terrible; ▪ *Ant*

auspicious, favorable, promising, propitious.

dirty [adj1] soiled, unclean
▪ **Syn** bedraggled, begrimed, black, contaminated, defiled, disheveled, dusty, filthy, foul, fouled, greasy, grimy, lousy, muddy, nasty, polluted, slimy, sloppy, slovenly, smudged, sooty, spotted, squalid, stained, sullied; ▪ **Ant** clean, hygienic, pure, sanitary, spotless, sterile, washed.

dirty [adj2] obscene, pornographic
▪ **Syn** base, blue, coarse, filthy, immoral, impure, indecent, lewd, low, mean, nasty, off-color, raunchy, ribald, risque, salacious, scatological, sordid, vile, vulgar; ▪ **Ant** clean, moral, upright.

dirty [v] cause to be soiled
▪ **Syn** begrime, blotch, blur, botch, coat, contaminate, corrupt, debase, decay, defile, discolor, encrust, foul, grime, mess up, muddy, pollute, smear, smoke, smudge, soil, spatter, spoil, spot, stain, taint, tarnish; ▪ **Ant** clean, cleanse, purify, sterilize, tidy.

disable [v] render inoperative; cripple
▪ **Syn** batter, damage, debilitate, disarm, disqualify, enfeeble, handicap, harm, hurt, immobilize, impair, incapacitate, invalidate, maim, paralyze, pinion, prostrate, ruin, sabotage, sap, shatter, spoil, undermine, weaken, wreck; ▪ **Ant** aid, assist, enable, help, improve, strengthen.

disabled [adj] incapacitated
▪ **Syn** broken-down, decrepit, disarmed, helpless, hurt, infirm, laid-up, maimed, mangled, mutilated, paralyzed, powerless, run-down, sidelined, stalled, useless, weak, weakened, worn-out, wounded, wrecked; ▪ **Ant** able, fit, healthy, operative, unharmed, working.

disadvantageous [adj] detrimental, inconvenient ▪ **Syn** adverse, contrary, damaging, deleterious, depreciative, depreciatory, detracting, harmful, hurtful, ill-timed, inexpedient, injurious; ▪ **Ant** advantageous, convenient, favorable, helpful, well-timed.

disaffected [adj] alienated, estranged
▪ **Syn** antagonistic, discontented, dissatisfied, hostile, indifferent, mutinous, rebellious, seditious; ▪ **Ant** contented, happy, satisfied, serene.

disagree [v1] be different
▪ **Syn** clash, conflict, contradict, counter,

depart, deviate, differ, discord, dissent, diverge, run counter to, vary, war; ▪ **Ant** agree, coincide, harmonize.

disagree [v2] argue; hold differing opinion ▪ **Syn** altercate, battle, bicker, brawl, contend, contest, controvert, debate, differ, discept, dispute, dissent, divide, feud, fight, haggle, object, oppose, palter, quarrel, quibble, rip, row, scrap, spar, sue, take issue; ▪ **Ant** accept, acquiesce, agree, concur, consent.

disagreeable [adj1] bad-tempered, irritable ▪ **Syn** bellicose, cantankerous, contentious, contrary, cross, difficult, disputatious, ill-natured, obnoxious, offensive, out of sorts, peevish, petulant, querulous, rude, surly, ugly; ▪ **Ant** agreeable, friendly, happy, nice, obliging, pleasant.

disagreeable [adj2] disgusting, offensive ▪ **Syn** annoying, awful, bad, bothersome, displeasing, distasteful, distressing, objectionable, obnoxious, repellent, repugnant, repulsive, rotten, sour, upsetting; ▪ **Ant** agreeable, inoffensive, nice, pleasant, pleasing.

disallow [v] reject, prohibit
▪ **Syn** abjure, cancel, censor, debar, deny, disavow, disclaim, dismiss, disown, embargo, exclude, forbid, proscribe, rebuff, refuse, repudiate, shut out, veto, withhold; ▪ **Ant** allow, permit.

disappear [v] vanish; cease
▪ **Syn** abscond, clear, decamp, depart, die, disperse, dissipate, dissolve, ebb, end, escape, evanesce, evaporate, exit, expire, fade, fade away, flee, fly, go, leave, pass, recede, retire, retreat, sink, vacate, wane, withdraw; ▪ **Ant** appear, arise, arrive, come in, materialize.

disappoint [v] sadden, dismay; frustrate
▪ **Syn** baffle, balk, chagrin, dash, deceive, delude, disconcert, disenchant, disgruntle, dishearten, disillusion, dissatisfy, dumbfound, embitter, fail, fall flat, fall short of, foil, founder, hamper, hinder, miscarry, mislead, thwart, torment, vex; ▪ **Ant** delight, excite, fulfill, gratify, please, satisfy, succeed.

disappointed [adj] let down, saddened
▪ **Syn** beaten, chapfallen, crestfallen, defeated, depressed, despondent, disconcerted, discontented, discouraged, disenchanted, disgruntled, disillusioned, distressed, downcast, downhearted, frustrated, hopeless, thwarted, upset, van-

quished, worsted; ▪ **Ant** delighted, excited, happy, pleased, satisfied.

disapprove [v] *condemn*
▪ **Syn** blame, censure, chastise, criticize, damn, decry, denounce, deplore, deprecate, detract, disesteem, dislike, dismiss, find fault with, frown on, oppose, refuse, reject, remonstrate, reprehend, reprobate, reprove, spurn; ▪ **Ant** agree, approve, endorse, like, love, sanction.

disarming [adj] *charming*
▪ **Syn** bewitching, convincing, ingratiating, irresistible, likable, persuasive, saccharine, seductive, winning; ▪ **Ant** annoying, despicable, disgusting, irritating, repulsive, vexing.

disarray [n] *disorder, confusion, mess*
▪ **Syn** anarchy, ataxia, chaos, clutter, discomposure, disharmony, dishevelment, disorganization, jumble, muddle, snarl, tangle, upset; ▪ **Ant** arrangement, harmony, order, orderliness, organization.

disaster [n] *accident, trouble*
▪ **Syn** adversity, affliction, bad luck, bale, bane, blight, blow, calamity, casualty, cataclysm, catastrophe, crash, debacle, defeat, depression, emergency, exigency, failure, fall, fiasco, flood, grief, hard luck, harm, hazard, holocaust, misadventure, mischance, misfortune, mishap, reverse, ruin, ruination, setback, slip, stroke, tragedy, upset, woe; ▪ **Ant** blessing, good fortune, good luck, miracle, prosperity, success, triumph, win, wonder.

disastrous [adj] *detrimental, devastating* ▪ **Syn** adverse, cataclysmic, catastrophic, destructive, dire, fatal, harmful, ill-fated, ruinous, terrible, tragic; ▪ **Ant** blessed, fortunate, lucky, miraculous, prosperous, successful, triumphant, winning, wondrous.

disavow [v] *reject*
▪ **Syn** abjure, contradict, deny, disclaim, disown, forswear, gainsay, impugn, negate, refuse, renege, repudiate; ▪ **Ant** agree, approve, sanction, vouch for, vow.

disbelieve [v] *doubt*
▪ **Syn** discount, discredit, distrust, eschew, mistrust, question, reject, repudiate, scoff at, scorn, suspect; ▪ **Ant** believe, trust.

disbelieving [adj] *suspicious, doubting*
▪ **Syn** cynical, incredulous, leery, mistrustful, questioning, quizzical, skeptical;

▪ **Ant** believing, trusting, trusting, unquestioning, unsuspicious.

disburse [v] *spend money*
▪ **Syn** acquit, contribute, deal, defray, dispense, disperse, distribute, divide, expend, give, measure out, outlay, partition, pay out; ▪ **Ant** deposit, hoard, hold, retain, save, set aside.

discard [v] *get rid of*
▪ **Syn** abandon, abdicate, abjure, banish, cancel, cast aside, desert, dispatch, dispose of, dispossess, ditch, divorce, eject, eliminate, expel, forsake, jettison, oust, part with, reject, relinquish, remove, shed, throw away, throw out, toss, write off; ▪ **Ant** embrace, keep, retain.

discern [v] *catch sight of; recognize and understand* ▪ **Syn** apprehend, ascertain, behold, descry, detect, distinguish, divine, espy, extricate, figure out, focus, foresee, judge, know, make out, note, notice, observe, perceive, pick out, read, remark, see, spot, take in, view; ▪ **Ant** disregard, neglect, overlook.

discernible [adj] *recognizable; distinct*
▪ **Syn** apparent, appreciable, audible, clear, detectable, distinguishable, noticeable, observable, palpable, perceptible, tangible, visible; ▪ **Ant** indistinct, invisible, obscured, unnoticeable, unrecognizable.

discerning [adj] *discriminating*
▪ **Syn** acute, clever, gnostic, ingenious, insightful, judicious, knowing, knowledgeable, perceptive, perspicacious, sagacious, sage, sensitive, sharp, shrewd, subtle, wise; ▪ **Ant** disregardful, neglectful, negligent, overlooking, undiscerning, undiscriminating.

discharge [v1] *set free*
▪ **Syn** absolve, acquit, clear, dismiss, emancipate, exonerate, expel, free, liberate, loose, loosen, manumit, oust, pardon, release; ▪ **Ant** bind, detain, hold, imprison, keep.

discharge [v2] *dismiss from responsibility* ▪ **Syn** absolve, ax, boot out, bounce, cashier, disburden, discard, disencumber, dispense, displace, eject, excuse, exempt, expel, fire, lay off, oust, relieve, remove, replace, spare, supersede, supplant, terminate; ▪ **Ant** assign, contract, delegate, employ, engage, hire.

discharge [v3] *unload*
▪ **Syn** carry away, disburden, empty, off-

load, remove; ▪ *Ant* burden, lade, load, pack, store.

disciple [*n*] *believer, follower*
▪ *Syn* apostle, attendant, catechumen, cohort, convert, devotee, enthusiast, fanatic, groupie, learner, proselyte, pupil, satellite, sectary, student, supporter, votary, witness; ▪ *Ant* god, guru, instructor, leader, teacher.

discipline [*n1*] *regimen, training*
▪ *Syn* control, drill, inculcation, indoctrination, limitation, method, practice, restraint, self-control, self-mastery, strictness, subordination, willpower; ▪ *Ant* chaos, confusion, disorder, disorganization, neglect, negligence, permissiveness.

discipline [*n2*] *punishment*
▪ *Syn* castigation, chastisement, comeuppance, correction, punition, rod; ▪ *Ant* award, reward.

disclaim [*v*] *deny*
▪ *Syn* abandon, abjure, abnegate, contradict, disavow, discard, disown, disparage, forswear, gainsay, negate, recant, retract, revoke, spurn; ▪ *Ant* accept, acknowledge, admit, allow, claim, own.

disclose [*v*] *reveal, make public*
▪ *Syn* acknowledge, admit, bare, betray, communicate, confess, divulge, expose, impart, leak, open, own, publish, reveal, show, tell, utter; ▪ *Ant* conceal, hide, secrete, withhold.

discolor [*v*] *fading, dirtying of hue*
▪ *Syn* besmear, defile, fade, mar, mark, rust, smear, soil, stain, streak, sully, tar, tarnish, tinge; ▪ *Ant* brighten, color.

discomfit [*v*] *defeat, frustrate; confuse*
▪ *Syn* abash, annoy, beat, bother, checkmate, confound, demoralize, discountenance, disturb, embarrass, faze, fluster, foil, irk, outwit, perplex, perturb, rattle, take aback, thwart, upset, vex, worst; ▪ *Ant* calm, placate, put at ease, relieve, soothe.

discomfort [*v*] *irritate; cause pain*
▪ *Syn* discomfit, disquiet, distress, disturb, embarrass, nettle, perturb, upset, vex; ▪ *Ant* aid, alleviate, comfort, ease, help, relieve.

discompose [*v*] *provoke, agitate*
▪ *Syn* annoy, bother, confuse, discomfit, disturb, embarrass, faze, fluster, harass, irk, irritate, nettle, perturb, ruffle, upset, vex; ▪ *Ant* calm, compose, settle, soothe.

disconcert [*v*] *shake up; confuse*
▪ *Syn* agitate, baffle, bewilder, confound,

discomfit, discountenance, embarrass, faze, frustrate, nonplus, perplex, puzzle, rattle, ruffle, throw off balance, upset, worry; ▪ *Ant* calm, comfort, soothe.

disconcerted [*adj*] *confused; shaken*
▪ *Syn* annoyed, bewildered, distracted, disturbed, embarrassed, fazed, flustered, nonplussed, perturbed, rattled, ruffled, taken aback, thrown, troubled, upset; ▪ *Ant* calm, composed, concerted, soothed, unworried.

disconnect [*v*] *take apart; uncouple*
▪ *Syn* abstract, cut, cut off, detach, disassociate, disengage, disjoin, dissever, dissociate, disunite, divide, part, separate, sever; ▪ *Ant* attach, connect, couple, hitch, hook, join, link, plug.

disconnected [*adj*] *confused; discontinuous* ▪ *Syn* broken, detached, disjointed, disordered, garbled, illogical, inchoate, incoherent, incohesive, interrupted, irrational, irregular, jumbled, loose, rambling, separated, wandering; ▪ *Ant* attached, coherent, connected, continuous, intelligible, joined, understandable.

disconsolate [*adj*] *depressed, unhappy*
▪ *Syn* black, blue, comfortless, crestfallen, crushed, dark, dejected, despairing, destroyed, doleful, downcast, forlorn, grief-stricken, heartbroken, hopeless, inconsolable, low, melancholy, miserable, sorrowful, woeful, wretched; ▪ *Ant* cheerful, consoled, happy, solaced, soothed.

discontented/discontent [*adj*] *unhappy, dissatisfied* ▪ *Syn* disaffected, disgruntled, displeased, disquieted, exasperated, fed up, fretful, griping, malcontent, miserable, perturbed, restless, upset, vexed; ▪ *Ant* content, contented, happy, patient, pleased, satisfied, uncomplaining.

discontinue [*v*] *prevent activity from going on* ▪ *Syn* abandon, cease, desist, disjoin, dissever, drop, end, finish, halt, intervene, kill, pause, quit, refrain from, suspend, terminate; ▪ *Ant* carry on, continue, restart, retry.

discontinuous [*adj*] *broken; intermittent* ▪ *Syn* alternate, desultory, disconnected, disjointed, disordered, fitful, incoherent, incohesive, interrupted, irregular, muddled, spasmodic; ▪ *Ant* connected, contiguous, continuous, regular, unbroken.

discordant [*adj*] *not in harmony; conflicting* ▪ *Syn* antagonistic, antipathetic, at odds, cacophonous, contradictory, contrary, different, discrepant, dissonant, divergent, grating, harsh, incompatible, incongruous, inconsistent, inconsonant, jangling, jarring, strident; ▪ *Ant* agreeable, agreeing, concordant, congenial, cooperating, harmonious, melodious.

discount [v1] *lower, reduce cost*
▪ *Syn* abate, allow, deduct, depreciate, diminish, mark down, modify, rebate, redeem, remove, subtract, undersell; ▪ *Ant* increase, mark up, raise.

discount [v2] *ignore; treat as insignificant* ▪ *Syn* belittle, depreciate, disbelieve, discredit, disregard, doubt, minimize, mistrust, neglect, omit, overlook, pass over, question, reject, scoff at, slight; ▪ *Ant* attend, pay attention, recognize.

discountenance [v] *reject, oppose*
▪ *Syn* condemn, deprecate, disapprove, discourage, disesteem, disfavor, dispute, object to, put down, resist; ▪ *Ant* approve, back, countenance, sanction, support.

discourage [v1] *dishearten, dispirit*
▪ *Syn* abash, afflict, bully, cast down, cow, dampen, dash, daunt, deject, demoralize, depress, dismay, disparage, distress, frighten, intimidate, irk, overawe, prostrate, repress, scare, trouble, try, unnerve, vex, weigh; ▪ *Ant* encourage, hearten, inspire, inspirit.

discourage [v2] *deter, dissuade; restrain* ▪ *Syn* curb, discountenance, frighten, hinder, hold back, impede, inhibit, obstruct, prevent, put off, repress, scare, withhold; ▪ *Ant* encourage, inspire, spur on.

discouraged [adj] *disheartened*
▪ *Syn* beat-down, blue, caved-in, crestfallen, dashed, daunted, depressed, deterred, dismayed, dispirited, downcast, pessimistic, sad; ▪ *Ant* encouraged, heartened, inspired, uplifted.

discouraging [adj] *upsetting*
▪ *Syn* bleak, daunting, depressing, disappointing, disheartening, dismal, dispiriting, dreary, gloomy, oppressive, repressing; ▪ *Ant* encouraging, heartening, inspiring, inspiriting.

discourteous [adj] *rude, impolite*
▪ *Syn* abrupt, bad-mannered, brusque, churlish, curt, disrespectful, fresh, ill-mannered, impertinent, impolite, insolent, offhand, rude; ▪ *Ant* civil,

courteous, gracious, mannered, mannerly, polite, refined, respectful, well-bred.

discover [v] *find, uncover*
▪ *Syn* ascertain, bring to light, catch, come across, detect, discern, disclose, distinguish, elicit, espy, glimpse, hear, identify, invent, learn, locate, notice, observe, perceive, pioneer, recognize, reveal, see, sense, spot; ▪ *Ant* lose, miss, pass by.

discredit [v1] *blame, detract from*
▪ *Syn* censure, degrade, disgrace, dishonor, disparage, expose, puncture, reproach, ruin, shoot, slander, slur, smear, vilify; ▪ *Ant* commend, credit, honor, praise.

discredit [v2] *doubt, question*
▪ *Syn* challenge, deny, disbelieve, discount, dispute, distrust, mistrust, reject, scoff at; ▪ *Ant* believe, credit, trust.

discreet [adj] *cautious, sensible*
▪ *Syn* alert, cagey, careful, chary, conservative, considerate, diplomatic, gingerly, guarded, judicious, moderate, noncommittal, observant, politic, prudent, reserved, restrained, safe, sagacious, strategic, tactful, thoughtful, vigilant, wary, watchful, wise; ▪ *Ant* careless, foolish, incautious, indiscreet, rash, reckless, thoughtless, undiscerning.

discrepancy [n] *conflict, disagreement*
▪ *Syn* contrariety, difference, discordance, disparity, dissimilitude, dissonance, distinction, divergence, error, incongruity, inconsistency, miscalculation, split, variation; ▪ *Ant* agreement, concordance, concurrence, consistency, harmony, parity.

discrepant [adj] *disagreeing*
▪ *Syn* at variance, conflicting, contradictory, contrary, different, differing, discordant, diverse, incompatible, incongruent, inconsistent; ▪ *Ant* agreeing, concurring, consistent, harmonious.

discrete [adj] *individual*
▪ *Syn* detached, different, disconnected, discontinuous, distinct, diverse, separate, several, various; ▪ *Ant* attached, blended, combined, joined, mingled.

discretionary [adj] *open to choice*
▪ *Syn* elective, facultative, open, optional, unrestricted; ▪ *Ant* compulsory, mandatory, obligatory.

discriminate [v] *differentiate, distinguish* ▪ *Syn* assess, compare, contrast, discern, evaluate, judge, know, note, perceive, remark, segregate, separate, sift, specify, tell apart, tell the difference; ▪ *Ant* confound, confuse, mix up.

discriminating [*adj*] *critical*
▪ *Syn* acute, astute, careful, choosy, discerning, distinctive, fastidious, finicky, fussy, judicious, keen, particular, prudent, refined, selective, sensitive, tasteful, wise; ▪ *Ant* uncritical, undiscriminating.

discussion [*n*] *talk with another or others* ▪ *Syn* argument, canvass, colloquy, confabulation, conference, conversation, debate, deliberation, dialogue, discourse, dispute, dissertation, examination, exchange, huddle, interview, meeting, review, symposium; ▪ *Ant* monologue, quiet, silence.

disdain [*v*] *scorn*
▪ *Syn* abhor, contemn, deride, despise, hate, ignore, misprize, refuse, repudiate, sneer at, spurn, undervalue; ▪ *Ant* admire, approve, esteem, favor, praise, respect.

disdainful [*adj*] *scornful*
▪ *Syn* aloof, antipathetic, arrogant, averse, cavalier, contemptuous, cool, derisive, egotistic, haughty, indifferent, insolent, overbearing, proud, supercilious, superior; ▪ *Ant* favoring, loving, praising, respectful, reverential, sympathetic.

diseased [*adj*] *unhealthy*
▪ *Syn* afflicted, ailing, indisposed, infected, infectious, infirm, rotten, sick, sickly, tainted, unsound; ▪ *Ant* fit, hale, healthy, well.

disembark [*v*] *get off transportation*
▪ *Syn* alight, anchor, arrive, debark, deplane, detrain, dismount, go ashore, land, put in; ▪ *Ant* embark, get on, leave.

disenchanted [*adj*] *let down*
▪ *Syn* blase, cynical, disillusioned, embittered, indifferent, jaundiced, knowing, sophisticated, soured, undeceived, worldly; ▪ *Ant* enchanted, encouraged, entranced, ingenuous, naive.

disengage [*v*] *free from connection*
▪ *Syn* abstract, disassociate, disconnect, disentangle, dissociate, extricate, liberate, loosen, release, separate, set free, withdraw; ▪ *Ant* attach, bind, connect, couple, engage, fasten, join, unite.

disentangle [*v*] *unwind, disconnect; solve* ▪ *Syn* clear up, disencumber, emancipate, extricate, free, open, resolve, simplify, sort out, sunder, work out; ▪ *Ant* entangle, entwine, twist, wind.

disgrace [*v*] *bring shame upon*
▪ *Syn* abase, besmirch, blot, debase, defile, degrade, expel, humble, humiliate, libel, lower, mock, reduce, ridicule, shame, slander, slur, snub, stain, stigmatize, sully, taint, tarnish; ▪ *Ant* esteem, exalt, honor, respect.

disgraceful [*adj*] *shameful, low*
▪ *Syn* contemptible, degrading, detestable, discreditable, dishonorable, disreputable, ignoble, ignominious, infamous, inglorious, mean, offensive, opprobrious, scandalous; ▪ *Ant* blameless, exalted, honorable, respectable.

disgruntled [*adj*] *unhappy; critical*
▪ *Syn* annoyed, discontented, displeased, dissatisfied, irritable, malcontent, peeved, petulant, put out, sullen, testy, vexed; ▪ *Ant* contented, happy, pleased, satisfied, uncritical.

disguise [*v*] *mask; misrepresent*
▪ *Syn* alter, assume, belie, camouflage, conceal, counterfeit, cover, deceive, fake, falsify, feign, front, gloss over, hide, masquerade, obfuscate, obscure, pretend, screen, secrete, shroud, simulate, varnish, veil; ▪ *Ant* expose, open, represent, reveal, uncover, unmask.

disguised [*adj*] *unrecognizable*
▪ *Syn* camouflaged, changed, cloaked, covered, covert, fake, false, feigned, hidden, masked, undercover; ▪ *Ant* bare, open, recognizable, revealed, uncovered, unmasked.

disgust [*v*] *cause aversion; repel*
▪ *Syn* abominate, bother, disenchant, displease, insult, nauseate, offend, outrage, pall, pique, put off, repulse, revolt, shock, sicken, turn off, upset; ▪ *Ant* attract, allure, appeal, entice, tempt.

disgusted [*adj*] *sickened; offended*
▪ *Syn* appalled, displeased, nauseated, nauseous, outraged, overwrought, queasy, repelled, repulsed, revolted, sick, squeamish; ▪ *Ant* attracted, delighted, desirous, happy, pleased.

disgusting [*adj*] *sickening; repulsive*
▪ *Syn* abominable, awful, beastly, cloying, detestable, foul, gruesome, hideous, horrific, loathsome, monstrous, nauseating, objectionable, odious, offensive, repugnant, revolting, shocking, vile, vulgar; ▪ *Ant* attractive, desirous, pleasant, pleasing.

dishearten [v] *depress, ruin one's hopes*
• **Syn** cast down, crush, deject, demoralize, depress, discourage, dismay, disparage, humble, humiliate, indispose, put down, shake; • **Ant** encourage, hearten, inspirit.

disheveled [adj] *wrinkled, unkempt in appearance* • **Syn** bedraggled, dirty, ill-kempt, rumpled, slipshod, slovenly, tousled; • **Ant** fastidious, neat, ordered, orderly, tidy, unwrinkled.

dishonest [adj] *lying, untruthful*
• **Syn** corrupt, crooked, deceitful, double-crossing, fraudulent, mendacious, misleading, perfidious, recreant, shady, sinister, traitorous, treacherous, tricky, unctuous, villainous; • **Ant** aboveboard, ethical, fair, frank, honest, moral, open, principled, scrupulous, trustworthy, truthful.

dishonor [v] *shame, degrade*
• **Syn** abase, attaint, blacken, blot, corrupt, debase, debauch, defame, defile, discredit, disgrace, libel, slander, sully; • **Ant** credit, esteem, honor, upgrade.

dishonorable [adj] *shameful, corrupt*
• **Syn** base, contemptible, crooked, deceitful, despicable, devious, disgraceful, disreputable, fraudulent, ignoble, ignominious, infamous, inglorious, low, miscreant, offensive, opprobrious, scandalous, shady, treacherous; • **Ant** blameless, ethical, honorable, incorrupt, principled, respectable, trustworthy, worthy.

disillusioned [adj] *disappointed*
• **Syn** blasé, broken, disabused, disenchanted, embittered, enlightened, freed, indifferent, knowing, mondaine, punctured, shattered, sophisticated, undeceived, worldly; • **Ant** enchanted, encouraged, enthralled, enthusiastic.

disinclined [adj] *unwilling*
• **Syn** afraid, antipathetic, balking, dubious, hesitating, indisposed, loath, objecting, opposed, protesting, reluctant, resistant; • **Ant** bent, desirous, disposed, enthusiastic, inclined, leaning, willing.

disinfect [v] *make clean, pure*
• **Syn** antisepticize, clean, cleanse, decontaminate, deodorize, fumigate, purify, sanitize, sterilize; • **Ant** dirty, pollute.

disingenuous [adj] *insincere*
• **Syn** artful, cunning, deceitful, dishonest, false, guileful, indirect, mendacious, oblique, sly, tricky, underhanded, wily;

• **Ant** candid, frank, honest, ingenuous, naive, sincere.

disinherit [v] *cut off in will of bequeathal*
• **Syn** deprive, disaffiliate, disown, dispossess, divest, evict, exclude, neglect, repudiate; • **Ant** bequeath, give.

disintegrate [v] *fall apart; reduce to pieces* • **Syn** atomize, break down, crumble, decay, decompose, disperse, fade away, pulverize, putrefy, rot, shatter, splinter, wither; • **Ant** combine, meld, unite.

disinterested [adj] *detached, uninvolved* • **Syn** aloof, candid, casual, dispassionate, impartial, impersonal, neutral, nonpartisan, outside, perfunctory, remote, withdrawn; • **Ant** biased, concerned, interested, involved, passionate, prejudiced.

disjointed [adj] *loose, disconnected*
• **Syn** aimless, confused, discontinuous, fitful, incohesive, irrational, jumbled, muddled, rambling, separated, spasmodic; • **Ant** attached, coherent, connected, contiguous, jointed, ordered, united.

dislike [v] *be antagonistic toward something; hate* • **Syn** abhor, abominate, avoid, be averse to, condemn, deplore, despise, detest, disapprove, eschew, execrate, loathe, object to, resent, scorn, shun; • **Ant** approve, like, love, relish.

dislocate [v] *displace*
• **Syn** break, disarticulate, disconnect, disengage, disjoint, disorder, disrupt, disunite, jumble, misplace, move, remove, rummage, separate, shift, transfer, unhinge, upset; • **Ant** keep together, order, unite.

dislodge [v] *knock loose*
• **Syn** dislocate, displace, disturb, eject, evict, extricate, force out, oust, remove, uproot; • **Ant** bury, embed, establish, lodge, plant, root, seat, situate.

disloyal [adj] *unfaithful*
• **Syn** alienated, apostate, disaffected, estranged, faithless, false, perfidious, recreant, seditious, subversive, traitorous, treacherous; • **Ant** faithful, loyal, true, trustworthy.

dismal [adj] *bleak, dreary, gloomy*
• **Syn** afflictive, cheerless, dark, depressing, desolate, dim, dispiriting, dolorous, dull, forlorn, funereal, ghastly, hopeless, joyless, lonesome, lugubrious, melancholy, monotonous, morbid, murky, op-

pressive, overcast, somber, tenebrous; ▪ *Ant* bright, cheerful, glad, happy, hopeful, light, pleasant.

dismantle [v] *take apart*
▪ *Syn* break down, disassemble, dismember, dismount, fell, level, raze, ruin, subvert, tear down, wreck; ▪ *Ant* assemble, build, combine, construct, put together, raise.

dismay [v] *disappoint, fill with consternation* ▪ *Syn* abash, agitate, appall, bewilder, confound, daunt, discomfit, discompose, disconcert, embarrass, mystify, nonplus, paralyze, perplex, puzzle, rattle, shake, throw, unnerve, upset; ▪ *Ant* assure, encourage, make happy.

dismember [v] *cut into pieces*
▪ *Syn* amputate, anatomize, disassemble, disjoint, dismantle, dissect, divide, mutilate, part, rend, sever, sunder; ▪ *Ant* heal, join, mend, rehabilitate, restore, salvage.

dismiss [v1] *send away, remove; free*
▪ *Syn* abolish, banish, clear, deport, detach, discard, dispense with, dispose of, expel, force out, outlaw, reject, release, relinquish, rid, shed, supersede; ▪ *Ant* accept, accept, hold, keep, maintain, preserve, welcome.

dismiss [v2] *remove from job, responsibility* ▪ *Syn* defrock, discharge, displace, drop, fire, furlough, impeach, lay off, oust, pension, recall, retire, suspend, terminate; ▪ *Ant* appoint, employ, engage, hire, keep, secure.

dismiss [v3] *put out of one's mind*
▪ *Syn* banish, contemn, discard, dispel, disregard, drop, lay aside, reject, relegate; ▪ *Ant* accept, admit, allow.

dismount [v] *get off something higher*
▪ *Syn* alight, debark, deplane, descend, detrain, disembark, get down, light; ▪ *Ant* get up, mount.

disobedient [adj] *defiant, mischievous* ▪ *Syn* contrary, contumacious, disorderly, fractious, headstrong, intractable, naughty, obstreperous, perverse, wayward, willful; ▪ *Ant* accepting, behaving, compliant, obedient, observant, submitting.

disobey [v] *disregard rules; refuse to conform* ▪ *Syn* balk, contravene, counteract, defy, evade, flout, ignore, infringe, insurrect, misbehave, mutiny, neglect, overstep, resist, revolt, riot, shirk, strike, transgress, violate, withstand; ▪ *Ant*

conform, go along, obey, oblige, regard, submit.

disoblige [v] *displease, annoy*
▪ *Syn* affront, bother, discommode, disturb, inconvenience, insult, offend, put out, slight, trouble, upset, vex; ▪ *Ant* agree, oblige, please.

disobliging [adj] *rude, annoying*
▪ *Syn* awkward, disagreeable, discourteous, ill-natured, rude, uncongenial, uncooperative, unpleasant; ▪ *Ant* accommodating, agreeable, civil, cooperative, courteous, mannered, mannerly, polite.

disorder [v] *mix up, disarrange*
▪ *Syn* clutter, confound, confuse, derange, discompose, dishevel, disjoint, dislocate, disorganize, disrupt, disturb, embroil, rummage, rumple, scatter, shuffle, tumble, unsettle, upset; ▪ *Ant* arrange, conform, neaten, order, regulate, systematize.

disordered [adj] *in a mess*
▪ *Syn* confused, disarranged, disjointed, dislocated, disorganized, incoherent, jumbled, misplaced, moved, muddled, roiled, ruffled, shuffled, stirred up, tangled, tousled, tumbled; ▪ *Ant* arranged, methodical, neat, ordered, orderly, organized, systematic, systematized, trim.

disorderly [adj1] *messy, untidy*
▪ *Syn* chaotic, cluttered, heterogeneous, indiscriminate, irregular, jumbled, mixed up, scattered, scrambled; ▪ *Ant* arranged, methodical, neat, ordered, orderly, organized, systematized, trim.

disorderly [adj2] *causing trouble; unlawful* ▪ *Syn* boisterous, disruptive, fractious, intemperate, noisy, obstreperous, raucous, refractory, termagant, unruly, wayward; ▪ *Ant* behaved, conforming, disciplined, manageable, orderly, wellbehaved.

disorganize [v] *disrupt arrangement; make shambles of* ▪ *Syn* break down, disarrange, disarray, disband, discompose, dishevel, disorder, disperse, disturb, jumble, litter, muddle, perturb, scatter, scramble, toss, upset; ▪ *Ant* compose, neaten, order, organize, plan, systematize, tidy.

disorganized [adj] *unmethodical; messed up* ▪ *Syn* chaotic, confused, disorderly, haphazard, jumbled, mixed up, muddled; ▪ *Ant* methodical, neat, ordered, organized, planned, regulated, systematic, tidy.

disoriented [*adj*] *confused, unstable*
▪ *Syn* adrift, astray, bewildered, lost, mixed-up, perplexed, unbalanced, unsettled; ▪ *Ant* balanced, oriented, settled, understanding.

disown [*v*] *refuse to acknowledge*
▪ *Syn* abandon, abjure, abnegate, cast off, deny, reject, renounce, retract; ▪ *Ant* accept, acknowledge, allow, avow, claim.

disparage [*v*] *criticize; detract from*
▪ *Syn* belittle, decry, defame, depreciate, deride, derogate, malign, put down, ridicule, scorch, scorn, slander, tear down, traduce, underestimate, vilify, write off; ▪ *Ant* approve, commend, compliment, flatter, laud, praise, sanction.

disparate [*adj*] *at odds, different*
▪ *Syn* at variance, contrasting, discordant, discrepant, dissimilar, distant, distinct, divergent, diverse, inconsistent, inconsonant, poles apart, separate, various; ▪ *Ant* alike, commensurate, equal, equivalent, like, same, similar.

dispassionate [*adj*] *unfeeling, impartial*
▪ *Syn* aloof, calm, cold-blooded, collected, composed, cool, detached, disinterested, impersonal, indifferent, moderate, neutral, nonpartisan, objective, serene, temperate, tough; ▪ *Ant* biased, discriminatory, emotional, excited, feeling, involved, moved, partial, passionate, prejudiced, subjective.

dispatch [*v*] *hurry, send fast*
▪ *Syn* accelerate, consign, dismiss, express, forward, hasten, issue, quicken, remit, ship, speed, transmit; ▪ *Ant* hold, hold back, keep, prohibit, retain.

dispel [*v*] *drive away thought, belief*
▪ *Syn* allay, banish, cancel, dismiss, disperse, dissipate, distribute, eject, eliminate, expel, oust, repel, resolve, rout, scatter; ▪ *Ant* accumulate, collect, garner, gather, recall.

dispensable [*adj*] *not necessary; able to be thrown away* ▪ *Syn* disposable, expendable, removable, superfluous, trivial, unimportant, unnecessary, useless; ▪ *Ant* essential, imperative, indispensable, irreplaceable, necessary, required, useful.

dispense [*v*] *dole out supply*
▪ *Syn* allocate, allot, apportion, assign, deal, disburse, distribute, divide, give, hand out, lot, measure, mete out, partition, portion, prepare, share, supply; ▪ *Ant* receive, take.

dispense with [*v*] *omit; do away with*
▪ *Syn* abolish, cancel, dispose of, disregard, do without, forgo, ignore, relinquish, waive; ▪ *Ant* accept, keep, regard, retain, take, use.

disperse [*v*] *distribute; scatter*
▪ *Syn* banish, break up, circulate, diffuse, dispel, disseminate, dissipate, dole out, eject, partition, radiate, scatter, spray, strew, vanish; ▪ *Ant* arrange, assemble, collect, garner, gather.

dispirited [*adj*] *dejected, sad*
▪ *Syn* crestfallen, despondent, disheartened, downcast, glum, low, melancholy, morose, spiritless, woebegone; ▪ *Ant* encouraged, enthused, happy, heartened, inspirited.

displace [*v*] *remove from position of responsibility* ▪ *Syn* banish, deport, discard, discharge, dismiss, exile, expatriate, fire, oust, supersede, supplant, take over, transport, usurp; ▪ *Ant* crown, inaugurate, induct, install, invest.

display [*v*] *show for public viewing, effect* ▪ *Syn* advertise, arrange, brandish, bring to view, demonstrate, disclose, emblazon, evidence, evince, exhibit, expand, expose, extend, feature, flaunt, illustrate, impart, manifest, model, open, parade, perform, present, promote, promulgate, publish, represent, reveal, showcase, show off, sport; ▪ *Ant* conceal, cover, hide, secrete, withhold.

displease [*v*] *make unhappy*
▪ *Syn* aggravate, anger, annoy, antagonize, bother, chagrin, disappoint, discontent, disgruntle, disgust, enrage, exasperate, fret, frustrate, gall, hurt, incense, irk, irritate, nettle, offend, perplex, pique, provoke, put out, rile, upset, vex; ▪ *Ant* appease, calm, compose, delight, humor, make happy, oblige, please, satisfy.

dispose [*v*] *place, order; deal with*
▪ *Syn* adjust, arrange, array, determine, distribute, fix, govern, group, incline, induce, influence, locate, marshal, motivate, move, organize, prepare, promote, prompt, put, range, rank, regulate, set, settle, shepherd, stand, systematize; ▪ *Ant* disarrange, disorder, displace, disturb, mismanage.

disposed [*adj*] *inclined to a type of behavior* ▪ *Syn* apt, biased, fain, given, liable, likely, partial, predisposed, prone, ready, subject, willing; ▪ *Ant* indisposed, unlikely, unready, unwilling.

dispose of [*v1*] *throw away*
▪ *Syn* destroy, discard, dump, eliminate, jettison, relinquish, scrap, sell, throw out, transfer, unload; ▪ *Ant* hold, keep, retain.

dispose of [*v2*] *settle a matter*
▪ *Syn* cut, cut off, deal with, decide, determine, end, finish, put away, take care of; ▪ *Ant* begin, continue, start.

disproportionate [*adj*] *out of balance*
▪ *Syn* asymmetric, excessive, incommensurate, inordinate, irregular, lopsided, off-balance, overbalanced, superfluous; ▪ *Ant* balanced, equal, even, proportionate.

disprove [*v*] *prove false*
▪ *Syn* belie, confound, confute, contradict, contravene, controvert, deny, discredit, explode, expose, invalidate, negate, overthrow, overturn, puncture, rebut, refute, traverse; ▪ *Ant* confirm, credit, prove, validate.

disputable [*adj*] *debatable; open to discussion* ▪ *Syn* arguable, controversial, doubtful, dubious, moot, questionable, uncertain; ▪ *Ant* certain, inarguable, indisputable, unquestionable.

disputatious [*adj*] *argumentative*
▪ *Syn* cantankerous, captious, caviling, contentious, litigious, polemical, pugnacious, quarrelsome; ▪ *Ant* agreeable, calm, peaceful, tranquil.

dispute [*v*] *argue*
▪ *Syn* altercate, bicker, brawl, challenge, confute, contend, contest, debate, deny, discept, discuss, disprove, doubt, gainsay, hassle, impugn, negate, quarrel, question, quibble, rebut, refute, wrangle; ▪ *Ant* agree, concede, concur, give in, go along.

disqualify [*v*] *make unfit for; make ineligible* ▪ *Syn* bar, debar, disable, disenable, disentitle, disfranchise, except, exclude, impair, incapacitate, invalidate, paralyze, preclude, prohibit, rule out, suspend; ▪ *Ant* allow, capacitate, fit, make eligible, permit, qualify.

disquiet [*v*] *worry; make uneasy*
▪ *Syn* agitate, annoy, bother, concern, discompose, distress, disturb, fluster, fret, harass, perplex, perturb, pester, plague, trouble, unhinge, unsettle, upset, vex; ▪ *Ant* calm, ease, please, settle, soothe.

disregard [*v*] *ignore; make light of*
▪ *Syn* brush aside, brush off, contemn, discount, disdain, disobey, disparage, fail, forget, miss, neglect, omit, overlook, scorn, slight, vilipend; ▪ *Ant* attend, esteem, note, pay attention, regard, respect.

disreputable [*adj*] *dishonorable, lowly*
▪ *Syn* abject, bad, base, contemptible, despicable, disgraceful, disorderly, dissolute, ignominious, infamous, libidinous, licentious, mean, notorious, opprobrious, pitiable, scandalous, shabby, shady, shameful, shocking, shoddy, sordid, sorry, vicious, vile; ▪ *Ant* decent, ethical, honorable, principled, reputable, respected.

disrespectful [*adj*] *insulting, rude*
▪ *Syn* bad-mannered, blasphemous, bold, contemptuous, discourteous, flippant, ill-mannered, impertinent, impious, impolite, impudent, insolent, irreverent, profane, sacrilegious, unfilial; ▪ *Ant* civil, courteous, gracious, mannered, mannerly, nice, respectful.

disrobe [*v*] *take off one's clothes*
▪ *Syn* bare, denude, dismantle, divest, doff, remove, shed, strip, unclothe, uncover, undress; ▪ *Ant* clothe, put on.

disrupt [*v*] *upset, disorganize*
▪ *Syn* agitate, bollix, confuse, disarray, discompose, disorder, disturb, muddle, rattle, rummage, shake, spoil, throw, unsettle; ▪ *Ant* arrange, organize, ready.

disruptive [*adj*] *causing trouble, confusion* ▪ *Syn* confusing, disorderly, distracting, disturbing, obstreperous, rowdy, troublesome, unruly, unsettling, upsetting; ▪ *Ant* calming, disciplined, settling, soothing, well-behaved.

dissatisfied [*adj*] *discontented, unhappy*
▪ *Syn* annoyed, bothered, critical, disaffected, disappointed, discontent, disgruntled, displeased, fretful, frustrated, irked, jaundiced, malcontent, offended, vexed; ▪ *Ant* appeased, contented, fulfilled, gratified, happy, pleased, satisfied.

dissect [*v*] *cut up; take apart*
▪ *Syn* anatomize, cut, dichotomize, disjoin, disjoint, dismember, dissever, divide, exscind, exsect, operate, part, prosect, quarter, section, sever, slice, sunder; ▪ *Ant* connect, join, mend, sew.

dissemble [*v*] *disguise, pretend*
▪ *Syn* affect, camouflage, cloak, conceal, counterfeit, cover up, dissimulate, fake, falsify, feign, hide, mask, pass, shroud,

signify, simulate; ▪ *Ant* admit, allow, reveal, show.

disseminate [v] *distribute, scatter*
▪ *Syn* advertise, announce, blaze, blazon, broadcast, circulate, declare, diffuse, disperse, dissipate, proclaim, promulgate, propagate, publicize, publish, radiate, sow, spread, strew; ▪ *Ant* collect, contain, gather.

dissent [v] *disagree*
▪ *Syn* argue, balk, buck, contradict, decline, demur, differ, divide, object, oppose, pettifog, protest, refuse, vary, wrangle; ▪ *Ant* agree, approve, assent, authorize, concur, consent, endorse, ratify, sanction.

disservice [n] *unkindness*
▪ *Syn* bad turn, detriment, disfavor, harm, hurt, injury, injustice, insult, outrage, prejudice, wrong; ▪ *Ant* benevolence, favor, giving, good turn, kindness, service.

dissident [adj] *disagreeing, differing*
▪ *Syn* discordant, dissenting, heretical, heterodox, nonconformist, schismatic, sectarian, unorthodox; ▪ *Ant* agreeing, conforming.

dissimilar [adj] *not alike; not capable of comparison* ▪ *Syn* antithetical, antonymous, contradictory, contrary, different, disparate, distant, divergent, diverse, heterogeneous, individual, opposite, unique, various; ▪ *Ant* alike, compatible, equal, matched, related, same, similar.

dissimulate [v] *conceal, disguise*
▪ *Syn* camouflage, cloak, deceive, dissemble, fake, feign, hide, mask, pretend; ▪ *Ant* be honest, disclose, expose, reveal.

dissipate [v1] *expend, spend*
▪ *Syn* consume, deplete, fritter away, lavish, misuse, squander, waste; ▪ *Ant* accumulate, collect, gather, hoard, save.

dissipate [v2] *disappear*
▪ *Syn* dispel, disperse, dissolve, evanesce, evaporate, scatter, spread, vanish; ▪ *Ant* accumulate, amass, appear.

dissociate [v] *part company with; separate* ▪ *Syn* alienate, detach, disband, disconnect, disengage, disjoin, disrupt, distance, disunite, divide, divorce, estrange, isolate, quit, scatter, segregate; ▪ *Ant* associate, attach, connect, join.

dissolute [adj] *immoral*
▪ *Syn* abandoned, corrupt, debauched, degenerate, depraved, dissipated, intemperate, lascivious, lax, lecherous, lewd,

libertine, licentious, profligate, raffish, rakish, reprobate, slack, sybaritic, wanton, wayward, wicked, wild; ▪ *Ant* chaste, good, moral, pure, resolute, respectful, virtuous.

dissolve [v1] *melt from solid to liquid; mix in* ▪ *Syn* defrost, deliquesce, diffuse, flux, fuse, liquefy, render, run, soften, thaw; ▪ *Ant* coagulate, concentrate, solidify, unmix.

dissolve [v2] *disappear, disintegrate*
▪ *Syn* break down, break up, crumble, decline, decompose, diffuse, disband, disperse, dissipate, dwindle, evanesce, evaporate, fade, melt away, perish, separate, vanish, waste away; ▪ *Ant* appear, assemble, integrate, put together, unite.

dissolve [v3] *annul, discontinue*
▪ *Syn* abrogate, adjourn, annihilate, cancel, collapse, decimate, demolish, destroy, destruct, discharge, disorganize, disunite, divorce, end, eradicate, invalidate, loose, overthrow, postpone, quash, repeal, ruin, separate, sever, shatter, shoot, suspend, terminate, vacate, void, wreck; ▪ *Ant* construct, continue, marry, resolve.

dissonant [adj1] *different, conflicting*
▪ *Syn* anomalous, differing, dissonant, discordant, discrepant, dissentient, incompatible, incongruent, incongruous, inconsistent, inconsonant, irreconcilable, irregular; ▪ *Ant* coinciding, compatible, complementary, consonant, similar.

dissonant [adj2] *unharmonious*
▪ *Syn* cacophonous, discordant, grating, harsh, jangling, jarring, out of tune, raucous, strident, tuneless; ▪ *Ant* concordant, harmonious, melodious, musical.

dissuade [v] *talk out of*
▪ *Syn* advise against, caution against, counsel, deprecate, derail, deter, discourage, disincline, divert, exhort, expostulate, faze, hinder, prevent, remonstrate, thwart, warn; ▪ *Ant* incite, persuade, talk into.

distant [adj1] *faraway*
▪ *Syn* abroad, apart, away, beyond range, far, far-flung, far-off, inaccessible, in background, indirect, in distance, isolated, obscure, outlying, out-of-the-way, remote, secluded, sequestered, telescopic; ▪ *Ant* adjacent, close, near, nearby, neighboring.

distant [adj2] *aloof*
▪ *Syn* abstracted, arrogant, ceremonious,

cold, cool, formal, haughty, modest, proud, remote, reserved, restrained, reticent, retiring, shy, solitary, stiff, withdrawn; ▪ *Ant* approachable, friendly, kind, sociable, sympathetic, warm.

distasteful [*adj*] *repulsive, unpleasant*
▪ *Syn* abhorrent, abominable, afflictive, bitter, detestable, disagreeable, galling, hateful, loathsome, obnoxious, odious, offensive, painful, repugnant; ▪ *Ant* agreeable, appetizing, delectable, delicious, desirable, palatable, pleasant, pleasing.

distend [*v*] *bulge, swell*
▪ *Syn* amplify, augment, balloon, bloat, bulge, dilate, distort, enlarge, expand, increase, inflate, lengthen, puff, stretch, widen; ▪ *Ant* cave in, contract, deflate, fall, shrink.

distinct [*adj1*] *apparent, obvious*
▪ *Syn* audible, categorical, clear, decided, definite, enunciated, evident, incisive, lucid, manifest, marked, noticeable, patent, perspicuous, recognizable, sharp, specific, trenchant, well-defined; ▪ *Ant* ambiguous, hazy, indistinct, obscure, undefined, vague.

distinct [*adj2*] *different; unconnected*
▪ *Syn* detached, disparate, dissimilar, diverse, especial, individual, particular, peculiar, separate, separated, special, specific, unique, various; ▪ *Ant* connected, like, resembling, similar.

distinctive [*adj*] *different, unique*
▪ *Syn* characteristic, diacritic, diagnostic, distinct, distinguishing, excellent, extraordinary, idiosyncratic, individual, offbeat, original, peculiar, singular, special, superior, typical, unreal, weird; ▪ *Ant* common, normal, resembling, same, similar, standard.

distinguished [*adj*] *famous, outstanding*
▪ *Syn* acclaimed, celebrated, distingué, eminent, esteemed, famed, foremost, great, honored, illustrious, memorable, name, noble, nonpareil, notable, noteworthy, peerless, prominent, remarkable, reputable, royal, salient, singular, special, stately, striking, superior, unforgettable, venerable, well-known; ▪ *Ant* common, insignificant, ordinary, standard, unknown.

distract [*v*] *divert attention; confuse*
▪ *Syn* abstract, addle, agitate, amuse, befuddle, beguile, bewilder, confound, detract, disturb, divert, engross, entertain,

fluster, frenzy, mislead, occupy, perplex, puzzle, sidetrack, stall; ▪ *Ant* clarify, explain, focus.

distraught [*adj*] *very upset, worked-up*
▪ *Syn* addled, agitated, bothered, concerned, distressed, frantic, harassed, hysterical, muddled, overwrought, perturbed, rattled, troubled, wild, worried; ▪ *Ant* calm, serene, soothed, untroubled.

distress [*v*] *worry, upset*
▪ *Syn* afflict, agonize, ail, bother, disquiet, disturb, grieve, harass, harry, hound, hurt, injure, irk, irritate, oppress, pain, peeve, pester, sadden, strain, stress, torment, torture, trouble, try, vex, weigh; ▪ *Ant* assist, calm, comfort, help, soothe.

distressed [*adj*] *upset*
▪ *Syn* agitated, antsy, anxious, bothered, concerned, distracted, distrait, distraught, harassed, inconsolable, jittery, jumpy, perturbed, saddened, shaky, tormented, troubled, worried, wretched; ▪ *Ant* calm, collected, comforted, glad, happy, joyful.

distribute [*v*] *allocate, deliver, spread*
▪ *Syn* administer, allot, apportion, appropriate, assign, bestow, circulate, consign, convey, deal, deliver, diffuse, disburse, dispense, disperse, dispose, endow, give, issue, mete out, parcel, partition, prorate, ration, share, sow, strew; ▪ *Ant* collect, gather, hoard, hold, keep, maintain, preserve, store.

distrust [*v*] *be suspicious, skeptical of*
▪ *Syn* be wary of, disbelieve, discredit, doubt, mistrust, question, suspect; ▪ *Ant* be confident, believe, credit, trust.

distrustful [*adj*] *disbelieving*
▪ *Syn* cagey, cautious, chary, cynical, doubtful, dubious, fearful, leery, skeptical, suspicious, wary; ▪ *Ant* assured, believing, certain, faithful, trustful, trusting, unsuspecting.

disturb [*v1*] *bother, upset*
▪ *Syn* agitate, alarm, badger, disrupt, distress, excite, fluster, gall, harass, interrupt, intrude, irk, irritate, pain, perturb, pester, pique, provoke, ruffle, shake, trouble, unnerve, vex; ▪ *Ant* appease, calm, comfort, pacify, quiet, reassure, soothe.

disturb [*v2*] *disorder; dislocate*
▪ *Syn* confuse, derange, disarrange, disarray, discompose, disorganize, displace, distort, interfere with, jumble, mess up, mix up, move, muddle, remove,

replace, shift, tamper, unsettle, upset; ▪ **Ant** arrange, locate, order, organize, sort.

dive [v] *descend, usually going underwater* ▪ **Syn** dip, fall, jump, leap, lunge, nose-dive, pitch, plumb, plummet, spring, swoop, vanish; ▪ **Ant** ascend, go up, jump, vault.

diverge [v1] *go in different directions* ▪ **Syn** bifurcate, branch, depart, deviate, digress, divaricate, fork, part, radiate, separate, split, spread, stray, swerve, veer, wander; ▪ **Ant** agree, converge, join, parallel.

diverge [v2] *be different from; be at odds* ▪ **Syn** conflict, contrast, depart, deviate, differ, disagree, dissent, oppose; ▪ **Ant** agree, concur.

divergent [adj] *differing* ▪ **Syn** aberrant, anomalous, antithetical, conflicting, contradictory, disparate, dissimilar, diverse, factious, opposite, separate, various; ▪ **Ant** agreeing, convergent, similar, similar.

diverse [adj] *different; various* ▪ **Syn** assorted, contrasting, differing, discrete, disparate, dissimilar, distinct, diversified, manifold, multifarious, opposite, several, sundry; ▪ **Ant** alike, commensurable, conforming, identical, like, parallel, similar, uniform.

diversify [v] *spread out; branch out* ▪ **Syn** alter, assort, change, expand, mix, modify, transform, variegate, vary; ▪ **Ant** conform, stay the same.

divert [v1] *turn in a different direction* ▪ **Syn** alter, avert, change, deflect, modify, pivot, redirect, sheer, swerve, switch, veer, wheel; ▪ **Ant** be direct, keep to, maintain, stay.

divert [v2] *amuse, entertain* ▪ **Syn** beguile, delight, gladden, gratify, please, recreate, regale, relax, tickle; ▪ **Ant** anger, bore, fatigue, irritate, upset, weary.

divest [v] *dispossess; take off* ▪ **Syn** bare, bleed, deprive, disinherit, dismantle, disrobe, doff, oust, plunder, remove, strip, unload; ▪ **Ant** clothe, cover, dress, invest, possess, take.

divide [v1] *separate, disconnect* ▪ **Syn** abscind, bisect, branch, cleave, cut, dichotomize, disengage, disjoin, disunite, divorce, halve, isolate, part, quarter, rend, rupture, section, segregate, sever, split, tear; ▪ **Ant** append, attach,

collect, combine, connect, couple, gather, join, link, unite.

divide [v2] *distribute* ▪ **Syn** allocate, allot, apportion, disburse, dispense, factor, parcel, partition, prorate, ration, share, shift, slice; ▪ **Ant** hold, keep, maintain, retain.

divide [v3] *put in order; classify* ▪ **Syn** arrange, categorize, grade, group, separate, sort; ▪ **Ant** disarrange, disorganize.

divide [v4] *disagree, alienate* ▪ **Syn** differ, dissent, disunite, estrange, part, separate, set against, split, vary; ▪ **Ant** accord, agree, convince, persuade.

divinity [n] *godliness; god* ▪ **Syn** deity, divine nature, goddess, godhead, guardian spirit, higher power, holiness, prime mover, sanctity, spirit; ▪ **Ant** devil, evil.

divorce [v] *split up a marriage* ▪ **Syn** annul, break up, dissolve, disunite, divide, nullify, part, separate, sever, split, sunder; ▪ **Ant** join, marry, unite.

divulge [v] *make known; confess* ▪ **Syn** admit, betray, broadcast, communicate, declare, disclose, discover, exhibit, expose, gossip, impart, leak, mouth, proclaim, promulgate, publish, reveal, spill, spring, tattle, tell, uncover; ▪ **Ant** conceal, hide, keep, secrete.

dizzy [adj] *lightheaded, confused* ▪ **Syn** addled, befuddled, bewildered, blind, dazed, dazzled, distracted, disturbed, dumbfounded, faint, giddy, hazy, light, muddled, puzzled, reeling, shaky, staggering, tipsy, upset, vertiginous, whirling, wobbly, woozy; ▪ **Ant** clear, clear-headed, steady, unconfused.

do [v] *carry out* ▪ **Syn** accomplish, achieve, act, complete, create, determine, effect, end, execute, fulfill, make, move, operate, perform, produce, succeed, take on, transact, undertake, work; ▪ **Ant** defer, destroy, fail, idle, lose, miss, neglect, pass, put off, undo.

do away with [v] *get rid of; destroy* ▪ **Syn** abolish, cancel, discard, discontinue, eliminate, exterminate, finish, kill, liquidate, murder, remove, slaughter, slay; ▪ **Ant** build, construct, get, keep.

docile [adj] *compliant, submissive* ▪ **Syn** accommodating, acquiescent, amenable, biddable, complacent, ductile, easygoing, gentle, mild, obliging, pliant, quiet, resigned, soft, tame, teachable, tractable, willing, yielding; ▪ *Ant* determined, headstrong, inflexible, intractable, obstinate, opinionated, stubborn, uncooperative, unyielding.

dock [v] *land on the waterfront*
▪ *Syn* anchor, berth, drop anchor, moor, put in, rendezvous, tie up, unite; ▪ *Ant* set sail, ship out.

doctor [v1] *fix up, treat*
▪ *Syn* administer, attend, fix, medicate, mend, overhaul, rebuild, recondition, reconstruct, repair, supply; ▪ *Ant* harm, hurt, injure.

doctor [v2] *adulterate, pervert*
▪ *Syn* alter, change, debase, dilute, disguise, falsify, gloss, load, misrepresent, tamper with; ▪ *Ant* clean, purify.

doctrinaire [adj] *dogmatic, opinionated*
▪ *Syn* authoritarian, biased, bigoted, dictatorial, dogged, fanatical, impractical, inflexible, insistent, magisterial, mulish, obstinate, one-sided, pertinacious, rigid, stubborn; ▪ *Ant* amenable, flexible, manageable, obedient, submissive.

doddering [adj] *aged, feeble*
▪ *Syn* anile, decrepit, faltering, floundering, infirm, senile, shaky, tottering, trembling, unsteady, weak; ▪ *Ant* agile, young, youthful.

dodge [v] *avoid*
▪ *Syn* deceive, ditch, duck, elude, equivocate, escape, evade, fence, hedge, malinger, parry, shake, shift, shirk, short-circuit, shuffle, sidestep, skirt, slide, slip, swerve, tergiversate, trick, turn aside; ▪ *Ant* confront, encounter, face, meet, stand up to.

do for [v] *help*
▪ *Syn* abet, aid, assist, benefact, care for, look after, provide for, steady, support; ▪ *Ant* deny, hinder, hurt, injure, refuse.

dog [v] *chase after; bother*
▪ *Syn* haunt, hound, plague, pursue, shadow, tag, tail, track, trail, trouble; ▪ *Ant* leave alone, let go.

dogged [adj] *determined, persistent*
▪ *Syn* adamant, firm, indefatigable, inexorable, inflexible, mulish, obdurate, obstinate, persevering, pertinacious, relentless, resolute, rigid, staunch, steadfast, stubborn, tenacious; ▪ *Ant* indifferent, irresolute, undetermined, yielding.

dogmatic [adj1] *dictatorial, opinionated*
▪ *Syn* arbitrary, arrogant, bigoted, categorical, despotic, doctrinaire, domineering, egotistical, emphatic, fanatical, imperious, intolerant, magisterial, narrow-minded, obstinate, peremptory, prejudiced, stubborn, tenacious, tyrannical, unequivocal; ▪ *Ant* amenable, doubting, flexible, indecisive, manageable, obedient, questioning, skeptical, submissive.

dogmatic [adj2] *based on absolute truth*
▪ *Syn* a priori, authoritarian, authoritative, axiomatic, canonical, categorical, deducible, doctrinal, eternal, ex cathedra, formal, imperative, inevitable, oracular, orthodox, peremptory, positive, pragmatic, prophetic, reasoned, systematic, theoretical, unqualified; ▪ *Ant* ambiguous, doubtful, dubious, equivocal, fluctuating, indecisive, uncertain, vacillating.

do in [v] *destroy; exhaust*
▪ *Syn* assassinate, bankrupt, dispatch, eliminate, execute, fatigue, finish, kill, murder, ruin, shatter, slaughter, slay, tire, wear out, weary, wreck; ▪ *Ant* conserve, create, invent, restore, salvage.

doldrums [n] *depression*
▪ *Syn* apathy, boredom, dejection, disinterest, ennui, gloom, indifference, inertia, lassitude, listlessness, malaise, stupor, tedium, torpor; ▪ *Ant* elation, gladness, glee, happiness, high spirits, joy.

doleful [adj] *depressing*
▪ *Syn* afflicted, cheerless, crestfallen, dejected, depressed, dispirited, downcast, dreary, forlorn, gloomy, lugubrious, melancholy, mournful, plaintive, rueful, sad, somber, woeful, wretched; ▪ *Ant* blithe, cheerful, elated, glad, gleeful, happy, joyful.

dole out [v] *allocate, distribute*
▪ *Syn* administer, allot, apportion, assign, deal, dispense, disperse, divide, give, hand out, lot, measure, mete out, parcel, partition, share; ▪ *Ant* collect, gather, hoard, hold.

dolorous [adj] *miserable, anguished*
▪ *Syn* afflicted, calamitous, deplorable, dire, distressing, doleful, grievous, harrowing, heart-rending, lamentable, lugubrious, melancholy, mournful, painful, regrettable, rueful, sad, woebegone, woeful, wretched; ▪ *Ant* cheery, happy, hopeful, lighthearted.

domestic [adj1] *household*
▪ *Syn* domiciliary, family, home, home-

like, home-loving, homely, indoor, stay-at-home; ▪ **Ant** business, industrial, office, public.

domestic [adj2] *not foreign*
▪ **Syn** home-grown, homemade, indigenous, internal, intestine, intramural, municipal, national, native; ▪ **Ant** alien, foreign, imported.

dominant [adj1] *superior, controlling*
▪ **Syn** ascendant, assertive, authoritative, commanding, demonstrative, despotic, first, foremost, imperative, imperious, main, paramount, powerful, predominant, preeminent, preponderant, presiding, prevalent, principal, regnant, sovereign, supreme, surpassing, transcendent; ▪ **Ant** humble, inferior, modest, reserved, retiring, unaggressive, unassuming, uncontrolling.

dominant [adj2] *main, primary*
▪ **Syn** capital, chief, influential, major, outstanding, paramount, predominant, prevailing, principal, prominent; ▪ **Ant** inferior, secondary, subordinate.

dominate [v] *govern, rule*
▪ **Syn** boss, control, dictate, domineer, eclipse, head, influence, lead, monopolize, overrule, prevail, reign, subjugate, sway, tyrannize; ▪ **Ant** follow, go along, submit, surrender, yield.

domineer [v] *oppress; assume authority*
▪ **Syn** bend, bluster, browbeat, dominate, hector, intimidate, menace, overbear, predominate, reign, rule, threaten, tyrannize; ▪ **Ant** follow, submit, surrender, yield.

domineering [adj] *oppressive, authoritarian* ▪ **Syn** arrogant, autocratic, bossy, coercive, despotic, dictatorial, egotistic, high-handed, imperative, magisterial, overbearing, peremptory, tyrannical; ▪ **Ant** submissive, subservient, surrendering, timid, yielding.

donate [v] *make a gift of*
▪ **Syn** accord, award, bequeath, bestow, confer, contribute, devote, give, grant, present, provide, subscribe; ▪ **Ant** keep, renege, withhold.

done [adj1] *accomplished, finished*
▪ **Syn** brought about, compassed, completed, concluded, consummated, effected, executed, exhausted, fixed, fulfilled, over, performed, rendered, spent, succeeded, terminated, through, wrought; ▪ **Ant** incomplete, undone, unfinished, unperfected.

done [adj2] *thoroughly cooked*
▪ **Syn** baked, boiled, brewed, broiled, browned, crisped, fried, ready, stewed; ▪ **Ant** rare, raw, undone.

done for [adj] *beaten, defeated*
▪ **Syn** broken, conquered, destroyed, doomed, finished, ruined, undone, vanquished, wrecked; ▪ **Ant** accomplished, successful.

done in [adj] *exhausted*
▪ **Syn** dead, depleted, done, effete, fagged, spent, tired, used up, weary, worn-out; ▪ **Ant** rested, vigorous, vital.

doomed [adj] *condemned, hopeless*
▪ **Syn** convicted, cursed, damned, destroyed, done, ill-fated, lost, menaced, reprobate, ruined, sentenced, starcrossed, sunk, wrecked; ▪ **Ant** delivered, fortunate, hopeful, lucky, redeemed.

dopey [adj] *stupid*
▪ **Syn** comatose, dense, dumb, foolish, heavy, hebetudinous, idiotic, lethargic, senseless, silly, simple, slow, sluggish, thick, torpid; ▪ **Ant** brainy, intelligent, quick, sensible, smart.

dormant [adj] *inactive; sleeping*
▪ **Syn** abeyant, asleep, comatose, fallow, hibernating, inert, inoperative, latent, lethargic, passive, quiescent, slumbering, suspended, torpid; ▪ **Ant** active, awake, lively, operative.

dote on/dote upon [v] *lavish affection on* ▪ **Syn** admire, adore, cherish, fancy, hold dear, idolize, love, pet, prize, treasure, worship; ▪ **Ant** ignore, loathe, neglect.

doting [adj] *indulgent*
▪ **Syn** adoring, affectionate, devoted, fatuous, fond, foolish, loving; ▪ **Ant** aloof, detached, indifferent.

double [adj] *in a pair*
▪ **Syn** bifold, binary, coupled, double-barreled, dual, dualistic, duplex, duplicate, geminate, paired, repeated, twofold; ▪ **Ant** distinct, separate, single.

double [v] *make two of; make twice as large* ▪ **Syn** amplify, augment, dualize, duplicate, enlarge, fold, grow, increase, magnify, multiply, plait, pleat, plicate, redouble, repeat, replicate, supplement; ▪ **Ant** decrease, dissect, divide, halve.

double-dealing [adj] *cheating, deceitful* ▪ **Syn** crooked, dishonest, duplicitous, fraudulent, hypocritical, insincere, lying, perfidious, sneaky, swindling, treacherous, tricky, underhanded, wily;

▪ *Ant* forthright, honest, trustworthy, truthful.

doubt [*v*] *lack confidence in; question*
▪ *Syn* be apprehensive of, be dubious, be undetermined, challenge, demur, disbelieve, discredit, dispute, distrust, fear, fluctuate, have qualms, hesitate, imagine, impugn, insinuate, mistrust, query, question, scruple, surmise, suspect, vacillate, waver, wonder at; ▪ *Ant* be certain, believe, rely, trust.

doubtful [*adj1*] *questionable, unclear*
▪ *Syn* ambiguous, chancy, debatable, dicey, dubious, equivocal, hazy, impugnable, inconclusive, indefinite, indeterminate, obscure, shady, speculative, suspicious, uncertain, unsure; ▪ *Ant* certain, clear, confirmed, decided, definite, exact, positive, resolved, settled, unquestionable.

doubtful [*adj2*] *not believing*
▪ *Syn* agnostic, baffled, confused, distrustful, dubious, equivocal, faithless, faltering, hesitant, in a quandary, indecisive, irresolute, lost, perplexed, puzzled, questioning, skeptical, suspicious, tentative, troubled, vacillating, wavering; ▪ *Ant* believing, certain, confident, convinced, faithful, sure, trusting.

doubtless [*adj*] *certainly; most likely*
▪ *Syn* absolutely, assuredly, clearly, doubtlessly, for sure, indisputably, of course, positively, precisely, surely, truly, unequivocally, unquestionably; ▪ *Ant* doubtedly, dubious, improbably, perhaps, probably, questionable, seemingly, uncertain, unlikely.

do up [*v*] *physically prepare; fix*
▪ *Syn* clean, doctor, finish, mend, overhaul, package, patch, rebuild, recondition, reconstruct, repair, revamp, wash, wrap; ▪ *Ant* hurt, injure, ruin.

dour [*adj*] *gloomy, grim*
▪ *Syn* bleak, dismal, dreary, forbidding, glum, harsh, morose, saturnine, severe, sour, sullen, surly; ▪ *Ant* bright, cheerful, cheery, friendly, happy.

douse [*v*] *drench, extinguish with liquid*
▪ *Syn* blow out, deluge, drown, dunk, immerse, plunge, put out, quench, saturate, smother, snuff, soak, steep, submerge, submerse, wet; ▪ *Ant* dehydrate, dry, ignite, parch.

dovetail [*v*] *link, fit together*
▪ *Syn* accord, agree, coincide, conform, correspond, fit, harmonize, interlock,

jibe, join, match, mortise, square, tally, tenon, unite; ▪ *Ant* conflict, differ, disconnect, disunite, unlink.

dowdy [*adj*] *poorly dressed; old-fashioned* ▪ *Syn* antiquated, bedraggled, dated, homely, outdated, outmoded, plain, run-down, shabby, slatternly, stodgy, vintage, wrinkled; ▪ *Ant* chic, classy, fashionable, modern, stylish, well-dressed.

down [*adj1/adv*] *below; physically lower*
▪ *Syn* bottomward, earthward, groundward, inferior, nether, subjacent, under, underneath; ▪ *Ant* above, aloft, higher, superior, upwards.

down [*adj2*] *unhappy*
▪ *Syn* cast down, chapfallen, crestfallen, dejected, depressed, disheartened, dispirited, low, miserable, sad, slack, sluggish; ▪ *Ant* cheerful, cheery, happy, heartened.

down-and-out [*adj*] *poverty-stricken*
▪ *Syn* beaten, beggared, defeated, derelict, destitute, finished, impoverished, needy, outcast, penniless, ruined, vagabond, vagrant; ▪ *Ant* rich, wealthy, well-to-do.

downcast [*adj*] *depressed, unhappy*
▪ *Syn* blue, brooding, chapfallen, crestfallen, daunted, dejected, despondent, disheartened, dismayed, dispirited, doleful, dull, forlorn, gloomy, glum, heartsick, listless, low, miserable, moody, morose, oppressed, sad, troubled, woebegone; ▪ *Ant* cheerful, elated, glad, happy, heartened, satisfied.

downgrade [*v*] *lower in opinion or rank*
▪ *Syn* abase, decrease, degrade, demerit, demote, denigrate, depreciate, devalue, disparage, humble, minimize, reduce, undervalue; ▪ *Ant* improve, promote, raise, upgrade.

downhearted [*adj*] *depressed, unhappy*
▪ *Syn* dejected, despondent, disconsolate, discouraged, disheartened, dispirited, down, downcast, low, low-spirited, sad, sorrowful, spiritless, woebegone; ▪ *Ant* cheered, happy, heartened, uplifted.

down-to-earth [*adj*] *reasonable, practical* ▪ *Syn* common, commonsense, hard, hard-boiled, matter-of-fact, no-nonsense, plainspoken, pragmatic, rational, realistic, sane, sensible, sober; ▪ *Ant* dreamy, excitable, excited, fantastic, idealistic, impractical.

downside [*n*] *negative aspect or aspects of a situation* ▪ *Syn* defect, disadvantage, drawback, fault, flaw, inconvenience, minus, problem, trouble; ▪ *Ant* advantage, beauty, benefit, bright side, good part, perk, perquisite, plus, positive, upside.

downsize [v] *to decrease in size, especially a workforce* ▪ *Syn* curtail, cut, cut down, cut back, decrease, deduct, diminish, phase down, phase out, reduce, retrench, roll back, roll down, scale, scale back, scale down, shrink, step down, trim, trim away, tune down; ▪ *Ant* add to, amplify, augment, develop, hire, expand, grow, increase, inflate, spread out.

downtime [n] *time during which an activity is stopped* ▪ *Syn* break, breathing spell, free time, freedom, halt, interim, interlude, intermission, letup, lull, pause, recess, repose, respite, rest, spare time, spell, stay, suspension, time to burn, time to kill, time out; ▪ *Ant* animation, business, bustle, exertion, frenzy, hustle, on the clock, on the job, whirlwind.

downtrodden [adj] *afflicted, abused* ▪ *Syn* abject, destitute, exploited, helpless, maltreated, mistreated, needy, oppressed, overcome, persecuted, subjugated, subservient, suppressed, tyrannized; ▪ *Ant* respected, satisfied, supported, uplifted.

drab [adj] *dull, colorless* ▪ *Syn* arid, bleak, boring, characterless, cheerless, desolate, dingy, dismal, faded, flat, gloomy, gray, lackluster, shabby, somber, subfuse, vapid; ▪ *Ant* bright, brilliant, colorful, inspired.

drag [v] *move very slowly* ▪ *Syn* crawl, creep, delay, lag, lag behind, limp along, linger, loiter, procrastinate, shamble, shuffle, stagnate, straggle, tarry; ▪ *Ant* hasten, hurry, rush.

dragging [adj] *tiresome, monotonous* ▪ *Syn* boring, drawn-out, dull, humdrum, lengthy, long, prolonged, protracted, tedious, wearisome; ▪ *Ant* energizing, lively.

drag on/drag out [v] *extend time of action* ▪ *Syn* continue, draw out, endure, extend, lengthen, persist, prolong, protract, spin out, stretch out; ▪ *Ant* accelerate, complete, expedite.

drain [v1] *remove liquid; remove supply* ▪ *Syn* bankrupt, bleed, catheterize, consume, deplete, devitalize, draft, draw off, drink up, dry, empty, exhaust, expend,

sap, siphon, suck; ▪ *Ant* augment, bolster, fill, pour, renew, replace.

drain [v2] *seep, discharge liquid* ▪ *Syn* decline, decrease, diminish, dwindle, effuse, exude, filter off, flow, flow out, leak, ooze, osmose, percolate, reduce, run off, taper off, trickle, well; ▪ *Ant* fill, replenish, supply.

drained [adj] *used up; exhausted* ▪ *Syn* dead, depleted, dragging, effete, spent, washed-out, weary, worn-out; ▪ *Ant* energized, full, lively, vigorous.

dramatic [adj] *exciting, moving* ▪ *Syn* affecting, climactic, effective, emotional, expressive, histrionic, powerful, startling, striking, theatrical, thrilling, tragic, vivid; ▪ *Ant* comedic, normal, ordinary, undramatic, unexciting, unmoving, usual.

drape [v] *hang over, adorn* ▪ *Syn* array, cloak, clothe, cover, display, don, dress, enclose, envelop, enwrap, fold, hang, line, model, roll, sprawl, spread, suspend, swathe, wrap; ▪ *Ant* bare, expose, strip, undrape.

drastic [adj] *severe, extreme* ▪ *Syn* desperate, dire, exorbitant, extravagant, forceful, harsh, immoderate, radical, strong; ▪ *Ant* calm, collected, easy, mild.

draw [v1] *move something by pulling* ▪ *Syn* carry, convey, cull, drag, haul, lug, pull, rake, tap, tow, trail, trawl, tug, wind in; ▪ *Ant* drive, exhale, propel, push, repel, repulse, shove, thrust.

draw [v2] *allure, influence* ▪ *Syn* attract, captivate, charm, enchant, entice, induce, magnetize, persuade, prompt, win over; ▪ *Ant* alienate, estrange, push away, rebuff, reject, repel, repulse, turn off.

draw [v3] *take out, extend* ▪ *Syn* choose, drain, elongate, extort, extract, lengthen, pick, respire, select, stretch, suck, take; ▪ *Ant* abridge, curtail, put in, shorten.

draw back [v] *retract from position* ▪ *Syn* pull back, recede, recoil, reel in, retreat, sheathe, shrink, withdraw; ▪ *Ant* forge, go forward, start.

drawl [v] *lengthen, draw out* ▪ *Syn* chant, drag out, drone, extend, intone, prolong, protract; ▪ *Ant* attenuate, clip, shorten.

drawn [adj] *looking tense, fatigued* ▪ *Syn* fraught, haggard, harrowed, peaked, pinched, sapped, starved, strained, taut, thin, tired, worn; ▪ *Ant* hale, relaxed, robust, unstressed, vigorous.

draw out [v] *prolong*
▪ *Syn* continue, drag, draw, elongate, extend, lead on, lengthen, prolongate, protract, pull, spin, stretch; ▪ *Ant* abbreviate, clip, shorten.

dread [adj] *horrible, terrifying*
▪ *Syn* alarming, awe-inspiring, awful, dire, frightening, frightful, terrible; ▪ *Ant* pleasant, pleasing, welcomed, wonderful.

dread [v] *anticipate with horror*
▪ *Syn* apprehend, cringe, fear, quake, shrink from, shudder, tremble; ▪ *Ant* encourage, want, welcome.

dreadful [adj] *horrible, frightening*
▪ *Syn* abominable, alarming, atrocious, awful, bad, beastly, dire, fearful, frightful, ghastly, grievous, grim, hideous, horrific, monstrous, rotten, terrible, wicked; ▪ *Ant* pleasant, pleasing, welcomed, wonderful.

dreamy [adj] *illusory, romantic*
▪ *Syn* abstracted, astral, dreamlike, fanciful, idealistic, imaginary, musing, otherworldly, pensive, preoccupied, quixotic, speculative, unreal, utopian, visionary, whimsical; ▪ *Ant* down-to-earth, practical, pragmatic.

dreary [adj] *gloomy, lifeless*
▪ *Syn* black, bleak, boring, colorless, comfortless, depressing, dingy, dismal, dispiriting, drab, dull, forlorn, funereal, glum, humdrum, joyless, lonely, lonesome, melancholy, monotonous, mournful, oppressive, pedestrian, raw, routine, sad, somber, tedious, wearisome, wintry, wretched; ▪ *Ant* bright, brilliant, clear, effulgent, happy, light, lively, pleasant, stimulating.

drench [v] *wet thoroughly*
▪ *Syn* deluge, douse, drown, dunk, flood, inundate, saturate, soak, sop, submerge; ▪ *Ant* desiccate, dry, parch.

dress [v1] *put on clothing*
▪ *Syn* adorn, apparel, attire, clothe, cover, deck, don, drape, fit out, furbish, garb, ornament, outfit, robe, suit up, trim, wear; ▪ *Ant* bare, disrobe, lay bare, unclothe, undress.

dress [v2] *physically prepare; groom*
▪ *Syn* arrange, comb, decorate, dispose, make ready, ornament, set, straighten,

trim; ▪ *Ant* disarray, mess up, rumple, wrinkle.

dress [v3] *cover a wound*
▪ *Syn* attend to, bandage, bind, cauterize, cleanse, heal, plaster, sew up, sterilize, treat; ▪ *Ant* open, uncover, undress.

dress down [v] *scold*
▪ *Syn* berate, call on the carpet, castigate, censure, lash, rail, ream, rebuke, reprimand, reprove, upbraid; ▪ *Ant* compliment, flatter, praise.

dress up [v] *put on one's best clothes*
▪ *Syn* array, attire, beautify, embellish, preen, prettify, primp, slick, smarten, titivate; ▪ *Ant* dress casually, dress down.

dressy [adj] *formal, fashionable*
▪ *Syn* chic, classy, elaborate, elegant, fancy, ornate, ritzy, smart, stylish; ▪ *Ant* casual, dowdy, inelegant, informal, unstylish.

dribble [v] *trickle*
▪ *Syn* drip, drivel, drizzle, drool, drop, leak, ooze, run, salivate, seep, slaver, slobber, spout, squirt; ▪ *Ant* flood, gush, pour, stream.

drift [v] *move aimlessly*
▪ *Syn* amble, coast, flicker, flit, float, flutter, gather, gravitate, hover, linger, meander, ride, sail, saunter, skim, slide, stray, wander; ▪ *Ant* aim, decide, direct, guide, set.

drip [v] *drop, trickle*
▪ *Syn* dribble, drizzle, exude, filter, plop, rain, splash, sprinkle, trill, weep; ▪ *Ant* flow, pour, surge.

drive [v] *move or urge on*
▪ *Syn* actuate, animate, arouse, coerce, compel, force, goad, hasten, herd, impel, induce, instigate, kick, motivate, nag, oblige, pressure, prod, prompt, propel, provoke, push, rouse, shepherd, spur, stimulate; ▪ *Ant* check, curb, discourage, dissuade, halt, repress, retard, stop.

driving [adj] *forceful*
▪ *Syn* active, compelling, dynamic, energetic, enterprising, galvanic, lively, propulsive, sweeping, vigorous, violent; ▪ *Ant* apathetic, lethargic, listless, weak.

drizzle [v] *fall as fine rain*
▪ *Syn* dribble, drip, drop, mist, mizzle, shower, spit, spray, sprinkle; ▪ *Ant* deluge, inundate, pour down.

droll [adj] *amusing, farcical*
▪ *Syn* absurd, campy, comical, diverting, eccentric, entertaining, funny, humorous,

jocular, ludicrous, odd, preposterous, quaint, quizzical, ridiculous, riotous, risible, waggish, whimsical; ▪ *Ant* dramatic, grave, serious, solemn, tedious, traumatic.

drone [n] *person who is lazy*
▪ *Syn* idler, leech, loafer, lounger, parasite, slug, sluggard; ▪ *Ant* overachiever, workaholic.

drone [v] *make a monotonous noise continuously* ▪ *Syn* bombinate, buzz, chant, drawl, hum, intone, nasalize, purr, sound, strum, thrum, vibrate, whirr; ▪ *Ant* howl, shriek, silence.

droop [v] *hang down; languish*
▪ *Syn* bend, dangle, fade, flag, lean, loll, lop, sag, settle, sink, sling, slouch, slump, subside, wilt, wither; ▪ *Ant* flourish, inflate, perk up, revive, rise.

droopy [adj] *limp*
▪ *Syn* bent, flabby, floppy, languid, languorous, pendulous, sagging, slouchy, stooped, wilting; ▪ *Ant* full, inflated, raised, turgescent.

drop [n1] *steep decline; hole*
▪ *Syn* abyss, chasm, declivity, depth, descent, dip, fall, plunge, precipice, slope; ▪ *Ant* incline, mound, mountain, rise.

drop [n2] *decrease*
▪ *Syn* cut, decline, descent, dip, downfall, downslide, downswing, downtrend, downturn, fall, lapse, lowering, reduction, sag, slide, slump, tumble; ▪ *Ant* ascent, increase, rise, upswing.

drop [v1] *fall in globules*
▪ *Syn* bead, bleed, distill, drain, dribble, drip, emanate, leak, ooze, percolate, precipitate, seep, splash, trickle; ▪ *Ant* downpour, pour.

drop [v2] *let go of; fall*
▪ *Syn* collapse, dive, duck, dump, knock, lower, pitch, plummet, plump, plunge, release, relinquish, shed, shoot, sink, slump, topple, tumble; ▪ *Ant* ascend, mount, rise, soar, take up.

drop [v3] *abandon; ignore*
▪ *Syn* abort, break with, call off, cancel, desert, dismiss, disown, jilt, leave, lose, quit, reject, relinquish, separate, shake, stop, terminate; ▪ *Ant* continue, do, mount, pursue, take up.

drop off [v1] *decrease*
▪ *Syn* decline, diminish, dwindle, fall away, fall off, lessen, sag, slacken, slide, slip, slump; ▪ *Ant* climb, go up, increase, rally, rise.

drop off [v2] *fall asleep*
▪ *Syn* catnap, doze, drowse, nod, snooze; ▪ *Ant* awake, wake.

drop out [v] *stop doing an activity*
▪ *Syn* abandon, back out, cease, forsake, give up, leave, quit, renege, retreat, withdraw; ▪ *Ant* begin, carry out, engage, join.

drown [v] *submerge in liquid; submerge and die* ▪ *Syn* asphyxiate, deluge, douse, drench, engulf, flood, immerse, inundate, obliterate, overwhelm, plunge, prostrate, sink, soak, sop, souse, stifle, submerge, suffocate, whelm out; ▪ *Ant* drain, dry, float, rescue, save.

drowsy [adj] *sleepy*
▪ *Syn* comatose, dazed, dopey, dozing, dreamy, drugged, heavy, indolent, languid, lazy, lethargic, lulling, sleepy, sluggish, slumberous, somnolent, soothing, soporific, tired, torpid; ▪ *Ant* alert, awake, dynamic, energized, lively, stimulating, vigilant.

drudge [v] *work very hard*
▪ *Syn* dig, labor, perform, plod, plow, slave, slog, sweat, toil, travail; ▪ *Ant* avoid, be lazy, dodge, idle, loaf, lounge.

drugged [adj] *under the influence of medication* ▪ *Syn* benumbed, comatose, dazed, doped, narcotized, stupefied, unconscious; ▪ *Ant* clean, straight, undrugged.

drum up [v] *gather support for something*
▪ *Syn* beg, bid for, canvass, discover, obtain, petition, round up, solicit; ▪ *Ant* dissuade, repulse, turn off.

drunk [adj] *intoxicated by alcohol*
▪ *Syn* drunken, inebriated, tipsy, under the influence; ▪ *Ant* sober, straight.

dry [adj1] *moistureless*
▪ *Syn* anhydrous, arid, baked, bare, dehydrated, depleted, desert, desiccated, drained, draughty, dusty, evaporated, exhausted, impoverished, parched, sapless, shriveled, torrid; ▪ *Ant* damp, dripping, humid, juicy, moist, soaked, soggy, watery, wet.

dry [adj2] *dull, uninteresting*
▪ *Syn* boring, bromidic, dreary, impassive, insipid, monotonous, phlegmatic, plain, simple, tedious, tiresome, trite, wearisome; ▪ *Ant* exciting, interesting, juicy, lively, untiring.

dry [v] *take moisture out of*
▪ *Syn* bake, blot, dehumidify, dehydrate, desiccate, drain, empty, evaporate, ex-

haust, exsiccate, harden, kiln, mummify, parch, scorch, sear, shrivel, torrefy, towel, wipe, wither, wizen; ▪ **Ant** dampen, douse, soak, water, wet.

dubious [*adj1*] *doubtful*
▪ **Syn** chancy, debatable, disputable, equivocal, far-fetched, improbable, indecisive, moot, open, questionable, reluctant, skeptical, suspicious; ▪ **Ant** certain, definite, dependable, doubtless, positive, reliable, sure, trustworthy, trusty.

dubious [*adj2*] *vague, unclear*
▪ **Syn** ambiguous, debatable, indefinite, indeterminate, obscure, open, problematic; ▪ **Ant** certain, clear, definite, unambiguous.

duck [*v*] *drop down; avoid*
▪ **Syn** bend, bob, bow, crouch, dip, elude, escape, evade, fence, lower, plunge, shirk, shun, shy, sidestep, stoop, submerge; ▪ **Ant** face, jump, meet.

ductile [*adj*] *pliant, flexible*
▪ **Syn** adaptable, amenable, extensile, malleable, moldable, pliable, submitting, supple, tractable, yielding; ▪ **Ant** hard, inflexible, intractable, stiff, unyielding.

due [*adj1*] *unpaid; owed*
▪ **Syn** chargeable, collectible, expected, in arrears, mature, outstanding, overdue, payable, receivable; ▪ **Ant** paid, satisfied, settled.

due [*adj2*] *appropriate, proper*
▪ **Syn** becoming, condign, deserved, earned, fair, fitting, good, justified, merited, obligatory, requisite, rhadamanthine, rightful, suitable; ▪ **Ant** improper, inappropriate, insufficient, unjustified, unmerited, unrightful, unsuitable.

due [*adv*] *directly*
▪ **Syn** dead, direct, exactly, right, straight, straightly, undeviatingly; ▪ **Ant** deviously, indirectly, roundabout.

dull [*adj1*] *unintelligent*
▪ **Syn** brainless, dense, feeble-minded, half-witted, ignorant, insensate, low, moronic, obtuse, shallow, simple-minded, slow, stupid, thick, vacuous, witless; ▪ **Ant** bright, clever, intelligent, keen, sharp, smart, witty.

dull [*adj2*] *insensitive*
▪ **Syn** blank, callous, dead, empty, even, flat, heavy, indifferent, inert, jejune, languid, listless, placid, prosaic, quiet, regular, routine, slack, spiritless, stagnant, stolid, torpid, vacuous; ▪ **Ant** lively, passionate, quick, sensitive, vivacious.

dull [*adj3*] *boring, uninteresting*
▪ **Syn** arid, colorless, commonplace, dead, dry, familiar, flat, hackneyed, insipid, monotonous, ordinary, plain, routine, stale, stock, tiresome, trite, usual, vapid, worn-out; ▪ **Ant** active, exciting, inspiring, interesting, lively.

dull [*adj4*] *not sharp*
▪ **Syn** blunt, blunted, edentate, flat, obtuse, pointless, round, square, toothless, turned; ▪ **Ant** honed, knifelike, pointed, serrated, sharp.

dull [*adj5*] *drab, lackluster in effect on senses* ▪ **Syn** dim, dingy, dun, faded, feeble, flat, hazy, indistinct, leaden, lifeless, muted, overcast, plain, somber, subdued; ▪ **Ant** bright, clear, light, luminous, lustrous.

duly [*adv*] *accordingly, properly*
▪ **Syn** appropriately, befittingly, correctly, decorously, on time, punctually, rightfully, suitably; ▪ **Ant** improperly, unduly, unsuitably.

dumb [*adj1*] *unable to speak*
▪ **Syn** impaired, inarticulate, mute, quiet, silent, soundless, speechless, tongue-tied, voiceless, wordless; ▪ **Ant** articulate, communicative, speaking.

dumb [*adj2*] *stupid, unintelligent*
▪ **Syn** dense, dim-witted, doltish, dull, foolish, moronic, simple-minded; ▪ **Ant** bright, intelligent, sharp, smart.

dumbfound [*v*] *astound, confuse*
▪ **Syn** amaze, astonish, bewilder, boggle, confound, flabbergast, nonplus, overwhelm, puzzle, stagger, startle, stun, surprise, take aback, throw; ▪ **Ant** clear up, explain, explicate.

dumbfounded [*adj*] *astounded, confused* ▪ **Syn** agape, aghast, amazed, astonished, bewildered, confounded, flabbergasted, nonplused, overwhelmed, puzzled, shocked, stumped, stunned, surprised, taken aback, thrown; ▪ **Ant** aware, expectant, unsurprised.

dump [*v*] *drop, throw away*
▪ **Syn** cast, chuck, clear out, deposit, discard, discharge, dispose of, empty, evacuate, jettison, junk, leave, scrap, throw out; ▪ **Ant** hold, keep, maintain, save.

duplicate [*adj*] *matching*
▪ **Syn** alike, corresponding, dualistic, duple, duplex, equal, equivalent, identical, indistinguishable, matched, same, selfsame, tantamount, twin, twofold; ▪ **Ant** different, unmatching.

durable [adj] sturdy, long-lasting
- **Syn** abiding, constant, dependable, enduring, fast, firm, fixed, impervious, perdurable, resistant, sound, stable, substantial, tough; ▪ **Ant** fragile, impermanent, poorly made, temporary, undependable, unsturdy, weak.

dusky [adj] dark-hued; murky
- **Syn** bleak, crepuscular, dim, dull, funereal, gloomy, obscure, overcast, sable, shadowy, swarthy, tenebrous, veiled; ▪ **Ant** bright, clear, illuminated, light.

dusty [adj] filled with or covered with powdery particles ▪ **Syn** arenaceous, chalky, crumbly, dirty, friable, granular, grubby, sandy, sooty; ▪ **Ant** clean, clear.

dutiful [adj] obedient
- **Syn** compliant, deferential, devoted, obligatory, punctilious, respectful, reverential, submissive; ▪ **Ant** betraying, disobedient, faithless, irresponsible, undutiful, unfaithful, unrespectful.

dwarf [adj] miniature, tiny
- **Syn** baby, diminutive, low, petite, pocket, small, undersized; ▪ **Ant** big, giant, huge, large.

dwarf [v] minimize
- **Syn** detract from, dim, diminish, dominate, hinder, lower, overshadow, predominate, stunt, suppress, tower above, tower over; ▪ **Ant** maximize, oversize.

dwell on/dwell upon [v] linger over; be engrossed in ▪ **Syn** consider, continue, elaborate, emphasize, expatiate, tarry over; ▪ **Ant** forget, ignore, miss, pass.

dwindle [v] waste away; taper off
- **Syn** abate, bate, close, contract, decay, decline, decrease, die away, die down, die out, diminish, drain, drop, ebb, fade, fall, lessen, pine, shrink, shrivel, sink, subside, taper, wane, weaken, wither; ▪ **Ant** develop, enlarge, expand, extend, grow, increase, save, swell.

dye [v] change the color of something
- **Syn** color, pigment, stain, tincture, tinge, tint; ▪ **Ant** bleach, fade, whiten.

dying [adj] failing, expiring
- **Syn** decaying, declining, disintegrating, doomed, ebbing, fading, fated, final, in extremis, moribund, mortal, passing, perishing, sinking, vanishing, withering; ▪ **Ant** creating, developing, growing, living, reviving.

dynamic [adj] active, vital
- **Syn** aggressive, charismatic, compelling, driving, effective, electric, energetic, forceful, high-powered, influential, intense, lively, lusty, magnetic, potent, powerful, productive, progressive, strenuous, vehement, vigorous, vitalizing; ▪ **Ant** apathetic, boring, dull, inactive, passive, unexciting.

dysfunctional [adj] impaired
- **Syn** broken, debilitated, decayed, defective, deteriorated, flawed, inhibited, maladjusted, malfunctional, sick, undermined, unfit, wounded, ▪ **Ant** functioning, healthy, socialized, together, well, well-adjusted, working.

E

each [adj] every
- **Syn** all, any, exclusive, individual, particular, respective, separate, single, specific; ▪ **Ant** every other, none, some.

each [pron] each one
- **Syn** each other, every last one, every one, one, one another; ▪ **Ant** none.

eager [adj] anxious, enthusiastic
- **Syn** ambitious, antsy, appetent, ardent, athirst, avid, breathless, craving, desirous, earnest, fervent, fervid, greedy, heated, impatient, intent, keen, longing, pining, restive, restless, solicitous, thirsty, vehement, voracious, wild, wishful, yearning, zealous; ▪ **Ant** apathetic, disinterested, dispassionate, impassive, indifferent, unconcerned, unenthusiastic.

early [adj1] in the beginning
- **Syn** ancient, antecedent, antediluvian, antiquated, budding, fresh, initial, new, original, preceding, premier, prevenient, previous, primal, prime, primeval, primitive, primordial, prior, pristine, proleptical, raw, recent, undeveloped, young; ▪ **Ant** conclusive, final, last, late, terminal.

early [adj2] sooner than expected
- **Syn** advanced, ahead of time, anticipatory, beforehand, direct, immediate, matinal, preceding, precipitant, precocious, premature, previous, prompt, punctual, quick, seasonable, soon, speedy, untimely; ▪ **Ant** anticipated, expected, later, slow, tardy.

earmark [v] reserve
- **Syn** allocate, designate, label, maintain, mark out, name, set aside, slot, tab, tag; ▪ **Ant** throw away, use, waste.

earn [v1] *make money*
- *Syn* acquire, attain, bring in, collect, consummate, derive, draw, effect, gain, gather, get, gross, make, net, obtain, perform, procure, profit, rate, realize, reap, receive, secure, turn, win; *Ant* cost, lose, spend, throw away.

earn [v2] *deserve a reward*
- *Syn* be entitled to, be worthy of, gain, harvest, merit, net, rate, reap, score, warrant, win; *Ant* forfeit, lose.

earnest [adj1] *very enthusiastic*
- *Syn* ardent, devoted, diligent, eager, fervent, fervid, heartfelt, impassioned, keen, passionate, persevering, sedulous, sincere, urgent, vehement, warm, whole-hearted, zealous; *Ant* flippant, lethargic, nonchalant, offhand, unconcerned, unenthusiastic.

earnest [adj2] *serious; very important*
- *Syn* determined, firm, fixed, grave, intent, meaningful, no-nonsense, resolute, sincere, sober, solemn, staid, steady, thoughtful; *Ant* flippant, frivolous, insincere, thoughtless, trivial, unimportant.

earthly [adj1] *concerning land or its inhabitants* *Syn* alluvial, carnal, corporeal, earthy, global, human, material, mortal, mundane, physical, profane, secular, sublunary, tellurian, temporal, terraqueous, terrene, terrestrial, worldly; *Ant* astral, celestial, divine, heavenly, immaterial, spiritual, unearthly.

earthly [adj2] *conceivable*
- *Syn* feasible, imaginable, likely, mortal, possible, potential, practical, probable; *Ant* improbable, inconceivable.

earthy [adj] *unsophisticated*
- *Syn* coarse, crude, easygoing, folksy, homely, homey, mundane, natural, pragmatic, rough, simple; *Ant* cultured, elegant, refined, sophisticated.

ease [v1] *alleviate, help*
- *Syn* abate, aid, allay, ameliorate, assist, assuage, calm, comfort, cure, disburden, doctor, expedite, facilitate, free, further, improve, lessen, lighten, mitigate, mollify, nurse, pacify, palliate, promote, quiet, release, relent, relieve, simplify, slacken, smooth, soften, soothe, speed, still, tranquilize; *Ant* annoy, increase, irritate, perplex, vex, worsen.

ease [v2] *guide, move carefully*
- *Syn* disentangle, edge, extricate, facilitate, handle, inch, induce, insert, maneu-

ver, relax, remove, right, slacken, slide, slip, steer; *Ant* make difficult, vex.

easily [adv1] *without difficulty*
- *Syn* calmly, comfortably, conveniently, dexterously, effortlessly, facilely, fluently, freely, handily, lightly, plainly, quickly, readily, simply, smoothly, steadily, well; *Ant* arduously, difficultly, laboriously.

easily [adv2] *without a doubt*
- *Syn* absolutely, actually, assuredly, beyond question, by far, certainly, clearly, decidedly, definitely, doubtless, far and away, indeed, indisputably, indubitably, no doubt, plainly, positively, really, surely, truly; *Ant* doubtedly, dubitably, unquestionably.

easy [adj1] *not difficult*
- *Syn* accessible, apparent, basic, cinch, clear, effortless, elementary, facile, light, manageable, manifest, mere, obvious, painless, paltry, plain, simple, slight, smooth, snap, yielding; *Ant* arduous, burdensome, complex, complicated, demanding, difficult, hard, intricate, involved, laborious.

easy [adj2] *leisurely, relaxed*
- *Syn* calm, carefree, comfortable, content, cursive, cushy, effortless, fluent, gentle, languid, mild, peaceful, pleasant, quiet, secure, serene, slow, smooth, snug, soft, temperate, tranquil; *Ant* demanding, difficult, exhausting, hard, oppressive, trying, uneasy.

easy [adj3] *tolerant, permissive*
- *Syn* accommodating, amenable, benign, biddable, charitable, clement, compliant, condoning, exploitable, flexible, forbearing, gentle, gullible, indulgent, kindly, lax, lenient, mild, moderate, naive, pardoning, submissive, temperate, trusting; *Ant* difficult, impossible, intolerant, ornery, strict.

easy [adj4] *good-humored*
- *Syn* affable, amiable, carefree, casual, complaisant, diplomatic, friendly, gentle, good-natured, gregarious, informal, mild, natural, obliging, open, pleasant, relaxed, secure, smooth, sociable, tolerant, urbane; *Ant* anxious, difficult, unhappy, wooden.

easygoing [adj] *complacent, permissive*
- *Syn* amenable, breezy, calm, carefree, casual, composed, easy, flexible, informal, insouciant, lazy, lenient, liberal, mild, moderate, nonchalant, offhand, pa-

tient, placid, relaxed, self-possessed, serene, tolerant, tranquil; ▪ *Ant* agitated, critical, demanding, hurried, hyped, intolerant, nervous, strict, upset, worried.

eat [v] *erode, wear away; use up*
▪ *Syn* condense, corrode, crumble, decay, decompose, disappear, disintegrate, dissipate, dissolve, drain, exhaust, gnaw, liquefy, melt, rot, rust, spill, squander, vanish, waste away; ▪ *Ant* build, maintain, preserve.

eatable [adj] *able to be consumed*
▪ *Syn* appetizing, comestible, culinary, dietary, digestible, edible, esculent, nutritious, nutritive, palatable, safe, savory; ▪ *Ant* inedible, uneatable, unpalatable, unwholesome.

eavesdrop [v] *listen without permission*
▪ *Syn* bug, listen in, monitor, overhear, pry, snoop, spy, tap, wire, wiretap; ▪ *Ant* ignore.

ebb [v] *subside; decline*
▪ *Syn* abate, deteriorate, die out, diminish, dwindle, ease off, fade away, fall away, flag, languish, lessen, melt, peter out, recede, relent, retire, retreat, shrink, sink, slacken, wane, weaken, withdraw; ▪ *Ant* flow, increase, mount, progress, rise.

ebullient [adj] *enthusiastic*
▪ *Syn* agitated, buoyant, effervescent, effusive, elated, exuberant, gushing, high-spirited, irrepressible, vivacious, zestful; ▪ *Ant* apathetic, constrained, disinterested, impassive, unenthusiastic.

eccentric [adj] *bizarre, unusual*
▪ *Syn* aberrant, abnormal, anomalous, capricious, cockeyed, crazy, curious, erratic, freakish, idiosyncratic, irregular, kooky, nutty, odd, offbeat, outlandish, peculiar, queer, quirky, singular, strange, weird, whimsical, wild; ▪ *Ant* boring, bromidic, common, conventional, dull, normal, ordinary, plain, regular, standard, traditional, usual.

echo [v] *repeat, copy*
▪ *Syn* ape, imitate, impersonate, mimic, mirror, parallel, parrot, react, reflect, reiterate, reproduce, resemble, resound, respond, reverberate, ring, second, vibrate; ▪ *Ant* be at odds with, contradict, deny, differ from, oppose.

eclectic [adj] *comprehensive, general*
▪ *Syn* assorted, broad, catholic, dilettantish, diverse, diversified, heterogeneous, inclusive, liberal, mingled, mixed, mul-

tifarious, multiform, selective, universal, varied, wide-ranging; ▪ *Ant* incomprehensive, narrow, particular, specific, unvaried.

eclipse [v] *obscure, veil*
▪ *Syn* adumbrate, cloud, darken, dim, extinguish, overshadow, shadow, shroud; ▪ *Ant* clear, explain, illuminate, lay out.

economical [adj1] *conservative with resources; careful* ▪ *Syn* chary, circumspect, closefisted, cost-effective, efficient, frugal, meager, mean, miserly, money-saving, parsimonious, penurious, practical, prudential, spare, stingy, thrifty, tight, watchful, work-saving; ▪ *Ant* careless, expensive, extravagant, lavish, uncareful, uneconomical, wasteful.

economical [adj2] *inexpensive*
▪ *Syn* cheap, cut-rate, low, low-priced, low-tariff, marked down, moderate, modest, on sale, reasonable, reduced; ▪ *Ant* expensive, uneconomical, unreasonable.

economize [v] *save money*
▪ *Syn* be frugal, be prudent, conserve, cut back, cut down, keep within one's means, manage, retrench, save, scrimp, skimp, stint; ▪ *Ant* spend, squander, throw away.

ecstatic [adj] *very happy, blissful*
▪ *Syn* beatific, crazy, delirious, dreamy, elated, enraptured, enthusiastic, entranced, euphoric, fervent, floating, frenzied, joyful, joyous, overjoyed, rapturous, ravished, rhapsodic, thrilled, wild; ▪ *Ant* despairing, sorrowful, tormented, troubled, unhappy.

eco-rich [adj] *possessing an abundance of natural resources* ▪ *Syn* bountiful, clean, flowing, full, green, natural, plentiful, pure, rich; ▪ *Ant* barren, contaminated, deficient, depleted, dry, empty, polluted, scant, scarce, spoiled, toxic, wasted.

edge [v] *sharpen*
▪ *Syn* file, grind, hone, polish, sharpen, strop, whet; ▪ *Ant* blunt, dull, thicken.

edgy [adj] *nervous*
▪ *Syn* anxious, excitable, excited, high-strung, ill at ease, impatient, irascible, irritable, restive, restless, skittish, tense, touchy, uneasy, uptight; ▪ *Ant* calm, composed, easygoing, laid-back.

edible [adj] *able to be eaten*
▪ *Syn* comestible, digestible, eatable, es-

culent, fit, good, nourishing, nutritious, nutritive, palatable, savory, succulent, tasty, toothsome, wholesome; ▪ **Ant** harmful, inedible, poisonous, unpalatable.

educated [adj] learned, experienced
▪ **Syn** accomplished, coached, cultivated, cultured, developed, enlightened, enriched, erudite, expert, finished, informed, initiated, instructed, knowledgeable, lettered, literary, literate, polished, prepared, professional, refined, scholarly, schooled, scientific, taught, trained, tutored, well-informed, well-read, well-taught, well-versed; ▪ **Ant** ignorant, illiterate, inexperienced, uncultured, uneducated, unsophisticated.

eerie [adj] spooky
▪ **Syn** awesome, bizarre, fantastic, fearful, frightening, ghostly, mysterious, scary, spectral, strange, supernatural, superstitious, uncanny, unearthly, weird; ▪ **Ant** funny, natural, normal, ordinary, silly.

effect [v] carry out, accomplish
▪ **Syn** achieve, actualize, actuate, begin, cause, complete, conceive, conclude, consummate, create, enact, enforce, execute, fulfill, generate, implement, induce, initiate, invoke, make, perform, procure, produce, realize, render, secure, sell, turn out, yield; ▪ **Ant** fail, impede, neglect, restrict.

effective [adj1] productive, persuasive
▪ **Syn** adequate, capable, cogent, compelling, competent, convincing, effectual, efficacious, efficient, energetic, forceful, forcible, impressive, operative, potent, powerful, practical, resultant, serviceable, sound, sufficient, trenchant, useful, valid, virtuous; ▪ **Ant** fruitless, futile, impotent, incapable, ineffective, unproductive, useless, weak.

effective [adj2] in use at the time
▪ **Syn** active, actual, current, direct, dynamic, in force, operative, real; ▪ **Ant** inoperative, useless.

effectual [adj] influential; authoritative
▪ **Syn** adequate, capable, conclusive, decisive, determinative, effective, efficacious, efficient, forcible, potent, powerful, practicable, productive, qualified, serviceable, sound, strong, successful, useful, valid, workable; ▪ **Ant** impotent, incapable, ineffectual, unproductive, unsuccessful, useless, weak.

effeminate [adj] having the quality or characteristics of a woman ▪ **Syn** female, feminine, womanlike, womanly; ▪ **Ant** manly, masculine.

effervescent [adj1] fizzing, foaming
▪ **Syn** airy, boiling, bouncy, bubbling, bubbly, carbonated, expansive, fermenting, fizzy, foamy, frothing, frothy, resilient, sparkling, volatile; ▪ **Ant** flat, stale.

effervescent [adj2] enthusiastic, vivacious ▪ **Syn** animated, bouncy, bubbly, buoyant, ebullient, excited, exhilarated, exuberant, gleeful, happy, high-spirited, hilarious, irrepressible, jolly, joyous, lively, merry, mirthful, sprightly, vital; ▪ **Ant** dull, flat, inactive, serious, sober, unenthusiastic.

effete [adj1] spoiled, exhausted
▪ **Syn** corrupt, debased, decadent, decayed, declining, decrepit, degenerate, dissipated, dissolute, drained, enervated, enfeebled, feeble, immoral, ineffectual, obsolete, overrefined, overripe, soft, spent, vitiated, wasted, weak, worn out; ▪ **Ant** capable, tireless, vigorous, vital, wholesome.

effete [adj2] unproductive
▪ **Syn** barren, fruitless, impotent, infertile, sterile, unfruitful; ▪ **Ant** fecund, productive, prolific, useful, working.

efficacious [adj] efficient, productive
▪ **Syn** adequate, capable, competent, effective, effectual, influential, operative, potent, powerful, puissant, serviceable, successful, useful; ▪ **Ant** incapable, inefficacious, inefficient, unproductive, unsuccessful, useless.

efficient [adj] adept, effective
▪ **Syn** able, accomplished, active, adequate, apt, businesslike, capable, clever, competent, conducive, decisive, deft, dynamic, economic, economical, effectual, efficacious, energetic, experienced, expert, fitted, handy, organized, potent, powerful, practiced, productive, proficient, profitable, qualified, ready, shrewd, skilled, skillful, systematic, talented, tough, useful, valuable, virtuous, well-organized; ▪ **Ant** helpless, impotent, incompetent, ineffective, inefficient, powerless, unable, weak.

effortless [adj] easy
▪ **Syn** cursive, facile, flowing, fluent, light, offhand, painless, simple, smooth; ▪ **Ant** complicated, demanding, difficult, effortful, hard, labored.

effulgent [adj] *glowing, luminous*
▪ **Syn** beaming, blazing, bright, brilliant, dazzling, fluorescent, incandescent, lambent, lucent, lustrous, radiant, refulgent, resplendent, shining, splendid, vivid; ▪ **Ant** dark, dusky, gloomy, murky.

effusive [adj] *gushing, profuse*
▪ **Syn** demonstrative, ebullient, enthusiastic, expansive, extravagant, exuberant, fulsome, lavish, prolix, talkative, verbose, wordy; ▪ **Ant** constrained, reserved, restrained, sparing, sparse.

egg on [v] *push to do something*
▪ **Syn** agitate, arouse, drive, encourage, excite, exhort, goad, incite, instigate, pique, prick, prod, prompt, propel, rally, spur, stimulate, stir up, urge, whip up; ▪ **Ant** discourage, dissuade, hold back, talk out of.

egocentric [adj] *thinking very highly of oneself* ▪ **Syn** conceited, egoistic, egoistical, egomaniacal, egotistical, individualist, megalomaniac, narcissistic, pompous, self-absorbed, self-centered, selfish, self-loving, self-serving, vainglorious; ▪ **Ant** altruistic, humble, modest, reserved, selfless, shy, submissive, timid, unassuming.

egotistic/egoistic [adj] *thinking very highly of oneself* ▪ **Syn** affected, boastful, bragging, conceited, egocentric, egomaniacal, haughty, individualistic, inflated, narcissistic, obsessive, opinionated, pompous, proud, self-absorbed, self-admiring, self-centered, self-important, subjective, swollen, vainglorious; ▪ **Ant** altruistic, humble, modest, reserved, selfless, shy, submissive, timid, unassuming.

egregious [adj] *outstandingly bad; outrageous* ▪ **Syn** arrant, atrocious, deplorable, extreme, flagrant, glaring, grievous, heinous, infamous, insufferable, intolerable, monstrous, nefarious, notorious, preposterous, rank, scandalous, shocking, stark; ▪ **Ant** little, minor, secondary, slight.

eject [v] *throw or be thrown out*
▪ **Syn** banish, cast out, debar, discharge, disgorge, dislodge, dismiss, dispossess, ditch, ejaculate, eliminate, eradicate, evict, expel, expulse, fire, force out, irrupt, oust, reject, spew, spout, turn out, unloose, vomit; ▪ **Ant** accept, admit, inject, receive, swallow, take in.

elaborate [adj] *intricate; involved*
▪ **Syn** complex, complicated, decorated, detailed, embellished, exact, extensive, extravagant, fancy, fussy, garnished, highly wrought, imposing, labored, labyrinthine, luxurious, minute, ornamented, ornate, painstaking, perfected, precise, refined, showy, skillful, sophisticated, studied, thorough; ▪ **Ant** general, normal, plain, regular, simple, uncomplicated, unelaborate, uninvolved, usual.

elaborate [v] *make detailed; expand*
▪ **Syn** amplify, bedeck, clarify, complicate, decorate, develop, embellish, enhance, evolve, expatiate, expound, flesh out, garnish, improve, ornament, particularize, refine, specify, unfold, work out; ▪ **Ant** abridge, condense, contract, simplify.

elastic [adj1] *pliant, rubbery*
▪ **Syn** adaptable, bouncy, ductile, extendible, extensible, flexible, limber, lithe, malleable, moldable, plastic, pliable, resilient, springy, stretchable, stretchy, supple, tempered, yielding; ▪ **Ant** inelastic, inflexible, rigid, stiff, tense, unyielding.

elastic [adj2] *adaptable, tolerant*
▪ **Syn** accommodating, adjustable, airy, animated, buoyant, ebullient, effervescent, expansive, flexible, gay, high-spirited, lively, recuperative, resilient, soaring, spirited, sprightly, supple, variable, vivacious, volatile, yielding; ▪ **Ant** difficult, inflexible, intolerant, unadaptable, ungiving.

elated [adj] *very happy*
▪ **Syn** animated, aroused, blissful, delighted, ecstatic, enchanted, enraptured, euphoric, exalted, excited, exhilarated, exultant, gleeful, high, intoxicated, joyful, joyous, jubilant, overjoyed, transported; ▪ **Ant** depressed, down, sad, sorrowful, unhappy.

elder [adj] *born earlier*
▪ **Syn** ancient, earlier, first-born, older, senior; ▪ **Ant** last-born, younger, youngest.

elderly [adj] *in old age*
▪ **Syn** aged, aging, ancient, hoary, old, retired, venerable; ▪ **Ant** juvenile, young, youthful.

elect [v] *select as representative; choose*
▪ **Syn** accept, admit, appoint, ballot, conclude, designate, determine, judge, mark, name, nominate, opt for, pick, prefer, resolve, tap, vote for; ▪ **Ant** abjure, reject, vote down, vote out.

elective [*adj*] *able to be chosen*
- *Syn* discretionary, electoral, facultative, optional, selective, voluntary; ▪ *Ant* compulsory, obligatory, required.

electric/electrical [*adj*] *charged; energetic* ▪ *Syn* AC, DC, dynamic, electrifying, exciting, magnetic, rousing, stimulating, stirring, tense, thrilling, voltaic; ▪ *Ant* boring, uncharged, unenergetic, unexciting.

electrify [*v*] *thrill, stimulate*
- *Syn* animate, charge, commove, disturb, energize, enthuse, excite, fire, frenzy, galvanize, invigorate, jar, jolt, magnetize, power, provoke, rouse, send, shock, stagger, startle, stir, strike, stun; ▪ *Ant* bore, dull, weary.

elegant [*adj*] *beautiful, tasteful*
- *Syn* appropriate, classic, comely, courtly, cultivated, cultured, dignified, exquisite, fancy, fine, genteel, graceful, grand, handsome, ingenious, luxurious, majestic, noble, opulent, ornate, polished, recherche, refined, select, stately, stylized, sumptuous, superior; ▪ *Ant* crude, inelegant, rough, ugly, unfashionable, unrefined, unsophisticated, untasteful.

elementary [*adj*] *simple, basic*
- *Syn* ABCs, abecedarian, basal, basic, beginning, clear, easy, elemental, essential, fundamental, initial, introductory, original, plain, primary, rudimentary, simplified, straightforward, substratal, underlying; ▪ *Ant* abstruse, advanced, complex, complicated, compound, difficult, hard, intricate, involved, secondary.

elevate [*v1*] *lift up*
- *Syn* erect, heighten, hoist, levitate, lift, pump, raise, ramp, rear, stilt, tilt, uphold, uplift, upraise; ▪ *Ant* decrease, depress, drop, lessen, lower, push down.

elevate [*v2*] *promote; augment*
- *Syn* advance, aggrandize, appoint, boost, build up, dignify, enhance, ennoble, exalt, further, glorify, heighten, honor, increase, intensify, magnify, swell, upgrade; ▪ *Ant* condemn, demote, denounce, deprecate, disdain, lessen, lower, spurn.

elevate [*v3*] *raise spirits*
- *Syn* animate, boost, brighten, cheer, elate, excite, exhilarate, glorify, hearten, inspire, raise, refine, rouse, sublimate, uplift; ▪ *Ant* depress, disgrace, distress, lower, shame, trouble, upset.

elevated [*adj1*] *highly moral or dignified*
- *Syn* ethical, exalted, formal, grand, grandiloquent, heavy, high, high-minded, honorable, inflated, lofty, noble, righteous, stately, sublime, upright, upstanding, virtuous; ▪ *Ant* base, immoral, lowly, undignified.

elevated [*adj2*] *raised up*
- *Syn* aerial, high, lifted, raised, stately, tall, towering, upheaved, uplifted, upraised, uprisen; ▪ *Ant* base, decreased, dropped, lessened, lowered, lowly, sunken.

elicit [*v*] *draw out*
- *Syn* badger, bring, bring out, call forth, cause, derive, educe, evince, evoke, evolve, exact, extort, extract, fetch, obtain, rattle, wrest, wring; ▪ *Ant* cover, forgo, hide, keep, repress, suppress.

eligible [*adj*] *fit, worthy*
- *Syn* acceptable, appropriate, becoming, desirable, discretionary, elective, employable, fitted, licensed, likely, preferable, privileged, proper, qualified, satisfactory, seemly, suitable, suited; ▪ *Ant* improper, inappropriate, ineligible, unfit, unsuitable, unsuited, unworthy.

eliminate [*v*] *remove, throw out*
- *Syn* annihilate, cancel, cast out, defeat, discard, dismiss, dispose of, disqualify, disregard, drive out, eject, eradicate, evict, expel, ignore, invalidate, kill, liquidate, murder, omit, oust, reject, terminate, waive; ▪ *Ant* accept, choose, include, keep, ratify, receive, sanction, welcome.

elite [*adj*] *best, first-class*
- *Syn* aristocratic, best, choice, elect, exclusive, greatest, noble, pick, selected, super, top, topflight, top-notch, upper-class, world-class; ▪ *Ant* common, low-class, lower, lower-class, ordinary, poor, worst.

elongate [*v*] *make longer*
- *Syn* drag out, draw, draw out, extend, fill, lengthen, prolong, protract, spin out, stretch; ▪ *Ant* constrict, contract, shorten.

eloquent [*adj*] *having a skillful way with words* ▪ *Syn* affecting, ardent, articulate, expressive, fervent, fervid, fluent, forceful, glib, grandiloquent, graphic, impassioned, impressive, magniloquent, meaningful, moving, outspoken, passionate, persuasive, poignant, potent, powerful, revealing, rhetorical, sententious, significant, stirring, suggestive, telling, touching, vivid, vocal, voluble, well-expressed; ▪ *Ant* dull, inarticulate.

elucidate [v] *explain in detail*
▪ *Syn* annotate, clarify, clear, decode, enlighten, exemplify, explicate, expound, gloss, illuminate, illustrate, interpret, prove, unfold; ▪ *Ant* confuse, darken, distract, mystify, obscure.

elude [v] *avoid; escape*
▪ *Syn* baffle, bilk, circumvent, confound, ditch, dodge, duck, eschew, evade, flee, fly, foil, frustrate, get around, outrun, outwit, shirk, shuck, shun, shy, stall, stump, thwart; ▪ *Ant* attract, confront, encounter, entice, face, invite, meet, take on.

elusive [adj] *evasive, mysterious*
▪ *Syn* ambiguous, cagey, deceitful, deceptive, equivocal, fleeting, fugacious, fugitive, illusory, imponderable, incomprehensible, indefinable, intangible, misleading, occult, phantom, shifty, slippery, subtle, starved, transient, transitory, tricky, volatile; ▪ *Ant* actual, plain, substantial, tangible.

emaciated [adj] *undernourished; thin*
▪ *Syn* atrophied, attenuated, bony, cadaverous, famished, gaunt, haggard, lank, lean, meager, peaked, pinched, scrawny, skeletal, skinny, starved, underfed, wasted, wizened; ▪ *Ant* fat, heavy, overnourished, overweight, plump.

emanate [v] *come forth; give off*
▪ *Syn* arise, derive, discharge, egress, emerge, emit, exhale, exit, exude, flow, initiate, issue, originate, proceed, radiate, rise, spring, stem; ▪ *Ant* absorb, culminate, take, terminate, withdraw.

emancipate [v] *set free*
▪ *Syn* deliver, discharge, disencumber, disenthrall, enfranchise, free, liberate, loose, loosen, manumit, release, unchain, unfetter; ▪ *Ant* enslave, hold, imprison, incarcerate.

embark [v] *get on transportation vehicle*
▪ *Syn* board, enplane, enter, entrain, launch, set out, set sail; ▪ *Ant* disembark, land, stay.

embark on [v] *begin undertaking, journey* ▪ *Syn* broach, commence, engage, enter, initiate, launch, open, plunge into, set about, start, take up, undertake; ▪ *Ant* cease, conclude, end, finish, terminate.

embarrass [v] *cause mental discomfort*
▪ *Syn* abash, agitate, bewilder, chagrin, confuse, discomfit, discomfort, discompose, disconcert, discountenance, distress, disturb, faze, fluster, irk, mortify, perturb, plague, rattle, shame, tease, upset; ▪ *Ant* comfort, gladden, help, please, relieve.

embarrassing [adj] *humiliating, shaming* ▪ *Syn* awkward, compromising, disagreeable, discomfiting, discommoding, disconcerting, equivocal, incommodious, inopportune, mortifying, perplexing, sensitive, shameful, sticky, ticklish, touchy, troublesome, uncomfortable, unseemly; ▪ *Ant* advantageous, comfortable, shameless.

embed [v] *sink, implant*
▪ *Syn* bury, deposit, dig in, fasten, fix, impact, ingrain, inlay, insert, install, lodge, pierce, plant, plunge, press, root, set; ▪ *Ant* dig up, eradicate, root out.

embellish [v] *make beautiful; decorate*
▪ *Syn* adorn, amplify, bedeck, emblaze, enhance, enrich, festoon, garnish, gild, magnify, ornament, trim; ▪ *Ant* deface, disfigure, mar, simplify, spoil, strip.

embezzle [v] *steal money, often from employer* ▪ *Syn* abstract, appropriate, defalcate, filch, forge, loot, misapply, misappropriate, misuse, peculate, pilfer, purloin, skim, thieve; ▪ *Ant* compensate, give, pay, reimburse, return.

embitter [v] *upset, alienate*
▪ *Syn* acerbate, acidulate, aggravate, anger, annoy, bitter, bother, disaffect, disillusion, envenom, exacerbate, exasperate, irritate, poison, sour; ▪ *Ant* calm, comfort, make happy, pacify.

embody [v1] *represent; materialize*
▪ *Syn* actualize, demonstrate, epitomize, evince, exhibit, express, hypostatize, illustrate, incarnate, manifest, objectify, personify, realize, reify, show, symbolize, typify; ▪ *Ant* disembody, exclude.

embody [v2] *include, integrate*
▪ *Syn* absorb, amalgamate, assimilate, blend, codify, collect, combine, comprehend, comprise, consolidate, encompass, fuse, incorporate, merge, organize, subsume, systematize, unify; ▪ *Ant* disembody, disintegrate, exclude, exclude.

embrace [v1] *hold tightly in one's arms*
▪ *Syn* clasp, cling, clutch, cradle, cuddle, encircle, enfold, entwine, envelop, fold, grasp, grip, hug, lock, nuzzle, press, seize, snuggle, wrap; ▪ *Ant* let go, release.

embrace [v2] *include in one's beliefs; take into account* ▪ **Syn** accept, admit, adopt, comprise, encompass, espouse, incorporate, involve, receive, seize, subsume, take in, welcome; ▪ **Ant** disbelieve, distrust, exclude, reject, shun.

emend [v] *correct*
▪ **Syn** alter, amend, edit, improve, polish, rectify, redact, retouch, revise, right, touch up; ▪ **Ant** damage, mar, worsen.

emerge [v] *come out, arise*
▪ **Syn** appear, arrive, come forth, dawn, develop, egress, emanate, flow, gush, issue, loom, materialize, originate, proceed, rise, show, spring, spurt, steam, stem, surface, transpire, turn up; ▪ **Ant** disappear, dissolve, evaporate, fade, go away, leave.

emergent [adj] *arising or resulting*
▪ **Syn** appearing, budding, developing, efflorescent, emanant, emerging, rising; ▪ **Ant** declining, dependent.

emigrate [v] *move to new country*
▪ **Syn** depart, migrate, move abroad, quit, remove, transmigrate; ▪ **Ant** remain, stay.

eminent [adj] *very important; famous*
▪ **Syn** august, celebrated, conspicuous, distinguished, dominant, elevated, esteemed, exalted, famed, grand, great, high, high-ranking, illustrious, lofty, name, noble, notable, noteworthy, outstanding, paramount, prestigious, prominent, renowned; ▪ **Ant** common, inferior, undistinguished, unimportant.

emit [v] *diffuse, discharge*
▪ **Syn** belch, breathe, disembogue, drip, eject, emanate, erupt, evacuate, excrete, exhale, expectorate, expel, expend, expire, extrude, exude, issue, jet, loose, ooze, pass, perspire, pour, pronounce, purge, radiate, reek, secrete, send out, shoot, spew, spill, spit, squirt, transmit, utter, vent, voice, void, vomit, yield; ▪ **Ant** conceal, contain, refrain, repress, retain, suppress, withhold.

emotional [adj] *demonstrative about feelings* ▪ **Syn** ardent, emotive, enthusiastic, excitable, feeling, fervent, fervid, fiery, heartwarming, heated, impassioned, impetuous, impulsive, irrational, moving, passionate, poignant, responsive, roused, sensitive, sentient, sentimental, spontaneous, susceptible, temperamental, tender, touching, warm, zealous; ▪ **Ant** cold, dispassionate, dull, insensitive.

emotionless [adj] *unfeeling, undemonstrative* ▪ **Syn** blank, chill, cold, cool, deadpan, detached, dispassionate, distant, flat, frigid, heartless, icy, immovable, impassive, impersonal, indifferent, matter-of-fact, remote, reserved, toneless, undemonstrative, unemotional, unfeeling, unimpassioned, with straight face; ▪ **Ant** demonstrative, emotional, feeling, passionate, sympathetic.

emphasize [v] *stress, give priority to*
▪ **Syn** accent, accentuate, affirm, articulate, assert, charge, dramatize, dwell on, enlarge, enunciate, highlight, impress, indicate, italicize, maintain, mark, pinpoint, press, pronounce, punctuate, underline, underscore, weight; ▪ **Ant** depreciate, forget, ignore, play down, understate.

emphatic [adj] *insistent, unequivocal*
▪ **Syn** absolute, assertive, categorical, certain, decided, definitive, dogmatic, explicit, express, flat, forceful, forcible, important, marked, momentous, positive, potent, powerful, pronounced, resounding, significant, sober, solemn, stressed, strong, sure, trenchant, vigorous; ▪ **Ant** equivocal, hesitant, indefinite, indefinite, indistinct, insignificant, reserved, understated.

empirical/empiric [adj] *practical; based on experience* ▪ **Syn** experiential, experimental, factual, observational, observed, pragmatic, provisional; ▪ **Ant** conjectural, hypothetical, impractical, speculative, theoretical, unobserved.

employ [v1] *make use of*
▪ **Syn** apply, engage, exercise, exert, exploit, fill, manipulate, occupy, operate, spend, use, utilize; ▪ **Ant** ignore, misuse, shun, waste.

employ [v2] *give money in exchange for work performed* ▪ **Syn** commission, contract, engage, enlist, hire, obtain, place, procure, retain, secure; ▪ **Ant** fire, lay off, let go.

employed [adj] *working*
▪ **Syn** active, busy, engaged, hired, laboring, occupied, operating, selected; ▪ **Ant** idle, inactive, unemployed, unengaged, unoccupied.

empower [v] *authorize*
▪ **Syn** accredit, allow, capacitate, charge, commission, delegate, enable, entitle, en-

trust, grant, invest, license, permit, privilege, qualify, sanction, vest, warrant; ▪ *Ant* disenfranchise, refuse, reject, revoke.

empty [*adj1*] *containing nothing*
▪ *Syn* abandoned, bare, barren, blank, clear, dead, deflated, depleted, deserted, desolate, despoiled, destitute, devoid, dry, evacuated, exhausted, forsaken, hollow, lacking, stark, unfilled, vacant, vacated, vacuous, void, waste; ▪ *Ant* complete, entire, filled, full, inhabited, replete, sated, satisfied.

empty [*adj2*] *fruitless, ineffective*
▪ *Syn* banal, barren, cheap, dead, deadpan, expressionless, fatuous, flat, frivolous, futile, hollow, inane, insipid, jejune, meaningless, nugatory, otiose, paltry, petty, unsubstantial, vacuous, vain, valueless, vapid, worthless; ▪ *Ant* abundant, copious, effective, fruitful, meaningful, productive, sincere, sufficient.

empty [*adj3*] *hungry*
▪ *Syn* famished, ravenous, starving, unfed, unfilled; ▪ *Ant* filled, full, sated, satisfied.

empty [*v*] *remove contents*
▪ *Syn* clear, decant, deplete, discharge, disgorge, drain, dump, eject, escape, evacuate, exhaust, expel, gut, leak, leave, purge, release, tap, unburden, unload, use up, vacate, void; ▪ *Ant* fill, pack, stuff.

empty-headed [*adj*] *flighty, scatterbrained* ▪ *Syn* brainless, dizzy, featherbrained, frivolous, giddy, harebrained, ignorant, inane, silly, skittish, stupid, vacant, vacuous; ▪ *Ant* cognizant, intelligent, sensible, slick, smart.

enable [*v*] *allow, authorize, or make possible* ▪ *Syn* approve, capacitate, commission, empower, facilitate, implement, let, license, make possible, permit, qualify, ready, sanction, warrant; ▪ *Ant* block, disallow, halt, hinder, inhibit, oppose, prevent, stop.

enact [*v1*] *act out; accomplish*
▪ *Syn* achieve, act, depict, discourse, do, execute, perform, personate, play, playact, portray, represent; ▪ *Ant* fail, hinder, repeal, stop.

enact [*v2*] *authorize, legislate*
▪ *Syn* appoint, command, decree, dictate, establish, execute, fix, formulate, institute, ordain, pass, proclaim, ratify, sanc-

tion, set, transact; ▪ *Ant* hinder, prevent, refuse, repeal, veto.

enactment [*n*] *law; authorization*
▪ *Syn* command, commandment, decree, dictate, edict, execution, legislation, order, ordinance, proclamation, ratification, regulation, statute; ▪ *Ant* block, disallowance, hindrance, stop, veto.

enamored [*adj*] *in love*
▪ *Syn* amorous, attracted, besotted, bewitched, captivated, charmed, devoted, dotty, enchanted, enraptured, entranced, fascinated, infatuated, loving, smitten; ▪ *Ant* repelled, repulsed, sickened.

enchant [*v*] *delight, mesmerize*
▪ *Syn* allure, beguile, captivate, charm, draw, enamor, enrapture, enthrall, entice, entrance, fascinate, hex, hypnotize, magnetize, please, spell, spellbind, thrill, wile; ▪ *Ant* bother, disenchant, disgust, repel, repulse.

enchanting [*adj*] *fascinating, delightful*
▪ *Syn* appealing, attractive, beguiling, bewitching, captivating, endearing, entrancing, glamorous, intriguing, lovely, pleasant, pleasing, ravishing, seductive, winsome; ▪ *Ant* disenchanting, disgusting, repellent, repulsive.

encircle [*v*] *circumscribe*
▪ *Syn* band, cincture, circle, circuit, compass, cover, enclose, encompass, enfold, envelop, girdle, halo, inclose, invest, ring, surround, wreathe; ▪ *Ant* let go, unloose.

enclose [*v*] *put inside, surround*
▪ *Syn* box up, cage, circumscribe, confine, coop, corral, encase, encircle, encompass, fence, hedge, imbue, immure, impound, imprison, insert, jail, limit, mew, pen, restrict, wall in, wrap; ▪ *Ant* free, let go, release, unloose.

encompass [*v*] *include, contain*
▪ *Syn* admit, comprehend, comprise, cover, embody, embrace, hold, incorporate, involve, subsume; ▪ *Ant* exclude, ignore, leave out, omit.

encounter [*v1*] *happen upon*
▪ *Syn* alight upon, chance upon, come across, confront, descry, detect, espy, experience, face, find, front, happen on, hit upon, meet, sustain, turn up, undergo; ▪ *Ant* avoid, evade, retreat, run away.

encounter [*v2*] *fight, attack*
▪ *Syn* affront, battle, collide, combat, conflict, confront, contend, engage, face,

grapple, meet, strive, struggle; ▪ *Ant* let go, surrender, yield.

encourage [v1] *stimulate spiritually*
▪ *Syn* animate, applaud, boost, buoy, cheer, embolden, energize, enliven, fortify, galvanize, goad, hearten, incite, inspire, inspirit, instigate, praise, push, rally, restore, revitalize, revivify, rouse, spur, steel, stimulate, stir; ▪ *Ant* dampen, deject, depress, depress, deter, discourage, dispirit, dissuade.

encourage [v2] *give support; help*
▪ *Syn* abet, advocate, aid, approve, assist, back, befriend, bolster, boost, brace, comfort, countenance, develop, ease, endorse, favor, fortify, foster, further, improve, promote, push, reassure, reinforce, relieve, sanction, second, serve, solace, spur, strengthen, subsidize, succor, support, sustain, uphold; ▪ *Ant* block, confuse, deter, discourage, hinder.

encroach [v] *invade another's property, business* ▪ *Syn* appropriate, arrogate, crash, entrench, impinge, infringe, interfere, interpose, intervene, intrude, invade, meddle, overstep, trench, trespass, usurp; ▪ *Ant* avoid, keep off, pass over.

encumber [v] *burden*
▪ *Syn* block, charge, clog, cramp, discommode, hamper, handicap, hinder, impede, incommode, inconvenience, lade, load, obstruct, oppress, overburden, overload, retard, saddle, tax, trammel, weigh down, weight; ▪ *Ant* aid, alleviate, assist, ease, help, relieve.

encyclopedic [adj] *comprehensive*
▪ *Syn* all-inclusive, broad, catholic, complete, discursive, exhaustive, extensive, general, thorough, universal, vast, wide-ranging; ▪ *Ant* brief, incomplete, summary, uncomprehensive.

end [v1] *bring to an end*
▪ *Syn* abolish, abort, accomplish, achieve, cease, close, complete, conclude, consummate, crown, culminate, desist, determine, discontinue, dissolve, drop, expire, finish, halt, interrupt, perorate, postpone, quit, relinquish, resolve, settle, stop, terminate, wrap; ▪ *Ant* begin, commence, create, start.

end [v2] *die or kill*
▪ *Syn* abolish, annihilate, cease, depart, destroy, die, expire, exterminate, extinguish, lapse, put to death, ruin, run out, wane; ▪ *Ant* bear, create, give birth.

endanger [v] *put in jeopardy*
▪ *Syn* chance, expose, hazard, imperil, jeopardize, menace, peril, risk, threaten, venture; ▪ *Ant* aid, assist, comfort, help, protect, save, take care.

endear [v] *attract attention*
▪ *Syn* attach, bind, captivate, charm, engage, win; ▪ *Ant* alienate, disenchant, estrange, repulse.

endeavor [v] *attempt to achieve something* ▪ *Syn* aim, aspire, assay, essay, grind, hustle, intend, labor, offer, plug, push, seek, strain, strive, struggle, sweat, try, undertake, venture; ▪ *Ant* be idle, ignore, laze, procrastinate, put off.

endless [adj] *not stopping, not finishing*
▪ *Syn* amaranthine, boundless, ceaseless, constant, continual, continuous, countless, deathless, enduring, eternal, everlasting, illimitable, immeasurable, immortal, incalculable, incessant, indeterminate, infinite, interminable, limitless, measureless, monotonous, multitudinous, numberless, perpetual, unbounded, unbroken, undivided, undying; ▪ *Ant* bounded, completing, ending, finishing, limited, passing, stopping, terminable.

endorse [v] *support, authorize*
▪ *Syn* accredit, advocate, affirm, approve, attest, authenticate, back, bless, certify, champion, commend, confirm, countenance, defend, favor, guarantee, praise, ratify, recommend, sanction, second, stand behind, sustain, underwrite, uphold, vouch for, warrant, witness; ▪ *Ant* ban, censure, disapprove, oppose, protest, reject, repel.

endow [v] *give large gift*
▪ *Syn* accord, award, bequeath, bestow, confer, donate, empower, enable, endue, enhance, enrich, establish, favor, finance, found, fund, furnish, grant, heighten, invest, leave, organize, promote, provide, settle on, sponsor, subscribe, subsidize, supply, support, vest in, will; ▪ *Ant* impoverish, pauperize, receive, take.

endurable [adj] *tolerable*
▪ *Syn* bearable, livable, sufferable, supportable, sustainable; ▪ *Ant* intolerable, unendurable.

endure [v1] *bear hardship*
▪ *Syn* abide, accustom oneself to, allow, bear, brave, brook, countenance, experi-

ence, face, know, permit, stand, stick, be subject to, submit to, suffer, support, sustain, take, tolerate, undergo, weather, withstand; ▪ *Ant* avoid, break, bypass, collapse, escape, evade, give in, resign, sidestep, succumb.

endure [v2] *continue; be durable*
▪ *Syn* abide, bide, carry on, cling, exist, hold, last, linger, live, live on, perdure, persist, prevail, remain, stand, stay, survive, sustain, wear; ▪ *Ant* cease, crumble, discontinue, perish.

enemy [n] *someone hated or competed against* ▪ *Syn* adversary, antagonist, archenemy, assailant, attacker, betrayer, competitor, contender, criminal, detractor, disputant, emulator, foe, guerrilla, informer, invader, murderer, opponent, opposition, prosecutor, rebel, revolutionary, rival, saboteur, seditionist, spy, terrorist, traducer, traitor, vilifier, villain; ▪ *Ant* aide, ally, assistant, confidante, friend, helper.

energetic [adj] *full of life; forceful*
▪ *Syn* active, aggressive, animated, brisk, demoniac, dynamic, enterprising, forcible, fresh, hardy, high-powered, indefatigable, industrious, kinetic, lively, lusty, peppy, potent, powerful, rugged, snappy, spirited, sprightly, spry, stalwart, strenuous, strong, sturdy, tireless, tough, unflagging, vigorous, vital, vivacious; ▪ *Ant* idle, inactive, lazy, lethargic, lifeless, slow, sluggish, tired.

energize [v] *activate; give more life*
▪ *Syn* animate, arm, build up, empower, enliven, fortify, innervate, inspirit, invigorate, motivate, prime, quicken, reinforce, stimulate, strengthen, sustain, trigger, vitalize, work up; ▪ *Ant* deactivate, debilitate, flag, sap, tire, weaken, weary.

enervate [v] *tire, wear out*
▪ *Syn* debilitate, devitalize, disable, enfeeble, exhaust, fatigue, incapacitate, jade, paralyze, prostrate, sap, unnerve, unstring, vitiate, wash out, weaken, wear, weary; ▪ *Ant* activate, animate, empower, energize, invigorate, liven, strengthen.

enervated [adj] *exhausted, worn out*
▪ *Syn* deteriorated, done in, feeble, languid, languorous, limp, listless, paralyzed, prostrate, run-down, sapped, spent, spiritless, tired, undermined, weak; ▪ *Ant* activated, active, animated,

energized, enthusiastic, invigorated, lively, strengthened.

enfeeble [v] *make very weak*
▪ *Syn* attenuate, blunt, cripple, debilitate, deplete, devitalize, diminish, disable, exhaust, fatigue, incapacitate, sap, undermine, weaken, wear out; ▪ *Ant* fortify, harden, strengthen.

enfold [v] *embrace, hug*
▪ *Syn* cinch, clasp, clinch, clutch, cover, drape, encase, enclose, encompass, enshroud, envelop, envelope, enwrap, fold, girdle, grab, hold, invest, press, shroud, squeeze, surround, swathe, veil, wrap, wrap up; ▪ *Ant* drop, let go, release.

enforce [v] *put a rule, plan in force*
▪ *Syn* accomplish, administer, administrate, apply, carry out, coerce, constrain, crack down, demand, dictate, discharge, dragoon, drive, effect, exact, execute, exert, fortify, fulfill, implement, impose, lash, lean on, necessitate, oblige, perform, press, prosecute, reinforce, require, sanction, spur, support, urge, whip; ▪ *Ant* abandon, disregard, drop, forego, forget, give up, neglect, overlook, relax.

engage [v1] *hire for job, use*
▪ *Syn* appoint, bespeak, book, charter, commission, contract, employ, enlist, lease, place, rent, reserve, retain, secure, sign on, sign up, take on; ▪ *Ant* banish, discharge, dismiss, eject, expel, fire, let go, oust, release.

engage [v2] *occupy oneself; engross*
▪ *Syn* absorb, allure, arrest, busy, captivate, catch, charm, draw, employ, enamor, enchant, enthrall, fascinate, imbue, immerse, interest, involve, join, monopolize, partake, participate, practice, preoccupy, undertake; ▪ *Ant* decline, elude, escape, evade, refuse, reject, shun.

engage [v3] *promise to marry*
▪ *Syn* affiance, betroth, commit, contract, pledge, plight, troth, vow; ▪ *Ant* break off, break up.

engage [v4] *start a fight; attack*
▪ *Syn* assail, assault, battle, combat, encounter, face, fight, launch, meet, strike, take on; ▪ *Ant* give up, surrender, yield.

engage [v5] *interconnect; bring into operation* ▪ *Syn* activate, apply, attach, dovetail, energize, fasten, interact, interlace, interlock, intermesh, interplay, join, lock, mesh; ▪ *Ant* cancel, defuse, disconnect.

engaged [*adj1*] *promised to be married*
▪ *Syn* affianced, betrothed, committed, intended, matched, pledged, plighted, spoken for; ▪ *Ant* available, free, uncommitted, uninvolved.

engaged [*adj2*] *operating; busy*
▪ *Syn* absorbed, at work, committed, deep, employed, engrossed, immersed, intent, interested, involved, occupied, preoccupied, pursuing, rapt, signed, tied up, unavailable, working; ▪ *Ant* disengaged, free, idle, inoperable, not working.

engaging [*adj*] *charming*
▪ *Syn* agreeable, alluring, appealing, attractive, captivating, enchanting, enticing, entrancing, fascinating, fetching, glamorous, interesting, intriguing, inviting, likable, lovable, magnetic, mesmeric, pleasant, pleasing, prepossessing, sweet, winning, winsome; ▪ *Ant* boring, repulsive, tiresome, undesirable, unlikable.

engender [*v*] *cause to happen; cause an action* ▪ *Syn* arouse, beget, breed, bring forth, create, develop, excite, foment, generate, give birth to, hatch, incite, induce, instigate, occasion, precipitate, procreate, produce, rouse, spawn, stimulate, stir, work up; ▪ *Ant* destroy, extinguish, finish, halt, kill, stop.

engross [*v*] *hold one's attention*
▪ *Syn* absorb, apply, arrest, assimilate, attract, busy, consume, corner, engage, engulf, enrapture, enthrall, fascinate, fill, grip, hold, immerse, involve, monopolize, occupy, preoccupy, soak; ▪ *Ant* distract, forget, ignore, reject, repulse, turn off.

engrossed [*adj*] *preoccupied; attentive to* ▪ *Syn* absorbed, busy, captivated, caught up, consumed, deep, engaged, enthralled, fascinated, gripped, hooked, immersed, industrious, intent, intrigued, lost, occupied, rapt, riveted, sedulous, submerged; ▪ *Ant* bored, detached, disinterested, inattentive, indifferent, oblivious, uninterested.

engrossing [*adj*] *very interesting*
▪ *Syn* absorbing, all-consuming, captivating, compelling, consuming, controlling, enthralling, exciting, fascinating, gripping, intriguing, obsessing, preoccupying, provoking, riveting, stimulating; ▪ *Ant* boring, repellent, repulsive, uninteresting.

enhance [*v*] *improve, embellish*
▪ *Syn* adorn, aggrandize, amplify, appreciate, augment, beautify, boost, build up, complement, elevate, enlarge, exalt, heighten, increase, intensify, lift, magnify, reinforce, strengthen, swell, upgrade; ▪ *Ant* decrease, detract, lower, minimize, reduce, worsen.

enigmatic/enigmatical [*adj*] *mysterious* ▪ *Syn* ambiguous, cryptic, dark, equivocal, indecipherable, inexplicable, inscrutable, obscure, occult, oracular, perplexing, puzzling, recondite, secret; ▪ *Ant* clear, obvious, plain.

enjoin [*v1*] *order, command*
▪ *Syn* advise, appoint, bid, caution, charge, counsel, decree, demand, dictate, forewarn, impose, instruct, ordain, prescribe, rule, tell, urge, warn; ▪ *Ant* acquiesce, agree, comply, conform, obey, submit, yield.

enjoin [*v2*] *forbid*
▪ *Syn* ban, bar, deny, disallow, inhibit, interdict, outlaw, preclude, prohibit, proscribe, restrain, taboo; ▪ *Ant* allow, exhort, let, permit.

enjoy [*v1*] *take pleasure in, from something* ▪ *Syn* adore, appreciate, delight in, fancy, like, love, luxuriate in, pleasure in, rejoice in, relish, revel in, savor, thrill to; ▪ *Ant* condemn, detest, dislike, hate, scorn.

enjoy [*v2*] *have the benefit or use of*
▪ *Syn* boast, command, experience, have, hold, maintain, occupy, own, possess, process, retain, use; ▪ *Ant* lack, need, want.

enjoyable [*adj*] *pleasing; to one's liking*
▪ *Syn* agreeable, amusing, delectable, delicious, delightful, entertaining, fun, genial, gratifying, likable, pleasant, pleasurable, satisfying, welcome; ▪ *Ant* disagreeable, displeasing, unenjoyable, unhappy, unpleasant, unsatisfying.

enlarge [*v*] *make or grow bigger; increase* ▪ *Syn* aggrandize, amplify, augment, boost, broaden, build, bulk, develop, diffuse, dilate, distend, elaborate, elongate, embroider, exaggerate, expand, expatiate, extend, grow, heighten, inflate, lengthen, magnify, mount, multiply, rise, spread, stretch, swell, upsurge, wax, widen; ▪ *Ant* abridge, compress, condense, curtail, decrease, diminish, lessen, lower, reduce, shrink.

enlighten [v] *explain thoroughly; make aware* ▪ *Syn* acquaint, advise, apprise, brief, catechize, counsel, direct, disclose, divulge, edify, educate, elucidate, guide, illuminate, illumine, inculcate, indoctrinate, inform, instruct, persuade, preach, reveal, save, school, teach, tell, train, update, uplift; ▪ *Ant* bewilder, confound, confuse, delude, mislead, mystify, obscure, puzzle.

enlightened [adj] *informed, educated* ▪ *Syn* aware, broad-minded, civilized, cultivated, knowledgeable, learned, liberal, literate, open-minded, reasonable, refined, savvy, sharp, sophisticated; ▪ *Ant* confounded, confused, in the dark, misled, perplexed, uneducated, unenlightened, uninformed.

enlist [v] *sign up for responsibility* ▪ *Syn* admit, appoint, assign, call up, conscript, draft, embody, employ, engage, enroll, enter, hire, hitch, impress, incorporate, initiate, join up, levy, list, mobilize, muster, oblige, procure, record, recruit, register, secure, serve, sign on, volunteer; ▪ *Ant* avoid, dodge, quit, shun.

enliven [v] *inspire, vitalize* ▪ *Syn* animate, brighten, buoy, cheer, divert, entertain, excite, exhilarate, fire up, galvanize, gladden, hearten, inspirit, invigorate, quicken, refresh, rejuvenate, rouse, spark, spice, stimulate, vivify, wake up; ▪ *Ant* bore, dull, enervate, exhaust, fatigue, subdue, tire.

en masse [adv] *all at once* ▪ *Syn* all in all, all together, altogether, as a body, as a whole, as one, bodily, ensemble, generally, in a body, in a group, jointly, on the whole, together; ▪ *Ant* one at a time, singly.

enmesh [v] *involve in situation* ▪ *Syn* box in, catch, draw in, embroil, ensnare, entangle, entrap, hook, implicate, incriminate, net, snare, snarl, tangle, trap; ▪ *Ant* exclude, leave out.

enmity [n] *hatred, animosity* ▪ *Syn* acrimony, antagonism, antipathy, aversion, bitterness, detestation, dislike, hate, hostility, ill will, loathing, malevolence, malice, rancor, spite, spleen, venom; ▪ *Ant* affinity, cordiality, fellowship, friendship, good will, kindness, love.

ennui [n] *boredom* ▪ *Syn* apathy, blahs, blues, dejection, depression, doldrums, fatigue, languor, lassitude, listlessness, melancholy, sadness, satiety, tedium, weariness; ▪ *Ant* energy, enthusiasm, excitement, liveliness, vigor.

enormous [adj] *very large* ▪ *Syn* astronomic, colossal, excessive, gargantuan, gigantic, gross, huge, immense, mammoth, massive, monstrous, mountainous, prodigious, stupendous, tremendous, vast, whopping; ▪ *Ant* diminutive, insignificant, little, minute, small, tiny.

enough [adj] *plenty* ▪ *Syn* abundant, acceptable, adequate, ample, bounteous, bountiful, comfortable, competent, complete, copious, decent, full, lavish, plenteous, plentiful, replete, satisfactory, sufficient, suitable; ▪ *Ant* deficient, inadequate, insufficient.

enrage [v] *make very angry* ▪ *Syn* aggravate, anger, exasperate, incense, incite, inflame, infuriate, ire, irritate, madden, needle, provoke, rile, umbrage; ▪ *Ant* appease, calm, compose, pacify, placate, please, soothe.

enrapture [v] *captivate* ▪ *Syn* allure, attract, beguile, bewitch, charm, delight, elate, enamor, enchant, enthrall, entrance, fascinate, gladden, gratify, please, ravish, rejoice, score, send, spellbind, transport; ▪ *Ant* disgust, displease, offend, repel.

enrich [v] *improve, embellish* ▪ *Syn* adorn, aggrandize, ameliorate, augment, better, build, cultivate, decorate, develop, endow, enhance, grace, ornament, pad, parlay, refine, supplement, upgrade; ▪ *Ant* decrease, deplete, impoverish, reduce, take.

enroll [v1] *sign up for membership* ▪ *Syn* accept, admit, call up, employ, engage, enlist, enter, join, matriculate, recruit, register, serve, sign on, subscribe; ▪ *Ant* avoid, dodge, ignore, pass, reject, withdraw.

enroll [v2] *list, record* ▪ *Syn* affix, bill, book, catalog, chronicle, enlist, enter, file, fill out, index, inscribe, mark, matriculate, note, poll, register, schedule, slate; ▪ *Ant* cancel, dismiss, neglect.

en route [adj/adv] *on the way to destination* ▪ *Syn* along the way, bound, in passage, in transit, midway, progressing, travelling; ▪ *Ant* derailed, detained, off the path, sidetracked.

ensconce [*v*] *hide; tuck away*
▪ *Syn* bury, cache, conceal, ditch, establish, fix, install, locate, nestle, protect, screen, secrete, set, shelter, shield, situate, stash, station; ▪ *Ant* dislocate, reveal, take out, uncover, unveil.

enshrine [*v*] *hold as sacred*
▪ *Syn* apotheosize, bless, cherish, consecrate, dedicate, exalt, hallow, idolize, preserve, revere, sanctify, treasure; ▪ *Ant* defile, desecrate, disrespect.

enslave [*v*] *make someone a slave*
▪ *Syn* bind, capture, chain, confine, disenfranchise, dominate, fetter, hobble, hold, incarcerate, indenture, jail, oppress, restrain, secure, shackle, subjugate, suppress, tether, tie, yoke; ▪ *Ant* emancipate, enfranchise, free, let go, liberate.

ensnare [*v*] *trap*
▪ *Syn* capture, catch, embroil, enmesh, entangle, hook, inveigle, lure net, rope in, snag, trick; ▪ *Ant* free, let go, liberate, release.

ensue [*v*] *start to happen; come to pass*
▪ *Syn* appear, arise, attend, befall, derive, develop, emanate, eventuate, flow, follow, issue, occur, proceed, result, stem, succeed, supervene; ▪ *Ant* antecede, precede.

ensuing [*adj*] *subsequent or resultant*
▪ *Syn* after, consequent, following, later, next, posterior, postliminary, subsequent, subsequential; ▪ *Ant* antecedent, preceding, preliminary.

entangle [*v*] *involve, mix up*
▪ *Syn* bewilder, burden, catch, complicate, compromise, confuse, corner, dishevel, embroil, enchain, enmesh, ensnare, fetter, hamper, hook, impede, intertwine, jumble, knot, muddle, perplex, rope in, snag, snare, trammel, trap, twist; ▪ *Ant* clear, disentangle, exclude, explain, extricate, free, untangle.

enter [*v1*] *come, put into a place*
▪ *Syn* arrive, immigrate, infiltrate, ingress, insert, insinuate, invade, penetrate, pierce, probe; ▪ *Ant* depart, exit, go, issue, leave, withdraw.

enter [*v2*] *embark on; take part in*
▪ *Syn* begin, commence, enlist, enroll, inaugurate, join, join up, open, sign on, sign up, start, subscribe; ▪ *Ant* abstain, forget, refrain, stop.

enter [*v3*] *record, list*
▪ *Syn* admit, docket, inject, inscribe, insert, intercalate, interpolate, introduce, log, note, post, register, set down, take down; ▪ *Ant* delete, erase.

enterprise [*n*] *resourcefulness, energy*
▪ *Syn* activity, ambition, audacity, boldness, courage, daring, eagerness, enthusiasm, force, hustle, industry, initiative, pluck, push, readiness, self-reliance, spirit, vigor, zeal; ▪ *Ant* apathy, idleness, indolence, passiveness, passivity.

enterprising [*adj*] *resourceful, energetic*
▪ *Syn* active, aggressive, ambitious, aspiring, audacious, bold, busy, diligent, driving, eager, enthusiastic, hardworking, hungry, industrious, intrepid, keen, lively, progressive, ready, self-starting, spirited, venturesome, vigorous, zealous; ▪ *Ant* apathetic, inactive, indolent, lethargic, passive.

entertain [*v1*] *amuse*
▪ *Syn* beguile, captivate, charm, cheer, delight, distract, divert, elate, engross, enliven, enthrall, gladden, gratify, humor, indulge, inspire, inspirit, interest, occupy, please, satisfy, stimulate, tickle; ▪ *Ant* bore, tire.

entertain [*v2*] *accommodate visitors*
▪ *Syn* admit, board, chaperon, dine, feed, foster, harbor, house, invite, lodge, nourish, quarter, receive, recreate, regale, room, treat, welcome; ▪ *Ant* refuse, reject, turn away.

entertain [*v3*] *think about seriously*
▪ *Syn* cherish, cogitate on, conceive, consider, contemplate, deliberate, foster, harbor, heed, imagine, maintain, ponder, recognize, support, think over; ▪ *Ant* disregard, forget, reject.

entertaining [*adj*] *amusing, pleasing*
▪ *Syn* absorbing, affecting, clever, compelling, delightful, enjoyable, fascinating, fun, gay, humorous, interesting, lively, moving, piquant, pleasurable, poignant, provocative, stimulating, stirring, thrilling, witty; ▪ *Ant* boring, dull, laborious, sad, tiring, unpleasant.

enthrall [*v*] *captivate*
▪ *Syn* absorb, beguile, bewitch, charm, enchant, engage, enrapture, enslave, entrance, fascinate, grab, grip, hook, hypnotize, intrigue, mesmerize, preoccupy, rivet, spellbind, subdue, subject, subjugate; ▪ *Ant* bore, dull, tire, turn off, weary.

enthusiastic [adj] interested, excited
• **Syn** ardent, athirst, avid, eager, exuberant, fervent, forceful, hearty, intent, keen, lively, obsessed, passionate, rhapsodic, spirited, tantalized, titillated, vehement, vigorous, warm, wholehearted, willing, zealous; • **Ant** apathetic, disinterested, doubting, indifferent, lethargic, pessimistic, reluctant, unenthusiastic, unexcited, weary.

entice [v] allure; persuade
• **Syn** attract, bait, beguile, cajole, coax, decoy, draw, entrap, inveigle, lead on, lure, seduce, tempt, toll, wheedle; • **Ant** disgust, dissuade, repel, repulse, turn away, turn off.

entire [adj] complete, whole
• **Syn** absolute, all, consolidated, continuous, full, gross, intact, integral, integrated, outright, perfect, plenary, sound, thorough, total, unified; • **Ant** abridged, inchoate, incomplete, limited, part, partial.

entirely [adv] completely
• **Syn** absolutely, alone, altogether, exclusively, fully, only, perfectly, plumb, quite, solely, thoroughly, totally, uniquely, utterly, well, wholly, without exception, without reservation; • **Ant** incompletely, partially.

entity [n1] object that exists
• **Syn** article, being, body, creature, existence, individual, item, material, matter, organism, presence, quantity, something, subsistence, substance, thing; • **Ant** abstract, concept, idea.

entity [n2] nature of a being
• **Syn** actuality, essence, existence, integral, quiddity, quintessence, reality, subsistence, substance, sum, system, totality; • **Ant** abstract.

entrance [v] captivate, hypnotize
• **Syn** anesthetize, attract, bewitch, charm, delight, enchant, enrapture, enthrall, fascinate, mesmerize, ravish, spellbind, transport; • **Ant** bore, disgust, repel, repulse, turn off.

entrap [v] capture, involve
• **Syn** beguile, catch, decoy, embroil, enmesh, ensnare, entangle, entice, hook, implicate, inveigle, lure, net, seduce, snare, tempt, trap, trick; • **Ant** clear, disentangle, exclude, free, liberate, release.

entreat [v] plead with
• **Syn** appeal to, ask, beg, beseech, blandish, coax, conjure, crave, enjoin, exhort, implore, importune, invoke, pester, petition, plague, pray, press, request, supplicate, urge, wheedle; • **Ant** answer, command, demand.

entrench [v] establish, make inroads
• **Syn** anchor, confirm, define, dig in, embed, ensconce, fence, fix, fortify, found, ground, hole up, implant, ingrain, install, lodge, plant, protect, root, seat, set, settle, strengthen; • **Ant** cast out, eradicate, expel, remove, root out.

entwine [v] twist around
• **Syn** braid, coil, corkscrew, curl, embrace, encircle, enmesh, entangle, interlace, intertwine, interweave, knit, lace, plait, spiral, surround, twine, weave, wind, wreathe; • **Ant** straighten, unravel, untwist, unwind.

enunciate [v] speak clearly
• **Syn** announce, articulate, declare, deliver, enounce, express, modulate, outline, phonate, proclaim, pronounce, say, sound, state, submit, utter, vocalize, voice; • **Ant** mispronounce, muffle, mumble.

envelop [v] encase, hide
• **Syn** blanket, cloak, conceal, contain, cover, drape, embrace, encircle, enclose, encompass, engulf, fence, gird, girdle, guard, hem, immure, obscure, protect, roll, sheathe, shield, shroud, superimpose, surround, swaddle, swathe, veil, wrap; • **Ant** free, let go, let loose, open, release, uncover, unwrap.

enviable [adj] desired, blessed
• **Syn** advantageous, desirable, excellent, favored, fortunate, good, lucky, privileged; • **Ant** disadvantaged, undesirable, undesired, unenviable, unlucky.

envious [adj] jealous, resentful
• **Syn** appetent, covetous, craving, desiring, desirous, fain, greedy, grudging, invidious, jaundiced, malicious, spiteful, umbrageous, wishful, yearning; • **Ant** benign, comfortable, confident, content, generous, kind, pleased, unenvious.

envy [v] desire an advantage possessed by another • **Syn** begrudge, covet, crave, grudge, hanker, hunger, long, lust, object to, resent, thirst, want, yearn; • **Ant** be confident, be content, be satisfied.

ephemeral [adj] momentary, passing
• **Syn** brief, episodic, evanescent, fleeting, flitting, fugacious, fugitive, impermanent, short, short-lived, temporary,

transient, transitory, volatile; ▪ **Ant** enduring, eternal, everlasting, interminable, lasting, long, permanent, perpetual.

epicurean [adj] *loving food and finer things* ▪ **Syn** gluttonous, gourmet, hedonistic, libertine, lush, luxurious, pleasure-seeking, self-indulgent, sensual, sensuous, sybaritic, voluptuous; ▪ **Ant** austere, disciplined, humble, modest, plain, restrained, simple, Spartan.

epidemic [adj] *widespread* ▪ **Syn** catching, communicable, contagious, endemic, general, infectious, pandemic, prevailing, prevalent, rampant, rife, sweeping, wide-ranging; ▪ **Ant** contained, limited.

epilogue [n] *afterword* ▪ **Syn** coda, conclusion, finale, follow-up, peroration, postlude, postscript, sequel, summation; ▪ **Ant** foreword, introduction, preface.

episodic [adj] *intermittent; composed of several tales* ▪ **Syn** anecdotal, digressive, disconnected, discursive, disjointed, incidental, irregular, occasional, picaresque, rambling, roundabout, segmented, sporadic, wandering; ▪ **Ant** connected, lasting, permanent, regular, unbroken.

equable [adj] *steady, calm* ▪ **Syn** composed, consistent, constant, even, even-tempered, imperturbable, level-headed, orderly, placid, regular, serene, smooth, stable, temperate, tranquil, unflappable, uniform, unruffled, unvarying; ▪ **Ant** changeable, excitable, fluctuating, irregular, spasmodic, vacillating, variable, varying, wavering.

equal [adj1] *alike* ▪ **Syn** balanced, commensurate, comparable, coordinate, correspondent, duplicate, egalitarian, equivalent, homologous, identical, indistinguishable, invariable, level, look-alike, matched, parallel, proportionate, same, tantamount, uniform, unvarying; ▪ **Ant** different, not alike, unequal, unlike, unmatched, variable, varying.

equal [adj2] *fair, unbiased* ▪ **Syn** dispassionate, egalitarian, equitable, even-handed, impartial, just, nonpartisan, objective, unprejudiced; ▪ **Ant** biased, discriminatory, disproportionate, unequal, unequitable, unfair, unjust.

equal [v] *make even, be even with* ▪ **Syn** agree, approach, balance, be commensurate, be level, compare, comprise, coordinate, correspond, emulate, equalize, equate, equipoise, level, match, measure up, meet, parallel, reach, rival, square with, tally, tie; ▪ **Ant** disproportion, imbalance, vary.

equalize [v] *make the same; balance* ▪ **Syn** adjust, compare, coordinate, democratize, emulate, equate, establish, even, even up, handicap, level, match, parallel, regularize, smooth, square, standardize, trim; ▪ **Ant** disproportion, imbalance, vary.

equanimity [n] *levelheadedness* ▪ **Syn** aplomb, ataraxia, calm, composure, cool, equability, imperturbability, patience, phlegm, placidity, sangfroid, self-possession, serenity, steadiness, tranquillity; ▪ **Ant** agitation, alarm, anxiety, discomposure, excitableness, upset, worry.

equate [v] *balance; think of together* ▪ **Syn** agree, assimilate, associate, average, compare, equalize, even, level, liken, match, offset, pair, paragon, parallel, relate, square, tally, treat; ▪ **Ant** disagree, imbalance.

equilibrium [n] *balance; evenness* ▪ **Syn** calm, calmness, composure, cool, counterbalance, counterpoise, equanimity, equipoise, poise, serenity, stability, stasis, steadiness, symmetry; ▪ **Ant** imbalance, unevenness.

equitable [adj] *impartial* ▪ **Syn** cricket, decent, disinterested, due, ethical, even-handed, fair, honest, impersonal, just, level, moral, nondiscriminatory, nonpartisan, objective, proper, proportionate, reasonable, right, square, stable; ▪ **Ant** biased, disproportionate, partial, prejudiced, unequitable, unfair, unjust, unreasonable.

equivalent [adj] *same, similar* ▪ **Syn** agnate, akin, alike, analogous, commensurate, comparable, convertible, correlative, correspondent, duplicate, equal, even, homologous, identical, indistinguishable, interchangeable, like, parallel, proportionate, reciprocal, substitute, synonymous, tantamount; ▪ **Ant** changed, different, dissimilar, mismatched, unequal, unlike.

equivocal [adj] *doubtful, uncertain* ▪ **Syn** ambiguous, ambivalent, borderline, dubious, evasive, indefinite, indeterminate, indistinct, misleading, oblique, obscure, open, problematic, questionable, suspect, suspicious, tenebrous, unclear, undecided, vague; ▪ *Ant* certain, clear, definite, determined, obvious, plain, sure, unequivocal, unquestionable.

equivocate [v] *avoid an issue*
▪ *Syn* cavil, con, dodge, elude, evade, falsify, hedge, lie, mince words, prevaricate, quibble, sidestep, tergiversate; ▪ *Ant* articulate, face, meet, speak honestly.

eradicate [v] *destroy; remove*
▪ *Syn* abate, abolish, annihilate, demolish, efface, eliminate, expunge, exterminate, extirpate, liquidate, obliterate, purge, raze, scrub, uproot, wash out; ▪ *Ant* aid, assist, bear, create, establish, fix, generate, help, institute, plant.

erase [v] *remove; rub out*
▪ *Syn* abolish, annul, black out, blot, cancel, cut, delete, dispatch, efface, eliminate, excise, expunge, extirpate, kill, negate, nullify, obliterate, remove, strike, strike out; ▪ *Ant* add, insert, put in.

erect [adj] *straight up*
▪ *Syn* arrect, cocked, firm, perpendicular, raised, rigid, stiff, straight, upright, vertical; ▪ *Ant* prone, prostrate, recumbent.

erect [v] *build or raise*
▪ *Syn* assemble, cock, compose, construct, create, elevate, fabricate, fashion, forge, form, frame, heighten, hoist, lift, make, manufacture, mount, pitch, put up, raise, rear, shape, stand, throw up, upraise, uprear; ▪ *Ant* demolish, raze, topple.

erode [v] *deteriorate; wear away*
▪ *Syn* abrade, bite, corrode, crumble, destroy, disintegrate, eat, gnaw, grind down, spoil, wear down; ▪ *Ant* build, construct, fix, rebuild.

erosion [n] *deterioration; wearing away*
▪ *Syn* abrasion, attrition, consumption, corrosion, decrease, desedimentation, despoliation, destruction, disintegration, wear; ▪ *Ant* building, construction, rebuilding, strengthening.

erotic [adj] *sexy*
▪ *Syn* amorous, aphrodisiac, carnal, concupiscent, earthy, erogenous, fervid, fleshly, impassioned, lascivious, lecherous, lewd, obscene, prurient, raunchy, raw, romantic, rousing, salacious, seductive, sensual, sexual, spicy, steamy, stimulating, suggestive, titillating, venereal, voluptuous; ▪ *Ant* bland, cold, dull, frigid, unerotic.

errant [adj] *wrong; deviant*
▪ *Syn* aberrant, devious, drifting, erratic, fallible, heretic, meandering, misbehaving, mischievous, miscreant, naughty, offending, rambling, ranging, roaming, roving, shifting, sinning, stray, straying, unorthodox, wandering, wayward; ▪ *Ant* correct, reliable, righteous.

erratic [adj] *unpredictable; wandering*
▪ *Syn* aberrant, abnormal, anomalous, arbitrary, bizarre, capricious, devious, dicey, eccentric, fitful, fluctuant, idiosyncratic, inconsistent, irregular, meandering, nomadic, peculiar, planetary, stray, vagarious, volatile, wayward, weird, whimsical; ▪ *Ant* certain, consistent, definite, dependable, predictable, regular, reliable, steady, sure, unchanging.

erroneous [adj] *wrong, incorrect*
▪ *Syn* amiss, askew, awry, defective, fallacious, false, faulty, flawed, invalid, misguided, mistaken, off, specious, spurious, unfounded, untrue, way off; ▪ *Ant* accurate, correct, right, sound, true, valid.

ersatz [adj] *artificial*
▪ *Syn* bogus, copied, counterfeit, fake, false, imitation, manufactured, phony, pretended, sham, simulated, spurious, substitute, synthetic; ▪ *Ant* genuine, real.

erstwhile [adj] *former*
▪ *Syn* bygone, late, old, once, one-time, past, preceding, previous, quondam; ▪ *Ant* current, latter, present.

erudite [adj] *well-educated, cultured*
▪ *Syn* brainy, cultivated, educated, highbrow, knowledgeable, learned, lettered, literate, savvy, scholarly, scholastic, well-read, wise to; ▪ *Ant* common, ignorant, uncultured, uneducated.

erupt [v] *give forth, eject with force*
▪ *Syn* appear, belch, boil, burst, detonate, discharge, emit, eruct, explode, extravasate, gush, hurl, jet, rupture, spew, spit, spout, spurt, vent, vomit; ▪ *Ant* contain, hold, hold back, retain, subside.

escalate [v] *increase, be increased*
▪ *Syn* amplify, ascend, broaden, climb, enlarge, expand, extend, grow, heighten, intensify, magnify, mount, raise, rise, scale, step up; ▪ *Ant* decrease, diminish, lessen, lower, weaken.

escape [v] *break away from*
▪ *Syn* abscond, avoid, break, circumvent, depart, desert, dodge, duck, elope, elude, evade, flee, leave, pass, run, shun, skip, vanish; ▪ *Ant* capture, remain, stay.

eschew [v] *have nothing to do with*
 ▪ *Syn* abandon, abjure, abstain, avoid, duck, elude, evade, forgo, forswear, refrain, renounce, sacrifice, shun; ▪ *Ant* embrace, like, love.

escort [v] *act as a companion, guard*
 ▪ *Syn* accompany, attend, carry, chaperon, conduct, convoy, direct, guide, lead, partner, pilot, route, see, shepherd, usher; ▪ *Ant* abandon, desert, drop, leave, lose, maroon, neglect.

esoteric [adj] *mysterious, obscure*
 ▪ *Syn* abstruse, arcane, cabalistic, cryptic, Delphic, heavy, hidden, inner, mystical, occult, Orphic, private, profound, recondite, secret, Sibylline; ▪ *Ant* common, familiar, known, obvious, plain, public, simple.

especial [adj] *exceptional, particular*
 ▪ *Syn* chief, distinguished, dominant, exclusive, express, extraordinary, individual, marked, notable, noteworthy, outstanding, paramount, peculiar, predominant, principal, set, signal, singular, special, supreme, surpassing, unique; ▪ *Ant* common, general, normal, ordinary, unexceptional, unspecific, usual.

espouse [v1] *stand up for; support*
 ▪ *Syn* accept, adopt, advocate, approve, back, champion, defend, embrace, maintain, uphold; ▪ *Ant* deny, forsake, reject, repudiate.

espouse [v2] *marry*
 ▪ *Syn* betroth, unite, wed; ▪ *Ant* divorce.

essay [v] *try, attempt*
 ▪ *Syn* aim, assay, endeavor, labor, offer, seek, strive, struggle, test, toil, travail, undertake, venture; ▪ *Ant* be idle, forget, neglect, pass.

essential [adj1] *important, vital*
 ▪ *Syn* capital, cardinal, chief, crucial, fundamental, imperative, indispensable, leading, main, necessary, principal, required, requisite; ▪ *Ant* accessory, auxiliary, inessential, minor, nonessential, secondary, subsidiary, unimportant.

essential [adj2] *basic, fundamental*
 ▪ *Syn* absolute, basal, cardinal, complete, congenital, connate, constitutional, deep-seated, elemental, elementary, inborn, inbred, inherent, innate, intrinsic, key, main, material, primary, prime, primitive, principal, quintessential, substratal, underlying; ▪ *Ant* atypical, minor, secondary, subordinate.

establish [v1] *set up, organize*
 ▪ *Syn* authorize, base, build, constitute, create, decree, enact, endow, ensconce, erect, found, ground, inaugurate, inculcate, institute, land, moor, originate, place, practice, rivet, root, secure, stabilize, start, station; ▪ *Ant* abrogate, destroy, disestablish; extirpate, invalidate, ruin, unsettle.

establish [v2] *authenticate; demonstrate*
 ▪ *Syn* ascertain, authorize, base, certify, circumstantiate, confirm, constitute, corroborate, decree, determine, discover, enact, formulate, learn, legislate, predicate, prescribe, prove, ratify, rest, show, stay, substantiate, validate, verify; ▪ *Ant* confuse, confute, disprove, invalidate, rebut.

esteem [v] *think highly of*
 ▪ *Syn* admire, appreciate, apprize, cherish, consider, hold dear, honor, idolize, like, love, prize, respect, revere, treasure, value, venerate, worship; ▪ *Ant* abhor, abuse, dislike, disregard, disrespect, hate, insult, mock, ridicule.

estimable [adj] *honorable, worthy*
 ▪ *Syn* admirable, august, commendable, decent, esteemed, excellent, good, honored, laudable, meritorious, name, noble, palmary, praiseworthy, reputable, respectable, sterling, valuable, venerable; ▪ *Ant* bad, dishonorable, inestimable, insignificant, poor, unworthy.

estrange [v] *destroy the affections of*
 ▪ *Syn* alienate, antagonize, disaffect, disunite, divorce, leave, part, separate, sever, split, sunder, wean, withdraw, withhold; ▪ *Ant* conciliate, engage, marry, reconcile, unite.

eternal [adj] *without pause; endless*
 ▪ *Syn* abiding, ageless, always, amaranthine, boundless, ceaseless, constant, continual, enduring, everlasting, forever, incessant, infinite, interminable, lasting, never-ending, perdurable, perpetual, persistent, timeless; ▪ *Ant* brief, changeable, changing, ending, ephemeral, stopping, temporary, terminable, transient.

eternally [adv] *endlessly*
 ▪ *Syn* always, continually, ever, evermore, forever, forevermore, in perpetuum, perpetually; ▪ *Ant* briefly, temporarily, transiently.

ethereal [adj] *delicate, heavenly*
 ▪ *Syn* aerial, airy, celestial, dainty, di-

vine, empyreal, empyrean, exquisite, fairy, filmy, ghostly, gossamer, impalpable, intangible, light, rarefied, spiritual, sublime, supernal, tenuous, unearthly, vaporous; ▪ *Ant* earthly, heavy, indelicate, substantial, thick, worldly.

ethical [*adj*] *moral, righteous*
▪ *Syn* conscientious, correct, decent, equitable, fitting, good, honorable, humane, just, moralistic, noble, principled, proper, respectable, right, square, upright, virtuous; ▪ *Ant* corrupt, dishonest, immoral, improper, nefarious, unethical, unjust, unrighteous.

eulogize [*v*] *praise, glorify*
▪ *Syn* acclaim, applaud, bless, celebrate, commend, compliment, exalt, extol, flatter, hymn, idolize, laud, magnify, panegyrize; ▪ *Ant* calumniate, condemn, criticize, vilify.

euphoria [*n*] *extreme happiness*
▪ *Syn* bliss, dreamland, ecstasy, elation, exaltation, exhilaration, exultation, frenzy, glee, health, high spirits, intoxication, joy, jubilation, rapture, relaxation, transport; ▪ *Ant* anxiety, depression, despair, misery, sorrow, unhappiness, woe.

evacuate [*v*] *clear an area; empty*
▪ *Syn* abandon, cut out, decamp, depart, desert, discharge, displace, eject, expel, forsake, leave, quit, relinquish, remove, vacate, withdraw; ▪ *Ant* come in, enter, fill, load, occupy.

evade [*v*] *get away from*
▪ *Syn* avoid, bypass, circumvent, deceive, dodge, duck, escape, eschew, fence, flee, hedge, lie, parry, pussyfoot, shift, shirk, shun, shy, sidestep, tergiversate; ▪ *Ant* confront, face, meet, take on.

evaporate [*v*] *dry up, dissolve*
▪ *Syn* clear, concentrate, dehumidify, dehydrate, dematerialize, desiccate, disappear, dispel, disperse, dissipate, dry, evanesce, fade, melt, parch, pass, vanish, vaporize; ▪ *Ant* dampen, soak, wet.

evasive [*adj*] *deceitful, tricky*
▪ *Syn* ambiguous, cagey, casuistic, deceptive, devious, dissembling, elusive, equivocating, false, indirect, misleading, oblique, prevaricating, shifty, slippery, sly, unclear, vague; ▪ *Ant* direct, forthright, honest, ready, straight, straightforward.

even [*adj1*] *flat, uniform*
▪ *Syn* balanced, consistent, direct, equal,

flush, homogenous, horizontal, level, metrical, parallel, planate, plumb, proportional, regular, right, same, smooth, square, stable, steady, true; ▪ *Ant* broken, different, disparate, irregular, rough, uneven.

even [*adj2*] *calm, undisturbed*
▪ *Syn* composed, cool, equable, equanimous, even-tempered, imperturbable, peaceful, placid, serene, stable, steady, tranquil, unruffled; ▪ *Ant* agitated, excitable, troubled.

even [*adj3*] *commensurate; having no advantage* ▪ *Syn* balanced, coequal, comparable, coterminous, equivalent, exact, identical, level, matching, parallel, proportionate, same, similar, square, tied, uniform; ▪ *Ant* irregular, unequal, uneven.

even [*adj4*] *fair, impartial*
▪ *Syn* balanced, disinterested, dispassionate, equal, equitable, honest, just, matching, nonpartisan, square, unprejudiced; ▪ *Ant* biased, partial, unfair.

even [*v*] *balance, make smooth*
▪ *Syn* align, equal, equalize, flatten, flush, grade, level, match, plane, regularize, roll, smooth, square, stabilize, steady; ▪ *Ant* break, furrow, lump, roughen.

evening [*n*] *latter part of the day*
▪ *Syn* close, dark, decline, dim, dusk, eve, even, eventide, late afternoon, nightfall, sundown, sunset, twilight; ▪ *Ant* dawn, morning, sunrise.

eventful [*adj*] *significant, busy*
▪ *Syn* active, consequential, critical, crucial, decisive, exciting, fateful, full, historic, important, lively, memorable, momentous, notable, noteworthy, outstanding, remarkable, signal, significant; ▪ *Ant* dull, insignificant, normal, ordinary, trivial, uneventful, usual.

eventual [*adj*] *future, concluding*
▪ *Syn* closing, consequent, contingent, dependent, endmost, ensuing, final, hindmost, inevitable, last, later, latter, overall, possible, prospective, resulting, secondary, terminal, ulterior, ultimate; ▪ *Ant* past, previous, prior.

eventually [*adv*] *in the course of time*
▪ *Syn* after all, at last, finally, hereafter, someday, sometime, ultimately, yet; ▪ *Ant* at once, immediately, never.

everlasting [*adj*] *infinite, never-ending*
▪ *Syn* amaranthine, ceaseless, deathless,

eternal, immortal, incessant, interminable, limitless, perdurable, perpetual, timeless; ▪ *Ant* ceasing, concluding, ending, sporadic, temporary, terminating, transient.

everyday [*adj*] *common*
▪ *Syn* accustomed, average, commonplace, conventional, customary, daily, dull, familiar, frequent, habitual, informal, lowly, mainstream, mundane, normal, ordinary, per diem, plain, prosaic, quotidian, routine, stock, usual, wonted, workaday; ▪ *Ant* abnormal, different, exceptional, special, uncommon, unexpected, unfamiliar, unusual.

everywhere [*adv*] *in all places*
▪ *Syn* all around, all over, in all quarters, in every direction, inside and out, omnipresent, overall, throughout, ubiquitous, ubiquitously, universally, wherever; ▪ *Ant* here and there, nowhere.

evict [*v*] *throw out from residence*
▪ *Syn* chase, dislodge, dismiss, dispossess, eject, expel, extrude, force out, oust, put out, remove, shut out, turn out; ▪ *Ant* admit, board, harbor, include, lease, receive, rent, take in, welcome.

evidence [*v*] *prove*
▪ *Syn* attest, bespeak, betoken, confirm, connote, demonstrate, denote, designate, display, evince, exhibit, expose, illustrate, indicate, manifest, mark, ostend, proclaim, reveal, show, signify, testify to, witness; ▪ *Ant* contradict, disguise, disprove, refute.

evident [*adj*] *apparent, clear*
▪ *Syn* axiomatic, clear-cut, conspicuous, distinct, incontestable, incontrovertible, indisputable, logical, manifest, noticeable, obvious, palpable, patent, perceptible, plain, tangible, unambiguous, unmistakable, visible; ▪ *Ant* disputable, hidden, indefinite, obscure, secret, uncertain, unclear, unknown, vague.

evidently [*adv*] *apparently, clearly*
▪ *Syn* doubtless, doubtlessly, incontestably, incontrovertibly, indisputably, manifestly, obviously, officially, ostensibly, outwardly, patently, plainly, seemingly, undoubtedly, unmistakably; ▪ *Ant* doubtfully, mistakably, obscurely, questionably, vaguely.

evil [*adj*] *sinful, immoral*
▪ *Syn* atrocious, bad, baneful, base, beastly, calamitous, corrupt, damnable, depraved, destructive, execrable, flagitious, foul, hateful, heinous, iniquitous, injurious, loathsome, low, malevolent, malicious, nefarious, obscene, offensive, pernicious, poison, rancorous, reprobate, repugnant, repulsive, spiteful, ugly, vicious, vile, wicked, wrathful, wrong; ▪ *Ant* auspicious, decent, good, honest, moral, righteous, sinless, upright, virtuous.

evoke [*v*] *induce, stimulate*
▪ *Syn* arouse, awaken, call, conjure, educe, elicit, evince, evolve, excite, extort, extract, invoke, provoke, raise, rally, recall, rouse, stir up, summon, waken; ▪ *Ant* halt, quell, repress, silence, stifle, stop, suppress.

evolve [*v*] *develop, progress*
▪ *Syn* advance, derive, disclose, educe, elaborate, emerge, enlarge, excogitate, expand, grow, increase, mature, obtain, open, result, ripen, unfold; ▪ *Ant* block, decrease, halt, stop.

exacerbate [*v*] *make worse or more severe* ▪ *Syn* aggravate, annoy, exasperate, heighten, increase, inflame, intensify, irritate, madden, provoke, vex, worsen; ▪ *Ant* appease, calm, comfort, pacify, soothe.

exact [*adj1*] *accurate, precise*
▪ *Syn* careful, clear, clear-cut, correct, definite, distinct, explicit, faultless, identical, literal, methodical, particular, perfect, right, sharp, specific, true, unequivocal, unerring, veracious, verbal, verbatim; ▪ *Ant* approximate, false, imprecise, inaccurate, incorrect, indefinite, inexact, wrong.

exact [*adj2*] *careful, painstaking*
▪ *Syn* conscientious, demanding, finicky, heedful, meticulous, punctilious, punctual, rigorous, scrupulous, severe, strict; ▪ *Ant* approximate, careless, uncareful, unreliable.

exact [*v*] *demand, call for*
▪ *Syn* assess, bleed, call, challenge, claim, coerce, command, compel, constrain, extort, extract, force, gouge, impose, levy, oblige, pinch, postulate, require, requisition, solicit, squeeze, wrench, wrest, wring; ▪ *Ant* give, offer, remit, tender.

exacting [*adj*] *demanding*
▪ *Syn* burdensome, critical, difficult, exigent, fussy, hard, harsh, hypercritical, imperious, onerous, oppressive, painstaking, particular, picky, precise, rigid, rig-

orous, severe, stern, strict, stringent, taxing, tough, trying, weighty; ▪ *Ant* easy, lenient, temperate, tolerant.

exactly [*adv*] *accurately, particularly*
▪ *Syn* absolutely, altogether, completely, definitely, explicitly, expressly, faithfully, indeed, just, literally, methodically, precisely, quite, right, scrupulously, severely, specifically, square, strictly, totally, truthfully, unequivocally, unerringly, veraciously, wholly; ▪ *Ant* approximately, inaccurately, inexactly, roughly.

exaggerate [*v*] *overstate, embellish*
▪ *Syn* amplify, boast, boost, brag, build up, caricature, color, corrupt, distort, embroider, emphasize, enlarge, exalt, expand, fabricate, falsify, heighten, hike, inflate, intensify, lie, magnify, misreport, overdo, overdraw, overemphasize, overestimate, puff, romanticize, scam, stretch; ▪ *Ant* depreciate, minimize, play down, reduce, understate.

exaggerated [*adj*] *overstated, embellished* ▪ *Syn* abstract, artificial, excessive, extravagant, fabulous, false, fantastic, farfetched, hyperbolic, impossible, melodramatic, overblown, overdone, overkill, overwrought, preposterous, pretentious, schmaltzy, sensational, spectacular, steep, strained, stylized, tall, unrealistic; ▪ *Ant* depreciated, minimized, played down, reduced, understated, unembellished, unexaggerated.

exalt [*v*] *promote, praise*
▪ *Syn* acclaim, advance, aggrandize, apotheosize, applaud, bless, boost, commend, dignify, distinguish, ennoble, erect, eulogize, extol, glorify, halo, honor, idolize, intensify, laud, magnify, raise, revere, sublime, transfigure, worship; ▪ *Ant* castigate, condemn, criticize, debase, denounce, humiliate.

exalted [*adj*] *praised; held in high esteem*
▪ *Syn* astral, august, dignified, elevated, eminent, first, grand, highest, high-ranking, honorable, illustrious, immodest, lofty, magnificent, noble, outstanding, overblown, pompous, prestigious, self-important, sublime, superb, superior, top-ranking; ▪ *Ant* condemned, criticized, debased, denounced, humble, humiliated, lowly, minor.

exasperate [*v*] *upset, provoke*
▪ *Syn* aggravate, agitate, anger, annoy,

disturb, embitter, enrage, gall, incense, inflame, infuriate, irk, irritate, madden, nettle, peeve, pique, rankle, rile, rouse, vex; ▪ *Ant* calm, comfort, ease, placate, please, soothe.

excavate [*v*] *dig up*
▪ *Syn* burrow, cut, delve, dig, empty, gouge, grub, hollow, mine, quarry, scoop, scrape, shovel, spade, trench, tunnel, uncover, unearth; ▪ *Ant* bury, cover, fill, stuff, up.

exceed [*v*] *be superior to; surpass*
▪ *Syn* beat, best, better, cap, eclipse, excel, go beyond, outrun, outshine, outstrip, overstep, overtake, overtax, pass, surmount, top, transcend; ▪ *Ant* be inferior, fail, fall behind.

excel [*v*] *be superior; surpass*
▪ *Syn* beat, best, better, cap, eclipse, exceed, go beyond, outdo, outrival, outshine, outstrip, pass, predominate, shine, show talent, surmount, top, transcend; ▪ *Ant* be inferior, fail.

excellent [*adj*] *superior, wonderful*
▪ *Syn* accomplished, capital, certified, champion, choice, distinctive, distinguished, estimable, exceptional, exemplary, finest, first-class, first-rate, good, great, incomparable, invaluable, magnificent, meritorious, notable, outstanding, peerless, premium, priceless, prime, select, sterling, superlative, supreme, top-notch, transcendent, world-class; ▪ *Ant* bad, imperfect, inferior, mediocre, poor, second-class, second-rate, shoddy, undistinguished, unworthy.

except [*v*] *leave out*
▪ *Syn* ban, bar, bate, count out, debar, disallow, eliminate, exclude, exempt, expostulate, inveigh, object, omit, pass over, protest, reject, rule out, suspend, taboo; ▪ *Ant* admit, allow, include, incorporate.

exceptional [*adj1*] *irregular*
▪ *Syn* aberrant, abnormal, anomalous, atypical, deviant, distinct, extraordinary, inconsistent, notable, noteworthy, odd, peculiar, phenomenal, rare, remarkable, scarce, singular, special, strange, unheard-of, unimaginable, unique, unprecedented, unthinkable, unusual; ▪ *Ant* common, conventional, expected, general, normal, ordinary, regular, unexceptional, usual.

exceptional [*adj2*] *excellent, wonderful*
▪ *Syn* extraordinary, fine, first-class, first-

rate, good, high, marvelous, outstanding, phenomenal, premium, prodigious, remarkable, singular, special, superior, world-class; ▪ *Ant* inferior, mediocre, ok, unexceptional, unprodigious.

excessive [adj] *too much; overdone*
▪ *Syn* boundless, disproportionate, enormous, exaggerated, exorbitant, extra, extravagant, extreme, immoderate, indulgent, inordinate, intemperate, limitless, needless, overboard, overkill, overmuch, plethoric, prodigal, profligate, recrementitious, redundant, self-indulgent, steep, superabundant, superfluous, supernatural, unbounded, undue; ▪ *Ant* insufficient, moderate, reasonable, underdone.

exchange [v] *trade*
▪ *Syn* alternate, bandy, bargain, barter, change, commute, deal in, displace, interchange, invert, market, reciprocate, replace, reverse, revise, shift, shuffle, substitute, swap, switch, traffic, transact, transfer, transpose; ▪ *Ant* hold, keep.

excise [v] *remove, delete*
▪ *Syn* amputate, black out, cross out, cut, destroy, edit, elide, eradicate, erase, expunge, exscind, exsect, exterminate, extirpate, extract, gut, slash, strike, trim; ▪ *Ant* add, put in.

excitable [adj] *easily upset or inspired*
▪ *Syn* demonstrative, edgy, emotional, enthusiastic, fiery, hasty, high-strung, hot-headed, hysterical, impatient, impetuous, irascible, nervous, overzealous, quick-tempered, rash, restless, sensitive, short fused, skittish, susceptible, temperamental, testy, touchy, vehement, volatile, volcanic; ▪ *Ant* calm, easy, easygoing, insensitive, laid-back, passive, unexcitable, uninspired.

excite [v] *inspire; upset*
▪ *Syn* agitate, amaze, anger, animate, arouse, astound, awaken, disturb, energize, evoke, fire, fluster, foment, galvanize, goad, incite, induce, inflame, instigate, jar, jolt, kindle, move, precipitate, provoke, quicken, rouse, start, stimulate, thrill, titillate, touch off, vex, waken, warm, whet, worry; ▪ *Ant* bore, calm, compose, deaden, lull, moderate, pacify, quiet, repress, tranquilize.

excited [adj] *inspired; upset*
▪ *Syn* aflame, agitated, animated, annoyed, awakened, charged, delighted, disturbed, eager, enthusiastic, feverish, frantic, hyperactive, hysterical, inflamed, moved, nervous, overwrought, passionate, piqued, provoked, ruffled, stimulated, stirred, thrilled, tumultous/tumultuous, wild, worked up; ▪ *Ant* bored, calm, composed, easygoing, laidback, unenthused, unenthusiastic, unexcited, uninspired.

exciting [adj] *inspiring, exhilarating*
▪ *Syn* arresting, astonishing, bracing, breathtaking, dangerous, dramatic, electrifying, exhilarating, fine, flashy, hectic, impelling, intoxicating, intriguing, lively, moving, overpowering, overwhelming, provocative, racy, rousing, sensational, stimulating, stirring, thrilling, titillating, wild; ▪ *Ant* boring, moderate, unenthused, unenthusiastic, unexciting, uninspiring, unpromising, unstimulating.

exclaim [v] *shout out*
▪ *Syn* assert, bellow, blurt, burst out, call, call out, cry, cry out, declare, ejaculate, emit, holler, proclaim, roar, shout, vociferate, yell; ▪ *Ant* be quiet, be silent, murmur, whisper.

exclude [v] *expel, forbid*
▪ *Syn* ban, bar, blacklist, block, boycott, count out, debar, disallow, eject, eliminate, evict, expel, force out, ignore, obviate, occlude, omit, ostracize, oust, prohibit, proscribe, reject, remove, repudiate, sideline, suspend, veto; ▪ *Ant* accept, add, admit, allow, include, incorporate, take on, welcome.

exclusive [adj] *unshared, restricted*
▪ *Syn* aristocratic, circumscribed, clannish, cliquish, closed, confined, discriminative, fashionable, full, independent, limited, narrow, particular, preferential, private, privileged, prohibitive, restrictive, segregated, select, single, snobbish, sole, unique, whole; ▪ *Ant* common, divided, inclusive, part, partial, public, shared, unlimited, unrestricted.

exclusive of [prep] *except for*
▪ *Syn* aside from, bar, barring, bating, besides, but, excepting, excluding, omitting, outside of, restricting, ruling out, save; ▪ *Ant* including, inclusive of.

excogitate [v] *think about seriously*
▪ *Syn* consider, contemplate, contrive, deliberate, derive, develop, devise, educe, evolve, frame, invent, mind, perpend, ponder, ruminate, study, think out, weigh; ▪ *Ant* disregard, ignore, neglect, slight.

excommunicate [v] *banish*
▪ *Syn* anathematize, ban, cast out, curse, denounce, dismiss, eject, exclude, expel, oust, proscribe, remove, repudiate, unchurch; ▪ *Ant* allow, include, permit, welcome.

excoriate [v] *denounce, criticize*
▪ *Syn* attack, berate, blister, castigate, censure, chastise, condemn, flay, lambaste, lash, rebuke, reproach, reprove, revile, scathe, scold, scorch, slash, upbraid, vilify; ▪ *Ant* compliment, laud, praise.

excruciating [adj] *torturous, painful*
▪ *Syn* acute, agonizing, burning, chastening, consuming, extreme, grueling, harrowing, insufferable, intense, piercing, racking, searing, severe, stabbing, tormenting, violent; ▪ *Ant* bearable, endurable, helpful, pleasant, pleasing, soothing.

exculpate [v] *forgive*
▪ *Syn* absolve, acquit, amnesty, clear, condone, discharge, disculpate, dismiss, excuse, exonerate, free, justify, pardon, rationalize, remit, vindicate; ▪ *Ant* blame, condemn, denounce, sentence.

excusable [adj] *allowable*
▪ *Syn* condonable, defensible, exculpatory, fair, forgivable, justifiable, minor, moderate, okay, pardonable, permissible, reasonable, slight, specious, temperate, tenable, understandable, vindicable, warrantable; ▪ *Ant* blameable, criminal, heinous, inexcusable, unallowable, unforgivable, unjustifiable.

excuse [v] *forgive, absolve; justify*
▪ *Syn* acquit, appease, clear, condone, defend, discharge, exculpate, exempt, exonerate, free, indulge, liberate, mitigate, overlook, pardon, purge, rationalize, release, relieve, shrive, spare, tolerate, vindicate; ▪ *Ant* accuse, blame, censure, charge, chastise.

execrate [v] *hate*
▪ *Syn* abhor, abominate, accurse, anathematize, censure, condemn, curse, damn, denounce, deplore, despise, detest, excoriate, imprecate, loathe, objurgate, reprehend, reprobate, reprove, revile, vilify; ▪ *Ant* admire, commend, like, love.

execute [v] *carry out a task*
▪ *Syn* accomplish, achieve, act, administer, cause, complete, consummate, discharge, effect, enact, enforce, finish, fulfill, govern, implement, meet, perform, prosecute, render, transact; ▪ *Ant* abandon, disregard, fail, forget, ignore, leave, miss, neglect, shirk.

executive [n] *person who manages organization* ▪ *Syn* administrator, boss, businessperson, chief, commander, director, entrepreneur, government, governor, head, hierarchy, industrialist, leader, leadership, management, official, supervisor, tycoon; ▪ *Ant* flunky, hired hand, laborer, menial, subordinate, underling, worker.

exemplary [adj] *ideal*
▪ *Syn* admirable, blameless, classical, commendable, correct, estimable, excellent, good, guiltless, honorable, inculpable, laudable, meritorious, model, paradigmatic, praiseworthy, punctilious, quintessential, righteous, sterling, typical, virtuous, worthy; ▪ *Ant* erring, incorrect, reprehensible, unideal, wrong.

exempt [adj] *freed from responsibility*
▪ *Syn* absolved, cleared, discharged, excepted, excluded, excused, free, immune, liberated, outside, privileged, released, spared, special; ▪ *Ant* accountable, answerable, liable, nonexempt, responsible.

exempt [v] *relieve, absolve*
▪ *Syn* clear, discharge, dispense, except, excuse, exonerate, free, grant immunity, liberate, pass by, privilege from, release, spare, write off; ▪ *Ant* blame.

exercise [v] *put to use*
▪ *Syn* apply, bestow, drill, employ, execute, exert, handle, operate, practice, rehearse, sharpen, utilize, wield; ▪ *Ant* disregard, ignore, neglect, not use.

exertion [n] *hard work*
▪ *Syn* action, activity, application, employment, endeavor, industry, labor, operation, pains, strain, struggle, toil, travail, utilization; ▪ *Ant* idleness, inertia, laziness.

exhale [v] *breathe out*
▪ *Syn* breathe, discharge, eject, emanate, emit, evaporate, expel, issue, outbreathe, respire, steam, vaporize; ▪ *Ant* breathe in, inhale, inspire.

exhaust [v1] *tire or wear out*
▪ *Syn* debilitate, drain, enervate, enfeeble, fag, fatigue, frazzle, impoverish, overexert, overwork, prostrate, tire, weaken, weary; ▪ *Ant* animate, invigorate, refresh.

exhaust [v2] *consume, use up*
▪ *Syn* bankrupt, deplete, devour, dis-

perse, drain, draw, dry, eat, empty, expend, finish, impoverish, spend, squander, void, wash up, waste; ▪ *Ant* refresh, replenish.

exhausted [*adj*] *extremely tired*
▪ *Syn* bleary, bone-weary, bushed, crippled, debilitated, disabled, drained, effete, enervated, frazzled, limp, rundown, spent, tired out, weak, worn out; ▪ *Ant* animated, energetic, fresh, invigorated, lively, vigorous.

exhaustive [*adj*] *all-inclusive, complete*
▪ *Syn* all-embracing, all-encompassing, catholic, comprehensive, encyclopedic, extensive, far-reaching, full-blown, full-scale, in-depth, intensive, profound, radical, sweeping, thorough, total; ▪ *Ant* cursory, excluding, incomplete, shallow, superficial, unfinished.

exhibit [*v*] *put on view; present*
▪ *Syn* advertise, air, brandish, demonstrate, disclose, display, disport, evidence, evince, expose, express, feature, flash, flaunt, illustrate, indicate, manifest, mark, offer, ostend, parade, proclaim, reveal, roll out, show, showcase, show off; ▪ *Ant* conceal, cover, disguise, hide.

exhilarate [*v*] *make very happy*
▪ *Syn* animate, boost, buoy, cheer, commove, delight, elate, enliven, exalt, excite, gladden, inspire, inspirit, invigorate, lift, quicken, rejoice, send, stimulate, thrill, uplift, vitalize; ▪ *Ant* agitate, deject, depress, discourage, sadden, upset, worry.

exhilarating [*adj*] *stimulating, cheering*
▪ *Syn* bracing, breathtaking, electric, elevating, exalting, exciting, gladdening, inspiring, inspiriting, intoxicating, invigorating, quickening, rousing, stimulating, stimulative, stirring, thrilling, tonic, uplifting, vitalizing; ▪ *Ant* agitating, boring, depressing, discouraging, upsetting, worrying.

exhort [*v*] *urge, warn*
▪ *Syn* admonish, advise, beseech, caution, counsel, encourage, enjoin, entreat, goad, incite, persuade, plead, press, pressure, prod, prompt, spur, stimulate; ▪ *Ant* discourage, dissuade, forbid, prohibit.

exhume [*v*] *dig up, especially the dead*
▪ *Syn* disclose, disembalm, disentomb, disinhume, disinter, exhumate, resurrect, reveal, uncharnel, unearth; ▪ *Ant* bury, entomb, inter.

exigent [*adj1*] *urgent, pressing*
▪ *Syn* acute, burning, clamant, crucial, imperative, importunate, insistent, menacing, necessary, threatening; ▪ *Ant* ordinary, unpressured, usual.

exigent [*adj2*] *difficult, taxing*
▪ *Syn* arduous, burdensome, demanding, exacting, grievous, hard, harsh, onerous, oppressive, rigorous, severe, stringent, tough, weighty; ▪ *Ant* easy, effortless, facile, simple.

exiguous [*adj*] *scanty*
▪ *Syn* bare, confined, diminutive, inadequate, limited, little, meager, narrow, negligible, paltry, petty, poor, restricted, scant, skimpy, slender, slight, sparse, tenuous, thin; ▪ *Ant* adequate, ample, plenty.

exile [*v*] *deport from place*
▪ *Syn* banish, cast out, displace, dispossess, drive out, eject, evacuate, expatriate, expel, expulse, extradite, ostracize, oust, outlaw, proscribe, relegate, transport, turn out; ▪ *Ant* import, take in, welcome.

exist [*v*] *be living*
▪ *Syn* abide, be, be extant, be latent, be present, breathe, continue, endure, happen, last, lie, live, move, obtain, occur, prevail, remain, stand, stay, subsist, survive; ▪ *Ant* die, pass away, perish.

exit [*v*] *leave a place*
▪ *Syn* bid farewell, depart, go, issue, move, quit, retire, retreat, withdraw; ▪ *Ant* arrive, come in, enter, go in.

exodus [*n*] *leaving*
▪ *Syn* departure, egress, emigration, evacuation, exit, flight, journey, migration, retreat, withdrawal; ▪ *Ant* arrival, entrance, influx.

exonerate [*v*] *excuse, clear of responsibility or blame* ▪ *Syn* absolve, acquit, disburden, discharge, dismiss, except, exculpate, excuse, exempt, free, justify, liberate, pardon, release, relieve, sanitize, vindicate; ▪ *Ant* accuse, blame, charge, condemn, incarcerate, incriminate, sentence.

exorbitant [*adj*] *extravagant, excessive*
▪ *Syn* dear, enormous, exacting, expensive, extortionate, high, inordinate, outrageous, preposterous, pricey, towering, undue, unwarranted, wasteful; ▪ *Ant* cheap, inexpensive, low, moderate, reasonable, sensible.

exotic [adj] *not native or usual; mysterious* ▪ **Syn** alien, alluring, avant garde, bizarre, colorful, curious, different, enticing, external, extraneous, extraordinary, extrinsic, fascinating, foreign, glamorous, imported, introduced, outlandish, outside, peculiar, romantic, strange, striking; ▪ **Ant** familiar, normal, ordinary, usual.

expand [v1] *extend, augment* ▪ **Syn** aggrandize, amplify, bolster, broaden, burgeon, develop, distend, enlarge, explicate, fatten, fill out, heighten, increase, inflate, lengthen, magnify, mushroom, open, open out, pad, spread, stretch, swell, thicken, upsurge, widen; ▪ **Ant** abbreviate, contract, lessen, lower, shorten, shrink.

expand [v2] *go into detail* ▪ **Syn** amplify, build up, develop, dilate, discourse, elaborate, embellish, enlarge, expatiate, expound, extend, spell out, sweeten; ▪ **Ant** abbreviate, abridge, confine, limit, shorten.

expansive [adj1] *broad, comprehensive* ▪ **Syn** all-embracing, ample, big, elastic, extensive, far-reaching, great, inclusive, large, stretching, thorough, voluminous, wide, widespread; ▪ **Ant** constricted, limited, narrow, restricted.

expansive [adj2] *talkative* ▪ **Syn** affable, communicative, demonstrative, effusive, extroverted, friendly, generous, genial, gregarious, loquacious, open, outgoing, sociable, warm; ▪ **Ant** constrained, quiet, reserved, silent, withdrawn.

expatriate [v] *throw out of country or voluntarily move to another country* ▪ **Syn** banish, deport, displace, exile, expel, expulse, ostracize, oust, proscribe, transport; ▪ **Ant** allow, repatriate, welcome.

expectant [adj] *anticipating* ▪ **Syn** alert, anticipative, anxious, apprehensive, awaiting, breathless, eager, hopeful, hoping, prepared, ready, vigilant, waiting, watchful; ▪ **Ant** apathetic, indifferent, unconcerned, unimpressed, uninterested, unmoved.

expedient [adj] *worthwhile, appropriate* ▪ **Syn** ad hoc, advantageous, advisable, appropriate, beneficial, convenient, desirable, effective, feasible, fitting, helpful, judicious, opportune, practicable, pragmatic, prudent, seasonable, suitable, tactical, timely, useful, wise; ▪ **Ant** deleterious, detrimental, futile, inappropriate, inexpedient, unprofitable, vain.

expedite [v] *make happen faster* ▪ **Syn** accelerate, advance, assist, dispatch, facilitate, forward, hasten, hurry, precipitate, press, promote, quicken, rush, speed, speed up, urge; ▪ **Ant** block, cease, check, delay, halt, hinder, slow, stop.

expeditious [adj] *immediate, speedy* ▪ **Syn** active, breakneck, brisk, effective, effectual, fleet, hasty, instant, nimble, prompt, punctual, quick, ready, swift; ▪ **Ant** dilatory, slow, sluggish.

expel [v1] *discharge* ▪ **Syn** belch, discharge, disgorge, dislodge, ejaculate, eruct, erupt, evacuate, exhaust, exudate, exude, irrupt, pass, remove, spew, vomit; ▪ **Ant** absorb, admit, take in.

expel [v2] *throw out, banish* ▪ **Syn** ban, bar, cast out, chase, discharge, dismiss, displace, dispossess, drum out, eject, evict, exclude, exile, expulse, fire, kick out, oust, proscribe, suspend, turn out; ▪ **Ant** admit, allow, permit, take in, welcome.

expend [v] *exhaust; spend* ▪ **Syn** consume, disburse, dispense, distribute, employ, finish, give, lay out, outlay, pay, use up; ▪ **Ant** hoard, hold, keep, save.

expendable [adj] *not important* ▪ **Syn** dispensable, disposable, excess, inessential, replaceable, superfluous; ▪ **Ant** essential, important, indispensable, necessary, useful.

expensive [adj] *high-priced* ▪ **Syn** costly, dear, excessive, exorbitant, extravagant, high, immoderate, inordinate, invaluable, lavish, overpriced, plush, posh, rich, valuable; ▪ **Ant** cheap, economical, inexpensive, low-priced, moderate, reasonable.

experienced [adj] *knowledgeable, knowing* ▪ **Syn** accomplished, accustomed, adept, capable, competent, cultivated, expert, familiar, instructed, mature, old, practical, practiced, pro, professional, qualified, seasoned, skillful, sophisticated, tested, trained, tried, versed, vet, veteran, well-versed, wise, worldly; ▪ **Ant** green, ignorant, immature, inexperienced, unfamiliar, unknowledgeable, unseasoned, unsophisticated.

experimental [*adj*] *exploratory*
▪ *Syn* beginning, developmental, empirical, experiential, laboratory, momentary, pilot, preliminary, preparatory, primary, probationary, provisional, speculative, temporary, tentative, test, trial; ▪ *Ant* established, proven, tested, tried.

expert [*n*] *specialist*
▪ *Syn* adept, artist, authority, buff, connoisseur, doyen, graduate, maven, phenomenon, pro, professional, proficient, virtuoso, wizard; ▪ *Ant* amateur, apprentice, dilettante, novice.

expert [*adj*] *knowledgeable, proficient*
▪ *Syn* able, adept, adroit, apt, crack, deft, dexterous, experienced, facile, handy, practiced, professional, qualified, schooled, sharp, skilled, skillful, slick, trained, virtuoso; ▪ *Ant* amateur, inexpert, unknowledgeable, unskilled, untrained.

expire [*v1*] *come to an end*
▪ *Syn* cease, close, conclude, decease, depart, die, elapse, end, finish, go, lapse, pass, perish, quit, stop, terminate; ▪ *Ant* bear, begin, commence, start.

expire [*v2*] *breathe out*
▪ *Syn* emit, exhale, expel, outbreathe; ▪ *Ant* breathe in, inhale.

explain [*v*] *make clear; give a reason for*
▪ *Syn* account for, analyze, annotate, clarify, construe, decipher, define, demonstrate, describe, diagram, disclose, elucidate, excuse, explicate, expound, illustrate, interpret, justify, manifest, paraphrase, rationalize, read, refine, render, resolve, reveal, solve, teach, tell, translate, unfold, unravel, untangle; ▪ *Ant* complicate, confuse, mystify, obfuscate, obscure, perplex.

explanatory [*adj*] *descriptive*
▪ *Syn* allegorical, analytical, annotative, critical, declarative, demonstrative, diagrammatic, discursive, explicative, expository, graphic, hermeneutic, illuminative, illustrative, informative, instructive, justifying, summary, supplementary; ▪ *Ant* confusing, mysterious, obscure, perplexing, puzzling, vague.

explicate [*v*] *clarify, expand*
▪ *Syn* amplify, construe, demonstrate, develop, dilate, elucidate, expatiate, explain, illustrate, interpret, untangle, work out; ▪ *Ant* cloud, complicate, confuse, mystify, obscure, tangle.

explicit [*adj*] *specific, unambiguous*
▪ *Syn* absolute, accurate, categorical, certain, clear-cut, definite, direct, distinct, exact, express, frank, lucid, obvious, perspicuous, plain, positive, precise, stated, straightforward, understandable; ▪ *Ant* ambiguous, confused, cryptic, equivocal, implicit, indefinite, obscure, vague.

explode [*v1*] *blow up*
▪ *Syn* backfire, blast, burst, collapse, detonate, discharge, erupt, flare up, fracture, jet, rupture, shatter, shiver, split, thunder; ▪ *Ant* fail, fizzle, implode.

explode [*v2*] *discredit*
▪ *Syn* belie, confute, debunk, deflate, discard, disprove, invalidate, puncture, refute, repudiate; ▪ *Ant* demonstrate, establish, evidence, prove.

explosive [*adj*] *volatile, dangerous*
▪ *Syn* charged, convulsive, detonating, ebullient, eruptive, fiery, forceful, fulminant, hazardous, impetuous, meteoric, overwrought, perilous, raging, rampant, stormy, tense, ugly, vehement, violent, wild; ▪ *Ant* calm, peaceful, safe, stable.

exponent [*n*] *person who supports, advocates* ▪ *Syn* advocate, backer, booster, champion, defender, expounder, interpreter, partisan, propagandist, spokesperson, supporter, upholder; ▪ *Ant* critic, detractor, enemy, foe, opponent.

export [*v*] *sell or trade abroad*
▪ *Syn* consign, convey, freight, ship, smuggle, transport, transship; ▪ *Ant* buy, import.

expose [*v1*] *reveal*
▪ *Syn* advertise, air, bare, betray, brandish, broadcast, crack, debunk, denude, disclose, divulge, exhibit, feature, flaunt, leak, manifest, open, present, prove, report, reveal, show; ▪ *Ant* conceal, cover, hide.

expose [*v2*] *subject to danger*
▪ *Syn* endanger, hazard, imperil, jeopardize, peril, risk; ▪ *Ant* guard, protect, save, shield.

exposed [*adj1*] *made public*
▪ *Syn* apparent, bare, caught, debunked, denuded, disclosed, discovered, divulged, evident, exhibited, manifest, naked, open, peeled, revealed, shown, solved, stripped, visible; ▪ *Ant* concealed, guarded, private, protected, secret.

exposed [*adj2*] *in danger*
▪ *Syn* accessible, liable, menaced, open,

sensitive, subject, susceptible, threatened, vulnerable; ▪ **Ant** guarded, protected, safe, sheltered, shielded.

express [adj1] *certain, precise*
▪ **Syn** accurate, categorical, clear, clearcut, considered, definitive, direct, distinct, especial, exact, explicit, intended, outright, particular, specific, unmistakable, unqualified, uttered, voiced, voluntary; ▪ **Ant** imprecise, indefinite, obscure, uncertain, vague.

express [adj2] *direct, speedy*
▪ **Syn** accelerated, fast, high-speed, nonstop, quick, rapid, swift; ▪ **Ant** indirect, roundabout, slow.

expressionless [adj] *having a blank look on face* ▪ **Syn** deadpan, dull, empty, impassive, inexpressive, inscrutable, lackluster, stolid, straight-faced, stupid, vacant, vacuous, wooden; ▪ **Ant** animated, demonstrative, expressive, responsive.

expressive [adj] *telling, revealing*
▪ **Syn** alive, allusive, articulate, brilliant, colorful, demonstrative, dramatic, eloquent, emphatic, graphic, ingenious, lively, mobile, passionate, pathetic, pictorial, poignant, pointed, pregnant, representative, revelatory, significant, spirited, stirring, striking, suggestive, vivid, warm; ▪ **Ant** cold, expressionless, inexpressive, passive, stiff, undemonstrative.

expressly [adv] *definitely, unambiguously* ▪ **Syn** absolutely, categorically, clearly, decidedly, distinctly, explicitly, manifestly, outright, plainly, pointedly, positively, specifically; ▪ **Ant** ambiguously, equivocally.

expropriate [v] *seize*
▪ **Syn** accroach, annex, appropriate, arrogate, assume, commandeer, confiscate, dispossess, impound, preempt, requisition, sequester, take, take over; ▪ **Ant** cede, distribute, give, relinquish.

expulsion [n] *banishing*
▪ **Syn** banishment, debarment, deportment, discharge, dismissal, dispossession, ejection, eviction, exclusion, exile, expatriation, ostracism, proscription, purge, relegation, removal, suspension; ▪ **Ant** import, recall, restoration, welcoming.

expunge [v] *destroy, obliterate*
▪ **Syn** abolish, annihilate, annul, black, cancel, cut, delete, discard, efface, eradicate, exterminate, extinguish, extirpate,

gut, kill, omit, raze, remove, strike out, trim; ▪ **Ant** bear, build, construct, create, renew, restore.

expurgate [v] *censor, cut*
▪ **Syn** bowdlerize, cleanse, decontaminate, purge, purify, sanitize, screen, squash, sterilize; ▪ **Ant** allow, permit.

exquisite [adj1] *beautiful, excellent, finely detailed* ▪ **Syn** choice, cultivated, delicate, discerning, elegant, ethereal, fastidious, fine, impeccable, lovely, matchless, meticulous, outstanding, peerless, polished, precious, recherche, refined, select, splendid, superb, superlative; ▪ **Ant** crude, flawed, horrible, horrifying, imperfect, inferior, poor, ugly.

exquisite [adj2] *intense*
▪ **Syn** acute, concentrated, consummate, desperate, excruciating, extreme, fierce, keen, piercing, poignant, sharp, vehement, violent; ▪ **Ant** dull, ordinary, slight, subdued.

extant [adj] *in existence*
▪ **Syn** actual, alive, around, being, contemporary, current, existent, immediate, instant, living, present, present-day, real, remaining, subsisting, surviving, undestroyed; ▪ **Ant** dead, extinct, gone.

extemporaneous/extemporary [adj]
unrehearsed, improvised ▪ **Syn** ad hoc, ad lib, casual, expedient, extempore, free, impromptu, improvisatory, informal, made-up, makeshift, offhand, snap, spontaneous; ▪ **Ant** deliberate, designed, planned, prepared, read, rehearsed, written.

extemporize [v] *improvise*
▪ **Syn** ad-lib, devise, improvisate, invent, make up; ▪ **Ant** plan, prepare, read, rehearse.

extend [v1] *make larger, longer*
▪ **Syn** add to, aggrandize, amplify, augment, boost, broaden, continue, crane, develop, dilate, draw, elongate, enhance, enlarge, expand, heighten, increase, last, lengthen, magnify, mantle, multiply, open, pad, prolong, prolongate, protract, spread, spread out, stall, stretch, supplement, take, unfold, unfurl, unroll, widen; ▪ **Ant** abridge, condense, contract, curtail, cut, decrease, lessen, lower, reduce, shorten, shrink.

extend [v2] *offer*
▪ **Syn** accord, advance, allocate, allot, award, bestow, confer, donate, give,

grant, impart, pose, present, proffer, submit, tender, yield; ▪ **Ant** hold, keep, maintain, rescind, take back.

extended [*adj1*] *lengthened*
▪ **Syn** continued, drawn-out, elongated, enlarged, lengthy, long, prolonged, protracted, spread; ▪ **Ant** abbreviated, abridged, compressed, condensed, contracted, curtailed, cut, lessened, reduced, shortened.

extended [*adj2*] *widespread, comprehensive* ▪ **Syn** broad, enlarged, expanded, expansive, extensive, far-flung, far-reaching, large-scale, outspread, spread, sweeping, thorough, wide; ▪ **Ant** abbreviated, abridged, narrow, reduced.

extensive [*adj*] *far-reaching, thorough*
▪ **Syn** all-inclusive, big, boundless, broad, capacious, commodious, comprehensive, exclusive, general, great, hefty, huge, inclusive, indiscriminate, large, lengthy, major, pervasive, prevalent, protracted, roomy, sizable, spacious, sweeping, universal, vast, voluminous, wide, wide-ranging, widespread; ▪ **Ant** limited, narrow, restricted, short, uncomprehensive.

exterior [*adj*] *outside*
▪ **Syn** exoteric, external, extraneous, extrinsic, foreign, marginal, outdoor, outermost, outlying, outward, over, peripheral, superficial, surface; ▪ **Ant** central, interior, middle.

exterminate [*v*] *kill*
▪ **Syn** abolish, annihilate, decimate, destroy, eliminate, eradicate, execute, extinguish, extirpate, massacre, obliterate, slaughter; ▪ **Ant** bear, create, foster, generate.

external [*adj*] *outside, extrinsic*
▪ **Syn** alien, apparent, exterior, extraneous, foreign, independent, outermost, peripheral, superficial, surface, visible; ▪ **Ant** inside, internal, intrinsic.

extinct [*adj*] *dead, obsolete*
▪ **Syn** abolished, archaic, bygone, deceased, defunct, ended, exterminated, extinguished, fallen, gone, late, lifeless, outmoded, passé, superseded, terminated, vanquished, void; ▪ **Ant** active, alive, current, existing, extant, living.

extinguish [*v1*] *put out a fire*
▪ **Syn** blow out, choke, douse, drown, quench, smother, stifle, suffocate, trample; ▪ **Ant** fire, ignite, kindle, light.

extinguish [*v2*] *kill; quash*
▪ **Syn** abolish, annihilate, check, crush, destroy, eliminate, eradicate, erase, expunge, exterminate, extirpate, obliterate, quell, remove, stamp out, suppress; ▪ **Ant** bear, create, encourage, inflame.

extirpate [*v*] *destroy; uproot*
▪ **Syn** abate, abolish, annihilate, demolish, deracinate, efface, eliminate, excise, expunge, exsect, extinguish, kill, raze, remove, root out; ▪ **Ant** foster, generate, propagate.

extol [*v*] *sing the praises of*
▪ **Syn** acclaim, applaud, bless, boost, brag about, celebrate, commend, eulogize, exalt, glorify, hymn, laud, magnify, panegyrize, praise, rave; ▪ **Ant** blame, criticize.

extra [*adj*] *accessory; excess*
▪ **Syn** additional, ancillary, auxiliary, extraneous, further, leftover, more, needless, optional, redundant, reserve, spare, superfluous, supernumerary, supplementary, surplus; ▪ **Ant** basic, elementary, essential, fundamental, integral, necessary.

extract [*v*] *physically remove, draw out*
▪ **Syn** avulse, catheterize, cull, derive, distill, draw, elicit, eradicate, evoke, evulse, exact, express, extirpate, extort, extricate, garner, gather, get, glean, obtain, pluck, pry, pull, reap, secure, select, separate, siphon, squeeze, take, tear, uproot, withdraw, wrest, wring; ▪ **Ant** add, embed, inject, insert, put in.

extraneous [*adj1*] *unneeded; irrelevant*
▪ **Syn** accidental, additional, extra, foreign, immaterial, inadmissible, incidental, needless, peripheral, redundant, superfluous, supplementary; ▪ **Ant** appropriate, basic, essential, integral, necessary, needed, pertinent, relevant.

extraneous [*adj2*] *foreign*
▪ **Syn** adventitious, alien, exotic, external, extrinsic, strange; ▪ **Ant** intrinsic, national, native.

extraordinary [*adj*] *strange and wonderful* ▪ **Syn** amazing, bizarre, curious, exceptional, fantastic, inconceivable, marvelous, outstanding, particular, peculiar, phenomenal, remarkable, singular, special, stupendous, terrific, unheard-of, unique, unprecedented, unusual, weird; ▪ **Ant** common, commonplace, customary, familiar, normal, ordinary, usual.

extravagant [adj] indulgent, wasteful
▪ **Syn** costly, exaggerated, excessive, exorbitant, expensive, fanciful, fantastic, flamboyant, flashy, grandiose, immoderate, imprudent, inordinate, lavish, ornate, outrageous, overpriced, pretentious, prodigal, profligate, steep; ▪ **Ant** close, economical, frugal, moderate, provident, reasonable, saving, stingy, thrifty.

extreme [adj1] very great
▪ **Syn** acute, consummate, great, high, intense, maximal, maximum, severe, sovereign, supreme, top, ultimate, utmost, uttermost; ▪ **Ant** limited, mild, moderate.

extreme [adj2] beyond reason and convention ▪ **Syn** absolute, desperate, drastic, egregious, exceptional, extraordinary, fanatical, flagrant, gross, harsh, immoderate, inordinate, irrational, outrageous, preposterous, radical, remarkable, sheer; ▪ **Ant** conventional, mild, moderate, ordinary, traditional.

extreme [adj3] faraway
▪ **Syn** far-off, farthest, final, furthermost, last, outermost, remotest, terminal, ultimate, utmost, uttermost; ▪ **Ant** close, near.

extremely [adv] greatly, intensely
▪ **Syn** acutely, drastically, exceedingly, exceptionally, extraordinarily, highly, immensely, inordinately, intensely, markedly, mortally, notably, over, parlous, powerful, quite, radically, rarely, remarkably, severely, strikingly, surpassingly, terribly, totally, unduly, utterly; ▪ **Ant** commonly, mildly, moderately.

extremist [n] person zealous about belief
▪ **Syn** agitator, die-hard, fanatic, radical, revolutionary, revolutionist, ultraist, zealot; ▪ **Ant** conservative, moderate.

extricate [v] get out of situation; relieve of responsibility ▪ **Syn** clear, deliver, detach, disburden, disencumber, disengage, extract, free, liberate, loose, release, remove, rescue, sever, withdraw; ▪ **Ant** embroil, entangle, entangle, involve.

extrinsic [adj] foreign
▪ **Syn** acquired, alien, exotic, exterior, external, extraneous, gained, imported, outer, outside, outward, superficial; ▪ **Ant** essential, integral, interior, intrinsic, necessary.

exuberant [adj1] energetic, enthusiastic
▪ **Syn** animated, ardent, buoyant, cheerful, chipper, ebullient, effervescent, frolicsome, gay, high-spirited, lively, passionate, sparkling, spirited, vigorous, vivacious, zestful; ▪ **Ant** depressed, discouraged, lifeless, subdued, unenthusiastic, unexcited.

exuberant [adj2] profuse
▪ **Syn** abundant, affluent, copious, diffuse, effusive, exaggerated, excessive, fecund, fertile, fruitful, fulsome, lavish, lush, luxuriant, opulent, overflowing, plenteous, plentiful, prodigal, prolific, rampant, rich, riotous, superabundant, superfluous, teeming; ▪ **Ant** insufficient, lacking, needing, wanting.

exude [v] display, emit
▪ **Syn** bleed, discharge, emanate, emit, excrete, expel, issue, leak, manifest, ooze, pass, percolate, radiate, secrete, seep, trickle, weep; ▪ **Ant** conceal, hide.

exult [v1] be joyful
▪ **Syn** celebrate, cheer, delight, glory, jubilate, rejoice; ▪ **Ant** be sad, grieve, lament, mourn.

exult [v2] boast
▪ **Syn** bluster, brag, bully, crow, gloat, glory, revel, triumph, vaunt; ▪ **Ant** conceal, hide.

exultant [adj] very happy
▪ **Syn** delighted, ecstatic, elated, flushed, gleeful, high, joyful, joyous, jubilant, overjoyed, revelling, transported, triumphant; ▪ **Ant** depressed, discouraged, sad, sorrowful, unhappy.

eye [v] gaze at, scrutinize
▪ **Syn** consider, contemplate, gape, inspect, leer, ogle, peruse, regard, study, survey, view, watch; ▪ **Ant** ignore, look away.

eyesore [n] mess, ugliness
▪ **Syn** atrocity, blemish, blight, blot, deformity, disfigurement, disgrace, distortion, dump, horror, monstrosity, sight; ▪ **Ant** beauty, eyeful, sight.

F

fable [n] fantasy, story
▪ **Syn** allegory, apologue, bestiary, fabrication, fairy tale, fiction, figment, invention, legend, myth, parable, romance, tale, tall story, yarn; ▪ **Ant** fact, history, truth.

fabled [adj] *legendary, famous*
- *Syn* fabulous, famed, fanciful, fictional, mythical, mythological, storied; ▪ *Ant* authentic, real, unheard of, unknown.

fabricate [v] *manufacture*
- *Syn* assemble, build, compose, concoct, construct, contrive, create, devise, erect, fashion, form, formulate, frame, invent, join, make, mix, organize, produce, shape, structure; ▪ *Ant* break, demolish, destroy, ruin, wreck.

fabrication [n] *lie*
- *Syn* artifact, concoction, deceit, fable, falsehood, fib, fiction, figment, forgery, invention, lie, myth, untruth, work, yarn; ▪ *Ant* actuality, fact, truth, veracity.

fabulous [adj] *amazing, wonderful*
- *Syn* astonishing, astounding, breathtaking, extravagant, fantastic, incredible, legendary, marvelous, outrageous, phenomenal, prodigious, remarkable, spectacular, striking, stupendous, super, terrific, wonderful; ▪ *Ant* believable, common, credible, normal, ordinary, simple.

facade [n] *appearance, often deceptive*
- *Syn* bluff, color, disguise, exterior, face, fake, front, guise, look, mask, pretense, semblance, show, veneer; ▪ *Ant* character, interior, personality, substance.

face [v] *come up against situation*
- *Syn* accost, affront, bear, beard, brave, brook, confront, contend, cope with, countenance, dare, defy, encounter, endure, meet, oppose, resist, stand, suffer, sustain, take, tolerate, venture, withstand; ▪ *Ant* avoid, evade, hide, retreat, run, withdraw.

facetious [adj] *tongue-in-cheek, kidding*
- *Syn* amusing, clever, comical, droll, dry, farcical, funny, humorous, ironic, irreverent, jesting, jocose, jocular, merry, playful, ridiculous, sarcastic, satirical, smart, sportive, waggish, wisecracking, witty, wry; ▪ *Ant* formal, grave, serious, somber.

facile [adj] *easy; easily accomplished*
- *Syn* adept, adroit, breezy, cursory, deft, dexterous, effortless, fluent, light, obvious, proficient, quick, ready, simple, smooth, superficial; ▪ *Ant* arduous, complicated, confusing, difficult, hard, involved, laborious, profound.

facilitate [v] *assist the progress of*
- *Syn* aid, ease, expedite, forward, fur-

ther, help, promote, simplify, smooth, speed, speed up; ▪ *Ant* block, check, delay, detain, hinder, prohibit, stop.

facsimile [n] *reproduction*
- *Syn* carbon, clone, copy, double, duplicate, duplication, likeness, look-alike, mimeo, miniature, mirror, photocopy, photostat, print, replica, replication, stat, transcript, twin; ▪ *Ant* model, original, pattern.

fact [n] *verifiable truth; reality*
- *Syn* actuality, authenticity, basis, certainty, certitude, evidence, experience, genuineness, gospel, intelligence, law, palpability, permanence, scene, scripture, solidity, stability, substantiality, verity; ▪ *Ant* fabrication, fiction, illusion, lie.

faction [n1] *group sharing a belief or cause* ▪ *Syn* band, bloc, cabal, camp, caucus, cell, circle, club, coalition, confederacy, coterie, design, division, entente, gang, guild, insiders, intrigue, junta, knot, lobby, machine, minority, mob, network, offshoot, outfit, partnership, party, ring, schism, sect, sector, set, side, splinter group, team, unit, wing; ▪ *Ant* entirety, total, whole.

faction [n2] *conflict, strife*
- *Syn* disagreement, discord, disharmony, dissension, disunity, division, divisiveness, friction, infighting, rebellion, sedition, tumult, turbulence; ▪ *Ant* agreement, conformity, peace, unity.

factious [adj] *conflicting, warring*
- *Syn* belligerent, contentious, contumacious, disputatious, dissident, divisive, estranged, hostile, insurgent, insurrectionary, litigious, malcontent, mutinous, partisan, quarrelsome, rebellious, refractory, rival, sectarian, seditious, turbulent; ▪ *Ant* agreeing, cooperating, cooperative, peaceful, united.

factual [adj] *real, correct*
- *Syn* absolute, accurate, actual, authentic, certain, circumstantial, close, credible, exact, faithful, genuine, hard, legitimate, literal, objective, positive, precise, specific, sure, true, valid, veritable; ▪ *Ant* biased, erroneous, false, fanciful, imprecise, wrong.

faculty [n] *ability, skill*
- *Syn* adroitness, aptness, bent, capacity, dexterity, facility, forte, gift, instinct, knack, leaning, penchant, predilection, proclivity, propensity, quality, readiness, reason, sense, talent, wits; ▪ *Ant*

inability, incompetence, ineptness, lack, need.

fad [n] *craze*
▪ **Syn** affectation, caprice, conceit, dernier cri, eccentricity, fancy, fashion, frivolity, furor, innovation, kink, mania, mode, passion, quirk, rage, sport, style, thing, trend, vogue, whim, whimsy; ▪ **Ant** custom, standard, tradition.

fade [v1] *lose color*
▪ **Syn** achromatize, blanch, bleach, clear, decolorize, dim, discolor, dissolve, dull, etiolate, evanish, evaporate, neutralize, pale, tarnish, vanish, wash out; ▪ **Ant** brighten, color, intensify, sharpen, strengthen.

fade [v2] *dwindle, die out*
▪ **Syn** abate, clear, decline, deteriorate, diminish, disappear, dissolve, droop, ebb, evanesce, evaporate, fall, flag, fold, hush, languish, lessen, melt, moderate, perish, quiet, rarefy, sink, taper, thin, tire, vanish, wane, weaken, wither; ▪ **Ant** enhance, flourish, improve, recover, strengthen.

faded [adj] *bleached; used*
▪ **Syn** achromatic, ashen, dim, dingy, discolored, dull, etiolated, indistinct, lackluster, lusterless, murky, pale, pallid, run-down, seedy, shabby, shopworn, tacky, tattered, threadbare, tired, wan, washed out, worn; ▪ **Ant** brightened, colored, strengthened, vivid.

fail [v1] *be unsuccessful*
▪ **Syn** abort, backslide, blunder, decline, fall, flop, flounder, fold, founder, miss, slip; ▪ **Ant** accomplish, achieve, earn, gain, merit, obtain, prosper, reach, succeed, win.

fail [v2] *abandon, forsake*
▪ **Syn** back out, blink, desert, disappoint, discount, disregard, fault, forget, funk, ignore, let down, neglect, omit, overlook, overpass, slight, slip; ▪ **Ant** capture, complete, deliver, finish, obtain, procure.

fail [v3] *lose money*
▪ **Syn** become insolvent, be ruined, break, close, crash, defalcate, default, end, finish, fold, go bankrupt, overdraw, terminate; ▪ **Ant** boom, earn, gain, obtain, prosper, succeed, win.

failing [adj] *not well, weak*
▪ **Syn** declining, defeated, deficient, faint, feeble, inadequate, insufficient, scant, scanty, scarce, short, shy, vain, wanting;

▪ **Ant** healthy, rebounding, strong, thriving, well.

faint [adj1] *having little effect on senses*
▪ **Syn** bated, bland, blurred, deadened, delicate, dim, dull, faded, feeble, gentle, hazy, hushed, imperceptible, indistinct, lenient, light, low, mild, moderate, muted, obscure, pale, quiet, remote, shadowy, slight, softened, stifled, subdued, tenuous, thin, vague, wan, weak; ▪ **Ant** clear, distinct, evident, heavy, loud, strong.

faint [adj2] *weak*
▪ **Syn** delicate, dizzy, drooping, enervated, exhausted, faltering, fatigued, feeble, fragile, languid, lethargic, light-headed, woozy; ▪ **Ant** hearty, steady, strong.

fair [adj1] *impartial, unprejudiced*
▪ **Syn** aboveboard, candid, civil, decent, equitable, even-handed, frank, honest, honorable, impartial, just, lawful, legitimate, moderate, nonpartisan, objective, principled, reasonable, respectable, righteous, scrupulous, sincere, straightforward, temperate, trustworthy; ▪ **Ant** biased, partial, prejudiced, unfair, unjust, unreasonable.

fair [adj2] *light-complexioned, light-haired* ▪ **Syn** blond, blonde, fair-haired, fair-skinned, flaxen-haired, pale, pale-faced, pallid, pearly, sallow, tow-haired, tow-headed; ▪ **Ant** brunet, dark.

fair [adj3] *mediocre, satisfactory*
▪ **Syn** adequate, average, commonplace, decent, intermediate, mean, medium, moderate, okay, ordinary, passable, reasonable, respectable, satisfactory, tolerable, usual; ▪ **Ant** bad, choice, exceptional, poor.

fair [adj4] *beautiful*
▪ **Syn** attractive, beauteous, bonny, charming, comely, dainty, delicate, enchanting, exquisite, good-looking, handsome, lovely, pretty, pulchritudinous; ▪ **Ant** repulsive, ugly.

fair [adj5] *bright, cloudless (weather)*
▪ **Syn** balmy, calm, clarion, clear, clement, dry, favorable, fine, mild, placid, pleasant, rainless, sunny, sunshiny, tranquil; ▪ **Ant** cloudy, foul, inclement, rainy, stormy.

fairly [adv1] *somewhat*
▪ **Syn** adequately, averagely, enough, kind of, moderately, more or less, passably, pretty well, quite, rather, rea-

sonably, sort of, tolerably; ▪ *Ant* exceptionally, extremely, immoderately, very.

fairly [*adv2*] *justly*
▪ *Syn* deservedly, equitably, honestly, honorably, impartially, objectively, properly, reasonably; ▪ *Ant* unfairly, unjustly.

faithful [*adj1*] *loyal, reliable*
▪ *Syn* allegiant, attached, circumspect, conscientious, constant, dependable, devoted, dutiful, fast, firm, genuine, honest, honorable, incorruptible, patriotic, resolute, scrupulous, sincere, staunch, steadfast, steady, straight, sure, tried, true, trustworthy, trusty, truthful, upright, veracious; ▪ *Ant* disloyal, false, fickle, perfidious, treacherous.

faithful [*adj2*] *authentic, accurate*
▪ *Syn* close, credible, exact, just, precise, right, similar, strict, true, trusty, veracious, veridical; ▪ *Ant* different, distorted, false, inaccurate, inexact.

faithless [*adj*] *disloyal*
▪ *Syn* capricious, changeable, changeful, cheating, deceitful, dishonest, doubting, dubious, false, fickle, fluctuating, inconstant, perfidious, recreant, skeptical, traitorous, treacherous, wavering; ▪ *Ant* believing, constant, faithful, loyal, reliable, true.

fake [*adj*] *false, imitation*
▪ *Syn* affected, artificial, assumed, bogus, concocted, counterfeit, fabricated, fictitious, forged, fraudulent, invented, make-believe, mock, phony, pretended, reproduction, sham, simulated, spurious; ▪ *Ant* genuine, original, real, true, truthful.

fall [*v1*] *descend; become lower*
▪ *Syn* abate, backslide, buckle, cascade, cave in, collapse, crash, decline, decrease, depreciate, diminish, dip, dive, drag, droop, drop, dwindle, ease, ebb, flag, flop, gravitate, land, lapse, lessen, lower, nose-dive, pitch, plummet, plunge, recede, regress, relapse, settle, sink, slip, slump, stumble, subside, topple, trip, tumble, wane; ▪ *Ant* ascend, climb, go up, rise, scale, soar.

fall [*v2*] *be overthrown by enemy; surrender* ▪ *Syn* back down, be destroyed, bend, be taken, capitulate, collapse, defer to, die, drop, go down, obey, perish, resign, slump, submit, succumb, yield; ▪ *Ant* advance, attain, conquer, overcome, overthrow, prevail, reach, triumph, win.

fallacious [*adj*] *false, wrong*
▪ *Syn* beguiling, deceptive, delusive, erroneous, fictitious, fraudulent, incorrect, invalid, irrational, misleading, mistaken, sophistic, spurious; ▪ *Ant* correct, real, true, truthful, veritable.

fall back [*v*] *retreat*
▪ *Syn* back, draw back, recede, recoil, retire, retrocede, retrograde, surrender, withdraw, yield; ▪ *Ant* advance, forge, forward, progress.

fallen [*adj*] *disgraced, ruined*
▪ *Syn* collapsed, decayed, dishonored, immoral, loose, ruinous, shaken, shamed, sinful, unchaste; ▪ *Ant* honorable, honored, lauded.

fallible [*adj*] *able or prone to err*
▪ *Syn* careless, deceptive, errable, errant, erring, faulty, frail, heedless, human, ignorant, imperfect, liable, mortal, questionable, weak; ▪ *Ant* certain, correct, definite, inerrant, infallible, perfect, reliable, strong, sure, unerring.

fall out [*v*] *argue*
▪ *Syn* altercate, bicker, clash, differ, disagree, fight, quarrel, spar, squabble; ▪ *Ant* agree, concur.

fallow [*adj*] *inactive*
▪ *Syn* dormant, idle, inert, neglected, quiescent, resting, slack, uncultivated, unproductive, unseeded, untilled, unused, vacant; ▪ *Ant* active, cultivated, developed, fertile, prolific, used.

fall to [*v*] *set about doing*
▪ *Syn* apply oneself, begin, commence, jump in, start, undertake; ▪ *Ant* be idle, forget, ignore, laze, neglect, procrastinate.

false [*adj1*] *wrong, made up*
▪ *Syn* apocryphal, bogus, concocted, deceitful, distorted, erroneous, fallacious, fictitious, fishy, illusive, imaginary, inaccurate, incorrect, invalid, lying, mendacious, misleading, mistaken, phony, sham, sophistical, spurious; ▪ *Ant* accurate, actual, correct, factual, genuine, known, precise, real, right, substantiated, true, valid.

false [*adj2*] *dishonest, hypocritical*
▪ *Syn* apostate, base, beguiling, canting, corrupt, crooked, deceitful, delusive, devious, dishonorable, duplicitous, false-hearted, forsworn, malevolent, malicious, mean, perfidious, perjured, renegade, roguish, traitorous, treacherous, treasonable, venal, villainous,

wicked; ▪ *Ant* faithful, genuine, honest, just, reliable, right, straight, true, truthful.

false [adj3] *fake, counterfeit*
▪ *Syn* artificial, assumed, bent, brummagem, colored, contrived, copied, disguised, fabricated, factitious, feigned, forged, hollow, imitation, made-up, make-believe, manufactured, mock, ostensible, phony, pretended, shady, simulated, spurious, substitute, synthetic, unreal, wrong; ▪ *Ant* actual, genuine, real, valid, veritable.

falsely [adv] *deceitfully*
▪ *Syn* basely, crookedly, dishonorably, disloyally, faithlessly, falseheartedly, malevolently, maliciously, perfidiously, traitorously, treacherously, underhandedly; ▪ *Ant* faithfully, honestly, truthfully.

falter [v] *stumble, stutter*
▪ *Syn* bobble, break, flounder, fluctuate, halt, hesitate, lurch, quaver, reel, rock, roll, scruple, shake, stagger, stammer, teeter, topple, totter, tremble, vacillate, waver, whiffle, wobble; ▪ *Ant* continue, endure, maintain, persist, remain, stay.

fame [n] *celebrity*
▪ *Syn* acclaim, credit, distinction, eclat, eminence, esteem, exaltation, favor, glory, honor, illustriousness, kudos, laurels, notoriety, popularity, prominence, recognition, regard, renown, report, reputation, standing, stardom, station; ▪ *Ant* discredit, disgrace, dishonor, disrepute, ignominy, infamy, oblivion, obscurity.

familiar [adj1] *common, well-known*
▪ *Syn* accustomed, commonplace, customary, domestic, everyday, habitual, homespun, informal, intimate, known, mundane, ordinary, plain, prosaic, proverbial, recognizable, repeated, routine, simple, stock, usual, wonted, workaday; ▪ *Ant* foreign, new, rare, strange, uncommon, unfamiliar, unknown.

familiar [adj2] *knowledgeable*
▪ *Syn* abreast, acquainted, apprised, au courant, au fait, aware, cognizant, conscious, conversant, informed, introduced, mindful, savvy, versant, versed in; ▪ *Ant* ignorant, unacquainted, unaware, unknowledgeable.

familiar [adj3] *friendly, bold*
▪ *Syn* affable, amicable, close, comfortable, confidential, cordial, cozy, easy, forward, free, fresh, genial, impudent,

informal, intimate, intrusive, near, neighborly, nervy, obtrusive, officious, open, presuming, presumptuous, relaxed, smart, sociable, thick, tight; ▪ *Ant* aloof, ceremonious, cold, cool, distant, reserved, unfamiliar, unfriendly.

famine [n] *hunger*
▪ *Syn* dearth, destitution, drought, misery, paucity, poverty, scarcity, starvation, want; ▪ *Ant* abundance, bounty, feast, plenty, sufficiency.

famished [adj] *starving*
▪ *Syn* empty, hollow, hungering, hungry, ravening, ravenous, starved, voracious; ▪ *Ant* full, gorged, sated, satiated, satisfied.

famous [adj] *legendary, notable to many*
▪ *Syn* acclaimed, celebrated, distinguished, eminent, foremost, grand, honored, illustrious, influential, leading, lionized, memorable, notorious, preeminent, prominent, recognized, renowned, reputable, signal, well-known; ▪ *Ant* inconspicuous, obscure, unknown, unnotable, unremarkable.

fanatical [adj] *overly enthusiastic*
▪ *Syn* bigoted, dogmatic, enthusiastic, extreme, fervent, immoderate, impassioned, monomaniacal, obsessive, opinionated, passionate, possessed, prejudiced, rabid, radical, single-minded, zealous; ▪ *Ant* disinterested, dispassionate, impartial, moderate, unenthusiastic.

fanciful [adj] *imaginary, romantic*
▪ *Syn* absurd, aerial, bizarre, capricious, chimerical, extravagant, fabulous, fairytale, fantastic, fictive, illusory, imaginative, imagined, incredible, legendary, mythical, notional, poetic, preposterous, shadowy, supposititious, visionary, whimsical, wild; ▪ *Ant* ordinary, prosaic, real, serious.

fancy [adj] *extravagant, ornamental*
▪ *Syn* adorned, baroque, complicated, custom, decorated, decorative, deluxe, elaborate, elegant, embellished, florid, frilly, garnished, gaudy, intricate, lavish, ornamented, ornate, ostentatious, resplendent, rich, rococo, showy, sumptuous; ▪ *Ant* natural, plain, simple, unornamented.

fancy [v] *love, desire*
▪ *Syn* approve, be attracted to, be captivated by, be enamored of, be in love with, care for, crave, desire, dream of, endorse, favor, like, long for, lust after,

prefer, relish, sanction, take to, yearn for; ▪ *Ant* detest, dislike, hate, loathe.

fantastic [*adj1*] *strange, different; imaginary* ▪ *Syn* absurd, artificial, capricious, chimerical, crazy, exotic, fanciful, far-fetched, foreign, hallucinatory, illusive, implausible, incredible, ludicrous, mad, nonsensical, outlandish, phantasmagorical, preposterous, queer, ridiculous, singular, suppositious, whimsical; ▪ *Ant* common, commonplace, convential, customary, familiar, ordinary, plain, usual.

fantastic [*adj2*] *enormous* ▪ *Syn* cracking, extreme, great, huge, massive, monstrous, monumental, overwhelming, prodigious, severe, stupendous, towering, tremendous; ▪ *Ant* little, minute, small, tiny.

fantastic [*adj3*] *wonderful, excellent* ▪ *Syn* awesome, best, best ever, first-class, first-rate, great, marvelous, sensational, superb; ▪ *Ant* bad, poor, unpleasant.

fantasy [*n*] *imagination, dream* ▪ *Syn* apparition, appearance, chimera, creativity, delusion, fabrication, fancy, flight, hallucination, invention, mirage, nightmare, originality, reverie, trip, vagary, vision; ▪ *Ant* fact, reality, truth.

far [*adj/adv*] *at a great distance* ▪ *Syn* afar, a good way, a long way, deep, distant, faraway, far-off, far-removed, long, outlying, remote, removed; ▪ *Ant* close, near, nigh.

faraway [*adj*] *remote, distant* ▪ *Syn* absent, abstracted, distant, dreamy, far, far-off, far-removed, lost, outlying, preoccupied, removed, well away; ▪ *Ant* close, near, proximate.

farcical [*adj*] *absurd* ▪ *Syn* amusing, camp, comical, derisory, funny, gelastic, laughable, ludicrous, nonsensical, outrageous, preposterous, ridiculous, slapstick, stupid; ▪ *Ant* real, reasonable, sensible, serious, tragic.

farewell [*n*] *departing saying; departure* ▪ *Syn* adieu, adieus, adieux, adios, bye-bye, cheerio, ciao, goodbye, hasta la vista, leave-taking, parting, salutation, sendoff, so long, valediction; ▪ *Ant* greeting, hello, salutation, welcome.

far-fetched [*adj*] *hard to believe* ▪ *Syn* bizarre, doubtful, dubious, eccentric, fantastic, illogical, implausible, improbable, incredible, labored, prepos-

terous, queer, recondite, strained, strange, suspicious; ▪ *Ant* believable, likely, plausible, realistic.

far-reaching [*adj*] *broad, widespread* ▪ *Syn* extensive, far-ranging, pervasive, sweeping, wide; ▪ *Ant* insignificant, narrow, trivial, unimportant.

far-sighted [*adj*] *looking ahead wisely* ▪ *Syn* acute, canny, cautious, clairvoyant, commonsensical, discerning, judicious, levelheaded, perceptive, politic, prescient, provident, prudent, sagacious, sage, shrewd, wise; ▪ *Ant* incautious, rash, shortsighted, unthinking, unwise.

farther [*adj/adv*] *at a greater distance* ▪ *Syn* beyond, further, longer, more remote, yon, yonder; ▪ *Ant* closer, nearer.

farthest [*adj/adv*] *most distant* ▪ *Syn* extreme, furthermost, furthest, last, lattermost, outermost, remotest, ultimate, utmost, uttermost; ▪ *Ant* closest, nearest.

fascinate [*v*] *captivate, hold spellbound* ▪ *Syn* absorb, allure, attract, beguile, bewitch, charm, compel, draw, enamor, enchant, enrapture, ensnare, enthrall, hypnotize, infatuate, intoxicate, intrigue, lure, mesmerize, overwhelm, pique, ravish, rivet, seduce, thrill, transfix, transport, win; ▪ *Ant* bore, disenchant, disenthrall, disinterest, repel, tire.

fascinating [*adj*] *interesting, spellbinding* ▪ *Syn* alluring, appealing, attractive, captivating, compelling, delightful, enchanting, engaging, enticing, gripping, intriguing, irresistible, ravishing, riveting, seductive, siren; ▪ *Ant* boring, dull, repulsive, uninteresting.

fascination [*n*] *strong interest* ▪ *Syn* allure, appeal, attraction, charisma, charm, enchantment, enthrallment, glamour, lure, magnetism, obsession, piquancy, power, spell, trance; ▪ *Ant* boredom, disinterest.

fascism [*n*] *political system of dictatorship* ▪ *Syn* absolutism, authoritarianism, autocracy, despotism, Nazism, one-party system, totalitarianism; ▪ *Ant* democracy, socialism.

fashionable [*adj*] *stylish, up-to-date* ▪ *Syn* chic, contemporary, current, dashing, favored, genteel, in vogue, modern, new, newfangled, now, popular, prevailing, rakish, smart, swank, trendsetting; ▪ *Ant* dated, old-fashioned, out, passé, unfashionable, unpopular.

fast [*adj1*] *speedy*
▪ *Syn* accelerated, brisk, dashing, electric, expeditious, flashing, fleeting, flying, hasty, hot, hurried, nimble, posthaste, presto, pronto, quick, racing, rapid, ready, supersonic, swift, velocious, winged; ▪ *Ant* plodding, slow, tardy, unhurried.

fast [*adj2*] *fixed, immovable*
▪ *Syn* adherent, close, constant, durable, fastened, firm, fortified, glued, held, indelible, inextricable, lasting, loyal, permanent, resistant, secure, set, stable, staunch, steadfast, tenacious, true, wedged; ▪ *Ant* flexible, impermanent, insecure, loose, movable, unattached, unfixed.

fast [*adj3*] *immoral, promiscuous*
▪ *Syn* bawdy, careless, debauched, dissolute, extravagant, frivolous, indecent, lascivious, libertine, libidinous, licentious, profligate, reckless, salacious, self-indulgent, sportive, wanton, wild; ▪ *Ant* chaste, good, moral, upright.

fast [*v*] *go without food*
▪ *Syn* abstain, deny oneself, diet, famish, forbear, go hungry, refrain, starve; ▪ *Ant* eat, glut, gorge, stuff.

fast [*adv*] *speedily*
▪ *Syn* apace, expeditiously, fleetly, hastily, hurriedly, posthaste, presto, promptly, pronto, quick, quickly, rapidly, soon, swift, swiftly; ▪ *Ant* behind, slow, slowly.

fasten [*v*] *make secure; join together*
▪ *Syn* adhere, affix, attach, band, bind, bolt, bond, button, catch, cement, cleave, cohere, couple, establish, fix, girth, glue, grip, hitch, hold, infix, jam, knot, link, lock, lodge, moor, mortise, nail, rivet, rope, seal, secure, set, solder, stick, truss, unite, wedge, weld; ▪ *Ant* detach, disconnect, loosen, open, release, sever, unchain, unfasten, unlock.

fastidious [*adj*] *very careful, meticulous*
▪ *Syn* choosy, critical, demanding, discriminating, exacting, finicky, fussy, nitpicky, overdelicate, overnice, particular, punctilious, stickling; ▪ *Ant* casual, indifferent, uncareful, uncouth, uncritical, undemanding.

fat [*adj1*] *overweight*
▪ *Syn* big, broad, bulky, corpulent, distended, fleshy, gargantuan, heavy, hefty, husky, inflated, large, obese, paunchy, plump, porcine, portly, rotund, solid,

stout; ▪ *Ant* cadaverous, gaunt, skinny, slender, slight, slim, thin.

fat [*adj2*] *containing oily substance*
▪ *Syn* adipose, fatty, greasy, oily, oleaginous, suety, unctuous; ▪ *Ant* lean.

fat [*adj3*] *productive, rich*
▪ *Syn* affluent, fertile, flourishing, fruitful, good, lucrative, lush, profitable, prosperous, remunerative, thriving; ▪ *Ant* barren, impoverished, poor, scanty, unproductive.

fatal [*adj*] *deadly, lethal*
▪ *Syn* baneful, calamitous, cataclysmic, catastrophic, destructive, final, ill-fated, incurable, inevitable, killing, lethal, malignant, mortal, noxious, pernicious, pestilent, pestilential, poisonous, ruinous, terminal, virulent; ▪ *Ant* advantageous, healthful, life-giving, nourishing, vital, wholesome.

fate [*n*] *predetermined course*
▪ *Syn* break, chance, circumstance, destiny, doom, effect, end, ending, fortune, future, horoscope, issue, karma, lot, luck, Moira, nemesis, outcome, portion, predestination, providence, termination, upshot; ▪ *Ant* accident, chance, choice, decision, freedom, independence, will.

fateful [*adj1*] *significant*
▪ *Syn* acute, apocalyptic, conclusive, critical, crucial, decisive, determinative, direful, doomful, eventful, important, momentous, ominous, portentous, resultful; ▪ *Ant* insignificant, trivial, unimportant.

fateful [*adj2*] *deadly*
▪ *Syn* calamitous, cataclysmic, catastrophic, destructive, disastrous, fatal, lethal, mortal, ominous, ruinous; ▪ *Ant* healthful, healthy, life-giving.

fathom [*v*] *discern, understand*
▪ *Syn* appreciate, apprehend, catch, comprehend, dig, divine, estimate, follow, gauge, grasp, interpret, know, measure, penetrate, perceive, plumb, probe, recognize, savvy, sound; ▪ *Ant* confound, confuse, misunderstand, not get.

fatigue [*v*] *tire, wear out*
▪ *Syn* debilitate, deplete, disable, drain, enervate, exhaust, fag, fizzle, flag, languish, prostrate, sag, sink, succumb, tucker, weaken, wear, weary; ▪ *Ant* energize, envigorate, refresh, rejuvenate.

fatigued [*adj*] *tired*
▪ *Syn* bedraggled, blasé, enervated, exhausted, languid, languorous, listless,

overtired, prostrate, weary, worn, worn-out; ▪ *Ant* alert, energized, keen, lively, refreshed, vivacious.

fatten [v] *grow or make bigger; nourish*
▪ *Syn* augment, bloat, broaden, build up, cram, distend, expand, fill, increase, overfeed, plump, round out, spread, stuff, swell, thicken, thrive, wax; ▪ *Ant* attenuate, thin, undernourish.

fatty [adj] *full of adipose tissue*
▪ *Syn* blubbery, fatlike, greasy, larda-ceous, lardy, oily, oleaginous, rich, suety, unctuous; ▪ *Ant* defatted, lean, low-fat, thin.

fatuous [adj] *stupid*
▪ *Syn* absurd, asinine, dense, dull, fool-ish, idiotic, imbecile, inane, insensate, ludicrous, mindless, moronic, puerile, sappy, silly, simple, vacuous, witless; ▪ *Ant* aware, bright, intelligent, keen, sensible, smart.

faultless [adj] *having nothing wrong with it* ▪ *Syn* accurate, blameless, clean, crimeless, errorless, exemplary, exqui-site, flawless, foolproof, guiltless, ideal, immaculate, impeccable, innocent, in-tact, irreproachable, model, perfect, pure, sinless, spotless, stainless, whole; ▪ *Ant* blemished, flawed, imperfect, sullied, tainted.

faulty [adj] *not working; incorrect*
▪ *Syn* amiss, awry, bad, blemished, botched, cracked, damaged, defective, distorted, erroneous, fallacious, flawed, impaired, lame, leaky, lemon; maimed, malformed, malfunctioning, marred, warped; ▪ *Ant* accurate, correct, exact, perfect, precise, sound, strong, working.

favor [v1] *pamper, reward; help*
▪ *Syn* abet, accommodate, advance, aid, assist, befriend, esteem, facilitate, fur-ther, gratify, humor, indulge, oblige, pro-mote, spare, spoil, value; ▪ *Ant* foil, hinder, hurt, thwart.

favor [v2] *prefer, like*
▪ *Syn* accept, advocate, appreciate, ap-probate, approve, back, champion, choose, commend, countenance, encour-age, endorse, esteem, eulogize, fancy, honor, incline, patronize, pick, praise, prefer, prize, sanction, support, value; ▪ *Ant* disfavor, dislike, object to.

favorable [adj1] *approving, friendly*
▪ *Syn* acclamatory, affirmative, agree-able, amicable, approbative, benevolent, benign, complimentary, encouraging, en-thusiastic, inclined, kind, laudatory, positive, praiseful, predisposed, recom-mendatory, sympathetic, understanding, welcoming; ▪ *Ant* bad, disagreeable, ill-disposed, unfavorable, unfriendly, un-promising.

favorable [adj2] *good, timely, advanta-geous* ▪ *Syn* appropriate, auspicious, ben-eficial, benign, bright, convenient, encouraging, fair, fortunate, gratifying, helpful, lucky, opportune, pleasant, pro-pitious, providential, seasonable, suit-able, toward, useful, welcome, well-timed, worthy; ▪ *Ant* bad, derogatory, detrimental, harmful, hindering, hurtful, injurious, unfavorable.

favorably [adv] *genially, in a kindly manner* ▪ *Syn* agreeably, amiably, ap-provingly, cordially, courteously, enthu-siastically, fairly, generously, graciously, helpfully, kindly, positively, recep-tively, usefully, willingly; ▪ *Ant* con-temptuously, disdainfully, unfavorably, unfriendly.

favored [adj] *popular*
▪ *Syn* advantaged, blessed, chosen, elite, favorite, lucky, preferred, privileged, rec-ommended, selected, well-liked; ▪ *Ant* disfavored, rejected, unpopular.

favorite [adj] *preferred*
▪ *Syn* admired, adored, beloved, cher-ished, choice, dear, esteemed, favored, intimate, liked, main, precious, prized, revered, treasured; ▪ *Ant* disdained, dis-liked, hated, loathed.

favoritism [n] *bias, partiality*
▪ *Syn* discrimination, inclination, ineq-uity, nepotism, partisanship, preference; ▪ *Ant* fairness, impartiality, justice.

fawn [v] *ingratiate oneself; serve*
▪ *Syn* abase oneself, blandish, bow, ca-jole, cater to, court, cower, crawl, creep, cringe, crouch, debase oneself, defer, flatter, grovel, invite, jolly, kneel, pan-der, scrape, slaver, stoop, submit, yield; ▪ *Ant* ignore, insult.

fawning [adj] *deferential, groveling*
▪ *Syn* abject, adulatory, compliant, cring-ing, humble, ingratiating, obsequious, parasitic, prostrate, servile, slavish, sniv-eling, spineless, submissive, subservient, sycophant, sycophantic; ▪ *Ant* aloof, cool, disinterested, proud, unfriendly.

faze [v] *embarrass*
▪ *Syn* abash, annoy, appall, bother, con-found, confuse, daunt, discomfit, dis-

concert, discountenance, dismay, dumbfound, horrify, irritate, muddle, mystify, nonplus, perplex, puzzle, rattle, vex; ▪ *Ant* calm, comfort, compose, ease, quiet, relieve, soothe.

fearful [*adj1*] *alarmed, apprehensive*
▪ *Syn* aflurrmed, afraid, agitated, anxious, chicken, discomposed, disturbed, fainthearted, frightened, hesitant, intimidated, jumpy, panicky, pusillanimous, quivery, scared, shaky, skittish, timid, tremulous, worried; ▪ *Ant* bold, brave, confident, courageous, inapprehensive, unafraid, unfearful.

fearful [*adj2*] *horrifying*
▪ *Syn* appalling, atrocious, awful, baleful, bloodcurdling, creepy, dire, dreadful, eerie, formidable, frightful, ghastly, grisly, gruesome, hideous, horrendous, lurid, macabre, monstrous, morbid, overwhelming, redoubtable, shocking, sinister, sublime, terrible, tremendous; ▪ *Ant* benign, encouraging, pleasant, reassuring.

fearless [*adj*] *brave, unafraid*
▪ *Syn* assured, aweless, bodacious, bold, brassy, cheeky, confident, courageous, daring, dauntless, doughty, gallant, gutsy, heroic, indomitable, intrepid, lionhearted, nervy, plucky, sanguine, sure, temerarious, valiant, valorous; ▪ *Ant* afraid, apprehensive, fearful, timid.

feasible [*adj*] *possible, doable*
▪ *Syn* achievable, attainable, expedient, fitting, likely, performable, practicable, practical, profitable, realizable, reasonable, suitable, viable, workable; ▪ *Ant* impossible, inconceivable, unfeasible, unlikely, unpractical, unreasonable.

feast [*v*] *eat a great amount or very well*
▪ *Syn* banquet, dine, entertain, gorge, gormandize, indulge, overindulge, regale, stuff, treat; ▪ *Ant* abstain, fast.

feat [*n*] *achievement*
▪ *Syn* accomplishment, act, conquest, consummation, coup, deed, effort, enterprise, execution, performance, stunt, tour de force, triumph, venture, victory; ▪ *Ant* failure, idleness, inaction.

feature [*v*] *give prominence to*
▪ *Syn* accentuate, advertise, emphasize, italicize, mark, present, promote, star, stress, underline, underscore; ▪ *Ant* disregard, ignore, minimize.

febrile [*adj*] *feverish*
▪ *Syn* delirious, fevered, fiery, flushed,

hallucinatory, hot, inflamed, pyretic; ▪ *Ant* cold, freezing, frigid.

feckless [*adj*] *without purpose*
▪ *Syn* aimless, carefree, fustian, futile, hopeless, incautious, irresponsible, meaningless, reckless, shiftless, useless, weak, wild, worthless; ▪ *Ant* competent, effective, effectual, efficient, purposeful, responsible, strong, useful.

fecund [*adj*] *productive*
▪ *Syn* fertile, fructiferous, fruitful, pregnant, proliferant, prolific, propagating, rich, teeming; ▪ *Ant* impotent, infertile, sterile, unfruitful, unproductive.

fed up [*adj*] *disgusted with*
▪ *Syn* annoyed, blas, bored, depressed, discontented, dismal, down, gloomy, glum, jaded, surfeited, tired, weary; ▪ *Ant* happy, overjoyed, pleased, satisfied.

feeble [*adj*] *not strong; ineffective*
▪ *Syn* aged, ailing, debilitated, decrepit, enervated, etiolated, exhausted, failing, faint, fragile, frail, helpless, impotent, inefficient, infirm, insufficient, lame, languid, low, paltry, poor, powerless, puny, sapless, sickly, slight, tame, thin, vitiated, weak, weakened; ▪ *Ant* able, effective, hardy, healthy, hearty, powerful, solid, sound, strong.

feed [*v*] *give nourishment; augment*
▪ *Syn* banquet, bolster, cater, cram, deliver, dine, dispense, encourage, fatten, feast, fill, find, foster, fuel, furnish, gorge, maintain, minister, nourish, nurse, nurture, provide, provision, regale, satisfy, stock, strengthen, stuff, supply, support, sustain, victual; ▪ *Ant* starve, stifle, thwart.

feel [*v*] *believe*
▪ *Syn* assume, be convinced, conclude, conjecture, consider, credit, deduce, deem, esteem, gather, guess, hold, infer, intuit, judge, know, presume, repute, sense, suppose, surmise, suspect, think; ▪ *Ant* challenge, disbelieve, doubt, question.

feigned [*adj*] *pretended*
▪ *Syn* affected, artificial, assumed, counterfeit, fabricated, fake, false, fictitious, imaginary, imagined, imitation, phony, pretended, simulated, spurious; ▪ *Ant* genuine, real, sincere.

felicitate [*v*] *congratulate*
▪ *Syn* commend, compliment, praise, recommend, salute; ▪ *Ant* condemn, reject.

felicitous [adj] appropriate, suitable
▪ **Syn** applicable, apposite, apropos, apt, fit, fitting, germane, happy, inspired, just, meet, neat, opportune, pat, pertinent, proper, propitious, relevant, seasonable, timely, well-chosen, well-timed; ▪ **Ant** awkward, clumsy, improper, inappropriate, infelicitous, inopportune, unsuitable.

fell [v] chop down
▪ **Syn** cleave, cut, dash, demolish, down, drop, flatten, gash, ground, hack, hew, level, mangle, prostrate, raze, rive, sever, shoot, slash, split, sunder, tumble; ▪ **Ant** build, construct, erect, raise.

fellow [n] colleague, friend
▪ **Syn** assistant, associate, cohort, companion, compeer, comrade, concomitant, coordinate, coworker, equal, match, mate, member, partner, peer; ▪ **Ant** antagonist, competitor, enemy, foe.

fellowship [n] sociability, association
▪ **Syn** affability, alliance, amity, camaraderie, club, communion, companionship, company, comradeship, conviviality, familiarity, guild, intimacy, kindliness, league, order, society, togetherness; ▪ **Ant** antagonism, hostility, unfriendliness.

feminism [n] doctrine advocating social, political, and economic rights of women equal to those of men ▪ **Syn** equal rights, female liberation movement, gynocentrism, liberation movement, womanism, women's liberation, women's rights, women's rights, women's studies; ▪ **Ant** gender bias, male chauvinism, traditionalism.

fence [v1] enclose, separate an area
▪ **Syn** bound, cage, circumscribe, confine, coop, corral, defend, encircle, fortify, guard, hedge, hem, immure, mew, pen, protect, rail, secure, surround, wall; ▪ **Ant** release, set free, uncoop.

fence [v2] dodge; beat around the bush
▪ **Syn** avoid, baffle, cavil, duck, equivocate, evade, feint, foil, hedge, maneuver, parry, prevaricate, quibble, shift, shirk, sidestep, tergiversate; ▪ **Ant** challenge, confront, face, meet.

fend [v] defend
▪ **Syn** bulwark, cover, dodge, guard, oppose, parry, protect, repel, resist, safeguard, screen, secure, shield; ▪ **Ant** capitulate, submit, surrender, yield.

fend for [v] take care of
▪ **Syn** look after, provide for, subsist, support, survive, sustain; ▪ **Ant** ignore, neglect.

fend off [v] keep at bay
▪ **Syn** avert, avoid, deflect, keep at a distance, parry, rebuff, rebuke, rebut, refuse, reject, repel, repulse, resist, snub, spurn, stave off, ward off; ▪ **Ant** allure, attract.

ferment [n] agitation, uprising
▪ **Syn** clamor, commotion, convulsion, disquiet, disruption, disturbance, excitement, fever, flap, frenzy, furor, fuss, imbroglio, outcry, stir, storm, turbulence, turmoil, unrest, upheaval, uproar; ▪ **Ant** calm, contentedness, happiness, peace, pleasure.

ferocious [adj] violent, barbaric
▪ **Syn** barbarous, bloodthirsty, brutal, cruel, feral, fierce, grim, lupine, merciless, murderous, pitiless, predatory, rapacious, relentless, ruthless, sanguinary, savage, truculent, vehement, vicious, voracious, wild; ▪ **Ant** gentle, innocent, kind, mild, nonviolent, tame, tender.

fertile [adj] ready to bear, produce
▪ **Syn** abundant, bearing, bountiful, breeding, fecund, flowering, fruitful, generative, gravid, hebetic, loamy, lush, plentiful, pregnant, procreant, productive, prolific, puberal, pubescent, rank, rich, spawning, uberous, vegetative; ▪ **Ant** barren, fruitless, impotent, infertile, sterile, unproductive, useless.

fervent/fervid [adj] enthusiastic, excited
▪ **Syn** animated, ardent, blazing, devout, eager, earnest, emotional, enthused, fiery, glowing, heartfelt, intense, passionate, responsive, tender, vehement, wholehearted, zealous; ▪ **Ant** cool, discouraged, dispirited, frigid, impassive, unenthusiastic, unexcited.

fester [v] intensify; become inflamed
▪ **Syn** aggravate, blister, canker, chafe, decay, gall, putrefy, rankle, rot, smolder, suppurate, ulcer, ulcerate; ▪ **Ant** dissipate, heal, lessen, soothe.

festive [adj] decorated, celebratory
▪ **Syn** carnival, cheery, convivial, gala, gay, happy, holiday, jolly, joyous, jubilant, lighthearted, merry, mirthful, perky, swinging, upbeat; ▪ **Ant** depressed, drab, gloomy, somber, undecorated.

fetching [adj] alluring, attractive
▪ **Syn** beautiful, captivating, charming, cute, enchanting, enticing, intriguing, luring, pleasing, sweet, tempting, winsome; ▪ **Ant** repellent, repulsive, ugly, unattractive.

fetid [adj] *foul, rancid*
▪ **Syn** corrupt, fusty, loathsome, lousy, malodorous, mephitic, noisome, noxious, offensive, putrid, rank, repugnant, repulsive, rotten, smelly; ▪ **Ant** aromatic, clean, fragrant, pure, sweet.

fetter [v] *tie up, hold*
▪ **Syn** bind, chain, check, clog, confine, cuff, curb, encumber, hamper, handcuff, hinder, hobble, leash, manacle, repress, restrain, restrict, shackle, tie, trammel; ▪ **Ant** free, let go, loose, loosen, release.

feud [v] *fight bitterly; fall out*
▪ **Syn** bicker, brawl, clash, contend, dispute, duel, quarrel, row, squabble, war; ▪ **Ant** agree, make peace, socialize.

feverish [adj1] *having high temperature*
▪ **Syn** aguey, burning, febrile, fevered, fiery, flushed, hectic, hot, inflamed, pyretic; ▪ **Ant** chilled, chilly, cold, freezing.

feverish [adj2] *excited, agitated*
▪ **Syn** burning, distracted, frenetic, frenzied, furious, heated, hectic, impatient, nervous, obsessive, overwrought, passionate, restless; ▪ **Ant** calm, collected, content, cool, easygoing, unexcited.

few [adj] *hardly any*
▪ **Syn** exiguous, imperceptible, lean, meager, minor, minute, negligible, paltry, petty, piddling, scant, scarce, slight, slim, sparse, straggling, thin, trifling; ▪ **Ant** abundance, considerable, many, much.

few [pron] *scarcely any*
▪ **Syn** not many, scattering, several, smattering, some, spattering, sprinkling; ▪ **Ant** many, much, numerous.

fiasco [n] *catastrophe*
▪ **Syn** abortion, blunder, breakdown, debacle, disaster, embarrassment, error, failure, farce, flap, flop, mess, route, ruin, stunt; ▪ **Ant** coup, miracle, smash, success, wonder.

fiat [n] *order, proclamation*
▪ **Syn** authorization, command, decree, dictate, dictum, edict, endorsement, mandate, ordinance, permission, precept, sanction, ukase, warrant; ▪ **Ant** ban, interdiction, objection, question, request.

fib [v] *tell a lie*
▪ **Syn** concoct, equivocate, fabricate, falsify, invent, lie, make up, palter, prevaricate; ▪ **Ant** be honest, be straight, tell truth.

fickle [adj] *vacillating, blowing hot and cold* ▪ **Syn** arbitrary, capricious, double-crossing, faithless, fitful, inconstant, irresolute, lubricious, mercurial, mutable, quicksilver, temperamental, ticklish, variable, volatile, whimsical; ▪ **Ant** constant, faithful, reliable, stable, steady.

fictitious [adj] *untrue, made-up*
▪ **Syn** assumed, chimerical, concocted, created, delusive, fabricated, false, fanciful, fantastic, fashioned, feigned, imaginary, invented, mock, mythical, phony, romantic, simulated, spurious, supposititious, synthetic; ▪ **Ant** actual, certain, confirmed, factual, genuine, proven, real, sincere, sure, true, truthful.

fidelity [n1] *faithfulness in a relationship*
▪ **Syn** allegiance, attachment, constancy, dependability, devotion, faith, fealty, integrity, loyalty, piety, reliability, staunchness, steadfastness, trustworthiness; ▪ **Ant** disloyalty, faithlessness, infidelity, lying, treachery.

fidelity [n2] *conformity to standard or original* ▪ **Syn** adherence, adhesion, attachment, closeness, constancy, correspondence, exactitude, faithfulness, loyalty, precision, realism, scrupulousness, verism; ▪ **Ant** inconstancy, nonconformity, unsteadiness, vacillation, wavering.

fidget [v] *move restlessly*
▪ **Syn** bustle, chafe, fiddle, fret, fuss, hitch, jump, play, squirm, stir, toss, trifle, twiddle, twitch, worry; ▪ **Ant** be still, relax, rest.

fidgety [adj] *restlessly moving*
▪ **Syn** apprehensive, impatient, jerky, jittery, jumpy, nervous, nervy, restive, restless, twitchy; ▪ **Ant** quiet, relaxed, restful, resting, still, unmoving.

fiend [n] *dastardly person*
▪ **Syn** beast, brute, degenerate, demon, devil, evil spirit, hellcat, hellion, imp, Mephistopheles, monster, ogre, Satan, savage, serpent, troll; ▪ **Ant** angel, friend.

fierce [adj] *violent, menacing*
▪ **Syn** awful, barbarous, bloodthirsty, brutal, cruel, dangerous, enraged, feral, ferocious, furious, horrible, howling, impetuous, infuriated, intense, malevolent, malign, murderous, passionate, relentless, savage, stormy, tempestuous, terrible, threatening, truculent, vehement, venomous, wild; ▪ **Ant** calm, gentle, kind, meek, nonviolent, peaceful, tame, tender, unthreatening.

fiercely [*adv*] *violently, menacingly*
▪ *Syn* angrily, brutally, ferociously, forcefully, furiously, impetuously, madly, malevolently, mightily, passionately, riotously, savagely, severely, stormily, tempestuously, threateningly, turbulently, vehemently, venomously, viciously, wildly; ▪ *Ant* gently, kindly, mildly, quietly, tamely.

fiery [*adj*] *passionate; on fire*
▪ *Syn* ablaze, blazing, burning, choleric, combustible, conflagrant, enthusiastic, febrile, feverish, fierce, flaming, flaring, glowing, heated, hot-blooded, igneous, ignited, impassioned, impetuous, inflamed, intense, madcap, peppery, precipitate, spirited, vehement, violent; ▪ *Ant* cold, cool, dull, flat, impassive, subdued.

fight [*v1*] *engage in physical encounter*
▪ *Syn* altercate, assault, attack, battle, bicker, brawl, challenge, clash, contend, cross swords, dispute, duel, feud, grapple, joust, meet, oppugn, quarrel, resist, rowdy, scrap, scuffle, skirmish, spar, struggle, tussle, war, wrangle, wrestle; ▪ *Ant* agree, make peace, reconcile, surrender, yield.

fight [*v2*] *oppose an action or belief*
▪ *Syn* argue, buck, combat, contest, defy, force, hassle, maintain, oppose, resist, struggle, travail, traverse, wage, withstand, wrangle; ▪ *Ant* agree, believe, support, uphold.

fight back/fight off [*v*] *defend oneself*
▪ *Syn* check, contain, control, curb, fend off, hold back, oppose, repel, reply, repress, repulse, resist, restrain, retaliate, stave off, ward off; ▪ *Ant* give in, give up, surrender, yield.

fighting [*adj*] *aggressive, warlike*
▪ *Syn* argumentative, bellicose, belligerent, brawling, combative, contentious, disputatious, ferocious, hawkish, hostile, jingoistic, militant, pugnacious, quarrelsome, sparring, truculent, warmongering; ▪ *Ant* passive, peaceful, peace-loving, tolerant.

figment [*n*] *creation in one's mind*
▪ *Syn* chimera, daydream, dream, fable, fabrication, falsehood, fancy, fantasy, fiction, illusion, improvisation, invention, lie, nightmare; ▪ *Ant* certainty, fact, reality.

figurative [*adj*] *not literal, but symbolic*
▪ *Syn* allegorical, denotative, descriptive, emblematic, fanciful, flowery, illustrative, metaphoric, metaphorical, ornate, pictorial, poetical, representative, signifying; ▪ *Ant* literal, real, straightforward.

figure [*v1*] *calculate, compute*
▪ *Syn* add, cast, cipher, count, enumerate, estimate, number, reckon, run down, sum, summate, tally, total, work out; ▪ *Ant* estimate, guess.

figure [*v2*] *understand; decide, infer*
▪ *Syn* cipher, clear up, comprehend, conclude, crack, decipher, decode, determine, discover, disentangle, fathom, follow, opine, puzzle out, reason, resolve, rule, see, settle, solve, suppose, think; ▪ *Ant* conceal, obfuscate, obscure, scramble.

filch [*v*] *steal*
▪ *Syn* embezzle, misappropriate, purloin, rob, scrounge, sneak, snipe, swipe, take, thieve; ▪ *Ant* contribute, give.

file [*v*] *put in place, order*
▪ *Syn* alphabetize, arrange, catalog, catalogue, categorize, classify, deposit, docket, document, enter, index, list, record, register, slot, tabulate; ▪ *Ant* disarrange, disorder.

filibuster [*n*] *obstruction of progress, especially in verbal argument* ▪ *Syn* delay, hindrance, interference, opposition, postponement, procrastination; ▪ *Ant* catalyst, impetus, incentive, progression.

fill [*v*] *to completely occupy a given space*
▪ *Syn* choke, clog, congest, cram, distend, furnish, glut, gorge, heap, impregnate, inflate, jam-pack, load, meet, overspread, pack, plug, replenish, satiate, saturate, shoal, stock, store, stretch, stuff, supply, swell, top; ▪ *Ant* deplete, drain, empty, exhaust, spend, take, use, void.

filmy [*adj1*] *finespun, fragile*
▪ *Syn* chiffon, dainty, delicate, diaphanous, fine, fine-grained, flimsy, gauzy, gossamer, sheer, tiffany, transparent, wispy; ▪ *Ant* heavy, opaque, solid, substantial.

filmy [*adj2*] *covered with mist; blurry*
▪ *Syn* bleary, blurred, cloudy, dim, hazy, membranous, milky, misty, opalescent, opaque, pearly; ▪ *Ant* clean, clear, see-through, translucent, transparent.

filter [*v*] *separate to refine; seep through*
▪ *Syn* clarify, clean, distill, drain, escape, exude, filtrate, leak, metastasize, ooze, osmose, penetrate, percolate, permeate,

purify, refine, screen, sieve, sift, strain, trickle, winnow; ▪ *Ant* collect, combine, mix, thicken.

filthy [*adj1*] *dirty, polluted*
▪ *Syn* begrimed, black, blackened, disheveled, fecal, feculent, foul, impure, miry, muddy, offensive, putrid, repulsive, revolting, scummy, sleazy, slimy, slipshod, sloppy, slovenly, smoky, soiled, sooty, squalid, verminous, vile; ▪ *Ant* clean, immaculate, pure, sterile, unpolluted.

filthy [*adj2*] *vulgar, obscene*
▪ *Syn* base, bawdy, coarse, contemptible, corrupt, depraved, despicable, foul, indecent, lewd, low, mean, nasty, offensive, pornographic, ornate, raunchy, scatological, scurvy, smutty, suggestive, vicious, vile; ▪ *Ant* chaste, clean, decent, decorous, proper, pure.

final [*adj1*] *ending, last*
▪ *Syn* closing, concluding, crowning, end, eventual, hindmost, last-minute, latest, latter, supreme, terminal, ultimate; ▪ *Ant* beginning, commencing, first, initial, opening, starting.

final [*adj2*] *conclusive, definitive*
▪ *Syn* absolute, decided, decisive, definite, determinate, finished, incontrovertible, irrefutable, irrevocable, settled; ▪ *Ant* inconclusive, interim, introductory, preliminary, temporary.

finale [*n*] *ending of an event*
▪ *Syn* afterpiece, cessation, close, conclusion, culmination, denouement, end, epilogue, peroration, summation, termination; ▪ *Ant* beginning, debut, first act, opening, prologue, start.

finalize [*v*] *finish, complete action*
▪ *Syn* agree, conclude, consummate, decide, settle, wrap up; ▪ *Ant* begin, introduce, open, start.

finally [*adv*] *beyond any doubt*
▪ *Syn* assuredly, certainly, conclusively, decisively, definitely, enduringly, inescapably, inexorably, irrevocably, lastly, permanently; ▪ *Ant* doubtfully, dubiously, inconclusively.

find [*v1*] *catch sight of, lay hands on*
▪ *Syn* catch, come across, come upon, detect, discern, discover, encounter, espy, expose, identify, locate, make out, meet, notice, observe, perceive, pinpoint, recognize, run across, run into, sight, spot, track down; ▪ *Ant* fail, lose, misplace, miss, overlook, pass by.

find [*v2*] *achieve, win*
▪ *Syn* acquire, attain, earn, gain, get, meet, meet with, obtain, procure; ▪ *Ant* fail, fall short, forfeit, lose.

find out [*v*] *discover, learn*
▪ *Syn* ascertain, detect, determine, divine, hear, identify, note, observe, perceive, realize, see, uncover; ▪ *Ant* conceal, cover, disregard, hide, miss.

fine [*n*] *penalty in money*
▪ *Syn* amends, amercement, assessment, damages, forfeit, mulct, punishment, reparation; ▪ *Ant* amends, award, compensation, reimbursement, reward.

fine [*adj1*] *excellent, accomplished*
▪ *Syn* capital, choice, exceptional, exquisite, fashionable, first-rate, great, magnificent, ornate, outstanding, pleasant, rare, select, skillful, splendid, superior, top; ▪ *Ant* atrocious, bad, inferior, poor, wretched.

fine [*adj2*] *cloudless, sunshiny (weather)*
▪ *Syn* balmy, bright, clarion, clear, clement, dry, fair, pleasant, rainless, sunny; ▪ *Ant* cloudy, dark, rainy, stormy.

fine [*adj3*] *dainty, delicate; sheer*
▪ *Syn* diaphanous, ethereal, filmy, flimsy, fragile, gauzy, gossamer, granular, impalpable, light, lightweight, porous, powdery, quality, slender, thin, threadlike, transparent; ▪ *Ant* coarse, rough, thick.

fine [*adj4*] *discriminating, exact*
▪ *Syn* abstruse, acute, clear, critical, delicate, distinct, enigmatic, esoteric, fastidious, hairline, hairsplitting, keen, minute, nice, obscure, precise, pure, recondite, refined, sharp, sterling, tasteful, tenuous, trifling; ▪ *Ant* awkward, broad, crude, general, uncouth, undiscriminating, unrefined.

fine [*v*] *penalize in monetary way*
▪ *Syn* alienate, amerce, confiscate, exact, extort, levy, mulct, punish, sconce, seize, sequestrate, tax; ▪ *Ant* award, compensate, reimburse, reward.

finesse [*v*] *maneuver, manipulate*
▪ *Syn* angle, beguile, bluff, exploit, operate, play; ▪ *Ant* bobble, mishandle.

finger [*v*] *choose, designate*
▪ *Syn* appoint, determine, identify, indicate, locate, make, name, nominate, point out, specify, tap; ▪ *Ant* ignore, pass over, reject.

finicky [*adj*] *overparticular*
▪ *Syn* choosy, critical, dainty, difficult, fastidious, finical, fussy, nice, nit-

picking, overnice, particular, picky, scrupulous, squeamish, stickling; ▪ *Ant* easy, lax, negligent, open, slack, uncritical.

finish [*v1*] *bring to a conclusion; get done* ▪ *Syn* accomplish, achieve, cease, clinch, close, complete, conclude, culminate, determine, discharge, do, effect, end, execute, finalize, fold, fulfill, halt, make, perfect, settle, shut down, stop, terminate, wrap; ▪ *Ant* begin, commence, initiate, introduce, start, undertake.

finish [*v2*] *consume, use up* ▪ *Syn* deplete, devour, dispatch, dispose of, drain, drink, eat, empty, exhaust, expend, spend, use; ▪ *Ant* keep, maintain, save, store.

finish [*v3*] *defeat; kill* ▪ *Syn* annihilate, assassinate, destroy, dispatch, dispose of, down, execute, exterminate, liquidate, overcome, rout, ruin, slaughter, slay; ▪ *Ant* bear, create, generate.

finished [*adj1*] *cultivated, refined* ▪ *Syn* accomplished, classic, consummate, cultured, elegant, expert, flawless, impeccable, polished, proficient, skilled, smooth, suave, urbane, versatile; ▪ *Ant* crude, uncultivated, unfinished, unrefined, unsophisticated.

finished [*adj2*] *complete, done* ▪ *Syn* accomplished, achieved, closed, compassed, completed, consummated, decided, dispatched, disposed of, effected, ended, executed, finalized, fulfilled, lapsed, perfected, performed, realized, resolved, satisfied, stopped, terminated, through; ▪ *Ant* crude, incomplete, in progress, rough, unfinished.

finite [*adj*] *subject to limitations* ▪ *Syn* bound, circumscribed, confined, definable, definite, demarcated, determinate, exact, fixed, limited, precise, restricted, specific, terminable; ▪ *Ant* endless, infinite, interminable, unlimited, unrestricted.

fire [*v1*] *cause to burn* ▪ *Syn* burn, enkindle, ignite, kindle, light, set ablaze, set aflame, set alight; ▪ *Ant* extinguish, quench, smother.

fire [*v2*] *excite, arouse* ▪ *Syn* animate, electrify, enthuse, galvanize, heighten, impassion, incite, inflame, inspire, inspirit, intoxicate, irritate, provoke, quicken, rouse, stir, thrill; ▪ *Ant* bore, dismay, dull.

fire [*v3*] *dismiss from responsibility* ▪ *Syn* discharge, drop, eject, expel, lay off, oust, terminate; ▪ *Ant* appoint, designate, elect, engage, hire, name.

firm [*adj1*] *inflexible* ▪ *Syn* close, concrete, dense, hard, hardened, heavy, impenetrable, impermeable, impervious, refractory, rigid, set, solid, solidified, stiff, thick, tough; ▪ *Ant* elastic, flexible, loose, porous, slack, soft, supple, weak, yielding.

firm [*adj2*] *stable, unmoving* ▪ *Syn* anchored, bolted, braced, cemented, closed, durable, embedded, fast, fixed, immobile, motionless, mounted, nailed, petrified, riveted, rooted, secure, set, settled, sound, spiked, stationary, steady, strong, sturdy, substantial, taut, tenacious, tight, welded; ▪ *Ant* fluctuating, moving, shaky, unsettled, unstable, wavering.

firm [*adj3*] *unalterable, definite* ▪ *Syn* abiding, adamant, bent, consistent, constant, determined, enduring, established, explicit, fixed, inflexible, intent, obdurate, persistent, prevailing, resolute, set, settled, specific, stated, stipulated, strict, sure, tenacious, true; ▪ *Ant* alterable, changeable, indefinite, irresolute.

firmly [*adv*] *with determination* ▪ *Syn* adamantly, decisively, doggedly, indefatigably, intently, obdurately, obstinately, persistently, pertinaciously, purposefully, resolutely, staunchly, steadfastly, stolidly, strictly, stubbornly, tenaciously; ▪ *Ant* changeably, indefinitely, waveringly, weakly.

first [*adj1*] *earliest in order* ▪ *Syn* antecedent, basic, beginning, cardinal, early, elementary, fundamental, head, inaugural, inceptive, incipient, initial, key, opening, original, pioneer, primary, prime, primeval, rudimentary; ▪ *Ant* final, last, terminal, ultimate.

first [*adj2*] *highest in importance* ▪ *Syn* arch, champion, chief, dominant, eminent, foremost, greatest, head, leading, main, outstanding, paramount, predominant, premier, primary, ruling, supreme; ▪ *Ant* last, least, subordinate.

first [*adv*] *at the beginning* ▪ *Syn* at the outset, before all else, beforehand, initially, originally, to begin with, to start with; ▪ *Ant* finally, last, later, subsequently.

first-class/first-rate [*adj*] *superior, excellent* ▪ *Syn* capital, choice, dandy, fine, shipshape, sound, supreme, top, very good; ▪ *Ant* bad, inferior, lesser, poor, second-class/second-rate.

firsthand [*adj*] *direct*
▪ *Syn* eyewitness, immediate, primary, straight; ▪ *Ant* hearsay, impersonal, indirect.

fishy [*adj*] *doubtful, suspicious*
▪ *Syn* ambiguous, dubious, equivocal, far-fetched, implausible, improbable, odd, queer, questionable, shady, suspect; ▪ *Ant* aboveboard, honest, likely, probable, real, truthful, unquestionable, unsuspicious.

fit [*adj1*] *suitable, appropriate*
▪ *Syn* able, adapted, apt, befitting, capable, comme il faut, competent, correct, correspondent, due, equipped, expedient, feasible, just, likely, meet, opportune, practicable, proper, qualified, ready, right, rightful, seemly, timely, well-suited, worthy; ▪ *Ant* false, inadequate, inappropriate, incorrect, unfit, unsuitable, unsuited, unworthy, wrong.

fit [*adj2*] *healthy, in good physical shape*
▪ *Syn* able-bodied, competent, hale, muscled, robust, slim, sound, toned, trim, well, wholesome; ▪ *Ant* inadequate, poor, weak.

fitful [*adj*] *irregular, sporadic*
▪ *Syn* broken, capricious, changeable, desultory, erratic, fluctuating, haphazard, inconstant, intermittent, interrupted, periodic, random, restive, restless, shifting, spasmodic, variable; ▪ *Ant* constant, continous, even, regular, stable, undisturbed, unvarying.

fitted [*adj1*] *appropriate, right*
▪ *Syn* adapted, conformable, cut out for, equipped, matched, proper, qualified, suitable, suited, tailor-made; ▪ *Ant* inappropriate, incorrect, unfit, unprepared, unqualified, wrong.

fitted [*adj2*] *equipped*
▪ *Syn* accoutered, appointed, armed, furnished, implemented, outfitted, provided, set up, supplied; ▪ *Ant* ill-equipped, lacking, needing, unfitted, unprepared.

fitting [*adj*] *appropriate, suitable*
▪ *Syn* applicable, apt, becoming, comme il faut, correct, decent, decorous, desirable, due, felicitous, happy, just, meet, proper, right, seemly; ▪ *Ant* improper, in-

appropriate, incorrect, unfitting, unseemly, unsuitable.

fix [*v1*] *establish, make firm*
▪ *Syn* affix, anchor, bind, cement, connect, consolidate, couple, embed, entrench, fasten, glue, harden, implant, inculcate, ingrain, install, link, locate, lodge, moor, pin, plant, position, rivet, root, secure, set, settle, solidify, steady, stick, tie; ▪ *Ant* alter, change, destroy, disarrange, dislodge, disorganize, displace, unsettle.

fix [*v2*] *mend, repair*
▪ *Syn* adjust, amend, correct, debug, doctor, emend, overhaul, patch, rebuild, recondition, reconstruct, regulate, restore, retread, revamp, revise, sort, tune up; ▪ *Ant* break, corrupt, destroy, unfix.

fix [*v3*] *prepare, plan ahead*
▪ *Syn* arrange, dispose, frame, prearrange, precontrive, predesign, preorder, preplan, set up; ▪ *Ant* forget, ignore, neglect.

fix [*v4*] *focus on*
▪ *Syn* concenter, concentrate, direct, fasten, fixate, level at, put, rivet; ▪ *Ant* ignore, look away.

fixed [*adj1*] *permanent, steady*
▪ *Syn* anchored, attached, established, fast, firm, hooked, immobile, immovable, locked, quiet, rigid, rooted, secure, settled, solid, stable, steadfast, still, tenacious; ▪ *Ant* changeable, impermanent, unfixed, unsteady.

fixed [*adj2*] *intent, resolute; established*
▪ *Syn* abiding, arranged, certain, circumscribed, confirmed, decided, defined, definitive, firm, inveterate, limited, narrow, planned, prearranged, precise, resolved, restricted, rooted, settled, stated, steadfast, steady, still, stipulated, sure; ▪ *Ant* changeable, flexible, indefinite, irresolute, unfixed, variable, wandering, wavering.

fixed [*adj3*] *repaired*
▪ *Syn* in order, in working order, mended, put right, rebuilt, refitted, repaired, sorted, whole; ▪ *Ant* broken, in disrepair, unfixed.

fix up [*v*] *prepare, beautify*
▪ *Syn* dress up, furnish, primp, provide, rehabilitate, repair, smarten; ▪ *Ant* corrupt, damage, deface, defile, disfigure.

fizzle [*v*] *collapse, fall through*
▪ *Syn* abort, die, end, fail, fold, miscarry, misfire, wane; ▪ *Ant* build, develop, progress.

flabby [adj] baggy, fat
▪ *Syn* drooping, flaccid, hanging, limp, loose, pendulous, sagging, shapeless, slack, sloppy, tender, toneless, yielding; ▪ *Ant* firm, lean, slim, strong, taut, thin, tight.

flaccid [adj] drooping
▪ *Syn* debilitated, enervated, enfeebled, flabby, flimsy, lax, limp, loose, nerveless, quaggy, sapped, slack, soft, weak, weakened; ▪ *Ant* firm, rigid, stiff, taut, tight.

flag [v] decline, fall off
▪ *Syn* abate, deteriorate, die, droop, ebb, fade, fail, faint, fall, languish, pine, sag, sink, slump, succumb, wane, weaken, weary, wilt; ▪ *Ant* do well, freshen, increase, recover, rise, strengthen.

flagrant [adj] flaunting, blatant; without shame ▪ *Syn* arrant, atrocious, bold, brazen, conspicuous, dreadful, egregious, flagitous, flaming, glaring, heinous, immodest, infamous, noticeable, notorious, obvious, open, ostentatious, outrageous, rank, scandalous, shocking; ▪ *Ant* concealed, disguised, excusable, hidden, mild, moral, obscure, restrained, secret.

flair [n] talent, style
▪ *Syn* ability, aptitude, aptness, bent, chic, dash, elegance, faculty, feel, genius, gift, glamour, head, knack, panache, presence, taste, turn; ▪ *Ant* awkwardness, inability, incapacity, ineptitude, ineptness.

flak [n] complaint, criticism
▪ *Syn* abuse, censure, disapproval, disparagement, fault-finding, hostility, opposition; ▪ *Ant* compliment, praise.

flamboyant [adj] extravagant, theatrical
▪ *Syn* baroque, bombastic, colorful, dashing, dazzling, elaborate, flashy, florid, gaudy, glamorous, luscious, luxuriant, ostentatious, pretentious, resplendent, rich, rococo, showy, splashy, sporty; ▪ *Ant* calm, moderate, modest, natural, restrained, simple, subdued, tasteful.

flaming [adj] very angry, vehement
▪ *Syn* ardent, aroused, blazing, bright, burning, fervent, frenzied, hot, impassioned, intense, passionate, raging, scintillating, vivid; ▪ *Ant* cold, dispassionate, indifferent, objective.

flammable [adj] easily set on fire
▪ *Syn* burnable, combustible, ignitable, incendiary, inflammable; ▪ *Ant* fire-proof, flameproof, incombustible, non-flammable.

flap [n] commotion
▪ *Syn* agitation, banging, confusion, fluster, flutter, tumult, turbulence, turmoil; ▪ *Ant* calm, peace, quietude.

flashy [adj] flamboyant, in poor taste
▪ *Syn* blatant, brazen, cheap, chintzy, flaunting, florid, garish, gaudy, glaring, glitzy, loud, meretricious, ornate, ostentatious, showy, snazzy, sparkling, tasteless, tawdry, tinsel, vulgar; ▪ *Ant* plain, simple, subdued, tasteful, unobtrusive.

flat [adj1] level, smooth
▪ *Syn* collapsed, decumbent, deflated, empty, even, fallen, flush, horizontal, leveled, oblate, outstretched, planate, procumbent, prone, prostrate, reclining, recumbent, splay, supine, tabular; ▪ *Ant* broken, elevated, raised, rough, rounded, rugged, uneven.

flat [adj2] dull, lackluster to the senses
▪ *Syn* banal, bland, colorless, drab, flavorless, inane, insipid, jejune, lifeless, matte, monotonous, muted, prosaic, prosy, sapless, spiritless, stale, tasteless, tedious, vapid, weak; ▪ *Ant* bubbly, effervescent, palatable, savory, sharp.

flat [adj3] absolute, positive
▪ *Syn* categorical, direct, downright, explicit, final, fixed, indubitable, peremptory, plain, straight, unconditional; ▪ *Ant* equivocal, indefinite, qualified.

flatten [v] level out
▪ *Syn* abrade, compress, crush, debase, deflate, depress, fell, floor, flush, grade, ground, iron out, lay, lay low, level, plane, prostrate, raze, roll, smash, smooth, squash, straighten, subdue, trample; ▪ *Ant* break, elevate, raise, roughen, round.

flatter [v1] compliment excessively
▪ *Syn* adulate, blandish, cajole, charm, con, court, glorify, grovel, humor, inveigle, jolly, massage, overpraise, praise, salve, sell, stroke, wheedle; ▪ *Ant* belittle, castigate, condemn, criticize, denounce, insult, offend.

flatter [v2] complement, enhance
▪ *Syn* adorn, beautify, become, decorate, embellish, enrich, finish, grace, ornament, perfect, set off, suit; ▪ *Ant* clash, deface, distort, mar, spoil.

flatulent [adj] pretentious, long-winded
▪ *Syn* bombastic, inflated, oratorical,

overblown, pompous, prolix, shallow, superficial, swollen, tedious, tumescent, tumid, turgid, windy, wordy; ▪ **Ant** brief, unpretentious.

flaunt [v] *exhibit, show off*
▪ **Syn** advertise, air, boast, broadcast, declare, display, expose, flash, gasconade, parade, proclaim, reveal, showcase, show off, sport, vaunt; ▪ **Ant** conceal, hide, refrain.

flavor [n] *odor and taste*
▪ **Syn** aroma, essence, extract, gusto, piquancy, pungency, relish, sapor, savor, seasoning, smack, tang, tartness, taste, twang, vim, wallop, zest, zing; ▪ **Ant** flatness, insipidity, odorlessness, scentlessness, tastelessness, vapidity.

flawless [adj] *spotless, intact*
▪ **Syn** absolute, entire, faultless, immaculate, impeccable, irreproachable, perfect, sound, whole; ▪ **Ant** blemished, damaged, defective, disfigured, flawed, imperfect.

fledgling [n] *beginner in activity*
▪ **Syn** apprentice, chick, colt, learner, neophyte, nestling, newcomer, novice, rookie, trainee; ▪ **Ant** authority, expert, professional.

flee [v] *run away to escape*
▪ **Syn** abscond, avoid, break, decamp, depart, desert, elude, escape, evade, fly, jump, leave, retreat, run, scamper, scoot, vanish; ▪ **Ant** face, meet, stand, stay, wait.

fleet [adj] *quick in movement*
▪ **Syn** agile, brisk, expeditious, expeditive, fast, flying, hasty, lively, meteoric, nimble, nimble-footed, rapid, speedy, swift, winged; ▪ **Ant** clumsy, slow, sluggish, torpid.

fleeting [adj] *brief, transient*
▪ **Syn** cursory, ephemeral, evanescent, flitting, fugacious, impermanent, momentary, passing, short-lived, sudden, temporary, transitory, vanishing, volatile; ▪ **Ant** constant, continual, endless, enduring, lasting, lengthy, long, long-lived, permanent, perpetual.

fleshly [adj1] *lecherous, desiring sex*
▪ **Syn** animalistic, bodily, carnal, erotic, gross, lascivious, lewd, lustful, profane, sensual, venereal, voluptuous; ▪ **Ant** immaterial, religious, spiritual.

fleshly [adj2] *bodily*
▪ **Syn** corporal, corporeal, earthly, human, material, mundane, physical, secular, somatic, terrestrial, worldly; ▪ **Ant** mentally, spiritual.

fleshy [adj] *overweight*
▪ **Syn** adipose, ample, brawny, corpulent, fat, gross, heavy, hefty, husky, obese, plump, porcine, portly, pulpy, sarcous, stout, weighty; ▪ **Ant** emaciated, scrawny, skinny, thin, underweight.

flex [v] *bend*
▪ **Syn** angle, bend, contract, crook, curve, mold, ply, spring, stretch, tighten, tilt, yield; ▪ **Ant** extend, stiffen, straighten.

flexible [adj1] *pliable, bendable*
▪ **Syn** adjustable, bending, ductile, elastic, extensile, formable, impressionable, limber, lithe, malleable, plastic, pliant, soft, spongy, springy, stretchable, supple, tensile, tractable, willowy, yielding; ▪ **Ant** brittle, inflexible, resistant, rigid, rigid, stiff, unyielding.

flexible [adj2] *adaptable, responsive*
▪ **Syn** acquiescent, adjustable, amenable, biddable, complaisant, compliant, discretionary, docile, gentle, manageable, open, tractable, variable; ▪ **Ant** dogmatic, obstinate, ornery, stern, stubborn.

flighty [adj] *fickle, irresponsible*
▪ **Syn** capricious, changeable, effervescent, empty-headed, frivolous, giddy, impetuous, lightheaded, lively, mercurial, scatterbrained, silly, thoughtless, volatile, whimsical, wild; ▪ **Ant** responsible, sedate, stable, steady.

flimsy [adj1] *not strong; light, thin*
▪ **Syn** chiffon, delicate, diaphanous, feeble, fragile, frail, gauzy, gossamer, insubstantial, meager, papery, rickety, shaky, sheer, slight, superficial, tacky, transparent, weak, wobbly; ▪ **Ant** firm, heavy, solid, sound, strong, sturdy, substantial, thick, tough.

flimsy [adj2] *unconvincing, implausible*
▪ **Syn** assailable, baseless, feeble, groundless, illogical, inane, inconceivable, incredible, inept, lame, poor, superficial, thin, trifling, trivial, weak; ▪ **Ant** convincing, plausible, reasonable, serious, strong.

flinch [v] *shy away, wince*
▪ **Syn** avoid, balk, blanch, blink, cower, cringe, crouch, duck, elude, escape, eschew, evade, flee, quail, recede, recoil, retreat, shirk, shrink, shun, swerve, withdraw; ▪ **Ant** confront, defy, face, meet.

flippant [adj] *irreverent*
▪ **Syn** brassy, breezy, cocky, disrespect-

ful, flighty, fresh, frivolous, glib, impertinent, impudent, insolent, offhand, pert, playful, rude, superficial; ▪ *Ant* considerate, courteous, respectful, reverent, serious.

flirtatious [*adj*] *provocative, teasing*
▪ *Syn* amorous, arch, coquettish, coy, dallying, enticing, libidinous, philandering, sportive; ▪ *Ant* cool, modest, shy, unprovocative.

float [*v*] *lie on the surface*
▪ *Syn* be buoyant, bob, drift, glide, hang, hover, poise, ride, sail, skim, slide, swim, waft, wash; ▪ *Ant* drown, settle, sink, submerge.

flock [*v*] *congregate*
▪ *Syn* collect, converge, crowd, gather, group, herd, huddle, mass, throng, troop; ▪ *Ant* disperse, separate, spread.

flood [*n*] *overwhelming flow, quantity*
▪ *Syn* abundance, alluvion, bore, bounty, cataclysm, cataract, current, deluge, downpour, excess, flow, flux, glut, inundation, multitude, Niagara, overflow, plenty, pour, profusion, rush, spate, stream, surge, surplus, tide, torrent, tsunami, wave; ▪ *Ant* dearth, drought, lack, scarcity.

floor [*n*] *bottom of a room; level of a multistory building* ▪ *Syn* attic, basement, boards, carpet, cellar, deck, flat, ground, landing, level, mezzanine, rug, stage, story, tier; ▪ *Ant* ceiling, dome, roof.

flop [*v*] *fail miserably*
▪ *Syn* close, flummox, fold, founder, misfire; ▪ *Ant* accomplish, achieve, prosper, succeed.

florid [*adj1*] *very elaborate*
▪ *Syn* aureate, baroque, decorative, embellished, flamboyant, flowery, fussy, garnished, high-flown, luscious, magniloquent, ornamented, ornate, pretentious, rich, sonorous; ▪ *Ant* austere, bare, inelaborate, natural, plain, undecorated.

florid [*adj2*] *flushed, ruddy*
▪ *Syn* blowzy, flush, glowing, high-colored, pink, reddened, rubicund, sanguine; ▪ *Ant* pale, pallid, white.

flourish [*v*] *grow, prosper*
▪ *Syn* arrive, batten, bloom, blossom, boom, burgeon, develop, expand, flower, increase, multiply, score, succeed, thrive, wax; ▪ *Ant* cease, decline, fade, fail, hinder, languish, stunt.

flourishing [*adj*] *prospering, going well*
▪ *Syn* blooming, burgeoning, expanding,

exuberant, growing, lush, luxuriant, mushrooming, profuse, rampant, robust, successful, thriving, vigorous; ▪ *Ant* ceasing, decreasing, failing, languishing, stunted, undeveloping.

flout [*v*] *show contempt for*
▪ *Syn* affront, defy, deride, disregard, gibe, gird, insult, jeer, mock, outrage, quip, repudiate, ridicule, scoff, scorn, slight, sneer, spurn, taunt; ▪ *Ant* honor, respect, revere.

flow [*v*] *issue, surge, run out*
▪ *Syn* cascade, circulate, continue, course, deluge, ebb, emanate, exude, flood, glide, gurgle, inundate, jet, leak, move, ooze, pass, percolate, pour, proceed, progress, pullulate, regurgitate, ripple, roll, run, rush, sluice, splash, spurt, stream, swirl, teem, tumble, void; ▪ *Ant* dribble, drip, drizzle, seep, trickle.

flower [*n2*] *best, choicest part*
▪ *Syn* choice, cream, elite, finest point, freshness, height, pick, pride, prime, prize, top; ▪ *Ant* dregs, residue, worst.

flower [*v*] *bloom, flourish*
▪ *Syn* batten, blossom, blow, burgeon, effloresce, mature, open, prosper, thrive, unfold; ▪ *Ant* close, die, droop, fade, sag, shrink, shrivel.

flowery [*adj*] *ornate, especially referring to speech or writing* ▪ *Syn* aureate, baroque, bombastic, declamatory, embellished, euphemistic, fancy, florid, grandiloquent, high-flown, magniloquent, ornamented, prolix, redundant, rhetorical, rococo, sonorous, verbose, windy, wordy; ▪ *Ant* concise, pithy, plain, succinct.

fluctuate [*v*] *vacillate, change*
▪ *Syn* alter, alternate, ebb and flow, flutter, hesitate, oscillate, shift, swing, undulate, vary, veer, vibrate, wave, waver; ▪ *Ant* hold, persist, remain, stay.

fluent [*adj*] *articulate*
▪ *Syn* chatty, cogent, copious, declamatory, effusive, eloquent, facile, garrulous, glib, loquacious, persuasive, prompt, quick, ready, smooth, smooth-spoken, talkative, verbose, voluble, well-versed; ▪ *Ant* hesitant, inarticulate, tongue-tied, unprepared.

fluid [*adj1*] *liquid*
▪ *Syn* aqueous, flowing, fluent, juicy, liquefied, lymphatic, melted, molten, running, runny, serous, watery; ▪ *Ant* congealed, firm, solid.

fluid [adj2] *adaptable, changeable*
- **Syn** adjustable, changeful, flexible, fluctuating, malleable, mercurial, mobile, mutable, protean, shifting, variable; **Ant** definite, fixed, settled, stable.

fluky [adj] *chance*
- **Syn** accidental, casual, chancy, coincidental, contingent, fortuitous, incalculable, incidental, lucky, odd, variable; **Ant** certain, designed, intended, planned, sure.

flurry [v] *agitate, confuse*
- **Syn** bewilder, bother, discompose, disconcert, disquiet, excite, fluster, frustrate, fuss, galvanize, hassle, hurry, perplex, perturb, quicken, ruffle, stimulate, upset; **Ant** calm, comfort, quiet, settle.

flush [adj1] *flat*
- **Syn** even, horizontal, level, planate, plane, smooth, square, true; **Ant** rough, uneven.

flush [adj2] *overflowing, abundant*
- **Syn** affluent, close, full, generous, lavish, liberal, opulent, prodigal, rich, wealthy, well-off; **Ant** destitute, lacking.

flush [v] *become or make pink or red*
- **Syn** blush, burn, color, crimson, flame, glow, go red, mantle, pink, pinken, redden, rose, rouge, suffuse; **Ant** blanch, pale, whiten.

flushed [adj] *pink, glowing*
- **Syn** ablaze, animated, aroused, blushing, burning, crimson, elated, embarrassed, enthused, exhilarated, feverish, florid, full-blooded, high, hot, intoxicated, red, rosy, rubicund, ruddy, sanguine; **Ant** ashen, livid, pale, pallid, wan.

fluster [v] *upset, perturb*
- **Syn** agitate, bother, confound, confuse, discompose, disquiet, disturb, excite, flurry, frustrate, hassle, muddle, nonplus, puzzle, rattle, ruffle; **Ant** calm, comfort, settle.

flux [n] *state of constant change*
- **Syn** alteration, change, flow, fluctuation, fluidity, instability, modification, motion, mutability, mutation, transition; **Ant** constancy, stability, steadiness.

fly [v1] *run or pass swiftly*
- **Syn** barrel, bolt, breeze, career, dart, dash, elapse, flee, flit, glide, hasten, hurry, hustle, pass, race, roll, rush, scamper, scoot, shoot, speed, sprint, tear;

Ant crawl, creep, drag, drift, linger, loiter, tarry.

fly [v2] *escape, flee*
- **Syn** abscond, avoid, bolt, break, clear, decamp, disappear, flee, hide, skip, steal away, take off, withdraw; **Ant** confront, face, remain, stay.

fly-by-night [adj] *undependable*
- **Syn** brief, dubious, impermanent, questionable, shady, shifty, short-lived, treacherous; **Ant** dependable, reliable, reputable, responsible, trustworthy.

foamy [adj] *bubbly*
- **Syn** barmy, burbling, carbonated, ebullient, effervescent, fizzy, frothy, lathery, seething, simmering, spumescent, spumy, sudsy, yeasty; **Ant** flat.

focus [v] *aim attention at*
- **Syn** adjust, attract, center, centralize, concenter, concentrate, convene, converge, direct, fasten, fix, fixate, join, meet, pinpoint, put, rivet, sharpen; **Ant** ignore, neglect.

foe [n] *person who is opponent* –
- **Syn** adversary, antagonist, enemy, hostile party, rival; **Ant** ally, comrade, friend.

fog [n] *mental unclarity*
- **Syn** befuddlement, blindness, confusion, daze, haze, maze, mist, obscurity, perplexity, stupor, trance, vagueness; **Ant** clarity, cognizance, perspicuity, understanding.

fog [v] *muddle, obscure*
- **Syn** addle, becloud, befuddle, bewilder, cloud, confuse, darken, eclipse, mist, muddy, obfuscate, perplex, puzzle, stupefy; **Ant** brighten, clear up, explain.

foggy [adj] *hazy, obscure*
- **Syn** blurred, clouded, cloudy, dark, dim, filmy, fuzzy, gray, indistinct, misty, murky, mushy, nebulous, smoggy, vague, vaporous, vapory; **Ant** clear, transparent.

foible [n] *personal imperfection*
- **Syn** characteristic, defect, eccentricity, failing, frailty, idiosyncrasy, kink, mannerism, oddity, peculiarity, quirk, shortcoming, singularity, vice, weakness; **Ant** forte, strength, virtue.

foil [v] *circumvent, nip in the bud*
- **Syn** balk, bilk, check, counter, curb, defeat, disconcert, ditch, dodge, duck, elude, frustrate, hinder, juke, nullify, outwit, prevent, rattle, stop, stymie, thwart;

▪ *Ant* abet, advance, aid, assist, further, help.

fold [*v1*] *lay in creases*
▪ *Syn* bend, corrugate, crease, crimp, crumple, curl, double, furrow, groove, hem, intertwine, knit, lap, overlap, plait, pleat, plicate, pucker, ridge, ruche, ruck, ruffle, telescope, tuck, wrinkle; ▪ *Ant* flatten, unbend.

fold [*v2*] *encase, enclose*
▪ *Syn* do up, enfold, entwine, envelop, involve, wrap, wrap up; ▪ *Ant* free, let out, loose, loosen.

fold [*v3*] *fail, close*
▪ *Syn* break, bust, collapse, crash, crumple, give, go bankrupt, impoverish, pauper, pauperize, shut down, yield; ▪ *Ant* achieve, revive, succeed.

follow [*v1*] *trail, pursue physically*
▪ *Syn* accompany, attend, catenate, chase, convoy, give chase, go after, hunt, persecute, run down, search, seek, shadow, stalk, stick to, tag, tail, track; ▪ *Ant* go before, guide, lead, precede, steer.

follow [*v2*] *act in accordance with*
▪ *Syn* abide by, adhere to, adopt, attend, comply, conform, emulate, heed, imitate, keep, match, mind, mirror, model on, note, obey, observe, regard, serve, support, take after, watch; ▪ *Ant* avoid, disregard, scorn, transgress, violate.

follow [*v3*] *understand*
▪ *Syn* accept, appreciate, apprehend, catch, comprehend, fathom, grasp, realize, see; ▪ *Ant* misconstrue, misinterpret, mistake, misunderstand.

following [*adj*] *happening, being next or after* ▪ *Syn* afterward, afterwards, back, by and by, coming, coming after, coming next, consecutive, consequent, consequential, ensuing, henceforth, hinder, later, latter, next, posterior, presently, proximate, sequent, sequential, serial, seriate, subsequent, succeeding, successive; ▪ *Ant* first, leading, preceding.

follow through [*v*] *bring to a conclusion*
▪ *Syn* complete, conclude, consummate, pursue, see through; ▪ *Ant* leave, not finish.

folly [*n*] *nonsense, ridiculous idea*
▪ *Syn* absurdity, craziness, daftness, fatuity, foolishness, idiocy, impracticality, imprudence, indiscretion, irrationality, lunacy, madness, obliquity, rashness, recklessness, senselessness, silliness, stupidity, triviality, vice; ▪ *Ant* judgment, knowledge, prudence, seriousness, understanding, wisdom.

foment [*v*] *instigate, provoke*
▪ *Syn* abet, agitate, arouse, brew, cultivate, encourage, excite, foster, goad, incite, nurture, promote, quicken, raise, set, spur, start, stimulate, stir up; ▪ *Ant* cease, dampen, discourage, dissuade, quell, stop, suppress.

fond [*adj*] *having a liking or taste for someone or something* ▪ *Syn* affectionate, amorous, caring, devoted, doting, enamored, indulgent, keen on, loving, partial to, responsive, romantic, sentimental, sympathetic, tender, warm; ▪ *Ant* averse, hating, hostile, indifferent.

fool around [*v*] *waste time*
▪ *Syn* dawdle, idle, lark; ▪ *Ant* labor, toil, work.

fooled [*adj*] *tricked*
▪ *Syn* conned, deceived, deluded, duped, misled; ▪ *Ant* clear, cognizant, enlightened, wise.

foolhardy [*adj*] *impetuous, rash*
▪ *Syn* adventuresome, adventurous, audacious, bold, daredevil, daring, headstrong, imprudent, incautious, irresponsible, madcap, precipitate, reckless, temerarious, venturesome, venturous; ▪ *Ant* careful, cautious, discreet, thoughtful, wary.

foolish [*adj*] *nonsensical, idiotic*
▪ *Syn* absurd, asinine, brainless, crazy, daft, fantastic, fatuous, ill-advised, ill-considered, imprudent, incautious, indiscreet, injudicious, insane, irrational, ludicrous, lunatic, mad, moronic, preposterous, ridiculous, senseless, shortsighted, silly, simple, stupid, weak, witless; ▪ *Ant* careful, cautious, circumspect, prudent, sensible, serious, thoughtful, wise.

foot [*n*] *base of an object*
▪ *Syn* bottom, footing, foundation, lowest point, nadir, pier; ▪ *Ant* apex, head, lid, top.

forbear [*v*] *resist the temptation*
▪ *Syn* abstain, avoid, bridle, cease, curb, decline, desist, escape, eschew, evade, forgo, inhibit, omit, pause, refrain, restrain, sacrifice, shun, stop, withhold; ▪ *Ant* continue, indulge, involve, partake, use.

forbearing [*adj*] *tolerant*
▪ *Syn* charitable, clement, considerate,

easy, forgiving, gentle, humane, indulgent, lenient, longanimous, long-suffering, merciful, mild, moderate, patient, thoughtful; ▪ *Ant* impatient, intolerant, merciless, strict, uncontrolled.

forbid [v] *outlaw, prohibit an action*
▪ *Syn* ban, block, cancel, censor, check, debar, deny, deprive, disallow, embargo, enjoin, exclude, forestall, forfend, halt, hinder, hold up, impede, inhibit, interdict, obstruct, obviate, oppose, preclude, prevent, proscribe, restrain, restrict, rule out, stop, veto, withhold; ▪ *Ant* allow, approve, authorize, permit, sanction.

forbidden [adj] *outlawed, prohibited*
▪ *Syn* banned, closed, contraband, off limits, proscribed, refused, verboten, vetoed; ▪ *Ant* allowed, approved, authorized, permitted, sanctioned.

forbidding [adj] *ominous, daunting*
▪ *Syn* disagreeable, frightening, glowering, grim, hostile, menacing, odious, offensive, repellent, repulsive, sinister, threatening, tough; ▪ *Ant* approachable, friendly, undaunting.

forced [adj] *compulsory, strained*
▪ *Syn* affected, artificial, bound, coerced, coercive, compelled, constrained, contrived, enforced, false, labored, mandatory, obligatory, peremptory, rigid, stiff, strained; ▪ *Ant* effortless, natural, sincere, spontaneous, voluntary.

forceful [adj] *effective, powerful*
▪ *Syn* cogent, commanding, compelling, dominant, dynamic, electric, mighty, persuasive, pithy, potent, powerhouse, puissant, strong, telling, titanic, vigorous, violent, weighty; ▪ *Ant* feeble, impotent, ineffective, meek, weak.

forcible [adj] *powerful, aggressive*
▪ *Syn* active, armed, assertive, coercive, energetic, forceful, impressive, intense, mighty, militant, persuasive, potent, puissant, strong, telling, vigorous, violent, weighty; ▪ *Ant* feeble, weak.

fore [adv] *in the front*
▪ *Syn* ahead, antecedently, before, beforehand, forward, in advance, near, precedently, previous; ▪ *Ant* aft, back, hindmost, rear.

foreboding [n] *misgiving, bad omen*
▪ *Syn* anxiety, apprehension, chill, dread, fear, foreshadowing, forewarning, portent, prediction, premonition, presage, presentiment, prognostic, prophecy,

warning; ▪ *Ant* assurance, confidence, good omen.

forefront/foreground [n] *prominence*
▪ *Syn* beginning, center, focus, fore, front, lead, vanguard; ▪ *Ant* back, background, rear, unimportance.

foregoing [adj] *coming before; previous*
▪ *Syn* above, aforementioned, aforesaid, antecedent, anterior, former, past, precedent, preceding, prior; ▪ *Ant* after, final, following, succeeding.

foreign [adj1] *from another country, experience* ▪ *Syn* adopted, alien, borrowed, derived, different, distant, exotic, external, extralocal, extraneous, extrinsic, far, far-fetched, far-off, immigrant, imported, outside, overseas, remote, strange, transoceanic; ▪ *Ant* familiar, local, national, native.

foreign [adj2] *irrelevant*
▪ *Syn* extraneous, extrinsic, heterogeneous, immaterial, inapposite, incongruous, inconsistent, inconsonant, irrelative, unrelated; ▪ *Ant* characteristic, intrinsic, pertinent, regular, relevant.

foremost [adj] *first in rank, order*
▪ *Syn* arch, champion, chief, first, fore, front, head, highest, inaugural, initial, leading, original, paramount, preeminent, premier, primary, prime, principal, supreme; ▪ *Ant* final, inferior, last, least, lowest, secondary, subordinate, unimportant.

forerunner [n] *example, sign*
▪ *Syn* antecedent, antecessor, augury, exemplar, foretoken, forewarning, indication, mark, model, omen, pattern, portent, precursor, predecessor, premonition, presage, prognostic, prototype, sign, token, warning; ▪ *Ant* conclusion, consequence, effect, result.

foresight [n] *mental preparedness*
▪ *Syn* canniness, care, caution, circumspection, clairvoyance, discernment, discretion, economy, forethought, insight, perception, premeditation, prenotion, prescience, prospect, providence, prudence, sagacity; ▪ *Ant* hindsight, ignorance, indiscretion, thoughtlessness.

forever [adj1] *for all time; everlasting*
▪ *Syn* always, durably, endlessly, enduringly, eternally, everlastingly, evermore, immortally, infinitely, in perpetuum, interminably, lastingly, permanently, perpetually; ▪ *Ant* brief, never, occasionally, temporary.

forever [adj2] *not ceasing, continually*
▪ *Syn* all the time, constantly, endlessly, incessantly, interminably, perpetually, regularly; ▪ *Ant* ceasing, ending, intermittently, never.

foreword [n] *introduction to document*
▪ *Syn* exordium, overture, preamble, preface, preliminary, prelude, prelusion, proem, prolegomenon, prologue; ▪ *Ant* addendum, epilogue, postscript.

forfeit [v] *give up something in sacrifice*
▪ *Syn* abandon, be deprived of, drop, give over, lose, relinquish, renounce, sacrifice, surrender; ▪ *Ant* gain, obtain, profit, win.

forget [v1] *not be able to remember*
▪ *Syn* blow, dismiss, disremember, to remember, misrecollect, obliterate; ▪ *Ant* learn, recall, recollect, remember.

forget [v2] *leave behind*
▪ *Syn* discount, disregard, drop, ignore, neglect, omit, overlook, pass over, skip, slight, transgress, trespass; ▪ *Ant* carry, remember, take.

forgetful [adj] *tending not to remember*
▪ *Syn* absent, absentminded, abstracted, amnemonic, amnesic, bemused, careless, distracted, dreamy, heedless, lax, mooning, neglectful, negligent, nirvanic, oblivious, preoccupied, remiss, slack, sloppy; ▪ *Ant* attentive, mindful, recalling, remembering, retentive.

forgive [v] *stop blaming and grant pardon* ▪ *Syn* absolve, acquit, amnesty, clear, commute, condone, efface, exculpate, excuse, exempt, exonerate, extenuate, forget, overlook, palliate, pardon, pocket, purge, release, relent, remit, reprieve, respite; ▪ *Ant* accuse, blame, censure, charge, punish.

forgo [v] *give up, do without*
▪ *Syn* abandon, abjure, abstain, cede, desist, eschew, forsake, pass, quit, refrain, resist, sacrifice, surrender, waive, yield; ▪ *Ant* continue, indulge, keep, use.

forgotten [adj] *out of one's mind*
▪ *Syn* abandoned, buried, bygone, erased, gone, lapsed, lost, obliterated, omitted, past, repressed, suppressed; ▪ *Ant* recalled, recollected, remembered.

fork [v] *go separate ways*
▪ *Syn* angle, bifurcate, branch, branch off, branch out, divaricate, diverge, divide, part, split; ▪ *Ant* couple, join, link, splice.

forked [adj] *going separate ways*
▪ *Syn* angled, bifid, bifurcated, branch-

ing, dichotomous, divaricate, divided, furcated, pronged, split, tined, tridented; ▪ *Ant* joined, unbranched, united.

forlorn [adj] *hopeless, inconsolable*
▪ *Syn* abandoned, bereft, cheerless, depressed, desolate, despondent, disconsolate, forsaken, lonely, lonesome, lost, miserable, oppressed, pitiful, solitary, tragic, woebegone, wretched; ▪ *Ant* cheerful, comforted, consolable, elated, happy, hopeful, joyful, pleased.

form [v] *bring into existence; make, produce* ▪ *Syn* arrange, assemble, build, cast, concoct, constitute, create, cultivate, cut, design, develop, devise, erect, establish, fashion, found, invent, manufacture, model, mold, organize, outline, pattern, project, shape, structure, trace, work; ▪ *Ant* break, demolish, destroy, hurt, ruin.

formal [adj1] *established, orderly*
▪ *Syn* approved, ceremonial, conventional, decorous, explicit, express, fixed, methodical, official, precise, prescribed, proper, punctilious, regular, rigid, ritual, ritualistic, set, stately, systematic; ▪ *Ant* casual, disorderly, informal, relaxed.

formal [adj2] *stiff, affected, correct*
▪ *Syn* aloof, ceremonious, decorous, exact, nominal, polite, precise, punctilious, reserved, seemly, sententious; ▪ *Ant* informal, normal, relaxed, unaffected.

formality [n] *convention, custom*
▪ *Syn* academism, ceremony, form, gesture, liturgy, officialism, procedure, rite, ritual, rule, service, solemnity, stereotype, tradition; ▪ *Ant* ease, informality.

former [adj] *previous in time or order*
▪ *Syn* above, aforementioned, antecedent, anterior, bygone, departed, earlier, erstwhile, first, foregoing, late, old, once, past, preceding, prior, quondam, sometime; ▪ *Ant* after, current, ensuing, following, future, present, prospective, subsequent, succeeding.

formidable [adj1] *horrible, terrifying*
▪ *Syn* appalling, awful, daunting, dire, dreadful, fearful, frightful, horrific, imposing, menacing, redoubtable, shocking, terrible, threatening; ▪ *Ant* feeble, friendly, harmless, nice, pleasant, powerless, weak.

formidable [adj2] *difficult, overwhelming* ▪ *Syn* arduous, challenging, colossal, hard, impressive, intimidating, laborious, mammoth, mighty, onerous, overpowering, puissant, staggering, strenuous, toilsome, tremendous; ▪ *Ant* easy, pleasant, simple, trivial.

formless [*adj*] *disorganized, vague*
▪ *Syn* amorphous, chaotic, crude, inchoate, indefinite, indeterminate, indistinct, nebulous, obscure, raw, rough, shapeless; ▪ *Ant* coherent, defined, distinct, formed, organized, shaped, specific.

forsake [*v*] *abandon, turn one's back on*
▪ *Syn* abdicate, cast off, desert, disclaim, forgo, forswear, jettison, jilt, leave, quit, renounce, resign, spurn, surrender, yield; ▪ *Ant* go back, rediscover, return, revert.

forsaken [*adj*] *abandoned*
▪ *Syn* cast off, derelict, deserted, desolate, destitute, disowned, forlorn, friendless, ignored, isolated, jilted, lonely, lorn, marooned, outcast, solitary; ▪ *Ant* cherished, helped, nurtured, prized, wanted.

forswear [*v*] *abandon, disavow*
▪ *Syn* abjure, deny, disclaim, disown, drop, forgo, forsake, give up, recall, recant, reject, renounce, repudiate, retract, swear off, take back, withdraw; ▪ *Ant* confirm, go back to, reaffirm, revert.

forte [*n*] *person's strong point*
▪ *Syn* ability, aptitude, competence, effectiveness, efficiency, eminency, faculty, medium, metier, speciality, strength, talent; ▪ *Ant* fault, weakness.

forthcoming [*adj*] *expected, imminent*
▪ *Syn* anticipated, approaching, available, coming, destined, expected, fated, future, impending, inevitable, nearing, oncoming, open, pending, prospective, ready, upcoming; ▪ *Ant* bygone, distant, former, gone, past, remote.

forthright [*adj*] *straightforward, honest*
▪ *Syn* aboveboard, bald, blunt, candid, categorical, direct, forward, frank, open, outspoken, plain, plain-spoken, sincere, straight; ▪ *Ant* deceitful, devious, dishonest, furtive, secret, untruthful.

forthwith [*adv*] *immediately*
▪ *Syn* abruptly, at once, away, directly, instantly, now, quickly, straightaway, suddenly; ▪ *Ant* later, subsequently.

fortify [*v1*] *make strong and secure; add to* ▪ *Syn* brace, build up, bulwark, buttress, embattle, garrison, gird, prepare, prop, protect, ready, reinforce, secure, strengthen, support; ▪ *Ant* debilitate, decrease, undermine, weaken.

fortify [*v2*] *encourage, reassure*
▪ *Syn* brace, cheer, confirm, embolden, energize, enliven, hearten, invigorate, rally, refresh, reinforce, renew, restore, rouse, stiffen, stir, strengthen, sustain; ▪ *Ant* demoralize, discourage, dissuade, weaken.

fortitude [*n*] *strength of mind; guts*
▪ *Syn* boldness, bravery, courage, dauntlessness, determination, endurance, fearlessness, hardihood, intrepidity, mettle, moxie, nerve, perseverance, pith, pluck, resolution, stamina, stoutheartedness, strength, tenacity, valor; ▪ *Ant* cowardice, helplessness, weakness.

fortuitous [*adj*] *lucky, accidental*
▪ *Syn* arbitrary, casual, chance, contingent, fortunate, haphazard, happy, incidental, odd, providential, random, serendipitous; ▪ *Ant* calculated, deliberate, designed, intentional, planned, unlucky.

fortunate [*adj*] *having good luck*
▪ *Syn* advantageous, affluent, auspicious, blessed, charmed, favorable, favored, felicitous, fortuitous, golden, lucky, opportune, promising, prosperous, providential, rosy, successful, thriving, timely, victorious, wealthy, well-off; ▪ *Ant* adverse, baleful, calamitous, sad, unfortunate, unlucky, untoward.

forward [*adj1*] *advancing, early*
▪ *Syn* advanced, leading, onward, precocious, premature, progressive, propulsive, well-developed; ▪ *Ant* backward, later, past, retrogressive, reversing.

forward [*adj2*] *in front, first*
▪ *Syn* advance, anterior, fore, foremost, front, head, leading, ventral; ▪ *Ant* back, last.

forward [*adj3*] *brash, impertinent*
▪ *Syn* aggressive, assuming, audacious, bold, brazen, confident, familiar, fresh, impudent, overassertive, overweening, pert, presumptuous, pushing, rude, self-assertive, smart, wise; ▪ *Ant* meek, modest, reserved, shy, timid.

forward [*v*] *aid, expedite*
▪ *Syn* advance, assist, back, champion, cultivate, encourage, favor, foster, further, hasten, help, hurry, promote, serve, speed, support, uphold; ▪ *Ant* block, cease, halt, hinder, impede, stop.

forward [*adv*] *toward the front in order, time* ▪ *Syn* ahead, alee, along, ante, antecedently, before, beforehand, fore, forth, in advance, onward, precedently, previously, vanward; ▪ **Ant** back, backward, past.

foster [v] *promote, support*
▪ **Syn** advance, back, champion, cherish, cultivate, encourage, feed, foment, forward, further, harbor, nurse, nurture, serve, stimulate, uphold; ▪ **Ant** condemn, discourage, oppose, restrain.

foul [adj1] *disgusting, dirty*
▪ **Syn** abhorrent, abominable, base, contaminated, despicable, egregious, fetid, filthy, hateful, horrid, impure, loathsome, malodorous, nasty, nefarious, noisome, offensive, putrid, repulsive, revolting, rotten, squalid, tainted, vile, wicked; ▪ **Ant** clean, fragrant, pleasing, pure, wonderful.

foul [adj2] *vulgar, offensive*
▪ **Syn** abusive, blasphemous, coarse, dirty, filthy, indecent, lewd, low, nasty, obscene, profane, raunchy, scatological, scurrilous; ▪ **Ant** clean, innocent, inoffensive, moral.

foul [adj3] *corrupt, dishonest*
▪ **Syn** caitiff, crooked, dirty, fraudulent, inequitable, monstrous, shady, underhand, underhanded, vicious; ▪ **Ant** fair, good, honest, incorrupt, just, scrupulous.

foul [v] *make or become dirty*
▪ **Syn** befoul, begrime, besmear, besmirch, contaminate, defile, desecrate, dirty, pollute, profane, smear, smudge, soil, spot, stain, sully, taint, tarnish; ▪ **Ant** clean, purify, sterilize.

foul up [v] *make a mess of*
▪ **Syn** botch, bungle, confuse, jumble, mismanage, muddle, snarl, tumble; ▪ **Ant** fix, mend, organize.

found [v] *bring into being*
▪ **Syn** begin, commence, constitute, create, endow, erect, establish, fashion, fix, form, inaugurate, initiate, institute, launch, organize, plant, raise, settle, start; ▪ **Ant** close, conclude, destroy, end.

founder [v] *go under, fail*
▪ **Syn** abort, break down, collapse, fall, lurch, miscarry, misfire, sink, sprawl, stagger, stumble, submerge, submerse, trip; ▪ **Ant** accomplish, achieve, succeed.

foxy [adj] *shrewd*
▪ **Syn** astute, canny, crafty, cunning, deceitful, devious, dishonest, experienced, insidious, intelligent, knowing, retiary, slick, sly, subtle, tricky, vulpine, wily; ▪ **Ant** artless, frank, guileless, ingenuous, naive.

fracas [n] *disturbance, fight*
▪ **Syn** affray, altercation, battle, brawl, dispute, feud, fray, hassle, melee, quarrel, riot, row, rumpus, scrimmage, scuffle, squabble, trouble, tumult, uproar; ▪ **Ant** accord, agreement, calm, harmony, peace.

fraction [n] *part*
▪ **Syn** bite, chunk, cut, division, end, fragment, half, piece, portion, section, share, slice; ▪ **Ant** entirety, total, whole.

fractious [adj] *grouchy, cross*
▪ **Syn** captious, fretful, froward, intractable, irritable, mean, peevish, petulant, querulous, recalcitrant, restive, testy, thin-skinned, touchy, wayward, wild; ▪ **Ant** agreeable, complaisant, docile, happy, nice, patient.

fragile [adj] *breakable, dainty*
▪ **Syn** brittle, crisp, crumbly, decrepit, delicate, feeble, fine, flimsy, fracturable, frail, friable, infirm, slight, weak; ▪ **Ant** durable, firm, resilient, strong, sturdy, tough, unbreakable.

fragment [n] *part, chip*
▪ **Syn** ace, atom, bit, bite, chunk, crumb, cut, end, fraction, grain, hunk, iota, minim, morsel, particle, piece, portion, remnant, scrap, share, shiver, shred, slice, sliver; ▪ **Ant** entirety, total, whole.

fragmentary [adj] *broken, incomplete*
▪ **Syn** disconnected, discrete, disjointed, fractional, incoherent, part, partial, piecemeal, scattered, scrappy, sketchy; ▪ **Ant** all, complete, total, unbroken, whole.

fragrant [adj] *smelling pleasant*
▪ **Syn** ambrosial, aromatic, delightful, odoriferous, odorous, perfumed, perfumy, redolent, savory, spicy, sweet, sweet-scented, sweet-smelling; ▪ **Ant** malodorous, noxious, putrid, stale, stinking.

frail [adj] *breakable, weak*
▪ **Syn** brittle, dainty, delicate, feeble, flimsy, fragile, frangible, infirm, puny, shatterable, sickly, tenuous, thin, vulnerable, weakly, wispy; ▪ **Ant** firm, strong, substantial, unbreakable.

frank [adj] *completely honest*
▪ **Syn** artless, blunt, candid, direct, downright, easy, forthright, guileless, ingenuous, matter-of-fact, natural, open, outright, plain, real, sincere, straightforward, truthful; ▪ **Ant** devious, dishonest, evasive, insincere, secretive.

frantic [adj] *distressed, distracted*
▪ **Syn** agitated, berserk, corybantic, delir-

ious, distraught, excited, fraught, frenetic, frenzied, hectic, insane, mad, overwrought, raging, violent, wild; ▪ *Ant* calm, collected, composed, docile, peaceful, tranquil.

fraternize [*v*] *socialize with*
▪ *Syn* associate, concur, consort, cooperate, hang out, join, league, mingle, mix, open up, unite; ▪ *Ant* avoid, disagree, ignore, shun.

fraudulent [*adj*] *deceptive, false*
▪ *Syn* counterfeit, crafty, crooked, deceitful, devious, duplicitous, fake, mock, phony, spurious, swindling, treacherous, tricky; ▪ *Ant* authentic, genuine, honest, honorable, real, valid.

fraught [*adj*] *full of*
▪ *Syn* abounding, attended, bristling, charged, filled, heavy, laden, replete, stuffed; ▪ *Ant* devoid, empty, lacking.

frazzle [*v*] *wear out*
▪ *Syn* exhaust, fray, knock out, prostrate, rip, shred, tear, tire, wear; ▪ *Ant* conserve, maintain, preserve, renew, restore.

freakish [*adj*] *abnormal, unusual*
▪ *Syn* aberrant, bizarre, capricious, erratic, fantastic, grotesque, odd, outlandish, preternatural, queer, strange, vagarious, weird, whimsical, wild; ▪ *Ant* common, conventional, general, natural, normal, ordinary, standard, usual.

free [*adj1*] *without charge*
▪ *Syn* complimentary, gratis, gratuitous, handout, unpaid, unrecompensed; ▪ *Ant* costly, expensive, high-priced, priced.

free [*adj2*] *unrestrained personally*
▪ *Syn* casual, disengaged, easy, familiar, forward, frank, informal, lax, liberal, loose, open, permitted, relaxed; ▪ *Ant* bound, confined, hindered, limited, restrained.

free [*adj3*] *unrestrained politically*
▪ *Syn* autonomous, democratic, emancipated, independent, individualistic, liberated, self-governing, self-ruling, separate, sovereign, sui juris; ▪ *Ant* barred, bound, constrained, enslaved, prevented, suppressed.

free [*adj4*] *not busy; unoccupied*
▪ *Syn* at leisure, available, clear, empty, extra, idle, loose, spare, vacant; ▪ *Ant* busy, engaged, occupied, scheduled, tied-up.

free [*adj5*] *generous, unsparing*
▪ *Syn* big, bounteous, bountiful, charitable, eager, handsome, hospitable, lavish,

liberal, munificent, prodigal, unstinging, willing; ▪ *Ant* mean, penurious, tight-fisted.

free [*v1*] *liberate, let go*
▪ *Syn* absolve, acquit, bail, clear, deliver, discharge, dismiss, extricate, loose, manumit, pardon, parole, redeem, release, relieve, reprieve, rescue, save; ▪ *Ant* chain, confine, enslave, fetter, hold, incarcerate, restrain, subjugate.

free [*v2*] *take burden from*
▪ *Syn* cast off, clear, deliver, discharge, disembarrass, disencumber, disengage, disentangle, empty, excuse, exempt, extricate, relieve, rescue, rid, unlade; ▪ *Ant* burden, compel, limit, suppress.

freely [*adv*] *easily, smoothly done*
▪ *Syn* abundantly, amply, bountifully, copiously, effortlessly, facilely, lavishly, liberally, lightly, loosely, open-handedly, readily, well; ▪ *Ant* awkwardly, laboriously, stiffly.

freeze [*v*] *make cold enough to become solid* ▪ *Syn* benumb, bite, chill, congeal, frost, glaciate, harden, ice over, refrigerate, solidify, stiffen; ▪ *Ant* boil, heat, melt, warm.

freezing [*adj*] *very cold*
▪ *Syn* arctic, bitter, cold, cutting, frigid, frosty, gelid, glacial, hawkish, icy, nippy, numbing, penetrating, polar, raw, shivery, wintry; ▪ *Ant* boiling, heated, hot, scorching.

frenetic [*adj*] *maniacal*
▪ *Syn* corybantic, delirious, demented, distraught, excited, fanatical, frantic, frenzied, furibund, furious, insane, mad, obsessive, overwrought, rabid, wild; ▪ *Ant* balanced, calm, composed, tranquil.

frenzied [*adj*] *uncontrolled*
▪ *Syn* agitated, berserk, convulsive, corybantic, delirious, excited, feverish, frantic, furious, hysterical, mad, maniacal, rabid, wild; ▪ *Ant* calm, controlled, placid, serene.

frequent [*adj*] *common, repeated*
▪ *Syn* customary, everyday, expected, familiar, general, habitual, manifold, perpetual, persistent, ubiquitous, usual, various; ▪ *Ant* inconstant, infrequent, irregular, occasional, rare, sporadic, uncommon, unrepeated, unusual.

frequently [*adv*] *commonly, repeatedly*
▪ *Syn* customarily, generally, habitually, many times, much, often, ordinarily, over and over, periodically, recurrently, regu-

larly, successively, usually, very often; ▪ *Ant* infrequently, not much, rarely, seldom, uncommonly.

fresh [*adj1*] *new, just produced*
▪ *Syn* crisp, current, immature, late, latest, modern, modernistic, neoteric, novel, now, original, radical, raw, recent, up-to-date, young, youthful; ▪ *Ant* old, stale, tired, used.

fresh [*adj2*] *refreshing to the senses*
▪ *Syn* bracing, bright, brisk, clean, clear, cool, crisp, fair, invigorating, pure, quick, sharp, sparkling, stiff, stimulating, vivid; ▪ *Ant* musty, polluted, stale.

fresh [*adj3*] *energetic, healthy*
▪ *Syn* active, alert, bright, clear, dewy, florid, glowing, hardy, invigorated, keen, lively, rosy, sprightly, spry, stimulated, verdant, vigorous, vital, wholesome, young; ▪ *Ant* exhausted, lifeless, tired, weary, worn.

fresh [*adj4*] *inexperienced*
▪ *Syn* artless, callow, natural, new, raw, uncultivated, untried, unversed, young, youthful; ▪ *Ant* experienced, skilled, trained.

fresh [*adj5*] *sassy, brazen*
▪ *Syn* bold, familiar, flippant, forward, impertinent, impudent, insolent, pert, presumptuous, rude, wise; ▪ *Ant* courteous, gentle, kind, polite, respectful.

fret [*v1*] *worry, be annoyed*
▪ *Syn* agonize, anguish, bleed, bother, brood, chafe, fume, fuss, grieve, stew; ▪ *Ant* abide, bear, endure.

fret [*v2*] *upset someone*
▪ *Syn* abrade, agitate, bother, distress, disturb, goad, harass, irk, nag, nettle, peeve, ruffle, trouble, vex; ▪ *Ant* appease, pacify, placate, please, soothe.

fretful [*adj*] *irritable*
▪ *Syn* captious, caviling, contrary, critical, edgy, faultfinding, fractious, mean, peevish, petulant, querulous, splenetic, testy, touchy, worried; ▪ *Ant* calm, cheered, easygoing, happy, laid-back, patient, pleased, relaxed.

friction [*n*] *disagreement*
▪ *Syn* animosity, antagonism, bickering, conflict, discontent, discord, factionalism, hassle, hostility, incompatibility, opposition, quarrel, resistance, rivalry, strife, trouble; ▪ *Ant* agreement, harmony, peace.

friend [*n1*] *confidant, companion*
▪ *Syn* acquaintance, ally, associate, co-

hort, colleague, comrade, cousin, crony, familiar, intimate, mate, partner, playmate, sidekick; ▪ *Ant* adversary, enemy, foe, rival.

friend [*n2*] *benefactor*
▪ *Syn* adherent, advocate, ally, associate, backer, partisan, patron, supporter, well-wisher; ▪ *Ant* detractor, opponent.

friendless [*adj*] *without companion or confidant* ▪ *Syn* abandoned, alienated, alone, deserted, estranged, forsaken, isolated, ostracized, shunned, solitary; ▪ *Ant* attached, befriended, beloved, liked, loved.

friendly [*adj*] *intimate, companionable*
▪ *Syn* affable, affectionate, amiable, auspicious, beneficial, benevolent, civil, close, convivial, cordial, genial, helpful, intimate, kind, kindly, loving, neighborly, outgoing, peaceable, propitious, receptive, sociable, solicitous, sympathetic, welcoming; ▪ *Ant* aloof, antagonistic, cold, cool, uncompanionable, unfriendly, unreceptive, unsociable.

frighten [*v*] *shock, scare*
▪ *Syn* agitate, alarm, astound, chill, cow, daunt, demoralize, disconcert, disquiet, faze, horrify, intimidate, petrify, repel, spook, startle, terrify, terrorize; ▪ *Ant* calm, comfort, embolden, encourage, reassure.

frightened [*adj*] *very scared*
▪ *Syn* abashed, afraid, aghast, alarmed, anxious, fearful, frozen, jittery, jumpy, numb, panicky, petrified, startled, terrified, terrorized, terror-stricken, uptight; ▪ *Ant* bold, confident, dauntless.

frightful/frightening [*adj*] *scary, shocking* ▪ *Syn* atrocious, chilling, daunting, dire, dreadful, formidable, ghastly, hair-raising, harrowing, hideous, horrendous, lurid, menacing, morbid, ominous, portentous, repellent, spooky, terrible, traumatic; ▪ *Ant* calming, comforting, pleasing.

frigid [*adj1*] *extremely cold*
▪ *Syn* antarctic, arctic, chilly, cool, freezing, frost-bound, frosty, frozen, gelid, glacial, hyperboreal, ice-cold, icy, wintry; ▪ *Ant* burning, hot, warm.

frigid [*adj2*] *unresponsive*
▪ *Syn* aloof, austere, chilly, cold, cool, forbidding, formal, frosty, icy, indifferent, lifeless, passionless, passive, repellent, rigid, stiff; ▪ *Ant* amicable,

amorous, ardent, lovable, loving, responsive, warm.

fringe [n] *border, trimming*
■ *Syn* borderline, brim, brink, edge, flounce, hem, limit, mane, margin, outskirts, perimeter, periphery, ruffle, skirt, tassel, verge; ■ *Ant* center, inside, interior, middle.

frisky [adj] *full of spirit*
■ *Syn* active, antic, bouncy, dashing, frolicsome, gamesome, high-spirited, jumpy, lively, playful, prankish, romping, spirited, sportive, wicked, zesty, zippy; ■ *Ant* depressed, down, lifeless, sedate, stolid.

fritter [v] *waste away*
■ *Syn* cast away, consume, dally, dissipate, frivol, idle, lavish, misspend, squander, throw away, trifle, waste; ■ *Ant* conserve, hold, save, store.

frivolous [adj] *trivial, silly*
■ *Syn* childish, facetious, flippant, gay, idiotic, juvenile, light, minor, paltry, peripheral, petty, playful, pointless, puerile, senseless, shallow, silly, sportive, superficial, trivial, volatile, whimsical; ■ *Ant* grave, mature, practical, sensible, serious, solemn, thoughtful, wise.

frolicsome [adj] *playful*
■ *Syn* antic, coltish, frisky, fun, gamesome, gay, gleeful, happy, impish, jocular, jovial, kittenish, lively, merry, mischievous, roguish, rollicking, sportive, sprightly; ■ *Ant* restrained, serious, staid, stiff.

front [n] *forward, beginning part of something* ■ *Syn* anterior, bow, breast, exterior, facade, facing, foreground, head, lead, obverse, proscenium, top, vanguard; ■ *Ant* back, end, rear, stern.

front [adj] *lead, beginning*
■ *Syn* advanced, ahead, anterior, facial, first, fore, foremost, forward, frontal, head, headmost, leading, obverse, topmost, vanward, ventral; ■ *Ant* back, ending, final, finishing, rear.

frontier [n] *unexplored, unoccupied area of land* ■ *Syn* backcountry, backwater, backwoods, bush, hinterland, outback, outskirts; ■ *Ant* interior, metropolis, settled region.

frosty [adj] *very cold*
■ *Syn* antarctic, arctic, chill, chilly, frigid, frozen, gelid, glacial, hoar, icy, rimy, shivery, wintry; ■ *Ant* heated, hot, warm.

frown [v] *scowl*
■ *Syn* glare, gloom, glower, grimace, lower, pout, sulk; ■ *Ant* beam, grin, smile.

frown on [v] *disapprove*
■ *Syn* deprecate, discommend, discountenance, discourage, disesteem, disfavor, dislike, object; ■ *Ant* approve, condone, encourage, support.

frozen [adj] *very cold*
■ *Syn* antarctic, arctic, chilled, frigid, frosted, icebound, iced, ice-covered, iced, icy, numb; ■ *Ant* boiled, heated, hot, melted, thawed.

frugal [adj] *economical*
■ *Syn* abstemious, careful, chary, conserving, discreet, meager, meticulous, parsimonious, provident, prudent, saving, scrimping, sparing, stingy, thrifty, wary; ■ *Ant* extravagant, generous, lavish, spendthrifty, wasteful.

fruitful [adj] *productive*
■ *Syn* abundant, blooming, blossoming, copious, effective, fecund, fertile, flourishing, plenteous, plentiful, profitable, profuse, prolific, reproducing, rich, spawning; ■ *Ant* barren, futile, impotent, pointless, sterile, unfruitful, unproductive.

fruitless [adj] *bringing no advantage, product* ■ *Syn* abortive, barren, empty, futile, gainless, idle, pointless, profitless, sterile, useless, vain; ■ *Ant* copious, effective, fruitful, plentiful, potent, productive, profitable, successful, useful.

frustrate [v] *thwart, disappoint*
■ *Syn* annul, arrest, baffle, balk, cancel, check, conquer, counter, counteract, cramp, defeat, depress, discourage, dishearten, foil, forestall, hinder, impede, inhibit, negate, nullify, obstruct, outwit, overcome, prevent, prohibit, ruin; ■ *Ant* advance, aid, assist, cooperate, encourage, facilitate, help, promote, support.

frustrated [adj] *disappointed, thwarted*
■ *Syn* cramped, defeated, discontented, discouraged, disheartened, embittered, foiled, irked, resentful, unsated; ■ *Ant* encourage, fulfilled, inspirited, stimulated, uplifted.

fuel [v] *give energy to*
■ *Syn* charge, fan, feed, fire, gas, incite, inflame, nourish, service, supply, sustain; ■ *Ant* dampen, de-energize, deplete, discourage.

fugitive [adj] fleeing, transient
■ Syn avoiding, brief, criminal, elusive, ephemeral, errant, erratic, escaping, evading, fleeting, fugacious, impermanent, momentary, passing, short-lived, transitory, volatile, wanted; ■ Ant confronting, durable, facing, permanent, stable.

fulfill [v] bring to completion
■ Syn accomplish, achieve, answer, carry out, complete, conclude, conform, discharge, do, effect, execute, finish, implement, keep, meet, obey, observe, perfect, perform, realize, render, satisfy, suffice, suit; ■ Ant disregard, fail, miss, neglect.

full [adj1] brimming, filled
■ Syn abundant, awash, bursting, chock-full, crowded, glutted, gorged, imbued, impregnated, laden, lavish, loaded, overflowing, packed, plenteous, profuse, replete, sated, saturated, stocked, stuffed, suffused, teeming, voluminous, weighted; ■ Ant devoid, empty, incomplete, vacant, void.

full [adj2] thorough
■ Syn absolute, all-inclusive, broad, choate, circumstantial, complete, comprehensive, copious, detailed, entire, exhaustive, extensive, generous, integral, maximum, minute, particular, plenary, whole; ■ Ant incomplete, partial.

full [adj3] deep in sound
■ Syn clear, distinct, loud, resonant, rich, rounded, throaty; ■ Ant faint, light, low.

full-bodied [adj] robust
■ Syn concentrated, full-flavored, heavy, lusty, mellow, potent, redolent, rich, strong; ■ Ant diluted, watered-down, weak.

full-grown/full-fledged [adj] developed, ripe, ready ■ Syn adult, grown, grown-up, mature, of age, perfected, prime, ripened; ■ Ant new, small, underdeveloped, undeveloped, unripe, young.

full-scale [adj] total, all-out
■ Syn all-encompassing, comprehensive, exhaustive, extensive, in-depth, major, proper, sweeping, thorough, thoroughgoing, total, wide-ranging; ■ Ant incomplete, incomprehensive, limited, partial, restrained.

fully [adv1] completely, in all respects
■ Syn absolutely, entirely, intimately, outright, perfectly, positively, quite, thoroughly, totally, utterly, wholly; ■ Ant incompletely, partially, partly.

fully [adv2] sufficiently, adequately
■ Syn abundantly, amply, comprehensively, enough, plentifully, satisfactorily, well; ■ Ant barely, hardly, inadequately, insufficiently, partly.

fulminate [v] criticize harshly
■ Syn animadvert, berate, castigate, censure, curse, declaim, denounce, execrate, intimidate, menace, protest, rage, rail, reprobate, thunder, upbraid, vilify, vituperate; ■ Ant compliment, defend, flatter, praise, support.

fulsome [adj] sickening, excessive
■ Syn adulatory, bombastic, cloying, extravagant, fawning, flattering, glib, grandiloquent, ingratiating, inordinate, insincere, nauseating, offensive, oleaginous, overdone, saccharine, sanctimonious, sycophantic, unctuous; ■ Ant earnest, genuine, reasonable, sincere.

fun [adj] enjoyable
■ Syn amusing, boisterous, convivial, diverting, lively, merry, pleasant, witty; ■ Ant bad, sad, unhappy, woeful.

functional [adj] working
■ Syn operative, practicable, practical, serviceable, useful, utile, utilitarian; ■ Ant broken, idle, malfunctioning.

fund [v] provide money for
■ Syn back, bankroll, capitalize, endow, finance, float, patronize, promote, stake, subsidize, support; ■ Ant divest, take, withdraw.

fundamental [adj] basic, important
■ Syn axiomatic, basal, cardinal, constitutional, elemental, essential, first, integral, intrinsic, key, major, necessary, organic, original, paramount, primary, radical, rudimentary, structural, substrative, theoretical, underlying, vital; ■ Ant additional, advanced, auxiliary, extra, minor, secondary, subordinate, superfluous, trivial, unimportant.

funereal [adj] depressing
■ Syn black, bleak, dark, deathlike, dismal, doleful, dreary, elegiac, gloomy, grim, lamenting, lugubrious, melancholy, mournful, oppressive, sad, sepulchral, somber, woeful; ■ Ant cheerful, festive, happy, joyful, lively, upbeat.

funny [adj1] comical, humorous
■ Syn absurd, antic, capricious, clever, comic, droll, entertaining, gay, hilarious, hysterical, jocose, jocular, laughable, lu-

dicrous, merry, mirthful, playful, rich, ridiculous, riotous, risible, screaming, silly, sportive, waggish, whimsical, witty; ▪ *Ant* dramatic, melancholy, sad, serious, solemn, tragic.

funny [*adj2*] *odd, peculiar*
▪ *Syn* bizarre, curious, dubious, fantastic, mysterious, perplexing, puzzling, queer, remarkable, strange, suspicious, unusual, weird; ▪ *Ant* common, normal, standard, usual.

furious [*adj1*] *extremely angry, very mad*
▪ *Syn* crazed, demented, enraged, fierce, fuming, incensed, infuriated, irrational, livid, maddened, rabid, raging, steamed, vehement, vicious, violent, wrathful; ▪ *Ant* cheerful, elated, happy, pleased.

furious [*adj2*] *stormy, turbulent*
▪ *Syn* agitated, blustery, boisterous, excessive, extreme, fierce, flaming, impetuous, intense, raging, savage, tempestuous, violent, wild; ▪ *Ant* calm, mild, moderate, peaceful, quiet.

furnish [*v1*] *decorate, supply*
▪ *Syn* accoutre, apparel, appoint, arm, array, clothe, endow, equip, fit, gear, outfit, provide, provision, purvey, rig, stock, store, turn out; ▪ *Ant* dismantle, leave plain, strip, unfurnish.

furnish [*v2*] *give; reveal information*
▪ *Syn* afford, bestow, deliver, dispense, endow, feed, grant, hand, hand over, offer, present, provide, supply, transfer; ▪ *Ant* conceal, hide, retain, secrete.

furor [*n*] *disturbance, excitement*
▪ *Syn* agitation, bustle, commotion, frenzy, fury, hysteria, lunacy, mania, outburst, rage, ruckus, tumult, uproar, whirl; ▪ *Ant* calm, peace, tranquility.

further [*v*] *advance, lend support*
▪ *Syn* aid, assist, champion, contribute, encourage, engender, expedite, forward, foster, generate, hasten, help, patronize, plug, promote, serve, speed, succor; ▪ *Ant* block, cease, check, curtail, delay, frustrate, halt, hinder, impede, obstruct, prevent, protest, stop.

furthest [*adj*] *most distant*
▪ *Syn* extreme, farthest, furthermost, outermost, outmost, remotest, ultimate, uttermost; ▪ *Ant* closest, nearest.

furtive [*adj*] *sneaky, secretive*
▪ *Syn* artful, cautious, circumspect, clandestine, covert, disguised, elusive, guileful, hidden, insidious, masked, scheming, skulking, sly, stealthy, surreptitious, wily; ▪ *Ant* aboveboard, forthright, honest, open, truthful.

fuse [*v*] *meld, intermix*
▪ *Syn* agglutinate, amalgamate, bind, cement, coalesce, combine, deliquesce, dissolve, federate, integrate, join, merge, run, smelt, solder, thaw, unite, weld; ▪ *Ant* diffuse, disconnect, divide, separate.

fuss [*n*] *disturbance, trouble*
▪ *Syn* ado, agitation, bother, bustle, commotion, controversy, difficulty, excitement, fight, flap, furor, hassle, objection, perturbation, quarrel, row, ruckus, scene, squabble, stir, storm, turmoil, upset, worry; ▪ *Ant* accord, calm, harmony, peace.

fussy [*adj*] *meticulous, particular*
▪ *Syn* careful, choosy, dainty, discriminating, exacting, fastidious, heedful, overparticular, painstaking, picky, punctilious, querulous, stickling; ▪ *Ant* lax, uncritical, undemanding.

futile [*adj*] *hopeless, pointless*
▪ *Syn* abortive, barren, delusive, empty, exhausted, fruitless, hollow, idle, nugatory, otiose, sterile, trivial, useless, vain, worthless; ▪ *Ant* fruitful, hopeful, productive, profitable, significant.

future [*n*] *time to come*
▪ *Syn* afterward, destiny, eternity, expectation, fate, futurity, hereafter, infinity, millennium, morrow, offing, outlook, posterity, prospect, tomorrow; ▪ *Ant* antiquity, past, yesterday, yesteryear.

future [*adj*] *to come; expected*
▪ *Syn* approaching, coming, destined, eventual, fated, forthcoming, imminent, impending, likely, near, next, planned, prospective, scheduled, subsequent, ulterior, ultimate; ▪ *Ant* bygone, former, past, previous.

fuzzy [*adj1*] *fluffy*
▪ *Syn* downy, flossy, frizzy, furry, hairy, linty, napped, pilate, velutinous, woolly; ▪ *Ant* slick, smooth.

fuzzy [*adj2*] *out of focus*
▪ *Syn* bleary, blurred, foggy, hazy, ill-defined, indefinite, misty, muffled, obscure, shadowy, vague; ▪ *Ant* clear, distinct, focused, sharp.

G

gabby [adj] talkative
▪ *Syn* chattering, chatty, effusive, garrulous, glib, gossiping, gushing, jabbering, loquacious, prattling, prolix, talky, verbose, voluble, wordy; ▪ *Ant* closemouthed, quiet, secretive, silent.

gaily [adv] happily, brightly
▪ *Syn* blithely, brilliantly, cheerfully, gleefully, joyfully, laughingly, lightheartedly, merrily, spiritedly; ▪ *Ant* sadly, solemnly, unhappily.

gain [v] acquire, win
▪ *Syn* accomplish, achieve, advance, annex, attain, augment, benefit, boost, capture, clear, collect, complete, consummate, earn, enlarge, enlist, expand, fulfill, gather, get, glean, grow, harvest, improve, increase, land, make, net, obtain, parlay, procure, produce, profit, progress, promote, reach, realize, reap, secure, succeed; ▪ *Ant* exhaust, forfeit, lose, miss, pass, spend, waste.

gainful [adj] very productive, profitable
▪ *Syn* advantageous, beneficial, fruitful, generous, lucrative, lush, moneymaking, paying, remunerative, rewarding, rich, satisfying, substantial, useful, worthwhile; ▪ *Ant* damaging, disadvantageous, unproductive, unprofitable, useless.

gainsay [v] contradict
▪ *Syn* combat, contravene, controvert, cross, deny, disclaim, disprove, dispute, fight, impugn, negate, oppose, refute, repudiate, resist, traverse; ▪ *Ant* admit, agree, concur, go along.

gall [v] upset, irritate
▪ *Syn* aggravate, annoy, bedevil, bother, burn, chafe, chide, disturb, exasperate, fret, grate, harass, harry, inflame, irk, nag, peeve, pester, plague, provoke, rile, rub, ruffle, scrape, torment, trouble, vex; ▪ *Ant* amuse, cheer, delight, encourage, enliven, exhilarate, please.

gallant [adj] brave, splendid
▪ *Syn* attentive, bold, chivalrous, considerate, courageous, courteous, courtly, daring, dashing, dauntless, dignified, doughty, fearless, glorious, gracious, grand, heroic, honorable, intrepid, lofty, magnanimous, noble, polite, quixotic, stately, stouthearted, suave, thoughtful, urbane, valiant,

valorous; ▪ *Ant* afraid, cowardly, fearful, timid, unmannerly.

galling [adj] very upsetting
▪ *Syn* acid, aggravating, annoying, bitter, bothersome, distasteful, exasperating, harassing, humiliating, irksome, irritating, nettlesome, painful, plaguing, provoking, rankling, unpalatable, vexing; ▪ *Ant* cheering, comforting, pleasing, satisfying, soothing.

gallop [v] bolt, race with slight jumping motion ▪ *Syn* amble, canter, career, course, dart, dash, fly, hasten, hurdle, hurry, jump, leap, lope, pace, run, rush, shoot, speed, spring, sprint, stride, trot; ▪ *Ant* amble, crawl, creep, saunter, walk.

galvanize [v] inspire, stimulate
▪ *Syn* animate, arouse, astonish, awaken, commove, electrify, energize, excite, innervate, invigorate, jolt, motivate, move, pique, provoke, quicken, shock, spur, startle, stir, stun, thrill, vitalize, wake; ▪ *Ant* depress, deter, discourage, dissuade, retard.

gamble [v] take a chance on winning
▪ *Syn* back, bet, brave, challenge, chance, dare, defy, endanger, face, game, hazard, imperil, jeopardize, lot, play, plunge, risk, set, speculate, stake, venture, wager; ▪ *Ant* be careful, design, ensure, guard, insure, plan, safeguard.

game [adj1] brave, willing
▪ *Syn* bold, courageous, dauntless, desirous, disposed, dogged, eager, fearless, gallant, hardy, heroic, inclined, intrepid, prepared, ready, resolute, spirited, spunky, unflinching, valiant, valorous; ▪ *Ant* afraid, cautious, cowardly, disinclined, fearful, unprepared, unwilling.

game [adj2] debilitated
▪ *Syn* ailing, bad, crippled, deformed, disabled, incapacitated, injured, lame, maimed, weak; ▪ *Ant* able, capable, working.

gaping [adj] wide open
▪ *Syn* broad, cavernous, chasmal, great, open, vast, wide, yawning; ▪ *Ant* closed, shut.

garb [v] fit with clothes
▪ *Syn* apparel, array, attire, clad, clothe, cover, deck, drape, dress, garment, raiment, robe; ▪ *Ant* disrobe, divest, unclothe.

garble [v] mix up, misrepresent
▪ *Syn* belie, color, confuse, corrupt, dis-

tort, doctor, falsify, jumble, misinterpret, misquote, mutilate, obscure, pervert, slant, twist, warp; ▪ *Ant* clarify, decipher, order, pronounce, represent, translate.

gargantuan [adj] *very large*
▪ *Syn* big, colossal, elephantine, enormous, gigantic, huge, immense, jumbo, leviathan, mammoth, massive, monstrous, monumental, prodigious, titanic, tremendous, vast; ▪ *Ant* little, miniscule, small, tiny.

garish [adj] *flashy, tasteless*
▪ *Syn* brassy, brazen, cheap, chintzy, gaudy, loud, meretricious, ostentatious, raffish, showy, tawdry, tinsel, vulgar; ▪ *Ant* discreet, modest, normal, plain, simple, tasteful.

garner [v] *collect, accumulate*
▪ *Syn* amass, assemble, cumulate, deposit, extract, glean, harvest, hoard, reap, stockpile, store, treasure; ▪ *Ant* disperse, dissipate, divide, separate, spread.

garnish [v] *embellish, improve*
▪ *Syn* adorn, beautify, bedeck, decorate, dress up, enhance, fix up, grace, ornament, trim; ▪ *Ant* decrease, denude, divest, leave plain, strip.

garrulous [adj] *talkative*
▪ *Syn* babbling, chattering, chatty, effusive, glib, gushing, loquacious, mouthy, prattling, prolix, prosy, verbose, wordy; ▪ *Ant* mum, quiet, reserved, silent, still, taciturn.

gather [v1] *come or bring together*
▪ *Syn* accumulate, aggregate, assemble, capture, choose, cluster, concentrate, congregate, converge, corral, cull, draw, flock, garner, group, heap, herd, marshal, mass, pick, pluck, rally, stockpile, swarm, throng, unite; ▪ *Ant* allot, deal, disperse, distribute, divide, scatter, separate, spread.

gather [v2] *be led to believe; infer*
▪ *Syn* assume, believe, conclude, deduce, draw, expect, find, hear, imagine, judge, learn, make, presume, reckon, suppose, surmise, take, think, understand; ▪ *Ant* misunderstand.

gather [v3] *gain, increase*
▪ *Syn* build, deepen, enlarge, expand, grow, heighten, intensify, rise, swell, thicken, wax; ▪ *Ant* decrease, dissipate, wane.

gauche [adj] *tactless, unsophisticated*
▪ *Syn* awkward, bumbling, clumsy,

crude, green, halting, ignorant, ill-mannered, maladroit, oafish, uncouth; ▪ *Ant* elegant, graceful, mannerly, polished, refined, sophisticated, tactful, tasteful.

gaudy [adj] *bright and vulgar*
▪ *Syn* brazen, chintzy, flashy, florid, garish, gay, jazzy, loud, meretricious, obtrusive, ostentatious, pretentious, raffish, showy, splashy, tasteless, tawdry, tinsel; ▪ *Ant* calm, drab, dull, modest, plain, refined, simple, sophisticated.

gaunt [adj] *skinny*
▪ *Syn* angular, attenuated, bare, bony, cadaverous, emaciated, grim, haggard, lank, lean, meager, peaked, pinched, rawboned, scrawny, skeletal, spare, thin, wasted; ▪ *Ant* plump, thick, well-nourished.

gauzy [adj] *see-through, gossamer in texture* ▪ *Syn* delicate, diaphanous, filmy, flimsy, light, lucid, pellucid, sheer, thin, tiffany, translucent, transparent; ▪ *Ant* cloudy, foggy, heavy, obscured, opaque, substantial, thick.

gawky [adj] *clumsy*
▪ *Syn* awkward, bumbling, clownish, gauche, lumbering, maladroit, oafish, rude, rustic, splay, uncouth, ungainly; ▪ *Ant* athletic, graceful, lithe.

gay [adj1] *happy*
▪ *Syn* animated, blithe, bouncy, cheery, convivial, festive, frolicsome, gamesome, gleeful, hilarious, insouciant, jocund, jovial, keen, lighthearted, merry, mirthful, playful, rollicking, sparkling, spirited, sportive, sunny, vivacious, wild; ▪ *Ant* depressed, discouraged, sad, unhappy, upset, worried.

gay [adj2] *colorful, vivid*
▪ *Syn* bright, brilliant, flamboyant, fresh, garish, intense, rich, showy; ▪ *Ant* colorless, drab, dull, lifeless, plain.

gay [adj3] *homosexual*
▪ *Syn* homoerotic, homophile, lesbian, Sapphic; ▪ *Ant* heterosexual.

general [adj1] *common, accepted*
▪ *Syn* accustomed, broad, commonplace, customary, everyday, familiar, generic, habitual, humdrum, inclusive, normal, ordinary, prevalent, public, regular, routine, typical, usual, widespread; ▪ *Ant* abnormal, exceptional, extraordinary, individual, novel, rare, uncommon, unique, unusual.

general [adj2] inexact, approximate
▪ **Syn** ill-defined, imprecise, inaccurate, indefinite, loose, vague; ▪ **Ant** circumscribed, definite, exact, individual, limited, singular, specific.

general [adj3] comprehensive
▪ **Syn** ample, blanket, broad, catholic, collective, diffuse, ecumenical, encyclopedic, extensive, far-reaching, generic, global, inclusive, indiscriminate, miscellaneous, overall, panoramic, sweeping, total, ubiquitous, universal, wide; ▪ **Ant** circumscribed, limited, particular.

generality [n] vague notion
▪ **Syn** abstraction, abstract principle, generalization, half-truth, law, loose statement, observation, principle, sweeping statement, universality; ▪ **Ant** detail, specific, specificity.

generally [adv] mainly, in most cases
▪ **Syn** altogether, approximately, as a rule, broadly, by and large, chiefly, customarily, extensively, habitually, largely, mostly, normally, ordinarily, predominantly, primarily, principally, roughly, roundly, thereabouts, typically, universally, widely; ▪ **Ant** exactly, particularly, rarely, seldom, specifically.

generate [v] produce, create
▪ **Syn** accomplish, achieve, bear, beget, cause, develop, effect, engender, form, found, give birth to, give rise to, hatch, inaugurate, induce, initiate, make, multiply, muster, occasion, originate, parent, perform, procreate, propagate, provoke, reproduce, spawn, terminate; ▪ **Ant** break, destroy.

generic [adj] common, general
▪ **Syn** all-encompassing, blanket, collective, comprehensive, inclusive, nonexclusive, sweeping, universal, wide; ▪ **Ant** exclusive, individual, particular, specific.

generous [adj1] giving, big-hearted
▪ **Syn** altruistic, beneficent, charitable, equitable, fair, good, helpful, hospitable, just, kind, kindhearted, lavish, liberal, lofty, magnanimous, munificent, noble, open-handed, philanthropic, prodigal, profuse, reasonable, thoughtful, willing; ▪ **Ant** greedy, mean, miserly, selfish, stingy, tight.

generous [adj2] plentiful
▪ **Syn** abundant, affluent, ample, aplenty, bounteous, copious, full, handsome, lavish, liberal, luxuriant, overflowing, plen-

teous, rich, unstinting; ▪ **Ant** depleted, scanty, sparse, wanting.

genesis [n] beginning, creation
▪ **Syn** alpha, birth, commencement, dawn, engendering, formation, generation, inception, origin, propagation, provenience, root, start; ▪ **Ant** conclusion, end, finale, finish, termination.

genetic [adj] hereditary
▪ **Syn** ancestral, congenital, inherited; ▪ **Ant** acquired.

genial [adj] extremely nice and happy
▪ **Syn** affable, agreeable, amiable, blithe, cheerful, congenial, convivial, easygoing, favorable, friendly, gentle, glad, good-natured, gracious, hearty, jolly, kind, merry, neighborly, pleasant, sociable, upbeat, warm, warm-hearted; ▪ **Ant** aloof, cold, cool, cranky, harsh, irritable, moody, morose.

genius [n] gift of high intellect
▪ **Syn** ability, acumen, aptitude, astuteness, brilliance, capability, faculty, grasp, ingenuity, intelligence, originality, prowess, sagacity, talent, wisdom; ▪ **Ant** dullness, ignorance, inability, incompetence, ineptitude.

genteel [adj] polite, elegant
▪ **Syn** affected, aristocratic, artificial, civil, cultivated, distingué, formal, mannerly, polished, pompous, pretentious, priggish, refined, stylish, urbane, well-behaved, well-bred, well-mannered; ▪ **Ant** boorish, callous, coarse, common, crude, rough, rude, rugged, vulgar.

gentle [adj1] having a mild or kind nature ▪ **Syn** benign, biddable, compassionate, considerate, docile, easy, kindly, lenient, meek, merciful, moderate, pacific, peaceful, pliable, quiet, soft, softhearted, sympathetic, temperate, tender, tractable, trained, warmhearted; ▪ **Ant** crude, harsh, rough, violent, wild.

gentle [adj2] mild, temperate in effect on senses ▪ **Syn** balmy, bland, calm, clement, delicate, easy, faint, feeble, halcyon, hushed, imperceptible, light, mild, muted, quiet, soft, subdued, tranquil; ▪ **Ant** harsh, intense, loud, odorous, powerful, putrid, rough, sharp, strong.

genuine [adj1] authentic, real
▪ **Syn** absolute, accurate, authenticated, bona fide, certified, demonstrable, existent, factual, honest, legitimate, natural, official, original, palpable, pure, sound, sterling, tested, true, valid, veritable;

▪ *Ant* artificial, counterfeit, fake, false, fraudulent, illegitimate, sham, unreal.

genuine [*adj2*] *unaffected; honest*
▪ *Syn* actual, artless, candid, earnest, frank, heartfelt natural, open, real, righteous, sincere, true, trustworthy; ▪ *Ant* affected, deceiving, deceptive, dishonest, feigned, insincere, misleading, phony.

germane [*adj*] *appropriate*
▪ *Syn* ad rem, akin, allied, applicatory, apropos, apt, cognate, connected, fitting, kindred, material, pertinent, related, relevant, suitable; ▪ *Ant* extraneous, inappropriate, incongruous, irrelevant.

germinate [*v*] *grow*
▪ *Syn* bud, develop, generate, live, originate, pullulate, shoot, sprout, swell, vegetate; ▪ *Ant* halt, slow, stop, thwart.

get [*v1*] *come into possession of; achieve*
▪ *Syn* accomplish, acquire, annex, attain, capture, clear, come by, compass, draw, earn, educe, elicit, evoke, extort, extract, fetch, gain, glean, grab, have, inherit, land, make, net, obtain, parlay, procure, pull down, pull in, realize, reap, secure, take, win; ▪ *Ant* abandon, fail, forsake, lose, miss, pass.

get [*v2*] *fall victim to*
▪ *Syn* accept, be afflicted with, catch, contract, receive, sicken, succumb, take; ▪ *Ant* be immune to, overtake, overthrow, resist.

get [*v3*] *seize*
▪ *Syn* apprehend, arrest, capture, defeat, grab, occupy, overpower, secure, take, trap; ▪ *Ant* free, give in, release, surrender, yield.

get [*v4*] *understand*
▪ *Syn* catch, catch on, comprehend, fathom, follow, gain, hear, know, learn, memorize, notice, perceive, receive, see, take in, work out; ▪ *Ant* misconstrue, misunderstand.

get [*v5*] *arrange, manage to obtain desired goal* ▪ *Syn* adjust, contrive, dispose, make, order, prepare, ready, straighten, succeed; ▪ *Ant* fail, mismanage.

get [*v6*] *have an emotional effect on*
▪ *Syn* affect, bend, bias, carry, dispose, entertain, excite, gratify, impress, influence, move, predispose, stimulate, stir, strike, sway, touch; ▪ *Ant* benumb, blunt, deaden, dull, harden, numb.

get [*v7*] *irritate, upset*
▪ *Syn* aggravate, annoy, bother, burn, exasperate, gall, irk, nettle, peeve, pique, provoke, rile, try, vex; ▪ *Ant* calm, please, soothe.

get ahead [*v*] *excel, succeed*
▪ *Syn* advance, be successful, climb, do well, flourish, get on, make good, outdo, progress, prosper, surpass, thrive; ▪ *Ant* fail, fall behind.

get along [*v*] *make progress*
▪ *Syn* cope, develop, flourish, make out, manage, progress, shift, succeed, thrive; ▪ *Ant* cease, halt, regress, stop.

get at [*v*] *convince, induce*
▪ *Syn* argue into, beg, coax, draw into, influence, persuade, pressure, sway, talk into, urge, wheedle, win over; ▪ *Ant* discourage, dissuade.

get back [*v1*] *regain*
▪ *Syn* reclaim, recoup, recover, repossess, retrieve, salvage; ▪ *Ant* forfeit, lose, miss, pass.

get back [*v2*] *return*
▪ *Syn* arrive home, come back, come home, reappear, revert, revisit, turn back; ▪ *Ant* depart, go away, leave.

get down [*v*] *dismount*
▪ *Syn* alight, come down, descend, disembark, get off, lower, step down; ▪ *Ant* ascend, climb, get up, mount, scale.

get on [*v1*] *be compatible*
▪ *Syn* agree, be friendly, concur, get along, harmonize, hit it off; ▪ *Ant* argue, bicker, disagree.

get on [*v2*] *put clothing on*
▪ *Syn* assume, attire, don, draw on, dress, slip into, throw on, wear; ▪ *Ant* denude, disrobe, doff, remove, unclothe.

get out [*v*] *escape*
▪ *Syn* avoid, break out, clear out, depart, dodge, duck, egress, evacuate, evade, flee, go, leave, run away, shirk, split, take off, vacate, withdraw; ▪ *Ant* capture, grab, seize.

get to [*v*] *arrive*
▪ *Syn* advance, come, come to, converge, draw near, land, make it, reach, show, turn up; ▪ *Ant* depart, leave.

get together [*v*] *meet; accumulate*
▪ *Syn* assemble, collect, congregate, convene, converge, gather, join, meet, muster, rally, unite; ▪ *Ant* disperse, distribute, divide, scatter, separate.

ghastly [*adj*] *horrifying, dreadful; pale*
▪ *Syn* abhorrent, appalling, ashen, bloodless, cadaverous, corpselike, deathlike, dim, frightening, funereal, ghostly,

ghoulish, grim, haggard, hideous, horrid, lurid, macabre, mortuary, nauseating, offensive, pallid, repellent, sepulchral, shocking, spectral, supernatural, terrifying, unearthly, wan, wraithlike; ▪ *Ant* appealing, delightful, pleasant, pleasing, robust, ruddy, wonderful.

giant [*adj*] *very large*
▪ *Syn* big, colossal, cyclopean, enormous, gargantuan, gigantic, huge, hulking, immense, mammoth, mountainous, prodigious, titanic, vast; ▪ *Ant* dwarf, little, miniature, miniscule, minor, small, teeny, tiny.

gibe [*v*] *ridicule*
▪ *Syn* deride, disrespect, flout, jeer, mock, scoff, scorn, sneer, taunt; ▪ *Ant* admire, commend, laud, praise.

giddy [*adj*] *silly, impulsive*
▪ *Syn* bemused, brainless, capricious, careless, dizzy, erratic, fickle, flustered, heedless, inconstant, irresolute, reckless, thoughtless, vacillating, volatile, whimsical, wild; ▪ *Ant* calm, careful, earnest, levelheaded, sensible, serious, stable, steady.

gifted [*adj*] *talented, intelligent*
▪ *Syn* able, accomplished, adroit, brilliant, capable, clever, expert, hotshot, ingenious, phenomenal, skilled, smart; ▪ *Ant* dull, incapable, inept, untalented.

gigantic [*adj*] *very large*
▪ *Syn* colossal, elephantine, enormous, gargantuan, giant, huge, immense, mammoth, massive, monstrous, prodigious, stupendous, titan, tremendous, vast; ▪ *Ant* dwarfed, little, microscopic, miniature, miniscule, puny, small, teeny, tiny.

gingerly [*adj*] *careful*
▪ *Syn* calculating, cautious, chary, delicate, discreet, fastidious, guarded, hesitant, reluctant, safe, squeamish, timid, wary; ▪ *Ant* careless, daring, impetuous, rash, rough.

gingerly [*adv*] *carefully*
▪ *Syn* cautiously, circumspectly, daintily, delicately, fastidiously, guardedly, hesitantly, reluctantly, suspiciously, timidly, warily; ▪ *Ant* boldly, carelessly, heedlessly, rashly, roughly, uncautiously.

gird [*v*] *encircle; strengthen*
▪ *Syn* band, bind, blockade, bolster, buttress, cincture, circle, enclose, encompass, fortify, girdle, prepare, ready, reinforce, ring, secure, surround; ▪ *Ant* erode, let go, weaken.

give [*v1*] *contribute, supply, transfer*
▪ *Syn* accord, administer, award, bequeath, bestow, cede, confer, consign, deliver, dispense, donate, endow, entrust, furnish, grant, hand out, lease, parcel out, pass down, permit, present, provide, relinquish, sell, subsidize, turn over, vouchsafe, will; ▪ *Ant* hold, keep, retain, take, withdraw, withhold.

give [*v2*] *communicate*
▪ *Syn* air, announce, broadcast, carry, deliver, emit, furnish, impart, issue, notify, present, pronounce, render, state, transmit, utter, ventilate; ▪ *Ant* conceal, keep, refrain, withhold.

give [*v3*] *yield, collapse*
▪ *Syn* allow, bend, bow to, cave, concede, crumble, fall, flex, fold, go, open, recede, relent, relinquish, retreat, sag, sink, slacken, surrender, weaken; ▪ *Ant* fight, hold up, withstand.

give away [*v1*] *reveal*
▪ *Syn* betray, disclose, discover, divulge, expose, inform, leak, let slip, spill, tell, uncover; ▪ *Ant* conceal, hide, keep secret, mask.

give away [*v2*] *unselfishly transfer*
▪ *Syn* award, bestow, devote, donate, hand out, present; ▪ *Ant* keep, keep back, reain, withhold.

give in/give up [*v*] *admit defeat*
▪ *Syn* abandon, capitulate, cede, collapse, comply, concede, despair, drop, fold, quit, relinquish, resign, submit, surrender, waive, yield; ▪ *Ant* fight, hold out, stand up to, withstand.

glacial [*adj1*] *extremely cold*
▪ *Syn* arctic, biting, chilly, cold, freezing, frigid, frosty, frozen, gelid, icy, piercing, polar, raw; ▪ *Ant* balmy, hot, mild, warm.

glacial [*adj2*] *unfriendly*
▪ *Syn* aloof, antagonistic, cool, distant, frigid, hostile, icy, inaccessible, remote, reserved, standoffish, withdrawn; ▪ *Ant* amicable, friendly, responsive, warm.

glad [*adj*] *happy, delightful*
▪ *Syn* animated, bright, cheery, contented, delighted, exhilarated, felicitous, gay, genial, gleeful, gratifying, hilarious, joyous, lighthearted, merry, mirthful, overjoyed, pleasant, radiant, sparkling, tickled; ▪ *Ant* blue, dejected, despondent, melancholy, morose, sad, sorrowful, unhappy.

glamorous [adj] *sophisticated in style*
▪ **Syn** alluring, attractive, bewitching, captivating, classy, dazzling, elegant, entrancing, flashy, glossy, lovely, magnetic, seductive, siren, smart; ▪ **Ant** drab, dull, lackluster, plain, ugly.

glance [v] *look at briefly*
▪ **Syn** browse, check out, flip through, gaze, glimpse, leaf through, peek, peep, peer, run through, scan, see, take in, view; ▪ **Ant** inspect, scrutinize, stare, study.

glare [v1] *give a dirty look*
▪ **Syn** bore, fix, frown, gape, gawk, gaze, glower, lower, menace, peer, pierce, scowl, stare, wither; ▪ **Ant** glance, grin, smile.

glaring [adj1] *obvious, unconcealed*
▪ **Syn** blatant, brazen, conspicuous, crying, egregious, evident, flagrant, gross, inordinate, manifest, noticeable, obtrusive, overt, patent, protrusive, rank, visible; ▪ **Ant** concealed, discreet, hidden, subtle.

glaring [adj2] *bright, dazzling; flashy*
▪ **Syn** blazing, blinding, brazen, chintzy, florid, garish, glowing, loud, meretricious, shining, tawdry; ▪ **Ant** dark, dull, plain, soft.

glassy [adj] *polished, smooth*
▪ **Syn** burnished, clear, glazed, glossy, hyaline, icy, lustrous, shiny, sleek, slippery, transparent, vitreous; ▪ **Ant** dull, rough, rugged, uneven.

glaze [v] *varnish, lacquer*
▪ **Syn** buff, burnish, coat, cover, enamel, furbish, gloss, overlay, polish, rub, shine; ▪ **Ant** coarsen, roughen, strip.

gleeful [adj] *very happy*
▪ **Syn** blithe, cheerful, delighted, elated, exultant, frolicsome, gay, jocund, jolly, jubilant, lighthearted, merry, mirthful, overjoyed, pleased, triumphant; ▪ **Ant** discouraged, sad, sorrowful, unhappy, upset, worried.

glib [adj] *slick, smooth-talking*
▪ **Syn** artful, articulate, eloquent, facile, fluent, garrulous, loquacious, plausible, quick, ready, smooth, suave, urbane, vocal, voluble; ▪ **Ant** halting, quiet, sincere, stuttering, tongue-tied.

glide [v] *move smoothly and quickly on surface* ▪ **Syn** coast, descend, drift, flit, float, flow, glissade, roll, run, sail, skim, skirr, slide, slink, slither, soar, stream, waft, wing; ▪ **Ant** bump, lurch, stagger.

glimpse [v] *look briefly*
▪ **Syn** catch sight of, check out, descry, espy, eye, flash, peek, sight, spot, spy, view; ▪ **Ant** inspect, observe, scrutinize, stare.

gloat [v] *feel triumphant satisfaction*
▪ **Syn** celebrate, exult, glory, rejoice, relish, triumph, vaunt; ▪ **Ant** commiserate, sympathize.

global [adj] *worldwide, all-encompassing* ▪ **Syn** all-around, all-inclusive, blanket, catholic, comprehensive, cosmic, cosmopolitan, earthly, ecumenical, encyclopedic, exhaustive, general, international, mundane, overall, pandemic, planetary, spherical, sweeping, thorough, total, universal, world; ▪ **Ant** individual, limited, local, parochial, provincial, regional, restricted.

gloomy [adj1] *dark, black*
▪ **Syn** bleak, caliginous, cheerless, cloudy, crepuscular, desolate, dim, dismal, dreary, dull, dusky, forlorn, funereal, lightless, murky, obscure, overcast, sepulchral, shadowy, somber, tenebrous; ▪ **Ant** bright, illuminated, light, radiant, sunny.

gloomy [adj2] *feeling down, blue*
▪ **Syn** broody, chapfallen, cheerless, crestfallen, dejected, depressed, despondent, dispirited, dour, down, downcast, forlorn, glum, joyless, low, melancholy, mirthless, moody, moping, morose, pessimistic, sad, saturnine, sullen, weary, woebegone; ▪ **Ant** animated, blithe, cheerful, content, encouraged, happy, joyful, merry, sparkling, vivacious.

gloomy [adj3] *sad, depressing*
▪ **Syn** acheronian, bad, black, bleak, cheerless, cold, comfortless, depressive, discouraging, disheartening, dismal, dispiriting, drab, dreary, funereal, joyless, lugubrious, morose, oppressive, saddening, somber, tenebrific; ▪ **Ant** cheerful, encouraging, exhilarating, happy, uplifting.

glorify [v1] *praise*
▪ **Syn** acclaim, bless, celebrate, commend, cry up, eulogize, exalt, extol, hike, honor, hymn, laud, lionize, magnify, panegyrize, put up; ▪ **Ant** castigate, condemn, criticize, debase, defile, degrade.

glorify [v2] *adore, idolize*
▪ **Syn** adorn, aggrandize, apotheosize, augment, beatify, bless, canonize, deify,

dignify, distinguish, elevate, ennoble, enshrine, erect, exalt, honor, immortalize, lift up, magnify, pay homage to, raise, revere, sanctify, transfigure, uprear, venerate, worship; ▪ *Ant* desecrate, humiliate, lower, mock, profane, shame.

glorious [*adj*] *adored, idiolized; divine*
▪ *Syn* august, beautiful, brilliant, celebrated, dazzling, distinguished, elevated, eminent, esteemed, exalted, grand, great, heavenly, heroic, honored, illustrious, immortal, magnificent, majestic, marvelous, noble, preeminent, radiant, renowned, resplendent, shining, splendid, sublime, superb, triumphant, venerable, wonderful; ▪ *Ant* atrocious, awful, bad, contemptible, disgraceful, shameful.

gloss [*v*] *conceal truth*
▪ *Syn* belie, camouflage, cover up, disguise, doctor, extenuate, falsify, hide, justify, mask, misrepresent, palliate, rationalize, smooth over, soft-pedal, varnish, veil, whiten; ▪ *Ant* clear up, emphasize, exaggerate, explain, reveal.

glossy [*adj*] *shiny*
▪ *Syn* brilliant, glazed, gleaming, glistening, lustrous, polished, reflecting, shining, silken, sleek, slick, smooth; ▪ *Ant* drab, dull, mate, muted.

glower [*v*] *frown*
▪ *Syn* glare, gloom, look, lower, scowl, stare, sulk, watch; ▪ *Ant* grin, laugh, smile.

glowing [*adj*] *very happy, enthusiastic*
▪ *Syn* adulatory, ardent, avid, blazing, burning, complimentary, ecstatic, eulogistic, fervent, fervid, impassioned, keen, laudatory, panegyrical, passionate, rave, rhapsodic, zealous; ▪ *Ant* cool, dispassionate, dull, halfhearted.

glut [*n*] *overabundance*
▪ *Syn* excess, nimiety, plenitude, saturation, superabundance, superfluity, surfeit, surplus; ▪ *Ant* dearth, insufficiency, lack, need, paucity, want.

glut [*v*] *choke; oversupply*
▪ *Syn* burden, clog, cloy, congest, deluge, devour, flood, gorge, inundate, jade, load, overfeed, pall, raven, satiate, stuff, surfeit; ▪ *Ant* abstain, deny, diet, fast, moderate, reduce, repress, suppress.

gnarled [*adj*] *knotted*
▪ *Syn* bent, contorted, crooked, deformed, distorted, knotty, knurled, rugged, tortured, twisted, weather-beaten,

wrinkled; ▪ *Ant* flat, level, smooth, straight.

go [*v1*] *advance, proceed physically*
▪ *Syn* approach, cruise, depart, exit, fare, get away, hie, journey, lam, leave, move, pass, progress, push off, push on, quit, repair, run along, run away, set off, take flight, travel, wend, withdraw; ▪ *Ant* abide, arrive, come, remain, stay, stop.

go [*v2*] *agree, harmonize*
▪ *Syn* accord, belong, blend, chime, complement, conform, correspond, enjoy, fit, like, match, mesh, relish, set, square, suit; ▪ *Ant* clash, conflict, disagree, mismatch.

goad [*v*] *egg on, incite*
▪ *Syn* animate, annoy, bully, coerce, drive, encourage, exhort, force, harass, hound, impel, instigate, irritate, lash, move, press, prod, provoke, push, rowel, sound, spur, tease, thrust, trigger, urge, work up, worry; ▪ *Ant* curb, deter, discourage, dissuade, restrain.

go ahead [*v*] *proceed*
▪ *Syn* advance, begin, continue, dash ahead, edge forward, move on, progress, shoot ahead; ▪ *Ant* cease, discontinue, finish, halt, regress, revert, stop.

go-ahead [*n*] *authorization*
▪ *Syn* assent, consent, leave, okay, permission; ▪ *Ant* ban, denial, refusal, veto.

go along/go along with [*v*] *agree, cooperate* ▪ *Syn* accompany, acquiesce, assent, collaborate, concur, conspire, follow; ▪ *Ant* balk, disagree, fight, refuse.

gobble [*v*] *eat hurriedly*
▪ *Syn* devour, gorge, guzzle, ingurgitate, swallow; ▪ *Ant* nibble, pick.

godless [*adj*] *not religious*
▪ *Syn* agnostic, atheistic, depraved, evil, heathen, impious, infidel, irreligious, nonreligious, profane, wicked; ▪ *Ant* devout, godly, holy, religious.

godly [*adj*] *religious*
▪ *Syn* angelic, celestial, deific, devout, divine, god-fearing, good, holy, pious, prayerful, righteous, saintlike, saintly, virtuous; ▪ *Ant* godless, hellish, impious, irreligious, sacrilegious, sinful, ungodly, wicked.

go down [*v*] *lose, fall*
▪ *Syn* be beaten, be defeated, cave in, collapse, crumple, drop, fold, founder, go under, keel, lessen, pitch, plunge, reduce, sag, set, sink, slump, submerge, submit, succumb, topple, tumble; ▪ *Ant*

ascend, burgeon, climb, gain, go up, increase, rise.

golden [adj] beautiful, advantageous
▪ **Syn** auspicious, best, blissful, delightful, excellent, favorable, glorious, happy, joyful, joyous, opportune, precious, promising, resplendent, rich, shining, valuable; ▪ **Ant** black, bleak, gloomy, hostile, ill-fated, poor, threatening, wretched.

gone [adj] not present, no longer in existence ▪ **Syn** absent, astray, consumed, dead, deceased, defunct, departed, displaced, dissipated, dissolved, dried up, elapsed, ended, extinct, finished, flown, lacking, lost, missing, moved, over, past, quit, removed, retired, spent, transferred, vanished, withdrawn; ▪ **Ant** active extant, around, current, existing, living, present.

good [adj1] pleasant, fine
▪ **Syn** acceptable, agreeable, capital, commendable, congenial, excellent, exceptional, favorable, first-class, first-rate, great, marvelous, nice, pleasing, positive, prime, satisfactory, sound, splendid, superb, valuable, welcome, wonderful, worthy; ▪ **Ant** awful, bad, detestable, disagreeable, harsh, unpleasant, worthless.

good [adj2] moral, virtuous
▪ **Syn** admirable, blameless, charitable, dutiful, estimable, ethical, exemplary, guiltless, honest, honorable, incorrupt, inculpable, obedient, praiseworthy, pure, reputable, respectable, righteous, sound, tractable, upright, well-behaved, worthy; ▪ **Ant** corrupt, evil, immoral, noxious, reprehensible, sinful, vile, wicked.

good [adj3] competent, skilled
▪ **Syn** able, accomplished, adept, adroit, au fait, capable, clever, dexterous, efficient, expert, proficient, proper, qualified, reliable, satisfactory, serviceable, skillful, suitable, suited, talented, thorough; ▪ **Ant** clumsy, incompetent, inept, unskilled.

good [adj4] useful, adequate
▪ **Syn** acceptable, advantageous, all right, ample, appropriate, beneficial, commendatory, convenient, decent, favorable, fruitful, healthful, helpful, needed, opportune, profitable, propitious, respectable, right, salubrious, salutary, satisfying, seemly, serviceable, suitable, tolerable, toward, wholesome; ▪ **Ant**

damaging, detrimental, inadequate, objectionalbe, rotten, unsuitable, wrong.

good [adj5] reliable; untainted
▪ **Syn** dependable, flawless, fresh, intact, loyal, safe, solid, sound, stable, trustworthy, vigorous, whole; ▪ **Ant** blemished, decayed, noxious, rotten, spoiled, tainted.

good [adj6] kind, giving
▪ **Syn** altruistic, benevolent, charitable, friendly, gracious, humane, kindhearted, merciful, obliging, philanthropic, tolerant; ▪ **Ant** bad, cold, heartless, mean, vicious.

good [adj7] authentic, real
▪ **Syn** bona fide, genuine, honest, justified, legitimate, loyal, orthodox, sound, strict, true, trustworthy, valid, well-founded; ▪ **Ant** fake, forged, phony.

good [adj8] well-behaved
▪ **Syn** considerate, decorous, dutiful, kindly, mannerly, obedient, polite, proper, respectful, seemly, thoughtful, tractable, well-mannered; ▪ **Ant** bad, misbehaving, mischievous, naught.

good [adj9] considerable
▪ **Syn** adequate, ample, big, extensive, full, great, immeasurable, large, lucrative, respectable, sizable, substantial, sufficient, worthwhile; ▪ **Ant** inconsequential, inconsiderable, meager, slight, trivial.

good-humored [adj] funny, happy
▪ **Syn** affable, amiable, buoyant, cheerful, complaisant, congenial, easy, genial, good-natured, lenient, merry, mild, obliging, pleasant, smiling; ▪ **Ant** ill-humored, irritable, morose, sad, surly.

good-looking [adj] attractive
▪ **Syn** beauteous, beautiful, clean-cut, comely, fair, handsome, impressive, lovely, pretty, pulchritudinous; ▪ **Ant** dull, homely, ugly.

good-natured [adj] easygoing, easily pleased ▪ **Syn** acquiescent, agreeable, amiable, benevolent, breezy, complaisant, cordial, easy, even-tempered, friendly, gracious, helpful, kindly, lenient, moderate, nice, obliging, tolerant, warmhearted, well-disposed; ▪ **Ant** bad, contrary, cross, mean, peerish.

good will/goodwill [n] kindliness
▪ **Syn** altruism, amity, benevolence, charity, comity, cordiality, favor, friendliness, generosity, helpfulness, kindness, rapport, sympathy, tolerance; ▪ **Ant**

animosity, ill will, malevolence, meanness.

go on [v] *continue*
▪ *Syn* act, advance, bear, behave, carry on, endure, keep on, last, persist, proceed, ramble, stay, take place; ▪ *Ant* cease, falter, give up, halt, stop.

go out [v] *become extinguished*
▪ *Syn* burn out, cease, darken, die, die out, dim, expire, fade out, flicker; ▪ *Ant* flare up, inflame, kindle.

gorge [v] *eat voraciously*
▪ *Syn* cloy, cram, devour, feed, fill, glut, gobble, gormandize, jade, jam, overeat, overindulge, pack, satiate, swallow; ▪ *Ant* abstain, diet, fast, nibble.

gorgeous [adj] *beautiful, magnificent*
▪ *Syn* attractive, bright, dazzling, elegant, fine, good-looking, handsome, impressive, lavish, lovely, luxuriant, luxurious, pleasing, plush, pulchritudinous, ravishing, resplendent, splendid, stunning, sublime, sumptuous, superb; ▪ *Ant* bleak, cheap, hideous, homely, shoddy, ugly.

gossamer [adj] *gauzy, thin*
▪ *Syn* airy, cobweb, delicate, diaphanous, fine, flimsy, light, sheer, silky, tiffany, translucent, transparent; ▪ *Ant* coarse, heavy, rugged, thick.

go through [v1] *endure*
▪ *Syn* bear, brave, experience, suffer, support, survive, swallow, tolerate, undergo, withstand; ▪ *Ant* surrender, yield.

go through [v2] *use up*
▪ *Syn* consume, deplete, exhaust, pay out, spend, squander; ▪ *Ant* hoard, save, store.

go under [v] *fail; submerge*
▪ *Syn* go bankrupt, default, die, drown, fall, fold, founder, go down, sink, submerge, submit, succumb, suffocate, surrender; ▪ *Ant* accomplish, achieve, endure, prevail, succeed, triumph.

govern [v1] *take control; rule*
▪ *Syn* administer, assume command, control, dictate, direct, execute, guide, head, lead, manage, order, oversee, pilot, render, run, steer, supervise, tyrannize; ▪ *Ant* comply, obey, surrender, yield.

govern [v2] *influence; hold in check*
▪ *Syn* bridle, check, contain, control, curb, direct, discipline, dispose, dominate, guide, handle, inhibit, manage, regulate, restrain, rule, shepherd, steer, subdue, tame; ▪ *Ant* acquiesce, allow, consent, give way, permit.

grab [v] *latch on to*
▪ *Syn* capture, catch, clutch, grapple, grasp, grip, hook, land, nab, nail, pluck, seize, snatch, take; ▪ *Ant* drop, let go, release.

grace [v] *beautify, embellish*
▪ *Syn* adorn, bedeck, crown, deck, decorate, dignify, distinguish, elevate, enhance, enrich, favor, garnish, glorify, honor, laureate, ornament, set off; ▪ *Ant* disfigure, disgrace, mar.

graceful [adj] *agile, charming, lovely*
▪ *Syn* adroit, balletic, beautiful, comely, dainty, delicate, dexterous, elastic, elegant, exquisite, fair, fine, handsome, limber, lithe, natural, nimble, pleasing, pliant, poised, refined, seemly, shapely, smooth, springy, statuesque, supple, symmetrical, tasteful; ▪ *Ant* awkward, careless, graceless, inept, uncouth, ungainly, ungraceful.

graceless [adj] *clumsy, unsophisticated*
▪ *Syn* awkward, barbarous, boorish, coarse, forced, gauche, ill-mannered, inept, loutish, oafish, rough, rude, tasteless; ▪ *Ant* elegant, refined, sophisticated.

gracious [adj] *kind, giving*
▪ *Syn* accommodating, affable, approachable, beneficent, benign, charitable, compassionate, complaisant, congenial, cordial, courteous, easy, forthcoming, friendly, gallant, genial, good-hearted, good-natured, hospitable, kindly, lenient, loving, merciful, obliging, polite, sociable, unctuous, urbane, well-mannered; ▪ *Ant* discourteous, hateful, mean, nasty, rude, sarcastic, severe, vulgar.

gradual [adj] *happening slowly, evenly*
▪ *Syn* by degrees, continuous, creeping, even, gentle, moderate, progressive, regular, slow, steady, successive; ▪ *Ant* abrupt, hurried, infrequent, intermittent, sudden.

grand [adj1] *impressive, great*
▪ *Syn* august, dignified, elevated, eminent, fine, first-rate, grandiose, illustrious, imposing, large, lofty, magnificent, marvelous, monumental, ostentatious, outstanding, palatial, smashing, splendid, stately, striking, sublime, sumptuous, superb, terrific; ▪ *Ant* bad, common, inferior, low, paltry, pitiful, poor.

grand [adj2] *most important*
▪ *Syn* chief, dignified, grave, head, highest, leading, lofty, main, majestic, mighty, preeminent, principal, regal, su-

preme, transcendent; ▪ *Ant* incidental, inferior, insignificant, trivial, unimportant.

grandiloquent [*adj*] *pretentious, flowery (communication)* ▪ *Syn* aureate, bombastic, declamatory, euphistic, fustian, high-flown, inflated, magniloquent, oratorical, overblown, pompous, rhetorical, sonorous, swollen, verbose; ▪ *Ant* direct, matter-of-fact, plain, simple, unadorned, unpretentious.

grandiose [*adj*] *theatrical, extravagant* ▪ *Syn* affected, ambitious, bombastic, cosmic, egotistic, flamboyant, fustian, grand, high-flown, impressive, magnificent, ostentatious, pretentious, royal, showy, splashy, stately, vast; ▪ *Ant* calm, moderate, small, trifling, unpretentious.

grant [*v*] *authorize, allow* ▪ *Syn* accede, accept, accord, acknowledge, acquiesce, admit, agree to, allocate, allow, assume, avow, award, bestow, bless, cede, concede, confer, consent, convey, donate, drop, impart, invest, own, permit, present, profess, relinquish, stake, suppose, surrender, transfer, transmit, vouchsafe, yield; ▪ *Ant* condemn, deny, dissent, object, refuse, veto.

graphic [*adj1*] *clear, explicit* ▪ *Syn* clear-cut, cogent, comprehensible, concrete, definite, descriptive, detailed, distinct, expressive, illustrative, incisive, intelligible, lively, lucid, perspicuous, precise, realistic, telling, vivid; ▪ *Ant* abstract, equivocal, hazy, implicit, obscure, vague.

graphic [*adj2*] *pictorial, visible* ▪ *Syn* delineated, depicted, diagrammatic, drawn, iconographic, illustrated, outlined, painted, photographic, pictorial, portrayed, representational, sketched, traced, visual; ▪ *Ant* abstract, conceptual, verbal.

grapple [*v*] *grab, wrestle* ▪ *Syn* attack, battle, clash, clasp, clutch, combat, confront, contend, deal with, encounter, engage, face, fight, grasp, hold, hug, nab, nail, scuffle, snatch, struggle, tackle, tussle; ▪ *Ant* free, let go, loose, release.

grasp [*v1*] *grab* ▪ *Syn* catch, clasp, clutch, corral, enclose, grapple, hold, hook, land, snatch, take; ▪ *Ant* drop, let go, release.

grasp [*v2*] *understand* ▪ *Syn* accept, appreciate, apprehend,

catch, cognize, comprehend, envisage, fathom, get, have, know, perceive, realize, see, take; ▪ *Ant* misapprehend, misconstrue, misunderstand.

grasping [*adj*] *greedy* ▪ *Syn* acquisitive, avaricious, covetous, desirous, extortionate, miserly, penurious, prehensile, rapacious, selfish, usurious, venal; ▪ *Ant* altruistic, ascetic, generous, liberal.

grate [*v*] *irritate* ▪ *Syn* aggravate, annoy, chafe, exasperate, fret, gall, irk, nettle, peeve, provoke, rankle, vex; ▪ *Ant* calm, mollify, pacify, please, soothe.

grateful [*adj1*] *appreciative* ▪ *Syn* beholden, gratified, indebted, obliged, pleased, thankful; ▪ *Ant* heedless, thankless, unappreciative, ungrateful.

grateful [*adj2*] *pleasing, nice* ▪ *Syn* agreeable, comforting, delightful, desirable, favorable, good, pleasant, refreshing, rejuvenating, restorative, satisfying, solacing, welcome; ▪ *Ant* abusive, distasteful, mean, obnoxious, rude.

gratify [*v*] *give pleasure; satisfy* ▪ *Syn* arride, content, delectate, delight, enchant, favor, gladden, humor, indulge, oblige, pamper, please, thrill; ▪ *Ant* annoy, disappoint, disturb, frustrate, offend, pain, upset.

grating [*adj*] *irritating; scraping* ▪ *Syn* disagreeable, discordant, dry, grinding, harsh, irksome, jarring, offensive, rasping, raucous, shrill, strident; ▪ *Ant* calming, mellifluous, melodic, pleasing, soothing.

gratuitous [*adj1*] *free* ▪ *Syn* chargeless, complimentary, costless, for nothing, gratis, spontaneous, unasked-for, voluntary, willing; ▪ *Ant* compensated, costly, expensive, paid.

gratuitous [*adj2*] *not necessary* ▪ *Syn* baseless, groundless, indefensible, needless, reasonless, superfluous, unessential, unjustified, unmerited, unwarranted, wanton; ▪ *Ant* deserved, essential, needed, reasonable, warranted.

grave [*adj1*] *serious; gloomy* ▪ *Syn* dignified, dour, dull, earnest, grim, heavy, leaden, long-faced, meaningful, muted, ponderous, quiet, sad, sage, saturnine, sedate, sober, solemn, somber, staid, subdued, thoughtful; ▪ *Ant* cheerful, flippant, frivolous, funny, happy, ridiculous, silly.

grave [adj2] *crucial, dangerous*
▪ *Syn* acute, afflictive, consequential, critical, deadly, destructive, dire, exigent, fatal, fell, grievous, hazardous, important, major, momentous, ominous, perilous, pressing, serious, severe, significant, threatening, urgent, vital, weighty; ▪ *Ant* harmless, inconsequential, petty, trivial, unimportant.

gravitate [v] *be drawn towards; fall to*
▪ *Syn* approach, be attracted, be influenced, be pulled, descend, drift, drop, fall, incline, lean, move, precipitate, settle, sink, tend; ▪ *Ant* retreat, run away.

great [adj1] *very large*
▪ *Syn* abundant, ample, big, bulky, colossal, considerable, enormous, excessive, extended, extensive, extreme, gigantic, huge, humongous, immense, inordinate, mammoth, oversize, prodigious, pronounced, protracted, strong, stupendous, terrible, towering, tremendous, vast, voluminous; ▪ *Ant* little, miniature, minute, puny, short, small, tiny.

great [adj2] *important, celebrated*
▪ *Syn* august, capital, commanding, dignified, distinguished, eminent, exalted, famed, famous, fine, glorious, grand, heroic, honorable, illustrious, impressive, leading, lofty, magnanimous, noble, outstanding, paramount, principal, prominent, renowned, stately, superior, superlative, talented; ▪ *Ant* infamous, insignificant, powerless, unimportant, unknown, weak.

great [adj3] *excellent, skillful*
▪ *Syn* able, absolute, adept, admirable, adroit, awesome, best, consummate, dynamite, exceptional, expert, fantastic, fine, good, marvelous, perfect, positive, proficient, terrific, transcendent, tremendous, unmitigated, wonderful; ▪ *Ant* ignorant, menial, poor, stupid, weak.

greatly [adv] *considerably*
▪ *Syn* abundantly, conspicuously, eminently, enormously, exceedingly, exceptionally, extremely, highly, hugely, immeasurably, immensely, incalculably, incomparably, incredibly, indeed, infinitely, inimitably, intensely, largely, markedly, mightily, most, much, notably, powerfully, remarkably, strikingly, superlatively, supremely, surpassingly, tremendously, vastly, very; ▪ *Ant* in-

considerably, insignificantly, little, mildly, somewhat, unremarkably.

greedy [adj] *desiring excessively*
▪ *Syn* acquisitive, avaricious, avid, carnivorous, close, covetous, craving, desirous, devouring, eager, edacious, esurient, gluttonous, gormandizing, grasping, hungry, impatient, insatiable, intemperate, omnivorous, prehensile, rapacious, ravenous, selfish, stingy, voracious; ▪ *Ant* abstemious, benevolent, charitable, extravagant, generous, liberal, philanthropic.

green [adj1] *young, new, blooming*
▪ *Syn* bosky, budding, burgeoning, callow, developing, flourishing, foliate, fresh, grassy, growing, half-formed, immature, juvenile, leafy, lush, maturing, pullulating, raw, recent, sprouting, supple, tender, verdant, visculent, youthful; ▪ *Ant* decayed, full-grown, old, ripe, seasoned, withered.

green [adj2] *inexperienced*
▪ *Syn* callow, credulous, fresh, gullible, ignorant, immature, ingenuous, innocent, naive, new, raw, unconversant, young, youthful; ▪ *Ant* experienced, expert, polished, skilled, sophisticated, well-versed.

green [adj3] *referring to practices or policies that do not negatively affect the environment* ▪ *Syn* biodegradable, ecological, environmental, environmentally safe, environment-friendly; ▪ *Ant* dangerous, destructive, harmful, industrially irresponsible, noxious, poisonous, reckless, synthetic, toxic.

greenhorn [n] *inexperienced person*
▪ *Syn* amateur, apprentice, beginner, ignoramus, ingenue, learner, naïf, neophyte, newcomer, new hand, novice, recruit; ▪ *Ant* expert, professional.

greet [v] *welcome*
▪ *Syn* acknowledge, address, approach, attend, bow, call to, flag, hail, herald, meet, nod, pay respects, receive, recognize, salute, say hello, shake hands, speak to, stop; ▪ *Ant* ignore, pass, say farewell, say goodbye, shun.

gregarious [adj] *friendly*
▪ *Syn* affable, companionable, convivial, cordial, fun, outgoing, sociable, social; ▪ *Ant* cold, cool, introverted, unfriendly, unhospitable, unsociable.

grieve [v1] *mourn, feel deep distress*
▪ *Syn* ache, bear, bemoan, bewail, carry on, complain, cry, deplore, endure,

keen, lament, regret, rue, sorrow, suffer, wail, weep; ▪ *Ant* be glad, be happy, rejoice.

grieve [v2] *upset, distress someone*
▪ *Syn* afflict, aggrieve, agonize, constrain, crush, hurt, injure, pain, sadden, wound; ▪ *Ant* comfort, console, delight, gladden, please, satisfy.

grievous [adj] *severe, painful; serious*
▪ *Syn* afflicting, agonizing, calamitous, damaging, dire, dreadful, egregious, flagrant, grave, heartrending, heinous, injurious, intolerable, lamentable, monstrous, mournful, onerous, oppressive, pathetic, sorrowful, taxing, tragic, upsetting, villainous, wounding; ▪ *Ant* beneficial, good, harmless, innocuous, pleasant.

grim [adj] *hopeless, horrible in manner, appearance* ▪ *Syn* austere, barbarous, bleak, churlish, cruel, dogged, ferocious, fierce, forbidding, foreboding, formidable, frightful, funereal, ghastly, gloomy, glowering, gruesome, harsh, hideous, horrid, inexorable, intractable, merciless, morose, ominous, relentless, ruthless, scowling, severe, shocking, sinister, somber, sour, splenetic, surly, terrible, truculent, unrelenting, unyielding; ▪ *Ant* benign, bright, cheerful, genial, happy, hopeful, joyful, sunny.

grimace [v] *make a pained expression*
▪ *Syn* contort, deform, distort, frown, make a face, mouth, scowl, smirk, sneer; ▪ *Ant* grin, smile.

grimy [adj] *dirty*
▪ *Syn* begrimed, besmirched, filthy, foul, messy, nasty, smeared, soiled, sooty, sordid, squalid; ▪ *Ant* clean, pure, sterile.

grind [v] *sharpen*
▪ *Syn* abrade, file, give an edge to, gnash, grate, grit, polish, rub, sand, scrape, smooth, whet; ▪ *Ant* dull, take the edge off.

grind down [v] *oppress*
▪ *Syn* afflict, annoy, harass, hound, persecute, plague, trouble, tyrannize, vex; ▪ *Ant* free, liberate.

grip [v1] *hold tightly*
▪ *Syn* clap a hand on, clasp, clench, clinch, clutch, grasp, nab, seize, snag, snatch, take, take hold of; ▪ *Ant* let go, release.

grip [v2] *entrance, enchant*
▪ *Syn* catch up, compel, engross, enthrall, fascinate, hold, hypnotize, involve, mesmerize, rivet, spellbind; ▪ *Ant* bore, disgust, repel.

gripe [v1] *complain*
▪ *Syn* carp, fuss, groan, grouch, grouse, grumble, moan, murmur, mutter, nag, squawk, whine; ▪ *Ant* compliment, praise.

gripe [v2] *pain, annoy*
▪ *Syn* ache, bother, compress, cramp, disturb, hurt, irritate, pinch, press, squeeze, vex; ▪ *Ant* please, soothe.

grisly [adj] *horrifying*
▪ *Syn* abominable, appalling, bloody, disgusting, dreadful, eerie, frightful, ghastly, gruesome, hideous, horrible, lurid, macabre, sanguine, shocking, sickening, terrifying; ▪ *Ant* nice, pleasant, pleasing, pretty.

gritty [adj1] *granular*
▪ *Syn* abrasive, branlike, calculous, crumbly, dusty, grainy, gravelly, in particles, loose, permeable, pulverant, rasping, rough, sabulous, sandy, scratchy; ▪ *Ant* fine, smooth.

gritty [adj2] *brave*
▪ *Syn* courageous, determined, dogged, hardy, mettlesome, resolute, spirited, steadfast, tenacious, tough; ▪ *Ant* afraid, cowardly, fainthearted, spineless, timid.

groggy [adj] *dizzy, stunned*
▪ *Syn* befuddled, confused, dazed, drunken, faint, hazy, reeling, shaky, staggering, stupefied, swaying, tired, weak, whirling, wobbly; ▪ *Ant* clear, clearheaded, cognizant, steady.

gross [n] *total, whole*
▪ *Syn* aggregate, all, entirety, sum, totality; ▪ *Ant* net, part.

gross [adj1] *large, fat*
▪ *Syn* adipose, big, bulky, corpulent, dense, fleshy, great, heavy, hulking, husky, massive, obese, porcine, portly, stout, thick, unwieldy, weighty; ▪ *Ant* bony, narrow, skinny, slender, slim, thin.

gross [adj2] *whole*
▪ *Syn* aggregate, all, before deductions, before tax, complete, entire, in sum, outright, total; ▪ *Ant* net, part, partial.

gross [adj3] *crude, vulgar*
▪ *Syn* boorish, callous, carnal, coarse, crass, dull, fleshly, foul, ignorant, indelicate, lewd, low, lustful, obscene, offensive, rank, raunchy, ribald, rude, scatological, tasteless, ugly, uncouth; ▪ *Ant* clean, decent, moral, polite, tasteful.

gross [adj4] *obvious, apparent*
▪ *Syn* arrant, blatant, downright, egregious, flagrant, glaring, immoderate, manifest, sheer, shocking, unmitigated, unqualified, utter; ▪ *Ant* hidden, modified, obscured, vague.

gross [v] *bring in as total*
▪ *Syn* earn, make, take in; ▪ *Ant* clear, loose, net.

grotesque [adj] *ugly, misshapen*
▪ *Syn* aberrant, absurd, bizarre, deformed, distorted, eerie, freakish, incongruous, ludicrous, malformed, monstrous, preposterous, queer, ridiculous, strange, surrealistic, weird, whimsical; ▪ *Ant* beautiful, natural, nice, pretty, shapely.

grouchy [adj] *complaining, irritable*
▪ *Syn* cross, grumbling, irascible, peevish, petulant, querulous, surly, testy; ▪ *Ant* complimentary, content, happy, pleased, praising, satisfied.

ground [v] *restrict; drop in place*
▪ *Syn* bar, beach, bring down, dock, down, fell, floor, knock down, land, level, prevent, strand; ▪ *Ant* free, let go, liberate.

groundless [adj] *without reason, justification* ▪ *Syn* baseless, chimerical, empty, flimsy, gratuitous, unauthorized, unfounded, unjustified; ▪ *Ant* called-for, grounded, justified, proven, reasonable, warranted.

group [v1] *bring together*
▪ *Syn* arrange, assemble, bunch, cluster, congregate, corral, gather, huddle, link, organize, systematize; ▪ *Ant* disband, disperse, scatter, spread.

group [v2] *classify, sort*
▪ *Syn* arrange, assemble, associate, assort, bracket, categorize, class, dispose, file, gather, marshal, order, organize, range, rank; ▪ *Ant* jumble, mix up.

grovel [v] *abase, demean oneself*
▪ *Syn* beg, beseech, blandish, cower, crawl, humble oneself, implore, kneel, pamper, snivel, stoop, wheedle; ▪ *Ant* boast, domineer, mock, scorn.

grow [v] *become larger, evolve*
▪ *Syn* advance, amplify, arise, augment, branch out, breed, build, cultivate, develop, expand, extend, flourish, germinate, heighten, increase, luxuriate, maturate, multiply, originate, produce, propagate, raise, rise, spread, spring up, sprout, stem, swell, thrive, vegetate, widen; ▪ *Ant* decline, decrease, diminish,

halt, lessen, reduce, stop, stunt, subside, wither.

grub [v1] *dig, uncover*
▪ *Syn* beat, break, burrow, clean, clear, comb, delve, excavate, ferret, forage, hunt, poke, prepare, probe, pull up, rake, ransack, root, rummage, scour, search, shovel, spade, unearth, uproot; ▪ *Ant* bury, cover, hide.

grub [v2] *work very hard*
▪ *Syn* drudge, grind, labor, moil, plod, slave, slog, sweat, toil; ▪ *Ant* idle, laze, tinker.

grubby [adj] *dirty, disheveled*
▪ *Syn* besmeared, black, filthy, foul, grimy, impure, messy, nasty, scruffy, shabby, sloppy, slovenly, soiled, sordid, squalid, unkempt, unwashed; ▪ *Ant* clean, cleanly, dressed-up, neat, scrubbed, tidy.

grudge [v] *feel resentful; give unwillingly*
▪ *Syn* begrudge, be reluctant, complain, covet, deny, envy, hold back, mind, pinch, refuse, resent, stint; ▪ *Ant* cherish, favor, forgive, lavish.

grueling [adj] *difficult, taxing*
▪ *Syn* arduous, backbreaking, brutal, chastening, crushing, demanding, excruciating, exhausting, fatiguing, fierce, grinding, hard, harsh, laborious, punishing, racking, severe, stiff, strenuous, tiring, torturous, trying; ▪ *Ant* easy, facile, simple.

gruesome [adj] *horrible, awful*
▪ *Syn* abominable, appalling, daunting, frightful, ghastly, grim, grisly, hideous, horrendous, loathsome, lurid, macabre, monstrous, repulsive, shocking, terrifying, ugly; ▪ *Ant* appealing, attractive, beautiful, pleasant, pretty.

gruff [adj1] *bad-tempered, rude*
▪ *Syn* abrupt, bearish, blunt, brusque, churlish, curt, dour, fierce, impolite, nasty, offhand, rough, saturnine, short, sour, surly, truculent; ▪ *Ant* civil, courteous, even-tempered, gracious, happy, nice, polite.

gruff [adj2] *rasping in sound*
▪ *Syn* cracked, croaking, grating, guttural, harsh, hoarse, husky, low, rough, throaty; ▪ *Ant* mellifluous, pleasant, smooth, soft, sweet.

grumble [v] *complain*
▪ *Syn* carp, fuss, gripe, groan, grouse, moan, protest, repine, scold, whine; ▪ *Ant* applaud, compliment, praise.

grumpy [adj] in a bad mood
▪ **Syn** bad-tempered, crotchety, disgruntled, irritable, peevish, petulant, querulous, sullen, surly, testy, truculent; ▪ **Ant** good-humored, happy, nice, pleasant.

guaranteed [adj] made certain
▪ **Syn** affirmed, ascertained, assured, bonded, deem, certified, endorsed, for a fact, insured, pledged, sealed, secured, warranted; ▪ **Ant** indefinite, insecure, uncertain, unsure.

guard [v] protect, watch
▪ **Syn** attend, baby-sit, bulwark, chaperone, conduct, convoy, cover, defend, escort, fend, keep, look after, mind, observe, patrol, preserve, safeguard, screen, secure, shepherd, superintend, supervise, tend, watch over; ▪ **Ant** disregard, endanger, forget, ignore, neglect, threaten.

guarded [adj] suspicious
▪ **Syn** attentive, cagey, calculating, canny, careful, cautious, chary, circumspect, discreet, gingerly, leery, noncommittal, overcautious, prudent, reserved, restrained, reticent, safe, vigilant, wary, watchful; ▪ **Ant** careless, daring, incautious, rash, reckless.

guess [v] try to figure out; imagine
▪ **Syn** believe, chance, conjecture, deduce, deem, divine, estimate, fathom, figure, hypothesize, infer, judge, opine, penetrate, pick, postulate, predicate, predict, presume, pretend, reason, reckon, select, solve, speculate, suggest, suppose, surmise, survey, suspect, theorize, think; ▪ **Ant** calculate, know, measure, prove.

guide [v] direct, lead
▪ **Syn** accompany, advise, attend, chaperon, command, conduct, control, convoy, counsel, educate, engineer, escort, govern, handle, influence, instruct, manage, maneuver, marshal, navigate, oversee, pilot, regulate, route, rule, see, shepherd, show, steer, superintend, supervise, sway, teach, train, usher; ▪ **Ant** abandon, leave, misguide, mislead, neglect.

guileless [adj] honest
▪ **Syn** aboveboard, artless, candid, frank, genuine, ingenuous, innocent, naive, natural, open, simple, simpleminded, sincere, straightforward, truthful, unaffected, undesigning, unsophisticated, unstudied; ▪ **Ant** artful, clever, crafty, cunning, deceitful, dishonest, guileful, tricky.

guiltless [adj] blameless, not responsible
▪ **Syn** clean, clear, crimeless, exemplary, faultless, free, good, immaculate, impeccable, inculpable, innocent, irreproachable, pure, righteous, sinless, spotless, virtuous; ▪ **Ant** blameful, corrupt, guilty, immoral, sinful, wrong.

guilty [adj] blameworthy; found at fault
▪ **Syn** accusable, at fault, censurable, censured, chargeable, condemned, conscience-stricken, contrite, convicted, criminal, culpable, damned, delinquent, doomed, erring, evil, felonious, impeached, incriminated, iniquitous, judged, liable, licentious, offending, proscribed, regretful, remorseful, reprehensible, responsible, rueful, sentenced, sheepish, sinful, sorry, wicked, wrong; ▪ **Ant** guiltless, innocent, moral, right, sinless, truthful.

gullible [adj] naive, trusting
▪ **Syn** believing, biting, credulous, foolish, innocent, silly, simple, sucker, susceptible, trustful, unskeptical, unsophisticated, unsuspecting; ▪ **Ant** astute, discerning, knowledgeable, perceptive, suspicious, unbelieving, untrusting, wise.

gulp [v] eat, drink fast
▪ **Syn** consume, devour, dispatch, dispose, eat, englut, imbibe, ingurgitate, pour, quaff, stuff, swig, swill, take in; ▪ **Ant** nibble.

gumption [n] nerve, initiative
▪ **Syn** ability, acumen, astuteness, cleverness, discernment, enterprise, good sense, industry, judgment, perspicacity, resourcefulness, sagaciousness, savvy, sense, shrewdness, spirit, wisdom, wit; ▪ **Ant** cowardice, naivety.

gush [v1] pour out
▪ **Syn** burst, cascade, emanate, flow, issue, jet, pour, roll, sluice, spout, spring, spurt, stream, surge, well; ▪ **Ant** dribble, ooze, trickle.

gush [v2] speak with overwhelming enthusiasm ▪ **Syn** blather, chatter, effervesce, effuse, jabber, overstate, prattle, rave; ▪ **Ant** be quiet, be silent.

gusto [n] great enthusiasm
▪ **Syn** appetite, appreciation, brio, delectation, enjoyment, exhilaration, fervor, heart, liking, palate, relish, savor, taste, verve, zeal, zest; ▪ **Ant** apathy, distaste, reluctance, unenthusiasm.

gusty [adj] windy
▪ **Syn** airy, blowy, blustering, blustery,

breezy, hearty, robust, squally, stormy, tempestuous; ▪ *Ant* calm, quiet, still.

gut [*adj*] *intuitive*
▪ *Syn* basic, deep-seated, emotional, heartfelt, innate, instinctive, internal, intimate, involuntary, natural, spontaneous, visceral, viscerous; ▪ *Ant* cerebral, material, physical.

gutless [*adj*] *timid*
▪ *Syn* abject, coward, cowardly, craven, feeble, irresolute, pusillanimous, submissive, unmanly, weak; ▪ *Ant* bold, brave, courageous, gutsy, resolute.

gutsy [*adj*] *bold, brave*
▪ *Syn* courageous, determined, gallant, indomitable, intrepid, mettlesome, plucky, resolute, staunch, valiant; ▪ *Ant* cowardly, fearful, gutless, timid.

guttural [*adj*] *deep in sound*
▪ *Syn* glottal, grating, gravelly, gruff, harsh, hoarse, husky, inarticulate, low, rasping, throaty; ▪ *Ant* dulcet, high-pitched, nasal.

guzzle [*v*] *drink down fast*
▪ *Syn* cram, devour, englut, gormandize, imbibe, ingurgitate, quaff, soak, swig, tipple; ▪ *Ant* nip, sample, sip, taste.

gyp [*v*] *defraud, cheat*
▪ *Syn* bilk, chicane, cozen, deceive, dupe, fake, hoax, swindle, trick; ▪ *Ant* be fair, give, offer.

H

habitual [*adj*] *usual, established*
▪ *Syn* accepted, accustomed, chronic, common, conventional, customary, familiar, fixed, ingrained, inveterate, iterative, methodical, normal, ordinary, perfunctory, perpetual, practiced, recurrent, regular, routine, set, standard, systematic, traditional, wonted; ▪ *Ant* exceptional, infrequent, intermittent, irregular, occasional, rare, seldom, strange, uncommon, unusual.

hacker [*n*] *someone proficient at computers, especially a hobbyist* ▪ *Syn* application progammer, computer architect, computer designer, computer jock, key puncher, operator, programmer, system software specialist, systems engineer, systems programmer, systems analyst, technician; ▪ *Ant* computer illiterate.

hackneyed [*adj*] *clichéd, tired*
▪ *Syn* antiquated, banal, commonplace, conventional, everyday, outdated, overworked, quotidian, stale, stereotyped, stock, timeworn, trite, well-worn; ▪ *Ant* fresh, innovative, new, novel, original, uncommon.

haggard [*adj*] *worn, weakened*
▪ *Syn* ashen, careworn, drawn, emaciated, exhausted, faded, fagged, fatigued, pallid, pinched, tired, wan, wasted, weak, wearied; ▪ *Ant* energetic, fresh, healthy, hearty, robust, strong, vigorous.

haggle [*v*] *bicker, quarrel*
▪ *Syn* argue, bargain, barter, chaffer, deal, dispute, palter, quibble, squabble, wrangle; ▪ *Ant* agree, comply, concur.

hail [*v1*] *call to, yell for*
▪ *Syn* accost, address, flag, greet, hello, salute, signal, speak to, wave down, welcome; ▪ *Ant* avoid, ignore, shun, whisper.

hail [*v2*] *honor, salute*
▪ *Syn* acclaim, acknowledge, applaud, cheer, commend, compliment, exalt, glorify, greet, kudize, praise, recognize, recommend, welcome; ▪ *Ant* disdain, dishonor, disparage, slight.

hail [*v3*] *rain down on*
▪ *Syn* barrage, batter, bombard, pelt, rain, shower, storm, volley; ▪ *Ant* dribble, drip, drizzle.

hairless [*adj*] *without hair growth on body part* ▪ *Syn* bald, beardless, clean-shaven, depilated, glabrate, glabrous, shaved, shaven, shorn, smooth, smooth-faced, tonsured; ▪ *Ant* furry, hairy, hirsute, whiskered.

hairy [*adj1*] *having much hair*
▪ *Syn* bearded, bushy, downy, fleecy, flocculent, fluffy, furry, fuzzy, hirsute, lanate, piliferous, shaggy, tufted, villous, woolly; ▪ *Ant* bald, balding, clean, hairless, shaven, shorn.

hairy [*adj2*] *dangerous*
▪ *Syn* chancy, difficult, hazardous, perilous, risky, scary, treacherous, wicked; ▪ *Ant* calm, harmless, reliable, safe, secure.

hale [*adj*] *strong and healthy*
▪ *Syn* able-bodied, blooming, fit, flourishing, healthy, hearty, husky, right, robust, sane, sound, stout, strapping, strong, trim, vigorous, well, well-conditioned, wholesome; ▪ *Ant* infirm, sick, unhealthy, weak.

half [*adj*] *partial*
▪ *Syn* bisected, divided, fractional,

halved, incomplete, limited, moderate, partly; ■ *Ant* aggregate, sum, total, whole.

half-baked/half-witted [*adj*] *stupid; not thought through* ■ *Syn* brainless, crazy, dumb, feebleminded, foolish, idiotic, ill-conceived, impractical, moronic, poorly planned, senseless, shortsighted, silly, sophomoric, underdeveloped, witless; ■ *Ant* intelligent, smart, thoughtful, wise.

halfhearted [*adj*] *without enthusiasm* ■ *Syn* apathetic, cool, impassive, indifferent, irresolute, lackluster, listless, lukewarm, neutral, passive, perfunctory, spiritless, tame, tepid; ■ *Ant* desirous, enthusiastic, interested, warm, wholehearted.

halfway [*adv*] *not complete; in the middle* ■ *Syn* comparatively, incompletely, medially, middling, midway, moderately, nearly, partially, partly, rather, restrictedly, to a degree, to some extent; ■ *Ant* completely, totally, wholly.

hallowed [*adj*] *holy, revered* ■ *Syn* anointed, beatified, blessed, consecrated, dedicated, enshrined, holy, honored, sacred, sanctified; ■ *Ant* desecrated, irreligious, profane, unhallowed, unholy, unsanctified.

hallucination [*n*] *dream, delusion* ■ *Syn* aberration, apparition, fantasy, illusion, mirage, phantasm, phantasmagoria, phantom, vision; ■ *Ant* experience, fact, reality, truth.

halt [*v*] *stop, cause to stop* ■ *Syn* adjourn, arrest, balk, bar, block, check, close down, cut short, desist, deter, draw up, end, frustrate, hamper, hold back, impede, interrupt, obstruct, stall, stand still, suspend, terminate, wait; ■ *Ant* carry on, continue, forge, forward, proceed, push.

halting [*adj*] *hesitant* ■ *Syn* awkward, bumbling, clumsy, doubtful, faltering, indecisive, inept, irresolute, lumbering, maladroit, stammering, stumbling, stuttering, tentative, unhandy, vacillating, wavering; ■ *Ant* certain, decisive, definite, flowing, smooth, sure.

halve [*v*] *cut in half* ■ *Syn* bisect, divide equally, reduce by fifty percent, share equally, split in two; ■ *Ant* double, increase by 100 percent.

hamper [*v*] *impede, restrict* ■ *Syn* baffle, balk, bar, block, check, clog, curb, down, encumber, entangle, fetter, frustrate, handicap, hinder, inconvenience, inhibit, leash, obstruct, prevent, retard, stymie, thwart, tie up, trammel; ■ *Ant* aid, allow, assist, encourage, expedite, help, permit, promote.

handful [*adj*] *a small quantity* ■ *Syn* few, scattering, smattering, some, spattering, sprinkling; ■ *Ant* lot, many, mass.

handicap [*v*] *give disadvantage* ■ *Syn* burden, cripple, encumber, hamper, hinder, hold back, impede, limit, restrict, retard; ■ *Ant* aid, assist, benefit, further, give advantage, help, promote.

handle [*v*] *manage, take care of* ■ *Syn* administer, advise, bestow, command, conduct, control, direct, dispense, dominate, employ, exercise, govern, manipulate, operate, play, run, steer, supervise, utilize, wield, work; ■ *Ant* disregard, mismanage, misuse, neglect.

hand out [*v*] *give to others* ■ *Syn* bestow, deal out, deliver, devote, disburse, dish out, dispense, disseminate, distribute, donate, mete, present, provide; ■ *Ant* keep, receive, retain, take, withhold.

hand over [*v*] *give back; release* ■ *Syn* abandon, cede, consign, deliver, dispense, donate, entrust, give up, leave, present, provide, relegate, surrender, turn over, waive, yield; ■ *Ant* hold, keep, retain, withhold.

handsome [*adj1*] *attractive* ■ *Syn* august, beautiful, becoming, comely, dapper, elegant, fair, fine, good-looking, impressive, lovely, majestic, pulchritudinous, sharp, spruce, stately, stylish, suave, well-proportioned; ■ *Ant* homely, ugly, unattractive.

handsome [*adj2*] *abundant* ■ *Syn* ample, bountiful, considerable, extensive, full, generous, large, lavish, liberal, magnanimous, munificent, plentiful, sizable, unsparing; ■ *Ant* frugal, poor, small, stingy.

handy [*adj1*] *nearby* ■ *Syn* accessible, adjacent, available, central, close, close by, convenient, near, ready, within reach; ■ *Ant* faraway, inconvenient, out of the way, remote, unhandy.

handy [*adj2*] *easy to use* ■ *Syn* adaptable, beneficial, convenient, functional, helpful, manageable, practicable, profitable, serviceable, useful; ▪ *Ant* awkward, hard, inconvenient, unhandy, unwieldly, useless.

handy [adj3] *adept physically*
▪ *Syn* able, adroit, clever, deft, expert, fit, ingenious, nimble, proficient, ready, skilled; ▪ *Ant* awkward, bumbling, bungling, clumsy, inept, unhandy.

hang [v] *suspend or be suspended*
▪ *Syn* adhere, attach, bow, cling, cover, dangle, depend, drape, fasten, fix, hold, hover, impend, nail, overhang, remain, stick, suspend, swing, wave; ▪ *Ant* detach, take down.

hang about/hang around/hang out
[v] *associate with; loiter or be residing in*
▪ *Syn* abide, dally, frequent, haunt, linger, loiter, reside, resort, roam, tarry; ▪ *Ant* avoid, condemn, eschew, shun.

hang on [v] *continue, endure*
▪ *Syn* be tough, carry on, cling, clutch, grasp, grip, hold, hold fast, hold out, persevere, persist, remain; ▪ *Ant* cease, give up, let go, stop.

hanker after/hanker for [v] *desire strongly* ▪ *Syn* ache, covet, crave, hunger, itch, long, lust, pine, sigh, thirst, want, wish, yearn, yen; ▪ *Ant* abhor, detest, dislike, hate, loathe.

hanky-panky [n] *mischief*
▪ *Syn* chicane, chicanery, deception, devilry, double-dealing, fourberie, fraud, knavery, machinations, subterfuge, trickery; ▪ *Ant* faithfulness, honesty, integrity, probity.

haphazard [adj] *without plan or organization* ▪ *Syn* accidental, aimless, arbitrary, chance, desultory, disorderly, erratic, fluke, incidental, indiscriminate, loose, offhand, purposeless, random, slipshod, spontaneous; ▪ *Ant* careful, designed, intentional, methodical, organized, planned, straight, systematic, thought-out.

hapless [adj] *unfortunate*
▪ *Syn* cursed, hexed, ill-fated, ill-starred, infelicitous, jinxed, loser, luckless, miserable, unhappy, untoward, woeful, wretched; ▪ *Ant* fortuitous, fortunate, lucky, well-off.

happily [adv1] *with joy, pleasure*
▪ *Syn* agreeably, blithely, brightly, cheerfully, delightedly, exultantly, freely, gaily, gleefully, heartily, jovially, joyfully, joyously, laughingly, lightheartedly, lovingly, merrily, willingly, with relish, with zeal; ▪ *Ant* grudgingly, resentfully, unhappily, with disgust, with scorn.

happily [adv2] *successfully*
▪ *Syn* appropriately, aptly, auspiciously, favorably, felicitously, fortunately, propitiously, prosperously, providentially, satisfyingly, seasonably, swimmingly, well; ▪ *Ant* unhappily, unluckily, unsuccessfully.

happy [adj1] *in high spirits; satisfied*
▪ *Syn* blessed, blissful, blithe, cheerful, chipper, chirpy, convivial, delighted, ecstatic, elated, exultant, gay, glad, gleeful, gratified, intoxicated, jolly, joyful, joyous, jubilant, laughing, light, lively, merry, mirthful, overjoyed, peaceful, playful, pleasant, pleased, sparkling, sunny, thrilled, tickled, up, upbeat; ▪ *Ant* depressed, discouraged, dissatisfied, miserable, morose, pained, sad, sorrowful, unhappy.

happy [adj2] *lucky, appropriate*
▪ *Syn* accidental, advantageous, appropriate, apt, auspicious, befitting, casual, convenient, correct, effective, efficacious, enviable, favorable, felicitous, fitting, fortunate, incidental, just, lucky, meet, nice, opportune, promising, proper, propitious, providential, right, satisfactory, seasonable, successful, suitable, timely, well-timed; ▪ *Ant* forsaken, hopeless, troubled, unfortunate, unhappy, unlucky.

happy-go-lucky [adj] *carefree and untroubled* ▪ *Syn* blithe, casual, cheerful, cool, easy, easygoing, feckless, free-minded, heedless, improvident, insouciant, irresponsible, lighthearted, nonchalant, reckless, unconcerned; ▪ *Ant* disconsolate, discontented, dissatisfied, distressed, troubled, upset, worried.

harass [v] *badger*
▪ *Syn* annoy, attack, bedevil, beleaguer, despoil, distress, exasperate, harry, heckle, intimidate, irk, maraud, pester, plague, raid, strain, torment, try, vex, weary; ▪ *Ant* aid, alleviate, assist, assuage, facilitate, help, support.

harbor [v] *hide, protect*
▪ *Syn* accommodate, board, bunk, conceal, defend, domicile, entertain, guard, house, lodge, nurse, nurture, provide refuge, put up, quarter, relieve, safeguard, screen, secrete, secure, shelter, shield; ▪ *Ant* eject, evict, exile, expel, let out, shut out, uncover.

hard [adj1] *rocklike*
- **Syn** adamantine, callous, compact, compacted, compressed, concentrated, consolidated, dense, firm, hardened, impenetrable, indurate, inflexible, packed, rigid, rocky, set, solid, stiff, stony, strong, thick, tough; **Ant** flexible, malleable, pliable, pliant, soft, yielding.

hard [adj2] *difficult, exhausting*
- **Syn** arduous, backbreaking, burdensome, complicated, demanding, effortful, fatiguing, formidable, grinding, irksome, laborious, onerous, rigorous, scabrous, severe, strenuous, toilsome, tough, troublesome, wearisome, wearying; **Ant** easy, facile, mild, simple.

hard [adj3] *cruel, ruthless*
- **Syn** acrimonious, antagonistic, bleak, brutal, callous, distressing, dour, exacting, grim, harsh, hostile, inclement, obdurate, painful, rancorous, rigorous, rugged, severe, stringent, tough, unrelenting, vengeful; **Ant** just, kind, merciful, mild, nice, pleasant, sensitive, sympathetic.

hard [adj4] *true, indisputable*
- **Syn** absolute, actual, bare, cold, definite, genuine, plain, positive, practical, pragmatic, realistic, sure, undeniable, unvarnished, verified; **Ant** disputable, doubtful, inexact, questionable, uncertain, untrue.

hard [adv1] *with great force*
- **Syn** actively, briskly, earnestly, energetically, ferociously, forcefully, furiously, intensely, keenly, madly, relentlessly, rigorously, savagely, strongly, turbulently, urgently, vigorously, violently, wildly, with all one's might; **Ant** gently, lightly, mildly, softly, weakly.

hard [adv2] *with determination*
- **Syn** assiduously, closely, determinedly, diligently, doggedly, earnestly, exhaustively, industriously, intensely, intently, painstakingly, persistently, strenuously, thoroughly, unremittingly, untiringly; **Ant** casually, idly, lazily, lethargically, unenthusiastically.

hard [adv3] *with difficulty*
- **Syn** agonizingly, arduously, cumbrously, distressingly, exhaustingly, gruelingly, laboriously, painfully, ponderously, roughly, strenuously, vigorously, with great effort; **Ant** easily, moderately, simply, smoothly, with ease.

hard [adv4] *with resentment*
- **Syn** bitterly, hardly, keenly, rancorously, reluctantly, resentfully, sorely; **Ant** indulgently, mildly, tolerantly.

hard [adv5] *in a fixed manner*
- **Syn** close, fast, firm, firmly, fixedly, solidly, steadfastly, tight, tightly; **Ant** loosely, unfixedly, yielding.

hard-core [adj] *dedicated*
- **Syn** devoted, extreme, faithful, intransigent, obstinate, resolute, rigid, staunch, steadfast, stubborn, uncompromising, unwaivering, unyielding; **Ant** indulgent, lax, mild, moderate, tolerant.

harden [v1] *make or become solid*
- **Syn** amalgamate, bake, brace, buttress, cake, callous, coagulate, congeal, consolidate, crystallize, dry, firm, fortify, fossilize, freeze, indurate, jell, ossify, petrify, solidify, steel, stiffen, strengthen, temper, thicken, toughen, vitrify; **Ant** dissolve, liquefy, melt, soften.

harden [v2] *accustom*
- **Syn** acclimate, adapt, adjust, climatize, coarsen, conform, deaden, develop, habituate, indurate, numb, paralyze, roughen, season, steel, stiffen, strengthen, teach, train; **Ant** debilitate, indulge, sap, soften, spoil, weaken.

hardened [adj] *unfeeling*
- **Syn** accustomed, benumbed, callous, disdainful, habituated, heartless, impenetrable, inaccessible, obdurate, resistant, steeled, toughened, unbending; **Ant** caring, compassionate, considerate, feeling, kind, sympathetic.

hardhearted [adj] *cold, cruel*
- **Syn** brutish, callous, hard, heartless, indifferent, inhuman, insensitive, merciless, obdurate, pitiless, stony; **Ant** compassionate, kind, sensitive, softhearted, tender, warm.

hardly [adv] *scarcely; with difficulty*
- **Syn** almost, barely, faintly, gradually, imperceptibly, just, little, only, practically, rarely, scantly, seldom, sparsely, sporadically; **Ant** amply, frequently, markedly, noticeably, often, quite, very.

hard-nosed/hardheaded [adj] *pragmatic, stubborn* **Syn** headstrong, intractable, mulish, obstinate, pertinacious, perverse, practical, pragmatic, resolute, shrewd, sober, stand pat, tough, unsentimental, unyielding, willful; **Ant** easy, easy-going, laid-back, merciful.

hardy [adj] *strong, tough*
- **Syn** able, able-bodied, acclimatized, capable, enduring, firm, fit, fresh, hale, hardened, healthy, hearty, inured, lusty,

mighty, muscular, powerful, resistant, robust, rugged, seasoned, solid, sound, stalwart, staunch, sturdy, substantial, tenacious, toughened, unflagging, vigorous, well; ▪ *Ant* feeble, infirm, invalid, sick, tender, unhealthy, weak.

harebrained [*adj*] *stupid, unthinking*
▪ *Syn* absurd, asinine, barmy, bizarre, careless, changeable, crazy, flighty, foolish, frivolous, giddy, heedless, inane, irresponsible, mindless, preposterous, rash, reckless, wild; ▪ *Ant* brainy, intelligent, prudent, reasonable, sensible, smart, thoughtful, wise.

harm [*v*] *injure; cause evil*
▪ *Syn* abuse, blemish, bruise, cripple, crush, damage, dilapidate, discommode, disserve, do violence to, get, hurt, illtreat, impair, incommode, inconvenience, maim, maltreat, mangle, mar, misuse, molest, mutilate, nick, outrage, prejudice, put down, ruin, sabotage, scathe, shatter, shock, spoil, stab, tarnish, total, trample, traumatize, undermine, vandalize, vitiate, wound, wreck, wrench, wrong; ▪ *Ant* aid, assist, benefit, care, fix, help, improve, mend.

harmful [*adj*] *injurious, hurtful*
▪ *Syn* adverse, bad, baleful, baneful, calamitous, corroding, corrupting, crippling, damaging, deleterious, destructive, detrimental, harassing, inimical, internecine, malefic, menacing, nocuous, noxious, pernicious, pestiferous, pestilential, risky, ruinous, sinful, sinister, subversive, toxic, undermining, virulent; ▪ *Ant* aiding, healthy, helpful, safe, salubrious, unharmful, wholesome.

harmless [*adj*] *not injurious or dangerous* ▪ *Syn* gentle, guiltless, innocent, innocuous, innoxious, inoffensive, inoperative, kind, manageable, naive, nonirritating, painless, powerless, reliable, safe, sanitary, simple, sound, sure, trustworthy; ▪ *Ant* bad, destructive, evil, harmful, hurtful, injurious, offensive, sinful, toxic, wicked.

harmonious [*adj*] *agreeable, corresponding; friendly* ▪ *Syn* accordant, amicable, balanced, compatible, concordant, congruous, correspondent, dulcet, euphonious, in chorus, in unison, like, matching, mellifluous, musical, peaceful, similar, simpatico, sonorous, sweetsounding, symmetrical, symphonic, tuneful; ▪ *Ant* cacaphonous, disagreeable,

discordant, dissonant, harsh, inharmonious, opposed, unfriendly, unlike.

harmonize [*v*] *correspond, match*
▪ *Syn* accord, adapt, adjust, agree, arrange, attune, blend, carol, cohere, combine, compose, cooperate, coordinate, correlate, correspond, integrate, orchestrate, reconcile, reconciliate, relate, set, suit, symphonize, synthesize, tune, unify, unite; ▪ *Ant* clash, conflict, disagree, fight, oppose.

harness [*v*] *rein in; control*
▪ *Syn* bind, bridle, channel, check, cinch, collar, constrain, curb, domesticate, employ, exploit, fasten, fetter, govern, hitch, hold, leash, limit, muzzle, saddle, secure, strap, tackle, tame, tie, utilize, yoke; ▪ *Ant* free, release, unharness.

harrowing [*adj*] *dangerous, frightening*
▪ *Syn* agonizing, alarming, chilling, distressing, disturbing, excruciating, heartbreaking, heartrending, nerve-racking, painful, racking, terrifying, tormenting, torturing, torturous, traumatic; ▪ *Ant* calming, easy, pleasant, pleasing.

harry [*v*] *pester, annoy*
▪ *Syn* attack, badger, bedevil, beleaguer, chivy, disturb, fret, gnaw, harass, hassle, irk, irritate, molest, persecute, perturb, pester, plague, plunder, ravage, sack, tease, torment, trouble, vex, worry; ▪ *Ant* aid, assist, help, support.

harsh [*adj1*] *rough, crude (to the senses)*
▪ *Syn* acrid, asperous, astringent, bitter, cacophonous, coarse, cracked, craggy, discordant, dissonant, disturbing, earsplitting, flat, glaring, grating, grim, guttural, hard, hoarse, jagged, jangling, jarring, rasping, raucous, rigid, rugged, rusty, screeching, severe, sharp, sour, strident, tuneless; ▪ *Ant* easy, even, gentle, melodious, mild, peaceful, pleasing, smooth, soft.

harsh [*adj2*] *nasty, abusive*
▪ *Syn* austere, bitter, brutal, comfortless, cruel, cussed, discourteous, dour, grim, gruff, hard, hard-boiled, mean, pitiless, punitive, relentless, rude, ruthless, severe, sharp, stern, stringent, tough, uncivil, unfeeling, ungracious, unkind, unpleasant, unrelenting, wicked; ▪ *Ant* courteous, kind, nice, polite.

harvest [*v*] *produce, gather*
▪ *Syn* accumulate, acquire, amass, bin, cache, collect, crop, cull, cut, garner,

glean, harrow, hoard, mow, pick, plow, pluck, reap, stash, store, stow; ▪ *Ant* plant, seed, sow.

hassle [*v*] *bother, harass*
▪ *Syn* annoy, argue, argufy, badger, bedevil, beleaguer, bicker, dispute, dun, harry, hound, pester, plague, quibble, squabble, worry, wrangle; ▪ *Ant* agree, concur, make peace.

hasten [*v*] *speed something; hurry*
▪ *Syn* accelerate, advance, bolt, bound, bustle, dash, dispatch, expedite, express, flee, fly, gallop, goad, hustle, leap, pace, plunge, precipitate, press, push, quicken, race, run, rush, scamper, scoot, scurry, scuttle, skip, speed, sprint, spurt, tear, trot, urge; ▪ *Ant* go slow, lag, linger, loiter, plod, procrastinate, rest, tarry.

hastily [*adv*] *with great speed*
▪ *Syn* agilely, apace, carelessly, double-quick, expeditiously, fast, heedlessly, hurriedly, impetuously, impulsively, nimbly, posthaste, precipitately, prematurely, promptly, quickly, rapidly, rashly, recklessly, speedily, straightaway, subito, suddenly, swiftly, thoughtlessly, too quickly, unpremeditatedly; ▪ *Ant* delayed, slowly.

hasty [*adj*] *speedy; without much thought*
▪ *Syn* abrupt, agile, brash, brief, brisk, careless, cursory, eager, expeditious, fast, fiery, fleet, fleeting, foolhardy, headlong, heedless, hurried, ill-advised, impatient, impetuous, impulsive, incautious, inconsiderate, passing, perfunctory, precipitate, prompt, quick, rapid, rash, reckless, rushed, short, sudden, superficial, swift, thoughtless, urgent; ▪ *Ant* delayed, lazy, leisurely, lingering, loitering, patient, slow, sluggish, tardy.

hate [*v*] *dislike very strongly*
▪ *Syn* abhor, abominate, anathematize, contemn, curse, deprecate, deride, despise, detest, disapprove, disdain, disfavor, dislike, disparage, execrate, feel malice to, loathe, object to, recoil from, scorn, shun, spurn; ▪ *Ant* adore, cherish, esteem, like, love, tolerate, treasure.

hateful [*adj*] *nasty, obnoxious*
▪ *Syn* abhorrent, abominable, accursed, awful, bitter, cursed, damned, despicable, detestable, disgusting, evil, execrable, forbidding, foul, gross, heinous, horrid, infamous, invidious, loathsome, malevolent, malign, mean, odious, offensive, pestiferous, repellent, repugnant, repulsive, resentful, revolting, spiteful, vicious, vile; ▪ *Ant* affectionate, friendly, kind, likable, lovable, nice, pleasant, pleasing, polite.

haughty [*adj*] *arrogant*
▪ *Syn* assuming, conceited, contemptuous, detached, disdainful, distant, egotistic, egotistical, high, imperious, indifferent, lofty, overbearing, overweening, proud, reserved, scornful, snobbish, supercilious, superior; ▪ *Ant* humble, meek, servile, shy, timid.

haunt [*v*] *spend a lot of time at*
▪ *Syn* affect, frequent, habituate, infest, repair, resort, visit; ▪ *Ant* avoid, eschew, shun.

have [*v1*] *be in possession*
▪ *Syn* carry, enjoy, have in hand, hold, include, own, possess, retain; ▪ *Ant* lack, need, want.

have [*v2*] *contain*
▪ *Syn* comprehend, comprise, embody, embrace, encompass, include, involve, subsume, take in; ▪ *Ant* exclude.

hazardous [*adj*] *dangerous, unpredictable* ▪ *Syn* chancy, difficult, haphazard, insecure, parlous, perilous, precarious, risky, touchy, uncertain, unhealthy, unsound; ▪ *Ant* certain, guarded, predictable, protected, safe, secure.

hazy [*adj1*] *cloudy*
▪ *Syn* bleared, bleary, blurred, blurry, clouded, crepuscular, dim, dull, dusky, faint, foggy, frosty, fuliginous, misty, murky, nebulous, obfuscated, obfuscous, obscure, opaque, overcast, rimy, shadowy, smoggy, smoky, steaming, thick, vague, vaporous, veiled; ▪ *Ant* bright, clear, cloudless, definite, distinct, sunny.

hazy [*adj2*] *confused*
▪ *Syn* dazed, dizzy, dreamy, groggy, indefinite, indistinct, muddled, murky, nebulous, obscure, stuporous, tranced, vague, whirling; ▪ *Ant* certain, clear, definite, distinct, explained, focused, sure.

head [*adj*] *most important; chief*
▪ *Syn* arch, champion, first, foremost, front, highest, leading, main, pioneer, preeminent, premier, prime, principal, stellar, supreme, topmost; ▪ *Ant* auxiliary, inferior, lower, second, secondary, trivial, unimportant.

head [*v*] *manage, oversee*
▪ *Syn* address, be in charge, command, control, direct, dominate, govern, guide,

lead, pioneer, precede, rule, run, supervise; ▪ *Ant* follow, obey.

headlong [*adj*] *dangerous, reckless*
▪ *Syn* abrupt, brash, breakneck, daredevil, foolhardy, hasty, impetuous, impulsive, precipitate, rash, sudden, tempestuous, thoughtless; ▪ *Ant* careful, cautious, considered, deliberate, wary.

headstrong [*adj*] *stubborn*
▪ *Syn* contrary, determined, hard-nosed, heedless, intractable, mulish, obstinate, perverse, reckless, refractory, self-willed, strong-minded, willful; ▪ *Ant* calm, docile, governable, moderate, obedient, submissive, tame, tolerant.

headway [*n*] *progress*
▪ *Syn* advance, advancement, anabasis, ground, improvement, increase, march, proficiency, progression, promotion, way; ▪ *Ant* block, hindrance, reduction, regression, stoppage.

heady [*adj*] *thrilling, intoxicating*
▪ *Syn* exciting, exhilarating, inebriating, overwhelming, potent, powerful, provocative, spirituous, stimulating, strong; ▪ *Ant* boring, dull, weak, wearying.

heal [*v*] *cure, recover*
▪ *Syn* alleviate, ameliorate, conciliate, fix, improve, knit, medicate, meliorate, mend, patch up, reanimate, rebuild, rehabilitate, rejuvenate, remedy, renew, repair, restore, resuscitate, revive, salve, soothe, treat; ▪ *Ant* harm, hurt, injure, worsen, wound.

healthful/healthy [*adj1*] *good for one's physical wellness* ▪ *Syn* advantageous, aseptic, beneficial, body-building, bracing, cathartic, clean, compensatory, conducive, corrective, desirable, fresh, healing, helpful, hygienic, innocuous, invigorating, mitigative, nourishing, nutritious, nutritive, profitable, pure, restorative, salubrious, salutary, sanatory, sanitary, sustaining, tonic, useful, wholesome; ▪ *Ant* bad, corrupt, deleterious, detrimental, diseased, noxious, pernicious, rotten, sickening.

healthy [*adj2*] *in good condition*
▪ *Syn* able-bodied, active, athletic, blooming, firm, fit, flourishing, fresh, hale, hardy, healthful, hearty, in good shape, lively, lusty, muscular, normal, physically fit, potent, robust, sound, stout, strong, sturdy, tough, trim, vigorous, virile, well, whole; ▪ *Ant* delicated, diseased, fragile, frail, ill, indisposed, infirm, poor, sick, sickly, worn.

heap [*v*] *amass, collect in pile*
▪ *Syn* accumulate, add, arrange, augment, bank, bunch, concentrate, deposit, dump, fill, fill up, gather, group, hoard, increase, load, lump, mass, mound, pack, pile, stack, stockpile, store, swell; ▪ *Ant* dispel, disperse, dissipate, scatter.

hear [*v*] *become aware of information*
▪ *Syn* apperceive, ascertain, be advised, be informed, catch, catch on, descry, determine, discover, find out, gather, glean, learn, receive, see, understand, unearth; ▪ *Ant* disregard, ignore, miss, overlook.

hearsay [*n*] *unsubstantiated information*
▪ *Syn* comment, cry, gossip, report, rumor, scandal, talk; ▪ *Ant* evidence, proof, reality, testimony, truth.

heartbreaking [*adj*] *disappointing*
▪ *Syn* afflictive, agonizing, bitter, calamitous, cheerless, deplorable, distressing, grievous, lamentable, moving, pitiful, poignant, regrettable, sad, touching, tragic; ▪ *Ant* exhilarating, heartwarming, joyous, propitious, wonderful.

hearten [*v*] *raise someone's spirits*
▪ *Syn* animate, buoy, cheer, comfort, console, embolden, encourage, energize, enliven, incite, inspire, inspirit, reassure, revivify, rouse, steel, stimulate, stir, strengthen; ▪ *Ant* bring down, dampen, depress, discourage, dishearten.

heartfelt [*adj*] *genuine*
▪ *Syn* ardent, bona fide, cordial, deep, devout, earnest, fervent, heart-to-heart, hearty, honest, profound, sincere, true, unfeigned, warm, wholehearted; ▪ *Ant* false, insincere, unreal.

heartless [*adj*] *without feeling; cold*
▪ *Syn* brutal, callous, cruel, hard, harsh, inhuman, merciless, obdurate, pitiless, ruthless, savage, uncaring, unemotional, unfeeling; ▪ *Ant* caring, compassionate, considerate, feeling, kind, nice, sensitive, sympathetic, warmhearted.

hearty [*adj1*] *energetic, enthusiastic*
▪ *Syn* ardent, avid, cheerful, eager, earnest, ebullient, effusive, exuberant, gay, impassioned, intense, jovial, passionate, profuse, responsive, vivacious, wholehearted, zealous; ▪ *Ant* apathetic, emotionless, lethargic, reserved, restrained.

hearty [*adj2*] *healthy, full*
▪ *Syn* active, ample, energetic, filling, glowing, good, hale, hardy, nourishing, robust, sizable, solid, sound, square, strong, substantial, vigorous, well; ▪ *Ant* feeble, small, unhealthy, weak.

heat [v] *make or become hot*
▪ *Syn* bake, boil, broil, chafe, char, enflame, enkindle, fire, flame, fry, glow, grill, ignite, incandesce, incinerate, inflame, kindle, melt, perspire, roast, scald, scorch, sear, seethe, set on fire, singe, smelt, steam, swelter, toast, warm; ▪ *Ant* chill, cool, freeze.

heated [adj1] *angry*
▪ *Syn* acrimonious, ardent, avid, bitter, excited, fervent, fervid, feverish, fiery, frenzied, furious, hectic, impassioned, indignant, intense, irate, ireful, mad, passionate, raging, stormy, tempestuous, vehement, violent, wrathful; ▪ *Ant* calm, cool, dispassionate, mild, peaceful.

heated [adj2] *warmed*
▪ *Syn* baked, baking, boiling, broiled, broiling, burned, burning, burnt, cooked, fiery, fired, fried, hot, parched, scalding, scorched, scorching, sizzling, toasted; ▪ *Ant* cooled, frozen.

heathen [adj] *not believing in Christian god* ▪ *Syn* agnostic, atheistic, barbarian, godless, idolatrous, infidel, irreligious, nonbelieving, non-Christian, pagan, profane, skeptical; ▪ *Ant* believing, godly, religious.

heavenly [adj] *very pleasant*
▪ *Syn* alluring, ambrosial, angelic, beatific, blissful, celestial, cherubic, delectable, delightful, divine, empyrean, enjoyable, exquisite, glorious, lovely, luscious, lush, paradisaical, rapturous, ravishing, scrumptious, seraphic, sublime, supernal, supernatural, sweet, wonderful; ▪ *Ant* distasteful, hellish, miserable, repugnant, wretched.

heavy [adj1] *having great weight*
▪ *Syn* awkward, big, bulky, copious, corpulent, cumbrous, fat, fleshy, gravid, hefty, huge, laden, large, massive, obese, ponderous, portly, substantial, weighty; ▪ *Ant* airy, light, lightweight, little, slight, small.

heavy [adj2] *difficult, severe*
▪ *Syn* abstruse, arduous, burdensome, complicated, esoteric, formidable, grave, hard, intolerable, laborious, onerous, oppressive, profound, recondite, solemn, strenuous, tedious, toilsome, vexatious, wearisome, weighty; ▪ *Ant* easy, inconsequential, insignificant, trivial, unimportant.

heavy [adj3] *depressed or depressing, gloomy* ▪ *Syn* cloudy, crestfallen, damp, dark, dejected, despondent, disconsolate, dismal, dull, grieving, leaden, lowering, melancholy, oppressive, overcast, sad, sorrowful, stifling; ▪ *Ant* gay, happy, joyful.

heavy [adj4] *listless, slow*
▪ *Syn* apathetic, comatose, dull, hebetudinous, indifferent, lethargic, sluggish, slumberous, torpid; ▪ *Ant* light, moving, quick, smoooth.

heckle [v] *jeer*
▪ *Syn* badger, bait, bother, bully, chivy, discomfit, disconcert, disrupt, disturb, embarrass, faze, gibe, interrupt, pester, plague, rattle, ridicule, taunt, tease, torment, worry; ▪ *Ant* encourage, help, promote, support.

hectic [adj] *frantic, turbulent*
▪ *Syn* chaotic, confused, disordered, exciting, fervid, fevered, flurrying, frenetic, frenzied, furious, heated, restless, tumultuous, wild; ▪ *Ant* calm, leisurely, serene, tranquil, unhurried.

hedge [v] *avoid, dodge*
▪ *Syn* duck, equivocate, evade, prevaricate, quibble, shuffle, sidestep, stall, temporize, tergiversate; ▪ *Ant* confront, face, meet.

hedonist [n] *person who seeks pleasure above other values* ▪ *Syn* bon vivant, debauchee, epicurean, glutton, libertine, pleasuremonger, pleasureseeker, profligate, sensualist, sybarite, thrill-seeker, voluptuary; ▪ *Ant* ascetic, moralist, puritan.

heed [v] *give care, thought to*
▪ *Syn* attend, be aware, consider, follow, listen, mind, note, pay attention, regard, see, spot, watch; ▪ *Ant* disregard, ignore, neglect, overlook, slight.

heedless [adj] *careless*
▪ *Syn* disregardful, feckless, foolhardy, impetuous, imprudent, negligent, oblivious, reckless, sloppy, thoughtless, uncaring; ▪ *Ant* attentive, careful, caring, cautious, concerned, considerate, heedful, observant, thoughtful, wary.

hefty [adj] *big, bulky*
▪ *Syn* ample, brawny, burly, cumbersome, extensive, fat, heavy, husky, large, major, massive, ponderous, robust, sizable, sturdy, substantial, tremendous, unwieldy, vigorous, weighty; ▪ *Ant* slight, small, thin, tiny.

heinous [adj] *horrifying, monstrous*
▪ *Syn* abhorrent, abominable, accursed, atrocious, awful, bad, beastly, crying,

cursed, evil, execrable, flagitious, flagrant, frightful, grave, hateful, hideous, horrendous, infamous, iniquitous, nefarious, odious, offensive, outrageous, revolting, scandalous, shocking, unspeakable, vicious, villainous; ▪ *Ant* glorious, good, lovely, magnificent, wonderful.

hell [*n*] *place where devil lives; bad situation* ▪ *Syn* abyss, affliction, agony, anguish, difficulty, grave, Hades, hellfire, infernal regions, inferno, limbo, lower world, misery, nether world, nightmare, ordeal, pandemonium, perdition, pit, purgatory, suffering, torment, trial, underworld, wretchedness; ▪ *Ant* bliss, ecstasy, happiness, heaven, joy, paradise.

help [*v1*] *aid, assist*
▪ *Syn* abet, accommodate, advocate, back, befriend, benefit, bolster, boost, cheer, cooperate, encourage, endorse, further, intercede, maintain, patronize, promote, prop, push, relieve, sanction, save, second, serve, stand by, stimulate, succor, support, sustain, uphold; ▪ *Ant* block, check, counteract, harm, hinder, hurt, injure, obstruct, stop.

help [*v2*] *improve*
▪ *Syn* alleviate, ameliorate, amend, attend, better, cure, doctor, ease, facilitate, heal, meliorate, mitigate, nourish, palliate, relieve, remedy, restore, revive, treat; ▪ *Ant* decrease, harm, hinder, hurt, injure, worsen.

helpful [*adj*] *beneficial, beneficent*
▪ *Syn* accommodating, advantageous, benevolent, caring, considerate, constructive, cooperative, efficacious, essential, favorable, fortunate, friendly, instrumental, invaluable, kind, neighborly, profitable, serendipitous, serviceable, supportive, symbiotic, sympathetic, timely, useful, utilitarian, valuable; ▪ *Ant* disadvantageous, harmful, hurtful, injurious, unconstructive, unhelpful, useless, worthless.

helpless [*adj*] *incapable, incompetent; vulnerable* ▪ *Syn* abandoned, debilitated, defenseless, destitute, exposed, feeble, forsaken, impotent, infirm, invalid, powerless, shiftless, tapped, weak; ▪ *Ant* able, capable, competent, enterprising, independent, resourceful, skilled, strong.

helter-skelter [*adj/adv*] *carelessly, confused* ▪ *Syn* at random, cluttered, disorderly, haphazard, hastily, headlong, hurriedly, impetuously, incautiously, irregular, randomly, rashly, recklessly, wildly; ▪ *Ant* carefully, methodical, organized, straight, systematic.

hem [*n*] *border, edge*
▪ *Syn* brim, brink, edging, fringe, margin, perimeter, periphery, piping, rim, selvage, skirt, verge; ▪ *Ant* body, center, interior.

herd [*v*] *gather; shepherd*
▪ *Syn* assemble, associate, collect, congregate, corral, drive, flock, force, goad, guide, huddle, lead, muster, poke, punch, rally, run, spur; ▪ *Ant* disperse, scatter.

hereafter [*adv*] *from now on*
▪ *Syn* after this, eventually, hence, henceforth, hereupon, in the future, ultimately; ▪ *Ant* before, hertofore, previously.

hereditary [*adj*] *inherited; transmitted at birth* ▪ *Syn* ancestral, bequeathed, family, genealogical, genetic, handed down, heritable, inborn, inbred, inheritable, inherited, lineal; ▪ *Ant* acquired, learned.

heretical [*adj*] *unorthodox*
▪ *Syn* agnostic, apostate, atheistic, differing, dissenting, dissident, freethinking, heterodox, iconoclastic, idolatrous, miscreant, revisionist, schismatic, sectarian, skeptical, unbelieving; ▪ *Ant* conformist, conventional, orthodox, traditional.

hermeneutical [*adj*] *interpretive*
▪ *Syn* critical, demonstrative, explanatory, explicative, expository, illustrative, investigative, revealing; ▪ *Ant* burying, concealing, covering up, disguising, masking, mystifying.

heroic [*adj*] *brave*
▪ *Syn* bold, courageous, daring, dauntless, doughty, elevated, epic, fearless, gallant, grand, grandiose, intrepid, lionhearted, mythological, noble, stouthearted, valiant, valorous; ▪ *Ant* afraid, cowardly, fearful, meek, timid, villainous.

hesitant [*adj*] *uncertain, waiting*
▪ *Syn* afraid, averse, diffident, doubtful, halfhearted, halting, indecisive, reluctant, shy, skeptical, slow, tentative, timid, vacillating, wavering; ▪ *Ant* certain, decisive, definite, resolute, sure, unhesitant, unwavering.

hesitate [*v*] *wait; be uncertain*
▪ *Syn* alternate, balk, dally, dawdle, demur, dither, doubt, equivocate, falter, flounder, fluctuate, hedge, linger, oscillate, pause, shift, straddle, stumble,

swerve, tergiversate, vacillate, waver, weigh; ▪ *Ant* attack, carry on, continue, go, go ahead, persevere, resolve.

heterogeneous [*adj*] *assorted, miscellaneous* ▪ *Syn* amalgamate, composite, confused, conglomerate, contrary, contrasted, different, discordant, discrepant, disparate, dissimilar, divergent, diverse, diversified, incongruous, independent, jumbled, mingled, mixed, mongrel, mosaic, motley, multifarious, multiplex, odd, opposed, variant, varied, variegated; ▪ *Ant* homogeneous, identical, pure, single, unchanging, uniform.

hiatus [*n*] *pause, interruption* ▪ *Syn* aperture, blank, breach, break, chasm, discontinuity, gap, interim, interval, lacuna, lapse, opening, rift, space; ▪ *Ant* continuation, continuity.

hidden [*adj*] *unseen, secret* ▪ *Syn* abstruse, clandestine, covert, cryptic, dark, esoteric, hermetic, imperceivable, indiscernible, latent, mysterious, obscure, occult, private, recondite, secluded, veiled, withheld; ▪ *Ant* bare, disclosed, exhibited, exposed, open, out, revealed, seen, showing.

hide [*v*] *conceal; remain unseen* ▪ *Syn* adumbrate, bury, cache, camouflage, cover, disguise, eclipse, ensconce, harbor, hush up, keep secret, lock up, mask, obscure, plant, protect, reserve, screen, shelter, shield, shroud, suppress, veil, withhold; ▪ *Ant* bare, disclose, divulge, exhibit, expose, lay bare, let out, open, reveal, show, tell, uncover, unmask.

hideous [*adj*] *grotesque, horrible* ▪ *Syn* abominable, appalling, detestable, disgusting, dreadful, frightful, grisly, gruesome, horrendous, loathsome, monstrous, odious, repulsive, revolting, shocking, sickening, terrible, ugly, weird; ▪ *Ant* attractive, beautiful, charming, delightful, pleasing.

high [*adj1*] *tall; at a great distance aloft* ▪ *Syn* aerial, alpine, altitudinous, elevated, eminent, formidable, giant, gigantic, great, huge, immense, large, lofty, sky-high, sky-scraping, soaring, steep, towering, tremendous, upraised; ▪ *Ant* dwarfed, low, lowly, short, stunted.

high [*adj2*] *extreme* ▪ *Syn* excessive, exorbitant, expensive, extraordinary, extravagant, grand, great, high-priced, steep, stiff, strong; ▪ *Ant* average, low, mild, moderate, reasonable.

high [*adj3*] *important* ▪ *Syn* arch, capital, chief, exalted, grave, influential, leading, noble, powerful, prominent, ruling, significant, superior; ▪ *Ant* dishonorable, inferior, low, unimportant, worthless.

high [*adj4*] *very happy* ▪ *Syn* boisterous, bouncy, cheerful, elated, excited, exuberant, joyful, lighthearted, merry; ▪ *Ant* depressed, down, low, upset.

high [*adj5*] *intoxicated, drugged* ▪ *Syn* delirious, doped, drunk, euphoric, inebriated, tipsy; ▪ *Ant* sober, straight.

high [*adj6*] *shrill, strong (on the senses)* ▪ *Syn* acute, loud, penetrating, piercing, piping, sharp, strident, treble; ▪ *Ant* low, soft, weak.

highlight [*n*] *memorable part* ▪ *Syn* best part, climax, feature, focal point, focus, high point, main feature, peak; ▪ *Ant* disappointment, low point, zenith.

high-strung [*adj*] *nervous* ▪ *Syn* edgy, excitable, fidgety, impatient, jittery, jumpy, nervy, restless, stressed, tense, unrestful; ▪ *Ant* calm, easygoing, laid-back, peaceful, tranquil.

hike [*v*] *raise, increase* ▪ *Syn* advance, boost, jack, jump, lift, pull up, upgrade; ▪ *Ant* decrease, lower, reduce.

hilarious [*adj*] *very funny* ▪ *Syn* amusing, comical, convivial, entertaining, frolicsome, gay, humorous, laughable, mirthful, rollicking, scream, uproarious, witty; ▪ *Ant* grave, serious, somber, tragic, unfunny.

hinder [*v*] *prevent, slow down* ▪ *Syn* arrest, balk, bar, block, bottleneck, burden, check, choke, clog, contravene, counteract, cramp, curb, debar, delay, deter, encumber, fetter, frustrate, hamper, handicap, impede, inhibit, interfere, interrupt, obstruct, offset, oppose, preclude, prevent, prohibit, resist, retard, stay, stop, terminate, thwart, trammel; ▪ *Ant* advance, aid, allow, assist, encourage, facilitate, forward, further, help, permit, promote, push.

hint [*v*] *suggest; indicate* ▪ *Syn* acquaint, adumbrate, advise, allude to, angle, broach, connote, cue, drop, expose, foreshadow, impart, imply, infer, inform, insinuate, intimate, mention, point, prefigure, press, prompt, recall, refer to, shadow, signify, solicit, whisper; ▪ *Ant* announce, assert, declare, proclaim.

hire [v] *commission for responsibility, use* ▪ *Syn* appoint, authorize, book, bring in, charter, contract for, delegate, draft, employ, engage, enlist, exploit, lease, let, obtain, occupy, pick, place, pledge, procure, promise, rent, retain, secure, select, sign on, sublease, sublet, use, utilize; ▪ *Ant* discharge, dismiss, fire, lay off, let go.

historic [adj] *momentous, remarkable* ▪ *Syn* celebrated, consequential, famous, important, memorable, notable, outstanding, significant, well-known; ▪ *Ant* trivial, unimportant, unremarkable.

historical [adj] *recorded as actually having happened* ▪ *Syn* actual, archival, authentic, chronicled, commemorated, documented, factual, real, verifiable; ▪ *Ant* apocryphal, fabulous, fictional, legendary.

history [n] *past events, experiences* ▪ *Syn* ancient times, antiquity, past, yesterday, yesteryear; ▪ *Ant* current times, future.

hit [n] *entertainment success* ▪ *Syn* achievement, bang, click, favorite, knockout, sellout, sensation, smash, triumph, winner; ▪ *Ant* failure, flop, loss.

hit [v] *accomplish* ▪ *Syn* achieve, arrive at, attain, gain, influence, occur, overwhelm, reach, secure, strike, touch; ▪ *Ant* fail, lose, surrender.

hitch [v] *join, fasten* ▪ *Syn* attach, chain, connect, couple, harness, hook, lash, make fast, moor, strap, tether, tie, unite, yoke; ▪ *Ant* disjoin, unchain, unfasten, unhitch, unlock.

hoard [v] *put away, accumulate* ▪ *Syn* acquire, amass, buy up, cache, collect, deposit, garner, keep, pile up, save, scrimp, stash, stockpile, store, stow away, treasure; ▪ *Ant* expend, spend, squander, throw away, waste.

hoarse [adj] *raspy in voice* ▪ *Syn* blatant, breathy, cracked, croaky, croupy, dry, grating, gravelly, gruff, guttural, husky, scratching, stertorous, strident, throaty, uneven, whispering; ▪ *Ant* clear, mellow, smooth, soft, soothing.

hoax [v] *trick* ▪ *Syn* bluff, chicane, con, deceive, delude, dupe, fake out, fleece, fool, frame, gammon, gull, swindle; ▪ *Ant* enlighten, undeceive.

hobble [v] *cripple, restrict* ▪ *Syn* cramp, cramp one's style, crimp, fasten, fetter, hamper, hinder, leash, shackle, trammel; ▪ *Ant* assist, free, let go, release.

hobby [n] *pleasurable pastime* ▪ *Syn* amusement, avocation, craft, diversion, fancy, game, interest, leisure activity, obsession, play, relaxation, sideline, specialty, sport, weakness, whim; ▪ *Ant* job, profession, vocation, work.

hogwash [n] *nonsense* ▪ *Syn* absurdity, debris, foolishness, hokum, refuse, ridiculousness, rot, rubbish, trash; ▪ *Ant* sense, truth.

hoist [v] *lift* ▪ *Syn* elevate, erect, heave, pick up, raise, rear, take up, uphold, uplift, upraise, uprear; ▪ *Ant* drop, fall, hold down, lower, push.

hold [v1] *have in one's hands, possession; grasp* ▪ *Syn* adhere, arrest, bind, carry, catch, check, clasp, cleave, cling, clutch, cradle, embrace, grip, handle, imprison, keep, maintain, own, possess, press, retain, secure, seize, stick, take, vise, withhold; ▪ *Ant* drop, give, let go, release.

hold [v2] *believe* ▪ *Syn* assume, aver, consider, credit, deem, entertain, esteem, feel, judge, maintain, presume, reckon, regard, sense, swear by, think, view; ▪ *Ant* abandon, disavow, disbelieve, disclaim, forsake, refute.

hold [v3] *continue, endure* ▪ *Syn* apply, exist, last, operate, persevere, persist, remain, resist, stand up, stay, stay staunch, wear; ▪ *Ant* cease, desert, halt, quit, stop.

hold [v4] *support* ▪ *Syn* bear, bolster, brace, buttress, carry, lock, prop, shore up, shoulder, stay, sustain, take, underpin, uphold; ▪ *Ant* break, give way.

hold up [v] *postpone* ▪ *Syn* delay, detain, hinder, impede, interfere, interrupt, pause, prorogue, retard, stay, stop, suspend, waive; ▪ *Ant* allow, continue, forward, permit, promote.

hollow [adj1] empty, hollowed out
▪ **Syn** alveolate, arched, carved out, cavernous, cleft, concave, cupped, curved, deep-set, depressed, dimpled, excavated, indented, infundibular, notched, pitted, striated, sunken, vacant, vaulted, void; ▪ **Ant** convex, full, protuberant, raised, solid.

hollow [adj2] deep, resonant in sound
▪ **Syn** cavernous, dull, echoing, flat, ghostly, low, muffled, muted, resounding, reverberant, ringing, roaring, rumbling, sepulchral, sounding, thunderous, toneless, vibrant, vibrating; ▪ **Ant** high, light, soft, vibrant.

hollow [adj3] meaningless
▪ **Syn** empty, fruitless, futile, idle, nugatory, otiose, pointless, specious, useless, vain, worthless; ▪ **Ant** earnest, meaningful, sincere, substantial.

hollow [adj4] false, artificial
▪ **Syn** cynical, deceitful, faithless, flimsy, hypocritical, treacherous, unsound, weak; ▪ **Ant** frank, genuine, honest, real, sincere, truthful.

hollow [v] empty out; make concave
▪ **Syn** channel, corrugate, dent, dig, excavate, furrow, gorge, groove, indent, notch, pit, scoop, shovel, trench; ▪ **Ant** fill, make convex, raise.

holy [adj] religious, sacred
▪ **Syn** angelic, blessed, chaste, consecrated, devout, divine, faithful, god-fearing, godly, good, hallowed, immaculate, just, moral, perfect, pious, prayerful, pure, reverent, righteous, sacrosanct, saintlike, sanctified, seraphic, spiritual, sublime, unworldly, virtuous; ▪ **Ant** depraved, evil, immoral, irreligious, irreverent, sacrilegious, sinful, unholy, unsacred, vile, wicked.

homage [n] devotion, admiration
▪ **Syn** adoration, adulation, allegiance, deference, faithfulness, fealty, fidelity, genuflection, loyalty, obeisance, reverence, tribute, worship; ▪ **Ant** dishonor, disloyalty, disrespect, faithlessness, scorn, treachery.

home [adj] domestic
▪ **Syn** family, homely, homey, household, internal, local, national, native; ▪ **Ant** business, commercial, foreign.

homeless [adj] displaced
▪ **Syn** abandoned, desolate, destitute, displaced, dispossessed, estranged, exiled, forsaken, itinerant, outcast, refugee, vagabond, vagrant, wandering; ▪ **Ant** housed, settled.

homely [adj] ordinary, comfortable
▪ **Syn** comfy, cozy, domestic, everyday, familiar, friendly, homespun, homey, informal, modest, natural, plain, simple, snug, welcoming; ▪ **Ant** elegant, grand, pretentious, showy, sophisticated.

homogenous [adj] similar, comparable
▪ **Syn** akin, alike, analogous, cognate, homologous, identical, kindred, like, uniform, unvarying; ▪ **Ant** different, discrete, dissimilar, heterogeneous, miscellaneous, varied.

honest [adj] truthful, candid
▪ **Syn** authentic, conscientious, decent, direct, equitable, ethical, fair, forthright, frank, genuine, honorable, impartial, ingenuous, just, open, outright, plain, proper, real, reliable, reputable, scrupulous, sincere, straight, straightforward, true, trustworthy, trusty, truthful, upright, veracious; ▪ **Ant** deceptive, devious, dishonest, false, fraudulent, lying, misleading, treacherous, untrustworthy, untruthful.

honor [v] recognize, treat with respect
▪ **Syn** acclaim, admire, adore, aggrandize, appreciate, celebrate, commemorate, commend, compliment, decorate, dignify, distinguish, ennoble, erect, esteem, exalt, glorify, hallow, keep, laud, lionize, magnify, observe, praise, prize, respect, revere, sanctify, value, venerate, worship; ▪ **Ant** betray, denounce, disgrace, dishonor, disrespect, reproach, shame.

hook [v] grab, catch
▪ **Syn** clasp, crook, curve, enmesh, ensnare, entrap, fasten, fix, hasp, lasso, net, pin, secure, snare, trap; ▪ **Ant** let go, release, unhook, unlatch, unlock.

hope [v] long for, dream about
▪ **Syn** anticipate, aspire, await, believe, cherish, contemplate, desire, expect, have faith, hold, pray, presume, suppose, surmise, suspect, trust, watch for, wish; ▪ **Ant** despair, disbelieve, fear.

hopeful [adj1] optimistic, expectant
▪ **Syn** anticipating, assured, blithe, cheerful, confident, content, eager, elated, emboldened, enthusiastic, expecting, faithful, high, inspirited, lighthearted, reassured, sanguine, satisfied, serene, trusting, upbeat; ▪ **Ant** despairing, despondent, discouraged, fearful, gloomy, hopeless, low, pessimistic, sad.

hopeful [adj2] *promising, auspicious*
▪ *Syn* advantageous, beneficial, cheerful, conducive, encouraging, enlivening, expeditious, fair, favorable, fortunate, golden, good, halcyon, heartening, inspiring, opportune, pleasant, probable, propitious, providential, reassuring, suitable, sunny, timely, uplifting, well-timed; ▪ *Ant* desperate, hopeless, inauspicious, pointless, unpromising, wretched.

hopeless [adj] *futile; pessimistic*
▪ *Syn* bad, cynical, dejected, demoralized, despairing, despondent, disconsolate, downhearted, forlorn, helpless, ill-fated, impossible, impracticable, irrevocable, lost, sad, sunk, tragic, unfortunate, useless, vain, woebegone; ▪ *Ant* auspicious, bright, encouraging, expectant, hopeful, optimistic, promising, propitious, rosy.

horizontal [adj] *lying flat*
▪ *Syn* accumbent, aligned, even, flush, level, parallel, plane, recumbent, regular, smooth, straight, uniform; ▪ *Ant* upright, vertical.

horrible/horrendous/horrid [adj] *repulsive, very unpleasant* ▪ *Syn* abhorrent, abominable, appalling, awful, beastly, cruel, detestable, disgusting, dreadful, eerie, execrable, fearful, frightful, ghastly, grim, gruesome, heinous, hideous, loathsome, lurid, nasty, obnoxious, offensive, repellent, revolting, scary, shocking, terrible, terrifying; ▪ *Ant* agreeable, delightful, magnificent, pleasant, pleasing, wonderful.

horrify [v] *scare*
▪ *Syn* affright, alarm, appall, consternate, daunt, disgust, dismay, frighten, intimidate, outrage, petrify, shake, shock, sicken, terrify, terrorize; ▪ *Ant* delight, gladden, please, reassure, soothe.

hospitable [adj] *sociable, accommodating* ▪ *Syn* accessible, amenable, amicable, bountiful, charitable, companionable, convivial, cooperative, cordial, courteous, friendly, generous, genial, gracious, kind, liberal, magnanimous, neighborly, obliging, open, receptive, responsive, tolerant, welcoming; ▪ *Ant* hostile, inhospitable, isolated, solitary, unaccommodating, uncordial, unfriendly, unkind, unsociable.

host/hostess [n1] *person who entertains, performs* ▪ *Syn* anchor, emcee, entertainer, innkeeper, keeper, manager,

master of ceremonies, moderator, owner, presenter, proprietor; ▪ *Ant* guest, visitor.

host [n2] *large group*
▪ *Syn* army, array, cloud, crowd, crush, drove, flock, gathering, horde, legion, multitude, myriad, rout, score, swarm, throng; ▪ *Ant* handful, small group, sprinkling.

hostile [adj] *antagonistic, mean*
▪ *Syn* adverse, argumentative, bellicose, belligerent, bitter, competitive, contentious, contrary, disapproving, dour, hateful, ill-disposed, inimical, malevolent, malicious, malignant, militant, nasty, opposed, oppugnant, pugnacious, rancorous, spiteful, surly, unfavorable, viperous, virulent, vitriolic, warlike; ▪ *Ant* agreeable, friendly, gentle, kind, nice, pacifistic, welcoming.

hot [adj1] *very high in temperature*
▪ *Syn* baking, blazing, blistering, burning, calescent, close, febrile, fevered, fiery, flaming, heated, igneous, parching, recalescent, scalding, scorching, sizzling, steaming, sweltering, thermogenic, torrid, tropic, tropical, warm; ▪ *Ant* cold, cool, freezing, frigid, gelid, icy.

hot [adj2] *spicy to taste*
▪ *Syn* acrid, biting, peppery, piquant, pungent, racy, sharp, spicy, zestful; ▪ *Ant* bland, insipid, mild, moderate.

hot [adj3] *passionate, vehement*
▪ *Syn* angry, ardent, enthusiastic, excited, fervent, fiery, ill-tempered, impassioned, impetuous, inflamed, intense, irascible, lustful, raging, stormy, temperamental, violent; ▪ *Ant* calm, cool, indifferent, unfeeling.

hot [adj4] *new, in vogue*
▪ *Syn* approved, dandy, favored, fresh, in demand, keen, marvelous, popular, recent, trendy; ▪ *Ant* old, old-fashioned, out, unpopular.

hot [adj5] *sexually excited*
▪ *Syn* aroused, carnal, concupiscent, erotic, lascivious, lewd, libidinous, lustful, passionate, prurient, salacious, sensual; ▪ *Ant* frigid, turned off.

household [adj] *domestic*
▪ *Syn* domiciliary, everyday, family, home, homely, homey, ordinary, plain; ▪ *Ant* business, commercial, industrial.

hover [v] *hang, float over*
▪ *Syn* be suspended, dance, drift, flicker, flit, flutter, fly, hang about, linger, poise, waver; ▪ *Ant* lie, rest, settle.

howl [n] *long, painful cry*
▪ *Syn* bark, bay, bellow, clamor, hoot, keen, lament, moan, outcry, quest, roar, scream, shriek, ululate, wail, weep, whimper, whine, yell, yelp, yip, yowl; ▪ *Ant* murmur, mutter, whisper.

hub [n] *center, focal point*
▪ *Syn* core, focus, heart, middle, pivot, polestar, seat; ▪ *Ant* exterior, exteriority, outside.

hubbub [n] *commotion, disorder*
▪ *Syn* babel, bedlam, clamor, confusion, din, disturbance, fuss, hassle, jangle, noise, pandemonium, racket, tumult, uproar, whirl; ▪ *Ant* calm, order, peace.

huffy [adj] *angry, in a bad mood*
▪ *Syn* angered, annoyed, crabbed, cross, crotchety, disgruntled, fractious, grumpy, irked, miffed, moody, nettled, peeved, petulant, piqued, provoked, querulous, riled, short, snappish, surly, testy, touchy, vexed, waspish; ▪ *Ant* cheerful, delighted, happy, joyful.

hug [v] *hold close, cling to*
▪ *Syn* cherish, clasp, cuddle, embrace, enbosom, envelop, grasp, hold onto, keep close, love, nestle, nurse, seize, squeeze; ▪ *Ant* push away, release.

huge [adj] *extremely large*
▪ *Syn* behemothic, bulky, colossal, cyclopean, elephantine, enormous, gargantuan, gigantic, great, humongous, immense, jumbo, leviathan, mammoth, massive, mountainous, planetary, prodigious, stupendous, towering, tremendous, vast, walloping; ▪ *Ant* dwarf, little, miniature, minute, small, teeny, tiny.

humane [adj] *kind, compassionate*
▪ *Syn* accommodating, altruistic, benevolent, broad-minded, charitable, clement, considerate, cordial, democratic, forgiving, generous, good-natured, gracious, helpful, humanitarian, kindhearted, magnanimous, merciful, obliging, open-minded, philanthropic, sympathetic, tolerant, understanding, unselfish, warmhearted; ▪ *Ant* cruel, fierce, inhumane, merciless, uncivilized, uncompassionate, unkind, unsympathetic, violent.

humanitarian [adj] *giving, compassionate* ▪ *Syn* altruistic, beneficent, benevolent, charitable, eleemosynary, generous, good, humane, idealistic, kindly, philanthropic, public-spirited; ▪ *Ant* egoistic, egotistic, inhumanitarian, stingy, uncompassionate, ungiving.

humble [adj1] *meek, unassuming*
▪ *Syn* bashful, blushing, courteous, deferential, demure, docile, fearful, modest, obliging, obsequious, polite, quiet, reserved, respectful, reverential, self-conscious, sheepish, simple, timorous, tractable; ▪ *Ant* assertive, boasting, brave, conceited, egotistical, insolent, pretentious, proud, showy.

humble [adj2] *poor, inferior*
▪ *Syn* base, beggarly, common, humdrum, ignoble, inglorious, insignificant, little, lowly, meager, measly, menial, ordinary, paltry, petty, pitiful, plebeian, simple, sordid, trivial, vulgar, wretched; ▪ *Ant* luxurious, refined, rich, superior.

humble [v] *shame, put down*
▪ *Syn* abase, bemean, chasten, confound, debase, deflate, degrade, demean, discomfit, disgrace, embarrass, humiliate, mortify, reduce, silence, squelch, subdue, upset; ▪ *Ant* build up, praise, promote.

humid [adj] *very damp, referring to weather* ▪ *Syn* boiling, clammy, close, dank, moist, muggy, oppressive, sodden, soggy, steamy, sticky, stifling, stuffy, sultry, sweaty, sweltering, watery, wet; ▪ *Ant* arid, dry.

humiliate [v] *embarrass, put down*
▪ *Syn* abase, abash, bemean, blister, break, cast down, chagrin, chasten, confound, confuse, conquer, debase, degrade, demean, denigrate, discomfit, discountenance, disgrace, dishonor, humble, lower, mortify, pan, shame, smear, snub, subdue, vanquish, wither; ▪ *Ant* build up, elevate, laud, praise.

humorous [adj] *funny, comical*
▪ *Syn* amusing, comic, droll, entertaining, facetious, farcical, hilarious, jocose, jocular, laughable, ludicrous, merry, playful, ribald, waggish, whimsical, witty; ▪ *Ant* depressing, dramatic, gloomy, morose, sad, serious, tragic, uncomical, unfunny.

hump [n] *swelling, projection*
▪ *Syn* bulge, bump, convexity, dune, elevation, hill, hummock, humpback, hunch, hunchback, knap, knob, knurl, kyphosis, mound, prominence, protrusion, protuberance, ridge, swell; ▪ *Ant* concavity, depression, hollow, pit.

hunch [n] *feeling, idea*
▪ *Syn* anticipation, apprehension, augury, boding, clue, expectation, foreboding, glimmer, hint, impression, inkling, in-

stinct, intuition, notion, omination, portent, premonition, prescience, presentiment, qualm, suspicion, thought; ▪ *Ant* certainty, proof, reality, truth.

hunch [v] *cower, crouch*
▪ *Syn* bend, bow, curve, huddle, hump, lean, squat, stoop, tense; ▪ *Ant* stand, straighten.

hungry [adj] *starving; desirous*
▪ *Syn* athirst, avid, carnivorous, covetous, craving, eager, edacious, esurient, famished, greedy, hankering, insatiate, keen, omnivorous, rapacious, ravenous, starved, voracious, yearning; ▪ *Ant* full, replete, satiated, satisfied, stuffed.

hunt [v] *look, search for*
▪ *Syn* cast about, delve, drag, examine, ferret out, inquire, investigate, probe, prowl, quest, question, ransack, rummage, scour, seek, trace, trail, winnow; ▪ *Ant* ignore, neglect.

hurl [v] *throw forcefully*
▪ *Syn* bung, cast, chuck, chunk, fire, fling, gun, heave, launch, let fly, lob, peg, pitch, project, propel, send, sling, toss; ▪ *Ant* capture, catch, clutch, grab, grasp, seize.

hurried [adj] *quick, rushed*
▪ *Syn* abrupt, breakneck, brief, cursory, fast, hasty, headlong, hectic, impetuous, perfunctory, precipitous, rushing, short, slapdash, speedy, sudden, superficial, swift; ▪ *Ant* easily, leisurely, slow, unhurried, unrushed.

hurry [v] *act, move speedily*
▪ *Syn* accelerate, barrel, breeze, burst, bustle, dash, drive, expedite, fly, goad, haste, hasten, hustle, jog, move, nip, push, quicken, race, rip, rocket, run, rush, sally, scoot, scurry, smoke, speed, spur, urge, whisk, whiz, zip; ▪ *Ant* dally, dawdle, delay, procrastinate, rest, slow, stall, wait.

hurt [adj] *physically or mentally injured*
▪ *Syn* aching, aggrieved, agonized, battered, bleeding, bruised, crushed, cut, damaged, disfigured, grazed, harmed, impaired, lacerated, mauled, mutilated, offended, pained, piqued, resentful, rueful, sad, scraped, shook, sore, stricken, suffering, tender, tortured, umbrageous, wounded; ▪ *Ant* comforted, cured, healed, healthy, pleased, remedied, well.

hurt [v1] *cause physical pain; experience pain* ▪ *Syn* abuse, ache, afflict, ail, belt, bite, bruise, burn, cramp, cut, damage,

do violence, flail, flog, harm, impair, injure, kick, lacerate, lash, maltreat, maul, pain, pinch, pummel, punch, slap, slug, smart, stab, sting, tear, throb, torture, total, trouble, whip, wing, wound; ▪ *Ant* aid, assist, assuage, cure, heal, help, relieve, remedy, soothe.

hurt [v2] *cause mental pain*
▪ *Syn* abuse, afflict, aggrieve, burn, chafe, discomfit, displease, distress, excruciate, faze, grieve, injure, lambaste, martyr, pain, punish, sadden, torment, torture, try, upset, vex, vitiate, wound; ▪ *Ant* calm, placate, please, relieve, soothe.

hurtful [adj] *injurious, cruel*
▪ *Syn* afflictive, bad, cutting, damaging, deleterious, destructive, detrimental, evil, harmful, malicious, nasty, noxious, ominous, pernicious, spiteful, unkind, upsetting, wounding; ▪ *Ant* aiding, assisting, harmless, helpful, helping, innocuous, kind, nice, relieving.

hurtle [v] *plunge, charge*
▪ *Syn* bump, collide, fly, lunge, push, race, rush, scoot, scramble, shoot, speed, spurt, tear; ▪ *Ant* crawl, creep, drag, inch.

hush-hush [adj] *secret*
▪ *Syn* clandestine, classified, closet, confidential, covert, dark, private, restricted, surreptitious, top-secret, undercover; ▪ *Ant* known, public, revealed, told.

hush up [v] *keep secret*
▪ *Syn* burke, conceal, cover, cover up, keep dark, sit on, smother, squash, stifle, suppress; ▪ *Ant* expose, reveal, tell.

husky [adj1] *deep, scratchy in sound*
▪ *Syn* croaking, growling, gruff, guttural, harsh, hoarse, loud, rasping, raucous, rough, throaty; ▪ *Ant* low, quiet, soft.

husky [adj2] *big, burly*
▪ *Syn* brawny, hefty, mighty, muscular, powerful, rugged, sinewy, stalwart, stocky, stout, strapping, strong, sturdy, thickset, well-built; ▪ *Ant* little, small, thin.

hustle [v] *hurry; work hurriedly*
▪ *Syn* apply oneself, bustle, fly, force, haste, hasten, impel, jog, press, push, race, rush, shove, speed, thrust; ▪ *Ant* dally, delay, procrastinate, slow, wait.

hut [n] *tiny, often roughly built, house*
▪ *Syn* bungalow, cabana, cabin, camp, cot, cottage, den, dugout, hutch, lean-to, lodge, refuge, shack, shanty, shed, shelter; ▪ *Ant* castle, manor, mansion, palace.

hybrid [n] *composite, mixture*
▪ *Syn* amalgam, bastard, combination, compound, cross, crossbreed, incross, miscegenation, mongrel; ▪ *Ant* homogeneous, pure, purebred, thoroughbred, unmixed.

hygienic [adj] *clean*
▪ *Syn* aseptic, disinfected, germ-free, healthful, pure, salubrious, salutary, sanitary, sterile, wholesome; ▪ *Ant* contaminated, dirty, diseased, filthy, foul, infected, unclean, unpure, unsterile.

hyperbole [n] *exaggeration*
▪ *Syn* amplification, distortion, embellishment, embroidering, enlargement, magnification, metaphor, overstatement; ▪ *Ant* understatement.

hypnotic [adj] *spellbinding, sleep-inducing* ▪ *Syn* anesthetic, anodyne, calmative, mesmerizing, narcotic, opiate, somnolent, soporific, trance-inducing; ▪ *Ant* exciting, exhilarating, inciteful, inspiring, stimulating.

hypnotize [v] *put in trance; spellbind*
▪ *Syn* anesthetize, captivate, charm, drug, entrance, fascinate, induce, magnetize, mesmerize, narcotize, soothe, stupefy; ▪ *Ant* excite, exhilarate, incite, inspire, stimulate.

hypocritical [adj] *deceitful, pretending*
▪ *Syn* affected, artificial, assuming, bland, canting, captious, caviling, deceptive, deluding, dissembling, duplicitous, faithless, false, feigning, fraudulent, glib, hollow, insincere, jivey, left-handed, lying, moralistic, oily, pharisaical, phony, pietistic, pious, sanctimonious, self-righteous, smooth, smooth-spoken, snide, specious, spurious, unctuous, unnatural; ▪ *Ant* actual, authentic, forthright, honest, just, real, reliable, righteous, sincere, truthful, upright.

hypothetical [adj] *guessed, assumed*
▪ *Syn* academic, casual, concocted, conditional, conjecturable, conjectural, contestable, contingent, debatable, disputable, doubtful, equivocal, imaginary, indefinite, indeterminate, postulated, presumptive, presupposed, provisory, putative, questionable, refutable, speculative, stochastic, supposed, suppositional, suppositious, suspect, theoretical, vague; ▪ *Ant* calculated, certain, confirmed, factual, measured, proved, proven, real, reliable, truthful.

hysterical [adj] *very upset, excited*
▪ *Syn* agitated, berserk, convulsive, crazed, crazy, delirious, distracted, distraught, emotional, fiery, frantic, frenzied, fuming, furious, impassioned, impetuous, incensed, irrepressible, mad, maddened, nervous, neurotic, overwrought, panic-stricken, passionate, possessed, rabid, raging, rampant, raving, seething, spasmodic, uproarious, vehement, violent, wild; ▪ *Ant* calm, controlled, restrained, serene.

I

icky [adj] *not pleasant*
▪ *Syn* disgusting, horrible, loathsome, nasty, noisome, offensive, repellent, revolting, sickening, vile; ▪ *Ant* agreeable, good, nice, pleasing.

icy [adj1] *frozen; slippery when frozen*
▪ *Syn* antarctic, biting, chilly, cold, freezing, frigid, frostbound, frosty, gelid, glacial, iced, polar, raw, rimy, shivering, sleeted; ▪ *Ant* fiery, hot, unfrozen, watery.

icy [adj2] *aloof*
▪ *Syn* chill, cold, distant, emotionless, forbidding, frigid, frosty, glacial, hostile, indifferent, steely, stony, unemotional, unfriendly, unwelcoming; ▪ *Ant* cordial, friendly, genial, gracious, warm.

ideal [adj1] *model, perfect*
▪ *Syn* absolute, archetypal, classic, classical, complete, consummate, excellent, exemplary, fitting, flawless, optimal, paradigmatic, prototypical, quintessential, representative, supreme; ▪ *Ant* flawed, imperfect, incorrect, problematic, wrong.

ideal [adj2] *conceptual; impractical*
▪ *Syn* abstract, chimerical, dreamlike, fanciful, high-flown, hypothetical, imaginary, mental, notional, quixotic, theoretical, transcendental, visionary; ▪ *Ant* actual, common, material, practical, pragmatic, real.

identical [adj] *alike, equal*
▪ *Syn* corresponding, double, duplicate, equivalent, exact, indistinguishable, interchangeable, like, look-alike, matching, same, tantamount, twin, very, very same; ▪ *Ant* different, dissimilar, distinct, diverse, opposite, unequal, unlike.

identify [v] *recognize; label*
▪ *Syn* analyze, catalog, classify, describe, determine, diagnose, distinguish, establish, find, name, pick out, pinpoint,

place, select, separate, spot; ▪ *Ant* confuse, mistake.

idiotic [*adj*] *very stupid*
▪ *Syn* asinine, crazy, daft, dull, dumb, fatuous, foolhardy, foolish, imbecile, imbecilic, inane, insane, lunatic, moronic, senseless, silly; ▪ *Ant* brainy, clever, intelligent, sage, sensible, smart.

idle [*adj1*] *not used; out of action*
▪ *Syn* abandoned, asleep, barren, dead, deserted, down, empty, inert, leisured, mothballed, motionless, passive, quiet, redundant, resting, rusty, sleepy, stationary, still, unused, vacant, void, waste; ▪ *Ant* active, busy, employed, productive, used, working.

idle [*adj2*] *lazy*
▪ *Syn* at rest, indolent, lackadaisical, resting, shiftless, slothful, sluggish; ▪ *Ant* ambitious, busy, diligent, hustling, productive.

idle [*adj3*] *worthless, ineffective*
▪ *Syn* abortive, bootless, empty, frivolous, fruitless, futile, groundless, hollow, insignificant, irrelevant, nugatory, otiose, pointless, rambling, superficial, trivial, unavailing, useless, vain; ▪ *Ant* effective, important, productive, worthwhile.

idleness [*n*] *laziness, inaction*
▪ *Syn* dormancy, hibernation, inactivity, indolence, inertia, lethargy, loafing, loitering, otiosity, pottering, sloth, sluggishness, stupor, torpor, truancy, vegetating; ▪ *Ant* action, ambition, busyness, diligence, employment, hustle, industry, labor, occupation, work.

idolize [*v*] *think of very highly; worship*
▪ *Syn* admire, adore, apotheosize, canonize, deify, dote on, exalt, glorify, love, revere, venerate; ▪ *Ant* abhor, despise, loathe.

idyllic [*adj*] *perfect; extremely pleasant*
▪ *Syn* arcadian, bucolic, charming, comfortable, halcyon, heavenly, ideal, idealized, pastoral, peaceful, picturesque, pleasing, rustic, unspoiled; ▪ *Ant* bad, disagreeble, flawed, imperfect.

iffy [*adj*] *uncertain*
▪ *Syn* capricious, chancy, conditional, dicey, doubtful, erratic, incalculable, problematic, unsettled, whimsical; ▪ *Ant* certain, decided, definite, predictable, reliable, sure.

ignite [*v*] *set on fire*
▪ *Syn* burn, burst into flames, catch fire, enkindle, fire, flare up, inflame, kindle,

light, set alight, set fire to, start up, take fire, touch off; ▪ *Ant* douse, extinguish, put out, quench, snuff.

ignoble [*adj*] *lowly, unworthy*
▪ *Syn* abject, base, coarse, common, contemptible, corrupt, craven, degenerate, despicable, heinous, infamous, lewd, low, mean, menial, petty, rotten, shabby, vile, vulgar, wicked, wretched; ▪ *Ant* dignified, grand, high, honorable, noble, reputable, respectable, worthy.

ignorant [*adj*] *unaware, unknowing*
▪ *Syn* benighted, dense, illiterate, imbecilic, innocent, insensible, mindless, moronic, naive, nescient, oblivious, obtuse, shallow, thick, uninitiated, unwitting, witless; ▪ *Ant* aware, educated, experienced, informed, intelligent, knowledgeable, literate, schooled.

ignore [*v*] *disregard on purpose*
▪ *Syn* avoid, be oblivious to, discount, disdain, evade, fail, forget, neglect, omit, overlook, pass over, reject, scorn, slight; ▪ *Ant* acknowledge, heed, look at, mark, note, notice, pay attention, recognize, regard.

ill [*adj1*] *sick*
▪ *Syn* afflicted, ailing, diseased, down, indisposed, infirm, peaked, poorly, queasy, rotten, run-down; ▪ *Ant* good, hale, healthy, hearty, sound, strong, well.

ill [*adj2*] *bad, evil*
▪ *Syn* adverse, antagonistic, damaging, deleterious, detrimental, foreboding, foul, harmful, harsh, hostile, inauspicious, inimical, injurious, malevolent, malicious, nocuous, noxious, ominous, ruinous, sinister, surly, threatening, vile, wicked; ▪ *Ant* favorable, fortunate, good, kind, lucky, promising.

ill-advised [*adj*] *unwise, not thought out*
▪ *Syn* brash, confused, foolhardy, hasty, impolitic, imprudent, injudicious, misguided, rash, reckless, thoughtless, wrong; ▪ *Ant* cautious, reasonable, sensible, well-advised, wise.

ill at ease [*adj*] *uncomfortable, nervous*
▪ *Syn* anxious, awkward, discomfited, disquieted, disturbed, edgy, faltering, fidgety, hesitant, insecure, restless, self-conscious, shy, suspicious, tense, uneasy; ▪ *Ant* at ease, comfortable, content, relaxed.

illegal [*adj*] *against the law*
▪ *Syn* actionable, banned, contraband, criminal, crooked, felonious, forbidden,

illegitimate, illicit, outlawed, prohibited, proscribed, racket, shady, sub rosa, taboo, verboten, violating, wrongful; ▪ *Ant* allowed, authorized, ethical, good, lawful, legal, legitimate, moral, permissible, right.

illegible [*adj*] *unreadable*
▪ *Syn* cacographic, cramped, faint, hieroglyphic, indecipherable, indistinct, obscure, scrawled, unclear; ▪ *Ant* decipherable, legible, readable, understandable.

illegitimate [*adj*] *not legal*
▪ *Syn* contraband, illegal, illicit, invalid, misbegotten, spurious, supposititious, unauthorized, unconstitutional, unsanctioned; ▪ *Ant* authorized, blessed, ethical, justifiable, legal, legitimate, moral, sanctioned, warranted.

ill-fated/ill-starred [*adj*] *doomed*
▪ *Syn* blighted, catastrophic, disastrous, hapless, ill-omened, inauspicious, luckless, ruined, untoward; ▪ *Ant* auspicious, fortuitous, fortunate, happy, lucky.

illicit [*adj*] *not legal; forbidden*
▪ *Syn* adulterous, clandestine, crooked, felonious, furtive, guilty, illegitimate, immoral, improper, lawless, prohibited, wrong, wrongful; ▪ *Ant* authorized, good, legal, legitimate, licit, moral, proper, right.

illiterate [*adj*] *unable to read and write well; lacking education* ▪ *Syn* benighted, catachrestic, ignorant, inerudite, solecistic, unenlightened, uninstructed, unlearned, unread, unschooled, untaught, untutored; ▪ *Ant* educated, learned, literate, taught.

ill-mannered [*adj*] *badly behaved*
▪ *Syn* bad-mannered, boorish, churlish, coarse, discourteous, disrespectful, impertinent, impolite, insolent, loud, loutish, raw, rough, rude, uncouth, vulgar; ▪ *Ant* behaved, civil, gracious, mannered, mannerly, polite.

ill-natured [*adj*] *bad-tempered*
▪ *Syn* catty, churlish, crabby, cross, crotchety, disobliging, dyspeptic, hot-tempered, irritable, malevolent, malicious, nasty, perverse, petulant, spiteful, sullen, surly, temperamental, touchy; ▪ *Ant* agreeable, amenable, amiable, friendly, good-natured, good-tempered, pleasant.

illness [*n*] *disease; bad health*
▪ *Syn* affliction, ailment, attack, break-down, collapse, complaint, confinement, convalescence, disorder, fit, flu, indisposition, infirmity, malady, malaise, prostration, relapse, sickness, syndrome, virus; ▪ *Ant* good health, health, well-being, wellness.

illogical [*adj*] *not making sense*
▪ *Syn* absurd, casuistic, fallacious, fatuous, groundless, hollow, implausible, invalid, irrational, meaningless, preposterous, senseless, spurious, wacky; ▪ *Ant* correct, logical, meaningful, rational, reasonable, right, sensible, sound.

ill-timed [*adj*] *not occurring at suitable time* ▪ *Syn* awkward, improper, inappropriate, inconvenient, inept, inopportune, malapropos, unbecoming, unfavorable, unseasonable, unseemly; ▪ *Ant* appropriate, apt, convenient, opportune, suitable, timely, welcome, well-timed.

illuminate [*v1*] *make light*
▪ *Syn* brighten, fire, floodlight, highlight, ignite, irradiate, kindle, lighten, light up, spot, spotlight; ▪ *Ant* blur, cloud, darken, obscure, shadow.

illuminate [*v2*] *make clear; educate*
▪ *Syn* clarify, clear up, construe, define, dramatize, edify, elucidate, enlighten, explain, expound, express, finish, give insight, gloss, illustrate, instruct, interpret; ▪ *Ant* baffle, cloud, complicate, confound, obscure.

illusory/illusive [*adj*] *deceptive, false*
▪ *Syn* apparent, chimerical, deceitful, delusory, fake, fallacious, fanciful, fictional, hallucinatory, ideal, imaginary, misleading, ostensible, seeming, semblant, supposititious, visionary, whimsical; ▪ *Ant* actual, certain, factual, real, sure, true, valid.

illustrate [*v*] *demonstrate, clarify*
▪ *Syn* allegorize, clear up, delineate, depict, elucidate, emphasize, epitomize, evidence, evince, explain, expose, expound, highlight, illuminate, imitate, interpret, ostend, picture, portray, represent, reveal, show, specify, symbolize, typify, vivify; ▪ *Ant* cloak, conceal, hide, obscure.

illustrative [*adj*] *explanatory*
▪ *Syn* allegorical, comparative, corroborative, descriptive, diagrammatic, emblematic, explicatory, expository, figurative, graphic, iconographic, indicative, interpretive, metaphoric, pictorial, representative, typical; ▪ *Ant* atypical, complicated, confusing, involved.

illustrious [adj] *famous, prominent*
▪ *Syn* celebrated, distinguished, eminent, esteemed, exalted, famed, glorious, lofty, noble, outstanding, remarkable, renowned, signal, splendid, star, sublime, well-known; ▪ *Ant* ignoble, infamous, lowly, unimportant, unknown, unremarkable.

ill will [n] *hatred; hard feelings*
▪ *Syn* acrimony, animosity, antagonism, antipathy, aversion, blame, dislike, enmity, envy, feud, grudge, hate, hostility, malevolence, malice, objection, rancor, resentment, spite, spleen, venom; ▪ *Ant* cordiality, friendliness, friendship, good feelings, good will.

imaginable [adj] *believable, possible*
▪ *Syn* apprehensible, calculable, comprehensible, conceivable, conjecturable, credible, likely, plausible, sensible, supposable, thinkable; ▪ *Ant* impossible, improbable, incomprehensible, unbelieveable, unimaginable, unthinkable.

imaginary [adj] *fictitious, invented*
▪ *Syn* apocryphal, apparitional, assumed, chimerical, dreamlike, fabulous, fanciful, fantastic, fictional, hallucinatory, illusory, imagined, legendary, mythological, notional, phantasmal, quixotic, spectral, theoretical, visionary, whimsical; ▪ *Ant* existing, factual, genuine, physical, real, substantial, true.

imaginative [adj] *creative, inventive*
▪ *Syn* artistic, avant-garde, clever, enterprising, fanciful, ingenious, inspired, offbeat, original, quixotic, romantic, utopian, visionary, vivid, whimsical; ▪ *Ant* dull, mundane, ordinary, pedestrian, prosaic, uncreative, unimaginative, unresourceful.

imbecile [adj] *stupid, foolish*
▪ *Syn* asinine, dim-witted, dull, fatuous, feebleminded, half-witted, idiotic, inane, ludicrous, moronic, simpleminded, thick, witless; ▪ *Ant* intelligent, smart, wise.

imbibe [v] *drink, often heavily*
▪ *Syn* absorb, consume, down, gorge, ingest, ingurgitate, irrigate, partake, quaff, sip, swallow; ▪ *Ant* abstain, forbear.

imbroglio [n] *misunderstanding; fight*
▪ *Syn* altercation, argument, bickering, brawl, complication, dispute, entanglement, involvement, quandary, quarrel, row, spat, squabble; ▪ *Ant* accord, agreement, concord, peacemaking.

imbue [v] *infuse, saturate*
▪ *Syn* bathe, diffuse, impregnate, inculcate, infix, ingrain, inoculate, instill, invest, leaven, permeate, pervade, steep, suffuse; ▪ *Ant* drain, take out.

imitate [v] *pretend to be; do an impression of* ▪ *Syn* affect, ape, assume, borrow, caricature, clone, copy, counterfeit, do, duplicate, emulate, feign, follow, impersonate, mimic, mock, parallel, parody, pretend, reflect, resemble, sham, simulate, spoof, travesty; ▪ *Ant* be original, clash, differ, oppose, reverse.

imitative [adj] *simulated, unoriginal*
▪ *Syn* artful, copied, copycat, counterfeit, deceptive, derivative, emulative, forged, mimic, mock, plagiarized, reflective, secondhand; ▪ *Ant* different, genuine, original.

immaculate [adj1] *very clean; unspoiled*
▪ *Syn* bright, clean, exquisite, flawless, impeccable, neat, pure, spotless, stainless, taintless, trim; ▪ *Ant* contaminated, dirty, filthy, foul, tainted, unclean, unsterile.

immaculate [adj2] *innocent, uncorrupted* ▪ *Syn* above reproach, chaste, clean, decent, guiltless, incorrupt, modest, perfect, pure, sinless, spotless, stainless, virtuous; ▪ *Ant* corrupt, defiled, immoral, impure, polluted, sinful.

immaterial [adj1] *irrelevant*
▪ *Syn* extraneous, foreign, impertinent, inapposite, inconsequential, irrelative, meaningless, trifling, trivial, unimportant, unnecessary; ▪ *Ant* applicable, appropriate, essential, important, material, meaningful, relevant, substantial.

immaterial [adj2] *not existing in physical form* ▪ *Syn* aerial, airy, apparitional, bodiless, celestial, discarnate, disembodied, dreamy, ethereal, ghostly, heavenly, impalpable, intangible, metaphysical, psychic, shadowy, spectral, spiritlike, supernatural, unearthly, wraithlike; ▪ *Ant* bodily, corporeal, material, physical, real, solid, substantial.

immature [adj] *young, inexperienced*
▪ *Syn* adolescent, baby, callow, childish, crude, half-grown, imperfect, infantile, jejune, juvenile, kid, premature, puerile, raw, sophomoric, unfledged, unformed, unripe, unseasoned, youthful; ▪ *Ant* adult, developed, experienced, grown, mature, old, sophisticated.

immeasurable [adj] *infinite, incalculable* ▪ **Syn** bottomless, boundless, countless, endless, extensive, illimitable, immense, inestimable, inexhaustible, large, limitless, measureless, unbounded, unfathomable, vast; ▪ **Ant** bounded, calculable, finite, limited, measurable, specific.

immediate [adj] *instantaneous; without delay* ▪ **Syn** at once, critical, current, existing, extant, first, instant, live, now, paramount, present, pressing, prompt, urgent; ▪ **Ant** consequent, eventual, ultimate.

immediate [adj2] *near, next* ▪ **Syn** adjacent, close, contiguous, direct, firsthand, near-at-hand, nearby, nearest, nigh, primary, proximal, proximate, recent; ▪ **Ant** away, distant, far, peripheral, remote.

immediately [adv] *at once, right away* ▪ **Syn** anon, directly, forthwith, hereupon, instantaneously, instantly, now, promptly, rapidly, right now, shortly, unhesitatingly, urgently, without delay, without hesitation; ▪ **Ant** eventually, later, never, tardily.

immemorial [adj] *ancient, old* ▪ **Syn** age-old, archaic, forever, longstanding, of yore, olden, prehistoric, primeval, rooted, time-honored, traditional; ▪ **Ant** current, lately, memorable, new, recent, young.

immense [adj] *extremely large* ▪ **Syn** boundless, colossal, enormous, eternal, extensive, giant, gross, huge, immeasurable, interminable, limitless, mammoth, massive, mighty, monumental, prodigious, stupendous, tremendous, vast; ▪ **Ant** diminutive, little, miniature, minute, small, tiny.

immerse [v] *become deeply involved* ▪ **Syn** absorb, busy, engage, engross, interest, involve, occupy, soak, take up; ▪ **Ant** disinvolve, ignore, neglect.

immersed [adj] *deeply involved with* ▪ **Syn** absorbed, busy, consumed, engaged, engrossed, intent, mesmerized, occupied, rapt, spellbound; ▪ **Ant** absent, abstracted, neglectful, negligent, oblivious.

immigrate [v] *enter a foreign area intending to live there* ▪ **Syn** arrive, colonize, come in, go in, migrate, settle; ▪ **Ant** depart, emigrate, leave.

imminent [adj] *at hand, on the way* ▪ **Syn** approaching, close, coming, expected, fast-approaching, forthcoming, gathering, immediate, impending, inescapable, inevitable, looming, menacing, near, nigh, on the verge, threatening; ▪ **Ant** distant, doubtful, far, future, later, remote.

immobile [adj] *motionless, fixed* ▪ **Syn** anchored, frozen, immovable, nailed, pat, quiescent, rigid, riveted, rooted, stable, stagnant, static, stationary, steadfast, stiff, stock-still, stolid; ▪ **Ant** mobile, movable, moving, unfixed.

immoderate [adj] *excessive, extreme* ▪ **Syn** dizzying, exaggerated, exorbitant, extravagant, inordinate, overindulgent, steep, towering, unbridled, undue, unjustified, wanton; ▪ **Ant** calm, justified, mild, moderate, reasonable, restrained.

immoral [adj] *evil, degenerate* ▪ **Syn** abandoned, bad, corrupt, debauched, depraved, dishonest, impure, indecent, iniquitous, lewd, licentious, nefarious, obscene, pornographic, rakish, reprobate, saturnalian, sinful, vile, wicked; ▪ **Ant** chaste, good, moral, noble, principled, pure, right, scrupulous, virtuous.

immortal [adj] *death-defying, imperishable* ▪ **Syn** abiding, amaranthine, ceaseless, constant, deathless, enduring, eternal, everlasting, indestructible, interminable, lasting, perdurable, perennial, permanent, perpetual, timeless, undying; ▪ **Ant** destructible, ephemeral, fugitive, human, mortal, perishable.

immovable [adj] *fixed, stubborn* ▪ **Syn** adamant, constant, fast, firm, hard-nosed, immobile, immutable, impassive, inflexible, intransigent, obdurate, resolute, rooted, secure, stable, stationary, steadfast, stuck, unshakable, unwavering, unyielding; ▪ **Ant** changeable, flexible, mobile, movable, moving, unfixed.

immune [adj] *invulnerable or exempted* ▪ **Syn** allowed, clear, exempt, favored, free, licensed, not affected, protected, resistant, safe, unaffected, unsusceptible; ▪ **Ant** liable, subject, susceptible, unguarded, unprotected, vulnerable.

immunity [n] *privilege, exemption, protection* ▪ **Syn** amnesty, charter, exoneration, franchise, freedom, impunity, indemnity, invulnerability, license, prerogative, resistance, right; ▪ **Ant** defenselessness, liability, responsibility, susceptibility, vulnerability.

immutable [*adj*] *unchangeable*
 ▪ *Syn* abiding, ageless, changeless, constant, enduring, fixed, inflexible, invariable, permanent, perpetual, stable, steadfast, unmodifiable; ▪ *Ant* alterable, changeable, flexible, mutable, variable.

impair [*v*] *harm, hinder*
 ▪ *Syn* damage, debilitate, destroy, deteriorate, devalue, disqualify, hurt, injure, invalidate, mar, spoil, undermine, vitiate, weaken; ▪ *Ant* aid, assist, help, improve.

impalpable [*adj*] *intangible, unsubstantial* ▪ *Syn* airy, delicate, disembodied, fine, imperceptible, incorporeal, nebulous, tenuous, thin, vague; ▪ *Ant* believable, observable, palpable, perceptible, substantial, tangible, understandable.

impart [*v*] *make known*
 ▪ *Syn* admit, announce, break, communicate, convey, disclose, divulge, expose, inform, pass on, relate, reveal, tell, transmit; ▪ *Ant* conceal, hide, obscure, veil.

impartial [*adj*] *fair, unprejudiced*
 ▪ *Syn* detached, equitable, evenhanded, fair-minded, impersonal, just, neutral, nonpartisan, objective, open-minded, unslanted; ▪ *Ant* biased, bigoted, discriminating, partial, prejudiced, unfair, unjust.

impasse [*n*] *stalemate*
 ▪ *Syn* cessation, dead end, deadlock, dilemma, fix, gridlock, jam, pause, plight, predicament, quandary, standoff, standstill; ▪ *Ant* agreement, breakthrough, conclusion.

impassioned [*adj*] *excited, vehement*
 ▪ *Syn* animated, ardent, blazing, burning, deep, fervent, fervid, fierce, fiery, furious, glowing, inflamed, intense, melodramatic, moving, mushy, overemotional, passionate, romantic, rousing, sentimental, stirring, torrid, violent, zealous; ▪ *Ant* apathetic, calm, cool, detached, impassive, indifferent, unconcerned, unexcited.

impassive [*adj*] *aloof, cool*
 ▪ *Syn* apathetic, callous, cold, dispassionate, dry, hardened, heartless, imperturbable, indifferent, matter-of-fact, nonchalant, phlegmatic, placid, reserved, reticent, sedate, self-contained, spiritless, stoic, stolid, taciturn, unfeeling, unmoved, unruffled, wooden; ▪ *Ant* emotional, feeling, passionate, responsive, sensitive, susceptible, warm.

impatient [*adj*] *unable, unwilling to wait*
 ▪ *Syn* abrupt, antsy, anxious, ardent, athirst, avid, breathless, brusque, chafing, choleric, curt, demanding, eager, edgy, feverish, fretful, hasty, impetuous, indignant, intolerant, irritable, itchy, keen, restless, snappy, testy, vehement; ▪ *Ant* controlled, easygoing, enduring, forbearing, laid-back, patient, tolerant, waiting, willing.

impeach [*v*] *denounce, censure*
 ▪ *Syn* accuse, arraign, blame, challenge, charge, criminate, criticize, discredit, impugn, incriminate, inculpate, indict, query, question, reprehend, reprimand, reprobate, try; ▪ *Ant* absolve, endorse, exculpate, exonerate.

impeccable [*adj*] *above suspicion; flawless* ▪ *Syn* accurate, clean, correct, exact, exquisite, faultless, immaculate, infallible, irreproachable, perfect, precise, pure, right, stainless, unimpeachable; ▪ *Ant* blemished, corrupt, culpable, defective, deficient, flawed, suspicious, wrong.

impecunious [*adj*] *poverty-stricken*
 ▪ *Syn* beggared, destitute, homeless, impoverished, indigent, insolvent, needy, penniless, penurious, poor, unprosperous; ▪ *Ant* affluent, moneyed, prosperous, rich, wealthy.

impede [*v*] *obstruct, hinder*
 ▪ *Syn* bar, block, check, clog, curb, dam, delay, deter, disrupt, faze, hamper, hold up, interfere, oppose, rattle, restrain, retard, slow, stop, stymie, thwart; ▪ *Ant* advance, aid, assist, facilitate, forward, help, support.

impel [*v*] *prompt, incite*
 ▪ *Syn* boost, compel, drive, excite, foment, goad, induce, influence, instigate, jog, mobilize, motivate, oblige, power, push, spur, start, stimulate, thrust, urge; ▪ *Ant* curb, delay, dissuade, repress, restrain, slow, suppress.

impending [*adj*] *forthcoming*
 ▪ *Syn* approaching, at hand, brewing, coming, gathering, imminent, looming, menacing, nearing, ominous, portending, proximate, threatening; ▪ *Ant* distant, far-off, later, never, remote.

impenetrable [*adj1*] *dense*
 ▪ *Syn* bulletproof, impassable, impermeable, impervious, inviolable, solid, substantial, thick; ▪ *Ant* clear, penetrable, permeable, porous, soft, thin, vulnerable.

impenetrable [adj2] *incomprehensible*
▪ *Syn* arcane, baffling, cabalistic, dark, Delphic, enigmatic, hidden, indiscernible, inexplicable, inscrutable, mysterious, mystic, obscure, sibylline, unfathomable; ▪ *Ant* clear, comprehensible, intelligible, lucid, obvious, penetrable, understandable.

imperative [adj1] *necessary*
▪ *Syn* acute, burning, clamant, clamorous, compulsory, critical, crucial, essential, exigent, immediate, important, importunate, indispensable, insistent, instant, obligatory, pressing, urgent, vital; ▪ *Ant* inessential, optional, secondary, unnecessary, voluntary.

imperative [adj2] *authoritative*
▪ *Syn* autocratic, bidding, bossy, commanding, dictatorial, dominant, domineering, harsh, imperious, magisterial, ordering, overbearing, peremptory, powerful, stern; ▪ *Ant* discretionary, lenient, mild, voluntary.

imperceptible [adj] *hard to sense; faint*
▪ *Syn* ephemeral, evanescent, fine, impalpable, inaudible, inconspicuous, indiscernible, indistinct, invisible, microscopic, minute, momentary, slight, trivial, undetectable, vague; ▪ *Ant* apparent, conspicuous, distinct, evident, noticeable, obvious, perceptible, striking.

imperfect [adj] *flawed*
▪ *Syn* amiss, broken, damaged, defective, disfigured, faulty, immature, impaired, marred, rudimentary, sketchy, warped; ▪ *Ant* complete, excellent, faultless, finished, perfect, pure, sound, unblemished, unflawed.

imperil [v] *cause to be in danger*
▪ *Syn* chance it, compromise, endanger, expose, gamble, hazard, jeopardize, menace, peril, risk; ▪ *Ant* guard, protect, save, shield.

imperious [adj] *bossy, overbearing*
▪ *Syn* arrogant, autocratic, commanding, despotic, dictatorial, exacting, haughty, high-handed, imperative, magisterial, obligatory, oppressive, peremptory, tyrannical; ▪ *Ant* fawning, helpless, humble, obedient, obsequious, servile, subservient, weak.

impersonal [adj] *cold, unfriendly*
▪ *Syn* abstract, bureaucratic, businesslike, colorless, cool, detached, dispassionate, emotionless, equitable, fair, formal, impartial, indifferent, neutral, objective, remote; ▪ *Ant* friendly, informal, personable, personal, warm.

impertinence [n] *boldness*
▪ *Syn* assurance, audacity, disrespect, effrontery, gall, guff, impropriety, impudence, incivility, insolence, nerve, pertness, presumption, rudeness; ▪ *Ant* humility, manners, politeness.

impertinent [adj] *bold, disrespectful*
▪ *Syn* arrogant, brash, brazen, discourteous, forward, fresh, ill-mannered, impolite, intrusive, offensive, presumptuous, prying, rude, sassy, smart; ▪ *Ant* civil, gracious, kind, mannered, nice, polite, refined, respectful.

imperturbable [adj] *calm, collected*
▪ *Syn* assured, complacent, composed, cool, nonchalant, sedate, self-possessed, self-satisfied, smug, stoical, thick-skinned, tranquil, unflappable; ▪ *Ant* excitable, excitable, irritable, jittery, perturbable, touchy.

impervious [adj] *unable to be penetrated*
▪ *Syn* hermetic, immune, impassable, impenetrable, impermeable, inaccessible, invulnerable, resistant, sealed, tight, watertight; ▪ *Ant* exposed, open, penetrable, responsive, sensitive, vulnerable.

impetuous [adj] *acting without thinking*
▪ *Syn* abrupt, ardent, eager, fervid, fierce, furious, hasty, hurried, impassioned, impulsive, passionate, precipitous, rash, rushing, spontaneous, swift, vehement, violent; ▪ *Ant* calm, cautious, circumspect, considerate, reflective, sensible, thoughtful, wary, wise.

impetus [n] *stimulus, force*
▪ *Syn* catalyst, energy, goad, impulse, incentive, incitement, momentum, motivation, power, pressure, push, spur, stimulant, urge; ▪ *Ant* block, check, hindrance.

impious [adj] *not religious*
▪ *Syn* agnostic, apostate, atheistic, blasphemous, canting, diabolic, disobedient, disrespectful, godless, hardened, iconoclastic, iniquitous, profane, reprobate, sacrilegious, sinful, unctuous, wayward, wicked; ▪ *Ant* devout, dutiful, holy, pious, religious, reverent, righteous.

impish [adj] *mischievous*
▪ *Syn* casual, devilish, fiendish, flippant, fresh, frolicsome, giddy, jaunty, naughty, offhand, pert, prankish, puckish, roguish, saucy, sportive, waggish; ▪ *Ant* behaved, subdued, unmischievous.

implacable [adj] *merciless, cruel*
▪ *Syn* grim, inflexible, intractable, pitiless, rancorous, relentless, remorseless, uncompromising, unrelenting, unyielding, vindictive; ▪ *Ant* appeasable, forbearing, indulgent, kind, merciful.

implausible [adj] *not likely*
▪ *Syn* doubtful, dubious, farfetched, flimsy, impossible, improbable, inconceivable, suspect, unbelievable, unconvincing, unsubstantial, weak; ▪ *Ant* believable, likely, plausible, possibly, probably, reasonable.

implement [v] *start, put into action*
▪ *Syn* actualize, carry out, complete, effect, enforce, execute, fulfill, invoke, materialize, perform, put into effect, realize, resolve; ▪ *Ant* cancel, cease, delay, halt, hinder, pause, stop.

implicate [v] *imply, incriminate*
▪ *Syn* accuse, associate, blame, charge, cite, compromise, concern, connect, embroil, entangle, frame, hint, impute, include, involve, inculpate, insinuate, link, mire, name, relate, stigmatize, suggest, tangle; ▪ *Ant* acquit, defend, exclude, pardon, support.

implicit [adj] *included without question, inherent, absolute* ▪ *Syn* complete, definite, firm, fixed, implied, inferential, inferred, latent, practical, steadfast, tacit, total, understood, unspoken, virtual, wholehearted; ▪ *Ant* declared, explicit, expressed, qualified, specific.

implied [adj] *hinted at*
▪ *Syn* adumbrated, alluded to, connoted, foreshadowed, hidden, implicit, indicated, indirect, inferred, inherent, insinuated, latent, meant, occult, parallel, perceptible, potential, suggested, tacit, understood; ▪ *Ant* declared, explicated, expressed, stated.

implore [v] *beg*
▪ *Syn* appeal, beseech, conjure, crave, entreat, importune, plead, pray, solicit, supplicate, urge; ▪ *Ant* command, demand, order.

imply [v] *indicate, mean*
▪ *Syn* betoken, connote, denote, designate, entail, evidence, hint, import, include, insinuate, intend, intimate, involve, mention, refer, signify, suggest; ▪ *Ant* define, explicate, express, state.

impolite [adj] *having bad manners*
▪ *Syn* boorish, churlish, discourteous, disrespectful, ill-mannered, indecorous, loutish, oafish, rude, sullen; ▪ *Ant* civil, courteous, gracious, mannerly, polite.

impolitic [adj] *unwise, careless*
▪ *Syn* brash, imprudent, inadvisable, inconsiderate, inexpedient, maladroit, rash, stupid, tactless, untimely; ▪ *Ant* careful, cautious, diplomatic, discreet, judicious, politic, wise.

important [adj1] *valuable, substantial*
▪ *Syn* big, considerable, conspicuous, critical, crucial, decisive, earnest, exceptional, exigent, far-reaching, foremost, grave, great, heavy, imperative, importunate, large, marked, meaningful, momentous, necessary, paramount, ponderous, pressing, principal, relevant, salient, significant, urgent, vital, weighty; ▪ *Ant* insignificant, little, paltry, small, trivial.

important [adj2] *eminent, influential, outstanding* ▪ *Syn* distinctive, esteemed, foremost, grand, high-ranking, honored, illustrious, leading, majestic, notable, powerful, prominent, remarkable, seminal, signal, solid, superior, talented, well-known; ▪ *Ant* insignificant, powerless, unimportant, unknown, worthless.

imported [adj] *brought in from another place* ▪ *Syn* alien, exotic, foreign, introduced, rare, shipped, transported; ▪ *Ant* home-grown, local, native.

importunate [adj] *demanding, insistent*
▪ *Syn* burning, clamant, crying, disturbing, exigent, imperative, instant, persevering, persistent, pertinacious, pressing, solicitous, troublesome, urgent; ▪ *Ant* undemanding, unimportant.

impose [v] *set, dictate*
▪ *Syn* burden, command, compel, constrain, decree, demand, encroach, enforce, enjoin, establish, exact, fix, foist, force, inflict, institute, introduce, levy, oblige, obtrude, ordain, place, prescribe, promulgate, require, trespass, visit, wreck; ▪ *Ant* guard, lift, protect, remove, shelter, shield.

imposing [adj] *impressive*
▪ *Syn* august, big, commanding, dignified, effective, grandiose, imperial, magnificent, monumental, noble, ominous, overwhelming, pretentious, regal, stately, striking, towering; ▪ *Ant* common, modest, ordinary, poor, subordinate, trivial, unimportant, unimposing, unimpressive.

imposition [n] *burden*
▪ *Syn* charge, command, constraint, demand, duty, encroachment, encum-

brance, intrusion, levy, pressure, presumption, restraint, tax; ▪ *Ant* advantage, aid, benefit, blessing, help, profit.

impossible [*adj*] *beyond the bounds of possibility* ▪ *Syn* absurd, futile, hopeless, impervious, inconceivable, preposterous, unimaginable, unthinkable, useless; ▪ *Ant* achievable, believable, likely, obtainable, possible, probable, reasonable, tenable.

imposture [*n*] *fraud, trick*
▪ *Syn* artifice, cheat, con, deceit, fabrication, fake, forgery, gambit, hoax, illusion, make-believe, masquerade, phony, ploy, quackery, ruse, sham, sleight, swindle, wile; ▪ *Ant* honesty, reality, truth.

impotent [*adj*] *disabled; unable to perform action* ▪ *Syn* barren, crippled, effete, enervated, feeble, frigid, gutless, helpless, incompetent, infirm, nerveless, paralyzed, powerless, sterile, weak; ▪ *Ant* able, capable, effective, fertile, forceful, potent, productive, strong.

impoverished [*adj*] *poor, exhausted*
▪ *Syn* bankrupt, barren, clean, depleted, destitute, empty, hurting, impecunious, indigent, needy, penurious, poverty-stricken, ruined, spent, strapped; ▪ *Ant* affluent, enriched, full, plentiful, rich.

impractical/impracticable [*adj*] *unrealistic* ▪ *Syn* abstract, chimerical, idealistic, illogical, impossible, inefficacious, otherworldly, quixotic, romantic, speculative, theoretical, unattainable, unwise, useless, visionary, wild; ▪ *Ant* feasible, practicable, practical, probable, realistic, reasonable, sensible, tenable, viable.

impressionable [*adj*] *easily taught; gullible* ▪ *Syn* affectable, impressible, ingenuous, open, perceptive, receptive, responsive, sensitive, suggestible, susceptible, vulnerable, waxlike; ▪ *Ant* impenetrable, impervious, insusceptible, obstinate, stubborn, unresponsive.

impressive [*adj*] *powerful, influential*
▪ *Syn* affecting, august, awe-inspiring, consequential, dramatic, effective, forcible, grand, imposing, inspiring, momentous, moving, notable, penetrating, profound, remarkable, rousing, stirring, striking, thrilling, towering; ▪ *Ant* inconsequential, ineffective, insignificant, unimportant, unimpressive, weak.

imprison [*v*] *confine; put in jail*
▪ *Syn* apprehend, cage, check, circumscribe, commit, detain, hold, immure, incarcerate, intern, jail, keep, lock up, nab, occlude, pen, restrain, stockade, trammel; ▪ *Ant* free, let go, liberate, release.

improbable [*adj*] *not likely*
▪ *Syn* doubtful, dubious, fanciful, farfetched, implausible, inconceivable, questionable, rare, slim, unlikely, unsubstantial; ▪ *Ant* believable, likely, ostensible, plausible, possible, probable, tenable.

impromptu [*adj/adv*] *unrehearsed, improvised* ▪ *Syn* ad-lib, extemporaneous, extempore, extemporized, offhand, spontaneous, spur-of-the-moment, vamped; ▪ *Ant* deliberate, designed, planned, premeditated, prepared, rehearsed, scripted.

improper [*adj1*] *not suitable*
▪ *Syn* abnormal, awkward, discordant, discrepant, erroneous, false, ill-advised, ill-timed, imprudent, inaccurate, inapplicable, inapposite, inappropriate, incongruous, incorrect, inexpedient, infelicitous, irregular, ludicrous, malapropos, odd, preposterous, unsuited, wrong; ▪ *Ant* appropriate, apt, correct, fitting, opportune, proper, right, suitable.

improper [*adj2*] *vulgar, immoral*
▪ *Syn* dirty, impolite, indecent, indecorous, lewd, malodorous, naughty, risqué, salacious, untoward, wrong, wrongful; ▪ *Ant* decent, formal, good, moral, proper.

impropriety [*n*] *bad taste, mistake*
▪ *Syn* barbarism, blunder, faux pas, gaucherie, immodesty, impudence, indecency, indecorum, rudeness, solecism, unseemliness, vulgarity; ▪ *Ant* correctness, propriety, suitability, tastefulness.

improve [*v*] *make or become better*
▪ *Syn* advance, ameliorate, amend, augment, better, boost, convalesce, correct, develop, elevate, emend, help, increase, lift, meliorate, polish, progress, purify, raise, rectify, refine, reform, revamp, revise, sharpen, update, upgrade; ▪ *Ant* damage, decline, decrease, diminish, harm, hurt, injure, weaken, worsen.

improvident [*adj*] *careless, spendthrift*
▪ *Syn* extravagant, heedless, imprudent, lavish, negligent, profligate, profuse, reckless, shiftless, shortsighted, thriftless, wasteful; ▪ *Ant* careful, economical, miserly, provident, prudent, thrifty.

improvise [v] *make up*
• *Syn* ad-lib, brainstorm, coin, concoct, contrive, devise, dream up, extemporize, fake, invent, spark; • *Ant* design, devise, plan, premeditate.

improvised [adj] *made-up*
• *Syn* ad-lib, extemporaneous, extempore, impromptu, makeshift, offhand, spontaneous; • *Ant* designed, planned, premediated, rehearsed.

imprudent [adj] *without much thought; unwise* • *Syn* brash, careless, foolhardy, heedless, ill-advised, impolitic, improvident, inexpedient, rash, temerarious, thoughtless; • *Ant* careful, cautious, discreet, judicious, prudent, wise.

impudent [adj] *bold, shameless*
• *Syn* arrant, audacious, barefaced, blatant, brassy, contumelious, fresh, immodest, insolent, pert, presumptuous, rude, unabashed, wise; • *Ant* deferential, humble, meek, modest, polite, retiring.

impugn [v] *criticize, challenge*
• *Syn* assail, attack, blast, contradict, contravene, deny, dispute, gainsay, negate, oppose, question, resist, traduce, trash, traverse; • *Ant* defend, flatter, praise, support.

impulsive [adj] *tending to act without thought* • *Syn* abrupt, careless, emotional, hasty, headlong, impetuous, instinctive, mad, offhand, passionate, precipitate, quick, rash, spontaneous, sudden; • *Ant* cautious, considering, deliberate, heedful, predictable, premeditative, thoughtful, wise.

impunity [n] *freedom*
• *Syn* dispensation, exception, exemption, immunity, liberty, license, permission, privilege, security; • *Ant* blame, culpability, liability, retribution.

impure [adj] *not clean mentally, physically; mixed* • *Syn* admixed, alloyed, contaminated, corrupt, debased, defiled, dirty, filthy, infected, lewd, nasty, obscene, polluted, squalid, tainted, vitiated, wicked; • *Ant* chaste, clean, decent, impeccable, modest, moral, pure, sterile, wholesome.

impute [v] *attribute*
• *Syn* accredit, accuse, adduce, assign, blame, censure, charge, hint, indict, insinuate, intimate, lay, refer, reference, stigmatize; • *Ant* defend, guard, help, protect.

inaccessible [adj] *out of reach*
• *Syn* aloof, away, beyond, distant, elusive, far, faraway, far-off, impassable, impervious, insurmountable, remote, unreachable, unworkable; • *Ant* accessible, approachable, attainable, obtainable, reachable.

inaccurate [adj] *erroneous*
• *Syn* careless, counterfactual, defective, discrepant, fallacious, false, faulty, imprecise, incorrect, in error, mistaken, off, specious, untrue, wrong; • *Ant* accurate, correct, exact, faithful, right.

inactive [adj] *not engaged in action; inert; lazy* • *Syn* abeyant, disengaged, dormant, idle, immobile, indolent, latent, lax, lethargic, motionless, ossified, passive, quiescent, sedentary, slothful, sluggish, somnolent, static, torpid; • *Ant* active, busy, industrious, involved, occupied, operative, working.

inadequate [adj] *defective, insufficient, incompetent* • *Syn* bare, barren, deficient, depleted, dry, failing, faulty, feeble, imperfect, impotent, inapt, incapable, incompetent, incomplete, lacking, lousy, low, meager, minus, miserly, poor, scanty, scarce, short, small, spare, sparse, sterile, stinted, thin, weak; • *Ant* able, adequate, ample, competent, enough, sufficient.

inadmissible [adj] *not appropriate*
• *Syn* exceptionable, immaterial, improper, inappropriate, inept, irrelevant, malapropos, objectionable; • *Ant* acceptable, admissible, allowable, appropriate.

inadvertent [adj] *accidental*
• *Syn* careless, chance, feckless, heedless, irreflective, negligent, reckless, thoughtless, unintentional, unwitting; • *Ant* advertent, attentive, deliberate, intentional, planned.

inadvisable [adj] *not recommended*
• *Syn* careless, foolish, ill-advised, impolitic, incautious, pointless, rash, unsensible, unwise, wrong; • *Ant* advisable, judicious, prudent, recommended, wise.

inalienable [adj] *absolute, inherent*
• *Syn* basic, entailed, inviolable, natural, nonnegotiable, sacrosanct, unassailable, untransferable; • *Ant* acquired, alienable, changeable, impermanent, transitory.

inane [adj] *stupid*
• *Syn* absurd, asinine, daft, empty, fatuous, foolish, idiotic, innocuous, insipid, jejune, laughable, meaningless, pointless,

puerile, ridiculous, senseless, silly, trifling, vacuous, vapid, worthless; ▪ **Ant** meaningful, profound, thoughtful, wise.

inanimate [adj] not alive, not organic
▪ **Syn** cold, dead, defunct, dull, extinct, idle, inert, inoperative, insensate, insentient, lifeless, mineral, motionless, soulless, spiritless; ▪ **Ant** active, alive, animate, living, organic.

inapplicable [adj] not relevant
▪ **Syn** extraneous, foreign, immaterial, impertinent, inappurtenant, inapropos, irrelative, irrelevant, remote, unsuited; ▪ **Ant** applicable, germane, related, relevant, suitable.

inappropriate [adj] not proper, suitable
▪ **Syn** bad form, disproportionate, illfitted, ill-suited, inapplicable, inapropos, incongruous, inept, irrelevant, malapropos, tasteless, unbecoming, wrong; ▪ **Ant** appropriate, correct, fitting, proper, suitable.

inapt [adj] not suitable
▪ **Syn** awkward, banal, clumsy, dull, flat, gauche, ill-suited, improper, inappropriate, inept, insipid, jejune, maladroit, malapropos; ▪ **Ant** adept, apt, competent, felicitous, happy, proficient, suitable, suited.

inarticulate [adj] unable to speak well; not clearly spoken ▪ **Syn** blurred, dumb, faltering, halting, hesitant, inaudible, incoherent, incomprehensible, muffled, mum, mumbling, obscure, reticent, stammering, tongue-tied, unclear, unintelligible, vague, wordless; ▪ **Ant** articulate, communicative, expressive, glib, verbal, vocal.

inattentive [adj] negligent, not paying attention ▪ **Syn** absentminded, blind, careless, distracted, diverted, dreamy, faraway, heedless, indifferent, listless, musing, neglectful, oblivious, preoccupied, rapt, thoughtless, undiscerning; ▪ **Ant** attentive, aware, careful, heedful, mindful, observant.

inaugurate [v] begin; install
▪ **Syn** break in, commence, commission, dedicate, initiate, institute, introduce, jump, launch, ordain, set up, start, usher in; ▪ **Ant** adjourn, close, conclude, end, finish, stop.

inauspicious [adj] ominous, unpromising ▪ **Syn** baleful, black, dire, discouraging, evil, foreboding, ill-omened, impending, sinister, threatening, untimely; ▪ **Ant** auspicious, favorable, fortunate, lucky, promising, propitious.

inborn/inbred [adj] coming from birth; natural ▪ **Syn** congenital, connate, connatural, deep-seated, essential, hereditary, indigenous, ingenerate, ingrained, inherent, inherited, innate, instinctive, intrinsic, intuitive, native; ▪ **Ant** acquired, conditioned, earned, learned.

incalculable [adj] countless, limitless
▪ **Syn** boundless, enormous, immense, incomputable, innumerable, unreckonable, vast; ▪ **Ant** calculable, countable, finite, limited, measurable.

incandescent [adj] glowing
▪ **Syn** beaming, brilliant, effulgent, fulgent, intense, lambent, luminous, phosphorescent, radiant, shining; ▪ **Ant** dark, dim, dusky, gloomy, tenebrous.

incapable [adj] not adequate; helpless
▪ **Syn** disqualified, feeble, impotent, inadequate, incompetent, inept, insufficient, naive, poor, powerless, unfit, unqualified, weak; ▪ **Ant** capable, competent, effective, proficient, qualified, skillful, strong.

incapacitate [v] put out of action
▪ **Syn** cripple, damage, disable, disarm, disqualify, hinder, hurt, immobilize, lame, maim, paralyze, prostrate, take out, undermine, weaken; ▪ **Ant** allow, capacitate, enable, facilitate, mobilize, permit.

incarcerate [v] put in jail, confinement
▪ **Syn** commit, confine, constrain, detain, hold, immure, impound, imprison, intern, jail, restrain, restrict; ▪ **Ant** free, let go, liberate, release.

incautious [adj] not careful
▪ **Syn** bold, brash, careless, hasty, heedless, ill-advised, impetuous, improvident, imprudent, impulsive, inconsiderate, injudicious, negligent, precipitate, rash, reckless, thoughtless; ▪ **Ant** careful, cautious, discreet, guarded, thoughtful, vigilant, wary.

incendiary [adj] causing trouble, damage ▪ **Syn** dangerous, demagogic, dissentious, inflammatory, malevolent, provocative, seditious, subversive, treacherous; ▪ **Ant** calming, modulating, peacemaking, soothing, temperate.

incense [v] make very angry
▪ **Syn** anger, bother, disgust, enrage, exasperate, excite, inflame, infuriate, ire, irritate, madden, provoke, rile; ▪ **Ant** calm, comfort, please.

incensed [adj] *very angry*
• *Syn* enraged, exasperated, fuming, furious, indignant, infuriated, irate, ireful, mad, maddened, peeved, riled, rousted, wrathful; • *Ant* cheerful, happy, joyous, pleased.

incentive [n] *lure, inducement*
• *Syn* allure bait, catalyst, determinant, encouragement, enticement, goad, impetus, incitement, inspiration, instigation, motivation, persuasion, provocation, reason, spring, spur, stimulus, temptation, urge, whip; • *Ant* block, deterrent, dissuasion, hindrance, turn-off.

inception [n] *beginning*
• *Syn* birth, commencement, dawn, fountain, inauguration, initiation, origin, outset, provenance, rise, source, start, wellspring; • *Ant* conclusion, end, ending, finish, termination.

incessant [adj] *never-ending, persistent*
• *Syn* ceaseless, constant, continual, endless, eternal, everlasting, interminable, monotonous, perpetual, relentless, timeless; • *Ant* broken, ceasing, ending, intermittent, interrupted.

inchoate [adj] *undeveloped, beginning*
• *Syn* amorphous, embryonic, formless, immature, inceptive, incipient, just begun, nascent, preliminary, rudimentary, shapeless; • *Ant* developed, finished, formed, grown, mature, shaped.

incidental [adj] *related; minor*
• *Syn* accidental, adventitious, ancillary, casual, chance, coincidental, concomitant, concurrent, occasional, odd, random, secondary, subordinate, subsidiary; • *Ant* basic, essential, fundamental, important, vital.

incipient [adj] *developing*
• *Syn* basic, beginning, commencing, elementary, embryonic, fundamental, inceptive, inchoate, introductory, nascent, originating; • *Ant* achieved, completed, developed, grown, mature, realized.

incisive [adj] *very intelligent*
• *Syn* acute, bright, clever, keen, penetrating, perspicacious, profound, sharp, trenchant; • *Ant* diffuse, dull, feeble, incompetent, stupid.

incite [v] *encourage, provoke*
• *Syn* abet, agitate, arouse, coax, drive, excite, exhort, foment, further, goad, impel, induce, influence, inspirit, instigate, motivate, persuade, push, rouse, spur, stimulate, taunt, trigger, urge; • *Ant*

delay, deter, discourage, inhibit, prohibit.

inclement [adj] *bitter, nasty (weather)*
• *Syn* brutal, cold, foul, harsh, intemperate, raw, rough, severe, stormy, tempestuous, violent, wintry; • *Ant* clear, mild, nice, sunny.

inclination [n] *tendency, bent*
• *Syn* affection, attachment, attraction, bias, disposition, drift, fancy, impulse, leaning, liking, mind, partiality, penchant, prejudice, propensity, susceptibility, taste, temperament, urge, velleity, weakness, whim; • *Ant* abhorrence, antipathy, disinclination, dislike.

include [v] *contain; involve*
• *Syn* admit, allow for, append, bear, build, carry, constitute, count, cover, embrace, encompass, entail, hold, incorporate, insert, interject, interpolate, number, receive, subsume; • *Ant* eliminate, exclude, neglect, omit, preclude, reject.

inclusive [adj] *all-encompassing, all-embracing* • *Syn* all-around, all together, broad, comprehensive, encyclopedic, full, general, global, overall, sweeping, whole; • *Ant* exclusive, incomprehensive, narrow.

incognito [adj] *in disguise*
• *Syn* anonymous, camouflaged, concealed, disguised, hidden, isolated, masked, masquerading, obscure, unknown, unrecognized; • *Ant* known, open, seen, unhidden.

incoherent [adj] *unintelligible*
• *Syn* breathless, confused, disconnected, disjointed, faltering, incohesive, jumbled, muddled, muttered, rambling, stammering, stuttering, wandering; • *Ant* coherent, consistent, intelligible, logical, rational, understandable.

income [n] *money earned by work or investments* • *Syn* assets, benefits, cash, compensation, dividends, earnings, gains, gross, livelihood, means, net, pay, profit, revenue, royalty, salary, wage; • *Ant* bills, debt, disbursement, expenses.

incomparable [adj] *superlative*
• *Syn* exceptional, inimitable, matchless, peerless, perfect, supreme, transcendent, ultimate, unparalleled, unrivalled, unsurpassable; • *Ant* average, common, inferior, lowly, ordinary, poor.

incompatible [adj] *antagonistic, contradictory* • *Syn* adverse, antithetical, contrary, discordant, discrepant, factious, incongruous, inconsonant, irreconcilable, jarring, mismatched, opposed, opposite, warring; ▪ *Ant* compatible, congenial, consonant, harmonious, loving, suited, well-matched.

incompetent [*adj*] *unskillful, unable*
▪ *Syn* amateur, amateurish, awkward, bungling, clumsy, floundering, helpless, inadequate, incapable, incapacitated, inept, inexperienced, inexpert, maladroit, raw, unequipped, unfit, unhandy, unskilled, untrained, useless; ▪ *Ant* able, adept, capable, competent, dexterous, effective, efficient, experienced, expert, proficient, skillful.

incomplete [*adj*] *unfinished, wanting*
▪ *Syn* abridged, broken, crude, defective, expurgated, fragmentary, garbled, half-done, inadequate, insufficient, lacking, meager, partial, rough, rudimentary, sketchy, undeveloped; ▪ *Ant* accomplished, complete, finished, perfect, whole.

incomprehensible [*adj*] *not understandable* ▪ *Syn* baffling, cryptic, enigmatic, impenetrable, inconceivable, inscrutable, mysterious, mystifying, obscure, perplexing, puzzling, sibylline; ▪ *Ant* clear, comprehensible, fathomable, intelligible, understandable.

inconceivable [*adj*] *beyond reason, belief* ▪ *Syn* extraordinary, fantastic, implausible, impossible, incredible, phony, rare, staggering, strange, unheard-of, unimaginable; ▪ *Ant* believable, conceivable, fathomable, imaginable, reasonable.

inconclusive [*adj*] *up in the air*
▪ *Syn* ambiguous, incomplete, indecisive, indeterminate, open, uncertain, undecided, unsettled, vague; ▪ *Ant* certain, conclusive, decisive, definite, sure.

incongruous [*adj*] *out of place; absurd*
▪ *Syn* alien, bizarre, contradictory, discordant, extraneous, fantastic, foreign, illogical, inconsistent, jumbled, twisted, unrelated, unsuitable; ▪ *Ant* compatible, congruous, consistent, corresponding, fitting, harmonious, matched, suitable, uniform.

inconsequential/inconsiderable
[*adj*] *of no significance* ▪ *Syn* casual, exiguous, immaterial, inappreciable, light, little, measly, negligible, paltry, picayune, scanty, skimpy, small, trifling, trivial, unimportant, worthless; ▪ *Ant* ample, consequential, considerable, important, significant, sufficient.

inconsiderate [*adj*] *insensitive to others*
▪ *Syn* boorish, brash, careless, discourteous, hasty, impolite, indelicate, reckless, rude, self-centered, tactless, thoughtless, uncharitable; ▪ *Ant* considerate, generous, gracious, kind, nice, sensitive, tactful, thoughtful.

inconsistent [*adj*] *contradictory, irregular* ▪ *Syn* at odds, capricious, contrary, discordant, discrepant, erratic, fickle, illogical, incongruent, lubricious, mercurial, temperamental, variable, warring; ▪ *Ant* certain, consistent, consonant, predictable, regular, steady, unchanging.

inconsolable [*adj*] *brokenhearted*
▪ *Syn* dejected, desolate, despairing, discouraged, distressed, forlorn, heartbroken, heartsick, sad; ▪ *Ant* calmed, comforted, consolable, soothed.

inconspicuous [*adj*] *hidden, unnoticeable* ▪ *Syn* camouflaged, concealed, dim, faint, hidden, muted, ordinary, plain, quiet, retiring, secretive, subtle, tenuous, unassuming, unobtrusive, unostentatious; ▪ *Ant* conspicuous, distinct, exposed, noticeable, obvious, open.

incontrovertible [*adj*] *beyond dispute*
▪ *Syn* accurate, authentic, certain, established, incontestable, indisputable, irrefutable, positive, sure, undeniable, unequivocable, unquestionable; ▪ *Ant* changeable, controvertible, questionable, uncertain, variable.

inconvenience [*v*] *bother, trouble*
▪ *Syn* aggravate, discommode, discompose, disrupt, disturb, exasperate, irk, meddle, try, upset; ▪ *Ant* aid, assist, be convenient, benefit, help.

inconvenient [*adj*] *bothersome, troublesome* ▪ *Syn* annoying, awkward, cumbersome, detrimental, difficult, disadvantageous, disturbing, embarrassing, inexpedient, tiresome, troublesome, unhandy, untimely, unwieldy, vexatious; ▪ *Ant* aiding, beneficial, convenient, helpful, opportune.

incorporate [*v*] *include, combine*
▪ *Syn* absorb, add to, amalgamate, assimilate, associate, blend, coalesce, consolidate, embody, form, fuse, imbibe, integrate, join, link, merge, mix, organize, pool, start, subsume, unite; ▪ *Ant* divide, drop, exclude, separate.

incorrect [adj] wrong
• **Syn** counterfactual, erroneous, false, faulty, flawed, imprecise, improper, inaccurate, inappropriate, mistaken, specious; • **Ant** correct, exact, right, true.

incorrigible [adj] bad, hopeless
• **Syn** beastly, hardened, incurable, intractable, inveterate, irredeemable, recidivous, useless, wicked; • **Ant** good, manageable, nice, obedient, reformable.

incorruptible [adj] honest, honorable
• **Syn** above suspicion, just, loyal, moral, pure, reliable, straight, trustworthy, upright; • **Ant** bad, corruptible, dishonest, venal.

increase [v] add or grow
• **Syn** advance, aggrandize, amplify, augment, boost, broaden, build up, develop, dilate, distend, enhance, enlarge, escalate, extend, further, heighten, inflate, magnify, mount, progress, proliferate, pullulate, raise, sharpen, spread, step up, swell, teem, thicken, widen; • **Ant** decline, decrease, deplete, diminish, drop, lose, lower, shrink, subtract, wane.

incredible [adj] beyond belief
• **Syn** absurd, far-fetched, improbable, inconceivable, outlandish, phony, preposterous, questionable, ridiculous, suspect, unimaginable, untenable; • **Ant** believable, credible, plausible, possible, realistic, tenable.

incredible [adj2] marvelous
• **Syn** amazing, astonishing, astounding, awe-inspiring, awesome, extraordinary, fabulous, glorious, wonderful; • **Ant** bad, common, ordinary, poor, terrible, usual.

incredulous [adj] unbelieving
• **Syn** aporetic, distrustful, doubtful, hesitant, questioning, quizzical, skeptical, suspicious, wary; • **Ant** believing, convinced, credulous, gullible, trusting.

incurable [adj] unfixable, unchangeable
• **Syn** cureless, deadly, fatal, hopeless, inoperable, serious, terminal; • **Ant** curable, healable, medicable, operable, remedial, reparable.

indebted [adj] under an obligation
• **Syn** accountable, bound, chargeable, duty-bound, honor-bound, liable, obliged, responsible, thankful; • **Ant** paid, settled, unobligated.

indecent [adj] obscene, vulgar; offensive
• **Syn** coarse, crude, filthy, foul, improper, indecorous, lewd, licentious, malodorous, outrageous, pornographic, raw, ridiculous, rough, salacious, shameless, shocking, tasteless, untoward, vile, vulgar, wicked; • **Ant** chaste, clean, decent, decorous, modest, pure, seemly, virtuous.

indecisive [adj] uncertain, indefinite
• **Syn** changeable, doubtful, faltering, halting, hesitant, indeterminate, irresolute, tentative, unclear, vacillating, waffling, wavering; • **Ant** certain, conclusive, decisive, definite, deliberate, determined, sure.

indefatigable [adj] untiring
• **Syn** active, assiduous, determined, diligent, energetic, industrious, inexhaustible, painstaking, persevering, persistent, relentless, sedulous, tireless, unflagging, vigorous; • **Ant** faltering, fatigued, tired, weary.

indefensible [adj] inexcusable
• **Syn** bad, faulty, inexpiable, insupportable, unforgivable, unpardonable, untenable, wrong; • **Ant** defensible, excusable, justifiable, justified.

indefinite [adj] ambiguous, vague
• **Syn** broad, doubtful, dubious, equivocal, evasive, general, ill-defined, imprecise, indistinct, inexact, loose, obscure, shadowy, unlimited, wide; • **Ant** certain, clear, defined, definite, distinct, specific, sure.

indelible [adj] not able to be erased, indestructible • **Syn** enduring, ineffaceable, ingrained, lasting, memorable, permanent, stirring, unforgettable; • **Ant** delible, destructible, erasable, impermanent.

indelicate [adj] obscene, vulgar
• **Syn** base, brash, callow, coarse, crude, earthy, embarrassing, immodest, improper, lewd, offensive, risqué, rude, suggestive, tasteless, uncouth; • **Ant** decent, delicate, inoffensive, nice, pure, tactful.

independent [adj] liberated, free
• **Syn** absolute, autonomous, freewheeling, individualistic, self-contained, self-governing, self-reliant, self-sufficient, self-supporting, separated, sovereign; • **Ant** dependent, subordinate, subservient.

indestructible [adj] lasting, unable to be destroyed • **Syn** abiding, durable, enduring, everlasting, immortal, imperishable, indelible, inextinguishable, permanent, perpetual, undying; • **Ant**

breakable, breakable, changeable, destructible, perishable.

indeterminate [*adj*] *uncertain, vague*
▪ **Syn** borderless, general, imprecise, inconclusive, indistinct, inexact, undefined, unstipulated; ▪ **Ant** certain, definite, determined, exact, fixed, measurable, specific, sure.

indicate [*v*] *signify, display*
▪ **Syn** attest, augur, bespeak, betoken, connote, demonstrate, denote, evince, express, finger, hint, illustrate, imply, intimate, make, manifest, name, prove, read, register, reveal, show, signal, signify, slot, specify, suggest, symbolize, testify, witness; ▪ **Ant** conceal, hide, mislead.

indict [*v*] *accuse*
▪ **Syn** arraign, censure, charge, criminate, impeach, incriminate, inculpate, prosecute, summon, tax; ▪ **Ant** absolve, acquit, exculpate, exonerate.

indifferent [*adj*] *unfeeling, uninterested*
▪ **Syn** aloof, apathetic, blasé, callous, cold, detached, dispassionate, distant, equitable, heartless, impartial, impervious, listless, neutral, nonchalant, objective, phlegmatic, scornful, stoical; ▪ **Ant** caring, compassionate, concerned, feeling, interested, involved, sympathetic.

indigenous [*adj*] *native, inborn*
▪ **Syn** aboriginal, congenital, domestic, endemic, homegrown, inbred, inherent, innate, natural, original, primitive, unacquired; ▪ **Ant** alien, exotic, foreign, imported.

indigent [*adj*] *poor*
▪ **Syn** beggared, destitute, homeless, impecunious, impoverished, needy, penniless, penurious, poverty-stricken; ▪ **Ant** affluent, rich, wealthy.

indignant [*adj*] *very angry*
▪ **Syn** annoyed, disgruntled, displeased, exasperated, fuming, furious, incensed, irate, livid, mad, miffed, peeved, piqued, provoked, resentful, riled, scornful, upset, wrathful; ▪ **Ant** delighted, happy, pleased.

indignity [*n*] *embarrassment, humiliation* ▪ **Syn** abuse, affront, contumely, discourtesy, dishonor, disrespect, grievance, injury, insult, insult, obloquy, opprobrium, outrage, reproach, slight, slur, snub, taunt; ▪ **Ant** deference, dignity, esteem, honor, regard, respect.

indirect [*adj*] *roundabout; unintended*
▪ **Syn** ambiguous, circular, collateral, complicated, devious, discursive, erratic, implied, incidental, meandering, oblique, obscure, rambling, secondary, sinuous, tortuous, twisting, underhand, vagrant, wandering, winding, zigzag; ▪ **Ant** direct, forthright, straight, straightforward.

indiscretion [*n*] *mistake*
▪ **Syn** bumble, crudeness, error, faux pas, folly, foolishness, foul-up, gaffe, gaucherie, imprudence, lapse, misjudgment, recklessness, stumble, thoughtlessness, unseemliness; ▪ **Ant** care, discreetness, discretion, right, tact.

indiscriminate [*adj*] *random, chaotic*
▪ **Syn** aimless, assorted, broad, confused, desultory, extensive, general, haphazard, heterogeneous, jumbled, miscellaneous, multifarious, promiscuous, shallow, superficial, sweeping, varied, wide; ▪ **Ant** chosen, critical, definite, discriminatory, methodical, particular, selective, specific, systematic.

indispensable [*adj*] *necessary*
▪ **Syn** basal, cardinal, crucial, essential, fundamental, imperative, key, necessitous, needful, prerequisite, primary, required, vital; ▪ **Ant** dispensable, needless, nonessential, redundant, superfluous, unnecessary.

indisposed [*adj1*] *not well*
▪ **Syn** ailing, below par, confined, down, ill, infirm, poorly, sick, sickly; ▪ **Ant** healthy, hearty, sound, well.

indisposed [*adj2*] *unwilling*
▪ **Syn** afraid, antagonistic, antipathetic, averse, hesitant, hostile, inimical, loath, reluctant; ▪ **Ant** bent, disposed, inclined, tending, willing.

indisputable [*adj*] *beyond doubt*
▪ **Syn** absolute, actual, certain, evident, incontestable, incontrovertible, irrefutable, positive, real, sure, true, unassailable; ▪ **Ant** disputable, doubtful, dubious, indefinite, questionable, refutable, uncertain, unreliable, unsure, vague.

indistinct [*adj*] *obscure, ambiguous*
▪ **Syn** bleary, blurred, confused, dark, doubtful, fuzzy, hazy, ill-defined, indefinite, indeterminate, indistinguishable, murky, shadowy, unclear, unintelligible, vague, weak; ▪ **Ant** apparent, certain, defined, definite, discernible, distinct, evident, explicit, plain, positive, sure.

indistinguishable [*adj*] *alike*
▪ **Syn** duplicate, equivalent, identical, like, same, tantamount, twin; ▪ **Ant**

different, distinguishable, separate, unalike, unlike.

individual [*adj*] *distinctive, exclusive*
▪ *Syn* characteristic, diacritic, distinct, express, idiosyncratic, lone, original, peculiar, personalized, reserved, respective, secluded, separate, singular, solitary, special, unique; ▪ *Ant* collective, common, general, group, ordinary.

individually [*adv*] *separately*
▪ *Syn* alone, apart, by oneself, distinctively, exclusively, independently, one at a time, one by one, personally, singly; ▪ *Ant* as one, in unison, together.

indolent [*adj*] *lazy*
▪ *Syn* easygoing, faineant, idle, inactive, lackadaisical, languid, listless, resting, shiftless, slothful, slow, torpid; ▪ *Ant* active, busy, diligent, energetic, enthusiastic, hard-working, industrious, intent.

indomitable [*adj*] *steadfast, unyielding*
▪ *Syn* dogged, impassable, insurmountable, invincible, invulnerable, obstinate, pertinacious, ruthless, staunch, unconquerable, willful; ▪ *Ant* beatable, conquerable, feeble, unstable, weak, yielding.

induce [*v*] *cause to happen; encourage*
▪ *Syn* abet, activate, actuate, breed, cajole, cause, coax, draw, effect, generate, impel, incite, influence, instigate, make, motivate, occasion, persuade, press, procure, produce, prompt, sway, urge, wheedle; ▪ *Ant* discourage, halt, hinder, prevent.

induct [*v*] *take into an organization*
▪ *Syn* conscript, draft, enlist, inaugurate, initiate, install, instate, introduce, invest, recruit, sign on, swear in; ▪ *Ant* blackball, expel, reject, turn away.

indulgent [*adj*] *lenient, giving*
▪ *Syn* charitable, complaisant, easygoing, favorable, forbearing, gratifying, kindly, liberal, merciful, mild, permissive, tolerant, understanding; ▪ *Ant* intolerant, rigorous, severe, stern, strict.

industrious [*adj*] *hardworking*
▪ *Syn* assiduous, busy, conscientious, diligent, dynamic, eager, involved, laborious, operose, persevering, productive, sedulous, tireless, zealous; ▪ *Ant* idle, inactive, indolent, lackadaisical, lazy, lethargic, slack, unemployed, unproductive.

inebriated [*adj*] *drunk*
▪ *Syn* bombed, boozy, inebriate, intoxicated, tipsy, under the influence; ▪ *Ant* sober, straight.

ineffable [*adj*] *too great for words*
▪ *Syn* celestial, divine, empyreal, ethereal, heavenly, ideal, impossible, indescribable, inexpressible, nameless, sacred, spiritual, transcendental, unspeakable, unutterable; ▪ *Ant* definable, describable, utterable.

ineffective/ineffectual [*adj*] *weak, useless* ▪ *Syn* abortive, barren, bootless, feckless, fruitless, futile, idle, impotent, inadequate, incompetent, inefficient, inept, inferior, lame, neutralized, nugatory, paltry, powerless, spineless, vain, void, worthless; ▪ *Ant* competent, effective, effectual, efficient, powerful, strong, successful, useful.

inefficient [*adj*] *not working well; wasteful* ▪ *Syn* careless, disorganized, extravagant, faulty, feeble, improvident, inept, inexpert, prodigal, slack, slipshod, slovenly, unfit, weak; ▪ *Ant* able, capable, competent, effectual, efficient, expert, useful.

inelegant [*adj*] *clumsy, crude*
▪ *Syn* awkward, coarse, crass, gauche, graceless, indelicate, labored, oafish, rough, rude, uncouth, vulgar; ▪ *Ant* elegant, glamorous, graceful, refined, sophisticated.

ineligible [*adj*] *not qualified*
▪ *Syn* disqualified, inappropriate, objectionable, ruled out, unacceptable, unfit, unqualified, unsuitable; ▪ *Ant* acceptable, eligible, equipped, qualified, suitable.

inept [*adj1*] *clumsy, unskilled; incompetent* ▪ *Syn* artless, awkward, bungling, gauche, inadept, incapable, incompetent, undexterous, unproficient; ▪ *Ant* adroit, competent, dexterous, fit, skilled, skillful.

inept [*adj2*] *not suitable; improper*
▪ *Syn* absurd, ill-timed, inappropriate, infelicitous, malapropos, pointless, ridiculous, undue, unseemly, unsuitable; ▪ *Ant* acceptable, germane, proper, suitable.

inequality [*n*] *prejudice; lack of balance*
▪ *Syn* asperity, bias, contrast, difference, discrimination, disparity, imparity, injustice, partisanship, variation; ▪ *Ant* balance, equality, equivalence, evenness, parity, similarity.

inert [*adj*] *not moving; lifeless*
▪ *Syn* apathetic, asleep, dormant, drowsy, dull, idle, immobile, inactive, indolent, languid, lazy, listless, numb, paralyzed, passive, phlegmatic, quiescent, quiet, sleepy, sluggard, slumberous, static, still,

stolid, torpid; ▪ **Ant** active, alive, animated, lively, mobile, moving, working.

inertia [n] *disinclination to move; lifelessness* ▪ **Syn** apathy, indolence, languor, lassitude, paralysis, passivity, sloth, stillness, stupor, torpidity, torpor; ▪ **Ant** activity, animation, life, liveliness, moving.

inevitable [adj] *certain; unavoidable* ▪ **Syn** assured, binding, destined, determined, doomed, fated, foreordained, imminent, impending, ineluctable, inexorable, irrevocable, necessary, obligatory, prescribed, settled, unalterable; ▪ **Ant** avoidable, doubtful, escapable, fortuitous, preventable, uncertain, unlikely, unsure.

inexcusable [adj] *not forgivable* ▪ **Syn** blamable, blameworthy, censurable, indefensible, intolerable, outrageous, reprehensible, unforgivable, unpardonable, wrong; ▪ **Ant** excusable, forgivable, justifiable, venial.

inexorable [adj] *cruel, pitiless* ▪ **Syn** adamant, dogged, harsh, immobile, implacable, inflexible, ironclad, merciless, obstinate, relentless, remorseless, resolute, severe, uncompromising, unmovable, unrelenting, unyielding; ▪ **Ant** flexible, indulgent, lenient, merciful, remorseful, yielding.

inexpensive [adj] *not high-priced* ▪ **Syn** bargain, budget, cheap, cut-rate, economical, low, low-cost, modest, nominal, popular, reasonable, reduced; ▪ **Ant** costly, dear, expensive, high-cost, high-priced.

inexperienced [adj] *unskilled, unfamiliar* ▪ **Syn** amateur, callow, fresh, inept, inexpert, naive, new, rookie, rude, sophomoric, untried, young; ▪ **Ant** educated, experienced, expert, familiar, schooled, seasoned, skilled, trained, versed.

inexplicable [adj] *beyond comprehension, explanation* ▪ **Syn** baffling, enigmatic, incomprehensible, inscrutable, insoluble, mysterious, obscure, peculiar, puzzling, strange, unaccountable, undefinable, unfathomable, unsolvable; ▪ **Ant** clear, comprehensible, explainable, explicable, intelligible, obvious.

infallible [adj] *unerring, always dependable* ▪ **Syn** accurate, apodictic, certain, correct, effective, efficacious, exact, faultless, foolproof, impeccable, omniscient, perfect, positive, reliable, satisfactory, sure, true, trustworthy, unim-

peachable; ▪ **Ant** erring, fallible, faulty, imperfect, questionable.

infamous [adj] *shameful, bad in reputation* ▪ **Syn** abominable, atrocious, base, contemptible, corrupt, degenerate, despicable, egregious, evil, flagitious, heinous, ignominious, iniquitous, loathsome, miscreant, nefarious, notorious, odious, rotten, scandalous, scurvy, wicked; ▪ **Ant** dignified, glorious, good, innocent, moral, perfect, principled, pure, reputable, respectable, righteous, virtuous.

infant/infantile [adj] *very young* ▪ **Syn** baby, babyish, callow, childlike, developing, early, emergent, growing, immature, juvenile, kid, naive, nascent, newborn, puerile, tender, unfledged, unripe, weak, youthful; ▪ **Ant** adult, grown-up, mature.

infatuated [adj] *in love with; obsessed* ▪ **Syn** beguiled, besotted, captivated, enamored, enraptured, fascinated, intoxicated, possessed, seduced, smitten, spellbound; ▪ **Ant** disenchanted, repelled, repulsed.

infectious [adj] *catching, spreading* ▪ **Syn** communicable, contagious, diseased, epidemic, infective, mephitic, noxious, pestilential, poisonous, toxic, transmittable, virulent, vitiating; ▪ **Ant** antiseptic, harmless, noninfectious, uncommunicable, uncontagious.

inferior [adj1] *low or lower in rank, importance* ▪ **Syn** bottom-rung, junior, lesser, lower, menial, minor, secondary, smaller, subordinate, subsidiary, underneath; ▪ **Ant** higher, senior, superior, upper.

inferior [adj2] *poor, second-rate* ▪ **Syn** average, bad, base, common, déclassé, fair, imperfect, lousy, low-grade, middling, ordinary, paltry, secondclass, substandard, wretched; ▪ **Ant** best, better, excellent, extraordinary, fine, first-class, first-rate, foremost, prime, superior.

infernal [adj] *damned* ▪ **Syn** accursed, chthonian, confounded, demonic, devilish, diabolical, execrable, fiendish, hellish, malevolent, monstrous, nether, satanic, subterranean, sulphurous, wicked; ▪ **Ant** heavenly, otherworldly, supernal.

infertile [adj] *not bearing fruit, young* ▪ **Syn** barren, depleted, drained, effete, exhausted, impotent, sterile, unfertile, unfruitful, unproductive; ▪ *Ant* fecund, fertile, fruitful, potent, productive.

infidelity [n] *disloyalty, especially sexual*
▪ *Syn* adultery, affair, betrayal, cheating, duplicity, faithlessness, inconstancy, lewdness, perfidy, treachery; ▪ *Ant* faithfulness, fidelity, loyalty.

infinite [adj] *limitless, without end*
▪ *Syn* absolute, all-embracing, boundless, enduring, eternal, immense, incessant, interminable, measureless, never-ending, perpetual, supreme, total, vast, wide; ▪ *Ant* bounded, calculable, confined, countable, definite, ephemeral, finite, fleeting, limited, measurable.

infinitesimal [adj] *very small*
▪ *Syn* atomic, imperceptible, inappreciable, inconsiderable, insignificant, little, microscopic, miniature, minuscule, minute, negligible, tiny, unnoticeable; ▪ *Ant* big, huge, large, significant, substantial.

infirm [adj] *sick, weak*
▪ *Syn* ailing, anemic, anile, debilitated, decrepit, delicate, enfeebled, failing, faint, faltering, feeble, flimsy, fragile, frail, halting, ill, lame, shaky, vacillating, wavering, weakly, wobbly; ▪ *Ant* firm, healthy, hearty, robust, sound, stable, strong.

inflame [v] *anger, aggravate*
▪ *Syn* agitate, annoy, arouse, disturb, embitter, enrage, exacerbate, excite, fire, fire up, foment, gall, grate, heat, ignite, impassion, incense, infuriate, intensify, intoxicate, kindle, light, madden, provoke, rile, rouse, stimulate, vex, worsen; ▪ *Ant* alleviate, appease, cool, pacify, placate, put out, quench, soothe, tranquilize.

inflammable [adj] *ready to burn*
▪ *Syn* burnable, combustible, dangerous, flammable, hazardous, ignitable, incendiary, risky, unsafe; ▪ *Ant* fireproof, incombustible, nonflammable, noninflammable.

inflammatory [adj] *instigative, angering*
▪ *Syn* anarchic, demagogic, explosive, fiery, incendiary, incitive, inflaming, insurgent, provocative, rabid, rebellious, revolutionary, riotous, seditious; ▪ *Ant* calming, mitigating, placating, pleasing, tranquilizing.

inflate [v] *blow up, increase*
▪ *Syn* aerate, aggrandize, amplify, augment, bloat, boost, dilate, distend, enlarge, escalate, exaggerate, exalt, expand, magnify, maximize, overestimate, pyramid, raise, spread, stretch, widen; ▪ *Ant* compress, contract, deflate, empty, flatten, shrink.

inflated [adj] *exaggerated*
▪ *Syn* amplified, augmented, bombastic, diffuse, distended, enlarged, euphuistic, flowery, fustian, grandiloquent, magnified, overblown, pompous, pretentious, puffed, rhapsodical, swollen, tumescent, turgid, verbose, windy; ▪ *Ant* concise, deflated, pithy, shrunken, succinct.

inflexible [adj1] *stubborn*
▪ *Syn* adamant, adamantine, determined, dogged, hard, immovable, implacable, inexorable, intractable, iron, obdurate, obstinate, relentless, resolute, rigid, staunch, steadfast, stringent; ▪ *Ant* flexible, pliable, reasonable, relenting, willing, yielding.

inflexible [adj2] *hardened, stiff*
▪ *Syn* hard, immalleable, inelastic, rigid, set, starched, taut, unbending; ▪ *Ant* bendable, elastic, flexible, pliable, pliant, resilient, soft.

inflict [v] *impose something*
▪ *Syn* administer, apply, bring upon, command, deal out, deliver, dispense, exact, force upon, give, levy, mete out, require, strike, visit, wreak; ▪ *Ant* alleviate, shelter, shield, spare, suspend.

influence [v] *lead to believe, do*
▪ *Syn* affect, alter, arouse, bias, change, compel, direct, form, guide, impel, impress, incline, manipulate, mold, predispose, prejudice, prompt, regulate, rouse, seduce, shape, train, urge; ▪ *Ant* dissuade, hinder, impede, restrain.

influential [adj] *effective, powerful*
▪ *Syn* authoritative, controlling, dominant, efficacious, forcible, important, instrumental, leading, meaningful, moving, persuasive, potent, significant, strong, substantial, weighty; ▪ *Ant* impotent, ineffective, ineffectual, powerless, unimportant, uninfluential, weak.

influx [n] *flow, rush*
▪ *Syn* arrival, convergence, entrance, incursion, inflow, inundation, invasion, penetration; ▪ *Ant* egress, exit, exodus, outflow, outpouring.

inform [v] *communicate knowledge, information* ▪ *Syn* acquaint, advise, brief, clue, edify, educate, enlighten, familiarize, forewarn, illuminate, leak, level, notify, post, relate, snitch, squeal, tattle, tip, update, warn; ▪ *Ant* conceal, hide, keep quiet, secrete.

informal [*adj*] *casual, simple*
▪ *Syn* breezy, colloquial, congenial, easy, everyday, familiar, free, homey, intimate, loose, low-pressure, mellow, natural, open, ordinary, relaxed, urbane; ▪ *Ant* buttoned-up, ceremonious, dressed-up, formal, official, rigid, stiff.

informative [*adj*] *educational*
▪ *Syn* advisory, communicative, descriptive, edifying, elucidative, enlightening, explanatory, forthcoming, illuminating, instructive, newsy, revealing, significant; ▪ *Ant* unilluminating, unimportant, uninformative, useless.

informed [*adj*] *cognizant, conversant*
▪ *Syn* abreast, acquainted, briefed, enlightened, erudite, familiar, knowledgeable, learned, reliable, savvy, up-to-date, versed, well-read; ▪ *Ant* ignorant, unaware, uninformed, unknowledgeable.

infrequent [*adj*] *not happening regularly*
▪ *Syn* exceptional, isolated, limited, meager, occasional, odd, rare, scant, scarce, seldom, sparse, sporadic, stray; ▪ *Ant* common, frequent, habitual, often, usual.

infringe [*v*] *violate*
▪ *Syn* breach, break, disobey, encroach, infract, intrude, lift, meddle, obtrude, presume, steal, trespass; ▪ *Ant* comply, discharge, obey, observe.

infuriate [*v*] *make very angry*
▪ *Syn* aggravate, anger, enrage, exasperate, incense, ire, madden, provoke, rile, umbrage; ▪ *Ant* make happy, please.

ingenious [*adj*] *very clever; brilliant*
▪ *Syn* able, adroit, artistic, bright, crafty, creative, dexterous, gifted, imaginative, innovative, intelligent, original, resourceful, shrewd, skillful; ▪ *Ant* artless, awkward, clumsy, ignorant, incompetent, inept.

ingenuous [*adj*] *honest, trustful*
▪ *Syn* artless, candid, frank, guileless, innocent, naive, open, plain, simple, straightforward, trusting, unsophisticated, unstudied; ▪ *Ant* affected, artificial, deceitful, dishonest, sly.

ingrained [*adj*] *deep-rooted*
▪ *Syn* built-in, confirmed, congenital, deep-seated, fixed, fundamental, hereditary, inbred, indelible, ineradicable, inherent, innate, intrinsic, rooted; ▪ *Ant* exterior, external, superficial, surface.

ingratiating [*adj*] *fawning, servile*
▪ *Syn* charming, crawling, deferential, disarming, flattering, humble, insinuating, obsequious, saccharine, serving, silken, sycophantic, unctuous; ▪ *Ant* abrasive, disgusting, repellent.

inhabit [*v*] *reside or take up residence in*
▪ *Syn* abide, dwell, indwell, live, lodge, occupy, park, people, populate, reside, roost, settle, squat, stay, tenant; ▪ *Ant* depart, leave, move, vacate.

inhale [*v*] *breathe in*
▪ *Syn* drag, draw in, gasp, inspire, puff, pull, respire, smell, sniff, snort; ▪ *Ant* breathe out, exhale, expire.

inherent [*adj*] *basic, hereditary*
▪ *Syn* built-in, congenital, deep-seated, elementary, fixed, genetic, immanent, inborn, indigenous, innate, integral, internal, intrinsic, latent, natural, original, subjective, unalienable; ▪ *Ant* acquired, added, external, extrinsic, incidental, learned.

inhibit [*v*] *restrict, prevent*
▪ *Syn* arrest, avert, bar, bit, bridle, cramp, curb, discourage, enjoin, forbid, frustrate, hinder, hold back, impede, obstruct, prohibit, restrain, stop, stymie, suppress; ▪ *Ant* abet, aid, allow, approve, assist, encourage, free, help.

inhibited [*adj*] *very shy*
▪ *Syn* constrained, frustrated, guarded, passionless, repressed, reticent, self-conscious, subdued, uptight, withdrawn; ▪ *Ant* aggressive, bold, demonstrative, forward, immodest, self-confident.

inhospitable [*adj*] *unfriendly*
▪ *Syn* brusque, cold, discourteous, hostile, rude, short, unreceptive, unsociable, unwelcoming; ▪ *Ant* cordial, friendly, generous, genial, hospitable, kind, obliging.

inhuman/inhumane [*adj*] *animal, savage* ▪ *Syn* barbaric, bestial, brutal, cold-blooded, cruel, devilish, diabolical, fiendish, grim, hateful, heartless, implacable, malicious, malign, merciless, pitiless, remorseless, ruthless, truculent, vicious; ▪ *Ant* animate, compassionate, human/humane, kind, sensate, sympathetic.

inimical [*adj*] *antagonistic, contrary*
▪ *Syn* adverse, antipathetic, destructive, harmful, inimicable, injurious, noxious, opposed, pernicious, repugnant; ▪ *Ant* amiable, beneficial, friendly, hospitable, kind, salutary.

inimitable [adj] incomparable
 • **Syn** consummate, matchless, nonpareil, peerless, supreme, unequalled, unique, unmatched, unparalleled, unsurpassable; • **Ant** common, comparable, indistinctive, matchable, ordinary.

iniquity [n] sin, evil
 • **Syn** abomination, baseness, crime, evildoing, heinousness, immorality, miscreancy, misdeed, offense, sinfulness, wickedness, wrongdoing; • **Ant** fairness, good, goodness, justice, rectitude, virtue.

initial [adj] beginning, primary
 • **Syn** antecedent, earliest, elementary, embryonic, first, foremost, fundamental, germinal, headmost, inaugural, inceptive, inchoate, leading, nascent, opening, original, pioneer; • **Ant** closing, final, last, terminal, ultimate.

initiate [v] start, introduce
 • **Syn** admit, begin, commence, enter, inaugurate, induct, invest, launch, open, pioneer, set up, trigger, usher in; • **Ant** close, conclude, end, finish, terminate.

initiative [n] eagerness to do something
 • **Syn** ambition, drive, dynamism, energy, enterprise, enthusiasm, inventiveness, leadership, originality, punch, resourcefulness, vigor; • **Ant** apathy, indifference, lethargy.

injure [v] hurt, harm
 • **Syn** abuse, batter, blemish, break, contort, cripple, damage, deface, disable, disfigure, foul, impair, maim, maltreat, mar, mutilate, pain, ruin, spoil, torture, undermine, vitiate, wax, weaken; • **Ant** aid, assist, cure, fix, heal, help, mend.

injurious [adj] hurtful
 • **Syn** abusive, adverse, baneful, corrupting, deadly, deleterious, detrimental, evil, harmful, iniquitous, mischievous, nocent, nocuous, opprobrious, pernicious, prejudicial, ruinous, slanderous, unjust, wrongful; • **Ant** advantageous, aiding, beneficial, constructive, curing, healing, helpful, salutary.

injustice [n] unfair treatment; bias
 • **Syn** abuse, breach, crime, discrimination, encroachment, favoritism, grievance, infraction, iniquity, malfeasance, maltreatment, negligence, oppression, outrage, partiality, prejudice, ruin, transgression, violation, wrongdoing; • **Ant** equality, equity, ethics, fairness, impartiality, justice, lawfulness, morality.

innate [adj] inherited, native
 • **Syn** congenital, connate, constitutional, deep-seated, elemental, essential, hereditary, inborn, inbred, intrinsic, intuitive, natural; • **Ant** acquired, extrinsic, learned.

inner [adj1] central, middle physically
 • **Syn** close, constitutional, essential, focal, inside, interior, internal, intimate, intrinsic, inward, nuclear; • **Ant** exterior, external, outer, outside.

inner [adj2] mental, private
 • **Syn** central, concealed, deep-rooted, deep-seated, emotional, essential, focal, hidden, individual, inherent, innate, inside, interior, internal, intimate, intrinsic, intuitive, inward, personal, psychological, repressed, secret, spiritual, subconscious, visceral; • **Ant** exterior, obvious, outer, physical, public.

innocent [adj1] blameless
 • **Syn** above suspicion, angelic, chaste, clean, clear, crimeless, exemplary, faultless, good, guiltless, honest, immaculate, impeccable, inculpable, irreproachable, lawful, legal, legitimate, licit, pristine, pure, righteous, safe, sinless, spotless, stainless, unimpeachable, virtuous; • **Ant** bad, blamable, corrupt, culpable, evil, guilty, sinful.

innocent [adj2] harmless, naive
 • **Syn** artless, childlike, credulous, frank, fresh, guileless, gullible, ignorant, ingenuous, innocuous, open, raw, safe, simple, soft, square, unworldly, well-intentioned, well-meant, wide-eyed, youthful; • **Ant** cunning, experienced, impure, knowledgeable, worldly.

innocuous [adj] harmless
 • **Syn** banal, bland, flat, inane, insipid, jejune, painless, safe, sapless, unobjectionable, weak; • **Ant** bad, deleterious, destructive, harmful, hurtful, injurious, malicious.

innovative [adj] creative
 • **Syn** avant-garde, contemporary, deviceful, ingenious, inventive, new, original, originative, state-of-the-art; • **Ant** customary, habitual, old, traditional, uncreative, unimaginative.

innumerable [adj] many, infinite
 • **Syn** beyond number, countless, incalculable, multitudinous, myriad, numerous, uncountable, unnumbered, untold; • **Ant** computable, countable, definite, few, finite, known, numbered, numerable.

inoffensive [adj] *not obnoxious; harmless* ▪ *Syn* bland, innocuous, innoxious, mild, neutral, peaceable, pleasant, quiet, retiring, safe, unobjectionable, unobtrusive; ▪ *Ant* damaging, harmful, malicious, noxious, offensive, provocative.

inopportune [adj] *not appropriate or suitable* ▪ *Syn* contrary, disadvantageous, ill-timed, inappropriate, inauspicious, malapropos, troublesome, unpropitious, unseasonable, untimely; ▪ *Ant* appropriate, auspicious, opportune, suitable, timely.

inordinate [adj] *excessive, extravagant* ▪ *Syn* disproportionate, dizzying, exorbitant, extravagant, gratuitous, immoderate, overindulgent, preposterous, superfluous, undue, untempered, wanton, wasteful; ▪ *Ant* moderate, reasonable, restrained, warranted.

inquire [v] *ask; look into* ▪ *Syn* analyze, catechize, examine, grill, inspect, interrogate, prospect, pry, query, question, scrutinize, search, seek, sift, study; ▪ *Ant* answer, reply, respond, retort.

inquiring [adj] *wondering, curious* ▪ *Syn* analytical, catechistic, examining, fact-finding, heuristic, inquisitive, interrogative, investigative, nosy, probing, prying, questioning, quizzical, searching, Socratic, speculative, studious; ▪ *Ant* disinterested, incurious, indifferent, unskeptical.

inquisitive [adj] *curious* ▪ *Syn* analytical, challenging, impertinent, inquiring, intrusive, meddlesome, nosy, presumptuous, prying, questioning, scrutinizing, speculative; ▪ *Ant* incurious, indifferent, unconcerned, uninterested.

insane [adj] *mentally ill; foolish* ▪ *Syn* bizarre, crazed, daft, demented, deranged, fatuous, frenzied, idiotic, impractical, irresponsible, lunatic, mad, maniacal, paranoid, preposterous, psychopathic, psychotic, rabid, screwy, senseless, touched, unhinged, wild; ▪ *Ant* balanced, healthy, rational, reasonable, sane, sound, well.

insatiable [adj] *voracious, wanting* ▪ *Syn* clamorous, demanding, exigent, gluttonous, importunate, insistent, pressing, quenchless, rapacious, ravenous, unappeasable, urgent, yearning; ▪ *Ant* fulfilled, full, pleased, satiable, satisfied.

inscrutable [adj] *hidden, mysterious; blank* ▪ *Syn* ambiguous, arcane, cabalistic, difficult, enigmatic, impenetrable, inexplicable, mystic, secret, sphinxlike, unaccountable, unfathomable, unintelligible; ▪ *Ant* clear, comprehensible, evident, intelligible, manifest, obvious, palpable, plain.

insecure [adj1] *uncertain, worried* ▪ *Syn* afraid, anxious, apprehensive, diffident, hesitant, jumpy, shaky, troubled, unsure, vague; ▪ *Ant* assured, certain, confident, confident, secure, sure.

insecure [adj2] *dangerous, precarious* ▪ *Syn* defenseless, exposed, frail, hazardous, insubstantial, loose, perilous, precarious, rickety, rocky, rootless, shaky, vacillating, vulnerable, wavering, weak, wobbly; ▪ *Ant* guarded, protected, reliable, safe, secure, sound, stable.

insensitive [adj1] *indifferent, callous* ▪ *Syn* aloof, crass, hardened, heartless, imperceptive, impervious, obtuse, stony, tactless, unfeeling, unresponsive; ▪ *Ant* caring, concerned, feeling, impressionable, mindful, responsive, sensitive, susceptible.

insensitive [adj2] *numb* ▪ *Syn* anesthetized, asleep, benumbed, dead, deadened, insensible, senseless, unfeeling; ▪ *Ant* aware, feeling, sensate, tender, touched.

inseparable [adj] *unable to be divided* ▪ *Syn* attached, conjoined, connected, entwined, inalienable, indivisible, inseverable, intertwined, interwoven, molded, secure, unified, united, whole; ▪ *Ant* dividable, divisible, separable, severable.

insert [v] *put, tuck into* ▪ *Syn* admit, embed, enter, fill in, imbed, implant, include, infix, infuse, inject, inlay, insinuate, instill, interject, interlope, interpolate, interpose, introduce, intrude, obtrude, place, root, set, stick; ▪ *Ant* detach, extract, remove, take out, withdraw.

inside [adj1] *in the middle; interior* ▪ *Syn* central, inner, innermost, internal, intramural, inward, surrounded; ▪ *Ant* exterior, external, outer, outside.

inside [adj2] *secret* ▪ *Syn* classified, closet, confidential, esoteric, exclusive, hush-hush, internal, limited, private, restricted; ▪ *Ant* known, open, public.

inside [adv] within
- **Syn** indoors, under cover, within doors, within walls; **Ant** exterior, outside.

insidious [adj] sneaky, tricky
- **Syn** artful, astute, crafty, crooked, cunning, deceitful, deceptive, duplicitous, ensnaring, foxy, guileful, Machiavellian, perfidious, secret, sneaking, stealthy, surreptitious, treacherous, tricky, wily; **Ant** candid, fair, honest, ingenuous, open, sincere.

insight [n] intuitiveness, awareness
- **Syn** acumen, comprehension, discernment, intuition, judgment, observation, penetration, sagacity, sapience, shrewdness, understanding, vision, wisdom; **Ant** ignorance, obtuseness, stupidity.

insignificant [adj] not important; of no consequence **Syn** casual, immaterial, inconsequential, infinitesimal, lesser, meager, meaningless, minuscule, negligible, nondescript, nugatory, paltry, pointless, scanty, secondary, senseless, trifling, trivial; **Ant** consequential, important, momentous, significant, substantial, valuable.

insincere [adj] dishonest, pretended
- **Syn** backhanded, deceitful, disingenuous, dissimulating, evasive, faithless, false, hollow, hypocritical, lying, mendacious, perfidious, pretentious, shifty, snide; **Ant** candid, forthright, frank, honest, open, sincere, truthful.

insinuate [v] force one's way into
- **Syn** edge in, foist, infiltrate, infuse, insert, interject, interpose, introduce, slip in, wedge in; **Ant** alienate, remove, retreat, withdraw.

insipid [adj1] dull, uninteresting
- **Syn** anemic, banal, beige, bland, colorless, drab, dry, feeble, flat, inane, innocuous, jejune, lifeless, mundane, ordinary, prosaic, slight, subdued, tame, tedious, tired, vapid, watery; **Ant** exciting, exhilarating, imaginative, interesting, inventive, pleasing, spirited, stimulating.

insipid [adj2] tasteless
- **Syn** bland, distasteful, flat, flavorless, mild, savorless, stale, unpalatable, vapid, watered-down, watery; **Ant** appetizing, delicious, poignant, savory, tasty.

insist [v] order and expect; claim
- **Syn** assert, aver, be firm, contend, demand, hold, importune, maintain, persist, press, reiterate, stand firm, swear, urge, vow; **Ant** ask, beg, deny, plead, request.

insistent [adj] demanding
- **Syn** assertive, clamorous, dire, dogged, emphatic, forceful, imperative, importunate, incessant, obstinate, peremptory, persistent, pressing, resolute, unrelenting, urgent; **Ant** disinterested, indifferent, lenient, tolerant.

insolent [adj] bold, disrespectful
- **Syn** abusive, arrogant, brazen, contemptuous, dictatorial, discourteous, fresh, imperative, impertinent, impolite, magisterial, nervy, offensive, overbearing, peremptory, procacious, rude, smart; **Ant** deferential, humble, modest, polite, respectful, servile.

insoluble [adj] mysterious, unable to be solved or answered **Syn** baffling, difficult, impenetrable, mystifying, obscure, unaccountable, unfathomable, unresolved, unsolved; **Ant** explainable, explicable, obvious, open, solvable.

insolvent [adj] financially ruined
- **Syn** bankrupt, broken, failed, foreclosed, indebted, lost, undone; **Ant** affluent, moneyed, rich, solvent, wealthy.

insouciant [adj] easygoing, casual
- **Syn** airy, breezy, buoyant, careless, gay, heedless, jaunty, lighthearted, nonchalant, sunny, thoughtless, unconcerned, untroubled; **Ant** anxious, careful, cautious, guarded, high-strung, nervous.

inspect [v] examine, check
- **Syn** audit, canvass, interrogate, investigate, notice, observe, probe, question, review, scope, scrutinize, study, survey, vet, watch; **Ant** forget, ignore, neglect, overlook.

inspire [v] encourage, stimulate
- **Syn** affect, animate, arouse, cause, embolden, enliven, exalt, excite, exhilarate, galvanize, hearten, imbue, inflame, influence, inspirit, invigorate, motivate, occasion, provoke, quicken, reassure, spur, stimulate, stir, sway, trigger, urge, work up; **Ant** deter, discourage, disenchant, dissuade.

instability [n] imbalance, inconstancy
- **Syn** alternation, anxiety, capriciousness, disquiet, fickleness, fluctuation, impermanence, insecurity, irresolution, mutability, oscillation, precariousness, restlessness, transience, vacillation, vola-

tility, vulnerability, wavering; ▪ *Ant* balance, consistency, constancy, equilibrium, regularity, soundness, stability, steadfastness.

install [*v*] *set up, establish*
▪ *Syn* build in, ensconce, fix, furnish, inaugurate, institute, invest, lodge, place, position, put in, station; ▪ *Ant* dislodge, remove.

instant [*adj*] *immediate, urgent*
▪ *Syn* clamant, contemporary, current, dire, direct, exigent, existent, fast, imperative, importunate, present, prompt, quick; ▪ *Ant* delayed, eventual, late, later.

instantaneous [*adj*] *immediate*
▪ *Syn* direct, fast, instant, momentary, quick, rapid, spontaneous, transitory; ▪ *Ant* delayed, eventual, late, later.

instantly [*adv*] *right now*
▪ *Syn* at once, directly, forthwith, immediately, instantaneously, now, right away, spontaneously, this minute, without delay; ▪ *Ant* eventually, later.

instigate [*v*] *influence, provoke*
▪ *Syn* abet, actuate, encourage, foment, goad, hint, impel, incite, insinuate, kindle, move, persuade, prompt, rouse, scheme, spur, stimulate, urge; ▪ *Ant* deter, halt, prevent, quell, repress, restrain, stop.

instill [*v*] *implant, introduce*
▪ *Syn* catechize, diffuse, disseminate, engender, engraft, imbue, impregnate, impress, inculcate, indoctrinate, infiltrate, infuse, inoculate, insinuate, inspire, interject, program, propagandize, suffuse, transfuse; ▪ *Ant* dislodge, eradicate, remove, uproot.

instinctive [*adj*] *reflex, automatic*
▪ *Syn* accustomed, habitual, impulsive, inborn, ingrained, innate, intrinsic, involuntary, mechanical, native, natural, rooted, spontaneous, typical, visceral; ▪ *Ant* acquired, conscious, deliberate, learned, meditated, reasonable, sensible, voluntary.

institute [*v*] *begin; put into operation*
▪ *Syn* appoint, bow, commence, constitute, enact, establish, fix, inaugurate, initiate, launch, ordain, organize, pioneer, settle, start; ▪ *Ant* cease, halt, prevent, stop, terminate.

instrumental [*adj*] *influential, assisting*
▪ *Syn* active, auxiliary, conducive, contributory, helpful, serviceable, subsid-

iary, useful; ▪ *Ant* ineffectual, negligible, unhelpful, useless.

insubordinate [*adj*] *rebellious*
▪ *Syn* contrary, contumacious, defiant, disaffected, disorderly, dissentious, factious, insurgent, intractable, mutinous, perverse, recalcitrant, refractory, seditious, turbulent, unruly; ▪ *Ant* behaved, compliant, disciplined, docile, obedient, submissive.

insubstantial [*adj*] *weak, imaginary*
▪ *Syn* aerial, airy, chimerical, decrepit, ephemeral, false, fanciful, feeble, flimsy, frail, idle, intangible, metaphysical, petty, puny, slender, slight, tenuous, thin; ▪ *Ant* material, real, strong, substantial, tangible.

insufferable [*adj*] *horrible, intolerable*
▪ *Syn* detestable, dreadful, impossible, outrageous, painful, unacceptable, unendurable, unspeakable; ▪ *Ant* delightful, endurable, pleasant, sufferable, tolerable.

insufficient [*adj*] *not enough; lacking*
▪ *Syn* bereft, defective, deficient, destitute, devoid, drained, dry, failing, faulty, imperfect, inadequate, incomplete, meager, scant, scarce, short, short of, shy, thin, wanting; ▪ *Ant* adequate, ample, competent, enough, satisfactory, sufficient.

insular [*adj*] *narrow-minded*
▪ *Syn* bigoted, circumscribed, closed, confined, contracted, detached, isolated, limited, narrow, parochial, provincial, restricted, secluded, sequestered; ▪ *Ant* broad-minded, catholic, cosmopolitan, liberal, unbiased, unprejudiced.

insult [*v*] *abuse, offend*
▪ *Syn* abase, affront, aggravate, annoy, blister, curse, debase, degrade, deride, flout, humiliate, injure, jeer, libel, mock, outrage, provoke, revile, ridicule, scoff, slander, slight, sneer, snub, taunt, tease, vex; ▪ *Ant* compliment, flatter, honor, praise.

insure [*v*] *protect, secure*
▪ *Syn* assure, cinch, cover, guarantee, guard, hedge, indemnify, register, safeguard, shield, underwrite, warrant; ▪ *Ant* imperil, jeopardize.

insurgent [*adj*] *rebellious*
▪ *Syn* anarchical, contumacious, disobedient, factious, insubordinate, mutinous, revolting, revolutionary, riotous, seditious; ▪ *Ant* loyal, obedient, patriotic, subordinate.

insurmountable [adj] *impossible to overcome* ▪ *Syn* hopeless, impassable, impregnable, inaccessible, indomitable, ineluctable, insuperable, invincible, overwhelming, unbeatable; ▪ *Ant* attainable, beatable, defeatable, possible, surmountable.

insurrection [n] *rebellion*
▪ *Syn* coup, disorder, insurgence, insurgency, mutiny, revolt, revolution, riot, rising, sedition, uprising; ▪ *Ant* compliance, obedience, submission, subordination.

intact [adj] *undamaged; all in one piece*
▪ *Syn* complete, entire, flawless, imperforate, indiscrete, perfect, sound, together, unblemished, uncut, undefiled, unharmed, unhurt, unimpaired, uninjured, unmarred, unscathed, untouched, unviolated, whole; ▪ *Ant* broken, damaged, defective, harmed, hurt, injured, violated.

intangible [adj] *indefinite, obscured*
▪ *Syn* abstruse, airy, dim, elusive, ethereal, evasive, hypothetical, impalpable, imperceptible, inappreciable, incorporeal, invisible, unreal, rare, slight, uncertain, unobservable, unsubstantial, unsure, vague; ▪ *Ant* apparent, definite, obvious, palpable, perceptible, tangible.

integral [adj1] *necessary, basic*
▪ *Syn* component, constituent, elemental, essential, fundamental, indispensable, intrinsic, requisite; ▪ *Ant* extrinsic, peripheral, secondary, supplemental, unnecessary.

integral [adj2] *complete*
▪ *Syn* aggregate, entire, full, indivisible, intact, perfect, undivided, whole; ▪ *Ant* accessory, fractional, fragmentary, part, partial, supplementary.

integrate [v] *mix, merge*
▪ *Syn* amalgamate, assimilate, blend, coalesce, combine, concentrate, conjoin, consolidate, coordinate, fuse, incorporate, interface, intermix, join, knit, link, mesh, reconcile, symphonize, synthesize, unite, wed; ▪ *Ant* disperse, divide, scatter, segregate, separate.

integrity [n] *honor, uprightness*
▪ *Syn* candor, forthrightness, goodness, honesty, incorruptibility, principle, probity, rectitude, righteousness, sincerity, virtue; ▪ *Ant* corruption, deceit, disgrace, dishonesty, dishonor, duplicity.

intellectual [adj] *studious*
▪ *Syn* bookish, cerebral, creative, intelligent, inventive, learned, mental, phrenic, rational, scholarly, thoughtful; ▪ *Ant* foolish, ignorant, illiterate, simple, stupid.

intelligent [adj] *very smart*
▪ *Syn* acute, alert, astute, bright, brilliant, capable, clever, comprehending, discerning, enlightened, exceptional, imaginative, inventive, keen, original, penetrating, perceptive, perspicacious, profound, quick-witted, rational, sage, sharp, smart, thinking, understanding, well-informed, wise, witty; ▪ *Ant* foolish, idiotic, ignorant, imbecile, irrational, stupid, unintelligent.

intelligible [adj] *understandable*
▪ *Syn* apprehensible, clear, comprehensible, distinct, fathomable, knowable, lucid, open, plain, unmistakable; ▪ *Ant* ambiguous, confusing, equivocal, obscure, perplexing, unintelligible.

intense [adj] *forceful, severe; passionate*
▪ *Syn* acute, agonizing, ardent, biting, bitter, burning, concentrated, consuming, cutting, deep, energetic, exquisite, fanatical, fervent, fierce, hard, heightened, impassioned, keen, marked, piercing, pungent, sharp, stinging, supreme, undue, violent, zealous; ▪ *Ant* calm, casual, dull, gentle, low-key, mild, moderate, relaxed, subdued, weak.

intensify [v] *make more forceful, severe*
▪ *Syn* accent, accentuate, aggrandize, augment, boost, brighten, concentrate, darken, emphasize, enhance, escalate, exacerbate, exalt, heighten, increase, magnify, point, quicken, raise, redouble, reinforce, rise, rouse, sharpen, step up, strengthen, stress, whet; ▪ *Ant* allay, calm, diminish, lessen, lower, mitigate, slow, soothe, weaken.

intensive [adj] *exhaustive*
▪ *Syn* accelerated, complete, comprehensive, concentrated, deep, demanding, fast, hard, in-depth, profound, radical, severe, thorough, thoroughgoing; ▪ *Ant* cursory, incomplete, incomprehensive, superficial, surface.

intent [adj] *determined, resolute*
▪ *Syn* absorbed, alert, attending, bent, committed, concentrated, decided, eager, earnest, engrossed, firm, fixed, immersed, industrious, intense, occupied, piercing, resolved, set, steadfast, watch-

ful; **Ant** abstracted, distracted, irresolute, wandering.

intentional [*adj*] *deliberate*
- **Syn** advised, aforethought, calculated,
designful, done on purpose, intended,
meditated, prearranged, premeditated,
proposed, studied, voluntary, willful,
witting; **Ant** accidental, inadvertent, unintentional, unplanned.

inter [*v*] *bury*
- **Syn** cover up, entomb, inhume, inurn,
lay to rest, sepulcher, tomb; **Ant** dig
up, disinter, exhume.

intercept [*v*] *head off; interrupt*
- **Syn** ambush, appropriate, arrest, block,
catch, curb, deflect, hijack, interlope,
obstruct, prevent, seize, stop; **Ant** abet,
forward, hasten, help, relay, transmit.

interchangeable [*adj*] *identical, trans-
posable* **Syn** changeable, commutable,
compatible, converse, convertible, correspondent, equivalent, exchangeable,
fungible, mutual, reciprocal, same, sub-
stitutable, synonymous; **Ant** different,
dissimilar, opposite.

interest [*v*] *hold the attention of*
- **Syn** affect, amuse, appeal, appeal to,
arouse, attract, concern, divert, engage,
engross, entertain, enthrall, excite, fascinate, grab, hook, intrigue, involve, lure,
move, pique, please, snare, tantalize,
tempt, titillate; **Ant** bore, bother, disenchant, disinterest.

interested [*adj*] *concerned, curious*
- **Syn** absorbed, affected, attentive, attracted, concerned, drawn, engrossed,
fascinated, implicated, impressed, intent,
keen, lured, moved, obsessed, occupied,
partial, partisan, predisposed, prejudiced,
responsive, roused, stimulated, struck,
taken, touched; **Ant** aloof, apathetic,
detached, disinterested, incurious, unconcerned.

interesting [*adj*] *appealing, entertaining*
- **Syn** absorbing, affecting, alluring,
amusing, arresting, captivating, charismatic, compelling, delightful, enchanting, engaging, engrossing, enthralling,
entrancing, fascinating, fine, gripping,
impressive, intriguing, lovely, magnetic,
pleasing, provocative, riveting, stimulating, striking, thought-provoking, winning; **Ant** boring, dull, flat, tedious,
tiresome, unexciting, unstimulating.

interfere [*v*] *meddle, intervene*
- **Syn** baffle, balk, conflict, discommode,

foil, frustrate, hamper, hinder, impede,
incommode, inconvenience, intercede,
interpose, intrude, jam, obstruct, prevent,
remit, stop, suspend, tamper, thwart,
trammel, trouble; **Ant** aid, assist, help.

interim [*adj*] *temporary*
- **Syn** acting, ad interim, improvised, intervening, makeshift, pro tem, pro tempore, provisional, stopgap; **Ant**
continual, permanent.

interior [*adj*] *inside, central*
- **Syn** autogenous, domestic, endogenous,
home, innermost, internal, intimate, inward, private, remote, secret, visceral,
within; **Ant** exterior, external, outer,
outside, outward.

interject [*v*] *throw in; interrupt*
- **Syn** add, implant, include, infiltrate,
infuse, ingrain, insinuate, interpolate,
intersperse, introduce, intrude, parenthe-
size, splice; **Ant** extract, remove, withdraw.

intermediate [*adj*] *middle, in-between*
- **Syn** average, between, common, fair,
halfway, indifferent, intermediary, intervening, mean, median, mediocre, medium, middling, moderate, neutral,
standard, transitional; **Ant** advanced,
end, extreme, first, last.

interminable [*adj*] *infinite*
- **Syn** boundless, ceaseless, constant, continuous, endless, eternal, everlasting, immeasurable, incessant, interminate,
limitless, never-ending, permanent, perpetual, protracted, timeless, unceasing,
uninterrupted; **Ant** bounded, brief, ending, finite, short, terminable.

intermingle [*v*] *blend, mix*
- **Syn** amalgamate, associate, combine,
commingle, fuse, interblend, interfuse,
intermix, interweave, join, merge, mesh,
network, pool, wed; **Ant** divide, separate, unmix.

intermission [*n*] *break, recess*
- **Syn** abeyance, breather, cessation, interim, interlude, interruption, lull, pause,
quiescence, respite, spell, suspension,
time, time-out; **Ant** continuance, prolongation.

intermittent [*adj*] *irregular, sporadic*
- **Syn** alternate, arrested, broken,
checked, cyclic, discontinuous, epochal,
fitful, infrequent, iterant, metrical, occasional, periodic, recurrent, seasonal,
spasmodic; **Ant** constant, continual,
continuing, perpetual, regular.

internal [*adj*] *within*
- *Syn* circumscribed, civic, constitutional, domestic, enclosed, home, inherent, innate, interior, intestine, intimate, intramural, intrinsic, municipal, native, private, subjective, visceral; - *Ant* exterior, external, foreign, outer.

international [*adj*] *worldwide*
- *Syn* cosmopolitan, ecumenical, foreign, global, intercontinental, world; - *Ant* domestic, local, national.

interpolate [*v*] *add*
- *Syn* admit, annex, append, enter, include, inject, insert, insinuate, interjaculate, interject, interlope, interpose, introduce, intrude; - *Ant* erase, remove, subtract.

interpret [*v*] *make sense of; define*
- *Syn* annotate, clarify, construe, decipher, decode, delineate, depict, elucidate, enact, exemplify, explain, explicate, gather, illustrate, image, improvise, paraphrase, read, render, represent, solve, translate, understand, view; - *Ant* confuse, misinterpret, mistake, misunderstand.

interrogate [*v*] *ask pointed questions*
- *Syn* catechize, cross-examine, cross-question, examine, grill, inquire, investigate, pump, query, question, quiz; - *Ant* answer, reply, respond, retort.

interrupt [*v*] *break in, check*
- *Syn* arrest, barge in, crash, cut, delay, discontinue, disjoin, disturb, divide, edge in, halt, hinder, horn in, impede, infringe, intrude, obstruct, prevent, punctuate, sever, stay, stop, suspend; - *Ant* advance, continue, resume.

interstice [*n*] *opening, crack*
- *Syn* aperture, chink, cleft, cranny, crevice, fissure, gap, hole, interval, slit, space; - *Ant* closing, closure, seam.

intertwine/interweave [*v*] *twist around*
- *Syn* associate, braid, connect, convolute, crisscross, entwine, interknit, interweathe, link, mesh, network, relate, reticulate, tangle, tat, weave; - *Ant* untwine, untwist.

intervene [*v*] *mediate*
- *Syn* arbitrate, divide, interfere, intermediate, interpose, interrupt, intrude, involve, meddle, negotiate, obtrude, part, reconcile, separate, settle, sever, step in; - *Ant* ignore, leave alone, remove oneself, withdraw.

intimate [*adj1*] *friendly, devoted*
- *Syn* affectionate, bosom, cherished, close, confidential, cozy, dear, dearest, faithful, fast, fond, loving, mellow, near, nearest, nice, regular, snug, trusted, warm; - *Ant* cool, distant, formal, incompatible, unfriendly.

intimate [*adj2*] *private, personal*
- *Syn* confidential, deep, exhaustive, firsthand, in-depth, innate, innermost, interior, internal, intrinsic, privy, profound, secret, special, visceral; - *Ant* formal, open, public.

intimate [*v*] *suggest; tip off*
- *Syn* air, allude, communicate, connote, express, hint, impart, imply, infer, insinuate, leak, profess; - *Ant* assert, declare, proclaim, state.

intimidate [*v*] *frighten, threaten*
- *Syn* alarm, bully, coerce, compel, daunt, dishearten, dispirit, dragoon, enforce, force, oblige, ruffle, scare, spook, strong-arm, subdue, terrify, terrorize, threaten; - *Ant* assist, encourage, help.

intolerable [*adj*] *unacceptable; beyond bearing* - *Syn* excruciating, extreme, impossible, insufferable, offensive, painful, unbearable, undesirable, unendurable; - *Ant* acceptable, bearable, tolerable.

intolerant [*adj*] *impatient, prejudiced*
- *Syn* antipathetic, averse, biased, bigoted, chauvinistic, contemptuous, dictatorial, dogmatic, fanatical, inflexible, irate, jaundiced, narrow-minded, obdurate, xenophobic; - *Ant* fair, forbearing, impartial, indulgent, lenient, patient, tolerant, unprejudiced.

intoxicated [*adj1*] *drunk*
- *Syn* boozed, drunken, inebriated, muddled, sloppy, tipsy, under the influence; - *Ant* sober, straight.

intoxicated [*adj2*] *extremely happy*
- *Syn* absorbed, affected, beside oneself, captivated, delirious, ecstatic, enraptured, euphoric, excited, exhilarated, galvanized, infatuated, moved, piqued, quickened, stimulated; - *Ant* gloomy, morose, sad, unhappy.

intoxicating [*adj*] *causing great happiness* - *Syn* exhilarating, eye-popping, heady, inspiring, provocative, rousing, stimulating, thrilling; - *Ant* boring, dull, saddening, sobering.

intractable/intransigent [*adj*] *difficult, stubborn* - *Syn* awkward, cantankerous, headstrong, immovable, indomitable, insoluble, mulish, obdurate, obstinate, pertinacious, recalcitrant, refractory, self-willed, tenacious, undisciplined, ungovernable, wayward, wild, willful; ▪ *Ant* amenable, compliant, docile, easy, facile, manageable, pliable.

intrepid [adj] *brave, nervy*
▪ *Syn* audacious, bold, courageous, dauntless, fearless, game, heroic, impavid, lionhearted, nerveless, plucky, resolute, stalwart, undaunted, valiant, valorous; ▪ *Ant* afraid, cowardly, fearful, meek, timid.

intricate [adj] *complicated, elaborate*
▪ *Syn* abstruse, baroque, complex, difficult, entangled, fancy, hard, involved, labyrinthine, obscure, perplexing, rococo, sophisticated, tortuous, tricky; ▪ *Ant* direct, methodical, simple, systematic, understandable.

intrigue [v] *arouse curiosity*
▪ *Syn* appeal, attract, bait, captivate, draw, enchant, entertain, fascinate, grab, hook, interest, pique, pull, rivet, titillate; ▪ *Ant* bore, weary.

intrinsic [adj] *basic, inborn*
▪ *Syn* built-in, central, congenital, connate, constitutional, deep-seated, elemental, essential, fundamental, hereditary, inbred, inherent, innate, intimate, material, native, natural, particular, peculiar, real, true, underlying; ▪ *Ant* accidental, acquired, extrinsic, incidental, learned.

introduce [v1] *begin, institute*
▪ *Syn* admit, bring forward, commence, establish, found, inaugurate, initiate, launch, organize, pioneer, present, set up, unveil; ▪ *Ant* close, end, finish.

introduce [v2] *add, insert*
▪ *Syn* carry, enter, import, inject, inlay, inset, insinuate, instill, interpolate, interpose, ship, transport, work in; ▪ *Ant* erase, extract, subtract, take away.

introductory [adj] *preliminary, first*
▪ *Syn* anterior, basic, beginning, elementary, inaugural, incipient, initiatory, original, precursory, prefatory, preparatory, primary, provisional, rudimentary, starting; ▪ *Ant* concluding, ending, final, finishing, last, terminal.

introvert [n] *person who retreats mentally* ▪ *Syn* autist, brooder, egoist, egotist, narcissist, solitary; ▪ *Ant* extrovert.

intrude [v] *trespass, interrupt*
▪ *Syn* barge in, bother, cut in, disturb, encroach, infringe, insinuate, interject, interlope, interpolate, interpose, introduce, invade, meddle, obtrude, overstep, pester, push in, thrust, violate; ▪ *Ant* leave, leave alone, withdraw.

intuitive [adj] *instinctive*
▪ *Syn* automatic, direct, emotional, habitual, immediate, inherent, instinctual, natural, perceptive, spontaneous, understood, visceral; ▪ *Ant* calculated, meditated, rational, reasoned, taught.

inundate [v] *drown, overwhelm*
▪ *Syn* deluge, dunk, engulf, flood, glut, immerse, overflow, overrun, submerge, swamp, whelm; ▪ *Ant* dehydrate, dessicate, drain, dry, parch.

invade [v] *attack and encroach*
▪ *Syn* assail, assault, breach, entrench, foray, infest, infringe, loot, maraud, occupy, overswarm, penetrate, permeate, pillage, plunder, ravage, storm, trespass, violate; ▪ *Ant* evacuate, retreat, surrender, yield.

invalid [adj1] *worthless; unfounded*
▪ *Syn* bad, baseless, fallacious, false, ill-founded, illogical, inoperative, irrational, nugatory, null, sophistic, unsound, untrue, void, wrong; ▪ *Ant* legitimate, sound, valid, worthwhile, worthy.

invalid [adj2] *sickly*
▪ *Syn* ailing, bedridden, debilitated, disabled, down, feeble, frail, ill, infirm, peaked, poorly, run-down, sick, weak; ▪ *Ant* healthy, strong, vigorous, well.

invalidate [v] *render null and void*
▪ *Syn* abolish, abrogate, annihilate, cancel, counteract, discredit, negate, neutralize, nullify, offset, overrule, overthrow, revoke, undermine; ▪ *Ant* approve, authorize, certify, permit, validate.

invaluable [adj] *priceless*
▪ *Syn* beyond price, costly, dear, expensive, helpful, inestimable, precious, serviceable, valuable; ▪ *Ant* paltry, valueless, worthless.

invariable [adj] *not changing*
▪ *Syn* consistent, fixed, immovable, inflexible, monotonous, perpetual, regular, rigid, static, unalterable, unmodifiable; ▪ *Ant* changeable, changing, variable, varying, wavering.

invasion [n] *attack, encroachment*
▪ *Syn* aggression, assault, breach, entrenchment, foray, forced infringement, inroad, intrusion, maraud, onslaught, raid, transgression, usurpation, violation; ▪ *Ant* evacuation, retreat, surrender, withdrawal.

invective [n] *verbal abuse*
▪ *Syn* accusation, billingsgate, blame, castigation, censure, condemnation, denunciation, epithet, jeremiad, obloquy,

philippic, reproach, revilement, tirade, vilification, vituperation; ▪ **Ant** compliment, flattery, praise.

inveigh [v] *blame, denounce*
▪ **Syn** admonish, berate, censure, condemn, denounce, expostulate, object, protest, rail, recriminate, remonstrate, reproach, scold, scorch, tongue-lash, upbraid, vituperate; ▪ **Ant** commend, flatter, praise.

inventive [adj] *creative*
▪ **Syn** adroit, avant-garde, constructive, demiurgic, fertile, formative, fruitful, gifted, imaginative, ingenious, inspired, original, originative, productive, resourceful; ▪ **Ant** uncreative, uninventive, unoriginal, unproductive.

invest [v1] *contribute money to make money* ▪ **Syn** advance, back, buy into, buy stock, devote, endow, imbue, infuse, intrust, lend, plunge, provide, spend, supply; ▪ **Ant** divest, divest, take out, withdraw.

invest [v2] *give power or authority*
▪ **Syn** adopt, authorize, bequeath, charge, consecrate, empower, endow, endue, enthrone, establish, inaugurate, induct, initiate, install, instate, license, ordain, sanction, vest; ▪ **Ant** deny, divest, reserve, take away, withhold.

investigate [v] *check into thoroughly*
▪ **Syn** consider, delve, dig, examine, inspect, interrogate, poke, probe, prospect, pry, question, reconnoiter, research, scrutinize, search, sift, spy, study; ▪ **Ant** conjecture, guess, ignore.

inveterate [adj] *long-standing, established* ▪ **Syn** abiding, accustomed, chronic, customary, deep-rooted, enduring, fixed, habitual, incorrigible, indurated, innate, long-lasting, obstinate, old, permanent, persistent, set, stubborn, sworn; ▪ **Ant** incipient, short-lived, superficial.

invidious [adj] *hateful*
▪ **Syn** abominable, calumnious, defamatory, detestable, insulting, libelous, maligning, obnoxious, odious, repugnant, scandalous, slanderous, vilifying; ▪ **Ant** delightful, likable, lovable.

invigorate [v] *stimulate*
▪ **Syn** activate, animate, brace, energize, exhilarate, freshen, galvanize, harden, inspirit, perk up, quicken, refresh, reinforce, rejuvenate, restore, revitalize, rouse, strengthen, trigger, vitalize, vivify;

▪ **Ant** bore, depress, dishearten, dull, enervate.

invigorating [adj] *stimulating*
▪ **Syn** aesthetic, bracing, energizing, exhilarating, fresh, healthful, interesting, lively, quickening, rejuvenating, restorative, salubrious, tonic, uplifting, vitalizing; ▪ **Ant** boring, depressing, dull, enervating, unstimulating, wearying.

invincible [adj] *indestructible*
▪ **Syn** bulletproof, impassable, insuperable, inviolable, powerful, strong, unconquerable, unsurmountable, untouchable; ▪ **Ant** beatable, breakable, conquerable, destructible, vulnerable.

invisible [adj] *unable to be seen; hidden*
▪ **Syn** concealed, covert, disguised, impalpable, inconspicuous, indiscernible, masked, microscopic, obliterated, obscured, screened, veiled; ▪ **Ant** apparent, detectable, noticeable, observable, obvious, seen, visible.

invite [v] *ask to do something socially*
▪ **Syn** appeal to, bid, call, encourage, entreat, issue, lure, petition, ply, pray, propose, request, solicit, suggest, urge, welcome; ▪ **Ant** rebuff, reject, repulse.

inviting [adj] *alluring, captivating*
▪ **Syn** appealing, attractive, beguiling, charming, delightful, enticing, fascinating, intriguing, magnetic, open, provocative, tempting, warm, welcoming, winsome; ▪ **Ant** disenchanting, disgusting, forbidding, repelling, uninviting.

involuntary [adj] *automatic; not done willingly* ▪ **Syn** automatic, compulsory, forced, grudging, habitual, impulsive, instinctive, obligatory, reflex, spontaneous, unconscious, uncontrolled, unintended, unwitting; ▪ **Ant** conscious, intentional, unforced, voluntary, willing.

involve [v] *draw in; include*
▪ **Syn** absorb, affect, bind, catch, commit, comprise, concern, connect, contain, embroil, entail, entangle, incorporate, incriminate, inculpate, link, mire, necessitate, prove, rivet, tangle, touch; ▪ **Ant** disengage, exclude, extricate, free, liberate, remove.

involved [adj1] *complicated*
▪ **Syn** complex, confusing, convoluted, difficult, elaborate, intricate, labyrinthine, mazy, ramified, sophisticated, tangled, tortuous, winding; ▪ **Ant** easy, facile, simple, uncomplicated.

involved [adj2] *implicated in action*
• *Syn* affected, caught, embroiled, enmeshed, entangled, hooked, incriminated, occupied, participating, tangled;
• *Ant* blameless, exculpated, exonerated, removed.

inward [adj1] *ingoing*
• *Syn* entering, inbound, incoming, inflowing, inpouring, penetrating, through;
• *Ant* outgoing, outward.

inward [adj2] *private*
• *Syn* confidential, hidden, inner, innermost, inside, interior, internal, intimate, personal, privy, secret; • *Ant* exterior, outward, public.

iota [n] *small bit*
• *Syn* atom, crumb, grain, hint, jot, mite, molecule, ounce, particle, scintilla, scrap, smidgen, speck, trace, whit; • *Ant* bulk, heap, lot, mass, pack, pile.

irascible [adj] *crabby*
• *Syn* angry, bristly, cantankerous, choleric, cranky, fractious, grouchy, hot-tempered, irritable, petulant, querulous, quick-tempered, snappish, surly, testy, uptight; • *Ant* amiable, cheerful, good-natured, happy.

irate [adj] *angry*
• *Syn* angered, enraged, fuming, furious, incensed, infuriated, livid, mad, piqued, riled, wrathful, wroth; • *Ant* calm, cheerful, happy, pleased.

iridescent [adj] *rainbow-colored*
• *Syn* lustrous, many-colored, nacreous, opalescent, opaline, pearly, polychromatic, prismatic, shimmering; • *Ant* colorless, dingy, dull, flat, neutral.

irk [v] *aggravate; rub the wrong way*
• *Syn* abrade, annoy, bother, discommode, disturb, fret, gall, harass, inconvenience, irritate, miff, nettle, peeve, provoke, rasp, rile, ruffle, trouble, vex;
• *Ant* cheer, delight, please.

iron [adj] *hard, tough; inflexible*
• *Syn* adamantine, cruel, dense, ferric, firm, heavy, implacable, indomitable, obdurate, relentless, rigid, steely, stubborn, thick; • *Ant* bending, flexible, pliant, soft, weak, yielding.

ironic/ironical [adj] *sarcastic*
• *Syn* acrid, backbiting, bitter, caustic, contemptuous, contradictory, cutting, cynical, derisive, disparaging, incisive, keen, mocking, paradoxical, quick-witted, sardonic, scathing, sneering, trenchant, wry; • *Ant* considerate, def-

erential, direct, sincere, straightforward.

irrational [adj] *illogical, senseless*
• *Syn* aberrant, absurd, crazy, disjointed, distraught, fallacious, freaky, incoherent, insane, invalid, mad, nonsensical, preposterous, ridiculous, silly, specious, unreasonable, unsound, wild; • *Ant* logical, rational, reasonable, reflective, sensible, sound, stable.

irreconcilable [adj] *hostile, conflicting*
• *Syn* clashing, discordant, dissonant, implacable, incompatible, incongruous, inharmonious, intransigent, opposed, reluctant; • *Ant* appeasable, compromising, reconcilable.

irrefutable [adj] *beyond question*
• *Syn* accurate, apodictic, certain, evident, final, inarguable, incontrovertible, indubitable, ironclad, obvious, positive, proven, unanswerable, unassailable, undeniable; • *Ant* arguable, disputable, doubtful, dubious, moot, questionable, refutable, uncertain.

irregular [adj1] *random, variable*
• *Syn* aberrant, capricious, changeable, desultory, eccentric, erratic, faltering, fluctuating, fragmentary, haphazard, inconstant, infrequent, intermittent, occasional, patchy, random, recurrent, spasmodic, sporadic, uneven; • *Ant* methodical, orderly, regular, systematic, uniform.

irregular [adj2] *abnormal, peculiar*
• *Syn* aberrant, anomalous, capricious, deviant, divergent, eccentric, exceptional, odd, queer, singular, strange, unique, unusual; • *Ant* common, conventional, normal, standard, usual.

irregular [adj3] *bumpy, uneven*
• *Syn* amorphous, asymmetrical, bent, crooked, devious, eccentric, hilly, jagged, lopsided, meandering, notched, off-balance, pitted, protuberant, rough, scarred, serrate, variable, wobbly, zigzagged; • *Ant* aligned, balanced, equal, even, flat, level, smooth, symmetrical.

irrelevant [adj] *beside the point*
• *Syn* extraneous, foreign, immaterial, impertinent, inapropos, inconsequential, insignificant, outside, pointless, remote, trivial; • *Ant* applicable, appropriate, germane, necessary, pertinent, related, relevant.

irreparable [adj] *unable to be fixed*
• *Syn* broken, destroyed, hopeless, im-

possible, incorrigible, incurable, irredeemable, irreplaceable, irretrievable, irreversible, ruined; ▪ *Ant* fixable, mendable, repairable, reparable.

irrepressible [*adj*] *effervescent, vivacious* ▪ *Syn* bubbling, buoyant, ebullient, enthusiastic, rebellious, rhapsodical, uncontainable, uncontrollable, unmanageable, unruly, unstoppable; ▪ *Ant* depressed, despondent, grave, hopeless, restrained, serious.

irreproachable [*adj*] *completely innocent* ▪ *Syn* beyond reproach, blameless, exemplary, faultless, guiltless, impeccable, inculpable, perfect, reproachless, righteous, unblemished, unimpeachable, virtuous; ▪ *Ant* blamable, imperfect, reprehensible.

irresistible [*adj*] *compelling; inescapable* ▪ *Syn* alluring, fascinating, imperative, indomitable, ineluctable, inevitable, inexorable, invincible, overpowering, overwhelming, potent, powerful, ravishing, seductive, sexy, tempting, urgent; ▪ *Ant* avoidable, escapable, resistible.

irresolute [*adj*] *indecisive* ▪ *Syn* changing, doubtful, faltering, fearful, fluctuating, halting, hesitant, infirm, shaky, tentative, undecided, vacillating, wavering, weak, wobbly; ▪ *Ant* decisive, definite, determined, obstinate, resolute, stubborn, unyielding, willful.

irresponsible [*adj*] *careless, reckless* ▪ *Syn* capricious, carefree, feckless, flighty, giddy, immoral, incautious, lax, rash, reckless, shiftless, thoughtless, unpredictable, unreliable, unstable, untrustworthy, wild; ▪ *Ant* accountable, careful, liable, reliable, responsible, trustworthy.

irreverent [*adj*] *disrespectful* ▪ *Syn* aweless, contemptuous, derisive, flippant, fresh, iconoclastic, impudent, insolent, mocking, profane, rude, sacrilegious; ▪ *Ant* religious, respectful, reverent.

irrevocable [*adj*] *fixed, unchangeable* ▪ *Syn* certain, constant, established, final, immutable, indelible, inevitable, irreversible, permanent, settled, unalterable; ▪ *Ant* alterable, changeable, reversible, revocable.

irritable [*adj*] *bad-tempered, crabby* ▪ *Syn* annoyed, bearish, cantankerous, cross, crotchety, disputatious, dyspeptic, exasperated, fiery, fractious, grouchy, hot, huffy, ill-humored, irascible, moody,

oversensitive, peevish, petulant, prickly, querulous, quick-tempered, tense, touchy; ▪ *Ant* affable, cheerful, easy-going, happy, nice.

irritate [*v1*] *upset, anger* ▪ *Syn* abrade, affront, aggravate, annoy, bother, chafe, distemper, enrage, exasperate, grate on, harass, incense, inflame, infuriate, irk, madden, nettle, offend, peeve, pique, provoke, rankle, rile, roil, sour, try, vex; ▪ *Ant* aid, appease, assuage, delight, help, mollify, please.

irritate [*v2*] *hurt, chafe* ▪ *Syn* aggravate, burn, erupt, fret, inflame, intensify, itch, pain, redden, rub, sensitize, sharpen, sting, swell; ▪ *Ant* balm, ease, soothe.

isolate [*v*] *cut off, set apart* ▪ *Syn* abstract, confine, detach, disconnect, divide, insulate, quarantine, remove, segregate, separate, sequester, sever, sunder; ▪ *Ant* combine, include, incorporate, integrate, join, mingle.

isolated [*adj*] *unique or sporadic; private* ▪ *Syn* abandoned, alone, anomalous, apart, confined, deserted, detached, exceptional, forsaken, hidden, lonely, outlying, random, screened, secluded, segregated, sequestered, single, solitary, special, stranded, withdrawn; ▪ *Ant* central, incorporated, nearby, public.

issue [*v1*] *broadcast or distribute* ▪ *Syn* air, allot, announce, assign, bring out, circulate, consign, declare, deliver, dispatch, dispense, emit, give out, promulgate, publish, put in circulation, put out, release, send, send out, transmit; ▪ *Ant* collect, gather, hold, keep, retract, withdraw.

issue [*v2*] *emit, emerge; come from* ▪ *Syn* appear, arise, emanate, exude, flow, ooze, originate, proceed, rise, send forth, spring, spurt, stem, vent, well; ▪ *Ant* hold, keep, repress, retain, suppress.

itinerant [*adj*] *roaming* ▪ *Syn* afoot, ambulatory, floating, gypsy, journeying, migratory, nomadic, peripatetic, roving, shifting, traveling, vagabond, wandering, wayfaring; ▪ *Ant* permanent, settled, stationary.

J

jaded [adj] *exhausted, indifferent*
▪ *Syn* blasé, bored, dulled, fagged, fatigued, sated, spent, surfeited, tired, weary, worn, worn-down, worn-out; ▪ *Ant* fresh, lively, naive, refreshed.

jagged [adj] *ragged, notched*
▪ *Syn* asperous, barbed, craggy, denticulate, harsh, indented, pointed, ridged, rugged, scabrous, serrated, snaggy, toothed, uneven, unsmooth; ▪ *Ant* even, smooth.

jail [v] *incarcerate*
▪ *Syn* book, cage, confine, constrain, detain, hold, immure, impound, lock up, prison, sentence; ▪ *Ant* free, liberate, parole, release.

jangle [n] *cacophony of noises*
▪ *Syn* babel, clangor, clash, din, dissonance, jar, pandemonium, racket, roar, tintamarre, tumult, uproar; ▪ *Ant* quiet, silence.

jar [v1] *shock, jolt*
▪ *Syn* agitate, bounce, bump, clash, disturb, hit, irritate, jerk, jiggle, jolt, offend, quake, rattle, rock, shake, tremor, vibrate; ▪ *Ant* calm, quiet, soothe.

jar [v2] *clash, disharmonize*
▪ *Syn* clash, contend, discord, grate, grind, irk, irritate, jangle, nettle, oppose, outrage, quarrel, shock; ▪ *Ant* accord, agree, harmonize, match.

jaundiced [adj] *tainted, prejudiced*
▪ *Syn* biased, bigoted, bitter, colored, distorted, hostile, intolerant, opprobrious, partisan, preconceived, skeptical, suspicious, tendentious, warped, yellow; ▪ *Ant* clean, detached, fresh, impartial, neutral, unbiased, unprejudiced.

jaunty [adj] *lively*
▪ *Syn* airy, animated, breezy, buoyant, carefree, debonair, easy, frisky, frolicsome, gamesome, gay, high-spirited, impetuous, impudent, jovial, light, perky, playful, provocative, self-confident, sportive, sprightly, spruce, swaggering, vivacious; ▪ *Ant* depressed, lethargic, lifeless, sedate, sober, staid.

jaw [v] *criticize*
▪ *Syn* abuse, baste, berate, blame, censure, rail, rate, revile, scold, upbraid, vituperate; ▪ *Ant* commend, compliment, praise.

jazzy [adj] *fancy*
▪ *Syn* exciting, flashy, gaudy, lively, smart, spirited, vivacious, wild, zestful; ▪ *Ant* conservative, simple, unfancy.

jealous [adj] *desirious; wary*
▪ *Syn* anxious, apprehensive, begrudging, covetous, demanding, doubting, envious, grasping, green-eyed, guarded, intolerant, invidious, jaundiced, mistrustful, monopolizing, protective, questioning, resentful, skeptical, solicitous, vigilant, watchful, zealous; ▪ *Ant* confident, content, generous, satisfied, tolerant, trusting, unresentful.

jeer [v] *heckle*
▪ *Syn* banter, contemn, deride, fleer, flout, gibe, hector, hoot, jab, jest, mock, quip, ridicule, scoff, sneer, snipe, taunt; ▪ *Ant* applaud, cheer, encourage.

jell [v] *coagulate*
▪ *Syn* clot, cohere, congeal, crystallize, finalize, form, freeze, gelate, gelatinize, harden, materialize, set, solidify, stiffen, thicken; ▪ *Ant* deliquesce, liquidate, liquify, melt, run.

jet [adj] *black*
▪ *Syn* atramentous, coal-black, dark, ebon, ebony, inky, midnight, obsidian, pitch-black, pitch-dark, raven, sable; ▪ *Ant* ashen, chalky, ivory, pale, white.

jettison [v] *eject; throw overboard*
▪ *Syn* abdicate, cast off, discard, dump, expel, heave, hurl, maroon, reject, shed, throw away; ▪ *Ant* salvage, save, take in, take on.

jibe [v] *agree*
▪ *Syn* accord, conform, correspond, dovetail, fit, fit in, go, harmonize, match, resemble, square, tally; ▪ *Ant* clash, conflict, differ, disagree.

jinx [n] *curse*
▪ *Syn* black magic, charm, enchantment, hex, nemesis, plague, spell; ▪ *Ant* advantage, benefit, boon, luck.

jitters [n] *nervousness*
▪ *Syn* anxiety, dither, fidgets, jumps, nerves, shakes, shivers, tenseness; ▪ *Ant* calmness, composure, ease, poise, repose.

jocular/jocose/jocund [adj] *funny, playful* ▪ *Syn* amusing, blithe, cheerful, comical, crazy, daffy, frolicsome, gay, humorous, jesting, jovial, joyous, laughable, lighthearted, ludicrous, merry, mischievous, sportive, teasing, wacky, whimsical; ▪ *Ant* earnest, grave, morose, serious, solemn, somber.

join [*v1*] *unite*
- *Syn* add, annex, append, associate, attach, blend, bracket, cement, coalesce, combine, concrete, couple, entwine, fasten, fuse, incorporate, intermix, knit, leash, link, marry, mate, pair, span, tie, weld, yoke; ■ *Ant* disjoin, divide, part, separate, sever, sunder.

join [*v2*] *affiliate with organization*
- *Syn* align, associate, consort, cooperate, enlist, enroll, enter, follow, mingle with, side with, sign on, sign up; ■ *Ant* leave, quit, resign, withdraw.

joint [*adj*] *shared, combined*
- *Syn* collective, common, communal, concerted, conjoint, conjunct, consolidated, cooperative, intermutual, mutual, public, united; ■ *Ant* individual, personal, separate, single, solitary.

jointly [*adv*] *as one*
- *Syn* coincidentally, collectively, combined, concomitantly, concurrently, cooperatively, en masse, harmoniously, in concert, in conjunction, inseparably, intimately, in unison, mutually, reciprocally, similarly, simultaneously, together; ■ *Ant* individually, separately, singly.

jolly [*adj*] *laughing, joyful*
- *Syn* blithe, bouncy, carefree, cheerful, chipper, convivial, delightful, enjoyable, entertaining, festive, frolicsome, funny, gay, gladsome, gleeful, happy, hilarious, jocund, jovial, joyous, jubilant, lighthearted, merry, mirthful, playful, pleasant, sportive, sprightly; ■ *Ant* dour, grave, sad, serious, solemn, unhappy.

journey [*v*] *travel*
- *Syn* circuit, cruise, fare, fly, go, hie, hop, jaunt, jet, junket, pass, peregrinate, proceed, process, push on, ramble, range, repair, roam, rove, safari, tour, traverse, trek, voyage, wander, wend; ■ *Ant* stay, stop, wait.

jovial [*adj*] *very happy*
- *Syn* affable, animated, blithe, buoyant, cheery, chipper, convivial, delightful, enjoyable, festive, gay, gleeful, good-natured, hilarious, humorous, jocose, jocund, jubilant, larking, lighthearted, merry, mirthful, pleasant, sociable; ■ *Ant* dour, gloomy, lugubrious, morose, sad, unhappy.

joyful/joyous [*adj*] *very happy*
- *Syn* cheerful, cheery, delighted, ecstatic, effervescent, elated, enraptured, festive, gay, glad, jocund, jolly, jovial, jubilant, lighthearted, merry, overjoyed, pleasurable, rapturous, satisfied, transported, upbeat; ■ *Ant* sad, sorrowful, unhappy, woeful.

joyless [*adj*] *very unhappy*
- *Syn* black, bleak, blue, dejected, depressed, dismal, dispirited, doleful, downcast, dreary, droopy, gloomy, low, melancholic, miserable, mopey, mournful, sad, somber; ■ *Ant* cheerful, delighted, happy, joyful.

jubilant [*adj*] *very happy*
- *Syn* elated, euphoric, excited, exultant, glad, joyous, overjoyed, pleased, rejoicing, rhapsodic, thrilled, triumphal; ■ *Ant* depressed, despondent, doleful, melancholy, sad, sorrowful, unhappy.

judicious [*adj*] *wise, thoughtful*
- *Syn* accurate, acute, astute, careful, cautious, considerate, diplomatic, discerning, discreet, expedient, far-sighted, informed, keen, perceptive, politic, profound, quick-witted, rational, reasonable, sagacious, sane, sapient, seemly, sensible, sharp, shrewd, sober, sophisticated, thorough, wary, well-advised; ■ *Ant* foolish, hasty, idiotic, injudicious, irrational, nonsensical, reckless, senseless, thoughtless, unwise.

juicy [*adj1*] *moist*
- *Syn* dank, dewy, dripping, liquid, luscious, lush, mellow, oily, pulpy, sappy, sauced, slippery, slushy, soaked, sodden, succulent, syrupy, viscid, watery, wet; ■ *Ant* arid, dessicated, dry.

juicy [*adj2*] *exciting, interesting*
- *Syn* colorful, fascinating, intriguing, piquant, provocative, racy, risqué, sensational, spicy, suggestive, tantalizing, vivid; ■ *Ant* dull, unexciting, uninteresting, vapid.

jumble [*v*] *mix up, confuse*
- *Syn* clutter, confound, derange, disarrange, disarray, dishevel, disorder, disorganize, disturb, entangle, foul up, mess up, mistake, mix, muddle, rummage, shuffle, snarl, tangle, tumble; ■ *Ant* arrange, clear up, order, organize.

jumbo [*adj*] *gigantic*
- *Syn* colossal, cyclopean, giant, huge, immense, large, mammoth, mighty, oversized, prodigious; ■ *Ant* little, mini, miniature, small, tiny.

jump [*v*] *increase*
- *Syn* advance, ascend, boost, escalate, gain, hike, jack up, mount, put up, raise,

rise, surge, up; ▪ *Ant* decline, decrease, drop.

jumpy [*adj*] *nervous*
▪ *Syn* agitated, anxious, apprehensive, excitable, excited, fidgety, frisky, jittery, restless, sensitive, shaky, skittish, spooked, tense, timorous, unrestful; ▪ *Ant* calm, collected, composed, easygoing, laid-back, poised.

junior [*adj*] *subordinate, younger*
▪ *Syn* inferior, lesser, lower, minor, second, secondary; ▪ *Ant* elder, older, senior, superior.

just [*adj1*] *fair, impartial*
▪ *Syn* aloof, condign, conscientious, decent, dispassionate, due, equal, ethical, evenhanded, fair-minded, good, honest, lawful, objective, pure, reliable, right, rightful, rigid, scrupulous, true, trustworthy, uncolored, upright, virtuous; ▪ *Ant* biased, crooked, inequitable, partial, partisan, unfair, unjust.

just [*adj2*] *accurate, precise*
▪ *Syn* cogent, correct, exact, faithful, good, normal, proper, regular, sound, strict, true, undistorted, veracious, well-founded, well-grounded; ▪ *Ant* imprecise, inaccurate, inappropriate, unjust, unjustified, wrong.

just [*adj3*] *suitable, appropriate*
▪ *Syn* apt, befitting, condign, deserved, due, felicitous, fit, fitting, legitimate, meet, merited, proper, reasonable, requisite, right, rightful, well-deserved; ▪ *Ant* inappropriate, unfitting, unjust, unsuitable, unsuited.

justifiable [*adj*] *reasonable, well-founded* ▪ *Syn* acceptable, admissible, allowable, condonable, defensible, excusable, fair, fit, lawful, licit, pardonable, proper, reasonable, remissible, rightful, sound, suitable, tenable, understandable, valid, vindicable, warrantable; ▪ *Ant* unjustifiable, unreasonable, unwarranted.

justly [*adv*] *fairly*
▪ *Syn* accurately, befittingly, correctly, decently, duly, duteously, dutifully, equally, equitably, evenhandedly, fittingly, honestly, honorably, impartially, lawfully, legally, legitimately, properly, reasonably, respectably, righteously, rightfully, rightly, uprightly, well; ▪ *Ant* improperly, unfairly, unjustly.

jut [*v*] *extend*
▪ *Syn* beetle, bulge, elongate, impend, lengthen, overhang, poke, pop, pouch,

project, protrude, stand out, stick out; ▪ *Ant* indent, recede.

juvenile [*n*] *young person*
▪ *Syn* adolescent, boy, child, girl, infant, minor, youngster, youth; ▪ *Ant* adult.

juvenile [*adj*] *childish*
▪ *Syn* adolescent, babyish, blooming, budding, callow, developing, formative, fresh, green, growing, immature, infantile, jejune, junior, naive, pubescent, puerile, teenage, tender, vernal, young, youthful; ▪ *Ant* adult, experienced, grown-up, mature.

K

keen [*adj1*] *enthusiastic*
▪ *Syn* agog, ardent, avid, breathless, devoted, eager, earnest, ebullient, fervid, impassioned, impatient, intense, lively, perfervid, spirited, thirsty, vivacious, warm, zealous; ▪ *Ant* apathetic, dispassionate, reluctant, unenthusiastic, uninterested.

keen [*adj2*] *sharp, piercing*
▪ *Syn* acid, acute, caustic, cutting, edged, fine, honed, incisive, intense, penetrating, pointed, quick-witted, sardonic, satirical, tart, trenchant; ▪ *Ant* blunt, dull, obtuse, pointless.

keep [*v1*] *hold, maintain*
▪ *Syn* accumulate, amass, conserve, control, detain, enjoy, garner, grip, have, heap, manage, own, pile, possess, reserve, retain, save, stack, store, withhold; ▪ *Ant* consume, disperse, give, give up, hand over, let go, release.

keep [*v2*] *tend; provide for*
▪ *Syn* administer, board, care for, defend, endure, feed, foster, guard, look after, maintain, nurture, ordain, provide for, provision, run, safeguard, shield, support, sustain, victual, watch over; ▪ *Ant* abandon, ignore, neglect.

keep [*v3*] *prevent*
▪ *Syn* arrest, avert, block, check, curb, delay, detain, deter, hamper, hinder, inhibit, limit, obstruct, restrain, retard, shackle, stop, withhold; ▪ *Ant* expedite, hurry, speed.

keep [*v4*] *commemorate; pay attention to*
▪ *Syn* bless, celebrate, consecrate, fulfill, hold, honor, laud, observe, perform, praise, regard, respect, sanctify, solemnize; ▪ *Ant* break, dishonor, ignore, omit.

keep at [v] *continue, endure*
▪ *Syn* be steadfast, carry on, drudge, grind, labor, last, maintain, persevere, persist, remain, slave, stay, stick, toil; ▪ *Ant* discontinue, give in, give up.

key [adj] *essential, important*
▪ *Syn* basic, chief, crucial, decisive, fundamental, indispensable, leading, main, major, material, pivotal, primary, principal, vital; ▪ *Ant* inessential, insignificant, nonessential, unimportant.

kick [v] *complain*
▪ *Syn* anathematize, carp, combat, condemn, criticize, curse, damn, execrate, expostulate, fight, fuss, gripe, grumble, inveigh, mumble, object, oppose, protest, rebel, remonstrate, repine, resist, wail, whine; ▪ *Ant* accept, compliment, praise, tolerate.

kick out [v] *get rid of*
▪ *Syn* ax, chase, chuck, discharge, dismiss, drop, eject, evict, expel, extrude, fire, oust, out, reject, remove, throw out, toss out; ▪ *Ant* accept, admit, allow, contract, engage, hire, hold, keep.

kid [n] *young person*
▪ *Syn* baby, bairn, boy, child, daughter, girl, infant, juvenile, lad, son, teenager, tot, youngster, youth; ▪ *Ant* adult, grown-up.

kill [v] *turn off; cancel*
▪ *Syn* annul, cease, counteract, deaden, defeat, extinguish, forbid, halt, neutralize, nullify, prohibit, quash, quell, recant, refuse, revoke, ruin, shut off, smother, stifle, still, stop, suppress, veto; ▪ *Ant* begin, initiate, start, turn on.

kind [adj] *generous, good*
▪ *Syn* affectionate, altruistic, amicable, benevolent, big, bounteous, charitable, clement, congenial, considerate, friendly, gentle, good-hearted, humane, indulgent, kindhearted, lenient, mild, neighborly, obliging, philanthropic, softhearted, sympathetic, thoughtful, tolerant, understanding; ▪ *Ant* bad, bitter, cruel, inconsiderate, malicious, mean, merciless, savage, unfriendly, unkind.

kindhearted [adj] *compassionate, helpful* ▪ *Syn* altruistic, amicable, considerate, generous, good-natured, gracious, humane, kind, merciful, responsive, softhearted, sympathetic, tender, warmhearted; ▪ *Ant* cruel, harsh, incompassionate, mean, nasty, unsympathetic.

kindle [v1] *start a fire*
▪ *Syn* blaze, burn, fire, flame, flare, glow, ignite, inflame, light, set alight, set fire; ▪ *Ant* extinguish, put out, quell, quench.

kindle [v2] *excite, incite*
▪ *Syn* agitate, animate, arouse, awaken, bestir, challenge, exasperate, foment, induce, inspire, provoke, rally, rouse, sharpen, stimulate, thrill, waken, whet; ▪ *Ant* disenchant, smother, stifle.

kindly [adj] *compassionate, helpful*
▪ *Syn* attentive, benevolent, cordial, friendly, generous, gentle, good-hearted, gracious, humane, merciful, mild, neighborly, pleasant, polite, sociable, sympathetic, thoughtful, warm; ▪ *Ant* disagreeable, inconsiderate, unkindly, unsympathetic.

kindly [adv] *with compassion*
▪ *Syn* affectionately, agreeably, benignly, charitably, considerately, courteously, genially, good-naturedly, graciously, heedfully, politely, solicitously, sympathetically, tenderly, thoughtfully, understandingly; ▪ *Ant* disagreeably, inconsiderately, spitefully, unkindly.

kindred [adj] *corresponding, matching*
▪ *Syn* affiliated, agnate, akin, alike, allied, analogous, cognate, congeneric, congenial, connate, connatural, consanguine, homogeneous, incident, parallel, related, similar; ▪ *Ant* alien, different, irrelevant, noncorresponding, unaffiliated.

kinky [adj1] *twisted*
▪ *Syn* coiled, crimped, curled, curly, frizzled, frizzy, knotted, matted, matty, rolled, tangled; ▪ *Ant* straight, unkinked, untwisted.

kinky [adj2] *bizarre, perverted*
▪ *Syn* degenerated, depraved, deviant, eccentric, far-out, licentious, odd, outlandish, outre, peculiar, perverted, queer, quirky, strange, unusual, warped, weird; ▪ *Ant* clean, conventional, decent, ethical, normal, ordinary, unperverted, usual.

kittenish [adj] *frisky, playful*
▪ *Syn* childish, coquettish, coy, flirtatious, frolicsome, fun-loving, impish, jaunty, mischievous, roguish, sportive; ▪ *Ant* grim, lethargic, stern, stiff, unplayful.

knack [n] *ability, talent*
▪ *Syn* aptitude, bent, capacity, command, dexterity, expertise, facility, flair, forte, genius, gift, ingenuity, know-how, pro-

pensity, quickness, readiness, savvy, skillfulness, trick, turn; ▪ *Ant* clumsiness, inability, ineptitude, lack, want.

knit [*v*] *intertwine*
▪ *Syn* affix, ally, bind, cable, connect, crochet, fasten, heal, interlace, intermingle, join, link, loop, mend, net, purl, spin, tie, unite, weave, web; ▪ *Ant* smooth, uncrease, unknit, untie.

knock [*v*] *criticize harshly*
▪ *Syn* abuse, belittle, blame, carp, cavil, censure, denounce, deprecate, lambaste, reprehend, reprobate, slam; ▪ *Ant* compliment, praise.

knock off [*v*] *stop action; accomplish*
▪ *Syn* achieve, cease, complete, desist, discontinue, eliminate, finish, halt, over, quit, surcease, terminate; ▪ *Ant* continue, pursue, start.

knot [*v*] *weave, complicate*
▪ *Syn* bind, cord, entangle, knit, loop, secure, tat, tether, tie; ▪ *Ant* unknot.

knotty [*adj*] *troublesome*
▪ *Syn* baffling, complex, difficult, effortful, elaborate, formidable, hard, intricate, labyrinthine, mazy, puzzling, rough, sophisticated, tough, tricky; ▪ *Ant* easy, plain, simple, uncomplicated, untroublesome.

know [*v1*] *understand information*
▪ *Syn* apperceive, appreciate, apprehend, comprehend, discern, experience, fathom, grasp, ken, learn, notice, perceive, realize, recognize, see; ▪ *Ant* misconstrue, misinterpret, misunderstand.

know [*v2*] *be familiar with*
▪ *Syn* associate, experience, feel, identify, savor, see, sustain, taste, undergo; ▪ *Ant* be ignorant, forget.

know-how [*n*] *skill, talent*
▪ *Syn* ability, adroitness, aptitude, capability, command, craft, cunning, dexterity, expertise, flair, ingenuity, knack, mastery, proficiency, savoir-faire, wisdom; ▪ *Ant* ignorance, incompetence, inexperience, lack, want.

knowing [*adj*] *experienced, aware*
▪ *Syn* astute, awake, bright, brilliant, clever, cognizant, conscious, discerning, expert, insightful, judicious, observant, perceptive, qualified, quick, sage, sentient, sharp, smart, sophic, tuned-in, vigilant, watchful, well-informed, wise, witting, worldly; ▪ *Ant* inexperienced, naive, unaware, uncognizant, uninformed, unknowing.

knowledgeable [*adj*] *aware, educated*
▪ *Syn* abreast, acquainted, alert, appreciative, apprised, au courant, au fait, clever, cognizant, conscious, conversant, discerning, erudite, experienced, familiar, informed, insightful, intelligent, learned, lettered, perceptive, posted, savvy, scholarly, sensible, sharp, smart, sophic, understanding, versed, well-informed, well-rounded, wise; ▪ *Ant* ignorant, unaware, uneducated, uninformed.

known [*adj*] *famous, popular*
▪ *Syn* accepted, acknowledged, celebrated, certified, conscious, established, familiar, noted, notorious, obvious, patent, plain, proverbial, published, received, recognized, well-known; ▪ *Ant* obscure, unknown.

kudos [*n*] *praise, acclaim*
▪ *Syn* applause, credit, distinction, eminence, esteem, fame, flattery, glory, honor, laudation, notability, plaudits, prestige, prominence, regard, renown; ▪ *Ant* blame, censure, criticism.

L

labored [*adj*] *unclear, strained*
▪ *Syn* affected, arduous, awkward, clumsy, contrived, forced, hard, heavy, maladroit, overdone, overwrought, ponderous, stiff, strenuous, studied, unnatural; ▪ *Ant* easy, facile, natural, relaxed.

laborious [*adj*] *hard, difficult*
▪ *Syn* arduous, backbreaking, burdensome, heavy, onerous, operose, ponderous, strenuous, tiresome, tough, wearing, wearisome; ▪ *Ant* easy, effortless, simple, trivial.

lace [*v*] *fasten, intertwine*
▪ *Syn* bind, close, fortify, interlace, interweave, plat, spike, strap, thread, tie, twine; ▪ *Ant* unfasten, unlace, untie, untwine.

lack [*n*] *deficiency, need*
▪ *Syn* absence, dearth, default, defect, deficit, depletion, deprivation, destitution, exigency, exiguity, inadequacy, inferiority, insufficiency, loss, meagerness, necessity, paucity, poverty, privation, scarcity, shortage, shortfall, stint, want; ▪ *Ant* abundance, excess, extra, plenty, plethora, profusion, satisfaction, surplus, wealth.

lackadaisical [adj] careless, indifferent
▪ *Syn* disinterested, dreamy, dull, enervated, faineant, halfhearted, idle, inattentive, indolent, inert, laid-back, languid, languishing, languorous, lazy, lethargic, limp, listless, passive, spiritless; ▪ *Ant* active, ambitious, animated, caring, energetic, enthusiastic, excited.

lacking [adj] wanting, deficient
▪ *Syn* defective, deprived of, flawed, impaired, incomplete, missing, needed, short, without; ▪ *Ant* abundant, ample, enough, profuse, sufficient.

lackluster [adj] dull, lifeless
▪ *Syn* colorless, commonplace, dark, dim, drab, dull, leaden, muted, prosaic, sombre, unimaginative, uninspired, vapid; ▪ *Ant* bright, enthusiastic, lively, spirited, vivid.

laconic [adj] short, to the point
▪ *Syn* breviloquent, brief, brusque, compact, concise, crisp, curt, pithy, succinct, terse; ▪ *Ant* garrulous, locquacious, longwinded, verbose, wordy.

laden [adj] loaded down
▪ *Syn* burdened, charged, encumbered, fraught, full, hampered, loaded, oppressed, taxed, weighed down; ▪ *Ant* empty, light, unladen, unloaded.

lag [v] move slowly; delay
▪ *Syn* dally, dawdle, drag, ebb, fall off, falter, hang back, idle, linger, loiter, plod, retard, slacken, slow up, straggle, tarry, trail, wane; ▪ *Ant* advance, hurry along, lead, run, rush.

lambaste [v] punish, beat
▪ *Syn* assail, attack, berate, castigate, criticize, denounce, excoriate, flog, pan, pummel, rebuke, reprimand, roast, scathe, scourge, smear, strike, thrash, upbraid, wallop, whip; ▪ *Ant* applaud, commend, laud, praise.

lame [adj1] unable to walk properly
▪ *Syn* bruised, crippled, disabled, game, handicapped, hobbled, infirm, limping, pained, stiff, weak; ▪ *Ant* able, agile, mobile, walking.

lame [adj2] feeble, weak
▪ *Syn* faltering, faulty, flimsy, inadequate, insufficient, poor, thin; ▪ *Ant* able, capable, convincing, effectual, efficient, persuasive, strong.

lament [v] to mourn or grieve deeply
▪ *Syn* bemoan, bewail, cry, deplore, grieve, howl, hurt, moan, mourn, regret, rue, sob, sorrow, wail, weep; ▪ *Ant* celebrate, exult, rejoice.

lamentable [adj] upsetting, miserable
▪ *Syn* awful, calamitous, deplorable, dire, grievous, heartbreaking, lousy, melancholy, pitiful, plaintive, rueful, sad, stinking, woeful, wretched; ▪ *Ant* cheering, encouraging, favorable, fortunate, good, lucky, satisfactory.

lampoon [v] ridicule, make fun of
▪ *Syn* caricature, jape, mock, parody, ridicule, satirize; ▪ *Ant* applaud, approve, praise, support.

land [v1] arrive, come to rest on
▪ *Syn* alight, berth, come ashore, descend, disembark, dock, ground, light on, set down, settle, steer, take down, touch down; ▪ *Ant* ascend, take off.

land [v2] achieve, acquire
▪ *Syn* bring in, gain, get, obtain, pick up, procure, secure, win; ▪ *Ant* fail, lose.

landlord [n] owner of property leased
▪ *Syn* freeholder, host/hostess, lessor, property owner, proprietor; ▪ *Ant* boarder, leaser, renter, tenant.

languid [adj] drooping, dull, listless
▪ *Syn* apathetic, dopey, enervated, feeble, heavy, indifferent, infirm, lackadaisical, lazy, leaden, lethargic, limp, nebbish, pining, sluggish, supine, torpid, weak, weary; ▪ *Ant* active, alert, animated, energetic, lively, spirited, vivacious.

languish [v] droop; become dull, listless
▪ *Syn* brood, despond, dwindle, ebb, fade, fag, fizzle out, grieve, hanker, long, pine, rot, tucker, waste away, weaken, wilt, yearn; ▪ *Ant* flourish, grow, improve, strengthen.

lanky [adj] tall and thin
▪ *Syn* angular, attenuated, bony, extenuated, gangly, gaunt, lean, meager, rawboned, scrawny, slender, spindly, stringy, weedy; ▪ *Ant* full, short, squat, stocky.

lapse [v] become void; fall back into previous pattern ▪ *Syn* backslide, cease, decline, degenerate, deteriorate, end, pass, recidivate, relapse, retrograde, revert, subside, terminate, weaken; ▪ *Ant* continue, go on, restart.

large [adj] big, abundant
▪ *Syn* ample, bulky, considerable, copious, enormous, excessive, full, generous, gigantic, hefty, huge, immense, liberal, massive, monumental, plentiful, roomy, sizable, substantial, voluminous, wide; ▪ *Ant* brief, little, meager, miniature, narrow, paltry, slim, small, tiny.

lascivious [adj] displaying excessive interest in sex ▪ *Syn* bawdy, carnal, coarse, crude, fleshly, incontinent, lecherous, lewd, libidinous, licentious, lustful, orgiastic, pornographic, prurient, raw, ribald, scurrilous, sensual, steamy, vulgar, wanton; ▪ *Ant* chaste, decent, moral.

lash [v] *criticize harshly*
▪ *Syn* abuse, attack, baste, berate, blister, castigate, censure, exprobate, flay, lambaste, ridicule, satirize, scold, upbraid; ▪ *Ant* commend, compliment, laud, praise.

last [adj] *final; newest*
▪ *Syn* aftermost, antipodal, climactic, conclusive, crowning, definitive, end, eventual, farthest, furthest, hindmost, latest, outermost, terminal, ulterior, utmost; ▪ *Ant* beginning, first, front, initial, introductory, oldest, primary, starting.

lasting [adj] *enduring, unending*
▪ *Syn* abiding, constant, continual, deep-rooted, durable, endless, eternal, everlasting, forever, indissoluble, lifelong, old, permanent, perpetual, persisting, stable; ▪ *Ant* ending, ephemeral, fleeting, passing, short-lived, temporary, transient.

latch [v] *fasten with lock*
▪ *Syn* bar, bolt, cinch, close, close up, lock, make fast, secure; ▪ *Ant* loose, loosen, unfasten, unlatch, unlock.

late [adj1] *not on time*
▪ *Syn* backward, behind, delayed, held up, lagging, overdue, postponed, put off, remiss, slow, tardy; ▪ *Ant* early, on time, prompt, punctual.

late [adj2] *new*
▪ *Syn* advanced, fresh, just out, modern, recent; ▪ *Ant* antique, old, old-fashioned.

late [adj3] *dead*
▪ *Syn* bygone, deceased, defunct, extinct, former, lifeless, once, past, preceding, previous; ▪ *Ant* existing, extant, live.

lately [adv] *new, recently*
▪ *Syn* afresh, anew, in recent times, just now, latterly, new, newly, of late; ▪ *Ant* at first, in the past, old, originally.

latent [adj] *dormant, hidden*
▪ *Syn* abeyant, concealed, covert, idle, immature, implied, inert, inherent, intrinsic, lurking, passive, secret, sleeping, smoldering, suppressed, suspended, tacit, underdeveloped, underlying, veiled; ▪ *Ant* active, apparent, clear, exposed, expressed, live, manifest, obvious, open, public.

later [adj] *coming after*
▪ *Syn* after, ensuing, following, next, postliminary, proximate, subsequent, succeeding, ulterior; ▪ *Ant* before, earlier, prior.

later [adv] *happening after*
▪ *Syn* after, afterward, behind, in a while, in time, latterly, next, subsequently, succeeding, thereafter; ▪ *Ant* before, earlier.

lateral [adj] *sideways*
▪ *Syn* crabwise, edgeways, flanking, oblique, side, side-by-side, sidelong, skirting; ▪ *Ant* centered, central, perpendicular.

latter [adj] *latest, concluding*
▪ *Syn* final, following, hindmost, lag, last, last-mentioned, later, modern, recent, second, terminal; ▪ *Ant* earliest, former, preceding.

laud [v] *acclaim, praise*
▪ *Syn* admire, approve, bless, boost, build up, celebrate, commend, compliment, extol, flatter, glorify, honor, panegyrize, revere, reverence, venerate, worship; ▪ *Ant* abuse, castigate, criticize, denigrate, scorn.

laudable [adj] *admirable*
▪ *Syn* commendable, creditable, deserving, estimable, excellent, meritable, meritorious, praisable, praiseworthy, stellar, thankworthy, worthy; ▪ *Ant* bad, base, blameable, contemptible, reprehensible.

laudatory [adj] *complimentary*
▪ *Syn* acclamatory, adulatory, approbatory, approving, commendatory, encomiastic, eulogistic, flattering, panegyrical, praiseful; ▪ *Ant* blaming, castigating, critical.

laughable [adj] *easily made fun of*
▪ *Syn* absurd, amusing, asinine, campy, comic, derisive, diverting, droll, entertaining, facetious, farcical, funny, gelastic, hilarious, humorous, inane, jocose, ludicrous, mirthful, mocking, nonsensical, preposterous, ridiculous, risible, scream, witty; ▪ *Ant* grave, serious, solemn.

launch [v1] *send off*
▪ *Syn* barrage, bombard, cast, catapult, discharge, dispatch, drive, eject, fire, heave, hurl, pitch, propel, send forth, sling, throw, toss; ▪ *Ant* beach, ground, hold, keep.

launch [v2] *begin, initiate*
▪ *Syn* bow, commence, embark upon, inaugurate, instigate, institute, introduce, jump, open, originate, start; ▪ *Ant* cease, end, finish, stop.

lavish [*adj*] *profuse; splendid*
▪ *Syn* abundant, bountiful, copious, effusive, excessive, extravagant, exuberant, free, generous, grand, immoderate, impressive, improvident, liberal, lush, luxuriant, munificent, openhanded, opulent, plentiful, plush, posh, profusive, prolific, sumptuous, swanky, unrestrained, wasteful; ▪ *Ant* economical, frugal, meager, scanty, scarce, small, spare.

lavish [*v*] *pamper, shower*
▪ *Syn* be generous, be wasteful, deluge, dissipate, expend, fritter, give, heap, pour, scatter, spend, squander, waste; ▪ *Ant* economize, hoard, limit, starve, stint, withhold.

lawful [*adj*] *allowable, legitimate*
▪ *Syn* authorized, bona fide, canonical, commanded, condign, constitutional, decreed, due, enacted, enforced, enjoined, established, judicial, juridical, jurisprudent, just, justifiable, legal, legalized, legislated, legitimate, legitimatized, licit, mandated, official, ordained, permissible, proper, protected, rightful, ruled, statutory, valid, vested, warrantable, warranted; ▪ *Ant* illegal, illegitimate, illicit, prohibited, taboo, unauthorized, unlawful.

lawless [*adj*] *reckless, ungoverned*
▪ *Syn* anarchic, anarchical, anarchistic, chaotic, contumacious, criminal, disobedient, evil, heterodox, nihilistic, noncompliant, piratical, rebellious, recusant, revolutionary, riotous, savage, seditious, traitorous, violent, warlike, wild; ▪ *Ant* disciplined, governed, law-abiding, lawful, legal, legitimate, licit, proper, restrained, rightful, valid.

lax [*adj*] *slack, remiss*
▪ *Syn* careless, delinquent, derelict, forgetful, indefinite, lenient, neglectful, negligent, oblivious, slipshod, sloppy, unmindful, vague, yielding; ▪ *Ant* exact, hard, precise, rigid, scrupulous, stern, strict, tight.

lay [*adj*] *amateur, not trained in a religious or other profession* ▪ *Syn* inexpert, nonprofessional, nonspecialist, ordinary, secular, temporal, unsacred; ▪ *Ant* clerical, ecclesiastical, ordained, professional.

lay [*v*] *put, place*
▪ *Syn* arrange, deposit, establish, fix, locate, order, organize, plant, position, repose, rest, set, set down, settle, spread, stick, systematize; ▪ *Ant* lift, take.

lay into [*v*] *criticize, attack*
▪ *Syn* assail, battle, belabor, invade, lambaste, set upon; ▪ *Ant* compliment, praise.

lay off [*v1*] *stop doing*
▪ *Syn* cease, desist, end, give a rest, give up, halt, leave alone, leave off, let up, quit, rest; ▪ *Ant* begin, start.

lay off [*v2*] *relieve of responsibility*
▪ *Syn* discharge, dismiss, drop, fire, let go, oust, pay off, retire early; ▪ *Ant* employ, hire.

lay out [*v*] *spend money*
▪ *Syn* disburse, expend, give, invest, lend, outlay, pay, put out, put up; ▪ *Ant* hoard, save.

lay up/lay by [*v*] *set aside, store*
▪ *Syn* accumulate, amass, build up, cumulate, garner, hoard, keep, preserve, salt away, save, spare, store up; ▪ *Ant* squander, use, waste.

lazy [*adj*] *inactive, sluggish*
▪ *Syn* apathetic, careless, dallying, dull, idle, inert, lackadaisical, laggard, languid, lethargic, neglectful, passive, remiss, shiftless, slack, sleepy, slothful, somnolent, supine, torpid; ▪ *Ant* active, attentive, diligent, energetic, hardworking, industrious, lively.

lead [*v1*] *guide physically*
▪ *Syn* chaperone, coerce, compel, conduct, direct, drive, escort, impel, induce, manage, persuade, pilot, precede, prevail, protect, route, see, shepherd, show, squire, steer, traverse, usher, watch over; ▪ *Ant* follow, tail, trail.

lead [*v2*] *guide mentally; influence*
▪ *Syn* affect, bring, cause, command, contribute, direct, draw, govern, helm, incline, induce, manage, motivate, persuade, produce, prompt, shepherd, spur, supervise, tend; ▪ *Ant* comply, consent, follow, obey.

lead [*v3*] *surpass*
▪ *Syn* be ahead, exceed, excel, outdo, outstrip, precede, preface, transcend, usher; ▪ *Ant* fall behind, follow, lag, trail.

leading [*adj*] *chief, superior*
▪ *Syn* arch, best, champion, dominant, famous, first, foremost, greatest, highest, inaugural, main, notorious, outstanding, popular, preeminent, premier, prominent, ruling, stellar, top, well-known; ▪ *Ant* inferior, last, subordinate, supplementary, unimportant.

leafy [*adj*] *abundant in foliage*
▪ *Syn* abundant, green, shaded, shady,

umbrageous, verdant, wooded; ▪ *Ant* bare, denuded, leafless.

league [v] *associate*
▪ *Syn* ally, amalgamate, band, collaborate, combine, concur, confederate, conjoin, consolidate, cooperate, federate, join forces, unite; ▪ *Ant* disassociate, divide, part, secede, separate.

leak [v] *seep; make known*
▪ *Syn* come out, disclose, divulge, drool, escape, give away, make public, on, ooze, pass, reveal, slip, spill, tell, trickle; ▪ *Ant* conceal, hide, hold, suppress.

lean [adj] *bare, thin*
▪ *Syn* angular, bony, emaciated, gangly, gaunt, haggard, lanky, meager, rangy, rawboned, scanty, scrawny, sinewy, skinny, spare, sparse, svelte, sylphlike, wiry, wizened; ▪ *Ant* fat, fleshy, full, plump, rich, stout, sturdy.

lean [v] *count, depend on*
▪ *Syn* believe in, confide, have faith, put faith in, rely, trust; ▪ *Ant* disregard, forget.

leap [v] *jump, jump over; increase*
▪ *Syn* ascend, bound, caper, clear, escalate, hop, hurdle, mount, rise, rocket, saltate, soar, spring, surge, vault; ▪ *Ant* crawl, run, walk.

learn [v1] *acquire information*
▪ *Syn* apprentice, attain, commit to memory, gain, grasp, lucubrate, master, memorize, pore over, prepare, read, review, study, take in, train in; ▪ *Ant* forget, instruct, teach.

learn [v2] *discover, find out*
▪ *Syn* ascertain, catch on, detect, determine, discern, gain, gather, hear, see, uncover, understand, unearth; ▪ *Ant* miss, overlook.

learned [adj] *well-informed*
▪ *Syn* academic, accomplished, bookish, cultivated, cultured, educated, erudite, grounded, intellectual, literate, omniscient, pansophic, professorial, sage, sapient, scholarly, well-educated, well-read, well-rounded; ▪ *Ant* ignorant, illiterate, lowbrow, uneducated, uninformed.

leash [v] *rein, hold*
▪ *Syn* bridle, check, control, curb, fasten, fetter, hamper, hobble, restrain, secure, shackle, suppress, tether, tie, tie up, trammel; ▪ *Ant* let go, release, vent.

least [adj] *slightest, smallest*
▪ *Syn* feeblest, fewest, infinitesimal, lowest, meanest, microcosmic, microscopic, minimal, minimum, minute, minutest, molecular, nadir, poorest, tiniest, trivial, unimportant; ▪ *Ant* crucial, largest, maximal, most.

leathery [adj] *flexible, tough*
▪ *Syn* coriaceous, rough, rugged, strong, tough, wrinkled; ▪ *Ant* soft, supple.

leave [v1] *depart, abandon physically*
▪ *Syn* cut out, decamp, elope, embark, escape, exit, flee, fly, forsake, go, issue, migrate, move, move out, part, quit, relinquish, retire, sally, set out, slip out, start, step down, take off, vacate, vanish, walk out, withdraw; ▪ *Ant* appear, come, continue, stay.

leave [v2] *abandon, renounce*
▪ *Syn* cede, desert, desist, drop, evacuate, forbear, forsake, maroon, quit, refrain, relinquish, resign, stop, surrender, terminate, waive, yield; ▪ *Ant* continue, hold, keep, persist.

leave off [v] *stop*
▪ *Syn* abstain, break off, cease, desist, discontinue, end, give up, halt, quit, refrain, surcease; ▪ *Ant* begin, continue, restart.

lecherous [adj] *lustful, lewd*
▪ *Syn* carnal, concupiscent, corrupt, lascivious, libertine, libidinous, licentious, lubricous, prurient, salacious, satyric, sensual, wanton; ▪ *Ant* chaste, clean, prudish, puritanical.

lecture [v] *criticize lengthily*
▪ *Syn* admonish, berate, castigate, censure, chide, flay, harangue, moralize, preach, reprimand, reprove, scold, sermonize, tell off; ▪ *Ant* compliment, laud, praise.

leery [adj] *suspicious*
▪ *Syn* careful, cautious, chary, distrustful, doubting, dubious, shy, skeptical, uncertain, unsure, wary; ▪ *Ant* certain, sure, unwary.

left [adj] *politically radical*
▪ *Syn* leftist, left-wing, liberal, progressive, revolutionary, socialist; ▪ *Ant* conservative, right.

leftover [adj] *remaining, excess*
▪ *Syn* extra, residual, surplus, unconsumed, uneaten, untouched, unused, unwanted; ▪ *Ant* core, main, principle.

legal [adj] *allowable, permissible*
▪ *Syn* authorized, constitutional, contractual, decreed, due, enforcible, fair, granted, just, lawful, licit, ordained, precedented, proper, protected, rightful, sanctioned, statutory, straight, valid, war-

ranted; ▪ *Ant* illegal, illegitimate, illicit, unlawful, wrong.

legalize [v] *allow, validate*
▪ *Syn* approve, authorize, codify, decree, decriminalize, enact, legislate, legitimate, license, ordain, permit, regulate, sanction; ▪ *Ant* deny, prohibit, refuse, veto.

legendary [adj1] *fictitious but well known* ▪ *Syn* allegorical, apocryphal, created, dubious, fabled, fanciful, imaginary, invented, mythical, mythological, romantic, storied, traditional; ▪ *Ant* authenticated, factual, historical, real, true.

legendary [adj2] *famous*
▪ *Syn* celebrated, famed, illustrious, immortal, renowned, well-known; ▪ *Ant* infamous, unimportant.

legible [adj] *easy to read*
▪ *Syn* clear, coherent, decipherable, easily read, intelligible, lucid, neat, plain, readable, sharp, understandable; ▪ *Ant* illegible, unreadable.

legion [n] *mass, force of people*
▪ *Syn* army, brigade, company, division, drove, group, host, multitude, myriad, number, phalanx, rout, scores, throng, troop; ▪ *Ant* few, handful, none, scattering.

legion [adj] *numerous*
▪ *Syn* countless, many, multifarious, multitudinous, myriad, numberless, populous, several, sundry, various, voluminous; ▪ *Ant* few, numbered.

legitimate [adj] *authentic, valid, legal*
▪ *Syn* accepted, accredited, admissible, authorized, correct, customary, fair, genuine, just, lawful, licit, official, orthodox, proper, received, recognized, rightful, sanctioned, statutory, true, verifiable, warranted; ▪ *Ant* false, fraudulent, illegal, illegitimate, invalid, unlawful, unwarranted.

leisurely [adj] *casual, unhurried*
▪ *Syn* comfortable, dilatory, easy, free, gentle, languid, lax, lazy, relaxed, restful, slow, slow-moving; ▪ *Ant* hasty, hectic, hurried.

leisurely [adv] *casually, unhurriedly*
▪ *Syn* at one's leisure, calmly, dilatorily, easily, gradually, indolently, langorously, lingeringly, slowly, torpidly, without haste; ▪ *Ant* fast, hectically, hurriedly, rapidly.

lend [v] *loan, accommodate*
▪ *Syn* add, advance, afford, allow, bestow, confer, contribute, entrust, extend, furnish, give, grant, impart, oblige, permit, provide, stake, supply, trust; ▪ *Ant* borrow, deprive, withhold.

lengthen [v] *extend*
▪ *Syn* augment, continue, distend, drag out, elongate, expand, increase, let out, pad, proceed, prolong, protract, reach, stretch; ▪ *Ant* abbreviate, curtail, cut, shorten.

lengthy [adj] *extended*
▪ *Syn* drawn out, elongated, interminable, long, long-winded, overlong, padded, prolix, prolonged, protracted, verbose, windy, wordy; ▪ *Ant* abbreviated, curtailed, shortened, terse.

lenient [adj] *permissive*
▪ *Syn* assuasive, benign, charitable, compassionate, complaisant, easygoing, favoring, gentle, indulgent, kindly, mild, obliging, soft, sympathetic, tender, tolerant, yielding; ▪ *Ant* hard, harsh, intolerant, limiting, restrictive, rigorous, severe.

less [adj] *smaller, inferior*
▪ *Syn* diminished, excepting, lacking, lower, minor, negative, reduced, secondary, shortened, subordinate; ▪ *Ant* greater, larger, more, superior.

lessen [v] *lower, reduce*
▪ *Syn* abate, abridge, crop, curtail, cut back, decrease, degrade, dilute, diminish, dwindle, ease, impair, lighten, minimize, mitigate, narrow, roll back, shrink, taper, truncate, weaken; ▪ *Ant* build, enlarge, extend, increase, multiply, raise, strengthen.

lesser [adj] *inferior, secondary*
▪ *Syn* less important, low, lower, minor, slighter, small, subjacent, subordinate, undersized; ▪ *Ant* greater, higher, major, primary, superior.

let [v1] *allow*
▪ *Syn* approve, authorize, cause, certify, concede, enable, endorse, give, grant, license, permit, sanction, tolerate, warrant; ▪ *Ant* forbid, hinder, hold, impede, inhibit, keep, obstruct, prevent.

let [v2] *rent out object, property*
▪ *Syn* charter, hire, lease, sublease, sublet; ▪ *Ant* buy, sell.

let down [v] *disappoint*
▪ *Syn* abandon, depress, disenchant, disillusion, dissatisfy, fail, fall short, lower, take down; ▪ *Ant* benefit, fulfill, satisfy.

lethal [adj] *deadly*
▪ *Syn* dangerous, deathly, destructive,

devastating, fatal, harmful, hurtful, malignant, mortal, mortiferous, murderous, necrotic, noxious, pernicious, pestilent, pestilential, poisonous, virulent; ▪ *Ant* beneficial, harmless, helpful, life-giving, wholesome.

lethargic [adj] *lazy, sluggish*
▪ *Syn* apathetic, debilitated, dilatory, dopey, dormant, drowsy, dull, enervated, heavy, idle, impassive, indifferent, inert, lackadaisical, laggard, languid, languorous, listless, passive, phlegmatic, sleepy, slothful, slow, slumberous, somnolent, spiritless, stolid, stupefied, stupid, supine, torpid; ▪ *Ant* active, animated, busy, energetic, lively, vital, vivacious.

let off [v] *make not subject to punishment or action* ▪ *Syn* absolve, discharge, dispense, drop, excuse, exempt, exonerate, forgive, let go, pardon, release, relieve, remove, spare; ▪ *Ant* blame, incarcerate, punish.

let on [v] *acknowledge, admit*
▪ *Syn* allow, avow, betray, concede, confess, disclose, divulge, give away, grant, hint, imply, indicate, let out, make known, own, reveal, say, suggest, tell, uncover, unveil; ▪ *Ant* deny, disacknowledge.

let up [v] *pause*
▪ *Syn* abate, cease, decrease, die down, die out, diminish, ease up, ebb, fall, moderate, release, relent, slacken, slow down, stop, subside, wane; ▪ *Ant* accelerate, continue, expand, increase, surge.

level [adj] *smooth, balanced*
▪ *Syn* aligned, calm, commensurate, consistent, constant, equable, even, flat, flush, horizontal, like, matched, parallel, plane, proportionate, regular, stable, steady, trim, uniform; ▪ *Ant* bumpy, ragged, uneven, vertical, warped.

level [v1] *make even*
▪ *Syn* equalize, even, even off, even out, flatten, flush, grade, lay, make equal, make flat, smooth, smoothen, straighten, surface; ▪ *Ant* jag, roughen.

level [v2] *destroy, demolish*
▪ *Syn* bring down, devastate, fell, flatten, floor, ground, knock down, pull down, raze, ruin, smooth, tear down, wreck; ▪ *Ant* build, construct, erect, raise.

level [v3] *aim, direct*
▪ *Syn* cast, excuse, incline, lay, point, slant, train, turn, zero in on; ▪ *Ant* point away, turn.

levelheaded [adj] *reasonable, calm*
▪ *Syn* balanced, collected, composed, cool, dependable, even-tempered, judicious, prudent, rational, sane, self-possessed, together, unflappable, wise; ▪ *Ant* nervous, senseless, unreasonable, upset.

levity [n] *funniness, silliness*
▪ *Syn* absurdity, amusement, facetiousness, festivity, flightiness, flippancy, folly, foolishness, frivolity, giddiness, happiness, high spirits, hilarity, jocularity, lightheartedness, mirth, pleasantry, repartee, trifling, volatility, wit; ▪ *Ant* dignity, gravity, seriousness, solemnity.

lewd [adj] *vulgar, indecent*
▪ *Syn* bawdy, blue, coarse, foul-mouthed, impure, indelicate, lecherous, libertine, naughty, obscene, pornographic, profligate, rakish, ribald, scurrilous, smutty, taboo, vile, wanton, wicked; ▪ *Ant* clean, decent, modest, moral, proper.

liable [adj1] *answerable, responsible*
▪ *Syn* accountable, bound, chargeable, obligated, subject, tied; ▪ *Ant* excusable, freed, irresponsible, unaccountable.

liable [adj2] *open, likely*
▪ *Syn* apt, disposed, exposed, given, inclined, penetrable, prone, sensitive, subject, susceptible, tending, vulnerable; ▪ *Ant* immune, unlikely.

libel [v] *purposefully lie about someone*
▪ *Syn* asperse, blacken, blister, burlesque, calumniate, caricature, crack, defame, denigrate, derogate, knock, malign, revile, roast, scandalize, scorch, sizzle, slur, smear, tear down, traduce, travesty, vilify; ▪ *Ant* defend, justify, vindicate.

libelous [adj] *derogatory*
▪ *Syn* aspersive, backbiting, calumnious, debasing, defamatory, false, injurious, maligning, opprobrious, pejorative, sarcastic, scurrilous, traducing, untrue, vilifying, vituperative; ▪ *Ant* complimentary, laudatory, praising.

liberal [adj1] *progressive*
▪ *Syn* avant-garde, broad-minded, catholic, enlightened, flexible, general, high-minded, indulgent, lenient, libertarian, permissive, radical, rational, receptive, reformist, tolerant; ▪ *Ant* conservative, narrow, narrow-minded, orthodox, reactionary, right-wing.

liberal [adj2] *giving, generous*
▪ *Syn* altruistic, beneficent, benevolent, bountiful, exuberant, free, kind, lavish, loose, magnanimous, munificent, open-

handed, philanthropic; **Ant** economical, greedy, mean, selfish, stingy, thrifty.

liberal [adj3] *abundant, profuse*
Syn ample, aplenty, bounteous, copious, generous, handsome, lavish, munificent, plentiful, rich; **Ant** lacking, poor, wanting.

liberate [v] *give freedom*
Syn deliver, emancipate, free, loose, manumit, redeem, release, rescue, save, unbind, unchain; **Ant** hold back, limit, prevent, restrain.

libidinous [adj] *lustful*
Syn carnal, coarse, debauched, fast, impure, lascivious, lecherous, obscene, prurient, salacious, sensual, wanton, wicked; **Ant** chaste, clean, decent, moral.

license [v] *authorize*
Syn allow, certify, commission, empower, enable, let, permit, privilege, sanction, suffer, warrant; **Ant** ban, prohibit, refuse, withhold.

licentious [adj] *immoral, uncontrolled*
Syn amoral, carnal, corrupt, debauched, depraved, disorderly, dissolute, fast, immoral, impure, incontinent, lascivious, lax, lecherous, lewd, libertine, libidinous, lubricious, lustful, profligate, promiscuous, relaxed, reprobate, salacious, satyric, scabrous, sensual, swinging, uncurbed, unruly, wanton; **Ant** chaste, controlled, good, innocent, law-abiding, moral, puritanical.

lick [v] *defeat, sometimes by hitting*
Syn beat, best, clobber, conquer, down, flog, hit, master, outdo, rout, slap, spank, strike, surmount, surpass, thrash, top, trim, trounce, vanquish, wallop, whip; **Ant** lose, submit, succumb, surrender, yield.

lie [v2] *be prostrate, flat*
Syn laze, loll, lounge, nap, recline, repose, rest, retire, sprawl, stretch out, turn in; **Ant** be upright, stand, straighten.

lifeless [adj1] *not living, not containing living things* **Syn** bare, barren, cold, comatose, dead, deceased, defunct, departed, empty, exanimate, extinct, inanimate, inert, inorganic, insensate, insensible, late, sterile; **Ant** alive, animate, conscious, inhabited, living.

lifeless [adj2] *dull, spiritless*
Syn cold, colorless, drab, dull, flat, hollow, insipid, lackluster, lethargic, list-less, lusterless, passive, prosaic, prosy, slothful, sluggish, spent, static, torpid; **Ant** dynamic, energetic, lively, spirited, vital.

lifelong [adj] *lasting*
Syn constant, continuing, enduring, inveterate, lifetime, livelong, long-lasting, long-lived, long-standing, old, perennial, permanent, persistent; **Ant** casual, short-lived, temporary, tenuous, transitory.

lift [v1] *move upwards; ascend*
Syn arise, boost, bring up, buoy up, climb, draw up, elevate, erect, heft, hike, hike up, hoist, jack up, jump up, mount, move up, pick up, raise, rise, soar, take up, uphold, uplift, upraise, vanish; **Ant** descend, drop, lower.

lift [v2] *repeal, revoke*
Syn annul, cancel, countermand, dismantle, end, recall, relax, remove, rescind, reverse, stop, terminate; **Ant** establish, impose, impose, set down.

lift [v3] *steal*
Syn appropriate, cop, copy, crib, filch, hook, nip, pilfer, pinch, pirate, plagiarize, pocket, purloin, snitch, swipe, take, thieve; **Ant** give, receive, return.

lift [v4] *promote, improve*
Syn advance, ameliorate, boost, build up, dignify, elevate, enhance, exalt, raise, support, upgrade; **Ant** demote, depress, dispirit, weaken.

light [adj1] *illuminated*
Syn ablaze, aglow, bright, brilliant, burnished, clear, cloudless, flashing, fluorescent, glossy, glowing, lambent, lucent, luminous, lustrous, phosphorescent, polished, radiant, refulgent, resplendent, shining, shiny, sunny, vivid; **Ant** black, clouded, dark, darkened, dim, gloomy, obscure.

light [adj2] *blond, fair*
Syn bleached, fair-skinned, light-hued, light-skinned, light-toned, pale, pastel, tow-headed; **Ant** brunette, dark, dusky.

light [adj3] *not heavy*
Syn agile, airy, buoyant, delicate, easy, effervescent, featherweight, fluffy, frothy, graceful, light-footed, lithe, meager, petty, sheer, sylphlike, thin, trifling, weightless; **Ant** burdensome, heavy, ponderous, substantial, weighted.

light [adj4] *small in amount, content*
Syn casual, digestible, faint, fragmentary, frivolous, gentle, mild, minute, moderate, puny, restricted, scanty,

sparse, thin, trivial, unimportant, unsubstantial, weak, wee; ▪ *Ant* considerable, heavy, massive, sufficient.

light [*adj5*] *simple, easy*
▪ *Syn* effortless, facile, manageable, moderate, smooth; ▪ *Ant* demanding, difficult, exacting, heavy, laborious, taxing.

light [*adj6*] *funny, cheery*
▪ *Syn* airy, amusing, blithe, carefree, cheerful, diverting, dizzy, entertaining, flighty, gay, giddy, high, lighthearted, merry, perky, sunny, trifling, upbeat, witty; ▪ *Ant* grave, serious, solemn.

light [*v1*] *illuminate*
▪ *Syn* animate, brighten, cast, fire, highlight, ignite, illumine, inflame, irradiate, kindle, lighten, shine, spot, spotlight; ▪ *Ant* darken, dull, obscure.

light [*v2*] *start on fire*
▪ *Syn* burn, fire, flame, ignite, inflame, kindle, set fire to, spark; ▪ *Ant* drench, extinguish, put out, quench.

light [*v3*] *step down; land*
▪ *Syn* alight, come down, deplane, detrain, disembark, drop, perch, rest, roost, settle, stop, touch down; ▪ *Ant* ascend, climb, mount.

lighten [*v1*] *reduce weight, load*
▪ *Syn* alleviate, ameliorate, assuage, buoy, disburden, disencumber, ease, eradicate, facilitate, free, jettison, lessen, mitigate, mollify, reduce, relieve, shift, thin; ▪ *Ant* burden, increase, intensify, load down, weigh down.

lighten [*v2*] *cheer up; inspire*
▪ *Syn* brighten, cheer, elate, encourage, gladden, hearten, lift, perk up, revive; ▪ *Ant* bring down, burden, depress, upset.

light-headed [*adj*] *silly; feeling faint*
▪ *Syn* delirious, dizzy, faint, frivolous, giddy, hazy, reeling, rocky, superficial, swimming, trifling, vertiginous, whirling; ▪ *Ant* sober, solid.

lighthearted [*adj*] *carefree, untroubled*
▪ *Syn* blithe, buoyant, cheerful, effervescent, frolicsome, gay, gleeful, high-spirited, insouciant, jocund, joyful, lively, merry, playful, resilient, spirited, sunny, upbeat, vivacious; ▪ *Ant* depressed, gloomy, heavy-hearted, melancholy, troubled, upset, worried.

lightly [*adv*] *gently, effortlessly*
▪ *Syn* airily, breezily, carelessly, casually, delicately, ethereally, faintly, freely, gingerly, leniently, moderately, nimbly, quietly, readily, simply, softly, subtly,

tenderly; ▪ *Ant* arduously, effortlessly, firmly, heavily, ponderously.

light out [*v*] *run away*
▪ *Syn* abscond, depart, escape, leave, make off, quit, set out, strike out, take off; ▪ *Ant* stay, wait.

lightweight [*adj*] *inconsequential*
▪ *Syn* featherweight, foolish, incompetent, insignificant, of no account, paltry, petty, slight, trifling, trivial, weightless; ▪ *Ant* big, consequential, heavyweight, important, major.

likable [*adj*] *nice, pleasant*
▪ *Syn* agreeable, amiable, appealing, attractive, charismatic, charming, engaging, enjoyable, friendly, genial, good, good-natured, pleasing, sweet, sweet-natured, sympathetic, winning, winsome; ▪ *Ant* disagreeable, hateful, mean, odious, repellent.

like [*adj*] *similar*
▪ *Syn* according to, akin, analogous, approximating, close, cognate, comparable, congenerous, consistent, consonant, corresponding, equivalent, homologous, jibing, matching, near, parallel, related, such, uniform; ▪ *Ant* different, dissimilar, dissimilar, diverse, unlike.

like [*v1*] *enjoy, be fond of*
▪ *Syn* admire, appreciate, approve, delight in, esteem, fancy, love, prize, rejoice in, relish, revel in, savor; ▪ *Ant* abhor, dislike, hate, loathe.

like [*v2*] *choose, feel inclined*
▪ *Syn* care to, choose to, desire, elect, fancy, feel disposed, feel like, have a preference for, incline toward, prefer, select, want, will, wish; ▪ *Ant* dislike, ignore.

likely [*adj*] *probable, apt, hopeful*
▪ *Syn* acceptable, achievable, attainable, believeable, credible, destined, disposed, expected, fair, favorite, feasible, imaginable, liable, ostensible, plausible, predisposed, prone, rational, reasonable, seeming, tending, verisimilar, workable; ▪ *Ant* implausible, inapt, unforeseeable, unlikely.

likewise [*adj*] *also, similarly*
▪ *Syn* additionally, along, as well, besides, correspondingly, in addition, in the same way, moreover, so, too, withal; ▪ *Ant* contrariwise, opposing, opposite, reverse.

limber [*adj*] *flexible*
▪ *Syn* agile, deft, elastic, graceful, lissome, lithe, loose, nimble, plastic, pli-

able, pliant, resilient, springy, spry, supple; ▪ *Ant* rigid, stiff, straight, tense, wooden.

limbo [*n*] *state of uncertainty*
▪ *Syn* edge, nothingness, nowhere, oblivion; ▪ *Ant* certainty, certitude, sureness, surety.

limit [*v*] *confine, restrict*
▪ *Syn* appoint, assign, bar, bind, bottle up, cap, check, circumscribe, constrict, contract, cramp, curb, define, delimit, demarcate, fix, hinder, inhibit, lessen, narrow, prescribe, ration, restrain, set, specify; ▪ *Ant* free, let go, release, unbound.

limitation [*n*] *restraint, disadvantage*
▪ *Syn* bar, block, check, circumspection, condition, constraint, control, curb, definition, impediment, inhibition, injunction, modification, obstruction, qualification, reservation, restriction, stint, stricture; ▪ *Ant* advantage, extent, freedom, infinity, range, release.

limited [*adj1*] *restricted, definite*
▪ *Syn* bound, circumscribed, confined, curbed, defined, determinate, fixed, hampered, local, narrow, particular, qualified, restrained, sectional, topical; ▪ *Ant* indefinite, limitless, unbounded, unlimited, unrestricted.

limited [*adj2*] *inadequate, short*
▪ *Syn* cramped, diminished, faulty, little, mean, minimal, narrow, paltry, poor, reduced, restricted, set, small; ▪ *Ant* adequate, ample, satisfactory, sufficient.

limitless [*adj*] *never-ending, infinite*
▪ *Syn* bottomless, boundless, endless, immense, incomprehensible, indefinite, innumerable, measureless, uncalculable, unfathomable, untold, vast, wide-open; ▪ *Ant* calculable, ending, exhaustible, finite, limited, measureable.

limp [*adj*] *not stiff; weak*
▪ *Syn* bending, debilitated, drooping, enervated, feeble, flaccid, flexible, floppy, impressible, infirm, languid, lax, loose, pliant, relaxed, slack, soft, supple, tired, wearied, worn out, yielding; ▪ *Ant* hard, inflexible, rigid, stiff, straight, strong, unbending.

limpid [*adj*] *clear, comprehensible*
▪ *Syn* bright, comprehensible, crystalline, definite, distinct, intelligible, lucid, obvious, pellucid, perspicuous, see-through, thin, translucent, transparent; ▪ *Ant* ambiguous, dark, dim, muddy, murky, obscure, vague.

line [*n*] *person's calling, interest*
▪ *Syn* activity, area, business, department, employment, field, forte, job, occupation, profession, specialization, trade, vocation, work; ▪ *Ant* entertainment, fun.

linger [*v1*] *loiter, delay*
▪ *Syn* amble, crawl, dally, dawdle, falter, hesitate, hobble, idle, lag, loll, mosey, plod, poke, remain, saunter, shuffle, tarry, trail, trifle, vacillate, wait; ▪ *Ant* go, hasten, hurry, leave, run, rush.

linger [*v2*] *continue, endure*
▪ *Syn* abide, bide, cling, hang on, last, persist, remain, stand, stay, survive, wait; ▪ *Ant* halt, stop.

link [*v*] *connect*
▪ *Syn* associate, attach, bind, bracket, combine, conjoin, conjugate, couple, fasten, group, incorporate, interface, join, meld with, network, plug into, relate, slap on, tag on, team up with, tie, tie in with, unite, yoke; ▪ *Ant* detach, disconnect, divide, separate, unfasten, unlink.

lip [*n1*] *edge, brink*
▪ *Syn* border, brim, flange, labium, labrum, margin, nozzle, portal, projection, rim, spout; ▪ *Ant* inside, interior, middle.

lip [*n2*] *insolence*
▪ *Syn* back talk, effrontery, impertinence, rudeness, sauciness; ▪ *Ant* civility, deference, kindness, mannerliness, respect.

liquid [*adj*] *fluid, flowing, melting*
▪ *Syn* aqueous, damp, deliquescent, dissolved, dulcet, fluent, ichorous, juicy, liquefied, liquiform, luscious, mellifluent, mellifluous, mellow, molten, runny, sappy, serous, smooth, succulent, thawed, viscous, watery, wet; ▪ *Ant* close, condensed, congealed, dense, firm, hard, solid.

liquidate [*v1*] *pay; change into cash*
▪ *Syn* cash, clear, convert, discharge, exchange, honor, pay off, quit, realize, reimburse, repay, satisfy, sell off, settle, square; ▪ *Ant* invest, keep, retain, save.

liquidate [*v2*] *destroy, dissolve*
▪ *Syn* abolish, annihilate, annul, cancel, dispatch, eliminate, exterminate, kill, murder, purge, remove, terminate, vaporize; ▪ *Ant* build, construct, create.

list [*v*] *lean, slant*
▪ *Syn* cant, careen, heel, incline, pitch, recline, slope, tilt, tip; ▪ *Ant* lie, straighten.

listen [*v*] *hear and pay attention*
▪ *Syn* attend, audit, catch, eavesdrop,

give heed to, hearken, hear out, mind, monitor, overhear, pay attention, receive, take notice, tune in, welcome; ▪ **Ant** disregard, ignore, speak, talk.

listless [adj] *spiritless, without energy* ▪ **Syn** abstracted, apathetic, bored, careless, dormant, dull, enervated, faint, heavy, heedless, impassive, inert, insouciant, languorous, leaden, lethargic, lifeless, limp, mopish, neutral, passive, phlegmatic, slack, slow, sluggish, supine, torpid, vacant; ▪ **Ant** active, alert, attentive, bright, eager, energetic, lively.

literacy [n] *ability to read* ▪ **Syn** articulateness, cultivation, education, knowledge, learning, proficiency, refinement, scholarship; ▪ **Ant** illiteracy.

literal [adj] *word for word; exact, real* ▪ **Syn** accurate, actual, apparent, authentic, bona fide, critical, faithful, genuine, gospel, natural, original, scrupulous, strict, true, undeviating, unvarnished, veracious, verbal, verbatim, veritable; ▪ **Ant** exaggerated, false, figurative, imaginative, inexact, loose, sloppy, unreliable, wrong.

literally [adv] *word for word; exactly* ▪ **Syn** actually, completely, correctly, direct, directly, faithfully, literatim, plainly, really, rightly, rigorously, simply, straight, strictly, truly, verbatim, veritably; ▪ **Ant** figuratively, loosely.

literary [adj] *concerning books, intellectual* ▪ **Syn** belletristic, bookish, classical, erudite, formal, learned, literate, scholarly, well-read; ▪ **Ant** illiterate, uneducated, unenlightened.

lithe [adj] *flexible, graceful and slender* ▪ **Syn** agile, limber, lissome, loose, nimble, pliable, pliant, slight, slim, spare, supple, thin; ▪ **Ant** awkward, fat, rigid, stiff, thick.

litter [v] *make a mess* ▪ **Syn** clutter, confuse, derange, dirty, disarrange, disarray, disorder, jumble, mess up, scatter, strew; ▪ **Ant** clean, clean up, neaten, organize, tidy.

little [adj1] *small in size, amount* ▪ **Syn** bantam, brief, diminutive, elfin, imperceptible, infinitesimal, junior, limited, meager, microscopic, miniature, minute, petite, scant, skimpy, slight, sparse, tiny, toy, truncated, wee; ▪ **Ant** big, considerable, enormous, giant, great, huge, immense, large, massive.

little [adj2] *not important* ▪ **Syn** casual, light, minor, minute, negligible, paltry, petty, small, trifling, trivial; ▪ **Ant** great, important, magnificent, significant.

little [adj3] *narrow-minded* ▪ **Syn** base, bigoted, contemptible, hidebound, illiberal, limited, narrow, petty, provincial, self-centered, set, small-minded, vulgar; ▪ **Ant** magnanimous, open, open-minded.

little [adv] *infrequently, not much* ▪ **Syn** barely, hardly, not often, rarely, scarcely, seldom, somewhat; ▪ **Ant** frequently, more, much.

livable [adj] *adequate, acceptable* ▪ **Syn** bearable, endurable, fit, inhabitable, passable, satisfactory, sustainable, tenantable, tolerable, worthwhile; ▪ **Ant** inadequate, intolerable, unacceptable, unbearable, unendurable, unlivable, unsuitable.

live [adj1] *existent* ▪ **Syn** alive, animate, aware, breathing, conscious, living, vital; ▪ **Ant** dead, nonexistent.

live [adj2] *energetic, vigorous* ▪ **Syn** active, alert, brisk, current, dynamic, effectual, hot, lively, operative, pertinent, running, topical, unsettled, vital, vivid, working; ▪ **Ant** apathetic, dispirited, dormant, lethargic.

live [v] *exist* ▪ **Syn** abide, be, breathe, continue, endure, last, lead, maintain, move, persist, prevail, remain, subsist, survive; ▪ **Ant** cease, depart, die.

livelihood [n] *occupation* ▪ **Syn** art, business, craft, employment, income, job, living, means, profession, source of income, subsistence, sustenance, trade, vocation, work; ▪ **Ant** avocation, entertainment, fun.

lively [adj] *energetic, active, busy* ▪ **Syn** agile, alert, animated, blithe, bright, brisk, buoyant, bustling, cheerful, effervescent, enterprising, festive, frolicsome, gay, happy, industrious, involved, jocund, jumping, keen, merry, nimble, perky, quick, rousing, snappy, sparkling, spirited, spry, stimulating, vigorous, vivacious; ▪ **Ant** apathetic, dispirited, inactive, lethargic, lifeless, sleepy.

livid [adj1] *pale, ashen* ▪ **Syn** ashy, blanched, bloodless, colorless, discolored, dusky, gloomy, greyish, grisly, leaden, lurid, murky, pallid, pasty, wan, waxen; ▪ **Ant** blushing, brilliant, flushed, radiant, rosy.

livid [adj2] *extremely angry*
▪ *Syn* beside oneself, boiling, enraged, exasperated, flaming, fuming, furious, incensed, indignant, infuriated, mad, offended, outraged; ▪ *Ant* assuaged, blissful, content, delighted, mollified.

living [adj] *existing, active*
▪ *Syn* alert, alive, animated, around, awake, breathing, brisk, contemporary, continuing, current, developing, dynamic, existent, extant, in use, live, lively, ongoing, operative, persisting, strong, subsisting, ticking, vigorous, vital, warm; ▪ *Ant* dead, dormant, inactive.

load [v] *burden, saddle, pressure*
▪ *Syn* bear, carry, charge, choke, cram, encumber, fill, flood, hamper, heap, lade, mass, pile, pile it on, place, pour in, stack, store, stow, stuff, surfeit, swamp, trouble, weigh, weight; ▪ *Ant* aid, assist, benefit, bless, discharge, empty, help, relieve, support.

loaf [v] *be idle, lazy*
▪ *Syn* dally, dream, drift, evade, goldbrick, idle, laze, lie, loiter, loll, lounge, malinger, piddle, relax, saunter, shirk, slack, stall, trifle, vegetate, waste time; ▪ *Ant* achieve, do, energize, labor, slave, toil, work hard.

loan [v] *give money, possession temporarily*
▪ *Syn* accommodate, advance, allow, credit, lend, provide, score, scratch, stake, touch; ▪ *Ant* borrow.

loath [adj] *against, averse*
▪ *Syn* afraid, counter, disinclined, hesitant, indisposed, opposed, reluctant, remiss, resisting; ▪ *Ant* desirous, eager, for, keen, willing.

loathe [v] *dislike very strongly*
▪ *Syn* abhor, abominate, decline, despise, detest, execrate, hate, refuse, reject, repudiate, revolt, spurn; ▪ *Ant* admire, crave, fancy, like, long for, love, relish.

loathsome [adj] *hateful*
▪ *Syn* abhorrent, abominable, beastly, deplorable, detestable, execrable, gross, horrible, invidious, lousy, nasty, odious, pestiferous, repugnant, repulsive, revolting, vile; ▪ *Ant* admirable, delightful, liking, loveable, respectful.

lobby [v] *press for political action*
▪ *Syn* advance, boost, campaign for, drum, exert influence, further, influence, persuade, pitch, plug, politick, press, pressure, promote, push, put pressure on, request, solicit, solicit votes, spot, sway,

thump, urge; ▪ *Ant* dissuade, impede, restrain.

local [adj] *of a community, restricted to immediate area* ▪ *Syn* civic, confined, district, divisional, geographical, homegrown, insular, legendary, neighborhood, parish, parochial, provincial, regional, sectarian, territorial, vernacular; ▪ *Ant* foreign, international, national, nonnative.

locate [v1] *find*
▪ *Syn* detect, determine, discover, establish, hit upon, pinpoint, place, position, read, search out, spot, station, strike, track down, uncover, unearth; ▪ *Ant* lose, miss.

locate [v2] *settle*
▪ *Syn* dig in, dwell, establish, fix, inhabit, park, place, reside, set, situate, squat, stand; ▪ *Ant* depart, forsake, leave, move, vacate.

lock [v] *fasten, clasp*
▪ *Syn* bar, bolt, button, clench, close, encircle, enclose, engage, grapple, join, latch, link, mesh, press, seal, secure, unite; ▪ *Ant* open, unclasp, unfasten, unlock.

lodge [v] *become fixed or wedged*
▪ *Syn* abide, catch, come to rest, entrench, fix, imbed, implant, infix, ingrain, install, plant, remain, root, stay, stick; ▪ *Ant* dislodge, loosen, remove.

lofty [adj1] *high, elevated*
▪ *Syn* airy, high, raised, sky-high, skyward, soaring, spiring, tall, towering; ▪ *Ant* low, short, stunted.

lofty [adj2] *grand, stately*
▪ *Syn* commanding, distinguished, exalted, illustrious, majestic, noble, renowned, striking, sublime, superior, utopian, visionary; ▪ *Ant* below, beneath, cheap, debased, humble, ignoble, low, mean, modest, unobtrusive.

lofty [adj3] *arrogant, high and mighty*
▪ *Syn* cavalier, condescending, disdainful, grandiose, haughty, high-minded, insolent, overbearing, patronizing, pretentious, proud, snooty, supercilious; ▪ *Ant* cordial, friendly, humble, modest, receptive, unassuming.

logical [adj] *probable, reasonable*
▪ *Syn* analytical, cogent, coherent, compelling, congruent, convincing, deducible, discerning, fair, germane, inferential, justifiable, legitimate, lucid, necessary, obvious, perspicuous, plausible, rational, sensible, sound, valid, well-organized, wise; ▪ *Ant* foolish, illogical,

improbable, irrational, nonsensical, unlikely, unreasonable.

loiter [v] *hang around; stroll*
▪ *Syn* amble, dabble, dawdle, drag, hover, idle, lag, loaf, lounge, pause, poke, procrastinate, ramble, saunter, shuffle, tarry, traipse, waste time; ▪ *Ant* hasten, hurry, rush, scamper, scurry, vamoose.

lone [adj] *by oneself; only*
▪ *Syn* abandoned, alone, deserted, forsaken, isolated, lonesome, one, particular, secluded, separate, singular, solitary, solo, unaccompanied, unique; ▪ *Ant* accompanied, escorted, multiple, paired.

lonely [adj1] *feeling friendless, forlorn*
▪ *Syn* abandoned, apart, companionless, disconsolate, estranged, forsaken, isolated, lone, lonesome, outcast, reclusive, rejected, secluded, troglodytic, withdrawn; ▪ *Ant* befriended, loved, popular.

lonely [adj2] *out-of-the-way*
▪ *Syn* deserted, desolate, godforsaken, isolated, obscure, private, quiet, remote, removed, secluded, sequestered, solitary, unfrequented; ▪ *Ant* close, crowded, frequented, inhabited, populous, swarming, teeming.

lonesome [adj] *forlorn, friendless*
▪ *Syn* alienated, alone, aloof, cheerless, companionless, deserted, desolate, dreary, gloomy, homesick, insular, isolated, lone, lonely, solitary; ▪ *Ant* befriended, gregarious, loved, sociable, unlonesome.

long [adj1] *extended in space or time*
▪ *Syn* continued, deep, drawn out, elongated, enduring, enlarged, extensive, faraway, far-off, great, lasting, lingering, prolonged, remote, spread out, stretched, sustained, towering; ▪ *Ant* abbreviated, abridged, brief, momentary, quick, short, short-lived.

long [adj2] *interminable, excessive in length* ▪ *Syn* boundless, diffuse, drawnout, limitless, lingering, overlong, prolix, protracted, sustained, tardy, unending, verbose, wordy; ▪ *Ant* ephemeral, evanescent, fleeting, short.

long [v] *desire, crave*
▪ *Syn* ache, aim, aspire, covet, dream of, hanker, have a yen for, hunger, itch, lust, miss, pine, sigh, suspire, thirst, want, wish, yearn; ▪ *Ant* despise, disdain, dislike, hate, renounce, spurn.

longing [adj] *desirous*
▪ *Syn* anxious, ardent, avid, craving, eager, hungry, pining, ravenous, wishful, wistful, yearning; ▪ *Ant* despising, disinterested, hating, loathing.

look [v] *examine visually*
▪ *Syn* admire, attend, behold, beware, consider, contemplate, eye, focus, gape, glance, heed, inspect, mark, mind, notice, observe, ogle, peep, pore over, regard, scan, scrutinize, see, spy, tend, view, watch; ▪ *Ant* be blind, close one's eyes to, disregard, ignore, miss, overlook.

look down on [v] *hold in contempt*
▪ *Syn* abhor, contemn, despise, disdain, scorn, scout, sneer, spurn; ▪ *Ant* approve, honor, laud, look up to, praise.

look out [v] *be wary*
▪ *Syn* be alert, be on guard, beware, check out, hearken, listen, mind, notice, pay attention, scope, size up, spot, spy, watch out; ▪ *Ant* disregard, ignore, neglect.

look up [v] *improve*
▪ *Syn* advance, ameliorate, come along, convalesce, gain, get better, mend, perk up, pick up, progress, recuperate, shape up, show improvement; ▪ *Ant* decline, fail, falter, worsen.

loom [v] *appear, often imposingly*
▪ *Syn* approach, become visible, be imminent, brew, come on, dawn, dominate, emanate, emerge, figure, foreshadow, gather, hover, impend, lower, menace, near, portend, soar, threaten, tower; ▪ *Ant* disappear, dissolve, drop, fade away, melt away, vanish.

loose [adj1] *not tight; unconstrained*
▪ *Syn* apart, baggy, clear, detached, disconnected, flabby, flaccid, floating, free, hanging, lax, movable, relaxed, separate, slack, wobbly; ▪ *Ant* bound, chained, constrained, curbed, leashed, restricted, taut, tight.

loose [adj2] *indefinite, vague*
▪ *Syn* careless, disordered, ill-defined, imprecise, inaccurate, inexact, negligent, obscure, rambling, random, remiss, slack; ▪ *Ant* accurate, clear, definite, meticulous, precise, strict.

loose [adj3] *promiscuous*
▪ *Syn* capricious, careless, corrupt, debauched, disreputable, dissipated, easy, fast, heedless, immoral, imprudent, inconstant, lax, lewd, licentious, negligent, profligate, reckless, wanton; ▪ *Ant* abstemious, clean, decent, disciplined, moral, virtuous.

loose/loosen [v] *set free; unbind*
▪ *Syn* deliver, detach, discharge, disconnect, disengage, ease off, emancipate,

free, let go, liberate, loosen, mitigate, relax, release, separate, slacken, work loose; ▪ *Ant* bind, cage, chain, imprison, limit, manacle, restrict, tighten.

lopsided [*adj*] *leaning, falling to one side; larger on one side* ▪ *Syn* askew, asymmetrical, awry, cockeyed, disproportionate, irregular, off-balance, tilting, top-heavy, warped; ▪ *Ant* balanced, even, level, steady, straight, symmetrical.

loquacious [*adj*] *talkative*
▪ *Syn* babbling, chattering, chatty, fluent, garrulous, gossipy, jabbering, prolix, verbose, voluble, wordy; ▪ *Ant* concise, quiet, restrained, silent, subdued, terse.

lose [*v1*] *be deprived of; mislay*
▪ *Syn* be reduced, displace, dissipate, drain, exhaust, expend, fail, fall short, forfeit, forget, give up, lavish, misplace, oust, pass up, relinquish, squander, suffer, use up, waste, yield; ▪ *Ant* hold on to, keep, maintain, preserve, recover, save.

lose [*v2*] *be defeated*
▪ *Syn* be humbled, be outdistanced, capitulate, come up short, decline, drop, fall, lose out, miss, succumb, suffer defeat, yield; ▪ *Ant* achieve, succeed, win.

lose [*v3*] *escape, avoid*
▪ *Syn* clear, dodge, duck, elude, evade, leave behind, outrun, rid, shake, slip away, stray; ▪ *Ant* confront, face, meet.

lost [*adj1*] *missing, off-track*
▪ *Syn* absent, adrift, astray, at sea, disappeared, disoriented, forfeited, gone, gone astray, hidden, irretrievable, irrevocable, lacking, mislaid, misplaced, missed, obscured, off-course, strayed, vanished, wandering, wayward, without; ▪ *Ant* found, recovered.

lost [*adj2*] *extinct, destroyed*
▪ *Syn* abolished, annihilated, bygone, consumed, dead, demolished, devastated, dissipated, eradicated, exterminated, forgotten, frittered, gone, lapsed, obliterated, out-of-date, past, perished, ruined, squandered, wasted, wrecked; ▪ *Ant* alive, existent, existing, living.

lost [*adj3*] *distracted, dreaming*
▪ *Syn* absent, absentminded, absorbed, abstracted, bemused, bewildered, distrait, dreamy, engrossed, entranced, faraway, musing, perplexed, preoccupied, rapt, spellbound, wasted; ▪ *Ant* attentive, aware, cognizant.

loud [*adj1*] *blaring, noisy*
▪ *Syn* booming, cacophonous, clamorous,

crashing, deafening, deep, ear-piercing, ear-splitting, emphatic, forte, full, intense, obstreperous, pealing, piercing, powerful, raucous, resonant, resounding, ringing, roaring, rowdy, sonorous, stentorian, strident, strong, thundering, tumultuous, turbulent, uproarious, vehement, vehement, vociferous; ▪ *Ant* inaudible, low, quiet, soft, subdued.

loud [*adj2*] *offensive, gaudy*
▪ *Syn* brash, brassy, brazen, chintzy, coarse, crass, crude, flamboyant, flashy, garish, glaring, gross, lurid, meretricious, obnoxious, obtrusive, ostentatious, raucous, rude, showy, tasteless, tawdry, vulgar; ▪ *Ant* conservative, inoffensive, sedate, soft, tasteful.

lousy [*adj*] *very bad*
▪ *Syn* awful, base, contemptible, despicable, dirty, disliked, execrable, harmful, hateful, horrible, inferior, low, mean, miserable, outrageous, poor, rotten, shoddy, slovenly, terrible, unpopular, vicious, vile; ▪ *Ant* good, great, magnificent, wonderful.

lovable [*adj*] *very likable; endearing*
▪ *Syn* adorable, alluring, attractive, captivating, charming, cuddly, desirable, enchanting, enthralling, entrancing, fascinating, fetching, pleasing, ravishing, seductive, sweet, winning; ▪ *Ant* hateful, loathsome, offensive, repellent.

love [*v*] *adore, like very much*
▪ *Syn* admire, adulate, be attached to, be captivated by, be crazy about, be enamored of, be enchanted by, be fascinated with, be fond of, be in love with, canonize, care for, cherish, choose, deify, delight in, dote on, esteem, exalt, fall for, fancy, glorify, have affection for, hold dear, hold high, idolize, long for, prefer, prize, thrive with, treasure, venerate, worship; ▪ *Ant* dislike, hate, scorn.

lovely [*adj*] *beautiful, charming; agreeable* ▪ *Syn* admirable, alluring, attractive, beauteous, bewitching, captivating, comely, delectable, delicious, exquisite, exquisite, fair, good-looking, gorgeous, knockout, nice, pleasing, pretty, splendid, sweet, winning; ▪ *Ant* awful, disagreeable, drab, homely, repugnant, ugly, unsightly.

loving [*adj*] *expressing adoration*
▪ *Syn* admiring, affectionate, amatory, appreciative, ardent, benevolent, caring, concerned, devoted, doting, earnest, en-

amored, expressive, faithful, fervent, fond, generous, idolatrous, impassioned, kind, loyal, passionate, reverent, romantic, sentimental, tender, thoughtful, warm, worshipful, zealous; ▪ *Ant* cold, contemptuous, hateful, hostile, mean.

low [*adj1*] *close to the ground; short*
▪ *Syn* bottommost, crouched, decumbent, depressed, flat, ground-level, inferior, junior, level, little, lowering, low-hanging, low-set, minor, nether, profound, shallow, small, squat, stunted, subjacent, subsided, sunken, under; ▪ *Ant* above, elevated, high, tall.

low [*adj2*] *reduced; mediocre*
▪ *Syn* cheap, depleted, inferior, insignificant, low-grade, marked down, moderate, modest, nominal, paltry, poor, scant, shoddy, substandard, trifling, worthless; ▪ *Ant* above, elevated, high, increased, prominent.

low [*adj3*] *crude, vulgar*
▪ *Syn* abject, base, blue, coarse, common, contemptible, depraved, despicable, disgraceful, ignoble, menial, miserable, nasty, obscene, offensive, raw, rough, rude, scurvy, vile, woebegone, woeful, wretched; ▪ *Ant* decent, honest, honorable, moral, reputable, respectable, upright.

low [*adj4*] *living in, coming from poor circumstances* ▪ *Syn* base, baseborn, humble, ignoble, lowborn, lowly, mean, meek, obscure, plain, poor, rude, simple; ▪ *Ant* affluent, comfortable, high, moneyed, prosperous, rich, wealthy.

low [*adj5*] *depressed*
▪ *Syn* crestfallen, dejected, despondent, disheartened, downcast, downhearted, forlorn, gloomy, glum, miserable, moody, morose, sad, spiritless, unhappy; ▪ *Ant* cheerful, gay, happy.

low [*adj6*] *not feeling well*
▪ *Syn* ailing, debilitated, exhausted, faint, feeble, frail, ill, indisposed, poorly, prostrate, reduced, sick, sickly, stricken, unwell, weak; ▪ *Ant* healthy, strong, well.

low [*adj7*] *not loud*
▪ *Syn* faint, gentle, hushed, muffled, muted, quiet, soft, sub3Syn apathetic, chilly, cool, halfdued, whispered; ▪ *Ant* high-pitched, noisy, raucous, strong.

lower [*adj*] *under, inferior*
▪ *Syn* decreased, diminished, lesser, nether, pared down, reduced, secondary, second-class, smaller, subjacent, subordi-

nate, under; ▪ *Ant* higher, important, increased, superior.

lower [*v1*] *let down; fall*
▪ *Syn* cast down, couch, droop, drop, let down, reduce, set down, sink, submerge, take down; ▪ *Ant* elevate, increase, raise.

lower [*v2*] *reduce, minimize*
▪ *Syn* abate, clip, curtail, cut, decrease, decry, deflate, demote, devalue, diminish, downsize, lessen, mark down, pare, prune, roll back, scale down, slash, tone down, undervalue, write off; ▪ *Ant* elevate, heighten, increase, rise.

low-key [*adj*] *subdued*
▪ *Syn* easygoing, loose, low-pitched, muffled, muted, played down, quiet, relaxed, restrained, sober, softened, subtle, toned down, understated; ▪ *Ant* energized, high-pitched, high-strung, nervous, pumped up.

lowly [*adj*] *inferior, plain*
▪ *Syn* average, base, common, commonplace, humble, ignoble, mean, meek, modest, mundane, obscure, ordinary, plebeian, poor, proletarian, prosaic, retiring, reverential, servile, simple, submissive, subordinate, unassuming; ▪ *Ant* conceited, elevated, higher, lofty, noble, proud, superior.

loyal [*adj*] *faithful, dependable*
▪ *Syn* allegiant, ardent, attached, believing, constant, devoted, dutiful, firm, patriotic, resolute, staunch, steadfast, steady, true, trustworthy, trusty, unfailing, unswerving, unwavering; ▪ *Ant* disloyal, false, perfidious, treasonous.

lucid [*adj1*] *evident, obvious, clear*
▪ *Syn* apprehensible, clear-cut, comprehensible, crystal clear, distinct, explicit, fathomable, intelligible, knowable, limpid, luminous, pellucid, plain, translucent, transparent, transpicuous, understandable; ▪ *Ant* ambiguous, confused, indistinct, obscure, unclear, vague.

lucid [*adj2*] *brilliant, shining*
▪ *Syn* beaming, bright, effulgent, gleaming, incandescent, lambent, luminous, lustrous, radiant, refulgent, resplendent; ▪ *Ant* cloudy, dark, gloomy, murky, shadowy.

lucid [*adj3*] *clearheaded, sensible*
▪ *Syn* all there, compos mentis, in right mind, normal, rational, reasonable, right, sane, sober, sound; ▪ *Ant* confused, crazy, insane, irrational, neurotic, paranoid, puzzled.

luckily [adv] happily
▪ Syn by chance, favorably, fortuitously, fortunately, opportunely, propitiously, providentially; ▪ Ant unhappily, unluckily.
lucky [adj] fortunate, opportune
▪ Syn advantageous, beneficial, blessed, charmed, favored, felicitous, golden, happy, hopeful, promising, prosperous, serendipitous, timely, well; ▪ Ant bad, inopportune, unfavorable, unfortunate, unlucky, unpropitious, unsuccessful.
lucrative [adj] productive, well-paid
▪ Syn advantageous, beneficial, fruitful, gainful, money-making, paying, profitable, remunerative, worthwhile; ▪ Ant low-paying, unprofitable.
ludicrous [adj] absurd, ridiculous
▪ Syn antic, bizarre, burlesque, comical, droll, fantastic, foolish, gelastic, grotesque, incongruous, outlandish, preposterous, silly, zany; ▪ Ant logical, reasonable, sensible, serious.
lukewarm [adj1] slightly heated
▪ Syn blood-warm, milk-warm, room temperature, temperate, tepid, warm, warmish; ▪ Ant boiling, chilly, cool, cooled.
lukewarm [adj2] indifferent, unenthusiastic ▪ Syn apathetic, chilly, cool, half-hearted, hesitant, indecisive, irresolute, phlegmatic, tepid, uncommitted, unconcerned; ▪ Ant enthusiastic, interested, responsive, warm.
lull [v] calm
▪ Syn abate, allay, balm, becalm, cease, compose, decrease, die down, diminish, dwindle, ebb, fall, hush, let up, lullaby, pacify, quell, quiet, quiet down, settle, slacken, soothe, still, subdue, subside, temper, wane; ▪ Ant arouse, energize, excite, provoke.
lumbering [adj] clumsy, awkward
▪ Syn blundering, bovine, clunking, elephantine, gauche, halting, inept, lumpish, maladroit, overgrown, ponderous, splay, ungainly, unwieldy, wooden; ▪ Ant agile, gliding, lithe.
luminescent [adj] glowing, shining
▪ Syn bright, effulgent, fluorescent, luminous, phosphorescent, radiant; ▪ Ant dull, obscured.
luminous [adj1] bright, glowing
▪ Syn beaming, brilliant, clear, effulgent, illuminated, incandescent, lambent, lucent, lucid, lustrous, radiant, refulgent, resplendent, shining, transparent, vivid; ▪ Ant dark, dim, dull, gloomy.

luminous [adj2] obvious, understandable ▪ Syn apprehensible, brilliant, clear, comprehensible, evident, fathomable, graspable, intelligible, knowable, lucid, perspicacious, perspicuous; ▪ Ant obscure, unclear, unintelligible, vague.
lump [n] clump, mass
▪ Syn agglomeration, ball, bulk, bunch, cluster, gob, group, hunk, knot, lot, mountain, pile, portion, section, swelling, tumescence, tumor, wad, wedge; ▪ Ant granule, particle.
lunatic [adj] crazy, mad
▪ Syn absurd, cracked, crazed, daft, demented, deranged, foolish, idiotic, insane, irrational, loco, maniacal, nonsensical, preposterous, psychotic, stupid, zany; ▪ Ant healthy, sane, sensible.
lunge [v] pounce, dive for
▪ Syn bound, burst, charge, cut, dash, drive, fall upon, hit, jab, jump, leap, lurch, pitch, plunge, stab, surge, thrust; ▪ Ant drag, pull, recoil, retreat, withdraw.
lurch [v] move toward with jerk
▪ Syn blunder, bumble, careen, dodge, falter, flounder, jerk, lean, move to the side, pitch, reel, rock, seesaw, slide, stagger, stumble, teeter, totter, weave, wobble, yaw; ▪ Ant retreat, stabilize, steady, stride.
lure [v] attract, seduce
▪ Syn bait, beckon, beguile, captivate, charm, decoy, draw, ensnare, entice, fascinate, grab, hook, inveigle, invite, lead on, pull, rope, steer, tempt, vamp; ▪ Ant antagonize, disenchant, disgust, dissuade, repulse, repulse, turn off.
lurid [adj] shocking, gruesome
▪ Syn bloody, extreme, fiery, ghastly, graphic, grisly, hideous, horrifying, livid, macabre, obscene, revolting, rough, savage, sensational, sinister, startling, terrible, terrifying, violent, vivid; ▪ Ant clean, humble, lighthearted, modest, pale.
lurk [v] hide; move stealthily
▪ Syn conceal oneself, creep, crouch, go furtively, gumshoe, lie in wait, prowl, skulk, slide, slink, slip, snake, sneak, snoop, stay hidden, steal, wait; ▪ Ant barge, parade, strut, swagger.
luscious [adj] delicious, delectable
▪ Syn adorable, ambrosial, appetizing, choice, darling, flavorsome, honeyed, juicy, lush, mellow, mouth-watering, nectarious, opulent, piquant, rich, savory, scrumptious, succulent, toothsome,

voluptuous; ▪ *Ant* bitter, bland, nasty, poor, tart, unappetizing, unsavory.

lush [*adj*] *profuse and delightful*
▪ *Syn* abundant, delectable, deluxe, extravagant, flourishing, green, heavenly, juicy, lavish, luscious, luxurious, opulent, palatial, plush, prolific, rich, ripe, scrumptious, sensuous, succulent, sumptuous, teeming, verdant, voluptuous; ▪ *Ant* austere, bare, barren, sparse.

lust [*v*] *desire strongly*
▪ *Syn* ache, covet, crave, hanker, hunger for, itch, long, need, pine, thirst, want, wish, yearn, yen; ▪ *Ant* disdain, dislike, spurn.

lustrous [*adj*] *glossy, shining*
▪ *Syn* bright, burnished, dazzling, effulgent, glace, gleaming, glinting, glistening, glowing, incandescent, lambent, lucent, luminous, polished, radiant, refulgent, shimmering, shiny, sparkling, splendid, waxy; ▪ *Ant* dark, dingy, drab, dull, lusterless, matte.

lusty [*adj*] *energetic, healthy*
▪ *Syn* brawny, dynamic, hale, hearty, potent, powerful, red-blooded, robust, rugged, stalwart, stout, strapping, strenuous, strong, sturdy, tough, vigorous, virile, vital; ▪ *Ant* infirm, lackluster, lethargic, listless, unhealthy, weak.

luxuriant [*adj*] *profuse, plush*
▪ *Syn* abundant, ample, copious, elaborate, extravagant, exuberant, fancy, flamboyant, flourishing, lavish, luscious, lush, opulent, overflowing, palatial, plenteous, plentiful, prodigal, productive, profusive, prolific, rampant, rich, sumptuous, teeming, thriving; ▪ *Ant* barren, meager, plain, poor, sparse, unadorned.

luxurious [*adj*] *affluent, indulgent*
▪ *Syn* costly, deluxe, epicurean, extravagant, fancy, grandiose, gratifying, hedonistic, immoderate, imposing, lavish, lush, magnificent, majestic, opulent, ostentatious, palatial, pampered, plush, posh, pretentious, rich, sensuous, splendid, stately, sumptuous, voluptuous, well-appointed; ▪ *Ant* ascetic, austere, frugal, poor, spartan.

lying [*adj*] *dishonest*
▪ *Syn* deceitful, deceptive, delusory, dissembling, dissimulating, equivocating, false, fibbing, guileful, knavish, mendacious, misleading, misrepresenting, misstating, perfidious, prevaricating, shifty, treacherous, tricky, unreliable, untruthful; ▪ *Ant* candid, direct, frank, honest, truthful.

M

macabre [*adj*] *very eerie; deathlike*
▪ *Syn* cadaverous, deathly, dreadful, frightening, ghastly, ghoulish, grim, gruesome, hideous, horrible, lurid, morbid, offensive, scary, spooky, terrible, unearthly, weird; ▪ *Ant* appealing, common, living, normal, pleasant.

mad [*adj1*] *crazy, insane*
▪ *Syn* aberrant, absurd, crazed, delirious, demented, deranged, fantastic, foolhardy, frenetic, illogical, imprudent, irrational, ludicrous, lunatic, nonsensical, preposterous, raving, senseless, unhinged; ▪ *Ant* balanced, rational, reasonable, sane, sound, stable.

mad [*adj2*] *very angry*
▪ *Syn* agitated, enraged, exasperated, fuming, furious, incensed, infuriated, livid, raging, resentful, uncontrolled, wild, wrathful; ▪ *Ant* appeased, calm, cheered, collected, happy.

mad [*adj3*] *enthusiastic; in love*
▪ *Syn* ardent, avid, crazy, daft, devoted, enamoured, fanatical, impassioned, infatuated, keen, wild, zealous; ▪ *Ant* disenchanted, nonchalant, unenthusiastic.

madcap [*adj*] *crazy, impulsive*
▪ *Syn* brash, foolhardy, harebrained, heedless, ill-advised, imprudent, incautious, lively, rash, reckless, stupid, thoughtless, wild; ▪ *Ant* circumspect, reasonable, sane.

madden [*v*] *make very angry*
▪ *Syn* anger, annoy, bother, distract, drive insane, enrage, exasperate, incense, infuriate, possess, unbalance, upset, vex; ▪ *Ant* appease, gladden, make happy, soothe.

made-up [*adj*] *invented*
▪ *Syn* fabricated, false, fictional, imaginary, make-believe, mythical, specious, trumped-up, unreal, untrue; ▪ *Ant* original, real, true.

madly [*adj*] *wildly, fiercely*
▪ *Syn* crazily, deliriously, desperately, devotedly, distractedly, energetically, exceedingly, excessively, excitedly, extremely, foolishly, frantically, furiously, hastily, insanely, intensely, irrationally, ludicrously, nonsensically, passionately, rabidly, rashly, recklessly, senselessly, speedily, stormily, tumultuously/tumultuously, turbulently, unreasonably, violently; ▪ *Ant* calmly, normally.

magic/magical [*adj*] *bewitching, charming* ▪ *Syn* charismatic, clairvoyant, conjuring, demoniac, diabolic, eerie, enchanting, ensorcelled, entrancing, fascinating, ghostly, haunted, imaginary, marvelous, mysterious, mystic, necromantic, occult, otherworldly, parapsychological, runic, sorcerous, spectral, spellbinding, spooky, telekinetic, thaumaturgic, unusual, weird, witchlike, wizardly, wonderful; ▪ *Ant* everyday, normal, ordinary.

magnanimous [*adj*] *very giving and kind* ▪ *Syn* all heart, altruistic, beneficent, benevolent, big, bountiful, charitable, chivalrous, considerate, forgiving, free, generous, great, handsome, high-minded, kindly, knightly, liberal, lofty, loose, munificent, noble, openhanded, princely, selfless; ▪ *Ant* parsimonious, petty, small, stingy, suspicious, unforgiving.

magnate [*n*] *very important person, usually in business* ▪ *Syn* aristocrat, baron, businessman/woman, capitalist, captain of industry, chief, czar, figure, financier, industrialist, leader, merchant, mogul, name, noble, notable, peer, personage, plutocrat, tycoon; ▪ *Ant* lowly individual, peon, underling.

magnetic [*adj*] *drawing, attractive* ▪ *Syn* alluring, appealing, arresting, attractive, bewitching, captivating, charismatic, charming, enchanting, entrancing, fascinating, hypnotic, inviting, irresistible, mesmerizing, pulling, seductive; ▪ *Ant* repellent, repulsive.

magnificent [*adj*] *glorious, wonderful* ▪ *Syn* brilliant, chivalric, commanding, elegant, elevated, exalted, excellent, fine, glittering, gorgeous, grand, grandiose, imperial, imposing, impressive, lavish, lofty, lordly, luxurious, magnanimous, magnific, majestic, noble, opulent, outstanding, plush, posh, princely, proud, radiant, regal, resplendent, rich, smashing, splendid, standout, stately, striking, sublime, sumptuous, superb, superior, superlative, towering, transcendent; ▪ *Ant* bad, ignoble, modest, offensive, ordinary, poor, tawdry, ugly.

magnify [*v*] *enlarge, intensify, exaggerate* ▪ *Syn* aggrandize, amplify, augment, blow up, boost, build up, deepen, dignify, embellish, enhance, ennoble, exalt, expand, extend, glorify, heighten, hike up, increase, inflate, intensate, jack up, jump up, mount, multiply, overdo, overplay, overrate, pad, pyramid, redouble, rise, rouse, run up, step up, sweeten,

swell; ▪ *Ant* decrease, diminish, lessen, miniaturize, play down, weaken.

maiden [*adj*] *first, earliest* ▪ *Syn* beginning, fresh, inaugural, initial, initiatory, introductory, new, original, pioneer, primary, unbroached, untapped, untried, unused; ▪ *Ant* concluding, final, latest.

maim [*v*] *cripple, put out of action* ▪ *Syn* batter, break, crush, damage, disable, disfigure, dismember, hack, impair, incapacitate, lame, mangle, mar, maul, mutilate, spoil, truncate, wound; ▪ *Ant* aid, cure, heal, help, repair.

main [*adj*] *principal, predominant* ▪ *Syn* capital, cardinal, central, controlling, crucial, essential, foremost, fundamental, head, leading, major, outstanding, paramount, premier, primary, prime, star, stellar, supreme, vital; ▪ *Ant* auxiliary, extra, insignificant, minor, secondary, subordinate, unimportant.

mainly [*adv*] *for the most part* ▪ *Syn* above all, chiefly, essentially, first and foremost, in the main, largely, mostly, overall, predominantly, primarily, principally, substantially, to the greatest extent, usually; ▪ *Ant* least of all, minimally, partially, secondarily, slightly, subordinately.

mainstay [*n*] *chief support* ▪ *Syn* anchor, backbone, brace, bulwark, buttress, pillar, prop, staff, stay, strength, supporter, sustainer, upholder; ▪ *Ant* weak link.

maintain [*v1*] *care for, keep up* ▪ *Syn* carry on, continue, finance, keep, look after, manage, nurture, perpetuate, persevere, protect, provide, repair, save, sustain, take care of, uphold; ▪ *Ant* conclude, desert, end, ignore, neglect.

maintain [*v2*] *assert, claim; argue for* ▪ *Syn* advocate, affirm, allege, asseverate, attest, aver, avow, back, champion, contend, declare, defend, emphasize, fight for, hold, insist, justify, persist, plead for, profess, protest, rectify, report, say, stand by, state, stress, uphold, vindicate; ▪ *Ant* condemn, disavow, discard, retract.

majestic [*adj*] *impressive, splendid* ▪ *Syn* august, awesome, ceremonious, dignified, elevated, exalted, grand, grandiose, imperial, imposing, kingly, lofty, magnific, magnificent, marvelous, monumental, noble, pompous, princely, regal, royal, stately, stunning, sublime, sumptuous, superb; ▪ *Ant* humble, low, lowly, modest, shabby, undistinguished.

major [*adj1*] *bigger*
▪ *Syn* better, chief, considerable, dominant, extreme, greater, hefty, higher, large, larger, leading, main, most, primary, senior, sizable, superior, supreme, ultra, upper, uppermost; ▪ *Ant* lesser, little, minor, small.

major [*adj2*] *important*
▪ *Syn* big, chief, critical, crucial, grave, great, influential, main, major-league, meaningful, notable, outstanding, overshadowing, preeminent, principal, serious, significant, star, stellar, top, vital, weighty; ▪ *Ant* ancillary, insignificant, minor, secondary, subordinate, unimportant.

make [*v1*] *create, build*
▪ *Syn* assemble, beget, bring about, cause, compose, conceive, construct, dream up, effect, engender, fabricate, fashion, generate, hatch, initiate, lead to, manufacture, originate, parent, prepare, procreate, produce, put together, secure, shape, sire, spawn, synthesize; ▪ *Ant* crush, destroy, raze, ruin.

make [*v2*] *induce, compel*
▪ *Syn* bring about, cause, coerce, constrain, dragoon, drive, effect, force, impel, oblige, press, pressure, prevail upon, require, secure, tamper; ▪ *Ant* ask, discourage, dissuade, halt, plead, prevent, stop.

make [*v3*] *designate, appoint*
▪ *Syn* advance, assign, constitute, create, delegate, elect, install, nominate, ordain, proffer, select, tap, tender; ▪ *Ant* demote, renounce.

make [*v4*] *enact, execute*
▪ *Syn* carry out, conduct, declare, decree, effect, establish, fix, formulate, legislate, pass, perform, practice, prepare, prosecute, wage; ▪ *Ant* cancel, deny, disallow, repeal, veto.

make [*v5*] *earn, acquire*
▪ *Syn* bring in, clear, gain, get, harvest, hustle, net, obtain, pull, rate, realize, reap, receive, secure, take in; ▪ *Ant* lose.

make [*v6*] *arrive, aim at*
▪ *Syn* advance, arrive at, attain, catch, head, meet, move, proceed, progress, reach, set out, strike out, take off; ▪ *Ant* leave, miss, withdraw from.

make-believe [*adj*] *imagined, unreal*
▪ *Syn* false, fantasized, fictional, fraudulent, imaginary, mock, pretend, pretended, sham, simulated; ▪ *Ant* real, true, unimagined.

make off [*v*] *flee, run away*
▪ *Syn* abscond, clear, cut and run, decamp, escape, go, make away, quit, retire, run for it, scamper, scoot, withdraw; ▪ *Ant* apprehend, capture, retain, stay.

make out [*v1*] *understand*
▪ *Syn* accept, catch, comprehend, decipher, deduce, derive, fathom, gather, grasp, infer, judge, perceive, recognize, see, take in, work out; ▪ *Ant* misconceive, misunderstand.

make out [*v2*] *get by, succeed*
▪ *Syn* accomplish, achieve, do with, endure, fare, flourish, get along, manage, muddle through, prosper, score, thrive; ▪ *Ant* fail.

makeshift [*adj*] *temporary*
▪ *Syn* alternative, expedient, provisional, stopgap, substitute; ▪ *Ant* complete, finished, permanent.

make up [*v1*] *create*
▪ *Syn* blend, coin, combine, concoct, contrive, devise, dream up, fabricate, formulate, frame, hatch, invent, knock off, originate, prepare, pretend, put together, ready, trump up; ▪ *Ant* destroy, tell truth.

make up [*v2*] *reconcile*
▪ *Syn* come to terms, conciliate, counterbalance, make amends, make peace, mend, pacify, recompense, requite, settle, shake hands; ▪ *Ant* disagree.

maladroit [*adj1*] *awkward, clumsy*
▪ *Syn* blundering, bungling, clunky, floundering, heavy-handed, inept, inexpert, lumbering, stumbling, ungraceful, unskillful; ▪ *Ant* able, capable, skillful.

maladroit [*adj2*] *tactless*
▪ *Syn* brash, gauche, impolitic, inconsiderate, inelegant, insensitive, thoughtless, undiplomatic, untactful, untoward; ▪ *Ant* diplomatic, sensitive, tactful.

malaise [*n*] *depression, sickness*
▪ *Syn* angst, debility, decrepitude, discomfort, disquiet, distress, doldrums, enervation, feebleness, illness, infirmity, lassitude, melancholy, pain, sickliness, unhealthiness, weakness; ▪ *Ant* strength, well being.

malediction [*n*] *curse*
▪ *Syn* anathema, commination, curse, cuss, damnation, denunciation, execration, expletive, imprecation, jinx, oath; ▪ *Ant* blessing, compliment, praise.

malevolent [*adj*] *hateful*
▪ *Syn* bad-natured, evil, hellish, hostile, lousy, malicious, murderous, pernicious,

rancorous, sinister, spiteful, tough, vengeful, vindictive, waspish, wicked; ▪ *Ant* amiable, benevolent, benign, harmless, kind, liking, loving.

malformed [*adj*] *distorted*
▪ *Syn* abnormal, contorted, crooked, deformed, distorted, grotesque, irregular, misshapen, twisted, warped; ▪ *Ant* perfect, regular, undistorted.

malicious [*adj*] *hateful*
▪ *Syn* awful, bad-natured, baleful, beastly, bitter, deleterious, detrimental, envious, evil, evil-minded, ill-disposed, injurious, jealous, low, malevolent, malign, malignant, mean, mischievous, nasty, noxious, ornery, pernicious, petty, poisonous, rancorous, resentful, spiteful, vengeful, venomous, vicious, virulent, wicked; ▪ *Ant* benevolent, friendly, good, kind, likeable, sympathetic, thoughtful.

malign [*adj*] *hurtful, injurious*
▪ *Syn* antagonistic, antipathetic, baleful, baneful, deleterious, evil, harmful, hateful, inimical, malevolent, malignant, noxious, pernicious, rancorous, sinister, vicious, wicked; ▪ *Ant* aiding, benign, helpful, nice.

malign [*v*] *slander, defame*
▪ *Syn* abuse, accuse, befoul, besmirch, blacken, calumniate, curse, decry, defile, disparage, harm, insult, misrepresent, mudsling, opprobriate, pollute, revile, scandalize, slur, smear, spatter, stain, taint, tarnish, traduce, vilify, villainize, vituperate; ▪ *Ant* commend, praise, uphold.

malignant [*adj*] *diseased*
▪ *Syn* deadly, destructive, fatal, internecine, lethal, mortal, pestilential, poisonous; ▪ *Ant* benign, harmless.

malleable [*adj*] *pliable*
▪ *Syn* adaptable, compliant, ductile, flexible, governable, impressionable, moldable, plastic, pliant, soft, supple, tractable, transformable, workable, yielding; ▪ *Ant* firm, rigid, stiff, unbending.

malodorous [*adj*] *foul-smelling*
▪ *Syn* decayed, decomposed, fetid, foul, infested, lousy, musty, nauseating, noxious, offensive, pestilential, putrid, rancid, reeking, smelly, stenchful, strong, tainted, vile; ▪ *Ant* aromatic, fragrant, perfumed, savory, sweet.

mammoth [*adj*] *huge*
▪ *Syn* behemothic, colossal, elephantine, enormous, gargantuan, giant, high, immense, jumbo, large, leviathan, massive, monstrous, monumental, prodigious, stupendous, titanic, vast; ▪ *Ant* little, miniature, small, tiny.

manage [*v1*] *be in charge, control*
▪ *Syn* administer, advocate, boss, captain, care for, command, conduct, counsel, direct, dominate, execute, govern, guide, handle, head, influence, instruct, maintain, manipulate, mastermind, minister, officiate, operate, oversee, pilot, preside, regulate, rule, run, run the show, steer, superintend, supervise, take care of, use, watch, watch over, wield; ▪ *Ant* follow, serve under.

manage [*v2*] *accomplish*
▪ *Syn* achieve, arrange, bring about, bring off, carry out, con, contrive, cope with, deal with, effect, engineer, execute, finagle, fix, push around, succeed, swing, upstage, work; ▪ *Ant* botch, bumble, fail, muff.

manager [*n*] *person who runs organization* ▪ *Syn* administrator, boss, comptroller, conductor, controller, director, executive, governor, handler, head, impresario, officer, official, organizer, overseer, producer, proprietor, superintendent, supervisor; ▪ *Ant* employee.

mandate [*n*] *authority, order*
▪ *Syn* authorization, behest, bidding, charge, command, commission, decree, dictate, directive, edict, fiat, imperative, injunction, instruction, precept, sanction, warrant; ▪ *Ant* denial, veto.

mandatory [*adj*] *required, necessary*
▪ *Syn* binding, commanding, compelling, compulsatory, compulsory, de rigueur, essential, forced, imperative, involuntary, irremissible, obligatory, requisite; ▪ *Ant* optional, unnecessary, voluntary.

maneuver [*v*] *direct physically*
▪ *Syn* deploy, dispense, drive, exercise, guide, handle, manipulate, move, navigate, negotiate, pilot, ply, steer, swing, wield; ▪ *Ant* follow.

mangle [*v*] *mutilate, deform*
▪ *Syn* batter, butcher, contort, damage, distort, flay, hack, hash, impair, injure, lacerate, maim, maul, ruin, slay, slice, spoil, tear, wound, wreck; ▪ *Ant* cure, heal, help, preserve.

mangy [*adj*] *scruffy*
▪ *Syn* decrepit, dirty, impoverished, indigent, mean, poor, shabby, shoddy, sick, squalid, tattered; ▪ *Ant* kempt, neat.

manic/maniacal [*adj*] *overexcited, crazy* ▪ *Syn* berserk, crazed, demented, deranged, excited, frenzied, insane, lunatic, mad, raving, unbalanced, wild; ▪ *Ant* balanced, calm, depressed, low, sane, sluggish.

manifest [adj] *clear, obvious*
- *Syn* apparent, bold, conspicuous, distinct, divulged, evident, evinced, glaring, noticeable, open, palpable, patent, plain, prominent, revealed, shown, straightforward, unambiguous, unmistakable, visible; *Ant* ambiguous, concealed, obscure, unclear, vague.

manifest [v] *exhibit, make plain*
- *Syn* confirm, declare, demonstrate, display, embody, evince, expose, externalize, flash, illustrate, incarnate, mark, materialize, objectify, personify, proclaim, prove, reveal, set forth, showcase, signify, sport, strut, suggest, utter, vent, voice; *Ant* bury, conceal, cover, obscure, withhold.

manifold [adj] *abundant, many*
- *Syn* assorted, complex, copious, different, diverse, diversified, multifarious, multifold, multiple, multitudinous, multivarious, numerous, sundry, varied, various; *Ant* few, one, single, sole, uniform.

manipulate [v1] *maneuver, handle physically* *Syn* employ, feel, form, manage, mold, operate, ply, shape, swing, use, wield, work; *Ant* leave alone.

manipulate [v2] *change to suit one's desire* *Syn* beguile, conduct, control, direct, engineer, exploit, finagle, finesse, guide, handle, influence, jockey, machinate, maneuver, massage, mold, negotiate, play, push around, shape, steer, upstage, use; *Ant* leave alone.

mannered [adj] *affected, put-on*
- *Syn* artificial, artsy, conscious, posed, pretentious, self-conscious, stilted, unnatural; *Ant* natural, unpretentious.

mannerly [adj] *polite, well-behaved*
- *Syn* charming, civil, civilized, considerate, courteous, decorous, genteel, gracious, polished, refined, respectful, well-bred, well-mannered; *Ant* crass, crude, gross, impolite, misbehaved, rude.

mansion [n] *very large house*
- *Syn* abode, building, castle, chateau, dwelling, estate, habitation, hall, home, manor, palace, residence, seat, villa; *Ant* hovel, hut, shack.

manual [adj] *done by hand*
- *Syn* hand-operated, physical; *Ant* automated, automatic.

manufacture [v] *build, produce*
- *Syn* accomplish, assemble, carve, cast,

complete, compose, construct, create, execute, fabricate, fashion, forge, form, frame, machine, make, make up, mass-produce, mill, mold, process, put together, shape, synthesize, throw together, tool, turn out; *Ant* destroy, ruin.

many [adj] *profuse, abundant*
- *Syn* abounding, alive with, bounteous, bountiful, copious, countless, crowded, divers, frequent, innumerable, legion, manifold, multifarious, multifold, multiplied, multitudinous, myriad, numberless, numerous, plentiful, populous, prevalent, profuse, rife, sundry, teeming, uncounted, varied, various; *Ant* few, scarce.

mar [v] *hurt, damage*
- *Syn* blemish, blight, blot, bruise, deface, deform, detract, disfigure, harm, impair, injure, maim, mangle, mutilate, ruin, scar, scratch, spoil, stain, sully, taint, tarnish, vitiate, warp, wreck; *Ant* aid, heal, help.

marginal [adj] *borderline; slight*
- *Syn* insignificant, minimal, minor, negligible, on the edge, peripheral, small; *Ant* central, interior, internal.

marine/maritime [adj] *concerning the sea* *Syn* aquatic, coastal, deep-sea, hydrographic, littoral, maritime, nautical, naval, Neptunian, oceanic, oceanographic, pelagic, seafaring, seaside, shore; *Ant* dryland, freshwater, land, terrestrial.

mariner [n] *person who makes living on the sea* *Syn* captain, crew, mate, navigator, sailor, seafarer, shipmate; *Ant* landlubber.

marital [adj] *concerning marriage*
- *Syn* conjugal, connubial, married, matrimonial, nuptial, spousal, wedded; *Ant* unmarried, unwed.

mark [v1] *blemish, stain*
- *Syn* blot, blotch, brand, bruise, chalk, dent, nick, scar, score, scratch, smudge, splotch, streak, stroke, trace; *Ant* clean, erase, remove, repair.

mark [v2] *characterize*
- *Syn* bespeak, brand, check off, demonstrate, designate, distinguish, earmark, evidence, evince, exhibit, feature, identify, illustrate, indicate, label, manifest, ostend, point out, qualify, remark, set apart, show, signify, singularize, stamp; *Ant* camouflage, conceal, conver, disguise, hide, mask, screen, veil.

mark [v3] *see, notice*
- *Syn* attend, behold, chronicle, discern,

distinguish, eye, hearken, mind, note, observe, pay attention, pay heed, perceive, regard, register, remark, take notice of, view, watch, write down; ▪ *Ant* disregard, ignore, overlook.

marked [*adj*] *apparent, obvious*
▪ *Syn* arresting, clear, considerable, conspicuous, distinct, evident, manifest, notable, outstanding, patent, prominent, remarkable, salient, striking; ▪ *Ant* ambiguous, obscure, unapparent, unnoticeable, vague.

markedly [*adv*] *distinctly*
▪ *Syn* clearly, considerably, conspicuously, decidedly, evidently, greatly, manifestly, notably, obviously, patently, remarkably, signally, strikingly, to a great extent; ▪ *Ant* imperceptibly, indistinctly, invisibly, unmarkedly.

market [*v*] *package and sell goods*
▪ *Syn* advertise, barter, display, exchange, merchandise, offer for sale, retail, vend, wholesale; ▪ *Ant* buy.

marketable [*adj*] *easily sold; in demand*
▪ *Syn* commercial, fit, for sale, merchandisable, profitable, salable, sellable, selling, sought after, sound, vendible, wanted; ▪ *Ant* undesirable, unmarketable.

maroon [*v*] *abandon*
▪ *Syn* beach, cast ashore, cast away, desert, forsake, isolate, leave, strand; ▪ *Ant* care, help, maintain, rescue, save.

marry [*v*] *become husband and wife in legal ceremony* ▪ *Syn* ally, associate, become one, bond, combine, conjugate, contract, couple, espouse, get married, join, knit, link, match, mate, merge, pledge, plight one's troth, promise, take vows, tie, unify, unite, wed, yoke; ▪ *Ant* divorce.

marshal [*v*] *organize, guide*
▪ *Syn* align, arrange, assemble, collect, deploy, direct, dispose, gather, group, lead, line up, methodize, mobilize, muster, order, rally, rank, shepherd, systematize, usher; ▪ *Ant* disorganize, scatter.

martial [*adj*] *having to do with armed hostilities* ▪ *Syn* aggressive, bellicose, belligerent, combative, hostile, military, pugnacious, soldierly, warlike; ▪ *Ant* civil, civilian, peaceful.

marvel [*v*] *be amazed*
▪ *Syn* be awed, be surprised, feel surprise, gape, gaze, goggle, stand in awe, stare, wonder; ▪ *Ant* expect.

marvelous [*adj1*] *hard to believe; amazing* ▪ *Syn* astonishing, astounding, awesome, awful, bewildering, breathtaking, confounding, extraordinary, fabulous, fantastic, implausible, improbable, incomprehensible, inconceivable, incredible, miraculous, phenomenal, prodigious, remarkable, singular, spectacular, staggering, strange, striking, stunning, stupendous, supernatural, surprising, unbelievable, unimaginable, unlikely, unusual, wonderful, wondrous; ▪ *Ant* believable, expected, ordinary, plain.

marvelous [*adj2*] *superb, great*
▪ *Syn* agreeable, colossal, divine, enjoyable, excellent, fabulous, fantastic, glorious, keen, magnificent, outrageous, pleasant, pleasurable, sensational, smashing, spectacular, splendid, stupendous, super, supreme, swell, terrific, wonderful; ▪ *Ant* inconsiderable, insignificant, paltry, worthless.

mask [*v*] *disguise*
▪ *Syn* beard, camouflage, cloak, conceal, cover, cover up, dress up, hide, obscure, safeguard, screen, secrete, shield, veil; ▪ *Ant* reveal, uncover, unmask.

masquerade [*v*] *disguise*
▪ *Syn* attitudinize, dissimulate, impersonate, mask, pass as, pass for, pose, posture, pretend, revel; ▪ *Ant* reveal, unmask.

massacre [*v*] *kill, often in great numbers*
▪ *Syn* annihilate, butcher, decimate, depopulate, exterminate, kill, mass murder, murder, slaughter, slay; ▪ *Ant* create, give birth.

massive [*adj*] *very large*
▪ *Syn* big, bulky, colossal, cracking, cumbersome, cumbrous, elephantine, enormous, extensive, gargantuan, gigantic, grand, great, gross, heavy, hefty, huge, hulking, immense, imposing, impressive, mammoth, mighty, monster, monumental, mountainous, ponderous, prodigious, solid, stately, substantial, titanic, towering, tremendous, unwieldy, vast, walloping, weighty; ▪ *Ant* little, miniature, small, tiny.

master [*n*] *person in charge, female or male* ▪ *Syn* administrator, boss, captain, chief, chieftain, commander, commanding officer, conqueror, controller, director, employer, general, governor, guide, head, instructor, judge, manager, overseer, owner, pedagogue, preceptor, principal, pro, ruler, skipper, spiritual leader, superintendent, supervisor, taskmaster, teacher, tutor; ▪ *Ant* crew, servant, subject, vassal.

master [*adj1*] *expert*
▪ *Syn* adept, experienced, masterly, proficient, skilled, skillful; ▪ *Ant* amateur.

master [*adj2*] *main*
▪ *Syn* chief, foremost, grand, leading, major, original, paramount, predominant, preponderant, prevalant, prime, principal, regnant, sovereign, supreme; ▪ *Ant* auxiliary, copy, duplicate, lesser, minor, subordinate.

master [*v1*] *learn; become proficient*
▪ *Syn* acquire, comprehend, excel in, gain mastery, grasp, grind, pick up, study, understand; ▪ *Ant* misapprehend, misconceive, misunderstand.

masterful [*adj1*] *expert, skilled*
▪ *Syn* adept, adroit, clever, consummate, crack, deft, dexterous, excellent, first-rate, master, masterly, preeminent, proficient, skillful, supreme, transcendent; ▪ *Ant* amateurish, bungling, incompetent, unproficient, unskilled.

match [*n1*] *counterpart, equal*
▪ *Syn* adversary, analogue, approximation, companion, competitor, complement, copy, correlate, countertype, double, equivalent, fellow, lookalike, mate, opponent, parallel, peer, replica, rival, twin; ▪ *Ant* difference, imbalance.

match [*n2*] *couple*
▪ *Syn* affiliation, alliance, combination, duet, espousal, marriage, mating, pair, pairing, partnership, union; ▪ *Ant* mismatch.

matching [*adj*] *corresponding, equal*
▪ *Syn* analogous, comparable, coordinating, double, duplicate, equivalent, identical, like, paired, parallel, same, twin; ▪ *Ant* different, uncorrespondent, unequal.

matchless [*adj*] *unequaled, unique*
▪ *Syn* consummate, incomparable, inimitable, nonpareil, paramount, peerless, superior, superlative, supreme, unapproached, unmatched, unparalleled, unrivaled; ▪ *Ant* common, commonplace, mediocre, regular, second-class, surpassed, usual.

mate [*v*] *marry and breed*
▪ *Syn* cohabit, copulate, couple, crossbreed, generate, join, match, merge, pair, procreate, serve, tie, wed; ▪ *Ant* abstain, uncouple.

material [*adj1*] *bodily, tangible*
▪ *Syn* actual, appreciable, carnal, concrete, corporeal, earthly, fleshly, incarnate, nonspiritual, objective, palpable, perceptible, physical, real, sensible, substantial, true, worldly; ▪ *Ant* ethereal, incorporeal, intangible, mental.

material [*adj2*] *important, relevant*
▪ *Syn* applicable, apropos, cardinal, consequential, considerable, essential, fundamental, germane, intrinsic, key, meaningful, momentous, pertinent, primary, serious, significant, substantial, vital, weighty; ▪ *Ant* immaterial, irrelevant, unimportant, unsubstantial.

materialistic [*adj*] *preoccupied with physical things* ▪ *Syn* acquisitive, earthy, greedy, mundane, possessive, profane, secular, temporal, terrestrial, unspiritual; ▪ *Ant* idealistic, spiritual, thrifty.

materialize [*v*] *come into being*
▪ *Syn* appear, become concrete, coalesce, come about, come to pass, develop, embody, emerge, evolve, happen, manifest, metamorphose, occur, personify, realize, substantiate, take form, take shape, typify, unfold, visualize; ▪ *Ant* disappear, dissolve, evaporate, fade away, vanish.

matriculate [*v*] *begin, enroll*
▪ *Syn* enter, join, register, sign up for; ▪ *Ant* graduate.

matrimony [*n*] *being joined in marriage*
▪ *Syn* alliance, conjugality, connubiality, marital rites, marriage, match, nuptials, union, wedding, wedding ceremony, wedlock; ▪ *Ant* divorce.

matted [*adj*] *tangled*
▪ *Syn* disordered, kinky, knotted, rumpled, snarled, tousled, twisted, uncombed; ▪ *Ant* silken, smooth, unknotted, untangled.

matter [*n*] *substance*
▪ *Syn* amount, being, body, constituents, corporeality, corporeity, element, entity, individual, material, materialness, object, phenomenon, physical world, protoplasm, quantity, stuff, substantiality, sum, thing; ▪ *Ant* nothing, nothingness, soul, spirit, zero.

matter [*v*] *be of consequence, importance*
▪ *Syn* affect, be important, be of value, be substantive, carry weight, count, express, have influence, imply, import, involve, make a difference, mean, mean something, signify, value, weigh; ▪ *Ant* be inconsequential, be insignificant, be unimportant, make no difference.

matter-of-fact [adj] *realistic, unembellished* ▪ **Syn** calm, deadpan, direct, earthy, emotionless, factual, flat, frank, impassive, impersonal, mundane, objective, phlegmatic, plain, practical, pragmatic, prosaic, straight-forward, unaffected, unimpassioned, unsentimental, unvarnished; ▪ **Ant** emotional, imaginative, lively, speculative, theoretical.

mature [adj] *adult, grown-up* ▪ **Syn** cultivated, cultured, developed, full-blown, full-fledged, full-grown, fully grown, grown, in full bloom, in one's prime, mellow, mellowed, of age, prepared, prime, ready, ripe, ripened, seasoned, settled, sophisticated; ▪ **Ant** green, immature, inexperienced, juvenile, young, youthful.

maudlin [adj] *teary, overemotional* ▪ **Syn** bathetic, befuddled, confused, emotional, gushing, insipid, lachrymose, mawkish, romantic, sentimental, tearful, weak, weepy; ▪ **Ant** calm, matter-of-fact, realistic, unimaginative.

maul [v] *mangle, abuse* ▪ **Syn** bang, bash, batter, beat, beat up, bludgeon, claw, drub, flagellate, flail, handle roughly, hit, hurt, ill-treat, lacerate, lash, maltreat, manhandle, molest, muscle, paw, pelt, pound, pummel, rough up, skin, thrash, trample, wax, whip; ▪ **Ant** guard, maintain, protect, take care.

maverick [n] *person who takes chances, departs from accepted course* ▪ **Syn** bohemian, dissenter, eccentric, extremist, malcontent, nonconformist, radical; ▪ **Ant** conformist, conservative, follower.

mawkish [adj] *sentimental, emotional* ▪ **Syn** bathetic, cloying, feeble, gushing, maudlin, romantic, sloppy, teary; ▪ **Ant** calm, serious, unemotional.

maximum [adj] *highest, utmost* ▪ **Syn** best, biggest, greatest, largest, maximal, most, outside, paramount, superlative, supreme, top, topmost, ultimate; ▪ **Ant** least, lowest, minimum, smallest.

maybe [adv] *possibly* ▪ **Syn** conceivable, conceivably, could be, credible, feasible, imaginably, it could be, might be, obtainable, perchance, perhaps, weather permitting; ▪ **Ant** certainly, definitely, surely.

mayhem [n] *chaos, confusion* ▪ **Syn** anarchy, commotion, destruction, disorder, fracas, havoc, pandemonium, trouble, violence; ▪ **Ant** calm, harmony, peace.

meager [adj1] *small, inadequate; poor* ▪ **Syn** bare, barren, deficient, exiguous, flimsy, inappreciable, inconsiderable, insubstantial, insufficient, little, mere, paltry, puny, scant, scanty, scrimpy, shabby, short, skimpy, slender, slight, spare, sparse, tenuous, wanting, weak; ▪ **Ant** adequate, large, liberal, plenty, substantial, sufficient.

meager [adj2] *very thin* ▪ **Syn** angular, anorexic, bony, emaciated, gangly, gaunt, hungry, lank, lean, lithe, narrow, rawboned, scrawny, skinny, slender, slim, spare, starved, tenuous, underfed, willowy, withered; ▪ **Ant** big, fat, full, large, wide.

mean [n] *average* ▪ **Syn** balance, center, commonplace, happy medium, median, middle, middle course, midpoint, norm, par; ▪ **Ant** extreme, ultimate.

mean [adj1] *stingy* ▪ **Syn** avaracious, cheap, close-fisted, greedy, mercenary, mingy, miserly, niggard, niggardly, parsimonious, penurious, rapacious, scrimpy, selfish, tight; ▪ **Ant** generous, kind, unselfish.

mean [adj2] *hostile, rude* ▪ **Syn** bad-tempered, callous, cantankerous, churlish, despicable, difficult, disagreeable, evil, formidable, hard, ignoble, infamous, knavish, liverish, malicious, nasty, perfidious, scurrilous, sour, unpleasant, vicious, vile; ▪ **Ant** agreeable, compassionate, humane, kind, nice, noble, polite, sympathetic.

mean [adj3] *poor; of or in inferior circumstances* ▪ **Syn** base, beggarly, common, humble, ignoble, inferior, limited, low, lowborn, lowly, miserable, modest, narrow, ordinary, paltry, petty, pitiful, plebeian, proletarian, second-rate, servile, squalid, tawdry, undistinguished, unwashed, vulgar, wretched; ▪ **Ant** lucky, profuse, rich, superior.

meander [v] *wander, zigzag* ▪ **Syn** change, drift, extravagate, gallivant, get sidetracked, peregrinate, ramble, range, recoil, roam, rove, snake, stray, stroll, traipse, turn, twine, twist, wind; ▪ **Ant** go directly, stay on path.

meaningful [adj] *significant* ▪ **Syn** clear, concise, consequential, considerable, deep, eloquent, essential, exact, explicit, expressive, heavy, important, intelligible, material, momentous, pointed, pregnant, purposeful, relevant, sententious, serious, substantial, succinct, suggestive, useful, valid, weighty, worthwhile; ▪ **Ant** insignificant, meaningless, useless, worthless.

meaningless [adj] *without use, value, worth* ▪ **Syn** absurd, aimless, blank, empty, feckless, fustian, good-for-nothing, hollow, inane, inconsequential, nonsensical, nugatory, pointless, purposeless, senseless, trifling, unimportant, useless, vacant, vain, valueless, vapid, worthless; ▪ **Ant** meaningful, significant, useful, valuable, worthwhile.

means [n] *wealth, resources*
▪ **Syn** affluence, assets, backing, bankroll, budget, capital, estate, fortune, holdings, income, money, pocket, possessions, property, purse, revenue, riches, savings, securities, substance, wherewithal; ▪ **Ant** paucity, poorness, shame.

measly [adj] *skimpy*
▪ **Syn** beggarly, contemptible, insignificant, meager, mean, miserable, miserly, paltry, pathetic, petty, picayune, pitiful, poor, puny, scanty, stingy, trifling, trivial, ungenerous, unimportant, valueless, worthless; ▪ **Ant** abundant, plenty, satisfactory, sufficient.

measurable [adj] *determinable*
▪ **Syn** assessable, calculable, computable, fathomable, gaugeable, material, mensurable, perceptible, quantifiable, quantitative, significant, surveyable, weighable; ▪ **Ant** imperceptible, incalculable, insignificant, undeterminable, unmeasurable.

measure [v] *calculate, judge*
▪ **Syn** adapt, adjust, align, appraise, assess, calibrate, check, compute, delimit, demarcate, determine; estimate, evaluate, figure, gauge, gradate, grade, graduate, limit, mark, mark out, mete, pace off, plumb, portion, quantify, rank, rate, read, reckon, rule, scale, size up, square, survey, tailor, time, value, weigh; ▪ **Ant** estimate, guess.

meat [n] *core, gist*
▪ **Syn** essence, heart, kernel, marrow, matter, nub, nucleus, pith, point, sense, short, substance, thrust, upshot; ▪ **Ant** exterior, exteriority, outside.

meaty [adj] *significant*
▪ **Syn** epigrammatic, factual, full of content, interesting, meaningful, pithy, pointed, profound, rich, substantial, weighty; ▪ **Ant** insignificant, thin.

mechanical [adj] *done by machine; machinelike* ▪ **Syn** automated, cold, emotionless, fixed, habitual, impersonal, involuntary, lifeless, matter-of-fact, monotonous, perfunctory, programmed, routine, spiritless, standardized, unconscious, unfeeling, unthinking, useful; ▪ **Ant** by hand, conscious, feeling, manual.

meddle [v] *intervene, interfere*
▪ **Syn** barge in, chime in, dabble in, encroach, encumber, fool with, hinder, impede, interlope, intervene, intrude, invade, mix in, molest, obtrude, pry, snoop, tamper, trespass; ▪ **Ant** avoid, dodge, ignore, stay out of.

meddlesome [adj] *interfereing*
▪ **Syn** curious, encumbering, hindering, impeding, interposing, intruding, intrusive, mischievous, nosy, obstructive, prying, pushy, tampering, troublesome; ▪ **Ant** avoiding, dodging, indifferent, standoffish.

median [n/adj] *middle*
▪ **Syn** average, center, centermost, central, equidistant, halfway, intermediary, intermediate, mean, medial, mid, middlemost, midmost, midpoint, midway, par; ▪ **Ant** extreme, outside.

mediate [v] *try to bring to an agreement*
▪ **Syn** arbitrate, bring to terms, conciliate, deal, intercede, interpose, intervene, moderate, negotiate, propitiate, reconcile, referee, resolve, step in, trade off, umpire; ▪ **Ant** argue, contend, disagree, fight.

mediator [n] *person who negotiates agreement* ▪ **Syn** advocate, agent, arbiter, arbitrator, broker, conciliator, fixer, interceder, intermediary, intermediator, judge, medium, moderator, negotiator, peacemaker, referee, umpire; ▪ **Ant** arguer, fighter.

medicine/medication [n] *substance that helps cure, alleviate, or prevent illness* ▪ **Syn** antibiotic, antidote, antitoxin, balm, biologic, capsule, cure, dose, drug, elixir, inoculation, liniment, lotion, ointment, pharmaceutical, pill, potion, prescription, remedy, salve, serum, tablet, tincture, tonic, vaccination, vaccine; ▪ **Ant** bane, poison, toxin.

medieval [adj] *having to do with the Middle Ages; very old* ▪ **Syn** antediluvian, antiquated, antique, archaic, feudal, Gothic, old, old-fashioned, primitive, unenlightened; ▪ **Ant** modern.

mediocre [*adj*] *average, commonplace*
▪ *Syn* colorless, common, conventional, dull, fair, indifferent, mainstream, mean, medium, ordinary, pedestrian, second-rate, standard, tolerable, undistinguished, unexceptional; ▪ *Ant* exceptional, extraordinary, inferior, superior, uncommon, unusual.

meditate [*v*] *think deeply about*
▪ *Syn* brood over, cogitate, consider, contemplate, deliberate, design, devise, figure, mull over, plan, ponder, puzzle over, reflect, ruminate, scheme, speculate, study, think, think over, view, weigh; ▪ *Ant* act, commit oneself, decide, perform.

medium [*adj*] *midway, average*
▪ *Syn* common, commonplace, fair, intermediate, mean, medial, median, middle, middling, moderate, neutral, normal, ordinary, par, passable, standard, tolerable; ▪ *Ant* extreme, limit.

meek [*adj*] *very shy; compliant*
▪ *Syn* acquiescent, deferential, docile, forbearing, gentle, humble, lenient, mild, passive, resigned, soft, spineless, spiritless, subdued, submissive, tame, timid, tolerant, unassuming, weak, yielding; ▪ *Ant* bold, brave, immodest, impertinent, uninhibited.

meet [*adj*] *fitting*
▪ *Syn* applicable, appropriate, apt, conformed, equitable, fair, felicitous, fit, good, just, proper, reconciled, right, suitable, timely; ▪ *Ant* improper, inappropriate, unfitting, unseemly.

meet [*v1*] *happen on*
▪ *Syn* brush against, bump into, chance on, collide, come across, come up against, confront, contact, cross, encounter, engage, face, find, front, get together, greet, meet face to face, rendezvous with, run across, run into, run up against, salute, see; ▪ *Ant* avoid, elude, miss.

meet [*v2*] *connect, join*
▪ *Syn* abut, adhere, adjoin, border, coincide, connect, converge, cross, intersect, link, link up, reach, touch, unite; ▪ *Ant* disconnect, disjoin, divide, separate.

meet [*v3*] *perform, carry out*
▪ *Syn* answer, approach, come up to, comply, cope with, discharge, equal, execute, fit, fulfill, gratify, handle, match, measure up, rival, satisfy, suffice, tie, touch; ▪ *Ant* fail, fall short, renege.

meet [*v4*] *come together, convene*
▪ *Syn* appear, assemble, be introduced, be present, be presented, collect, congregate, converge, enter in, flock, foregather, gather, get together, get to know, join, make acquaintance, muster, rendezvous; ▪ *Ant* adjourn, scatter.

melancholy [*adj*] *sad, depressed*
▪ *Syn* dejected, despondent, disconsolate, dispirited, doleful, downcast, downhearted, funereal, gloomy, grim, heavyhearted, joyless, lachrymose, low-spirited, lugubrious, mirthless, moody, pensive, saddened, somber, sorrowful, trite, unhappy, wistful, woebegone; ▪ *Ant* cheerful, happy, joyful.

melange [*n*] *mixture*
▪ *Syn* assortment, combo, farrago, gallimaufry, hodgepodge, jumble, medley, miscellany, mishmash, mix, mixed bag, pasticcio, pastiche, patchwork, potpourri, salmagundi, soup, stew; ▪ *Ant* singularity.

meld [*v*] *blend, bring together*
▪ *Syn* amalgamate, associate, blend, compound, dissolve, fuse, intermingle, marry, merge, mingle, mix, unite; ▪ *Ant* divide, separate.

melee [*n*] *battle, fight*
▪ *Syn* affray, brawl, broil, brush, clash, fracas, fray, row, ruckus, ruction, rumpus, scrimmage, scuffle, skirmish, tussle, words; ▪ *Ant* agreement, peace.

mellow [*adj*] *ripe, mature; softened*
▪ *Syn* aged, cultured, cured, dulcet, flavorful, full-flavored, fully developed, juicy, matured, mellifluous, perfect, ripened, rounded, sapid, savory, seasoned, sweet, tuneful; ▪ *Ant* hard, immature, sour, tart, unripe.

mellow [*v*] *ripen, mature*
▪ *Syn* age, arrive, develop, grow, grow up, improve, maturate, milden, mollify, perfect, ripe, season, settle down, soften, sweeten; ▪ *Ant* brutalize, harden.

melodious/melodic [*adj*] *harmonious, musical* ▪ *Syn* accordant, assonant, canorous, dulcet, euphonic, harmonic, mellifluous, pleasing, resonant, silvery, sweet-sounding, symphonic, symphonious, tuneful, well-tuned; ▪ *Ant* cacophonous, discordant, grating, harsh, inharmonious, unmelodic, unmusical.

melodramatic [*adj*] *extravagant in speech, behavior* ▪ *Syn* artificial, exaggerated, histrionic, overdramatic, over-emotional, sensational, spectacular, stagy, theatrical; ▪*Ant* calm, normal, untheatrical.

melody [*n*] *harmony, tune*
▪ *Syn* aria, assonance, carillon, chant, chime, concord, consonance, descant, diapason, euphony, inflection, lay, lyric, measure, music, musicality, refrain, resonance, run, song, strain, theme, tunefulness, unison; ▪*Ant* cacophony, disharmony.

melt [*v1*] *liquefy; dissolve*
▪ *Syn* deliquesce, disintegrate, evaporate, fade, flow, flux, fuse, heat, merge, render, smelt, soften, thaw, warm; ▪*Ant* coagulate, condense, solidify.

melt [*v2*] *give in, yield*
▪ *Syn* become lenient, disarm, forgive, mollify, relax, relent, show mercy, soften, touch; ▪*Ant* harden, make callous, resist.

memorable [*adj*] *noteworthy, significant*
▪ *Syn* celebrated, enduring, extraordinary, famous, great, historic, illustrious, important, indelible, lasting, meaningful, momentous, notable, signal, standout, striking, terrific, top-drawer, unforgettable; ▪*Ant* forgettable, insignificant, pedestrian, unimpressive, unnoteworthy.

memorial [*adj*] *commemorative*
▪ *Syn* canonizing, celebrative, commemoratory, consecrative, dedicatory, deifying, enshrining, in tribute, memorializing, monumental; ▪*Ant* abusive, dishonorable.

menace [*v*] *bother, frighten*
▪ *Syn* alarm, browbeat, bully, compromise, endanger, hazard, impend, imperil, intimidate, jeopardize, loom, lower, overhang, peril, portend, risk, scare, spook, terrorize, threaten, torment; ▪*Ant* aid, assist, help.

menacing [*adj*] *intimidating, ominous*
▪ *Syn* alarming, approaching, dangerous, frightening, imminent, impending, looming, louring, lowering, minacious, overhanging, threatening; ▪*Ant* aiding, assisting, helping, unthreatening.

mend [*v*] *correct, improve, fix*
▪ *Syn* ameliorate, amend, better, convalesce, darn, doctor, get better, heal, knit, overhaul, patch, ready, rebuild, reconstruct, rectify, recuperate, redress, refurbish, rejuvenate, remedy, renovate, restore, revamp, service, sew; ▪*Ant*

break, damage, destroy, hurt, lacerate, ruin, tear, weaken.

mendacious [*adj*] *dishonest*
▪ *Syn* deceitful, equivocating, fallacious, fraudulent, insincere, knavish, lying, perfidious, prevaricating, shifty, spurious, untruthful, wrong; ▪*Ant* frank, honest, open, sincere, truthful.

menial [*adj*] *lowly, servile*
▪ *Syn* abject, base, baseborn, common, degrading, demeaning, fawning, grovelling, humdrum, ignominious, low, obsequious, routine, sorry, subservient, sycophantic, unskilled; ▪*Ant* aristocratic, arrogant, elevated, noble, overbearing, skilled, superior, talented.

mental [*adj1*] *concerning the mind*
▪ *Syn* abstract, brainy, cerebral, deep, ideological, imaginative, intellectual, phrenic, psychic, psychological, rational, reasoning, spiritual, subconscious, subjective, subliminal, thinking, thoughtful; ▪*Ant* body, physical.

mental [*adj2*] *insane*
▪ *Syn* deranged, disturbed, fruity, lunatic, mad, mentally ill, mindless, non compos mentis, psychotic, unbalanced, unstable; ▪*Ant* balanced, sane.

mention [*v*] *refer to*
▪ *Syn* acknowledge, acquaint, adduce, advert, allude to, bring up, broach, call attention to, cite, declare, designate, detail, disclose, discuss, divulge, enumerate, hint at, impart, infer, intimate, introduce, make known, name, notice, notify, observe, point out, point to, quote, recount, remark, report, reveal, speak about, speak of, specify, state, suggest, tell, touch on; ▪*Ant* disregard, drop, forget, ignore, neglect, omit, overlook, slight.

mercenary [*adj*] *greedy for money*
▪ *Syn* acquisitive, avaricious, corrupt, covetous, grasping, money-grubbing, selfish, sordid, stingy, unethical, unprincipled, unscrupulous, venal; ▪*Ant* generous, idealistic, philanthropic, unselfish.

merchandise [*v*] *sell goods*
▪ *Syn* advertise, buy and sell, deal in, distribute, market, promote, publicize, retail, trade, traffic in, vend, wholesale; ▪*Ant* buy.

merchant [*n*] *person who sells goods*
▪ *Syn* broker, consigner, dealer, exporter, handler, jobber, marketer, operator, retailer, seller, shipper, shopkeeper, store-

keeper, trader, trafficker, tycoon, vendor, wholesaler; ▪ *Ant* buyer, customer.

merciful [*adj*] *kind, sparing*
▪ *Syn* benign, charitable, compassionate, easygoing, forgiving, generous, gentle, gracious, humane, humanitarian, indulgent, kindly, lenient, liberal, mild, pardoning, pitying, sympathetic, tender, tolerant; ▪ *Ant* cruel, merciless, pitiless, unforgiving, unkind, unmerciful.

merciless [*adj*] *mean, heartless*
▪ *Syn* barbarous, callous, compassionless, cruel, cutthroat, fierce, gratuitous, grim, hard, harsh, implacable, inexorable, iron-fisted, mortal, pitiless, ruthless, severe, unappeasable, unfeeling, unflinching, unpitying, unsparing, unyielding, wanton; ▪ *Ant* giving, kind, lenient, merciful, nice, sympathetic.

mercurial [*adj*] *flighty, temperamental*
▪ *Syn* buoyant, capricious, changeable, erratic, flaky, flighty, fluctuating, impulsive, inconstant, irregular, irrepressible, lively, mobile, movable, quicksilver, spirited, unpredictable, unstable, variable, volatile; ▪ *Ant* phlegmatic, unchangeable, unperturbable, unvarying.

meretricious [*adj*] *gaudy, pretentious*
▪ *Syn* blatant, bogus, brazen, chintzy, counterfeit, garish, glaring, insincere, loud, misleading, ornate, phony, showy, spurious, superficial, tawdry, tinsel, trashy; ▪ *Ant* bona fide, genuine, real, undecorated, unembellished.

merge [*v*] *bring or come together*
▪ *Syn* absorb, amalgamate, assimilate, become partners, blend, cement, centralize, coalesce, combine, compound, conglomerate, consolidate, converge, fuse, incorporate, join, marry, meld, melt into, mingle, mix, pool, submerge, synthesize, tag, tie in, unite; ▪ *Ant* divide, part, separate.

meridian [*n*] *summit, climax*
▪ *Syn* acme, apex, apogee, crest, culmination, extremity, high noon, high-water mark, peak, pinnacle, zenith; ▪ *Ant* bottom, depths, low, nadir, perigee.

meritorious [*adj*] *honorable, commendable*
▪ *Syn* admirable, choice, creditable, deserving, estimable, excellent, exemplary, golden, good, laudable, meritable, noble, praisable, praiseworthy, right, righteous, thankworthy, virtuous, worthy; ▪ *Ant* corrupt, dishonorable, immoral, improper, unworthy, wrong.

merry [*adj*] *very happy; festive*
▪ *Syn* amusing, blithe, blithesome, boisterous, boon, carefree, cheerful, comic, comical, convivial, enjoyable, entertaining, facetious, festive, frolicsome, fun-loving, funny, gay, glad, gleeful, hilarious, humorous, jocund, jolly, joyful, joyous, lighthearted, lively, mirthful, perky, pleasant, rollicking, saturnalian, sportive, sunny, unconstrained, uproarious, vivacious, wild, winsome; ▪ *Ant* grave, sad, serious, sorrowful, unhappy, upset.

mesh [*v*] *entangle, connect*
▪ *Syn* agree, catch, coincide, combine, come together, coordinate, dovetail, engage, enmesh, ensnare, fit, fit together, harmonize, interlock, knit, net, snare, tangle, trap; ▪ *Ant* disconnect, unmesh, untangle.

mesmerize [*v*] *captivate*
▪ *Syn* catch up, control, deaden, drug, ensorcell, enthrall, entrance, fascinate, grip, hold spellbound, hypnotize, magnetize, numb, spellbind, stupefy; ▪ *Ant* disenchant, turn off.

mess around [*v*] *fiddle; goof off*
▪ *Syn* amuse oneself, dabble, dawdle, doodle, fool around, loiter, play, play around, potter, puddle, putter, tinker, trifle; ▪ *Ant* labor, toil, work.

messenger [*n*] *person carrying information to another* ▪ *Syn* agent, ambassador, bearer, carrier, commissionaire, courier, crier, delegate, detachment, detail, dispatcher, emissary, envoy, flag-bearer, forerunner, harbinger, herald, intermediary, internuncio, mediator, minister, post, prophet, runner; ▪ *Ant* receiver.

mess up [*v*] *disorder, dirty*
▪ *Syn* befoul, besmirch, bobble, botch, bungle, clutter, confuse, damage, derange, destroy, disarrange, discompose, dishevel, disorganize, disturb, foul, jumble, litter, louse up, muddle, pollute, ruin, rummage, scramble, smear, soil, spoil, unsettle, upset; ▪ *Ant* arrange, order, organize, tidy.

messy [*adj*] *cluttered, dirty*
▪ *Syn* careless, chaotic, confused, disheveled, disordered, disorganized, grimy, littered, muddled, rumpled, sloppy, slovenly, unkempt, untidy; ▪ *Ant* clean, fastidious, ordered, organized, uncluttered.

metamorphosis [n] *conversion, transformation* ▪ **Syn** alteration, change, changeover, development, evolution, mutation, rebirth, transfiguration, translation, transmogrification, transmutation, transubstantiation; ▪ **Ant** stagnation.

metaphor [n] *figure of speech, implied comparison* ▪ **Syn** allegory, analogy, emblem, hope, image, metonymy, personification, similitude, symbol, trope; ▪ **Ant** plain speech.

metaphysical [adj] *not physical; without physical presence* ▪ **Syn** abstract, abstruse, bodiless, deep, difficult, esoteric, fundamental, impalpable, intangible, mystical, nonphysical, preternatural, profound, recondite, spiritual, superhuman, supermundane, supernatural, theoretical, transcendental, unearthly, universal; ▪ **Ant** concrete, down-to-earth, material, objective, physical, real, solid, substantial, tangible.

meteoric [adj] *brief, sudden* ▪ **Syn** dazzling, ephemeral, flashing, fleeting, momentary, overnight, rapid, spectacular, speedy, swift, transient; ▪ **Ant** gradual, obscure, slow.

methodical/methodic [adj] *organized, precise* ▪ **Syn** analytical, by the numbers, careful, deliberate, disciplined, efficient, exact, logical, methodized, meticulous, neat, orderly, painstaking, planned, regular, scrupulous, systematic, together, well-regulated; ▪ **Ant** chaotic, confused, disorderly, disorganized, haphazard, imprecise, unmethodical/unmethodic.

meticulous [adj] *detailed, perfectionist* ▪ **Syn** accurate, cautious, conscientious, exact, fastidious, fussy, microscopic, painstaking, particular, picky, punctilious, scrupulous, strict, thorough; ▪ **Ant** careless, messy, sloppy, undetailed.

metropolitan [adj] *concerning a city* ▪ **Syn** cosmopolitan, municipal, urban, urbane; ▪ **Ant** pastoral, rural.

mettle [n] *boldness, strength of character* ▪ **Syn** animation, ardor, backbone, caliber, courage, daring, dauntlessness, energy, fire, force, gallantry, gameness, indomitability, moxie, nerve, pluck, resolve, spirit, spunk, stamina, temper, valor, vigor, vitality; ▪ **Ant** cowardice, weakness.

microscopic [adj] *very tiny, almost undetectable* ▪ **Syn** atomic, diminutive, imperceptible, infinitesimal, invisible, little, minuscule, minute, negligible; ▪ **Ant** big, huge, large, macroscopic.

middle [adj] *central* ▪ **Syn** average, between, center, centermost, equidistant, halfway, inner, inside, intermediate, intervening, mainstream, mean, medial, median, medium, middlemost, midmost, smack in the middle; ▪ **Ant** border, extreme, outer, outside.

middling [adj] *adequate, OK* ▪ **Syn** average, common, conventional, decent, fair, intermediate, mediocre, medium, moderate, modest, okay, ordinary, passable, tolerable, traditional, unexceptional, unremarkable; ▪ **Ant** exceptional, extraordinary.

midget [adj] *very short, small* ▪ **Syn** baby, diminutive, dwarf, dwarfish, Lilliputian, miniature, minikin, pocket, pygmy, tiny; ▪ **Ant** big, giant, huge, large, tall.

midst [n] *middle, core* ▪ **Syn** bosom, center, deep, depths, halfway, heart, hub, interior, mean, medium, midpoint, nucleus, thick; ▪ **Ant** exterior, exteriority, outside.

miff [v] *annoy* ▪ **Syn** aggrieve, bother, displease, hurt, irk, irritate, nettle, offend, pester, pique, provoke, put out, upset, vex; ▪ **Ant** appease, mollify, please.

mightily [adv1] *very much, extremely* ▪ **Syn** decidedly, exceedingly, greatly, highly, hugely, intensely, mighty, much, notably, surpassingly, very; ▪ **Ant** little.

mightily [adv2] *forcefully* ▪ **Syn** arduously, energetically, forcibly, hard, hardly, lustily, powerfully, strenuously, strongly, vigorously, with all one's strength; ▪ **Ant** feebly, impotently, weakly.

mighty [adj1] *forceful, powerful* ▪ **Syn** doughty, hardy, indomitable, lusty, omnipotent, potent, powerhouse, robust, stalwart, stout, strapping, strong, sturdy, vigorous, wieldy; ▪ **Ant** delicate, powerless, weak.

mighty [adj2] *gigantic, monumental* ▪ **Syn** august, colossal, considerable, dynamic, eminent, enormous, grand, great, heroic, illustrious, imposing, impressive, irresistible, large, magnificent, majestic, notable, prodigious, renowned, stupendous, titanic, towering, tremendous, vast; ▪ **Ant** insignificant, small, tiny, unimportant.

migrant/migratory [adj] moving, traveling ▪ **Syn** changing, drifting, emigrating, errant, gypsy, immigrant, immigrating, impermanent, itinerant, mobile, nomadic, peripatetic, ranging, roving, seasonal, shifting, temporary, transient, transmigratory, unsettled, vagabond, vagrant, wandering; ▪ **Ant** resident, stationary.

mild [adj1] gentle, temperate, nonirritating ▪ **Syn** balmy, benign, benignant, bland, breezy, calm, clement, cool, demulcent, easy, faint, flat, genial, lenient, light, lukewarm, medium, mellow, moderate, mollifying, pacific, peaceful, placid, smooth, soft, soothing, tempered, tepid, untroubled, warm, weak; ▪ **Ant** fierce, harsh, rough, violent.

mild [adj2] easygoing, pleasant in personality ▪ **Syn** amiable, calm, clement, complaisant, deferential, docile, easy, forbearant, forbearing, gentle, goodnatured, humane, indulgent, jejune, kind, lenient, meek, mellow, merciful, mildmannered, moderate, obeisant, obliging, pacific, patient, placid, serene, soft, subdued, submissive, tame, temperate, tender, tranquil, unassuming, vapid, warm; ▪ **Ant** agitated, flappable, nervous.

militant [adj] aggressive, combative ▪ **Syn** active, assertive, bellicose, belligerent, combative, contentious, martial, offensive, pugnacious, pushy, quarrelsome, scrappy, self-assertive, truculent, up in arms, vigorous, warlike, warring; ▪ **Ant** compliant, peaceful, peaceloving, submissive, tolerant.

military [adj] soldierlike; concerning the armed forces ▪ **Syn** aggressive, armed, army, chauvinistic, combative, fighting, martial, militant, militaristic, noncivil, soldierly, warlike, warmongering; ▪ **Ant** civilian.

milk [v] tap; exploit ▪ **Syn** bleed, drain, draw off, elicit, empty, exhaust, extort, extract, fleece, impose on, press, pump, siphon, suck, take advantage, use, wring; ▪ **Ant** hoard, save.

milky [adj] white, cloudy ▪ **Syn** alabaster, clouded, frosted, lacteal, lacteous, lactescent, milk-white, opalescent, opaline, opaque, pearly, whitish; ▪ **Ant** clear, pristine.

mince [v] euphemize, hold back in communication ▪ **Syn** alleviate, decrease, diminish, extenuate, lessen, minimize, moderate, palliate, soften, spare, tone down, weaken; ▪ **Ant** reveal, tell all.

mincing [adj] affected, pretentious ▪ **Syn** artificial, fastidious, finicky, fussy, insincere, particular, persnickety, precious, stilted, unnatural; ▪ **Ant** extroverted, unaffected, unpretentious.

mind [v1] comply, obey ▪ **Syn** adhere to, attend, behave, do as told, follow, follow orders, heed, listen, mark, note, notice, observe, pay attention, pay heed, regard, respect, take heed, watch; ▪ **Ant** disobey, disregard, ignore.

mind [v2] attend, tend ▪ **Syn** baby-sit, be attentive, behold, care for, discern, discipline, ensure, give heed to, govern, guard, have charge of, listen up, look, make certain, mark, note, notice, observe, oversee, perceive, regard, see, sit, superintend, supervise, watch; ▪ **Ant** ignore, neglect.

mind [v3] be careful ▪ **Syn** be cautious, be concerned, be on guard, be solicitous, be wary, have a care, take care, tend, trouble, watch; ▪ **Ant** forget, neglect, throw caution to the wind.

mind [v4] remember ▪ **Syn** bethink, bring to mind, cite, recall, recollect, remind, reminisce, retain; ▪ **Ant** forget.

mindful [adj] attentive, aware ▪ **Syn** alert, apprehensive, cautious, chary, conscientious, conversant, heedful, in the know, knowledgeable, observant, regardful, solicitous, thoughtful, vigilant, wary, watchful; ▪ **Ant** absentminded, careless, heedless, inattentive, unaware.

mindless [adj] oblivious, stupid; automatic ▪ **Syn** asinine, brutish, careless, daydreaming, foolish, forgetful, gratuitous, heedless, idiotic, inattentive, mooning, moronic, neglectful, obtuse, rash, senseless, silly, thoughtless, unaware, unintelligent, unthinking, witless; ▪ **Ant** careful, considerate, intelligent, mindful, sane, thinking, thoughtful.

mine [v] dig up ▪ **Syn** burrow, delve, dig for, drill, excavate, extract, hew, pan, quarry, shovel, unearth; ▪ **Ant** bury.

mingle [v] physically join ▪ **Syn** admix, alloy, blend, coalesce, commingle, compound, intermix, make up, marry, meld, merge, mix, unite, wed; ▪ *Ant* disjoin.

miniature [adj] *tiny*
▪ *Syn* baby, diminutive, elfin, Lilliputian, little, minuscule, minute, model, petite, pint-sized, pocket, reduced, scaled-down, small, toy, wee; ▪ *Ant* big, full-size, giant, huge, large.

minimal [adj] *littlest, slightest*
▪ *Syn* basic, least, least possible, lowest, minimum, nominal, smallest, token; ▪ *Ant* maximum, most.

minimize [v] *make smaller; underrate*
▪ *Syn* abbreviate, attenuate, belittle, cheapen, curtail, decrease, decry, deprecate, derogate, detract, diminish, discount, disparage, lessen, make little of, miniaturize, pan, play down, prune, put down, reduce, run down, shrink, underestimate, underplay; ▪ *Ant* enlarge, maximize, overestimate, overrate.

minimum [adj] *least, lowest*
▪ *Syn* least possible, littlest, merest, minimal, slightest, smallest, tiniest; ▪ *Ant* largest, maximum, most.

minister [v] *help, serve*
▪ *Syn* accommodate, administer, aid, attend, cater to, cure, doctor, do for, foster, heal, nurse, succor, take care of, tend, treat, wait on, watch over; ▪ *Ant* hurt, injure.

minor [n] *person under legal age of maturity* ▪ *Syn* adolescent, baby, boy, child, girl, infant, junior, juvenile, lad, little one, schoolboy, schoolgirl, teenager, underage, youngster, youth; ▪ *Ant* adult.

minor [adj] *insignificant, small*
▪ *Syn* casual, inconsequential, inconsiderable, inferior, junior, lesser, light, negligible, paltry, secondary, smaller, small-time, subordinate, trivial, unimportant, younger; ▪ *Ant* adult, greater, large, major, significant.

mint [adj] *brand-new*
▪ *Syn* excellent, first-class, fresh, intact, original, perfect, unblemished, undamaged, unmarred, untarnished, virgin; ▪ *Ant* ancient, damaged, imperfect, old, used.

minute [adj1] *very small*
▪ *Syn* atomic, diminutive, exact, exiguous, fine, inconsiderable, infinitesimal, insignificant, invisible, little, microbic, microscopic, minimal, minuscule, molecular, piddling, puny, slender, tiny, wee; ▪ *Ant* big, giant, gigantic, huge, large, mighty.

minute [adj2] *unimportant*
▪ *Syn* immaterial, inconsiderable, insignificant, light, little, minor, negligible, nonessential, paltry, petty, picayune, piddling, puny, slight, small, trifling, trivial; ▪ *Ant* consequential, considerable, important, substantial, trivial.

minute [adj3] *exact, precise*
▪ *Syn* careful, clocklike, close, critical, detailed, elaborate, exhaustive, full, itemized, meticulous, painstaking, particular, particularized, punctilious, scrupulous, specialized, thorough; ▪ *Ant* imprecise, inexact, rough.

miraculous [adj] *surprisingly wonderful*
▪ *Syn* amazing, astonishing, astounding, extraordinary, fabulous, heavy, incredible, marvelous, numinous, phenomenal, preternatural, prodigious, spectacular, staggering, strange, superhuman, supernatural, thaumaturgic, unaccountable, unbelievable, unearthly, unreal, wondrous; ▪ *Ant* normal, usual.

mirth [n] *great joy*
▪ *Syn* amusement, cheer, festivity, frivolity, frolic, fun, glee, hilarity, jocularity, jollity, joviality, joyousness, levity, lightheartedness, merriment, pleasure, revelry, sport; ▪ *Ant* blues, depression, distress, sadness, unhappiness.

misadventure [n] *bad luck, mishap*
▪ *Syn* accident, blunder, calamity, cataclysm, catastrophe, debacle, disaster, error, ill fortune, lapse, misfortune, reverse, setback, slip, tragedy, woe; ▪ *Ant* blessing, good fortune, good luck, success, triumph.

misanthropic [adj] *unsociable, cynical*
▪ *Syn* antisocial, cynical, egotistical, eremitic, inhumane, malevolent, misanthropical, misogynic, reclusive, selfish, solitary, standoffish, unfriendly; ▪ *Ant* amiable, humanitarian, philanthropic, sociable.

misapprehend [v] *get the wrong idea, impression* ▪ *Syn* blunder, confuse, err, misconceive, misconstrue, misinterpret, misread, mistake, misunderstand; ▪ *Ant* apprehend, comprehend, understand.

misappropriate [v] *use wrongly; steal*
▪ *Syn* abuse, appropriate, defalcate, embezzle, misapply, misspend, misuse, peculate, plunder, pocket, rob, swindle; ▪ *Ant* use wisely.

misbegotten [*adj*] *illegitimate, illicit*
▪ *Syn* dishonest, disreputable, illegal, poor, shady, spurious, stolen, unlawful, unrespectable; ▪ *Ant* lawful, legal, legitimate, licit.

misbehave [*v*] *act in inappropriate manner* ▪ *Syn* act up, be at fault, be bad, be dissolute, be guilty, be immoral, be indecorous, be insubordinate, be mischievous, carry on, cut up, deviate, do evil, do wrong, fail, get into mischief, go astray, go wrong, make trouble, misconduct, offend, sin, transgress, trespass; ▪ *Ant* behave, obey.

miscalculate [*v*] *make a mistake*
▪ *Syn* blunder, err, go wrong, misconstrue, miscount, misinterpret, misjudge, misread, misreckon, misunderstand, mix up, overestimate, slip up, stumble, underestimate, underrate, undervalue; ▪ *Ant* do correctly, figure correctly, succeed.

miscarriage [*n*] *failure*
▪ *Syn* botch, breakdown, defeat, error, interruption, malfunction, misadventure, mischance, misfire, mishap, miss, mistake, nonsuccess, perversion, undoing; ▪ *Ant* success.

miscellaneous [*adj*] *diversified, various*
▪ *Syn* assorted, confused, different, disordered, disparate, divergent, divers, diverse, heterogeneous, indiscriminate, jumbled, many, mingled, mixed, motley, muddled, odd, scattered, scrambled, sundry, varied, variegated; ▪ *Ant* homogenous, identical, uniform.

mischievous [*adj*] *devilish, wicked*
▪ *Syn* arch, artful, bothersome, deleterious, destructive, detrimental, evil, exasperating, frolicsome, harmful, ill-behaved, impish, injurious, insidious, irksome, malicious, naughty, nocuous, perilous, pernicious, risky, roguish, rude, sly, spiteful, sportive, teasing, tricky, troublesome, vexing, vicious, wayward; ▪ *Ant* behaved, good, nice, obedient.

misconception [*n*] *wrong idea, impression* ▪ *Syn* delusion, error, fallacy, fault, misapprehension, misconstruction, misinterpretation, mistake, mistaken belief, misunderstanding; ▪ *Ant* comprehension, perception, truth, understanding.

misconduct [*n*] *bad or unethical behavior* ▪ *Syn* delinquency, dereliction, impropriety, malfeasance, malpractice, misbehavior, mischief, misdemeanor, misdoing, mismanagement, naughtiness, offense, rudeness, transgression, wrong-doing; ▪ *Ant* behavior, manners, obedience, probity.

misconstrue [*v*] *get a wrong or false impression* ▪ *Syn* distort, exaggerate, misapprehend, misconceive, misinterpret, misjudge, misread, misunderstand, pervert, take the wrong way; ▪ *Ant* discern, get, perceive, understand.

miscreant [*adj*] *evil, immoral*
▪ *Syn* corrupt, criminal, degenerate, depraved, flagitious, infamous, iniquitous, nefarious, perverse, reprobate, unhealthy, unprincipled, vicious, villainous, wicked; ▪ *Ant* good, moral, nice.

miser [*n*] *person who hoards money, possessions* ▪ *Syn* churl, curmudgeon, hoarder, misanthrope, misanthropist, niggard, skin-flint, tightwad; ▪ *Ant* profligate, spender, spendthrift, waster, wastrel.

miserable [*adj1*] *unhappy, depressed*
▪ *Syn* ailing, anguished, brokenhearted, crestfallen, dejected, desolate, despondent, disconsolate, doleful, downcast, forlorn, gloomy, heartbroken, hurt, melancholy, mournful, pained, pathetic, racked, rueful, sad, strained, suffering, tormented, tragic, woebegone, wounded, wretched; ▪ *Ant* cheerful, elated, happy, joyful, merry.

miserable [*adj2*] *destitute, shabby*
▪ *Syn* abject, contemptible, deplorable, despicable, detestable, disgraceful, impoverished, indigent, inferior, lamentable, low, meager, mean, needy, paltry, pathetic, penniless, piteous, pitiable, poor, poverty-stricken, scanty, shameful, sordid, sorry, squalid, tragic, vile, worthless, wretched; ▪ *Ant* comfortable, respectable.

miserly [*adj*] *greedy, stingy*
▪ *Syn* abject, avaricious, beggarly, churlish, close, close-fisted, covetous, grasping, illiberal, mean, niggardly, parsimonious, penurious, sordid, ungenerous; ▪ *Ant* generous, giving, liberal.

misfortune/mishap [*n*] *bad luck; disaster* ▪ *Syn* accident, adversity, anxiety, burden, calamity, catastrophe, contretemps, crunch, debacle, disadvantage, disappointment, failure, hardship, harm, inconvenience, infelicity, loss, misadventure, mischance, misery, nuisance, reverse, setback, tragedy, trial, tribulation, trouble, unpleasantness, visitation, worry; ▪ *Ant* advantage, benefit, blessing, fortune, good luck.

misgiving [n] *uncertainty*
▪ *Syn* anxiety, apprehension, apprehensiveness, distrust, doubt, fear, foreboding, hesitation, mistrust, premonition, presentiment, qualm, reservation, suspicion, unease, worry; ▪ *Ant* certainty, confidence, doubtlessness, sureness, trust.

misguided [adj] *ill-advised, deluded*
▪ *Syn* deceived, disinformed, erroneous, foolish, imprudent, indiscreet, inexpedient, injudicious, misdirected, misinformed, misled, misplaced, mistaken, uncalled for, unwise, wrong; ▪ *Ant* prudent, well-guided.

mishandle/mismanage [v] *mess up*
▪ *Syn* be incompetent, be inefficient, blow, blunder, bungle, confound, err, foul up, fumble, harm, misapply, misdirect, misgovern, mistreat, misuse, overlook, pervert; ▪ *Ant* handle, manage.

misinform [v] *give wrong information intentionally* ▪ *Syn* deceive, disinform, lead astray, lie, misdirect, misguide, mislead, misstate, pervert, prevaricate, signify; ▪ *Ant* inform, tell all.

misjudge [v] *get the wrong idea*
▪ *Syn* be misled, be partial, err, miscalculate, misconceive, misconstrue, misreckon, mistake, misunderstand, overestimate, presume, presuppose, suppose, underestimate, underrate; ▪ *Ant* figure, judge well, understand.

mislead [v] *give someone the wrong idea, information* ▪ *Syn* bait, beguile, bluff, cheat, cozen, deceive, defraud, delude, fool, gull, hoax, inveigle, juggle, lead astray, lure, misinform, misrepresent, outwit, pervert, rook, scam, seduce, take in, trick, victimize; ▪ *Ant* advise, counsel, guard, lead, protect.

misleading [adj] *deceptive, confusing*
▪ *Syn* ambiguous, beguiling, bewildering, confounding, deceiving, deluding, delusive, evasive, fallacious, inaccurate, perplexing, spurious, tricky, wrong; ▪ *Ant* honest, truthful.

misplace [v] *lose; be unable to find*
▪ *Syn* confuse, forget whereabouts of, lose track of, misfile, mislay, miss, mix, muss, remove, scatter, unsettle; ▪ *Ant* find.

misrepresent/misquote [v] *lie, distort*
▪ *Syn* adulterate, angle, belie, build up, cloak, color, con, confuse, cover up, disguise, distort, embellish, embroider, exaggerate, falsify, garble, mangle, mask, misinterpret, overstate, palter, pervert, prevaricate, promote, skew, slant, stretch, twist, warp; ▪ *Ant* be forthright, be honest, explain.

miss [v] *fail, make a mistake*
▪ *Syn* blow, blunder, botch, disregard, drop, err, fall short, forget, fumble, ignore, lose, miscarry, misfire, mislay, misplace, mistake, muff, neglect, omit, overlook, overshoot, pass over, pass up, skip, slight, slip, trip, trip up, undershoot; ▪ *Ant* do well, obtain, succeed.

missing [adj] *gone, absent*
▪ *Syn* astray, away, disappeared, lacking, left behind, left out, lost, mislaid, misplaced, not present, omitted, removed, short, unaccounted for, wanting; ▪ *Ant* found, here, present.

misspent [adj] *wasted*
▪ *Syn* dissipated, idle, imprudent, misapplied, prodigal, profitless, squandered, thrown away; ▪ *Ant* fruitful, productive, profitable, unwasted.

misstep [n] *mistake, wrong move*
▪ *Syn* blunder, bungle, error, failure, false step, gaffe, indiscretion, lapse, miscue, miss, slip, stumble, trip; ▪ *Ant* good deed, success.

mistake [v] *mix up, misunderstand*
▪ *Syn* addle, bungle, confound, confuse, deceive oneself, err, fail, misconceive, misconstrue, misinterpret, misjudge, omit, overestimate, overlook, snarl, tangle, underestimate; ▪ *Ant* be certain, be sure, comprehend, interpret, perceive, understand.

mistaken [adj] *wrong, incorrect*
▪ *Syn* at fault, confounded, confused, deceived, deluded, duped, fallacious, false, ill-advised, inaccurate, misconstrued, misguided, misinformed, misunderstanding, tricked, under wrong impression, warranted, wrongly identified; ▪ *Ant* correct, exact, fair, just, precise, right, sound, true.

mistreat [v] *treat badly or wrongly*
▪ *Syn* abuse, backbite, bash, brutalize, harm, injure, knock around, maltreat, manhandle, maul, mess up, misuse, molest, push around, rough up, wound, wrong; ▪ *Ant* coddle, favor, pamper, pet, please, satisfy, treat well.

mistrust [v] *doubt*
▪ *Syn* apprehend, beware, be wary, challenge, disbelieve, dispute, distrust, fear, have doubts, question, scruple, suspect, suspicion; ▪ *Ant* be certain, believe, have faith, rely on, trust.

misty [*adj*] *filmy, obscure*
▪ **Syn** bleary, blurred, closed in, clouded, cloudy, dark, dewy, dim, enveloped, foggy, fuzzy, hazy, indistinct, murky, mushy, nebulous, opaque, overcast, shrouded, socked in, unclear, vague, vaporous; ▪ **Ant** clear, unclouded.

misunderstand [*v*] *get the wrong idea*
▪ **Syn** be bewildered, be confused, be perplexed, confound, confuse, fail, misapply, misapprehend, miscalculate, miscomprehend, misconceive, misconstrue, misinterpret, misjudge, misread, misreckon, mistake, take amiss; ▪ **Ant** comprehend, construe, get, grasp, interpret, perceive, understand.

misuse [*v*] *abuse; apply wrongly*
▪ **Syn** brutalize, corrupt, exploit, ill-treat, maltreat, manhandle, maul, mess up, misapply, misemploy, mistreat, molest, outrage, pervert, prostitute, shake up, squander, waste, wrong; ▪ **Ant** appreciate, respect, treasure, use correctly.

mitigate [*v*] *check, diminish; lighten*
▪ **Syn** abate, allay, alleviate, appease, assuage, dull, ease, extenuate, lessen, moderate, modify, mollify, pacify, palliate, placate, quiet, reduce, relieve, remit, soften, soothe, subdue, temper, tone down, tranquilize, weaken; ▪ **Ant** aggravate, heighten, incite, increase, intensify, strengthen, worsen.

mix [*v1*] *combine, join*
▪ **Syn** admix, adulterate, alloy, amalgamate, associate, blend, braid, coalesce, commingle, commix, compound, conjoin, cross, embody, fuse, hybridize, incorporate, infiltrate, infuse, instill, interbreed, intermingle, interweave, jumble, knead, link, lump, merge, mingle, mix up, put together, saturate, stir, suffuse, synthesize, tangle, transfuse, unite, weave, work in; ▪ **Ant** detach, disconnect, divide, remove, separate, sever.

mix [*v2*] *socialize*
▪ **Syn** associate, come together, consort, fraternize, get along, hang out, hobnob, join, mingle; ▪ **Ant** disengage, dissociate, segregate, separate.

mixed [*adj*] *assorted, combined*
▪ **Syn** alloyed, amalgamated, assorted, blended, brewed, composite, crossbred, different, diverse, embodied, fused, heterogeneous, hybrid, interbred, joint, merged, miscellaneous, multifarious, varied, woven; ▪ **Ant** homogenous, lone, pure, single, singular, ummixed, uncombined.

mix up [*v*] *confuse*
▪ **Syn** addle, befuddle, bewilder, confound, disorganize, disrupt, distract, disturb, dizzy, fluster, jumble, mistake, muddle, perplex, puzzle, upset; ▪ **Ant** clear up, explain, explicate.

mob [*v*] *come upon by pushing; surround*
▪ **Syn** attack, cram, crowd, fill, hustle, jam, jostle, overrun, pack, riot, set upon, swarm, throng; ▪ **Ant** avoid, ignore, leave alone, shun.

mobile [*adj*] *movable, traveling*
▪ **Syn** adaptable, ambulatory, changeable, fluid, free, itinerant, liquid, locomotive, migratory, moving, mutable, nomadic, peripatetic, roaming, roving, unstable, versatile, wandering; ▪ **Ant** fixed, immobile, permanent, stable, stationary, unmovable.

mobilize [*v*] *ready for action, movement*
▪ **Syn** activate, animate, call to arms, catalyze, circulate, drive, gather, impel, marshal, muster, organize, propel, put in motion, rally, set in motion, set off; ▪ **Ant** check, demobilize, disband, end, halt, hold back, retire, stop.

mock [*adj*] *artificial, fake*
▪ **Syn** counterfeit, dummy, faked, forged, fraudulent, imitation, imitative, make-believe, phony, simulated, spurious, substitute; ▪ **Ant** authentic, genuine, real.

mock [*v1*] *ridicule*
▪ **Syn** buffoon, burlesque, caricature, chaff, deride, flout, hoot, insult, jape, jeer, kid, laugh at, make fun of, needle, parody, rally, scoff, scorn, show contempt, sneer, taunt, tease, travesty; ▪ **Ant** flatter, honor, praise.

mock [*v2*] *deceive*
▪ **Syn** beguile, belie, betray, challenge, cheat, defeat, defy, delude, disappoint, dupe, elude, foil, fool, frustrate, juggle, mislead, thwart; ▪ **Ant** tell truth.

model [*adj*] *typical, ideal*
▪ **Syn** archetypal, classic, classical, commendable, exemplary, illustrative, imitative, miniature, paradigmatic, prototypical, quintessential, representative, standard, typical; ▪ **Ant** flawed, imperfect, unworthy.

moderate [*adj1*] *calm, temperate*
▪ **Syn** abstinent, balanced, bearable, careful, cautious, conservative, cool, deliber-

ate, disciplined, dispassionate, equable, even, impartial, inexpensive, judicious, limited, low-key, mild, neutral, nonpartisan, pacific, reserved, sober, steady, straight, tame, tolerant, tranquil, untroubled; • *Ant* excessive, extreme, immoderate, outrageous, uncontrolled, unlimited, unreasonable, unrestrained, violent, wild.

moderate [*adj2*] *fair, average, so-so*
• *Syn* bland, inconsequential, inconsiderable, indifferent, intermediate, mediocre, medium, ordinary, paltry, passable, trifling, trivial, unexceptional; • *Ant* considerate, extravagant, extreme, immoderate, liberal, significant.

moderate [*v*] *restrain, control*
• *Syn* abate, appease, assuage, check, constrain, decrease, lessen, mitigate, modulate, pacify, play down, quiet, reduce, regulate, relieve, repress, slacken, soft-pedal, subdue, tame, temper, tone down, wane; • *Ant* egg on, free, incite, let go, liberate, unleash.

moderately [*adv*] *to a degree, to some extent* • *Syn* a little, fairly, gently, in moderation, in reason, kind of, not exactly, passably, pretty, rather, reasonably, slightly, some, something, somewhat, sort of, temperately, tolerable, tolerably, tolerantly; • *Ant* immoderately, unlimitedly.

modern [*adj*] *new, up-to-date*
• *Syn* avant-garde, contemporary, current, fresh, late, latest, modernistic, modernized, modish, neoteric, newfashioned, novel, now, present, present-day, prevailing, prevalent, recent, stylish, today, up-to-the-minute; • *Ant* ancient, antiquated, obsolete, old, old-fashioned, outdated, passe, stale.

modernize [*v*] *bring up to date; remodel*
• *Syn* improve, refresh, regenerate, rejuvenate, remake, renew, renovate, restore, revamp, revive, update; • *Ant* antique, date, outmode, regress, wear.

modest [*adj1*] *shy*
• *Syn* bashful, blushing, chaste, coy, demure, diffident, humble, lowly, meek, moderate, quiet, reticent, seemly, self-conscious, sheepish, simple, temperate, unassertive, unassuming, unassured, unboastful, withdrawing; • *Ant* arrogant, assured, bold, brave, conceited, egotistical, proud, self-confident, unabashed, unashamed.

modest [*adj2*] *limited, ordinary*
• *Syn* average, discreet, economical, humble, inexpensive, moderate, plain, reasonable, simple, unadorned, unaffected, unembroidered, unexceptional, unpretentious, unstudied; • *Ant* extraordinary, immodest, ostentatious, presumptuous, unlimited.

modicum [*n*] *bit, small amount*
• *Syn* atom, crumb, dash, drop, fraction, fragment, grain, inch, iota, jot, little, mite, molecule, ounce, particle, pinch, scrap, shred, smidge, speck, tinge, touch, trifle, whit; • *Ant* lot.

modify [*v1*] *alter, change*
• *Syn* adapt, adjust, convert, customize, doctor, mutate, refashion, remodel, reshape, revise, rework, transfigure, transform, transmute, turn, vary; • *Ant* keep, leave alone, retain, stagnate.

modify [*v2*] *lessen, reduce*
• *Syn* abate, curb, decrease, limit, lower, mitigate, moderate, modulate, qualify, relax, restrain, restrict, slacken, soften, temper, tone down; • *Ant* grow, increase.

modish [*adj*] *very fashionable*
• *Syn* chic, contemporary, current, dashing, fresh, happening, last-word, latest, smart, stylish, swank, trendy, up-to-date, up-to-the-minute, vogue; • *Ant* old-fashioned, unfashionable, unstylish.

modulate [*v*] *adjust, harmonize*
• *Syn* attune, balance, fine-tune, inflect, regulate, revamp, switch, temper, tone, tune, tweak, vary; • *Ant* aggravate, excite, intensify.

moist [*adj*] *wet, wettish*
• *Syn* clammy, damp, dampish, dank, dewy, dripping, drippy, drizzly, humid, irriguous, muggy, soggy, teary, watery; • *Ant* dry.

moisten [*v*] *make wet, damp*
• *Syn* bathe, bedew, dampen, dip, drench, humidify, lick, mist, moisturize, rinse, saturate, shower, splash, splatter, spray, sprinkle, squirt, steam, steep, wash, water, water down, wet; • *Ant* dry.

mold [*v*] *form, give shape*
• *Syn* build, construct, devise, erect, fashion, forge, form, frame, make, pat, plan, plant, plot, put together, scheme, sculpt, shape, whittle; • *Ant* dismantle.

molest [*v1*] *physically abuse*
• *Syn* accost, assail, attack, disturb, en-

croach, fondle, harm, hinder, hurt, ill-treat, injure, interfere, intrude, maltreat, manhandle, meddle, misuse, rape; ▪*Ant* be careful, benefit, guard, help, protect, soothe.

molest [*v2*] *bother, annoy*
▪ *Syn* abuse, bait, bedevil, confuse, disturb, encroach, frighten, harass, heckle, obtrude, persecute, perturb, pester, plague, pursue, scare, tease, torment, trouble, vex, worry; ▪*Ant* assist, cheer, make happy, please.

mollify [*v*] *pacify, soothe*
▪ *Syn* abate, allay, alleviate, ameliorate, appease, assuage, calm, conciliate, cushion, diminish, ease, lessen, lull, mellow, mitigate, pacify, placate, quell, reduce, relieve, soften, temper; ▪*Ant* agitate, depress, exasperate, harass, incite, provoke, trouble, upset, worry.

momentarily [*adv*] *for a very short time*
▪ *Syn* briefly, for a little while, for an instant, for a second, for a short time, for a short while, immediately, instantly, now, right now, temporarily; ▪*Ant* lengthily, permanently.

momentary [*adj*] *brief, fleeting*
▪ *Syn* cursory, ephemeral, evanescent, flashing, fugitive, hasty, impermanent, like lightning, passing, quick, shifting, short, short-lived, spasmodic, temporary, transient, transitory, vanishing, volatile; ▪*Ant* lasting, long-lasting, permanent, staying.

momentous [*adj*] *very important; serious* ▪ *Syn* big, consequential, critical, crucial, decisive, earth-shattering, epochal, eventful, fateful, grave, heavy, historic, material, meaningful, memorable, notable, outstanding, pivotal, significant, vital, weighty; ▪*Ant* immaterial, insignificant, trifling, trivial, unimportant.

moneyed [*adj*] *rich*
▪ *Syn* affluent, opulent, prosperous, upper-class, upscale, uptown, wealthy; ▪*Ant* destitute, poor.

moneymaking [*adj*] *producing profit*
▪ *Syn* advantageous, gainful, going, good, lucrative, paying, profitable, remunerative, successful, thriving, well-paying; ▪*Ant* unprofitable.

mongrel [*n*] *animal of mixed background*
▪ *Syn* bastard, cross, crossbreed, cur, half-blood, half-breed, hybrid, mixed breed, mixture, mule, mutt; ▪*Ant* pedigree, purebred, thoroughbred.

monitor [*v*] *listen, watch carefully*
▪ *Syn* advise, audit, check, control, counsel, follow, observe, oversee, record, scan, supervise, survey, track; ▪*Ant* forget, ignore, neglect.

monkey [*v*] *fiddle, tamper with*
▪ *Syn* interfere, interlope, intermeddle, meddle, mess, play, pry, tinker, trifle; ▪*Ant* leave alone.

monologue [*n*] *speech by one person*
▪ *Syn* address, descant, discourse, disquisition, harangue, lecture, sermon, soliloquy, speech, talk; ▪*Ant* conversation, dialogue.

monopolize [*v*] *dominate, control*
▪ *Syn* absorb, acquire, corner, employ, engross, exercise control, have, hold, keep to oneself, manage, own, patent, possess, syndicate, take over, take up; ▪*Ant* distribute, divide, scatter, share.

monotonous [*adj*] *all the same, remaining the same* ▪ *Syn* banal, boring, colorless, dreary, droning, dull, flat, pedestrian, plodding, prosaic, recurrent, repetitive, soporific, tedious, tiresome, toneless, unchanging, uniform, uninflected, uninteresting, unrelieved, unvaried, unvarying, wearisome, wearying; ▪*Ant* changing, exciting, innovative, lively, stimualting, variable, versatile.

monstrous [*adj1*] *unnatural, shocking*
▪ *Syn* aberrant, abnormal, atrocious, cruel, desperate, devilish, disgraceful, dreadful, egregious, evil, fiendish, flagitious, freakish, frightful, grotesque, gruesome, heinous, hideous, horrendous, horrifying, infamous, loathsome, macabre, miscreated, morbid, obscene, odious, outrageous, preposterous, rank, satanic, scandalous, terrible, vicious, villainous; ▪*Ant* average, common, expected, natural, ordinary, standard.

monstrous [*adj2*] *very large*
▪ *Syn* colossal, elephantine, enormous, gargantuan, gigantic, great, huge, immense, mammoth, massive, monumental, prodigious, stupendous, titanic, towering, tremendous, vast, whopping; ▪*Ant* little, miniature, small, tiny.

monumental [*adj*] *impressive, overwhelming* ▪ *Syn* awe-inspiring, classic, enduring, fantastic, gigantic, grand, great, historic, immortal, important, lasting, memorable, mighty, outstanding, prodigious, significant, stupendous, tremendous, unforgettable, vast; ▪*Ant* insignificant, trivial, unimportant, unimposing, unimpressive.

moody [adj] *crabby, temperamental*
▪ *Syn* angry, cantankerous, crestfallen, cross, dismal, doleful, dour, erratic, fickle, fitful, frowning, gloomy, huffy, ill-tempered, irascible, lugubrious, melancholy, mercurial, offended, pensive, petulant, piqued, saturnine, short-tempered, splenetic, testy, touchy; ▪ *Ant* balanced, cheerful, happy, overjoyed.

moon [v] *dream about; desire*
▪ *Syn* daydream, idle, languish, mope, pine, waste time, yearn; ▪ *Ant* abhor, despise, dislike, hate.

moor [v] *anchor, fasten securely*
▪ *Syn* anchor, berth, catch, chain, dock, fix, lash, make fast, picket, secure, tether, tie, tie up; ▪ *Ant* loose, push off, set adrift, unhitch.

moot [adj] *doubtful, arguable*
▪ *Syn* at issue, contestable, controversial, debatable, disputable, dubious, open, open to debate, problematic, questionable, suspect, uncertain, undecided, unresolved, unsettled; ▪ *Ant* decided, definite, proven, resolved, self-evident.

mope [v] *pout, be dejected*
▪ *Syn* ache, be gloomy, brood, chafe, despair, despond, droop, fret, grieve, grumble, grump, idle, lament, languish, lose heart, moon, pine, regret, repine, sink, sulk, yearn; ▪ *Ant* be elated, be excited, be happy, be satisfied.

moral [adj] *ethical, honest*
▪ *Syn* conscientious, correct, decent, elevated, exemplary, good, honorable, incorruptible, just, laudable, meritorious, noble, principled, proper, respectable, righteous, saintly, scrupulous, square, trustworthy, upright, virtuous, worthy; ▪ *Ant* amoral, bad, corrupt, dishonest, evil, immoral, sinful, unethical, unprincipled, vile.

morass [n] *bog; mess*
▪ *Syn* chaos, confusion, fen, jam, jungle, knot, labyrinth, marsh, maze, mesh, mix-up, muddle, quagmire, skein, snarl, swamp, tangle, web; ▪ *Ant* order, organization.

morbid [adj] *gloomy, nasty, sickly*
▪ *Syn* abnormal, brooding, dark, depressed, despondent, dreadful, grim, grisly, hideous, irascible, macabre, malignant, melancholy, moody, pathological, pessimistic, saturnine, somber, unhealthy, unwholesome; ▪ *Ant* cheer-

ful, happy, healthy, optimistic, pleased, sound.

more [adj] *additional, greater*
▪ *Syn* added, aggrandized, also, augmented, enhanced, expanded, extended, extra, farther, fresh, further, heavier, higher, in addition, increased, innumerable, larger, likewise, major, massed, new, numerous, over and above, supplementary; ▪ *Ant* fewer, less.

more [adv] *to a greater extent*
▪ *Syn* additionally, along with, also, as well, besides, better, beyond, further, furthermore, in addition, likewise, longer, moreover, over, too, withal; ▪ *Ant* fewer, less.

morning [n] *first part of the day*
▪ *Syn* after midnight, AM, ante meridiem, aurora, before lunch, before noon, break of day, dawn, daybreak, daylight, dayspring, foreday, forenoon, morningtide, morrow, sunrise, sunup; ▪ *Ant* afternoon, dusk, evening, PM, post meridiem, sundown, sunset.

moron [n] *very stupid person*
▪ *Syn* addlepate, cretin, dimwit, dolt, dunce, fool, halfwit, idiot, ignoramus, imbecile, simpleton; ▪ *Ant* brain, genius, mastermind.

morose [adj] *very depressed, pessimistic*
▪ *Syn* cantankerous, churlish, dolorous, dour, down, frowning, gloomy, gruff, harsh, ill-tempered, irritable, low, melancholy, moody, mournful, perverse, sad, saturnine, sour, surly, taciturn, testy; ▪ *Ant* cheerful, friendly, happy, lighthearted, optimistic, uplifted.

morsel [n] *tiny piece*
▪ *Syn* bit, bite, chunk, crumb, cut, drop, fragment, grain, nibble, nosh, particle, sample, scrap, segment, slice, snack, soupcon, taste, tidbit, treat; ▪ *Ant* lot.

mortal [adj] *deadly*
▪ *Syn* death-dealing, deathly, destructive, dire, fatal, grave, great, grievous, grim, lethal, malignant, merciless, murderous, noxious, pestilential, poisonous, relentless, remorseless, ruthless, severe, terminal, terrible, unrelenting; ▪ *Ant* invigorating, lifegiving, permanent, refreshing.

mortify [v] *embarrass*
▪ *Syn* abase, abash, affront, annoy, belittle, chasten, confound, crush, deflate, discipline, discomfit, disgrace, displease, harass, humble, humiliate, put to shame,

ridicule, shame, vex, worry; ▪ **Ant** compliment, flatter, praise, satisfy.

most [adj] best, greatest
▪ **Syn** better, biggest, greater, highest, largest, maximum, ultimate, utmost, uttermost; ▪ **Ant** least, lowest, minimum, smallest.

most [adv] nearly all; extremely
▪ **Syn** about, all but, almost, approximately, close, eminently, exceedingly, in the majority, mightily, much, nearly, nigh, practically, remarkably, super, surpassingly, too, very, well-nigh; ▪ **Ant** least.

motion [v] gesture, direct
▪ **Syn** beckon, flag, gesticulate, guide, invite, move, nod, sign, signal, signalize, wave; ▪ **Ant** be still.

motionless [adj] calm, not moving
▪ **Syn** apoplectic, at a standstill, at rest, becalmed, dead, fixed, frozen, halted, immotile, inanimate, inert, lifeless, numb, paralyzed, quiescent, quiet, stable, stagnant, stalled, static, stationary, steadfast, still, stock-still, torpid, transfixed, unmovable, unmoved, unmoving; ▪ **Ant** active, busy, lively, mobile, moving.

motivate [v] stimulate, instigate
▪ **Syn** actuate, arouse, cause, dispose, draw, drive, excite, fire, galvanize, give incentive, goad, impel, incite, incline, induce, innervate, innerve, inspire, lead, move, persuade, pique, prompt, propel, provoke, quicken, rouse, spark, spur, suggest, sway, trigger, whet; ▪ **Ant** daunt, depress, discourage, dissuade.

motley [adj] mixed, varied
▪ **Syn** assorted, conglomerate, dappled, disparate, dissimilar, diversified, heterogeneous, kaleidoscopic, miscellaneous, mixed, mottled, multicolor, multiform, polychromatic, prismatic, variegated, various; ▪ **Ant** homogenous, like, same, similar, uniform, unmixed, unvaried.

mottled [adj] speckled
▪ **Syn** blotchy, checkered, dappled, flecked, freckled, maculate, marbled, motley, piebald, pied, skewbald, spotted, streaked, tabby, variegated; ▪ **Ant** plain, unflecked.

mound [n] heap, hill
▪ **Syn** anthill, bank, bulwark, drift, dune, embankment, hillock, knoll, mass, molehill, mountain, pile, rise, stack, tumulus; ▪ **Ant** depression, dip, ditch, valley.

mount [v1] climb
▪ **Syn** arise, ascend, bestride, clamber up, escalate, get up on, lift, rise, scale, soar, tower, up, vault; ▪ **Ant** alight, descend, dismount, drop, fall.

mount [v2] increase, grow
▪ **Syn** accumulate, augment, build, deepen, enhance, escalate, heighten, intensify, multiply, pile up, redouble, rouse, swell, upsurge, wax; ▪ **Ant** decline, decrease, drop, fall, slump, subside.

mountain [n] very large hill
▪ **Syn** alp, bank, bluff, butte, cliff, crag, dome, drift, elevation, eminence, height, mesa, mound, mount, palisade, peak, pike, precipice, range, ridge, sierra, tor; ▪ **Ant** crevasse, valley.

mourn [v] be sad over loss
▪ **Syn** ache, agonize, anguish, bemoan, bewail, cry, deplore, fret, grieve, hurt, keen, lament, long for, miss, moan, pine, rain, regret, rue, sorrow, suffer, wail, weep, yearn; ▪ **Ant** be happy, be joyful, exult, triumph.

mousy [adj] drab; quiet
▪ **Syn** bashful, colorless, diffident, dull, indeterminate, ineffectual, plain, self-effacing, shy, timid, timorous, unassertive, unassuming; ▪ **Ant** brazen, extroverted, flamboyant, self-confident.

movable [adj] transportable
▪ **Syn** adaptable, adjustable, ambulatory, conveyable, deployable, detachable, mobile, motile, moving, not fastened, not fixed, on wheels, portable, removable, shiftable, transferable, unattached, unfastened, unstationary, unsteady; ▪ **Ant** fixed, immoveable, permanent, unmovable.

move [v1] be in motion, put in motion
▪ **Syn** advance, budge, carry, climb, depart, disturb, drift, flow, fly, get away, get going, glide, go, go away, head for, hurry, impel, jump, leap, leave, locomote, march, migrate, off-load, position, proceed, progress, propel, quit, relocate, scram, shift, ship, shove, skip out, split, stir, take off, transfer, transport, transpose, travel, traverse, walk, withdraw; ▪ **Ant** fix, pause, remain, stay, stop.

move [v2] motivate, influence
▪ **Syn** activate, actuate, advocate, affect, agitate, bring, bring up, cause, convert, draw up, drive, excite, get going, give

rise to, impel, impress, incite, induce, inspire, inspirit, instigate, introduce, lead, persuade, prevail upon, prompt, propel, propose, push, recommend, rouse, shift, stimulate, stir, strike, submit, suggest, sway, touch, turn, urge; • *Ant* discourage, dishearten, dissuade.

moving [*adj1*] *affecting, exciting*
• *Syn* affective, arousing, awakening, compelling, dynamic, emotional, emotive, expressive, gripping, heartrending, impressive, inspirational, inspiring, motivating, persuasive, poignant, provoking, rallying, rousing, significant, stimulating, stirring, stunning, touching; • *Ant* unaffecting, unemotional, unexciting, unmoving.

moving [*adj2*] *mobile*
• *Syn* advancing, changing, evolving, locomotive, motile, motor, movable, nomadic, portable, shifting, unfixed, unstable, unsteadfast, unsteady; • *Ant* fixed, immobile, permanent, stationary, unmoving.

much [*adj*] *plenty*
• *Syn* abundant, adequate, ample, considerable, copious, countless, endless, enough, extravagant, full, galore, generous, great, immeasurable, lavish, many, plentiful, profuse, satisfying, sizable, substantial, sufficient, very many, voluminous; • *Ant* few, little, scarce, small.

much [*adv*] *greatly, a lot*
• *Syn* considerably, decidedly, eminently, exceedingly, exceptionally, extremely, frequently, highly, notably, oft, often, regularly, repeatedly, surpassingly, very; • *Ant* hardly, little, rarely.

muddle [*v*] *confuse, disorganize*
• *Syn* addle, befuddle, botch, bungle, clutter, complicate, confound, daze, disorient, disturb, fluster, foul up, jumble, mess, mix up, mumble, perplex, perturb, rattle, ruffle, scramble, shuffle, spoil, stir up, tangle, throw, throw off, tumble; • *Ant* clear up, educate, enlighten, explain, explicate, order, organize.

muddy [*adj*] *dark and cloudy; dirty*
• *Syn* addled, bemired, bespattered, blurred, confused, dingy, dull, filthy, fuzzy, greasy, grimy, hazy, impure, indistinct, obscure, opaque, sloppy, slushy, smoky, sodden, soggy, soiled, swampy, turbid, unclean, unclear; • *Ant* bright, clean, clear.

muffle [*v*] *suppress, make quiet*
• *Syn* conceal, cover, cushion, dampen, deaden, decrease, drown, dull, gag, hide, hush, mellow, muzzle, silence, smother, soften, squelch, stifle, subdue; • *Ant* encourage, express, incite, inflame, provoke, reveal, uncover, unleash.

muffled [*adj*] *quietened*
• *Syn* deadened, dim, dull, faint, flat, indistinct, muted, obscure, silenced, stifled, strangled, subdued, suppressed; • *Ant* clear, unblocked.

muggy [*adj*] *humid*
• *Syn* close, damp, dank, moist, oppressive, soggy, sticky, stuffy, sultry, wettish; • *Ant* cool, dry.

mull [*v*] *think about seriously*
• *Syn* brood over, chaw, contemplate, deliberate, examine, figure, linger, meditate, muse on, ponder, pore over, reflect, review, ruminate, study, think over, turn over, weigh; • *Ant* disregard, ignore, neglect.

multicolored [*adj*] *having various hues*
• *Syn* checkered, dappled, flecked, kaleidoscopic, marbled, motley, mottled, particolored, piebald, polychrome, prismatic, speckled, spotted, varicolored, veined, versicolor; • *Ant* monochrome.

multiculturalism [*n*] *doctrine acknowledging contributions and interests of many cultures* • *Syn* cross-culturalism, cultural diversity, diversity, ethnic inclusiveness, ethnic mosaic, multiracialism, pluralism; • *Ant* exclusivity, homogeneity, insularity, isolationism, nativism, racial purism, sameness, separation, singularity, uniformity, xenophobia.

multiple/multifarious [*adj*] *diversified, miscellaneous* • *Syn* assorted, collective, conglomerate, diverse, diversiform, heterogeneous, indiscriminate, legion, manifold, motley, multiform, numerous, populous, several, sundry, variegated, voluminous; • *Ant* single, singular, unvaried.

multiply [*v*] *increase; reproduce*
• *Syn* add, augment, breed, double, enlarge, expand, generate, heighten, magnify, procreate, produce, propagate, repeat, square; • *Ant* abate, decrease, divide, lessen, reduce.

multitudinous [*adj*] *many, considerable*
• *Syn* abounding, abundant, copious, countless, innumerable, legion, multifarious, myriad, numerous, populous, pro-

fuse, sundry, teeming, uncountable, untold, various, voluminous; ▪ *Ant* few, limited.

mumble [*v*] *speak low and inarticulately*
▪ *Syn* grumble, hem and haw, maunder, murmur, mutter, ramble, speak, stammer, utter, whisper; ▪ *Ant* articulate, enunciate, speak clearly.

mundane [*adj*] *ordinary*
▪ *Syn* banal, commonplace, day-to-day, everyday, lowly, normal, pedestrian, prosaic, routine, terrestrial, workday, worldly; ▪ *Ant* exciting, extraordinary, heavenly, supernatural, wonderful.

municipal [*adj*] *of a city; possessing local self-government* ▪ *Syn* borough, city, civic, community, corporate, domestic, home, incorporated, local, metropolitan, native, public, town, urban; ▪ *Ant* federal, international, national.

munificent [*adj*] *giving, generous*
▪ *Syn* benevolent, big-hearted, bounteous, bountiful, charitable, free, kind, liberal, magnanimous, openhanded, philanthropic, princely, rich, unsparing, unstinting; ▪ *Ant* careful, greedy, mean, selfish, stingy.

murder [*v*] *kill*
▪ *Syn* asphyxiate, assassinate, behead, butcher, decapitate, electrocute, eliminate, eradicate, execute, extinguish, finish, garotte, guillotine, hang, knife, liquidate, lynch, massacre, shoot, slaughter, slay, smother, snuff, strangle, take a life; ▪ *Ant* guard, preserve, protect, save.

murderous [*adj*] *very difficult*
▪ *Syn* arduous, brutal, cruel, destructive, devastating, exhausting, ferocious, harrowing, hellish, killing, lethal, ruinous, sapping, strenuous, unpleasant; ▪ *Ant* easy, facile, pleasant.

murky [*adj*] *gloomy, obscure*
▪ *Syn* black, cheerless, cloudy, dark, dim, dismal, drab, dreary, foggy, gray, impenetrable, muddy, nasty, nebulous, overcast, sad, somber, squalid, stormy, tenebrous, turbid, unclean; ▪ *Ant* bright, clear, light, luminous, sparkling, unobscured.

murmur [*v*] *make low, continuous sound*
▪ *Syn* babble, buzz, drone, hum, mumble, mutter, purl, purr, stage-whisper, stammer, utter, whisper; ▪ *Ant* shout, speak clearly, yell.

muscular [*adj*] *powerfully built*
▪ *Syn* able-bodied, athletic, brawny, burly, hefty, hulky, mighty, powerful,

robust, stalwart, stout, strapping, strong, sturdy, tough, vigorous, well-built; ▪ *Ant* delicate, flabby, infirm, skinny, weak.

muse [*v*] *think about, dream*
▪ *Syn* brood, cogitate, contemplate, deliberate, meditate, mull over, percolate, ponder, puzzle over, reflect, ruminate, speculate, think over, turn over, weigh; ▪ *Ant* act upon, ignore, neglect.

mushroom [*v*] *sprout; grow quickly*
▪ *Syn* blow up, burgeon, explode, flourish, grow rapidly, increase, luxuriate, proliferate, shoot up, spread, spring up; ▪ *Ant* decrease, devolve, shrink, shrivel.

mushy [*adj1*] *doughy, soft*
▪ *Syn* gelatinous, jelled, muddy, pulpous, pulpy, semiliquid, semisolid, slushy, spongy; ▪ *Ant* hard, stiff.

mushy [*adj2*] *romantic, corny*
▪ *Syn* bathetic, effusive, emotional, maudlin, mawkish, saccharine, sentimental, sugary, syrupy, tear-jerking, weepy, wet; ▪ *Ant* unfeeling, unromantic.

musical [*adj*] *harmonic, lyrical*
▪ *Syn* agreeable, choral, dulcet, euphonious, harmonious, lilting, mellow, melodic, melodious operatic, orchestral, rhythmic, songful, sweet, symphonic, tuned, tuneful; ▪ *Ant* cacophonous, discordant, dissonant, inharmonious, unmusical.

muss [*v*] *dishevel, disorder*
▪ *Syn* clutter, crumple, disorganize, disrupt, disturb, jumble, mess up, mix up, muddle, ruffle, rummage, rumple, tangle, tousle, upset, wrinkle; ▪ *Ant* fix up, order, organize, straighten, tidy.

must [*n*] *necessity, essential*
▪ *Syn* commitment, condition, devoir, duty, fundamental, imperative, need, obligation, precondition, prerequisite, requirement, requisite, sine qua non; ▪ *Ant* accessory, extra, nonessential.

muster [*v*] *gather, come together*
▪ *Syn* assemble, call together, call up, collect, congregate, congress, convene, convoke, enroll, enter, group, join up, marshal, meet, mobilize, organize, raise, rally, rendezvous, round up, sign on, sign up, summon; ▪ *Ant* adjourn, disperse, divide, remove, separate, throw away.

musty [*adj1*] *stuffy, aged*
▪ *Syn* airless, ancient, crumbling, dank, decayed, decrepit, fetid, malodorous, moldy, noisome, old, putrid, rotten, squalid, stale, stuffy; ▪ *Ant* clean, clear, fresh, new, sweet-smelling.

musty [*adj2*] *worn-out, clichéd*
▪ **Syn** ancient, antiquated, banal, common, dull, hackneyed, hoary, obsolete, old-fashioned, stale, stereotypical, threadbare, trite, worn; ▪ **Ant** fresh, new, unused.

mutation [*n*] *metamorphosis*
▪ **Syn** alteration, anomaly, change, deviation, evolution, innovation, modification, novelty, permutation, transformation, vicissitude; ▪ **Ant** inaction, stagnation.

mute [*adj*] *unable to speak*
▪ **Syn** aphasiac, aphonic, dumb, inarticulate, muffled, mum, quiet, silent, speechless, tongue-tied, unexpressed, unsounded, unspeaking, unspoken, voiceless, wordless; ▪ **Ant** articulate, loquacious, speaking, vocal.

mute [*v*] *muffle, tone down sound*
▪ **Syn** benumb, dampen, deaden, decrease the volume, drown, gag, hush, lower, moderate, muzzle, reduce, silence, soften, subdue, turn down; ▪ **Ant** express, provoke, raise the volume, turn up, voice.

mutilate [*v*] *maim, damage*
▪ **Syn** adulterate, amputate, batter, bowdlerize, butcher, cripple, cut to pieces, damage, dismember, hurt, injure, lacerate, lame, mar, scratch; ▪ **Ant** fix, mend, repair.

mutiny [*v*] *defy, revolt*
▪ **Syn** be insubordinate, disobey, insurrect, kick over, rebel, resist, rise against, rise up, strike; ▪ **Ant** obey, observe, serve.

mutter [*v*] *grumble, mumble*
▪ **Syn** complain, croak, groan, grouse, growl, grunt, moan, muddle, murmur, snarl, sputter, whisper; ▪ **Ant** speak clearly.

mutual [*adj*] *shared, common*
▪ **Syn** associated, bilateral, collective, communal, connected, correlative, interactive, interdependent, joint, reciprocal, related, requited, respective, returned, united; ▪ **Ant** detached, dissociated, distinct, separate, unshared.

mutually [*adv*] *together*
▪ **Syn** all at once, as a group, by agreement, by contract, commonly, conjointly, cooperatively, en masse, in collaboration, in conjunction, jointly, reciprocally, respectively; ▪ **Ant** dissimilarly, distinctly.

muzzle [*v*] *gag, quiet*
▪ **Syn** censor, choke, cork, curb, hush, muffle, prevent, quieten, repress, restrain, restrict, shush, silence, squelch, stifle, still, stop, suppress, trammel; ▪ **Ant** free, let go, liberate.

myopic [*adj*] *able only to see things near at hand* ▪ **Syn** biased, blind, halfsighted, nearsighted, presbyopic, shortsighted; ▪ **Ant** far-sighted.

myriad [*adj*] *innumerable*
▪ **Syn** countless, endless, heaping, immeasurable, incalculable, infinite, multiple, multitudinous, numberless, uncounted, untold, variable; ▪ **Ant** calculable, few, limited, measurable.

mysterious [*adj*] *secret, concealed*
▪ **Syn** abstruse, alchemistic, arcane, baffling, cabalistic, covert, cryptic, curious, dark, enigmatic, esoteric, hidden, inexplicable, magical, mystifying, necromantic, obscure, occult, oracular, perplexing, recondite, sphinxlike, spiritual, strange, unfathomable, unnatural, veiled, weird; ▪ **Ant** apparent, clear, known, manifest, obvious, plain, public, straightforward, tangible.

mystic/mystical [*adj*] *secret, esoteric*
▪ **Syn** abstruse, arcane, cabalistic, cryptic, enigmatical, esoteric, hidden, impenetrable, inscrutable, magic, magical, metaphysical, mysterious, necromantic, nonrational, numinous, oecult, otherworldly, paranormal, preternatural, quixotic, spiritual, supernatural, transcendental, unaccountable, unknowable, visionary; ▪ **Ant** knowable, natural, palpable, undisguised.

mystify [*v*] *bewilder, confuse*
▪ **Syn** baffle, confound, deceive, elude, lie, perplex, puzzle, trick; ▪ **Ant** clear up, enlighten, explain, explicate.

mythical/mythological [*adj*] *make-believe, fairy-tale* ▪ **Syn** allegorical, fabled, fabricated, fabulous, false, fanciful, fictitious, fictive, folkloric, imaginary, invented, legendary, made-up, mythic, nonexistent, traditional, unreal, untrue, visionary, whimsical; ▪ **Ant** factual, historical, real, true.

mythology [*n*] *folklore*
▪ **Syn** belief, conviction, folk tales, legend, lore, mythicism, mythos, stories, tradition; ▪ **Ant** actuality, history, reality, truth.

N

nab [*v*] *seize*
▪ **Syn** apprehend, arrest, capture, catch,

clutch, detain, grab, take into custody;
▪ *Ant* let go, release.

nag [v] *harass, bother*
▪ *Syn* annoy, badger, bait, berate, carp at, find fault, fuss, goad, harry, heckle, henpeck, hound, importune, irk, needle, pester, pick at, plague, ride, scold, torment, upbraid, urge, vex, worry; ▪ *Ant* assuage, please.

nail [v1] *fasten, fix with pointed object*
▪ *Syn* attach, beat, bind, drive, hammer, hit, hold, join, pin, pound, secure, spike, strike, tack; ▪ *Ant* unfasten, unnail.

nail [v2] *capture, arrest*
▪ *Syn* apprehend, bag, catch, detain, nab, secure, seize; ▪ *Ant* let go, liberate, release.

naive [adj] *childlike, trusting*
▪ *Syn* aboveboard, artless, callow, candid, credulous, forthright, frank, fresh, guileless, gullible, harmless, ignorant, innocent, innocuous, instinctive, jejune, natural, open, plain, simple-minded, sincere, spontaneous, trusting, unaffected, unjaded, unpretentious, unsuspecting, unworldly, virgin; ▪ *Ant* experienced, leery, skeptical, wise.

naked [adj1] *without covering*
▪ *Syn* au naturel, bald, bare, bared, bareskinned, barren, defenseless, denuded, disrobed, divested, exposed, leafless, natural, nude, open, stripped, threadbare, unclad, vulnerable; ▪ *Ant* clothed, concealed, dressed, protected, veiled.

naked [adj2] *manifest, evident*
▪ *Syn* artless, blatant, disclosed, dry, matter-of-fact, obvious, open, overt, palpable, plain, pure, revealed, sheer, simple, stark, unadorned, unexaggerated, unqualified, unvarnished; ▪ *Ant* hidden, private, secret.

name [v] *choose, designate*
▪ *Syn* announce, appoint, cite, commission, delegate, denote, elect, identify, classify, list, make, mark, mention, nominate, point to, recognize, select, signify, specify, tab, tag; ▪ *Ant* ignore, neglect, pass over.

nameless [adj] *unknown, anonymous*
▪ *Syn* incognito, innominate, obscure, pseudonymous, unacknowledged, undistinguished, unfamed, unheard-of, unnoted; ▪ *Ant* designated, distinguished, eminent, famous, known, named, prominent, renowned.

narcissistic [adj] *concerned only with oneself* ▪ *Syn* conceited, egotistical,

self-centered, self-involved, self-loving, stuck-up, vain, vainglorious; ▪ *Ant* outgoing, sacrificing, unselfish.

narrate [v] *describe, detail*
▪ *Syn* characterize, chronicle, delineate, depict, disclose, enumerate, expatiate, forth, give an account of, make known, portray, proclaim, recount, rehearse, relate, repeat, report, set forth, spin, tell, tell a story, unfold; ▪ *Ant* conceal, hide, suppress.

narrative [adj] *storylike, chronological*
▪ *Syn* anecdotal, fictional, fictive, historical, narrated, recounted, reported, retold, sequential; ▪ *Ant* rambling.

narrow [adj1] *confined, restricted*
▪ *Syn* attenuated, circumscribed, compressed, constricted, cramped, definite, exclusive, fine, incapacious, limited, linear, meager, near, paltry, pinched, precarious, scant, select, shrunken, slender, slim, spare, strait, tapered, thin, threadlike, tight; ▪ *Ant* broad, generous, liberal, unconfined, unrestricted, wide.

narrow [adj2] *intolerant, small-minded*
▪ *Syn* biased, conservative, conventional, dogmatic, hidebound, illiberal, inexorable, inflexible, narrow-minded, obdurate, partial, prejudiced, reactionary, stupid; ▪ *Ant* accepting, broad-minded, liberal, tolerant.

narrow [adj3] *cheap, stingy*
▪ *Syn* avaricious, close, mean, mercenary, ungenerous; ▪ *Ant* generous, spendthrift, wasting.

narrow [v] *reduce, simplify*
▪ *Syn* circumscribe, constrict, contract, diminish, limit, taper, tighten; ▪ *Ant* broaden, complicate, expand, increase, intensify.

narrowly [adv] *just, closely*
▪ *Syn* almost, barely, by narrow margin, carefully, close, nearly, only just, painstakingly, scarcely, scrutinizingly; ▪ *Ant* carelessly, imprecisely.

narrow-minded [adj] *biased, intolerant*
▪ *Syn* bigoted, conventional, hidebound, illiberal, insular, narrow, opinionated, parochial, prejudiced, provincial, reactionary, small-minded, strait-laced, unenlarged; ▪ *Ant* broad-minded, liberal, tolerant, unbiased.

nasty [adj1] *disgusting, offensive*
▪ *Syn* awful, beastly, dirty, fierce, filthy, foul, gross, grubby, hellish, horrid, impure, loathsome, malodorous, nauseating, noisome, objectionable, odious,

ornery, repugnant, revolting, sickening, soiled, squalid, stinking, unappetizing, unclean, vile, vulgar; ▪ *Ant* great, magnificent, pleasing, wonderful.

nasty [*adj2*] *indecent, smutty*
▪ *Syn* coarse, dirty, filthy, foul, immodest, immoral, improper, impure, lascivious, lewd, licentious, obscene, pornographic, ribald, scatological, unseemly, vulgar, wicked; ▪ *Ant* clean, decent, moral.

nasty [*adj3*] *bad-tempered, mean*
▪ *Syn* abusive, annoying, beastly, critical, cruel, distasteful, evil, hateful, malevolent, malicious, malignant, ornery, ruthless, sarcastic, sordid, spiteful, unpleasant, vicious, vile, wicked; ▪ *Ant* agreeable, friendly, happy, kind, pleasant.

nasty [*adj4*] *injurious, dangerous*
▪ *Syn* bad, critical, damaging, harmful, noxious, painful, poisonous, serious, severe, ugly; ▪ *Ant* aiding, assisting, helpful, helping, safe.

national [*adj*] *concerning a country with a government* ▪ *Syn* civic, communal, countrywide, domestic, ethnic, federal, general, governmental, home, imperial, interstate, nationwide, politic, public, royal, societal, sovereign, state, sweeping, vernacular, widespread; ▪ *Ant* local.

native [*adj1*] *innate, inherent*
▪ *Syn* built-in, congenital, connate, connatural, constitutional, endemic, essential, fundamental, genuine, hereditary, implanted, inborn, inbred, indigenous, ingrained, inherited, instinctive, intrinsic, inveterate, inwrought, natal, natural, original, real, unacquired, wild; ▪ *Ant* alien, foreign, outside.

native [*adj2*] *domestic, home*
▪ *Syn* aboriginal, belonging, endemic, homegrown, homemade, indigenous, inland, internal, local, mother, municipal, national, original, primary, primeval, primitive, regional, related, vernacular; ▪ *Ant* foreign, outside.

natural [*adj1*] *normal, everyday*
▪ *Syn* accustomed, characteristic, commonplace, congenital, counted on, customary, essential, familiar, general, habitual, inborn, indigenous, innate, instinctive, intuitive, looked for, matter-of-course, natal, ordinary, prevalent, probable, regular, relied on, typical, unacquired, uniform, universal, usual;

▪ *Ant* abnormal, different, uncommon, unnatural.

natural [*adj2*] *open, unaffected*
▪ *Syn* artless, being oneself, candid, credulous, direct, easy, frank, genuine, inartificial, ingenuous, instinctive, naive, plain, primitive, provincial, real, rustic, simple, sincere, straightforward, trusting, unassumed, unembarrassed, unforced, unpolished, unpretentious; ▪ *Ant* affected, artificial, pretended, unnatural.

natural [*adj3*] *organic, unrefined*
▪ *Syn* agrarian, agrestal, crude, native, plain, pure, raw, unbleached, uncultivated, undomesticated, unmixed, unpolished, unprocessed, whole, wild; ▪ *Ant* artificial, fixed, modified, refined, unnatural.

naturally [*adv*] *as anticipated*
▪ *Syn* artlessly, by birth, by nature, characteristically, commonly, consistently, customarily, easily, freely, generally, habitually, instinctively, normally, openly, ordinarily, readily, simply, typically, unaffectedly, uniformly, unpretentiously, usually; ▪ *Ant* affectedly, unnaturally.

natural medicine [*n*] *a system of health treatment using non-invasive techniques*
▪ *Syn* acupuncture, alternative medicine, complementary medicine, herbal medicine, holistic medicine, homeopathy, hydropathy, hypnotherapy, iridology, massage therapy, naturopathy, reflexology, shiatsu; ▪ *Ant* allopathy, conventional medicine, traditional medicine.

naughty [*adj1*] *bad, misbehaved*
▪ *Syn* annoying, contrary, disobedient, disorderly, evil, exasperating, fiendish, froward, headstrong, impish, indecorous, mischievous, obstreperous, playful, rascally, recalcitrant, roguish, rough, rowdy, teasing, ungovernable, unruly, wanton, wayward, wicked, willful, wrong; ▪ *Ant* behaved, controlled, good, obedient.

naughty [*adj2*] *obscene, vulgar*
▪ *Syn* adult, bawdy, improper, lascivious, lewd, pornographic, ribald, risqué; ▪ *Ant* clean, good, moral, pure.

nauseate [*v*] *make sick; disgust*
▪ *Syn* bother, disturb, horrify, offend, reluct, repel, repulse, revolt, sicken; ▪ *Ant* delight, impress, please, soothe.

nauseous [*adj*] *disgusting*
▪ *Syn* abhorrent, brackish, detestable, distasteful, ill, loathsome, offensive,

queasy, repugnant, repulsive, revolting, seasick, sick, sickening, squeamish; ▪ *Ant* nice, pleasing, soothing.

near [*adj1*] *close by physically*
▪ *Syn* abreast, abutting, adjoining, alongside, approximal, at close quarters, beside, bordering, close, close-at-hand, conterminous, contiguous, convenient, handy, immediate, nearby, neighboring, not remote, practically, proximate, side-by-side, touching; ▪ *Ant* away, distant, far, remote.

near [*adj2*] *close in time; forthcoming*
▪ *Syn* approaching, approximate, at hand, coming, comparative, expected, imminent, impending, looming, next, relative; ▪ *Ant* deferred, distant, expired, far, postponed, remote.

near [*adj3*] *familiar*
▪ *Syn* affecting, akin, allied, attached, close, connected, dear, friendly, intimate, related, touching; ▪ *Ant* far, gone, past, unfamiliar.

nearby [*adj*] *adjoining*
▪ *Syn* adjacent, close, close-at-hand, close-by, contiguous, convenient, handy, immediate, neighboring, proximate, ready; ▪ *Ant* far, faraway.

nearby [*adv*] *within reach*
▪ *Syn* about, at close quarters, close, close at hand, hard, near, not far away; ▪ *Ant* far, faraway.

nearing [*adj*] *approaching*
▪ *Syn* advancing, approximating, coming, forthcoming, imminent, impending, oncoming, threatening, upcoming; ▪ *Ant* departing, gone, leaving, past.

neat [*adj1*] *arranged well, uncluttered*
▪ *Syn* accurate, correct, dainty, elegant, fastidious, finicky, immaculate, in good shape, methodical, natty, orderly, precise, proper, regular, sleek, smart, spotless, systematic, tidy, well-groomed, well-kept; ▪ *Ant* disorderly, messed up, sloppy, slovenly, unkempt.

neat [*adj2*] *clever, practiced*
▪ *Syn* able, adroit, agile, artful, deft, efficient, effortless, expert, finished, graceful, handy, nimble, precise, quick, ready, skillful, stylish, well-judged; ▪ *Ant* disorganized, unpracticed.

nebulous [*adj*] *confused, obscure*
▪ *Syn* ambiguous, amorphous, cloudy, dim, hazy, imprecise, indistinct, misty, shapeless, unformed, vague; ▪ *Ant* apparent, definite, obvious, plain.

necessarily [*adv*] *inevitably, certainly*
▪ *Syn* accordingly, automatically, by definition, cardinally, compulsorily, exigently, incontrovertibly, indubitably, inexorably, naturally, of necessity, positively, significantly, undoubtedly, unquestionably, vitally; ▪ *Ant* unnecessarily.

necessary [*adj1*] *essential*
▪ *Syn* all-important, basic, binding, cardinal, chief, compelling, compulsory, crucial, decisive, elementary, exigent, expedient, fundamental, imperative, incumbent on, indispensable, mandatory, momentous, needed, needful, obligatory, paramount, prerequisite, pressing, prime, principal, quintessential, required, requisite, significant, specified, unavoidable, urgent, vital, wanted; ▪ *Ant* inessential, unimportant, unnecessary, useless.

necessary [*adj2*] *inevitable*
▪ *Syn* assured, certain, fated, imminent, ineluctable, ineludible, inerrant, inescapable, inevasible, inexorable, infallible, returnless, unavoidable, undeniable, unescapable; ▪ *Ant* contingent, needless, optional, voluntary.

need [*v*] *want something*
▪ *Syn* be deficient, be deprived, be inadequate, be in want, covet, crave, desire, do without, exact, feel the necessity for, hanker, have occasion to, hunger, hurt for, lack, long, miss, necessitate, pine, require, suffer privation, thirst, wish, yearn, yen for; ▪ *Ant* do not want, have.

needle [*v*] *tease, annoy*
▪ *Syn* aggravate, badger, bait, bother, examine, gnaw, goad, harass, irritate, nettle, plague, prick, prod, question, rile, ruffle, spur, taunt, worry; ▪ *Ant* praise.

needless [*adj*] *unnecessary, groundless*
▪ *Syn* causeless, expendable, gratuitous, nonessential, pointless, redundant, superfluous, uncalled-for, unrequired, useless; ▪ *Ant* grounded, necessary, needed.

needy [*adj*] *deprived, impoverished*
▪ *Syn* beggared, destitute, disadvantaged, impecunious, indigent, necessitous, penniless, plague-stricken, underprivileged, unprosperous; ▪ *Ant* affluent, rich, wealthy.

nefarious [*adj*] *bad, sinful*
▪ *Syn* abominable, base, corrupt, degenerate, depraved, evil, flagrant, foul, glaring, heinous, infamous, iniquitous, miscreant, monstrous, odious, opprobri-

ous, putrid, rank, rotten, shameful, treacherous, vile, wicked; ▪ *Ant* good, honorable, respectable, virtuous, worthy.

negate [v] *contradict, countermand*
▪ *Syn* abate, abolish, abrogate, annihilate, belie, cancel, controvert, deny, disaffirm, disallow, disprove, frustrate, gainsay, impugn, invalidate, kill, neutralize, nullify, oppose, put down, rebut, refute, repeal, rescind, retract, revoke, traverse, undo, vitiate; ▪ *Ant* allow, approve, permit.

negative [adj] *bad, contradictory*
▪ *Syn* abrogating, adverse, against, annulling, antagonistic, anti, balky, colorless, con, contrary, contravening, counteractive, cynical, denying, detrimental, disallowing, disavowing, dissentient, dissenting, gainsaying, gloomy, impugning, invalidating, jaundiced, naysaying, neutralizing, nugatory, nullifying, opposing, pessimistic, privative, recusant, refusing, rejecting, removed, repugnant, resisting, resistive, unaffirmative, unenthusiastic, unfavorable, uninterested, unwilling, weak; ▪ *Ant* good, positive.

neglect [n1] *disregard*
▪ *Syn* carelessness, coolness, delinquency, disdain, disregardance, disrespect, heedlessness, inadvertence, inattention, inconsideration, indifference, laxity, laxness, oversight, scorn, slight, thoughtlessness, unconcern; ▪ *Ant* care, obedience, observance, regard, respect, watchfulness.

neglect [n2] *failure, default*
▪ *Syn* carelessness, chaos, delay, delinquency, dereliction, dilapidation, forgetfulness, lapse, laxity, laxness, limbo, neglectfulness, negligence, omission, oversight, pretermission, remissness, slackness, slovenliness; ▪ *Ant* accomplishment, achievement, completion, finish, success.

neglect [v1] *be indifferent, leave alone*
▪ *Syn* affront, brush aside, brush off, contemn, depreciate, despise, detest, discount, disdain, dismiss, disregard, ignore, overlook, pass by, pass over, pass up, pay no attention to, pretermit, rebuff, reject, scant, scorn, slight, slur, spurn, underestimate; ▪ *Ant* cherish, concern, guard, nurture, protect, take care of, watch.

neglect [v2] *fail to do; forget*
▪ *Syn* bypass, discard, disregard, elide, evade, miss, omit, overlook, postpone,

procrastinate, shirk, skip, trifle; ▪ *Ant* accomplish, achieve, complete, do, finish, succeed.

neglectful [adj] *careless, failing*
▪ *Syn* behindhand, delinquent, disregardful, heedless, inattentive, lax, lazy, negligent, regardless, remiss, slack, thoughtless, unmindful; ▪ *Ant* attentive, careful, caring, mindful, successful.

negligent [adj] *careless, indifferent*
▪ *Syn* behindhand, cursory, delinquent, derelict, disregardful, forgetful, heedless, inadvertent, inconsiderate, lax, neglectful, offhand, regardless, slack, slovenly, thoughtless, unheedful, unmindful, unthinking; ▪ *Ant* attentive, careful, caring, mindful, successful.

negligible [adj] *insignificant*
▪ *Syn* imperceptible, inconsequential, minor, minute, outside, petty, remote, slender, slight, slim, small, trifling, trivial, unimportant; ▪ *Ant* important, major, significant.

negotiate [v] *traverse, cross*
▪ *Syn* clear, get around, get over, get past, hurdle, leap over, overleap, pass, pass through, surmount, vault; ▪ *Ant* remain, stay.

neighborly [adj] *friendly*
▪ *Syn* amiable, civil, companionable, considerate, cordial, genial, gregarious, harmonious, helpful, hospitable, kind, obliging, sociable, well-disposed; ▪ *Ant* cold, distant, unfriendly, unneighborly, unsociable.

neologism [n] *new word*
▪ *Syn* coinage, neology, new phrase, slang; ▪ *Ant* time-worn.

nerve [v] *strengthen, hearten*
▪ *Syn* animate, brace, cheer, embolden, encourage, enhearten, fortify, inspirit, invigorate, steel; ▪ *Ant* discourage, dishearten, fear, weaken.

nerveless [adj1] *calm, cool*
▪ *Syn* collected, composed, controlled, impassive, imperturbable, intrepid, patient, self-possessed, tranquil, unemotional; ▪ *Ant* disconcerted, nervous.

nerveless [adj2] *scared to death*
▪ *Syn* afraid, cowardly, debilitated, enervated, fearful, feeble, nervous, petrified, timid, weak; ▪ *Ant* brave, courageous, nervy, unafraid.

nervous [adj] *anxious, fearful*
▪ *Syn* afraid, agitated, annoyed, apprehensive, bothered, concerned, distressed,

disturbed, edgy, excitable, fidgety, fitful, flustered, hesitant, hysterical, irritable, neurotic, overwrought, querulous, restive, ruffled, sensitive, shrinking, shy, skittish, snappish, solicitous, taut, tense, timid, timorous, troubled, uneasy, unrestful, upset, uptight, volatile, weak, worried; ▪ *Ant* brave, calm, unafraid, unnervous, unworried.

nervy [*adj*] *bold, pushy*
▪ *Syn* crass, crude, forward, impudent, inconsiderate, pert, rude, smart, wise; ▪ *Ant* afraid, modest, shy, timid, unwilling.

net [*adj*] *profiting*
▪ *Syn* after deductions, after taxes, clear, excluding, exclusive, final, irreducible, pure, remaining, take-home, undeductible; ▪ *Ant* unprofitable.

net [*v1*] *capture*
▪ *Syn* catch, enmesh, ensnare, entangle, trap; ▪ *Ant* free, let go, release.

net [*v2*] *gain after expenses*
▪ *Syn* accumulate, bring in, clean up, clear, earn, make, profit, realize, reap; ▪ *Ant* gross.

nettle [*v*] *provoke, upset*
▪ *Syn* annoy, chafe, disgust, disturb, exasperate, fret, goad, harass, huff, incense, insult, irritate, miff, pester, pet, pique, rile, roil, ruffle, stew, tease, tiff, vex; ▪ *Ant* appease, mollify, please.

neurotic [*adj*] *mentally maladjusted*
▪ *Syn* aberrant, abnormal, anxious, compulsive, distraught, disturbed, erratic, hysteric, inhibited, manic, nervous, obsessive, overwrought, psychoneurotic, unhealthy, unstable, upset, uptight; ▪ *Ant* adjusted, balanced, sane, stable.

neutral [*adj1*] *impartial, noncommittal*
▪ *Syn* aloof, bystanding, cool, detached, disengaged, dispassionate, evenhanded, fair-minded, impersonal, indifferent, nonaligned, nonchalant, nonpartisan, pacifistic, relaxed, unaligned, unbiased, uncommitted, unconcerned, undecided, unprejudiced; ▪ *Ant* biased, committal, partial, predisposed, prejudiced.

neutral [*adj2*] *flat, dull to senses*
▪ *Syn* abstract, achromatic, colorless, drab, expressionless, indeterminate, indistinct, intermediate, toneless, undefined, vague, vanilla; ▪ *Ant* bright, loud, strong.

neutralize [*v*] *counteract*
▪ *Syn* abrogate, annul, balance, cancel,

counterbalance, counterpoise, countervail, defeat, frustrate, invalidate, negative, nullify, offset, overcome, override, redress, subdue, undo; ▪ *Ant* activate, animate, dynamize, stimulate, vitalize.

never [*adv*] *not at any time*
▪ *Syn* at no time, forget it, nevermore, not at all, not ever, not in any way, not in the least, not under any condition; ▪ *Ant* always, forever.

never-ending [*adj*] *continual, unceasing*
▪ *Syn* amaranthine, boundless, ceaseless, continuous, eternal, everlasting, immortal, incessant, interminable, nonstop, perpetual, persistent, relentless, timeless, unbroken, unchanging; ▪ *Ant* ceasing, ending, halting, intermittent, interrupted.

new [*adj1*] *recent, fresh*
▪ *Syn* advanced, au courant, contemporary, current, dewy, fashionable, inexperienced, latest, modern, neoteric, novel, original, recent, strange, topical, ultramodern, unfamiliar, unique, unknown, unseasoned, up-to-date, virgin, youthful; ▪ *Ant* deteriorated, old, old-fashioned, outdated, worn.

new [*adj2*] *additional*
▪ *Syn* added, another, else, extra, farther, fresh, further, increased, more, other, supplementary; ▪ *Ant* common, existent, existing, hackneyed, usual.

new [*adj3*] *modernized, restored*
▪ *Syn* altered, changed, improved, redesigned, refreshed, regenerated, renewed, revived; ▪ *Ant* old, old-fashioned, outdated, out-of-date, unstylish.

new [*adv*] *recently*
▪ *Syn* afresh, anew, freshly, lately, newly, of late; ▪ *Ant* old, past.

newcomer [*n*] *person who has just arrived in area* ▪ *Syn* alien, arrival, beginner, foreigner, freshman/woman, immigrant, latecomer, maverick, neophyte, novice, outsider, rookie, settler, stranger; ▪ *Ant* native, old hack.

newfangled [*adj*] *quite recent*
▪ *Syn* contemporary, fashionable, fresh, in vogue, modern, modernistic, neoteric, new, new-fashioned, novel, popular, unique; ▪ *Ant* old, old-fashioned, old hack, outmoded.

newly [*adv*] *very recently*
▪ *Syn* anew, freshly, just, lately, latterly, of late; ▪ *Ant* past.

news [*n*] *information, revelation*
▪ *Syn* account, announcement, broadcast,

bulletin, cable, communication, copy, data, discovery, dispatch, enlightenment, expos, headlines, hearsay, knowledge, leak, lowdown, message, narration, news flash, recital, release, report, statement, story, telecast, telegram; ▪ *Ant* history.

next [*adj*] *coming immediately after in space, time, order* ▪ *Syn* abutting, adjacent, adjoining, alongside, back-to-back, beside, close, closest, coming, consequent, ensuing, following, later, meeting, neighboring, proximate, side-by-side, subsequent, succeeding, touching; ▪ *Ant* earlier, preceding, previous.

next [*adv*] *immediately after in time, space, order* ▪ *Syn* after, afterward, afterwhile, behind, by and by, closely, coming up, following, later, latterly, next off, subsequently, thereafter; ▪ *Ant* earlier, preceding, previous.

nibble [*v*] *bite, pick at*
▪ *Syn* crop, eat, gnaw, munch, snack; ▪ *Ant* gorge.

nice [*adj1*] *likable, agreeable*
▪ *Syn* amiable, approved, attractive, becoming, charming, commendable, co-pacetic, cordial, courteous, ducky, fair, favorable, genial, gentle, good, gracious, helpful, inviting, kind, lovely, obliging, pleasant, polite, seemly, simpatico, swell, welcome, well-mannered, winning; ▪ *Ant* bad, disagreeable, horrible, nasty, repulsive, unlikable, unpleasant.

nice [*adj2*] *precise, neat, refined*
▪ *Syn* accurate, becoming, befitting, choosy, correct, critical, dainty, decent, discerning, discriminating, exacting, fastidious, finicking, genteel, meticulous, particular, proper, refined, respectable, right, scrupulous, seemly, strict, subtle, virtuous, well-bred; ▪ *Ant* disordered, imprecise, unmannerly, unrefined.

nifty [*adj*] *marvelous*
▪ *Syn* chic, clever, dandy, enjoyable, keen, neat, pleasing, quick, sharp, smart, spruce, stylish, swell, terrific; ▪ *Ant* bad, displeasing, unhandy, unpleasant.

nightly [*adj/adv*] *each evening; after dark*
▪ *Syn* at night, by night, every night, in the night, night after night, nights, nighttime, nocturnal, nocturnally; ▪ *Ant* daily.

nightmare [*n*] *bad dream or experience*
▪ *Syn* dream, fancy, fantasy, hallucination, horror, illusion, incubus, ordeal, phantasm, succubus, torment, trial, tribulation, vision; ▪ *Ant* daymare.

nihilism [*n*] *refusal to believe*
▪ *Syn* abnegation, agnosticism, anarchy, atheism, denial, disbelief, disorder, lawlessness, nonbelief, rejection, renunciation, repudiation, skepticism, terrorism; ▪ *Ant* belief, faith, obedience, optimism.

nil [*adj*] *nonexistent*
▪ *Syn* naught, nihil, none, nothing, nought, zero; ▪ *Ant* existent, existing.

nimble [*adj*] *dexterous, smart*
▪ *Syn* active, adept, adroit, agile, alert, bright, brisk, clever, deft, handy, light, lissome, lithe, lively, proficient, prompt, quick, quick-witted, ready, skillful, sprightly, spry, swift, vigilant, wide-awake; ▪ *Ant* awkward, clumsy, lumbering, slow, undexterous, unhandy.

nip [*v1*] *bite; take small part*
▪ *Syn* catch, clip, compress, grip, munch, nibble, pinch, snag, tweak, twinge, twitch; ▪ *Ant* gorge.

nip [*v2*] *stop; thwart*
▪ *Syn* arrest, balk, blight, check, dash, end, frustrate; ▪ *Ant* allow, encourage, permit.

noble [*adj1*] *aristocratic*
▪ *Syn* gentle, highborn, imperial, kingly, lordly, nobiliary, patrician, princely, queenly, titled, wellborn; ▪ *Ant* ignoble, lowly, servile, unaristocratic, unsophisticated.

noble [*adj2*] *dignified, excellent*
▪ *Syn* august, beneficent, big, bounteous, courtly, cultivated, distinguished, elevated, eminent, first-rate, gracious, grand, great, high-minded, honorable, humane, imposing, impressive, lofty, lordly, magnanimous, meritorious, preeminent, refined, reputable, stately, sublime, upright, virtuous, worthy; ▪ *Ant* ignoble, undignified, unrefined, unsophisticated.

nobody/nonentity [*n*] *person of little importance* ▪ *Syn* cipher, insignificancy, menial, nothing, upstart, zip; ▪ *Ant* somebody.

nocturnal [*adj*] *happening at night*
▪ *Syn* after dark, late, night, night-loving, nightly, nighttime; ▪ *Ant* by day, daily, diurnal.

nod [*v*] *fall asleep*
▪ *Syn* become inattentive, be sleepy, doze, drift, drift off, droop, drowse, nap, sleep, slump; ▪ *Ant* perk up, wake up.

noiseless [*adj*] *quiet*
▪ *Syn* hushed, hushful, inaudible, mute,

muted, silent, soundless, speechless, still, voiceless, wordless; ▪ *Ant* clamorous, noisy.

noisome [*adj*] *immoral, bad, offensive* ▪ *Syn* baneful, dangerous, deadly, deleterious, fetid, foul, harmful, hurtful, injurious, insalubrious, insalutary, loathsome, malodorous, nauseating, pernicious, pestilential, poisonous, putrid, rank, repulsive, sickening, smelly, unhealthy, unwholesome, vile; ▪ *Ant* good, just, moral, upright.

noisy [*adj*] *very loud and unharmonious in sound* ▪ *Syn* boisterous, booming, cacophonous, clamorous, clangorous, clattery, deafening, ear-splitting, jumping, loudmouth, obstreperous, piercing, rackety, rambunctious, rowdy, strident, tumultuous/tumultuous, turbulent, turned up, uproarious, vociferous; ▪ *Ant* noiseless, quiet, silent, still.

nomadic [*adj*] *itinerant* ▪ *Syn* drifting, gypsy, itinerate, migrant, migratory, pastoral, perambulant, perambulatory, peripatetic, roaming, roving, traveling, vagabond, vagrant, wandering, wayfaring; ▪ *Ant* native, settled.

nominal [*adj1*] *supposed, theoretical* ▪ *Syn* alleged, apparent, as advertised, formal, given, honorary, in effect only, in name only, mentioned, named, ostensible, pretended, professed, puppet, purported, seeming, self-styled, simple, so-called, stated, suggested, titular; ▪ *Ant* actual, real, true.

nominal [*adj2*] *insignificant* ▪ *Syn* cheap, inconsiderable, inexpensive, low, low-priced, meaningless, minimal, small, symbolic, token, trifling, trivial, unnecessary; ▪ *Ant* important, significant.

nominate [*v*] *designate, select* ▪ *Syn* appoint, assign, call, choose, commission, decide, draft, elect, empower, intend, make, name, offer, present, propose, put up, recommend, slate, slot, suggest, tender, term; ▪ *Ant* ignore, pass over.

nonchalant [*adj*] *easygoing, laid back* ▪ *Syn* airy, blasé, calm, careless, casual, composed, detached, easy, effortless, happy, impassive, imperturbable, insouciant, lackadaisical, light, loose, lukewarm, mellow, neutral, offhand, placid, serene, smooth, trifling, uncaring, unconcerned, unemotional,

unflappable; ▪ *Ant* intense, jumpy, nervous, unnerved.

noncommittal [*adj*] *unwilling to decide* ▪ *Syn* ambiguous, circumspect, constrained, discreet, equivocal, evasive, guarded, hush-hush, incommunicable, indefinite, judicious, neutral, playing-it-cool, politic, reserved, temporizing, tentative, unrevealing, vague, wary; ▪ *Ant* committal, decisive, definite, judgemental, willing.

noncompliant [*adj*] *unwilling to go along with something* ▪ *Syn* belligerent, contumacious, declining, divergent, impatient, negative, objecting, rebellious, recalcitrant, refractory, restive, truculent; ▪ *Ant* compliant, obedient, subservient, willing.

nonconformist [*adj*] *unwilling to behave, believe as most do* ▪ *Syn* dissident, dropout, heretical, heterodox, iconoclastic, maverick, oddball, offbeat, original, rebel, sectarian, swinger, unorthodox; ▪ *Ant* conforming, conformist, obeying, orthodox.

nondescript [*adj*] *undistinguished, commonplace* ▪ *Syn* characterless, colorless, common, dull, empty, featureless, indescribable, indeterminate, ordinary, unclassifiable, unclassified, unexceptional, uninspiring, uninteresting, unmemorable, unremarkable, vague; ▪ *Ant* describable, different, distinguished, illustrative, remarkable, superior, uncommon.

none [*prep*] *not one thing* ▪ *Syn* nil, nobody, no one, no one at all, no part, not a bit, not any, not anyone, not anything, not a soul, not a thing, nothing, not one, zero; ▪ *Ant* some.

nonessential [*adj*] *not needed or important* ▪ *Syn* dispensable, excessive, expendable, extraneous, inessential, insignificant, peripheral, petty, superfluous, trivial, unimportant, unnecessary; ▪ *Ant* essential, important, necessary, needed.

nonexistent [*adj*] *fictional, not real* ▪ *Syn* absent, airy, baseless, blank, chimerical, dead, defunct, departed, dreamlike, dreamy, empty, ethereal, extinct, extinguished, fancied, flimsy, gone, gossamery, groundless, hallucinatory, hypothetical, illusory, imaginary, imagined, immaterial, legendary, lost, missing, mythical, null, passed away, perished, shadowy, tenuous, ungrounded, unsubstantial, vague, void, without foundation;

• **Ant** actual, existent, existing, real, true.

nonpartisan [adj] *impartial; not political* • **Syn** detached, equitable, fair, independent, just, neutral, nonaligned, objective, unaffected, unbiased, uninvolved, unprejudiced; • **Ant** biased, decided, partial, partisan, political, prejudiced.

nonplus [v] *confuse, perplex* • **Syn** astonish, astound, baffle, boggle, confound, daze, discomfit, disconcert, dismay, dumbfound, embarrass, faze, fluster, frustrate, muddle, mystify, overcome, paralyze, puzzle, rattle, stagger, stump, take aback; • **Ant** clear up, educate, enlighten, explain.

nonsense [n] *craziness, ridiculousness* • **Syn** absurdity, babble, drivel, fatuity, flightiness, foolishness, fun, gibberish, giddiness, imprudence, inanity, jazz, jest, ludicrousness, madness, palaver, prattle, pretense, ranting, rashness, senselessness, silliness, thoughtlessness; • **Ant** clarity, common sense, fact, intelligibility, sense, truth, understanding.

nonstop [adj] *continuous, direct* • **Syn** ceaseless, constant, endless, incessant, interminable, relentless, steady, unbroken, unfaltering, unremitting; • **Ant** incontinuous, indirect, intermittent, stopping, terminating.

nonviolent [adj] *peaceful* • **Syn** irenic, nonbelligerent, pacifist, passive, peaceable, quiet, resistant, without violence; • **Ant** hateful, mean, violent, wicked, wild.

noon [n] *the middle of a day* • **Syn** apex, high noon, meridian, midday, noonday, noontide, noontime, twelve noon, twelve o'clock; • **Ant** midnight.

normal [adj1] *common, usual* • **Syn** accustomed, acknowledged, average, commonplace, conventional, customary, general, habitual, mean, median, methodical, natural, orderly, ordinary, popular, prevalent, regular, routine, standard, traditional, typic, typical, unexceptional; • **Ant** abnormal, irregular, odd, strange, uncommon, unconventional, unusual.

normal [adj2] *sane, rational* • **Syn** healthy, in good health, lucid, reasonable, right, right-minded, sound, together, well-adjusted, whole, wholesome; • **Ant** abnormal, eccentric, insane, irrational, irregular, odd, unbalanced.

normally [adv] *usually* • **Syn** as a rule, commonly, habitually, in accordance with, ordinarily, regularly, typically; • **Ant** abnormally, never.

north [adj/adv] *toward the top pole of the earth* • **Syn** arctic, boreal, cold, frozen, hyperborean, northbound, northerly, northern, northmost, northward, polar, septentrional, toward North Pole, tundra; • **Ant** south.

nosy [adj] *very curious; prying* • **Syn** eavesdropping, inquisitive, inquisitorial, inquisitory, interested, interfering, intermeddling, intrusive, meddlesome, personal, searching, snooping, snoopy; • **Ant** indifferent, uncaring, unconcerned, uninterested.

notable [adj] *very important; famous* • **Syn** celebrated, conspicuous, distinguished, eminent, extraordinary, famed, great, illustrious, manifest, marked, memorable, nameable, noteworthy, noticeable, notorious, observable, outstanding, preeminent, pronounced, remarkable, renowned, serious, uncommon, well-known; • **Ant** commonplace, inconsequential, insignificant, ordinary, unimportant, unnoticeable, unremarkable.

notably [adv] *especially* • **Syn** conspicuously, distinctly, exceedingly, exceptionally, greatly, highly, hugely, markedly, noticeably, outstandingly, particularly, prominently, remarkably, reputably, strikingly, uncommonly, very; • **Ant** insignificantly, unnotably, unremarkably.

notch [v] *indent* • **Syn** chisel, cleave, crenelate, crimp, cut, dent, gash, incise, jag, mark, mill, nick, scallop, score, scratch; • **Ant** flush.

note [n] *attention, heed* • **Syn** cognizance, mark, mind, notice, observance, observation, regard, remark; • **Ant** heedlessness, ignorance, neglect, unobservance.

note [v] *observe, perceive* • **Syn** catch, clock, denote, descry, discern, distinguish, enter, heed, indicate, jot down, mark, mention, notice, put down, record, set down, transcribe, view, write down; • **Ant** ignore, neglect.

noted [adj] *famous, eminent* • **Syn** acclaimed, celeb, celebrated, conspicuous, distinguished, esteemed, illustrious, leading, notable, notorious, popular, prominent, recognized, renowned, somebody, well-known; ▪ *Ant* insignificant, unimportant, unknown.

noteworthy [*adj*] *important*
▪ *Syn* conspicuous, evident, exceptional, extraordinary, major-league, manifest, meaningful, memorable, mind-blowing, murder, nameable, notable, noticeable, observable, outstanding, patent, prominent, remarkable, serious, significant, super, terrific, unique, unusual, utmost; ▪ *Ant* common, inconsequential, insignificant, ordinary, unimportant.

notice [*v*] *observe, perceive*
▪ *Syn* acknowledge, advert, allude, catch, clock, descry, detect, discern, distinguish, espy, heed, look at, mark, mind, note, pick up on, recognize, refer, regard, remark, see, spot, take in; ▪ *Ant* ignore, miss, neglect, overlook.

noticeable [*adj*] *conspicuous, evident*
▪ *Syn* apparent, appreciable, arresting, arrestive, clear, distinct, eye-catching, manifest, marked, notable, noteworthy, observable, obvious, outstanding, palpable, patent, perceptible, plain, pointed, prominent, remarkable, salient, sensational, signal, spectacular, striking, unmistakable; ▪ *Ant* forgotten, inconspicuous, obscure, overlooked, unnoticeable.

notify [*v*] *inform*
▪ *Syn* acquaint, advise, air, alert, announce, apprise, assert, blazon, brief, broadcast, cable, caution, circulate, clue in, convey, cue, debrief, declare, disclose, disseminate, divulge, enlighten, express, fill in, give, herald, hint, let in on, let know, make known, mention, pass out, post, proclaim, promulgate, publish, radio, report, reveal, send word, speak, spread, state, suggest, talk, teach, telephone, tell, tip off, vent, warn, wire, write; ▪ *Ant* conceal, hide, suppress.

notion [*n*] *whim, desire*
▪ *Syn* caprice, conceit, fancy, humor, imagination, impulse, inclination, wish; ▪ *Ant* need.

notoriety [*n*] *reputation*
▪ *Syn* celebrity, dishonor, disrepute, fame, infamy, obloquy, opprobrium, renown, scandal; ▪ *Ant* obscurity.

nourish [*v*] *feed, care for*
▪ *Syn* attend, cherish, comfort, cultivate, encourage, foster, furnish, maintain,

nurse, nurture, promote, provide, supply, support, sustain, tend; ▪ *Ant* abandon, deprive, neglect, starve.

nourishing [*adj*] *healthful*
▪ *Syn* alimentative, beneficial, health-giving, healthy, nutrient, nutrimental, nutritious, nutritive, wholesome; ▪ *Ant* bad, unhealthy, unwholesome.

novel [*adj*] *new, original*
▪ *Syn* atypical, avant-garde, contemporary, different, fresh, innovative, modernistic, neoteric, offbeat, peculiar, rare, recent, singular, strange, uncommon, unfamiliar, unique, unusual; ▪ *Ant* common, customary, familiar, old, ordinary, overused, used, usual, worn.

novice [*n*] *person just learning something*
▪ *Syn* amateur, apprentice, beginner, fledgling, freshman/woman, greenhorn, gremlin, learner, neophyte, newcomer, postulant, prentice, probationer, proselyte, pupil, recruit, rookie, starter, student, trainee, undergraduate; ▪ *Ant* expert, professional.

now [*adv*] *presently*
▪ *Syn* any more, at once, at the moment, at this time, away, directly, first off, forthwith, here and now, immediately, in a minute, instantly, just now, momentarily, promptly, right away, right now, straightaway, these days, this day, today; ▪ *Ant* future, later, past.

noxious [*adj*] *deadly, injurious*
▪ *Syn* baneful, corrupting, dangerous, deleterious, detrimental, fetid, foul, harmful, injurious, insalubrious, noisome, pestiferous, pestilential, poisonous, putrid, sickly, stinking, toxic, unhealthful, unhealthy, unwholesome, venomous, virulent; ▪ *Ant* curing, good, healthy, helpful, hygienic, pure, sterile, wholesome.

nuance [*n*] *slight difference; shading*
▪ *Syn* distinction, gradation, hint, implication, nicety, refinement, shade, shadow, soupon, subtlety, suggestion, suspicion, tinge, touch, trace; ▪ *Ant* old.

nub [*n*] *core, gist*
▪ *Syn* basic, crux, essence, kernel, nubbin, nucleus, pith, point, short, substance, upshot; ▪ *Ant* exterior, outside.

nucleus [*n*] *core; basis for something's beginning* ▪ *Syn* bud, center, crux, embryo, foundation, germ, heart, kernel, matter, nub, pivot, principle, seed, spark; ▪ *Ant* exterior, exteriority, outside.

nude [*adj*] *without clothes, covering*
▪ *Syn* bald, bare, bare-skinned, disrobed, exposed, garmentless, in birthday suit, naked, raw, skin, stark, stripped, unattired, unclad, unclothed, uncovered, undraped, undressed; ▪ *Ant* clothed, covered.

nuisance [*n*] *annoyance; annoying person* ▪ *Syn* besetment, blister, bore, bother, botheration, botherment, creep, exasperation, frump, gadfly, inconvenience, infliction, irritant, irritation, louse, offense, pain, pest, pester, pesterer, plague, problem, terror, trouble, vexation; ▪ *Ant* delight, happiness, pleasantry, pleasure.

null [*adj*] *ineffectual, valueless*
▪ *Syn* absent, bad, barren, characterless, imaginary, ineffective, inefficacious, inoperative, invalid, negative, nonexistent, nothing, powerless, unavailing, unreal, unsanctioned, useless, vain, void, worthless; ▪ *Ant* effective, effectual, valid, valuable, worthwhile, worthy.

nullify [*v*] *cancel, revoke*
▪ *Syn* abate, abolish, abrogate, annihilate, annul, ax, compensate, confine, counteract, counterbalance, countervail, disannul, invalidate, limit, negate, neutralize, offset, renege, repeal, rescind, restrict, undo, veto, vitiate, void; ▪ *Ant* affirm, pass, sanctify, validate.

numb [*adj*] *deadened, insensitive*
▪ *Syn* aloof, anesthetized, apathetic, asleep, benumbed, callous, casual, comatose, dazed, dead, detached, disinterested, frozen, immobilized, incurious, indifferent, insensate, insensible, insentient, lethargic, listless, numbed, paralyzed, phlegmatic, remote, senseless, stupefied, stuporous, torpid, unconcerned, unconscious, uncurious, unfeeling, uninterested; ▪ *Ant* lively, responsive, sensitive.

numb [*v*] *deaden*
▪ *Syn* anesthetize, benumb, blunt, chill, desensitize, dull, freeze, frost, immobilize, obtund, paralyze, stun, stupefy; ▪ *Ant* enliven.

number [*v*] *count, calculate*
▪ *Syn* account, add, add up, aggregate, amount, come, computer, count off, enumerate, estimate, figure in, figure out, include, keep tabs, numerate, reckon, run, run down, run into, run to, sum, take account of, tale, tally, tell, total; ▪ *Ant* estimate, guess.

numbered [*adj*] *limited in number*
▪ *Syn* categorized, checked, counted, designated, doomed, enumerated, fixed, included, indicated, marked, specified, told, totalled; ▪ *Ant* infinite, unlimited, unnumbered.

numberless [*adj*] *infinite*
▪ *Syn* countless, endless, incalculable, innumerable, jillion, many, multitudinous, myriad, numerous, umpteen, uncountable, uncounted, unnumbered, untold; ▪ *Ant* counted, finite, limited, numbered.

numeric/numerical [*adj*] *concerning mathematics* ▪ *Syn* algebraic, algorithmic, arithmetic, arithmetical, binary, differential, digital, exponent, exponential, fraction, fractional, integral, logarithm, logarithmic, mathematical, numeral, numerary, statistical; ▪ *Ant* alphabetic, alphabetical.

numerous [*adj*] *many, abundant*
▪ *Syn* big, copious, diverse, great, infinite, large, legion, multifarious, multitudinal, multitudinous, plentiful, populous, profuse, rife, several, sundry, thick, various, voluminous; ▪ *Ant* deficient, few, lacking, little, small.

nurse [*v*] *care for, tend*
▪ *Syn* aid, attend, cherish, cradle, cultivate, encourage, father, feed, forward, foster, harbor, humor, immunize, inoculate, keep alive, look after, medicate, minister to, mother, nourish, nurture, pamper, preserve, serve, succor, take care of, vaccinate, wait on, watch over; ▪ *Ant* ignore, neglect.

nurture [*n*] *development, nourishment*
▪ *Syn* breeding, care, diet, discipline, education, feed, food, instruction, nutriment, provisions, rearing, sustenance, training, upbringing, viands, victuals; ▪ *Ant* deprivation, ignorance, neglect, starvation.

nurture [*v*] *feed, care for*
▪ *Syn* back, bolster, bring up, cherish, cultivate, develop, discipline, educate, foster, instruct, nourish, nurse, nursle, provide, raise, rear, school, support, sustain, tend, train, uphold; ▪ *Ant* deprive, ignore, neglect, starve.

nutritious [*adj*] *healthy*
▪ *Syn* balanced, beneficial, good, healthful, invigorating, nourishing, nutrient, salubrious, salutary, strengthening, wholesome; ▪ *Ant* bad, insubstantial, unhealthful, unhealthy, unwholesome.

nuts/nutty [adj] *mentally deranged*
▪ *Syn* absurd, bedlamite, crazy, daffy, demented, eccentric, foolish, harebrained, insane, irrational, keen, kooky, loony, lunatic, mad, ridiculous, touched, unusual, zealous; ▪ *Ant* balanced, calm, sane, well.

O

oaf [n] *person who is clumsy, stupid*
▪ *Syn* beast, blunderer, brute, clod, dolt, dunce, fool, idiot, imbecile, loser; ▪ *Ant* genius, intellectual, sage.

obdurate [adj] *pigheaded, stubborn*
▪ *Syn* adamant, callous, dogged, firm, harsh, heartless, immovable, inexorable, inflexible, mean, obstinate, perverse, rigid, tough, unbending, uncooperative, unshakable, unsympathetic, unyielding; ▪ *Ant* amenable, gentle, submissive, yielding.

obedient [adj] *well-behaved; submissive*
▪ *Syn* acquiescent, amenable, attentive, biddable, compliant, controllable, devoted, docile, dutiful, faithful, governable, honoring, law-abiding, loyal, obeisant, obliging, pliant, resigned, respectful, reverential, subservient, tame, tractable, under control, well-trained, willing, yielding; ▪ *Ant* contrary, disobedient, insolent, misbehaving, mutinous, obstinate, rebellious.

obeisance [n] *salutation*
▪ *Syn* allegiance, bow, curtsy, deference, fealty, genuflection, homage, honor, loyalty, praise, respect, reverence; ▪ *Ant* disregard, disrespect, irreverance, treachery.

obese [adj] *very overweight*
▪ *Syn* adipose, avoirdupois, corpulent, fat, heavy, outsize, paunchy, plump, porcine, portly, pudgy, rotund, stout; ▪ *Ant* emaciated, gaunt, lank, skinny, underweight.

obey [v] *conform, give in*
▪ *Syn* abide by, accede, accept, accord, acquiesce, act upon, adhere to, agree, assent, carry out, comply, concur, do one's bidding, do what one is told, follow, fulfill, heed, mind, observe, serve, submit, surrender, take orders; ▪ *Ant* be insubordinate, defy, disobey, mutiny, rebel.

obituary [n] *notice of person's death*
▪ *Syn* announcement, death notice, eulogy, mortuary tribute, necrology, obit, register; ▪ *Ant* birth announcement.

object [n] *aim, recipient*
▪ *Syn* focus, receiver, target, victim; ▪ *Ant* subject.

object [v] *disagree, argue against*
▪ *Syn* balk, challenge, criticize, demur, deprecate, disapprove, disavow, discountenance, dispute, dissent, except, expostulate, gripe, grouse, inveigh, oppose, protest, rail, raise objection, rant, rave, remonstrate, take exception; ▪ *Ant* accept, acquiesce, agree, concur, consent, go along.

objectionable [adj] *not nice; unpleasant*
▪ *Syn* abhorrent, deplorable, disagreeable, distasteful, exceptionable, illfavored, inadmissible, indecorous, insufferable, intolerable, invidious, loathsome, noxious, obnoxious, offensive, reprehensible, repugnant, repulsive, unfit, unpalatable, unseemly, unwelcome; ▪ *Ant* appropriate, good, nice, pleasant, seemly, welcome.

objective [adj] *fair, impartial*
▪ *Syn* cool, detached, disinterested, dispassionate, equitable, evenhanded, impersonal, judicial, just, nondiscriminatory, nonpartisan, unbiased, uninvolved, unprejudiced; ▪ *Ant* biased, partial, prejudiced, subjective, unfair.

objectively [adv] *impartially*
▪ *Syn* detachedly, dispassionately, equitably, evenhandedly, justly, neutrally, soberly, with impartiality, with objectivity, without favor, without prejudice; ▪ *Ant* emotionally, subjectively, unfairly.

obligate [v] *require*
▪ *Syn* astrict, bind, constrain, force, indebt, make indebted, oblige, restrain, restrict; ▪ *Ant* let off, liberate, release.

obligatory [adj] *essential, required*
▪ *Syn* binding, coercive, compulsatory, compulsory, de rigueur, enforced, imperative, mandatory, necessary, requisite, unavoidable; ▪ *Ant* nonessential, optional, unrequired, voluntary.

oblige [v1] *require*
▪ *Syn* bind, coerce, command, compel, constrain, force, impel, make, necessitate, obligate; ▪ *Ant* acquit, free, let off, release.

oblige [v2] *do a favor or kindness*
▪ *Syn* accommodate, aid, assist, benefit, contribute, convenience, favor, gratify,

help, indulge, please, serve; ▪ *Ant* be mean, disoblige, inconvenience.

obliging [*adj*] *friendly, helpful*
▪ *Syn* accommodating, agreeable, amiable, civil, complaisant, cooperative, courteous, eager to please, easygoing, good-humored, good-natured, hospitable, kind, lenient, polite, willing; ▪ *Ant* disobliging, inconsiderate, uncooperative, unfriendly, unhelpful.

oblique [*adj1*] *slanting; at an angle*
▪ *Syn* angled, askew, asymmetrical, awry, bent, cater-cornered, crooked, distorted, diverging, inclined, leaning, on the bias, pitched, sideways, skew, sloping, strained, tilted, tipped, turned, twisted; ▪ *Ant* horizontal, straight, vertical.

oblique [*adj2*] *indirect, evasive*
▪ *Syn* backhanded, circuitous, circular, circumlocutory, devious, implied, obliquitous, obscure, roundabout, sidelong, vague; ▪ *Ant* blunt, candid, direct, forthright, straightforward.

obliterate [*v*] *destroy*
▪ *Syn* annihilate, bog, cancel, defeat, eliminate, exterminate, extirpate, finish, kill, liquidate, mark out, obscure, ravage, scrub, shoot down, sink, smash, squash, take apart, waste; ▪ *Ant* build, construct, create, restore.

oblivious [*adj*] *unaware, ignorant*
▪ *Syn* absentminded, abstracted, amnesic, careless, disregardful, distracted, forgetting, gone, heedless, inattentive, insensible, neglectful, negligent, preoccupied, unconcerned, unconscious, undiscerning, uninformed, unknowing, unobservant, unwitting; ▪ *Ant* aware, cognizant, concerned, conscious, mindful, sensitive, understanding.

obnoxious [*adj*] *offensive, repulsive*
▪ *Syn* abhorrent, abominable, detestable, disagreeable, foul, hateful, horrid, insufferable, invidious, loathsome, mean, nauseating, objectionable, odious, pestiferous, repellent, reprehensible, revolting, sickening, unpleasant; ▪ *Ant* agreeable, charming, delightful, kind, likeable, nice, pleasant, soft.

obscene [*adj*] *indecent, offensive, immoral* ▪ *Syn* atrocious, bawdy, coarse, crude, disgusting, evil, filthy, foul, gross, heinous, hideous, immodest, lewd, loathsome, noisome, outrageous, profane, prurient, raw, repugnant, ribald, salacious,

scabrous, scurrilous, shocking, sickening, suggestive, unchaste, unclean, vile, wanton, wicked; ▪ *Ant* chaste, clean, decent, innocent, moral, upright.

obscure [*adj1*] *not easily understood*
▪ *Syn* abstruse, arcane, complicated, confusing, cryptic, dark, deep, enigmatic, esoteric, hidden, impenetrable, incomprehensible, inexplicable, inscrutable, intricate, involved, mysterious, occult, opaque, recondite, vague; ▪ *Ant* apparent, clear, evident, explicit, obvious, perceptible, understood.

obscure [*adj2*] *cloudy, shadowy*
▪ *Syn* blurred, caliginous, clouded, dark, dense, dim, dusk, dusky, faint, fuliginous, gloomy, indistinct, lightless, murky, obfuscated, shady, somber, tenebrous, umbrageous, unilluminated, unlit, veiled; ▪ *Ant* bright, clear, visible, well-defined.

obscure [*adj3*] *out-of-the-way, little-known* ▪ *Syn* abstruse, arcane, blind, cabalistic, covered, distant, enigmatic, esoteric, far-off, hidden, inaccessible, inconspicuous, lowly, minor, orphic, recondite, remote, reticent, secluded, secretive, seldom seen, undisclosed, unheard-of, unknown, unsung; ▪ *Ant* distinguished, eminent, famous, known, renowned.

obscure [*v*] *conceal, hide*
▪ *Syn* adumbrate, becloud, bedim, befog, belie, blear, block out, blur, camouflage, cloak, cloud, conceal, dim, disguise, eclipse, falsify, fog, gloom, haze, mask, mist, muddy, obfuscate, overshadow, screen, shade, shroud, veil, wrap; ▪ *Ant* expose, illuminate, loose, reveal.

obsequious [*adj*] *groveling, submissive*
▪ *Syn* abject, beggarly, compliant, cringing, crouching, deferential, enslaved, fawning, flattering, ingratiating, menial, obeisant, parasitic, parasitical, prostrate, respectful, servile, slavish, sniveling, stipendiary, subject, submissive, subordinate, subservient, sycophantic, unctuous; ▪ *Ant* arrogant, assertive, brazen, confident, haughty, imperious, presumptuous.

observable [*adj*] *apparent*
▪ *Syn* appreciable, clear, detectable, discernible, discoverable, evident, noticeable, obvious, open, palpable, patent, perceivable, perceptible, recognizable, sensible, tangible, visible; ▪ *Ant* hidden, imperceptible, unrecognizable.

observant [adj] *alert, watchful*
- *Syn* advertent, attentive, comprehending, considering, contemplating, correct, deducing, detecting, discerning, discriminating, heedful, intelligent, interested, keen, mindful, obedient, perceptive, quick, regardful, searching, sensitive, sharp, vigilant; - *Ant* careless, inattentive, indifferent, thoughtless, unaware, unmindful, unobservant, unwatchful.

observe [v1] *see, notice*
- *Syn* behold, catch, contemplate, detect, discern, discover, distinguish, espy, examine, inspect, look at, mark, mind, monitor, note, pay attention to, perceive, read, recognize, regard, scrutinize, spot, spy, study, survey, view, watch, witness; - *Ant* ignore, miss, overlook.

observe [v2] *celebrate, commemorate*
- *Syn* dedicate, hold, honor, keep, remember, respect, revere, reverence, solemnize, venerate; - *Ant* disregard, forget, miss, neglect.

observe [v3] *abide by, obey*
- *Syn* adhere, adopt, comply, comply with, conform, follow, fulfill, heed, honor, keep, mind, perform, respect; - *Ant* break, disobey, violate.

obsessed [adj] *consumed, driven about belief, desire* - *Syn* bedeviled, beset, bewitched, dominated, engrossed, fiendish, fixated, gripped, haunted, hooked, immersed in, infatuated, overpowered, possessed, seized, taken over, tormented, troubled; - *Ant* indifferent, unconcerned.

obsolete [adj] *no longer in use*
- *Syn* anachronistic, antediluvian, antiquated, archaic, bygone, dated, dead, discarded, extinct, old-fashioned, old-hat, outmoded, outworn, pass, stale, superannuated, timeworn, unfashionable; - *Ant* contemporary, current, in vogue, modern, new, present, up-to-date.

obstacle [n] *impediment, barrier*
- *Syn* bar, block, check, difficulty, encumbrance, hindrance, hurdle, interference, interruption, obstruction, restriction, snag, vicissitude; - *Ant* advantage, assistance, blessing, boon, clearance, help, support.

obstinate [adj] *stubborn, determined*
- *Syn* adamant, cantankerous, contumacious, dogmatic, firm, hardened, headstrong, indomitable, inflexible, intractable, obdurate, opinionated, pertinacious, perverse, recalcitrant, relentless,

resolved, self-willed, steadfast, strong-minded, tenacious, unyielding, willful; - *Ant* agreeable, amenable, cooperative, flexible, helpful, submissive, willing, yielding.

obstruct [v] *prevent, restrict*
- *Syn* arrest, barricade, block, check, choke, congest, curb, cut off, frustrate, hamper, hinder, hold up, impede, inhibit, mask, occlude, plug, restrain, retard, shield, stall, stop, throttle, thwart, trammel, weigh down; - *Ant* abet, aid, assist, boost, clear, expedite, help, promote, support.

obtain [v] *get, acquire*
- *Syn* access, accomplish, achieve, annex, capture, collect, corral, earn, effect, fetch, gain, gather, glean, hoard, inherit, invade, lay up, make use of, occupy, procure, purchase, reach, realize, reap, save, score, scrape together, secure, take, wangle, win; - *Ant* forfeit, forsake, lose, relinquish, sacrifice.

obtainable [adj] *achievable, available*
- *Syn* attainable, derivable, procurable, purchasable, ready, realizable, securable; - *Ant* unachievable, unavailable, unobtainable.

obtrusive [adj] *pushy, obvious*
- *Syn* bulging, forward, impertinent, importunate, intrusive, jutting, meddlesome, nosy, officious, presumptuous, prominent, protruding, protuberant, prying, sticking out; - *Ant* inconspicuous, modest, shy, unobtrusive.

obtuse [adj1] *stupid*
- *Syn* dense, dumb, imperceptive, insensitive, opaque, stolid, thick, uncomprehending, unintelligent; - *Ant* bright, clever, intelligent, quick, quick-witted, smart.

obtuse [adj2] *blunt, not sharp*
- *Syn* round, rounded; - *Ant* acute, pointed, sharp.

obviate [v] *make unnecessary*
- *Syn* avert, block, counter, counteract, deter, do away with, forestall, hinder, interpose, intervene, preclude, prevent, remove, restrain, rule out, stave off, ward; - *Ant* cause, impel, neccessitate, require.

obvious [adj] *apparent, understandable*
- *Syn* clear, conclusive, conspicuous, discernible, distinct, evident, explicit, glaring, indisputable, lucid, manifest, noticeable, observable, overt, palpable,

patent, perceptible, pronounced, public, recognizable, self-evident, straightforward, transparent, unconcealed, unmistakable, visible; ▪ *Ant* ambiguous, indefinite, invisible, obscure, unclear, vague.

occasional [*adj*] *irregular, sporadic*
▪ *Syn* casual, desultory, exceptional, exclusive, few, incidental, infrequent, intermittent, odd, particular, random, rare, scarce, seldom, special, sporadic, uncommon, unfrequent, unusual; ▪ *Ant* constant, frequent, incessant, regular, steady, usual.

occasionally [*adv*] *every now and then*
▪ *Syn* at intervals, at random, at times, every so often, from time to time, hardly, infrequently, irregularly, now and again, once in a while, on occasion, periodically, seldom, sometimes, sporadically, uncommonly; ▪ *Ant* always, constantly, incessantly, regularly, steadily, usually.

occlude [*v*] *block, prevent*
▪ *Syn* choke, clog, close, close out, congest, curb, fill, hinder, impede, leave out, lock out, obstruct, plug, seal, shut, stop up, throttle; ▪ *Ant* clear, open, ream, unclog, unplug.

occult ▪ [*adj*] *mysterious, secret; supernatural* ▪ *Syn* abstruse, arcane, cabalistic, concealed, deep, eerie, esoteric, hidden, invisible, mystical, obscure, orphic, preternatural, psychic, recondite, transmundane, unearthly, unknown, unrevealed, veiled, weird; ▪ *Ant* known, natural.

occupation [*n1*] *profession, business*
▪ *Syn* affair, calling, chosen work, craft, employment, job, line of work, métier, post, pursuit, trade, vocation, work; ▪ *Ant* avocation, hobby, pastime.

occupation [*n2*] *seizure, takeover*
▪ *Syn* attack, capture, conquest, entering, foreign rule, invasion, subjugation; ▪ *Ant* giving up, surrender.

occupied [*adj1*] *busy*
▪ *Syn* active, employed, engaged, engrossed, working; ▪ *Ant* idle, inactive, not busy, unoccupied.

occupied [*adj2*] *inhabited; in use*
▪ *Syn* busy, engaged, full, leased, populated, populous, rented, settled, taken, unavailable, utilized; ▪ *Ant* empty, free, uninhabited, unoccupied, vacant.

occupy [*v1*] *be busy with*
▪ *Syn* absorb, amuse, attend, busy, divert, employ, engage, engross, entertain, fill, hold attention, immerse, interest, involve, keep occupied, preoccupy, soak, take up, tie up, utilize; ▪ *Ant* be inactive, be lazy, idle.

occupy [*v2*] *reside; use*
▪ *Syn* be established, be in command, be in residence, cover, dwell, ensconce, establish, fill, hold, inhabit, involve, keep, live in, maintain, own, people, permeate, pervade, populate, possess, remain, stay, take up, tenant, utilize; ▪ *Ant* evacuate, leave, vacate.

occupy [*v3*] *seize, take over*
▪ *Syn* capture, conquer, garrison, hold, invade, keep, obtain, overrun, take possession; ▪ *Ant* free, liberate, yield.

odd/oddball [*adj1*] *unusual, abnormal*
▪ *Syn* atypical, avant-garde, bizarre, curious, deviant, different, eccentric, exceptional, idiosyncratic, offbeat, outlandish, peculiar, quaint, rare, remarkable, singular, strange, uncanny, uncommon, unique, weird, whimsical; ▪ *Ant* common, conventional, habitual, normal, ordinary, regular, standard, usual, usual.

odd [*adj2*] *single, unmatched; uneven*
▪ *Syn* alone, exceeding, individual, irregular, leftover, lone, over and above, remaining, singular, sole, solitary, spare, surplus, unconsumed, unitary; ▪ *Ant* matched, mated, paired.

odds [*n1*] *advantage*
▪ *Syn* allowance, benefit, difference, disparity, dissimilarity, distinction, draw, edge, handicap, head start, lead, overlay, start, superiority, vantage; ▪ *Ant* disadvantage, drawback, hindrance.

odds [*n2*] *probability*
▪ *Syn* balance, chances, favor, likelihood, superiority, toss-up; ▪ *Ant* improbability, unlikelihood.

odious [*adj*] *hateful, horrible*
▪ *Syn* abhorrent, abominable, charming, detestable, disgusting, execrable, foul, horrid, loathsome, mean, obnoxious, offensive, repulsive, revolting, unpleasant, vile; ▪ *Ant* agreeable, delightful, great, likeable, loveable, pleasing.

odorless [*adj*] *without fragrance*
▪ *Syn* flat, inodorous, odor-free, unaromatic, unfragrant, unperfumed, unscented, unsmelling; ▪ *Ant* aromatic, odorous, perfumed, scented, smelly.

odorous [*adj*] *having fragrance*
▪ *Syn* aromatic, balmy, effluvious, fetid, flavorsome, flowery, foul, fragrant, hon-

eyed, loud, malodorous, mephitic, miasmic, odoriferous, offensive, olfactive, perfumed, pungent, putrid, redolent, reeking, savory, scented, spicy, stagnant, stinking, sweet-scented, sweet-smelling, tumaceous; ▪ *Ant* odorless, unscented.

off [*adj1*] *gone; remote*
▪ *Syn* absent, canceled, finished, inoperative, negligible, not employed, not on duty, on vacation, outside, unavailable; ▪ *Ant* here, present.

off [*adj2*] *below par*
▪ *Syn* bad, decomposed, disappointing, disheartening, displeasing, low-quality, mortifying, poor, quiet, rancid, rotten, slack, sour, substandard, turned, unrewarding, unsatisfactory; ▪ *Ant* acceptable, on.

off [*adv*] *apart, away*
▪ *Syn* above, absent, afar, away from, divergent, elsewhere, far, farther away, gone away, in the distance, not here, out, over, removed, to one side, turning aside, up front, vanishing; ▪ *Ant* close, here, present.

offbeat [*adj*] *strange, very different*
▪ *Syn* bizarre, eccentric, far-out, fresh, idiosyncratic, novel, oddball, outré, uncommon, unconventional, unique, unorthodox, unusual, weird; ▪ *Ant* expected, normal, ordinary, usual.

off-color [*adj*] *risque*
▪ *Syn* indelicate, shady, suggestive, vulgar, wicked; ▪ *Ant* clean, prudent, tasteful.

offend [*v*] *displease, insult*
▪ *Syn* affront, aggrieve, antagonize, disgruntle, disgust, fret, gall, hurt, irritate, jar, miff, nauseate, nettle, outrage, pain, pique, provoke, rile, shock, sicken, slur, snub, transgress, upset, vex, wound; ▪ *Ant* beguile, captivate, charm, compliment, please.

offensive [*adj1*] *disrespectful, insulting; displeasing* ▪ *Syn* abhorrent, abusive, cutting, detestable, distasteful, dreadful, embarrassing, foul, ghastly, grisly, hideous, horrid, insolent, invidious, nauseating, objectionable, obnoxious, outrageous, repellent, reprehensible, repugnant, rude, shocking, terrible, uncivil; ▪ *Ant* agreeable, courteous, kind, polite, respectful.

offensive [*adj2*] *attacking*
▪ *Syn* aggressive, assailing, assaulting, belligerent, invading; ▪ *Ant* defending, defensive, guarding.

offer [*v1*] *present, propose for acceptance*
▪ *Syn* advance, bid, display, donate, exhibit, extend, furnish, give, grant, hold out, make available, move, ply, pose, press, proffer, propound, provide, put forth, put forward, put on the market, put up, put up for sale, sacrifice, show, submit, suggest, tender, volunteer; ▪ *Ant* take, take back, withdraw, withhold.

offer [*v2*] *propose*
▪ *Syn* adduce, advance, advise, allege, cite, make a motion, present, proposition, submit, suggest; ▪ *Ant* deny, refuse, withhold.

offhand [*adj1*] *abrupt, careless*
▪ *Syn* aloof, breezy, brusque, casual, cavalier, curt, easygoing, folksy, glib, informal, laid-back, mellow, perfunctory, unceremonious, unconcerned, uninterested; ▪ *Ant* calculated, careful, considered, deliberate, grand, planned, sober.

offhand [*adj2/adv*] *ad-lib, extemporaneous* ▪ *Syn* extemporary, extempore, impromptu, improvised, informal, spontaneous, unpremeditated, unrehearsed, unstudied, without preparation; ▪ *Ant* planned, practiced, premeditated.

official [*adj*] *authorized, legitimate*
▪ *Syn* accredited, approved, authentic, authoritative, canonical, certified, conclusive, correct, decided, decisive, definite, endorsed, established, fitting, legitimate, licensed, ordered, orthodox, recognized, sanctioned, true, valid; ▪ *Ant* unauthorized, unofficial, unsanctioned.

officiate [*v*] *oversee, manage*
▪ *Syn* act, chair, command, conduct, direct, emcee, govern, handle, preside, run, serve, superintend, umpire; ▪ *Ant* follow.

officious [*adj*] *self-important, dictatorial*
▪ *Syn* forward, impertinent, interfering, intrusive, meddlesome, meddling, obtrusive, opinionated, overzealous, pragmatic, pushy, rude; ▪ *Ant* modest, shy, timid, unobstrusive.

off-key [*adj*] *not harmonious*
▪ *Syn* anomalous, deviant, discordant, dissonant, divergent, inharmonious, irregular, jarring, unnatural; ▪ *Ant* concordant, harmonious, on-key.

offshoot [*n*] *development, product*
▪ *Syn* adjunct, appendage, branch, by-product, derivative, descendant, limb, outgrowth, spin-off, sprout; ▪ *Ant* origin, source.

offspring [*n*] *child, children*
▪ *Syn* baby, brood, cub, descendant, family, generation, heir, issue, lineage, offshoot, posterity, produce, progeniture, progeny, seed, spawn, succession, successor, young; ▪ *Ant* parent.

often [*adv*] *frequently*
▪ *Syn* again and again, a number of times, many a time, oftentimes, over and over, recurrently, time after time, time and again, usually; ▪ *Ant* infrequently, rarely, seldom.

ogre [*n*] *nasty person*
▪ *Syn* demon, devil, fiend, giant, monster, monstrosity, specter, troll; ▪ *Ant* angel, fairy, humanitarian.

oily [*adj*] *flattering*
▪ *Syn* cajoling, coaxing, compliant, glib, hypocritical, ingratiating, insinuating, obsequious, servile, slick, smooth, suave, supple, unctuous; ▪ *Ant* hateful, insulting, sincere, taciturn.

okay [*adj*] *acceptable, satisfactory*
▪ *Syn* adequate, all right, approved, convenient, correct, fair, fine, good, in order, middling, not bad, passable, permitted, surely, tolerable; ▪ *Ant* bad, incorrect, intolerable, unacceptable, unsatisfactory, unsuitable, wrong.

okay [*v*] *agree to*
▪ *Syn* accept, accredit, approve, authorize, certify, condone, confirm, consent to, endorse, give one's consent, notarize, pass, sanction, say yes to; ▪ *Ant* deny, disagree, refuse, reject, veto.

old [*adj1*] *advanced in age*
▪ *Syn* aged, ancient, elderly, experienced, geriatric, gray, impaired, infirm, mature, matured, not young, olden, oldish, seasoned, senior, superannuated, venerable, versed, veteran; ▪ *Ant* active, fresh, new, young, youthful.

old [*adj2*] *obsolete, outdated*
▪ *Syn* aboriginal, antediluvian, antiquated, antique, archaic, bygone, crumbling, dated, erstwhile, former, immemorial, late, of yore, olden, old-fashioned, outmoded, out-of-date, pass, primitive, primordial, quondam, relic, remote, stale, superannuated, traditional, venerable, worn-out; ▪ *Ant* contemporary, current, fresh, late, modern, new, recent, up-to-date.

old [*adj3*] *traditional, long-established*
▪ *Syn* age-old, constant, continuing, enduring, established, familiar, firm, invet-

erate, lifelong, long-lasting, long-lived, of long standing, perennial, perpetual, practiced, skilled, solid, staying, steady, time-honored, versed, veteran, vintage; ▪ *Ant* contemporary, current, modern, new.

older [*adj*] *most senior*
▪ *Syn* earlier, elder, eldest, first, firstborn, former, lower, of a former period, of an earlier time, preceding, prior, senior; ▪ *Ant* younger.

old-fashioned [*adj*] *outmoded, obsolete*
▪ *Syn* ancient, antiquated, antique, archaic, bygone, dated, demode, demoded, extinct, grown old, musty, obsolescent, outdated, out-of-date, outworn, past, primitive, superannuated, unstylish, vintage; ▪ *Ant* avant-garde, contemporary, current, in vogue, modern, new.

ominous [*adj*] *menacing, foreboding*
▪ *Syn* apocalyptic, augural, dark, dire, dismal, doomed, fateful, fearful, forbidding, gloomy, grim, haunting, hostile, ill-boding, ill-fated, impending, inauspicious, lowering, malefic, malificent, malign, minatory, perilous, portentous, precursive, premonitory, presaging, prescient, prophetic, sinister, suggestive, threatening, unfriendly, unlucky, unpromising; ▪ *Ant* auspicious, favorable, promising, propitious.

omit [*v*] *exclude, forget*
▪ *Syn* bar, bypass, cancel, cast aside, count out, cut out, delete, discard, dismiss, drop, edit, eliminate, exclude, leave out, miss, neglect, overlook, pass by, pass over, preclude, prohibit, reject, repudiate, skip, slight, snip, trim, void, withhold; ▪ *Ant* add, enter, include, inject, insert, recall, remember.

omnipotent [*adj*] *all-powerful*
▪ *Syn* almighty, divine, godlike, mighty, supreme, unlimited, unrestricted; ▪ *Ant* helpless, impotent, powerless, weak.

omniscient [*adj*] *all-knowing*
▪ *Syn* all-seeing, almighty, infinite, knowledgeable, pansophical, preeminent, wise; ▪ *Ant* fallible, ignorant, unaware.

once [*adj/adv*] *in the past; occurred one time only* ▪ *Syn* already, at one time, back, back when, before, bygone, earlier, erstwhile, formerly, heretofore, in the old days, in times past, late, long ago, old, once upon a time, one, on one occasion, previously, quondam, sometime, this time, time was, whilom; ▪ *Ant* continuously, incessantly, never, not at all.

oncoming [adj] *impending*
- **Syn** advancing, approaching, coming, expected, forthcoming, imminent, looming, nearing, onrushing, upcoming; **Ant** past, receding, retiring, withdrawing.

one [adj] *individual*
- **Syn** alone, definite, different, lone, odd, one and only, only, particular, peculiar, precise, separate, single, singular, sole, solitary, special, specific, uncommon, unique; **Ant** many, none, some.

onerous [adj] *very difficult; requiring hard labor* - **Syn** arduous, austere, backbreaking, burdensome, crushing, cumbersome, demanding, difficult, exacting, exhausting, fatiguing, formidable, grinding, grueling, harsh, intolerable, laborious, oppressive, overpowering, painful, ponderous, pressing, rigorous, strenuous, taxing, tiresome, toilsome, troublesome, vexatious, weighty; **Ant** common, easy, effortless, light, trivial.

ongoing [adj] *continuous*
- **Syn** advancing, continuing, current, developing, evolving, growing, heading, in progress, marching, open-ended, progressing, successful, unfinished, unfolding; **Ant** incontinuous, infrequent, intermittent, provisional, sporadic.

onlooker [n] *person observing an event*
- **Syn** beholder, bystander, eyewitness, looker-on, observer, sightseer, spectator, viewer, watcher, witness; **Ant** participant.

only [adj] *singular*
- **Syn** alone, apart, by oneself, exclusive, individual, isolated, lone, matchless, once in a lifetime, one and only, one shot, particular, peerless, single, sole, solitary, solo, unique, unparalleled, unrivaled; **Ant** innumerable, manifold, many, multitudinous, myriad, numerous, several.

only [adv] *barely; exclusively*
- **Syn** alone, at most, but, entirely, hardly, just, merely, nothing but, particularly, purely, simply, solely, totally, uniquely, utterly, wholly; **Ant** among, amongst, collectively, together.

onset [n] *beginning; attack*
- **Syn** aggression, assailment, assault, birth, charge, commencement, dawning, encounter, inception, incipience, offense, onslaught, origin, outbreak, outset, out-start, rush, seizure, start; **Ant** conclusion, defense, end, ending, finish, termination.

onslaught [n] *attack*
- **Syn** aggression, assailment, assault, blitz, charge, incursion, invasion, offense, offensive, onfall, onrush, onset; **Ant** defense, resistance.

onus [n] *burden*
- **Syn** blame, blot, blur, brand, charge, culpability, duty, encumbrance, fault, guilt, incubus, liability, obligation, odium, oppression, responsibility, stigma, task, tax, weight; **Ant** aid, benefit, blessing, help.

onward/onwards [adv] *ahead, beyond*
- **Syn** alee, along, forth, forward, in front, in front of, moving, on, on ahead; **Ant** backward, backwards.

opaque [adj1] *clouded, muddy*
- **Syn** blurred, cloudy, darkened, dim, dull, filmy, foggy, fuliginous, gloomy, hazy, impenetrable, lusterless, misty, muddied, murky, nubilous, obfuscated, shady, smoky, sooty, thick, turbid; **Ant** clear, lucid, sparkling, translucent, transparent, unclouded.

opaque [adj2] *hard to understand*
- **Syn** abstruse, amphibological, arcane, baffling, cryptic, difficult, enigmatic, equivocal, imperceptive, incomprehensible, nebulous, obscure, obtuse, perplexing, tenebrous, vague; **Ant** clear, crystal-clear, easy, intelligible, unambiguous, understandable.

open [adj1] *unfastened, unclosed*
- **Syn** accessible, airy, bare, clear, disclosed, emptied, expansive, exposed, extended, free, gaping, naked, navigable, passable, peeled, removed, revealed, spacious, stripped, unbarred, uncovered, unfurled, unimpeded, vacated, wide, yawning; **Ant** closed, enclosed, fastened, locked, shut.

open [adj2] *accessible; not forbidden*
- **Syn** admissible, allowable, approachable, attainable, available, employable, fit, free, general, nondiscriminatory, obtainable, permitted, practicable, public, reachable, securable, unconditional, unrestricted, vacant, within reach; **Ant** blocked, closed, inaccessible, obstructed, shut, unavailable.

open [adj3] *clear, obvious*
- **Syn** apparent, avowed, barefaced, blatant, conspicuous, downright, evident,

flagrant, frank, manifest, noticeable, overt, plain, visible, well-known; ▪ *Ant* ambiguous, closed, deceitful, unclear, vague.

open [*adj4*] *undecided*
▪ *Syn* ambiguous, arguable, controversial, debatable, doubtful, dubious, dubitable, equivocal, indecisive, in question, moot, problematic, questionable, uncertain, unresolved, unsettled; ▪ *Ant* certain, decided, definite, sure.

open [*adj5*] *honest, objective*
▪ *Syn* artless, candid, fair, frank, guileless, impartial, ingenuous, mellow, natural, objective, plain, receptive, sincere, straightforward, transparent, unbiased, uncommitted, unprejudiced; ▪ *Ant* deceitful, deceptive, dishonest, lying, shifty, subjective.

open [*vl*] *begin*
▪ *Syn* begin business, bow, commence, convene, embark, inaugurate, initiate, kick off, launch, meet, set in motion, sit, start; ▪ *Ant* close, conclude, end, finish, shut.

open [*v2*] *clear, breach, expose; spread*
▪ *Syn* bare, break in, break out, broach, burst, bust in, come apart, crack, disclose, display, disrupt, expand, fissure, free, gap, gape, hole, jimmy, kick in, lacerate, lance, penetrate, perforate, pierce, pop, puncture, release, reveal, rupture, separate, sliver, slit, slot, split, tap, throw wide, unbar, unblock, unbolt, unclose, unclothe, uncork, uncover, undo, unfasten, unfold, unfurl, unlatch, unlock, unroll, unseal, unshut, unstop, untie, unwrap, vent, ventilate, yawn, yawp; ▪ *Ant* block, bury, cover, exclude, hide, hinder, shut.

openly [*adv*] *honestly*
▪ *Syn* aboveboard, artlessly, blatantly, brazenly, candidly, face to face, flagrantly, forthrightly, frankly, fully, honestly, in broad daylight, in full view, ingenuously, in public, in the open, naively, naturally, plainly, publicly, readily, shamelessly, simply, straight, unabashedly, unashamedly, unhesitatingly, unreservedly, willingly, without pretense, without reserve; ▪ *Ant* secretly, shamefully.

operative [*adj*] *active, functioning; influential* ▪ *Syn* accessible, alive, current, dynamic, effective, efficient, employable, functional, important, indicative, in

force, in key, open, operational, practicable, relevant, running, serviceable, significant, standing, usable, workable, working; ▪ *Ant* inactive, ineffective, ineffectual, inoperative, unfunctional, unworking, useless, worthless.

opinionated [*adj*] *believing very strongly and conveying it* ▪ *Syn* adamant, arbitrary, assertive, biased, bigoted, bossy, conceited, dictatorial, doctrinaire, dogmatic, high-handed, inflexible, intransigent, obdurate, obstinate, one-sided, overbearing, positive, pragmatic, pragmatical, prejudiced, self-assertive, set-on, single-minded, stubborn, tilted, uncompromising, unyielding, weighted; ▪ *Ant* open-minded, responsive, unprejudiced.

opponent [*n*] *person with whom one competes* ▪ *Syn* adversary, antagonist, aspirant, assailant, challenger, competitor, counteragent, disputant, dissentient, enemy, entrant, foe, litigant, match, opposer, opposition, oppugnant, player, rival; ▪ *Ant* ally, associate, colleague, helper, supporter.

opportune [*adj*] *advantageous, lucky*
▪ *Syn* appropriate, apt, auspicious, convenient, favorable, felicitous, fit, fitting, fortuitous, fortunate, propitious, seasonable, suitable, timely, timeous, well-timed; ▪ *Ant* disadvantageous, ·inauspicious, inopportune, unlucky, unsuitable.

oppose [*vl*] *fight, obstruct*
▪ *Syn* argue, assail, assault, attack, bar, battle, bombard, check, combat, confront, counter, counterattack, cross, debate, defy, deny, dispute, encounter, expose, face, fight, gainsay, hinder, not countenance, prevent, protest, resist, reverse, run counter to, speak against, stand up to, take issue, take on, thwart, withstand; ▪ *Ant* abet, aid, assist, champion, favor, help, support.

oppose [*v2*] *compare, play off*
▪ *Syn* array, confront, contrast, counter, counterbalance, face, match, pit, set against, vie; ▪ *Ant* join, participate.

opposed/opposing [*adj*] *antagonistic, against* ▪ *Syn* antipathetic, antithetical, antonymous, at cross-purposes, averse, battling, combating, conflicting, contrary, controverting, counter, crossing, defensive, denying, disputing, dissentient, facing, gainsaying, hostile, incompatible, irreconcilable, objecting, obstructive, protesting, repelling, rival, up against, warring; ▪ **Ant** aiding, assisting, compatible, helping, similar.

opposite [adj] unlike, conflicting; completely different ▪ **Syn** adverse, antipodal, antithetical, contradictory, contrary, diametrically opposed, different, dissimilar, fronting, inimical, inverse, irreconcilable, obverse, opposed, polar, retrograde, reversed, separate, unalike, unsimilar, violative, vis-à-vis; ▪ **Ant** compatible, identical, like, similar.

oppress [v] depress, subdue
▪ **Syn** aggrieve, crush, despotize, dishearten, dispirit, distress, handicap, harass, harry, keep down, maltreat, outrage, overcome, overpower, overthrow, overwhelm, plague, press, prey on, put down, sadden, smother, strain, subjugate, suppress, trample, tyrranize, vex, weigh heavy upon, worry; ▪ **Ant** aid, boost, delight, encourage, gladden, help.

oppressive [adj1] overwhelming, repressive ▪ **Syn** bleak, brutal, burdensome, confining, cruel, demanding, depressing, despotic, dictatorial, disheartening, exacting, exigent, gloomy, grievous, grinding, harsh, heavy, inhuman, mean, onerous, overbearing, severe, somber, taxing, tyrannical, unjust, weighty; ▪ **Ant** calm, gentle, relieving.

oppressive [adj2] hot and humid
▪ **Syn** airless, close, heavy, muggy, overpowering, steamy, sticky, stifling, stuffy, suffocating, sultry, torrid; ▪ **Ant** cool, mild, temperate.

opprobrious [adj] abusive, hateful
▪ **Syn** abasing, calumniatory, contemptuous, damaging, defamatory, denigrating, depreciative, derogatory, detractive, disparaging, humiliating, injurious, insolent, insulting, libeling, malevolent, malign, notorious, offensive, pejorative, reproaching, reviling, scurrilous, spiteful, truculent, vile, vituperative, vulgar; ▪ **Ant** complimentary, flattering, kind, nice, praising.

opt [v] choose
▪ **Syn** cull, decide, elect, exercise choice, go for, make a selection, mark, pick, prefer, select, take; ▪ **Ant** overrule, refuse, reject, turn down.

optimistic [adj] believing positively
▪ **Syn** assured, bright, buoyant, cheerful, confident, encouraged, expectant, happy,

high, hopeful, idealistic, keeping the faith, merry, positive, promising, rosy, sanguine, trusting, upbeat, Utopian; ▪ **Ant** dejected, depressed, doubtful, gloomy, hopeless, pessimistic, sorrowful.

optimum [adj] best
▪ **Syn** ace, capital, choice, flawless, greatest, highest, ideal, matchless, maximum, most advantageous, most favorable, optimal, peak, peerless, perfect, select, superlative; ▪ **Ant** least, poorest, worst.

optional [adj] possible; available as choice ▪ **Syn** alternative, arbitrary, discretionary, elective, noncompulsory, nonobligatory, not required, open, unforced, unrestricted, up to the individual, volitional, voluntary; ▪ **Ant** compulsory, forced, necessary, required.

opulent [adj] rich, luxurious, profuse
▪ **Syn** abundant, affluent, copious, deluxe, extravagant, lavish, luxuriant, moneyed, ostentatious, palatial, plentiful, plush, prodigal, prolific, prosperous, rich, sumptuous; ▪ **Ant** depressed, destitute, poor.

oral [adj] spoken
▪ **Syn** articulate, lingual, narrated, recounted, related, said, sonant, sounded, told, uttered, verbal, viva voce, vocal, voiced; ▪ **Ant** printed, tacit, unspoken, written.

orb [n] globe
▪ **Syn** ball, circle, lamp, ring, rondure, round, sphere; ▪ **Ant** cube, square.

orchestrate [v] organize; cause to happen ▪ **Syn** arrange, concert, coordinate, integrate, manage, present, put together, score, set up, synthesize, unify; ▪ **Ant** disorganize, ignore.

ordain [v] establish, install
▪ **Syn** anoint, appoint, bless, call, commission, consecrate, decree, delegate, destine, dictate, elect, enjoin, frock, institute, invest, legislate, nominate, order, prescribe, pronounce, rule; ▪ **Ant** cancel, disallow, rescind, retract, reverse, void.

ordeal [n] trouble, suffering
▪ **Syn** affliction, agony, anguish, calamity, calvary, cross, crucible, difficulty, distress, nightmare, test, torment, torture, trial, tribulation, visitation; ▪ **Ant** elation, happiness, pleasure, rapture.

order [v1] command, authorize
▪ **Syn** adjure, bid, charge, contract for, decree, dictate, direct, enact, engage, enjoin, hire, instruct, obtain, ordain, pre-

scribe, request, require, reserve, secure, send away for, tell, warn; ▪ *Ant* beg, plead, request.

order [*v2*] *arrange, organize*
▪ *Syn* align, alphabetize, array, catalog, classify, codify, control, dispose, distribute, establish, file, formalize, group, hierarchize, index, lay out, line up, manage, marshal, neaten, place, regulate, right, set in order, sort out, streamline, systematize, tabulate, tidy; ▪ *Ant* disorder, disorganize, mess up, mix up, muddle.

orderly [*adj1*] *methodical, organized*
▪ *Syn* arranged, businesslike, careful, conventional, exact, fixed, methodic, neat, precise, regular, systematic, systematized, thorough, tidy, trim, uncluttered, uniform; ▪ *Ant* chaotic, complicated, disorderly, disorganized, unmethodical, unsystematic, untidy.

orderly [*adj2*] *well-behaved*
▪ *Syn* calm, controlled, decorous, disciplined, docile, law-abiding, manageable, nonviolent, obedient, peaceable, quiet, restrained, submissive, tranquil, well-mannered; ▪ *Ant* bad, misbehaving, unruly.

ordinarily [*adv*] *usually*
▪ *Syn* as a rule, commonly, customarily, frequently, generally, habitually, in general, normally, regularly; ▪ *Ant* infrequently, rarely, sometimes, sporadically.

ordinary [*adj*] *average; not distinctive; common* ▪ *Syn* commonplace, conventional, customary, dull, fair, familiar, generic, indifferent, mediocre, normal, pedestrian, plain, prosaic, quotidian, routine, second-rate, simple, standard, typical, usual, workaday; ▪ *Ant* abnormal, different, distinctive, extraordinary, novel, rare, remarkable, special.

organic [*adj*] *basic, natural*
▪ *Syn* animate, basal, biological, biotic, cellular, elemental, essential, fundamental, inherent, innate, integral, live, living, necessary, nuclear, original, plasmic, primary, prime, primitive, principal, structural, vital; ▪ *Ant* inorganic, man-made, unnatural.

organism [*n*] *living thing*
▪ *Syn* animal, being, body, creature, entity, morphon, person, plant, structure; ▪ *Ant* inanimate, object.

organize [*v*] *arrange, systematize*
▪ *Syn* catalog, classify, codify, combine, compose, coordinate, correlate, create, establish, fashion, form, formulate, frame, group, line up, marshal, mastermind, methodize, mold, put in order, put together, range, regulate, run, set up, shape, standardize, straighten, tabulate, tailor, take care of; ▪ *Ant* confuse, destroy, disarrange, disband, disorder, disorganize, dissolve.

orient [*v*] *familiarize*
▪ *Syn* acclimatize, adapt, adjust, conform, determine, locate, orientate; ▪ *Ant* confuse, disorient, lose.

original [*adj1*] *earliest*
▪ *Syn* aboriginal, authentic, beginning, early, embryonic, genuine, inceptive, infant, initial, introductory, maiden, master, opening, pioneer, primary, primeval, primitive, primordial, pristine, prototypal; ▪ *Ant* derivative, final, latest, newest.

original [*adj2*] *fresh, new*
▪ *Syn* avant garde, creative, formative, generative, imaginative, ingenious, innovative, inspiring, inventive, new, novel, productive, quick, ready, resourceful, seminal, strange, unconventional, unprecedented, untried, unusual; ▪ *Ant* banal, borrowed, commonplace, hackneyed, old, stale, traditional, used, worn.

originally [*adv*] *initially*
▪ *Syn* at first, at the outset, at the start, basically, by birth, by origin, first, formerly, in the beginning, in the first place, primarily, to begin with; ▪ *Ant* finally, secondarily.

originate [*v1*] *begin; spring*
▪ *Syn* arise, be born, begin, birth, come, come from, come into existence, commence, dawn, derive, emanate, emerge, flow, hail from, issue, proceed, result, rise, start, stem; ▪ *Ant* end, finish, terminate.

originate [*v2*] *create, introduce*
▪ *Syn* bring about, cause, coin, come up with, compose, conceive, develop, discover, evolve, form, formulate, found, generate, give birth to, hatch, inaugurate, initiate, innovate, institute, invent, launch, make, parent, pioneer, procreate, produce, set in motion, set up, sire, spark, spawn, start, think up, usher in; ▪ *Ant* copy, follow, imitate.

ornament [*v*] *decorate*
▪ *Syn* accessorize, adorn, array, beautify, bedeck, embellish, embroider, enrich, festoon, garnish, gild, grace, ornamental-

ize, polish, prettify, trim; ▪ *Ant* leave alone, make bare, strip.

ornamental [*adj*] *decorative*
▪ *Syn* accessory, adorning, attractive, decorative, elaborate, embellishing, enhancing, exquisite, fancy, festooned, florid, furbishing, garnishing, heightening, luxurious, ornate, showy; ▪ *Ant* plain, unembellished.

ornate [*adj*] *fancily decorated*
▪ *Syn* adorned, baroque, bedecked, busy, dazzling, elaborate, elegant, embroidered, fancy, flamboyant, flashy, flaunting, florid, flowery, fussy, gaudy, gilded, glamorous, glitzy, jeweled, lavish, magnificent, meretricious, opulent, ornamented, ostentatious, overdone, overelaborate, resplendent, rich, rococo, showy, sparkling, splashy, sumptuous, superficial, tawdry, variegated; ▪ *Ant* bare, plain, simple, unadorned.

orthodox [*adj*] *accepted, traditional*
▪ *Syn* acknowledged, approved, authoritative, canonical, conformist, conservative, conventional, customary, devout, doctrinal, established, legitimate, official, pious, proper, received, recognized, religious, sanctioned, standard, traditional, true, well-established; ▪ *Ant* heretical, heterodox, unconventional, unorthodox, untraditional.

oscillate [*v*] *change back and forth*
▪ *Syn* be unsteady, fluctuate, lurch, pendulate, pitch, reel, rock, seesaw, stagger, sway, teeter, thrash, totter, undulate, vacillate, vary, vibrate, waver, wobble; ▪ *Ant* remain, stay.

ossify [*v*] *become very hard from aging*
▪ *Syn* congeal, fossilize, freeze, harden, indurate, petrify, solidify, stiffen, thicken, turn to bone; ▪ *Ant* melt, soften.

ostensible [*adj*] *alleged, supposed*
▪ *Syn* apparent, avowed, demonstrative, exhibited, illusory, likely, manifest, notable, outward, plausible, professed, purported, quasi, seeming, specious, superficial; ▪ *Ant* actual, genuine, real.

ostensibly [*adv*] *apparently*
▪ *Syn* evidently, externally, officially, outwardly, professedly, seemingly, superficially, supposedly; ▪ *Ant* actually, truly.

ostentatious [*adj*] *flashy, showy*
▪ *Syn* boastful, conspicuous, exhibitionistic, extravagant, flamboyant, garish, grandiose, loud, obtrusive, pompous,

pretentious, splashy, swank, theatrical, vain; ▪ *Ant* conservative, modest, plain, quiet, reserved, sedate, simple.

ostracize [*v*] *exile, banish*
▪ *Syn* avoid, boycott, cast out, deport, displace, drop, exclude, excommunicate, expatriate, expel, oust, reject, shun, shut out, snub, throw out; ▪ *Ant* accept, embrace, welcome.

other [*adj1*] *additional, added*
▪ *Syn* alternative, another, auxiliary, extra, more, spare, supplementary; ▪ *Ant* included, related.

other [*adj2*] *different*
▪ *Syn* contrasting, disparate, dissimilar, distinct, divergent, diverse, opposite, otherwise, remaining, separate, unalike, unequal, unlike, unrelated, variant; ▪ *Ant* coinciding, same, similar.

otherwise [*adv*] *in another way; alternatively* ▪ *Syn* any other way, contrarily, differently, diversely, if not, in different circumstances, on the other hand, or else, or then, under other conditions, variously; ▪ *Ant* alike, correspondingly, similarly.

oust [*v*] *expel, get rid of*
▪ *Syn* banish, bereave, cast out, chase, dethrone, discharge, disinherit, divest, drive out, eject, evict, expulse, fire, force out, kick out, lay off, lose, ostracize, pack off, relegate, remove, rob, sack, throw out, topple, transport, turn out, unseat; ▪ *Ant* engage, indict, install, receive.

out [*adj*] *not possible; gone*
▪ *Syn* absent, at an end, cold, dated, dead, ended, exhausted, expired, finished, impossible, not allowed, oldfashioned, outmoded, pass, ruled out, unacceptable, unfashionable, used up; ▪ *Ant* accepted, here, in, new, outre, possible.

out [*adv*] *outside, outdoors*
▪ *Syn* out of doors, outward, without; ▪ *Ant* in, indoors, inside.

outbreak [*n*] *very sudden happening*
▪ *Syn* blowup, burst, commotion, convulsion, dawn, detonation, disruption, ebullition, effervescence, epidemic, eruption, explosion, fit, flare-up, gush, insurrection, mutiny, onset, outpouring, paroxysm, plague, rebellion, rending, revolution, sally, spasm, spurt, storm, surge, tumult, uprising, volley; ▪ *Ant* cessation, ebbing, waning.

outburst [n] *fit of temper*
▪ *Syn* attack, burst, discharge, eruption, explosion, flare, flare-up, frenzy, gush, gust, outbreak, outpouring, paroxysm, rapture, scene, spasm, storm, surge, tantrum, upheaval; ▪ *Ant* control, restraint, suppression.

outcast [n] *person who is unwanted, not accepted* ▪ *Syn* castaway, deportee, derelict, displaced person, exile, expatriate, fugitive, gypsy, refugee, reprobate, tramp, untouchable, vagabond, vagrant; ▪ *Ant* favorite, friend, idol.

outcome [n] *consequence, effect*
▪ *Syn* aftereffect, aftermath, causatum, conclusion, end, fallout, issue, reaction, result, score; ▪ *Ant* beginning, cause, origin, root, source.

outcry [n] *scream, exclamation*
▪ *Syn* clamor, commotion, complaint, convulsion, cry, ferment, howl, objection, outburst, protest, tumult, uproar, upturn, yell; ▪ *Ant* murmur, quiet, silence, whisper.

outdated/out-of-date [adj] *old-fashioned* ▪ *Syn* anachronous, antiquated, antique, archaic, dated, demode, dusty, musty, obsolete, old, outmoded, square, tired, unfashionable, vintage; ▪ *Ant* current, fashionable, modern, new, popular, up-to-date.

outdo [v] *better, overcome*
▪ *Syn* beat, best, defeat, eclipse, exceed, excel, lick, outclass, outdistance, outfox, outgun, outjockey, outmaneuver, outshine, outsmart, outstrip, surpass, top, transcend; ▪ *Ant* be inferior, fail, lose, stay within.

outdoor [adj/adv] *in the open air*
▪ *Syn* alfresco, healthful, in the open, natural, open-air, out-of-doors, out of the house, outside; ▪ *Ant* indoor.

outer [adj] *external, exposed*
▪ *Syn* beyond, exoteric, exterior, extrinsic, outermost, outlying, outmost, outside, outward, over, peripheral, remote, superficial, surface, without; ▪ *Ant* central, inner, interior.

outfit [v] *clothe, equip*
▪ *Syn* accoutre, appoint, arm, furnish, prepare, provide, provision, stock, suit, supply; ▪ *Ant* bare, deny, deprive, unclothe, withhold.

outgoing [adj1] *demonstrative, extroverted* ▪ *Syn* approachable, communicative, easy, friendly, genial, gregarious,

informal, kind, open, sociable, sympathetic, unrestrained, warm; ▪ *Ant* introverted, reclusive, shy, withdrawn.

outgoing [adj2] *leaving*
▪ *Syn* departing, former, last, outbound, outward-bound, past, retiring, withdrawing; ▪ *Ant* arriving, entering, incoming.

outgrowth [n1] *projection*
▪ *Syn* bulge, enlargement, excrescence, jut, node, offshoot, outcrop, prominence, protuberance, shoot, sprout, swelling; ▪ *Ant* cavity, hollow.

outgrowth [n2] *product, consequence*
▪ *Syn* aftereffect, branch, child, derivative, descendant, development, effect, emergence, end, issue, member, offshoot, offspring, outcome, result, yield; ▪ *Ant* cause, root, source.

outing [n *politically motivated exposure of another's secrets* ▪ *Syn* announcement, declaration, demystification, disclosure, proclamation, revealing, tossing, uncloseting, unmasking; ▪ *Ant* closeting, discretion, hiding, shield, silence, protection, privacy, secret.

outlandish [adj] *bizarre, very strange*
▪ *Syn* alien, awkward, barbarous, boorish, clumsy, curious, droll, eccentric, erratic, extravagant, fantastic, foreign, freakish, gauche, grotesque, odd, outrageous, peculiar, preposterous, quaint, queer, rude, singular, tasteless, unconventional, unusual, weird, whimsical, wild; ▪ *Ant* common, familiar, normal, ordinary, usual.

outlast [v] *endure beyond another*
▪ *Syn* hang on, outlive, outstay, outwear, prevail, remain, survive; ▪ *Ant* fail, fall apart, lose, peter out, shoot, succumb.

outlaw [v] *prohibit; make illegal*
▪ *Syn* ban, banish, bar, condemn, damn, disallow, embargo, enjoin, exclude, forbid, illegalize, inhibit, interdict, prevent, proscribe, stop; ▪ *Ant* allow, legalize, permit.

outlay [n] *expenses*
▪ *Syn* charge, cost, disbursement, expenditure, expense, investment, price tag, spending; ▪ *Ant* income, pay.

outlet [n] *place where one can enter, leave* ▪ *Syn* aperture, channel, crack, duct, egress, exit, hole, nozzle, opening, orifice, porthole, release, safety valve, spout, tear, vent, way out; ▪ *Ant* egress, entrance.

outline [*n*] *form, tracing of an object*
▪ *Syn* contour, delineation, figuration, periphery, shape, silhouette; ▪ *Ant* center, core.

outlook [*n1*] *point of view*
▪ *Syn* attitude, direction, perspective, standpoint, viewpoint, views, vision; ▪ *Ant* blindness, indifference.

outlook [*n2*] *probable future*
▪ *Syn* appearances, chance, expectation, forecast, likelihood, possibility, probability, prospect, prospects, risk; ▪ *Ant* hindsight.

outlying [*adj*] *in rural area; remote*
▪ *Syn* afar, backwoods, distant, external, exurban, faraway, far-off, outer, peripheral, provincial, removed, suburban; ▪ *Ant* central, inner, middle.

outmoded [*adj*] *obsolete, old-fashioned*
▪ *Syn* anachronistic, antediluvian, antiquated, archaic, bygone, dated, dead, extinct, fossilized, obsolescent, obsolete, out-of-style, superannuated, superseded, tired, unfashionable, unstylish, unusable, vintage; ▪ *Ant* current, modern, new, new-fangled, popular, up-to-date.

output [*n*] *something produced*
▪ *Syn* achievement, amount, crop, gain, harvest, making, manufacture, manufacturing, producing, product, production, productivity, profit, take, turnout, yield; ▪ *Ant* input.

outrage [*v*] *wrong, offend, abuse*
▪ *Syn* affront, aggrieve, desecrate, force, ill-treat, incense, infuriate, injure, insult, madden, misuse, oppress, persecute, scandalize, shock, spoil; ▪ *Ant* delight, make happy, please.

outrageous [*adj1*] *very bad*
▪ *Syn* abominable, atrocious, barbaric, beastly, brazen, contemptible, contumelious, corrupt, degenerate, disgraceful, egregious, flagitious, flagrant, gross, heinous, horrendous, horrible, ignoble, infamous, inhuman, iniquitous, malevolent, monstrous, nefarious, notorious, odious, opprobrious, scandalous, scurrilous, shameless, shaming, shocking, sinful, unbearable, ungodly, unspeakable, villainous, violent, wanton, wicked; ▪ *Ant* delightful, good, magnificent, pleasing, wonderful.

outrageous [*adj2*] *beyond reasonable limits* ▪ *Syn* excessive, exorbitant, extortionate, extravagant, immoderate, inordinate, offensive, preposterous, scandalous, shocking, uncivilized, unconscionable, unreasonable; ▪ *Ant* acceptable, mild, reasonable, sensible.

outright [*adj*] *complete, unconditional*
▪ *Syn* absolute, all, arrant, consummate, definite, direct, downright, entire, flat, straightforward, thorough, thoroughgoing, total, undeniable, unequivocal, unmitigated, unqualified, utter, whole, wholesale; ▪ *Ant* ambiguous, conditional, hesitating, incomplete, indefinite, partial, provisional, qualified.

outside [*adj1*] *external*
▪ *Syn* alfresco, alien, apart from, away from, exterior, external, extraneous, extreme, farther, farthest, foreign, furthest, open-air, out, outdoor, outer, outermost, outward, over, surface; ▪ *Ant* central, inside, internal, middle.

outside [*adj2*] *slight, slim*
▪ *Syn* distant, faint, far, marginal, negligible, off, remote, slender, small, unlikely; ▪ *Ant* certain, definite, good, likely, sure.

outspoken [*adj*] *explicit, unreserved*
▪ *Syn* abrupt, artless, blunt, candid, direct, forthright, frank, free, open, plain, plain-spoken, straightforward, strident, unceremonious, unequivocal, unreticent, vocal; ▪ *Ant* cautious, diplomatic, introverted, reserved, retiring, shy, tactful.

outstanding [*adj1*] *superior, excellent*
▪ *Syn* celebrated, distinguished, dominant, eminent, exceptional, famous, great, impressive, magnificent, major, meritorious, momentous, phenomenal, preeminent, principal, special, standout, star, stellar, superior, superlative, world-class; ▪ *Ant* average, bad, inferior, ordinary, poor, regular, unexceptional, unremarkable.

outstanding [*adj2*] *noticeable, striking*
▪ *Syn* arresting, arrestive, conspicuous, distinguished, eye-catching, important, leading, marked, memorable, notable, noteworthy, prominent, pronounced, remarkable, salient, signal; ▪ *Ant* inconspicuous, ordinary, unnoticeable, unstriking.

outstanding [*adj3*] *referring to an unpaid debt* ▪ *Syn* due, mature, ongoing, overdue, owing, payable, pending, remaining, unresolved, unsettled; ▪ *Ant* collected, paid, resolved, settled.

outward [*adj*] *visible; for appearances*
▪ *Syn* apparent, evident, exterior, exter-

nal, noticeable, observable, obvious, on the surface, open, ostensible, out, outer, outside, over, perceptible, superficial, surface, to the eye; **Ant** invisible, inward.

outwardly [adv] to all appearances
Syn apparently, evidently, externally, in appearance, officially, on the surface, ostensibly, seemingly, superficially, to the eye; **Ant** inside, internally, inwardly, privately.

outweigh [v] override, dominate
Syn cancel out, countervail, eclipse, exceed, outbalance, overshadow, predominate, preponderate, prevail, set off, surpass, take precedence, tip the scales; **Ant** balance, compensate.

ovation [n] clapping and cheers
Syn acclaim, acclamation, applause, bravos, cheering, hand, laudation, plaudits, praise, salvo, testimonial, tribute; **Ant** booing, heckling, hissing, jeering.

over [adj1] accomplished
Syn ancient history, at an end, bygone, completed, concluded, done, done with, ended, finished, gone, past, settled; **Ant** begun, current, in progress, started.

over [adj2/adv1] in addition
Syn additionally, beyond, excessively, extra, extremely, immensely, inordinately, left over, more, over and above, overly, remaining, superfluous, surplus, too, unduly, unused; **Ant** fewer, lacking, less, short.

over [adv2] above
Syn aloft, beyond, farther up, higher than, off, on top of, overhead, traversely, upstairs; **Ant** under.

overall [adj] complete, general
Syn all-embracing, blanket, comprehensive, global, inclusive, long-range, long-term, sweeping, thorough, total, umbrella; **Ant** incomplete, narrow, specific.

overall [adv] in general
Syn all over, chiefly, generally speaking, in the long run, largely, mainly, mostly, on the whole, predominantly, primarily, principally, throughout; **Ant** partially, subordinately.

overbearing [adj] arrogant, domineering **Syn** autocratic, bossy, cavalier, dictatorial, domineering, egotistic, haughty, imperious, lordly, magisterial, officious, overweening, paramount, proud, stuffy, supercilious, tyrannical; **Ant** com-

passionate, demure, kind, modest, nice, shy, unassertive.

overblown [adj] excessive, too much
Syn disproportionate, euphuistic, fulsome, grandiloquent, immoderate, magniloquent, overdone, pompous, profuse, superfluous, turgid, undue, verbose, windy; **Ant** underrated, undervalued.

overcast [adj] cloudy, darkened
Syn clouded, clouded over, dark, dismal, dreary, dull, gray, hazy, lowering, murky, nebulous, oppressive, somber, sunless, threatening; **Ant** bright, clear, sunny.

overcome [adj] overwhelmed; visibly moved **Syn** affected, at a loss for words, beaten, speechless, unable to continue; **Ant** indifferent, unbothered, unconcerned, unflappable, unmoved.

overcome [v] beat, defeat
Syn be victorious, conquer, drown, hurdle, outlive, overthrow, prevail, prostrate, render, shock, subjugate, surmount, survive, triumph over, vanquish, win; **Ant** give in, surrender, yield.

overconfident [adj] overly sure of oneself **Syn** brash, careless, foolhardy, heedless, hubristic, impudent, overweening, presumptuous, rash, reckless, self-assertive; **Ant** cautious, pessimistic.

overdo [v] go to extremes; carry too far
Syn amplify, belabor, do to death, exaggerate, fatigue, hype, magnify, overburden, overestimate, overindulge, overload, pressure, strain oneself, stretch; **Ant** ignore, neglect.

overdue [adj] late, behind schedule
Syn behindhand, behind time, belated, delinquent, due, long delayed, outstanding, owing, payable, tardy, unpunctual; **Ant** early, paid, premature.

overhead [adj/adv] up above
Syn above, aerial, aloft, atop, hanging, in the sky, on high, over, overhanging, roof, skyward, upper, upward; **Ant** below, underfoot.

overjoyed [adj] extremely happy
Syn charmed, delighted, elated, euphoric, joyful, jubilant, rapturous, ravished, thrilled, transported; **Ant** disappointed, sad, sorrowful, upset.

overlook [v1] disregard, neglect
Syn discount, disdain, fail to notice, forget, ignore, leave out, miss, omit, pass over, pay no attention, slight; **Ant**

attend, heed, honor, look at, notice, regard, respect.

overlook [v2] *make allowances for*
▪ *Syn* condone, disregard, excuse, forgive, go along with, handle, ignore, look the other way, stand for, stomach, take; ▪ *Ant* acknowledge, blame, heed.

overlook [v3] *supervise*
▪ *Syn* boss, chaperon, control, oversee, superintend, survey; ▪ *Ant* follow, serve.

overly [adv] *excessively*
▪ *Syn* exceedingly, extremely, immensely, immoderately, inordinately, over, overfull, overmuch, too much, unduly, very much; ▪ *Ant* inadequately, insufficiently.

overplay [v] *be very dramatic*
▪ *Syn* accentuate, dramatize, exaggerate, hyperbolize, labor at, magnify, overact, overdo, overemphasize, overstate, overstress, overuse, overwork, stretch; ▪ *Ant* play down, underestimate, underplay.

overpower [v] *beat; get the upper hand*
▪ *Syn* beat down, bury, clobber, conquer, crush, defeat, drown, immobilize, overcome, overwhelm, prostrate, quell, reduce, subdue, subjugate, trounce, vanquish; ▪ *Ant* surrender, yield.

overrate [v] *assign too much value, importance* ▪ *Syn* exaggerate, expect too much of, magnify, overassess, overestimate, overprize, overreckon, overvalue, rate too highly; ▪ *Ant* underrate, undervalue.

override/overrule [v] *cancel, reverse a decision* ▪ *Syn* alter, annul, control, countermand, direct, disallow, disregard, dominate, govern, ignore, influence, invalidate, make void, nullify, overturn, prevail over, quash, recall, repeal, rescind, revoke, supersede, sway, thwart, upset, vanquish, veto; ▪ *Ant* allow, approve, permit, support.

overriding [adj] *central, most important*
▪ *Syn* cardinal, dominant, final, main, major, paramount, pivotal, predominant, prime, principal, ruling, supreme, ultimate; ▪ *Ant* insignificant, least, unimportant.

overrun [v1] *defeat, invade*
▪ *Syn* beat, clobber, foray, lambaste, lick, massacre, occupy, overwhelm, put to flight, rout, thrash, trim, whip; ▪ *Ant* lose, surrender.

overrun [v2] *infest, spread over; exceed*
▪ *Syn* beset, choke, deluge, inundate, invade, overflow, overshoot, overstep, per-

meate, ravage, run on, run over, spill, surge, surpass, swarm, well over; ▪ *Ant* evacuate, retreat.

overseas [adj] *across an ocean*
▪ *Syn* abroad, across, away, foreign, in foreign land, transatlantic, transoceanic, transpacific; ▪ *Ant* at home, domestic, indigenous, native.

oversee [v] *manage, supervise*
▪ *Syn* boss, captain, chaperon, command, look after, overlook, shepherd, skipper, superintend, survey, watch; ▪ *Ant* follow, obey.

overt [adj] *obvious, unconcealed*
▪ *Syn* apparent, clear, definite, manifest, observable, open, patent, plain, public, undisguised, visible; ▪ *Ant* concealed, hidden, private, secret.

overtake [v] *catch; pass*
▪ *Syn* beat, better, come upon, engulf, gain on, get past, leave behind, outdistance, outdo, outstrip, overwhelm, reach, strike, take by surprise; ▪ *Ant* fall behind.

overthrow [v] *defeat, destroy*
▪ *Syn* abolish, beat, bring down, conquer, crush, demolish, dethrone, do away with, eradicate, exterminate, knock down, level, liquidate, master, oust, overpower, overrun, purge, raze, ruin, subdue, subjugate, terminate, topple, unseat, upset, vanquish; ▪ *Ant* give in, surrender, yield.

overture [n] *introduction, approach*
▪ *Syn* advance, bid, conciliatory move, exordium, foreword, invitation, offer, preamble, preface, prelude, presentation, prologue, proposition, signal, suggestion, tender; ▪ *Ant* conclusion, finish.

overweight [adj] *heavier than average*
▪ *Syn* ample, bulky, corpulent, fat, fleshy, hefty, massive, obese, outsize, overstuffed, plump, portly, pudgy, rotund, stout, weighty; ▪ *Ant* skinny, thin, underweight.

overwhelm [v1] *flood, beat physically*
▪ *Syn* bury, conquer, crush, defeat, drown, engulf, inundate, massacre, overcome, overpower, rout, smother, submerge, swamp, thrash; ▪ *Ant* capitulate, give up, surrender.

overwhelm [v2] *astonish, devastate*
▪ *Syn* bewilder, confound, confuse, demoralize, destroy, dumbfound, overcome, prostrate, puzzle, run circles around, shock, stagger, stun, surprise, swamp, upset, wreck; ▪ *Ant* encourage, leave indifferent.

overwrought [*adj*] *exhausted and excited* ▪ *Syn* agitated, distracted, emotional, excitable, frantic, nervous, neurotic, overexcited, overstrung, overworked, spent, tense, tired, uneasy, weary, wired, worked-up, worn, wound-up; ▪ *Ant* calm, collected, cool, rested, unruffled.

owe [*v*] *have an obligation* ▪ *Syn* be beholden, be bound, be contracted, be in arrears, be in debt, be indebted, be obligated, feel bound, have borrowed, incur, lost, ought to; ▪ *Ant* compensate, pay, resolve, settle.

own [*adj*] *belonging to individual* ▪ *Syn* endemic, individual, inherent, intrinsic, particular, peculiar, personal, private, resident; ▪ *Ant* another's, someone else's.

own [*v1*] *possess; be responsible for* ▪ *Syn* control, dominate, enjoy, fall heir to, have, have in hand, have rights, have title, hold, inherit, keep, occupy, reserve, retain; ▪ *Ant* dispossess, lack, lose, need, not have, sell.

own [*v2*] *acknowledge, admit* ▪ *Syn* allow, assent to, avow, concede, confess, declare, disclose, grant, own up, recognize, tell the truth; ▪ *Ant* deny, disavow, reject.

P

pace [*v*] *walk back and forth* ▪ *Syn* march, patrol, tread, walk up and down; ▪ *Ant* relax, sit, stroll.

pacify [*v*] *make peaceful; appease* ▪ *Syn* allay, assuage, conciliate, cool, dulcify, lull, mitigate, mollify, placate, propitiate, quell, relieve, silence, smooth over, soothe, subdue, temper, tranquilize; ▪ *Ant* aggravate, agitate, incite, irritate, upset.

pack [*v1*] *make ready for transport* ▪ *Syn* batch, bind, brace, bunch, bundle, burden, collect, dispose, fasten, gather, load, package, store, stow, tie, warehouse; ▪ *Ant* dismantle, unpack, untie.

pack [*v2*] *fill, compact* ▪ *Syn* choke, compress, contract, crowd, heap, insert, jam, load, mob, pile, press, ram, squeeze, stuff, tamp, throng, wedge; ▪ *Ant* allocate, disperse, dispose, distribute, unpack.

packed [*adj*] *very full* ▪ *Syn* awash, brimming, chock, congested, crammed, crowded, filled, jammed, loaded, mobbed, overloaded, seething, stuffed, swarming, tumid; ▪ *Ant* deserted, empty.

pact [*n*] *agreement* ▪ *Syn* alliance, arrangement, bargain, bond, compact, concordat, contract, covenant, deal, league, settlement, transaction, treaty, understanding; ▪ *Ant* disagreement, secession, separation.

pad [*v1*] *elaborate, amplify* ▪ *Syn* augment, embellish, enlarge, exaggerate, fill out, increase, inflate, lengthen, magnify, overdraw, protract, spin, stretch; ▪ *Ant* simplify, uncomplicate.

pad [*v2*] *walk quietly* ▪ *Syn* creep, hike, march, sneak, steal, traipse, trek; ▪ *Ant* plod, stamp, stomp, tramp, trudge.

pagan [*adj*] *irreligious* ▪ *Syn* agnostic, atheistic, heathen, heathenish, idolatrous, impious, infidel, polytheistic, profane, unchristian; ▪ *Ant* believing, enlightened, religious.

page [*v*] *call for over communications system* ▪ *Syn* announce, beep, call, call the name of, seek, send for, summon; ▪ *Ant* answer.

pain [*v*] *bother, trouble* ▪ *Syn* afflict, aggrieve, annoy, bite, chafe, chasten, constrain, discomfort, disquiet, distress, exasperate, gall, grieve, harass, harm, harrow, hurt, inflame, injure, irk, irritate, rile, sadden, smart, sting, strain, stress, suffer, throb, tingle, torment, torture, upset, vex, worry, wound; ▪ *Ant* aid, assist, assuage, help, please.

painful [*adj*] *physically or mentally agonizing* ▪ *Syn* awful, difficult, dire, disagreeable, distasteful, distressing, dreadful, excruciating, extreme, hard, harrowing, hurtful, hurting, inflamed, irritated, laborious, piercing, raw, saddening, sensitive, severe, sharp, smarting, sore, stinging, tender, terrible, throbbing, tormenting, troublesome, trying, uncomfortable, unpleasant, vexatious; ▪ *Ant* delightful, easy, painless, pleasant, soothing.

painstaking [*adj*] *meticulous, thorough* ▪ *Syn* assiduous, careful, conscientious, diligent, exacting, finicky, fussy, hardworking, heedful, industrious, particular, persevering, punctilious, punctual, scrupulous, sedulous, strenuous, thoroughgoing; ▪ *Ant* careless, easy, frivolous, haphazard, lazy, slapdash, thoughtless, unmindful.

paint [v] *apply colored tint, often to make design* ▪ *Syn* color, cover, daub, decorate, draft, limn, ornament, outline, picture, portray, represent, shade, sketch, stipple, swab, tint, touch up, wash; ▪ *Ant* strip.

pair [v] *make, become a twosome* ▪ *Syn* balance, bracket, combine, couple, join, marry, match, match up, mate, pair off, put together, team, twin, unite, wed, yoke; ▪ *Ant* divide, separate, sever.

pal [n] *friend* ▪ *Syn* associate, buddy, chum, companion, comrade, confidant, connate, crony, mate, sidekick; ▪ *Ant* enemy, foe.

palace [n] *royal or enormous home* ▪ *Syn* alcazar, castle, chateau, hall, manor, mansion, official residence, royal residence; ▪ *Ant* cottage, hovel, hut, shack.

palatable [adj] *delicious, agreeable* ▪ *Syn* acceptable, appetizing, delectable, divine, enjoyable, flavorsome, heavenly, luscious, mellow, mouthwatering, pleasant, satisfactory, savory, scrumptious, tasty, tempting, toothsome; ▪ *Ant* bitter, disagreeable, distasteful, sour, unsavory, untasty.

palatial [adj] *grand, opulent* ▪ *Syn* deluxe, grandiose, illustrious, imposing, impressive, lush, luxuriant, magnificent, majestic, noble, plush, regal, rich, spacious, splendid, stately, sumptuous; ▪ *Ant* cramped, minor, modest, simple, small, tiny, unpretentious.

pale [adj] *very light in color or effect* ▪ *Syn* anemic, ashen, blanched, bleached, bloodless, cadaverous, colorless, deathlike, doughy, faint, feeble, ghastly, gray, haggard, livid, pallid, pasty, sickly, spectral, thin, wan, washed-out, waxen, white; ▪ *Ant* bright, colorful, florid, flushed, glowing, radiant, rosy, rubicund.

pale [v] *become, make lighter or weakened* ▪ *Syn* blanch, dim, dull, fade, faint, go white, grow dull, lose color, lose luster, whiten; ▪ *Ant* blush, brighten, darken, flush, glow, radiate.

pall [v] *bore, tire* ▪ *Syn* become dull, become tedious, cloy, disgust, fill, glut, gorge, jade, sate, satiate, sicken, surfeit, weary; ▪ *Ant* animate, brighten, delight, excite, interest, make happy.

palliate [v] *gloss over; cover up* ▪ *Syn* alleviate, assuage, conceal, diminish, disguise, ease, exculpate, extenuate, hide, justify, lessen, lighten, mask, mitigate, moderate, mollify, prettify, qualify, relieve, soften, temper, varnish, veil, whiten; ▪ *Ant* arouse, exacerbate, increase.

palpable [adj] *clear, obvious, concrete* ▪ *Syn* apparent, blatant, certain, conspicuous, detectable, discernible, evident, manifest, noticeable, observable, perceptible, remarkable, solid, straightforward, striking, tactile, tangible, unmistakable, visible; ▪ *Ant* hidden, indistinct, intangible, obscure, unclear, vague.

palpitate [v] *beat at a rapid pace, like a heart* ▪ *Syn* flutter, pound, pulsate, pulse, quiver, shiver, throb, tremble, vibrate; ▪ *Ant* be still.

palsied [adj] *crippled* ▪ *Syn* arthritic, debilitated, disabled, diseased, neurasthenic, paralytic, paralyzed, shaking, shaky, sick, trembling, tremorous, weak; ▪ *Ant* healthy, steady, walking.

paltry [adj] *very poor; worthless* ▪ *Syn* base, beggarly, cheap, common, contemptible, derisory, inconsiderable, insignificant, limited, low, meager, measly, narrow, petty, piddling, pitiful, shabby, shoddy, slight, trifling, trivial, unconsequential, vile, wretched; ▪ *Ant* important, significant, substantial, valuable, worthy.

pamper [v] *serve one's every need, whim* ▪ *Syn* baby, caress, cater to, coddle, fondle, gratify, humor, indulge, overindulge, pet, please, regale, satisfy, spoil; ▪ *Ant* be mean, hurt, ignore, intimidate, mistreat, neglect, oppress, withhold.

pan [v] *criticize strongly* ▪ *Syn* censure, condemn, cut up, denounce, denunciate, disparage, flay, hammer, jeer at, knock, rap, reprehend, review unfavorably, roast, slam; ▪ *Ant* celebrate, compliment, eulogize, extol, praise.

panache [n] *person's flamboyant spirit* ▪ *Syn* brio, charisma, dash, flair, flamboyance, flourish, élan, style, swagger, verve, vigor; ▪ *Ant* apathy, indifference, repulsiveness, sluggishness, spiritlessness.

pandemonium [n] *craziness, commotion* ▪ *Syn* anarchy, babel, bedlam, bluster, chaos, clamor, clatter, confusion, din, hassle, jangle, noise, racket, riot, ruckus, rumpus, tumult, turbulence, turmoil, uproar; ▪ *Ant* calm, order, peace.

pander [*v*] *cater to, indulge*
▪ *Syn* cajole, gratify, please, satisfy, soften up, stroke; ▪ *Ant* deny, dissatisfy, refuse.

pang [*n*] *ache, twinge*
▪ *Syn* agony, anguish, discomfort, distress, gripe, misery, pain, spasm, stab, sting, stitch, throb, throe, wrench; ▪ *Ant* comfort, joy, pleasure, satisfaction.

panic [*v*] *become, make afraid or distressed* ▪ *Syn* alarm, become hysterical, be terror-stricken, clutch, come apart, overreact, scare, stampede, startle, terrify, unnerve; ▪ *Ant* be calm, be content.

pan out [*v*] *come to pass; succeed*
▪ *Syn* culminate, eventuate, happen, provide, render, result, work out, yield; ▪ *Ant* fail, not happen.

paper [*v*] *line with material*
▪ *Syn* cover, hang, paste up, plaster, wallpaper; ▪ *Ant* peal, strip, unline.

par [*n*] *average, equilibrium*
▪ *Syn* balance, coequality, equal footing, equality, equivalence, equivalency, level, mean, median, norm, parity, sameness, standard, usual; ▪ *Ant* extreme.

parade [*v*] *show off; march*
▪ *Syn* advertise, air, boast, brag, brandish, declare, demonstrate, display, exhibit, expose, flash, flaunt, prance, sport, strut, vaunt; ▪ *Ant* cloak, conceal, hide, mask, suppress.

paradigm [*n*] *example*
▪ *Syn* archetype, examplar, ideal, mirror, model, original, pattern, prototype, sample, standard; ▪ *Ant* abnormality, contradiction, incongruity.

paradise [*n*] *land, feeling of great pleasure; absence of evil* ▪ *Syn* bliss, delight, felicity, heaven, nirvana, promised land, Utopia, wonderland; ▪ *Ant* hell, misery, torment, wretchedness.

paradox [*n*] *contradiction, puzzle*
▪ *Syn* ambiguity, anomaly, enigma, inconsistency, mystery, oddity, opposite, reverse; ▪ *Ant* axiom, maxim, rule, truism.

parallel [*adj1*] *aligned, side-by-side*
▪ *Syn* alongside, coextensive, coordinate, equidistant, lateral; ▪ *Ant* crooked, non parallel, separate, skewed, zigzag.

parallel [*adj2*] *akin, similar*
▪ *Syn* alike, analogous, comparable, complementary, consonant, correspondent, equal, identical, like, matching, resembling, uniform; ▪ *Ant* different, dissimilar, divergent.

parallel [*v*] *be alike*
▪ *Syn* agree, assimilate, chime, collocate, compare, complement, conform, correlate, correspond, equate, imitate, keep pace, liken, match, paragon; ▪ *Ant* differ, distort, diverge, separate, skew.

paralyze [*v*] *immobilize, cripple*
▪ *Syn* anesthetize, arrest, astound, bemuse, daunt, daze, deaden, debilitate, disable, enfeeble, freeze, halt, incapacitate, knock out, lame, nonplus, numb, palsy, petrify, stun, stupefy, transfix, weaken; ▪ *Ant* animate, incite, mobilize, stimulate.

paramount [*adj*] *principal, superior*
▪ *Syn* ascendant, cardinal, chief, commanding, crowning, dominant, eminent, foremost, headmost, leading, main, outstanding, predominant, preeminent, premier, prevalent, primary, regnant, sovereign, supreme; ▪ *Ant* inferior, last, least, less, lesser, lowest, minor, secondary, smallest, trivial.

paraphrase [*v*] *interpret, translate*
▪ *Syn* express in other words, express in own words, recapitulate, rehash, render, rephrase, restate, reword, summarize, transcribe; ▪ *Ant* quote, reproduce, state, verbatim.

parcel [*n*] *part, piece*
▪ *Syn* bite, chunk, cut, division, member, moiety, portion, section, segment, slice; ▪ *Ant* entirely, whole.

parch [*v*] *dry, burn*
▪ *Syn* blister, brown, dehydrate, desiccate, dry up, evaporate, scorch, sear, shrivel, wither; ▪ *Ant* dampen, moisten, wet.

parched [*adj*] *very dry*
▪ *Syn* arid, burned, dehydrated, dried out, scorched, shriveled, thirsty, waterless, withered; ▪ *Ant* damp, moist, wet.

pardon [*v*] *forgive*
▪ *Syn* absolve, acquit, clear, condone, discharge, exculpate, exonerate, free, justify, liberate, overlook, release, remit, tolerate; ▪ *Ant* chastise, condemn, damn, ostracize, penalize, punish.

pare [*v*] *peel, trim*
▪ *Syn* carve, clip, crop, cut, decorticate, decrease, dock, flay, lop, lower, prune, reduce, shear, skin, strip, thin, uncover; ▪ *Ant* cover, increase, raise.

parent [n] *person, source of product*
• **Syn** ancestor, architect, author, begetter, cause, creator, father, forerunner, fountainhead, guardian, mother, originator, procreator, progenitor, prototype, root, sire, wellspring; • **Ant** child, offspring.

parenthetical [adj] *incidental*
• **Syn** bracketed, by the way, episodic, explanatory, extraneous, extrinsic, incidental, interposed, qualifying, related, subordinate; • **Ant** basic, central, consequential, important.

parity [n] *equality, balance*
• **Syn** affinity, agreement, analogy, closeness, conformity, congruity, consistency, correspondence, equivalence, likeness, nearness, parallelism, resemblance, sameness, similarity, similitude, uniformity, unity; • **Ant** dissimilitude, imbalance, inequality.

parochial [adj] *narrow-minded, restricted* • **Syn** biased, bigoted, conservative, insular, limited, narrow, petty, prejudiced, provincial, regional, sectarian, shallow, small-minded; • **Ant** broad, cosmopolitan, liberal, universal, unrestricted.

parody [n] *imitation, spoof*
• **Syn** burlesque, caricature, cartoon, farce, irony, jest, lampoon, mime, mimicry, mockery, pastiche, raillery, ridicule, satire, travesty; • **Ant** reality, tragedy, truth.

parry [v] *ward off, circumvent*
• **Syn** anticipate, avoid, bypass, deflect, dodge, elude, evade, fend off, forestall, preclude, prevent, rebuff, rebuke, resist, shun, sidestep, stave off; • **Ant** confront, deal with, face, meet.

parsimonious [adj] *penny-pinching*
• **Syn** avaricious, close, frugal, greedy, illiberal, miserly, penurious, prudent, scrimpy, selfish, sparing; • **Ant** extravagant, generous, lavish, liberal.

part [v1] *break, disconnect*
• **Syn** break up, cleave, come apart, detach, dichotomize, disjoin, dismantle, dissever, disunite, divide, factor, itemize, particularize, partition, portion, rend, section, segment, separate, sever, slice, split, strip, subdivide, sunder, tear; • **Ant** adhere, connect, join, unite.

part [v2] *leave, go away from someone*
• **Syn** break, break off, depart, ease out, go, part company, push off, quit, separate, split, take leave, withdraw; • **Ant** abide, arrive, come, linger.

partake [v] *eat, share*
• **Syn** consume, devour, engage, enter into, feed, ingest, participate, receive, sample, savor, sip, sit in, take; • **Ant** abstain, decline, refrain.

partial [adj1] *incomplete*
• **Syn** fractional, fragmentary, half done, halfway, inconclusive, limited, part, sectional, uncompleted, unfinished; • **Ant** complete, entire, total, whole.

partial [adj2] *biased, prejudiced*
• **Syn** colored, discriminatory, disposed, influenced, interested, jaundiced, minded, one-sided, partisan, predisposed, prepossessed, tendentious, warped; • **Ant** fair, just, objective, unbiased, unprejudiced.

partially [adv] *incompletely*
• **Syn** by degrees, by installments, fractionally, halfway, in part, in some measure, little by little, moderately, not wholly, partly, piece by piece, piecemeal, somewhat, to a certain degree, to a certain extent; • **Ant** all, completely, totally, wholly.

participate [v] *take part in activity*
• **Syn** be a party to, compete, concur, cooperate, engage, engage in, enter into, join in, lend a hand, partake, perform, play, share, strive, take an interest in; • **Ant** forbear, forswear, observe, watch.

particular [adj1] *exact, specific*
• **Syn** distinct, especial, express, full, individual, intrinsic, limited, local, meticulous, minute, painstaking, peculiar, scrupulous, selective, singular, thorough, topical; • **Ant** general, imprecise, indefinite, inexact, universal.

particular [adj2] *notable, uncommon*
• **Syn** especial, exceptional, marked, noteworthy, one, only, peculiar, remarkable, singular, sole, solitary, unique, unusual; • **Ant** common, general, ordinary, unimportant, usual.

particular [adj3] *finicky, demanding*
• **Syn** careful, choosy, critical, dainty, discriminating, exacting, fastidious, finical, fussy, hard to please, meticulous, tough; • **Ant** haphazard, indifferent, nonchalant, undemanding, undiscriminating.

particularly [adv] *specifically*
• **Syn** decidedly, distinctly, especially, exceptionally, explicitly, expressly, in particular, markedly, notably, princi-

pally, singularly, specially, surprisingly, uncommonly; ▪ *Ant* commonly, generally, usually.

parting [*adj*] *farewell*
▪ *Syn* departing, final, goodbye, last, valedictory; ▪ *Ant* greeting, introductory.

partisan [*adj*] *interested, factional*
▪ *Syn* biased, bigoted, colored, conspiratorial, denominational, devoted, exclusive, fanatic, jaundiced, one-sided, overzealous, partial, predisposed, prejudiced, sectarian, sympathetic, tendentious, unreasoning, zealous; ▪ *Ant* disinterested, objective, open-minded.

partition [*v*] *divide, separate*
▪ *Syn* apportion, cut, cut up, dispense, disperse, measure out, parcel out, portion, section, separate, share, slice, split, split up, subdivide; ▪ *Ant* attach, combine, join, unite.

partly [*adv*] *not completely*
▪ *Syn* at least, at most, bit by bit, by degrees, halfway, inadequately, in part, in some ways, insufficiently, little by little, measurably, noticeably, not strictly speaking, partially, piece by piece, piecemeal, relatively, slightly, somewhat, to a certain degree, to a certain extent; ▪ *Ant* completely, entirely, fully, totally, wholly.

partner [*n*] *person who takes part with another* ▪ *Syn* accomplice, ally, associate, bedfellow, buddy, cohort, collaborator, colleague, companion, comrade, confederate, confrere, consort, coworker, date, friend, helper, helpmate, mate, spouse; ▪ *Ant* enemy, foe.

pass [*adj*] *old-fashioned*
▪ *Syn* antiquated, belated, cursory, dated, dead, ephemeral, evanescent, extinct, fleeting, fugacious, fugitive, glancing, has-been, hasty, impermanent, momentary, obsolete, outdated, outmoded, out-of-date, outworn, quick, shallow, short, short-lived, slight, superficial, superseded, temporary, transient, transitory, yesterday; ▪ *Ant* current, fashionable, in, in vogue, modern, new.

pass [*v1*] *go by, elapse; move onwards*
▪ *Syn* come to pass, depart, develop, fare, flow, fly by, get ahead, glide, go, go past, happen, hie, journey, lapse, leave, move, occur, pass by, proceed, progress, push on, reach, rise, roll, run, slip away, take place, transpire, travel, wend; ▪ *Ant* halt, pause, reheat, stop, wait.

pass [*v2*] *surpass, beat*
▪ *Syn* exceed, excel, go beyond, go by, leave behind, outdistance, outdo, outshine, outstrip, surmount, top, transcend; ▪ *Ant* drag, fall behind, lose.

pass [*v3*] *succeed, graduate*
▪ *Syn* answer, get through, matriculate, pass muster, qualify, satisfy, suffice; ▪ *Ant* fail, fall behind.

pass [*v4*] *give, transfer*
▪ *Syn* buck, convey, deliver, exchange, hand, hand over, reach, relinquish, send, shoot, throw, transmit; ▪ *Ant* receive, take.

pass [*v5*] *cease*
▪ *Syn* close, decease, depart, die, disappear, discontinue, dwindle, ebb, end, expire, fade, perish, stop, succumb, terminate, vanish, wane; ▪ *Ant* begin, commence, continue, live.

pass [*v6*] *enact, legislate*
▪ *Syn* accept, adopt, approve, authorize, become law, become ratified, become valid, be established, carry, decree, engage, establish, ordain, pledge, promise, ratify, sanction, undertake, validate, vote in; ▪ *Ant* deny, refuse, veto.

pass [*v7*] *decide not to do*
▪ *Syn* decline, discount, disregard, fail, ignore, neglect, not heed, omit, overlook, refuse, skip, slight; ▪ *Ant* accept, be willing.

passable [*adj1*] *acceptable, admissible*
▪ *Syn* adequate, allowable, all right, average, common, fair, fair enough, mediocre, moderate, ordinary, presentable, respectable, tolerable; ▪ *Ant* excellent, exceptional, inadequate, superior, uncommon.

passable [*adj2*] *clear and able to be traveled* ▪ *Syn* accessible, attainable, beaten, crossable, easy, fair, graded, motorable, navigable, open, penetrable, reachable, traversable; ▪ *Ant* blocked, closed, obstructed.

pass away [*v*] *die*
▪ *Syn* decease, demise, depart, drop, expire, pass on, perish, succumb; ▪ *Ant* be born, live.

passing [*adj*] *brief, casual*
▪ *Syn* antiquated, belated, cursory, dated, dead, ephemeral, evanescent, extinct, fleeting, fugacious, fugitive, glancing, has-been, hasty, impermanent, momentary, obsolete, outdated, outmoded, out-of-date, outworn, quick, shallow, short, short-lived, slight, superficial, super-

seded, temporary, transient, transitory, yesterday; ▪ *Ant* lasting, lingering, long-lasting, permanent, perpetual.

passionate [*adj1*] *sensual, desirous*
▪ *Syn* amorous, ardent, aroused, concupiscent, desirous, erotic, lascivious, libidinous, loving, lustful, prurient, romantic, sexy, stimulated, sultry, wanton, wistful; ▪ *Ant* cold, cool, frigid, indifferent, uncaring, unpassionate.

passionate [*adj2*] *very excited; enthusiastic* ▪ *Syn* affecting, animated, ardent, blazing, burning, deep, dramatic, eager, eloquent, emotional, expressive, fervent, fervid, fierce, fiery, flaming, forceful, frenzied, glowing, headlong, heartfelt, heated, impassioned, impetuous, impulsive, intense, melodramatic, moving, poignant, precipitate, spirited, stimulated, stirring, strong, thrilling, vehement, violent, warm, wild, zealous; ▪ *Ant* apathetic, dull, unenthusiastic, unexcited, unpassionate.

passive [*adj*] *lifeless, inactive*
▪ *Syn* acquiescent, apathetic, compliant, cool, docile, enduring, flat, indifferent, inert, latent, long-suffering, motionless, nonviolent, patient, phlegmatic, quiescent, resigned, sleepy, static, submissive, tractable, unflappable, uninvolved, yielding; ▪ *Ant* active, aggresive, dynamic, forceful, lively.

pass off [*v*] *give because one does not want it* ▪ *Syn* eject, foist, palm, send forth, work off; ▪ *Ant* keep, maintain.

pass over [*v*] *ignore, disregard*
▪ *Syn* dismiss, fail, forget, miss, neglect, omit, overlook, pass by, skip; ▪ *Ant* attend, heed, take care, tap.

past [*adj1*] *preceding, done*
▪ *Syn* accomplished, ago, antecedent, completed, elapsed, ended, extinct, finished, forgotten, gone by, over, over and done, precedent, previous, prior, spent; ▪ *Ant* current, future, present.

past [*adj2*] *olden, former*
▪ *Syn* ancient, bygone, earlier, erstwhile, foregoing, late, latter, latter-day, long-ago, old, once, over, preceding, previous, prior, quondam, retired, sometime; ▪ *Ant* current, future, present.

pastel [*adj*] *muted in color*
▪ *Syn* delicate, light, pale, soft-hued, toned; ▪ *Ant* bright, loud, primary, vibrant, vivid.

pastiche [*n*] *work of art formed from disparate sources* ▪ *Syn* assortment, collage, collection, compilation, copy, hodgepodge, imitation, mishmosh*, paste-up, patchwork, potpourri, reappropriation, reproduction, synthesis; ▪ *Ant* model, novelty, original, pattern, prototype.

pastime [*n*] *leisure activity*
▪ *Syn* amusement, distraction, diversion, entertainment, fun, game, hobby, leisure, play, recreation, relaxation, sport; ▪ *Ant* business, profession, task, work.

pastoral [*adj*] *peaceful, especially referring to the countryside* ▪ *Syn* agrarian, Arcadian, bucolic, countrified, country, idyllic, outland, provincial, rural, rustic, simple, sylvan; ▪ *Ant* agitated, bustling, busy, cosmopolitan, urban.

pasty [*adj1*] *sticky*
▪ *Syn* adhesive, doughy, gelatinous, gluelike, gluey, glutinous, gooey, mucilaginous, starchy; ▪ *Ant* dry, powdery, smooth, unsticky.

pasty [*adj2*] *very pale*
▪ *Syn* anemic, ashen, bloodless, dull, pallid, sallow, sickly, unhealthy, wan, waxen; ▪ *Ant* blushing, flushed, healthy, vivid.

pat [*adj*] *relevant, suitable*
▪ *Syn* apropos, auspicious, felicitous, fitting, happy, neat, opportune, pertinent, suitable, timely, to the point; ▪ *Ant* imprecise, inexact, irrelevant, unacceptable, unsuitable, wrong.

pat [*adv*] *exactly, fittingly*
▪ *Syn* aptly, faultlessly, flawlessly, just right, opportunely, perfectly, precisely, relevantly, seasonably; ▪ *Ant* wrongly.

patch [*v*] *fix, mend*
▪ *Syn* cobble, overhaul, rebuild, recondition, reconstruct, reinforce, repair, revamp, sew; ▪ *Ant* break, damage, rend, tear.

patch up [*v*] *settle differences*
▪ *Syn* adjust, appease, compensate, conciliate, mediate, negotiate, placate, restore, settle, smooth; ▪ *Ant* argue, bicker, disagree, fight.

patchy [*adj*] *spotty, not consistent*
▪ *Syn* erratic, fitful, irregular, random, sketchy, uneven, variable, varying; ▪ *Ant* consistent, continuous, regular, unspotted.

patent [*adj*] *unconcealed, conspicuous*
▪ *Syn* apparent, blatant, clear, distinct, evident, flagrant, glaring, indisputable, limited, manifest, obvious, open, palpable, plain, prominent, rank, straightforward, transparent, unequivocal, un-

mistakable; ▪ *Ant* concealed, hidden, inconspicuous.

path [n] *course, way*
▪ *Syn* aisle, artery, avenue, beat, beaten path, boulevard, footpath, groove, highway, lane, line, pass, passage, pathway, road, roadway, route, street, thoroughfare, track, trail, walk, walkway; ▪ *Ant* barrier, blockage.

pathetic [adj] *sad, affecting*
▪ *Syn* commiserable, deplorable, distressing, feeble, heartbreaking, lamentable, miserable, paltry, petty, piteous, pitiful, plaintive, poignant, poor, rueful, sorry, touching, useless, woeful, wretched; ▪ *Ant* adequate, amusing, cheerful, entertaining, happy.

pathos [n] *deep sadness*
▪ *Syn* desolation, emotion, feeling, passion, pitifulness, plaintiveness, poignance, sentiment; ▪ *Ant* cheer, glee, happiness, joy.

patient [adj] *capable, willing to endure*
▪ *Syn* accommodating, composed, enduring, even-tempered, forbearing, forgiving, gentle, imperturbable, lenient, long-suffering, meek, mild, persevering, persistent, self-possessed, serene, stoical, submissive, tolerant, uncomplaining, untiring; ▪ *Ant* agitated, frustrated, impatient, intolerant, unwilling.

patrician [adj] *upper-class*
▪ *Syn* aristocratic, gentle, grand, highborn, high-class, noble, royal, well-born; ▪ *Ant* common, lower-class.

patriot [n] *person who loves his or her country* ▪ *Syn* good citizen, loyalist, nationalist, partisan, patrioteer, volunteer; ▪ *Ant* expatriate, subversive, traitor.

patrol [v] *guard, protect*
▪ *Syn* cruise, inspect, keep guard, keep watch, mount, police, pound, range, ride shotgun, safeguard, shotgun, watch; ▪ *Ant* ignore, neglect.

patronize [v1] *condescend*
▪ *Syn* assume a lofty attitude toward, deign, indulge, snub, stoop, treat as inferior, treat badly; ▪ *Ant* be humble, be modest, respect.

patronize [v2] *support a cause*
▪ *Syn* assist, back, befriend, foster, fund, help, maintain, promote, sponsor, subscribe to; ▪ *Ant* antagonize, contend, oppose.

patter [n] *casual talk; chatter*
▪ *Syn* argot, babble, cant, chatter, dialect, jabber, jargon, lingo,

monologue, patois, vernacular; ▪ *Ant* formal language.

pattern [v] *copy, imitate; decorate*
▪ *Syn* design, emulate, follow, form, model, mold, order, shape, style, trim; ▪ *Ant* be original.

paucity [n] *lack, scarcity*
▪ *Syn* absence, dearth, deficiency, famine, insufficiency, meagerness, paltriness, poverty, rarity, scantiness, scarceness, shortage, slenderness, slightness, smallness, sparseness; ▪ *Ant* abundance, affluence, plenty.

pauper [n] *person who is poor*
▪ *Syn* almsman, bankrupt, beggar, bum, dependent, destitute, homeless, indigent, insolvent, mendicant, poor person, supplicant; ▪ *Ant* magnate, millionaire, tycoon.

pause [v] *wait, delay*
▪ *Syn* cease, deliberate, hesitate, hold back, interrupt, put on hold, rest, sideline, stop briefly, suspend, waver; ▪ *Ant* continue, persist, restart.

pave [v] *cover with asphalt, concrete*
▪ *Syn* brick, cobblestone, flagstone, gravel, lay asphalt, lay concrete, macadamize, surface, tar, tile; ▪ *Ant* dig up, strip.

paw [v] *touch roughly*
▪ *Syn* clap, claw, clutch, dig, feel, grab, grate, grope, handle, hit, maul, molest, palpate, rake, rasp, rub, scratch, search, slap, smite; ▪ *Ant* caress, fondle, pat, stroke.

pawn [n] *person who is a fool*
▪ *Syn* creature, instrument, puppet, tool, toy, victim; ▪ *Ant* boss, chief, head, leader.

pay [v1] *give money for goods, services*
▪ *Syn* bear the cost, bequeath, bestow, compensate, disburse, grant, make payment, meet, offer, proffer, recompense, recoup, refund, reimburse, remit, render, reward, satisfy, settle, stake; ▪ *Ant* be in debt, collect, earn, owe, receive.

pay [v2] *be advantageous*
▪ *Syn* benefit, be worthwhile, repay, serve; ▪ *Ant* be futile, be worthless.

pay [v3] *profit, yield*
▪ *Syn* be profitable, be remunerative, bring in, make a return, make money, pay dividends, produce, provide a living, return, show gain, show profit, yield profit; ▪ *Ant* cost.

payable [adj] *to be paid*
▪ *Syn* due, mature, maturing, obligatory, outstanding, overdue, owed, owing, re-

ceivable, unpaid, unsettled; ▪ *Ant* paid, settled.

payoff [*n*] *conclusion, climax*
▪ *Syn* consequence, culmination, finale, judgment, outcome, result; ▪ *Ant* introduction, start.

peaceable [*adj*] *friendly, serene*
▪ *Syn* amiable, amicable, calm, complacent, conciliatory, gentle, irenic, mild, neighborly, pacific, pacifist, peaceloving, placid, quiet, restful, still, tranquil; ▪ *Ant* belligerent, cold, cool, mean, unfriendly.

peaceful [*adj*] *friendly, serene*
▪ *Syn* amicable, at peace, bloodless, calm, collected, composed, constant, equable, gentle, halcyon, harmonious, irenic, mellow, neutral, nonbelligerent, nonviolent, pacifistic, peaceable, peaceloving, placid, quiet, restful, smooth, sociable, steady, still, tranquil, undisturbed, unruffled, untroubled, without hostility; ▪ *Ant* clamorous, disturbed, excited, noisy, turbulent, unfriendly, violent.

peacemaker [*n*] *person who settles problem* ▪ *Syn* appeaser, arbitrator, conciliator, diplomat, mediator, negotiator, pacificator, pacifier, placater, statesperson; ▪ *Ant* agitator, instigator, insurgent.

peak [*v*] *reach highest point*
▪ *Syn* climax, crest, culminate, reach the top, reach the zenith; ▪ *Ant* fall, hit bottom, plunge.

peaked [*adj*] *pale, sick*
▪ *Syn* ailing, bilious, emaciated, ill, poorly, sickly, wan; ▪ *Ant* blushing, colorful, florid, flushed, healthy, robust, strapping.

peculiar [*adj1*] *characteristic, distinguishing* ▪ *Syn* appropriate, distinct, distinctive, endemic, exclusive, idiosyncratic, individual, intrinsic, local, particular, personal, private, restricted, special, specific, typical, unique; ▪ *Ant* common, conventional, general, normal.

peculiar [*adj2*] *bizarre, odd*
▪ *Syn* abnormal, curious, eccentric, exceptional, extraordinary, freakish, idiosyncratic, oddball, offbeat, quaint, queer, singular, strange, uncommon, unusual, weird, wonderful; ▪ *Ant* everyday, normal, ordinary, regular, standard, usual.

pedantic [*adj*] *ostentatiously learned*
▪ *Syn* abstruse, academic, arid, didactic, doctrinaire, donnish, dry, egotistic, erudite, fussy, learned, pedagogic, pompous, punctilious, scholastic, sententious, stilted; ▪ *Ant* pithy, straightforward, succinct, vague.

peddle [*v*] *sell door to door*
▪ *Syn* market, push, sell, shove, solicit, trade, vend; ▪ *Ant* acquire, buy, purchase.

pedestrian [*n*] *person traveling on foot*
▪ *Syn* ambler, hiker, passerby, stroller, walker; ▪ *Ant* driver, vehicle.

pedestrian [*adj*] *everyday, dull*
▪ *Syn* banal, boring, commonplace, dim, flat, inane, jejune, mediocre, monotone, mundane, ordinary, platitudinous, plodding, prosaic, stodgy, truistic, unimaginative, uninteresting; ▪ *Ant* different, exceptional, extraordinary, imaginative, interesting.

pedigree [*adj*] *purebred*
▪ *Syn* full-blooded, pedigreed, pureblood, thoroughbred; ▪ *Ant* base-born, lowly.

peek/peep [*v*] *sneak a look*
▪ *Syn* blink, glance, glimpse, have a gander, look, peer, snatch, snoop, spy, squint, stare, take a look; ▪ *Ant* contemplate, examine, inspect, observe, scrutinize, stall.

peel [*v*] *take off outer covering*
▪ *Syn* decorticate, delaminate, desquamate, excorticate, exfoliate, flake, flay, pare, pull off, scale, shave, skin, strip, tear off; ▪ *Ant* cover, wrap.

peerless [*adj*] *having no equal; superior*
▪ *Syn* all-time, alone, best, beyond compare, champion, excellent, faultless, greatest, incomparable, matchless, most, only, outstanding, superlative, supreme, unequaled, unique, unmatched, unparalleled, unrivaled, unsurpassed; ▪ *Ant* imperfect, inferior, lowly, mediocre, secondary, subordinate.

peeve [*v*] *bother, annoy*
▪ *Syn* aggravate, disturb, exasperate, gall, irk, irritate, nettle, pique, provoke, put out, rile, vex; ▪ *Ant* attract, charm, enchant, please.

peevish [*adj*] *irritable, testy*
▪ *Syn* acrimonious, bad-tempered, cantankerous, captious, carping, churlish, complaining, cranky, cross, fretful, grouchy, grumpy, huffy, ill-natured, morose, obstinate, ornery, petulant, querulous, short-tempered, snappy, splenetic, sullen, surly, touchy, whining; ▪ *Ant*

accepting, agreeable, friendly, good-natured, happy, pleasant.

peg [v] *attach*
▪ *Syn* clinch, fasten, fix, join, make fast, pin, secure, tighten; ▪ *Ant* detach, unfasten.

pejorative [adj] *negative, belittling*
▪ *Syn* debasing, deprecatory, derisive, derogatory, detractory, disparaging, irreverent, rude, slighting, uncomplimentary, unpleasant; ▪ *Ant* complimentary, positive, praising.

pell-mell [adj] *disordered*
▪ *Syn* chaotic, confused, disarrayed, disorganized, haphazard, muddled, tumultous/tumultuous; ▪ *Ant* ordered, organized.

pell-mell [adv] *hurriedly and carelessly*
▪ *Syn* foolishly, hastily, headlong, heedlessly, helter-skelter, impetuously, incontinently, indiscreetly, posthaste, precipitiously, rashly, recklessly, thoughtlessly; ▪ *Ant* carefully, cautiously.

pen [v1] *enclose*
▪ *Syn* box, cage, case, close in, confine, coop, corral, fence in, hedge, hem in, shut in; ▪ *Ant* free, let go, release.

pen [v2] *write*
▪ *Syn* autograph, commit to paper, compose, draft, draw up, engross, indict, jot down; ▪ *Ant* speak.

penalize [v] *punish*
▪ *Syn* amerce, castigate, chasten, chastise, condemn, correct, discipline, fine, handicap, impose penalty, judge, mulct, scold; ▪ *Ant* excuse, forgive, pardon, reward.

penchant [n] *fondness, inclination*
▪ *Syn* affection, affinity, attachment, bias, disposition, leaning, liking, partiality, predisposition, proclivity, proneness, propensity, tendency, weakness, yen; ▪ *Ant* dislike, hate, hatred, indifference.

pending [adj] *about to happen*
▪ *Syn* awaiting, continuing, dependent, forthcoming, hanging, imminent, impending, indeterminate, ominous, undecided, undetermined, unsettled; ▪ *Ant* improbable, unlikely.

penetrate [v1] *pierce; get through physically* ▪ *Syn* bore, break in, crack, drill, eat through, encroach, filter in, get in, gore, impale, infiltrate, ingress, invade, jab, knife, make a hole, make an entrance, pass through, perforate, permeate, prick, puncture, ream, saturate, seep,

spear, stab, suffuse, thrust, trespass; ▪ *Ant* bounce off, caroom, richochet.

penetrate [v2] *understand or be understood* ▪ *Syn* become clear, comprehend, decipher, discern, fathom, grasp, impress, perceive, touch, unravel, work out; ▪ *Ant* misconstrue, misinterpret, misunderstand.

penetrating [adj1] *stinging, harsh*
▪ *Syn* acrid, biting, caustic, crisp, cutting, edged, intrusive, penetrant, permeating, pervasive, piercing, pungent, redolent, sharp, strong, trenchant; ▪ *Ant* mild, sweet.

penetrating [adj2] *very intelligent*
▪ *Syn* acute, astute, critical, discerning, discriminating, incisive, keen, perceptive, perspicacious, profound, quick, quick-witted, sagacious, searching, sharp, sharp-witted, shrewd; ▪ *Ant* idiotic, senseless, stupid, unintelligent.

penitent [adj] *shamed, sorrowful*
▪ *Syn* abject, apologetic, atoning, compunctious, conscience-stricken, contrite, penitential, regretful, remorseful, repentant, rueful, sorry; ▪ *Ant* obdurate, remorseless, unashamed, unrepentent.

penniless [adj] *without any money*
▪ *Syn* bankrupt, destitute, impecunious, impoverished, indigent, lacking, moneyless, needy, penurious, poor, poverty-stricken, ruined; ▪ *Ant* affluent, rich, wealthy.

pensive [adj] *meditative, solemn*
▪ *Syn* absorbed, contemplative, dreamy, grave, melancholy, mournful, pondering, preoccupied, reflecting, reflective, ruminating, sad, serious, sober, sorrowful, speculative, thoughtful, wistful, withdrawn; ▪ *Ant* carefree, shallow.

pent-up [adj] *held within*
▪ *Syn* bottled-up, bridled, checked, constrained, curbed, held-back, held in check, inhibited, repressed, restrained, restricted, smothered, stifled, suppressed; ▪ *Ant* public, released.

pep [n] *vim, vigor*
▪ *Syn* animation, birr, energy, go, gusto, high spirits, life, liveliness, potency, spirit, verve, vitality, vivacity; ▪ *Ant* apathy, inactivity, lethargy, lifelessness, listlessness.

peppery [adj1] *highly seasoned*
▪ *Syn* fiery, hot, piquant, poignant, pungent, racy, snappy, spicy, zestful, zesty; ▪ *Ant* bland, dull, insipid, mild, tasteless.

peppery [adj2] *irritable; sarcastic*
▪ **Syn** acute, astringent, biting, caustic, choleric, cranky, fiery, hot-tempered, irascible, passionate, quick-tempered, sharp, stinging, testy, touchy, trenchant, waspish; ▪ **Ant** cheerful, happy.

pep up [v] *invigorate, inspire*
▪ **Syn** animate, enliven, exhilarate, quicken, stimulate, vitalize, vivify; ▪ **Ant** discourage, tire, wear.

perceive [v1] *notice, see*
▪ **Syn** apperceive, behold, descry, discern, distinguish, divine, espy, grasp, identify, look, make out, note, observe, realize, recognize, regard, remark, spot, spy; ▪ **Ant** miss, neglect, overlook.

perceive [v2] *understand*
▪ **Syn** appreciate, apprehend, comprehend, conclude, copy, deduce, distinguish, feel, gather, grasp, know, learn, read, recognize, see, sense, track; ▪ **Ant** misinterpret, misunderstand.

percentage [n] *portion, allotment*
▪ **Syn** allowance, bite, bonus, chunk, commission, cut, piece, proportion, quota, rate, ratio, section; ▪ **Ant** whole.

perceptible [adj] *noticeable, obvious*
▪ **Syn** apparent, appreciable, audible, clear, cognizable, detectable, discernible, distinct, evident, lucid, observable, palpable, perceivable, recognizable, sensible, tangible, understandable, visible; ▪ **Ant** ambiguous, imperceptible, invisible, obscure, silent, unnoticeable, vague.

perceptive [adj] *alert, sensitive*
▪ **Syn** acute, astute, aware, discerning, gnostic, incisive, intuitive, judicious, keen, knowing, observant, penetrating, percipient, perspicacious, quick, rational, responsive, sagacious, savvy, sharp, sophic, wise; ▪ **Ant** dense, insensitive, unaware, unobservant.

peremptory [adj] *overbearing, authoritative* ▪ **Syn** arbitrary, assertive, autocratic, bossy, categorical, commanding, dictatorial, dogmatic, domineering, firm, high-handed, imperative, intolerant, magisterial, obstinate, positive, rigorous, severe, stringent, tyrannical; ▪ **Ant** easygoing, laid-back, lax, moderate, passive, submissive.

perennial [adj] *enduring, perpetual*
▪ **Syn** abiding, annual, ceaseless, chronic, constant, deathless, durable, eternal, everlasting, immortal, incessant, lasting, lifelong, never-ending, old, perdurable, persistent, recurrent, seasonal, sustained, unceasing, unchanging, undying, yearly; ▪ **Ant** changing, ephemeral, intermittent, interrupted, temporary.

perfect [adj1] *flawless, superlative, whole* ▪ **Syn** absolute, beyond compare, consummate, crowning, culminating, defectless, excellent, faultless, flawless, foolproof, ideal, immaculate, impeccable, masterful, matchless, paradisiacal, peerless, pure, sheer, splendid, sublime, supreme, unblemished, unmarred, unmitigated, utopian, utter; ▪ **Ant** flawed, imperfect, incomplete, inferior, second-rate, unbroken.

perfect [adj2] *accurate, correct*
▪ **Syn** appropriate, certain, close, definite, distinct, exact, express, faithful, fit, ideal, model, precise, proper, right, sharp, strict, suitable, textbook, true, unerring, very; ▪ **Ant** imperfect, imprecise, inaccurate, wrong.

perfect [v] *polish; achieve*
▪ **Syn** accomplish, ameliorate, carry out, complete, consummate, crown, cultivate, develop, effect, elaborate, finish, fulfill, hone, idealize, improve, perform, put finishing touch on, realize, refine, smooth; ▪ **Ant** destroy, ruin.

perfectly [adv1] *absolutely*
▪ **Syn** altogether, completely, consummately, entirely, fully, positively, quite, thoroughly, totally, utterly, well, wholly; ▪ **Ant** imperfectly, incompletely, mistakenly, partially.

perfectly [adv2] *without flaw*
▪ **Syn** correctly, exquisitely, faultlessly, flawlessly, ideally, impeccably, superbly, superlatively, supremely, wonderfully; ▪ **Ant** faultily, poorly.

perforate [v] *make a hole in*
▪ **Syn** bore, drill, drive, hole, penetrate, permeate, pierce, pit, probe, punch, puncture, slit, stab; ▪ **Ant** close up.

perform [v] *carry out, accomplish*
▪ **Syn** achieve, act, be engaged in, behave, bring about, bring off, carry through, carry to completion, complete, comply, discharge, dispose of, do, effect, execute, finish, fulfill, implement, meet, move, operate, pull off, put through, realize, satisfy, transact, wind up, work; ▪ **Ant** fail, flounder, neglect.

perfume [n] *scent, often manufactured and packaged for personal use* ▪ **Syn** aroma, attar, balm, bouquet, cologne, eau de cologne, essence, fragrance, incense, oil, redolence, sachet, spice, sweetness; ▪ *Ant* odor, stench, stink.

perfunctory [*adj*] *automatic, unthinking*
▪ *Syn* apathetic, careless, cursory, disinterested, heedless, impersonal, inattentive, indifferent, lackadaisical, mechanical, negligent, offhand, routine, standard, stock, superficial, unconcerned, uninterested; ▪ *Ant* ardent, careful, diligent, precise, thoughtful, warmhearted.

perhaps [*adv*] *possibly*
▪ *Syn* as it may be, as the case may be, conceivably, feasibly, for all one knows, imaginably, maybe, perchance, reasonably; ▪ *Ant* certainly, definitely, improbably, never, unlikely.

perilous [*adj*] *very dangerous*
▪ *Syn* chancy, delicate, exposed, hazardous, insecure, precarious, risky, shaky, threatening, touchy, treacherous, uncertain, unsafe, unsound, unstable, unsteady, unsure, vulnerable; ▪ *Ant* safe, secure.

perimeter [*n*] *circumference, border*
▪ *Syn* ambit, borderline, boundary, bounds, brim, brink, circuit, compass, confines, edge, fringe, hem, limit, margin, outline, periphery, skirt, verge; ▪ *Ant* center, heart, hub, inside, interior, middle.

periodic [*adj*] *occuring from time to time*
▪ *Syn* alternate, annual, at various times, centennial, cyclical, epochal, every once in a while, every so often, fluctuating, hourly, infrequent, intermittent, isochronal, occasional, orbital, perennial, periodical, recurring, regular, rhythmic, seasonal, serial, sporadic; ▪ *Ant* constant, continual, lasting, permanent.

peripatetic [*adj*] *constantly traveling*
▪ *Syn* ambulant, itinerant, migrant, nomadic, perambulant, roaming, roving, vagabond, vagrant, wandering, wayfaring; ▪ *Ant* fixed, resident, settled, stationary.

peripheral [*adj*] *minor, outside*
▪ *Syn* beside the point, borderline, exterior, external, incidental, inessential, minor, outer, perimetric, secondary, superficial, surface, tangential, unimportant; ▪ *Ant* central, crucial, internal, major.

perish [*v*] *die, decline, decay*
▪ *Syn* be killed, break down, cease, collapse, crumble, decease, decompose, disappear, disintegrate, end, expire, fall, go under, lose life, pass away, pass on, rot, succumb, vanish, wither; ▪ *Ant* be born, flourish, prosper, revive, thrive.

perishable [*adj*] *liable to spoil, rot*
▪ *Syn* decaying, decomposable, destructible, easily spoiled, short-lived, unstable; ▪ *Ant* durable, long-lasting, stable.

perjure [*v*] *give false testimony*
▪ *Syn* deceive, delude, equivocate, falsify, forswear, lie under oath, mislead, prevaricate, swear falsely, trick; ▪ *Ant* attest, certify, prove.

perk up [*v*] *cheer*
▪ *Syn* ameliorate, brighten, cheer up, invigorate, liven up, look up, mend, pep up, rally, recover, recuperate, refresh, renew, revive; ▪ *Ant* depress, fatigue, tire, weaken.

perky [*adj*] *animated, happy*
▪ *Syn* active, alert, aware, bouncy, bright, brisk, bubbly, buoyant, cheerful, cheery, gay, jaunty, lively, spirited, sprightly, sunny, vivacious; ▪ *Ant* depressed, gloomy.

permanent [*adj*] *constant, lasting*
▪ *Syn* abiding, changeless, continual, diurnal, enduring, everlasting, fixed, forever, immutable, imperishable, indestructible, long-lasting, perduring, perpetual, persistent, set, stable, steadfast, unchanging; ▪ *Ant* ephemeral, finite, fleeting, short-lived, temporary, transitory.

permeable [*adj*] *absorbent, penetrable*
▪ *Syn* absorptive, accessible, passable, pervious, porous, spongelike, spongy; ▪ *Ant* impassable, inaccessible, inpenetrable.

permissible [*adj*] *allowable, legal*
▪ *Syn* acceptable, admissible, all right, approved, authorized, bearable, endorsed, lawful, legalized, legitimate, licit, permitted, proper, sanctioned, tolerable, tolerated, unforbidden, unprohibited; ▪ *Ant* banned, forbidden, illegal, prohibited.

permissive [*adj*] *very lenient*
▪ *Syn* acquiescent, agreeable, allowing, approving, easy-going, forbearing, free, indulgent, lax, liberal, open-minded, permitting, susceptible, tolerant; ▪ *Ant* intolerant, rigid, strict, withholding.

permit [*v*] *allow participation*
▪ *Syn* accede, accept, acquiesce, admit, authorize, bless, boost, charter, concede,

consent, empower, endorse, franchise, give leave, give permission, grant, have, indulge, leave, let pass, license, okay, pass, sanction, sign, suffer, tolerate, warrant; ▪ *Ant* deny, disallow, refuse, reject.

pernicious [*adj*] *bad, hurtful*
▪ *Syn* baleful, deleterious, destructive, devastating, evil, fatal, harmful, iniquitous, injurious, lethal, maleficent, malevolent, malignant, miasmatic, mortal, nefarious, noxious, offensive, pestiferous, poisonous, ruinous, sinister, toxic, venomous, virulent, wicked; ▪ *Ant* harmless, healthy, helpful, innocuous, kind, loveable, loving.

perpetrate [*v*] *be responsible for*
▪ *Syn* act, bring about, carry out, commit, do, effect, enact, execute, inflict, perform, pull, wreak; ▪ *Ant* abstain, omit.

perpetual [*adj*] *continual, lasting*
▪ *Syn* abiding, ceaseless, constant, continuous, endless, eternal, everlasting, immortal, incessant, never-ending, perdurable, perennial, permanent, persistent, recurrent, repeated, sempiternal, unceasing, unchanging, undying, unremitting; ▪ *Ant* brief, ephemeral, fleeting, momentary, temporary, transient.

perpetuate [*v*] *keep going*
▪ *Syn* bolster, conserve, continue, eternalize, immortalize, keep, keep alive, keep in existence, keep up, maintain, preserve, secure, support, sustain; ▪ *Ant* annihilate, cease, destroy, eschew, halt, prevent, stop.

perplex [*v*] *confuse, mix up*
▪ *Syn* astonish, astound, baffle, balk, befuddle, beset, bewilder, complicate, confound, discompose, dumbfound, encumber, fog, jumble, muck, muddle, mystify, nonplus, perturb, pose, puzzle, rattle, ravel, stump, surprise, tangle, thwart; ▪ *Ant* clarify, clear up, enlighten, explain.

persecute [*v*] *wrong, torment*
▪ *Syn* afflict, aggrieve, annoy, badger, crucify, exile, expel, harass, hector, illtreat, injure, maltreat, martyr, oppress, outrage, pester, plague, pursue, tease, torture, tyrannize, vex, victimize; ▪ *Ant* comfort, commend, console, reward, soothe.

persevere [*v*] *keep at; work hard*
▪ *Syn* be determined, be resolved, be stubborn, carry on, continue, endure, go

on, hold on, keep going, keep on, maintain, persist, press on, proceed, pursue, remain; ▪ *Ant* be lazy, give up, idle, leave, quit, stop.

persist [*v*] *carry on, carry through*
▪ *Syn* abide, be resolute, be stubborn, continue, endure, go on, hold on, insist, last, linger, obtain, perdure, persevere, prevail, pursue, recur, remain, repeat, strive; ▪ *Ant* cease, quit, stop, surrender, vacillate, waver.

persistent [*adj*] *determined; continuous* ▪ *Syn* assiduous, bound, constant, dogged, enduring, fixed, immovable, incessant, indefatigable, insistent, never-ending, obdurate, obstinate, perpetual, pertinacious, relentless, resolute, steadfast, stubborn, tenacious, tireless, unflagging, unrelenting, unremitting, unshakable; ▪ *Ant* lazy, relenting, surrendering, yielding.

persnickety [*adj*] *fussy, particular*
▪ *Syn* careful, choosy, fastidious, finicky, meticulous, picayune, picky; ▪ *Ant* haphazard, sloppy, unconcerned.

person [*n*] *human being*
▪ *Syn* being, body, character, creature, human, individual, life, mortal, personage, personality, self, somebody, soul, specimen, spirit; ▪ *Ant* non-sentient being.

personable [*adj*] *friendly, sociable*
▪ *Syn* affable, agreeable, amiable, attractive, charming, easygoing, gregarious, likable, nice, pleasant, pleasing, presentable, winning; ▪ *Ant* disagreeable, rude, sullen, unfriendly, unsociable.

personal [*adj*] *private, individual*
▪ *Syn* confidential, exclusive, intimate, particular, private, privy, secret, special; ▪ *Ant* general, public.

perspicacious [*adj*] *observant, perceptive* ▪ *Syn* acute, alert, astute, aware, clear-sighted, clever, discerning, judicious, keen, penetrating, percipient, sagacious, savvy, sharp, shrewd; ▪ *Ant* dense, dull, ignorant, unobservant, viscous.

perspicuous [*adj*] *clear, obvious*
▪ *Syn* apparent, clear-cut, comprehensible, distinct, easily understood, explicit, intelligible, limpid, lucent, lucid, luminous, pellucid, plain, self-evident, straightforward, transparent, unambiguous, unblurred, understandable; ▪ *Ant* obscure, unclear, vague.

persuade [v] *cause to believe; convince to do* ▪ **Syn** actuate, advise, affect, assure, blandish, bring around, cajole, coax, counsel, draw, enlist, entice, get, impel, incite, influence, inveigle, lead, lead to believe, move, prevail upon, prompt, proselytize, reason, seduce, sell, stroke, sway, talk into, turn on to, urge, wheedle, win over, woo; ▪ **Ant** discourage, dissuade, hinder, prohibit, repel, repress, stop, suppress.

persuasive [adj] *effective, influential* ▪ **Syn** actuating, alluring, cogent, compelling, convincing, credible, effectual, eloquent, enticing, forceful, impelling, inspiring, inveigling, logical, luring, moving, plausible, powerful, seductive, strong, swaying, telling, touching, unctuous, valid, weighty, wheedling, winning; ▪ **Ant** dampening, discouraging, disheartening, dissuasive, ineffective, ineffectual.

pert [adj] *lively, bold* ▪ **Syn** animated, audacious, brash, brisk, dapper, dashing, forward, fresh, gay, impertinent, impudent, insolent, jaunty, keen, perky, sassy, saucy, sprightly, vivacious; ▪ **Ant** dull, humble, lifeless.

pertinent [adj] *relevant, suitable* ▪ **Syn** admissible, ad rem, applicable, apposite, appropriate, apropos, apt, congruent, connected, fitting, germane, material, opportune, pertaining, proper, related, to the point; ▪ **Ant** foreign, inappropriate, irrelevant, unsuitable.

perturb [v] *upset, unsettle* ▪ **Syn** agitate, alarm, annoy, bewilder, confound, discompose, disconcert, disquiet, disturb, flurry, fluster, irritate, muddle, needle, perplex, pester, ruffle, trouble, vex, worry; ▪ **Ant** calm, please, soothe.

peruse [v] *check out; examine* ▪ **Syn** analyze, browse, glance over, look through, pore over, read, scan, scrutinize, skim, study; ▪ **Ant** neglect, overlook.

pervasive [adj] *extensive* ▪ **Syn** common, general, inescapable, omnipresent, permeating, pervading, rife, ubiquitous, universal, widespread; ▪ **Ant** limited, localized, narrow, occasional, spotty, uncommon.

perverse [adj] *mean, ornery; troublesome* ▪ **Syn** abnormal, bad-tempered, cantankerous, capricious, contradictory, contumacious, corrupt, cross, degenerate, delinquent, depraved, disobedient, erring, fractious, headstrong, intractable, intransigent, miscreant, nefarious, obdurate, petulant, rebellious, refractory, self-willed, spiteful, unyielding, villainous, wayward, wicked, willful; ▪ **Ant** agreeable, compliant, happy, natural, nice, nominal, reasonable, willing.

pervert [v] *twist, turn away from what is acceptable or correct* ▪ **Syn** abuse, adulterate, alloy, corrupt, debase, debauch, deprave, distort, divert, fake, falsify, garble, misrepresent, misstate, outrage, prostitute, ruin, seduce, spike, vitiate, warp; ▪ **Ant** leave alone, straighten.

perverted [adj] *immoral, evil* ▪ **Syn** aberrant, abused, contorted, corrupt, debased, debauched, depraved, deviant, distorted, grotesque, impaired, kinky, misguided, monstrous, outraged, polluted, queer, sick, tainted, twisted, vicious, vitiated, warped, wicked; ▪ **Ant** clean, good, healthy, moral.

pesky [adj] *bothersome* ▪ **Syn** annoying, disturbing, irksome, mean, nettlesome, peeving, provoking, troublesome, vexatious, vexing, wicked; ▪ **Ant** pleasing, untroubling.

pessimistic [adj] *expecting bad outcome* ▪ **Syn** bleak, cynical, dark, dejected, depressed, despairing, despondent, discouraged, distrustful, downhearted, fatalistic, foreboding, gloomy, hopeless, melancholy, misanthropic, morbid, morose, sullen, troubled, worried; ▪ **Ant** confident, optimistic, trusting.

pester [v] *bother, harass* ▪ **Syn** annoy, badger, bedevil, beleaguer, disturb, drive crazy, fret, harry, hassle, hector, hound, importune, irk, nag, nudge, plague, provoke, tantalize, tease, torment, worry; ▪ **Ant** delight, make happy, please.

pestilent/pestilential [adj] *dangerous, harmful* ▪ **Syn** baneful, contaminating, corrupting, deleterious, destructive, detrimental, evil, fatal, infectious, injurious, lethal, mortal, noxious, pernicious, pestiferous, ruinous, tainting, vicious; ▪ **Ant** clean, healthy, hygienic, safe, sanitary.

pet [adj] *favorite* ▪ **Syn** cherished, darling, dear, dearest, favored, loved, precious, preferred, special; ▪ **Ant** disfavored, hated.

peter out [v] *dwindle, decrease* ▪ **Syn** abate, diminish, drain, ebb, fade, give out, lessen, miscarry, rebate, recede, run dry, run out, stop, taper off, wane; ▪ *Ant* develop, grow, increase.

petite [*adj*] *very small*
▪ *Syn* baby, bantam, dainty, delicate, diminutive, elfin, little, miniature, slight, smallish, tiny; ▪ *Ant* extra-large, huge, tall.

petrify [*v1*] *make hard*
▪ *Syn* calcify, clarify, fossilize, harden, lapidify, mineralize, set, solidify, turn to stone; ▪ *Ant* melt, soften.

petrify [*v2*] *frighten*
▪ *Syn* alarm, astound, benumb, chill, confound, daze, dumbfound, horrify, immobilize, numb, paralyze, scare, startle, stun, stupefy, terrify, transfix; ▪ *Ant* calm, comfort, please, soothe.

petty [*adj*] *trivial, insignificant*
▪ *Syn* casual, frivolous, inconsequent, inconsiderable, irrelevant, junior, lesser, measly, minor, narrow-minded, negligible, paltry, secondary, shabby, shallow, slight, small-minded, subordinate, trifling, unimportant; ▪ *Ant* consequential, generous, important, major, necessary, prominent, significant, tolerant, useful.

petulant [*adj*] *crabby, moody*
▪ *Syn* bad-tempered, caviling, complaining, displeased, fault-finding, fractious, grouchy, grumbling, huffy, ill-humored, impatient, irritable, mean, peevish, pouting, querulous, snappish, sour, sulky, sullen, testy, touchy, ungracious, whiny; ▪ *Ant* complaisant, good-natured, gracious, happy, pleasant.

phenomenal [*adj*] *astounding, exceptional* ▪ *Syn* extraordinary, fantastic, marvelous, outstanding, prodigious, rare, remarkable, sensational, singular, uncommon, unique, unparalleled, unusual, wondrous; ▪ *Ant* normal, regular, unexceptional.

philanthropic [*adj*] *charitable, giving*
▪ *Syn* altruistic, beneficent, benevolent, big-hearted, bountiful, eleemosynary, generous, helpful, humane, humanitarian, kind, kindhearted, liberal, magnanimous, munificent, patriotic, public-spirited; ▪ *Ant* misanthropic, miserly, stingy, uncharitable.

philosophical/philosophic [*adj1*]
thinking deeply, rationally ▪ *Syn* abstract, cogitative, deep, erudite, judicious, logical, pensive, profound,

rational, reflective, sagacious, sapient, theoretical, thoughtful, wise; ▪ *Ant* irrational, narrow-minded, thoughtless, unreasonable.

philosophical/philosophic [*adj2*]
calm, serene ▪ *Syn* collected, commonsensical, composed, imperturbable, patient, resigned, stoical, tranquil, unagitated, unflappable, unmoved, unruffled; ▪ *Ant* emotional, excited, imprudent, rash.

phobia [*n*] *fear*
▪ *Syn* anxiety, aversion, awe, detestation, disgust, dread, fear, hatred, horror, irrationality, loathing, neurosis, obsession, repulsion, resentment, revulsion, terror; ▪ *Ant* fancy, liking, love, penchant.

phony [*adj*] *fake, false*
▪ *Syn* affected, artificial, assumed, bastard, bogus, counterfeit, forged, imitation, spurious, trick; ▪ *Ant* genuine, real, sincere, true.

physical [*adj1*] *tangible, material*
▪ *Syn* concrete, corporeal, natural, objective, palpable, phenomenal, real, solid, substantial, visible; ▪ *Ant* immaterial, intangible, spiritual.

physical [*adj2*] *concerning the body*
▪ *Syn* bodily, carnal, corporal, corporeal, earthly, mortal, somatic, visceral; ▪ *Ant* mental, psychological.

physician [*n*] *person trained in medical science* ▪ *Syn* doctor, general practitioner, healer, intern, medic, medical practitioner, medico, specialist, surgeon; ▪ *Ant* patient.

pick [*v1*] *choose, select*
▪ *Syn* cull, decide upon, elect, fix upon, hand-pick, mark, name, opt for, prefer, sort, tab, tag, take, tap, winnow; ▪ *Ant* refuse, reject.

pick [*v2*] *gather, harvest*
▪ *Syn* accumulate, choose, collect, cull, cut, draw, pluck, pull; ▪ *Ant* grow, plant.

pick at/pick on [*v*] *nag, provoke*
▪ *Syn* badger, bait, blame, bully, carp, cavil, criticize, find fault, foment, goad, hector, incite, instigate, quibble, start, tease, torment; ▪ *Ant* compliment, praise.

pick up [*v1*] *lift, raise*
▪ *Syn* elevate, gather, hoist, take up, uphold, uplift, upraise, uprear; ▪ *Ant* drop, lower.

pick up [*v2*] *obtain, find*
▪ *Syn* acquire, buy, cull, extract, gain, garner, gather, get, glean, learn, master, procure, purchase, score, secure, take; ▪ *Ant* have, spend, throw away.

pick up [*v3*] *improve*
▪ *Syn* gain, get better, get well, increase, mend, rally, recommence, recover, renew, swell, take up; ▪ *Ant* drop, weaken, worsen.

pick up [*v4*] *arrest for crime*
▪ *Syn* apprehend, detain, nab, take into custody; ▪ *Ant* free, release.

picky [*adj*] *choosy, finicky*
▪ *Syn* captious, carping, critical, dainty, fastidious, fault-finding, particular, persnickety; ▪ *Ant* accepting.

picnic [*n*] *very easy undertaking*
▪ *Syn* cinch, light work, no trouble, snap, sure thing; ▪ *Ant* difficulty, drudgery.

plummet [*v*] *fall hard and fast*
▪ *Syn* collapse, crash, decline, decrease, descend, dip, dive, downturn, drop, drop down, dump, fall, nose-dive, plunge, precipitate, sink, skid, stoop, swoop, tumble; ▪ *Ant* ascend, rise, shoot up.

plump [*adj*] *chubby, fat*
▪ *Syn* burly, buxom, corpulent, filled, fleshy, full, obese, portly, rotund, round, stout; ▪ *Ant* lean, skinny, thin.

plunder [*v*] *ravage, steal*
▪ *Syn* burn, depredate, despoil, devastate, forage, foray, gut, lay waste, loot, maraud, pillage, prey, raid, ransack, rifle, rob, sack, salvage, strip; ▪ *Ant* give, receive.

plunge [*v*] *dive or fall fast*
▪ *Syn* dash, descend, dip, go down, hurtle, immerge, immerse, jump, keel, lunge, lurch, nose-dive, pitch, plummet, plunk, propel, rush, sink, sound, submerge, submerse, swoop, throw oneself, thrust, topple, tumble; ▪ *Ant* ascend, emerge, increase, rise.

plurality [*n*] *large part of a group*
▪ *Syn* bulk, greater part, majority, most, nearly all, preponderance; ▪ *Ant* minority.

plus [*adj*] *added, extra*
▪ *Syn* additional, augmented, expanded, increased, supplementary, surplus; ▪ *Ant* detrimental, minus, negative.

plush [*adj*] *luxurious, rich*
▪ *Syn* deluxe, elegant, lavish, lush, opulent, palatial, sumptuous; ▪ *Ant* austere, barren, destitute, poor, spartan.

ply [*v*] *use, work at*
▪ *Syn* dispense, employ, exercise, exert, follow, function, handle, maneuver, manipulate, practice, pursue, utilize, wield; ▪ *Ant* be lazy, idle.

poach [*v*] *infringe upon; trespass*
▪ *Syn* appropriate, encroach, filch, fish illegally, hunt illegally, intrude, pilfer, plunder, rob, smuggle, steal; ▪ *Ant* keep off.

pocket [*adj*] *small, portable*
▪ *Syn* abridged, capsule, compact, concise, condensed, diminutive, dwarfish, epitomized, miniature, tiny; ▪ *Ant* big, huge, large, stationary.

pocket [*v*] *help oneself to something*
▪ *Syn* abstract, appropriate, conceal, enclose, filch, hide, lift, nab, pilfer, purloin, shoplift, steal, swipe, take; ▪ *Ant* bequeath, bestow, give.

poetic [*adj*] *with rhythm and beauty; related to poetic composition* ▪ *Syn* anapestic, dactylic, dramatic, elegiac, epic, epodic, iambic, idyllic, imaginative, lyrical, melodious, metrical, odic, rhythmical, romantic, songlike, tuneful; ▪ *Ant* matter of fact, prosaic, realistic, unimaginative.

poignant [*adj1*] *affecting, painful*
▪ *Syn* agitating, agonizing, bitter, distressing, heartbreaking, intense, moving, pathetic, piteous, sad, sentimental, sorrowful, touching, upsetting; ▪ *Ant* calm, numb, pleasant, soothing, trite, unaffecting.

poignant [*adj2*] *sharp, bitter*
▪ *Syn* acrid, acute, biting, caustic, keen, penetrating, peppery, piercing, piquant, pointed, pungent, sarcastic, severe, sharp, spicy, stinging, tangy, zesty; ▪ *Ant* banal, blah, blunt, dull.

pointed [*adj1*] *having a sharp end or part* ▪ *Syn* acicular, aciculate, acuminate, acuminous, acute, barbed, cornered, cuspidate, edged, keen, mucronate, peaked, piked, pointy, pronged, sharp, sharp-cornered, spiked; ▪ *Ant* blunt, dull, rounded.

pointed [*adj2*] *penetrating, biting*
▪ *Syn* acid, acute, barbed, boiled down, cutting, incisive, insinuating, keen, pertinent, pregnant, sarcastic, sharp, tart, telling, trenchant; ▪ *Ant* calming, inappropriate, mild, soothing.

pointless [*adj*] *ridiculous, senseless*
▪ *Syn* absurd, aimless, fruitless, futile,

impotent, inane, inconsequential, ineffective, ineffectual, insignificant, irrelevant, meaningless, nongermane, nonsensical, not pertinent, powerless, silly, stupid, trivial, unavailing, unnecessary, unproductive, unprofitable, vague, worthless; ▪ *Ant* appropriate, beneficial, fitting, meaningful, profitable, sensible.

point out [v] *call attention to*
▪ *Syn* advert, allude, bring up, denote, designate, indicate, mention, refer, remind, reveal, show, specify; ▪ *Ant* distract, ignore, overlook, pass over.

poise [v] *balance, suspend*
▪ *Syn* float, hang, hold, hover, position, stabilize, steady, support, wait; ▪ *Ant* drop, fall.

poison/poisonous [adj] *very harmful*
▪ *Syn* bad, baleful, baneful, corrupt, corruptive, dangerous, deadly, deleterious, destructive, detrimental, evil, fatal, hurtful, infective, lethal, malicious, malignant, mephitic, miasmatic, morbid, mortal, nocuous, noisome, noxious, peccant, pernicious, pestiferous, pestilential, septic, toxic, toxicant, toxiferous, venomous, vicious, viperous, virulent; ▪ *Ant* aiding, antidotal, curative, curing, healing, helpful.

poison [v] *contaminate, pollute*
▪ *Syn* adulterate, corrupt, debase, defile, deprave, destroy, envenom, fester, infect, injure, kill, make ill, murder, pervert, stain, subvert, taint, undermine, vitiate, warp; ▪ *Ant* purify, sterilize.

poke [v1] *interfere, snoop*
▪ *Syn* intrude, meddle, peek, pry, tamper; ▪ *Ant* ignore, leave alone.

poke [v2] *move along slowly*
▪ *Syn* dally, dawdle, delay, drag, idle, lag, loiter, tarry, trail; ▪ *Ant* hasten, hurry, rush, speed.

polar [adj1] *very cold*
▪ *Syn* arctic, freezing, frigid, frozen, glacial, icy, north; ▪ *Ant* torrid, tropic, tropical.

polar [adj2] *opposite, opposed*
▪ *Syn* antagonistic, antipodal, antipodean, antithetical, contradictory, contrary, converse, counter, diametric, reverse; ▪ *Ant* alike, same, similar.

polish [n] *cultivated look, performance*
▪ *Syn* breeding, class, cultivation, culture, elegance, finesse, finish, grace, politesse, refinement, style, suavity, urbanity; ▪ *Ant* awkwardness, boorishness, clumsiness, gaucheness, indecorum, rudeness, uncouthness.

polish [v1] *shine, buff*
▪ *Syn* brighten, burnish, clean, finish, furbish, glaze, gloss, rub, scour, scrub, sleek, slick, smooth, wax; ▪ *Ant* corrode, dull, erode, roughen.

polish [v2] *improve performance, look*
▪ *Syn* amend, better, brush up, cultivate, enhance, finish, furbish, mature, perfect, refine, round, sleek, slick, smooth, touch up; ▪ *Ant* deface, muddle, ruin, spoil.

polish off [v] *finish using*
▪ *Syn* consume, devour, dispatch, dispose of, eat, eat up, eliminate, liquidate, use up; ▪ *Ant* amass, collect, hoard, save.

polite [adj] *mannerly, civilized*
▪ *Syn* affable, amiable, civil, conciliatory, considerate, cordial, courteous, courtly, deferential, elegant, friendly, genteel, gracious, nice, obliging, pleasant, polished, refined, respectful, smooth, sociable, sympathetic, thoughtful, urbane, well-behaved, well-bred, well-mannered; ▪ *Ant* impolite, rude, tactless, uncivil, uncivilized, unmannerly, unrefined, unsophisticated.

politic [adj] *wise, tactful*
▪ *Syn* adroit, cool, delicate, diplomatic, discreet, expedient, judicious, perspicacious, prudent, sagacious, sensible, sharp, shrewd, smooth, tactical, urbane; ▪ *Ant* impolitic, indiscreet, injudicious, rash, tactless.

politically correct [adj] *sensitive to all forms of oppression* ▪ *Syn* bias-free, dogmatic, gay/lesbian affirmative, gender-free, inclusive, leftist, liberal, multicultural, nondiscriminatory, nonsexist, nonracist, pro-choice, reform, respectful, revisionary; ▪ *Ant* exclusive, insensitive, politically incorrect, reactionary.

pollute [v] *make dirty; corrupt*
▪ *Syn* adulterate, alloy, befoul, besmirch, contaminate, corrupt, debase, debauch, defile, deprave, desecrate, dirty, dishonor, foul, infect, make filthy, mar, poison, profane, soil, spoil, stain, sully, taint, violate; ▪ *Ant* clean, cleanse, purge, purify.

pompous [adj] *arrogant, egotistic*
▪ *Syn* affected, bloated, boastful, bombastic, conceited, flatulent, flaunting, flowery, fustian, grandiloquent, grandi-

ose, imperious, inflated, magisterial, magniloquent, narcissistic, orotund, ostentatious, overbearing, overblown, pontifical, portentous, presumptuous, pretentious, rhetorical, self-centered, self-important, selfish, showy, sonorous, supercilious, turgid, vain, vainglorious; ▪ *Ant* dull, modest, plain, simple, unassuming.

ponder [*v*] *think about seriously*
▪ *Syn* appraise, brood, cerebrate, cogitate, consider, contemplate, daydream, debate, deliberate, dwell, evaluate, examine, figure, meditate, mind, mull, mull over, muse, perpend, puzzle over, reason, reflect, revolve, ruminate, speculate, study, think out, think over, turn over, weigh; ▪ *Ant* disregard, forget, ignore, neglect, overlook.

ponderous [*adj1*] *heavy, cumbersome*
▪ *Syn* awkward, burdensome, clumsy, cumbrous, elephantine, graceless, huge, laborious, lumbering, massive, onerous, substantial, unhandy, unwieldy, weighty; ▪ *Ant* airy, buoyant, delicate, graceful, light, unburdensome, weightless.

ponderous [*adj2*] *dreary, tedious*
▪ *Syn* arid, barren, dry, dull, heavy, labored, lifeless, monotonous, pedantic, pedestrian, plodding, prolix, stilted, stodgy, vapid, verbose; ▪ *Ant* absorbing, fun, light, lively.

pool [*v*] *combine*
▪ *Syn* amalgamate, blend, join forces, league, merge, put together, share; ▪ *Ant* divide, section, separate, sever.

poor [*adj1*] *lacking sufficient money*
▪ *Syn* bankrupt, beggared, destitute, fortuneless, impoverished, insolvent, low, meager, necessitous, needy, pauperized, penniless, poverty-stricken, suffering, underprivileged, unprosperous; ▪ *Ant* affluent, moneyed, rich, wealthy.

poor [*adj2*] *deficient, inadequate*
▪ *Syn* base, below par, common, contemptible, dwarfed, exiguous, faulty, feeble, humble, imperfect, inferior, insignificant, insufficient, lacking, low-grade, meager, mediocre, miserable, paltry, pitiful, reduced, scanty, shabby, shoddy, skimpy, sparse, substandard, trivial, unsatisfactory, valueless, weak, worthless; ▪ *Ant* adequate, sufficient, superior, worthy.

poor [*adj3*] *weak, unfertile*
▪ *Syn* barren, depleted, exhausted, feeble,

impoverished, indisposed, infertile, infirm, puny, sick, sterile, unfruitful, unproductive, worthless; ▪ *Ant* fecund, fruitful, potent, strong.

poor [*adj4*] *unfortunate, unhappy*
▪ *Syn* commiserable, hapless, ill-fated, luckless, miserable, pathetic, piteous, pitiable, pitiful, rueful, unlucky, wretched; ▪ *Ant* fortunate, great, happy, lucky.

poorly [*adj*] *not well*
▪ *Syn* ailing, below par, failing, ill, indisposed, low, mean, sick, sickly, unwell; ▪ *Ant* hale, healthy, robust, well.

poorly [*adv*] *unsatisfactorily*
▪ *Syn* badly, crudely, defectively, inadequately, incompetently, inexpertly, inferiorly, insufficiently, meanly, shabbily, unsuccessfully; ▪ *Ant* adequately, satisfactorily, up to standard, well.

popular [*adj1*] *well-known, favorite*
▪ *Syn* accepted, attractive, beloved, celebrated, famous, in demand, in vogue, leading, likable, liked, lovable, notorious, pleasing, praised, preferred, prominent, sought-after, suitable, trendy, well-liked, well-received; ▪ *Ant* disliked, in disfavor, unknown, unpopular.

popular [*adj2*] *common, standard*
▪ *Syn* accepted, accessible, conventional, familiar, general, in demand, in use, ordinary, prevailing, prevalent, public, rampant, rife, ruling, stock, ubiquitous, universal, widespread; ▪ *Ant* different, uncommon, unconventional, unusual.

popularize [*v*] *make widely popular, accessible* ▪ *Syn* catch on, disseminate, familiarize, generalize, give currency, make available, promote, spread, universalize; ▪ *Ant* discredit, reject, shun.

populous [*adj*] *packed with inhabitants*
▪ *Syn* crawling, crowded, dense, heavily populated, jammed, legion, multifarious, multitudinous, swarming, teeming, thronged, voluminous; ▪ *Ant* deserted.

pore [*v*] *go over carefully*
▪ *Syn* brood, contemplate, dwell on, examine, look over, muse, peruse, ponder, read, regard, scrutinize, study; ▪ *Ant* flip through, overlook, scan.

pornographic [*adj*] *obscene*
▪ *Syn* adult, immoral, indecent, lewd, off-color, offensive, prurient, rough, salacious, sexy; ▪ *Ant* clean, innocent, moral, pure.

porous [*adj*] *having holes; absorbent*
• *Syn* absorptive, penetrable, permeable, pervious, spongelike, spongy; • *Ant* impermeable, solid.

portable [*adj*] *easily transported*
• *Syn* cartable, compact, convenient, conveyable, easily carried, handy, lightweight, manageable, portative, transportable, wieldy; • *Ant* awkward, clumsy, cumbersome.

portent [*n*] *miracle*
• *Syn* marvel, phenomenon, prodigy, sensation, stunner, wonder; • *Ant* doom.

portion [*v*] *divide into pieces*
• *Syn* allot, apportion, deal, dispense, distribute, parcel, part, partition, piece, prorate, quota, ration, section, share, shift; • *Ant* collect, combine, gather, join.

portly [*adj*] *bulky, fat*
• *Syn* ample, avoirdupois, burly, corpulent, fleshy, heavy, hefty, large, obese, overweight, plump, rotund, stout; • *Ant* skinny, slender, thin, trim.

pose [*v1*] *sit, stand in place*
• *Syn* arrange, model, position, posture, sit for, strike a pose, strut; • *Ant* go, move.

pose [*v2*] *pretend, fake*
• *Syn* act, affect, attitudinize, feign, impersonate, make believe, masquerade, playact, posture, profess, purport; • *Ant* be genuine, be natural.

pose [*v3*] *offer, put forward idea*
• *Syn* advance, ask, extend, give, hold out, posit, prefer, present, proffer, propose, proposition, propound, put, query, question, set, suggest, tender; • *Ant* hide, suppress, withhold.

posh [*adj*] *luxurious, upper-class*
• *Syn* chic, classy, deluxe, elegant, exclusive, fashionable, grand, high-class, luxury, opulent, rich, smart, swank, trendy; • *Ant* austere, destitute, lower-class, modest, poor.

position [*v*] *place physically in location*
• *Syn* arrange, array, dispose, fix, lay out, locate, put, set, settle, stand, stick; • *Ant* displace, disarrange, lose.

positive [*adj1*] *definite, certain*
• *Syn* absolute, affirmative, assured, categorical, clear, clear-cut, conclusive, concrete, confident, convinced, decisive, direct, downright, explicit, express, factual, firm, inarguable, incontrovertible, indisputable, outright, specific, sure,

thorough; • *Ant* disputable, doubtful, indefinite, negative, uncertain, unsure.

positive [*adj2*] *beneficial, helpful*
• *Syn* affirmative, constructive, effective, efficacious, forward-looking, practical, productive, progressive, reasonable, sound, useful; • *Ant* disadvantageous, negative, useless.

positively [*adv*] *absolutely, definitely*
• *Syn* assuredly, categorically, certainly, doubtlessly, easily, emphatically, firmly, indubitably, surely, undeniably, undoubtedly, unequivocally, unmistakably, unquestionably, with certainty, without qualification; • *Ant* doubtfully, perhaps, questionably.

possess [*v*] *have or obtain*
• *Syn* acquire, bear, be blessed with, be born with, be endowed with, control, dominate, enjoy, grab, hold, latch on to, lock up, maintain, occupy, own, retain, seize, take over, take possession; • *Ant* dispossess, lose, miss, not have.

possessed [*adj*] *obsessive, agitated, preoccupied* • *Syn* bedeviled, consumed, cursed, demented, enchanted, enthralled, frenetic, frenzied, haunted, insane, obsessed, violent; • *Ant* cool, dispassionate, normal.

possible [*adj*] *likely, attainable*
• *Syn* accessible, achievable, adventitious, conceivable, credible, doable, feasible, fortuitous, hopeful, hypothetical, imaginable, latent, obtainable, potential, practicable, probable, promising, realizable, thinkable, viable, within reach, workable; • *Ant* impossible, improbable, unattainable, unlikely, unrealizable.

possibly [*adv*] *by chance; in some way*
• *Syn* at all, by any chance, by any means, conceivably, could be, if possible, in any way, maybe, not impossibly, perchance, perhaps, probably, within realm of possibility; • *Ant* impossibly, perhaps, unlikely.

post [*v1*] *situate, position*
• *Syn* assign, establish, locate, place, put, set, station; • *Ant* displace.

post [*v2*] *advise, inform*
• *Syn* acquaint, apprise, brief, clue, fill in, notify, put wise to, report, tell, warn; • *Ant* withhold.

posterior [*adj1*] *rear*
• *Syn* after, back, behind, dorsal, hind, hinder, hindmost, in back of, last, retral; • *Ant* anterior, front.

posterior [adj2] *subsequent*
▪ *Syn* after, coming after, ensuing, following, later, latter, next, subsequential, succeeding; ▪ *Ant* before, front, preceding, previous.

posterity [n] *future generations*
▪ *Syn* children, descendants, family, heirs, issue, lineage, next generation, offspring, progeniture, progeny, scions, seed, succeeding generations, successors, unborn; ▪ *Ant* ancestry, heredity, past.

posthaste [adj/adv] *very fast*
▪ *Syn* at once, directly, expeditious, fast, fleet, hastily, headlong, promptly, pronto, quick, quickly, rapid, speedy, straightaway, swiftly; ▪ *Ant* eventually, ponderously, slow, slowly.

postpone [v] *put off till later time*
▪ *Syn* adjourn, defer, delay, hold off, hold over, hold up, lay over, prorogue, put on hold, shelve, suspend, table; ▪ *Ant* carry out, continue, do, expedite, forward, maintain, persevere.

postulate [v] *suppose, figure*
▪ *Syn* advance, affirm, assume, aver, estimate, guess, hypothesize, posit, predicate, presuppose, put forward, speculate, suppose, take for granted, theorize; ▪ *Ant* be certain, calculate, know.

posture [v] *display an attitude*
▪ *Syn* affect, attitudinize, display, fake, fake it, masquerade, pass for, pass off, playact, pose; ▪ *Ant* be natural, be truthful.

potent [adj] *effective, powerful, forceful*
▪ *Syn* almighty, authoritative, cogent, commanding, dominant, dynamic, efficacious, forcible, great, impressive, influential, lusty, mighty, persuasive, puissant, punchy, robust, strong, sturdy, trenchant, useful, vigorous, virile; ▪ *Ant* disabled, fragile, helpless, impotent, incapable, ineffective, weak.

potential [adj] *promising*
▪ *Syn* abeyant, budding, conceivable, dormant, embryonic, future, hidden, imaginable, implied, inherent, latent, likely, lurking, plausible, possible, prepatent, quiescent, thinkable, undeveloped, unrealized, within realm of possibility; ▪ *Ant* helpless, impossible, lacking, unpromising.

potpourri [n] *miscellany*
▪ *Syn* assortment, blend, collection, combination, combo, gallimaufry, goulash, hash, hodgepodge, medley, mélange, mishmash, mixed bag, mixture, motley, patchwork, soup, stew; ▪ *Ant* ingredient, singular.

pound [v] *impress; make someone listen*
▪ *Syn* din, drive, drub, drum, grave, hammer, stamp; ▪ *Ant* give up.

pout [v] *make a sad face; be sad*
▪ *Syn* be cross, be moody, be petulant, be sullen, frown, grouch, make a moue, mope, sulk; ▪ *Ant* grin, look happy, smile.

poverty-stricken [adj] *in great need; financially poor* ▪ *Syn* bankrupt, beggarly, destitute, distressed, impecunious, impoverished, indigent, in want, moneyless, necessitous, needy, penniless, penurious, unmoneyed, wanting; ▪ *Ant* affluent, rich, wealthy.

powdery [adj] *consisting of fine, loose grains* ▪ *Syn* arenaceous, arenose, branny, chalky, crumbling, crumbly, dry, dusty, fine, floury, friable, grainy, granular, gravelly, gritty, impalpable, loose, mealy, pulverized, pulverulent, sandy; ▪ *Ant* solid.

powerful [adj] *strong, effective*
▪ *Syn* able, authoritative, capable, cogent, commanding, compelling, competent, controlling, convincing, dominant, dynamic, effectual, efficacious, energetic, forceful, impressive, influential, mighty, omnipotent, persuasive, potent, preeminent, prevailing, puissant, robust, ruling, sovereign, stalwart, sturdy, supreme, telling, vigorous, weighty; ▪ *Ant* impotent, incapable, ineffective, unable, weak.

powerfully [adv] *with energy, authority*
▪ *Syn* effectively, energetically, forcefully, forcibly, hard, intensely, mightily, severely, strongly, vigorously, with might and main; ▪ *Ant* softly, weakly.

powerless [adj] *weak; unable*
▪ *Syn* debilitated, defenseless, disenfranchised, etiolated, feeble, frail, gutless, helpless, impotent, incapable, ineffectual, inert, paralyzed, prostrate, supine, unfit, vulnerable; ▪ *Ant* able, dominant, potent, powerful, strong.

practicable [adj] *within the realm of possibility* ▪ *Syn* accessible, achievable, applicable, attainable, doable, employable, feasible, operative, possible, serviceable, usable, utilizable, viable, workable; ▪ *Ant* impossible, impracticable, unattainable, unreasonable, unworkable.

practical [adj1] *realistic, useful*
▪ *Syn* applied, businesslike, commonsensical, doable, down-to-earth, efficient, empirical, factual, functional, handy, operative, orderly, possible, pragmatic, reasonable, sensible, serviceable, usable, utilitarian, virtual, workable; ▪ *Ant* impossible, impractical, unfeasible, unrealistic, unserviceable, unworkable, useless, worthless.

practical [adj2] *experienced, proficient*
▪ *Syn* accomplished, effective, qualified, seasoned, skilled, sophisticated, trained, versed, veteran, working, worldly; ▪ *Ant* incapable, inefficient, inexperienced, unseasoned, unskilled, useless.

practically [adv] *almost; very nearly*
▪ *Syn* about, all but, approximately, as good as, as much as, basically, close to, essentially, fundamentally, in effect, in essence, most, much, nearly, nigh, virtually, well-nigh; ▪ *Ant* absolutely, completely.

practice [v] *carry out; undertake*
▪ *Syn* apply, carry on, do, engage in, execute, follow, fulfill, function, perform, ply, pursue, put into effect, specialize in, work at; ▪ *Ant* cease, forget, halt, neglect, stop.

pragmatic [adj] *sensible*
▪ *Syn* businesslike, commonsensical, down-to-earth, efficient, hard, logical, matter-of-fact, practical, realistic, sober, unidealistic, utilitarian; ▪ *Ant* idealistic, romantic, unreasonable, untheoretical.

praise [v] *congratulate; adore*
▪ *Syn* acclaim, admire, adulate, advocate, aggrandize, applaud, approve, bless, boost, celebrate, cheer, cite, commend, compliment, dignify, distinguish, elevate, endorse, ennoble, eulogize, exalt, extol, flatter, glorify, hail, honor, laud, panegyrize, pay homage, pay tribute, proclaim, recommend, resound, tout, worship; ▪ *Ant* accuse, blame, censure, condemn, damn, denounce, reproach.

praiseworthy [adj] *deserving congratulations, adoration* ▪ *Syn* admirable, commendable, creditable, estimable, excellent, exemplary, fine, honorable, keen, laudable, meritable, meritorious, select, stellar, worthy; ▪ *Ant* dishonorable, disliked, disrespected, unworthy.

precarious [adj] *tricky, doubtful*
▪ *Syn* ambiguous, borderline, chancy, dangerous, delicate, dubious, equivocal, hazardous, impugnable, perilous, problematic, risky, rocky, sensitive, shaky, slippery, ticklish, touchy; ▪ *Ant* certain, definite, dependable, firm, stable, sure, undoubted.

precaution [n] *carefulness; preventative measure* ▪ *Syn* anticipation, canniness, caution, circumspection, discretion, foresight, forethought, insurance, prudence, regard, safeguard, safety measure, wariness; ▪ *Ant* carelessness, negligence.

precede [v] *go ahead of in space, time, order* ▪ *Syn* announce, antecede, anticipate, forerun, foreshadow, go before, herald, introduce, lead, pioneer, predate, preface, run ahead, scout, take precedence, usher; ▪ *Ant* follow, go after.

preceding [adj] *earlier, above*
▪ *Syn* above-mentioned, aforementioned, antecedent, before, erstwhile, foregoing, forerunning, former, heretofore, introductory, leading, one time, other, past, pioneering, precedent, precursive, prefatory, preliminary, preparatory, previous, prior; ▪ *Ant* after, below, following, later.

precious [adj1] *favorite, valued*
▪ *Syn* adored, beloved, cherished, darling, dear, dearest, idolized, inestimable, loved, pet, prized, treasured; ▪ *Ant* disfavored, useless, valueless, worthless.

precious [adj2] *expensive; rare*
▪ *Syn* choice, costly, dear, exquisite, fine, high-priced, invaluable, priceless, prizable, prized, recherché, rich, treasurable, valuable; ▪ *Ant* cheap, common, inexpensive.

precious [adj3] *extremely sophisticated and picky* ▪ *Syn* affected, alembicated, artful, artificial, choosy, dainty, delicate, fastidious, finicky, fussy, ostentatious, particular, pretentious, refined, sophisticated, studied; ▪ *Ant* simple, unsophisticated.

precipitate [v] *hurry, speed*
▪ *Syn* accelerate, advance, bring on, cast, dispatch, expedite, fling, further, hasten, launch, let fly, push forward, quicken, send forth, speed up, throw, trigger; ▪ *Ant* check, slow, wait.

precipitation [n] *moisture in air or falling from sky* ▪ *Syn* cloudburst, condensation, drizzle, hail, heavy dew, rain, rainfall, rainstorm, sleet, snow, storm, wetness; ▪ *Ant* dryness.

precipitous/precipitate [adj1] *very fast, sudden; impulsive; initial* ▪ **Syn** abrupt, brief, frantic, hasty, heedless, ill-advised, impatient, madcap, precipitant, quick, rash, reckless, refractory, rushing, subitaneous, swift, violent; ▪ **Ant** controlled, slow, thoughtful.

precipitate [adj2] *steep, falling sharply* ▪ **Syn** abrupt, arduous, craggy, dizzy, dizzying, high, perpendicular, precipitate, sharp, sheer; ▪ **Ant** gradual.

precis [n] *abridgment* ▪ **Syn** abstract, aperu, compendium, condensation, digest, outline, pandect, résumé, rundown, sketch, summary, survey, syllabus, synopsis; ▪ **Ant** entirety, expansion.

precise [adj1] *exact, accurate* ▪ **Syn** actual, categorical, circumscribed, clear-cut, decisive, determinate, explicit, express, fixed, literal, particular, restricted, rigorous, specific, strict, unequivocal, well-defined; ▪ **Ant** ambiguous, equivocal, false, imprecise, inaccurate, inexact, questionable.

precise [adj2] *meticulous, fastidious* ▪ **Syn** careful, exact, finicky, formal, fussy, genteel, inflexible, particular, picky, prim, prudish, punctilious, rigid, scrupulous, stickling, strait-laced, strict, stuffy, uncompromising; ▪ **Ant** careless, flexible, loose, negligent, slipshod.

precisely [adv] *exactly, just* ▪ **Syn** absolutely, accurately, correctly, definitely, expressly, for a fact, just so, literally, plumb, right, sharp, specifically, square, squarely, strictly, sure, yes; ▪ **Ant** ambiguously, imprecisely, questionably, unsure

preclude [v] *inhibit; make impossible* ▪ **Syn** avert, check, debar, deter, discontinue, exclude, forestall, hinder, impede, interrupt, obviate, prevent, prohibit, restrain, rule out, stave off, stop, ward; ▪ **Ant** allow, encourage, facilitate, permit, support.

precocious [adj] *exceptionally smart, ahead of age in understanding* ▪ **Syn** advanced, aggressive, bold, bright, forward, fresh, intelligent, mature, presumptuous, quick, sassy; ▪ **Ant** backward, retarded, slow.

preconception [n] *idea formed before event occurs or facts are received* ▪ **Syn** assumption, bias, delusion, inclination, notion, preconceived idea, predisposition, prejudgment, prejudice, presumption, presupposition; ▪ **Ant** factual knowledge, objectivity.

predecessor [n] *something, someone that comes before* ▪ **Syn** ancestor, antecedent, antecessor, forebear, foregoer, forerunner, former, precursor, previous, prior, prototype; ▪ **Ant** derivative, descendant, successor.

predetermined [adj] *decided in advance* ▪ **Syn** agreed, arranged, calculated, destined, determined, fated, fixed, foreordained, planned, prearranged, premeditated, preplanned, proposed, set, set up; ▪ **Ant** unarranged, undetermined, unplanned, unsettled.

predicament [n] *difficult situation* ▪ **Syn** asperity, circumstance, clutch, condition, crisis, deadlock, dilemma, exigency, hardship, imbroglio, impasse, juncture, muddle, perplexity, pinch, plight, quagmire, quandary, rigor, strait, vicissitude; ▪ **Ant** fix, good fortune, solution.

predictable [adj] *very easy to foretell* ▪ **Syn** anticipated, calculable, certain, expected, foreseeable, foreseen, likely, prepared, sure; ▪ **Ant** improbable, original, surprising, unpredictable.

predilection [n] *inclination, preference toward something* ▪ **Syn** bias, fancy, leaning, love, partiality, penchant, predisposition, proclivity, proneness, propensity, tendency, weakness; ▪ **Ant** antipathy, aversion, disinterest, dislike.

predispose [v] *influence to believe something* ▪ **Syn** activate, affect, bias, cultivate, dispose, impress, incline, indoctrinate, induce, inspire, prejudice, prepare, prime, prompt, stimulate, sway, urge; ▪ **Ant** discourage, dissuade.

predisposed [adj] *willing, inclined* ▪ **Syn** agreeable, amenable, biased, eager, enthusiastic, fain, given to, liable, likely, minded, partial, prone, ready, subject, susceptible; ▪ **Ant** disagreeing, disinclined, unprepared, unwilling.

predominant [adj] *ruling; most important* ▪ **Syn** all-powerful, ascendant, capital, chief, controlling, directing, dominant, effective, efficacious, governing, imperious, influential, leading, main, mighty, official, omnipotent, overpowering, paramount, predominate, prevalent, principal, prominent, reigning, sovereign, superior, transcendent, weighty; ▪ *Ant* inconsequential, minor, secondary, subordinate, trivial, unimportant.

preeminent [*adj*] *most important; superior* ▪ *Syn* capital, chief, dominant, excellent, foremost, incomparable, major, matchless, outstanding, paramount, peerless, principal, renowned, stellar, towering, ultimate, unequaled, unrivaled; ▪ *Ant* inferior, low, secondary, unimportant, unknown.

preempt [*v*] *take over in place of another* ▪ *Syn* annex, appropriate, assume, bump, commandeer, confiscate, expropriate, obtain, seize, sequester, take, usurp; ▪ *Ant* acquiesce, give up, renounce, surrender.

preface [*v*] *introduce* ▪ *Syn* begin, commence, launch, lead, lead up to, open, precede, prefix, usher; ▪ *Ant* conclude, end, finish.

prefer [*v*] *favor; single out* ▪ *Syn* adopt, advance, aggrandize, be partial to, choose, cull, desire, elect, fancy, fix upon, incline, mark, opt for, pick, promote, propone, proposition, put forward, raise, select, suggest, tag, wish; ▪ *Ant* dislike, eschew, hate, reject, spurn.

preferred [*adj*] *favorite, chosen* ▪ *Syn* adopted, approved, decided upon, elected, endorsed, fancied, favored, handpicked, liked, named, picked, popular, sanctioned, selected, set apart, singled out, taken, well-liked; ▪ *Ant* ill-favored, rejected, undesirable.

pregnant [*adj*] *significant, meaningful* ▪ *Syn* charged, consequential, creative, eloquent, expressive, fecund, imaginative, important, inventive, loaded, momentous, original, pointed, redolent, rich, seminal, sententious, suggestive, telling, weighty; ▪ *Ant* immaterial, insignificant, trivial.

prejudice [*v*] *influence another's beliefs without basis, information* ▪ *Syn* bias, damage, dispose, distort, harm, hinder, hurt, impair, incline, indoctrinate, injure, jaundice, mar, predispose, prejudge, prepossess, spoil, undermine, vitiate; ▪ *Ant* approve, be fair, be just, regard, respect, tolerate.

prejudicial [*adj*] *harmful, undermining* ▪ *Syn* biased, bigoted, detrimental, differential, disadvantageous, discriminatory, evil, hurtful, inimical, injurious, mischievous, nocuous, unjust; ▪ *Ant* approving, fair, just, objective, unbiased.

preliminary [*adj*] *introductory, initial* ▪ *Syn* basic, elemental, elementary, exploratory, first, fundamental, inductive, initiatory, opening, pilot, preceding, precursory, prefatory, preparatory, primal, primary, prior, qualifying, readying, test, trial; ▪ *Ant* closing, concluding, final.

prelude [*n*] *beginning of event* ▪ *Syn* commencement, exordium, foreword, introduction, overture, preamble, preface, preliminary, proem, prolegomenon, prologue, start; ▪ *Ant* coda, ending, epilogue, postlude.

premature [*adj1*] *earlier in occurrence than anticipated* ▪ *Syn* embryonic, inopportune, precipitate, unanticipated, undeveloped, unfledged, untimely; ▪ *Ant* backward, delayed, late, mature, overdue.

premature [*adj2*] *rash, impulsive* ▪ *Syn* hasty, ill-considered, inopportune, overhasty, precipitatious, untimely; ▪ *Ant* careful, cautious, prepared, slow.

premeditated [*adj*] *planned, intended* ▪ *Syn* advised, aforethought, calculated, conscious, considered, contrived, deliberate, designed, intentional, studied, thought-out, willful; ▪ *Ant* accidental, casual, spontaneous, unexpected.

premier [*adj*] *leading; original* ▪ *Syn* arch, beginning, champion, chief, earliest, first, foremost, head, inaugural, initial, main, opening, prime, principal; ▪ *Ant* inferior, minor.

premise [*n*] *hypothesis, argument* ▪ *Syn* assertion, assumption, basis, ground, posit, postulate, presumption, presupposition, proposition, supposition, thesis; ▪ *Ant* fact, reality, truth.

premium [*adj*] *excellent* ▪ *Syn* choice, exceptional, prime, select, selected, superior; ▪ *Ant* inferior, low, poor.

preoccupied [*adj*] *busy; mentally caught up in something* ▪ *Syn* absent, absentminded, absorbed, abstracted, bemused, daydreaming, distracted, distrait, engaged, engrossed, fascinated, forgetful, immersed, intent, lost, oblivious, obsessed, rapt, removed, spellbound; ▪ *Ant* aware, conscious, observant, thoughtful.

preparatory [*adj*] *introductory, basic* ▪ *Syn* before, elementary, in advance of, in anticipation of, inductive, opening, precautionary, prefatory, preliminary, prelusive, preparative, previous, primary, prior to; ▪ **Ant** auxiliary, supplementary.

prepare [v] *make or get ready*
▪ **Syn** adapt, adjust, anticipate, arrange, assemble, brace, concoct, construct, contrive, cook, develop, draw up, endow, fabricate, fashion, formulate, fortify, furnish, gird, lay the groundwork, make, outfit, plan, produce, put in order, qualify, ready, settle, strengthen, train, turn out, warm up; ▪ **Ant** disorganize, ignore, neglect.

prepared [adj] *ready in body or mind*
▪ **Syn** able, adapted, arranged, disposed, fit, groomed, inclined, in order, planned, predisposed, prepped, primed, qualified, rehearsed, set, stacked, willing; ▪ **Ant** ignorant, neglectful, unprepared.

preponderance [n] *great numbers; supremacy* ▪ **Syn** advantage, ascendancy, dominance, domination, greater part, predominance, prevalence, superiority, sway, weight; ▪ **Ant** disadvantage, inferiority, weakness.

prepossessing [adj] *attractive, handsome* ▪ **Syn** alluring, amiable, appealing, bewitching, captivating, charming, enchanting, engaging, fascinating, fetching, inviting, magnetic, pleasant, pleasing, striking, winning; ▪ **Ant** homely, unattractive, uninviting.

preposterous [adj] *ridiculous, bizarre*
▪ **Syn** absurd, asinine, crazy, excessive, exorbitant, extravagant, extreme, fantastic, foolish, impossible, incredible, insane, irrational, laughable, ludicrous, monstrous, nonsensical, outrageous, senseless, shocking, silly, stupid, unbelievable, unusual, wild; ▪ **Ant** reasonable, sensible.

prerequisite [adj] *necessary*
▪ **Syn** called for, essential, expedient, imperative, important, indispensable, mandatory, necessitous, obligatory, required, requisite, vital; ▪ **Ant** optional, unnecessary, voluntary.

prerogative [n] *right, privilege*
▪ **Syn** advantage, authority, birthright, choice, claim, droit, due, exemption, liberty, sanction; ▪ **Ant** duty, obligation.

present [adj1] *at this time*
▪ **Syn** at this moment, commenced, contemporary, current, existent, extant, for the time being, immediate, in duration, instant, just now, modern, nowadays, present-day, prompt, started, today, top-

ical, under consideration, up-to-date; ▪ **Ant** absent, former, future, past, previous.

present [adj2] *nearby, here*
▪ **Syn** accounted for, at hand, attendant, available, in attendance, in view, near, on board, on deck, on hand, on-the-spot, ready, within reach; ▪ **Ant** absent, away, distant.

present [v1] *introduce; demonstrate*
▪ **Syn** acquaint, advance, allege, cite, declare, display, exhibit, expose, expound, extend, make known, manifest, mount, offer, open to view, perform, proffer, put forward, raise, recount, relate, show, stage, state, submit, suggest, tender, trot out; ▪ **Ant** refrain, subdue, withhold.

present [v2] *give, hand over*
▪ **Syn** award, bestow, come up with, confer, devote, donate, entrust, furnish, gift, grant, hand out, offer, proffer, put at disposal, put forth; ▪ **Ant** acquire, procure, take.

presentable [adj] *respectable; fit to be seen* ▪ **Syn** acceptable, decent, fit, passable, prepared, proper, satisfactory, suitable, tolerable; ▪ **Ant** unacceptable, unfit, unsuitable.

presently [adv] *in a short while*
▪ **Syn** anon, before long, by and by, directly, immediately, in a minute, in a moment, now, nowadays, pretty soon, shortly, soon, today, without delay; ▪ **Ant** eventually, later, never.

preserve [v] *care for, maintain; continue*
▪ **Syn** bottle, can, conserve, cure, defend, evaporate, freeze, guard, keep, keep up, mummify, perpetuate, pickle, process, protect, put up, refrigerate, retain, safeguard, save, season, secure, shelter, shield, store, sustain, uphold; ▪ **Ant** destroy, hurt, ruin.

preside [v] *be in authority*
▪ **Syn** administer, advise, carry on, chair, conduct, control, direct, do the honors, govern, handle, head, head up, keep, lead, manage, officiate, operate, ordain, oversee, run, supervise; ▪ **Ant** follow, serve.

press [v1] *push on with force*
▪ **Syn** bear down, bear heavily, compress, condense, constrain, crowd, crush, cumber, depress, flatten, force down, impel, jam, mash, pack, pile, pin down, ram, reduce, scrunch, shove, squash, squeeze,

stuff, thrust, weigh; ▪ *Ant* liberate, pull, release.

press [*v2*] *pressure, trouble*
▪ *Syn* afflict, assail, beg, beset, besiege, come at, compel, constrain, demand, disquiet, enjoin, entreat, exhort, force, harass, implore, importune, lean on, oppress, petition, plague, plead, push, squeeze, sue, torment, urge, vex, weigh down, work on, worry; ▪ *Ant* appease, comfort, ignore, placate, relieve.

pressing [*adj*] *very important; urgent*
▪ *Syn* acute, burning, clamorous, compelling, constraining, critical, crucial, demanding, dire, exacting, exigent, forcing, high-priority, immediate, imperative, importunate, obliging, serious, urgent, vital; ▪ *Ant* insignificant, trivial, unimportant.

pressure [*v*] *bother, urge*
▪ *Syn* come at, compel, constrain, drive, impel, insist, press, push, rush, sell, squeeze; ▪ *Ant* ease, liberate, release.

prestigious [*adj*] *famous, influential*
▪ *Syn* celebrated, distinguished, eminent, esteemed, exalted, famed, great, illustrious, important, imposing, impressive, notable, prominent, renowned, reputable, respected; ▪ *Ant* humble, insignificant, modest, unimportant.

presumably [*adv*] *likely, reasonably*
▪ *Syn* apparently, credible, doubtless, doubtlessly, hypothetically, in all likelihood, in all probability, it would seem, most likely, on the face of it, presumptively, probably, seemingly, supposedly, surely, theoretically, unquestionably; ▪ *Ant* doubtfully, unlikely.

presume [*v1*] *make assumption; believe*
▪ *Syn* assume, be afraid, conclude, conjecture, consider, count on, depend, figure, gather, guess, infer, posit, postulate, premise, presuppose, speculate, suppose, surmise, take for granted, think, trust; ▪ *Ant* disbelieve.

presume [*v2*] *dare; take the liberty*
▪ *Syn* go so far, have the audacity, impose, infringe, intrude, make bold, undertake, venture; ▪ *Ant* assure, guarantee, protect.

presumptuous [*adj*] *very self-confident*
▪ *Syn* arrogant, audacious, bold, conceited, confident, egotistic, foolhardy, forward, fresh, insolent, overconfident, overfamiliar, overweening, pompous, presuming, pretentious, pushy, rash,

rude, self-assertive, self-satisfied, smug, supercilious; ▪ *Ant* humble, modest, polite, respectful.

pretend [*v1*] *fake, falsify*
▪ *Syn* act, affect, allege, assume, be deceitful, beguile, be hypocritical, bluff, cheat, counterfeit, cozen, deceive, delude, dissemble, dupe, feign, impersonate, masquerade, mislead, profess, purport, simulate; ▪ *Ant* tell truth.

pretend [*v2*] *play the part of*
▪ *Syn* act, assume the role, imagine, imitate, impersonate, make as if, make believe, make out like, make up, masquerade, mimic, play, playact, portray, pose, purport, represent, reproduce, suppose; ▪ *Ant* be frank, be genuine, be honest.

pretentious [*adj*] *snobbish, conceited*
▪ *Syn* affected, assuming, bombastic, conspicuous, euphuistic, exaggerated, flamboyant, flashy, flaunting, grandiloquent, grandiose, hollow, imposing, inflated, lofty, magniloquent, mincing, ostentatious, overblown, pompous, rhetorical, showy, snobbish, specious, splashy, swank, tumid, turgid, vainglorious; ▪ *Ant* humble, modest, unconceited.

preternatural [*adj*] *unusual, abnormal*
▪ *Syn* aberrant, anomalous, arcane, atypical, deviant, extraordinary, inexplicable, marvelous, mysterious, occult, odd, peculiar, strange, superhuman, supermundane, supernatural, unearthly, unnatural; ▪ *Ant* common, mundane, natural, normal, regular, usual.

pretext [*n*] *disguise; alleged reason*
▪ *Syn* affectation, alibi, appearance, bluff, cloak, excuse, front, guise, mask, masquerade, ploy, pretense, ruse, semblance, simulation, subterfuge; ▪ *Ant* disclosure, revelation.

pretty [*adj*] *attractive*
▪ *Syn* appealing, beauteous, beautiful, charming, comely, cute, dainty, delicate, elegant, fine, good-looking, graceful, handsome, lovely, pleasant, pleasing, pulchritudinous, tasteful; ▪ *Ant* graceless, plain, ugly.

prevail [*v*] *dominate, control*
▪ *Syn* abound, be prevalent, be victorious, be widespread, carry, command, conquer, domineer, exist generally, gain, master, obtain, overcome, predominate, prove, reign, succeed, triumph, win; ▪ *Ant* be deficient in, fall short, lose, surrender.

prevailing [*adj*] *general, dominant*
▪ **Syn** all-embracing, catholic, comprehensive, current, customary, ecumenical, established, familiar, influential, in vogue, main, operative, predominant, prevalent, principal, rampant, rife, ruling, set, sweeping, usual, widespread; ▪ **Ant** dated, old-fashioned, rare.

prevail upon/prevail on [*v*] *persuade, influence* ▪ **Syn** affect, convince, dispose, draw, get, impress, incline, induce, promote, prompt, sway, talk into, win over; ▪ **Ant** discourage, dissuade, leave alone.

prevalent [*adj1*] *accepted, widespread*
▪ **Syn** accustomed, common, customary, established, everyday, extensive, general, habitual, natural, popular, prevailing, rampant, stylish, typical, ubiquitous, usual, wonted; ▪ **Ant** infrequent, isolated, limited, uncommon.

prevalent [*adj2*] *governing, superior*
▪ **Syn** ascendant, compelling, dominant, overbearing, paramount, predominant, preponderant, prevailing, regnant, ruling, sovereign, successful; ▪ **Ant** inferior, subservient.

prevaricate [*v*] *deceive; stretch the truth*
▪ **Syn** belie, cavil, con, distort, dodge, exaggerate, fabricate, falsify, fib, hedge, invent, misrepresent, misspeak, palter, quibble, shift, shuffle; ▪ **Ant** tell truth.

prevent [*v*] *keep from happening or continuing* ▪ **Syn** avert, avoid, balk, check, counter, dam, debar, foil, forbid, forestall, frustrate, halt, hamper, head off, hinder, hold back, impede, inhibit, intercept, limit, obstruct, obviate, preclude, prohibit, put a stop to, repress, restrain, retard, stave off, stop, thwart, ward off; ▪ **Ant** allow, assist, incite, permit, urge.

previous [*adj*] *former, prior*
▪ **Syn** antecedent, anterior, earlier, erstwhile, foregoing, one-time, past, precedent, preceding, quondam, sometime; ▪ **Ant** ensuing, later, subsequent.

previously [*adv*] *earlier*
▪ **Syn** antecedently, at one time, back, before, beforehand, erstwhile, fore, formerly, forward, heretofore, hitherto, in advance, in anticipation, in days gone by, in the past, long ago, once, precedently, then, until now; ▪ **Ant** currently, presently.

prey on [*v*] *attack, terrorize*
▪ **Syn** blackmail, bleed, bully, depredate, distress, exploit, feed on, fleece, haunt,

intimidate, live off, oppress, plunder, raid, seize, take advantage of, tax, trouble, victimize, weigh, worry; ▪ **Ant** encourage, liberate, protect, reassure.

price [*n*] *consequences of action*
▪ **Syn** cost, expense, penalty, sacrifice, toll; ▪ **Ant** cause.

priceless [*adj1*] *precious, irreplaceable*
▪ **Syn** cherished, costly, dear, expensive, incomparable, inestimable, invaluable, prized, rare, rich, treasured, valuable, valued; ▪ **Ant** cheap, replaceable, useless, worthless.

priceless [*adj2*] *extremely funny*
▪ **Syn** absurd, amusing, comic, droll, hilarious, humorous, riotous, sidesplitting; ▪ **Ant** grave, serious.

prickly [*adj1*] *thorny or difficult*
▪ **Syn** annoying, barbed, bothersome, complicated, echinated, intricate, involved, knotty, nettlesome, pointed, sharp, ticklish, tricky, troublesome, trying; ▪ **Ant** easy, smooth, uncomplicated.

prickly [*adj2*] *irritable, bad-tempered*
▪ **Syn** cantankerous, edgy, fractious, grumpy, irritable, petulant, snappish, touchy, waspish; ▪ **Ant** happy, pleasant.

pride [*v*] *take pleasure in accomplishment*
▪ **Syn** be proud, boast, brag, crow, exult, felicitate, flatter oneself, gasconade, glory in, hold head high, overbear, prance, preen, presume, revel in, strut, swagger, swell, vaunt; ▪ **Ant** be self-deprecating, disavow, disclaim.

prim [*adj*] *particular, fussy*
▪ **Syn** ceremonious, choosy, conventional, correct, decorous, demure, fastidious, orderly, overmodest, precise, priggish, prissy, proper, prudish, puritanical, rigid, spruce, stickling, stiff, straight, strait-laced, tidy, uncluttered, upright, Victorian; ▪ **Ant** careless, informal, relaxed, untidy.

primarily [*adv1*] *generally; for the most part* ▪ **Syn** above all, basically, chiefly, especially, essentially, fundamentally, generally, largely, mainly, mostly, on the whole, overall, predominantly, principally; ▪ **Ant** secondarily.

primarily [*adv2*] *in the beginning*
▪ **Syn** at first, at the start, first and foremost, from the start, initially, in the first place, originally, primitively; ▪ **Ant** finally, wholely.

primary/prime [*adj1*] *best, principal*
▪ **Syn** capital, cardinal, chief, dominant,

first, greatest, heavy, highest, leading, main, paramount, stellar, top; ▪ *Ant* inferior, least, minor, second, secondary, subordinate.

primary/prime [*adj2*] *earliest*
▪ *Syn* aboriginal, beginning, direct, first, initial, maiden, original, pioneer, primal, primeval, primitive, primordial, pristine; ▪ *Ant* final, latest.

primary/prime [*adj3*] *basic, fundamental* ▪ *Syn* basal, beginning, bottom, central, elementary, essential, first, original, principal, radical, rudimentary, simple, ultimate, underlying; ▪ *Ant* auxiliary, secondary, supplemental.

prime [*v*] *get ready; prepare*
▪ *Syn* break in, brief, coach, cram, excite, galvanize, groom, inform, innervate, make ready, motivate, provoke, rehearse, stimulate, train; ▪ *Ant* deaden, dull, learn.

primeval [*adj*] *ancient*
▪ *Syn* earliest, early, first, old, original, prehistoric, primal, primary, primordial, pristine; ▪ *Ant* modern, new.

primitive [*adj1*] *ancient, original*
▪ *Syn* basic, earliest, elementary, first, fundamental, old, primary, primeval, primordial, pristine, substratal, underlying; ▪ *Ant* current, modern, new, present.

primitive [*adj2*] *barbaric, crude*
▪ *Syn* animal, austere, barbarous, brutish, fierce, natural, raw, rudimentary, savage, simple, uncivilized, uncultivated, untamed, vestigial, wild; ▪ *Ant* comfortable, cultured, modern, sophisticated.

primordial [*adj*] *earliest*
▪ *Syn* basic, early, elemental, fundamental, original, prehistoric, primal, primary, prime, primeval, primitive, pristine; ▪ *Ant* last, latest.

principal [*adj*] *most important*
▪ *Syn* arch, capital, cardinal, chief, crowning, dominant, essential, foremost, greatest, head, highest, key, leading, main, maximum, outstanding, paramount, peerless, premier, prevailing, primary, prominent, sovereign, stellar, supreme, transcendent; ▪ *Ant* auxiliary, extra, least, lesser, minor, secondary, trivial, unimportant.

principally [*adv*] *mainly*
▪ *Syn* above all, basically, cardinally, chiefly, dominantly, eminently, especially, essentially, first and foremost, fundamentally, generally, in the first place,

largely, materially, mostly, notably, particularly, predominantly, preeminently, substantially, supremely, to a great degree, vitally; ▪ *Ant* secondarily, trivially.

principle/principles [*n*] *belief, morality; morals* ▪ *Syn* attitude, code, conduct, conscience, ethic, faith, ideals, integrity, opinion, policy, rectitude, scruples, sense of duty, system, teaching, uprightness; ▪ *Ant* amorality, immorality.

prior [*adj*] *earlier*
▪ *Syn* aforementioned, antecedent, anterior, before, foregoing, former, past, precedent, preceding, preexistent, preexisting, previous; ▪ *Ant* after, following, later, subsequent.

prissy [*adj*] *particular and fussy*
▪ *Syn* effeminate, epicene, fastidious, finicky, genteel, persnickety, picky, precious, prim, prudish, puritanical, stickling, strait-laced, Victorian; ▪ *Ant* informal, relaxed, unconcerned.

private [*adj1*] *personal, intimate*
▪ *Syn* clandestine, confidential, discreet, exclusive, hushed, individual, nonpublic, particular, reserved, secret, special; ▪ *Ant* open, public, unrestricted.

private [*adj2*] *hidden, isolated*
▪ *Syn* clandestine, concealed, covert, discreet, quiet, removed, retired, secluded, secret, sequestered, solitary, withdrawn; ▪ *Ant* open, revealed, unconcealed.

privileged [*adj1*] *favored, elite*
▪ *Syn* advantaged, entitled, honored, indulged, powerful, ruling, special; ▪ *Ant* disadvantaged, poor, underprivileged.

privileged [*adj2*] *allowed, exempt*
▪ *Syn* authorized, chartered, eligible, empowered, entitled, excused, franchised, free, furnished, granted, licensed, palatine, qualified, sanctioned, special, vested; ▪ *Ant* prevented, prohibited, unexempt.

privileged [*adj3*] *confidential, secret*
▪ *Syn* exceptional, inside, not for publication, privy, special, top secret; ▪ *Ant* known, open, public.

privy [*adj1*] *secret*
▪ *Syn* buried, concealed, confidential, covert, hidden, obscured, personal, private, separate, shrouded, ulterior; ▪ *Ant* known, public, revealed.

privy [*adj2*] *aware*
▪ *Syn* acquainted, apprised, cognizant, conscious, informed, private, privileged, wise; ▪ *Ant* unaware, unknowing.

prize [*adj*] *best*
▪ *Syn* award-winning, champion, choice, elite, outstanding, pick, prime, top, topnotch, winning; ▪ *Ant* worst.

prize [*v*] *value highly*
▪ *Syn* appreciate, apprize, cherish, count, enshrine, esteem, guard, hold dear, rate, regard highly, treasure; ▪ *Ant* despise, dislike, feel indifference, hate.

probable [*adj*] *likely to happen*
▪ *Syn* apparent, believable, credible, earthly, feasible, most likely, ostensible, plausible, possible, presumable, presumed, rational, reasonable, seeming; ▪ *Ant* improbable, unlikely.

probably [*adv*] *likely to happen*
▪ *Syn* apparently, as likely as not, assumably, believably, feasibly, imaginably, in all likelihood, in all probability, like enough, maybe, most likely, one can assume, perchance, perhaps, plausibly, possibly, practicably, presumably, reasonably, seemingly, to all appearances; ▪ *Ant* improbably, unlikely.

probity [*n*] *fairness, honesty*
▪ *Syn* equity, fidelity, goodness, honor, integrity, justice, morality, rectitude, righteousness, sincerity, trustworthiness, truthfulness, virtue, worth; ▪ *Ant* deceit, dishonesty, unfairness.

problematic [*adj*] *open to doubt*
▪ *Syn* ambiguous, arguable, chancy, debatable, disputable, doubtful, dubious, dubitable, enigmatic, indecisive, moot, open, precarious, problematical, puzzling, questionable, suspect, tricky, uncertain, unsettled; ▪ *Ant* certain, settled, solvable, sure, undisputed.

proceed [*v1*] *physically or mentally carry on, carry out* ▪ *Syn* advance, continue, fare, get on with, go ahead, go on, hie, journey, make a start, march, move on, move out, pass, press on, progress, push on, repair, set in motion, travel, wend; ▪ *Ant* cease, halt, lose ground, regress, retreat, stop, withdraw.

proceed [*v2*] *flow from; originate*
▪ *Syn* arise, come, derive, emanate, ensue, extend, follow, head, issue, pass, result, rise, spring, stem; ▪ *Ant* end, return, terminate.

proceeds [*n*] *earnings from business*
▪ *Syn* gain, gate, income, interest, lucre, produce, product, profit, receipts, result, returns, revenue, reward, split, take, takings, till, yield; ▪ *Ant* loss.

process [*v*] *subject to series of action to achieve result* ▪ *Syn* deal with, alter, concoct, dispose of, fulfill, handle, make ready, prepare, refine, transform, treat; ▪ *Ant* forget, neglect.

proclaim [*v*] *advertise, make known*
▪ *Syn* affirm, announce, blast, blazon, broadcast, call, circulate, declare, demonstrate, enunciate, evince, exhibit, herald, illustrate, ostend, profess, publish, spout, utter, vent, voice; ▪ *Ant* conceal, hide, retract, suppress.

proclivity [*n*] *inclination, tendency*
▪ *Syn* bias, disposition, facility, inclining, leaning, penchant, predilection, predisposition, propensity, weakness; ▪ *Ant* disinclination.

procrastinate [*v*] *delay, put off doing*
▪ *Syn* adjourn, be dilatory, dally, dawdle, hesitate, linger, loiter, pause, postpone, protract, retard, stall, suspend, tarry, wait; ▪ *Ant* accelerate, advance, expedite; hasten, quicken.

procure [*v*] *acquire, obtain*
▪ *Syn* annex, appropriate, compass, corral, draw, earn, find, gain, grab, have, induce, persuade, pick up, prevail upon, promote, score, secure, wangle, win; ▪ *Ant* give away, have, lose.

prod [*v*] *urge, incite*
▪ *Syn* excite, goad, impel, instigate, jog, motivate, pique, prompt, propel, provoke, remind, rouse, spark, spur, stimulate, stir up, trigger; ▪ *Ant* discourage, dissuade.

prodigal [*adj1*] *wasteful*
▪ *Syn* dissipated, excessive, extravagant, immoderate, improvident, intemperate, lavish, profligate, reckless, spendthrift, squandering, wanton; ▪ *Ant* careful, thrifty.

prodigal [*adj2*] *luxurious, profuse*
▪ *Syn* abundant, bounteous, bountiful, copious, exuberant, lavish, lush, luxuriant, moneyed, munificent, opulent, profusive, sumptuous, teeming; ▪ *Ant* modest, plain, poor, spared, unadorned.

prodigious [*adj1*] *huge, enormous*
▪ *Syn* big, giant, gigantic, gross, immense, inordinate, large, mammoth, massive, mighty, monstrous, monumental, stupendous, towering, tremendous, vast; ▪ *Ant* little, small, tiny.

prodigious [*adj2*] *extraordinary, fabulous* ▪ *Syn* abnormal, amazing, astonishing, astounding, exceptional, fantastic, impressive, marvelous, miraculous, phenomenal, preternatural, remarkable, spectacular, staggering, startling, striking, stupendous, surprising, unreal, unusual, utmost, wonderful; ▪ *Ant* common, insignificant, ordinary, unremarkable.

produce [v] *generate, create*
▪ *Syn* afford, assemble, author, bear, beget, blossom, breed, bring forth, build, compose, conceive, construct, contribute, cultivate, deliver, design, develop, devise, effectuate, engender, erect, fabricate, form, frame, furnish, give birth, invent, make, manufacture, multiply, originate, parent, present, procreate, propagate, provide, put together, render, reproduce, supply, turn out, write, yield; ▪ *Ant* consume, destroy, ruin.

productive [adj] *fruitful, creative*
▪ *Syn* advantageous, beneficial, constructive, dynamic, effective, energetic, fecund, fertile, gainful, generative, inventive, plentiful, profitable, prolific, rewarding, rich, valuable, worthwhile; ▪ *Ant* fruitless, impotent, unproductive.

productivity [n] *output, work rate*
▪ *Syn* abundance, capacity, fecundity, fertility, potency, richness; ▪ *Ant* idleness, impotency, infertility.

profane [adj] *immoral, crude, disrespectful of religion* ▪ *Syn* abusive, atheistic, blasphemous, coarse, foul, godless, heathen, idolatrous, impious, impure, indecent, infidel, irreligious, irreverent, irreverential, mundane, nasty, obscene, pagan, profanatory, raunchy, sacrilegious, sinful, temporal, transient, transitory, unconsecrated, ungodly, unhallowed, unholy, unsanctified, vulgar, wicked, worldly; ▪ *Ant* clean, delicate, moral, proper, sacred.

profane [v] *defile, desecrate*
▪ *Syn* abuse, befoul, blaspheme, commit sacrilege, contaminate, curse, cuss, damn, debase, despoil, misuse, mock, pervert, pollute, prostitute, revile, scorn, sin, swear, tar, vice, violate, vitiate; ▪ *Ant* bless, cleanse, purify.

profess [v] *declare, assert*
▪ *Syn* acknowledge, act as if, admit, affirm, allege, announce, asseverate, aver, avouch, avow, claim, confess, confirm, croon, depose, maintain, make out, own, predicate, proclaim, purport, purport, state, vouch; ▪ *Ant* conceal, hide.

profession [n] *line of work requiring academic or practical preparation* ▪ *Syn* business, calling, career, chosen work, employment, engagement, field, occupation, office, position, post, service, specialty, sphere, trade, undertaking, vocation; ▪ *Ant* avocation, entertainment, fun, hobby.

professional [adj] *skilled, trained*
▪ *Syn* able, ace, acknowledged, adept, competent, efficient, experienced, expert, finished, known, learned, licensed, masterly, polished, practiced, proficient, qualified, sharp, skillful, well-qualified; ▪ *Ant* amateur, rookie, unprofessional, unskilled, untrained.

professor [n] *person who teaches college courses* ▪ *Syn* don, educator, faculty member, fellow, instructor, lecturer, pedagogue, pundit, sage, savant, teacher, tutor; ▪ *Ant* pupil, student.

proffer [v] *suggest, offer*
▪ *Syn* bestow, donate, extend, give, pose, present, propose, proposition, propound, submit, tender, volunteer; ▪ *Ant* discourage, dissuade, keep, reserve, withhold.

proficient [adj] *able, skilled*
▪ *Syn* accomplished, adept, apt, capable, clever, competent, consummate, conversant, effective, efficient, experienced, expert, gifted, masterful, masterly, qualified, savvy, sharp, skillful, talented, trained, versed; ▪ *Ant* clumsy, incompetent, inept, unable, unskilled.

profit [v] *gain; get or give an advantage*
▪ *Syn* aid, avail, benefit, be of advantage, better, capitalize on, cash in on, clean up, clear, earn, help, improve, prosper, realize, score, thrive, turn to advantage, use, utilize, work for; ▪ *Ant* lose.

profitable [adj] *advantageous; money-making* ▪ *Syn* beneficial, commercial, contributive, effective, favorable, fruitful, gainful, lucrative, paying, productive, rewarding, successful, sustaining, sweet, valuable, well-paying, worthwhile; ▪ *Ant* disadvantageous, unprofitable.

profligate [adj1] *immoral, corrupt*
▪ *Syn* abandoned, debauched, degenerate, depraved, dissolute, iniquitous, lax, libertine, loose, promiscuous, reprobate, shameless, unprincipled, vicious, wanton, wicked, wild; ▪ *Ant* decent, good, moral, nice, virtuous.

profligate [adj2] *wasteful*
• **Syn** extravagant, immoderate, improvident, lavish, prodigal, reckless, spendthrift, squandering; • **Ant** careful, economical, frugal, moderate.

profound [adj1] *intellectual, thoughtful*
• **Syn** abstruse, deep, discerning, enlightened, erudite, esoteric, heavy, hermetic, intellectual, learned, mysterious, occult, Orphic, philosophical, recondite, sage, scholarly, secret, serious, subtle, weighty, wise; • **Ant** frivolous, meaningless, shallow, superficial.

profound [adj2] *bottomless*
• **Syn** abysmal, buried, cavernous, deep, fathomless, subterranean, yawning; • **Ant** shallow, slight.

profound [adj3] *intense; emotional*
• **Syn** abject, acute, consummate, deep, deep-seated, exhaustive, extensive, far-reaching, great, heartfelt, intense, keen, pronounced, sincere, thorough, total, utter; • **Ant** external, mild, moderate, slight, unemotional.

profuse [adj] *abundant, excessive*
• **Syn** abounding, ample, aplenty, bountiful, copious, extravagant, extreme, exuberant, fulsome, generous, immoderate, lavish, liberal, openhanded, opulent, overflowing, plentiful, prodigal, profusive, prolific, riotous, sumptuous, superfluous, swarming, teeming; • **Ant** meager, scanty, sparse.

progeny [n] *offspring*
• **Syn** children, descendants, family, issue, lineage, posterity, progeniture, race, scions, seed, stock, young; • **Ant** ancestry, parent.

progress [v1] *move forward*
• **Syn** advance, continue, edge, forge ahead, gain ground, get along, get on, go forward, keep going, lunge, move on, proceed, shoot, speed, travel; • **Ant** back up, retreat, stop.

progress [v2] *improve, advance*
• **Syn** ameliorate, become better, better, blossom, boost, develop, gain, grow, increase, mature, upgrade; • **Ant** decline, decrease, deteriorate, retrogress.

progressive [adj] *liberal; growing*
• **Syn** advancing, broad-minded, continuing, developing, dynamic, enlightened, enterprising, escalating, forward-looking, graduated, increasing, modern, ongoing, open-minded, radical, reformist, revolutionary, tolerant, up-to-date,

wide; • **Ant** conservative, moderate, reactionary.

prohibit [v] *make impossible; stop*
• **Syn** ban, block, constrain, disallow, enjoin, forbid, halt, impede, inhibit, interdict, nix, obstruct, outlaw, preclude, prevent, restrain, restrict, shut out, veto; • **Ant** allow, favor, permit, push.

prohibited [adj] *forbidden*
• **Syn** banned, barred, closed down, contraband, illegal, illicit, not allowed, not approved, proscribed, refused, restricted, taboo, verboten, vetoed; • **Ant** allowed, permitted.

prohibitive [adj] *restrictive; beyond one's financial means* • **Syn** conditional, excessive, exorbitant, forbidding, high-priced, limiting, preposterous, preventing, repressive, restraining, suppressive; • **Ant** affordable, allowable, reasonable.

projection [n] *bulge, overhang*
• **Syn** bump, eaves, extension, hook, jut, knob, ledge, outthrust, point, prominence, protrusion, protuberance, ridge, rim, shelf, sill, step, swelling; • **Ant** depression, hollow.

proliferate [v] *increase quickly*
• **Syn** breed, burgeon, engender, escalate, expand, generate, grow rapidly, multiply, procreate, propagate, reproduce; • **Ant** decline, decrease, fall off.

prolific [adj] *fruitful, productive*
• **Syn** abounding, bountiful, breeding, copious, creative, fecund, fertile, generative, luxuriant, profuse, reproductive, rich, spawning, teeming, yielding; • **Ant** barren, fruitless, impotent, unproductive.

prolong [v] *extend, draw out*
• **Syn** continue, delay, hold, hold up, lengthen, perpetuate, protract, stall, stretch; • **Ant** abbreviate, curtail, expedite, shorten.

prominent [adj1] *sticking out; conspicuous* • **Syn** bulging, easily seen, extrusive, eye-catching, flashy, in the foreground, marked, noticeable, obtrusive, obvious, outstanding, pronounced, raised, remarkable, salient, signal, striking, to the fore, unmistakable; • **Ant** depressed, inconspicuous, invisible, obscured, sunken.

prominent [adj2] *very important; famous* • **Syn** celebrated, chief, distinguished, eminent, famed, foremost, great, leading, main, notable, noted, notorious, outstanding, popular, preeminent, renowned, respected, top, underlined, well-known, well-thought-of; ▪ *Ant* common, obscure, ordinary, unimportant, unknown.

promiscuous [*adj*] *very sexually active*
▪ *Syn* abandoned, debauched, dissipated, dissolute, immoral, indiscriminate, lax, libertine, licentious, of easy virtue, oversexed, profligate, wanton, wild; ▪ *Ant* chaste, cool, moral, pure, temperate.

promise [*v1*] *give word that something will be done* ▪ *Syn* accede, affiance, agree, assent, assure, bargain, betroth, bind, commit, consent, contract, declare, engage, ensure, espouse, guarantee, insure, mortgage, obligate, pass, pledge, plight, profess, secure, stipulate, subscribe, swear, take an oath, undertake, underwrite, vouch, vow, warrant; ▪ *Ant* break, denounce, deny, refute, renege.

promise [*v2*] *bring hope, possibility*
▪ *Syn* augur, betoken, bode, denote, encourage, give hope, hint, indicate, like, look, omen, presage, seem likely, suggest; ▪ *Ant* discourage.

promising [*adj*] *hopeful*
▪ *Syn* able, auspicious, bright, encouraging, favorable, gifted, happy, likely, lucky, propitious, reassuring, roseate, talented, up-and-coming; ▪ *Ant* discouraging, unpromising.

promote [*v1*] *help, advance*
▪ *Syn* advertise, advocate, back, bolster, boost, champion, encourage, endorse, espouse, forward, foster, further, get behind, nurture, patronize, publicize, push, recommend, sell, speak for, sponsor, stimulate, support, uphold, urge, work for; ▪ *Ant* discredit, hinder, hurt, impede, prevent.

promote [*v2*] *give a higher position in organization* ▪ *Syn* advance, better, dignify, elevate, exalt, favor, graduate, honor, increase, magnify, move up, prefer, raise, skip, upgrade; ▪ *Ant* degrade, demote, discredit.

prompt [*adj*] *early, responsive*
▪ *Syn* alert, brisk, eager, efficient, immediate, instantaneous, on time, punctual, quick, ready, swift, timely, unhesitating, vigilant, watchful; ▪ *Ant* hesitating, late, lax, negligent, remiss, slow, tardy.

prompt [*v*] *incite, cue*
▪ *Syn* advise, aid, arouse, bring up, call forth, cause, draw, elicit, evoke, exhort, give rise to, goad, help, hint, imply, indi-

cate, induce, instigate, jog, mention, motivate, move, occasion, persuade, propel, propose, provoke, refresh, spur, suggest, talk into, urge, win over; ▪ *Ant* discourage, repress, stifle, stop, suppress.

promptly [*adv*] *immediately*
▪ *Syn* at once, directly, fast, hastily, instantly, now, posthaste, pronto, punctually, quickly, rapidly, straightaway, swiftly, unhesitatingly; ▪ *Ant* late, negligently.

promulgate [*v*] *make known*
▪ *Syn* advertise, announce, broadcast, circulate, communicate, declare, decree, disseminate, drum, issue, make public, notify, proclaim, promote, spread; ▪ *Ant* conceal, hide.

prone [*adj1*] *lying down*
▪ *Syn* decumbent, face down, flat, horizontal, level, procumbent, prostrate, reclining, recumbent, resupine, supine; ▪ *Ant* erect, sitting, straight, upright.

prone [*adj2*] *liable, likely*
▪ *Syn* apt, bent, disposed, fain, given, inclined, minded, predisposed, subject, susceptible, tending, willing; ▪ *Ant* averse, disinclined, reluctant.

pronounce [*v1*] *produce words vocally*
▪ *Syn* accent, articulate, enunciate, phonate, sound, stress, utter, verbalize, vocalize, voice; ▪ *Ant* mumble, stammer.

pronounce [*v2*] *announce, declare*
▪ *Syn* affirm, assert, call, decree, judge, mouth, proclaim, trumpet; ▪ *Ant* conceal, hide.

pronounced [*adj*] *distinct, evident*
▪ *Syn* clear, clear-cut, conspicuous, definite, marked, notable, obvious, outstanding, striking, strong, unmistakable; ▪ *Ant* indistinct, obscure, unpronounced, vague.

proof [*n*] *evidence, authentication*
▪ *Syn* affidavit, case, confirmation, credentials, criterion, data, demonstration, deposition, establishment, facts, grounds, reason, substantiation, testament, trace, validation, verification, warrant, witness; ▪ *Ant* hypothesis, theory.

prop [*v*] *hold up or lean against*
▪ *Syn* bolster, brace, buoy, buttress, carry, maintain, rest, set, shore, stand, stay, strengthen, support, sustain, truss, underprop, uphold; ▪ *Ant* tear down, weaken, weigh down.

propaganda [*n*] *information that is designed to mislead or persuade* ▪ *Syn* advertising, brainwashing, disinformation, evangelism, inculcation, indoctrination, newspeak, promotion, proselytism, publicity; ▪ *Ant* truth.

propagate [v] *spread, make known*
▪ *Syn* broadcast, circulate, develop, disperse, disseminate, distribute, promulgate, publicize, radiate, scatter, strew, transmit; ▪ *Ant* silence, stifle, suppress.

propel [v] *throw; release into air*
▪ *Syn* drive, impel, launch, mobilize, press, push, set in motion, shove, start, thrust; ▪ *Ant* hinder, hold, keep.

propensity [n] *inclination, weakness*
▪ *Syn* ability, aptness, bias, capacity, competence, disposition, flash, leaning, liability, partiality, penchant, predilection, predisposition, proclivity, susceptibility, talent, tendency, yen; ▪ *Ant* antipathy, disinclination, dislike, hate, loathing.

proper [adj1] *suitable*
▪ *Syn* able, applicable, appropriate, becoming, capable, competent, desired, felicitous, fit, good, happy, just, legitimate, meet, qualified, right, suited, true, useful; ▪ *Ant* improper, unacceptable, unfit, wrong.

proper [adj2] *mannerly, decent*
▪ *Syn* becoming, befitting, comely, decorous, demure, genteel, moral, polite, precise, prim, punctilious, refined, respectable, right, seemly; ▪ *Ant* crass, crude, objectionable, unseemly, vulgar.

proper [adj3] *conventional, correct*
▪ *Syn* absolute, accurate, consummate, customary, decorous, established, formal, orthodox, precise, usual; ▪ *Ant* incorrect, substandard, unconventional.

propitious [adj1] *full of promise; good, favorable* ▪ *Syn* advantageous, auspicious, beneficial, bright, dexter, encouraging, favoring, fortunate, happy, lucky, opportune, promising, rosy, timely, well-timed; ▪ *Ant* adverse, inauspicious, unlucky, unpromising.

propitious [adj2] *friendly*
▪ *Syn* benevolent, benign, favorably inclined, gracious, kind, nice, well-disposed; ▪ *Ant* cold, cool, unfriendly.

proponent [n] *person who advocates, supports cause* ▪ *Syn* advocate, backer, champion, defender, enthusiast, expounder, friend, partisan, patron, protector, spokesperson, subscriber, supporter, upholder, vindicator; ▪ *Ant* enemy, foe, opponent.

proportionate/proportional [adj] *balanced, corresponding* ▪ *Syn* commensurate, comparative, compatible, correlative, correspondent, dependent, equitable, equivalent, even, just, reciprocal, relative, symmetrical, uniform; ▪ *Ant* disproportionate, imbalanced, irrelevant.

propose [v] *suggest, present for action*
▪ *Syn* adduce, advance, advise, ask, broach, counsel, introduce, invite, make a motion, nominate, offer, press, proffer, proposition, put forward, recommend, request, set forth, solicit, submit, tender, urge, volunteer; ▪ *Ant* condemn, deny, oppose, refuse, reject.

proprietor [n] *person who owns something* ▪ *Syn* landlord, land owner, owner, possessor, proprietary, titleholder; ▪ *Ant* customer, tenant.

propriety [n] *suitableness, appropriateness* ▪ *Syn* accordance, becomingness, concord, congruity, decorum, etiquette, fitness, harmony, legitimacy, modesty, morality, order, protocol, rectitude, reeding, respectability, seemliness, suitability; ▪ *Ant* immorality, impropriety, inappropriateness, misconduct.

prosaic [adj] *unimaginative*
▪ *Syn* banal, boring, colorless, commonplace, drab, dry, dull, everyday, factual, hackneyed, irksome, lackluster, pedestrian, platitudinous, plebeian, routine, square, stale, tedious, trite, vapid, workaday; ▪ *Ant* creative, imaginative, interesting, provocative.

proscribe [v] *condemn, exclude*
▪ *Syn* ban, banish, boycott, censure, damn, denounce, embargo, exile, expatriate, forbid, interdict, ostracize, outlaw, prohibit, reject, sentence; ▪ *Ant* admit, allow, approve, praise, sanction.

prosecute [v1] *bring action against in court* ▪ *Syn* arraign, bring to trial, contest, indict, involve in litigation, litigate, prefer charges, put on trial, seek redress, sue, summon, take to court, try; ▪ *Ant* exonerate, free, liberate, pardon.

prosecute [v2] *follow through, persevere* ▪ *Syn* carry on, conduct, continue, discharge, execute, follow through, follow up, manage, perform, pursue, see through, wage; ▪ *Ant* cease, halt, stop.

prospect [v] *look for; seek*
▪ *Syn* delve, dig, explore, go into, investigate, look into, probe, search, sift, survey; ▪ *Ant* miss, overlook.

prospective [*adj*] *anticipated, potential*
▪ **Syn** approaching, awaited, coming, destined, eventual, expected, forthcoming, hoped-for, impending, intended, likely, planned, promised, proposed, soon-to-be; ▪ **Ant** agreed, concurred, unlikely.

prosper [*v*] *be fortunate; succeed*
▪ **Syn** advance, augment, bear fruit, benefit, blossom, fare well, flourish, gain, increase, make money, multiply, produce, rise, thrive, yield; ▪ **Ant** be unfortunate, decrease, fail, lose.

prosperous [*adj1*] *successful, thriving*
▪ **Syn** affluent, blooming, booming, comfortable, flourishing, halcyon, lucky, moneyed, opulent, prospering, rich, robust, substantial, uptown, wealthy, well-off, well-to-do; ▪ **Ant** failing, losing, poor, unprosperous, unsuccessful.

prosperous [*adj2*] *promising, advantageous* ▪ **Syn** appropriate, auspicious, bright, convenient, desirable, favorable, felicitous, lucky, opportune, profitable, seasonable, timely, well-timed; ▪ **Ant** disadvantageous, unpromising, unprosperous.

prostrate [*adj1*] *flat, horizontal*
▪ **Syn** abject, bowed low, procumbent, prone, reclining, recumbent, supine; ▪ **Ant** erect, straight, upright, vertical.

prostrate [*adj2*] *tired, worn*
▪ **Syn** dejected, depressed, drained, exhausted, fallen, immobilized, incapacitated, inconsolable, overcome, paralyzed, wearied, worn out; ▪ **Ant** hale, healthy, strong.

prostrate [*v*] *fall on knees; submit*
▪ **Syn** abase, bow, bow down, cast before, cringe, fall at feet, give in, grovel, kneel, obey, surrender; ▪ **Ant** dominate, intimidate, tower over.

protect [*v*] *take care of; guard from harm*
▪ **Syn** assure, care for, champion, chaperon, conserve, cushion, defend, give refuge, harbor, insulate, keep, look after, preserve, safeguard, save, screen, secure, shelter, shield, stand guard, support, watch over; ▪ **Ant** attack, harm, hurt, injure.

protective [*adj*] *guarding, securing*
▪ **Syn** careful, conservative, custodial, defensive, insulating, possessive, protecting, safeguarding, sheltering, shielding, vigilant, warm, watchful; ▪ **Ant** attacking, harmful, hurtful, injurious, threatening.

protest [*v*] *complain, disapprove; argue against* ▪ **Syn** asseverate, attest, avouch, avow, buck, constate, contend, declare, demonstrate, demur, disagree, except, expostulate, fight, holler, insist, inveigh against, maintain, object, oppose, predicate, rebel, remonstrate, resist, revolt, testify; ▪ **Ant** accept, approve, praise.

protocol [*n*] *rules of conduct, behavior in certain situation* ▪ **Syn** code, compact, concordat, conventions, courtesy, covenant, custom, decorum, etiquette, formalities, good form, manners, obligation, order, pact, politesse, propriety, treaty; ▪ **Ant** bad manners, crudeness, impropriety.

protract [*v*] *extend, draw out*
▪ **Syn** delay, draw, elongate, hold up, lengthen, postpone, procrastinate, prolong, prolongate, put off, stall, stretch, stretch out; ▪ **Ant** abbreviate, curtail, shorten.

protrude [*v*] *stick out*
▪ **Syn** bulge, distend, extend, extrude, jut, jut out, obtrude, overhang, point, poke, pouch, pout, project, shoot out, stand out, start, stick up, swell; ▪ **Ant** depress, sink.

protuberance [*n*] *lump, outgrowth*
▪ **Syn** bulge, bump, excrescence, jut, jutting, knob, outthrust, process, projection, prominence, protrusion, swelling, tumor; ▪ **Ant** depression, ingrowth, sinkage.

proud [*adj1*] *pleased, pleasing*
▪ **Syn** appreciative, content, dignified, eminent, fiery, glad, glorious, grand, honored, illustrious, impressive, magnificent, majestic, noble, rewarding, satisfied, spirited, splendid, stately, sublime, valiant, well-pleased; ▪ **Ant** dishonorable, humble, sad, sorry.

proud [*adj2*] *arrogant, self-important*
▪ **Syn** boastful, cavalier, conceited, egotistical, haughty, imperious, lofty, masterful, narcissistic, overbearing, pompous, pretentious, scornful, supercilious, vainglorious; ▪ **Ant** deferential, humble, meek, modest.

prove [*v*] *establish facts; put to a test*
▪ **Syn** affirm, analyze, ascertain, attest, authenticate, back, certify, check, confirm, determine, document, establish, evince, explain, find, justify, manifest, result, settle, show, test, testify, try, uphold, validate, verify, warrant; ▪ **Ant**

contradict, hypothesize, rule out, theorize.

proverbial [adj] *conventional, traditional* ▪ **Syn** accepted, acknowledged, common, current, customary, familiar, general, self-evident, time-honored, typical, unquestioned, well-known; ▪ **Ant** abnormal, different, fresh, original, unconventional, untraditional.

provide [v] *supply, support* ▪ **Syn** administer, afford, arrange, bestow, cater, contribute, dispense, equip, feed, fix up, furnish, give, grant, impart, implement, keep, lend, maintain, outfit, prepare, procure, proffer, provision, ration, render, replenish, serve, supply, sustain, take care of, yield; ▪ **Ant** deprive, remove, take.

provident [adj] *careful, frugal* ▪ **Syn** cautious, discreet, economical, expedient, far-sighted, judicious, politic, prudent, saving, shrewd, sparing, thrifty, tight, unwasteful, vigilant, well-prepared, wise; ▪ **Ant** careless, improvident, spendthrift, wasteful.

providing/provided [conj] *as long as; with the understanding* ▪ **Syn** contingent upon, given, if, in case, in the event, on the assumption, on these terms, subject to, supposing, with the proviso; ▪ **Ant** independent of, unrelated to.

provincial [adj] *countrified; limited* ▪ **Syn** bigoted, bucolic, hidebound, homespun, insular, local, narrow, narrow-minded, parochial, pastoral, rustic, sectarian, small-minded, small-town, unsophisticated; ▪ **Ant** citified, cosmopolitan, liberal, modern.

provisional [adj] *contingent, tentative* ▪ **Syn** conditional, dependent, ephemeral, experimental, interim, limited, makeshift, passing, provisionary, qualified, temporary, transient, transitional; ▪ **Ant** certain, definite, permanent.

provocative [adj1] *aggravating* ▪ **Syn** annoying, challenging, disturbing, galling, goading, heady, insulting, intoxicating, offensive, outrageous, provoking, spurring, stimulating; ▪ **Ant** delightful, moderate, soothing.

provocative [adj2] *sexually stimulating* ▪ **Syn** alluring, arousing, enchanting, erotic, heady, interesting, intoxicating, seductive, stimulating, suggestive, tantalizing, tempting; ▪ **Ant** drab, repellent, unexciting.

provoke [v1] *make angry* ▪ **Syn** aggravate, anger, bother, chafe, enrage, exasperate, foment, grate, incense, infuriate, madden, nag, offend, perturb, pique, rile, ruffle, upset, vex; ▪ **Ant** assuage, calm, delight, mollify, please.

provoke [v2] *start, evoke; stimulate* ▪ **Syn** arouse, awaken, bestir, call forth, draw forth, electrify, elicit, excite, fire, galvanize, generate, incite, inspire, instigate, motivate, occasion, pique, prime, prompt, quicken, rally, roust, stir, suscitate, thrill, titillate, waken, whet; ▪ **Ant** bore, deaden, dull.

prowess [n1] *ability, skill* ▪ **Syn** accomplishment, address, adeptness, adroitness, attainment, command, deftness, dexterity, expertise, facility, genius, mastery, readiness, talent; ▪ **Ant** inability, incompetence, weakness.

prowess [n2] *bravery* ▪ **Syn** boldness, courage, daring, dauntlessness, fearlessness, gallantry, heroism, intrepidity, mettle, nerve, pluck, spunk, valiancy, valor; ▪ **Ant** cowardice, fear, timidity, weakness.

proximity [n] *nearness to something* ▪ **Syn** adjacency, appropinquity, closeness, concurrence, contiguity, immediacy, juxtaposition, nearness, propinquity, togetherness; ▪ **Ant** distance, remoteness.

prudent [adj] *wise, sensible in action and thought* ▪ **Syn** advisable, canny, cautious, circumspect, discerning, economical, far-sighted, judicious, politic, reasonable, sagacious, sane, shrewd, sound, sparing, thrifty, vigilant, wary; ▪ **Ant** careless, heedless, imprudent, incautious, unwise.

prudish [adj] *shy and strict in behavior* ▪ **Syn** austere, bigoted, conventional, demure, fastidious, genteel, illiberal, mincing, narrow-minded, overmodest, precise, prim, proper, puritanical, rigid, scrupulous, severe, stilted, strait-laced, stuffy; ▪ **Ant** bold, brave, extroverted, outgoing.

pry [v1] *interfere in someone else's business* ▪ **Syn** be inquisitive, ferret out, intrude, listen in, meddle, nose, poke, ransack, reconnoiter, search, snoop, spy, tap, wiretap; ▪ **Ant** disregard, ignore, overlook, refrain form noticing.

pry [v2] *force or break open* ▪ **Syn** crack, disengage, divide, extort, extract, jimmy, lever, press, separate, take up, tilt, twist, uplift, wrench, wrest, wring; ▪ *Ant* close.

pseudo [*adj*] *artificial, fake*
▪ *Syn* bogus, counterfeit, ersatz, false, imitation, mock, phony, pretended, simulated, spurious, wrong; ▪ *Ant* genuine, real, true.

pseudonym [*n*] *false name*
▪ *Syn* alias, ananym, anonym, assumed name, nickname, nom de guerre, nom de plume, pen name, professional name, stage name; ▪ *Ant* name.

psyche [*n*] *innermost self; personality*
▪ *Syn* anima, character, ego, essential nature, individuality, inner child, lan vital, mind, pneuma, soul, spirit, subconscious, true being; ▪ *Ant* body, physicality.

psychological [*adj*] *concerning the mind* ▪ *Syn* cerebral, cognitive, intellective, in the mind, mental, psychical, psychosomatic, subconscious, subjective, unconscious; ▪ *Ant* physical.

puberty [*n*] *young adulthood*
▪ *Syn* adolescence, high-school years, juvenescence, juvenility, pubescence, teenage years, teens, youth, youthfulness; ▪ *Ant* adulthood, childhood.

public [*adj1*] *community, general*
▪ *Syn* accessible, communal, conjunct, federal, free to all, governmental, mutual, open, popular, social, universal, unrestricted, urban, widespread, without charge; ▪ *Ant* particular, private, specific.

public [*adj2*] *known, acknowledged*
▪ *Syn* exposed, general, notorious, obvious, open, overt, patent, popular, prevalent, recognized, widespread; ▪ *Ant* private, unknown.

publicize [*v*] *make widely known; promote* ▪ *Syn* advance, advertise, announce, bill, broadcast, cry, extol, headline, immortalize, make a pitch for, pitch, promulgate, propagandize, spread, tout, write up; ▪ *Ant* conceal, hide, secret.

pucker [*v*] *draw together; wrinkle*
▪ *Syn* cockle, condense, contract, crinkle, crumple, fold, furrow, gather, knit, pleat, purse, ruffle, tighten; ▪ *Ant* iron out, loosen, open, smooth.

pudgy [*adj*] *slightly fat*
▪ *Syn* chubby, dumpy, hefty, plump, plumpish, rotund, round, stout, thick-bodied; ▪ *Ant* skinny, slight, thin.

puerile [*adj*] *childish*
▪ *Syn* babyish, callow, foolish, immature,

inane, inexperienced, infantile, jejune, juvenile, naive, petty, ridiculous, silly, trivial, unfledged, weak; ▪ *Ant* adult, mature, rational.

puff [*v*] *publicize*
▪ *Syn* admire, advertise, build, commend, congratulate, flatter, overpraise, praise, promote, push; ▪ *Ant* conceal, hide, secret.

puffy [*adj*] *swollen*
▪ *Syn* billowy, bloated, bulgy, distended, distent, enlarged, expanded, increased, inflamed, inflated, puffed up; ▪ *Ant* contracted, flat, shrunken, tight.

pugnacious [*adj*] *belligerent*
▪ *Syn* aggressive, antagonistic, bellicose, combative, contentious, defiant, disputatious, hot-tempered, irascible, militant, petulant, quarrelsome, rebellious, self-assertive, truculent, warlike; ▪ *Ant* calm, easy-going, kind, laid-back, peaceful.

pull [*v1*] *drawing something with force*
▪ *Syn* cull, dislocate, drag, extract, gather, rend, rip, strain, stretch, tug, twitch, uproot, wrench, yank; ▪ *Ant* push, shove.

pull [*v2*] *attract*
▪ *Syn* draw, entice, get, lure, magnetize, obtain, pick up, secure, win; ▪ *Ant* deter, repel, repulse.

pull down [*v*] *destroy; knock over*
▪ *Syn* annihilate, bulldoze, decimate, demolish, destruct, dismantle, raze, ruin, tear down, wreck; ▪ *Ant* build, construct.

pull in [*v1*] *arrest*
▪ *Syn* apprehend, bust, collar, detain, nab, nail, pick up, pinch, run in, take into custody; ▪ *Ant* exonerate, free, let go.

pull in [*v2*] *attract, obtain*
▪ *Syn* absorb, bring in, clear, draw, draw in, earn, gain, gross, make, net, pocket, suck; ▪ *Ant* repel, throw away.

pull off [*v*] *accomplish*
▪ *Syn* achieve, bring off, carry out, manage, score a success, secure, succeed, win; ▪ *Ant* fail.

pull out [*v*] *quit*
▪ *Syn* abandon, depart, evacuate, go, leave, retreat, shove off, stop, withdraw; ▪ *Ant* continue, persevere, start.

pull through [*v*] *recover*
▪ *Syn* come through, get better, get over, improve, rally, survive, triumph; ▪ *Ant* die, fail, lose.

pulp [*adj*] *cheap, vulgar, especially regarding reading material* ▪ *Syn* lurid, mushy, rubbish, sensational, trash, trashy; ▪ *Ant* clean, moral.

pulverize [v] *destroy*
▪ *Syn* annihilate, crush, decimate, dynamite, flatten, ruin, shatter, smash, vanquish, vaporize, wax, wreck; ▪ *Ant* build, construct, create.

pump [v] *question relentlessly*
▪ *Syn* cross-examine, grill, interrogate, probe, query, question, quiz; ▪ *Ant* answer, reply, respond.

punch [n] *energy, vigor*
▪ *Syn* bite, cogency, drive, effectiveness, force, impact, point, validity, verve; ▪ *Ant* idleness, lethargy, unenthusiasm.

punctilious [adj] *careful, finicky*
▪ *Syn* ceremonious, conventional, exact, formal, fussy, heedful, meticulous, observant, painstaking, persnickety, punctual, scrupulous, strict; ▪ *Ant* careless, easygoing, informal, negligent, uncaring.

punctual [adj] *on time*
▪ *Syn* accurate, careful, conscientious, conscionable, constant, dependable, early, expeditious, heedful, meticulous, on schedule, painstaking, precise, punctilious, quick, ready, recurrent, reliable, scrupulous, seasonable, strict, timely; ▪ *Ant* late, tardy.

puncture [v] *poke hole in*
▪ *Syn* bore, cut, cut through, deflate, drill, knife, lacerate, lance, nick, open, penetrate, perforate, pierce, prick, punch, riddle, rupture; ▪ *Ant* close, sew.

pundit [n] *person who is authority*
▪ *Syn* auger, buff, cognoscenti, expert, intellectual, learned one, maestro, maven, savant, scholar, thinker; ▪ *Ant* amateur, novice, tyro.

pungent [adj1] *highly flavored*
▪ *Syn* acid, acrid, aromatic, bitter, effluvious, hot, odoriferous, peppery, piquant, poignant, rich, seasoned, sharp, snappy, stinging, strong, tangy, tart, zesty; ▪ *Ant* blah, bland, dull, flavorless, tasteless.

pungent [adj2] *sharp, stinging in speech*
▪ *Syn* acrimonious, barbed, biting, caustic, incisive, keen, mordant, penetrating, peppery, piercing, poignant, provocative, racy, salty, sarcastic, scathing, snappy, spicy, stimulating, trenchant, zesty; ▪ *Ant* dull, mild, moderate.

punish [v] *penalize for wrongdoing*
▪ *Syn* castigate, chasten, correct, debar, defrock, discipline, exile, expel, fine, flog, immure, incarcerate, lash, lecture, misuse, oppress, paddle, reprove, sentence, teach a lesson; ▪ *Ant* award, excuse, exonerate, let go, pardon, praise, protect, reward.

punitive [adj] *concerning punishment*
▪ *Syn* castigating, correctional, disciplinary, in reprisal, in retaliation, penal, punishing, retaliative, retaliatory, vindictive; ▪ *Ant* beneficial, rewarding.

puny [adj] *small, insignificant*
▪ *Syn* diminutive, dwarfish, feeble, inconsequential, inferior, infirm, little, minor, paltry, petty, picayune, runt, stunted, tiny, trifling, underfed, weak, worthless; ▪ *Ant* big, giant, huge, large.

pupil [n] *person who is learning something* ▪ *Syn* adherent, attendant, beginner, catechumen, disciple, follower, freshman, junior, learner, neophyte, novice, satellite, scholar, student, undergraduate; ▪ *Ant* professor, teacher.

purchase [v] *buy, obtain* .
▪ *Syn* acquire, attain, come by, gain, invest, patronize, pay for, procure, realize, redeem, secure, take, take up, win; ▪ *Ant* divest, liquidate, sell.

pure [adj1] *unmixed, genuine*
▪ *Syn* authentic, classic, flawless, lucid, natural, pellucid, perfect, simple, total, transparent, true, unadulterated, undiluted; ▪ *Ant* impure, mixed, ungenuine.

pure [adj2] *clean, uncontaminated*
▪ *Syn* disinfected, germ-free, immaculate, pasteurized, pristine, refined, sanitary, spotless, sterile, taintless, unadulterated, unsoiled, untainted, untarnished, wholesome; ▪ *Ant* contaminated, dirty, polluted, tainted.

pure [adj3] *virginal, chaste*
▪ *Syn* blameless, celibate, clean, continent, decent, exemplary, fresh, good, guileless, honest, immaculate, inculpable, innocent, inviolate, irreproachable, modest, righteous, sinless, spotless, stainless, true, uncorrupted, upright, virgin, virtuous; ▪ *Ant* corrupt, dirty, immodest, indecent, obscene, unchaste, vulgar.

pure [adj4] *absolute, utter*
▪ *Syn* complete, confounded, mere, out-and-out, sheer, thorough, unmitigated, unqualified; ▪ *Ant* indefinite, uncertain.

pure [adj5] *theoretical*
▪ *Syn* abstract, academic, philosophical, speculative, tentative, unproved; ▪ *Ant* applied, practical.

purely [adv] *simply, absolutely*
▪ *Syn* all, all in all, altogether, barely,

completely, entirely, essentially, exactly, exclusively, just, merely, only, plainly, quite, solely, totally, utterly, wholly; ▪ *Ant* moderately, partially.

purge [v] *rid of; clean out; forgive*
▪ *Syn* abolish, absolve, clarify, cleanse, clear, depurate, dismiss, dispose of, eject, eradicate, erase, excrete, exonerate, expel, expiate, expunge, exterminate, forgive, oust, pardon, purify, remove, rout out, sweep out, wash, wipe out; ▪ *Ant* hold, keep, maintain.

purify [v] *free; make clean*
▪ *Syn* absolve, clarify, cleanse, clear, decontaminate, depurate, disinfect, exculpate, exonerate, expiate, filter, fumigate, lustrate, purge, rarify, refine, sanctify, sanitize, shrive, wash; ▪ *Ant* adulterate, corrupt, dirty, pollute.

purposeful [adj] *resolved to do something* ▪ *Syn* bent, bound, decided, determined, firm, fixed, intent, obstinate, persistent, resolute, single-minded, stalwart, staunch, steadfast, strong-willed, stubborn, telelogical, tenacious, unwavering; ▪ *Ant* aimless, thoughtless, undetermined, unplanned, wanton, wavering.

purposely [adv] *intentionally*
▪ *Syn* advisedly, by design, calculatedly, consciously, deliberately, designedly, explicitly, expressly, knowingly, on purpose, prepensely, purposedly, willfully, with intent; ▪ *Ant* impulsively, spontaneously, unintentionally.

purse [v] *press together*
▪ *Syn* close, cockle, contract, crease, knit, pucker, ruffle, tighten, wrinkle; ▪ *Ant* open, smooth.

pursue [v1] *chase, follow*
▪ *Syn* badger, bait, bug, chivy, give chase, go after, harass, harry, haunt, hound, hunt, hunt down, plague, prowl after, run after, run down, search for, search out, seek, shadow, stalk, trace, track down, trail; ▪ *Ant* retreat, run away.

pursue [v2] *have as one's goal*
▪ *Syn* aim for, aspire to, attempt, desire, seek, strive for, try for, work for, work toward; ▪ *Ant* eschew, ignore, shun.

pursue [v3] *persist, persevere*
▪ *Syn* adhere, apply oneself, carry on, conduct, continue, cultivate, engage in, hold to, keep on, maintain, perform, ply, practice, proceed, prosecute, see through,

tackle, wage, work at; ▪ *Ant* discontinue, give up, stop.

push [v1] *thrust, press with force*
▪ *Syn* accelerate, bear down, bump, butt, crowd, drive, elbow, exert, force, gore, hustle, impel, jam, jostle, launch, muscle, nudge, poke, pressure, propel, shift, shoulder, shove, stir, strain; ▪ *Ant* drag, pull, tow.

push [v2] *incite, urge*
▪ *Syn* browbeat, coerce, constrain, dragoon, encourage, exert influence, expedite, goad, hurry, impel, influence, inspire, motivate, oblige, persuade, press, pressure, prod, spur; ▪ *Ant* discourage, dissuade, repress, suppress.

push [v3] *advertise, promote*
▪ *Syn* advance, boost, make known, propagandize, publicize; ▪ *Ant* conceal, hide.

push off/push on [v] *leave; go to another place* ▪ *Syn* continue, depart, exit, go, hie, journey, keep going, launch, light out, pass, quit, repair, start, take off, travel, wend, withdraw; ▪ *Ant* arrive, come.

pushy [adj] *aggressive, offensive*
▪ *Syn* ambitious, assertive, bold, brash, bumptious, forceful, loud, militant, obnoxious, obtrusive, officious, presumptuous, pushful, pushing, self-assertive; ▪ *Ant* modest, quiet, shy, unassuming.

pussyfoot [v] *walk or act very carefully*
▪ *Syn* avoid, dodge, evade, hedge, sidestep, tergiversate, tergiverse, tiptoe, tread warily; ▪ *Ant* confront, decide, face.

put [v1] *position*
▪ *Syn* bring, concentrate, deposit, down, embed, establish, fasten, fix, focus, insert, invest, lay, nail, park, peg, plank down, plop, quarter, repose, rest, rivet, set, settle, situate, stick; ▪ *Ant* remove, take.

put [v2] *commit, assign*
▪ *Syn* condemn, constrain, doom, employ, force, impose, inflict, levy, make, oblige, require, set, subject, subject to; ▪ *Ant* change, displace, transfer.

putative [adj] *commonly believed*
▪ *Syn* accepted, alleged, assumed, conjectural, hypothetical, imputed, presumed, reported, reputed, supposed, suppositional, suppositious; ▪ *Ant* proven, real, true.

put away/put aside/put by [v1/v] *keep in reserve* ▪ *Syn* cache, deposit, lay aside, lay away, put by, save, set aside, stockpile, store, stow away; ▪ *Ant* spend, use up, waste.

put away [*v2*] *incarcerate*
▪ *Syn* certify, commit, confine, institutionalize, jail, lock up; ▪ *Ant* free, liberate.

put away [*v3*] *consume*
▪ *Syn* devour, eat up, gulp down, punish, put down, shift, swill; ▪ *Ant* abstain, refrain.

put away [*v4*] *kill*
▪ *Syn* assassinate, bury, cut off, destroy, dispatch, do away with, execute, finish, inter, liquidate, murder, plant, slay, tomb; ▪ *Ant* give birth, heal, protect.

put down [*v1*] *write into record*
▪ *Syn* enter, inscribe, jot down, log, record, set down, take down, transcribe, write down; ▪ *Ant* erase, extract.

put down [*v2*] *comment negatively*
▪ *Syn* belittle, condemn, deflate, derogate, disparage, humiliate, minimize, mortify, opprobriate, run down, shame, slight, snub, write off; ▪ *Ant* build up, compliment, flatter, praise.

put off [*v*] *defer, delay*
▪ *Syn* adjourn, dally, dawdle, hold off, lay over, linger, loiter, postpone, procrastinate, reschedule, retard, shelve, suspend, tarry, trail; ▪ *Ant* accomplish, achieve, carry out, do, succeed.

put on [*v*] *pretend*
▪ *Syn* act, affect, assume, bluff, confound, deceive, don, feign, make believe, masquerade, playact, pose, put on an act, sham, simulate, take on, trick; ▪ *Ant* be truthful.

put out [*v*] *upset, irritate; inconvenience*
▪ *Syn* aggravate, annoy, bother, burn, confound, discomfit, discountenance, displease, dissatisfy, disturb, embarrass, exasperate, gall, grate, harass, impose upon, incommode, inflame, nettle, perturb, rile, trouble, vex; ▪ *Ant* assuage, help, please.

putrid [*adj*] *rotten, stinking*
▪ *Syn* contaminated, corrupt, decayed, decomposed, fetid, foul, high, malodorous, noisome, putrefied, rancid, reeking, rotting, smelly, spoiled, tainted; ▪ *Ant* fresh, perfumed, sweet.

putter [*v*] *dawdle*
▪ *Syn* doodle, fiddle, fritter, loiter, mess, niggle, shuffle around; ▪ *Ant* execute, expedite.

put up [*v*] *build, erect*
▪ *Syn* construct, fabricate, forge, make, put together, raise, rear, shape; ▪ *Ant* destroy, ruin.

puzzle [*v1*] *baffle, confuse*
▪ *Syn* addle, amaze, befog, befuddle, bewilder, confound, disconcert, dumbfound, flabbergast, foil, frustrate, mystify, nonplus, obscure, perplex, rattle, stir, stump, throw; ▪ *Ant* clarify, elucidate, explain, illustrate, unravel.

puzzle [*v2*] *wonder about*
▪ *Syn* ask oneself, brood, cudgel, marvel, mull over, muse, ponder, study, think about, think hard; ▪ *Ant* ignore.

puzzled [*adj*] *confused*
▪ *Syn* baffled, bewildered, clueless, doubtful, foggy, lost, mystified, nonplussed, perplexed, rattled, shook, stumped, thrown, without a clue; ▪ *Ant* aware, certain, cognizant, sure.

puzzling [*adj*] *very confusing*
▪ *Syn* abstruse, ambiguous, baffling, bewildering, difficult, enigmatic, hard, inexplicable, knotty, labyrinthine, mystifying, obscure, perplexing, surprising; ▪ *Ant* comprehendible, intelligible, understandable.

Q

quack [*adj*] *counterfeit*
▪ *Syn* dishonest, dissembling, fake, false, fraudulent, phony, pretended, simulated, unprincipled; ▪ *Ant* genuine, original, real.

quaff [*v*] *drink down*
▪ *Syn* down, gulp, guzzle, imbibe, ingurgitate, partake, sip, sup, swallow, swig, swill, toss; ▪ *Ant* eject.

quagmire [*n1*] *bad situation*
▪ *Syn* dilemma, entanglement, fix, imbroglio, impasse, jam, mire, muddle, perplexity, predicament, quandary, scrape, trouble; ▪ *Ant* blessing, solution, success.

quail [*v*] *cower, shrink*
▪ *Syn* blanch, cringe, droop, faint, falter, flinch, quake, recoil, shake, shudder, tremble, wince; ▪ *Ant* face, meet.

quaint [*adj1*] *strange, odd*
▪ *Syn* bizarre, curious, droll, eccentric, fanciful, idiosyncratic, oddball, offbeat, original, peculiar, singular, unusual, whimsical; ▪ *Ant* common, conventional, regular, usual.

quaint [adj2] *old-fashioned; nostalgically attractive* ▪ *Syn* antiquated, archaic, baroque, charming, colonial, cute, enchanting, fanciful, ingenious, old-world, picturesque, whimsical; ▪ *Ant* current, new, new-fangled, up-to-date.

quake [v] *shake, vibrate* ▪ *Syn* convulse, cower, fluctuate, jar, move, pulsate, quiver, rock, shiver, shudder, tremble, tremor, twitter, waver, wobble; ▪ *Ant* be still.

qualified [adj1] *able, skillful* ▪ *Syn* accomplished, adept, capable, certified, competent, efficient, equipped, experienced, expert, fit, knowledgeable, licensed, practiced, proficient, proved, talented, tested, trained, tried, veteran; ▪ *Ant* incapable, inept, unqualified, unskilled.

qualified [adj2] *limited, restricted* ▪ *Syn* bounded, circumscribed, conditional, confined, contingent, definite, determined, equivocal, fixed, guarded, modified, partial, provisional, reserved; ▪ *Ant* open, unlimited, unrestricted.

qualify [v1] *make or become ready, prepared* ▪ *Syn* authorize, capacitate, certify, check out, commission, condition, empower, enable, endow, entitle, equip, fit, ground, measure up, meet, pass, permit, prepare, ready, sanction, score, suffice, suit, train; ▪ *Ant* be unprepared, disqualify.

qualify [v2] *lessen, restrict* ▪ *Syn* abate, adapt, alter, assuage, change, circumscribe, diminish, ease, lessen, limit, mitigate, moderate, modify, modulate, reduce, regulate, restrain, soften, temper, vary, weaken; ▪ *Ant* allow, be lenient.

qualm [n] *nagging doubt* ▪ *Syn* agitation, anxiety, apprehension, compunction, conscience, demur, disquiet, doubt, foreboding, hesitation, indecision, insecurity, misgiving, nervousness, objection, pang, presentiment, regret, reluctance, remorse, scruple, suspicion, twinge, unease; ▪ *Ant* approval, comfort, contentedness, inclination, willingness.

quandary [n] *delicate situation* ▪ *Syn* bewilderment, bind, clutch, difficulty, dilemma, doubt, embarrassment, impasse, mire, perplexity, plight, predicament, puzzle, strait, uncertainty; ▪ *Ant* advantage, certainty, ease, resolution, solution.

quarrel [v] *disagree* ▪ *Syn* altercate, argue, battle, bicker, brawl, break with, carp, caterwaul, cavil, clash, collide, differ, dispute, dissent, embroil, feud, fight, find fault, hassle, row, scrap, set to, spar, spat, squabble, struggle, take exception, tangle, vary, war, wrangle; ▪ *Ant* agree, assent, concur, make peace.

quarrelsome [adj] *being disagreeable* ▪ *Syn* argumentative, bad-tempered, bellicose, brawling, choleric, churlish, contentious, disputatious, dissentious, excitable, fiery, fractious, hasty, impassioned, irascible, ornery, peevish, petulant, querulous, ructious, snappy, tempestuous, truculent, unruly; ▪ *Ant* agreeable, forgiving, friendly, good-natured, happy, patient.

quarter [n] *forgiveness* ▪ *Syn* clemency, compassion, favor, grace, leniency, lenity, mercy, pity; ▪ *Ant* disfavor, mercilessness.

quash [v1] *destroy, defeat* ▪ *Syn* annihilate, beat, crush, extinguish, extirpate, overcome, overthrow, put down, quell, quench, repress, subdue, suppress, trash; ▪ *Ant* aid, assist, help, rebuild.

quash [v2] *nullify, cancel* ▪ *Syn* abrogate, annul, clamp down on, discharge, dissolve, invalidate, kill, negate, overrule, overthrow, repeal, rescind, reverse, revoke, set aside, shut down, squelch, undo, vacate, veto, vitiate, void; ▪ *Ant* allow, permit, sanction, start, support.

quasi [adj] *almost; to a certain extent* ▪ *Syn* apparent, apparently, fake, mock, near, nominal, partly, pretended, seeming, seemingly, semi-, so-called, supposedly, synthetic, virtual; ▪ *Ant* entire, total, true, whole.

queasy [adj] *not feeling well; not comfortable* ▪ *Syn* anxious, bilious, concerned, fidgety, groggy, ill, indisposed, nauseated, sick, sickly, squeamish, troubled, uncomfortable, upset; ▪ *Ant* comfortable, healthy, satisfied.

queer [adj1] *very odd; abnormal* ▪ *Syn* anomalous, atypical, bizarre, curious, disquieting, dubious, eccentric, eerie, funny, idiosyncratic, mysterious, oddball, outlandish, peculiar, puzzling, quaint, remarkable, shady, singular, strange, suspicious, touched, weird; ▪ *Ant* common, natural, normal, orthodox, regular, typical, usual.

queer [*adj2*] *not feeling well*
▪ *Syn* dizzy, faint, giddy, ill, light-headed, qualmish, reeling, sick, uneasy; ▪ *Ant* healthy, well.

quell [*v1*] *defeat, suppress*
▪ *Syn* annihilate, conquer, extinguish, kill, overcome, overpower, put down, quench, shut down, silence, stifle, stop, subdue, subjugate, vanquish; ▪ *Ant* defend, encourage, foster.

quell [*v2*] *alleviate, calm*
▪ *Syn* allay, appease, assuage, check, compose, deaden, ease, mitigate, mollify, pacify, quiet, reduce, silence, soothe, still; ▪ *Ant* aggravate, agitate, disturb, irritate, perturb.

quench [*v1*] *destroy, extinguish*
▪ *Syn* annihilate, choke, crush, dampen, decimate, demolish, destruct, dismantle, end, knock down, put out, quell, smother, stifle, suppress, wreck; ▪ *Ant* enflame, kindle, set, start.

quench [*v2*] *satisfy (used of thirst)*
▪ *Syn* allay, alleviate, assuage, glut, gorge, gratify, mitigate, moisten, relieve, sate, slake; ▪ *Ant* intensify, pique.

querulous [*adj*] *grouchy, hard to please*
▪ *Syn* bearish, bemoaning, cantankerous, captious, carping, censorious, complaining, critical, cross, crying, discontented, dissatisfied, edgy, fault-finding, fretful, grousing, grumbling, irritable, petulant, plaintive, scrappy, snappy, sour, testy, uptight, wailing, waspish, whining, whiny; ▪ *Ant* cheerful, complacent, easy-going, happy.

query [*v*] *ask; doubt*
▪ *Syn* catechize, challenge, dispute, distrust, enquire, examine, impeach, impugn, inquire, interrogate, quiz; ▪ *Ant* answer, reply.

question [*v*] *ask for answer*
▪ *Syn* ask about, challenge, cross-examine, enquire, examine, grill, inquire, interrogate, interview, investigate, make inquiry, petition, probe, pry, pump, query, quest, quiz, search, seek, solicit; ▪ *Ant* answer, reply.

questionable [*adj*] *doubtful, uncertain*
▪ *Syn* ambiguous, apocryphal, arguable, contingent, controversial, cryptic, debatable, disputable, dubious, dubitable, enigmatic, equivocal, hypothetical, indecisive, indefinite, indeterminate, moot, mysterious, obscure, occult, paradoxical, problematic, provisional, suspect, suspicious, under examination, unreliable, vague; ▪ *Ant* certain, definite, indisputable, proven, sure, undoubted, unquestionable.

queue [*n*] *sequence*
▪ *Syn* chain, concatenation, echelon, file, line, order, progression, rank, row, series, string, succession, tail, tier, train; ▪ *Ant* chaos, disorganization.

quibble [*v*] *disagree over minor issues*
▪ *Syn* altercate, argue over, bicker, carp, chicane, dispute, equivocate, hassle, paralogize, pretend, prevaricate, shift, spar, squabble, talk back, waffle, wrangle; ▪ *Ant* agree, approve, concur.

quick [*adj1*] *fast, speedy*
▪ *Syn* abrupt, accelerated, alert, animated, brief, brisk, cursory, energetic, fleet, hasty, headlong, impetuous, keen, lively, mercurial, nimble, perfunctory, rapid, snappy, spry, sudden, swift; ▪ *Ant* lazy, slow, sluggish.

quick [*adj2*] *very smart*
▪ *Syn* able, active, adroit, apt, bright, canny, clever, competent, deft, effective, intelligent, keen, nimble-witted, perceptive, perspicacious, quick-witted, receptive, savvy, sharp, shrewd, skillful, vigorous, wise; ▪ *Ant* ignorant, slow, stupid, uneducated.

quicken [*v*] *make faster; invigorate*
▪ *Syn* accelerate, awaken, energize, excite, expedite, galvanize, goad, hasten, hurry, increase, inspire, kindle, liven, motivate, pique, precipitate, promote, rouse, shake up, spur, step up, stimulate, stir, urge, vitalize, vivify; ▪ *Ant* dull, retard, slow, weaken.

quick-tempered [*adj*] *easily upset, angered* ▪ *Syn* choleric, hot-tempered, impulsive, irascible, irritable, peppery, petulant, quarrelsome, sensitive, short-tempered, shrewish, splenetic, temperamental, testy, waspish; ▪ *Ant* calm, cool, easy-going, even-tempered, laid-back.

quick-witted [*adj*] *very smart*
▪ *Syn* acute, alert, apt, bright, canny, clever, humorous, intelligent, keen, nimble-witted, perceptive, quick, ready, savvy, sharp-witted, shrewd, wise, witty; ▪ *Ant* dull, slow-witted, stupid, uneducated.

quiet [adj1] *without or with little sound*
▪ *Syn* close, hushed, inaudible, low-pitched, muffled, mute, noiseless, peaceful, quiescent, quieted, reserved, silent, still, taciturn; ▪ *Ant* boisterous, clamorous, loud, noisy.

quiet [adj2] *calm, peaceful*
▪ *Syn* collected, contented, gentle, halcyon, level, mild, pacific, reserved, restful, serene, smooth, still, tranquil; ▪ *Ant* agitated, excited, perturbed, troubled.

quiet [adj3] *simple, unobtrusive*
▪ *Syn* conservative, homely, inobtrusive, modest, plain, restrained, sober, subdued, tasteful; ▪ *Ant* complex, complicated, intricate, obtrusive.

quiet [v] *make silent, calm*
▪ *Syn* allay, appease, assuage, becalm, compose, console, gratify, hush, lull, moderate, muffle, pacify, quieten, reconcile, relax, shush, silence, soften, squelch, still, stroke, subdue, tranquilize; ▪ *Ant* agitate, disturb, stir.

quit [v1] *abandon, leave*
▪ *Syn* abdicate, bow out, decamp, desert, evacuate, exit, forsake, give up, pull out, relinquish, resign, retire, surrender, take off, vacate, withdraw, yield; ▪ *Ant* come, remain, stay.

quit [v2] *stop doing something*
▪ *Syn* abandon, break off, cease, discontinue, drop, end, give notice, give up, halt, leave, resign, secede, surcease, terminate, withdraw; ▪ *Ant* complete, continue, do, finish, persevere.

quite [adv] *completely*
▪ *Syn* absolutely, all in all, altogether, entirely, fully, in all respects, in fact, in reality, in toto, in truth, largely, perfectly, positively, really, thoroughly, totally, utterly, well, wholly, without reservation; ▪ *Ant* incompletely.

quiver [v] *shake, vibrate*
▪ *Syn* agitate, convulse, dither, jitter, oscillate, palpitate, pulsate, quake, quaver, shiver, shudder, thrill, throb, tremble, twitter; ▪ *Ant* be still.

quiz [v] *question*
▪ *Syn* ask, catechize, check, cross-examine, examine, inquire, interrogate, investigate, query, test; ▪ *Ant* answer, reply.

quizzical [adj] *appearing confused or curious* ▪ *Syn* amusing, bantering, curious, eccentric, incredulous, mocking, odd, probing, quaint, queer, sardonic, supercilious, suspicious, teasing, unusual; ▪ *Ant* indifferent, uninterested.

quotation/quote [n] *repetition of something spoken or written by someone* ▪ *Syn* citation, excerpt, extract, passage, recitation, reference, saying, selection; ▪ *Ant* paraphrase, recapitulation, restatement, summary.

R

rabid [adj] *very angry; maniacal*
▪ *Syn* berserk, crazy, delirious, deranged, enthusiastic, fanatical, fervent, frenetic, furious, hydrophobic, insane, intemperate, keen, mad, obsessed, poisoned, raging, ultraist, violent, virulent, wild, zealous; ▪ *Ant* calm, quiet, rational, sane, tame.

race [v] *run, speed in competition*
▪ *Syn* bolt, bustle, chase, course, dart, dash, fly, gallop, hasten, hie, hurry, hustle, post, rush, scramble, scud, scuttle, shoot, sprint, tear, whisk, wing; ▪ *Ant* crawl, creep, saunter, walk.

rack [v] *torture; strain*
▪ *Syn* afflict, agonize, crucify, distress, harass, harrow, martyr, oppress, pain, persecute, tear, torment, try, wrench, wring; ▪ *Ant* cheer, comfort, please, pleasure, soothe.

racket [n] *commotion; fight*
▪ *Syn* agitation, babel, clamor, clangor, commotion, din, disturbance, fracas, fuss, jangle, noise, outcry, pandemonium, riot, shouting, stir, tumult, turbulence, turmoil, uproar, vociferation, wrangle; ▪ *Ant* harmony, peace, quiet, silence.

racy [adj1] *energetic, zestful*
▪ *Syn* animated, bright, buoyant, clever, distinctive, entertaining, exciting, fiery, forceful, heady, keen, lively, peppery, playful, rich, saucy, sharp, snappy, sparkling, spicy, spirited, sportive, tangy, vigorous, vivacious, witty, zesty; ▪ *Ant* dull, idle, languid, lazy, morose.

racy [adj2] *risqué, vulgar*
▪ *Syn* bawdy, broad, erotic, immodest, indecent, indelicate, lewd, lurid, naughty, suggestive, wicked; ▪ *Ant* clean, decent, inoffensive, modest, moral, upright.

radiant [adj1] *bright, luminous*
▪ *Syn* beaming, brilliant, effulgent, gleaming, glittering, glowing, incandes-

cent, lambent, lucent, radiating, reful-gent, shining, sunny; ▪ **Ant** cloudy, dark, dim, dull.

radiant [adj2] *happy in appearance*
▪ **Syn** beaming, beatific, blissful, bright, cheery, delighted, ecstatic, gay, glad, glowing, joyful, joyous, rapturous; ▪ **Ant** downcast, frowning, glum, sad, somber.

radiate [v] *give off; scatter*
▪ **Syn** beam, branch out, diffuse, dissem-inate, distribute, diverge, emanate, emit, expand, gleam, glitter, illumine, irradi-ate, issue, light up, proliferate, propagate, ramify, send out, shed, shine, spread, spread out, sprinkle, strew, throw out, transmit, yield; ▪ **Ant** collect, converge, gather, unite.

radical [adj1] *fundamental, basic*
▪ **Syn** basal, bottom, cardinal, constitu-tional, deep-seated, essential, inherent, innate, intrinsic, native, natural, organic, original, primal, primary, primitive, pro-found, underlying, vital; ▪ **Ant** extrinsic, nonessential, superficial, trivial.

radical [adj2] *deviating by extremes*
▪ **Syn** anarchistic, excessive, extremist, fanatical, freethinking, iconoclastic, im-moderate, insurgent, militant, mutinous, nihilistic, progressive, rabid, rebellious, recalcitrant, revolutionary, seditious, se-vere, sweeping, thorough, uncompro-mising, violent; ▪ **Ant** conservative, moderate.

raffish [adj] *unmindful of social conven-tions* ▪ **Syn** careless, casual, coarse, dash-ing, disreputable, jaunty, meretricious, rakish, sporty, tasteless, tawdry, uncon-ventional, uncouth, vulgar; ▪ **Ant** be-haved, couth, elegant, proper, subdued, tasteful.

ragamuffin [n] *person who is poor, tat-tered* ▪ **Syn** beggar, gamin, hobo, loafer, orphan, scarecrow, street person, tramp, urchin, vagabond, vagrant, waif, wastrel; ▪ **Ant** sophisticate.

rage [v] *be very angry*
▪ **Syn** chafe, erupt, fret, fulminate, fume, go berserk, have a fit, have a tantrum, make a fuss over, rail at, rampage, rant, rave, roar, scold, scream, seethe, snap at, storm, surge, tear, yell; ▪ **Ant** be happy.

ragged [adj] *worn-out; in shreds*
▪ **Syn** badly dressed, battered, crude, des-ultory, dilapidated, frayed, frazzled, in rags, jagged, moth-eaten, notched, patched, poorly made, rent, rough, rug-ged, scraggy, seedy, shabby, shaggy, shoddy, shredded, tattered, threadbare, torn, unkempt; ▪ **Ant** even, kempt, new, smooth.

raid [v] *attack, pillage*
▪ **Syn** assail, assault, bombard, breach, charge, descend on, fall upon, fire on, forage, harass, invade, loot, maraud, march on, overrun, pirate, plunder, ran-sack, rob, sack, shell, spoliate, storm, sweep, waste; ▪ **Ant** aid, assist, guard, help, protect.

rail [v] *criticize harshly*
▪ **Syn** abuse, attack, berate, castigate, censure, complain, fulminate, fume, in-veigh, objurate, rant, rate, revile, scold, thunder, upbraid, vituperate, vociferate, whip; ▪ **Ant** compliment, praise.

rain [n] *downpour of water or other substance* ▪ **Syn** cloudburst, deluge, driz-zle, flood, hail, mist, monsoon, pour, precipitation, rainfall, rainstorm, shower, showers, sleet, spit, sprinkle, sprinkling, stream, torrent; ▪ **Ant** aridity, drought, dryness.

raise [v1] *lift; build from the ground*
▪ **Syn** boost, bring up, construct, erect, establish, heave, hoist, lever, lift up, mount, move up, promote, pull up, put up, rear, shove, stand up, take up, uplift; ▪ **Ant** demolish, destroy, drop, lower, raze.

raise [v2] *increase, augment*
▪ **Syn** advance, aggravate, amplify, boost, build up, enhance, enlarge, escalate, ex-aggerate, gather, heighten, hike, inflate, intensify, jack up, levy, magnify, mass, muster, perk up, promote, put up, rally, recruit, strengthen, up; ▪ **Ant** decrease, depress, diminish, lessen, lower, reduce.

raise [v3] *start up, motivate; introduce*
▪ **Syn** abet, activate, arouse, awaken, broach, cause, evoke, excite, foment, foster, incite, instigate, kindle, moot, mo-tivate, provoke, put forward, resurrect, set on, stir up, suggest, whip up; ▪ **Ant** calm, quell, soothe.

raise [v4] *nurture, care for*
▪ **Syn** breed, bring up, cultivate, develop, foster, grow, nourish, nurse, plant, pro-duce, provide, rear, sow, suckle, support, train, wean; ▪ **Ant** abandon, destroy, eradicate, ignore, neglect.

rakish [adj] *charming and immoral*
▪ **Syn** chic, dashing, debauched, de-praved, dissipated, fashionable, flashy,

gay, jaunty, licentious, natty, prodigal, profligate, raffish, saucy, sinful, wanton, wild; ▪ *Ant* clean, dowdy, moral, unstylish, upright.

rally [v1] *reorganize, unite*
▪ *Syn* assemble, bring together, convene, encourage, gather, kindle, marshal, mobilize, muster, organize, reassemble, redouble, regroup, round up, rouse, summon, surge, urge, wake, waken, whet; ▪ *Ant* disband, disperse, divide, scatter.

rally [v2] *revive; take a turn for the better*
▪ *Syn* bounce back, come along, enliven, grow stronger, improve, invigorate, make a comeback, perk up, pick up, pull through, recover, recuperate, refresh, shape up, surge, turn around; ▪ *Ant* lose, regress, weaken.

ram [v] *bang into; pack forcibly*
▪ *Syn* beat, butt, collide with, crash, crowd, dash, drive, drum, hammer, hit, jack, pack, pound, sink, slam, smash, strike, stuff, tamp, thrust, wedge; ▪ *Ant* tap.

ramble [v1] *wander about; travel aimlessly* ▪ *Syn* amble, cruise, digress, drift, excurse, gad, gallivant, meander, perambulate, peregrinate, roam, rove, saunter, snake, sprangle, stray, stroll, trail, traipse, wind, zigzag; ▪ *Ant* go straight, race, rush.

ramble [v2] *talk aimlessly, endlessly*
▪ *Syn* babble, blather, chatter, descant, digress, diverge, drift, maunder, meander, prose, protract, talk randomly, wander; ▪ *Ant* articulate, be direct.

rambling [adj1] *disconnected, wordy*
▪ *Syn* circuitous, confused, desultory, diffuse, discursive, disjointed, incoherent, incongruous, long-winded, periphrastic, prolix; ▪ *Ant* connected, direct, straightforward.

rambling [adj2] *sprawling, spread out*
▪ *Syn* at length, irregular, prolix, random, scattered, spreading, strewn, trailing, unplanned; ▪ *Ant* direct, straight.

rambunctious [adj] *loud, energetic*
▪ *Syn* boisterous, noisy, raucous, rowdy, rude, termagant, tumultous/tumultuous, turbulent, unruly; ▪ *Ant* introverted, meek, quiet, shy.

ramification [n] *consequence, development* ▪ *Syn* bifurcation, branching, complication, consequence, divarication, excrescence, extension, offshoot, outgrowth, radiation, result, sequel, upshot; ▪ *Ant* cause, root.

rampage [v] *go crazy; storm*
▪ *Syn* go berserk, rage, run amuck, run riot, run wild, tear; ▪ *Ant* be calm.

rampant [adj] *uncontrolled, out of hand*
▪ *Syn* aggressive, clamorous, epidemic, fanatical, flagrant, furious, growing, out of control, pandemic, profuse, raging, rife, spreading, turbulent, unbridled, unchecked, unruly, vehement, violent, widespread, wild; ▪ *Ant* checked, controlled, limited, restrained.

ramshackle [adj] *falling apart; in poor condition* ▪ *Syn* broken-down, crumbling, decrepit, dilapidated, flimsy, rickety, shaky, ▪ tottering, tumbledown, unsafe; ▪ *Ant* solid, stable, substantial.

rancid [adj] *rotten, strong-smelling*
▪ *Syn* contaminated, decomposing, evil-smelling, feculent, fetid, fusty, gamy, malodorous, musty, nasty, nidorous, noxious, offensive, putrid, rank, repulsive, sharp, smelly, sour, stinking, strong, tainted, turned, unhealthy; ▪ *Ant* fresh, pure, savory, sweet.

rancor [n] *bitterness, hatefulness*
▪ *Syn* acerbity, acrimony, animosity, antagonism, antipathy, dudgeon, enmity, grudge, harshness, hatred, hostility, ill will, malice, malignity, mordacity, pique, resentment, spite, spleen, umbrage, vengefulness, venom, vindictiveness, virulence; ▪ *Ant* affection, benevolence, kindness, love, respect, sympathy.

random [adj] *haphazard, chance*
▪ *Syn* accidental, aimless, arbitrary, casual, contingent, desultory, driftless, fortuitous, incidental, indiscriminate, odd, purposeless, stray; ▪ *Ant* definite, methodical, particular, premeditated, specific, systematic.

range [v1] *order, categorize*
▪ *Syn* align, arrange, assort, bias, bracket, catalog, classify, dispose, file, grade, group, incline, line up, predispose, rank; ▪ *Ant* disorder, disorganize.

range [v2] *wander, roam*
▪ *Syn* circumambulate, cruise, drift, explore, float, gallivant, meander, prowl, ramble, rove, spread, straggle, stray, traipse, traverse, trek; ▪ *Ant* make a beeline, remain.

range [v3] *extend; change within limits*
▪ *Syn* differ, diverge from, fluctuate, go, reach, run, stretch, vary, vary between; ▪ *Ant* limit, restrict.

rangy [*adj*] *long and lean*
▪ *Syn* gangling, gangly, lanky, leggy, long-legged, long-limbed, reedy, skinny, spindly, thin; ▪ *Ant* chubby, dumpy, fat, thick.

rank [*adj1*] *stinking, foul*
▪ *Syn* dank, disgusting, evil-smelling, feculent, fetid, funky, graveolent, loathsome, mephitic, nasty, nauseating, noisome, obnoxious, off, pungent, putrescent, reeking, sour, stale, strong, tainted, turned; ▪ *Ant* aromatic, perfumed, sweet, unspoiled.

rank [*adj2*] *abundant, luxurious*
▪ *Syn* dense, excessive, fertile, flourishing, fructiferous, lavish, luxuriant, overabundant, productive, profuse, prolific, rampant, rich, tropical, wild; ▪ *Ant* rare, scarce, sparse.

rank [*adj3*] *obscene, vulgar*
▪ *Syn* abusive, atrocious, coarse, crass, filthy, foul, indecent, nasty, outrageous, raunchy, scurrilous, shocking, wicked; ▪ *Ant* clean, moral.

rank [*v*] *line up; classify in system*
▪ *Syn* align, arrange, array, class, dispose, evaluate, grade, judge, list, marshal, order, peg, place in formation, position, put, range, sort, tab, value; ▪ *Ant* disorder, scatter.

rankle [*v*] *annoy, irritate*
▪ *Syn* aggravate, anger, bother, chafe, embitter, exasperate, fester, fret, gall, harass, irk, irritate, mortify, nettle, pester, rile, torment, vex; ▪ *Ant* delight, make happy, please.

ransack [*v*] *turn inside out in search; ravage* ▪ *Syn* appropriate, comb, despoil, ferret, filch, go through, hunt, loot, maraud, pilfer, pillage, plunder, poach, purloin, raid, rake, rifle, rummage, rustle, sack, search, spoil, strip, thieve; ▪ *Ant* care for, clean, neaten, tidy.

rant [*v*] *yell, rave*
▪ *Syn* bellow, bloviate, bluster, carry on, clamor, cry, declaim, fume, harangue, mouth, objurgate, orate, perorate, rage, rail, roar, scold, shout, vociferate; ▪ *Ant* mumble, whisper.

rap [*v*] *criticize*
▪ *Syn* castigate, censure, denounce, denunciate, reprehend, reprimand, reprobate, scold; ▪ *Ant* commend, extol, flatter, praise.

rapid [*adj*] *very quick*
▪ *Syn* accelerated, active, agile, brisk, expeditious, expeditive, express, fast, fleet, hasty, hurried, mercurial, nimble, precipitate, prompt, quick, ready, speedy, spry, swift, winged; ▪ *Ant* languishing, leisurely, slack, slow.

rapidly [*adv*] *very quickly*
▪ *Syn* at speed, briskly, expeditiously, fast, hastily, hurriedly, immediately, in a hurry, in a rush, in haste, precipitately, promptly, speedily, swiftly, with dispatch; ▪ *Ant* leisurely, slowly.

rapport [*n*] *understanding between people* ▪ *Syn* affinity, agreement, bond, concord, cotton, empathy, good vibrations, groove, harmony, interrelationship, link, relationship, sympathy, togetherness, unity; ▪ *Ant* coldness, unfriendliness.

rapprochement [*n*] *restoration of harmony* ▪ *Syn* agreement, cordiality, detente, friendliness, friendship, harmonizing, harmony, pacification, reconciliation, reunion, softening; ▪ *Ant* disagreement, trouble, upset.

rapt [*adj*] *absorbed, fascinated*
▪ *Syn* absent, abstracted, beguiled, bewitched, captivated, charmed, daydreaming, delighted, dreaming, engrossed, enraptured, hypnotized, immersed, intent, involved, lost, oblivious, occupied, overwhelmed, rapturous, ravished, spellbound, transported, unconscious; ▪ *Ant* bored, disenchanted, indifferent, uninterested.

rapture [*n*] *extreme happiness and delight in something* ▪ *Syn* beatitude, bliss, cheer, delectation, delight, ecstasy, elation, elysium, euphoria, exhilaration, felicity, gaiety, gladness, heaven, inspiration, jubilation, nirvana, paradise, passion, rhapsody, satisfaction; ▪ *Ant* distress, misery, revulsion, unhappiness.

rare [*adj1*] *exceptional, infrequent*
▪ *Syn* attenuated, extraordinary, few, isolated, limited, occasional, out of the ordinary, rarefied, recherché, scanty, scarce, scattered, seldom, sparse, sporadic, tenuous, uncommon, unique; ▪ *Ant* common, frequent, regular, typical, usual.

rare [*adj2*] *precious, excellent*
▪ *Syn* choice, elegant, exquisite, great, invaluable, matchless, peerless, priceless, recherché, rich, select, superb, superlative, unique; ▪ *Ant* cheap, ordinary, worthless.

rarely [*adv*] *not often; exceptionally*
▪ *Syn* almost never, barely, extraordinarily, hardly, infrequently, little, now and

then, once in blue moon, on rare occasions, scarcely ever, seldom, singularly, uncommonly; ▪ *Ant* always, frequently, regularly, usually.

rash [*adj*] *careless, impulsive*
▪ *Syn* adventurous, audacious, bold, brash, daring, fiery, foolhardy, harebrained, hasty, headstrong, heedless, ill-advised, impetuous, imprudent, madcap, passionate, precipitant, premature, reckless, thoughtless, venturesome, wild; ▪ *Ant* careful, cautious, planned, thoughtful.

rate [*v*] *be entitled to*
▪ *Syn* be accepted, be welcome, be worthy, deserve, earn, merit, prosper, succeed; ▪ *Ant* disqualify.

rather [*adv1*] *moderately*
▪ *Syn* a bit, a little, comparatively, fairly, kind of, more or less, passably, pretty, quite, reasonably, relatively, slightly, somewhat, sort of, tolerably, to some degree, to some extent; ▪ *Ant* extremely, violently.

rather [*adv2*] *significantly*
▪ *Syn* a good bit, considerably, noticeably, quite, somewhat, very, well; ▪ *Ant* insignificantly, little.

ratify [*v*] *affirm, authorize*
▪ *Syn* accredit, approve, bear out, bind, certify, confirm, consent, endorse, establish, license, sanction, substantiate, uphold, validate; ▪ *Ant* deny, disaffirm, disagree, renounce, revoke, veto.

ratio [*n*] *percentage, relation of part to whole* ▪ *Syn* arrangement, correlation, correspondence, equation, fraction, proportion, proportionality, quotient, rate, relationship, scale; ▪ *Ant* whole.

ration [*v*] *divide something into portions*
▪ *Syn* allocate, allot, budget, conserve, deal, distribute, divvy, dole, give out, issue, limit, measure out, parcel out, restrict, save, share; ▪ *Ant* collect, gather.

rational [*adj*] *realistic; of sound mind*
▪ *Syn* analytical, balanced, calm, cerebral, circumspect, deductive, deliberate, discerning, discriminating, enlightened, far-sighted, intellectual, judicious, knowing, levelheaded, logical, lucid, normal, objective, perspicacious, reasonable, sane, sensible, sober, sound, stable, thoughtful, well-advised; ▪ *Ant* insane, irrational, mad, unreasonable, unsound.

rattle [*v*] *disconcert, upset someone*
▪ *Syn* addle, bewilder, bother, confound, discomfit, discountenance, embarrass, faze, muddle, nonplus, perturb, shake, throw, unnerve; ▪ *Ant* appease, placate, relax, soothe.

raucous [*adj1*] *noisy, rough*
▪ *Syn* absonant, blaring, cacophonous, discordant, ear-piercing, grating, grinding, harsh, inharmonious, jarring, loud, piercing, rasping, sharp, stertorous, strident; ▪ *Ant* calm, quiet, soft, subdued.

raucous [*adj2*] *rowdy*
▪ *Syn* boisterous, disorderly, intemperate, rambunctious, termagant, tumultous/tumultuous, turbulent, unruly; ▪ *Ant* calm, quiet, subdued.

ravage [*v*] *destroy, ransack*
▪ *Syn* annihilate, consume, cream, crush, demolish, desecrate, devastate, exterminate, forage, gut, harry, impair, lay waste, leave in ruins, loot, overrun, pillage, pirate, plunder, raid, rape, raze, ruin, sack, smash, spoil, sweep away, total, trample, trash, waste, wreak havoc, wrest; ▪ *Ant* aid, assist, help, protect.

rave [*v*] *be very enthusiastic*
▪ *Syn* be delighted, be excited, be mad about, be wild about, effervesce, enthuse, gush, praise, rhapsodize; ▪ *Ant* condemn, denounce, discourage.

ravel [*v*] *come apart; unwind*
▪ *Syn* disentangle, free, loosen, unbraid, unravel, unsnarl, untangle, weave out; ▪ *Ant* knit, mend, put together, twist.

ravenous [*adj*] *very hungry; desirous*
▪ *Syn* avaricious, covetous, devouring, edacious, famished, gluttonous, greedy, insatiable, omnivorous, predatory, rapacious, starved, voracious; ▪ *Ant* full, satisfied.

ravine [*n*] *gap in earth's surface*
▪ *Syn* abyss, arroyo, break, canyon, chasm, clove, coulee, crevasse, fissure, flume, gorge, gulf, gully, notch, pass, valley, wash; ▪ *Ant* mountain, plain.

ravish [*v*] *enchant*
▪ *Syn* allure, attract, bewitch, captivate, charm, draw, enrapture, enthrall, fascinate, hold, hypnotize, magnetize, mesmerize, overjoy, please, spellbind, transport; ▪ *Ant* disenchant, displease, repulse, turn off.

raw [*adj1*] *not cooked, prepared*
▪ *Syn* bloody, callow, crude, fibrous,

fresh, green, hard, immature, natural, organic, roughhewn, rude, unbaked, uncooked, unprepared, unrefined; ▪ **Ant** cooked, done, well-done.

raw [adj2] *exposed, tender, referring to skin* ▪ **Syn** abraded, blistered, bruised, chafed, cut, grazed, naked, open, scraped, scratched, sensitive, skinned, sore, wounded; ▪ **Ant** healed, healthy.

raw [adj3] *inexperienced* ▪ **Syn** callow, fresh, ignorant, inexperienced, new, unseasoned, unskilled, untried, young; ▪ **Ant** experienced, sophisticated.

raw [adj4] *vulgar, nasty* ▪ **Syn** coarse, crass, crude, foul, indecent, inelegant, mean, obscene, pornographic, rude, uncouth, unrefined, unscrupulous; ▪ **Ant** clean, good, moral.

raw [adj5] *harsh, unpleasant, referring to weather* ▪ **Syn** biting, bitter, bleak, chilly, cold, damp, freezing, piercing, wet, wind-swept, windy; ▪ **Ant** clement, pleasant, warm.

raze [v] *flatten, knock down; wipe out* ▪ **Syn** batter, bulldoze, decimate, demolish, dynamite, efface, extirpate, level, mow down, obliterate, pull down, reduce, rub out, ruin, strike out, subvert, tear down, tear up, total, wipe out, wreck; ▪ **Ant** build, construct.

reach [v1] *arrive at* ▪ **Syn** arrive, attain, come to, get to, hit, land, make, make it, overtake, show, show up, sign in; ▪ **Ant** depart, go, leave.

reach [v2] *attain; rise* ▪ **Syn** accomplish, achieve, amount to, arrive at, climb to, come to, gain, move, rack up, realize, sink, win; ▪ **Ant** fail, lose.

reaction [n1] *response* ▪ **Syn** acknowledgment, answer, comeback, echo, feedback, opinion, reagency, reception, recoil, reflex, reply, retort, reverberation; ▪ **Ant** cause, query, question.

reactionary [adj] *conservative* ▪ **Syn** counter-revolutionary, obscurantist, regressive, retrogressive, rigid, traditionalist, traditionalistic; ▪ **Ant** liberal, progressive, radical.

readable [adj1] *understandable, legible* ▪ **Syn** clear, comprehensible, decipherable, explicit, fluent, graphic, intelligible, lucid, orderly, precise, regular, simple, straightforward, tidy; ▪ **Ant** illegible, unintelligible, unreadable.

readable [adj2] *pleasurable to peruse* ▪ **Syn** absorbing, clever, easy, eloquent, engaging, engrossing, enjoyable, entertaining, gratifying, gripping, interesting, pleasant, rewarding, satisfying, stimulating, well-written; ▪ **Ant** boring, tedious, vapid.

readily [adv] *quickly; effortlessly* ▪ **Syn** at once, cheerfully, eagerly, easily, facilely, freely, gladly, immediately, lightly, promptly, speedily, swimmingly, unhesitatingly, willingly, without delay, without difficulty, without hesitation; ▪ **Ant** unwillingly.

ready [adj1] *prepared; available* ▪ **Syn** accessible, apt, arranged, close to hand, completed, convenient, equal to, equipped, fit, handy, in line, in place, in position, near, on call, on hand, open to, organized, primed, qualified, ripe, set, waiting; ▪ **Ant** immature, slow, unavailable, unprepared, unready, unripe, unsuitable.

ready [adj2] *willing, inclined* ▪ **Syn** agreeable, apt, ardent, disposed, eager, enthusiastic, fain, game, glad, keen, predisposed, prompt, prone; ▪ **Ant** disinclined, unprepared, unwilling.

ready [adj3] *skillful, intelligent* ▪ **Syn** adept, apt, bright, clever, deft, dexterous, expert, handy, keen, masterly, prompt, quick-witted, resourceful, sharp, skilled; ▪ **Ant** immature, slow, uneducated, unprepared, unskilled, untrained.

ready [v] *prepare* ▪ **Syn** arrange, brace, brief, equip, fit, fix, fortify, get ready, gird, make, make ready, make up, order, organize, post, prep, provide, set, strengthen, warm up; ▪ **Ant** hold back, retard, slow.

real [adj] *genuine in existence* ▪ **Syn** absolute, actual, bona fide, certain, concrete, corporeal, de facto, embodied, evident, factual, honest, incarnate, indubitable, irrefutable, legitimate, material, palpable, perceptible, physical, present, rightful, sound, stable, substantial, tangible, unaffected, valid, veritable; ▪ **Ant** dishonest, fake, false, feigned, imaginary, invalid, untrue.

realistic [adj1] *sensible, matter-of-fact* ▪ **Syn** astute, businesslike, commonsense, down-to-earth, earthy, hard-boiled, level-headed, practical, pragmatic, prudent, rational, reasonable, sane, sensible, shrewd, sober, sound, utilitarian; ▪ *Ant* impractical, irrational, unrealistic.

realistic [*adj2*] *genuine*
▪ *Syn* authentic, faithful, graphic, lifelike, natural, original, representational, representative, true, true to life, truthful; ▪ *Ant* fanciful, insincere.

realize [*v1*] *appreciate, become aware of*
▪ *Syn* apprehend, be cognizant of, catch, comprehend, conceive, discern, envision, get, grasp, know, recognize, understand; ▪ *Ant* ignore, neglect.

realize [*v2*] *accomplish*
▪ *Syn* actualize, bring about, bring off, bring to fruition, carry through, complete, consummate, corporealize, effect, effectuate, fulfill, materialize, perfect, perform, reify; ▪ *Ant* fail.

realize [*v3*] *gain, earn*
▪ *Syn* accomplish, achieve, acquire, attain, bring in, clear, get, go for, make, make a profit, net, obtain, produce, reach, receive, take in, win; ▪ *Ant* lose.

really [*adj*] *without a doubt*
▪ *Syn* absolutely, actually, authentically, beyond doubt, certainly, de facto, genuinely, honestly, in actuality, indeed, indubitably, in fact, in reality, legitimately, literally, of course, positively, precisely, surely, truly, verily; ▪ *Ant* doubtfully.

reap [*v*] *collect, harvest*
▪ *Syn* acquire, bring in, cull, derive, gain, garner, glean, obtain, pick, pluck, procure, realize, receive, retrieve, secure, take in, win; ▪ *Ant* plant, sow.

rear [*adj*] *back, end*
▪ *Syn* after, astern, backward, behind, dorsal, following, hindmost, last, mizzen, posterior, retral, reverse, stern, tail; ▪ *Ant* beginning, foremost, front, leading.

rear [*v1*] *raise young*
▪ *Syn* breed, bring up, care for, cultivate, educate, foster, grow, nurse, nurture, propagate, train; ▪ *Ant* abandon, neglect.

rear [*v2*] *lift, rise*
▪ *Syn* bring up, elevate, hoist, pick up, raise, set upright, spring up, uplift, upraise; ▪ *Ant* drop, fall.

reasonable [*adj1*] *moderate, tolerable*
▪ *Syn* acceptable, analytical, circumspect, conservative, controlled, discreet, equitable, fair, feasible, fit, impartial, inexpensive, judicious, legitimate, low-cost, low-priced, modest, objective, plausible,

politic, proper, prudent, rational, restrained, sane, sapient, sensible, sound, temperate, understandable, valid, within reason; ▪ *Ant* expensive, intolerable, outrageous, unreasonable.

reasonable [*adj2*] *intelligent, practical*
▪ *Syn* advisable, arguable, believeable, clear-cut, cognitive, commonsensical, consistent, credible, judicious, justifiable, levelheaded, logical, perceiving, plausible, rational, reasoned, reflective, sane, sensible, sober, sound, tenable, thoughtful, thought-out, well-advised, wise; ▪ *Ant* implausible, impractical, nonsensical, stupid, unreasonable.

reassure [*v*] *restore confidence to*
▪ *Syn* assure, bolster, brace, buoy, cheer, comfort, console, convince, encourage, give confidence, guarantee, hearten, inspire, inspirit, perk up, relieve; ▪ *Ant* discourage, dishearten, unnerve.

rebel [*adj*] *not obeying*
▪ *Syn* insubordinate, insurgent, insurrectionary, mutinous, rebellious, revolutionary; ▪ *Ant* complaisant, compliant, obedient.

rebel [*v*] *refuse to obey*
▪ *Syn* be insubordinate, boycott, censure, combat, criticize, defy, denounce, disobey, fight, insurrect, mutiny, oppose, overthrow, overturn, remonstrate, renounce, resist, revolt, riot, secede, strike, take up arms, upset; ▪ *Ant* agree, comply, obey.

rebellious [*adj*] *disobedient, unmanageable* ▪ *Syn* alienated, bellicose, contumacious, defiant, disobedient, dissident, factious, fractious, insurgent, mutinous, pugnacious, quarrelsome, radical, recalcitrant, refractory, resistant, revolutionary, seditious, threatening, treasonable, turbulent; ▪ *Ant* compliant, governable, manageable, obedient.

rebuff [*n*] *turning away; ignoring*
▪ *Syn* brush-off, check, denial, discouragement, insult, opposition, rebuke, refusal, reprimand, repulse, slight, snub, turndown; ▪ *Ant* encouragement, inclusion, welcome.

rebuff [*v*] *turn away; give the cold shoulder* ▪ *Syn* beat off, check, chide, deny, discourage, dismiss, ignore, keep at bay, lash out at, neglect, oppose, pass up, put off, rebuke, refuse, reject, repudiate, repulse, resist, slight, snub, spurn, ward off; ▪ *Ant* include, take in, welcome.

rebuke [n] *reprimand; harsh criticism*
▪ **Syn** admonishment, admonition, castigation, censure, condemnation, disapproval, lecture, objurgation, ostracism, punishment, put-down, rating, rebuff, remonstrance, reprehension, reproach, scolding, snub, upbraiding; ▪ **Ant** compliment, flattery, praise.

rebut [v] *argue against; prove wrong*
▪ **Syn** confound, controvert, deny, disprove, evert, fend off, invalidate, negate, overturn, prove false, quash, refute, repel, top; ▪ **Ant** agree, approve, back down, concede.

recalcitrant [adj] *disobedient, uncontrollable* ▪ **Syn** contrary, contumacious, defiant, fractious, intractable, obstinate, rebellious, refractory, resistant, stubborn, undisciplined, unruly, wayward, wild, willful; ▪ **Ant** amenable, obedient, passive.

recall [v] *remember*
▪ **Syn** arouse, cite, elicit, evoke, extract, flash, recollect, remind, reminisce, renew, retain, retrospect, revive, ring a bell, rouse, stir, summon, waken; ▪ **Ant** forget, lose sight of.

recant [v] *take back something said*
▪ **Syn** abjure, abnegate, abrogate, annul, apostatize, back down, back off, call back, cancel, contradict, countermand, deny, disavow, disclaim, forswear, nullify, palinode, recall, renounce, repudiate, rescind, revoke, take back, unsay, void, withdraw; ▪ **Ant** confirm, emphasize, recapitulate, validate.

recapitulate [v] *go over something again*
▪ **Syn** epitomize, outline, paraphrase, recount, rehash, reiterate, repeat, rephrase, replay, restate, review, reword, summarize, sum up; ▪ **Ant** expand, expound.

recede [v] *withdraw; diminish*
▪ **Syn** abate, decrease, drain away, draw back, dwindle, ebb, fade, lessen, regress, retract, retreat, retrograde, retrogress, return, shrink, subside, taper, wane; ▪ **Ant** advance, forge, forward, increase.

receipts [n] *money earned in business venture* ▪ **Syn** cash flow, earnings, gain, gate, gross, income, net, proceeds, profit, return, revenue, revenue stream, royalty; ▪ **Ant** loss, losses.

receive [v] *accept delivery of something*
▪ **Syn** acquire, admit, appropriate, arrogate, assume, collect, come by, come into, derive, draw, earn, gain, gather, hold, inherit, make, obtain, pick up, procure, reap, redeem, secure; ▪ **Ant** deliver, expend, lose, reject.

receive [v2] *take in guest or member*
▪ **Syn** accept, accommodate, admit, allow entrance, bring in, greet, host, install, introduce, invite, let in, make comfortable, meet, show in, take in, usher in, welcome; ▪ **Ant** refuse, turn away.

recent [adj] *current*
▪ **Syn** contempo, contemporary, fresh, just out, late, latter, latter-day, modern, neoteric, new, newborn, novel, present-day, today, up-to-date, young; ▪ **Ant** earlier, old, old-fashioned, past, remote.

recently [adv] *currently*
▪ **Syn** afresh, anew, freshly, in recent past, in recent times, just a while ago, just now, lately, latterly, new, newly, not long ago, of late, short while ago, the other day; ▪ **Ant** before, later.

receptive [adj] *open to new ideas*
▪ **Syn** accessible, amenable, approachable, favorable, friendly, hospitable, interested, open-minded, perceptive, ready, responsive, sensitive, suggestible, swayable, sympathetic, welcoming, well-disposed; ▪ **Ant** biased, narrow-minded, unfriendly, unreceptive.

recess [v] *stop action*
▪ **Syn** adjourn, dissolve, drop, drop it, prorogate, prorogue, put on hold, rise, shake, sideline, take a break, terminate; ▪ **Ant** carry on, continue, persist, prolong.

recession [n] *reversal of action; reduction of business activity* ▪ **Syn** bust, collapse, decline, deflation, depression, downturn, return, slide, slump, stagnation; ▪ **Ant** advance, boom, inflation.

reciprocal [adj] *exchanged, alternate*
▪ **Syn** changeable, complementary, coordinate, correlative, corresponding, equivalent, exchangeable, interchangeable, interdependent, matching, mutual; ▪ **Ant** independent, one-way, unilateral.

reciprocate [v] *exchange, alternate; equal* ▪ **Syn** correspond, interchange, match, recompense, render, repay, reply, requite, respond, retaliate, return, share, swap, trade; ▪ **Ant** deny, refuse.

reckless [adj] *irresponsible in thought, deed* ▪ **Syn** adventuresome, audacious, brash, careless, daring, feckless, foolhardy, harebrained, heedless, ill-advised, imprudent, inattentive, mindless, negligent, precipitate, rash, temerarious, thoughtless, venturous, wild; ▪ *Ant* careful, cautious, responsible, wary.

recline [*v*] *lie down*
▪ *Syn* be recumbent, cant, list, loll, lounge, repose, rest, slant, slope, sprawl, stretch, stretch out, tilt, tip; ▪ *Ant* sit up, stand up.

recluse/reclusive [*adj*] *hermitlike, unsociable* ▪ *Syn* antisocial, ascetic, cloistered, eremetic, hermetic, isolated, misanthropic, monastic, reserved, retiring, secluded, seclusive, solitary, standoffish, withdrawn; ▪ *Ant* extroverted, friendly, sociable.

recognize [*v1*] *identify*
▪ *Syn* descry, diagnose, distinguish, espy, know, make out, note, notice, observe, perceive, pinpoint, place, recall, recollect, remark, remember, see, sight, spot, tag; ▪ *Ant* forget, miss, neglect, overlook.

recognize [*v2*] *acknowledge, understand; approve* ▪ *Syn* accept, admit, agree, allow, appreciate, assent, avow, comprehend, concede, confess, grant, greet, honor, make, own, perceive, realize, respect, salute, sanction, see; ▪ *Ant* disapprove, misunderstand.

recoil [*v*] *shrink away*
▪ *Syn* balk, blanch, blench, blink, carom, cringe, demur, draw back, duck, falter, flinch, hesitate, pull back, quail, quake, reel, resile, shake, shirk, shrink, shudder, shy away, step back, swerve, tremble, turn away, waver, wince, withdraw; ▪ *Ant* face, meet.

recollect [*v*] *remember*
▪ *Syn* arouse, awaken, bethink, call to mind, cite, flash, look back on, mind, place, recall, recognize, remind, reminisce, retain, revive, rouse, stir, summon, waken; ▪ *Ant* forget.

recommend [*v*] *advise, approve*
▪ *Syn* advance, advocate, applaud, back, celebrate, commend, compliment, endorse, enjoin, esteem, eulogize, exalt, exhort, extol, favor, glorify, hold up, laud, magnify, praise, prescribe, propose, put forward, sanction, second, speak well of, stand by, steer, suggest, urge, value, vouch for; ▪ *Ant* disapprove, discourage, dissuade, forbid.

recompense [*n*] *something returned, paid back* ▪ *Syn* amends, atonement, compensation, damages, emolument, expiation, indemnity, pay, payment, propitiation, redemption, redress, remuneration, reparation, repayment, restitution, reward, salvo, wages; ▪ *Ant* expenditure.

reconcile [*v1*] *make peace; adjust*
▪ *Syn* accommodate, appease, arbitrate, assuage, bring together, conciliate, fix up, harmonize, integrate, make up, mitigate, pacify, placate, propitiate, rectify, re-establish, restore harmony, reunite, settle, suit, tune, win over; ▪ *Ant* disagree, refuse.

reconcile [*v2*] *resign oneself to something* ▪ *Syn* accept, accommodate, resign, submit, yield; ▪ *Ant* defy, disagree, refuse, resist.

recondite [*adj*] *mysterious, obscure*
▪ *Syn* abstruse, arcane, cabalistic, cryptic, dark, deep, esoteric, hermetic, hidden, learned, mystical, occult, orphic, pedantic, profound, secret; ▪ *Ant* obvious, plain, simple, straightforward.

reconsider [*v*] *think about again*
▪ *Syn* amend, change one's mind, reassess, reevaluate, rehash, review, sleep on, think over, work over; ▪ *Ant* dismiss, ignore.

record [*v*] *write down; store information*
▪ *Syn* catalog, chronicle, document, enter, file, inscribe, jot down, keep account, list, log, mark, mark down, note, post, put in writing, register, report, set down, tabulate, take down, tape, transcribe, videotape; ▪ *Ant* delete, erase, expunge, obliterate, omit.

recount [*v*] *tell a story*
▪ *Syn* convey, depict, describe, detail, echo, itemize, narrate, portray, recite, rehash, relate, repeat, report, state, tell, unload, verbalize; ▪ *Ant* conceal, repress.

recoup [*v*] *recover, make up for*
▪ *Syn* compensate, get back, make redress for, make well, redeem, refund, regain, reimburse, remunerate, repay, requite, satisfy, win back; ▪ *Ant* downslide, forsake, lose, renege, rescind, worsen.

recover [*v1*] *find again*
▪ *Syn* bring back, compensate, get back, recoup, redeem, rediscover, regain, repair, replevy, rescue, restore, resume, retrieve, salvage, take back, win back; ▪ *Ant* lose, mislay, miss.

recover [*v2*] *improve in health*
▪ *Syn* better, come around, convalesce, gain, get well, grow, heal, mend, pull

through, rally, rebound, recuperate, rejuvenate, restore, return to form, revive; ▪ *Ant* decline, deteriorate, fail, relapse, wane.

recreation [*n*] *sports, games, special interests* ▪ *Syn* amusement, avocation, disport, diversion, ease, enjoyment, entertainment, exercise, festivity, frolic, game, hobby, jollity, pastime, play, playtime, pleasure, refreshment, relaxation, repose, sport, vacation; ▪ *Ant* drugery, grind, labor, toil, work.

recruit [*n*] *person beginning service* ▪ *Syn* apprentice, beginner, convert, draftee, fledgling, freshman, helper, initiate, learner, neophyte, newcomer, novice, proselyte, rookie, sailor, trainee, volunteer; ▪ *Ant* doyen, expert, old hand, old-timer, pro, professional, veteran.

rectify [*v*] *correct a situation; make something right* ▪ *Syn* adjust, amend, clean up, doctor, fix, improve, mend, put right, recalibrate, redress, remedy, repair, revise, right, square, straighten out, straighten up; ▪ *Ant* damage, ruin, weaken, worsen.

recuperate [*v*] *improve in health* ▪ *Syn* ameliorate, convalesce, get well, heal, look up, mend, pick up, pull through, rally, recover, regain health; ▪ *Ant* decline, deteriorate, fail, succumb, worsen.

recur [*v*] *happen again; repeat in one's mind* ▪ *Syn* come again, come back, iterate, persist, reappear, recrudesce, reiterate, repeat, return, revert, turn back; ▪ *Ant* halt, stop.

recurrent [*adj*] *repeating* ▪ *Syn* alternate, continued, cyclical, frequent, habitual, intermittent, isochronal, periodic, recurring, regular, reoccurring, repetitive, rolling; ▪ *Ant* halted, infrequent, permanent, prevented, stopped.

redden [*v*] *blush, make rosy* ▪ *Syn* color, crimson, dye, encarmine, encarnadine, flush, glow, pink, pinken, rose, rouge, ruby, ruddy, rust, suffuse, tint; ▪ *Ant* lighten, pale.

redeem [*v1*] *recover possession* ▪ *Syn* buy back, cash in, exchange, get back, make good, purchase, recapture, reclaim, regain, repay, replevin, repossess, restore, retrieve, settle, trade in, win back; ▪ *Ant* forfeit, lose, yield.

redeem [*v2*] *free; buy the freedom of* ▪ *Syn* deliver, disenthrall, emanci-

pate, extricate, liberate, loose, manumit, pay ransom, release, rescue, save, set free; ▪ *Ant* abandon, oppress, subjugate.

redeem [*v3*] *atone for; compensate* ▪ *Syn* absolve, acquit, compensate, countervail, defray, fulfill, hold to, keep, make amends, make up for, offset, outweigh, redress, rehabilitate, reinstate, restore, satisfy, save; ▪ *Ant* break, forsake, shun, violate.

redress [*v*] *change, rectify* ▪ *Syn* adjust, amend, annul, balance, cancel, compensate, correct, even out, make amends, mend, negate, neutralize, pay for, recalibrate, recompense, reform, remedy, repair, revise, square, vindicate; ▪ *Ant* regress, worsen.

reduce [*v1*] *make less; decrease* ▪ *Syn* abate, abridge, cheapen, contract, curtail, cut back, deflate, depreciate, diet, diminish, discount, dwindle, impoverish, lessen, lower, mark down, moderate, pare, recede, roll back, scale down, shave, shorten, slash, taper, tone down, trim, truncate, weaken, wind down; ▪ *Ant* expand, extend, grow, increase, raise, upgrade.

reduce [*v2*] *defeat, demote* ▪ *Syn* bear down, break, bring, conquer, cripple, crush, disable, enfeeble, master, overcome, ruin, subdue, subjugate, undermine, vanquish, weaken; ▪ *Ant* increase, promote, win.

reduce [*v3*] *humble, humiliate* ▪ *Syn* abase, break, bust, declass, degrade, demerit, demote, disgrade, downgrade, lower, take down a peg; ▪ *Ant* invigorate, raise, strengthen.

redundant [*adj*] *excessive; repetitious* ▪ *Syn* bombastic, diffuse, extravagant, inessential, loquacious, oratorical, palaverous, periphrastic, prolix, reiterating, superfluous, tautological, verbose, wordy; ▪ *Ant* concise, essential, spare.

refine [*v1*] *purify* ▪ *Syn* clarify, cleanse, distill, filter, process, rarefy, strain; ▪ *Ant* corrupt, dirty, pollute.

refine [*v2*] *perfect, polish* ▪ *Syn* civilize, clarify, cultivate, elevate, hone, improve, make clear, round, smooth, temper; ▪ *Ant* damage, ruin.

refined [*adj1*] *cultured, civilized* ▪ *Syn* aesthetic, courteous, cultivated, delicate, discriminating, elegant, enlightened, fastidious, fine, genteel, gracious, high-minded, polished, polite, restrained, sophisticated, sublime, subtle, tasteful, urbane, well-bred, well-mannered; ■ *Ant* common, crude, ill-bred, uncivilized.

refined [adj2] *cleaned of impurities*
■ *Syn* aerated, boiled down, clarified, clean, cleansed, distilled, drained, expurgated, filtered, processed, pure, purified, rarefied, strained, washed; ■ *Ant* corrupt, dirtied, polluted.

reflect [v1] *give back*
■ *Syn* be resonant, echo, emulate, flash, follow, give forth, imitate, match, mirror, rebound, repeat, repercuss, reply, reproduce, resonate, resound, return, reverberate, reverse, revert; ■ *Ant* absorb, keep, retain.

reflect [v2] *think about*
■ *Syn* cerebrate, cogitate, consider, contemplate, deliberate, meditate, mull over, muse, ponder, reason, ruminate, speculate, study, think, weigh, wonder; ■ *Ant* dismiss, disregard, ignore.

reflect [v3] *demonstrate, indicate*
■ *Syn* bear out, communicate, display, evince, exhibit, express, indicate, manifest, reveal; ■ *Ant* conceal, cover, hide, mask.

reflective [adj] *thoughtful*
■ *Syn* cogitating, contemplative, deliberate, meditative, pensive, pondering, reasoning, ruminative, speculative, studious; ■ *Ant* ignorant, unthoughtful.

reform [v] *correct, rectify*
■ *Syn* ameliorate, amend, better, cure, emend, improve, make amends, mend, rearrange, rebuild, reconstitute, reconstruct, refashion, rehabilitate, remedy, renovate, repair, resolve, restore, revise, transform; ■ *Ant* hurt, impair, worsen.

refrain [v] *do without; keep from doing*
■ *Syn* abstain, avoid, be temperate, cease, check, curb, desist, eschew, forbear, forgo, give up, halt, inhibit, keep, leave off, not do, pass up, quit, resist, restrain, stop, withhold; ■ *Ant* do, go ahead, jump in.

refresh [v] *make like new; give new life*
■ *Syn* brace, breathe new life into, cheer, enliven, exhilarate, freshen, inspirit, quicken, reanimate, reinvigorate, rejuvenate, replenish, revive, stimulate, update, vivify; ■ *Ant* deaden, exhaust, fatigue, weaken.

refrigerate [v] *chill, usually in storage*
■ *Syn* air-condition, cool, freeze, ice, keep cold, make cold; ■ *Ant* heat, warm.

refuge [n] *place to hide, have privacy*
■ *Syn* anchorage, asylum, cover, den, escape, fortress, harbor, hideaway, hideout, immunity, port, protection, recourse, resort, retreat, sanctuary, shelter, stronghold; ■ *Ant* danger, exposure, insecurity, liability, menace, peril, threat, vulnerability.

refund [v] *return money; rebate*
■ *Syn* balance, compensate, give back, indemnify, make amends, pay back, recompense, recoup, redeem, redress, reimburse, relinquish, remit, remunerate, repay, restore, settle; ■ *Ant* withhold.

refurbish [v] *spruce up*
■ *Syn* fix up, mend, modernize, overhaul, recondition, redo, reequip, refit, refresh, rehab, rehabilitate, rejuvenate, remodel, renew, renovate, repair, restore, retread, revamp, spruce, update; ■ *Ant* destroy, ruin.

refuse [v] *deny; say no*
■ *Syn* beg off, decline, demur, desist, disallow, disapprove, protest, reject, repel, reprobate, repudiate, shun, spurn, turn away, turn down, withdraw, withhold; ■ *Ant* accept, allow, approve, consent, grant, offer, sanction.

refute [v] *prove false; discredit*
■ *Syn* abnegate, cancel, cancel out, confute, contend, contradict, contravene, counter, debate, disclaim, disprove, dispute, evert, expose, invalidate, negate, oppose, parry, rebut, reply to, repudiate, take a stand against; ■ *Ant* endorse, prove, ratify, sanction, support.

regain [v] *get back, get back to*
■ *Syn* compass, get well, reach, reacquire, reattain, recapture, reclaim, recoup, recover, recruit, redeem, repossess, retake, retrieve, return to, save, take back, win back; ■ *Ant* forfeit, lose.

regal [adj] *fit for royalty*
■ *Syn* august, glorious, imposing, magnificent, majestic, monarchial, noble, proud, resplendent, royal, sovereign, splendid, stately, sublime; ■ *Ant* common, humble, minor, petty.

regard [v1] *look at; listen to*
■ *Syn* attend, behold, contemplate, eye, heed, look on, mark, mind, note, notice, observe, read, remark, respect, scan,

scrutinize, see, spy, stare at, view, watch, witness; ▪ *Ant* disregard, ignore, look away, shun.

regard [v2] *believe, judge*
▪ *Syn* account, adjudge, admire, assay, assess, consider, deem, esteem, estimate, look upon, rate, reckon, respect, revere, see, suppose, surmise, think, treat, value, view; ▪ *Ant* disbelieve, disregard.

regardful [adj] *attentive, observant*
▪ *Syn* advertent, arrect, aware, careful, considerate, deferential, dutiful, heedful, mindful, observative, respectful, thoughtful, watchful; ▪ *Ant* dismissive, inattentive, unobservant.

regardless [adv] *despite everything*
▪ *Syn* although, anyway, come what may, despite, for all that, in any case, in spite of everything, leaving aside, nevertheless, no matter what, nonetheless, notwithstanding, without considering, without regard to; ▪ *Ant* considering, with care.

regenerate [v] *breathe new life into*
▪ *Syn* exhilarate, inspirit, invigorate, reanimate, reawaken, reinvigorate, rejuvenate, renew, restore, revive, revivify, uplift; ▪ *Ant* destroy, extinguish, kill, ruin.

register [v1] *enter in list, record*
▪ *Syn* catalog, chronicle, enlist, enroll, file, inscribe, list, note, record, set down, subscribe, take down, weigh in; ▪ *Ant* eradicate, erase, expunge.

regress [v] *return to earlier way of doing things* ▪ *Syn* backslide, degenerate, deteriorate, ebb, fall away, fall back, lapse, lose ground, recede, relapse, retrogress, revert, sink, throw back, turn back; ▪ *Ant* develop, grow, progress.

regret [v] *be upset about*
▪ *Syn* be disturbed, bemoan, bewail, deplore, feel remorse, feel sorry, grieve, lament, look back, miss, moan, mourn, repent, repine, rue; ▪ *Ant* be content, be satisfied.

regretful [adj] *sad, sorry*
▪ *Syn* apologetic, ashamed, compunctious, contrite, disappointed, mournful, penitent, remorseful, repentant, rueful, sorrowful; ▪ *Ant* content, happy, satisfied, unremorseful.

regrettable [adj] *unfortunate, wrong*
▪ *Syn* calamitous, dire, disappointing, distressing, dreadful, grievous, heartbreaking, ill-advised, lamentable, piti-

able, pitiful, shameful, woeful; ▪ *Ant* blessed, fortunate, happy, lucky, right.

regular [adj1] *normal, common*
▪ *Syn* commonplace, customary, daily, established, everyday, general, habitual, normal, ordinary, orthodox, prevalent, routine, sanctioned, standard, time-honored, traditional, typical, unexceptional, usual; ▪ *Ant* abnormal, anomalous, eccentric, extraordinary, irregular, rare, uncommon, unusual.

regular [adj2] *orderly, consistent, balanced* ▪ *Syn* constant, cyclic, dependable, established, expected, fixed, harmonious, in order, level, measured, methodical, ordered, organized, patterned, periodic, probable, rational, recurrent, regulated, rhythmic, routine, serial, standardized, steady, systematic, uniform; ▪ *Ant* inconsistent, infrequent, irregular, occasional, variable.

regulate [v] *manage, organize*
▪ *Syn* adapt, balance, conduct, coordinate, direct, govern, guide, handle, legislate, measure, methodize, monitor, order, oversee, put in order, run, standardize, superintend, systematize, temper; ▪ *Ant* deregulate, disorganize, mismanage.

rehabilitate [v] *renovate, adjust*
▪ *Syn* convert, fix up, furbish, improve, mend, rebuild, recondition, reconstruct, refurbish, reinstate, reinvigorate, rejuvenate, renew, restore, save; ▪ *Ant* destroy, hurt, ruin.

rehearse [v] *prepare for performance*
▪ *Syn* act, depict, describe, drill, experiment, go over, hone, iterate, learn one's part, narrate, practice, ready, recapitulate, recite, recount, reenact, review, run lines, run through, state, study, tell, train, warm up, work out; ▪ *Ant* ad lib, wing.

reign [v] *have power over; prevail*
▪ *Syn* administer, be supreme, boss, command, dominate, domineer, govern, head up, helm, influence, manage, obtain, occupy, overrule, predominate, preponderate, rule, sit; ▪ *Ant* serve, submit.

reimburse [v] *pay back something owed*
▪ *Syn* balance, compensate, make reparations, offset, pay, recompense, remunerate, repay, requite, restore, return, square, square up; ▪ *Ant* fine, penalize.

rein [v] *restrain, control*
▪ *Syn* bridle, check, compose, cool, curb, halt, hold back, limit, repress, restrict, suppress; ▪ *Ant* free, let go, liberate.

reinforce [v] *strengthen, augment*
• **Syn** add to, back up, bolster, buttress, fortify, harden, increase, multiply, prop up, punch up, shore up, support, sustain, toughen, underline; • **Ant** debilitate, subtract, take away, undermine, weaken.

reinstate [v] *give back responsibility*
• **Syn** recall, redeem, reelect, reestablish, rehabilitate, rehire, reinvest, renew, replace, restore, return, revive; • **Ant** fire, let go.

reiterate [v] *say or do again*
• **Syn** double-check, echo, ingeminate, iterate, recapitulate, recheck, rehash, renew, repeat, reprise, restate, retell; • **Ant** deny, take back.

reject [v] *say no to*
• **Syn** cast aside, cast off, decline, deny, discard, discount, dismiss, eliminate, exclude, jettison, jilt, pass on, rebuff, repudiate, repulse, scoff, scrap, shun, slough, spurn, throw out, turn down, veto; • **Ant** accept, allow, approve, choose, ratify, sanction.

rejoice [v] *be very happy about something* • **Syn** celebrate, delight, enchant, enjoy, exult, feel happy, glory, joy, jump for joy, make merry, revel, triumph; • **Ant** be sad, lament, mourn.

rejuvenate [v] *make new again*
• **Syn** exhilarate, give new life to, make young again, modernize, reanimate, recondition, recover, refresh, refurbish, renovate, restitute, restore, spruce, spruce up, update; • **Ant** age, damage, exhaust, sap, weaken.

relapse [v] *deteriorate, weaken*
• **Syn** backslide, be overcome, degenerate, fade, fail, fall, lapse, recidivate, regress, retrogress, revert, sicken, sink, slip back, suffer, worsen; • **Ant** get better, heal, progress, strengthen.

relate [v1] *give an account of*
• **Syn** chronicle, depict, describe, detail, disclose, divulge, express, impart, itemize, narrate, recite, recount, report, retell, reveal, run through, set forth, spill, state, tell, track, verbalize; • **Ant** conceal, hide.

relate [v2] *correlate, pertain*
• **Syn** ally, appertain, ascribe, assign, be relevant to, concern, correspond to, have reference to, impute, join, link, pertain, refer, tie in with, touch, unite, yoke; • **Ant** detach, dissociate, separate.

related [adj] *connected, accompanying*
• **Syn** affiliated, akin, allied, analogous, associated, complementary, concomitant, correlated, correspondent, dependent, enmeshed, fraternal, germane, interconnected, interdependent, intertwined, linked, parallel, pertinent, reciprocal, relevant, similar; • **Ant** alien, different, disassociated, disconnected, dissimilar, foreign, unrelated.

relative [adj1] *comparative, respective*
• **Syn** allied, analogous, approximate, associated, concerning, conditional, connected, contingent, corresponding, dependent, in regard to, near, parallel, proportionate, reciprocal, referring, related, relating to, reliant, with respect to; • **Ant** unconnected, unrelated.

relative [adj2] *pertinent, applicable*
• **Syn** apposite, appropriate, appurtenant, apropos, contingent, dependent, germane, pertaining, referring, related, relevant; • **Ant** inappropriate, irrelevant, remote.

relax [v1] *be or feel at ease*
• **Syn** calm, collect oneself, compose oneself, laze, loosen up, recline, repose, rest, settle back, sit back, soften, tranquilize, unbend, unlax, unwind; • **Ant** agitate, excite, tense, worry.

relax [v2] *diminish, lessen*
• **Syn** abate, ease, ease off, ebb, lax, let up, loose, loosen, mitigate, moderate, modify, modulate, reduce, relieve, remit, slack, slacken, slow, slow down, untighten, weaken; • **Ant** increase, intensify, tighten.

relay [v] *pass on, transmit*
• **Syn** broadcast, carry, communicate, deliver, hand down, hand over, send, spread, transfer, turn over; • **Ant** check, hold on, keep.

release [v] *let go, let out*
• **Syn** absolve, acquit, bail out, cast loose, clear, commute, deliver, discharge, disengage, dispense, emancipate, exculpate, exempt, exonerate, extricate, free, let off, liberate, loose, loosen, manumit, set free, turn loose, vent, yield; • **Ant** fetter, imprison, keep, maintain, shackle.

relegate [v1] *assign, transfer*
• **Syn** commission, confide, consign, delegate, entrust, hand over, pass on, refer, turn over; • **Ant** keep, retain.

relegate [v2] *banish, downgrade*
• **Syn** demote, dismiss, displace, eject,

exile, expatriate, expel, ostracize, remove, throw out; ▪ *Ant* promote, upgrade.

relent [v] *die down; let up*
▪ *Syn* acquiesce, capitulate, come around, comply, drop, ease, ease off, forbear, give in, give up, give way, lay back, let go, melt, moderate, relax, show mercy, slacken, slow, soften, subside, wane, weaken, yield; ▪ *Ant* argue, increase, refuse.

relentless [adj1] *cruel, merciless*
▪ *Syn* adamant, determined, dogged, ferocious, fierce, grim, hard, harsh, implacable, inexorable, inflexible, obdurate, pitiless, remorseless, rigid, rigorous, ruthless, single-minded, stringent, vindictive; ▪ *Ant* forgiving, kind, merciful, remorseful, sympathetic, understanding.

relentless [adj2] *continuous, neverending* ▪ *Syn* incessant, nonstop, persistent, pertinacious, punishing, sustained, tenacious; ▪ *Ant* ending, intermittent, stopping.

relevant [adj] *appropriate; to the purpose* ▪ *Syn* accordant, applicable, apposite, apt, cognate, compatible, concerning, conformant, conforming, congruent, congruous, consistent, consonant, correlated, correspondent, fit, fitting, germane, harmonious, have direct bearing, material, pertaining to, pertinent, pointful, proper, related, relative, significant, suitable, suited, to the point; ▪ *Ant* extraneous, inappropriate, irrelevant.

reliable [adj] *trustworthy*
▪ *Syn* careful, conscientious, constant, dependable, devoted, faithful, firm, good, honest, impeccable, loyal, predictable, proved, reputable, responsible, safe, sincere, solid, sound, stable, steadfast, steady, sterling, strong, sure, tried, true, trusty, upright, veracious; ▪ *Ant* deceptive, irresponsible, unreliable, untrustworthy.

relieve [v1] *make less painful; let up on*
▪ *Syn* abate, allay, alleviate, appease, assuage, calm, comfort, console, diminish, ease, free, lighten, mitigate, moderate, mollify, palliate, qualify, quiet, relax, salve, soften, soothe, subdue, temper; ▪ *Ant* aggravate, harm, injure, irritate.

relieve [v2] *help; give assistance*
▪ *Syn* aid, assist, substitute for, succor, support, sustain, take over from, take the

place of; ▪ *Ant* burden, discourage, hurt, trouble, upset, worry.

relieve [v3] *remove blame, responsibility*
▪ *Syn* absolve, deliver, dismiss, excuse, exempt, free, let off, release, spare, unburden; ▪ *Ant* accuse, blame, condemn.

religion [n] *belief in God*
▪ *Syn* adoration, church, creed, cult, denomination, devotion, doctrine, faithfulness, godliness, morality, mythology, orthodoxy, persuasion, piety, prayer, sect, spirituality, theology; ▪ *Ant* agnosticism, atheism, disbelief, impiety, sacrilege.

religious [adj1] *concerning belief in God*
▪ *Syn* canonical, churchgoing, clerical, deistic, devout, divine, doctrinal, ecclesiastical, faithful, god-fearing, holy, ministerial, moral, noble, orthodox, pious, reverent, righteous, sacerdotal, scriptural, sectarian, spiritual, staunch, theistic, theological; ▪ *Ant* agnostic, atheistic, irreligious, ungodly.

religious [adj2] *conscientious, scrupulous* ▪ *Syn* exact, faithful, fastidious, meticulous, punctilious, rigid, rigorous, unerring, unswerving; ▪ *Ant* careless, erring, indolent, lazy, undetailed.

relinquish [v] *give up, let go*
▪ *Syn* abandon, abdicate, abnegate, cast off, desert, discard, forbear, forsake, quit, release, renounce, sacrifice, shed, surrender, swear off, vacate, waive, yield; ▪ *Ant* hold, keep, sustain, take.

relish [v] *look forward to; appreciate*
▪ *Syn* admire, be fond of, cherish, delight in, enjoy, fancy, go for, like, luxuriate in, prefer, revel in, savor, taste; ▪ *Ant* dislike, hate.

reluctant [adj] *unenthusiastic, unwilling*
▪ *Syn* afraid, cautious, circumspect, demurring, diffident, grudging, hesitant, indisposed, laggard, loath, opposed, queasy, recalcitrant, remiss, shy, squeamish, wary; ▪ *Ant* anxious, eager, enthusiastic, ready, willing.

rely [v] *have confidence in*
▪ *Syn* bank, be confident of, believe in, be sure of, count, depend, entrust, expect, have faith in, hope, lean, reckon, trust; ▪ *Ant* be independent, distrust, doubt.

remain [v] *stay, wait*
▪ *Syn* abide, bide, bivouac, continue, delay, dwell, endure, linger, nest, outlast, pause, perch, rest, roost, sit out, sojourn,

stay behind, stop, survive, tarry, visit, wait; ▪ *Ant* depart, forge, go, leave, move.

remark [*v*] *notice and comment*
▪ *Syn* animadvert, commentate, declare, heed, mark, mention, note, observe, pass comment, reflect, regard, say, see, speak, take note, take notice; ▪ *Ant* disregard, hold back, ignore, suppress.

remarkable [*adj*] *extraordinary, unusual*
▪ *Syn* arresting, curious, distinguished, exceptional, impressive, marked, momentous, notable, noteworthy, outstanding, peculiar, phenomenal, prominent, rare, salient, significant, strange, striking, uncommon, unique, wonderful, world class; ▪ *Ant* normal, ordinary, typical, unremarkable, usual.

remedial [*adj*] *healing, restorative*
▪ *Syn* beneficial, corrective, curative, purifying, recuperative, reformative, repairing, restitutive, restorative, sanative, soothing, therapeutic, tonic, wholesome; ▪ *Ant* damaging, harmful, hurtful, injurious.

remedy [*v*] *fix, cure*
▪ *Syn* aid, alleviate, ameliorate, amend, correct, doctor, emend, fix up, heal, improve, mitigate, palliate, put right, rectify, redress, relieve, renew, repair, set right, solve, soothe, straighten out, treat; ▪ *Ant* aggravate, exacerbate, harm, injure.

remember [*v*] *keep in mind; summon into mind* ▪ *Syn* bear in mind, brood over, call to mind, call up, cite, conjure up, dwell upon, fix in the mind, look back, memorialize, recall, recognize, recollect, relive, remind, reminisce, retain, retrospect, revive, summon up, think back, treasure; ▪ *Ant* disregard, forget, overlook.

remind [*v*] *awaken memories of something* ▪ *Syn* bring to mind, call to mind, cite, emphasize, hint, imply, intimate, mention, prod, prompt, put in mind, recall, recollect, refresh memory, remember, reminisce, retrospect, revive, stir up, stress, suggest; ▪ *Ant* forget.

reminisce [*v*] *go over in one's memory*
▪ *Syn* bethink, hark back, live in the past, look back, mind, mull, muse, ponder, recall, recollect, remember, remind, retain, retrospect, review, revive, think back; ▪ *Ant* forget, repress.

reminiscent [*adj*] *suggestive of something in the past* ▪ *Syn* bringing to mind, evocative, mnemonic, nostalgic, recollective, redolent, remindful, similar; ▪ *Ant* forgetful, oblivious.

remiss [*v*] *careless, thoughtless*
▪ *Syn* culpable, daydreaming, delinquent, derelict, dilatory, disregardful, fainéant, forgetful, heedless, inattentive, indifferent, indolent, lackadaisical, lax, lazy, neglectful, negligent, slack, slapdash, slipshod, sloppy, slothful, tardy, unmindful; ▪ *Ant* careful, mindful, scrupulous, thorough, thoughtful.

remit [*v1*] *send, transfer*
▪ *Syn* address, consign, dispatch, forward, mail, pay, post, settle, square, transmit; ▪ *Ant* hold, keep, withhold.

remit [*v2*] *stop, postpone*
▪ *Syn* absolve, alleviate, cancel, condone, defer, delay, desist, diminish, ease up, excuse, exonerate, forbear, forgive, halt, intermit, mitigate, moderate, modify, modulate, pardon, prorogue, put off, reduce, relax, release, repeal, reprieve, rescind, soften, stay, suspend, wane, weaken; ▪ *Ant* encourage, forge, forward.

remnant [*n*] *leftover part*
▪ *Syn* balance, bit, dregs, dross, end, fragment, heel, leavings, lees, leftovers, orts, particle, piece, portion, remainder, remains, residue, residuum, rest, rump, scrap, shred, strip, surplus, survival, vestige; ▪ *Ant* whole.

remonstrate [*v*] *argue against*
▪ *Syn* animadvert, blame, censure, challenge, combat, criticize, decry, dispute, except, expostulate, fight, find fault, frown upon, inveigh, nag, object, pick at, protest, recriminate, resist, scold, take exception, take issue; ▪ *Ant* agree, concede, give in.

remorseful [*adj*] *guilty, ashamed*
▪ *Syn* apologetic, chastened, compunctious, guilt-ridden, mournful, penitent, regretful, repentant, rueful, sad, self-reproachful, sorry; ▪ *Ant* callous, merciless, remorseless, ruthless, unashamed, unmerciful.

remorseless [*adj*] *without guilt in spite of wrongdoing* ▪ *Syn* barbarous, callous, fierce, grim, hard, hard-bitten, hardened, impenitent, inexorable, inhumane, insensitive, merciless, obdurate, pitiless, ruthless, sanguinary, savage, shameless, vindictive; ▪ *Ant* ashamed, guilty, remorseful, sad, sorry.

remote [*adj1*] *out-of-the-way; in the distance* ▪ *Syn* alien, back, distant, far, far-flung, far-off, foreign, frontier, isolated, lonely, lonesome, obscure, outlying, private, removed, secluded, secret; ▪ *Ant* close, convenient, near, nearby.

remote [*adj2*] *irrelevant, unrelated* ▪ *Syn* alien, apart, extrinsic, farfetched, foreign, immaterial, inappropriate, obscure, outside, strange, unconnected; ▪ *Ant* close, germane, immediate, related, relevant.

remote [*adj3*] *unlikely, improbable* ▪ *Syn* dubious, faint, implausible, meager, negligible, outside, poor, slender, slight, slim; ▪ *Ant* imminent, likely, possible, probable.

remote [*adj4*] *cold, detached; unapproachable* ▪ *Syn* abstracted, aloof, casual, disinterested, icy, indifferent, introverted, removed, reserved, standoffish, uncommunicative, uppity, withdrawn; ▪ *Ant* alert, approachable, attentive, friendly, gentle, warm.

remove [*v1*] *lift or move object; take off, away* ▪ *Syn* abolish, amputate, carry off, clear away, cut out, delete, detach, discard, dislodge, displace, eliminate, expel, oust, purge, relegate, separate, tear out, throw out, transport, unload, unseat, uproot, withdraw; ▪ *Ant* fix, place, remain, stay.

remove [*v2*] *do away with; kill* ▪ *Syn* assassinate, dispose of, do away with, do in, eliminate, eradicate, erase, execute, exterminate, liquidate, murder, obliterate, purge, take out; ▪ *Ant* give birth, plant, sow.

remunerate [*v*] *compensate, reward* ▪ *Syn* award, grant, guerdon, indemnify, pay, pay off, pay up, recompense, redress, reimburse, repay, requite, vouchsafe; ▪ *Ant* assess, charge, fine, tax.

rend [*v*] *opening, split* ▪ *Syn* break, chink, cleave, crack, divide, fracture, gash, perforate, rip, rupture, slash, slit, tatter, tear; ▪ *Ant* join, mend.

render [*v1*] *contribute* ▪ *Syn* allot, deliver, dispense, distribute, furnish, give, impart, make restitution, minister, pay, provide, relinquish, repay, restore, submit, supply, tender, yield; ▪ *Ant* keep, refuse, retain, withhold.

render [*v2*] *translate, explain* ▪ *Syn* construe, deliver, interpret, paraphrase, restate, reword, transcribe, transliterate, transpose; ▪ *Ant* cloud, confuse, obscure.

renegade [*adj*] *rebellious* ▪ *Syn* apostate, disloyal, dissident, heterodox, mutinous, outlaw, radical, reactionary, rebel, recreant, revolutionary, schismatic, traitorous; ▪ *Ant* loyal, obedient, submissive.

renew [*v*] *start over; extend* ▪ *Syn* begin again, continue, exhilarate, freshen, gentrify, modernize, overhaul, prolong, recommence, recreate, reestablish, refresh, refurbish, rehabilitate, replenish, restock, resuscitate, revitalize, spruce, stimulate, transform; ▪ *Ant* depreciate, forget, let lapse, stop, wear out.

renounce [*v*] *abandon, reject* ▪ *Syn* abdicate, abjure, abnegate, apostacize, arrogate, cast off, disavow, disown, eschew, forswear, give up, quit, recant, reject, repudiate, resign, spurn, swear off, tergiversate, tergiverse, waive, walk out on; ▪ *Ant* allow, approve, condone, defend, maintain.

renovate [*v*] *fix up, modernize* ▪ *Syn* make over, overhaul, recondition, reconstitute, reform, refurbish, rehabilitate, remodel, renew, restore, revamp, revitalize, revive, spruce, update; ▪ *Ant* demolish, destroy, ruin.

renown [*adj*] *fame* ▪ *Syn* acclaim, celebrity, éclat, distinction, eminence, glory, honor, illustriousness, luster, note, notoriety, prestige, prominence, reputation, repute, stardom; ▪ *Ant* anonymity, obscurity, unimportance.

renowned [*adj*] *famous* ▪ *Syn* acclaimed, celebrated, distinguished, eminent, esteemed, extolled, famed, great, illustrious, lauded, name, notable, noted, outstanding, prominent, signal, star, well-known; ▪ *Ant* anonymous, obscure, unimportant, unknown.

rent [*v*] *pay or charge fee for use, service, or privilege* ▪ *Syn* borrow, charter, contract, engage, hire, lease, lend, let, loan, put on loan, sublet; ▪ *Ant* buy, purchase.

renunciation [*n*] *abandonment, rejection* ▪ *Syn* abdication, abjuration, abnegation, disavowal, disclaimer, eschewal, forswearing, rebuff, relinquishment, renouncement, repeal, repudiation, self-abnegation, self-denial, self-sacrifice, spurning, veto; ▪ *Ant* acceptance, approval, condonement.

repair [*v1*] *fix, restore*
▪ *Syn* correct, emend, heal, improve, mend, overhaul, patch, patch up, put back together, rebuild, recondition, recover, rectify, redline, redress, reform, refresh, refurbish, rejuvenate, remedy, renew, renovate, restore, revamp, revive, sew; ▪ *Ant* break, damage, destroy, hurt, injure, ruin, spoil, wreck.

repair [*v2*] *leave; retire*
▪ *Syn* betake oneself, move, pass, push on, recur, refer, remove, turn in, withdraw; ▪ *Ant* maintain, remain, stay.

repartee [*n*] *pleasant conversation*
▪ *Syn* answer, badinage, banter, comeback, humor, irony, pleasantry, quip, rejoinder, reply, response, retort, sally, sarcasm, satire, wit, witticism, wittiness, wordplay; ▪ *Ant* argument, deliberation, disagreement.

repay [*v1*] *give back money or possession*
▪ *Syn* accord, award, compensate, indemnify, make amends, offset, rebate, recompense, refund, reimburse, return, reward, settle up; ▪ *Ant* deprive, extort, penalize, seize, steal, take.

repay [*v2*] *get even; obtain restitution for past injustice* ▪ *Syn* avenge, even the score, get back at, make reprisal, pay back, retaliate, revenge; ▪ *Ant* excuse, forgive, overlook.

repeal [*v*] *declare null and void*
▪ *Syn* abolish, abrogate, annul, back out, cancel, countermand, dismantle, invalidate, nullify, rescind, revoke, set aside, shoot down, vacate, void, withdraw; ▪ *Ant* approve, confirm, enact, pass, sanction, validate.

repeatedly [*adv*] *over and over again*
▪ *Syn* again, again and again, frequently, many a time, many times, much, oft, often, oftentimes, oftimes, regularly, time after time, time and again; ▪ *Ant* never, once.

repel [*v1*] *push away; repulse*
▪ *Syn* brush off, cast aside, deflect, dismiss, dispute, drive away, fend off, fight, foil, force back, hold off, oppose, parry, put down, put to flight, rebuff, rebut, refuse, resist, turn down, ward off, withstand; ▪ *Ant* attract, draw, invite.

repel [*v2*] *induce aversion*
▪ *Syn* disgust, nauseate, offend, reluct, repulse, revolt, sicken; ▪ *Ant* attract, draw, enchant, fascinate, please.

repentance [*n*] *feeling bad for past action* ▪ *Syn* anguish, attrition, bitterness, conscience, contrition, grief, guilt, penitence, regret, remorse, rue, self-reproach, sorrow; ▪ *Ant* complacency, contentment, happiness, impenitence, self-righteousness, smugness.

repercussion [*n*] *consequence*
▪ *Syn* chain reaction, effect, fallout, impact, influence, reaction, rebound, recoil, result, reverberation, side effect, spinoff; ▪ *Ant* cause.

repetitious [*adj*] *wordy, tedious*
▪ *Syn* alliterative, dull, echoic, iterant, long-winded, pleonastic, prolix, redundant, reiterative, resonant, tautological, verbose, windy; ▪ *Ant* concise, simple.

replenish [*v*] *fill, stock*
▪ *Syn* provision, refill, refresh, reload, renew, replace, restock, restore, stock, top; ▪ *Ant* deplete, exhaust, use up, waste.

replete [*adj*] *full, well-stocked*
▪ *Syn* abounding, awash, brimful, crammed, filled, glutted, jam-packed, luxurious, overflowing, packed, rife, sated, satiated, stuffed, swarming, teeming, thronged; ▪ *Ant* empty, hungry, needy, starving, unpopulated, wanting.

replica [*n*] *duplicate*
▪ *Syn* carbon, carbon copy, clone, facsimile, imitation, likeness, lookalike, miniature, model, photocopy, replication, reproduction, stat; ▪ *Ant* original.

reply [*n*] *answer*
▪ *Syn* acknowledgment, comeback, feedback, reaction, reciprocation, rejoinder, response, retort, return, riposte, wisecrack; ▪ *Ant* invitation, question, request.

reply [*v*] *answer*
▪ *Syn* acknowledge, counter, echo, feedback, get back to, react, reciprocate, rejoin, respond, retaliate, retort, return, riposte, write back; ▪ *Ant* question, request.

report [*v*] *communicate information, knowledge* ▪ *Syn* advise, air, announce, broadcast, circulate, cover, debrief, declare, describe, detail, disclose, document, · enunciate, impart, inform, inscribe, itemize, list, make known, make public, mention, narrate, note, notify, pass on, promulgate, provide details, publish, recite, record, recount, relate, relay, reveal, set forth, spread, state, summarize, tell; ▪ *Ant* conceal, suppress, withhold.

repose [v] *relax; recline*
▪ *Syn* lay down, lie, lie down, loaf, loll, lounge, place, rest, settle, settle down, slant, sleep, slumber, stretch, stretch out, take it easy; ▪ *Ant* be active, be busy, energize.

reprehensible [adj] *very bad; shameful*
▪ *Syn* amiss, blameworthy, condemnable, culpable, delinquent, demeritorious, errant, guilty, ignoble, objectionable, opprobrious, remiss, sinful, unholy, unworthy, wicked; ▪ *Ant* creditable, good, kind, respectable.

represent [v] *depict, show*
▪ *Syn* delineate, denote, display, draft, enact, evoke, exhibit, express, hint, illustrate, interpret, limn, mirror, narrate, outline, picture, portray, relate, render, reproduce, run down, sketch, suggest, track; ▪ *Ant* belie, color, distort, falsify, garble, misinterpret, misrepresent, pervert, twist, warp.

representative [adj] *characteristic, typical* ▪ *Syn* adumbrative, archetypal, classic, classical, emblematic, evocative, exemplary, ideal, illustrative, model, prototypical, quintessential, symbolic, symbolical; ▪ *Ant* aberrant, atypical, different, uncharacteristic.

repress [v] *keep back, hold in*
▪ *Syn* bottle, check, compose, control, crush, curb, hinder, hold back, inhibit, keep in, keep in check, muffle, overpower, quash, quelch, quell, rein, restrain, silence, smother, squelch, stifle, subdue, subjugate, suppress, swallow; ▪ *Ant* allow, let out, liberate, permit, unleash.

reprieve [v] *relieve of blame, responsibility* ▪ *Syn* abate, absolve, allay, alleviate, amnesty, excuse, forgive, grant a stay, let go, let off, mitigate, palliate, pardon, postpone, remit, respite; ▪ *Ant* accusation, blame.

reprimand [v] *blame, scold*
▪ *Syn* admonish, castigate, censure, check, chide, criticize, denounce, lecture, rebuke, reprehend, reprove, tell off, upbraid; ▪ *Ant* exonerate, forgive, reward.

reprisal [n] *revenge*
▪ *Syn* avengement, counterblow, counterstroke, requital, retaliation, retribution, vengeance; ▪ *Ant* kindness, sympathy.

reproach [v] *find fault with*
▪ *Syn* abuse, admonish, blame, call down, cavil, censure, chide, condemn, criticize, defame, discredit, disparage, lay on, rebuke, reprehend, reprimand, reprove, scold, trim, upbraid; ▪ *Ant* approve, praise.

reproduce [v1] *make more copies of*
▪ *Syn* clone, copy, duplicate, echo, imitate, knock off, match, mirror, parallel, photocopy, recount, recreate, redo, reenact, reflect, remake, repeat, replicate, represent, reprint, restamp, revive, transcribe, type; ▪ *Ant* destroy, stop.

reproduce [v2] *make something new; give birth* ▪ *Syn* bear, beget, breed, engender, fecundate, generate, hatch, impregnate, multiply, procreate, produce young, progenerate, proliferate, propagate, repopulate, sire, spawn; ▪ *Ant* abort, kill.

repudiate [v] *reject; turn one's back on*
▪ *Syn* abandon, abjure, apostatize, break with, cast, cast off, default, demur, deny, desert, disapprove, disavow, discard, disclaim, dishonor, disinherit, disown, forsake, recant, renounce, repeal, reprobate, rescind, retract, reverse, revoke, spurn, tergiversate, tergiverse; ▪ *Ant* admit, approve, embrace, espouse.

repugnant [adj] *bad, obnoxious; hostile*
▪ *Syn* abhorrent, abominable, adverse, antagonistic, antipathetic, conflicting, contradictory, disagreeable, disgusting, extrinsic, foul, hateful, inimical, invidious, loathsome, nasty, nauseating, noisome, objectionable, odious, offensive, repellent, revolting, sickening, vile; ▪ *Ant* attractive, favorable, friendly, pleasant.

repulse [v1] *push away*
▪ *Syn* beat off, drive back, fend off, hold off, push back, rebuff, rebut, reject, set back, ward off; ▪ *Ant* attract, enchant, encourage.

repulse [v2] *make sick*
▪ *Syn* disgust, rebuff, reject, reluct, repel, revolt, sicken, snub, spurn, turn down, turn off; ▪ *Ant* please, soothe.

repulsive [adj] *very disgusting, offensive*
▪ *Syn* abhorrent, abominable, distasteful, foul, hideous, horrid, loathsome, nasty,

nauseating, noisome, odious, off-putting, pugnacious, repellent, revolting, sickening, ugly, unsightly, vile; ■ *Ant* attractive, enchanting, inviting, pleasing.

reputable [*adj*] *worthy of respect*
■ *Syn* acclaimed, celebrated, distinguished, esteemed, famed, favored, high-principled, honorable, legitimate, notable, of good repute, prominent, reliable, renowned, sincere, trustworthy, upright, well-known; ■ *Ant* disreputable, notorious, unrespected, untrustworthy.

reputed [*adj*] *believed*
■ *Syn* alleged, assumed, considered, deemed, estimated, held, ostensible, putative, reckoned, regarded, reported, rumored, said, seeming, supposed, thought; ■ *Ant* actual, real, true.

request [*v*] *ask for*
■ *Syn* appeal, apply, beg, beseech, bespeak, call for, demand, desire, entreat, inquire, petition, promote, requisition, seek, solicit, sue, supplicate, touch; ■ *Ant* answer, rejoin, reply, respond, retort.

require [*v*] *need, want*
■ *Syn* crave, depend upon, desire, feel necessity for, have need, hurting for, lack, miss, stand in need, wish; ■ *Ant* dispense with, forego, have, not want.

required/requisite [*adj*] *necessary*
■ *Syn* appropriate, called for, compulsatory, compulsory, due, enforced, essential, imperative, indispensable, mandatory, needed, obligatory, prerequisite, prescribed, recommended, vital; ■ *Ant* nonessential, optional, unnecessary.

requisition [*v*] *ask for; apply for something needed* ■ *Syn* buy, call for, challenge, claim, demand, exact, order, postulate, put in for, request, require, solicit; ■ *Ant* answer, cede, give, grant, offer, relinquish, reply, resign, tender, waive.

requite [*v*] *compensate, give in return*
■ *Syn* indemnify, make amends, pay, quit, reciprocate, recompense, redeem, redress, reimburse, remunerate, repay, return, reward, satisfy, settle; ■ *Ant* forsake, refuse, renege, rescind.

rescind [*v*] *declare null and void*
■ *Syn* abolish, abrogate, annul, cancel, invalidate, overturn, quash, recall, renege, repeal, retract, revoke, set aside, void; ■ *Ant* allow, approve, permit, uphold, validate.

rescue [*v*] *save from danger*
■ *Syn* conserve, deliver, emancipate, extricate, free, liberate, manumit, preserve, recapture, recover, redeem, retrieve, salvage, set free, unleash; ■ *Ant* abandon, endanger, imperil.

research [*v*] *examine, study*
■ *Syn* analyze, consult, experiment, explore, inquire, investigate, look into, probe, read up on, scrutinize; ■ *Ant* ignore, neglect.

resemble [*v*] *look or be like*
■ *Syn* appear like, approximate, bear resemblance to, coincide, come close to, correspond to, duplicate, echo, favor, feature, match, mirror, parallel, relate, remind one of, seem like, simulate, sound like, take after; ■ *Ant* contradict, contrast, deviate, differ.

resent [*v*] *be angry about*
■ *Syn* begrudge, be insulted, be offended by, be vexed, dislike, feel bitter, frown at, grudge, object to, take exception, take offense, take umbrage; ■ *Ant* approve, like, welcome.

reserve [*v*] *keep, hold back*
■ *Syn* conserve, defer, delay, hoard, lay up, maintain, postpone, preserve, put away, put by, retain, save, set aside, stash, stockpile, store, stow away, withhold; ■ *Ant* distribute, give, offer.

reserved [*adj1*] *silent, unsociable; constrained* ■ *Syn* bashful, cautious, ceremonious, close, collected, composed, cool, demure, diffident, distant, eremitic, formal, mild, modest, noncommittal, placid, prim, quiet, reclusive, restrained, reticent, retiring, secretive, sedate, self-contained, serene, shy, soft-spoken, solitary, taciturn, withdrawn; ■ *Ant* extroverted, friendly, outgoing, sociable.

reserved [*adj2*] *held for future use*
■ *Syn* appropriated, arrogated, booked, claimed, engaged, kept, laid away, preempted, qualified, restricted, retained, roped off, set apart, set aside, spoken for, taken; ■ *Ant* given, offered.

residual [*adj*] *leftover*
■ *Syn* balance, continuing, enduring, extra, lingering, net, remaining, surplus, vestigial; ■ *Ant* base, core, fundamental, prime.

resign [*v*] *give up responsibility*
■ *Syn* abandon, abdicate, capitulate, cede, demit, drop, fold, forgo, forsake, give

notice, leave, quit, relinquish, renounce, retire, secede, sign off, stand down, step down, surrender, terminate, vacate, waive, walk out, yield; ▪ *Ant* agree, carry out, continue, take on.

resigned [adj] *enduring, passive*
▪ *Syn* acquiescent, adjusted, agreeable, amenable, compliant, deferential, docile, genial, long-suffering, manageable, obedient, patient, peaceable, philosophical, pliant, quiescent, reconciled, relinquishing, stoical, subdued, submissive, subservient, tame, tolerant, tractable, willing, yielding; ▪ *Ant* intolerant, resistent.

resilient [adj] *bouncy, flexible*
▪ *Syn* buoyant, effervescent, elastic, expansive, hardy, irrepressible, plastic, pliable, quick to recover, rebounding, springy, stretchy, strong, supple, tough, volatile; ▪ *Ant* hard, inflexible, rigid, stiff.

resist [v] *withstand, oppose*
▪ *Syn* battle, bear, brook, buck, check, combat, confront, contend, defy, dispute, duel, endure, fight back, forbear, forgo, hinder, hold off, hold out against, maintain, persevere, persist, put up a fight, refuse, remain, remain firm, stand up to, stonewall, struggle against, suffer, thwart, traverse, turn down, weather, withstand; ▪ *Ant* comply, conform, go along, surrender.

resolute [adj] *determined, strong-willed*
▪ *Syn* adamant, bold, constant, courageous, decided, dogged, faithful, firm, fixed, immutable, inflexible, intent upon, intrepid, loyal, obstinate, persevering, persistent, purposeful, relentless, resolved, serious, set, settled, staunch, steadfast, steady, strong, stubborn, tenacious, true, unbending, unflinching, unyielding, valiant; ▪ *Ant* cautious, cowardly, irresolute, vacillating, weak.

resolve [v] *make up one's mind; find solution* ▪ *Syn* agree, analyze, answer, choose, conclude, decide, decipher, design, determine, dissect, elect, elucidate, fathom, figure, fix, intend, propose, purpose, puzzle out, settle, solve, take a stand, undertake, will, work out, work through; ▪ *Ant* mull, question, waver, wonder.

resonant [adj] *vibrant in sound*
▪ *Syn* booming, consonant, deep, deep-toned, echoing, enhanced, full, heightened, intensified, loud, mellow, oro-

tund, plangent, powerful, profound, pulsating, resounding, reverberant, reverberating, rich, ringing, round, sonorant, sonorous, stentorian, thrilling, throbbing, thundering, thunderous; ▪ *Ant* faint, quiet.

resort [v] *have recourse to; make use of*
▪ *Syn* apply, avail oneself of, benefit by, bring into play, devote, employ, exercise, fall back on, make use of, put to use, recur, refer to, take up, try, turn, turn to, use, utilize, visit; ▪ *Ant* avoid, dodge.

resourceful [adj] *imaginative*
▪ *Syn* able, active, adventurous, aggressive, bright, capable, clever, creative, enterprising, ingenious, intelligent, inventive, original, quick-witted, sharp, talented, venturesome; ▪ *Ant* artless, dull, uncreative, unimaginative.

respect [v] *admire; obey*
▪ *Syn* abide by, adhere to, adore, appreciate, attend, comply with, defer to, esteem, follow, heed, honor, note, notice, recognize, regard, revere, set store by, show consideration, take into account, uphold, value, venerate; ▪ *Ant* condemn, disobey, scorn.

respectable [adj1] *good, honest*
▪ *Syn* admirable, august, befitting, comely, creditable, decent, decorous, dignified, estimable, fair, honorable, moderate, presentable, proper, redoubtable, reputable, respected, sublime, suitable, venerable, virtuous, worthy; ▪ *Ant* corrupt, dishonest, dishonorable, unworthy.

respectable [adj2] *substantial, ample*
▪ *Syn* appreciable, considerable, decent, fair, sensible, sizable, tidy, tolerable; ▪ *Ant* inadequate, miserly.

respectful [adj] *courteous, mannerly*
▪ *Syn* admiring, appreciative, civil, considerate, deferential, gracious, humble, obedient, obeisant, polite, recognizing, reverent, solicitous, well-mannered; ▪ *Ant* discourteous, mean, unmannerly.

respective [adj] *particular, specific*
▪ *Syn* corresponding, each, individual, own, personal, relevant, separate, several, singular, various; ▪ *Ant* indefinite.

respite [n] *pause, suspension in activity*
▪ *Syn* adjournment, break, cessation, deferment, delay, ease, exculpation, halt, hiatus, intermission, interregnum, interruption, lull, moratorium, postponement,

recess, reprieve, rest, stay;   **Ant** continuation.

resplendent [adj] bright, radiant
 Syn beaming, blazing, dazzling, effulgent, flaming, gleaming, glossy, glowing, irradiant, luminous, refulgent, shining, splendid, sublime;   **Ant** cloudy, dull, gloomy, withering.

respond [v] act in answer to something
 Syn acknowledge, answer, behave, come back, counter, get back to, react, reciprocate, rejoin, reply, retort, return;   **Ant** ask, question, request.

responsible [adj1] accountable, in charge   **Syn** answerable, at the helm, authoritative, bonded, bound, censurable, chargeable, compelled, constrained, contracted, culpable, duty-bound, fettered, hampered, important, in authority, incumbent, liable, obligated, obliged, pledged, sworn to, tied, under contract, under obligation;   **Ant** excused, exempt, free, immune, irresponsible.

responsible [adj2] trustworthy, mature
 Syn able, adult, capable, conscientious, dependable, dutiful, effective, efficient, faithful, firm, levelheaded, loyal, reliable, self-reliant, sensible, sound, stable, steadfast, trusty;   **Ant** immature, irresponsible, unreliable, untrustworthy.

responsive [adj] quick to react
 Syn active, alive, awake, aware, compassionate, conscious, forthcoming, impressionable, kindhearted, open, passionate, perceptive, reactive, receptive, respondent, sensitive, sharp, softhearted, susceptible, sympathetic, tender, warmhearted;   **Ant** apathetic, impassive, unresponsive.

rest [v] be calm; sleep
 Syn doze, dream, drowse, ease off, ease up, idle, laze, let up, loaf, loll, lounge, nap, nod, recline, refresh oneself, relax, repose, sit down, slack, sleep, slumber, snooze, spell, take a break, unwind, wind down;   **Ant** activate, be active, carry out, do, energize.

restitution [n] compensation, repayment
 Syn amends, dues, indemnification, indemnity, payment, quittance, rebate, recompense, redress, refund, reimbursement, remuneration, reparation, reprisal, requital, restoration, return, satisfaction;   **Ant** fee, fine, penalty.

restive [adj] impatient, nervous
 Syn agitated, contrary, edgy, fidgety,

fractious, fretful, froward, ill at ease, jittery, jumpy, nervy, obstinate, on edge, ornery, recalcitrant, refractory, restless, stubborn, tense, uneasy, uptight;   **Ant** calm, collected, patient, relaxed.

restless [adj] not content; moving about
 Syn agitated, anxious, bustling, disturbed, edgy, fidgety, fitful, fretful, irresolute, jumpy, nervous, on edge, perturbed, restive, roving, troubled, uneasy, wandering, worried;   **Ant** quiet, relaxed, restful.

restore [v1] fix, make new
 Syn cure, heal, improve, make healthy, make restitution, mend, modernize, reanimate, rebuild, recall, recondition, reconstitute, reconstruct, recover, re-establish, refresh, refurbish, rehabilitate, reinstate, rejuvenate, renew, renovate, repair, replace, rescue, retouch, revitalize, revive, touch up, update;   **Ant** damage, destroy, oppose, undermine.

restore [v2] give back
 Syn hand back, put back, replace, return, send back;   **Ant** banish, exile, oust.

restrain [v] keep under control; hold back   **Syn** arrest, bind, bridle, chain, check, circumscribe, confine, constrain, contain, control, curb, curtail, debar, detain, deter, fetter, gag, hamper, handicap, harness, hem in, hinder, hold, impound, imprison, inhibit, jail, keep, keep down, limit, lock up, manacle, muzzle, pinion, prescribe, prevent, pull back, repress, restrict, sit on, subdue, suppress, tie up;   **Ant** free, liberate, release.

restrained [adj] calm, quiet
 Syn calm and collected, conservative, controlled, cool, discreet, inobtrusive, laid-back, mild, moderate, muted, reasonable, reticent, retiring, self-controlled, steady, subdued, tasteful, temperate, under control, uptight, withdrawn;   **Ant** assured, bold, confident, extroverted, outgoing.

restrict [v] confine, limit situation or ability to participate   **Syn** bind, bound, chain, check, circumscribe, come down on, constrict, contain, contract, cramp, curb, decrease, define, delimit, demarcate, demark, diminish, encircle, hamper, handicap, hem in, hold back, impede, inhibit, moderate, modify, narrow, pin down, prelimit, put away, qualify, reduce, regulate, restrain, shorten, shrink, shut in, surround, temper, tether, tie; ▪ *Ant* enlarge, expand, free, let go, release.

result [v] *happen, develop*
▪ *Syn* accrue, appear, arise, attend, become of, be due to, come about, come from, come of, culminate, derive, effect, emanate, emerge, ensue, eventualize, eventuate, flow, follow, germinate, happen, issue, occur, originate, proceed, produce, rise, spring, stem, turn out, work out; ▪ *Ant* cause.

resume [v] *begin again*
▪ *Syn* pick up, proceed, reassume, recapitulate, recommence, recoup, regain, reinstitute, reoccupy, reopen, repossess, restart, retake, return to, take back, take up; ▪ *Ant* finish, halt, stop.

retain [v1] *hold on to physically or mentally* ▪ *Syn* absorb, contain, detain, enjoy, grasp, hand onto, have, hold, hold fast, keep, keep in mind, maintain, memorize, own, possess, preserve, recall, recognize, remember, reserve, save; ▪ *Ant* free, let go, lose, release, relinquish, spend.

retain [v2] *hire*
▪ *Syn* commission, contract, employ, engage, maintain, pay, reserve; ▪ *Ant* fire, let go, pass up.

retaliate [v] *get even with someone*
▪ *Syn* exact retribution, get back at, pay, pay back, reciprocate, recompense, revenge, settle, strike back, take revenge, turn upon, wreak vengeance; ▪ *Ant* forgive, pardon, sympathize.

retard [v] *hinder, obstruct*
▪ *Syn* arrest, balk, bog, brake, choke, clog, crimp, delay, detain, encumber, fetter, flag, hamper, handicap, hold back, impede, lessen, mire, postpone, reduce, set back, slacken, slow up, stall, take down; ▪ *Ant* advance, help, push, speed.

reticent [adj] *secretive, quiet*
▪ *Syn* bashful, close-mouthed, hesitant, mum, reserved, restrained, shy, silent, taciturn, tight-lipped, uncommunicative, unspeaking; ▪ *Ant* candid, communicative, talkative, voluble.

retire [v] *leave a place or responsibility*
▪ *Syn* decamp, depart, exit, get away, hand over, leave service, part, recede, relinquish, resign, sever connections, withdraw; ▪ *Ant* begin, enlist, enter, join.

retiring [adj] *shy, undemonstrative*
▪ *Syn* bashful, coy, demure, humble, meek, modest, quiet, reclusive, reserved, restrained, reticent, self-effacing, shrinking, timid, timorous, withdrawn; ▪ *Ant* demonstrative, extroverted, outgoing, self-confident.

retort [n] *snappy answer*
▪ *Syn* antiphon, back talk, comeback, counter, jest, quip, rejoinder, repartee, reprisal, response, return, riposte, wisecrack, witticism; ▪ *Ant* question, request.

retract [v] *take back; renege on*
▪ *Syn* abjure, back down, cancel, change one's mind, countermand, deny, disavow, disclaim, forswear, go back on, palinode, pull back, recall, recant, renounce, repeal, rescind, revoke, sheathe, take back, withdraw; ▪ *Ant* corroborate, emphasize, reaffirm, repeat.

retreat [v] *pull back, go away*
▪ *Syn* abandon, back down, back off, cave in, decamp, depart, draw back, ebb, escape, evacuate, fall back, fold, leave, move back, opt out, pull out, quail, quit, recede, recoil, regress, resign, retrocede, reverse, sequester, vacate, withdraw; ▪ *Ant* advance, engage, face, forge, meet.

retribution [n] *payback for another's action* ▪ *Syn* avengement, comeuppance, compensation, counterblow, justice, punishment, reckoning, recompense, redress, repayment, reprisal, retaliation, revenge, satisfaction, vengeance; ▪ *Ant* forgiveness, pardon, sympathy.

retrieve [v] *get back*
▪ *Syn* bring back, fetch, get back, reacquire, recapture, reclaim, recoup, recruit, regain, repair, repossess, rescue, restore, salvage, save, win back; ▪ *Ant* give, offer, relinquish.

retrospect [n] *afterthought*
▪ *Syn* hindsight, recollection, reconsideration, reexamination, remembering, remembrance, reminiscence, review; ▪ *Ant* forethought, prophesy, prospect.

return [v1] *go back, turn back*
▪ *Syn* bounce back, circle back, come back, double back, go again, hark back to, move back, reappear, recur, reel back, reexamine, reoccur, retire, retrace steps, revisit; ▪ *Ant* depart, leave.

return [v2] *give back, send back*
▪ *Syn* hand back, make restitution, pay back, rebate, reciprocate, recompense, refund, reimburse, reinstate, remit, ren-

der, restitute, restore, retaliate, roll back; ▪ *Ant* keep, retain, take.

return [v3] *earn*
▪ *Syn* bring in, make, net, pay, pay dividend, pay off, repay, score, show profit, yield; ▪ *Ant* pay.

reveal [v1] *disclose, tell*
▪ *Syn* acknowledge, admit, affirm, betray, broadcast, concede, confess, divulge, expose, give away, impart, inform, leak, make known, make public, notify, proclaim, publish, report, tell, utter; ▪ *Ant* conceal, hide, suppress.

reveal [v2] *show, uncover*
▪ *Syn* bare, disclose, display, exhibit, expose, flash, lay bare, manifest, open, unearth, unmask; ▪ *Ant* cover, hide.

revel [v] *take pleasure; celebrate*
▪ *Syn* bask, carouse, carry on, delight, enjoy, frolic, gloat, indulge, lark, make merry, rejoice, relish, rollick, savor, step out, thrive, wallow; ▪ *Ant* dislike, shrink from.

revelation [n] *disclosure, telling*
▪ *Syn* announcement, apocalypse, betrayal, communication, discovery, divulgement, earful, exhibition, exposure, flash, foreshadowing, leak, news, proclamation, prophecy, sign, vision; ▪ *Ant* concealment, cover-up, secret.

revelry [n] *merrymaking*
▪ *Syn* carousal, celebration, debauchery, entertainment, festival, festivity, fun, gaiety, jollity, party, reveling, saturnalia, spree; ▪ *Ant* mourning, sadness, sobriety.

revenge [v] *retaliate for wrong, grievance* ▪ *Syn* avenge, fight back, get back at, get even, make reprisal, pay back, punish, reciprocate, redress, repay, return, score, settle up, square, venge, vindicate; ▪ *Ant* forgive, pardon, sympathize.

revenue [n] *income, profit*
▪ *Syn* acquirement, annuity, cash flow, dividend, earnings, emolument, gain, interest, means, net, pay, proceeds, receipt, resources, salary, wages, yield; ▪ *Ant* debt, payment.

reverberate [v] *vibrate in sound*
▪ *Syn* echo, react, rebound, recoil, redound, resound, ring; ▪ *Ant* quieten.

revere [v] *have a high opinion of*
▪ *Syn* admire, adore, apotheosize, be in awe of, cherish, defer to, deify, enjoy, esteem, exalt, honor, love, magnify, pay homage, prize, regard, respect, treasure,

venerate, worship; ▪ *Ant* despise, disparage, disregard, disrespect.

reverie [n] *daydream*
▪ *Syn* absentmindedness, absorption, abstraction, contemplation, daydreaming, detachment, dreaminess, dreaming, fantasy, meditation, muse, musing, pensiveness, preoccupation, trance; ▪ *Ant* nightmare.

reverse [v] *cancel, change*
▪ *Syn* alter, annul, backpedal, backtrack, convert, countermand, dismantle, invalidate, lift, modify, negate, nullify, overrule, overset, overthrow, overturn, quash, recall, renege, repeal, rescind, retract, revoke, set aside, turn around, undo, upset; ▪ *Ant* ratify, stick to, uphold.

revert [v] *return to an earlier, less-developed condition* ▪ *Syn* backslide, degenerate, deteriorate, go back, hark back, lapse, recrudesce, recur, regress, relapse, resume, retrogress, return, throw back, turn back; ▪ *Ant* develop, grow, progress.

revive [v] *start again; bring back to life*
▪ *Syn* arouse, awaken, brighten, cheer, energize, enkindle, enliven, gladden, inspirit, invigorate, quicken, rally, reanimate, rekindle, renew, resurrect, resuscitate, revitalize, strengthen, wake up; ▪ *Ant* destroy, kill, suppress.

revoke [v] *take back; cancel*
▪ *Syn* abjure, abrogate, annul, backpedal, call back, countermand, deny, disclaim, dismiss, disown, erase, expunge, forswear, invalidate, negate, nullify, recall, remove, renounce, repeal, rescind, set aside, vacate, void, withdraw; ▪ *Ant* approve, authorize, enforce, restore.

revolt [v1] *rebel, rise up against*
▪ *Syn* arise, boycott, defect, defy, insurrect, mutiny, oppose, overthrow, overturn, rebel, renounce, resist, riot, strike, take up arms, turn against; ▪ *Ant* comply, obey, obey, submit, support.

revolt [v2] *disgust, nauseate*
▪ *Syn* make sick, offend, pain, reluct, repel, repulse, shock, sicken; ▪ *Ant* amuse, attract, delight, make happy.

revolting [adj] *disgusting, nauseating*
▪ *Syn* abhorrent, abominable, appalling, distasteful, foul, horrid, loathsome, nauseous, noisome, obscene, offensive, repellent, repugnant, repulsive, shocking, sickening, vile; ▪ *Ant* delightful, good, pleasant, pleasing.

revolution [n1] *drastic action or change, often in politics* ▪ **Syn** anarchy, bloodshed, cabal, coup, coup d'etat, disorder, foment, golpe, guerrilla activity, insubordination, insurgency, mutiny, overthrow, plot, rebellion, reformation, reversal, rising, shake-up, subversion, transformation, tumult, turnover, unrest, upheaval, uprising; ▪ **Ant** regression, retrogression, submission.

revulsion [n] *disgust, hatred* ▪ **Syn** abhorrence, abomination, aversion, detestation, dislike, distaste, hate, horror, loathing, recoil, repugnance, repulsion; ▪ **Ant** like, liking, love, loving.

reward [v] *pay; give prize* ▪ **Syn** compensate, honor, recompense, remunerate, repay, requite, stroke, tip; ▪ **Ant** penalize, punish, take away.

rewarding [adj] *beneficial, pleasing* ▪ **Syn** advantageous, edifying, fruitful, gainful, gratifying, productive, profitable, remunerative, satisfying, valuable, worthwhile; ▪ **Ant** troubling, upsetting.

rhetorical [adj] *wordy; flowery in speech* ▪ **Syn** articulate, bombastic, declamatory, embellished, exaggerated, flamboyant, florid, fluent, grandiloquent, hyperbolic, inflated, magniloquent, oratorical, ostentatious, overblown, overdone, overwrought, pompous, pretentious, showy, sonorous, swollen, tumescent, tumid, turgid, verbose, voluble; ▪ **Ant** concise, simple, straightforward.

ribald [adj] *vulgar, obscene* ▪ **Syn** base, bawdy, coarse, devilish, earthy, foul-mouthed, indecent, indecorous, lascivious, lewd, naughty, racy, raunchy, rogue, salacious, scabrous, scurrilous, unrefined; ▪ **Ant** chaste, clean, decent.

rich [adj1] *having a lot of money* ▪ **Syn** affluent, comfortable, easy, fat, flush, gilded, independent, moneyed, opulent, plush, propertied, prosperous, upscale, uptown, wealthy; ▪ **Ant** poor.

rich [adj2] *abundant, well-supplied* ▪ **Syn** abounding, ample, deluxe, elaborate, expensive, extravagant, fancy, fecund, fruitful, full, gorgeous, grand, lavish, lush, magnificent, ornate, palatial, plenteous, plush, posh, priceless, productive, prolific, resplendent, smart, swell, valuable, well-endowed; ▪ **Ant** depleted, impoverished, needy.

rich [adj3] *flavorful* ▪ **Syn** creamy, delicious, fatty, full-bodied, heavy, highly flavored, juicy, luscious, oily, satisfying, savory, succulent, sustaining, sweet, tasty; ▪ **Ant** bland, tasteless.

rich [adj4] *full in color or sound* ▪ **Syn** bright, canorous, deep, dulcet, eloquent, intense, mellifluous, resonant, rotund, significant, silvery, sonorous, strong, vibrant, vivid, warm; ▪ **Ant** flat, low, tinny, weak.

rich [adj5] *very funny* ▪ **Syn** absurd, amusing, comical, diverting, entertaining, farcical, hilarious, humorous, incongruous, ludicrous, odd, preposterous, queer, ridiculous, risible, strange; ▪ **Ant** serious.

rickety [adj] *unsound, broken-down* ▪ **Syn** broken, decrepit, dilapidated, feeble, fragile, frail, infirm, insecure, precarious, ramshackle, rocky, shaky, tottering, unsteady, wavering, wobbly; ▪ **Ant** sound, stable.

rid [v] *do away with; free* ▪ **Syn** abolish, clear, deliver, disburden, disencumber, eject, eliminate, eradicate, expel, exterminate, extirpate, fire, purge, relieve, roust, shed, uproot; ▪ **Ant** adopt, burden, encumber.

ride [v2] *dominate, oppress* ▪ **Syn** afflict, annoy, badger, bait, be arbitrary, disparage, grip, harass, harry, haunt, hector, hound, override, persecute, reproach, scold, torment, torture, tyrannize, upbraid; ▪ **Ant** amuse, soothe.

ridge [n] *raised part of solid* ▪ **Syn** backbone, corrugation, crease, elevation, esker, fold, furrow, hill, hogback, moraine, parapet, plica, range, rim, rimple, rivel, seam, spine, upland, wrinkle; ▪ **Ant** chasm, hollow, ravine, valley.

ridicule [v] *make contemptuous fun of something or someone* ▪ **Syn** banter, caricature, deride, expose, fleer, gibe, humiliate, jeer, josh, kid, lampoon, mimic, mock, needle, parody, rag, rail at, satirize, sneer, taunt, travesty, twit; ▪ **Ant** flatter, praise.

ridiculous [adj] *stupid, funny* ▪ **Syn** absurd, antic, bizarre, comical, droll, farcical, foolish, gelastic, hilarious, impossible, incredible, laughable, ludicrous, nonsensical, outrageous, preposterous, risible, silly, unbelievable; ▪ **Ant** believable, reasonable, sensible, serious.

rife [*adj*] *overflowing*
▪ *Syn* abounding, abundant, common, epidemic, extensive, frequent, general, multitudinous, numerous, pandemic, profuse, raging, rampant, regnant, ruling, swarming, teeming, ubiquitous, widespread; ▪ *Ant* low, scarce.

rifle [*v*] *ransack*
▪ *Syn* burglarize, burgle, despoil, gut, loot, pillage, plunder, rip, rob, rummage, sack, strip, take; ▪ *Ant* order, organize.

rift [*n1*] *break, crack*
▪ *Syn* breach, chink, cleavage, cleft, cranny, crevice, fault, fissure, flaw, fracture, gap, hiatus, interruption, opening, parting, rent, rime, space, split; ▪ *Ant* closing, closure.

rift [*n2*] *difference of opinion*
▪ *Syn* alienation, breach, clash, division, estrangement, misunderstanding, quarrel, rupture, schism, separation, split; ▪ *Ant* agreement, concordance.

right [*adj1*] *fair, just*
▪ *Syn* appropriate, condign, conscientious, deserved, equitable, ethical, fitting, good, honest, justifiable, legal, legitimate, merited, moral, proper, requisite, righteous, scrupulous, true, upright, virtuous; ▪ *Ant* corrupt, immoral, inequitable, unfair, unjust, wrong.

right [*adj2*] *accurate, precise*
▪ *Syn* absolute, admissible, authentic, bona fide, correct, exact, factual, faithful, genuine, immaculate, perfect, proper, punctilious, righteous, rigorous, satisfactory, solemn, sound, thoroughgoing, utter, valid, veritable; ▪ *Ant* imprecise, inaccurate, inadmissible, wrong.

right [*adj3*] *appropriate, fitting*
▪ *Syn* acceptable, becoming, befitting, comely, condign, correct, decorous, due, favorable, felicitous, fit, good, ideal, merited, proper, requisite, seemly, sufficient, suitable; ▪ *Ant* inappropriate, unfitting, unsuitable, unsuited, wrong.

right [*adj4*] *sane, healthy*
▪ *Syn* balanced, circumspect, compos mentis, discerning, enlightened, farsighted, fine, fit, hale, judicious, lucid, normal, penetrating, rational, reasonable, sound, wise; ▪ *Ant* insane, mad, unfit, unhealthy.

right [*adj5*] *conservative politically*
▪ *Syn* orthodox, reactionary, right wing, traditionalistic; ▪ *Ant* left, liberal.

right [*adj6*] *opposite of left*
▪ *Syn* clockwise, dexter, dextral, right-handed; ▪ *Ant* left, verso.

right [*v*] *fix, correct*
▪ *Syn* adjust, amend, debug, emend, fix, mend, overhaul, patch, put right, recalibrate, recompense, reconstruct, rectify, repair, reward, set straight, settle, shape up, square, straighten, turn around, vindicate; ▪ *Ant* break, upset, wrong.

right [*adv1*] *accurately, precisely*
▪ *Syn* absolutely, clear, completely, correctly, entirely, exactly, factually, genuinely, just, perfectly, quite, square, squarely, thoroughly, totally, truly, utterly, well, wholly; ▪ *Ant* inaccurately, incorrectly, wrongly.

right [*adv2*] *appropriately, suitably*
▪ *Syn* acceptably, adequately, aptly, fittingly, properly, satisfactorily, well; ▪ *Ant* inappropriately, unsuitably, wrongly.

right [*adv3*] *fairly, justly*
▪ *Syn* conscientiously, decently, ethically, honorably, impartially, lawfully, morally, objectively, properly, reliably, sincerely, squarely, virtuously; ▪ *Ant* unfairly, unjustly, wrongly.

right [*adv4*] *beneficially*
▪ *Syn* advantageously, favorably, for the better, fortunately, to advantage; ▪ *Ant* unfairly.

right [*adv5*] *directly, without delay*
▪ *Syn* at once, direct, due, first off, immediately, now, promptly, quickly, right away, straight, straightaway; ▪ *Ant* indirectly.

righteous [*adj*] *good, honest*
▪ *Syn* charitable, conscientious, devoted, devout, dutiful, equitable, ethical, exemplary, faithful, honorable, impartial, just, laudable, meritorious, moral, noble, philanthropic, praiseworthy, pure, reverent, saintly, scrupulous, trustworthy, upright, virtuous, worthy; ▪ *Ant* bad, corrupt, dishonest, immoral, unfair.

rightful [*adj*] *legitimate*
▪ *Syn* appropriate, apt, bona fide, canonical, condign, due, ethical, fair, fitting, honest, just, lawful, legal, moral, noble, official, permitted, principled, proper, suitable, true, valid, virtuous; ▪ *Ant* illegal, illegitimate, incorrect, wrongful.

rigid [*adj*] *stiff, strict, severe*
▪ *Syn* adamant, austere, changeless, def-

inite, exact, firm, fixed, harsh, inelastic, inexorable, inflexible, ntransigent, obdurate, rigorous, single-minded, solid, stern, stringent, uncompromising; ▪ *Ant* bending, flexible, lenient, limber, pliable, pliant, soft, yielding.

rigorous [*adj*] *severe; exact*
▪ *Syn* accurate, ascetic, austere, bitter, brutal, burdensome, correct, definite, dogmatic, exact, exacting, hard, harsh, inclement, inflexible, intemperate, meticulous, onerous, oppressive, precise, proper, punctilious, right, rigid, rugged, scrupulous, stern, stiff, strict, stringent; ▪ *Ant* easy, easygoing, lax, lenient, loose, mild.

rile [*v*] *anger, upset*
▪ *Syn* acerbate, aggravate, annoy, bother, disturb, exasperate, gall, grate, inflame, irk, irritate, nettle, peeve, pique, provoke, roil, vex; ▪ *Ant* calm, please, soothe.

rim [*n*] *border; top edge*
▪ *Syn* band, brim, brink, brow, circumference, confine, curb, end, fringe, hem, ledge, limit, line, lip, margin, outline, perimeter, periphery, ring, skirt, strip, terminus, top, verge; ▪ *Ant* center, middle.

riot [*v*] *protest; cause an uproar*
▪ *Syn* arise, debauch, dissipate, fight, go on rampage, racket, rampage, rebel, revolt, rise; ▪ *Ant* comply, cooperate, make peace.

rip [*v*] *tear, cut*
▪ *Syn* claw, cleave, fray, gash, hack, lacerate, rend, rive, score, shred, slash, slit, split; ▪ *Ant* close, mend, sew.

ripe [*adj1*] *fully developed; experienced*
▪ *Syn* accomplished, adult, aged, concummate, conditioned, enlightened, enriched, fit, full-blown, full-fledged, informed, learned, mature, matured, mellow, plump, prepared, prime, ready, seasoned, skilled, skillful, sound, timely, usable, versed, well-timed, wise; ▪ *Ant* immature, inexperienced, undeveloped, unripe.

ripe [*adj2*] *favorable, ideal*
▪ *Syn* auspicious, opportune, right, suitable, timely; ▪ *Ant* doomed, ill-starred, unfavorable, untimely.

rip off [*v*] *rob; trick*
▪ *Syn* abuse, appropriate, cheat, defraud, dupe, exploit, heist, pilfer, plunder, ransack, relieve, rifle, swindle, swipe, thieve, use; ▪ *Ant* give, offer.

rise [*v1*] *get up; ascend*
▪ *Syn* arise, climb, come up, get out of bed, levitate, lift, mount, move up, reach up, rocket, rouse, scale, soar, sprout, stand up, straighten up, surface, surge, surmount, sweep upward, tower; ▪ *Ant* descend, lower.

rise [*v2*] *increase, grow*
▪ *Syn* add to, advance, augment, build, deepen, enhance, enlarge, expand, heighten, improve, inflate, intensify, magnify, mount, multiply, raise, redouble, spread, stack up, swell, take off, upsurge, wax; ▪ *Ant* decline, decrease, lessen, lower, recede.

rise [*v3*] *progress in business*
▪ *Syn* advance, be elevated, be promoted, better oneself, flourish, get on, progress, prosper, succeed, thrive; ▪ *Ant* decline, drop, fall, slump.

rise [*v4*] *rebel*
▪ *Syn* insurrect, mount, mutiny, resist, revolt, riot, take up arms; ▪ *Ant* comply, cooperate, give in, go along.

risk [*v*] *take a chance*
▪ *Syn* adventure, brave, chance, compromise, confront, dare, defy, endanger, expose to danger, gamble, hazard, imperil, jeopardize, meet, menace, peril, plunge, put in jeopardy, speculate, tackle, venture, wager; ▪ *Ant* be certain.

risky [*adj*] *dangerous*
▪ *Syn* chancy, delicate, hazardous, insecure, perilous, precarious, sensitive, speculative, touchy, treacherous, tricky, wicked, wide-open; ▪ *Ant* assured, certain, safe, sure.

risque [*adj*] *improper, referring to sex*
▪ *Syn* amoral, crude, daring, earthy, erotic, foul, immodest, immoral, indecent, indecorous, lurid, naughty, obscene, out-of-line, provocative, racy, raw, ribald, salacious, sizzling, suggestive, vulgar, wanton, wicked; ▪ *Ant* acceptable, decent, moral, proper.

rival [*adj*] *opposing*
▪ *Syn* battling, combating, competing, competitive, conflicting, contesting, cutthroat, disputing, emulating, equal, opposed, striving, vying; ▪ *Ant* allied, associate.

rival [*v*] *oppose; be a match for*
▪ *Syn* approach, approximate, compare with, compete, contest, correspond, emulate, equal, match, measure up to, meet, near, tie, touch, vie with;

• *Ant* aid, assist, cooperate, help, support.

rob [v] *steal, deprive*
• *Syn* abscond, appropriate, bereave, burglarize, cheat, con, defraud, dispossess, embezzle, heist, hustle, loot, mug, peculate, pillage, plunder, purloin, raid, ransack, scrounge, swindle, swipe, take, thieve; • *Ant* give, offer.

robust [adj] *healthy, strong*
• *Syn* able-bodied, athletic, brawny, built, fit, flourishing, full-bodied, hardy, hearty, hefty, husky, lusty, muscular, potent, powerful, rugged, strapping, sturdy, thriving, vigorous; • *Ant* flabby, infirm, soft, unhealthy, weak.

rock [v] *move back and forth*
• *Syn* agitate, careen, convulse, heave, jiggle, jog, jolt, jounce, lurch, oscillate, pitch, quake, quaver, reel, roll, shake, sway, toss, totter, undulate, vibrate, wobble; • *Ant* hold, stabilize.

rocky [adj1] *rugged, stony*
• *Syn* bouldered, craggy, flinty, hard, inflexible, jagged, lapidarian, lithic, pebbly, petrous, rough; • *Ant* flat, smooth.

rocky [adj2] *doubtful, undependable*
• *Syn* dizzy, rickety, shaky, sick, sickly, staggering, tottering, tricky, weak, wobbly; • *Ant* dependable, happy, healthy.

roll [v2] *spread out*
• *Syn* even, flatten, grind, level, press, pulverize, smooth; • *Ant* collect, gather, pile.

roll [v4] *rock, sway*
• *Syn* billow, glide, heave, jibe, lean, lumber, lurch, pitch, ramble, range, reel, stagger, surge, swagger, swing, toss, tumble, undulate, waddle, wallow, wave, welter, yaw; • *Ant* stabilize, steady.

rollicking [adj] *fun-loving, lively*
• *Syn* antic, boisterous, carefree, cavorting, exuberant, frisky, frolicsome, glad, happy, jaunty, jovial, joyful, lighthearted, merry, playful, romping, spirited, sportive; • *Ant* dull, mirthless, serious, solemn.

romantic [adj] *sentimental, idealistic*
• *Syn* amorous, chimerical, daring, dreamy, erotic, extravagant, fanciful, fantastic, fascinating, fond, glamorous, idyllic, impractical, loving, mysterious, nostalgic, passionate, quixotic, starry-eyed, tender, unrealistic, utopian, visionary, whimsical, wild; • *Ant* pragmatic, realistic, unromantic.

romp [n] *fun; caper*
• *Syn* antic, cavort, dance, escapade, frisk, frolic, gambol, hop, lark, leap, play, rollick, rout, skip, sport; • *Ant* chore, duty.

roomy [adj] *having ample space*
• *Syn* ample, broad, capacious, commodious, extensive, generous, large, sizable, spacious, wide; • *Ant* cluttered, cramped, narrow.

root [n] *base, core*
• *Syn* basis, beginnings, cause, center, crux, essence, footing, foundation, fundamental, germ, groundwork, heart, inception, infrastructure, mainspring, marrow, nub, nucleus, origin, pith, quick, quintessence, radix, seat, seed, source, starting point, substance, substratum, well; • *Ant* derivation, derivative, sprout.

root [v] *dig and search*
• *Syn* burrow, delve, embed, ferret, forage, grub, grub up, hunt, ingrain, lodge, nose, place, poke, pry, rummage; • *Ant* cover.

rosy [adj1] *pink, reddish in color*
• *Syn* aflush, blooming, blushing, colored, coral, deep pink, fresh, glowing, healthy-looking, high-colored, incarnadine, roseate, rubicund; • *Ant* pale.

rosy [adj2] *cheerful, hopeful*
• *Syn* alluring, auspicious, bright, encouraging, favorable, glowing, likely, optimistic, pleasing, promising, reassuring; • *Ant* depressing, hopeless, sad.

rot [v] *corrode, deteriorate*
• *Syn* break down, crumble, decay, decline, decompose, degenerate, disintegrate, fester, languish, pervert, putrefy, retrograde, sink, spoil, stain, taint, turn, warp, waste away, wither, worsen; • *Ant* build, flourish, grow.

rotten [adj1] *decayed, decaying*
• *Syn* bad, corroded, crumbling, decomposing, disgusting, disintegrated, fecal, feculent, fetid, foul, infected, loathsome, mephitic, moldy, noisome, noxious, offensive, overripe, polluted, purulent, putrescent, putrid, rancid, rank, rotting, smelling, sour, spoiled, stinking, strong, tainted; • *Ant* fresh, good, new, pleasant, undecayed.

rotten [adj2] *dishonest, immoral*
• *Syn* bent, bribable, corrupt, crooked, debauched, degenerate, depraved, dirtied, dishonorable, faithless, impure, mer-

cenary, nefarious, perfidious, perverse, sullied, tainted, treacherous, vicious, villainous; ▪ *Ant* decent, good, honest, moral, trustworthy, uncorrupt.

rotten [*adj3*] *despicable, inferior, bad*
▪ *Syn* base, bruised, contemptible, deplorable, dirty, filthy, inadequate, low-grade, nasty, poor, regrettable, scurrilous, sour, substandard, unacceptable, unsatisfactory, unsound, vile, wicked, wrong; ▪ *Ant* pure, scrupulous, wholesome.

rough [*adj1*] *uneven, irregular*
▪ *Syn* asperous, brambly, bristly, broken, bumpy, chapped, choppy, coarse, cragged, cross-grained, harsh, jagged, knobby, nappy, nodular, ridged, rocky, scabrous, scraggy, stony, tangled, woolly, wrinkly; ▪ *Ant* even, level, polished, regular, smooth.

rough [*adj2*] *stormy; not quiet*
▪ *Syn* agitated, blustery, buffeting, choppy, coarse, discordant, furious, grating, gruff, harsh, inclement, inharmonious, jarring, raging, raucous, squally, tempestuous, turbulent; ▪ *Ant* calm, mild, moderate, temperate.

rough [*adj3*] *rude, impolite*
▪ *Syn* bearish, blunt, boisterous, boorish, brusque, churlish, coarse, crass, crusty, curt, discourteous, extreme, hard, ill-mannered, inconsiderate, indecorous, loud, loutish, mean, nasty, raw, rowdy, severe, short, tough, uncultured, unrefined, vulgar; ▪ *Ant* courteous, nice, polite, refined, sophisticated.

rough [*adj4*] *basic, incomplete*
▪ *Syn* crude, cursory, imperfect, raw, rudimentary, shapeless, spartan, unfinished, unhewn; ▪ *Ant* accurate, complete, definite, precise.

rough [*adj5*] *approximate*
▪ *Syn* amorphous, estimated, general, hazy, imprecise, inexact, proximate, rude, sketchy, vague; ▪ *Ant* accurate, definite, precise.

rough up [*v*] *beat up*
▪ *Syn* bash, batter, hit, knock about, knock around, maltreat, manhandle, mistreat, roughhouse, slap around, thrash; ▪ *Ant* aid, help, protect.

round [*adj1*] *ball-shaped; semicircular area* ▪ *Syn* annular, bowed, bulbous, curled, curvilinear, cylindrical, disk-shaped, globular, looped, orbed, ringed, rotund, spherical, spheroid, spiral; ▪ *Ant* angular, rectangular, square.

round [*adj2*] *complete*
▪ *Syn* entire, full, solid, unbroken, undivided, whole; ▪ *Ant* incomplete, lacking, unfinished.

round [*adj3*] *full-bodied, ample in size*
▪ *Syn* expansive, fleshy, generous, large, plump, plumpish, rotund; ▪ *Ant* inadequate, small, tiny.

round [*adj4*] *resonant, rich in sound*
▪ *Syn* consonant, full, mellifluous, orotund, plangent, resounding, ringing, rotund, sonorous, vibrant; ▪ *Ant* low, soft, weak.

round [*adj5*] *honest, direct*
▪ *Syn* blunt, candid, frank, free, outspoken, plain, straightforward, unmodified, vocal; ▪ *Ant* deceitful, dishonest, indirect.

round [*adv1*] *approximate*
▪ *Syn* about, all but, almost, around, close to, in the neighborhood of, just about, most, nearly, practically, roughly; ▪ *Ant* definite, exact, precise.

roundabout [*adj*] *indirect*
▪ *Syn* ambiguous, circuitous, circumlocutory, devious, discursive, evasive, meandering, oblique, periphrastic, tortuous; ▪ *Ant* direct, honest, straightforward.

round off [*v*] *finish*
▪ *Syn* bring to a close, cap, climax, close, complete, conclude, culminate, finish off, top off; ▪ *Ant* start.

round up [*v*] *collect, gather*
▪ *Syn* assemble, bring in, bring together, cluster, drive, group, herd, marshal, muster, rally; ▪ *Ant* disperse, scatter.

rouse [*v*] *stimulate, excite*
▪ *Syn* aggravate, agitate, anger, arouse, bestir, disturb, exhilarate, foment, galvanize, heighten, inflame, instigate, kindle, magnify, move, pique, provoke, quicken, rally, rile, startle, stir, trigger, urge, vivify, wake, whet, work up; ▪ *Ant* calm, disenchant, dull.

rout [*v*] *defeat overwhelmingly*
▪ *Syn* bash, beat, conquer, crush, destroy, discomfit, lambaste, outmaneuver, overpower, repulse, subdue, subjugate, trounce, vanquish, wallop, whip; ▪ *Ant* capitulate, succumb, surrender.

route [*v*] *send along a path*
▪ *Syn* address, conduct, consign, convey, direct, dispatch, escort, forward, guide, lead, pilot, remit, shepherd, steer, transmit; ▪ *Ant* hold, keep.

routine [*adj*] *habitual*
▪ *Syn* accustomed, conventional, customary, everyday, familiar, general, methodical, normal, ordinary, periodic, plain, quotidian, regular, standard, typical, usual, workaday; ▪ *Ant* exceptional, original, unfamiliar, unusual.

row [*n2*] *fight, ruckus*
▪ *Syn* affray, altercation, brawl, commotion, dispute, fracas, fuss, melee, quarrel, racket, riot, squabble, tiff, tumult, uproar, wrangle; ▪ *Ant* agreement, peace.

rowdy [*adj*] *boisterous, noisy*
▪ *Syn* disorderly, lawless, loud, loutish, mischievous, obstreperous, rambunctious, raucous, rude, turbulent, unruly, uproarious, wild; ▪ *Ant* calm, moderate, quiet, restrained.

royal [*adj*] *kingly, grand*
▪ *Syn* aristocratic, august, baronial, dignified, elevated, grandiose, high-born, illustrious, imperial, imposing, lofty, magnificent, majestic, monarchical, noble, regal, reigning, renowned, resplendent, sovereign, stately, supreme, worthy; ▪ *Ant* common, humble, lowly, small.

rub [*n*] *difficulty, problem*
▪ *Syn* catch, crimp, dilemma, drawback, hindrance, hitch, hurdle, impediment, obstacle, predicament, snag, traverse, trouble; ▪ *Ant* blessing, boon, solution.

rubbish [*n1*] *garbage*
▪ *Syn* debris, dregs, dross, junk, litter, offal, refuse, rubble, rummage, scrap, sweepings, trash, waste; ▪ *Ant* assets, valuable.

rubbish [*n2*] *nonsense*
▪ *Syn* bunkum, drivel, gibberish, hogwash; ▪ *Ant* sense, truth.

ruddy [*adj*] *pinkish, blushing*
▪ *Syn* blooming, blowsy, crimson, florid, flushed, full-blooded, glowing, healthy, pink, reddish, roseate, rosy, rubicund, sanguine, scarlet; ▪ *Ant* pale.

rude [*adj1*] *disrespectful, rough*
▪ *Syn* abrupt, abusive, bad-mannered, barbaric, blunt, boorish, brusque, churlish, coarse, crabbed, crude, curt, discourteous, gruff, impudent, insolent, loutish, obscene, peremptory, raw, surly, uncouth, vulgar; ▪ *Ant* kind, mannerly, polite, respectful.

rude [*adj2*] *crude, primitive*
▪ *Syn* artless, callow, coarse, inelegant, inexperienced, makeshift, primal, raw,

rudimentary, shapeless, slapdash, uncivilized, uncultivated, uneven; ▪ *Ant* polished, slick, well-built.

rude [*adj3*] *sudden*
▪ *Syn* abrupt, harsh, rough, sharp, startling, stormy, turbulent, unpleasant, violent; ▪ *Ant* gradual, smooth.

rudimentary [*adj*] *basic, fundamental*
▪ *Syn* abecedarian, basal, early, elemental, embryonic, formative, immature, initial, larval, primary, primitive, vestigial; ▪ *Ant* advanced, completely developed, finished, mature.

ruffle [*v1*] *mess up*
▪ *Syn* confuse, crease, crinkle, crumple, disarrange, discompose, dishevel, disorder, pucker, purse, rifle, rumple, tangle, tousle, wrinkle; ▪ *Ant* arrange, smooth.

ruffle [*v2*] *upset, irritate*
▪ *Syn* agitate, annoy, bother, confuse, disconcert, disturb, excite, flummox, fluster, harass, irk, nettle, peeve, perturb, rattle, stir, unsettle, vex, wear, worry; ▪ *Ant* calm, soothe.

rugged [*adj1*] *bumpy, weathered*
▪ *Syn* asperous, coarse, craggy, furrowed, harsh, hilly, irregular, jagged, mountainous, ragged, rocky, rough-hewn, scabrous, scraggy, stark, weather-beaten, worn, wrinkled; ▪ *Ant* even, flat, level, smooth.

rugged [*adj2*] *severe, violent*
▪ *Syn* bitter, brutal, difficult, hard, harsh, inclement, intemperate, rigorous, rough, stormy, tempestuous, turbulent; ▪ *Ant* calm, gentle, mild, moderate.

rugged [*adj3*] *uncouth, crude*
▪ *Syn* barbarous, blunt, boorish, churlish, graceless, ill-bred, loutish, rude, uncultured, unpolished, unrefined; ▪ *Ant* courteous, nice, refined, sophisticated.

rugged [*adj4*] *difficult, rigorous*
▪ *Syn* arduous, demanding, exacting, formidable, harsh, laborious, mean, operose, rough, strenuous, tough, trying, uncompromising; ▪ *Ant* easy, facile.

rugged [*adj5*] *big, strong*
▪ *Syn* brawny, burly, energetic, hale, hardy, healthy, husky, indefatigable, lusty, muscular, robust, sturdy, tough, unflagging, vigorous, well-built; ▪ *Ant* small, tiny, weak.

ruin [*v*] *devastate, destroy*
▪ *Syn* botch, break, bring down, crush, decimate, defeat, demolish, deplete, dese-

crate, exhaust, impoverish, injure, mangle, overthrow, overwhelm, pillage, rape, ravish, raze, sack, shatter, smash, total, use up, wreck; ▪ *Ant* build, construct, create, develop, grow.

ruinous [*adj*] *disastrous, devastating*
▪ *Syn* baneful, cataclysmic, catastrophic, crippling, damaging, dire, disastrous, fatal, harmful, immoderate, murderous, noxious, pernicious, shattering, wasteful; ▪ *Ant* advantageous, assisting, beneficial, helpful.

rule [*v*] *govern, manage*
▪ *Syn* administer, be in authority, be in power, command, conduct, control, dictate, direct, dominate, guide, lead, order, overrule, predominate, preponderate, preside, regulate, reign, sway; ▪ *Ant* serve, submit.

rule out [*v*] *exclude, reject*
▪ *Syn* abolish, ban, cancel, debar, dismiss, eliminate, except, forbid, forestall, forfend, obviate, preclude, prevent, prohibit, recant, revoke, suspend; ▪ *Ant* add, include, keep.

ruling [*adj1*] *dominant, governing*
▪ *Syn* cardinal, central, controlling, leading, overriding, pivotal, predominant, regnant, reigning, sovereign, supreme, upper, widespread; ▪ *Ant* minor, subjective, submissive, yielding.

ruminate [*v*] *think about seriously*
▪ *Syn* brood, chew over, cogitate, contemplate, deliberate, excogitate, figure, meditate, mull over, muse, ponder, reflect, revolve, speculate, think, turn over, weigh; ▪ *Ant* ignore, neglect.

rummage [*v*] *ransack, search*
▪ *Syn* comb, delve, disarray, disorganize, disrupt, explore, ferret out, fish, forage, grub, hunt, jumble, mess up, root, scour, seek, toss; ▪ *Ant* order, organize.

rumor [*n*] *unverifiable talk or opinion*
▪ *Syn* bruit, canard, fabrication, gossip, hearsay, hoax, innuendo, invention, lie, notoriety, repute, rumble, scandal, story, suggestion, supposition, tale, whisper; ▪ *Ant* fact, truth.

rumple [*v*] *crush, wrinkle*
▪ *Syn* crease, crimp, crinkle, crumple, dishevel, disorder, fold, muss, pucker, ruffle, scrunch, tousle; ▪ *Ant* flatten, iron, smooth.

run [*v1*] *move fast on foot*
▪ *Syn* bolt, bound, bustle, canter, course, dart, dash, gallop, hasten, hie, hurry, jog, race, rush, scorch, scramble, scurry, shag, speed, sprint, spurt, trot; ▪ *Ant* crawl, stand, walk.

run [*v2*] *move rapidly, flowingly*
▪ *Syn* bleed, cascade, course, deliquesce, drop, fall, flow, flux, glide, gush, issue, leak, liquefy, melt, pass, pour, roll, slide, spill, spout, spread, stream, turn to liquid; ▪ *Ant* cease, halt, stop.

run [*v3*] *manage, supervise*
▪ *Syn* administer, boss, conduct, control, coordinate, direct, head, lead, look after, mastermind, operate, ordain, oversee, regulate, superintend; ▪ *Ant* labor, obey, serve.

runaway [*adj*] *out of control*
▪ *Syn* delinquent, disorderly, escaped, fleeing, fugitive, loose, running, uncontrolled, wild; ▪ *Ant* controlled, stable, steady.

run down [*v*] *ridicule*
▪ *Syn* belittle, criticize, decry, defame, denigrate, depreciate, disparage, opprobriate, revile, speak ill of, vilify; ▪ *Ant* encourage, extol, praise.

run-down [*adj*] *shabby, in bad shape*
▪ *Syn* beat-up, broken-down, crumbling, debilitated, decrepit, desolate, dilapidated, dingy, enervated, fatigued, forsaken, neglected, peaked, ramshackle, rickety, seedy, tattered, tumble-down, weak, weary, worn-out; ▪ *Ant* durable, fresh, healthy, robust, sold.

run in [*v*] *arrest*
▪ *Syn* apprehend, bust, collar, detain, handcuff, jail, nab, pick up, pull in, take into custody; ▪ *Ant* exonerate, free, let go.

running [*adj*] *continuous, flowing, operating* ▪ *Syn* active, alive, constant, cursive, dynamic, easy, fluent, functioning, going, incessant, in operation, moving, operative, proceeding, smooth, unbroken, working; ▪ *Ant* broken, discontinuous, intermittent, occasional.

run out [*v*] *fail, be exhausted*
▪ *Syn* cease, close, come to a close, depart, dissipate, dry up, end, exhaust, expire, finish, give out, tire, waste, waste away, weaken, wear out; ▪ *Ant* energize, refresh, stimulate.

runt [*n*] *very small person*
▪ *Syn* dwarf, homunculus, Lilliputian, manikin, midget, pygmy; ▪ *Ant* behemoth, colossus, giant, monster, titan.

run through [v] *use up; waste*
- *Syn* blow, dissipate, exhaust, expend, finish, fritter away, lose, spend, squander, throw away; ▪ *Ant* hoard, save.

rupture [v1] *break open*
- *Syn* breach, burst, cleave, crack, disrupt, divide, erupt, fracture, hold, open, part, puncture, rend, rive, separate, sever, shatter, split, sunder, tear; ▪ *Ant* close, join, mend.

rupture [v2] *disagree; dissolve union*
- *Syn* break off, break up, disjoin, dissever, divide, divorce, part, separate, split, split up, sunder; ▪ *Ant* agree, reunite.

rural [adj] *country, not urban*
- *Syn* agrarian, Arcadian, backwoods, bucolic, countrified, georgic, idyllic, natural, pastoral, provincial, rustic, simple, sylvan; ▪ *Ant* city, cosmopolitan, metropolitan, suburban, urban.

rush [v1] *hurry, speed*
- *Syn* accelerate, barrel, bolt, career, charge, chase, dart, dash, dispatch, expedite, fleet, fling, flit, fly, hasten, hustle, press, push, quicken, race, run, scramble, scurry, sprint, streak, surge, tear; ▪ *Ant* retard, slow.

rush [v2] *charge, attack*
- *Syn* capture, overcome, storm, surge; ▪ *Ant* guard, protect.

rustic [adj1] *country, rural*
- *Syn* agrarian, Arcadian, bucolic, countrified, homely, homespun, homey, pastoral, picturesque, plain, primitive, provincial, simple, sylvan, verdant; ▪ *Ant* city, metropolitan, suburban, urban.

rustic [adj2] *crude, uncouth*
- *Syn* awkward, boorish, churlish, clodhopping, coarse, countrified, dull, foolish, graceless, ignorant, loutish, maladroit, rough, rude, unsophisticated; ▪ *Ant* couth, cultured, polished, refined, sophisticated.

rusty [adj2] *out of practice; inexperienced* ▪ *Syn* deficient, impaired, sluggish, stale, unqualified; ▪ *Ant* experienced, practiced, talented.

rut [n1] *groove, indentation*
- *Syn* furrow, gouge, hollow, pothole, rabbet, score, track, trench, trough; ▪ *Ant* bump, prominence.

rut [n2] *routine of daily life*
- *Syn* circuit, course, custom, groove, habit, pattern, practice, rote, system, treadmill; ▪ *Ant* divergence, irregularity.

ruthless [adj] *mean, heartless*
- *Syn* barbarous, callous, cruel, cutthroat, ferocious, fierce, grim, harsh, inexorable, ironfisted, malevolent, merciless, obdurate, pitiless, rancorous, remorseless, sadistic, savage, stony, unmerciful, unrelenting, vicious, vindictive, without pity; ▪ *Ant* compassionate, considerate, gentle, giving, kind, nice, sympathetic.

S

sable [adj] *very dark in color*
- *Syn* black, dark, dusky, ebony, gloomy, inky, jet, jetty, murky, pitch-black, pitch-dark, raven, somber; ▪ *Ant* fair, light, white.

sabotage [v] *incapacitate, damage*
- *Syn* block, bollix, cripple, destroy, disrupt, frustrate, hamper, hinder, obstruct, subvert, undermine, vandalize, wreck; ▪ *Ant* abet, aid, fix, help.

sack [v1] *remove from position of responsibility* ▪ *Syn* discharge, dismiss, drop, expel, fire, kick out, ship, terminate; ▪ *Ant* employ, hire.

sack [v2] *raid, plunder*
- *Syn* demolish, desecrate, destroy, devastate, devour, fleece, gut, lay waste, loot, maraud, pillage, ravage, ruin, spoil; ▪ *Ant* guard, protect, save.

sacred [adj1] *holy, blessed*
- *Syn* angelic, cherished, consecrated, divine, enshrined, godly, hallowed, numinous, pious, pure, revered, saintly, spiritual, venerable; ▪ *Ant* irreligious, lay, profane, ungodly, unholy, unsacred.

sacred [adj2] *protected*
- *Syn* dedicated, defended, guarded, immune, inviolable, invulnerable, sacrosanct, secure, shielded, untouchable; ▪ *Ant* open, unprotected, vulnerable.

sacrifice [v] *give up, let go*
- *Syn* cede, drop, eschew, forfeit, forgo, offer, part with, renounce, suffer, surrender, waive, yield; ▪ *Ant* hold, refuse.

sacrilege [n] *irreverence*
- *Syn* blasphemy, curse, desecration, heresy, impiety, mockery, offense, profanation, profanity, sin, violation; ▪ *Ant* piety, respect, reverence.

sad [adj1] *unhappy, depressed*
- *Syn* bereaved, cheerless, dejected, despondent, disconsolate, doleful, down, forlorn, glum, grief-stricken, heartbro-

ken, heartsick, languishing, low-spirited, melancholy, mournful, pensive, somber, sorrowful, troubled, weeping, wistful, woebegone; ▪ *Ant* cheerful, glad, happy, joyful.

sad [*adj2*] *unfortunate, distressing*
▪ *Syn* calamitous, deplorable, disastrous, dispiriting, dreary, funereal, grave, grievous, hapless, joyless, lamentable, lugubrious, pathetic, pitiable, poignant, regrettable, tearful, tragic, unhappy, wretched; ▪ *Ant* fortunate, great, happy, lucky.

sadden [*v*] *upset, depress*
▪ *Syn* cast down, dampen spirits, damper, desolate, discourage, dishearten, dispirit, grieve, make blue, oppress, press; ▪ *Ant* cheer, delight, gladden, make happy.

sadistic [*adj*] *cruel, perverted*
▪ *Syn* barbarous, brutal, fiendish, perverse, ruthless, vicious; ▪ *Ant* humane, kind, merciful.

safe [*adj1*] *free from harm*
▪ *Syn* free from danger, guarded, impervious, inviolable, invulnerable, out of danger, preserved, protected, secure, sheltered, tended, unassailable, unthreatened, vindicated, watched; ▪ *Ant* damaged, exposed, unprotected, vulnerable.

safe [*adj2*] *not dangerous*
▪ *Syn* clear, decontaminated, harmless, healthy, innocuous, innoxious, inoffensive, neutralized, nonpoisonous, nontoxic, pure, reliable, risk-free, secure, sound, trustworthy, wholesome; ▪ *Ant* dangerous, harmful, poisonous, unsafe.

safe [*adj3*] *cautious, conservative*
▪ *Syn* assure, bulwark, conserve, cover, defend, ensure, fend, guard, insure, look after, preserve, screen, secure, shield, watch over; ▪ *Ant* expose, imperil, jeopardize.

sag [*v*] *droop*
▪ *Syn* bag, bend, bow, bulge, cave in, dangle, decline, dip, drop, drop off, fail, fall, flag, flap, flop, give way, hang, hang down, languish, lean, settle, sink, slide, slip, slump, swag, wilt; ▪ *Ant* bulge, draw up, tighten.

sagacious [*adj*] *smart, judicious*
▪ *Syn* acute, apt, astucious, astute, canny, clear-sighted, clever, discerning, discriminating, gnostic, insightful, intelligent, keen, knowing, knowledgeable, perceptive, perspicacious, prudent, rational, sage, sapient, savvy, sensible, sharp, shrewd, smooth, sophic, wise; ▪ *Ant* careless, foolish, ignorant, stupid.

saintly [*adj*] *good, righteous*
▪ *Syn* angelic, beatific, blameless, blessed, devout, divine, god-fearing, godly, holy, pious, pure, religious, seraphic, sinless, upright, upstanding, virtuous, worthy; ▪ *Ant* bad, sinful, unholy, unrighteous, wicked.

sake [*n1*] *benefit, gain*
▪ *Syn* account, advantage, behalf, consideration, good, interest, profit, regard, respect, welfare, well-being; ▪ *Ant* detriment, disadvantage.

salary [*n*] *money paid for work done*
▪ *Syn* earnings, emolument, income, pay, payroll, recompense, remuneration, stipend, take, wage, wages; ▪ *Ant* debt, expenditure.

salient [*adj*] *noticeable, important*
▪ *Syn* arresting, conspicuous, impressive, jutting, marked, notable, obtrusive, outstanding, projecting, prominent, pronounced, protruding, remarkable, significant, striking; ▪ *Ant* inconspicuous, unimportant, unnoticeable.

sallow [*adj*] *pale, unhealthy*
▪ *Syn* ashen, bilious, colorless, dull, jaundiced, muddy, olive, pallid, pasty, sickly, wan, waxy, yellowish; ▪ *Ant* dark, flushed, healthy, ruddy.

salt away [*v*] *save, store up*
▪ *Syn* accumulate, amass, bank, cache, hide, hoard, invest, lay aside, put away, put in the bank, save, spare, stash, stockpile; ▪ *Ant* spend, throw away, waste.

salty [*adj2*] *spicy, colorful*
▪ *Syn* humorous, lively, piquant, racy, sharp, tangy, tart, witty, zestful; ▪ *Ant* blah, bland, dull.

salubrious [*adj*] *health-giving*
▪ *Syn* beneficial, good, healthful, healthy, hygienic, invigorating, salutary, sanitary, wholesome; ▪ *Ant* harmful, unhealthy, unwholesome.

salute/salutation [*n*] *greeting, recognition* ▪ *Syn* address, bow, kiss, obeisance, tribute, welcome; ▪ *Ant* farewell, goodbye.

salvage [v] *save, rescue*
▪ *Syn* deliver, glean, ransom, reclaim, recover, redeem, regain, restore, retrieve, salve; ▪ *Ant* destroy, discard, scatter, waste.

same [adj1] *alike, identical*
▪ *Syn* comparable, compatible, corresponding, double, duplicate, equal, equivalent, indistinguishable, interchangeable, in the same manner, like, likewise, related, similar, similarly, synonymous, tantamount; ▪ *Ant* different, inconsistent, other, unlike.

same [adj2] *unchanging*
▪ *Syn* changeless, consistent, constant, immutable, invariable, perpetual, regular, uniform; ▪ *Ant* changing, inconsistent, variable, wavering.

sanctify [v] *hold in highest esteem*
▪ *Syn* absolve, anoint, bless, cleanse, consecrate, dedicate, deify, enshrine, glorify, hallow, purify; ▪ *Ant* desecrate, dishonor, disrespect, pollute, profane.

sanctimonious [adj] *self-righteous*
▪ *Syn* bigoted, false, hypocritical, insincere, pharisaical, preachy, self-satisfied, smug, unctuous; ▪ *Ant* modest, sincere, tolerant.

sanction [v] *authorize, confirm*
▪ *Syn* accredit, allow, approve, back, bless, certify, commission, countenance, empower, endorse, license, permit, ratify, support, vouch for, warrant; ▪ *Ant* disapprove, prevent, refuse, veto.

sane [adj] *mentally sound; reasonable*
▪ *Syn* balanced, commonsensical, compos mentis, discerning, fair-minded, fit, healthy, intelligent, judicious, levelheaded, logical, lucid, moderate, normal, oriented, prudent, rational, right-minded, sapient, self-possessed, sensible, sober, sound, steady, together, well, wise; ▪ *Ant* crazy, insane, unreasonable, unsound, unstable.

sanguine [adj1] *happy; optimistic*
▪ *Syn* animated, assured, buoyant, cheerful, confident, enthusiastic, expectant, hopeful, lively, positive, secure, selfassured, self-confident, spirited, upbeat; ▪ *Ant* depressed, pessimistic, sad, unhappy.

sanguine [adj2] *reddish; flushed*
▪ *Syn* bloody, florid, flush, glowing, red, rubicund, ruddy, scarlet; ▪ *Ant* pale, pallid, sallow.

sanitary [adj] *clean, germ-free*
▪ *Syn* healthful, healthy, hygienic, purified, salubrious, sterile, uncontaminated, unpolluted, wholesome; ▪ *Ant* dirty, diseased, polluted, unsanitary.

sap [v] *squeeze out; weaken*
▪ *Syn* attenuate, bleed, blunt, cripple, debilitate, deplete, devitalize, disable, drain, enervate, enfeeble, erode, exhaust, impair, prostrate, ruin, subvert, undermine, vitiate, wear down; ▪ *Ant* build, increase, restore, strengthen.

sappy [adj] *foolish, sentimental*
▪ *Syn* absurd, balmy, bathetic, idiotic, illogical, maudlin, preposterous, silly, stupid; ▪ *Ant* levelheaded, realistic, serious.

sarcastic [adj] *nasty, mocking in speech*
▪ *Syn* acerbic, acid, acrimonious, arrogant, backhanded, biting, bitter, brusque, captious, carping, caustic, chaffing, contemptuous, cutting, cynical, derisive, disillusioned, disparaging, disrespectful, evil, hostile, irascible, mordant, needling, offensive, sardonic, satirical, scornful, scurrilous, sharp, sneering, taunting, trenchant, twitting; ▪ *Ant* complimentary, flattering, gracious.

satiate [v] *stuff, satisfy completely or excessively* ▪ *Syn* cloy, content, fill, glut, gorge, gratify, indulge, jade, nauseate, overdose, overfill, pall, sate, saturate, slake, surfeit; ▪ *Ant* deprive, dissatisfy, leave wanting.

satisfactory [adj] *acceptable, sufficient*
▪ *Syn* adequate, ample, assuasive, average, comfortable, competent, decent, fair, fulfilling, gratifying, passable, pleasing, satisfying, solid, suitable, tolerable, valid; ▪ *Ant* inadequate, insufficient, unacceptable, unfit, unsatisfactory, unsuitable.

satisfy [v1] *please, content*
▪ *Syn* assuage, cheer, comfort, content, delight, elate, fill, get by, gratify, humor, indulge, mollify, pacify, quench, sate, slake, suit; ▪ *Ant* anger, disappoint, upset, worsen.

satisfy [v2] *answer, persuade*
▪ *Syn* accomplish, appease, assuage, assure, comply with, conform to, dispel doubt, fulfill, furnish, inveigle, keep promise, meet, observe, perform, provide, qualify, reassure, suffice, win over; ▪ *Ant* dissuade, fail, frustrate.

satisfy [v3] *pay, compensate*
■ *Syn* answer, atone, clear up, disburse, indemnify, liquidate, make reparation, pay off, quit, recompense, remunerate, repay, reward, settle; ■ *Ant* extort, owe.

saturate [v] *drench, wet through*
■ *Syn* bathe, douse, imbue, immerse, infuse, overfill, penetrate, permeate, pervade, sate, soak, sop, souse, steep, suffuse, transfuse, waterlog; ■ *Ant* dehydrate, dry.

saucy [adj] *disrespectful*
■ *Syn* audacious, bold, brash, brazen, contumelious, flippant, fresh, impudent, insolent, meddlesome, nervy, obtrusive, pert, presumptuous, rude, sassy, volatile; ■ *Ant* kind, polite, respectful.

saunter [v] *stroll along*
■ *Syn* amble, dally, drift, loiter, meander, promenade, ramble, roam, rove, sashay, tarry, traipse, trill, wander; ■ *Ant* hie, run, speed.

savage [adj1] *wild, untamed*
■ *Syn* barbarian, bestial, brutal, crude, ferocious, fierce, harsh, lupine, native, original, primitive, rough, rude, rustic, uncivilized, undomesticated, vicious; ■ *Ant* calm, civilized, domesticated, tame.

savage [adj2] *cruel, vicious*
■ *Syn* atrocious, barbarous, beastly, bloodthirsty, brutish, cold-blooded, demoniac, destructive, devilish, diabolical, feral, ferocious, heartless, hellish, infernal, inhumane, malevolent, murderous, pitiless, rabid, raging, sadistic, truculent, violent, wolfish; ■ *Ant* kind, merciful, mild, soft, tender.

save [v1] *rescue*
■ *Syn* bail out, deliver, emancipate, extricate, free, liberate, ransom, recover, redeem, salvage; ■ *Ant* endanger, harm, hurt.

save [v2] *economize; set money aside for later use* ■ *Syn* amass, be frugal, be thrifty, cache, collect, conserve, deposit, economize, gather, hoard, keep, lay aside, pile up, reserve, scrimp, skimp, spare, stash, stockpile, store, treasure; ■ *Ant* squander, throw away, waste.

save [v3] *guard, protect*
■ *Syn* conserve, defend, keep safe, look after, maintain, preserve, safeguard, screen, shield, sustain, take care of; ■ *Ant* endanger, leave open, make vulnerable.

savior [n] *person who redeems, aids in time of difficulty* ■ *Syn* conservator, defender, deliverer, guardian angel, hero, knight, liberator, messiah, protector, rescuer, salvager, salvation; ■ *Ant* bane, satan, traitor.

savor [v] *delight in, enjoy*
■ *Syn* appreciate, experience, feel, gloat, know, like, luxuriate in, partake, relish, revel in, sample, sip, smack, smell, taste; ■ *Ant* dislike, refuse, shun.

savory [adj] *pleasing, delicious in flavor*
■ *Syn* agreeable, ambrosial, appetizing, aromatic, delectable, fragrant, full-flavored, luscious, mouthwatering, palatable, piquant, pungent, rich, sapid, sweet, tangy, tasty, tempting, toothsome; ■ *Ant* bland, displeasing, distasteful, offensive, tasteless, unappetizing.

say [v] *make declaration*
■ *Syn* allege, announce, assert, claim, communicate, convey, declare, deliver, express, jaw, maintain, make known, mention, opine, orate, pronounce, put into words, relate, remark, render, report, speak, state, tell, utter, verbalize, voice; ■ *Ant* be quiet.

scale [v1] *ascend, climb*
■ *Syn* clamber, escalade, escalate, go up, mount, surmount; ■ *Ant* descend.

scamper [v] *run, dash*
■ *Syn* bolt, dart, flee, fly, hasten, hie, light out, make off, romp, rush off, scoot, scurry, scuttle, speed away, tear, trot, whip; ■ *Ant* amble, stroll.

scandalous [adj] *disreputable*
■ *Syn* atrocious, backbiting, calumnious, defamatory, heinous, ignominious, libelous, maligning, odious, outrageous, shameful, shocking, slanderous, traducing, vilifying; ■ *Ant* decent, proper, reputable, respected.

scant/scanty [adj] *inadequate*
■ *Syn* barely sufficient, deficient, exiguous, failing, insufficient, limited, meager, minimal, narrow, poor, rare, restricted, scrimpy, skimpy, slender, spare, sparse, thin, tight, wanting; ■ *Ant* abundant, adequate, ample, plentiful, substantial.

scarce [adj] *insufficient, infrequent*
■ *Syn* deficient, failing, in short supply, limited, occasional, rare, scant, seldom, shortened, shy, sparse, sporadic, truncated, uncommon, wanting; ■ *Ant* abundant, frequent, plentiful, sufficient.

scarcely [adv] barely
• **Syn** hardly, imperceptibly, infrequently, just, just barely, only just, rarely, scantily, seldom, slightly; • **Ant** adequately, commonly, sufficiently.

scare [v] frighten someone
• **Syn** affright, alarm, awe, chill, daunt, freeze, intimidate, panic, paralyze, petrify, shock, spook, startle, terrify, terrorize; • **Ant** calm, comfort, reassure, soothe.

scared [adj] frightened
• **Syn** afraid, aghast, anxious, fearful, panicked, petrified, shaken, startled, terrified, terror-stricken; • **Ant** calm, confident, encouraged, unafraid.

scary [adj] frightening, terrifying
• **Syn** alarming, bloodcurdling, chilling, creepy, eerie, horrifying, intimidating, shocking, spooky, unnerving; • **Ant** calming, encouraging, soothing.

scathing [adj] nasty, critical in remarks
• **Syn** biting, brutal, caustic, cutting, harsh, mordacious, mordant, sarcastic, scorching, searing, severe, trenchant, withering; • **Ant** generous, kind, nice, praising.

scatter [v] strew, disperse
• **Syn** broadcast, cast, diffuse, dispel, dissipate, distribute, fling, intersperse, litter, separate, shower, spray, spread, sprinkle, sunder; • **Ant** collect, gather.

scatterbrained [adj] not thinking clearly
• **Syn** careless, dizzy, flighty, forgetful, giddy, illogical, inattentive, madcap, silly, thoughtless; • **Ant** aware, careful, sensible, thoughtful.

scenic [adj] beautiful, picturesque
• **Syn** breathtaking, dramatic, grand, impressive, panoramic, spectacular, striking; • **Ant** commonplace, dreary, gloomy.

scent [n] smell, aroma
• **Syn** aura, balm, bouquet, essence, fragrance, incense, odor, perfume, redolence, spice, tang; • **Ant** odor, stench, stink.

schedule [v] plan one's time
• **Syn** arrange, book, catalog, engage, list, note, organize, pencil in, program, record, register, set, set up, slate, time; • **Ant** disorder, disorganize.

scheming [adj] deceitful, sly
• **Syn** artful, calculating, conniving, cunning, designing, duplicitous, foxy, slippery, tricky, underhand, wily; • **Ant** honest, ingenuous, naive.

scholarly [adj] academic
• **Syn** bookish, cultured, educated, erudite, intellectual, learned, literate, schooled, studious, well-read; • **Ant** uneducated, unscholarly.

school [v] teach
• **Syn** advance, coach, cultivate, drill, educate, guide, indoctrinate, inform, instruct, prepare, show, train, tutor, verse; • **Ant** learn.

scientific [adj] systematic; discovered through experimentation • **Syn** accurate, controlled, deductive, exact, logical, mathematical, methodical, objective, precise; • **Ant** intuitive, transcedental, unscientific.

scintillating [adj] bright, stimulating
• **Syn** animated, brilliant, clever, dazzling, ebullient, flashing, gleaming, lively, shining, sparkling, sprightly, twinkling, witty; • **Ant** boring, dull, obtuse, stolid.

scion [n] offshoot, descendant
• **Syn** branch, brood, child, heir, issue, junior, offspring, progeny, seed, shoot, sprout, successor, twig; • **Ant** parent, progenitor, root.

scoff [v] make fun of; despise
• **Syn** belittle, contemn, deride, disbelieve, discredit, flout, gibe, jeer, laugh at, mock, reject, ridicule, scorn, sneer, tease; • **Ant** compliment, encourage, praise.

scold [v] find fault with
• **Syn** abuse, admonish, berate, blame, castigate, censure, chasten, chide, criticize, denounce, lecture, nag, objurgate, preach, rail, rebuke, recriminate, reprimand, reproach, taunt, upbraid, vilify; • **Ant** compliment, flatter, praise.

scorch [v] burn
• **Syn** bake, blacken, blister, broil, char, melt, parch, roast, scald, sear, shrivel, singe, swelter, wither; • **Ant** freshen, moisten.

score [v1] achieve, succeed
• **Syn** accomplish, amass, arrive, attain, flourish, gain, impress, prosper, reach, realize, secure, thrive, triumph, win; • **Ant** fail, lose.

score [v2] cut, nick
• **Syn** cleave, crosshatch, deface, furrow, gash, gouge, graze, groove, indent, line, mark, mill, notch, scrape, scratch, serrate, slash, slit; • **Ant** mend, smooth.

scorn [v] hold in contempt; look down on
• **Syn** avoid, confute, contemn, defy, de-

ride, despise, disdain, flout, gibe, ignore, mock, refute, reject, renounce, repudiate, ridicule, scoff at, shun, slight, sneer, spurn, taunt; ▪ *Ant* admire, approve, like, love.

scour [*v1*] *clean, polish thoroughly*
▪ *Syn* brush, buff, burnish, cleanse, furbish, mop, pumice, purge, rub, sand, scrub, wash, whiten; ▪ *Ant* dirty, rust.

scour [*v2*] *search thoroughly*
▪ *Syn* beat, comb, ferret out, forage, grub, hunt, look for, rake, ransack, rout, rummage, track down; ▪ *Ant* ignore, overlook.

scourge [*v*] *beat, punish, often physically* ▪ *Syn* belt, castigate, chastise, curse, discipline, excoriate, flail, harass, hit, lambaste, plague, scathe, thrash, trounce, whip; ▪ *Ant* guard, protect.

scout [*v*] *investigate, check out*
▪ *Syn* case, examine, explore, ferret, hunt, inspect, look for, observe, probe, reconnoiter, search, seek, stake out, survey, track down, watch; ▪ *Ant* ignore, overlook, shun.

scowl [*v*] *frown*
▪ *Syn* disapprove, glare, gloom, glower, grimace, lour, lower; ▪ *Ant* grin, smile.

scram [*v*] *leave quickly*
▪ *Syn* decamp, depart, disappear, go away, take off; ▪ *Ant* dally, wait.

scramble [*n*] *mix-up, confusion*
▪ *Syn* clutter, commotion, hassle, hustle, jumble, jungle, litter, melee, mishmash, muddle, rush, shuffle, tumble, tussle; ▪ *Ant* order, organization.

scrap [*v1*] *abandon; throw away*
▪ *Syn* chuck, demolish, discard, dismiss, ditch, drop, forsake, jettison, junk, reject, shed, slough, throw out, toss out, write off; ▪ *Ant* hoard, keep, save, store.

scrap [*v2*] *fight, argue*
▪ *Syn* bicker, caterwaul, fall out, quarrel, row, spat, squabble, tiff, wrangle; ▪ *Ant* agree, harmonize, make peace.

scrape [*v1*] *scratch, remove outer layer*
▪ *Syn* abrade, bark, bray, chafe, file, grate, graze, grind, irritate, pare, peel, rasp, rub, scour, scuff, shave, skin, thin, triturate; ▪ *Ant* smoothe.

scrape [*v2*] *be very frugal*
▪ *Syn* cut it close, get along, get by, pinch, save, scrimp, shave, skimp, stint, struggle; ▪ *Ant* spend, squander, waste.

scratch [*v1*] *cut; make a mark on*
▪ *Syn* claw, damage, etch, grate, graze, incise, lacerate, mark, prick, rasp, scarify, scrape; ▪ *Ant* heal, mend, smooth.

scratch [*v2*] *cancel*
▪ *Syn* annul, delete, eliminate, erase, strike, withdraw; ▪ *Ant* schedule, set up.

scrawny [*adj*] *unhealthily thin*
▪ *Syn* angular, bony, gaunt, lank, lanky, lean, rawboned, scraggy, skeletal, skinny, spare, undernourished, underweight; ▪ *Ant* chubby, fat, healthy, plump.

scream [*v*] *cry out*
▪ *Syn* bawl, bellow, blare, caterwaul, holler, howl, jar, roar, screak, screech, shout, shriek, shrill, sing out, squeal, voice, wail, yell, yip, yowl; ▪ *Ant* be quiet.

screen [*v*] *hide, protect*
▪ *Syn* blind, block out, camouflage, cloak, conceal, cover, cover up, defend, disguise, ensconce, guard, inumbrate, mask, obscure, safeguard, seclude, secrete, secure, shade, shelter, shield, shroud, shutter, stash, veil; ▪ *Ant* lay open, open, reveal, uncover.

scrub [*v1*] *clean with force*
▪ *Syn* abrade, brush, buff, cleanse, mop, polish, rub, scour, wash; ▪ *Ant* dirty, smudge, soil, sully.

scrub [*v2*] *cancel*
▪ *Syn* abandon, abolish, abort, call off, discontinue, drop; ▪ *Ant* organize, schedule, set up.

scruffy [*adj*] *rough, bedraggled*
▪ *Syn* badly groomed, messy, ragged, run-down, seedy, shabby, slovenly, tattered, threadbare; ▪ *Ant* kempt, smooth, tidy.

scrumptious [*adj*] *delicious*
▪ *Syn* ambrosial, appetizing, delectable, delightful, exquisite, heavenly, inviting, luscious, lush, magnificent, mouthwatering, rich, succulent, tasty, yummy; ▪ *Ant* distasteful, unappetizing.

scruple [*v*] *balk, have misgivings*
▪ *Syn* be loath, be reluctant, boggle, demur, doubt, falter, gag, have qualms, hesitate, question, shy, stumble, vacillate, waver; ▪ *Ant* assist, concur, cooperate.

scrupulous [*adj*] *extremely careful*
▪ *Syn* conscientious, exact, fastidious, heedful, honest, just, meticulous, moral, painstaking, precise, principled, punctilious, rigorous, strict, true, upright; ▪ *Ant* careless, negligent, unscrupulous.

scrutinize [v] *examine closely*
- **Syn** analyze, canvass, check, contemplate, dissect, explore, inspect, penetrate, perlustrate, pore over, probe, scan, scope, sift, stare, study, survey, view, watch, weigh; **Ant** disregard, glance at, neglect, overlook.

scuffle [n] *fight*
- **Syn** affray, brawl, commotion, disturbance, fracas, fray, jump, mix-up, ruckus, rumpus, scrap, shuffle, strife, tussle, wrangle; **Ant** harmony, peace.

scum [n] *superficial impurities, dirt*
- **Syn** algae, crust, dross, film, froth, residue, scruff, spume, waste; **Ant** cleanliness.

scurrilous [adj] *foul-mouthed, vulgar*
- **Syn** abusive, coarse, contumelious, defamatory, foul, indecent, insulting, invective, lewd, nasty, obscene, offensive, opprobrious, raunchy, ribald, salacious, scabrous, slanderous, truculent, vituperative; **Ant** clean, decent, polite, refined, upright.

scurry [v] *move along swiftly*
- **Syn** barrel, bustle, dart, dash, fly, hasten, hurry, race, rip, run, rush, scamper, scoot, scuttle, shoot, sprint, tear; **Ant** dawdle, loaf, walk.

sea [n] *large body of water; large mass*
- **Syn** abundance, brine, deep, expanse, lake, main, multitude, number, ocean, plethora, pond, profusion, sheet, surf, swell; **Ant** land, meagerness, terrain.

seal [v1] *make airtight*
- **Syn** close, cork, enclose, fasten, gum, paste, plaster, plug, quarantine, secure, shut, stopper, stop up, waterproof; **Ant** loosen, open, unseal.

seal [v2] *ensure, finalize*
- **Syn** assure, attest, authenticate, clinch, conclude, confirm, consummate, establish, ratify, settle, stamp, validate; **Ant** delay, put off, refuse.

seamy [adj] *corrupt, unwholesome*
- **Syn** bad, dark, degraded, disagreeable, disreputable, disturbing, low, nasty, rough, sordid, squalid, unpleasant; **Ant** respectable, upright, wholesome.

sear [v] *dry, burn*
- **Syn** blight, brand, brown, cauterize, cook, dehydrate, desiccate, dry out, exsiccate, harden, parch, scorch, shrivel, sizzle, tan, toast, wilt, wither; **Ant** freshen, moisten.

search [v] *seek to find something*
- **Syn** beat about, chase after, comb, examine, explore, ferret, forage, frisk, go in quest of, grope, grub, hunt, investigate, look, probe, pry, quest, rake, ransack, root, rummage, scour, scout, scrutinize, sift, smell around, study, track down; **Ant** find.

seasonable [adj] *timely, appropriate*
- **Syn** apropos, apt, auspicious, convenient, favorable, fit, opportune, pertinent, propitious, providential, relevant, seasonal, suitable, well-timed; **Ant** inappropriate, inclement, unfitting, unseasonable, unsuitable, untimely.

seat [v] *place in furniture, position*
- **Syn** accommodate, deposit, establish, fix, hold, install, locate, lounge, nestle, perch, plant, roost, set, settle, sit, squat, take; **Ant** displace, move, oust, remove.

secede [v] *pull away; split from*
- **Syn** abdicate, apostatize, break with, disaffiliate, quit, resign, separate, withdraw; **Ant** combine, come in, join, unite.

seclude [v] *isolate, hide*
- **Syn** cloister, closet, cover, embargo, enclose, immure, quarantine, retire, screen, segregate, sequester, shut off, withdraw; **Ant** integrate, join, mingle, socialize.

secluded [adj] *isolated, sheltered*
- **Syn** abandoned, alone, beleaguered, cloistered, covert, hermetic, hidden, insular, lonely, private, quarantined, remote, removed, reserved, secret, segregated, sequestered, solitary, withdrawn; **Ant** joining, mingling, open, public, sociable, socializing.

second [adj] *next; subordinate*
- **Syn** additional, alternative, double, duplicate, extra, following, further, inferior, lesser, lower, next, other, reproduction, runner-up, secondary, subsequent, succeeding, supporting; **Ant** first, primary.

second [v] *support, advance a suggestion* **Syn** aid, approve, assist, back, encourage, endorse, forward, further, give moral support, promote, stand by, uphold; **Ant** hinder, oppose, undermine.

secondary [adj1] *subordinate; less important* **Syn** accessory, alternate, auxiliary, backup, collateral, dependent, extra, inferior, lesser, lower, minor, relief, reserve, second, small, subject, subservient, subsidiary, supporting, tributary, under; ▪ *Ant* first-class, first-rate, primary, superior.

secondary [*adj2*] *derivative*
▪ *Syn* auxiliary, borrowed, dependent, derived, indirect, proximate, resultant, second-hand; ▪ *Ant* original, sole.

second-rate/second-class [*adj*] *inferior, cheap* ▪ *Syn* common, commonplace, déclassé, inferior, low-grade, low-quality, mean, mediocre, poor, substandard, tawdry; ▪ *Ant* excellent, first-class, first-rate; superior.

secret [*adj1*] *hidden, unrevealed*
▪ *Syn* abstruse, ambiguous, arcane, camouflaged, clouded, covert, cryptic, disguised, enigmatical, esoteric, furtive, mysterious, mystic, obscure, occult, private, recondite, secluded, shrouded, undercover, veiled; ▪ *Ant* clear, defined, explicit, forthright, honest, open, public, revealed, unconcealed.

secret [*adj2*] *underhand, clandestine*
▪ *Syn* backdoor, camouflaged, classified, confidential, covert, discreet, dissembled, furtive, incognito, inside, restricted, sneak, sub-rosa, surreptitious, top secret; ▪ *Ant* aboveboard, known, legal, legitimate, public.

secrete [*v1*] *hide*
▪ *Syn* bury, cache, conceal, cover up, disguise, ensconce, finesse, harbor, paper, plant, screen, seclude, shroud, stash, stow, veil, withhold; ▪ *Ant* reveal, show, tell.

secrete [*v2*] *give off, emit*
▪ *Syn* discharge, emanate, excrete, extravasate, extrude, exude, perspire, sweat; ▪ *Ant* fill, pour in.

secretive [*adj*] *uncommunicative*
▪ *Syn* cagey, close, covert, cryptic, enigmatic, furtive, hushed, reserved, reticent, taciturn, withdrawn; ▪ *Ant* communicative, forthright, honest, open.

secretly [*adv*] *in hidden manner*
▪ *Syn* clandestinely, confidentially, covertly, furtively, in confidence, insidiously, intimately, privately, privily, quietly, slyly, stealthily, sub rosa, surreptitiously, underhandedly; ▪ *Ant* openly, publicly.

sectarian [*adj*] *narrow-minded, exclusive* ▪ *Syn* bigoted, clannish, doctrinaire, dogmatic, factional, fanatical, hidebound, insular, limited, parochial, partisan, rigid, schismatic, skeptical; ▪ *Ant* broad, broad-minded, liberal, nonsectarian.

sectional [*adj*] *localized, divided*
▪ *Syn* exclusive, factional, local, narrow, partial, regional, separate, separatist; ▪ *Ant* general, universal, widespread.

secular [*adj*] *not spiritual or religious*
▪ *Syn* civil, earthly, laic, laical, lay, material, materialistic, nonclerical, nonreligious, of this world, profane, temporal, worldly; ▪ *Ant* godly, holy, religious, spiritual.

secure [*adj1*] *safe*
▪ *Syn* defended, guarded, immune, impregnable, out of harm's way, protected, safe, sheltered, shielded, unassailable; ▪ *Ant* endangered, insecure, unprotected, unsafe.

secure [*adj2*] *fastened, stable*
▪ *Syn* anchored, bound, fast, firm, fixed, fortified, immovable, iron, locked, nailed, set, solid, sound, staunch, steady, strong, sure, tenacious, tight; ▪ *Ant* loose, unfixed.

secure [*adj3*] *certain, definite*
▪ *Syn* absolute, assured, confident, established, firm, reassured, resolute, sanguine, settled, solid, sound, stable, steadfast, strong, well-founded; ▪ *Ant* indefinite, insecure, uncertain, undecided, unsure.

secure [*v1*] *obtain*
▪ *Syn* access, achieve, acquire, annex, assure, buy, capture, catch, ensure, gain, grasp, guarantee, hook, insure, land, lock, lock up, procure, take, win; ▪ *Ant* forfeit, give up, lose.

secure [*v2*] *attach, tie up*
▪ *Syn* adjust, anchor, batten down, bind, bolt, button, button down, catch, cement, chain, clamp, fasten, hitch, lock, make fast, moor, nail, padlock, pinion, tie down, tighten; ▪ *Ant* let go, loose, loosen, unfasten, untie.

secure [*v3*] *protect, make safe*
▪ *Syn* assure, cover, defend, ensure, fend, guarantee, guard, insure, safeguard, screen, shield; ▪ *Ant* endanger, harm, hurt, injure.

sedate [*adj*] *calm, collected*
▪ *Syn* composed, cool, decorous, deliberate, demure, dignified, dispassionate, earnest, grave, imperturbable, no-nonsense, placid, proper, quiet, seemly, serene, serious, sober, solemn, somber, staid, steady, tranquil; ▪ *Ant* agitated, excitable, excited, lively, upset.

sedative [*adj*] *soothing*
▪ *Syn* allaying, anodyne, calmative, calm-

ing, lenitive, relaxing, sleep-inducing, soporific, tranquillizing; ▪ *Ant* agitating, excitative, upsetting.

sedentary [*adj*] *motionless, lazy*
▪ *Syn* desk, desk-bound, idle, inactive, seated, settled, sitting, sluggish, stationary, torpid; ▪ *Ant* activated, active, energetic, mobile, moving.

seduce [*v*] *tempt, ensnare*
▪ *Syn* allure, bait, beguile, coax, corrupt, debauch, deflower, entice, entrap, hook, inveigle, invite, lure, mislead, pervert, pull, ravish, rope in, ruin, steer, tease, vamp; ▪ *Ant* disenchant, dissuade, repel.

seductive [*adj*] *alluring, sexy*
▪ *Syn* attractive, beguiling, captivating, charming, desirable, enchanting, enticing, flirtatious, inviting, irresistible, magnetic, provocative, ravishing, tempting; ▪ *Ant* drab, off-putting, prim, repellent.

see [*v2*] *appreciate, comprehend*
▪ *Syn* appraise, ascertain, behold, catch, determine, discern, distinguish, espy, fancy, follow, get, grasp, know, mark, mind, note, observe, perceive, ponder, realize, recognize, take in, understand, visualize, weigh; ▪ *Ant* ignore, neglect, overlook.

seedy [*adj*] *run-down, dilapidated*
▪ *Syn* beat up, bedraggled, decrepit, dingy, faded, flagging, grubby, messy, neglected, poor, ragged, ratty, shabby, sickly, squalid, tacky, tattered, threadbare, torn, unkempt, wilting, worn; ▪ *Ant* crisp, dapper, elegant, luxurious, posh.

seek [*v1*] *look for*
▪ *Syn* bob for, cast about, chase, comb, delve, dragnet, explore, ferret out, fish, follow, go after, hunt, investigate, prowl, pursue, quest, ransack, root, scout, search for, track down; ▪ *Ant* abandon, ignore.

seek [*v2*] *try, attempt*
▪ *Syn* aim, aspire to, assay, endeavor, essay, offer, pursue, strive, struggle, undertake; ▪ *Ant* neglect, relinquish.

seeming [*adj*] *apparent*
▪ *Syn* appearing, illusive, illusory, ostensible, outward, professed, quasi-, semblant, specious, surface; ▪ *Ant* genuine, real, true.

seemly [*adj*] *appropriate, suitable*
▪ *Syn* becoming, conforming, congruous, consonant, decent, decorous, fit, fitting, pleasing, proper, suited, timely; ▪ *Ant* improper, inappropriate, rude.

seep [*v*] *leak*
▪ *Syn* bleed, drain, drip, exude, ooze, percolate, permeate, sweat, transude, trickle, weep; ▪ *Ant* flood, gush, pour.

seethe [*v*] *be very angry*
▪ *Syn* boil, burn, ferment, foam, froth, fume, rage, simmer, smolder, spark; ▪ *Ant* be happy.

segment [*n*] *part of something*
▪ *Syn* articulation, bit, cut, division, member, moiety, parcel, piece, portion, section, sector, slice, subdivision, wedge; ▪ *Ant* entirety, whole.

segregate [*v*] *discriminate and separate*
▪ *Syn* close off, disconnect, dissociate, divide, insulate, isolate, quarantine, sequester, set apart, sever, split up; ▪ *Ant* combine, desegregate, gather, join, unite.

seize [*v1*] *grab, take*
▪ *Syn* catch, catch hold of, clasp, clench, clinch, compass, embrace, envelope, fasten, grapple, grasp, grip, hold fast, pinch, snag, snatch, squeeze; ▪ *Ant* give, let go, release.

seize [*v2*] *abduct; take by force*
▪ *Syn* ambush, annex, appropriate, arrogate, capture, conquer, exact, force, hijack, impound, kidnap, lift, nab, occupy, overcome, overwhelm, shanghai, snare, subdue, take captive, trap, usurp, wrench; ▪ *Ant* free, liberate, release.

seldom [*adv*] *infrequently*
▪ *Syn* a few times, every now and then, from time to time, hardly, hardly ever, irregularly, little, not often, occasionally, once in a while, rarely, scarcely, scarcely ever, sometimes, sporadically, uncommonly, whimsically; ▪ *Ant* frequently, often, usually.

select [*adj*] *excellent, elite, preferable*
▪ *Syn* best, choice, culled, delicate, discriminating, eclectic, exclusive, favored, handpicked, limited, picked, preferred, prime, privileged, rare, recherché, screened, special, superior, top-notch, winner; ▪ *Ant* inferior, poor, second-rate.

select [*v*] *pick out, prefer from among choices* ▪ *Syn* choose, cull, decide, elect, make, mark, name, opt, pick, pin down, single out, sort out, take, winnow; ▪ *Ant* refuse, reject.

selective [*adj*] *discriminating*
▪ *Syn* careful, choosy, discerning, discriminatory, fussy, judicious, particular, picky, scrupulous; ▪ *Ant* careless, promiscuous, undiscriminating.

self-centered [adj] *absorbed with oneself* ▪ **Syn** conceited, egocentric, egomaniacal, egotistical, inward-looking, narcissistic, self-absorbed, self-involved, selfish, self-seeking, self-serving, self-sufficient, vain; ▪ **Ant** benevolent, generous, giving, self-effacing.

self-confident [adj] *secure with oneself* ▪ **Syn** assured, bold, plucky, poised, sanguine, self-assured, self-reliant; ▪ **Ant** humble, insecure, meek, unsure.

self-conscious [adj] *insecure with oneself* ▪ **Syn** anxious, artificial, awkward, bashful, diffident, discomfited, embarrassed, ill-at-ease, mannered, nervous, stiff, stilted, uncertain, uncomfortable; ▪ **Ant** aggressive, assured, secure, sure.

self-control [n] *willpower over one's actions* ▪ **Syn** abstemiousness, aplomb, balance, constraint, discipline, discretion, poise, reserve, restraint, reticence, self-discipline; stoicism, strength of character; ▪ **Ant** instability, rashness, weakness.

self-evident/self-explanatory [adj] *obvious* ▪ **Syn** apparent, axiomatic, clear, comprehensible, incontrovertible, manifest, plain, undeniable, understandable, visible; ▪ **Ant** obscure, questionable.

selfish [adj] *thinking only of oneself* ▪ **Syn** egomaniacal, egotistical, mercenary, miserly, narcissistic, narrow-minded, parsimonious, prejudiced, self-centered, self-indulgent, stingy; ▪ **Ant** benevolent, caring, generous, kind.

self-respect/self-esteem [n] *pride in oneself* ▪ **Syn** amour-propre, conceit, confidence, dignity, egotism, self-assurance, self-regard, self-satisfaction, worth; ▪ **Ant** self-doubt, uncertainty.

self-righteous [adj] *smug* ▪ **Syn** affected, canting, egotistical, hypocritical, noble, pietistic, pious, preachy, sanctimonious, self-satisfied, superior; ▪ **Ant** caring, humble, thoughtful, understanding.

self-satisfied [adj] *proud, smug* ▪ **Syn** complacent, conceited, egotistic, self-congratulatory, vain; ▪ **Ant** humble, meek, unsure.

self-sufficient [adj] *able to take care of oneself* ▪ **Syn** competent, confident, efficient, independent, individual, on one's own, self-confident, self-supporting, self-sustaining; ▪ **Ant** incapable, needy.

sell [v1] *exchange an object for money* ▪ **Syn** advertise, auction, bargain, barter, contract, dispose, drum, hustle, merchandise, move, peddle, pitch, plug, push, retail, stock, trade, traffic, unload, vend, wholesale; ▪ **Ant** buy, purchase.

sell/sell out [v2] *betray* ▪ **Syn** beguile, bunk, cross, deceive, fail, give away, give up, mislead, play false, surrender, take in, violate; ▪ **Ant** be loyal, stand by, support.

send [v1] *transmit, transfer through a system* ▪ **Syn** address, assign, cast, communicate, convey, direct, dispatch, emit, expedite, express, fire, forward, give off, grant, hasten, hurl, impart, issue, mail, post, propel, relay, remit, shoot, televise, wire; ▪ **Ant** admit, receive.

send [v2] *please* ▪ **Syn** charm, delight, enrapture, enthrall, excite, intoxicate, please, ravish, stir, thrill, titillate; ▪ **Ant** displease.

senile [adj] *failing in physical and mental capabilities due to old age* ▪ **Syn** aged, ancient, anile, decrepit, doddering, doting, enfeebled, feeble, imbecile, infirm, old, senescent, shattered, sick, weak; ▪ **Ant** alert, sound, well.

senior [adj] *older or of higher rank* ▪ **Syn** chief, elder, higher, leading, next higher, superior; ▪ **Ant** behind, inferior, junior.

sensational [adj1] *startling, exaggerated* ▪ **Syn** amazing, arresting, breathtaking, dramatic, electrifying, exciting, lurid, melodramatic, noticeable, outstanding, piquant, remarkable, revealing, scandalous, shocking, signal, staggering, stimulating, thrilling, vulgar; ▪ **Ant** ordinary, run-of-the-mill, unexceptional, usual.

sense [v] *become aware of* ▪ **Syn** apperceive, appreciate, apprehend, believe, catch, deem, discern, divine, feel, grasp, hold, notice, observe, perceive, read, realize, savvy, suspect, take in, think, understand; ▪ **Ant** be numb, be unaware, overlook.

senseless [adj] *silly, meaningless* ▪ **Syn** absurd, asinine, batty, crazy, daft, fatuous, flaky, idiotic, illogical, inane, irrational, ludicrous, mad, moronic, nutty, pointless, purportless, ridiculous, simple, trivial; ▪ **Ant** feeling, intelligent, rational, reasonable, sensible, wise.

sensible [adj] *realistic, reasonable* ▪ **Syn** astute, attentive, au courant, canny, cognizant, commonsensical, discreet, discriminating, down-to-earth, informed, intelligent, judicious, knowing, logical, practical, prudent, rational, sagacious, sentient, shrewd, sober, sound, together, well-reasoned, wise; ▪ *Ant* indiscreet, senseless, unrealistic, unreasonable, unwise.

sensitive [*adj1*] *impressionable*
▪ *Syn* acute, delicate, emotional, feeling, hypersensitive, impressible, keen, nervous, oversensitive, perceptive, psychic, receptive, responsive, susceptible, tense, ticklish, touchy, umbrageous; ▪ *Ant* impassive, insensitive, thick-skinned, unsusceptible.

sensitive [*adj2*] *easily hurt*
▪ *Syn* delicate, easily harmed, painful, sore, tender; ▪ *Ant* heartless, indifferent, insensitive, numb, unfeeling.

sensual [*adj*] *physical, erotic*
▪ *Syn* animal, animalistic, carnal, fleshly, heavy, hedonic, lascivious, libidinous, lustful, moving, pleasing, sensuous, sexual, sexy, steamy, stimulating, stirring, tactile, voluptuous; ▪ *Ant* cerebral, spartan, spiritual.

sensuous [*adj*] *gratifying to senses*
▪ *Syn* carnal, epicurean, fleshly, hedonistic, luscious, passionate, physical, pleasurable, pleasure-loving, pleasure-seeking, self-indulgent, sensory, sumptuous, sybaritic, voluptuous; ▪ *Ant* despicable, distasteful.

sentimental [*adj*] *emotional, romantic*
▪ *Syn* affectionate, demonstrative, dewy-eyed, effusive, gushing, idealistic, impressionable, jejune, languishing, loving, maudlin, nostalgic, passionate, pathetic, simpering, soft, tearful, tender, touching, weepy; ▪ *Ant* hard-hearted, indifferent, pragmatic, unemotional.

separate [*adj1*] *disconnected*
▪ *Syn* abstracted, apart, asunder, detached, disassociated, disembodied, disjointed, distant, disunited, divided, divorced, independent, isolated, partitioned, put asunder, removed, scattered, severed, sundered; ▪ *Ant* combined, connected, joined, mixed, together, united.

separate [*adj2*] *alone, individual*
▪ *Syn* autonomous, different, discrete, distinct, distinctive, lone, one, only, particular, peculiar, single, sole, solitary, unique; ▪ *Ant* associated, together, united.

separate [*v1*] *remove something from group; keep or set apart* ▪ *Syn* break, break off, cleave, come apart, detach,

dichotomize, disconnect, disjoin, disjoint, dissect, dissever, divide, divorce, part, rupture, sever, split, sunder; ▪ *Ant* combine, join, mix, unite.

separate [*v2*] *part company in a romantic relationship or marriage* ▪ *Syn* alienate, bifurcate, break off, break up, de-domicile, depart, disunify, disunite, divorce, estrange, leave, part, pull out, split up; ▪ *Ant* marry.

separately [*adv*] *alone, individually*
▪ *Syn* apart, clearly, definitely, disjointly, distinctly, independently, one at a time, one by one, singly, solely; ▪ *Ant* together.

sequential [*adj*] *occurring in an order*
▪ *Syn* consecutive, continuous, following, regular, sequent, serial, subsequential, succedent, succeeding, successive; ▪ *Ant* disordered, nonsequential, out of order.

sequester [*v*] *isolate, seclude*
▪ *Syn* cloister, close off, cut off, enisle, hide, insulate, island, secrete, segregate, separate, set apart, set off, withdraw; ▪ *Ant* make public, reveal.

serene [*adj*] *calm, undisturbed*
▪ *Syn* at peace, collected, composed, content, dispassionate, easygoing, fair, halcyon, imperturbable, limpid, patient, pellucid, phlegmatic, placid, quiescent, quiet, resting, self-possessed, stoical, tranquil; ▪ *Ant* agitated, disturbed, excited, troubled.

serial [*adj*] *in continuing order*
▪ *Syn* consecutive, continual, continued, continuing, ensuing, following, sequent, sequential, succedent; ▪ *Ant* disordered.

serious [*adj1*] *somber, humorless*
▪ *Syn* austere, contemplative, deliberate, determined, earnest, genuine, grave, grim, honest, intent, meditative, nonsense, pensive, reflective, resolute, resolved, sedate, set, severe, sincere, sober, solemn, staid, steady, stern, thoughtful, weighty; ▪ *Ant* flippant, funny, happy, light.

serious [*adj2*] *crucial, weighty*
▪ *Syn* arduous, deep, difficult, fateful, fell, formidable, grave, grievous, grim, hard, heavy, important, laborious, major, momentous, operose, pressing, severe, significant, sobering, strenuous, threatening, tough, urgent, worrying; ▪ *Ant* light, minor, trivial, unimportant.

seriously [*adv1*] *not humorously*
▪ *Syn* actively, determinedly, earnestly,

fervently, gravely, in earnest, intently, passionately, purposefully, resolutely, sedately, sincerely, soberly, solemnly, sternly, thoughtfully, vigorously, zealously; ▪ *Ant* lightly.

seriously [adv2] *dangerously, critically*
▪ *Syn* acutely, badly, decidedly, deplorably, distressingly, gravely, grievously, harmfully, intensely, perilously, precariously, quite, regrettably, severely, sorely, threateningly, very; ▪ *Ant* casually, trivially.

serrated [adj] *jagged*
▪ *Syn* denticulate, indented, notched, ragged, sawtooth, saw-toothed, scored, serried, toothed; ▪ *Ant* smooth, straight.

serve [v1] *aid, help; supply*
▪ *Syn* arrange, assist, attend to, be of assistance, be of use, care for, deal, deliver, distribute, do for, give, handle, hit, minister to, mother, nurse, oblige, play, present, provide, provision, set out, succor, wait on, work for; ▪ *Ant* hinder, obstruct, oppose.

serve [v2] *act, do*
▪ *Syn* accept, attend, be employed by, carry on, discharge, follow, fulfill, function, hearken, labor, obey, observe, officiate, pass, perform, subserve, toil, work; ▪ *Ant* refrain, refuse.

serve [v3] *suffice; do the work of*
▪ *Syn* advantage, answer, answer the purpose, apply, avail, be acceptable, be adequate, be good enough, benefit, be of use, be useful, content, do, do duty as, fit, function, make, profit, satisfy, service, suit, work, work for; ▪ *Ant* be insufficient, dissatisfy.

serviceable [adj] *useful, functional*
▪ *Syn* advantageous, aiding, assistive, beneficial, convenient, durable, handy, helpful, operative, practical, profitable, usable, utile, utilitarian; ▪ *Ant* unhelpful, unprofitable, unserviceable, useless, weak, worthless.

servile [adj] *groveling, subservient*
▪ *Syn* abject, base, beggarly, craven, cringing, despicable, fawning, humble, ignoble, low, mean, obedient, obeisant, obsequious, passive, slavish, submissive, sycophantic, toadying, unctuous; ▪ *Ant* aggressive, dominant.

set [adj1] *decided*
▪ *Syn* agreed, appointed, arranged, certain, confirmed, customary, definite, determined, established, firm, fixed, in-

tent, pat, prearranged, predetermined, prescribed, regular, resolute, resolved, scheduled, settled, specified, stated, steadfast, stipulated, usual; ▪ *Ant* indefinite, undecided, unfixed.

set [adj2] *firm, hardened; inflexible*
▪ *Syn* entrenched, fixed, hard and fast, hidebound, immovable, jelled, located, placed, positioned, rigid, sited, situate, situated, solid, stable, stiff, strict, stubborn, unyielding; ▪ *Ant* flexible, movable, soft, tractable.

set [v1] *position, place*
▪ *Syn* affix, aim, anchor, bestow, cast, deposit, direct, ensconce, establish, fasten, fix, head, insert, install, lay, level, lock, lodge, make fast, make ready, mount, park, plant, plunk, point, post, prepare, put, rest, seat, settle, situate, station, stick, turn, wedge; ▪ *Ant* displace, lift, remove.

set [v2] *harden*
▪ *Syn* become firm, cake, clot, coagulate, condense, congeal, crystallize, fix, gel, gelatinize, jell, solidify, stiffen, thicken; ▪ *Ant* liquefy, soften.

set [v3] *start, incite*
▪ *Syn* abet, begin, commence, foment, initiate, instigate, provoke, put in motion, raise; ▪ *Ant* discourage, dissuade, end, finish, halt, hinder.

set back [v] *delay, hinder*
▪ *Syn* decelerate, detain, embog, hold up, impede, mire, retard, reverse, slow, slow down, slow up; ▪ *Ant* advance, forward.

settle [v1] *straighten out, resolve*
▪ *Syn* adjudicate, adjust, arrange, clear up, come to an agreement, concert, conclude, decide, determine, end, establish, figure, fix, judge, mediate, negotiate, order, reconcile, regulate, satisfy, verify, work out; ▪ *Ant* confuse, mix up, unsettle.

settle [v2] *calm, relieve*
▪ *Syn* allay, assure, becalm, compose, lull, pacify, quell, quiet, reassure, relax, soothe, still; ▪ *Ant* confuse, trouble, upset, worry.

settle [v3] *come to rest; fall*
▪ *Syn* alight, decline, descend, flop, immerse, land, lay, light, lodge, perch, place, plop, plunge, put, repose, roost, seat, set down, sink, sit, submerge, submerse, subside, touch down; ▪ *Ant* ascend, rise.

settle [v4] *make one's home*
▪ *Syn* abide, colonize, dwell, establish,

inhabit, keep house, live, locate, lodge, park, put down roots, reside, set up home, take up residence; ▪ *Ant* roam, rove.

set up [*v*] *start*
▪ *Syn* begin, build, constitute, construct, create, elevate, erect, establish, found, inaugurate, initiate, institute, introduce, launch, open, organize, originate, prearrange, prepare, put together, raise, rear, stimulate, subsidize, usher in; ▪ *Ant* conclude, end, finish.

sever [*v1*] *cut apart*
▪ *Syn* bisect, cleave, cut, detach, disconnect, disjoin, dissect, divide, part, rend, rive, separate, slice, split, sunder; ▪ *Ant* combine, join, mend, seal, seam, unite.

sever [*v2*] *dissociate*
▪ *Syn* abandon, break off, disjoint, dissolve, divide, divorce, put an end to, separate, terminate; ▪ *Ant* associate, unite.

several [*adj*] *assorted, various*
▪ *Syn* a few, a lot, certain, considerable, different, diverse, handful, indefinite, manifold, many, numerous, proportionate, quite a few, some, sundry; ▪ *Ant* combined, individual, joint, one.

severe [*adj1*] *uncompromising, stern*
▪ *Syn* astringent, biting, caustic, cruel, cutting, dour, firm, forbidding, grave, grim, harsh, inconsiderate, inexorable, obdurate, peremptory, pitiless, relentless, resolute, rigid, scathing, serious, sober, strict, unsparing; ▪ *Ant* amenable, compromising, easygoing, friendly, willing.

severe [*adj2*] *difficult, harsh*
▪ *Syn* acute, arduous, ascetic, bitter, despotic, distressing, drastic, effortful, exacting, fierce, forbidding, grave, grim, hard, heavy, implacable, intense, mordant, oppressive, pitiless, punishing, rigorous, serious, sharp, strenuous, stringent, taxing, tough, violent, weighty; ▪ *Ant* calm, easy, facile, mild, temperate.

severely [*adv*] *harshly*
▪ *Syn* acutely, badly, critically, extremely, firmly, gravely, hardly, intensely, markedly, painfully, rigorously, seriously, sharply, sorely, sternly, with an iron hand; ▪ *Ant* compassionately, lightly.

sew [*v*] *prepare fabric for clothing, covering* ▪ *Syn* baste, bind, embroider, fasten, piece, seam, stitch, tack, tailor, work; ▪ *Ant* rip, tear.

sexual [*adj*] *concerning reproduction, intercourse* ▪ *Syn* carnal, erotic, fleshly, generative, genital, intimate, loving, passionate, procreative, reproductive, sensual, venereal, voluptuous, wanton; ▪ *Ant* asexual, neuter, nonsexual, platonic.

sexy [*adj*] *being attractive to another*
▪ *Syn* arousing, erotic, flirtatious, inviting, libidinous, provocative, racy, risqué, seductive, sensual, suggestive, titillating, voluptuous; ▪ *Ant* tedious, unattractive, unexciting.

shabby [*adj1*] *broken-down; in poor shape* ▪ *Syn* bedraggled, crummy, decaying, decrepit, deteriorated, dilapidated, dingy, frayed, mangy, moth-eaten, neglected, poor, ramshackle, ratty, rickety, ruinous, run-down, seedy, shoddy, sleazy, tattered, threadbare, tired, worn; ▪ *Ant* kempt, neat, pristine, spruce.

shabby [*adj2*] *despicable*
▪ *Syn* beggarly, cheap, contemptible, disgraceful, dishonorable, disreputable, ignoble, ignominious, inconsiderate, inglorious, low, low-down, mean, mercenary, miserly, rotten, shady, shameful, shoddy, sordid, sorry, stingy, thoughtless, unkind, unworthy; ▪ *Ant* honorable, respectable.

shade [*v*] *shut out the light*
▪ *Syn* adumbrate, blacken, cloud, cloud over, conceal, darken, dim, eclipse, gray, hide, inumbrate, mute, obscure, protect, screen, shadow, shelter, shield, shutter, umbrage, veil; ▪ *Ant* brighten, expose, illuminate.

shadow [*v1*] *make dark*
▪ *Syn* adumbrate, becloud, cloud, darken, dim, gray, haze, inumbrate, obscure, overcast, screen, shelter, shield, umbrage, veil; ▪ *Ant* brighten, lighten.

shady [*adj1*] *dark, covered*
▪ *Syn* adumbral, bosky, cloudy, cool, dim, dusky, leafy, screened, shaded, shadowy, sheltered, vague; ▪ *Ant* bright, light, open.

shady [*adj2*] *disreputable, suspicious*
▪ *Syn* crooked, dishonest, dubious, fishy, ignominious, questionable, shifty, shoddy, slippery, suspect, unscrupulous, untrustworthy; ▪ *Ant* aboveboard, honorable, reputable, respectable.

shaggy [*adj*] *hairy, unkempt*
▪ *Syn* furry, hirsute, long-haired, ragged, ruffled, uncombed, unshorn; ▪ *Ant* kempt, shaven, smooth.

shake [v] *upset deeply*
- *Syn* appall, bother, consternate, daunt, discompose, disturb, frighten, impair, jar, move, rattle, throw, unnerve, upset, weaken; - *Ant* calm, placate, soothe.

shaky [adj1] *trembling*
- *Syn* faltering, infirm, jellylike, jittery, nervous, precarious, quaking, rickety, shaking, tottering, trembling, tremulous, unsteady, vacillating, wavering, wobbly; - *Ant* firm, steady, unwavering.

shaky [adj2] *doubtful*
- *Syn* dubious, indecisive, precarious, problematic, questionable, suspect, uncertain, unreliable, unsound, unsteady; - *Ant* certain, firm, indubious, sure.

shallow [adj1] *not deep*
- *Syn* cursory, depthless, empty, flat, hollow, shelf, slight, superficial, surface, trifling, trivial, unsound; - *Ant* bottomless, deep.

shallow [adj2] *unintelligent, ignorant*
- *Syn* cursory, empty, featherbrained, flighty, foolish, frivolous, hollow, idle, inane, lightweight, meaningless, petty, piddling, puerile, simple, superficial, trifling, trivial; - *Ant* aware, deep, intelligent, profound.

sham [adj] *artificial, counterfeit*
- *Syn* adulterated, affected, false, feigned, fraudulent, imitation, lying, misleading, mock, phony, pretend, simulated, spurious, substitute, synthetic; - *Ant* genuine, real, true, unfeigned.

sham [v] *trick; pull a hoax*
- *Syn* affect, ape, assume, bluff, copy, counterfeit, fake, feign, imitate, invent, lie, mislead, pretend, put on, simulate; - *Ant* tell truth.

shambles [n] *a mess*
- *Syn* anarchy, bedlam, botch, chaos, confusion, disarray, disorder, disorganization, hash, havoc, hodge-podge, madhouse, maelstrom, mess-up, mix-up, muddle; - *Ant* order, organization.

shame [v] *disgrace, embarrass*
- *Syn* abash, blot, confound, debase, defile, degrade, disconcert, discredit, dishonor, humble, humiliate, mortify, reproach, ridicule, smear, stain; - *Ant* honor, make proud, respect.

shameful [adj] *atrocious; disreputable*
- *Syn* base, contemptible, dastardly, debauched, diabolical, dishonorable, embarrassing, heinous, ignominious, immoral, indecent, lewd, low, mortifying,

notorious, obscene, outrageous, profligate, reprobate, ribald, scandalous, shocking, sinful, vile, vulgar, wicked; - *Ant* admirable, honorable, noble, reputable, respectable.

shameless [adj] *corrupt, indecent*
- *Syn* abandoned, arrant, audacious, bold, brassy, brazen, depraved, dissolute, flagrant, immodest, improper, impudent, incorrigible, lewd, outrageous, presumptuous, profligate, reprobate, wanton; - *Ant* decent, good, moral.

shape [v1] *form, create*
- *Syn* assemble, build, carve, cast, chisel, construct, crystallize, cut, determine, embody, fabricate, fashion, guide, hew, make, mint, mold, pattern, produce, stamp; - *Ant* deform, destroy.

shapeless [adj] *formless*
- *Syn* amorphic, anomalous, embryonic, inchoate, indefinite, indeterminate, indistinct, invisible, nebulous, vague, without form; - *Ant* contoured, formed, proportioned.

shapely [adj] *well-proportioned*
- *Syn* balanced, beautiful, comely, curvaceous, full-figured, graceful, proportioned, rounded, statuesque, sylphlike, well-formed, well-turned; - *Ant* deformed, disproportioned, misshapen.

share [v] *use in common with others*
- *Syn* accord, administer, allot, be a party to, deal, dispense, distribute, divide, dole out, mete out, parcel out, partake, partition, prorate, quota, ration, shift, slice, split, yield; - *Ant* hold, keep.

sharp [adj1] *knifelike, cutting*
- *Syn* aciculate, acuminate, acuminous, apical, barbed, briery, honed, jagged, keen, needlelike, peaked, pointed, pronged, razor-sharp, salient, serrated, spiked, spiny, stinging, thorny, tined, unblunted, whetted; - *Ant* blunt, dull, rounded.

sharp [adj2] *sudden*
- *Syn* abrupt, distinct, extreme, intense, marked; - *Ant* gradual, slow.

sharp [adj3] *perceptive, quick-witted*
- *Syn* adroit, alert, apt, astute, bright, canny, clever, discerning, fast, intelligent, keen, nimble, observant, penetrating, quick, ready, savvy, sensitive, smart; - *Ant* ignorant, unintelligent, unperceptive.

sharp [adj4] *dishonest, deceitful*
- *Syn* artful, bent, crafty, cunning, de-

signing, shady, shrewd, slick, slippery, sly, smart, wily; ▪ *Ant* aboveboard, forthright, frank, honest.

sharp [*adj5*] *severe, intense*
▪ *Syn* acute, agonizing, biting, cutting, distinct, drilling, excruciating, fierce, keen, knifelike, painful, paralyzing, penetrating, piercing, shooting, stabbing, stinging, violent; ▪ *Ant* calm, mild, moderate.

sharp [*adj6*] *distinct, well-defined*
▪ *Syn* audible, clear, clear-cut, crisp, definite, explicit, obvious, visible; ▪ *Ant* indefinite, indistinct, undefined.

sharp [*adj7*] *stylish*
▪ *Syn* chic, classy, dashing, distinctive, dressy, fashionable, fine, in style, smart, trendy; ▪ *Ant* dowdy, old-fashioned.

sharp [*adj8*] *hurtful, bitter in speech*
▪ *Syn* acrimonious, biting, caustic, double-edged, harsh, incisive, penetrating, pointed, sardonic, scathing, severe, stinging, tart, trenchant, virulent, vitriolic; ▪ *Ant* benevolent, kind, sweet, tender.

sharp [*adj9*] *having strong affect on animate senses* ▪ *Syn* acerbic, acid, acrid, astringent, bitter, brisk, burning, harsh, hot, odorous, piquant, pungent, tart, vinegary; ▪ *Ant* bland, dull, flat, mild, moderate, tasteless.

sharp [*adv*] *on time*
▪ *Syn* accurately, exactly, just, precisely, promptly, punctually, right, squarely; ▪ *Ant* late.

sharpen [*v*] *make knifelike*
▪ *Syn* acuminate, dress, edge, file, grind, hone, make acute, put an edge on, strop, taper, whet; ▪ *Ant* blunt, dull.

shatter [*v1*] *break into small pieces*
▪ *Syn* burst, crack, crash, explode, fracture, fragment, implode, overturn, pulverize, rive, smash, smatter, snap, splinter, split, wrack up, wreck; ▪ *Ant* fix, mend.

shatter [*v2*] *hurt someone badly*
▪ *Syn* crush, destroy, devastate, dumbfound, rattle, ruin, upset, wreck; ▪ *Ant* better, improve, increase.

shed [*v*] *cast off*
▪ *Syn* beam, cast, diffuse, disburden, exuviate, give forth, jettison, molt, radiate, scatter, scrap, shower, slough, sprinkle, take off, throw, yield; ▪ *Ant* put on.

sheen [*n*] *brightness, shine*
▪ *Syn* burnish, finish, glaze, gleam, glint,

gloss, luster, patina, polish, shimmer, shininess, wax; ▪ *Ant* dullness, filminess, tarnish.

sheepish [*adj*] *shy, embarrassed*
▪ *Syn* abashed, ashamed, chagrined, diffident, docile, guilty, mortified, retiring, self-conscious, shamefaced, silly, timid, timorous; ▪ *Ant* aggressive, bold, immodest.

sheer [*adj1*] *abrupt, steep*
▪ *Syn* erect, headlong, perpendicular, precipitate, precipitous, steep, upright; ▪ *Ant* gradual, sloping.

sheer [*adj2*] *utter, absolute*
▪ *Syn* arrant, complete, downright, infernal, outright, quite, rank, thoroughgoing, total, unadulterated, unmixed, unqualified, utter; ▪ *Ant* alloyed, fragmentary, mixed.

sheer [*adj3*] *see-through, thin*
▪ *Syn* airy, chiffon, diaphanous, filmy, fine, gauzy, gossamer, limpid, lucid, pellucid, slight, tiffany, translucent, transparent; ▪ *Ant* impermeable, opaque, thick.

shell [*n*] *structure; covering*
▪ *Syn* carapace, case, chassis, crust, frame, framework, hull, husk, integument, pericarp, plastron, pod, scale, shard, shuck, skeleton, skin; ▪ *Ant* center, interior, middle.

shell out [*v*] *give*
▪ *Syn* ante up, disburse, expend, hand over, lay out, outlay, pay, pay out, spend; ▪ *Ant* receive, take.

shelter [*v*] *provide safety, cover*
▪ *Syn* chamber, conceal, defend, enclose, guard, harbor, house, lodge, protect, safeguard, shield, take in, ward; ▪ *Ant* evict, expel, expose, lay bare, turn away, turn out.

shelve [*v*] *defer, postpone*
▪ *Syn* delay, hold, lay aside, prolong, put aside, put off, scrub, sideline, suspend, table, tie up, waive; ▪ *Ant* expedite, initiate, reactivate.

shield [*v*] *protect*
▪ *Syn* bulwark, chamber, conceal, cover up, defend, give cover, guard, harbor, house, safeguard, screen, secure, shelter, ward off; ▪ *Ant* endanger, reveal, uncover.

shift [*v*] *switch, fluctuate*
▪ *Syn* alter, change, deviate, dislocate, disturb, exchange, rearrange, recalibrate, relocate, reposition, shuffle, stir, swerve,

tack, transfer, transmogrify, transpose, turn, vacillate, veer, waffle; ▪ *Ant* remain, stagnate.

shifty [*adj*] *deceitful, untrustworthy*
▪ *Syn* cagey, conniving, crafty, crooked, cunning, devious, dishonest, equivocating, evasive, foxy, furtive, insidious, knavish, lying, mendacious, prevaricative, roguish, scheming, shady, slippery, sly, sneaky, treacherous, underhand, wily; ▪ *Ant* forthright, frank, honest, trustworthy.

shimmer [*n*] *gleam*
▪ *Syn* blinking, coruscation, flash, glimmer, glisten, glitter, iridescence, luster, phosphorescence, scintillation, sheen, spangle, sparkle, twinkle; ▪ *Ant* dullness, tarnish.

shine [*v1*] *give off or reflect light*
▪ *Syn* beam, burn, dazzle, flash, flicker, gleam, glimmer, glitter, glow, illuminate, incandesce, irradiate, luminesce, radiate, scintillate, shimmer, sparkle, twinkle; ▪ *Ant* darken, dull.

shine [*v2*] *polish, burnish*
▪ *Syn* brush, buff, finish, furbish, glaze, gloss, make brilliant, put a gloss on, rub, scour, sleek, wax; ▪ *Ant* dull, tarnish.

shiny [*adj*] *bright, glistening*
▪ *Syn* agleam, burnished, glossy, lustrous, polished, satiny, slick, sparkling, sunny; ▪ *Ant* dark, dull.

ship [*v*] *send, transport*
▪ *Syn* address, consign, direct, dispatch, drop, embark, export, forward, freight, haul, move, remit, route, shift, transfer, transmit; ▪ *Ant* hold, keep.

shirk [*v*] *avoid, get out of responsibility*
▪ *Syn* bypass, cheat, dodge, eschew, evade, malinger, off, parry, shun, sidestep, skulk, slink, sneak; ▪ *Ant* face, fulfill, meet, perform.

shocking [*adj*] *outrageous; very surprising* ▪ *Syn* abominable, appalling, awful, crying, disquieting, distressing, dreadful, formidable, frightful, ghastly, glaring, heinous, hideous, horrifying, loathsome, monstrous, nauseating, odious, repulsive, revolting, scandalous, shameful, sickening, stupefying, terrible, unspeakable; ▪ *Ant* acceptable, admirable, expected, gratifying, pleasant.

shoddy [*adj*] *in bad shape; contemptible*
▪ *Syn* borax, broken-down, cheap, dilapidated, dishonorable, disreputable, ignominious, inglorious, makeshift, mean, poor, run-down, seedy, shady, shameful, slipshod, tawdry; ▪ *Ant* excellent, fastidious, first-rate.

shoot [*v2*] *dash*
▪ *Syn* bolt, charge, chase, dart, flash, fling, fly, gallop, hurry, hurtle, race, run, rush, scoot, skirr, speed, spring, spurt, streak, tear; ▪ *Ant* saunter, walk.

shop [*v*] *look for merchandise to buy*
▪ *Syn* buy, hunt for, look for, market, patronize, purchase, windowshop; ▪ *Ant* market, sell, vend.

shore [*v*] *reinforce*
▪ *Syn* bolster, brace, bulwark, buttress, carry, hold, prop, strengthen, support, sustain, underpin; ▪ *Ant* overturn, topple, weaken.

short [*adj1*] *abridged*
▪ *Syn* abbreviated, aphoristic, bare, boiled down, brief, compendiary, compressed, condensed, curtailed, decreased, epigrammatic, laconic, pithy, precise, succinct, summarized, terse; ▪ *Ant* attenuated, long, protracted, unabridged.

short [*adj2*] *not tall*
▪ *Syn* abbreviated, chunky, compact, diminutive, dwarfed, little, petite, pocket, runty, skimpy, small, squat, stubby, stunted, tiny, undersized; ▪ *Ant* high, lengthy, long, tall.

short [*adj3*] *insufficient*
▪ *Syn* deficient, exiguous, inadequate, lacking, limited, meager, poor, scant, scanty, scarce, shy, skimpy, slender, slim, sparse, tight, wanting; ▪ *Ant* adequate, enough, sufficient.

short [*adj4*] *abrupt, discourteous*
▪ *Syn* blunt, breviloquent, brusque, curt, direct, gruff, impolite, offhand, rude, sharp, terse, testy, thoughtless, unceremonious; ▪ *Ant* courteous, kind, polite.

short [*adv*] *abruptly*
▪ *Syn* aback, by surprise, forthwith, sudden, suddenly, unexpectedly, without delay, without hesitation, without warning; ▪ *Ant* gently, gradually, slowly.

shorten [*v*] *diminish, decrease*
▪ *Syn* abbreviate, abridge, bob, chop, clip, compress, condense, contract, curtail, cut back, cut down, edit, elide, excerpt, lessen, lop, minimize, reduce, retrench, shrink, slash, snip, trim; ▪ *Ant* amplify, elongate, enlarge, grow, increase, lengthen.

short-lived [*adj*] *temporary*
▪ *Syn* brief, ephemeral, evanescent,

fleeting, fugacious, impermanent, momentary, passing, transient, transitory; ▪ *Ant* enduring, ethereal, lasting, lengthy, long-lived, permanent.

shortly [*adv*] *right away*
▪ *Syn* anon, before long, by and by, in a little while, presently, proximately, quickly, soon; ▪ *Ant* later.

short-sighted [*adj*] *unmindful of future consequences* ▪ *Syn* astigmatic, careless, foolish, headlong, ill-advised, imperceptive, impractical, improvident, imprudent, myopic, near-sighted, rash; ▪ *Ant* careful, long-sighted, prudent, thoughtful, wise.

shoulder [*vl*] *be responsible for*
▪ *Syn* accept, acknowledge, assume, bear, carry, sustain, take on, take upon oneself; ▪ *Ant* avoid, dodge, neglect, shirk.

shout [*n*] *loud outcry*
▪ *Syn* bark, bellow, call, cheer, clamor, cry, howl, roar, scream, shriek, squall, squawk, tumult, vociferation, yell; ▪ *Ant* murmur, mutter, whimper, whisper.

shove [*v*] *push without gentleness*
▪ *Syn* boost, buck, cram, crowd, dig, drive, elbow, hustle, impel, jab, jostle, nudge, poke, prod, shoulder, thrust; ▪ *Ant* drag, draw, haul, pull.

show [*vl*] *actively exhibit something*
▪ *Syn* air, bare, blazon, demonstrate, display, exhibit, expose, flash, flaunt, lay bare, mount, offer, parade, present, reveal, showcase, sport, stage, trot out, vaunt, wave; ▪ *Ant* conceal, hide, withhold.

show [*v2*] *passively exhibit something*
▪ *Syn* appear, assert, clarify, demonstrate, display, divulge, elucidate, evince, illustrate, indicate, manifest, mark, ostend, present, project, reach, reveal; ▪ *Ant* conceal, screen, veil.

show [*v3*] *grant*
▪ *Syn* accord, act with, bestow, confer, dispense, give; ▪ *Ant* withdraw, withhold.

show [*v4*] *accompany*
▪ *Syn* attend, conduct, direct, escort, guide, lead, pilot, route, see, shepherd, steer; ▪ *Ant* abandon, withdraw.

showdown [*n*] *confrontation*
▪ *Syn* breaking point, clash, climax, crisis, culmination, expos, moment of truth, unfolding; ▪ *Ant* accord, agreement, peace.

show off [*v*] *flaunt; brag*
▪ *Syn* advertise, boast, brandish, demonstrate, display, disport, exhibit, make a spectacle of, parade, spread out, swagger; ▪ *Ant* be modest, cower, shy away.

show up [*vl*] *arrive, attend*
▪ *Syn* appear, come, get, make an appearance, put in appearance, reach, show, stand out, turn up; ▪ *Ant* be absent, depart, leave, miss.

show up [*v2*] *expose, embarrass*
▪ *Syn* belittle, convict, debunk, discredit, highlight, invalidate, let down, mortify, pinpoint, reveal, shame; ▪ *Ant* compliment, praise.

showy [*adj*] *flamboyant, flashy*
▪ *Syn* dashing, garish, gaudy, loud, meretricious, ostentatious, overdone, pompous, pretentious, resplendent, sensational, splashy, sumptuous, tawdry; ▪ *Ant* dismal, drab, gloomy, moderate, restrained.

shred [*v*] *cut into ribbons*
▪ *Syn* cut, fray, frazzle, make ragged, reduce, shave, sliver, strip, tatter, tear; ▪ *Ant* mend, sew.

shrewd [*adj*] *clever, intelligent*
▪ *Syn* acute, artful, astute, calculating, cunning, discerning, far-sighted, judicious, keen, knowing, perceptive, perspicacious, prudent, quick-witted, savvy, sensible, smart, streetwise, tricky, underhand, wily, wise; ▪ *Ant* ingenuous, slow-witted, straightforward, unthinking.

shrill [*adj*] *high-pitched, harsh in sound*
▪ *Syn* acute, blaring, cacophonous, clanging, deafening, discordant, ear-piercing, high, metallic, noisy, penetrating, piercing, raucous, screeching, sharp, strident, thin; ▪ *Ant* low, soft.

shrink [*vl*] *become smaller*
▪ *Syn* compress, condense, constrict, decrease, diminish, dwindle, fail, lessen, narrow, reduce, shorten, shrivel, wane, wither; ▪ *Ant* develop, enlarge, expand, grow, stretch.

shrink [*v2*] *recoil, shy away*
▪ *Syn* blench, cower, cringe, demur, draw back, flinch, huddle, quail, recede, retreat, shudder, slink, wince, withdraw; ▪ *Ant* confront, face, meet, take on, welcome.

shrivel [*v*] *dehydrate, dry up*
▪ *Syn* contract, dwindle, fossilize, mummify, parch, shrink, stale, welter, wither,

wizen, wrinkle; ▪ *Ant* blossom, enlarge, expand, grow, regenerate.

shuffle [*v1*] *move along lazily*
▪ *Syn* drag, limp, muddle, pad, scrape, scuffle, shamble, straggle, stumble, trail; ▪ *Ant* high step, light step.

shuffle [*v2*] *rearrange, mix up*
▪ *Syn* break the deck, change the order, confuse, disarrange, disarray, disorganize, disrupt, disturb, intermix, jumble, mess up, shift; ▪ *Ant* arrange, order, organize.

shun [*v*] *avoid, ignore*
▪ *Syn* bilk, decline, disdain, dodge, duck, elude, eschew, evade, keep away from, neglect, pass up, reject, scorn, snub, stand aloof from; ▪ *Ant* accept, seek, solicit, welcome.

shut [*v*] *close*
▪ *Syn* bar, cage, confine, draw, enclose, exclude, fasten, fold, lock, push, seal, secure, shut down, slam; ▪ *Ant* open, unfasten, unlock.

shut off/shut out [*v*] *exclude; screen*
▪ *Syn* bar, beleaguer, blockade, conceal, debar, discontinue, evict, fence off, hide, keep out, lock out, mask, obstruct, ostracize, refuse, shroud, veil; ▪ *Ant* include, welcome.

shut up [*v*] *be or make quiet*
▪ *Syn* choke, fall silent, gag, hush, muzzle, quieten, quit chattering, silence, still, stop talking; ▪ *Ant* elicit, speak, talk.

shy [*adj1*] *quiet and self-conscious*
▪ *Syn* apprehensive, backward, bashful, cautious, circumspect, coy, demure, hesitant, humble, introverted, loath, modest, nervous, reserved, retiring, sheepish, shrinking, skittish, timid, wary; ▪ *Ant* confident, extroverted, unreserved.

shy [*adj2*] *lacking, failing*
▪ *Syn* deficient, inadequate, insufficient, scant, scanty, scarce, short, wanting; ▪ *Ant* adequate, enough, sufficient.

sick [*adj1*] *not healthy, not feeling well*
▪ *Syn* ailing, bedridden, confined, debilitated, declining, diseased, down, feverish, frail, ill, impaired, infected, infirm, invalid, laid-up, nauseated, peaked, queasy, run down, suffering, tottering, unhealthy, weak, wobbly; ▪ *Ant* fit as a fiddle, healthy, undiseased, well.

sick [*adj2*] *morbid, gross*
▪ *Syn* black, ghoulish, macabre, morose, sadistic; ▪ *Ant* clean, gentle, moral.

sick [*adj3*] *fed up, displeased*
▪ *Syn* blasé, bored, disgusted, jaded, revolted, satiated, tired, weary; ▪ *Ant* content, happy, pleased, satisfied.

sicken [*v*] *revolt, make ill*
▪ *Syn* affect, afflict, derange, disgust, nauseate, offend, repulse, turn, unsettle, upset; ▪ *Ant* cure, heal, help, make well, mend.

sickening [*adj*] *disgusting, awful*
▪ *Syn* diseased, distasteful, foul, loathsome, nauseating, noisome, offensive, putrid, repugnant, repulsive, rotten, tainted; ▪ *Ant* delightful, mild, nice, pleasing.

sickly [*adj1*] *not healthy*
▪ *Syn* ailing, below par, bilious, cranky, delicate, diseased, faint, feeble, indisposed, infirm, lackluster, languid, pallid, peaked, pining, poorly, rocky, run-down, wan, weak; ▪ *Ant* fine, healthy, hearty, well, wholesome.

sickly [*adj2*] *revolting*
▪ *Syn* bilious, cloying, insalubrious, mawkish, morbid, morose, nauseating, noisome, noxious; ▪ *Ant* gentle, nice.

side [*adj*] *minor; flanking*
▪ *Syn* ancillary, incidental, indirect, lateral, lesser, marginal, oblique, off-center, postern, roundabout, secondary, skirting, subordinate, subsidiary, superficial; ▪ *Ant* important, major, serious.

sideways [*adv*] *to the edge, exteriority*
▪ *Syn* alongside, aside, aslant, aslope, athwart, broadside, crabwise, edgeways, indirectly, laterally, obliquely, sidelong, sidewards, slanting, slantwise, sloping, to the side; ▪ *Ant* backward, direct, forward, headlong, head on.

sigh [*v*] *long for*
▪ *Syn* ache, crave, dream, hanker, hunger, languish, lust, mourn, pine, suspire, thirst, yearn; ▪ *Ant* forget, neglect.

sight [*v*] *see*
▪ *Syn* behold, discern, distinguish, espy, observe, perceive, spot, view, witness; ▪ *Ant* miss, overlook.

signal [*adj*] *extraordinary, outstanding*
▪ *Syn* arresting, conspicuous, distinctive, distinguished, eminent, exceptional, eye-catching, famous, illustrious, marked, memorable, momentous, notable, noteworthy, noticeable, peculiar, prominent, pronounced, remarkable, renowned, salient, significant, striking; ▪ *Ant* insignificant.

significant [adj1] *telling, meaningful*
▪ *Syn* cogent, compelling, convincing, eloquent, expressive, fecund, forceful, knowing, momentous, powerful, pregnant, rich, sententious, serious, sound, symbolic, valid, weighty; ▪ *Ant* ambiguous, meaningless, trivial, unimportant.

significant [adj2] *important, critical*
▪ *Syn* big, consequential, considerable, heavy, material, meaningful, momentous, notable, noteworthy, serious, substantial, vital, weighty; ▪ *Ant* minor, trivial, unimportant.

silence [v] *make or be quiet*
▪ *Syn* cut off, cut short, dampen, deaden, dull, dumb, extinguish, gag, hush, lull, muffle, mute, muzzle, overawe, quash, quell, quiet, quiet down, quieten, shut up, squelch, stifle, still, subdue, suppress; ▪ *Ant* be noisy, communicate, talk.

silent [adj1] *quiet; speechless*
▪ *Syn* closemouthed, curbed, dumb, hushed, inarticulate, laconic, mum, mute, noiseless, reserved, still, struck dumb, taciturn, tongue-tied, uncommunicative, voiceless, wordless; ▪ *Ant* clamorous, communicative, noisy, talkative.

silent [adj2] *understood, implied*
▪ *Syn* covert, implicit, inferred, intimated, tacit, unexpressed, unspoken, wordless; ▪ *Ant* explicit, tangible.

silhouette [n] *outline*
▪ *Syn* contour, delineation, etching, figuration, form, likeness, line, lineament, lineation, portrait, profile, shade, shadow, shape; ▪ *Ant* body.

silky [adj] *very smooth; like satin*
▪ *Syn* delicate, glossy, luxurious, plush, satiny, sleek, soft; ▪ *Ant* coarse, rough, rugged.

silly [adj] *absurd, giddy, foolish*
▪ *Syn* asinine, brainless, childish, flighty, foolhardy, frivolous, idiotic, inane, irrational, ludicrous, meaningless, nitwitted, nonsensical, preposterous, puerile, ridiculous, simpleminded, vacuous, witless; ▪ *Ant* mature, mundane, practical, sensible, serious, wise.

similar [adj] *very much alike*
▪ *Syn* agnate, akin, analogous, coinciding, collateral, complementary, congruent, consonant, correlative, homogeneous, in agreement, kindred, like, matching, parallel, reciprocal, same, the same; ▪ *Ant* alien, antithetical, different, disparate, opposite.

simple [adj1] *clear, understandable; easy* ▪ *Syn* effortless, elementary, facile, intelligible, lucid, manageable, mild, plain, self-explanatory, straightforward, transparent, uncomplicated; ▪ *Ant* complex, complicated, convoluted, difficult, exacting, intricate, unclear.

simple [adj2] *uncluttered, natural*
▪ *Syn* absolute, classic, discreet, folksy, homely, modest, not complex, plain, pure, rustic, sheer, Spartan, unadorned, unembellished, unpretentious; ▪ *Ant* cluttered, decorated, embellished, jumbled, ornate.

simple [adj3] *childlike, innocent*
▪ *Syn* amateur, artless, basic, direct, frank, guileless, honest, ingenuous, naive, natural, plain, sincere, square, stark, trusting; ▪ *Ant* mature, older, sophisticated.

simple [adj4] *feebleminded; not intelligent* ▪ *Syn* asinine, backward, brainless, credulous, dense, dim-witted, dull, dumb, feeble, gullible, half-witted, idiotic, inane, mindless, moronic, nitwitted, obtuse, slow, stupid, thick, witless; ▪ *Ant* aware, intelligent, on-the-ball, smart.

simplify [v] *make easy, intelligible*
▪ *Syn* abridge, analyze, boil down, break down, chasten, clarify, decipher, disentangle, elucidate, facilitate, interpret, lay out, make clear, order, reduce, spell out, streamline, unscramble; ▪ *Ant* complicate, confuse.

simply [adv1] *plainly, clearly*
▪ *Syn* artlessly, candidly, directly, frankly, guilelessly, honestly, ingenuously, matter-of-factly, naturally, openly, ordinarily, straightforwardly; ▪ *Ant* artfully, cunningly.

simply [adv2] *absolutely, completely*
▪ *Syn* altogether, in fact, really, totally, unreservedly, utterly, wholly; ▪ *Ant* incompletely, indefinitely.

simultaneous [adj] *happening at about the same time* ▪ *Syn* accompanying, at the same time, coeval, coexistent, coincident, concurrent, contemporaneous, synchronal, synchronous; ▪ *Ant* asynchronous, different, divided, following, preceding, separate.

sin [v] *commit illegal or immoral action*
▪ *Syn* break commandment, break law, cheat, commit crime, deviate, do wrong, err, fall, lapse, live in sin, misbehave,

offend, stray, transgress, trespass, wander; ▪ *Ant* behave, comply, obey.

sincere [*adj*] *straightforward, honest*
▪ *Syn* aboveboard, artless, bona fide, candid, earnest, faithful, frank, genuine, guileless, heartfelt, natural, open, plain, real, saintly, true, trustworthy, wholehearted; ▪ *Ant* dishonest, insincere, tricky, untrustworthy.

sincerely [*adv*] *seriously, honestly*
▪ *Syn* candidly, deeply, earnestly, frankly, from bottom of heart, genuinely, ingenuously, profoundly, really, truly, wholeheartedly, without equivocation; ▪ *Ant* dishonestly, falsely, untruthfully.

sinful [*adj*] *immoral, criminal*
▪ *Syn* amiss, bad, base, blameworthy, censurable, corrupt, culpable, damnable, depraved, erring, evil, guilty, immoral, iniquitous, low, reprehensible, reprobate, shameful, vicious, vile, wicked, wrong; ▪ *Ant* honest, moral, righteous, upright.

sing [*v*] *tattle on someone*
▪ *Syn* betray, fink, inform, snitch, talk, turn in; ▪ *Ant* protect.

single [*adj1*] *alone, distinct*
▪ *Syn* distinct, especial, exceptional, exclusive, individual, isolated, lone, one, only, particular, peerless, rare, separate, singular, solitary, specific, unique, without equal; ▪ *Ant* numerous, several, some, together.

single [*adj2*] *not married*
▪ *Syn* bachelor, divorced, eligible, free, separated, solo, spouseless, unattached, unmarried, unwed; ▪ *Ant* married, together, united, wed, wedded.

singly [*adv*] *individually*
▪ *Syn* apart, independently, one at a time, one by one, particularly, respectively, separately, severally; ▪ *Ant* together.

singular [*adj1*] *unique, odd*
▪ *Syn* atypical, avant-garde, bizarre, curious, eccentric, exceptional, noteworthy, outstanding, peculiar, queer, rare, remarkable, special, strange, weird; ▪ *Ant* commonplace, normal, ordinary, regular, usual.

singular [*adj2*] *alone, separate*
▪ *Syn* certain, definite, discrete, exclusive, individual, one, only, particular, respective, sole, solitary, unique; ▪ *Ant* common, familiar.

sinister [*adj*] *nasty, menacing*
▪ *Syn* adverse, apocalyptic, baleful, blackhearted, corrupt, dire, evil, foreboding, harmful, ill-boding, inauspicious, injurious, lowering, malefic, malevolent, menacing, ominous, pernicious, perverse, portentous, threatening, woeful; ▪ *Ant* heroic, honorable, noble.

sink [*v1*] *fall in, go under*
▪ *Syn* capsize, cave in, decline, descend, dip, disappear, droop, drown, fall, flounder, founder, go down, immerse, lower, plummet, plunge, sag, submerge, swamp, touch bottom; ▪ *Ant* float, rise.

sink [*v2*] *fall, decrease*
▪ *Syn* abate, collapse, drop, lapse, relapse, retrogress, slip, slump, subside, wane; ▪ *Ant* grow, increase, rise.

sink [*v3*] *deteriorate*
▪ *Syn* decay, decline, degenerate, deteriorate, disintegrate, dwindle, fade, flag, retrograde, rot, spoil, waste, weaken, worsen; ▪ *Ant* increase, rise, strengthen.

sink [*v4*] *be humble or humbled*
▪ *Syn* abase, bemean, be reduced to, cast down, debase, degrade, demean, humiliate, lower, stoop, succumb; ▪ *Ant* brave, fight.

sinuous [*adj*] *winding, twisting*
▪ *Syn* anfractuous, circuitous, coiling, convoluted, crooked, curved, devious, flexuous, indirect, meandering, serpentine, tortuous, undulating; ▪ *Ant* direct, straight, untwisted, unwinding.

sip [*v*] *drink slowly*
▪ *Syn* extract, imbibe, lap, nip, partake, quaff, sample, savor, sup, swallow, taste; ▪ *Ant* down, gulp, swig.

sit [*v2*] *hold a meeting*
▪ *Syn* assemble, be in session, come together, convene, deliberate, hold an assembly, meet, officiate, open, preside; ▪ *Ant* adjourn, disperse.

sizable [*adj*] *considerable, large*
▪ *Syn* ample, big, capacious, extensive, gross, hefty, king-size, massive, ponderous, respectable, spacious, strapping, substantial, voluminous; ▪ *Ant* inadequate, inconsiderable, insufficient, little, short, small, tiny.

skeleton [*n*] *structure of bones in animate being or supports in an object*
▪ *Syn* bones, bony structure, cage, design, draft, frame, framework, osteology, outline, scaffolding, sketch, support; ▪ *Ant* exterior, skin, surface.

skeptical [*adj*] *disbelieving, leery*
▪ *Syn* agnostic, cynical, dissenting, doubtful, dubious, freethinking, hesitating, in-

credulous, mistrustful, questioning, scoffing, suspicious, unconvinced; ▪ *Ant* believing, credulous, devoted, sure.

sketchy [*adj*] *rough, incomplete*
▪ *Syn* coarse, crude, depthless, faulty, imperfect, introductory, perfunctory, preliminary, rough, shallow, superficial, unfinished, vague; ▪ *Ant* complete, detailed, finished, full.

skillful [*adj*] *able, talented*
▪ *Syn* accomplished, adept, clever, competent, dexterous, expert, handy, masterful, practiced, primed, proficient, quick, ready, savvy, seasoned, sharp, trained, versed, veteran, whiz; ▪ *Ant* clumsy, green, incapable, inept, inexperienced, unable.

skim [*v*] *look through cursorily*
▪ *Syn* browse, brush over, dip, examine, flip through, glance, glance over, read swiftly, riff, riffle, scan, skip; ▪ *Ant* peruse, pore.

skimp [*v*] *be cheap or frugal about*
▪ *Syn* be mean with, be niggardly, be sparing, pinch, roll back, save, scant, scrape, scrimp, slight, spare, stint, withhold; ▪ *Ant* spend, use, waste.

skimpy [*adj*] *sparse, inadequate*
▪ *Syn* deficient, exiguous, insufficient, meager, miserly, niggardly, poor, scant, scrimp, short, shy, spare, stingy, thin, tight, wanting; ▪ *Ant* adequate, enough, generous, sufficient.

skin [*v*] *remove outer covering*
▪ *Syn* abrade, bare, cut off, decorticate, excoriate, exuviate, flay, graze, hull, husk, lay bare, pare, peel, pull off, remove, scalp, scrape, shave, shed, shuck, slough, strip, trim; ▪ *Ant* cover.

skinny [*adj*] *very thin*
▪ *Syn* angular, bony, emaciated, gaunt, lanky, lean, malnourished, rawboned, scraggy, scrawny, skeletal, slender, spare; ▪ *Ant* chubby, fat, heavy, large, overweight, plump, thick.

skip [*v1*] *bounce or jump over*
▪ *Syn* bob, bound, canter, caper, cavort, dance, flit, gambol, graze, hop, leap, prance, scamper, skim, skitter, tiptoe, trip; ▪ *Ant* drag, hobble, lumber, plod, shamble, shuffle, stagger, trudge, waddle.

skip [*v2*] *avoid, miss*
▪ *Syn* cut, disregard, eschew, leave out, miss out, neglect, omit, pass over, pass up, skim over; ▪ *Ant* include.

skirt [*v1*] *border; be on the edge*
▪ *Syn* bound, define, edge, flank, fringe, hem, lie along, lie alongside, margin, rim, surround, verge; ▪ *Ant* center.

skirt [*v2*] *avoid; get around*
▪ *Syn* burke, bypass, circumnavigate, circumvent, detour, dodge, duck, elude, equivocate, escape, evade, hedge, ignore, sidestep, skip, steer clear of; ▪ *Ant* face, meet, take on.

skittish [*adj*] *very nervous*
▪ *Syn* agitable, capricious, edgy, excitable, fearful, fidgety, flighty, frivolous, giddy, jumpy, light-headed, restive, spirited, volative; ▪ *Ant* calm, collected, easygoing, sedate, tranquil.

sky [*n*] *earth's atmosphere*
▪ *Syn* azure, celestial sphere, empyrean, firmament, heavens, upper atmosphere, vault, welkin; ▪ *Ant* earth.

slab [*n*] *chunk of solid object*
▪ *Syn* bar, billet, board, boulder, chip, cutting, hunk, ingot, lump, muck, piece, plate, portion, rod, slice, stave, strip, wedge; ▪ *Ant* bit, chip, fragment, scrap, sharing, shred, sliver, splinter.

slack [*adj1*] *loose, baggy; inactive*
▪ *Syn* easy, flabby, flaccid, flimsy, inert, laggard, lax, limp, passive, relaxed, slow-moving, supine, weak; ▪ *Ant* rigid, stiff, taut, tight.

slack [*adj2*] *lazy, negligent*
▪ *Syn* behindhand, careless, delinquent, derelict, disregardful, faineant, idle, inattentive, indolent, lackadaisical, lax, lethargic, neglectful, quiescent, regardless, slothful, slow, sluggish, stagnant, tardy; ▪ *Ant* active, alert, disciplined.

slack/slacken [*v*] *do little or nothing; loosen* ▪ *Syn* abate, decrease, diminish, dwindle, ease off, flag, idle, lay back, let up, loose, neglect, reduce, relax, shirk, slack off, taper, tire, wane; ▪ *Ant* stiffen, tighten.

slam [*v*] *criticize very harshly*
▪ *Syn* attack, castigate, damn, excoriate, flay, lambaste, lash into, pan, scathe, scourge, shoot down, slap, slash, vilify; ▪ *Ant* flatter, praise.

slander [*v*] *make a scandalous remark*
▪ *Syn* assail, attack, belie, besmirch, blaspheme, calumniate, curse, damage, defame, defile, denigrate, depreciate, dishonor, hurt, injure, libel, malign, muckrake, plaster, revile, scandalize, smear,

smirch, sully, tarnish, traduce, vilify; ▪ *Ant* defend, flatter, glorify, praise.

slang [*n*] *casual dialect*
▪ *Syn* argot, cant, colloquialism, informal speech, jargon, lingo, neologism, patter, pidgin, shoptalk, vernacular, vulgarity; ▪ *Ant* standard.

slant [*v1*] *angle off, slope*
▪ *Syn* aim, bank, beam, bend, bevel, cant, decline, descend, diverge, grade, heel, incline, lie obliquely, list, point, skew, splay, tilt, tip, train, veer; ▪ *Ant* even, level.

slant [*v2*] *change to suit; distort*
▪ *Syn* aim, angle, bias, color, focus, influence, orient, point, prejudice, train, twist, warp, weight; ▪ *Ant* leave alone, maintain.

slash [*v1*] *cut*
▪ *Syn* gash, hack, incise, injure, lacerate, pierce, rend, rip, score, sever, slice, slit, wound; ▪ *Ant* fix, mend, sew.

slash [*v2*] *reduce greatly*
▪ *Syn* abbreviate, abridge, clip, curtail, cut, cut back, cut down, drop, hack, lower, mark down, pare, retrench, shave, shorten; ▪ *Ant* increase, raise.

slaughter [*v*] *kill*
▪ *Syn* butcher, crush, decimate, defeat, destroy, finish, liquidate, maim, mangle, massacre, murder, mutilate, overwhelm, rout, slay, thrash, torture, vanquish, waste; ▪ *Ant* bear, create, give birth, spare, sustain.

slave [*v*] *work very hard*
▪ *Syn* be servile, drudge, grind, grovel, grub, muck, slog, toil; ▪ *Ant* idle, laze, loaf.

slay [*v*] *kill*
▪ *Syn* annihilate, assassinate, butcher, destroy, do away with, eliminate, execute, exterminate, finish, hit, liquidate, massacre, murder, neutralize, slaughter; ▪ *Ant* bear, create, give birth.

sleazy [*adj*] *disreputable*
▪ *Syn* base, broken-down, cheap, dilapidated, flimsy, limp, low, mean, paltry, poor, run-down, seedy, shoddy, squalid; ▪ *Ant* fine, genuine, reputable, respectable.

sleek [*adj*] *smooth, glossy*
▪ *Syn* glassy, glistening, lustrous, polished, satin, shiny, silken, silky; ▪ *Ant* dull, rough, unkempt.

sleep [*v*] *suspend consciousness*
▪ *Syn* catnap, doze, drowse, hibernate,

nap, nod, nod off, relax, repose, rest, retire, slumber, snooze, snore; ▪ *Ant* wake, waken.

sleepy [*adj*] *tired, dull*
▪ *Syn* asleep, comatose, dozy, drowsy, lethargic, listless, slow, sluggish, slumberous, somnolent, soporific, torpid, yawning; ▪ *Ant* animated, awake, energetic.

slender/slim [*adj1*] *thin, not heavy*
▪ *Syn* attenuate, fine, lean, lithe, narrow, slight, spare, svelte, sylphlike, threadlike, trim, willowy; ▪ *Ant* chubby, fat, heavy, overweight, plump, thick.

slender/slim [*adj2*] *inadequate, flimsy*
▪ *Syn* bare, deficient, feeble, inconsiderable, insufficient, little, meager, poor, remote, scant, scarce, short, shy, slight, spare, tenuous, thin, wanting, weak; ▪ *Ant* adequate, appreciable, solid, strong.

slice [*v*] *cut into portions, shares*
▪ *Syn* carve, cleave, dissect, dissever, divide, gash, hack, incise, pierce, segment, sever, shave, shred, slash, slit, split, strip, subdivide, sunder; ▪ *Ant* combine, unite.

slick [*adj1*] *smooth, polished*
▪ *Syn* glossy, greasy, lubricious, oily, oleaginous, shiny, sleek, slippery; ▪ *Ant* coarse, rough, unpolished.

slick [*adj2*] *smart, clever*
▪ *Syn* adroit, canny, deft, dextrous, foxy, glib, knowing, meretricious, quick, shrewd, smooth-spoken, sophisticated, specious, unctuous, urbane, wise; ▪ *Ant* honest, ingenuous, open.

slight [*adj1*] *insignificant, small*
▪ *Syn* insubstantial, meager, minor, negligible, off, paltry, petty, piddling, remote, scanty, trifling, trivial; ▪ *Ant* important, large, significant.

slight [*adj2*] *thin, small in build*
▪ *Syn* dainty, delicate, feeble, fragile, frail, light, reedy, skinny, slender, slim, spare; ▪ *Ant* fat, husky, large, muscular, strong, tall.

slight [*v*] *offend, insult*
▪ *Syn* affront, brush off, contemn, disparage, ignore, make light of, neglect, reject, scoff, scorn, shrug off, skip, slur, snub, treat with contempt; ▪ *Ant* compliment, flatter, praise.

slightly [*adv*] *a little*
▪ *Syn* hardly, hardly noticeable, imperceptibly, insignificantly, kind of, lightly, mar-

ginally, more or less, scarcely any, somewhat, to some degree, to some extent; ▪ *Ant* a lot, considerably, greatly.

slim [v] *lose weight*
▪ *Syn* diet, reduce, slenderize; ▪ *Ant* gain.

slimy [adj] *oozy, gooey*
▪ *Syn* clammy, glutinous, miry, mucky, mucous, muculent, muddy, scummy, viscous; ▪ *Ant* dry, pleasant.

slink/slither [v] *creep by*
▪ *Syn* coast, cower, glide, glissade, lurk, meander, prowl, shirk, sidle, skitter, skulk, slide, slip, snake, sneak, steal; ▪ *Ant* barge, clump, march, parade, stamp, stomp, stride, strut, swagger.

slip [v2] *err*
▪ *Syn* blunder, go wrong, make a mistake, miscalculate, misjudge, mistake, slip up, stumble, trip; ▪ *Ant* correct, perfect.

slippery [adj1] *smooth, slick*
▪ *Syn* glassy, glazed, glistening, greasy, icy, lubricious, perilous, satiny, silky, sleek, slimy, soapy, unctuous, waxy, wet; ▪ *Ant* dry, rough.

slippery [adj2] *uncertain, unreliable*
▪ *Syn* crafty, cunning, devious, duplicitous, elusive, foxy, mutable, shifty, smooth, sneaky, treacherous, variable; ▪ *Ant* certain, definite, reliable, stable.

slipshod [adj] *careless; not well done*
▪ *Syn* bedraggled, disheveled, faulty, haphazard, imperfect, inaccurate, inexact, loose, messy, neglected, negligent, sloppy, slovenly, tattered, threadbare, unkempt, untidy; ▪ *Ant* careful, neat, polished, refined, well-done.

slit [v] *cut open*
▪ *Syn* gash, incise, knife, lance, pierce, rip, sever, slash, slice, slot, split open, tear; ▪ *Ant* close, mend, sew.

sliver [n] *tiny piece, usually of wood or metal* ▪ *Syn* bit, flake, fragment, paring, shaving, shred, slice, slip, snip, snippet, splinter, thorn; ▪ *Ant* chunk, slat.

slop [v] *splash; make a mess*
▪ *Syn* drip, let run over, overflow, slosh, spatter, spill, splatter, spray; ▪ *Ant* clean up.

slope [v] *slant, tilt*
▪ *Syn* angle, ascend, bank, bevel, cant, descend, dip, drop, drop away, fall, heel, incline, lean, list, pitch, rake, recline, rise, shelve, skew, splay, tip; ▪ *Ant* even, flatten, level.

sloppy [adj] *messy*
▪ *Syn* bedraggled, botched, careless,

clumsy, disheveled, inattentive, muddy, poor, slapdash, slipshod, slovenly, unkempt, untidy, watery, wet; ▪ *Ant* clean, neat, orderly, tidy.

slouch [v] *slump over*
▪ *Syn* be lazy, bend, bow, crouch, droop, lean, loaf, loll, lounge, sag, stoop, wilt; ▪ *Ant* straighten up.

slovenly [adj] *dirty, disordered*
▪ *Syn* bedraggled, careless, disheveled, disorderly, heedless, loose, messy, mussy, negligent, slack, slapdash, slipshod, sloppy, tacky; ▪ *Ant* clean, conscientious, ordered, organized.

slow [adj1] *unhurried, lazy*
▪ *Syn* apathetic, creeping, dawdling, dilatory, disinclined, drowsy, easy, gradual, heavy, idle, inactive, inert, lackadaisical, laggard, lethargic, measured, passive, phlegmatic, plodding, slack, slothful, sluggish, snaillike, stagnant, supine, torpid, tortoiselike; ▪ *Ant* active, busy, fast, hurried, quick, rapid.

slow [adj2] *behind, late*
▪ *Syn* behindhand, belated, delayed, detained, dilatory, hindered, impeded, longdelayed, overdue, prolonged, protracted, stagnant, tardy; ▪ *Ant* in cue, on time, ready, waiting.

slow [adj3] *unintelligent*
▪ *Syn* backward, dense, dim, dim-witted, dull, dumb, dunce, imbecile, limited, moronic, obtuse, retarded, simple, stupid; ▪ *Ant* cognizant, intelligent, quick-witted, smart.

slow [v] *delay, restrict*
▪ *Syn* abate, bog down, brake, choke, curb, curtail, decelerate, detain, diminish, ease off, handicap, hinder, impede, mire, moderate, postpone, procrastinate, retard, set back, slacken, stall, stunt, temper; ▪ *Ant* accelerate, speed up.

sluggish [adj] *dull, slow-moving*
▪ *Syn* apathetic, comatose, down, dragging, heavy, hebetudinous, indolent, inert, languid, languorous, lethargic, lifeless, listless, phlegmatic, slack, slothful, slow, slumberous, stagnant, stiff, sullen, torpid; ▪ *Ant* active, alert, energetic, fast, lively, spirited.

slumber [n] *sleep*
▪ *Syn* coma, dormancy, doze, drowse, languor, lethargy, nap, repose, rest, snooze, stupor, torpor; ▪ *Ant* awakening, consciousness, wakefulness.

slump [v] *decline, sink*
▪ *Syn* bend, blight, cave in, collapse, crash, decay, deteriorate, droop, drop, fall, hunch, loll, pitch, plummet, plunge, sag, slide, slip, slouch, topple, tumble; ▪ *Ant* ascend, increase, rise.

slur [v1] *insult*
▪ *Syn* blacken, blemish, blister, blot, brand, calumniate, defame, denigrate, detract, discredit, disgrace, insinuate, libel, malign, reproach, slander, slight, snub, spatter, stain, traduce, vilify; ▪ *Ant* compliment, flatter, praise.

slur [v2] *mumble words*
▪ *Syn* garble, mispronounce, miss, skip, stutter; ▪ *Ant* articulate, enunciate, pronounce.

sly [adj] *clever, devious*
▪ *Syn* arch, artful, bluffing, cagey, calculating, canny, conniving, covert, cunning, deceitful, deceptive, designing, elusive, foxy, furtive, guileful, impish, mischievous, plotting, roguish, scheming, shifty, slick, sneaking, stealthy, treacherous, tricky, underhand, wily; ▪ *Ant* honest, open, scrupulous, simple, straight, straightforward.

smack [adv] *directly, exactly*
▪ *Syn* accurately, clearly, just, plumb, precisely, right, sharp, square, squarely, straight; ▪ *Ant* indirectly, inexactly, off.

small [adj1] *tiny in size, quantity*
▪ *Syn* baby, bantam, diminutive, dwarf, inconsiderable, little, meager, miniature, minute, modest, narrow, scanty, slight, small-scale, stunted, teeny, toy, undersized; ▪ *Ant* big, enormous, generous, huge, immense, large.

small [adj2] *unimportant*
▪ *Syn* inadequate, inconsiderable, ineffectual, inferior, insignificant, lesser, limited, minor, minute, narrow, negligible, paltry, petty, secondary, trifling, trivial; ▪ *Ant* distinguished, fine, important.

small [adj3] *narrow-minded, nasty*
▪ *Syn* base, grudging, ignoble, illiberal, limited, little, mean, narrow, petty, selfish, set, vulgar; ▪ *Ant* benevolent, broadminded, considerate, giving, kind.

smart [adj1] *intelligent*
▪ *Syn* acute, adept, apt, astute, bright, brilliant, canny, clever, effective, fresh, keen, knowing, nimble, pointed, quickwitted, resourceful, sharp, wise; ▪ *Ant* dull, stupid, unintelligent.

smart [adj2] *stylish, fashionable*
▪ *Syn* chic, dapper, dashing, exclusive, fine, in fashion, modish, natty, neat, snappy, spruce, swank, trendy, well turned-out; ▪ *Ant* dowdy, old, unfashionable, unstylish, worn.

smart [adj3] *brisk, lively*
▪ *Syn* active, bold, brazen, cracking, energetic, forward, jaunty, pert, quick, saucy, scintillating, spanking, spirited, sprightly, vigorous; ▪ *Ant* apathetic, lethargic, slow.

smart [v] *hurt, pain*
▪ *Syn* ache, be painful, bite, burn, prick, prickle, sting, suffer, throb, tingle; ▪ *Ant* assuage, help, soothe.

smash [v1] *break into pieces*
▪ *Syn* bang, belt, clobber, crack, crush, demolish, fracture, hit, pound, powder, pulverize, rive, shatter, slug, splinter, wallop; ▪ *Ant* fix, mend.

smash [v2] *defeat, destroy*
▪ *Syn* annihilate, break up, decimate, demolish, destruct, overthrow, overturn, raze, ruin, shatter, tear down, topple, tumble, wreck; ▪ *Ant* fail, lose.

smear [v2] *tarnish a reputation*
▪ *Syn* asperse, besmirch, blacken, calumniate, defame, defile, libel, malign, slander, slur, taint, traduce, vilify; ▪ *Ant* honor, laud, upgrade.

smelly [adj] *having a bad odor*
▪ *Syn* evil-smelling, fetid, foul, high, malodorous, mephitic, noisome, olid, putrid, rancid, rank, reeking, stinking, strong; ▪ *Ant* fragrant, good-smelling, perfumed.

smile [v] *put on a happy expression*
▪ *Syn* beam, express friendliness, express tenderness, grin, laugh, look pleased, simper, smirk; ▪ *Ant* frown, glower.

smoky [adj] *hazy, sooty*
▪ *Syn* begrimed, black, burning, caliginous, dingy, fumy, gray, grimy, murky, reeking, silvery, smoke-colored, smoldering, thick, vaporous; ▪ *Ant* clean, clear, unpolluted.

smolder [v] *burn, simmer*
▪ *Syn* boil, bubble, consume, ferment, fester, fulminate, fume, seethe, smoke, steam, stir; ▪ *Ant* be flat, freeze.

smooth [adj1] *level, unwrinkled; flowing*
▪ *Syn* bland, continuous, creamy, effortless, flat, fluent, fluid, gentle, horizontal, invariable, mild, peaceful, plain, polished, quiet, regular, rippleless, serene,

silky, sleek, stable, still, tranquil, unbroken, uniform, velvety; ▪ *Ant* broken, coarse, intermittent, irregular, rough, uneven, wrinkled.

smooth [*adj2*] *suave in behavior*
▪ *Syn* agreeable, bland, courteous, facile, glib, ingratiating, mild, persuasive, polite, slick, unctuous, urbane; ▪ *Ant* coarse, rough, uncool, unpolished.

smooth [*v1*] *make level*
▪ *Syn* burnish, even, flatten, grade, iron, lay, level, perfect, plane, polish, refine, sand, slick, varnish; ▪ *Ant* coarsen, roughen, wrinkle.

smooth [*v2*] *make peace*
▪ *Syn* allay, appease, assuage, calm, comfort, ease, facilitate, iron out, mitigate, mollify, palliate, soften, stroke; ▪ *Ant* aggravate, agitate, incite, irritate, upset.

smother [*v*] *extinguish; cover, hide*
▪ *Syn* asphyxiate, choke, conceal, cork, douse, envelop, inundate, kill, muffle, overwhelm, quash, quell, repress, restrain, shroud, squelch, stifle, strangle, suffocate, throttle; ▪ *Ant* kindle, light, open up, uncover.

smudge [*v*] *smear, dirty*
▪ *Syn* begrime, blacken, blur, foul, grime, mark, smirch, soil, spatter, taint; ▪ *Ant* clean, launder, wash.

smug [*adj*] *pleased with oneself*
▪ *Syn* conceited, egotistical, pompous, priggish, self-righteous, self-satisfied, stuffy, vainglorious; ▪ *Ant* insecure, modest, unsure.

smutty [*adj*] *obscene, vulgar*
▪ *Syn* bawdy, crude, dirty, foul, immoral, indecent, lewd, nasty, pornographic, prurient, raunchy, raw, risqué, salacious, salty, scatological, suggestive; ▪ *Ant* clean, decent, moral, puritanical, straitlaced.

snack [*n*] *tiny meal*
▪ *Syn* bite, break, light meal, lunch, luncheon, morsel, nibble, pickings, refreshment, tea, tidbit; ▪ *Ant* breakfast, dinner, lunch, meal.

snag [*n*] *complication in situation*
▪ *Syn* bar, barrier, Catch-22, clog, crimp, difficulty, glitch, hitch, hurdle, impediment, obstacle, obstruction, problem, scrape, spot; ▪ *Ant* advantage, convenience, ease.

snaky [*adj1*] *winding*
▪ *Syn* anfractuous, convoluted, entwined, flexuous, indirect, meandering, serpentine, sinuous, tortuous, twisting, writhing, zigzag; ▪ *Ant* straight, unwinding.

snaky [*adj2*] *devious, sly*
▪ *Syn* crafty, insidious, lurking, perfidious, slinking, subtle, treacherous, venomous, vipery; ▪ *Ant* forthright, honest, upfront.

snap [*v1*] *separate, break*
▪ *Syn* click, come apart, crack, fracture, give way, pop; ▪ *Ant* fix, mend, unite.

snap [*v2*] *bite, seize*
▪ *Syn* bite at, catch, clutch, grab, grasp, grip, lurch, nip, snatch, twitch, yank; ▪ *Ant* free, liberate, loose.

snappy [*adj1*] *nasty, irritable*
▪ *Syn* cross, disagreeable, edgy, fractious, hasty, huffy, petulant, quick-tempered, tart, testy, touchy, waspish; ▪ *Ant* affable, good humor, happy, pleasant.

snappy [*adj2*] *fashionable*
▪ *Syn* chic, classy, dapper, dashing, modish, natty, sharp, smart, stylish, trendy, up-to-the-minute, with style; ▪ *Ant* dowdy, old, outdated, tacky, unfashionable.

snappy [*adj3*] *fast*
▪ *Syn* abrupt, expeditious, fleet, harefooted, hasty, instant, on-the-spot, quick, rapid, speedy, swift; ▪ *Ant* delayed, lethargic, slow, sluggish, torpid.

snare [*v*] *catch, trap*
▪ *Syn* arrest, entangle, entrap, involve, land, lure, net, pull in, round up, seduce, seize, tempt; ▪ *Ant* disengage, free, let go, liberate, loosen.

snarl [*v1*] *grumble*
▪ *Syn* bark, bluster, bully, complain, fulminate, gnarl, gnash teeth, growl, mumble, mutter, snap, threaten, thunder, yelp; ▪ *Ant* beam, grin, laugh, show pleasure.

snarl [*v2*] *complicate, mess up*
▪ *Syn* confuse, embroil, enmesh, ensnarl, entangle, entwine, involve, muck, muddle, perplex, ravel, tangle; ▪ *Ant* fix, simplify, uncomplicate, untangle.

snatch [*v*] *grab away*
▪ *Syn* abduct, catch, clutch, gain, grasp, grip, jerk, jump, kidnap, make off with, nab, pluck, pull, rescue, seize, snag, spirit away, steal, take, wrench, wrest, yank; ▪ *Ant* give, receive.

sneaky [*adj*] *underhanded, dishonest*
▪ *Syn* base, contemptible, devious, disingenuous, duplicitous, furtive, guileful, indirect, low, mean, nasty, recreant, secretive, shifty, sly, surreptitious, tricky,

underhand, unscrupulous; ■ *Ant* above-board, candid, forthright, frank, honest, honorable, straightforward.

sneer [v] *mock, condemn*
■ *Syn* affront, belittle, burlesque, carica-ture, deride, disparage, flout, gibe, gird, insult, jeer, lampoon, leer, put down, quip at, ridicule, satirize, scorn, snigger, taunt, underrate; ■ *Ant* compliment, flat-ter, laud, praise.

snide [adj] *hateful, nasty*
■ *Syn* base, cynical, disparaging, hurtful, insinuating, malicious, sarcastic, sneer-ing, spiteful, unkind; ■ *Ant* gentle, kind, lovable, loving, nice.

sniff [v] *breathe in*
■ *Syn* detect, inhale, inspire, nose, scent, smell, snuff, snuffle; ■ *Ant* blow, exhale, expire, puff.

snobbish [adj] *stuck-up, conceited*
■ *Syn* arrogant, condescending, egotistic, haughty, ostentatious, patronizing, pomp-ous, supercilious, swanky, uppish; ■ *Ant* accepting, benevolent, friendly, humble, sociable, unpretentious, welcoming.

snoop [v] *nose around*
■ *Syn* interfere, intrude, meddle, mess with, peep, peer, poke, pry, snook, spy; ■ *Ant* eschew, ignore, neglect.

snooze [v] *sleep lightly*
■ *Syn* catnap, doze, drop off, drowse, nap, siesta, slumber; ■ *Ant* awaken, wake up.

snub [v] *give someone the cold shoulder*
■ *Syn* burr, cut, disregard, ignore, look coldly upon, mortify, neglect, ostracize, pass up, rebuff, scorn, scratch, shun, slight, swank, upstage; ■ *Ant* be friendly, include, socialize, welcome.

snug [adj] *cozy, warm*
■ *Syn* close, comfortable, comfy, homely, intimate, restful, sheltered, tight, trim; ■ *Ant* cold, cool, loose, uncomfortable, unprotected.

snuggle [v] *cuddle*
■ *Syn* bundle, burrow, curl up, grasp, huddle, hug, nestle, nuzzle, spoon; ■ *Ant* separate, stay away.

soak [v] *drench, wet*
■ *Syn* absorb, bathe, damp, dunk, flood, imbrue, immerse, infiltrate, infuse, mac-erate, moisten, percolate, permeate, satu-rate, seethe, sop, souse, steep, submerge, wash, water; ■ *Ant* dehydrate, dry.

soar [v] *climb, fly*
■ *Syn* arise, ascend, aspire, escalate, glide, lift, mount, rise, rocket, sail, shoot up, skyrocket, top, tower, up, uprear, wing; ■ *Ant* land.

sob [v] *cry hard*
■ *Syn* bawl, blubber, break down, howl, lament, shed tears, snivel, wail, weep, whimper; ■ *Ant* chortle, laugh.

sober [adj1] *not partaking of alcohol*
■ *Syn* abstemious, abstinent, ascetic, clear-headed, controlled, dry, nonindul-gent, restrained, steady, temperate; ■ *Ant* drunk, inebriated, intoxicated.

sober [adj2] *dull, staid, grave*
■ *Syn* composed, constrained, dispassion-ate, drab, earnest, imperturbable, level-headed, low-key, pacific, practical, quiet, rational, reserved, restrained, sedate, se-rious, somber, subdued, toned down, unruffled; ■ *Ant* excited, immoderate, ir-rational, joyful, lively.

so-called [adj] *supposed*
■ *Syn* alleged, commonly named, nomi-nal, ostensible, pretended, professed, purported, self-named, titular, wrongly named; ■ *Ant* actual, authentic, bona fide, genuine, real, true.

sociable [adj] *friendly, outgoing*
■ *Syn* accessible, affable, companionable, conversable, convivial, familiar, genial, gregarious, neighborly, regular, social, warm; ■ *Ant* forbidding, introverted, snobbish, unfriendly, unkind, withdrawn.

social [adj] *public, friendly*
■ *Syn* civil, collective, communal, convivi-al, cordial, entertaining, familiar, gra-cious, gregarious, hospitable, neighborly, organized, pleasant, popular, public, so-ciable, societal; ■ *Ant* hermetical, pri-vate, reclusive, secluded, solitary, un-friendly.

socialize [v] *be friendly at gatherings*
■ *Syn* associate, consort, entertain, frater-nize, get together, hobnob, join, keep com-pany, mingle, mix; ■ *Ant* exclude, shun.

sock [n/v] *hit hard*
■ *Syn* beat, belt, bop, buffet, chop, clout, cuff, punch, slap, smack, smash, whack; ■ *Ant* tap.

soft [adj1] *cushioned, squishy*
■ *Syn* comfortable, cozy, doughy, downy, elastic, flabby, fleecy, fleshy, flocculent, fluffy, gelatinous, impressible, limp, mal-leable, mushy, pulpy, rounded, satiny, supple, velvety, yielding; ■ *Ant* hard, in-flexible, rigid, unyielding.

soft [adj2] *faint, temperate*
■ *Syn* cool, delicate, diffuse, dulcet, faint,

gentle, lenient, low, mellifluous, mellow, mild, muted, pallid, pastel, pleasing, quiet, restful, shaded, subdued, sweet, tinted, toned down, understated, wan, whispered; ▪ *Ant* harsh, loud, noisy, rough, severe.

soft [*adj3*] *compassionate*
▪ *Syn* benign, easy, effortless, gentle, indulgent, kindly, lenient, pitying, sensitive, sentimental, sympathetic, tender-hearted, undemanding, weak; ▪ *Ant* callous, severe, stern, strict, tough, unsympathetic.

soft [*adj4*] *out of condition*
▪ *Syn* doughy, fat, flabby, flaccid, fleshy, limp, overindulged, pampered, weak; ▪ *Ant* firm, healthy, strong, taut, tight, well.

soft [*adj5*] *stupid*
▪ *Syn* daft, fatuous, feeble-minded, foolish, silly, simple, witless; ▪ *Ant* bright, clever, intelligent, quick, smart.

soften [*v*] *calm, soothe*
▪ *Syn* abate, allay, assuage, bend, cushion, ease, give, lessen, mellow, mitigate, mollify, palliate, quell, relax, subdue, temper, tenderize, tone down, weaken, yield; ▪ *Ant* discomfort, irritate, trouble, upset, worry.

soggy [*adj*] *damp or soaking*
▪ *Syn* clammy, dank, dripping, humid, moist, muggy, pasty, pulpy, saturated, soaked, sodden, sopping, spongy, sultry, waterlogged; ▪ *Ant* dehydrated, dry, fluffy.

soil [*v*] *make dirty*
▪ *Syn* bedraggle, besmirch, contaminate, debase, dirty, discolor, foul, grime, maculate, muddy, pollute, shame, smudge, spoil, sully, taint, tarnish; ▪ *Ant* brighten, clean, cleanse, purify, whiten.

solace [*v*] *give comfort, peace*
▪ *Syn* allay, alleviate, buck up, cheer, comfort, condole with, console, mitigate, soothe, upraise; ▪ *Ant* dishearten, hurt, trouble, upset, worry.

sole [*adj*] *alone, singular*
▪ *Syn* exclusive, individual, lone, only, only one, particular, remaining, separate, single, solitary, solo, unique, unshared; ▪ *Ant* joint, shared, together.

solely [*adv*] *only, alone*
▪ *Syn* barely, but, exclusively, individually, purely, simply, single-handedly, singly, singularly, totally, undividedly, wholly; ▪ *Ant* shared, together.

solemn [*adj1*] *quiet, serious*
▪ *Syn* austere, brooding, deliberate, dignified, downbeat, earnest, funereal, glum, grave, heavy, intense, moody, pensive, portentous, reflective, sedate, sober, somber, staid, stern, thoughtful, weighty; ▪ *Ant* frivolous, funny, jovial, laughing, light.

solemn [*adj2*] *impressive, sacred*
▪ *Syn* august, awe-inspiring, ceremonial, devotional, divine, formal, grand, grave, hallowed, imposing, magnificent, majestic, momentous, overwhelming, religious, reverential, ritual, sanctified, stately, venerable; ▪ *Ant* insignificant, irreligious, ordinary, sacrilegious, unimpressive, usual.

solicit [*v*] *plead for; try to sell*
▪ *Syn* apply, approach, ask, beg, beseech, bum, cadge, call, canvass, claim, crave, desire, entreat, hustle, implore, importune, inquire, panhandle, petition, postulate, pray, promote, proposition, query, refer, request, requisition, seek, sponge, sue for, supplicate, tout; ▪ *Ant* disapprove, refuse, reject.

solicitous [*adj*] *worried; concerned*
▪ *Syn* anxious, appetent, apprehensive, attentive, avid, caring, devoted, earnest, heedful, impatient, keen, loving, mindful, regardful, tender, troubled, uneasy, zealous; ▪ *Ant* easy-going, heedless, laidback, unafraid, unworried.

solid [*adj1*] *hard, dimensional*
▪ *Syn* close, compact, compacted, concentrated, concrete, consolidated, dense, firm, fixed, hunk, massed, material, rocklike, rooted, secure, set, sound, stable, sturdy, substantial, thick, tight, unshakable; ▪ *Ant* fluid, gaseous, hollow, insubstantial, liquid, soft, vaporous.

solid [*adj2*] *continuous, complete*
▪ *Syn* consecutive, consentient, continued, firm, like a rock, stable, steady, unalloyed, unanimous, unbroken, undivided, uninterrupted, united, unmixed; ▪ *Ant* broken, divided, incomplete, incontinuous, intermittent.

solid [*adj3*] *dependable, reliable*
▪ *Syn* cogent, constant, estimable, genuine, good, law-abiding, levelheaded, real, satisfying, sensible, serious, sober, sound, stalwart, steadfast, trustworthy, trusty, upright, upstanding, valid, worthy; ▪ *Ant* irresponsible, tenuous, unde-

pendable, unreliable, untrustworthy, vulnerable.

solitary [adj] alone, single; unsociable
▪ **Syn** aloof, antisocial, cloistered, companionless, desolate, distant, eremetic, friendless, introverted, isolated, lone, lorn, only, particular, reclusive, secluded, sequestered, solo, stag, standoffish, unaccompanied, unapproachable, unattended, uncompanionable, unique, unsocial, withdrawn; ▪ **Ant** gregarious, sociable.

solve [v] answer, resolve
▪ **Syn** clarify, construe, deal with, decipher, determine, divine, elucidate, expound, fathom, figure out, fix, get right, have, illuminate, reason, settle, think out, unfold, unravel, unriddle, work out; ▪ **Ant** pose, question, search, wonder.

somber [adj] sad, depressing
▪ **Syn** bleak, blue, caliginous, dark, depressive, dismal, dispiriting, drab, dreary, dull, funereal, gloomy, grave, joyless, lugubrious, melancholy, murky, sepulchral, solemn, staid, tenebrous, weighty; ▪ **Ant** bright, cheerful, colorful, happy, joyful.

somebody [n] person of fame, importance ▪ **Syn** celebrity, dignitary, luminary, notable, personage, person of note, public figure, star, superstar; ▪ **Ant** nobody, nonentity.

someday [adv] eventually
▪ **Syn** after a while, anytime, at a future time, finally, in a time to come, one day, one time or another, sometime, sooner or later, subsequently, ultimately, yet; ▪ **Ant** never.

somehow [adv] by some means
▪ **Syn** after a fashion, anyway, anywise, in some way, one way or another, somehow or another, somehow or other; ▪ **Ant** no way.

sometimes [adv] every now and then
▪ **Syn** at intervals, at times, every so often, frequently, from time to time, intermittently, now and again, occasionally, once in a while, on occasion, periodically, recurrently; ▪ **Ant** never, not at all.

somewhat [adv] to some extent
▪ **Syn** adequately, a little, bearably, fairly, incompletely, in part, insignificantly, kind of, moderately, more or less, not much, partially, quite, rather, slightly, some, sort of, to a degree, tolerably; ▪ **Ant** not at all.

somewhere [adv] in, at some place
▪ **Syn** about, around, elsewhere, in one place or another, scattered, someplace, someplace or another; ▪ **Ant** nowhere.

soon [adv] in the near future
▪ **Syn** anon, any minute now, before long, directly, early, expeditiously, fleetly, forthwith, in a little while, in due time, instantly, in time, posthaste, presently, promptly, rapidly, shortly, speedily; ▪ **Ant** distant, far, later, never.

soothe [v] calm, ease
▪ **Syn** allay, alleviate, appease, balm, calm down, cheer, console, dulcify, hush, lull, mitigate, mollify, pacify, quieten, relieve, smooth down, soften, stroke, subdue, tranquilize; ▪ **Ant** agitate, arouse, distress, upset, worry.

sophisticated [adj1] cosmopolitan, cultured ▪ **Syn** artificial, blasé, bored, citified, cultivated, cynical, disenchanted, experienced, jaded, knowing, mature, practiced, refined, schooled, seasoned, skeptical, suave, urbane, world-weary; ▪ **Ant** naive, provincial, simple, uncultured, unsophisticated.

sophisticated [adj2] complex, advanced
▪ **Syn** complicated, delicate, elaborate, highly developed, intricate, involved, knotty, labyrinthine, modern, refined, subtle; ▪ **Ant** easy, old-fashioned, simple, slow, unsophisticated.

sophomoric [adj] inexperienced, juvenile ▪ **Syn** brash, foolish, naive, puerile, reckless, young; ▪ **Ant** experienced, knowledgeable, mature, sophisticated.

soporific [adj] sleepy; sleep-inducing
▪ **Syn** anesthetic, balmy, calming, deadening, drowsy, dull, hypnotic, mesmerizing, narcotic, numbing, opiate, quietening, sedative, slumberous, somnolent, tranquilizing; ▪ **Ant** animated, awake, conscious, exciting, invigorating, stimulating.

sordid [adj] dirty, bad, low
▪ **Syn** abject, avaricious, base, corrupt, debauched, degraded, despicable, disreputable, filthy, foul, grasping, impure, low-down, mean, miserable, nasty, poor, scurvy, seedy, self-seeking, shabby, shameful, sleazy, slovenly, squalid, unclean, vile, wretched; ▪ **Ant** clean, honorable, pristine, pure, reputable.

sore [adj1] hurt physically
▪ **Syn** aching, afflicted, bruised, burning, chafed, distressing, hurting, inflamed,

pained, painful, raw, reddened, sensitive, severe, smarting, tender, ulcerated, vexatious; ▪ *Ant* healthy, pain-free.

sore [*adj2*] *angry; hurt mentally*
▪ *Syn* afflicted, aggrieved, annoying, critical, distressing, grieving, indignant, pained, peeved, resentful, sensitive, smarting, stung, troubled, upset, vexed; ▪ *Ant* delighted, happy, pleased.

sorrow [*v*] *be very upset, grieved*
▪ *Syn* agonize, bemoan, bewail, carry on, deplore, grieve, lament, mourn, regret, sob, take on, weep; ▪ *Ant* be happy, be joyful, delight, rejoice.

sorrowful [*adj*] *very upset; grieving*
▪ *Syn* afflicted, depressed, disconsolate, doleful, grievous, heavy-hearted, in mourning, in pain, lugubrious, melancholy, miserable, mournful, piteous, plaintive, rueful, sad, tearful, unhappy, woeful, wretched; ▪ *Ant* cheerful, delighted, happy, joyful, uplifted.

sorry [*adj1*] *remorseful, regretful*
▪ *Syn* apologetic, attritional, compunctious, conscience-stricken, guilt-ridden, melted, penitent, repentant, self-reproachful, shamefaced, softened, touched; ▪ *Ant* glad, happy, unremorseful.

sorry [*adj2*] *sad, heartbroken*
▪ *Syn* disconsolate, distressed, grieved, heavy-hearted, melancholy, pitiful, rueful, saddened, sorrowful, unhappy; ▪ *Ant* happy, heartened, joyful.

sorry [*adj3*] *despicable, pathetic*
▪ *Syn* abject, base, contemptible, deplorable, dismal, distressing, inadequate, miserable, paltry, pitiful, poor, sad, scurvy, shoddy, trifling, trivial, unimportant, vile, worthless, wretched; ▪ *Ant* good, hopeful, nice, uplifting, wonderful.

sort [*v*] *place in order*
▪ *Syn* arrange, assort, catalog, classify, cull, distribute, file, group, order, put in order, rank, riddle, sift, systematize, tab, typecast, winnow; ▪ *Ant* disorder, disorganize.

so-so [*adj*] *adequate, passable*
▪ *Syn* average, enough, fair, indifferent, mediocre, moderate, ordinary, respectable, tolerable; ▪ *Ant* different, distinguished, excellent, exceptional.

soul [*n1*] *psyche, inspiration, energy*
▪ *Syn* anima, animus, bottom, breast, cause, conscience, courage, disposition, ego, elan vital, essence, force, heart, individuality, life, marrow, nobility,

noumenon, personality, pith, pneuma, principle, quintessence, spirit, spiritual being, stuff, substance, thought, vital force, vitality, vivacity; ▪ *Ant* body, intellect, mind.

sound [*adj1*] *complete, healthy*
▪ *Syn* firm, fit, hearty, intact, perfect, right, sane, stable, sturdy, substantial, thorough, vibrant, vigorous, vital, well-constructed, whole, wholesome; ▪ *Ant* ailing, incomplete, infirm, unfit, unhealthy, unsound, weak.

sound [*adj2*] *logical, reasonable*
▪ *Syn* accurate, advisable, cogent, convincing, deep, exact, fair, impeccable, just, levelheaded, orthodox, profound, prudent, rational, right, satisfactory, sensible, sober, solid, telling, thoughtful, trustworthy, valid, well-founded, wise; ▪ *Ant* illogical, unbelievable, unfathomable, unreasonable, unsound.

sound [*adj3*] *accepted, established*
▪ *Syn* authoritative, canonical, dependable, fair, faithful, legal, loyal, orthodox, proper, proven, recognized, reliable, reputable, safe, sanctioned, secure, solid, stable, true, valid; ▪ *Ant* distrusted, refused, rejected.

sound bite [*n*] *very brief broadcast statement* ▪ *Syn* blurb, buzzword, clip, excerpt, newsbreak, news item, one-liner, outtake, photo opportunity piece, slogan, snippet, spot news; ▪ *Ant* documentary, full-length piece, manifesto, opus, policy statement, position paper, speech.

sour [*adj1*] *bad-tasting; gone bad*
▪ *Syn* acerb, acetic, acid, acidic, acrid, astringent, biting, bitter, briny, caustic, fermented, green, keen, musty, piquant, pungent, rancid, salty, sharp, stinging, tart, unpleasant, vinegary; ▪ *Ant* fresh, good, pleasant, sweet, tasty, unspoiled.

sour [*adj2*] *in a bad mood*
▪ *Syn* acid, acrimonious, bitter, churlish, cynical, disagreeable, discontented, displeasing, embittered, grouchy, ill-tempered, irritable, jaundiced, peevish, tart; ▪ *Ant* agreeable, cheerful, cordial, friendly, happy, sweet.

sour [*v*] *alienate*
▪ *Syn* acidify, curdle, disenchant, embitter, envenom, exacerbate, exasperate, make sour, spoil, turn, turn off; ▪ *Ant* encourage, excite, incite.

source [*n*] *beginning; point of supply*
▪ *Syn* antecedent, author, begetter, birth-

place, cause, commencement, dawn, derivation, expert, father, fountain, inception, mother, onset, opening, origin, parent, provenience, rise, root, start, wellspring; ▪ *Ant* consequence, effect, end, outcome, result.

souse [v] *make very wet*
▪ *Syn* brine, deluge, dip, douse, drench, drown, duck, dunk, immerse, impregnate, marinate, preserve, seethe, soak, sop, steep, submerge, submerse, waterlog, wet; ▪ *Ant* dehydrate, dry.

sovereign [adj] *dominant, effective*
▪ *Syn* absolute, ascendant, autonomous, chief, commanding, directing, efficacious, guiding, highest, imperial, independent, kingly, lofty, majestic, master, monarchial, overbearing, paramount, predominant, predominate, preponderant, principal, queenly, regal, regnant, reigning, royal, ruling, supreme; ▪ *Ant* inferior, limited, submissive, subordinate, subservient.

sow [v] *plant*
▪ *Syn* broadcast, disject, disseminate, grow, implant, inseminate, lodge, pitch, propagate, put in, raise, scatter, seed, strew, toss; ▪ *Ant* dig, harvest, reap.

spacious [adj] *extensive, expansive*
▪ *Syn* ample, big, boundless, broad, capacious, cavernous, commodious, enormous, generous, great, huge, immense, large, limitless, roomy, sizable, spacy, uncrowded, vast, voluminous, wide; ▪ *Ant* close, cramped, crowded, small.

span [v] *stretch over*
▪ *Syn* arch, bridge, connect, cover, cross, extend, ford, go across, link, pass over, range, reach, traverse, vault; ▪ *Ant* compress, concentrate, condense, shorten.

spare [adj1] *extra, reserve*
▪ *Syn* additional, backup, de trop, emergency, free, in reserve, lagniappe, leftover, odd, over, superfluous, surplus, unoccupied, unused; ▪ *Ant* necessary.

spare [adj2] *thin; sparse*
▪ *Syn* bony, economical, exiguous, frugal, gaunt, lanky, lean, meager, modest, poor, rangy, rawboned, scant, scrawny, shadow, skimpy, skinny, slim, sparing, sparse, stick, stilt, stingy, wiry; ▪ *Ant* fat, thick.

spare [v1] *do or manage without*
▪ *Syn* accommodate with, allow, bestow, dispense with, give, grant, indulge in, lay aside, lay up, let have, part with, pinch,

put by, relinquish, save, scrape, scrimp, skimp; ▪ *Ant* need.

spare [v2] *forgive; have mercy upon*
▪ *Syn* absolve, bail out, be lenient, be merciful, discharge, dispense, excuse, exempt, forbear, leave, let go, pardon, pity, privilege from, refrain from, release, relieve from, save from, spring; ▪ *Ant* condemn, destroy, harm, hurt, injure, punish.

sparing [adj] *careful, economical*
▪ *Syn* avaricious, canny, cost-conscious, frugal, money-conscious, parsimonious, provident, prudent, saving, stewardly, thrifty, tight-fisted, unwasteful, wary; ▪ *Ant* careless, generous, lavish, profuse, spendthrift.

spark [v] *start, inspire*
▪ *Syn* animate, excite, kindle, precipitate, set in motion, stimulate, stir, touch off, trigger; ▪ *Ant* cease, halt, stop.

sparkle [v] *glitter, shine*
▪ *Syn* beam, coruscate, dance, flash, flicker, gleam, glimmer, glint, glisten, glow, scintillate, shimmer, twinkle, wink; ▪ *Ant* darken, dull, fade.

sparse [adj] *very few and scattered*
▪ *Syn* dispersed, exiguous, inadequate, meager, occasional, rare, scanty, scarce, skimpy, spare, sporadic, thin, uncommon; ▪ *Ant* crowded, dense, full, lush, plentiful, populous.

spasmodic [adj] *twitching, erratic*
▪ *Syn* changeable, convulsive, desultory, fitful, irregular, jerky, periodic, shaky, sporadic, spotty, spurtive, uncertain; ▪ *Ant* consultant, resting, steady, uninterrupted.

spawn [v] *produce*
▪ *Syn* bring forth, create, father, generate, give rise to, hatch, issue, make, originate, parent, procreate, reproduce, sire; ▪ *Ant* abort, destroy.

speak [v1] *talk*
▪ *Syn* allege, articulate, break silence, communicate, convey, declare, deliver, discourse, expatiate, make known, modulate, mouth, perorate, put into words, say, sound, state, tell, utter, verbalize, voice, whisper, yammer; ▪ *Ant* be quiet, listen, repress.

speak [v2] *address; give a lecture*
▪ *Syn* argue, declaim, descant, discourse, get across, harangue, hold forth, orate, pitch, plead, prelect, recite, sermonize, stump, talk; ▪ *Ant* listen.

speak out/speak up [v] *make one's position known* ▪ *Syn* assert, come out with, declare, insist, make oneself heard, make plain, say loud and clear, sound off, speak loudly, stand up for; ▪ *Ant* be quiet, shut up.

special [adj] *distinguished, distinctive; important in own way* ▪ *Syn* certain, characteristic, choice, defined, determinate, different, earmarked, especial, exceptional, exclusive, extraordinary, first, gala, individual, marked, memorable, momentous, out of the ordinary, peculiar, rare, select, unique; ▪ *Ant* common, commonplace, indistinctive, normal, ordinary, undistinguished, unimportant, usual.

specialize [v] *concentrate on specific area* ▪ *Syn* be into, develop oneself in, have a weakness for, limit oneself to, practice exclusively, pursue, study intensively, train, work in; ▪ *Ant* broaden, generalize.

specially [adv] *particularly* ▪ *Syn* distinctively, especially, expressly, in specie, specifically, uniquely; ▪ *Ant* broadly, vaguely.

specific [adj] *particular, distinguishing* ▪ *Syn* categorical, characteristic, definite, definitive, distinct, especial, explicit, express, individual, limited, outright, peculiar, precise, reserved, specialized, unambiguous, unique; ▪ *Ant* approximate, general, hazy, indefinite, uncertain, vague.

specifically [adv] *expressly, particularly* ▪ *Syn* accurately, categorically, characteristically, clearly, concretely, definitely, distinctively, especially, exactly, explicitly, in detail, indicatively, pointedly, precisely, respectively, specially; ▪ *Ant* broadly, generally.

specify [v] *designate; decide definitely* ▪ *Syn* be specific, cite, come to the point, condition, define, detail, determine, enumerate, establish, indicate, individualize, inventory, itemize, lay out, limit, list, name, particularize, peg, pin down, point out, put finger on, set, settle, show clearly, specialize, spell out, stipulate, tab, tag, tick off; ▪ *Ant* approxiamte, generalize, guess.

specious [adj] *misleading* ▪ *Syn* apparent, apparently right, captious, casuistic, deceptive, delusive, erroneous, fallacious, false, hollow, illogical, inaccurate, incorrect, likely, nugatory, ostensible, plausible, presumable, presumptive, pretentious, probable, seeming, sophistic, sophistical, spurious, unsound, untrue, vain, wrong; ▪ *Ant* conclusive, real, true, valid.

speck [n] *tiny bit* ▪ *Syn* atom, blemish, crumb, defect, dot, fault, flaw, fleck, flyspeck, grain, iota, jot, mark, mite, modicum, molecule, mote, particle, shred, smidgen, speckle, splotch, spot, stain, trace, whit; ▪ *Ant* lot, mass.

speckled [adj] *dotted* ▪ *Syn* brindled, dappled, flaked, flecked, freckled, mosaic, motley, mottled, particolored, patchy, peppered, spotted, spotty, sprinkled, stippled, studded, variegated; ▪ *Ant* plain, solid, unspeckled.

spectacular [adj] *wonderful, impressive* ▪ *Syn* amazing, astonishing, astounding, breathtaking, daring, dazzling, dramatic, eye-catching, fabulous, fantastic, grand, histrionic, magnificent, marked, marvelous, miraculous, prodigious, remarkable, sensational, splendid, staggering, striking, stunning, stupendous, theatrical, thrilling, wondrous; ▪ *Ant* dull, normal, ordinary, regular, unspectacular, usual.

speculate [v1] *think about deeply and theorize* ▪ *Syn* brainstorm, cerebrate, cogitate, conjecture, consider, contemplate, deliberate, excogitate, figure, guess, guesstimate, hazard a guess, hypothesize, meditate, muse, read, reason, reflect, review, ruminate, scheme, size up, study, suppose, surmise, suspect, weigh, wonder; ▪ *Ant* ignore, neglect.

speculate [v2] *gamble, risk* ▪ *Syn* dare, hazard, play, plunge, take a chance, venture, wildcat; ▪ *Ant* abstain, play safe.

speech [n1] *talk* ▪ *Syn* articulation, communication, conversation, dialect, dialogue, diction, discussion, elocution, enunciation, expressing, expression, idiom, intercourse, jargon, language, lingo, locution, mother tongue, native tongue, oral communication, palaver, parlance, prattle, pronunciation, prose, speaking, spiel, tone, tongue, utterance, verbalization, vernacular, vocal expression, vocalization, voice; ▪ *Ant* muteness, quiet, silence.

speechless [adj] *without ability to talk* ▪ *Syn* aghast, amazed, aphonic, astounded, dazed, dumb, dumbfounded, dumbstruck, inarticulate, mum, mute, reserved, shocked, silent, uncommunicative, voiceless, wordless; ▪ *Ant* articulate, chatty, communicative, responsive.

speed [v] *move along quickly*
▪ *Syn* advance, aid, assist, barrel, belt, bomb, boost, career, cut along, dispatch, expedite, facilitate, flash, fly, gallop, gather momentum, get under way, go all out, go fast, hasten, hightail, hurry, impel, make haste, press on, promote, quicken, race, run, rush, sail, tear, urge, whiz, zoom; ▪ *Ant* creep, dawdle, delay, halt, slow.

speedy [adj] *fast, quick*
▪ *Syn* accelerated, agile, alacritous, brisk, expeditious, fleet, hasty, hurried, immediate, nimble, precipitate, prompt, quick-fire, rapid, ready, snappy, summary, supersonic, swift; ▪ *Ant* delayed, dilatory, sluggish, tardy.

spell [v2] *give rest, relief*
▪ *Syn* breathe, free, lay off, lie by, release, relieve, stand in for, take over, take the place of; ▪ *Ant* abuse, run ragged, use.

spellbound [adj] *enchanted, fascinated*
▪ *Syn* agape, amazed, bemused, bewitched, captivated, enthralled, gripped, held, hooked, mesmerized, open-mouthed, possessed, rapt, transfixed, transported, under a spell; ▪ *Ant* disenchanted, disinterested, indifferent.

spend [v1] *give, pay out*
▪ *Syn* allocate, bestow, confer, contribute, defray, disburse, dispense, dissipate, drain, employ, exhaust, expend, fritter, give, hand out, invest, lavish, liquidate, misspend, outlay, squander, use up; ▪ *Ant* earn, get, hoard, receive, save.

spend [v2] *use time; occupy*
▪ *Syn* employ, fill, fritter, idle, kill, let pass, misuse, pass, put in, squander, waste; ▪ *Ant* conserve, save.

spendthrift [n] *person careless with money* ▪ *Syn* dissipater, high roller, improvident, imprudent, prodigal, profligate, spender, sport, squanderer, waster, wastrel; ▪ *Ant* cheapskate, miser, pennypincher, saver.

spent [adj] *used up, gone; tired out*
▪ *Syn* bushed, consumed, depleted, dissipated, drained, effete, exhausted, expended, finished, limp, prostrate, shattered, thrown away, used, wasted, weary, worn out; ▪ *Ant* animated, energetic, robust.

sphere [n1] *globular object*
▪ *Syn* ball, circle, earth, globe, globule, orb, pellet, pill, rondure, round; ▪ *Ant* block, cube, square.

spicy [adj1] *pungent, flavorful*
▪ *Syn* ambrosial, appetizing, aromal, aromatic, distinctive, fiery, flavorsome, fragrant, fresh, herbaceous, highly seasoned, hot, keen, odoriferous, peppery, perfumed, piquant, redolent, savory, scented, seasoned, snappy, spirited, tangy, tasty, zesty, zippy; ▪ *Ant* bland, dull, flavorless, tasteless, unsavory.

spicy [adj2] *off-color, vulgar*
▪ *Syn* breezy, broad, erotic, indelicate, poignant, racy, ribald, risqué, scandalous, sensational, sophisticated, suggestive, titillating, unseemly, wicked; ▪ *Ant* moral, proper, prudish.

spill [v1] *slop, drop*
▪ *Syn* discharge, disgorge, dribble, drip, empty, flow, lose, overfill, overflow, overrun, overturn, pour, run over, spill over, splash, splatter, spray, sprinkle, spurt, squirt, stream, upset, well over; ▪ *Ant* clean up, pick up.

spill [v2] *reveal*
▪ *Syn* betray, blab, blow, disclose, divulge, give away, inform, squeal, tattle, tell; ▪ *Ant* conceal, hide.

spin [v] *go around, make go around*
▪ *Syn* gyrate, gyre, oscillate, pendulate, pirouette, purl, reel, revolve, rotate, spiral, swim, turn, twirl, twist, wheel, whirl; ▪ *Ant* stand, steady.

spineless [adj] *cowardly*
▪ *Syn* faint-hearted, fearful, feeble, forceless, frightened, impotent, inadequate, ineffective, ineffectual, invertebrate, irresolute, nerveless, pithless, soft, spiritless, squeamish, submissive, timid, vacillating, weak, weak-kneed, weak-willed; ▪ *Ant* bold, brave, courageous, fearless, strong, tough.

spiral [adj] *curling, winding*
▪ *Syn* circling, circular, circumvoluted, coiled, corkscrew, curled, helical, helicoid, radial, rolled, screw-shaped, scrolled, tendrillar, tortile, voluted, whorled, wound; ▪ *Ant* straight, uncurling, unwinding.

spirited [adj] *lively, vivacious*
▪ *Syn* active, alert, animate, animated, ardent, audacious, avid, bold, bouncy, brave, bright, burning, courageous, dauntless, eager, effervescent, energetic,

enthusiastic, fearless, fiery, full of life, game, gritty, high-spirited, intrepid, keen, mettlesome, nervy, passionate, peppery, peppy, plucky, resolute, sharp, snappy, sparkling, sprightly, spunky, valiant, vigorous, zealous, zesty; ▪ *Ant* apathetic, depressed, dispirited, lazy, lethargic, unhappy, unlively.

spiritless [*adj*] *depressed*
▪ *Syn* apathetic, broken, cast down, dejected, despondent, disconsolate, dispirited, down, downcast, downhearted, draggy, droopy, dull, enervated, inanimate, indifferent, lackadaisical, lackluster, languid, languorous, lifeless, limp, listless, melancholic, melancholy, slothful, subdued, submissive, tame, torpid; ▪ *Ant* energetic, happy, lively, spirited, uplifted.

spiritual [*adj*] *religious, otherworldly*
▪ *Syn* asomatous, devotional, discarnate, disembodied, ethereal, ghostly, holy, immaterial, incorporeal, metaphysical, pure, rarefied, refined, sacred, supernal, unphysical; ▪ *Ant* bodily, corporeal, irreligious, irreverent, physical, unspiritual.

spit [*v*] *eject saliva or substance*
▪ *Syn* discharge, drool, expectorate, hiss, sibilate, sizz, slobber, spatter, spew, sputter, throw out; ▪ *Ant* swallow.

spite [*v*] *offend, hurt*
▪ *Syn* annoy, begrudge, beset, discomfit, gall, grudge, harass, harm, injure, needle, nettle, persecute, pique, provoke, vex; ▪ *Ant* forgive, help, love, please, serve.

spiteful [*adj*] *hurtful, nasty*
▪ *Syn* angry, barbed, cruel, despiteful, dirty, evil, hateful, ill-disposed, malevolent, malicious, malignant, mean, ornery, rancorous, snide, splenetic, venomous, vicious, vindictive, wicked; ▪ *Ant* affectionate, altruistic, forgiving, loving.

splendid [*adj1*] *luxurious, expensive*
▪ *Syn* baroque, beautiful, brilliant, dazzling, flamboyant, glowing, grandiose, impressive, lavish, magnificent, marvelous, ornate, plush, radiant, refulgent, resplendent, rich, sumptuous, superb; ▪ *Ant* drab, poor, shabby, shoddy, somber, tawdry.

splendid [*adj2*] *excellent, illustrious*
▪ *Syn* admirable, brilliant, celebrated, distinguished, divine, eminent, exceptional, exquisite, fantastic, fine, first-class, glorious, gorgeous, grand, great, heroic,

impressive, magnificent, marvelous, matchless, outstanding, peerless, premium, rare, remarkable, renowned, resplendent, royal, splendiferous, splendorous, sterling, sublime, superb, superlative, supreme, unparalleled, unsurpassed, wonderful; ▪ *Ant* humble, mediocre, ordinary, regular, usual.

splice [*v*] *join, interweave*
▪ *Syn* braid, entwine, graft, hitch, interlace, intertwine, knit, marry, mate, mesh, plait, tie, unite, weave, wed, yoke; ▪ *Ant* cut, divide, separate, sever.

splinter [*v*] *break into thin, small pieces*
▪ *Syn* burst, disintegrate, fracture, fragment, pash, rive, shatter, shiver, smash, split; ▪ *Ant* combine, fix, mend.

split [*v1*] *break up, pull apart*
▪ *Syn* bifurcate, break, burst, cleave, come apart, come undone, crack, dichotomize, disband, disjoin, dissever, disunite, diverge, divide, divorce, fork, gape, go separate ways, hack, open, part, part company, put asunder, rend, rip, rive, separate, sever, slash, slit, snap, splinter, sunder, tear, whack; ▪ *Ant* combine, join, merge, pull together.

split [*v2*] *divide into parts*
▪ *Syn* allocate, allot, apportion, carve up, distribute, divide, halve, mete out, parcel out, partition, share, slice up; ▪ *Ant* combine, join, unite.

splurge [*v*] *spend lavishly*
▪ *Syn* be extravagant, binge, fling, indulge, spred; ▪ *Ant* hoard, save.

spoil [*v1*] *ruin, hurt*
▪ *Syn* blemish, damage, debase, deface, depredate, desecrate, disfigure, disgrace, harm, impair, injure, make useless, mar, plunder, queer, ravage, sack, tarnish, trash, upset, vitiate, waste, wreck; ▪ *Ant* enhance, help, improve.

spoil [*v2*] *baby, indulge*
▪ *Syn* baby, cater to, coddle, cosset, favor, humor, oblige, overindulge, pamper; ▪ *Ant* be indifferent, deprive, ignore, neglect.

spoil [*v3*] *decay, turn bad*
▪ *Syn* addle, become tainted, crumble, decompose, deteriorate, disintegrate, go bad, mildew, molder, putrefy, rot, taint; ▪ *Ant* conserve, preserve.

spoken [*adj*] *by word of mouth*
▪ *Syn* announced, articulate, communicated, expressed, lingual, mentioned, oral, phonetic, put into words, said, told,

unwritten, uttered, verbal, voiced; ▪ **Ant** heard, written.

spongy [adj] *cushioned, absorbent*
▪ **Syn** absorptive, cushiony, elastic, light, mushy, pulpous, pulpy, resilient, rubbery, springy, squishy, yielding; ▪ **Ant** hard, impermeable, inflexible.

sponsor [v] *help, promote*
▪ **Syn** back, bankroll, be responsible for, finance, fund, grubstake, guarantee, patronize, put up money, stake, subsidize, vouch for; ▪ **Ant** disapprove, discourage, hurt.

spontaneous [adj] *impulsive, willing*
▪ **Syn** automatic, extemporaneous, free spirited, impetuous, impromptu, improvised, instinctive, involuntary, natural, offhand, simple, up front, voluntary; ▪ **Ant** deliberate, intended, involuntary, planned, premeditated, studied.

spooky [adj] *frightening*
▪ **Syn** chilling, creepy, eerie, ghostly, mysterious, ominous, scary, spine-chilling, supernatural, uncanny, unearthly, weird; ▪ **Ant** natural, unfrightening.

sporadic [adj] *on and off*
▪ **Syn** desultory, few, fitful, infrequent, irregular, occasional, random, rare, scarce, scattered, seldom, spasmodic; ▪ **Ant** constant, continuous, dependable, irregular, steady.

sporting/sportive [adj] *playful and fair*
▪ **Syn** antic, coltish, frisky, frolicsome, game, gay, impish, jaunty, joyous, larkish, lively, merry, mischievous, reasonable, roguish, rollicking, sprightly, square, wild; ▪ **Ant** cheating, dishonest, serious, somber, unfair.

spot [v1] *mark, stain*
▪ **Syn** besmirch, bespatter, blot, blotch, dapple, dirty, dot, fleck, maculate, marble, mottle, soil, spatter, speck, speckle, stipple, streak, stripe, stud, sully, taint, tarnish; ▪ **Ant** clean, unspot.

spot [v2] *see, recognize*
▪ **Syn** catch, catch sight of, descry, detect, discern, discover, encounter, espy, ferret out, identify, locate, make out, observe, pinpoint, place, sight, trace, track; ▪ **Ant** ignore, overlook.

spotless [adj] *very clean; innocent*
▪ **Syn** above reproach, blameless, chaste, clean, decent, faultless, gleaming, hygienic, immaculate, pure, shining, stainless, virginal, white; ▪ **Ant** dirty, messy, soiled, spotted, stained, tarnished.

spotlight [v] *focus attention on*
▪ **Syn** accentuate, draw attention, feature, give prominence, highlight, illuminate, point up, publicize; ▪ **Ant** ignore, obscure, turn aside.

spotty [adj] *blotchy, irregular*
▪ **Syn** desultory, erratic, flickering, not uniform, patchy, pimply, spasmodic, sporadic, unequal, uneven; ▪ **Ant** clean, constant, regular, systematic, unbroken, uniform.

spout [v1] *spurt, emit*
▪ **Syn** cascade, discharge, eject, erupt, expel, exude, gush, jet, pour, roll, shoot, spill, spray, squirt, stream, surge; ▪ **Ant** drain.

spout [v2] *talk forcefully*
▪ **Syn** boast, brag, declaim, expatiate, gush, harangue, orate, pontificate, ramble, sermonize, spellbind, vapor, yell; ▪ **Ant** be quiet.

sprawl [v] *sit or lie spread out*
▪ **Syn** drape, extend, flop, loll, lounge, recline, sit, slouch, slump, spread, straddle, straggle, stretch, trail; ▪ **Ant** erect, sit, straighten.

spray [v] *sprinkle, diffuse*
▪ **Syn** atomize, drizzle, scatter, shoot, shower, smear, spatter, splash, spritz, squirt, throw around; ▪ **Ant** collect, gather.

spread [v1] *open or fan out*
▪ **Syn** array, branch off, broaden, cast, circulate, diffuse, disperse, diverge, even out, flatten, gloss, lengthen, open, outstretch, paint, pervade, proliferate, radiate, roll out, sprawl, spray, stretch, strew, suffuse, widen; ▪ **Ant** close, collect, compress, fold, gather, wind.

spread [v2] *publicize*
▪ **Syn** advertise, blazon, broadcast, cast, circulate, declare, diffuse, disseminate, distribute, make known, make public, proclaim, promulgate, propagate, publish, radiate, scatter, transmit; ▪ **Ant** conceal, hide.

spree [n] *wild activity*
▪ **Syn** bacchanalia, ball, bash, binge, caper, carousal, carouse, celebration, fling, frolic, jag, jamboree, junket, lark, orgy, party, rampage, revel, spending expedition, spending spree, splurge; ▪ **Ant** chore, duty, obligation.

sprightly [adj] *fun, vivacious*
▪ **Syn** active, agile, alert, animated, blithe, bouncy, breezy, brisk, cheerful,

chipper, clever, dapper, energetic, frolicsome, gay, hyper, jaunty, jolly, jumping, keen, keen-witted, lively, nimble, perky, quick, smart, snappy, spirited, spry, swinging; ▪ *Ant* dull, glum, inactive, lethargic, phlegmatic.

spring [*v1*] *jump, skip*
▪ *Syn* bolt, bounce, bound, hop, hurdle, leap, lop, lope, rebound, recoil, skitter, start, startle, trip, vault; ▪ *Ant* alight, crawl, creep, drop, fall, land.

spring [*v2*] *originate, emerge*
▪ *Syn* appear, arise, arrive, be derived, be descended, begin, birth, burgeon, come, come into being, come into existence, come out, commence, derive, descend, develop, emanate, flow, grow, hatch, head, issue, loom, mushroom, proceed, rise, shoot up, start, stem, upspring; ▪ *Ant* end, finish, terminate.

sprinkle [*v*] *scatter, disseminate*
▪ *Syn* baptize, christen, dampen, dot, dust, freckle, mist, moisten, pepper, powder, rain, shake, shower, speck, speckle, spit, spot, spray, spritz, squirt, strew, stud; ▪ *Ant* collect, gather.

sprint [*v*] *run very fast*
▪ *Syn* dart, dash, go at top speed, race, rush, scamper, scoot, scurry, shoot; ▪ *Ant* crawl, saunter, stroll, walk.

sprout [*v*] *develop*
▪ *Syn* bud, burgeon, germinate, grow, push, shoot, shoot up, spring, take root, vegetate; ▪ *Ant* die, shrink, shrivel, wither.

spruce [*adj*] *stylish, neat*
▪ *Syn* classy, clean, dainty, dapper, elegant, prim, smart, tidy, trim, well-groomed; ▪ *Ant* sloppy, tacky, unkempt, unstylish, untidy.

spruce up [*v*] *make neat, well-groomed*
▪ *Syn* brush, dress up, fix up, groom, prim, primp, sleek, slick, smarten, tidy, titivate; ▪ *Ant* dirty, mess up.

spry [*adj*] *active, vivacious*
▪ *Syn* agile, brisk, energetic, fleet, lithe, nimble, prompt, quick, robust, rocking, spirited, sprightly, supple, vigorous; ▪ *Ant* doddering, inactive, lethargic, sluggish, unaware, unenergetic.

spunk [*n*] *courage, nerve*
▪ *Syn* backbone, determination, doggedness, fortitude, gameness, mettle, pluck, resolution, spirit, toughness; ▪ *Ant* cowardice, squeamishness, timidity.

spur [*v*] *incite, prompt*
▪ *Syn* animate, arouse, awaken, countenance, drive, exhort, favor, goad, impel, key up, propel, push, rally, rouse, spark, stimulate, trigger, urge, work up; ▪ *Ant* disapprove, discourage, dissuade, hinder.

spurious [*adj*] *counterfeit, fake*
▪ *Syn* apocryphal, artificial, bogus, contrived, deceitful, faked, false, feigned, framed, illegitimate, imitation, mock, phony, pirate, simulated; ▪ *Ant* authentic, genuine, legitimate, true.

spurn [*v*] *turn away; ignore*
▪ *Syn* contemn, cut, decline, despise, disapprove, disdain, dismiss, disregard, drop, dump, flout, flush, hold in contempt, pass by, rebuff, refuse, reject, reprobate, repudiate, repulse, scoff, scorn, slight, sneer, snub, turn down; ▪ *Ant* accept, embrace, encourage, welcome.

spurt [*v*] *erupt*
▪ *Syn* burst, emerge, flow, flow out, gush, issue, jet, ooze, pour out, shoot, spew, spout, spritz, squirt, stream, surge, well; ▪ *Ant* drip, drizzle, ooze.

squabble [*v*] *argue*
▪ *Syn* argufy, bicker, brawl, clash, disagree, dispute, encounter, fight, hassle, quarrel, quibble, row, scrap, spat, wrangle; ▪ *Ant* agree, collaborate, concur.

squalid [*adj*] *poor, run-down*
▪ *Syn* abominable, base, broken-down, decayed, despicable, dingy, dirty, disgusting, disheveled, fetid, filthy, foul, grimy, gruesome, horrible, horrid, ignoble, impure, low, mean, moldy, muddy, musty, nasty, odorous, offensive, poverty-stricken, ramshackle, reeking, repellent, repulsive, seedy, shabby, shoddy, sloppy, slovenly, soiled, sordid, ugly, vile, wretched; ▪ *Ant* attractive, clean, rich, tidy, well-kept.

squander [*v*] *fritter away, use up*
▪ *Syn* be wasteful, consume, dissipate, expend, frivol, frivol away, go through, lavish, misspend, misuse, run through, scatter, spend, throw away, trifle, waste; ▪ *Ant* accumulate, conserve, hoard, save, set aside.

square [*adj1*] *honest, genuine*
▪ *Syn* aboveboard, decent, equitable, even, fair, fair-and-square, impartial, just, nonpartisan, objective, sporting, straightforward, upright; ▪ *Ant* deceiving, dishonest, fake.

square [*adj2*] *four-sided*
▪ **Syn** boxlike, equal-sided, equilateral, foursquare, orthogonal, quadrate, quadratic, quadratical, rectangular, rectilinear, right-angled, squared, squarish; ▪ **Ant** oblong, octagonal, oval, round.

square [*adj3*] *old-fashioned, conventional* ▪ **Syn** behind the times, bourgeois, conservative, dated, orthodox, out-of-date; ▪ **Ant** current, in vogue, new, popular, stylish, worldly.

square [*vl*] *correspond, agree*
▪ **Syn** accord, balance, check out, coincide, conform, fit, gee, jibe, match, reconcile, tally; ▪ **Ant** contradict, contrast, disagree.

square [*v2*] *pay off, satisfy*
▪ **Syn** balance, bribe, buy off, clear, clear off, clear up, discharge, fix, liquidate, make even, pay, pay up, quit, rig, settle, tamper with; ▪ **Ant** be holden, owe.

squash [*v*] *compress*
▪ **Syn** bruise, crush, distort, extinguish, flatten, jam, kill, macerate, pound, pulp, quash, scrunch, smash, squish, suppress, trample, triturate; ▪ **Ant** fan, open, uncompress.

squat [*adj*] *short and stocky*
▪ **Syn** blocky, broad, chunky, fat, heavy, heavyset, splay, thick, thick-bodied, thickset; ▪ **Ant** lanky, skinny, slender, tall, thin.

squat [*v*] *lower body by bending knees*
▪ **Syn** cower, crouch, hunch, hunker down, perch, roost, settle, sit, stoop; ▪ **Ant** straighten, stretch.

squawk [*v2*] *gripe*
▪ **Syn** complain, protest, squeal, yammer; ▪ **Ant** compliment, praise.

squeal [*v2*] *inform on*
▪ **Syn** betray, complain, protest, talk, tattle, tattletale, tell; ▪ **Ant** conceal, hide.

squeamish [*adj*] *nauseated; finicky*
▪ **Syn** captious, delicate, exacting, fastidious, hypercritical, mincing, particular, prim, qualmish, queasy, scrupulous, sickly, straitlaced, upset, vertiginous; ▪ **Ant** bold, brash, callous, insensitive, tough.

squeeze [*vl*] *exert pressure on sides, parts of something* ▪ **Syn** choke, clasp, clip, compress, contract, cram, crowd, embrace, enfold, grip, hold tight, hug, jam, nip, pack, pinch, quash, ram, scrunch, squash, stuff, thrust, wedge, wring; ▪ **Ant** expand, uncompress.

squeeze [*v2*] *try to get money out of*
▪ **Syn** bring pressure to bear, eke out, extort, extract, oppress, pressure, pressurize, wrench, wring; ▪ **Ant** donate, give.

squelch [*v*] *suppress, restrain*
▪ **Syn** black out, censure, crush, extinguish, kill, muffle, oppress, quelch, quench, repress, shush, sit on, smother, squash, stifle, strangle, thwart; ▪ **Ant** encourage, incite, release.

squint [*v*] *scrunch up eyes when viewing*
▪ **Syn** cock the eye, look, look askance, look cross-eyed, peek, peep, screw up eyes, squinch; ▪ **Ant** open wide.

squire [*v*] *accompany*
▪ **Syn** assist, attend, chaperon, chauffer, companion, date, escort; ▪ **Ant** abandon, leave.

squirm [*v*] *wiggle, fidget*
▪ **Syn** agonize, flounder, shift, skew, squiggle, twist, wind, worm, wriggle, writhe; ▪ **Ant** sit still.

stabilize [*v*] *make or keep in steady state; make resistant to change* ▪ **Syn** balance, ballast, bolt, brace, counterbalance, counterpoise, equalize, fasten, firm, fix, maintain, ossify, preserve, prop, secure, set, settle, stabilitate, steady, stiffen, support, sustain, uphold; ▪ **Ant** change, loosen, shake, vary, weaken, wobble.

stable [*adj*] *constant, fixed; resistant*
▪ **Syn** anchored, balanced, durable, enduring, established, firm, immutable, invariable, lasting, nailed, perdurable, poised, reliable, safe, secure, stalwart, stationary, steadfast, stout, sturdy, substantial, together, uniform, well-built, well-founded; ▪ **Ant** inconstant, shaky, unfixed, unstable, vacillating, wobbly.

stack [*v*] *pile up*
▪ **Syn** accumulate, amass, bank up, cock, drift, heap, hill, load, mound, pile, rick, stockpile; ▪ **Ant** disassemble.

stagger [*vl*] *walk falteringly*
▪ **Syn** alternate, careen, dither, falter, halt, hesitate, lurch, overlap, pitch, reel, stammer, swing, teeter, titubate, topple, totter, vacillate, waver, wheel, whiffle, wobble, zigzag; ▪ **Ant** march, steady, stride.

stagnant [*adj*] *motionless, dirty*
▪ **Syn** brackish, dead, dormant, filthy, foul, idle, immobile, inactive, inert, lifeless, listless, passive, putrid, quiet, sluggish, stale, standing, static, stationary,

still, unmoving; ▪ *Ant* circulating, clean, dynamic, flowing, fresh, moving, pure, running, unpolluted.

stagnate [*v*] *deteriorate by lack of action*
▪ *Syn* constipate, decay, decline, fester, hibernate, idle, languish, lie fallow, not move, putrefy, rot, rust, stall, stand, stand still, stifle, stultify, trammel, vegetate; ▪ *Ant* evolve, grow, progress, strengthen.

staid [*adj*] *restrained, set*
▪ *Syn* calm, collected, composed, cool, decorous, demure, dignified, earnest, formal, grave, quiet, sedate, self-restrained, serious, settled, sober, solemn, somber, starchy, steady, stuffy, weighty; ▪ *Ant* adventurous, capricious, exuberant, frivolous, jaunty, sporting.

stain [*v*] *dirty, taint*
▪ *Syn* bastardize, besmirch, blacken, contaminate, corrupt, debase, debauch, defile, demoralize, deprave, mark, pervert, smear, soil, sully, tar, tinge; ▪ *Ant* clean, clear, purge, redeem, uplift.

stale [*adj1*] *old, decayed*
▪ *Syn* dried, faded, fetid, fusty, malodorous, musty, rank, sour, stagnant, stenchy, tasteless, watery, weak, zestless; ▪ *Ant* crisp, fresh, new.

stale [*adj2*] *overused, out-of-date*
▪ *Syn* antiquated, banal, bent, cliché, commonplace, dead, drab, dull, effete, flat, fusty, hackneyed, insipid, mawkish, platitudinous, repetitious, shopworn, timeworn, trite, well-worn, zestless; ▪ *Ant* current, fresh, imaginative, new, original.

stalemate [*n*] *deadlock*
▪ *Syn* arrest, check, delay, draw, gridlock, impasse, pause, standoff, standstill, tie; ▪ *Ant* decision, headway, progress.

stall [*v*] *delay for own purposes*
▪ *Syn* arrest, brake, check, equivocate, fence, halt, hamper, interrupt, not move, postpone, prevaricate, quibble, shut down, stand off, stop, suspend, tarry, temporize; ▪ *Ant* advance, further, help, progress.

stalwart [*adj*] *strong, valiant*
▪ *Syn* athletic, bold, brave, brawny, courageous, daring, dauntless, fearless, indomitable, intrepid, lusty, manly, muscular, robust, rugged, solid, staunch, stout, strapping, sturdy, tough, valorous, vigorous; ▪ *Ant* cowardly, fearful, fragile, infirm, meek, weak.

stamina [*n*] *strength, vigor*
▪ *Syn* endurance, energy, force, fortitude,

gutsiness, heart, indefatigability, lustiness, power, resilience, resistance, staying power, tolerance, vim, vitality; ▪ *Ant* apathy, fragility, frailty, lack, lethargy, weakness.

stammer [*v*] *stutter in speech*
▪ *Syn* falter, halt, hesitate, jabber, lurch, pause, repeat, splutter, sputter, stop, stumble, wobble; ▪ *Ant* enunciate, pronounce.

stand [*v1*] *be or get upright*
▪ *Syn* be erect, be on feet, be vertical, cock, erect, jump up, mount, rank, rise; ▪ *Ant* lay, lie, recline, sit.

stand/stand for [*v2*] *endure, bear*
▪ *Syn* abide, allow, bear with, brook, cope, countenance, experience, handle, hang on, live with, put up with, resign oneself to, submit, suffer, sustain, tolerate, undergo, weather, withstand accepted, basic, canonical, customary, definitive, established, general, normal, official, orthodox, recognized, set, staple, stock, typical, usual; ▪ *Ant* collapse, falter, give way, succumb, waver, yield.

stand [*v3*] *be in force, exist*
▪ *Syn* be located, belong, be situated, be valid, continue, endure, fill, halt, hold, last, obtain, occupy, prevail, remain, rest, stay, stop; ▪ *Ant* refuse, reject, veto.

standard [*adj*] *regular, approved*
▪ *Syn* abide, allow, bear with, brook, cope, countenance, experience, handle, hang on, live with, put up with, resign oneself to, submit, suffer, sustain, tolerate, undergo, weather, withstand accepted, basic, canonical, customary, definitive, established, general, normal, official, orthodox, recognized, set, staple, stock, typical, usual; ▪ *Ant* abnormal, different, irregular, unorthodox, unusual.

standardize [*v*] *make regular, similar*
▪ *Syn* assimilate, bring into line, homogenize, mass produce, normalize, regiment, stereotype, systematize; ▪ *Ant* change, differ, differentiate, vary, waver.

standing [*adj*] *permanent*
▪ *Syn* continuing, existing, fixed, perpetual, regular, repeated; ▪ *Ant* fleeting, impermanent, temporary.

standoffish [*adj*] *cold, distant*
▪ *Syn* aloof, antisocial, cool, distant, eremitic, haughty, indifferent, misanthropic, reclusive, remote, solitary, withdrawn; ▪ *Ant* affable, extroverted, friendly, sociable, warm.

stand out [v] *be conspicuous, prominent*
- **Syn** attract attention, be distinct, beetle, bulge, bulk, catch the eye, emerge, jut, loom, overhang, poke, project, protrude, stick out; **Ant** dim, obscure.

standstill [n] *stop*
- **Syn** arrest, cessation, check, checkmate, deadlock, delay, gridlock, halt, impasse, inaction, pause, stalemate, standoff, wait; **Ant** advance, progress.

staple [adj] *necessary, basic*
- **Syn** chief, essential, fundamental, important, key, main, popular, predominant, primary, principal, standard; **Ant** auxiliary, extra, minor, secondary, unnecessary.

star [n] *person who is famous*
- **Syn** celebrity, favorite, headliner, hero, idol, lead, luminary, name, superstar; **Ant** average joe, commoner, nobody.

star [adj] *famous, illustrious*
- **Syn** brilliant, capital, celebrated, dominant, leading, outstanding, paramount, predominant, principal, prominent, talented, well-known; **Ant** minor, unimportant, unknown.

stare [v] *gape, watch*
- **Syn** eye, fix, focus, gawk, look, look fixedly, ogle, peer, rivet, take in; **Ant** glance, ignore, overlook.

stark [adj1] *utter, absolute*
- **Syn** abrupt, arrant, bald, blunt, complete, confounded, consummate, downright, flagrant, infernal, palpable, rank, severe, sheer, stiff, unmitigated; **Ant** indefinite.

stark [adj2] *bare, unadorned*
- **Syn** austere, bald, bleak, chaste, clear, cold, depressing, desolate, empty, forsaken, grim, harsh, naked, plain, raw, severe, vacant; **Ant** clothed, covered.

start [v1] *begin; come into existence*
- **Syn** activate, appear, arise, come into being, commence, create, depart, embark, engender, found, inaugurate, initiate, institute, introduce, launch, lay foundation, leave, open, originate, pioneer, rise, sally forth, set in motion, spring, turn on; **Ant** complete, conclude, die, end, finish, stop.

start [v2] *flinch*
- **Syn** blanch, bolt, bounce, bound, buck, dart, draw back, jerk, jump, leap, quail, recoil, shrink, squinch, startle, twitch, wince; **Ant** ignore, remain passive.

startle [v] *frighten, surprise*
- **Syn** affright, agitate, alarm, astonish, astound, awe, consternate, floor, fright, rock, scare, shake up, shock, spook, spring, stagger, start, stun, take aback, terrify, terrorize; **Ant** calm, comfort, compose.

starving/starved [adj] *deprived of food*
- **Syn** craving, dehydrated, drawn, emaciated, faint, famished, haggard, hungry, malnourished, peaked, peckish, pinched, ravenous, skinny, thin, undernourished; **Ant** fed, full, satisfied.

state [v] *declare, assert*
- **Syn** affirm, articulate, asseverate, bring out, come out with, deliver, describe, elucidate, enounce, expound, express, narrate, present, pronounce, propound, recount, relate, report, say, set forth, tell, utter, vent, voice; **Ant** ask, question.

stately [adj] *dignified, impressive*
- **Syn** august, ceremonious, deliberate, elegant, formal, gracious, haughty, imperial, lofty, luxurious, magnificent, majestic, monumental, noble, opulent, palatial, pompous, proud, regal, royal, solemn, stiff, superb; **Ant** common, ignoble, informal, undignified, unimpressive, unstately.

static [adj] *motionless, changeless*
- **Syn** at a standstill, constant, deadlocked, fixed, gridlocked, immobile, inert, latent, stable, stagnant, standing stationary, still, stopped, stuck, unvarying; **Ant** active, changeable, continuous, dynamic, mobile, moving, variable.

station [v] *place at a location*
- **Syn** appoint, assign, base, commission, establish, fix, garrison, install, lodge, park, plant, post; **Ant** displace, move, remove.

stationary [adj] *not moving; fixed*
- **Syn** anchored, inert, moored, motionless, permanent, stable, stagnant, static, stock-still, unmoving; **Ant** mobile, moving, restless, unfixed, unsteady.

statuesque [adj] *tall and dignifed*
- **Syn** beautiful, graceful, grand, imposing, majestic, regal, shapely, stately, trim, well-proportioned; **Ant** short, small.

stature [n] *importance*
- **Syn** ability, caliber, capacity, development, dignity, elevation, eminence, growth, merit, position, prestige, qualification, rank, standing, state, status,

value, virtue, worth; ▪ *Ant* inconsequence, insignificance, unimportance.

staunch [*adj*] *resolute, dependable*
▪ *Syn* ardent, constant, faithful, loyal,
sound, stalwart, steadfast, stout, strong,
sure, tough, tried-and-true, true-blue,
trustworthy; ▪ *Ant* irresolute, undependable, unreliable, weak.

stay [*v1*] *wait*
▪ *Syn* abide, bide, continue, dally, delay,
endure, hang, hang around, hang out,
lag, last, linger, loiter, nest, pause, perch,
remain, reside, settle, sojourn, stop, tarry;
▪ *Ant* advance, go, leave.

stay [*v2*] *hold in abeyance*
▪ *Syn* adjourn, curb, defer, detain, discontinue, halt, hinder, hold, impede, interrupt, obstruct, postpone, prevent, put off,
shelve, stall, suspend; ▪ *Ant* express,
free, hurry, loose, promote, release,
speed.

steadfast [*adj*] *loyal, steady*
▪ *Syn* abiding, allegiant, ardent, bound,
constant, dedicated, enduring, faithful,
fast, firm, intent, liege, never-failing, obdurate, persevering, relentless, resolute,
staunch, true, true-blue, unwavering,
wholehearted; ▪ *Ant* disloyal, faltering,
halfhearted, unreliable, wavering.

steady [*adj1*] *stable, fixed*
▪ *Syn* abiding, certain, changeless, constant, durable, enduring, equable, even,
firm, immovable, never-failing, patterned, regular, safe, solid, steadfast,
substantial, sure, unchanging, uniform,
unwavering; ▪ *Ant* unfixed, unstable, unsteady, weak, wobbly.

steady [*adj2*] *continuing*
▪ *Syn* ceaseless, consistent, constant, continuous, equable, eternal, even, faithful,
habitual, incessant, never-ending, nonstop, persistent, regular, rhythmic, stabile, uninterrupted; ▪ *Ant* broken, discontinuous, intermittent, sporadic, synco-
pated.

steady [*adj3*] *balanced, faithful in mind*
▪ *Syn* allegiant, ardent, calm, constant,
cool, dependable, equable, fast, imperturbable, levelheaded, liege, poised,
reliable, reserved, resolute, sedate,
self-possessed, sensible, serious-minded,
settled, sober, staid, staunch, steadfast,
wholehearted; ▪ *Ant* imbalanced, unfaithful, untrustworthy.

steal [*v1*] *take something without permission* ▪ *Syn* abduct, appropriate, black-

mail, burglarize, carry off, cheat,
defraud, embezzle, heist, hold up, keep,
kidnap, loot, misappropriate, pilfer, pillage, pirate, plunder, poach, purloin, ransack, rifle, shoplift, swindle, swipe, take,
thieve; ▪ *Ant* donate, give.

stealthy [*adj*] *quiet and secretive*
▪ *Syn* catlike, clandestine, covert, crafty,
cunning, enigmatic, feline, noiseless, private, secret, silent, skulking, slinking, sly,
sneaking, surreptitious, undercover, underhand, wily; ▪ *Ant* open, public.

steel [*v*] *prepare oneself*
▪ *Syn* animate, brace, cheer, embolden,
encourage, fortify, gird, harden, hearten,
inspirit, prepare, rally, ready, reinforce,
strengthen; ▪ *Ant* fail, weaken.

steep [*adj1*] *extreme in direction, course*
▪ *Syn* abrupt, arduous, breakneck, declivi-
tous, erect, headlong, high, lofty, perpendicular, precipitate, prerupt, raised,
sharp, straight-up; ▪ *Ant* flat, gentle,
graded, gradual, low.

steep [*adj2*] *very expensive*
▪ *Syn* excessive, exorbitant, extortionate,
extreme, high, immoderate, inordinate,
overpriced, stiff, towering, unreasonable;
▪ *Ant* inexpensive, moderate.

steep [*v*] *let soak*
▪ *Syn* bathe, damp, drench, fill, imbue,
immerse, infuse, macerate, marinate,
moisten, permeate, pervade, saturate,
soak, sodden, submerge, waterlog; ▪ *Ant*
dehydrate, drain, dry.

stem [*v1*] *come from*
▪ *Syn* arise, be bred, be brought about, be
caused, be generated, derive, develop,
emanate, flow, issue, originate, proceed,
rise, spring; ▪ *Ant* consequence, end,
goal, result.

stem [*v2*] *prevent, stop*
▪ *Syn* arrest, bring to a standstill, check,
contain, control, curb, dam, hinder, hold
back, oppose, resist, restrain, stay, withstand; ▪ *Ant* abet, aid, encourage, help.

stench [*n*] *foul odor*
▪ *Syn* fetor, malodor, mephitis, noisome-
ness, redolence, smell; ▪ *Ant* perfume,
sweetness.

step in [*v*] *become involved*
▪ *Syn* enter, intercede, interfere, intermediate, interpose, intervene, mediate, negotiate, take action; ▪ *Ant* abandon,
leave, wash hands.

step up [*v*] *accelerate*
▪ *Syn* augment, boost, escalate, hasten,

hurry, improve, increase, intensify, lift, quicken, raise, shake up, speed, speed up, up; ▪ *Ant* decelerate, halt, hinder, slow.

stereotype [*v*] *categorize as being example, standard* ▪ *Syn* define, dub, pigeonhole, standardize, type, typecast; ▪ *Ant* differentiate.

stereotyped [*adj*] *standard, conventional* ▪ *Syn* banal, cliché-ridden, dull, hackneyed, overused, platitudinous, stale, stock, trite, unoriginal, worn-out; ▪ *Ant* different, dissimilar, unconventional, unlike.

sterile [*adj*] *unproductive, clean* ▪ *Syn* antiseptic, barren, bleak, dead, desolate, disinfected, effete, fallow, fruitless, germ-free, hygienic, impotent, infertile, pasteurized, sanitary, septic, vain, waste; ▪ *Ant* dirty, fruitful, productive, prolific.

sterilize [*v*] *make clean* ▪ *Syn* alter, antisepticize, aseptify, change, clean, decontaminate, disinfect, fumigate, incapacitate, pasteurize, purify, sanitize; ▪ *Ant* contaminate, corrupt, defile, dirty, pollute.

stern [*adj*] *serious, authoritarian* ▪ *Syn* ascetic, austere, cruel, forbidding, grim, hard, implacable, inexorable, inflexible, mulish, relentless, rigid, severe, stubborn, tough; ▪ *Ant* cheerful, funny, lenient, light, smiling, tolerant.

stew [*n2*] *commotion; mental upset* ▪ *Syn* agitation, confusion, dither, flap, fretting, fuming, fuss, lather, pother, snit, sweat, tizzy, tumult, turbulence, turmoil, worry; ▪ *Ant* calm, control, ease, happiness.

stick [*v1*] *adhere, affix* ▪ *Syn* attach, bind, bond, braze, catch, cement, cleave, clog, cohere, fasten, fix, fuse, glue, hold, join, lodge, paste, remain, solder, unite, weld; ▪ *Ant* loosen, unfasten.

stick [*v2*] *position, lay* ▪ *Syn* deposit, drop, establish, fix, install, place, plant, plonk, plunk, put, set, settle, store, stuff; ▪ *Ant* dislodge, displace, remove.

stick [*v3*] *endure* ▪ *Syn* abide, bear, bear up under, brook, last, persist, see through, stand, stay, suffer, support, tolerate, weather; ▪ *Ant* disobey, forget, refuse.

stick out [*v*] *bulge* ▪ *Syn* beetle, come through, extend,

extrude, jut, obtrude, overhang, poke, project, protrude, push, show, stand out; ▪ *Ant* depress, hollow.

sticky [*adj1*] *gummy, adhesive* ▪ *Syn* agglutinative, clinging, gluey, glutinous, ropy, tacky, tenacious, viscid, viscous; ▪ *Ant* slick, slippery.

sticky [*adj2*] *humid and hot* ▪ *Syn* clammy, close, dank, muggy, oppressive, soggy, sultry, sweltering; ▪ *Ant* cool, dry.

sticky [*adj3*] *difficult, embarrassing* ▪ *Syn* awkward, delicate, discomforting, painful, rough, thorny, tricky, unpleasant; ▪ *Ant* easy, facile, pleasant.

stiff [*adj1*] *hard, inflexible* ▪ *Syn* annealed, arthritic, brittle, firm, frozen, hardened, immalleable, indurate, inelastic, jelled, ossified, petrified, refractory, rheumatic, rigid, solidified, starched, stony, taut, tense, tight, wooden; ▪ *Ant* flexible, pliable, pliant, soft.

stiff [*adj2*] *formal, standoffish* ▪ *Syn* artificial, austere, ceremonious, cold, forced, hardheaded, inflexible, intractable, labored, mannered, obstinate, pompous, priggish, prim, relentless, starchy, stilted, wooden; ▪ *Ant* casual, graceful, informal.

stiff [*adj3*] *difficult* ▪ *Syn* arduous, exacting, fatiguing, formidable, hard, laborious, rigorous, tough, trying, uphill; ▪ *Ant* easy, moderate, simple.

stiff [*adj4*] *extreme, severe* ▪ *Syn* austere, brisk, exact, hard, harsh, inexorable, inordinate, oppressive, pitiless, rigorous, sharp, strict, stringent, towering, vigorous; ▪ *Ant* casual, moderate, normal, relaxed.

stiffen [*v*] *make or become harder* ▪ *Syn* anneal, brace, cement, chill, condense, congeal, crystallize, freeze, gel, harden, ossify, petrify, set, solidify, stabilize, starch, thicken; ▪ *Ant* liquefy, loosen, melt.

stifle [*v*] *prevent, restrain* ▪ *Syn* asphyxiate, check, choke, constipate, cork, curb, extinguish, gag, hush, muffle, repress, restrain, shut up, silence, smother, squelch, stop, suffocate, suppress, trammel; ▪ *Ant* encourage, help, persuade.

stigma [*n*] *shame* ▪ *Syn* besmirchment, blame, brand, disfigurement, disgrace, dishonor, imputation, odium, onus, reproach, slur, taint; ▪ *Ant* glory, honor.

still [*adj*] *calm, motionless, quiet*
▪ *Syn* at rest, closed, close-mouthed, fixed, halcyon, hushed, inert, lifeless, noiseless, pacific, peaceful, placid, restful, sealed, serene, silent, smooth, soundless, stable, stagnant, static, stationary, stock-still, tranquil, whist; ▪ *Ant* agitated, moving, stirred, unquiet.

still [*v*] *make quiet, motionless, calm*
▪ *Syn* allay, alleviate, appease, arrest, balm, becalm, calm, choke, compose, gag, hush, lull, muffle, muzzle, pacify, quiet, quieten, settle, shut down, silence, smooth, soothe, squash, squelch, subdue, tranquilize; ▪ *Ant* agitate, disturb, irritate, move.

stilted [*adj*] *artificial, pretentious*
▪ *Syn* affected, aureate, bombastic, constrained, decorous, egotistic, euphuistic, forced, formal, high-flown, inflated, labored, magniloquent, mincing, overblown, pedantic, pompous, prim, rhetorical, sonorous, stiff, unnatural; ▪ *Ant* easygoing, genuine, graceful, relaxed.

stimulate [*v*] *excite, provoke*
▪ *Syn* activate, animate, arouse, commove, dynamize, elate, encourage, energize, enliven, exhilarate, fan, fire, foment, foster, galvanize, goad, grab, hook, impel, incite, inflame, innervate, inspire, instigate, motivate, move, perk, pique, prod, prompt, quicken, rouse, send, spark, spirit, spur, support, trigger, urge, vitalize, vivify, whet; ▪ *Ant* calm, depress, discourage.

sting [*v*] *prick, pain*
▪ *Syn* bite, burn, electrify, hurt, injure, needle, pique, poke, prickle, smart, tingle; ▪ *Ant* assuage, calm, caress, mollify, soothe.

stingy [*adj*] *penny-pinching, averse to spending money* ▪ *Syn* chary, cheap, churlish, close, close-fisted, costive, curmudgeonly, economical, frugal, grasping, grudging, ignoble, illiberal, ironfisted, mean, miserly, narrow, near, niggard, parsimonious, penurious, petty, saving, scrimping, selfish, skimping, sparing, thrifty, tightfisted; ▪ *Ant* generous, spendthrift, wasteful.

stink [*v1*] *smell badly*
▪ *Syn* be offensive, be rotten, have an odor, offend, smell up, stench; ▪ *Ant* perfume.

stink [*v2*] *be lousy, bad*
▪ *Syn* be abhorrent, be detestable, be held in disrepute, be no good, be offensive, be rotten, smell; ▪ *Ant* be excellent, be good.

stint [*v*] *economize; hold back*
▪ *Syn* be frugal, be parsimonious, be sparing, be stingy, grudge, limit, pinch, restrain, save, scrape, scrimp, spare, stash, withhold; ▪ *Ant* spend.

stipulate [*v*] *decide on conditions*
▪ *Syn* agree, arrange, bargain, condition, contract, designate, detail, engage, guarantee, impose, make, name, particularize, pin down, pledge, postulate, promise, provide, require, settle, specify, spell out, state; ▪ *Ant* imply, wish.

stir [*v1*] *mix up, agitate*
▪ *Syn* beat, blend, disturb, flutter, mix, move, move about, quiver, rustle, shake, toss, tremble, whip, whisk; ▪ *Ant* calm, soothe.

stir [*v2*] *incite, stimulate*
▪ *Syn* abet, agitate, animate, arouse, awaken, bestir, craze, drive, electrify, energize, excite, foment, galvanize, impel, inflame, inspire, kindle, motivate, move, prompt, provoke, quicken, raise, rally, rile, rouse, spark, spur, stimulate, stir up, thrill, trigger, urge, vitalize, wake, waken, whet; ▪ *Ant* calm, discourage.

stir [*v3*] *arise*
▪ *Syn* awake, awaken, bestir, be up and about, budge, exert, get moving, hasten, look alive, make an effort, mill about, move, rouse, wake, waken; ▪ *Ant* laze, rest, wait.

stock [*adj*] *commonplace*
▪ *Syn* banal, common, conventional, customary, dull, established, formal, hackneyed, ordinary, overused, regular, routine, set, standard, staple, stereotyped, traditional, trite, typical, usual, worn-out; ▪ *Ant* different, original, unusual.

stock [*v*] *supply with merchandise*
▪ *Syn* accumulate, amass, carry, deal in, equip, fill, gather, handle, have, hoard, keep, keep on hand, lay in, provide, reserve, save, stockpile, store, stow away, trade in; ▪ *Ant* deplete, drain, empty, use up, waste.

stocky [*adj*] *short and overweight; short and muscular* ▪ *Syn* corpulent, fat, heavyset, plump, solid, squat, sturdy, thick, thickset; ▪ *Ant* lanky, skinny, tall, thin, underweight.

stodgy [adj] dull, stuffy
- **Syn** boring, dim, dreary, formal, heavy, labored, monotonous, pedantic, pedestrian, plodding, ponderous, staid, tedious, turgid, weighty; **Ant** adventurous, exciting, ready, willing.

stoic/stoical [adj] philosophic, calm
- **Syn** aloof, cool, detached, dry, enduring, impassive, imperturbable, long-suffering, matter-of-fact, patient, phlegmatic, resigned, self-controlled, sober, stolid; **Ant** anxious, depressed, stressed, upset.

stolid [adj] apathetic, stupid
- **Syn** bovine, dense, doltish, dry, dumb, heavy, impassive, indifferent, lumpish, matter-of-fact, obtuse, passive, phlegmatic, slow, stoic, unemotional, wooden; **Ant** aware, intelligent, interested.

stomach [v] endure, tolerate
- **Syn** abide, bear, bear with, brook, digest, put up with, resign oneself, stand, submit to, suffer, swallow, sweat, take, tolerate; **Ant** condemn, refuse, reject.

stony [adj] hard, icy in appearance, response ▪ **Syn** adamant, callous, cold, cruel, expressionless, firm, frigid, hardened, heartless, indifferent, inflexible, merciless, obdurate, pitiless, rough, tough; **Ant** friendly, soft, warm.

stoop [v1] bow down
- **Syn** be bowed, bend, be servile, bow, cringe, crouch, descend, dip, duck, hunch, incline, kneel, lean, relax, sink, slant, squat; **Ant** straighten.

stoop [v2] condescend; lower oneself to another ▪ **Syn** accommodate, concede, debase oneself, deign, demean oneself, descend, oblige, patronize, resort, sink, thaw, unbend, vouchsafe; **Ant** rise above.

stop [v1] bring or come to a halt or end
- **Syn** break, break off, cease, close, cut short, desist, discontinue, draw up, end, finish, halt, hold, kill, pause, put an end to, quit, refrain, shut down, stall, stand, stay, terminate; **Ant** advance, begin, continue, go, start.

stop [v2] prevent, hold back
- **Syn** arrest, avoid, bar, block, bottle, check, choke, clog, close, cut off, disrupt, forestall, frustrate, gag, hinder, impede, intercept, interrupt, muzzle, obstruct, occlude, plug, rein in, repress, restrain, seal, shut down, shut off, shut out, silence, stall, staunch, stem, still, stopper, suspend, throw over, turn off, ward off; **Ant** allow, continue, encourage.

stopgap [adj] temporarily helping
- **Syn** band-aid, expedient, impromptu, improvised, makeshift, practical, provisional, substitute, temporary; **Ant** finished, permanent.

stoppage [n] halt, curtailment
- **Syn** abeyance, arrest, blockage, check, close, closure, cutoff, deduction, discontinuance, interruption, layoff, lockout, obstruction, occlusion, shutdown, sit-down, standstill, walkout; **Ant** beginning, continuation, go, start.

store [v] collect and put aside
- **Syn** accumulate, amass, bank, bin, bottle, bury, cache, can, cumulate, deposit, freeze, garner, hide, hive, hoard, hutch, keep, keep in reserve, lay away, pack, pack away, park, plant, put, put away, put by, reserve, save, stash, stock, stockpile, treasure, warehouse; **Ant** squander, use, waste.

stormy [adj] rough (referring to weather) ▪ **Syn** bitter, blustering, foul, furious, gusty, howling, menacing, pouring, raging, rainy, roaring, savage, threatening, torrid, turbulent, violent, wet, wild, windy; **Ant** calm, clear, clement, fair, mild.

story [n] lie
- **Syn** canard, fabrication, falsehood, falsity, fib, fiction, misrepresentation, prevarication, tale, untruth, white lie; **Ant** truth.

stout [adj1] overweight
- **Syn** big, bulky, corpulent, fat, fleshy, heavy, obese, plump, porcine, portly, rotund, substantial, thick-bodied, upholstered, weighty; **Ant** skinny, thin, underweight.

stout [adj2] strong, brawny
- **Syn** able-bodied, athletic, hardy, husky, muscular, robust, stalwart, staunch, strapping, sturdy, substantial, tough, vigorous; **Ant** weak.

stout [adj3] courageous
- **Syn** bold, brave, dauntless, fearless, gallant, heroic, intrepid, lionhearted, plucky, resolute, stalwart, undaunted, valiant, valorous; **Ant** afraid, timid, weak.

stow [v] reserve, store
- **Syn** bundle, deposit, load, pack, put away, secrete, stash, stuff, top off, tuck; **Ant** throw overboard, use, waste.

straggle [v] *wander, stray*
▪ *Syn* dawdle, lag, loiter, meander, poke, ramble, roam, rove, straddle, string out, trail; ▪ *Ant* hurry, run, rush.

straight [adj1] *aligned; not curved*
▪ *Syn* collinear, consecutive, direct, even, horizontal, inflexible, invariable, linear, perpendicular, precipitous, rectilinear, right, solid, square, through, true, upright, vertical; ▪ *Ant* curved, indirect, twisted.

straight [adj2] *honest, fair*
▪ *Syn* aboveboard, blunt, candid, decent, equitable, forthright, frank, good, honorable, just, law-abiding, moral, outright, plain, respectable, straightforward, trustworthy, upright; ▪ *Ant* corrupt, dishonest, unfair, unjust.

straight [adj3] *orderly*
▪ *Syn* arranged, correct, exact, neat, organized, put to rights, right, sorted, tidy; ▪ *Ant* disorderly, disorganized, messy.

straight [adj4] *unmixed*
▪ *Syn* concentrated, neat, plain, pure, strong, unadulterated, undiluted, unmodified, unqualified; ▪ *Ant* diluted, mixed.

straight [adj5] *conventional, square*
▪ *Syn* bourgeois, conservative, orthodox, traditional; ▪ *Ant* different, nonconformist, unconventional.

straight [adv1] *immediately, directly*
▪ *Syn* at once, direct, due, exactly, first off, in direct line, instantly, now, right, right away, straightaway; ▪ *Ant* later.

straight [adv2] *honestly*
▪ *Syn* candidly, frankly; ▪ *Ant* dishonestly, indirectly.

straighten [v] *put in neat or aligned order* ▪ *Syn* align, arrange, compose, even, level, make straight, neaten, order, put in order, rectify, set to rights, tidy; ▪ *Ant* bend, curve, move, twist.

straightforward [adj1] *honest*
▪ *Syn* aboveboard, candid, direct, forthright, frank, genuine, guileless, honorable, just, level, outspoken, plain, sincere, truthful, upright, upstanding, veracious; ▪ *Ant* deceitful, devious, dishonest.

straightforward [adj2] *simple, easy*
▪ *Syn* apparent, clear-cut, direct, distinct, elementary, evident, manifest, palpable, plain, routine, straight, through; ▪ *Ant* complicated, difficult, hard, indirect, involved.

strain [v1] *stretch, often to limit*
▪ *Syn* constrict, distend, distort, draw tight, exert, fatigue, injure, overexert, push to the limit, rack, sprain, task, tauten, tax, tighten, twist, wrench; ▪ *Ant* compress, concentrate.

strain [v2] *work very hard*
▪ *Syn* bear down, endeavor, exert, grind, hammer hustle, labor, moil, plug, push, strive, struggle, sweat, toil, try; ▪ *Ant* idle, laze, rest.

strain [v3] *cause mental stress*
▪ *Syn* distress, harass, hassle, irk, pain, pick at, push, stress, trouble, try; ▪ *Ant* calm, placate, soothe.

strained [adj] *forced, pretended*
▪ *Syn* artificial, awkward, choked, difficult, embarrassed, false, labored, self-conscious, stiff, taut, tense, uptight; ▪ *Ant* genuine, unforced.

strait [n] *crisis, difficulty*
▪ *Syn* bewilderment, bind, contingency, dilemma, distress, embarrassment, emergency, hardship, pass, perplexity, plight, predicament, rigor, vicissitude; ▪ *Ant* advantage, comfort, ease, luxury, solution, success.

stranded [adj] *marooned, abandoned*
▪ *Syn* aground, ashore, beached, cast away, grounded, helpless, shipwrecked, sidelined; ▪ *Ant* found.

strange [adj1] *deviating, unfamiliar*
▪ *Syn* aberrant, abnormal, atypical, bizarre, curious, different, eccentric, fantastic, idiosyncratic, irregular, marvelous, new, odd, off, peculiar, queer, rare, remarkable, singular, weird, wonderful; ▪ *Ant* common, familiar, normal, regular, standard, usual.

strange [adj2] *exotic, foreign*
▪ *Syn* alien, apart, awkward, detached, external, faraway, isolated, lost, new, novel, out of place, outside, remote, unexplored; ▪ *Ant* common, native.

strangle [v] *choke, stifle*
▪ *Syn* asphyxiate, gag, inhibit, kill, muffle, quelch, repress, restrain, shush, smother, squelch, subdue, suffocate, suppress, throttle; ▪ *Ant* clear, help, loose, unclog.

strapped [adj] *destitute*
▪ *Syn* beggared, fortuneless, impoverished, out of money, penniless, penurious, poor; ▪ *Ant* rich, wealthy.

strapping [adj] *big and strong*
▪ *Syn* brawny, burly, hefty, hulking, husky, powerful, powerhouse, robust, stalwart, stout, sturdy, tall, vigorous,

well-built; ▪ *Ant* attenuated, skinny, slight, small, thin.

strategic [*adj1*] *crucial*
▪ *Syn* cardinal, critical, decisive, imperative, important, key, necessary, vital; ▪ *Ant* unimportant, unnecessary.

strategic [*adj2*] *clever, calculated*
▪ *Syn* calculated, cunning, deliberate, diplomatic, planned, politic, tricky, vigilant; ▪ *Ant* nonstrategic, unplanned.

stray [*v1*] *deviate, err*
▪ *Syn* circumlocute, depart, digress, divagate, diverge, do wrong, excurse, ramble, sin, wander; ▪ *Ant* adhere, conform, obey, remain.

stray [*v2*] *wander; get lost*
▪ *Syn* deviate, drift, err, gallivant, go amiss, go astray, lose one's way, meander, ramble, range, roam, rove, straggle, swerve, traipse, turn, wander away, wander off; ▪ *Ant* go direct, go straight as an arrow.

stream [*v*] *flow*
▪ *Syn* cascade, continue, course, emerge, emit, flood, glide, gush, issue, move past, pour, roll, run, shed, sluice, spill, spout, spritz, spurt, surge; ▪ *Ant* recede, retreat, withdraw.

strengthen [*v1*] *make more forceful, powerful* ▪ *Syn* add, anneal, bolster, brace, build up, buttress, confirm, corroborate, empower, enhance, enlarge, extend, fortify, harden, heighten, increase, intensify, invigorate, make firm, mount, multiply, regenerate, reinforce, rejuvenate, renew, restore, step up, substantiate, support, sustain, temper, tone, toughen; ▪ *Ant* break down, devitalize, weaken.

strengthen [*v2*] *encourage, hearten*
▪ *Syn* animate, back up, bloom, brace, burgeon, cheer, embolden, enhearten, enliven, flourish, flower, fortify, gird, give weight, harden, inspirit, invigorate, nourish, prepare, prosper, rally, refresh, rejuvenate, restore, steel, temper; ▪ *Ant* discourage, dishearten, dissuade, weaken.

strenuous [*adj1*] *difficult; requiring hard work* ▪ *Syn* arduous, demanding, effortful, energy-consuming, exhausting, hard, laborious, operose, taxing, toilful, toilsome, tough, wicked; ▪ *Ant* easy, effortless, facile.

strenuous [*adj2*] *energetic, zealous*
▪ *Syn* active, aggressive, ardent, bold, determined, dynamic, eager, earnest, lusty, persistent, red-blooded, resolute, spirited, strong, tireless, vigorous, vital; ▪ *Ant* apathetic, lazy, lethargic.

stress [*v*] *accentuate, emphasize*
▪ *Syn* accent, belabor, dwell on, feature, lay emphasis on, make emphatic, play up, point up, repeat; ▪ *Ant* de-emphasize, play down.

stretch [*v*] *extend, elongate*
▪ *Syn* branch out, cover, crane, distend, draw out, expand, grow, inflate, lengthen, make taut, pad, prolong, protract, pull out, pyramid, rack, range, recline, span, spread, spread out, strain, string out, swell, tauten, tighten, widen; ▪ *Ant* compress, concentrate, loosen, relax, shrink, slacken.

strict [*adj1*] *authoritarian*
▪ *Syn* austere, disciplinary, exacting, firm, forbidding, grim, harsh, picky, prudish, punctilious, rigid, rigorous, scrupulous, severe, square, stringent, tough; ▪ *Ant* amenable, easygoing, flexible, lenient, tolerant, tractable, yielding.

strict [*adj2*] *accurate, absolute*
▪ *Syn* close, complete, exact, faithful, just, meticulous, particular, perfect, religious, right, scrupulous, undistorted, utter, veracious, veridical; ▪ *Ant* approximate, indefinite.

strident [*adj*] *harsh, shrill*
▪ *Syn* blatant, boisterous, clamorous, clashing, discordant, grating, hoarse, jangling, obstreperous, raucous, screeching, squeaky, stentorian, stridulant, vociferous; ▪ *Ant* dulcet, low, mellifluous, mild, moderate, soft, soothing.

strife [*n*] *struggle, battle*
▪ *Syn* altercation, animosity, bickering, brawl, clash, combat, contention, disagreement, discord, dissidence, disunity, factionalism, fighting, friction, quarrel, rivalry, warfare, wrangle; ▪ *Ant* calm, conciliation, harmony, peace, tranquility.

strike [*v1*] *hit hard*
▪ *Syn* bang, bash, beat, box, buffet, chastise, clash, clout, collide, crash, drive, force, hammer, impel, knock, percuss, pound, pummel, run into, slap, slug, smack, smite, thrust, wallop; ▪ *Ant* tap.

strike [*v2*] *find, discover*
▪ *Syn* achieve, arrive at, attain, catch, come across, come upon, effect, encounter, light upon, open up, reach; ▪ *Ant* lose, miss.

strike [v3] *devastate, affect*
▪ *Syn* afflict, assail, assault, attack, beset, deal a blow, fall upon, harrow, invade, rack, set upon, smite, storm, torment, torture, wring; ▪ *Ant* not touch, pass up.

strike out [v] *leave to begin new venture*
▪ *Syn* bear, begin, head, initiate, make, set out, start, start out; ▪ *Ant* remain, stay.

striking [adj] *extraordinary; beautiful*
▪ *Syn* arresting, astonishing, cogent, confounding, conspicuous, dazzling, dynamite, electrifying, fascinating, handsome, impressive, lofty, marked, noteworthy, outstanding, powerful, prominent, remarkable, salient, singular, staggering, startling, stunning, surprising, telling, wonderful; ▪ *Ant* commonplace, homely, pedestrian, unimpressive.

string along [v] *play with; keep dangling*
▪ *Syn* bluff, coquet, dally, deceive, dupe, flirt, fool, hoax, toy, trifle, wanton; ▪ *Ant* dump, let go, release.

stringent [adj] *rigid, tight*
▪ *Syn* acrimonious, binding, compelling, drawing, exacting, forceful, hard, harsh, inflexible, ironclad, picky, poignant, rigorous, severe, stiff, strict, tough, valid; ▪ *Ant* flexible, inexact, tolerant.

stringy [adj] *long, thin*
▪ *Syn* fibrous, gangling, gristly, lank, muscular, reedy, ropy, sinewy, spindling, spindly, threadlike, tough, wiry; ▪ *Ant* stubby, stumpy.

strip [v] *bare, uncover*
▪ *Syn* decorticate, denude, disrobe, excorticate, expose, hull, husk, lay bare, peel, remove, scale, shed, shuck, skin, take off, undress; ▪ *Ant* clothe, cover, dress.

strive [v] *try for, exert oneself*
▪ *Syn* aim, attempt, bear down, compete, contend, drive, endeavor, fight, go after, labor, make every effort, push, scramble, seek, strain, struggle, tackle, take on, toil, work; ▪ *Ant* forget, skip.

stroll [v] *walk along lazily*
▪ *Syn* amble, cruise, drift, gallivant, linger, promenade, ramble, roam, rove, saunter, toddle, traipse, tramp, wander; ▪ *Ant* run.

strong [adj1] *healthy, powerful*
▪ *Syn* able, athletic, durable, enduring, energetic, forceful, hale, hardy, hearty, mighty, muscular, robust, rugged, secure, solid, stalwart, staunch, strapping, tenacious, vigorous, well-built; ▪ *Ant* feeble, infirm, unhealthy, weak.

strong [adj2] *determined, resolute*
▪ *Syn* aggressive, brave, cogent, courageous, dedicated, deep, eager, fervent, fervid, fierce, firm, forceful, intense, iron-willed, keen, plucky, potent, resourceful, self-assertive, staunch, steadfast, tenacious, vehement, zealous; ▪ *Ant* agreeable, complacent, easygoing, irresolute, laid-back, uncaring, weak.

strong [adj3] *distinct, unmistakable*
▪ *Syn* clear-cut, cogent, compelling, convincing, marked, overpowering, persuasive, potent, secure, sharp, telling, trenchant, urgent, weighty, well-founded; ▪ *Ant* indistinct, mistakable, obscure, vague.

strong [adj4] *extreme*
▪ *Syn* acute, drastic, forceful, intense, keen, severe, sharp, strict; ▪ *Ant* mild, moderate.

strong [adj5] *forceful on the senses*
▪ *Syn* bold, bright, concentrated, fetid, full-bodied, heady, high, hot, inebriating, loud, malodorous, noisome, potent, powerful, pungent, robust, sharp, spicy, stark; ▪ *Ant* bland, delicate, mild, moderate, pale.

struggle [v1] *labor, work*
▪ *Syn* assay, attempt, cope, endeavor, grind, hassle, plug, scratch, strain, strive, tackle, toil, try, undertake; ▪ *Ant* idle, laze, rest.

struggle [v2] *fight, wrestle*
▪ *Syn* battle, brawl, buck, compete, contend, contest, grapple, hassle, romp, row, scrap, scuffle, shuffle, tangle; ▪ *Ant* surrender, yield.

strut [v] *walk pompously*
▪ *Syn* flaunt, flounce, mince, parade, play to audience, prance, show off, stalk, stride, swagger; ▪ *Ant* cower, cringe, slink, sneak.

stubborn [adj] *obstinate, unyielding*
▪ *Syn* adamant, contumacious, determined, dogged, firm, fixed, headstrong, inexorable, mulish, obdurate, opinionated, persevering, recalcitrant, relentless, self-willed, single-minded, tenacious, willful; ▪ *Ant* broad-minded, complacent, compliant, tractable, yielding.

stubby [adj] *short and thick*
▪ *Syn* fat, heavyset, squat, stocky, stout, stumpy, thick-bodied, thickset; ▪ *Ant* lanky, long, thin.

student [n] *person actively learning*
▪ *Syn* apprentice, coed, disciple, freshman, graduate, junior, learner, novice, observer, pupil, registrant, scholar, sophomore, undergraduate; ▪ *Ant* mentor, professor, teacher.

studied [adj] *intentional*
▪ *Syn* advised, affected, calculated, conscious, deliberate, examined, premeditated, prepared, thought-out, well-considered, willful; ▪ *Ant* natural, spontaneous, unintentional, unplanned.

studious [adj] *scholarly, attentive*
▪ *Syn* academic, contemplative, diligent, eager, earnest, hard-working, industrious, intellectual, learned, sedulous, serious, thoughtful, well-informed, well-read; ▪ *Ant* ignorant, inattentive, lazy, unscholarly.

study [v1] *contemplate, learn*
▪ *Syn* apply oneself, brood over, cogitate, consider, cram, examine, grind, inquire, learn, lucubrate, meditate, mind, mull over, ponder, read, read up, refresh, think over, tutor, weigh; ▪ *Ant* forget, ignore, neglect.

stuff [v] *load with*
▪ *Syn* clog up, compress, congest, cram, crowd, fill, force, glut, gorge, gormandize, jam, jam-pack, overfill, pack, pad, push, ram, satiate, stow; ▪ *Ant* empty, remove.

stuffy [adj1] *close, oppressive*
▪ *Syn* airless, breathless, confined, fetid, heavy, muggy, stagnant, stale, stifling, suffocating, sultry, thick; ▪ *Ant* airy, breezy, open, ventilated.

stuffy [adj2] *old-fashioned, prim*
▪ *Syn* bloated, conventional, dreary, fusty, genteel, humorless, magisterial, musty, narrow-minded, pompous, priggish, puritanical, self-important, staid, stilted, stodgy; ▪ *Ant* current, informal, modern, new.

stump [v] *confuse, bewilder*
▪ *Syn* baffle, confound, dumbfound, foil, mystify, nonplus, outwit, perplex, puzzle, stagger, stop, stymie; ▪ *Ant* explain, explicate, help.

stun/stupefy [v] *amaze, shock*
▪ *Syn* astonish, astound, bemuse, confound, daze, dumbfound, flabbergast, knock unconscious, muddle, overwhelm, paralyze, petrify, surprise; ▪ *Ant* anticipate, expect.

stunning [adj] *beautiful, marvelous*
▪ *Syn* beauteous, brilliant, comely, dazzling, devastating, excellent, fair, fine, gorgeous, handsome, impressive, lovely, remarkable, sensational, smashing, spectacular, striking, superior, top, wonderful; ▪ *Ant* homely, plain, run-of-the-mill.

stunted [adj] *kept from growing*
▪ *Syn* bantam, diminutive, dwarf, dwarfed, little, mite, runted, runty, scrub, short, small, tiny; ▪ *Ant* gigantic, lofty, tall.

stupendous [adj] *wonderful, amazing*
▪ *Syn* astonishing, breathtaking, colossal, dynamite, enormous, fabulous, great, huge, marvelous, monumental, overwhelming, phenomenal, prodigious, smashing, spectacular, stunning, superb, surprising, tremendous, vast, wondrous; ▪ *Ant* diminutive, puny, small, terrible.

stupid [adj] *not intelligent; irresponsible*
▪ *Syn* brainless, dazed, dense, dim, dumb, foolish, gullible, idiotic, inane, insensate, irresponsible, laughable, mindless, moronic, nonsensical, obtuse, pointless, puerile, rash, senseless, shortsighted, simpleminded, sluggish, stolid, stupefied, thick, trivial, witless; ▪ *Ant* cognizant, intelligent, responsible, smart.

stupor [n] *daze, unconsciousness*
▪ *Syn* anaesthesia, asphyxia, bewilderment, coma, dullness, faint, hebetude, hypnosis, inertia, languor, narcosis, numbness, petrifaction, somnolence, stupefaction, suspended animation, trance; ▪ *Ant* consciousness, sensibility.

sturdy [adj] *solid, durable, spirited*
▪ *Syn* athletic, bulky, determined, firm, hardy, muscular, powerful, resolute, robust, secure, solid, stalwart, staunch, steadfast, stout, strapping, strong, tenacious, tough, vigorous, well-built; ▪ *Ant* unstable, weak, wobbly.

stylish [adj] *fashionable*
▪ *Syn* chic, classy, dap, dapper, dashing, dressy, in, in fashion, in vogue, latest, new, nifty, polished, rakish, ritzy, sharp, showy, sleek, smart, swell, trendy, upscale, up-to-date, uptown, urbane, voguish; ▪ *Ant* old-fashioned, pass, unfashionable.

stymie [v] *frustrate, hinder*
▪ *Syn* balk, block, choke off, confound, corner, cramp, crimp, cut off, defeat, foil, hold off, hold up, impede, mystify, nonplus, obstruct, prevent, put on hold,

puzzle, shelve, stall, stump, thwart; ▪ *Ant* aid, assist, encourage, help.

suave [*adj*] *charming, smooth*
▪ *Syn* affable, civilized, cordial, courteous, cultivated, diplomatic, fulsome, genial, glib, ingratiating, obliging, pleasant, refined, sophisticated, unctuous, urbane, well-bred, worldly; ▪ *Ant* awkward, clumsy, unsophisticated.

subconscious [*adj*] *innermost in thought* ▪ *Syn* hidden, inner, intuitive, latent, mental, repressed, subliminal, suppressed, unconscious; ▪ *Ant* conscious, outer.

subdivision [*n*] *smaller entity of whole* ▪ *Syn* class, community, development, group, lower group, minor group, subclass, subsidiary, tract; ▪ *Ant* totality, whole.

subdue [*v*] *keep under control; moderate* ▪ *Syn* check, control, defeat, discipline, extinguish, gentle, humble, master, overcome, quash, quell, quiet, repress, restrain, soften, squelch, suppress, tame, temper, tone down, trample, triumph over, vanquish; ▪ *Ant* arouse, incite, release, rouse, start.

subdued [*adj*] *quiet, controlled* ▪ *Syn* chastened, crestfallen, dejected, dim, downcast, grave, hushed, low-key, mellow, muted, neutral, repressed, sad, softened, solemn, subtle, tasteful, tempered, toned down; ▪ *Ant* aroused, boisterous, communicative, excited, talkative.

subject [*adj*] *at the mercy of; answerable* ▪ *Syn* accountable, bound by, captive, collateral, conditional, contingent, dependent, directed, enslaved, governed, in danger of, liable, prone, satellite, sensitive, servile, subjugated, submissive, subordinate, susceptible, tentative, under, vulnerable; ▪ *Ant* independent, unconstrained.

subjective [*adj*] *emotional; based on inner experience rather than fact* ▪ *Syn* abstract, biased, fanciful, idiosyncratic, individual, instinctive, intuitive, nonobjective, nonrepresentative, personal, prejudiced; ▪ *Ant* objective, tangible, unbiased, unemotional.

subjugate [*v*] *overpower, defeat* ▪ *Syn* bear down, coerce, conquer, crush, enslave, force, hold sway, master, overcome, put down, quell, reduce, subdue, suppress, tame, triumph, vanquish; ▪ *Ant* free, liberate.

sublime [*adj*] *great, magnificent* ▪ *Syn* august, divine, dynamite, elevated, eminent, exalted, glorious, gorgeous, grand, heavenly, ideal, lofty, majestic, noble, proud, resplendent, sacred, stately, superb, transcendental; ▪ *Ant* lowly, poor, secondary, second-rate.

submerge [*v*] *dunk in liquid* ▪ *Syn* deluge, descend, dip, drench, drown, duck, engulf, flood, immerse, inundate, plunge, sink, submerse, swamp, whelm; ▪ *Ant* emerge, surface.

submissive [*adj*] *compliant* ▪ *Syn* abject, accommodating, acquiescent, complying, deferential, domesticated, dutiful, humble, ingratiating, lowly, malleable, menial, obedient, obsequious, passive, resigned, servile, subdued, tame, yielding; ▪ *Ant* arrogant, disobedient, fighting, intractable, rebellious, resistant, unyielding.

submit [*v1*] *comply, endure* ▪ *Syn* abide, acknowledge, acquiesce, agree, bend, bow, buckle, capitulate, cave, concede, defer, fold, give in, humor, indulge, knuckle, obey, relent, resign oneself, stoop, succumb, surrender, tolerate, withstand, yield; ▪ *Ant* disobey, fight, resist.

submit [*v2*] *present, offer; argue for* ▪ *Syn* advance, advise, affirm, argue, assert, claim, commit, contend, move, proffer, propose, propound, put, put forward, refer, state, suggest, tender, theorize, urge, volunteer; ▪ *Ant* conceal, dissuade, hide.

subordinate [*adj*] *lesser, supplementary* ▪ *Syn* adjuvant, ancillary, auxiliary, collateral, contributory, dependent, insignificant, junior, lower, minor, paltry, satellite, secondary, subsidiary, tributary, under; ▪ *Ant* chief, important, major, necessary, superior, vital.

subscribe [*v*] *agree* ▪ *Syn* accede, acquiesce, advocate, assent, back, bless, boost, consent, countenance, endorse, favor, obey, sanction, signature, support, take, undersign, underwrite; ▪ *Ant* be opposed, disagree, dissent.

subsequent [*adj*] *after* ▪ *Syn* consequential, ensuing, following, later, next, posterior, postliminary, resulting, serial, subsequential, succeeding, successive; ▪ *Ant* antecedent, earlier, former, previous, prior.

subsequently [adv] *afterward*
▪ *Syn* after, at a later date, behind, by and by, consequently, finally, in the aftermath, in the end, later, latterly, next; ▪ *Ant* earlier, former, prior.

subservient [adj1] *extremely compliant*
▪ *Syn* abject, acquiescent, cowering, cringing, deferential, docile, ignoble, inferior, menial, obeisant, resigned, servile, slavish, subject, submissive, sycophantic, toadying; ▪ *Ant* controlling, domineering, overbearing, rebellious.

subservient [adj2] *secondary, useful*
▪ *Syn* accessory, adjuvant, ancillary, auxiliary, collateral, contributory, inferior, minor, subordinate, subsidiary, supplemental; ▪ *Ant* unhelpful, unnecessary, useless.

subside [v] *die down; decrease*
▪ *Syn* abate, cave in, collapse, decline, de-escalate, die away, diminish, dwindle, ease off, ebb, fall, let up, lower, melt, moderate, quieten, recede, settle, slacken, taper, wane; ▪ *Ant* grow, increase, rise.

subsidiary [adj] *secondary, helpful*
▪ *Syn* accessory, ancillary, appurtenant, auxiliary, backup, branch, collateral, contributory, lesser, minor, subject, supplemental, supplementary; ▪ *Ant* chief, important, necessary.

subsist [v] *keep going, living*
▪ *Syn* breathe, continue, endure, exist, last, live, manage, move, remain, survive, sustain; ▪ *Ant* die, perish, starve.

substantial [adj1] *important, ample*
▪ *Syn* abundant, bulky, consequential, extraordinary, firm, generous, heavyweight, key, large, massive, material, plentiful, principal, significant, sizable, solid, sturdy, tidy, valuable, well-built, worthwhile; ▪ *Ant* insignificant, lightweight, meager, minor, poor, unimportant.

substantial [adj2] *material, real*
▪ *Syn* actual, concrete, corporeal, existent, objective, phenomenal, physical, righteous, sensible, solid, tangible, true, valid, visible, weighty; ▪ *Ant* ethereal, mental, spiritual.

substantial [adj3] *rich*
▪ *Syn* affluent, comfortable, easy, opulent, prosperous, snug, solid, solvent, wealthy, well, well-heeled, well-off, well-to-do; ▪ *Ant* impoverished, poor.

substantially [adv] *to a large extent*
▪ *Syn* considerably, essentially, extensively, heavily, in essence, in fact, in reality, in substance, in the main, largely, mainly, materially; ▪ *Ant* insignificantly, slightly.

substantiate [v] *back up a statement, idea* ▪ *Syn* affirm, approve, attest to, bear out, confirm, corroborate, establish, justify, manifest, objectify, personify, prove, ratify, reify, support, validate, verify; ▪ *Ant* controvert, disprove, refute, undermine.

substitute [n] *someone or something that takes the place of another* ▪ *Syn* agent, alternate, auxiliary, backup, delegate, expedient, fill-in, ghost writer, locum, proxy, relief, replacement, resort, stand-in, sub, surrogate, temporary, understudy; ▪ *Ant* original.

subtle [adj1] *nice, quiet, delicate*
▪ *Syn* attenuated, discriminating, ethereal, faint, finespun, hairline, implied, inconspicuous, inferred, ingenious, mental, penetrating, profound, refined, slight, suggestive, tenuous, thin, understated; ▪ *Ant* crude, direct, gross, heavy-handed, rough.

subtle [adj2] *clever, cunning*
▪ *Syn* analytical, artful, astute, complex, crafty, dexterous, exacting, foxy, guileful, insidious, keen, perceptive, scheming, shrewd, skillful, wily; ▪ *Ant* artless, awkward, bumbling, obvious.

subtract [v] *take away*
▪ *Syn* decrease, deduct, detract, diminish, discount, draw back, knock off, remove, take, take from, take off, take out, withdraw, withhold; ▪ *Ant* add, replenish.

suburb [n] *neighborhood outside of but reliant on nearby large city* ▪ *Syn* environs, fringe, outlying area, outpost, outskirts, precinct, purlieu, suburbia; ▪ *Ant* center, city, countryside, metropolis.

subversive [adj] *rebellious, destructive*
▪ *Syn* incendiary, inflammatory, insurgent, overthrowing, perversive, riotous, ruinous, seditious, treasonous, underground, undermining; ▪ *Ant* loyal, obedient.

subvert [v] *rebel, destroy*
▪ *Syn* capsize, corrupt, demolish, deprave, extinguish, invalidate, level, overthrow, pervert, poison, reverse, ruin, sabotage, topple, tumble, undermine, upset, vitiate, wreck; ▪ *Ant* comply support, encourage, promote, uphold.

succeed [v1] *attain good outcome*
▪ *Syn* accomplish, achieve, benefit, be

successful, conquer, distance, earn, flourish, fulfill, gain, get, master, obtain, outwit, overcome, prevail, prosper, realize, reap, recover, secure, surmount, triumph, vanquish, win; ▪ *Ant* default, fail, founder, miss.

succeed [*v2*] *come after; take the place of* ▪ *Syn* accede, assume, become heir to, come into, displace, ensue, enter upon, follow, inherit, postdate, replace, result, supersede, supplant, take over; ▪ *Ant* antedate, forerun, pave the way, precede.

succeeding/successive [*adj*] *following* ▪ *Syn* alternating, consecutive, ensuing, following after, next, next in line for, next off, next up, rotating, sequent, sequential, serial, subsequent, subsequential, succedent, successional; ▪ *Ant* antecedent, antedating, preceding, previous.

successful [*adj*] *favorable, profitable* ▪ *Syn* auspicious, booming, champion, extraordinary, flourishing, fortuitous, fruitful, lucrative, moneymaking, noteworthy, outstanding, prosperous, rewarding, strong, thriving, triumphant, victorious, wealthy; ▪ *Ant* unprofitable, unprosperous, unsuccessful.

succinct [*adj*] *brief, to the point* ▪ *Syn* blunt, breviloquent, brusque, compact, compendiary, concise, condensed, curt, laconic, pithy, short, summary, terse; ▪ *Ant* discursive, lengthy, long-winded, prolix, wordy.

succulent [*adj*] *juicy, delicious* ▪ *Syn* divine, heavenly, luscious, lush, mellow, moist, mouthwatering, pulpy, rich, sappy, tasty; ▪ *Ant* dessicated, dry, juiceless, withered.

succumb [*v*] *die or surrender* ▪ *Syn* accede, bow, buckle, capitulate, cave, croak, decease, defer, demise, expire, fall, fold, give in, go, go down, knuckle, pass away, perish, quit, submit, wilt, yield; ▪ *Ant* conquer, overcome, persevere, persist.

sudden [*adj*] *unexpected; happening quickly* ▪ *Syn* abrupt, accelerated, acute, expeditious, fast, flash, fleet, hasty, headlong, hurried, impetuous, impulsive, precipitate, precipitous, quick, rapid, rash, speeded, swift; ▪ *Ant* expected, slow.

suddenly [*adv*] *unexpectedly* ▪ *Syn* aback, abruptly, all at once, all of a sudden, forthwith, quickly, short,

swiftly, without warning; ▪ *Ant* expectedly, slowly.

suffering [*n*] *pain, agony* ▪ *Syn* adversity, affliction, anguish, difficulty, discomfort, distress, dolor, hardship, martyrdom, misery, misfortune, ordeal, passion, torment, torture; ▪ *Ant* happiness, health, joy.

suffice [*v*] *be adequate, enough* ▪ *Syn* answer, avail, be sufficient, content, do, get by, meet, meet requirement, satisfy, serve, suit; ▪ *Ant* disappoint, dissatisfy, fail, fall short.

sufficient [*adj*] *enough, adequate* ▪ *Syn* acceptable, agreeable, ample, comfortable, commensurate, copious, decent, due, galore, plentiful, satisfactory, sufficing, tolerable; ▪ *Ant* deficient, inadequate, insufficient, lacking, poor, wanting.

suffocate [*v*] *choke* ▪ *Syn* asphyxiate, drown, smother, stifle, strangle; ▪ *Ant* aid, foster, help, release.

suggest [*v1*] *convey advice, plan, desire* ▪ *Syn* advance, advocate, broach, commend, conjecture, exhort, move, offer, pose, proposition, recommend, steer, submit, theorize, tip; ▪ *Ant* declare, demand, order.

suggestive [*adj1*] *signifying* ▪ *Syn* evocative, expressive, intriguing, pregnant, redolent, reminiscent, symbolic, symptomatic; ▪ *Ant* empty, irrelevant, meaningless.

suggestive [*adj2*] *dirty, vulgar* ▪ *Syn* bawdy, broad, erotic, immodest, improper, indecent, indelicate, obscene, provocative, prurient, racy, ribald, risqué, rude, seductive, sexy, shady, tempting, titillating, unseemly, wicked; ▪ *Ant* clean, decent, delicate, moral, unprovocative.

suit [*v1*] *be acceptable, appropriate* ▪ *Syn* accord, agree, answer, become, befit, benefit, beseem, check, check out, conform, fulfill, go together, gratify, match, please, satisfy, serve, suffice, tally; ▪ *Ant* displease, dissatisfy.

suit [*v2*] *adapt, tailor* ▪ *Syn* accommodate, adjust, amuse, change, conform, entertain, fashion, fill, fit, fit in, gratify, modify, please, proportion, quadrate, readjust, reconcile, revise, satisfy, tailor-make; ▪ *Ant* be inappropriate to, disagree with.

suitable [*adj*] *appropriate, acceptable*
▪ *Syn* applicable, apposite, apt, befitting, copacetic, correct, due, expedient, felicitous, fitting, just, meet, opportune, pertinent, politic, proper, reasonable, right, satisfactory, seemly; ▪ *Ant* improper, inappropriate, irrelevant, unfitting, unsuitable.

sulk [*v*] *pout*
▪ *Syn* be morose, be silent, brood, frown, gloom, glower, gripe, grouse, look sullen, lower, scowl; ▪ *Ant* be happy, grin, smile.

sullen [*adj*] *brooding, upset*
▪ *Syn* bad-tempered, cheerless, churlish, cynical, dour, dull, fretful, frowning, gloomy, glowering, heavy, ill-humored, moody, morose, obstinate, peevish, pessimistic, petulant, pouting, querulous, somber, sourpussed, stubborn, sulking, surly, tenebrous; ▪ *Ant* bright, cheerful, grinning, happy.

sultry [*adj1*] *hot and humid*
▪ *Syn* baking, broiling, burning, close, hot, mucky, muggy, oppressive, scorching, sizzling, smothering, soggy, sticky, stifling, stuffy, suffocating, sweltering, sweltry, torrid, wet; ▪ *Ant* cool, dry.

sultry [*adj2*] *sensuous*
▪ *Syn* desirable, erotic, lurid, passionate, provocative, seductive, sexy, voluptuous; ▪ *Ant* cold, cool, frigid.

summarily [*adv*] *without delay*
▪ *Syn* arbitrarily, expeditiously, forthwith, immediately, on the spot, peremptorily, promptly, readily, speedily, swiftly, without waste; ▪ *Ant* lethargically, slowly.

summarize [*v*] *give a rundown*
▪ *Syn* abridge, compile, condense, cut, digest, encapsulate, inventory, outline, pare, précis, recapitulate, shorten, snip, synopsize, trim; ▪ *Ant* embroider, enlarge on, expand, flesh out.

summary [*adj*] *concise, to the point*
▪ *Syn* arbitrary, breviloquent, brief, compacted, compendiary, condensed, cursory, curt, hasty, laconic, perfunctory, rehashed, run-down, succinct, terse; ▪ *Ant* lengthy, long-winded, unabridged, wordy.

summon [*v*] *call to a place*
▪ *Syn* arouse, ask, beckon, bid, call, call forth, charge, command, conjure, convoke, draft, enjoin, gather, hail, invoke, mobilize, muster, order, petition, rally, rouse, send for, signal, subpoena, toll; ▪ *Ant* dismiss, send away.

sumptuous [*adj*] *luxurious, splendid*
▪ *Syn* awe-inspiring, beautiful, costly, dear, elegant, gorgeous, grand, impressive, lavish, luxuriant, magnificent, opulent, palatial, plush, pompous, posh, prodigal, profuse, rich, ritzy, superb, swank; ▪ *Ant* ordinary, plain.

sundry [*adj*] *miscellaneous*
▪ *Syn* assorted, different, divers, manifold, many, quite a few, several, some, varied, various; ▪ *Ant* homogeneous, regular, same, single, uniform.

sunny [*adj1*] *bright, clear (referring to weather)* ▪ *Syn* brilliant, clarion, cloudless, fine, light, luminous, pleasant, radiant, shiny, summery, sunlit, sunshiny; ▪ *Ant* cloudy, gloomy, rainy, stormy.

sunny [*adj2*] *happy*
▪ *Syn* beaming, blithe, buoyant, cheerful, chirpy, genial, joyful, lighthearted, lightsome, optimistic, pleasant, smiling, sunbeamy; ▪ *Ant* gloomy, sorrowful, sullen.

super [*adj*] *excellent*
▪ *Syn* divine, glorious, great, incomparable, keen, marvelous, neat, outstanding, peerless, sensational, smashing, superb, terrific, top-notch, wonderful; ▪ *Ant* commonplace, mediocre, prosaic.

superb [*adj*] *excellent, first-rate*
▪ *Syn* admirable, august, best, choice, elevated, exquisite, fine, glorious, grand, lofty, magnificent, matchless, noble, optimum, outstanding, peerless, resplendent, solid, splendid, standout, stunning, sublime, superlative, unrivaled, very best; ▪ *Ant* bad, inferior, poor, second-rate.

supercilious [*adj*] *arrogant, stuck-up*
▪ *Syn* bossy, condescending, contemptuous, disdainful, egotistic, haughty, imperious, lofty, overbearing, proud, scornful, superior, vainglorious; ▪ *Ant* humble, modest.

superficial [*adj*] *without depth, detail*
▪ *Syn* apparent, cosmetic, cursory, depthless, empty, external, frivolous, glib, hasty, lightweight, one-dimensional, ostensible, partial, passing, peripheral, seeming, shallow, sketchy, slight, smattery, surface, trivial; ▪ *Ant* analytical, careful, deep, detailed, earnest, genuine, profound, thorough.

superficially [*adv*] *lightly; without care*
▪ *Syn* apparently, at first glance, casually,

extraneously, flimsily, frivolously, hastily, ignorantly, ostensibly, partially; ▪ *Ant* carefully, deeply, thoroughly.

superfluous [adj] *extra, unnecessary*
▪ *Syn* abounding, dispensable, excess, exorbitant, expendable, gratuitous, inordinate, leftover, needless, nonessential, overflowing, profuse, redundant, spare, superfluent, surplus, useless; ▪ *Ant* important, necessary, needed.

superior [adj1] *better, greater, higher; excellent* ▪ *Syn* above, capital, choice, dandy, deluxe, distinguished, exceeding, excellent, exceptional, exclusive, expert, famous, fine, finer, first-class, first-rate, first-string, good, good quality, grander, high-caliber, high-class, major, more advanced, noteworthy, of higher rank, over, overlying, paramount, predominant, preferable, preferred, premium, prevailing, primary, remarkable, senior, surpassing, unrivaled; ▪ *Ant* inferior, lower, minor, poor.

superior [adj2] *arrogant, haughty*
▪ *Syn* bossy, cavalier, condescending, cool, disdainful, insolent, lofty, lordly, overbearing, patronizing, pretentious, proud, snobbish, supercilious; ▪ *Ant* humble, meek.

superlative [adj] *excellent, first-class*
▪ *Syn* accomplished, best, capital, consummate, crack, effusive, exaggerated, excessive, extreme, finished, greatest, highest, inflated, magnificent, matchless, optimum, outstanding, peerless, superb, supreme, surpassing, transcendent, winner, world-class; ▪ *Ant* poor, second-class, unexceptional.

supernatural [adj] *mysterious, not of this world* ▪ *Syn* abnormal, celestial, concealed, dark, fabulous, fairy, ghostly, heavenly, hidden, impenetrable, invisible, legendary, metaphysical, miraculous, mystic, mythical, mythological, numinous, obscure, occult, paranormal, phantom, phenomenal, preternatural, psychic, rare, secret, spectral, superior, supermundane, supranatural, transcendental, uncanny, unearthly, unknown, unusual; ▪ *Ant* earthly, existent, genuine, natural, real, true.

supersede [v] *take the place of; override*
▪ *Syn* abandon, annul, desert, discard, displace, forsake, oust, outmode, outplace, overrule, reject, remove, replace, repudiate, set aside, succeed, supplant,

suspend, take over, usurp; ▪ *Ant* accept, acknowledge.

supervise [v] *manage people, project*
▪ *Syn* administer, be responsible for, boss, chaperon, conduct, control, deal with, direct, handle, inspect, look after, overlook, oversee, preside over, run, superintend, survey; ▪ *Ant* follow, obey, serve.

supple [adj] *bendable*
▪ *Syn* adaptable, agile, bending, ductile, elastic, flexible, graceful, limber, lissome, lithe, lithesome, malleable, moldable, plastic, pliable, pliant, resilient, rubber, springy, stretchy, svelte, willowy, yielding; ▪ *Ant* hard, inflexible, rigid, stiff.

supplement [v] *add to*
▪ *Syn* augment, build up, buttress, complement, complete, enhance, enrich, extend, fill out, fill up, fortify, improve, increase, reinforce, step up, strengthen, subsidize, supply, top; ▪ *Ant* detract, subtract.

supply [v] *furnish, provide, give a resource* ▪ *Syn* afford, cater, contribute, deliver, dispense, drop, endow, equip, feed, fill, fulfill, grant, hand over, minister, outfit, produce, provide, provision, purvey, replenish, satisfy, stake, stock, store, transfer, turn over, victual, yield; ▪ *Ant* seize, take.

support [v1] *hold up*
▪ *Syn* base, be a foundation for, bear, bolster, bottom, brace, buttress, carry, cradle, crutch, embed, found, ground, hold, keep up, mainstay, poise, prop, reinforce, shore, shore up, shoulder, stand, stay, strut, sustain, undergird, upbear, uphold; ▪ *Ant* let down, let go, release.

support [v2] *take care of, provide for*
▪ *Syn* attend to, back, bankroll, buoy up, care for, cherish, encourage, feed, finance, fortify, foster, fund, guard, keep, look after, maintain, nourish, nurse, prop, raise, sponsor, stake, strengthen, stroke, subsidize, succor, sustain, underwrite, uphold; ▪ *Ant* abandon, neglect, shirk.

support [v3] *defend, advocate belief*
▪ *Syn* abet, advance, aid, assist, back, bear out, bolster, boost, carry, champion, cheer, comfort, countenance, endorse, establish, forward, foster, help, hold, justify, maintain, plead for, promote, pull for, put forward, rally round, second,

side with, stand behind, stand up for, stay, substantiate, sustain, uphold, verify; ▪ *Ant* contradict, disapprove, oppose.

support [v4] *endure*
▪ *Syn* abide, bear, bear with, brook, continue, countenance, handle, maintain, stand, submit, suffer, take, tolerate, undergo; ▪ *Ant* bypass, escape, surrender to.

suppose [v1] *assume, guess; believe*
▪ *Syn* conclude, conjecture, divine, dream, expect, figure, guess, hypothesize, imagine, opine, posit, predicate, presume, presuppose, pretend, speculate, surmise, suspect, theorize, think, understand; ▪ *Ant* calculate, know, measure.

suppress [v] *restrain, hold in check*
▪ *Syn* abolish, bottle, burke, censor, check, clamp, conceal, contain, cover up, crack down on, crush, curb, cut off, extinguish, hold back, hold down, hold in, keep in, keep secret, muffle, muzzle, overpower, put down, quash, quell, quench, repress, silence, smother, spike, stifle, stop, subdue, trample, withhold; ▪ *Ant* express, let go, release.

supreme [adj] *greatest, principal*
▪ *Syn* absolute, best, cardinal, chief, crowning, excellent, extreme, foremost, head, highest, incomparable, leading, master, matchless, maximum, paramount, peerless, perfect, predominant, preeminent, prevailing, prime, sovereign, superb, superlative, top, towering, transcendent, ultimate, utmost; ▪ *Ant* inferior, least, littlest, lowly, minor, poor.

sure [adj1] *certain, definite*
▪ *Syn* clear, constant, convinced, decided, enduring, fixed, genuine, incontrovertible, indisputable, never-failing, real, set, steady, telling, undeniable, unequivocal, valid; ▪ *Ant* doubtful, dubious, indefinite, uncertain, unsure, variable, wavering.

sure [adj2] *physically stable*
▪ *Syn* fast, firm, fixed, safe, secure, solid, staunch, steady, strong; ▪ *Ant* inaccurate, swerving, unsteady, unsure, wavering, wobbly.

sure [adj3] *inevitable*
▪ *Syn* assured, bound, certain, guaranteed, indisputable, inerrant, infallible, irrevocable, surefire, unavoidable; ▪ *Ant* doubtful, dubious, insecure, unsure.

sure [adj4] *self-confident*
▪ *Syn* assured, certain, composed, confi-

dent, decided, decisive, positive, self-assured, self-possessed; ▪ *Ant* humbled, insecure, uncertain.

surely [adv] *without doubt*
▪ *Syn* assuredly, absolutely, beyond doubt, certainly, decidedly, doubtlessly, evidently, explicitly, for certain, indeed, inevitably, infallibly, irrefutably, manifestly, plainly, to be sure, with certainty, without fail; ▪ *Ant* doubtfully, questionably, uncertain.

surface [adj] *external*
▪ *Syn* apparent, covering, depthless, exterior, outer, outside, outward, shallow, shoal, superficial, top; ▪ *Ant* central, core, interior, internal, median, middle.

surface [v] *come to the top of*
▪ *Syn* appear, arise, come to light, come up, crop up, emerge, flare up, materialize, rise, transpire; ▪ *Ant* dive, drop, fall, sink, submerge.

surfeit [n] *excess*
▪ *Syn* excess, overabundance, overflow, plenitude, plethora, profusion, remainder, satiety, satisfaction, saturation, superfluity, surplus; ▪ *Ant* paucity; lack, shortage, want.

surly [adj] *gruff, bearish*
▪ *Syn* boorish, brusque, churlish, cross, curmudgeonly, discourteous, dour, fractious, glum, ill-mannered, ill-natured, irritable, morose, perverse, rude, saturnine, sulky, sullen, testy; ▪ *Ant* amiable, cordial, gentle, pleasant.

surmise [v] *come to a conclusion*
▪ *Syn* assume, conclude, conjecture, consider, deduce, fancy, guess, hypothesize, imagine, infer, opine, presume, pretend, regard, speculate, suppose, suspect, theorize, think; ▪ *Ant* question, wonder.

surmount [v] *overcome, triumph over*
▪ *Syn* best, better, cap, clear, conquer, defeat, down, master, outdo, outstrip, overpower, pass, prevail over, rise above, subdue, surpass, vanquish, vault; ▪ *Ant* fail, lose, surrender, yield.

surpass [v] *outdo something or someone*
▪ *Syn* beat, best, cap, eclipse, exceed, go beyond, improve upon, outdistance, outperform, outshine, override, overshadow, pass, surmount, top, tower, transcend; ▪ *Ant* fail, fall behind, lose.

surplus [adj] *extra*
▪ *Syn* excess, leftover, remaining, spare, superfluent, superfluous, supernumerary, unused; ▪ *Ant* lacking, needing, wanting.

surprise [v1] *astonish; cause amazement*
▪ *Syn* amaze, astound, awe, bewilder, cause wonder, confound, confuse, consternate, daze, dazzle, discomfit, disconcert, dumbfound, electrify, flabbergast, floor, jar, jolt, leave aghast, nonplus, overwhelm, perplex, petrify, rattle, rock, shake up, shock, stagger, startle, strike with awe, stun, stupefy, take aback; ▪ *Ant* expect.

surprise [v2] *sneak up on; catch*
▪ *Syn* ambush, burst in on, capture, catch off guard, drop in on, lay for, spring on, startle, take, take by surprise, waylay; ▪ *Ant* alert, forewarn, warn.

surrender [v] *give up; resign*
▪ *Syn* abandon, capitulate, cede, concede, consign, deliver up, entrust, fall, fold, forego, give in, go under, hand over, knuckle, leave, let go, part with, quit, relinquish, renounce, submit, succumb, waive, yield; ▪ *Ant* keep, retain.

surreptitious [adj] *sneaky, secret*
▪ *Syn* clandestine, covert, fraudulent, furtive, hidden, private, skulking, slinking, sly, sneaking, stealthy, sub-rosa, undercover, underhand, veiled; ▪ *Ant* aboveboard, authorized, honest, open.

surrogate [n] *person or thing that acts as substitute* ▪ *Syn* agent, alternate, backup, delegate, deputy, expediency, expedient, fill-in, makeshift, proxy, refuge, replacement, representative, resort, resource, stand-in; ▪ *Ant* original, real.

survive [v] *continue to live*
▪ *Syn* bear, carry on, come through, endure, get through, handle, keep, last, live, live out, live through, outlast, persevere, persist, pull through, recover, remain, see through, suffer, sustain, weather, withstand; ▪ *Ant* cease, die, perish, succumb to.

susceptible [adj] *exposed, naive*
▪ *Syn* affected, aroused, disposed, gullible, impressionable, influenced, liable, open, predisposed, prone, ready, receptive, responsive, sensitive, sentient, soft, subject, swayed, sympathetic, tender, touched, vulnerable, wide open; ▪ *Ant* immune, resistant, resisting.

suspect [adj] *doubtful*
▪ *Syn* doubtable, dubious, incredible, problematic, questionable, ridiculous, suspicious; ▪ *Ant* innocent, known, trusted, trustworthy.

suspect [v] *distrust; guess*
▪ *Syn* assume, believe, conceive, conclude, conjecture, disbelieve, doubt, expect, imagine, mistrust, presume, reckon, speculate, surmise, think, understand, wonder; ▪ *Ant* believe, know, trust.

suspend [v] *delay, hold off*
▪ *Syn* adjourn, arrest, break up, check, defer, discontinue, halt, inactivate, interrupt, lay aside, postpone, protract, put off, retard, rule out, shelve, waive, withhold; ▪ *Ant* advance, continue, persist, push forward, sustain.

suspense [n] *anticipation*
▪ *Syn* anticipation, anxiety, apprehension, confusion, curiosity, dilemma, doubt, eagerness, expectancy, expectation, insecurity, irresolution, perplexity, tension, uncertainty, wavering; ▪ *Ant* certainty, knowledge.

suspicious [adj1] *distrustful*
▪ *Syn* apprehensive, careful, cautious, doubtful, incredulous, in doubt, leery, mistrustful, questioning, quizzical, skeptical, suspect, wary, watchful, wondering; ▪ *Ant* confident, trusting.

suspicious [adj2] *doubtful, fishy*
▪ *Syn* debatable, disputable, doubtable, dubious, equivocal, farfetched, irregular, open to doubt, peculiar, phony, problematic, queer, questionable, shady, suspect; ▪ *Ant* aboveboard, open, unquestionable.

sustain [v1] *keep up, maintain*
▪ *Syn* assist, back, bankroll, bear, befriend, bolster, brace, buoy, buttress, carry, comfort, confirm, continue, convey, defend, endorse, favor, feed, foster, help, keep alive, nourish, nurse, nurture, pack, preserve, prolong, prop, protract, provide for, ratify, relieve, save, shore up, stand by, stick up for, supply, support, tote, transfer, uphold, validate; ▪ *Ant* abandon, destroy, undermine.

sustain [v2] *endure, experience*
▪ *Syn* abide, bear, bear up under, bear with, brook, digest, hang in, stand up to, suffer, tolerate, undergo, withstand; ▪ *Ant* give up, succumb, surrender.

svelte [adj] *thin and well-built*
▪ *Syn* graceful, lean, lissome, slender, slinky, smooth, sylphlike, willowy; ▪ *Ant* chubby, corpulent, fat, thick.

swagger [v] *show off; walk pompously*
▪ *Syn* bluster, boast, brag, brandish, cock, flourish, gasconade, gloat, hector,

parade, pontificate, put on, strut, sweep, swell; ▪ **Ant** creep, slink, sneak.

swallow [v1] *consume*
▪ **Syn** devour, down, drink, eat, gulp, imbibe, ingest, ingurgitate, quaff, sip, slurp, take; ▪ **Ant** expel, regurgitate, spit out.

swallow [v2] *believe without much thought* ▪ **Syn** accept, be naive, buy, fall for; ▪ **Ant** disbelieve, doubt.

swamp [v] *overwhelm, flood*
▪ **Syn** besiege, crowd, drench, engulf, inundate, overflow, saturate, sink, submerge, swallow up, whelm; ▪ **Ant** deliver, pass up, rescue, save.

swank/swanky [adj] *plush, stylish*
▪ **Syn** classy, deluxe, exclusive, fancy, flamboyant, grand, lavish, ostentatious, posh, rich, showy, splashy, sumptuous, trendy; ▪ **Ant** dowdy, fruppy, modest, old-fashioned.

swap/swop [v] *exchange*
▪ **Syn** bandy, barter, change, interchange, substitute, switch, traffic, truck; ▪ **Ant** keep, maintain.

swarthy [adj] *dark-complexioned*
▪ **Syn** black, brown, brunet, dark, dark-skinned, exotic, swart, tan, tawny; ▪ **Ant** blonde, fair, light, pale.

sway [v1] *move back and forth*
▪ **Syn** bend, careen, fluctuate, incline, lean, oscillate, pendulate, rock, swagger, swing, undulate, vibrate, wave, weave, wobble; ▪ **Ant** remain still, stay, steady.

sway [v2] *influence, affect*
▪ **Syn** bias, brainwash, control, direct, govern, hook, impress, induce, inspire, move, overrule, predispose, reign, strike, touch, win over; ▪ **Ant** dissuade, impede, restrain.

sweat [v] *worry about*
▪ **Syn** agonize, brook, chafe, exert, fret, labor, suffer, take, toil, torture over; ▪ **Ant** be calm, ignore.

sweaty [adj] *damp with perspiration*
▪ **Syn** clammy, drenched, dripping, glowing, hot, moist, perspiring, soaked, sticky, stinky, sweating, wet; ▪ **Ant** dry.

sweeping [adj] *wide-ranging*
▪ **Syn** all-encompassing, all-inclusive, broad, comprehensive, exhaustive, general, inclusive, overall, radical, thorough, vast, wide; ▪ **Ant** exclusive, narrow, superficial.

sweet [adj1] *sugary*
▪ **Syn** candied, cloying, delicious, honeyed, like candy, luscious, nectarous, saccharine, sugared, sweetened, syrupy, toothsome; ▪ **Ant** acid, bitter, salty, sour.

sweet [adj2] *friendly, kind*
▪ **Syn** affectionate, amiable, appealing, beautiful, companionable, darling, dear, delectable, delightful, dulcet, engaging, generous, gentle, good-humored, lovable, pleasant, precious, sympathetic, tender, thoughtful, winning; ▪ **Ant** acrimonious, dour, grouchy, mean, unpleasant.

sweet [adj3] *nice-smelling*
▪ **Syn** ambrosial, aromatic, balmy, clean, fragrant, fresh, new, perfumed, pure, scented, wholesome; ▪ **Ant** malodorous, rancid, sour, unsavory.

sweet [adj4] *nice-sounding*
▪ **Syn** dulcet, euphonic, harmonious, mellifluous, melodious, musical, orotund, rich, silvery, sonorous, soothing, tuneful; ▪ **Ant** cacophonous, discordant, shrill.

sweeten [v1] *make happy; appease*
▪ **Syn** alleviate, assuage, conciliate, mollify, pacify, placate, propitiate, soften up, soothe; ▪ **Ant** displease, disrupt, trouble, undermine, worry.

swell [adj] *wonderful*
▪ **Syn** awesome, dandy, deluxe, desirable, excellent, exclusive, fashionable, fine, grand, keen, marvelous, neat, nifty, plush, posh, smart, stylish, super, terrific; ▪ **Ant** bad, horrible, shabby.

swell [v] *become larger*
▪ **Syn** amplify, balloon, become distended, belly, billow, bloat, bulge, dilate, distend, enlarge, expand, extend, fatten, grow, heighten, increase, mount, plump, protrude, puff up, rise, round out, surge, tumefy, well up; ▪ **Ant** compress, concentrate, contract, shrink.

sweltering [adj] *very hot*
▪ **Syn** airless, baking, broiling, close, fiery, humid, oppressive, scorching, sizzling, sticky, stuffy, sultry, sweltry, torrid; ▪ **Ant** cold, cool, freezing.

swerve [v] *turn aside, often to avoid collision* ▪ **Syn** bend, deflect, depart from, deviate, dip, diverge, err, incline, lurch, move, sheer, sidestep, swing, tack, veer, waver, wind; ▪ **Ant** make a beeline, straighten.

swift [adj] *very fast*
▪ **Syn** alacritous, barreling, breakneck, expeditious, express, fleet, hasty, nimble, precipitate, prónto, quick, rapid, speedy,

supersonic, unexpected; • *Ant* delayed, slow, sluggish.

swiftly/swift [*adv*] *very fast*
• *Syn* apace, expeditiously, fleetly, hastily, hurriedly, posthaste, promptly, quick, quickly, rapidly, speedily; • *Ant* slowly, sluggishly.

swimmingly [*adv*] *very well*
• *Syn* as planned, cosily, easily, effortlessly, favorably, happily, prosperously, smoothly, successfully, well, with no trouble; • *Ant* poorly, unsuccessfully.

swollen [*adj*] *enlarged*
• *Syn* bloated, bulgy, distended, distent, inflamed, inflated, puffed, puffy, tumescent, tumid; • *Ant* compressed, contracted, shrunken.

swoop [*v*] *descend quickly*
• *Syn* dive, fall, plummet, plunge, pounce, rush, slide, stoop, sweep; • *Ant* ascend.

symmetrical [*adj*] *well-proportioned*
• *Syn* balanced, commensurable, commensurate, equal, in proportion, proportional, regular, shapely, well-formed; • *Ant* asymmetrical, different, disproportioned, irregular, uneven.

sympathetic [*adj1*] *concerned, feeling*
• *Syn* affectionate, benign, caring, compassionate, considerate, interested, kind, loving, pitying, responsive, sensitive, soft, sympathizing, tender, thoughtful, understanding, vicarious, warm; • *Ant* callous, merciless, unconcerned, unfeeling.

sympathetic [*adj2*] *agreeable, friendly*
• *Syn* amenable, compatible, congenial, congruous, encouraging, favorably disposed, like-minded, receptive, simpatico, vicarious, well-disposed; • *Ant* cold, cool, disagreeable, unfriendly, unsociable, unsympathetic.

sympathize [*v*] *feel for, be compassionate* • *Syn* ache, agree, appreciate, be in accord, be in sympathy, be understanding, comfort, commiserate, emphathize, grieve with, offer consolation, pity, share another's sorrow, show kindliness, show tenderness, understand; • *Ant* disapprove, disregard, ignore.

synonymous [*adj*] *equivalent*
• *Syn* alike, apposite, coincident, compatible, convertible, correspondent, corresponding, equal, identical, identified, interchangeable, like, one and the same, same, similar, synonymic, tantamount; • *Ant* antonymous, different, dissimilar, opposite, polar, unequal.

synthesize [*v*] *combine; make whole*
• *Syn* amalgamate, arrange, blend, harmonize, incorporate, integrate, manufacture, orchestrate, symphonize, unify; • *Ant* decompose, dissect, divide, separate.

synthetic [*adj*] *artificial*
• *Syn* counterfeit, fabricated, factitious, fake, false, makeshift, man-made, manufactured, mock, phony, plastic, unnatural; • *Ant* genuine, natural, real.

systematic [*adj*] *orderly*
• *Syn* analytical, arranged, businesslike, complete, efficient, logical, methodic, methodical, ordered, organized, precise, regular, standardized, systematized, thoroughgoing, well-ordered; • *Ant* chaotic, confused, disorderly, sloppy.

systematize [*v*] *put in order*
• *Syn* arrange, array, contrive, design, devise, dispose, establish, frame, institute, marshal, methodize, order, organize, plan, project, pull together, regulate, schematize, shape up, standardize; • *Ant* confuse, disorder, disorganize, mix up.

T

table [*v*] *postpone a proposition*
• *Syn* defer, delay, enter, hold off, hold up, move, propose, put aside, put forward, put off, put on hold, shelve, submit, suggest; • *Ant* act on, decide, initiate, vote.

taboo [*adj*] *not allowed, permitted*
• *Syn* anathema, banned, disapproved, forbidden, illegal, outlawed, prohibited, restricted, ruled out; • *Ant* acceptable, allowed, mentionable.

tabulate [*v*] *figure, classify*
• *Syn* alphabetize, arrange, catalog, categorize, codify, digest, enumerate, grade, index, list, methodize, order, range, register, systematize; • *Ant* confuse, disorganize, jumble, mix.

tacit [*adj*] *taken for granted; not said aloud* • *Syn* alluded to, assumed, hinted at, implicit, implied, indirect, inferred, intimated, suggested, understood, unexpressed, wordless; • *Ant* explicit, express.

taciturn [*adj*] *uncommunicative*
• *Syn* aloof, antisocial, brooding, close, distant, dour, laconic, mum, mute, quiet, reserved, reticent, sententious, silent,

withdrawn; ▪ *Ant* communicative, fluent, talkative, wordy.

tack [*v*] *attach*
▪ *Syn* add, affix, annex, baste, fasten, hem, mount, nail, paste, sew, staple, tag, tie; ▪ *Ant* detach, separate, unfasten, untack.

tackle [*v1*] *make an effort*
▪ *Syn* apply oneself, attempt, devote oneself to, embark upon, launch, pitch into, set about, take on, undertake, work on; ▪ *Ant* avoid, dodge, evade, neglect, postpone.

tackle [*v2*] *jump on and grab*
▪ *Syn* attack, block, catch, clutch, down, grapple, intercept, nail, sack, seize, take, take hold of, throw down; ▪ *Ant* avoid, dodge.

tacky [*adj*] *cheap, tasteless*
▪ *Syn* broken-down, crude, dilapidated, faded, gaudy, inelegant, messy, ratty, run-down, slovenly, threadbare, unkempt, vulgar; ▪ *Ant* expensive, neat, tasteful.

tactful [*adj*] *thoughtful, careful*
▪ *Syn* adroit, aware, cautious, courteous, deft, delicate, diplomatic, discreet, gentle, judicious, observant, perceptive, poised, polished, polite, politic, prudent, sensitive, subtle, sympathetic, urbane, wise; ▪ *Ant* boorish, careless, indiscreet, rude.

tactless [*adj*] *unthinking, careless*
▪ *Syn* awkward, blundering, boorish, bungling, clumsy, discourteous, gauche, hasty, impolite, imprudent, indelicate, inept, injudicious, insensitive, maladroit, rash, thoughtless, vulgar; ▪ *Ant* careful, discreet, tactful, thoughtful.

tailor [*v*] *make fit; adjust*
▪ *Syn* accommodate, adapt, alter, conform, convert, custom-make, cut, cut to fit, fashion, fit, make to order, modify, mold, reconcile, shape, shape up, square, style, suit; ▪ *Ant* leave alone, let be.

taint [*v*] *dirty, contaminate; ruin*
▪ *Syn* besmirch, blacken, blemish, blight, blot, blur, brand, cloud, cook, corrupt, damage, debase, defile, deprave, discolor, discredit, disgrace, dishonor, foul, harm, hurt, infect, muddy, poison, pollute, putrefy, rot, shame, smear, soil, spike, spoil, stain, stigmatize, sully, tar, tarnish, trash; ▪ *Ant* clean, exalt, purify, strengthen.

take [*v1*] *get; help oneself to*
▪ *Syn* acquire, attain, capture, carry off, carve out, catch, clasp, clutch, earn, ensnare, entrap, gain possession, gather up, get hold of, grab, grasp, grip, haul in, lay hold of, obtain, pick up, prehend, pull in, reap, seize, snag, snatch, strike, take hold of, take in; ▪ *Ant* give, put.

take [*v2*] *steal*
▪ *Syn* abduct, abstract, accroach, annex, appropriate, arrogate, carry off, commandeer, confiscate, expropriate, misappropriate, pluck, preempt, purloin, salvage, seize, sequester, snag, snare, take in; ▪ *Ant* give up, restore, return, surrender, yield.

take [*v3*] *buy; reserve*
▪ *Syn* borrow, choose, cull, decide on, derive, elect, gain, hire, lease, obtain, pick, prefer, procure, rent, select, single out; ▪ *Ant* refuse, reject.

take [*v4*] *endure*
▪ *Syn* abide, accommodate, bear, brave, brook, go through, hold, live with, put up with, receive, stand, stomach, suffer, swallow, tolerate, undergo, weather, withstand; ▪ *Ant* avoid, be defeated by, dodge, surrender to.

take [*v5*] *consume*
▪ *Syn* devour, down, drink, eat, feed, feed on, imbibe, ingest, inhale, partake of, swallow; ▪ *Ant* abstain.

take [*v6*] *accept, adopt; use*
▪ *Syn* accommodate, appropriate, bring, effect, execute, exercise, luxuriate in, observe, perform, put in practice, relish, undertake, utilize, welcome; ▪ *Ant* disallow, refuse, reject.

take [*v7*] *understand*
▪ *Syn* accept, apprehend, be aware of, believe, catch, comprehend, deem, expect, follow, grasp, hold, interpret as, look upon, perceive, reckon, see, sense, suppose, think; ▪ *Ant* misconceive, misunderstand.

take [*v8*] *win; be successful*
▪ *Syn* beat, do the trick, have effect, operate, prevail, succeed, triumph, work; ▪ *Ant* fail, lose.

take [*v9*] *carry, transport; accompany*
▪ *Syn* attend, bear, bring, cart, convoy, drive, escort, ferry, go with, guide, haul, journey, lug, move, pack, ride, shoulder, tote, trek, truck, usher; ▪ *Ant* hold, keep, maintain.

take [*v10*] *captivate, enchant*
▪ *Syn* allure, attract, bewitch, charm, delight, draw, entertain, fascinate, magne-

tize, overwhelm, please, wile, win favor;
▪ *Ant* disenchant, repulse.

take [*v11*] *subtract*
▪ *Syn* deduct, discount, eliminate, knock off, remove, subtract, take away, take off, take out; ▪ *Ant* add, tack on.

take [*v12*] *cheat, deceive*
▪ *Syn* bilk, con, cozen, defraud, dupe, fiddle, gull, hoodwink, swindle, trick; ▪ *Ant* apprise, deal squarely with.

take [*v13*] *contract, catch*
▪ *Syn* be seized, derive, draw, get, sicken with, take sick with; ▪ *Ant* avoid, fight off, repel.

take down [*v*] *humble*
▪ *Syn* deflate, humiliate, let down, lower, mortify, pull down, put down, take apart; ▪ *Ant* build up, encourage.

take in [*v*] *understand*
▪ *Syn* absorb, assimilate, comprehend, digest, get, grasp, perceive, receive, savvy, see, soak up; ▪ *Ant* misconceive, misunderstand.

take off [*v*] *leave; leave the ground*
▪ *Syn* ascend, beat it, blast off, decamp, depart, disappear, exit, get out, lift off, pull out, quit, split, withdraw; ▪ *Ant* arrive, come, stay.

take on [*v*] *assume, accept*
▪ *Syn* acquire, adopt, annex, append, attempt, begin, commence, develop, embrace, endeavor, enlist, enroll, handle, launch, retain, set about, tackle, try, turn, undertake, venture; ▪ *Ant* refuse, reject.

take up [*v*] *begin or start again*
▪ *Syn* adopt, assume, become involved in, carry on, commence, continue, embrace, engage in, enter, espouse, follow through, get off, go on, initiate, kick off, open, pick up, proceed, recommence, renew, reopen, restart, resume, set to, start, tackle, take on, tee off, undertake; ▪ *Ant* complete, conclude, end, finish.

talk [*v1*] *produce words; inform*
▪ *Syn* articulate, babble, chat, chatter, communicate, converse, describe, drawl, drone, express, gab, give voice to, gossip, intone, parley, patter, prate, pronounce, rhapsodize, say, soliloquize, speak, spout, tell, utter, verbalize, voice; ▪ *Ant* be mute, be silent, listen.

talk [*v2*] *discuss with another*
▪ *Syn* argue, carry on conversation, collogue, commune, confabulate, confer, confide, consult, contact, deliberate, dialogue, exchange, hold discussion, in-

teract, interface, interview, join in conversation, palaver, parley, reach out, reason, relate, vent, visit; ▪ *Ant* be silent.

talk [*v3*] *address group*
▪ *Syn* discourse, give a talk, give speech, harangue, hold forth, induce, influence, lecture, orate, persuade, pitch, prelect, sermonize, speak; ▪ *Ant* attend, hear, listen.

talkative [*adj*] *excessively communicative* ▪ *Syn* articulate, chattering, effusive, eloquent, fluent, garrulous, loquacious, multiloquent, prolix, talky, verbal, verbose, vocal, voluble, wordy; ▪ *Ant* quiet, reserved, silent, uncommunicative.

tall [*adj1*] *high in stature, length*
▪ *Syn* alpine, big, elevated, great, high-reaching, lank, lofty, rangy, sky-high, skyscraping, soaring, towering; ▪ *Ant* diminutive, little, low, short, small.

tall [*adj2*] *exaggerated, unreasonable*
▪ *Syn* absurd, demanding, embellished, farfetched, hard, implausible, outlandish, preposterous, steep, unbelievable; ▪ *Ant* believable, reasonable, sensible.

tally [*v*] *add up; count, record*
▪ *Syn* catalog, compute, enumerate, inventory, itemize, keep score, mark, mark down, number, numerate, reckon, register, sum, tale, tell, total, write down; ▪ *Ant* subtract.

tame [*adj1*] *domesticated, compliant*
▪ *Syn* amenable, biddable, civilized, cultivated, docile, fearless, gentle, harmless, harnessed, kindly, manageable, meek, obedient, pliant, subdued, submissive, tractable, trained; ▪ *Ant* unmanageable, untamed, violent, wild.

tame [*adj2*] *dull, uninteresting*
▪ *Syn* bland, bloodless, boring, conventional, diluted, feeble, halfhearted, insipid, lifeless, monotonous, prosaic, routine, spiritless, tedious, vapid, weak, wearisome; ▪ *Ant* bright, exciting, interesting.

tame [*v*] *domesticate, make compliant*
▪ *Syn* break, bust, check, conquer, curb, discipline, enslave, gentle, housebreak, humble, master, mitigate, pacify, repress, subdue, subjugate, suppress, temper, tone down, train, vanquish; ▪ *Ant* animate, excite, heighten, provoke, sharpen.

tamper [*v*] *interfere, alter*
▪ *Syn* busybody, butt in, doctor, fiddle, fool, horn in, interfere, interlope, interpose, intrude, manipulate, meddle, pry,

tinker; ▪ *Ant* abstain from, leave alone, refrain.

tangible [*adj*] *real, concrete*
▪ *Syn* actual, appreciable, corporeal, definite, detectable, discernible, distinct, embodied, evident, factual, gross, incarnated, manifest, material, objective, observable, obvious, palpable, patent, perceivable, perceptible, phenomenal, physical, plain, positive, sensible, solid, stable, substantial, tactile, touchable, verifiable, visible, well-grounded; ▪ *Ant* abstract, conceptual, ethereal, imperceptible, intangible, unreal.

tangle [*v*] *knot, complicate*
▪ *Syn* catch, coil, confuse, derange, discompose, disorganize, embroil, enmesh, ensnare, entangle, entrap, hamper, implicate, interlace, interlock, intertwist, interweave, jam, kink, mat, mesh, obstruct, perplex, ravel, snarl, tie up, trap, twist, upset; ▪ *Ant* straighten, uncomplicate, untangle, untwist.

tantalize [*v*] *provoke, tease*
▪ *Syn* annoy, badger, baffle, bait, bedevil, beleaguer, charm, entice, fascinate, frustrate, gnaw, harass, harry, lead on, pester, plague, taunt, thwart, titillate, torment, torture, worry; ▪ *Ant* disenchant, gratify, repulse, satisfy, turn off.

tantamount [*adj*] *same*
▪ *Syn* alike, as good as, commensurate, equal, equivalent, identical, indistinguishable, like, parallel, same as, selfsame, synonymous, uniform; ▪ *Ant* different, opposite, polar, reverse.

tantrum [*n*] *fit*
▪ *Syn* anger, animosity, conniption, flareup, hysterics, outburst, temper, temper tantrum, wax; ▪ *Ant* calm, contentment, peace.

tap [*v1*] *hit lightly*
▪ *Syn* bob, palpate, pat, pat, peck, percuss, stroke, tip, touch; ▪ *Ant* slam, slap.

taper/taper off [*v*] *decrease to a point*
▪ *Syn* abate, bate, come to a point, die out, diminish, drain, dwindle, fade, lessen, narrow, recede, rescind, subside, thin, wane, weaken, wind down; ▪ *Ant* go up, increase, rise.

tardy [*adj*] *late*
▪ *Syn* behindhand, belated, delayed, delinquent, detained, dilatory, held up, jammed, laggard, overdue, procrastinating, sluggish; ▪ *Ant* early, on time, prompt, punctual, ready.

tarnish [*v*] *dirty, corrupt*
▪ *Syn* befoul, blemish, contaminate, damage, defile, disgrace, dull, harm, hurt, impair, lose luster, mar, muddy, pollute, rust, smear, smudge, soil, spot, stain, taint, vitiate; ▪ *Ant* clean, credit, enhance, glorify, polish.

tarry [*v*] *dawdle, delay*
▪ *Syn* abide, bide, dally, drag, filibuster, linger, loiter, pause, poke, remain, sojourn, stall, stop, tail, temporize, visit, wait; ▪ *Ant* carry on, complete, finish, go.

tart [*adj*] *bitter, sour in taste or effect*
▪ *Syn* accrbic, acetose, acid, acrimonious, astringent, barbed, biting, caustic, dry, harsh, nasty, pungent, scathing, snappy, snippy, tangy, testy, trenchant, vinegary; ▪ *Ant* sweet.

task [*v*] *assign, burden*
▪ *Syn* charge, encumber, entrust, exhaust, lade, load, oppress, overload, push, saddle, strain, tax, test, weary, weigh, weight; ▪ *Ant* absolve, aid, enhance, relieve, unburden.

taste [*v1*] *judge, try*
▪ *Syn* assay, differentiate, discern, distinguish, partake, perceive, relish, sample, savor, sense, sip, test, try; ▪ *Ant* abstain.

taste [*v2*] *experience*
▪ *Syn* appreciate, be exposed to, come up against, encounter, feel, have knowledge of, know, meet with, partake of, perceive, run up against, savor, undergo; ▪ *Ant* abstain, miss, refrain.

tasteful [*adj*] *nice, refined*
▪ *Syn* aesthetically pleasing, beautiful, chaste, classical, cultivated, delectable, exquisite, fastidious, fine, graceful, handsome, in good taste, pleasing, polished, posh, precise, quiet, restrained, rich, smart, stylish, subdued, swank; ▪ *Ant* gaudy, tasteless, tawdry, unrefined.

tasteless [*adj1*] *without flavor*
▪ *Syn* bland, boring, distasteful, flavorless, insipid, mild, plain, stale, tame, unappetizing, unsavory, vapid, watery, weak; ▪ *Ant* appetizing, flavorful, savory.

tasteless [*adj2*] *cheap, vulgar*
▪ *Syn* artificial, barbarous, crass, crude, flashy, gaudy, hideous, indecorous, indelicate, loud, ostentatious, showy, stupid, tacky, tawdry, trivial; ▪ *Ant* couth, moral, nice, tasteful.

tasty [*adj*] *delicious*
▪ *Syn* appetizing, delectable,. flavorful,

full-flavored, good-tasting, heavenly, luscious, mellow, palatable, piquant, sapid, scrumptious, tasteful, toothsome, yummy, zestful; ▪ *Ant* tasteless, unappetizing.

tattle [*v*] *gossip; tell rumor*
▪ *Syn* babble, chat, chatter, give away, gossip, jabber, leak, noise, prate, rumor, snitch, spill, squeal, talk, talk idly; ▪ *Ant* conceal, hide.

taunt [*v*] *provoke, reproach; tease*
▪ *Syn* affront, bother, deride, flout, insult, jeer, lout, mock, offend, put down, quiz, rally, ridicule, scorn, sneer, tantalize, torment, upbraid; ▪ *Ant* compliment, humor, praise, respect.

taut [*adj*] *rigid, tight*
▪ *Syn* close, firm, snug, strained, stressed, stretched, tense, tightly drawn, unbending, unyielding; ▪ *Ant* droopy, flabby, loose, relaxed, slack.

tawdry [*adj*] *cheap, tasteless*
▪ *Syn* brazen, crude, dirty, flashy, garish, glitzy, jazzy, loud, meretricious, obtrusive, poor, raffish, showy, tinsel, vulgar; ▪ *Ant* nice, sophisticated, tasteful.

tax [*v1*] *burden*
▪ *Syn* charge, drain, encumber, enervate, lade, make demands on, oppress, overburden, pressure, put pressure on, saddle, strain, task, try, wear out, weigh, weight; ▪ *Ant* alleviate, disburden, ease, lighten, relieve, unburden.

tax [*v2*] *accuse*
▪ *Syn* arraign, blame, censure, charge, criminate, impeach, impugn, impute, incriminate, inculpate, indict, reproach, reprove; ▪ *Ant* acquit, clear, exonerate, sue.

taxing [*adj*] *burdensome*
▪ *Syn* demanding, difficult, enervating, grievous, heavy, oppressive, punishing, sapping, tedious, tiring, trying, wearing, weighty; ▪ *Ant* easy, untroubling.

teach [*v*] *educate; instill knowledge*
▪ *Syn* advise, brief, catechize, coach, cram, demonstrate, direct, discipline, drill, edify, enlighten, exercise, explain, expound, give instruction, give lessons, ground, guide, illustrate, imbue, impart, implant, inculcate, indoctrinate, inform, initiate, instruct, lecture, nurture, prepare, school, sharpen, show, train, tutor; ▪ *Ant* absorb, learn, study.

tear [*v1*] *cut, rip an object*
▪ *Syn* claw, cleave, damage, fray, gash,

impair, injure, lacerate, mutilate, pull apart, rend, rift, rupture, scratch, shred, slash, slit, sunder, wrench, yank; ▪ *Ant* fix, mend, sew.

tear [*v2*] *move very fast*
▪ *Syn* bolt, career, charge, course, dash, fling, fly, gallop, hurry, race, run, rush, shoot, speed, spring, zoom; ▪ *Ant* amble, idle, stroll.

tearful [*adj*] *crying, very upset*
▪ *Syn* distressed, dolorous, in tears, lachrymose, lamenting, mournful, pathetic, poignant, sad, sobbing, sorrowful, teary, weeping, whimpering, woeful; ▪ *Ant* cheerful, happy.

tease [*v*] *aggravate, provoke*
▪ *Syn* annoy, badger, bedevil, beleaguer, chaff, devil, disturb, gibe, goad, harass, hector, importune, josh, mock, nudge, plague, rally, ridicule, slam, spoof, taunt, torment, vex, worry; ▪ *Ant* appease, flatter, humor, placate, soothe.

technical [*adj*] *concerning details, mechanics* ▪ *Syn* abstruse, industrial, mechanical, occupational, professional, restricted, scholarly, scientific, specialized, vocational; ▪ *Ant* accessible, commonplace, easily understood.

tedious [*adj*] *dull, monotonous*
▪ *Syn* arid, banal, boring, drab, dreary, enervating, insipid, irksome, laborious, lifeless, prosaic, slow, soporific, tiring, unexciting, uninteresting, vapid, wearisome; ▪ *Ant* entertaining, exciting, interesting.

teem [*v*] *be abundant, full*
▪ *Syn* abound, be crawling with, brim, bustle, crawl, crowd, flow, grow, jam, overflow, pack, produce, prosper, pullulate, rain, shower, swarm, swell, wallow in; ▪ *Ant* lack, need, want.

teeming [*adj*] *abundant, full*
▪ *Syn* alive, brimful, bursting, crammed, crawling, fruitful, multitudinous, numerous, overflowing, packed, plentiful, replete, swarming, thick, thronged; ▪ *Ant* empty, lacking, needing, wanting.

teeny/teensy [*adj*] *very small*
▪ *Syn* diminutive, microscopic, miniature, minuscule, minute, tiny; ▪ *Ant* big, enormous, huge, large.

teeter [*v*] *wobble back and forth*
▪ *Syn* dangle, falter, lurch, pivot, quiver, reel, seesaw, stammer, sway, topple, tremble, waver; ▪ *Ant* stabilize, steady.

tell [v1] *communicate*
▪ *Syn* acquaint, advise, authorize, bid, call upon, command, confess, declare, direct, divulge, enjoin, express, give facts, impart, inform, instruct, leak, let know, level, make known, notify, order, proclaim, put before, recite, report, reveal, say, speak, summon, utter; ▪ *Ant* conceal, hide, keep quiet, listen.

tell [v2] *narrate, describe*
▪ *Syn* chronicle, depict, express, give an account of, portray, recount, rehearse, relate, report, set forth, speak, state; ▪ *Ant* listen.

tell [v3] *understand, discern*
▪ *Syn* apprehend, ascertain, clinch, deduce, determine, differentiate, discover, discriminate, distinguish, divine, find out, identify, know, learn, make out, perceive, recognize, see; ▪ *Ant* confuse, misunderstand.

tell [v4] *calculate*
▪ *Syn* compute, count, count one by one, enumerate, number, numerate, reckon, tale, tally; ▪ *Ant* estimate, figure, guess.

telling [adj] *effective, significant*
▪ *Syn* cogent, considerable, conspicuous, convincing, crucial, decisive, effectual, forceful, important, impressive, influential, marked, operative, potent, powerful, solid, sound, striking, trenchant, valid, weighty; ▪ *Ant* ineffective, insignificant, secondary, trivial, unimportant.

tell off [v] *reprimand; criticize harshly*
▪ *Syn* berate, censure, chide, lecture, rail, rebuke, reproach, reprove, revile, scold, upbraid, vituperate; ▪ *Ant* compliment, praise.

temerity [n] *nerve, audacity*
▪ *Syn* boldness, carelessness, daring, effrontery, foolhardiness, forwardness, hardihood, hastiness, heedlessness, impertinence, imprudence, impudence, impulsiveness, indiscretion, intrepidity, intrusiveness, nerve, overconfidence, precipitancy, presumption, rashness, recklessness, rudeness; ▪ *Ant* care, caution, cowardice, forethought, hesitation.

temper [v1] *calm, moderate*
▪ *Syn* abate, allay, alleviate, assuage, cool, curb, dilute, ease, lessen, mitigate, modulate, mollify, pacify, palliate, relieve, restrain, soften, soothe, tone down, weaken; ▪ *Ant* aggravate, agitate, excite, infuriate, intensify, upset.

temper [v2] *harden*
▪ *Syn* anneal, bake, braze, cement, chill, congeal, dry, indurate, mold, petrify, set, solidify, starch, steel, stiffen, strengthen, toughen, toughen up; ▪ *Ant* flex, soften, weaken.

temperamental [adj] *angry most of the time; moody* ▪ *Syn* capricious, changeable, emotional, erratic, excitable, explosive, fickle, fiery, froward, headstrong, hypersensitive, impatient, inconsistent, irritable, mercurial, neurotic, ornery, petulant, sensitive, ticklish, touchy, uncertain, unreliable, unstable, variable, volatile, willful; ▪ *Ant* easygoing, happy, laid-back, peaceful, pleased.

temperate [adj1] *calm, moderate*
▪ *Syn* agreeable, balmy, checked, clement, collected, composed, conservative, constant, cool, curbed, discreet, dispassionate, equable, even, even-tempered, levelheaded, medium, mild, modest, pleasant, reasonable, regulated, restrained, self-controlled, sensible, sober, soft, stable, steady; ▪ *Ant* immoderate, stormy, violent.

temperate [adj2] *controlled, sober*
▪ *Syn* abstemious, abstentious, abstinent, continent, moderate, restrained, self-restraining; ▪ *Ant* drunk, excessive, inebriated.

tempestuous [adj] *wild, stormy*
▪ *Syn* agitated, blustery, emotional, excited, furious, gusty, heated, intense, passionate, raging, rough, rugged, storming, turbulent, violent, windy; ▪ *Ant* calm, gentle, mild, moderate.

temporal [adj1] *material, worldly*
▪ *Syn* banausic, earthly, fleshly, lay, mortal, nonspiritual, physical, secular, sensual, terrestrial; ▪ *Ant* mental, otherworldly, spiritual.

temporal [adj2] *momentary*
▪ *Syn* ephemeral, evanescent, fleeting, fugacious, fugitive, impermanent, momentary, passing, short-lived, temporary, transient, transitory; ▪ *Ant* endless, external, permanent, perpetual, unearthly.

temporary [adj] *lasting only a short while* ▪ *Syn* acting, ad hoc, ad interim, alternate, brief, changeable, ephemeral, evanescent, fleeting, fugitive, impermanent, limited, momentary, passing, pro tem, provisional, short-lived, substitute, supply, transient, volatile; ▪ *Ant* durable, enduring, everlasting, lasting, permanent, persisting, protracted.

tempt [v] *lure, entice*
▪ *Syn* allure, bait, captivate, coax, dare, draw, entrap, fascinate, incite, inveigle, lead on, motivate, persuade, promote, seduce, stimulate, tantalize, wheedle, whet; ▪ *Ant* discourage, repulse, turn off.

tempting [adj] *alluring, inviting*
▪ *Syn* appetizing, attractive, charming, divine, enticing, fascinating, fetching, heavenly, intriguing, luring, magnetic, provoking, rousing, scrumptious, seductive, tantalizing; ▪ *Ant* disenchanting, repulsive, revolting.

tenable [adj] *reasonable*
▪ *Syn* arguable, believable, condonable, credible, defensible, excusable, justifiable, plausible, rational, trustworthy, viable, vindicable, warrantable; ▪ *Ant* irrational, unjustifiable, untenable.

tenacious [adj1] *strong, unyielding*
▪ *Syn* adamant, bound, clinging, coherent, determined, firm, intransigent, iron, mulish, obstinate, persevering, pertinacious, resolute, stalwart, staunch, steadfast, strong-willed, stubborn, tough, true; ▪ *Ant* flexible, surrendering, weak, yielding.

tenacious [adj2] *sticky*
▪ *Syn* adhesive, clinging, fast, firm, gummy, inseparable, mucilaginous, retentive, secure, tight, viscose, viscous, waxy; ▪ *Ant* loose, slack, unattached.

tend [v] *care for*
▪ *Syn* administer, attend, cater to, cherish, cultivate, do for, feed, foster, guard, handle, keep, look after, maintain, manage, mind, minister to, nurse, nurture, protect, safeguard, see to, serve, shield, sit, superintend, supervise, take care of, wait on, watch, watch over; ▪ *Ant* abandon, ignore, neglect.

tender [adj1] *fragile, soft*
▪ *Syn* breakable, dainty, delicate, effete, feeble, frail, supple, weak; ▪ *Ant* hard, rough, tough.

tender [adj2] *young, inexperienced*
▪ *Syn* callow, childish, childlike, immature, impressionable, new, rookie, sensitive, unripe, vernal, vulnerable, youthful; ▪ *Ant* experienced, mature, older.

tender [adj3] *affectionate, loving*
▪ *Syn* amorous, benevolent, caring, compassionate, considerate, demonstrative, emotional, fond, gentle, humane, kind, lenient, merciful, mushy, poignant, responsive, sensitive, soft, solicitous, sympathetic, tenderhearted, thoughtful, tolerant, touching, warm, yielding; ▪ *Ant* brutal, callous, cruel, inconsiderate, sadistic.

tender [adj4] *painful, sore*
▪ *Syn* aching, acute, bruised, delicate, hypersensitive, inflamed, irritated, oversensitive, raw, sensitive, smarting, ticklish, touchy; ▪ *Ant* healthy, insensitive.

tenebrous [adj] *dark, ominous*
▪ *Syn* ambiguous, caliginous, dim, dusky, equivocal, gloomy, lightless, murky, obscure, shadowy, somber, sunless, vague; ▪ *Ant* inviting, light.

tense [adj1] *tight, stretched*
▪ *Syn* close, firm, rigid, stiff, strained, taut; ▪ *Ant* limp, limpid, loose, relaxed, slack.

tense [adj2] *under stress, pressure*
▪ *Syn* agitated, anxious, apprehensive, choked, clutched, concerned, edgy, excited, fidgety, jittery, jumpy, nervous, on edge, overanxious, overwrought, queasy, restive, restless, shaky, shot, strained, stressful, uneasy, worried; ▪ *Ant* calm, easygoing, laid-back, relaxed, uncaring.

tentative [adj1] *conditional, experimental* ▪ *Syn* acting, ad interim, conjectural, contingent, dependent, indefinite, makeshift, open for consideration, probationary, provisional, speculative, temporary, test, trial, unconfirmed; ▪ *Ant* certain, decisive, definite, final, sure.

tentative [adj2] *indefinite, uncertain*
▪ *Syn* diffident, disinclined, faltering, halting, hesitant, irresolute, reluctant, timid, vacillating, wobbly; ▪ *Ant* certain, conclusive, definite, sure.

tenuous [adj] *weak, thin*
▪ *Syn* airy, attenuated, delicate, doubtful, dubious, ethereal, fine, flimsy, gossamer, insignificant, insubstantial, light, narrow, nebulous, questionable, rare, rarefied, reedy, shaky, sketchy, slender, slight, slim, subtle, twiggy; ▪ *Ant* significant, stable, strong, substantial.

tepid [adj] *lukewarm*
▪ *Syn* apathetic, cool, disinterested, dull, halfhearted, indifferent, languid, lifeless, mild, milk-warm, moderate, slightly warm, spiritless, temperate, unenthusiastic, unlively, warm, warmish; ▪ *Ant* cold, excited, hot, passionate.

terminal [adj] *final, deadly*
  • *Syn* bounding, closing, concluding, eventual, extreme, fatal, hindmost, incurable, killing, lag, last, latest, latter, lethal, limiting, mortal, ultimate, utmost; • *Ant* nonfatal, opening, passing, starting.

terminate [v] *stop, finish*
  • *Syn* abort, adjourn, annul, bring to an end, cancel, close, come to an end, complete, conclude, cut off, discharge, discontinue, dismiss, dissolve, drop, eliminate, end, expire, extinguish, fire, halt, prorogate, prorogue, put an end to, recess, restrict, sack, scratch, scrub, wind down; • *Ant* begin, initiate, open, start.

terrestrial [adj] *earthly*
  • *Syn* earthbound, global, mundane, physical, profane, secular, sublunary, subsolar, temporal, terrene, worldly; • *Ant* aquatic, cosmic, heavenly, marine, otherworldly.

terrible [adj] *bad, horrible*
  • *Syn* abhorrent, appalling, atrocious, awe-inspiring, awesome, awful, beastly, dangerous, desperate, dire, disastrous, disturbing, dread, dreadful, extreme, fearful, frightful, ghastly, gruesome, harrowing, hateful, hideous, horrendous, horrible, horrid, horrifying, loathsome, monstrous, obnoxious, odious, offensive, petrifying, poor, repulsive, revolting, rotten, serious, severe, shocking, vile; • *Ant* gentle, mild, moderate, small.

terribly [adv] *very*
  • *Syn* awfully, badly, desperately, discouragingly, dreadfully, exceedingly, frightfully, gravely, horribly, intensely, markedly, notoriously, remarkably, seriously, thoroughly; • *Ant* easily, hardly, insignificantly, naturally.

terrific [adj1] *intense*
  • *Syn* appalling, awesome, dreadful, enormous, excessive, fearful, formidable, gigantic, great, harsh, huge, immense, large, monstrous, severe, tremendous, upsetting; • *Ant* calm, gentle, moderate.

terrific [adj2] *wonderful*
  • *Syn* amazing, breathtaking, divine, excellent, fabulous, fantastic, great, keen, magnificent, outstanding, sensational, super, superb, swell, very good; • *Ant* bad, distasteful, inferior, low, nasty, poor.

terrify [v] *scare*
  • *Syn* alarm, appall, awe, chill, dismay, freeze, fright, frighten, horrify, intimidate, paralyze, petrify, shock, spook,
startle, strike fear, stun, stupefy, terrorize; • *Ant* calm, delight, encourage, please, reassure.

terrorize [v] *upset, threaten*
  • *Syn* alarm, appall, awe, bludgeon, coerce, cow, dismay, dragoon, frighten, hector, horrify, intimidate, menace, oppress, petrify, scare, spook, startle, terrify; • *Ant* assuage, calm, help, please.

terse [adj] *brief, short*
  • *Syn* abrupt, aphoristic, breviloquent, brusque, clipped, compendious, concise, crisp, curt, elliptical, gnomic, incisive, laconic, neat, pithy, pointed, precise, sententious, snappy, succinct, summary, taut, to the point, trenchant; • *Ant* lengthy, long-winded, prolix, wordy.

testimony [n] *declaration about truth; proof* • *Syn* affidavit, attestation, confirmation, demonstration, documentation, evidence, facts, grounds, illustration, indication, manifestation, profession, statement, verification, witness; • *Ant* contradiction, denial, disavowal, disproof, rebuttal, refutation.

testy [adj] *irritable, touchy*
  • *Syn* annoyed, bad-tempered, cantankerous, choleric, cross, edgy, fretful, irascible, mean, ornery, peevish, peppery, quarrelsome, short-tempered, splenetic, waspish; • *Ant* happy, pleasant.

tether [v] *fasten*
  • *Syn* batten, bind, chain, fetter, leash, manacle, moor, picket, restrain, rope, secure, shackle, tie; • *Ant* free, liberate, unfasten.

thankful [adj] *appreciative*
  • *Syn* beholden, content, grateful, gratified, indebted, much obliged, obliged, overwhelmed, pleased, relieved, satisfied; • *Ant* critical, unappreciative.

thankless [adj1] *unappreciated*
  • *Syn* disagreeable, distasteful, fruitless, futile, miserable, unpleasant, vain, wretched; • *Ant* appreciated, contented, grateful, rewarded, satisfied, thankful.

thankless [adj2] *unappreciative, inconsiderate (in behavior)* • *Syn* careless, cruel, heedless, inappreciative, rude, self-centered, thoughtless; • *Ant* appreciative, considerate, grateful, thankful.

thaw [v] *unfreeze, warm*
  • *Syn* defrost, deliquesce, dissolve, flow, flux, liquefy, melt, open up, relent, run, soften, warm up; • *Ant* congeal, freeze, harden.

theatrical [adj] *dramatic*
• *Syn* affected, artificial, ceremonious, exaggerated, histrionic, mannered, meretricious, ostentatious, pompous, staged, superficial; • *Ant* natural, straight, unaffected.

then [adv] *before; at another time*
• *Syn* at that instant, at that moment, at that point, at that time, formerly, later, next, on that occasion, soon after, suddenly, thereupon, when, years ago; • *Ant* at this moment, now.

theological [adj] *religious, concerning a god-centered philosophy* • *Syn* apostolic, canonical, churchly, deistic, divine, doctrinal, ecclesiastical, metaphysical, scriptural, theistic; • *Ant* irreligious, lay, secular.

theoretical [adj] *hypothetical*
• *Syn* abstract, analytical, codified, contingent, ideological, metaphysical, pedantic, philosophical, postulated, quixotic, speculative, suppositional, tentative, transcendent, vague; • *Ant* certain, definite, factual, proven, real.

theorize [v] *hypothesize*
• *Syn* conjecture, formulate, guess, project, propound, speculate, submit, suggest, suppose, think; • *Ant* authenticate, bear out, demonstrate, establish, evince, prove.

therapeutic [adj] *healing*
• *Syn* ameliorative, analeptic, beneficial, corrective, curative, remedial, restorative, salubrious, salutary; • *Ant* damaging, harmful, hurtful, injurious.

thereafter [adv] *from that time forward*
• *Syn* after that, consequently, following, forever after, from that day forward, from that day on, from there on, thenceforth, thenceforward; • *Ant* before, previously.

thesis [n1] *belief, assumption to be tested*
• *Syn* apriorism, contention, hypothesis, idea, line, opinion, point, posit, postulation, premise, proposal, proposition, surmise, theory, view; • *Ant* certainty, fact, proof, reality.

thick [adj1] *deep, bulky*
• *Syn* broad, burly, chunky, consolidated, fat, firm, hard, heavy, massive, obese, pudgy, solid, stocky, thickset, wide; • *Ant* attenuated, narrow, slender, slight, thin.

thick [adj2] *concentrated, dense*
• *Syn* clotted, coagulated, compressed, condensed, congealed, crowded, firm, fixed, gummy, heavy, impenetrable, jelled, opaque, ossified, set, solidified, thickened, turbid, viscous; • *Ant* diluted, loose, thin, watery.

thick [adj3] *crowded, packed*
• *Syn* brimming, bursting, compressed, covered, crammed, full, heaped, impenetrable, multitudinous, populous, swarming, teeming, tight; • *Ant* penetrable, sparse, thin, uncrowded.

thick [adj5] *dense (referring to weather)*
• *Syn* cloudy, dull, foggy, heavy, impenetrable, indistinct, muddy, obscure, turbid; • *Ant* clear.

thick [adj6] *friendly*
• *Syn* close, confidential, cordial, devoted, familiar, inseparable, intimate, on good terms; • *Ant* unfriendly, unsociable.

thicken [v] *set; make more dense*
• *Syn* add, buttress, cake, condense, congeal, curdle, deepen, enlarge, expand, freeze, gel, harden, inspissate, jell, ossify, petrify, reinforce, solidify, widen; • *Ant* dilute, liquefy, melt, thin, water down.

thieving/thievish [adj] *criminal*
• *Syn* crooked, cunning, dishonest, fraudulent, larcenous, plunderous, rapacious, secretive, spoliative, stealthy; • *Ant* benevolent, honest, innocent, law-abiding, philanthropic.

thin [adj1] *fine, light, slender*
• *Syn* anorexic, cadaverous, delicate, emaciated, fragile, gangling, gangly, gaunt, haggard, lanky, meager, narrow, peaked, rangy, rawboned, shriveled, skeletal, slight, slim, spindly, starved, threadlike, wan, wasted, wizened; • *Ant* dense, fat, heavy, obese, thick.

thin [adj2] *transparent, fine*
• *Syn* attenuated, delicate, diaphanous, filmy, flimsy, gossamer, paper-thin, rarefied, refined, see-through, sheer, slight, subtle, translucent, wispy; • *Ant* dense, solid, thick.

thin [adj3] *deficient, weak*
• *Syn* diluted, implausible, inadequate, insubstantial, insufficient, lame, meager, poor, questionable, scant, scarce, shallow, slight, sparse, superficial, transparent, vapid; • *Ant* efficient, solid, strong.

thin [adj4] *diluted*
• *Syn* diffuse, dilute, dispersed, fine, light, rarefied, refined, runny, subtle, watery, weak; • *Ant* concentrated, thick.

thin [v] *make diluted or less dense*
▪ *Syn* attenuate, cut back, decrease, diminish, extenuate, irrigate, prune, rarefy, refine, shave, trim, weaken, weed out; ▪ *Ant* beef up, thicken.

think [v1] *believe; anticipate*
▪ *Syn* assume, conceive, conclude, credit, deem, determine, envisage, esteem, expect, fancy, foresee, gather, guess, hold, imagine, judge, presume, realize, reckon, see, sense, suppose, understand; ▪ *Ant* disbelieve, disregard, excogitate.

think [v2] *contemplate*
▪ *Syn* analyze, appreciate, brood, cerebrate, cogitate, comprehend, conceive, consider, deduce, deliberate, evaluate, examine, ideate, imagine, infer, intellectualize, judge, meditate, mull, mull over, muse, ponder, rationalize, reason, reflect, resolve, ruminate, speculate, study, turn over, weigh; ▪ *Ant* forget, ignore, neglect.

thinkable [adj] *believable, feasible*
▪ *Syn* cogitable, comprehensible, conceivable, convincing, imaginable, likely, possible, practical, reasonable, within the limits; ▪ *Ant* impossible, unbelievable, unfeasible, unlikely.

thirsty [adj1] *dry, desirous (especially for liquid)* ▪ *Syn* anxious, appetent, ardent, arid, athirst, avid, breathless, burning, craving, dehydrated, eager, hungry, inclined, keen, longing, parched, thirsting, yearning; ▪ *Ant* moist, quenched, satisfied, wet.

thorny [adj1] *sharp, pointed*
▪ *Syn* barbed, briery, bristling, bristly, prickly, spiked, spiky, spinous, spiny, stinging, thistly; ▪ *Ant* dull, smooth, unpointed.

thorny [adj2] *difficult, problematic*
▪ *Syn* awkward, bothersome, formidable, harassing, irksome, nettlesome, perplexing, prickly, severe, tough, tricky, trying, unpleasant, upsetting, vexatious, worrying; ▪ *Ant* easy, solvable, untroublesome.

thorough/thoroughgoing [adj1] *exhaustive* ▪ *Syn* absolute, all-embracing, careful, complete, comprehensive, detailed, efficient, full, intensive, meticulous, painstaking, scrupulous, sweeping, tough; ▪ *Ant* incomplete, partial, superficial, unfinished.

thorough/thoroughgoing [adj2] *absolute, utter* ▪ *Syn* arrant, complete, consummate, downright, entire, outright, perfect, pure, rank, sheer, total; ▪ *Ant* deficient, imperfect, inadequate.

thoroughbred [adj] *pure, unmixed*
▪ *Syn* full-blooded, graded, papered, pedigree, pedigreed, pure-blooded, purebred; ▪ *Ant* half-breed, impure, mixed.

thoroughly [adv1] *exhaustively*
▪ *Syn* assiduously, carefully, comprehensively, conscientiously, earnestly, fully, highly, in detail, intensely, meticulously, notably, painstakingly, scrupulously, unremittingly, wholly; ▪ *Ant* incompletely, inexhaustively, partially, superficially.

thoroughly [adv2] *utterly*
▪ *Syn* absolutely, completely, downright, entirely, fully, perfectly, quite, totally, wholly; ▪ *Ant* deficiently, inadequately.

thoughtful [adj1] *caring, mindful*
▪ *Syn* astute, attentive, aware, benign, canny, careful, cautious, charitable, chivalrous, circumspect, concerned, considerate, cooperative, courteous, deliberate, diplomatic, discreet, friendly, gallant, gracious, heedful, helpful, indulgent, kind, kindly, mindful, neighborly, observant, polite, prudent, responsive, sensitive, solicitous, tactful, unselfish, wary, well-bred, well thought-out; ▪ *Ant* careless, heedless, inattentive, inconsiderate.

thoughtful [adj2] *contemplative, introspective* ▪ *Syn* absorbed, analytical, attentive, calculating, cerebral, cogitative, deep, deliberative, discerning, earnest, engrossed, farsighted, grave, intellectual, intent, keen, levelheaded, logical, meditative, melancholy, museful, musing, pensive, philosophic, pondering, preoccupied, rapt, rational, reasonable, reasoning, reflecting, reflective, retrospective, ruminative, serious, sober, studious, subjective, thinking, wise, wistful; ▪ *Ant* facetious, idiotic, obtuse, shallow.

thoughtless [adj1] *inconsiderate*
▪ *Syn* asocial, blind, boorish, brash, discourteous, egocentric, hasty, heedless, impolite, inattentive, incautious, indelicate, indifferent, indiscreet, insensitive, negligent, primitive, rash, reckless, rude, self-centered, selfish, sharp, short, tactless; ▪ *Ant* considerate, kind, thinking, thoughtful, unselfish.

thoughtless [adj2] *absent-minded, unobservant* ▪ *Syn* careless, dull, foolish, heedless, ill-advised, imprudent, inattentive, inept, injudicious, mindless, neglectful, obtuse, puerile, regardless, remiss, senseless, vacuous, witless; • *Ant* attentive, heeding, mindful, observant, thoughtful.

threadbare [*adj1*] *worn, frayed*
• *Syn* damaged, dilapidated, faded, impaired, old, ragged, shabby, tattered, timeworn, used; • *Ant* fresh, new, unused.

threadbare [*adj2*] *trite, corny*
• *Syn* banal, cliché, cliché-ridden, commonplace, conventional, dull, familiar, hackneyed, imitative, musty, overused, stale, tedious, well-worn, worn-out; • *Ant* fresh, novel, original.

threaten [*v1*] *warn, pressure*
• *Syn* admonish, blackmail, browbeat, bully, caution, cow, enforce, forewarn, growl, intimidate, menace, portend, scare, spook, terrorize, torment; • *Ant* alleviate, help, protect, relieve.

threaten [*v2*] *endanger*
• *Syn* foreshadow, frighten, impend, imperil, jeopardize, loom, overhang, portend, presage, put at risk, put in jeopardy; • *Ant* guard, protect, save.

threatening [*adj*] *menacing, ominous*
• *Syn* alarming, apocalyptic, baneful, bullying, cautionary, dangerous, dire, fateful, grim, ill-boding, impending, looming, minacious, portending, sinister, terrorizing; • *Ant* auspicious, promising, reassuring.

threshold [*n*] *opening; beginning*
• *Syn* brink, dawn, door, edge, entrance, gate, inception, origin, point, start, verge, vestibule; • *Ant* conclusion, end, finish, termination.

thrifty [*adj*] *economical*
• *Syn* canny, careful, chary, close-fisted, conservative, frugal, mean, parsimonious, penny-pinching, preserving, provident, prudent, saving, sparing; • *Ant* extravagant, spendthrift, wasteful.

thrill [*v*] *excite, stimulate*
• *Syn* animate, arouse, delight, electrify, flush, galvanize, glow, inspire, move, palpitate, quicken, rouse, score, stir, titillate, tremble; • *Ant* bore, calm, depress, sedate.

thrilling [*adj*] *exciting*
• *Syn* breathtaking, electrifying, fabulous, gripping, magnificent, overwhelming, riveting, sensational, stirring, wild, wondrous; • *Ant* boring, dull, tedious.

thrive [*v*] *do well*
• *Syn* advance, bear fruit, bloom, blossom, burgeon, develop, flourish, grow, increase, progress, prosper, radiate, shine, succeed; • *Ant* decline, fail, languish, lose.

thriving [*adj*] *successful*
• *Syn* advancing, blooming, burgeoning, developing, flourishing, growing, healthy, prolific, prospering, roaring, robust, wealthy; • *Ant* declining, failing, languishing, losing.

throng [*n*] *large crowd*
• *Syn* assemblage, assembly, bunch, collection, congregation, drove, flock, gathering, horde, host, jam, mass, mob, multitude, pack, swarm; • *Ant* few, smattering, sprinkling.

throttle [*v*] *choke*
• *Syn* burke, control, gag, inhibit, silence, smother, stifle, strangle, suppress; • *Ant* free, release.

through [*adj1*] *done*
• *Syn* complete, completed, concluded, ended, finished, over, terminated; • *Ant* incomplete, unfinished.

through [*adj2*] *direct*
• *Syn* nonstop, rapid, regular, straight, straightforward, unbroken, uninterrupted; • *Ant* indirect, intermittent.

throughout [*adj*] *during the whole of*
• *Syn* all the time, completely, during, everywhere, far and wide, for the duration, from beginning to end, from start to finish, high and low, in all respects, in everything, inside and out, over, the whole time, to the end, up and down; • *Ant* here and there, infrequently, in some places, intermittently, now and then, occasionally, sometimes, sporadically.

throw [*v1*] *propel something through the air* • *Syn* bandy, barrage, bombard, cast, catapult, fire, flick, flip, hurl, impel, lapidate, launch, lob, peg, pelt, pitch, scatter, shower, sling, spray, stone, thrust, toss, volley, waft; • *Ant* catch, receive.

throw [*v2*] *confuse*
• *Syn* addle, astonish, baffle, befuddle, bewilder, confound, disconcert, distract, disturb, dumbfound, fluster, unsettle, upset; • *Ant* explain, help.

throw away [*v1*] *dispose of*
• *Syn* abandon, cast, discard, dismiss, eject, eliminate, evict, jettison, lose,

refuse, reject, shed, throw out; ▪ *Ant* hold, keep, retain.

throw away [*v2*] *waste*
▪ *Syn* blow, dissipate, fail to exploit, fritter, lose, refuse, reject, squander, trifle; ▪ *Ant* save, take advantage of, use.

throw off [*v*] *elude, escape*
▪ *Syn* abuse, deceive, evade, get away from, lose, outdistance, outrun, shake off, trick; ▪ *Ant* face, meet.

thrust [*v*] *push hard*
▪ *Syn* advance, assail, attack, bear down, buck, butt, cut, drive, embed, force, heave, impale, jab, jostle, lunge, nudge, peg, press, prod, push forward, ram, shove; ▪ *Ant* drag, draw, pull.

thunder [*v2*] *yell at*
▪ *Syn* bark, bellow, curse, declaim, fulminate, gnarl, growl, rail, roar, shout, snarl, threaten; ▪ *Ant* soothe, whisper.

thus [*adv1*] *in this manner*
▪ *Syn* along these lines, as follows, hence, in such a way, in this fashion, in this way, just like that, like so, thus and so, thusly, to such a degree; ▪ *Ant* otherwise, the other way.

thus [*adv2*] *accordingly*
▪ *Syn* consequently, ergo, for this reason, hence, on that account, so, then, therefore, thereupon; ▪ *Ant* but, despite, however, nevertheless.

thwart [*v*] *stop, hinder*
▪ *Syn* balk, bilk, circumvent, curb, dash, defeat, foil, frustrate, hold up, impede, obstruct, prevent, queer, restrain, stymie, trammel, upset; ▪ *Ant* aid, assist, encourage, forward, help.

tickle [*v*] *make laugh*
▪ *Syn* amuse, caress, delight, enchant, excite, gratify, pet, stimulate, stroke, titillate, vellicate; ▪ *Ant* annoy, displease, irritate, upset.

ticklish [*adj*] *difficult, tricky*
▪ *Syn* awkward, capricious, delicate, fickle, inconstant, mercurial, precarious, risky, sensitive, temperamental, thorny, variable, volatile; ▪ *Ant* easy, straightforward, unproblematic.

tidbit [*n*] *tiny portion*
▪ *Syn* bit, bite, delicacy, morsel, mouthful, snack, soupon, titbit, treat; ▪ *Ant* entirely, whole.

tide over [*v*] *help along*
▪ *Syn* aid, assist, keep one going, see through; ▪ *Ant* hinder, impede.

tidy [*adj1*] *clean, neat*
▪ *Syn* methodical, ordered, sleek, spruce, trim, well-groomed, well-ordered; ▪ *Ant* chaotic, dirty, disordered, disorganized, litered, messy, sloppy, slovenly.

tidy [*adj2*] *considerable*
▪ *Syn* ample, fair, generous, good, handsome, healthy, large, respectable, sizable, vast; ▪ *Ant* inconsequential, little, small, unsubstantial.

tidy [*v*] *make neat and orderly*
▪ *Syn* clean, fix up, groom, neaten, order, police, put in good shape, put in order, spruce, straighten, straighten up, tauten; ▪ *Ant* dirty, dishevel, disorder, disorganize, jumble, litter.

tie/tie up [*v*] *hamper, hinder*
▪ *Syn* bind, clog, confine, curb, delay, entrammel, fetter, hold, leash, limit, lock up, obstruct, restrain, restrict, shackle, stop, trammel bound, close-fitting, compact, constricted, contracted, cramped, crowded, dense, drawn, fast, firm, fixed, hidebound, inflexible, narrow, rigid, secure, set, skintight, solid, stable, steady, stiff, strained, stretched, strong, sturdy, taut, tenacious, tense, thick, tightened; ▪ *Ant* liberate, release, sever.

tie [*v1*] *connect, interlace*
▪ *Syn* anchor, attach, bind, cinch, do up, fasten, gird, join, knot, link, marry, rivet, rope, secure, splice, tether, truss, unite, wed; ▪ *Ant* detach, disconnect, loosen, unfasten, unlace.

tie [*v2*] *equal*
▪ *Syn* balance, draw, keep up with, match, measure up, meet, parallel, rival, touch; ▪ *Ant* fail, fall behind, go ahead, lose, succeed, surpass.

tight [*adj1*] *close, snug*
▪ *Syn* bind, clog, confine, curb, delay, entrammel, fetter, hold, leash, limit, lock up, obstruct, restrain, restrict, shackle, stop, trammel bound, close-fitting, compact, constricted, contracted, cramped, crowded, dense, drawn, fast, firm, fixed, hidebound, inflexible, narrow, rigid, secure, set, skintight, solid, stable, steady, stiff, strained, stretched, strong, sturdy, taut, tenacious, tense, thick, tightened; ▪ *Ant* comfortable, free, loose, open, slack.

tight [*adj2*] *sealed*
▪ *Syn* airtight, bolted, fast, firm, hermetic, hermetically sealed, impenetrable, impermeable, impervious, locked, ob-

structed, padlocked, plugged, proof, sealed, secure, shut, skintight, smothering, snapped, sound, stopped up, watertight; ▪ *Ant* open, porous, unsealed.

tight [*adj3*] *stingy*
▪ *Syn* cheap, close, grasping, mean, miserly, niggardly, parsimonious, penurious, sparing, tightfisted; ▪ *Ant* giving, spendthrift.

tight [*adj4*] *difficult, troublesome*
▪ *Syn* arduous, close, critical, dangerous, distressing, disturbing, exacting, hazardous, near, perilous, precarious, punishing, rough, sticky, tense, ticklish, tough, tricky, trying, upsetting, worrisome; ▪ *Ant* comfortable, easy, untroubled.

tight [*adj5*] *intoxicated*
▪ *Syn* drunk, drunken, inebriated, loaded, pickled, sloppy, tipsy, under the influence; ▪ *Ant* sober, straight.

tighten [*v*] *constrict*
▪ *Syn* bind, clench, close, compress, condense, contract, fasten, fix, grip, harden, narrow, pinch, pressure, screw, secure, squeeze, stiffen, strain, strangle, tense; ▪ *Ant* free, let go, loosen, relax, release.

tilt [*v1*] *lean, slant*
▪ *Syn* bend, cant, careen, dip, heel, incline, list, lurch, pitch, rake, recline, seesaw, set at an angle, shift, slope, slouch, swag, sway, tip, turn, yaw; ▪ *Ant* straighten.

tilt [*v2*] *attack, fight*
▪ *Syn* break, charge, clash, combat, contend, duel, encounter, joust, overthrow, spar, thrust; ▪ *Ant* surrender, yield.

timely [*adj*] *at the right time*
▪ *Syn* appropriate, convenient, favorable, fitting, judicious, likely, meet, opportune, promising, propitious, punctual, suitable, up-to-date, well-timed; ▪ *Ant* inappropriate, inopportune, unsuitable.

timid [*adj*] *shy*
▪ *Syn* afraid, apprehensive, bashful, cowardly, coy, daunted, demure, fearful, feeble, frightened, gentle, humble, intimidated, milquetoast, mousy, nervous, pusillanimous, retiring, shrinking, spiritless, timid, trembling, vacillating, wavering; ▪ *Ant* bold, brave, daring, extroverted, fearless.

tinge [*v*] *color*
▪ *Syn* dye, shade, stain, tincture, tinge, tint; ▪ *Ant* pale, whiten.

tinker [*v*] *fiddle with*
▪ *Syn* dabble, fix, play, play with, puddle,

putter, repair, take apart, toy, trifle with; ▪ *Ant* leave alone.

tint [*v*] *color with a certain shade*
▪ *Syn* dye, rinse, shade, stain, taint, tincture, tinge; ▪ *Ant* bleach, fade, whiten.

tiny [*adj*] *very small*
▪ *Syn* bitty, diminutive, dwarf, infinitesimal, insignificant, Lilliputian, little, microscopic, miniature, minikin, minuscule, minute, negligible, petite, pocket, puny, pygmy, slight, trifling; ▪ *Ant* big, enormous, gigantic, great, huge, large, vast.

tip [*v1*] *knock over; cause to lean*
▪ *Syn* bend, cant, capsize, careen, incline, lean, list, overset, overturn, shift, slant, slope, tilt, topple, topple over, turn over, upset, upturn; ▪ *Ant* right, straighten.

tipsy [*adj*] *inebriated*
▪ *Syn* addled, dazed, drunk, drunken, intoxicated, mellow, merry, tight, woozy; ▪ *Ant* sober.

tirade [*n*] *abuse, outburst*
▪ *Syn* berating, censure, condemnation, denunciation, fulmination, harangue, invective, lecture, malediction, ranting, revilement, screed, sermon, vituperation; ▪ *Ant* commendation, homage.

tire [*v*] *exhaust, weary*
▪ *Syn* annoy, bore, collapse, debilitate, dishearten, distress, drop, enervate, exasperate, fag, fail, fatigue, flag, give out, grow weary, overburden, overtax, pain, prostrate, sap, strain, tax, vex, weaken, wear, weary, wilt, worry; ▪ *Ant* activate, energize, fire up, invigorate, refresh.

tired [*adj*] *exhausted, weary*
▪ *Syn* drained, drooping, drowsy, enervated, exasperated, fagged, fatigued, flagging, haggard, narcoleptic, overtaxed, prostrated, run-down, sleepy, tuckered out, wasted, weary, worn; ▪ *Ant* energetic, fresh, invigorated, peppy, wide-awake.

tireless [*adj*] *determined*
▪ *Syn* active, energetic, enthusiastic, grind, incessant, indefatigable, jumping, perky, persevering, resolute, steadfast, strenuous, vigorous; ▪ *Ant* half-hearted, sporadic, unenthusiastic, wavering.

tiresome [*adj*] *irritating, exasperating*
▪ *Syn* annoying, arduous, burdensome, demanding, drudging, enervative, exacting, fatiguing, irksome, laborious, monotonous, oppressive, tedious, trying, vexatious, wearing; ▪ *Ant* easy, facile, fun, nice, stimulating.

titillate [v] *excite, stimulate*
▪ *Syn* amuse, arouse, entertain, grab, grapple, hook, interest, provoke, tantalize, tease, thrill, tickle, turn on; ▪ *Ant* allay, blunt, quench, satisfy.

together [adj] *composed*
▪ *Syn* calm, stable, well-adjusted, well-balanced, well-organized; ▪ *Ant* imbalanced, unstable, upset, worried.

together [adv1] *as a group; all at once*
▪ *Syn* all together, collectively, combined, concertedly, concomitantly, conjointly, en masse, in unison, jointly, mutually, side by side, simultaneously, unanimously, with one voice; ▪ *Ant* apart, individually, separately.

together [adv2] *in a row*
▪ *Syn* consecutively, continually, continuously, in succession, one after the other, on end, running, successively, without a break, without interruption; ▪ *Ant* intermittently, sporadically.

toil [v] *work hard*
▪ *Syn* drive, drudge, grind, labor, moil, plod, plug, push oneself, slave, strain, strive, struggle, sweat, tug, work; ▪ *Ant* idle, laze.

tolerable [adj] *acceptable, good enough*
▪ *Syn* adequate, allowable, average, bearable, decent, endurable, fair, mediocre, ordinary, passable, presentable, respectable, satisfactory, sufferable, sufficient, supportable, sustainable, tidy, unexceptional; ▪ *Ant* bad, unacceptable, unbearable.

tolerant [adj] *open-minded, easygoing*
▪ *Syn* advanced, benevolent, broad, catholic, charitable, clement, complaisant, easy, fair, forbearing, forgiving, humane, indulgent, lax, lenient, liberal, magnanimous, merciful, patient, permissive, progressive, radical, receptive, soft, sophisticated, sympathetic, understanding, unprejudiced; ▪ *Ant* biased, disapproving, intolerant, narrow-minded, prejudiced.

tolerate [v] *allow, indulge*
▪ *Syn* abide, accept, admit, authorize, bear, bear with, brook, condone, consent to, countenance, endure, go along with, humor, live with, permit, put up with, sanction, sit still for, stand, suffer, sustain, take; ▪ *Ant* check, disallow, disapprove, halt, stop, veto.

tome [n] *large, scholarly book*
▪ *Syn* classic, great work, magnum opus,

novel, opus, publication, reference book, schoolbook, textbook, title, tradebook, volume, work, writing; ▪ *Ant* abridgment, booklet, outline, pamphlet, précis, sketch, summary, synopsis.

tone down [v] *moderate*
▪ *Syn* cloud, dampen, darken, deepen, dim, mitigate, modulate, play down, reduce, restrain, shade, sober, soften, subdue, temper; ▪ *Ant* aggravate, increase, raise.

top [adj] *best, most important; highest*
▪ *Syn* apical, chief, crowning, dominant, elite, excellent, fine, first, foremost, head, lead, loftiest, maximal, outside, paramount, preeminent, principal, ruling, sovereign, supreme, top-notch, upper; ▪ *Ant* inept, inferior, low, second-rate, unknown.

top [v1] *surpass*
▪ *Syn* bash, beat, be first, best, better, eclipse, exceed, excel, go beyond, outdo, outfox, outshine, outstrip, overrun, transcend; ▪ *Ant* fall behind, lose, trail.

top [v2] *remove the upper part*
▪ *Syn* amputate, cream, curtail, cut off, decapitate, detruncate, file off, pare, prune, ream, scrape off, shave off, shear, shorten, skim, trim, truncate; ▪ *Ant* add, replace.

topical [adj1] *current*
▪ *Syn* contemporary, modern, newsworthy, up-to-date; ▪ *Ant* irrelevant, old, past, traditional.

topical [adj2] *restricted, local*
▪ *Syn* confined, insular, limited, localized, parochial, particular, regional, sectional; ▪ *Ant* general, universal, unrestricted.

topple [v] *fall or knock over; overthrow*
▪ *Syn* capsize, fall, founder, keel over, lurch, nose-dive, overturn, pitch, plunge, slump, teeter, totter, tumble, turn over, upset; ▪ *Ant* build, construct, place, put, straighten, tower.

topsy-turvy [adj] *mixed-up*
▪ *Syn* chaotic, cluttered, confused, disarranged, disheveled, disorganized, inside-out, inverted, jumbled, littered, muddled, overturned, riotous, tangled, upended, upside-down; ▪ *Ant* ordered, organized, straight.

torment [v] *be or make very upset*
▪ *Syn* abuse, afflict, bedevil, devil, excruciate, harass, harrow, hurt, irritate, molest, nag, pain, persecute, punish, rack,

smite, torture, vex, worry, wring; ▪ *Ant* comfort, delight, make happy, please.

torn [*adj1*] *cut open*
▪ *Syn* cleaved, divided, fractured, gashed, impaired, lacerated, ragged, rent, ripped, ruptured, severed, slashed, slit, split; ▪ *Ant* fixed, healed, mended.

torn [*adj2*] *undecided*
▪ *Syn* divided, irresolute, split, uncertain, unsure, vacillating, wavering; ▪ *Ant* certain, decided, resolute, sure.

torpid [*adj*] *lazy, slow*
▪ *Syn* apathetic, benumbed, comatose, dormant, faineant, heavy, idle, inactive, inert, lackadaisical, languorous, latent, lethargic, listless, motionless, numb, paralyzed, slothful, slumberous, stagnant, stuporous; ▪ *Ant* active, energetic, lively, moving, quick.

torrent [*n*] *heavy flow*
▪ *Syn* cascade, cataclysm, cloudburst, deluge, downpour, effusion, flood, flux, gush, inundation, niagara, overflow, pour, rush, spate, tide, waterfall; ▪ *Ant* dribble, drip, ooze.

torrid [*adj1*] *very hot*
▪ *Syn* blazing, blistering, boiling, fiery, heated, parched, scorched, sizzling, stifling, sultry, sweltering, tropical; ▪ *Ant* cold, gentle, mild, temperate.

torrid [*adj2*] *sensuous*
▪ *Syn* ardent, blazing, burning, erotic, fervent, flaming, intense, passionate, sexy, sultry; ▪ *Ant* cold, dispassionate, frigid, indifferent.

tortuous [*adj1*] *very twisted*
▪ *Syn* bent, circuitous, convoluted, flexuous, indirect, labyrinthine, meandering, roundabout, serpentine, snaky, twisting, vermiculate, winding, zigzag; ▪ *Ant* direct, plumb, straight, untwisted.

tortuous [*adj2*] *complicated*
▪ *Syn* ambiguous, convoluted, cunning, deceptive, devious, involved, misleading, perverse, roundabout, tricky; ▪ *Ant* easy, straightforward, uncomplicated.

torture [*v*] *upset or hurt severely*
▪ *Syn* abuse, afflict, agonize, beat, bother, crucify, distress, excruciate, grill, harrow, injure, irritate, lacerate, mangle, martyr, mistreat, mutilate, oppress, pain, persecute, rack, smite, torment, whip, wound, wrong; ▪ *Ant* alleviate, make happy, please, relieve.

toss [*v1*] *throw*
▪ *Syn* bung, cast, chuck, chunk, fire,

fling, flip, heave, hurl, launch, lob, peg, pitch, project, propel, sling, twirl, wing; ▪ *Ant* catch, clutch, retain, seize.

toss [*v2*] *move back and forth*
▪ *Syn* agitate, buffet, disturb, flounder, heave, joggle, jolt, lurch, move restlessly, oscillate, pitch, rise and fall, roll, seesaw, sway, swing, tumble, undulate, wave, wobble, writhe; ▪ *Ant* lie still.

total [*adj*] *complete, thorough*
▪ *Syn* absolute, all-out, comprehensive, downright, entire, full-blown, full-scale, gross, inclusive, integral, outright, perfect, plenary, sheer, sweeping, thoroughgoing, utter, whole; ▪ *Ant* incomplete, partial, unfinished.

total [*v*] *add up*
▪ *Syn* add, aggregate, calculate, comprise, consist of, equal, figure, number, reach, reckon, result in, run to, stack up, summate, sum up, tote, yield; ▪ *Ant* subtract, take away.

totalitarian [*adj*] *dictatorial*
▪ *Syn* absolute, authoritarian, autocratic, despotic, fascistic, monolithic, one-party, oppressive, total, totalistic, tyrannical; ▪ *Ant* anarchistic, democratic, popular.

totally [*adv*] *completely*
▪ *Syn* absolutely, all, all in all, altogether, comprehensively, consummately, entirely, exactly, exclusively, fully, just, perfectly, quite, thoroughly, unconditionally, utterly, wholeheartedly, wholly; ▪ *Ant* incompletely, partially, slightly, somewhat.

touch [*v1*] *make physical contact*
▪ *Syn* abut, adjoin, border, caress, communicate, contact, feel, fondle, glance, graze, handle, join, kiss, manipulate, massage, neighbor, palpate, paw, percuss, pet, rub, scrutinize, sip, smooth, stroke, tap; ▪ *Ant* cower, shrink, shy away.

touch [*v2*] *have an effect on*
▪ *Syn* affect, arouse, carry, disturb, excite, feel out, get to, grab, impress, influence, inspire, mark, melt, move, quicken, soften, stimulate, stir, strike, stroke, sway, upset; ▪ *Ant* bore, leave cold, leave unaffected.

touch [*v3*] *make mention*
▪ *Syn* allude to, bring in, cover, deal with, discuss, go over, mention, note, refer to, speak of, treat; ▪ *Ant* disregard, ignore, passover, secrete.

touched [adj1] *deeply moved emotionally* ▪ **Syn** affected, disturbed, impressed, softened, stirred, swayed, upset; ▪ **Ant** unemotional, unmoved, untouched.

touched [adj2] *crazy* ▪ **Syn** bizarre, daft, eccentric, fanatic, flighty, insane, neurotic, peculiar, pixilated, queer, unhinged; ▪ **Ant** sane, well.

touching [adj] *affecting, moving emotionally* ▪ **Syn** distressing, heartbreaking, impressive, pathetic, piteous, pitiful, poignant, sad, sentimental, stirring, tearjerking, tender; ▪ **Ant** unaffecting, unmoving.

touch up [v] *fix up; improve* ▪ **Syn** amend, enhance, gloss, modify, patch up, perfect, polish, remodel, renew, renovate, repair, retouch, revamp, rework, round off; ▪ **Ant** break, damage, harm, hurt.

touchy [adj] *easily offended* ▪ **Syn** bad-tempered, cantankerous, choleric, cranky, delicate, hazardous, hypersensitive, irascible, ornery, peevish, petulant, querulous, sensitive, splenetic, surly, temperamental, uptight, volatile; ▪ **Ant** callous, calm, easygoing, inured, laid-back, unflappable.

tough [adj1] *sturdy, strong* ▪ **Syn** brawny, conditioned, durable, fibrous, hardy, leathery, mighty, resilient, rigid, robust, rugged, seasoned, stout, strapping, tenacious, vigorous; ▪ **Ant** delicate, fragile, unstable, vulnerable, weak, wobbly.

tough [adj2] *obstinate, rough* ▪ **Syn** adamant, arbitrary, callous, exacting, ferocious, harsh, headstrong, immutable, merciless, narrow, obdurate, pugnacious, refractory, ruthless, severe, stern, strict, stubborn, taut, vicious, violent; ▪ **Ant** gentle, kind, lenient, permissive.

tough [adj3] *difficult, laborious* ▪ **Syn** arduous, burdensome, demanding, exacting, exhausting, hard, intricate, labored, onerous, perplexing, severe, strenuous, taxing, troublesome, trying; ▪ **Ant** controllable, easy, facile, simple, slight, soft.

toughen [v] *harden* ▪ **Syn** acclimate, acclimatize, anneal, develop, inure, season, steel, strengthen; ▪ **Ant** loosen, soften, weaken.

tourist [n] *person who visits a place* ▪ **Syn** day-tripper, excursionist, globetrotter, journeyer, sightseer, stranger, traveler, vacationist, voyager, wayfarer; ▪ **Ant** inhabitant, local, native.

tousled [adj] *disarrayed* ▪ **Syn** dirty, disarranged, disheveled, disordered, messy, ruffled, rumpled, sloppy, tangled, uncombed, unkempt; ▪ **Ant** kempt, neat, ordered, tidy.

tout [v] *brag about, show off* ▪ **Syn** acclaim, boost, glorify, herald, laud, plug, praise, proclaim, promote, publicize, push, trumpet; ▪ **Ant** belittle, denigrate, malign.

tow [v] *pull along* ▪ **Syn** drag, draw, ferry, haul, lug, propel, push, trail, trawl, tug, yank; ▪ **Ant** push, shove.

toward/towards [prep] *on the way to; near* ▪ **Syn** approaching, close to, en route, facing, headed for, in relation to, in the direction of, just before, moving, nearing, on the road to, pointing to, proceeding, shortly before, via, vis-à-vis; ▪ **Ant** away, from.

tower [v] *rise above* ▪ **Syn** ascend, be above, dominate, exceed, look down, look over, loom, mount, overlook, overtop, rear, soar, surmount, surpass, top, transcend; ▪ **Ant** descend, drop, fall, sink.

towering [adj] *huge, excessive* ▪ **Syn** colossal, extraordinary, fantastic, gigantic, high, immoderate, imposing, impressive, intense, lofty, magnificent, monumental, outstanding, paramount, skyscraping, stupendous, sublime, superior, surpassing, tremendous, ultimate; ▪ **Ant** commonplace, dwarfed, little, mediocre, minor, paltry, short, small, tiny.

toxic [adj] *poisonous* ▪ **Syn** baneful, deadly, harmful, lethal, mephitic, noxious, pernicious, pestilential, poison, septic, toxicant, venomous, virulent; ▪ **Ant** beneficial, harmless, nonpoisonous, wholesome.

toy [n] *entertainment article* ▪ **Syn** bauble, curio, doll, game, knickknack, novelty, plaything, trifle, trinket; ▪ **Ant** instrument, necessity, tool, utensil.

trace [v] *seek, follow* ▪ **Syn** determine, discern, ferret out, hunt, perceive, pursue, run down, search for, shadow, smell out, spoor, stalk, track, trail, unearth; ▪ **Ant** abandon, drop, relinquish.

track/track down [v] *follow, pursue* ▪ **Syn** chase, dig up, ferret out, find, go after, hunt, piece together, put together, run down, scout, shadow, stalk, stick to, tail, trace, travel, traverse, unearth; ▪ *Ant* abandon, ignore, relinquish.

tractable [adj] manageable
▪ *Syn* acquiescent, amenable, complaisant, compliant, docile, ductile, facile, flexible, game, governable, malleable, meek, obedient, plastic, pliable, pliant, subdued, submissive, tame, willing, workable, yielding; ▪ *Ant* intractable, obstinate, stubborn, uncontrollable, unmanageable, unruly.

trade [n] profession, work
▪ *Syn* art, business, calling, craft, employment, job, line, line of work, métier, occupation, position, pursuit, skill, vocation; ▪ *Ant* avocation, entertainment, fun, pastime.

traditional [adj] usual, established
▪ *Syn* acceptable, accustomed, acknowledged, ancestral, classic, classical, common, conventional, customary, doctrinal, fixed, folk, historic, immemorial, long-established, old, prescribed, rooted, sanctioned, taken for granted, time-honored, transmitted, universal, unwritten; ▪ *Ant* fresh, new, unestablished, unfixed, untraditional, unusual.

tragic [adj] catastrophic, very bad
▪ *Syn* adverse, anguished, calamitous, cataclysmic, deplorable, dire, disastrous, dreadful, fateful, grievous, grim, hapless, harrowing, ill-fated, lamentable, mournful, pathetic, pitiable, pitiful, ruinous, terrible, wretched; ▪ *Ant* advantageous, blessed, fortunate, successful, worthwhile.

trail [v] lag behind, follow
▪ *Syn* bedog, chase, dally, dawdle, draggle, droop, drop back, extend, fall back, falter, halt, hang, haul, lag, linger, loiter, plod, poke, shadow, stalk, tail, tarry, tow, trace, track, traipse, trudge; ▪ *Ant* be winning, lead, outpace, surpass, top.

train [v] prepare
▪ *Syn* accustom, coach, develop, discipline, drill, educate, enlighten, exercise, get in shape, ground, habituate, hone, improve, instruct, make ready, prime, qualify, rear, season, shape, study, tame, teach, tutor, update, warm up, work out; ▪ *Ant* forget, neglect.

traitor [n] person who is disloyal
▪ *Syn* apostate, betrayer, conspirator, deceiver, deserter, hypocrite, impostor, informer, miscreant, quisling, rebel, renegade, spy, tattletale, traducer; ▪ *Ant* defender, loyalist, nationalist, patriot.

tramp [v] walk heavily
▪ *Syn* footslog, march, plod, pound, range, slog, stamp, stodge, stomp, stump, thud, toil, tour, trample, tread, trek, tromp, trudge; ▪ *Ant* glide, stride, tiptoe.

trance [n] hypnotic state
▪ *Syn* abstraction, coma, daze, dream, glaze, insensibility, muse, petrifaction, rapture, reverie, spell, study, stupor, transfixion, unconsciousness; ▪ *Ant* awareness, consciousness, perception.

tranquil [adj] quiet, peaceful
▪ *Syn* at peace, balmy, calm, composed, easy, even, gentle, halcyon, hushed, measured, mild, moderate, pacific, pastoral, placid, pleasing, possessed, quiet, reasonable, sedate, serene, smooth, soothing, tame, temperate, whispering; ▪ *Ant* chaotic, loud, noisy, turbulent, violent, wild.

tranquilize [v] make calm, quiet
▪ *Syn* balm, calm, calm down, compose, hush, lull, pacify, quell, quiet, relax, sedate, soothe, still, subdue, unruffle; ▪ *Ant* aggravate, agitate, incite, stir up, upset.

transcend [v] go beyond; surpass
▪ *Syn* beat, best, better, eclipse, exceed, excel, leave behind, outdo, outrival, outstrip, outvie, overstep, rise above, top, transform; ▪ *Ant* fail, lose.

transcendent/transcendental [adj] extraordinary, superior ▪ *Syn* abstract, accomplished, beyond grasp, consummate, entire, exceeding, fantastic, ideal, infinite, intuitive, matchless, obscure, original, otherworldly, peerless, primordial, sublime, supernatural, surpassing, towering, transmundane, ultimate, unique; ▪ *Ant* commonplace, inferior, mediocre, ordinary, simple.

transfer [v] pass possession to
▪ *Syn* assign, bear, bring, carry, cart, cede, change, consign, convert, convey, deliver, dispatch, dispense, displace, disturb, ferry, forward, give, hand, hand over, haul, lug, metamorphose, pass on, post, relegate, relocate, send, shift, ship, sign over, supply, taxi, tote, transmit, transmogrify, transmute, transplant, transport, transpose, turn over; ▪ *Ant* hold, keep, retain.

transfix [v1] hold one's attention
▪ *Syn* bewitch, captivate, enchant, engross, fascinate, hold, hypnotize, mes-

merize, paralyze, rivet, root, spellbind, stun; ▪ *Ant* bore, exhaust, repel.

transform [*v*] *change completely*
▪ *Syn* alter, commute, convert, denature, make over, metamorphose, mold, mutate, reconstruct, remodel, renew, revamp, revolutionize, switch, transfer, transfigure, transmogrify, transpose; ▪ *Ant* leave alone, preserve.

transgression [*n*] *violation, misbehavior* ▪ *Syn* breach, contravention, crime, defiance, disobedience, encroachment, erring, error, fault, infraction, infringement, iniquity, lapse, misdeed, misdemeanor, offense, overstepping, sin, slip, trespass, vice, wrong, wrongdoing; ▪ *Ant* compliance, good manners, morality, obedience, right, virtue.

transient/transitory [*adj*] *temporary, brief* ▪ *Syn* changeable, deciduous, ephemeral, evanescent, flash, fleeting, flitting, flying, fugacious, fugitive, impermanent, insubstantial, migratory, momentary, moving, passing, provisional, short, short-lived, short-term, temporal, transmigratory, unstable, volatile; ▪ *Ant* enduring, incessant, lasting, long-lasting, neverending, permanent, persistent, undying.

translucent [*adj*] *clear*
▪ *Syn* clear-cut, crystal, crystalline, diaphanous, glassy, limpid, lucent, lucid, luminous, pellucid, see-through, semiopaque, semitransparent, translucid; ▪ *Ant* cloudy, muddy, opaque.

transmit [*v*] *communicate, send*
▪ *Syn* broadcast, carry, channel, conduct, convey, dispatch, forward, hand down, impart, issue, mail, radio, remit, send, ship, spread, transfer, transport; ▪ *Ant* get, receive, take.

transparent [*adj1*] *see-through*
▪ *Syn* cellophane, clear, crystal-clear, crystalline, diaphanous, filmy, gauzy, glassy, gossamer, hyaline, limpid, lucent, lucid, pellucid, permeable, plain, sheer, thin, tiffany, translucent, vitreous; ▪ *Ant* cloudy, dark, muddy, opaque.

transparent [*adj2*] *obvious, understandable* ▪ *Syn* apparent, artless, candid, direct, distinct, evident, explicit, frank, guileless, honest, ingenuous, manifest, open, patent, plain, recognizable, self-explanatory, straightforward, visible; ▪ *Ant* cloudy, questionable, unclear, unintelligible, vague.

transplant [*v*] *relocate*
▪ *Syn* displace, emigrate, graft, immigrate, move, readapt, recondition, remove, reorient, reset, resettle, revamp, shift, transfer, transpose, uproot; ▪ *Ant* preserve, remain, retain, save.

transport [*v*] *captivate, delight*
▪ *Syn* carry away, electrify, elevate, enchant, enrapture, entrance, excite, inflame, move, provoke, quicken, ravish, send, slay, spellbind, stimulate, stir, thrill, trance; ▪ *Ant* depress, disenchant, repulse.

trap [*v*] *catch, snare; trick*
▪ *Syn* ambuscade, ambush, beguile, circumvent, deceive, decoy, dupe, enmesh, ensnare, entangle, entrap, fool, grab, hook, inveigle, nab, net, overtake, seduce, snag, surprise, take, tangle, trammel; ▪ *Ant* let go, liberate, release.

trauma [*n*] *severe mental or physical pain* ▪ *Syn* agony, anguish, blow, confusion, damage, disturbance, hurt, injury, jolt, ordeal, outburst, shock, strain, stress, suffering, torture, upset, wound; ▪ *Ant* alleviation, healing, help, relief.

travel [*v*] *journey on a trip or tour*
▪ *Syn* adventure, cross, cruise, drive, explore, fly, go abroad, jaunt, knock around, make a journey, motor, move, proceed, progress, ramble, roam, rove, sail, scour, set forth, set out, sightsee, take a trip, tour, traverse, vacation, visit, voyage, walk, wander, wend; ▪ *Ant* put down roots, remain, settle, stay.

traverse [*v*] *resist, contradict*
▪ *Syn* balk, buck, check, combat, contest, contravene, counter, counteract, cross, deny, disaffirm, dispute, duel, fight, frustrate, gainsay, go against, hinder, impede, impugn, negate, negative, obstruct, oppose, repel, thwart, withstand; ▪ *Ant* back up, confirm.

travesty [*v*] *ridicule, spoof*
▪ *Syn* ape, burlesque, caricature, deride, distort, imitate, lampoon, make a mockery of, make fun of, mimic, mock, parody, pervert, satire; ▪ *Ant* applaud, celebrate, extol, laud.

treacherous [*adj1*] *dishonest, disloyal*
▪ *Syn* deceitful, deceptive, duplicitous, faithless, false, insidious, misleading, perfidious, recreant, traitorous, treasonable, tricky, unfaithful, untrustworthy; ▪ *Ant* forthright, honest, loyal, true.

treacherous [*adj2*] *dangerous*
▪ *Syn* alarming, difficult, faulty, hazardous, jeopardous, menacing, ominous, perilous, precarious, risky, shaky, slippery, ticklish, tricky, unsafe; ▪ *Ant* reliable, safe, secure.

treason [*n*] *disloyalty*
▪ *Syn* breach of faith, crime, disaffection, lèse majesté, mutiny, revolt, sedition, seditious act, seditiousness, subversion, traitorousness, treachery; ▪ *Ant* allegiance, fidelity, loyalty, patriotism.

treasure [*v*] *hold dear*
▪ *Syn* adore, appreciate, apprize, cherish, conserve, dote on, esteem, guard, idolize, love, preserve, prize, revere, reverence, save, value, venerate, worship; ▪ *Ant* disparage, disregard, scorn.

treat [*v1*] *doctor, medicate*
▪ *Syn* administer, apply treatment, attend, care for, cure, dose, dress, heal, medicament, minister to, nurse, operate, prescribe; ▪ *Ant* harm, hurt, injure.

treat [*v2*] *be concerned with; discuss*
▪ *Syn* advise, approach, arrange, comment, confabulate, confer, consider, consult, contain, criticize, deal with, deliberate, discuss, enlarge upon, explain, interpret, manipulate, reason, review, study, tackle, think, touch upon, weigh, write about; ▪ *Ant* ignore, neglect.

trek [*v*] *journey*
▪ *Syn* foot, hike, march, migrate, plod, range, roam, rove, slog, traipse, tramp, travel, trudge, walk; ▪ *Ant* remain, stay.

tremble [*v*] *shake, vibrate*
▪ *Syn* flutter, jar, jitter, oscillate, palpitate, quake, quaver, quiver, rock, shiver, shudder, teeter, throb, totter, tremor, wobble; ▪ *Ant* be calm, calm, steady.

tremendous [*adj*] *huge, overwhelming*
▪ *Syn* amazing, astounding, awesome, colossal, cracking, deafening, enormous, excellent, exceptional, fabulous, fantastic, fearful, frightful, gargantuan, huge, humongous, immense, large, mammoth, massive, monumental, prodigious, stupendous, terrible, towering, vast, whopping, wonderful; ▪ *Ant* insignificant, little, small, tiny, unimportant.

trenchant [*adj*] *sarcastic, scathing; incisive* ▪ *Syn* acerbic, acidulous, astringent, biting, caustic, crisp, critical, cutting, distinct, explicit, forceful, graphic, intense, keen, mordant, penetrating, piquant, pungent, salient, severe, sharp, tart, vigorous,

weighty, well-defined; ▪ *Ant* frivolous, gentle, impotent, vague, weak.

trendy [*adj*] *in fashion, style*
▪ *Syn* contemporary, fashionable, in, in vogue, latest, popular, stylish, up-to-the-minute, voguish; ▪ *Ant* classic, old-fashioned, passé.

trepidation [*n*] *anxiety, worry*
▪ *Syn* agitation, alarm, apprehension, consternation, dismay, disquiet, disturbance, dread, excitement, fear, fright, horror, jitters, nervousness, palpitation, panic, perturbation, shock, uneasiness, worriment; ▪ *Ant* calm, confidence, contentment, happiness, poise.

trespass [*v*] *infringe, offend*
▪ *Syn* crash, deviate, displease, do wrong by, encroach, entrench, err, interlope, intrude, invade, lapse, meddle, misbehave, mix in, obtrude, overstep, poach, sin, transgress, violate; ▪ *Ant* comply, obey.

trial [*adj*] *experimental*
▪ *Syn* balloon, exploratory, pilot, preliminary, probationary, provisional, tentative, test, testing; ▪ *Ant* definite, known, proven.

tributary [*adj*] *secondary; branch*
▪ *Syn* accessory, dependent, feeding, minor, satellite, shoot, side, sub, subject, subordinate, under; ▪ *Ant* original, primary, source.

tribute [*n*] *testimonial, praise*
▪ *Syn* accolade, acknowledgment, applause, appreciation, citation, commendation, compliment, encomium, eulogy, gift, gratitude, honor, memorial, offering, panegyric, recognition, recommendation, salutation, salvo; ▪ *Ant* accusation, blame, criticism, disrespect, scorn.

trick [*v*] *fool; play joke on*
▪ *Syn* bamboozle, cheat, con, deceive, defraud, delude, disinform, dupe, fake, fool, gull, hoax, hoodwink, impose upon, mislead, outwit, swindle, throw, trap, victimize; ▪ *Ant* be forthright, be serious.

trickle [*v*] *run out*
▪ *Syn* crawl, creep, distill, dribble, drip, drop, exude, flow, issue, leak, ooze, percolate, seep, stream, trill, weep; ▪ *Ant* flood, flow, surge.

tricky [*adj1*] *complicated, difficult*
▪ *Syn* catchy, complex, critical, delicate, intricate, involved, perplexing, precarious, problematic, quirky, risky, rocky, sensitive, sticky, ticklish, touchy, unstable; ▪ *Ant* easy, simple, uncomplicated.

tricky [adj2] *deceptive, sly*
- *Syn* artful, astute, cagey, catchy, clever, crafty, cunning, deceitful, deep, delusive, delusory, devious, dishonest, guileful, insidious, intelligent, keen, misleading, scheming, shady, sharp, shifty, shrewd, smooth, subtle, treacherous, wily, witted, wry; ▪ *Ant* aboveboard, frank, honest.

tried [adj] *reliable*
- *Syn* approved, certified, constant, demonstrated, dependable, faithful, proved, secure, staunch, steadfast, tested, trustworthy, trusty; ▪ *Ant* irresponsible, unreliable.

trifling [adj] *insignificant, worthless*
- *Syn* banal, empty, frivolous, hollow, idle, inane, inconsequential, insipid, jejune, loitering, measly, negligible, nugatory, picayune, piddling, silly, slight, trivial, vain, valueless, vapid; ▪ *Ant* crucial, important, significant, useful, worthwhile.

trigger [v] *cause to happen*
- *Syn* activate, bring about, cause, elicit, generate, give rise to, produce, prompt, provoke, set in motion, set off, spark, start; ▪ *Ant* block, check, halt, inhibit, repress, stop.

trim [adj1] *neat, orderly*
- *Syn* clean, compact, dapper, fit, in good shape, nice, slick, smart, spruce, streamlined, symmetrical, tidy, well-groomed; ▪ *Ant* disorderly, rough, sloppy, unkempt.

trim [adj2] *shapely*
- *Syn* beautiful, clean, comely, fit, graceful, in good shape, sleek, slender, slick, slim, statuesque, streamlined, svelte, well-balanced, well-proportioned, willowy; ▪ *Ant* chubby, fat, overweight.

trim [v1] *cut shorter*
- *Syn* abbreviate, barber, clip, curtail, cut, dock, edit, even up, lop, mow, pare, plane, prune, shave, shear, snip, tidy, truncate, whittle down; ▪ *Ant* develop, let grow.

trim [v2] *beat, defeat*
- *Syn* clobber, drub, lambaste, lick, smother, thrash, trounce, whip; ▪ *Ant* fail, lose.

trinket [n] *knickknack*
- *Syn* bagatelle, bauble, bead, bibelot, curio, gadget, hardware, junk, novelty, objet d'art, ornament, plaything, toy, trifle; ▪ *Ant* jewel, valuable.

trip [v] *fall, err*
- *Syn* buck, canter, confuse, disconcert, fall, fall over, founder, frolic, go wrong, hop, lapse, lope, lurch, miscalculate, misstep, pitch, plunge, skip, slide, slip, slip on, slip up, sprawl, spring, stumble, throw off, tumble, unsettle; ▪ *Ant* correct, fix.

trite [adj] *silly, commonplace*
- *Syn* banal, bathetic, bromidic, cliché, clichéd, common, drained, dull, exhausted, flat, hackneyed, jejune, ordinary, pedestrian, platitudinous, prosaic, routine, set, shopworn, stale, stereotyped, stock, threadbare, timeworn, tired, vapid, well-worn, worn-out; ▪ *Ant* desirable, important, impressive, original, pertinent, relevant, uncommon.

triumph [v1] *be very happy*
- *Syn* celebrate, crow, delight, exult, gloat, glory, jubilate, rejoice, revel, swagger; ▪ *Ant* bewail, grieve, mourn.

triumph [v2] *achieve, succeed*
- *Syn* best, conquer, dominate, flourish, master, overcome, overwhelm, prevail, prosper, sink, subdue, sweep, thrive, trounce, vanquish, win; ▪ *Ant* fail, forfeit, lose.

triumphant [adj] *successful*
- *Syn* boastful, celebratory, champion, conquering, dominant, elated, exultant, glorious, jubilant, on top, out front, prize-winning, proud, rejoicing, swaggering, victorious; ▪ *Ant* beaten, defeated, humbled.

trivial [adj] *not important*
- *Syn* atomic, commonplace, diminutive, evanescent, everyday, frivolous, immaterial, inconsequential, meager, minor, negligible, nugatory, paltry, scanty, slight, trifling, trite, worthless; ▪ *Ant* consequential, important, significant, useful, valuable, weighty, worthwhile.

tropical [adj] *warm and humid*
- *Syn* close, equatorial, hot, lush, steamy, sticky, stifling, sultry, sweltering, torrid, tropic; ▪ *Ant* arctic, freezing, frigid, polar.

trot [v] *move along briskly*
- *Syn* amble, canter, go, hurry, jog, lope, pad, rack, ride, run, scamper, step lively; ▪ *Ant* crawl, creep, gallop, plod, run.

trot out [v] *bring forward*
- *Syn* brandish, bring up, come out with, display, disport, drag up, exhibit, expose, flash, flaunt, parade, recite, rehearse, re-

iterate, relate, repeat, represent, show, show off; ▪ *Ant* conceal, hide.

trouble [*v1*] *bother, worry* ▪ *Syn* afflict, agitate, ail, annoy, burden, concern, discommode, discompose, disconcert, disoblige, disquiet, distress, disturb, fret, get to, grieve, harass, harry, impose on, inconvenience, irk, irritate, pain, perplex, perturb, pester, plague, sadden, stir up, strain, stress, torment, try, upset, vex; ▪ *Ant* delight, elate, please, soothe.

trouble [*v2*] *make an effort* ▪ *Syn* be concerned with, exert, go to the effort of; ▪ *Ant* aid, assist, help.

troublemaker [*n*] *person who causes a problem* ▪ *Syn* agent provocateur, agitator, hellion, incendiary, inciter, instigator, knave, meddler, mischief-maker, nuisance, rascal, recreant, rogue; ▪ *Ant* arbiter, pacifier, peacemaker.

troublesome [*adj*] *bothersome, worrisome* ▪ *Syn* alarming, annoying, arduous, burdensome, damaging, dangerous, demanding, difficult, disquieting, importunate, inconvenient, intractable, irksome, irritating, laborious, messy, painful, pesky, pestilential, problematic, refractory, rough, taxing, tiresome, tough, tricky, trying, uphill, upsetting, vexatious, wearisome, wicked, worrying; ▪ *Ant* cooperative, easy, helpful, nice.

trounce [*v*] *defeat overwhelmingly* ▪ *Syn* bash, beat, blank, bury, cap, clobber, conquer, crush, drub, overcome, overwhelm, rout, swamp, whip, win; ▪ *Ant* fail, forfeit, lose.

truce [*n*] *peaceful solution* ▪ *Syn* accord, agreement, amnesty, armistice, break, breather, cease-fire, cessation, de-escalation, halt, intermission, interval, letup, lull, moratorium, pause, peace, reconciliation, reprieve, respite, rest, stay, suspension, temporary peace, terms, treaty; ▪ *Ant* disagreement, fight, war.

truculent [*adj*] *belligerent, hateful* ▪ *Syn* aggressive, antagonistic, bad-tempered, barbarous, bellicose, brutal, bullying, caustic, contentious, contumelious, defiant, ferocious, hostile, inhumane, intimidating, mean, militant, opprobrious, ornery, pugnacious, quarrelsome, scurrilous, sharp, sullen, trenchant, vituperous; ▪ *Ant* amiable, cooperative, gentle, mild, tame.

trudge [*v*] *walk heavily* ▪ *Syn* clump, footslog, hike, lumber, march, plod, slog, step, stumble, stump, traipse, tramp, tread, trek, wade; ▪ *Ant* tiptoe.

true [*adj1*] *real, valid; concordant with facts* ▪ *Syn* accurate, appropriate, authentic, bona fide, correct, dependable, direct, exact, factual, fitting, genuine, honest, lawful, natural, normal, perfect, proper, right, rightful, sincere, straight, trustworthy, veracious, veritable, very; ▪ *Ant* corrupt, counterfeit, deceitful, false, fraudulent, invalid.

true [*adj2*] *loyal* ▪ *Syn* ardent, conscientious, creditable, dedicated, devoted, dutiful, estimable, faithful, firm, high-principled, honest, just, liege, pure, reliable, right, scrupulous, sincere, staunch, straight, strict, sure, trustworthy, worthy; ▪ *Ant* cheating, dishonest, disloyal, evil, faithless, untrustworthy.

true [*adv*] *honestly, accurately* ▪ *Syn* correctly, on target, perfectly, precisely, properly, rightly, truthfully, unerringly, veraciously, veritably; ▪ *Ant* dishonestly, inaccurately.

truly [*adv*] *really, doubtlessly* ▪ *Syn* absolutely, accurately, authentically, beyond doubt, beyond question, constantly, definitely, devotedly, exactly, firmly, genuinely, honestly, in fact, in truth, legitimately, loyally, positively, reliably, righteously, rightly, sincerely, staunchly, steadily, surely, truthfully, unequivocally, veritably, with devotion, without a doubt; ▪ *Ant* doubtfully, dubiously, indefinite.

truncate [*v*] *shorten* ▪ *Syn* abbreviate, abridge, clip, crop, curtail, cut, cut off, cut short, lop, pare, prune, shear, top, trim; ▪ *Ant* elongate, expand, lengthen, stretch.

trunk [*n*] *body, core* ▪ *Syn* block, bole, butt, column, log, soma, stalk, stem, stock, thorax, torso; ▪ *Ant* extremities.

trust [*v*] *believe, place confidence in* ▪ *Syn* accredit, assume, bank on, be convinced, bet on, build on, count on, depend on, expect, have faith in, imagine, lean on, look to, place confidence in, place trust in, presume, reckon on, rely upon, suppose, surmise, swear by, take, think likely; ▪ *Ant* disbelieve, distrust, mistrust.

trustworthy/trusty [adj] *reliable, believable* ▪ **Syn** authentic, authoritative, convincing, credible, dependable, ethical, exact, honest, honorable, level-headed, mature, open, plausible, principled, realistic, responsible, righteous, saintly, secure, sensible, square, steadfast, straight, tried, true, unfailing, upright, valid, veracious; ▪ **Ant** corrupt, dishonorable, undependable, unreliable.

truth [n] *honesty, loyalty*
▪ **Syn** candor, constancy, dedication, devotion, faith, faithfulness, fidelity, frankness, integrity, openness, sincerity, uprightness, veridicality, verity; ▪ **Ant** dishonesty, disloyalty, falsehood, misrepresentation.

truthful [adj] *accurate, honest*
▪ **Syn** believable, candid, exact, factual, frank, guileless, ingenuous, just, literal, open, plainspoken, precise, real, righteous, scrupulous, sincere, straightforward, trustworthy, veritable; ▪ **Ant** dishonest, hypocritical, inaccurate, lying, untruthful.

try [v1] *attempt*
▪ **Syn** aim, aspire, attack, bear down, compete, contend, contest, drive for, endeavor, exert oneself, go after, labor, make a bid, propose, risk, seek, strive, struggle, tackle, venture, vie for, work, wrangle; ▪ **Ant** abstain, avoid, balk, demur.

try [v2] *experiment, test*
▪ **Syn** appraise, assay, check, check out, evaluate, examine, inspect, investigate, judge, prove, sample, scrutinize, taste, try out, weigh; ▪ **Ant** abstain.

try [v3] *bother, afflict*
▪ **Syn** agonize, annoy, crucify, distress, excruciate, harass, irk, irritate, martyr, plague, rack, strain, stress, tax, torment, torture, upset, vex, weary, wring; ▪ **Ant** delight, please.

trying [adj] *difficult, bothersome*
▪ **Syn** aggravating, annoying, arduous, demanding, exacting, exasperating, exigent, fatiguing, hard, irksome, irritating, onerous, oppressive, pestilent, rough, severe, strenuous, taxing, tiresome, tough, tricky, troublesome, upsetting, vexing, wearisome, weighty; ▪ **Ant** easy, mild, moderate, soothing, unstressful.

tug [v] *pull*
▪ **Syn** drag, draw, haul, heave, jerk, lug, strain, toil, tow, traction, wrench, yank; ▪ **Ant** push, shove.

tumble [v] *fall or make fall awkwardly*
▪ **Syn** bowl down, bring down, descend, dip, disarrange, disarray, disorder, disturb, flop, go down, jumble, keel, keel over, knock down, knock over, lose footing, nose-dive, pitch, plummet, plunge, skid, slip, slump, spill, stumble, tip over, topple, toss, trip, upset; ▪ **Ant** ascend, construct, increase, rise, soar, tower.

tumultous/tumultuous [adj] *confused; in an uproar* ▪ **Syn** agitated, boisterous, clamorous, disorderly, disturbed, excited, hectic, lawless, noisy, obstreperous, passionate, raging, rambunctious, raucous, restless, riotous, rowdy, rumbunctious, stormy, termagant, turbulent, unrestrained, unruly, vociferous, wild; ▪ **Ant** calm, orderly, peaceful.

tunnel [v] *dig a passage through*
▪ **Syn** burrow, excavate, mine, penetrate, sap, scoop out, undermine; ▪ **Ant** block, fill in, plug.

turbulent [adj1] *unsettled, raging*
▪ **Syn** bitter, blustering, blustery, bumpy, choppy, fierce, foaming, furious, howling, inclement, noisy, restless, roaring, rough, rugged, storming, stormy, thunderous, tremulous, tumultous/tumultuous, violent, wild; ▪ **Ant** calm, mild, moderate, settled.

turbulent [adj2] *rebellious, unmanageable* ▪ **Syn** agitated, anarchic, angry, bitter, boisterous, chaotic, destructive, disorderly, excited, fierce, fiery, insubordinate, lawless, mutinous, obstreperous, passionate, quarrelsome, rabid, rambunctious, rampant, raucous, refractory, riotous, rough, rowdy, rude, seditious, shaking, storming, termagant, tumultous/tumultuous, vehement, violent, vociferous, wild; ▪ **Ant** calm, manageable, moderate, obedient, stable.

turmoil [n] *chaos*
▪ **Syn** agitation, bedlam, bustle, commotion, confusion, disorder, disquiet, distress, disturbance, dither, ferment, flurry, fuss, hassle, lather, mix-up, pandemonium, pother, restiveness, riot, row, ruckus, stir, strife, tumult, turbulence, unrest, uproar, violence, whirl; ▪ **Ant** calm, harmony, order, peace.

turn [v1] *reverse; change course*
▪ **Syn** about-face, alternate, backslide, change position, convert, curve, depart, detour, detract, deviate, digress, direct, diverge, double back, face about, go

back, inverse, invert, loop, pivot, rechannel, recoil, redirect, regress, relapse, retrace, return, revert, shift, shunt, shy away, sway, swerve, swing, switch, tack, twist, veer, volte-face, whip, whirl, zigzag; ▪ *Ant* advance, continue, progress, stay the course.

turn [*v2*] *sicken*
▪ *Syn* derange, discompose, disorder, nauseate, revolt, unbalance, undo, unsettle, upset; ▪ *Ant* attract, cheer, entice, soothe.

turn down [*v*] *reject*
▪ *Syn* decline, disapprove, dismiss, rebuff, refuse, reprobate, repudiate, say no, scorn, spurn; ▪ *Ant* accept, take.

turn in [*v*] *go to bed*
▪ *Syn* bed, go to sleep, lie down, nap, rest, retire, roll in; ▪ *Ant* awaken, get up, wake.

turn off [*v1*] *disgust*
▪ *Syn* alienate, bore, disenchant, disinterest, displease, irritate, nauseate, offend, repel, sicken; ▪ *Ant* attract, cheer, delight, enchant, fascinate.

turn off [*v2*] *stop from operating*
▪ *Syn* close, cut, cut out, douse, extinguish, halt, hit the switch, put out, shut, shut down, shut off, switch off, turn out, unplug; ▪ *Ant* begin, open, start, turn on.

turn on [*v1*] *excite, please*
▪ *Syn* arouse, attract, captivate, enchant, initiate, introduce, show, stimulate, stir up, titillate, work up; ▪ *Ant* bore, depress, disenchant, tire, turn off.

turn on [*v2*] *start the operation of*
▪ *Syn* activate, begin, energize, ignite, initiate, introduce, log on, put in gear, set in motion, start up, switch on; ▪ *Ant* close, end, finish, shut down, turn off.

turn out [*v*] *get out of bed*
▪ *Syn* arise, emerge, get up, pile out, rise, rise and shine, roll out, show up, wake, wake up; ▪ *Ant* nap, sleep.

turn over [*v1*] *give, transfer*
▪ *Syn* assign, confer, confide, consign, convey, delegate, deliver, entrust, feed, find, furnish, give over, hand over, pass on, relegate, relinquish, supply, surrender, yield; ▪ *Ant* receive, take, withhold.

turn over [*v2*] *think about seriously*
▪ *Syn* consider, contemplate, deliberate, give thought to, meditate, mull over, ponder, reflect on, roll, ruminate, wonder about; ▪ *Ant* dismiss, ignore, overlook.

turn up [*v1*] *come, arrive* ▪ *Syn* appear, attend, come, come in, enter, materialize,

reach, show; ▪ *Ant* abandon, go, leave.

turn up [*v2*] *discover or be discovered*
▪ *Syn* become known, be found, catch, descry, detect, disclose, encounter, espy, expose, find, learn, meet, reveal, spot, track, transpire, unearth; ▪ *Ant* lose, miss.

tutor [*v*] *teach someone privately*
▪ *Syn* clue, coach, direct, discipline, drill, edify, educate, guide, instruct, lecture, ready, school, train; ▪ *Ant* learn.

twilight [*n*] *onset of darkness at end of day* ▪ *Syn* afterglow, dimness, dusk, early evening, evening, gloaming, half-light, late afternoon, night, nightfall, sundown, sunset; ▪ *Ant* daybreak, sunrise.

twin [*adj*] *duplicate, similar*
▪ *Syn* bifold, binary, coupled, double, dual, identical, joint, like, matched, paired, parallel, same, twofold; ▪ *Ant* dissimilar, opposite, unlike.

twine [*v*] *coil, twist together*
▪ *Syn* bend, braid, corkscrew, curl, encircle, entwine, interlace, knit, loop, meander, plait, spiral, tangle, twist, undulate, weave, wreathe; ▪ *Ant* straighten, untwist.

twist [*v1*] *curl, spin*
▪ *Syn* coil, corkscrew, encircle, entwine, rick, screw, spiral, turn around, twine, twirl, weave, wiggle, wind, wrap, wreathe, wrench, wriggle, zigzag; ▪ *Ant* disentangle, straighten, uncurl, untwist, unwrap.

twist [*v2*] *misrepresent*
▪ *Syn* alter, belie, change, color, contort, distort, falsify, garble, misquote, misstate, pervert, warp; ▪ *Ant* clear up, elucidate, explain, explicate.

tycoon [*n*] *person who has a lot of money, power* ▪ *Syn* administrator, baron, boss, capitalist, entrepreneur, executive, financier, industrialist, investor, magnate, mogul; ▪ *Ant* employee, laborer, pauper.

type [*v*] *classify*
▪ *Syn* arrange, categorize, class, peg, put away, put down as, sort, standardize, stereotype, typecast; ▪ *Ant* disorganize, jumble.

typical [*adj*] *usual, conventional*
▪ *Syn* archetypal, average, characteristic, classic, common, emblematic, habitual, illustrative, indicative, model, normal, ordinary, orthodox, paradigmatic, prevalent, prototypical, quintessential, regular,

representative, standard, stock, suggestive, symbolic, typic; ▪ *Ant* atypical, different, rare, unconventional, unorthodox, unusual.

U

ubiquitous [*adj*] *ever-present*
▪ *Syn* all-over, everywhere, omnipresent, pervasive, ubiquity, universal, wall-to-wall, widespread; ▪ *Ant* rare, scarce, unusual.

ugly [*adj1*] *unattractive*
▪ *Syn* appalling, deformed, disfigured, frightful, grisly, grotesque, hideous, horrid, ill-favored, loathsome, monstrous, plain, repugnant, repulsive, revolting; ▪ *Ant* attractive, beautiful, lovely, pleasing.

ugly [*adj2*] *unpleasant, disagreeable*
▪ *Syn* base, despicable, dirty, disgusting, filthy, frightful, hideous, ignoble, low, mean, messy, nasty, nauseous, odious, pesky, repellent, repulsive, scandalous, sickening, sordid, terrible, vexatious, vile, wretched; ▪ *Ant* agreeable, good, kind, nice, pleasant, pleasing.

ugly [*adj3*] *dangerous, threatening*
▪ *Syn* angry, bellicose, dark, disagreeable, dour, evil, forbidding, gloomy, malevolent, menacing, nasty, ominous, rough, saturnine, sinister, truculent, vicious, violent, wicked; ▪ *Ant* auspicious, delicate, gentle, promising, safe.

ulterior [*adj*] *secret; pertaining to a hidden goal* ▪ *Syn* ambiguous, buried, concealed, covert, dark, enigmatic, guarded, hidden, obscure, remote, secondary, shrouded; ▪ *Ant* expressed, known, obvious, overt, public.

ultimate [*adj1*] *last, final*
▪ *Syn* capping, closing, concluding, conclusive, decisive, end, eventual, extreme, farthest, furthermost, furthest, hindmost, latest, latter, lattermost, most distant, terminal; ▪ *Ant* beginning, first, introductory, opening.

ultimate [*adj2*] *best, greatest*
▪ *Syn* extreme, highest, incomparable, maximum, paramount, significant, superlative, topmost, towering, transcendent, unmatchable, utmost; ▪ *Ant* least, lowest, minimum, worst.

ultimate [*adj3*] *fundamental*
▪ *Syn* absolute, basic, categorical, elemental, empyreal, primary, sublime, transcendental; ▪ *Ant* auxiliary, extra, inessential, secondary, unnecessary.

ultimately [*adv*] *eventually*
▪ *Syn* after all, at last, at long last, climactically, conclusively, finally, fundamentally, hereafter, in conclusion, in due time, in the end, someday, sooner or later, yet; ▪ *Ant* never.

ultra [*adj*] *extreme*
▪ *Syn* drastic, excessive, extremist, fanatical, immoderate, outlandish, outré, rabid, radical, revolutionary; ▪ *Ant* middle, moderate.

umbrage [*n*] *personal displeasure*
▪ *Syn* anger, annoyance, chagrin, exasperation, fury, grudge, huff, indignation, ire, offense, pique, rage, resentment, sense of injury, vexation, wrath; ▪ *Ant* amity, goodwill, harmony, pleasure.

unable [*adj*] *not having talent, skill*
▪ *Syn* clumsy, helpless, impotent, incapable, incapacitated, inefficient, inept, powerless, sidelined, weak; ▪ *Ant* able, adequate, capable, competent, fit, qualified, skillful, talented.

unabridged [*adj*] *not shortened*
▪ *Syn* complete, entire, full-length, intact, total, uncut, whole; ▪ *Ant* abridged, condensed, shortened.

unacceptable [*adj*] *not suitable or satisfactory* ▪ *Syn* below par, damaged, displeasing, ill-favored, improper, inadmissible, objectionable, offensive, reject, repugnant; ▪ *Ant* desirable, ok, satisfactory, suitable.

unaccompanied [*adj*] *alone*
▪ *Syn* by oneself, detached, individual, isolated, lone, on one's own, single, solitary, solo, stag, unescorted; ▪ *Ant* accompanied, chaperoned, escorted.

unaccountable [*adj*] *not explainable; mysterious* ▪ *Syn* arcane, astonishing, baffling, extraordinary, impenetrable, inexplicable, mystic, odd, peculiar, puzzling, strange, uncommon; ▪ *Ant* comprehensible, normal, ordinary, unusual.

unaccustomed [*adj1*] *not prepared, ready; new to* ▪ *Syn* inexperienced, not used to, novice, unacquainted, unfamiliar with, unskilled, untrained, unused to, unversed in; ▪ *Ant* experienced, practiced, prepared, ready.

unaccustomed [*adj2*] *new, strange*
▪ *Syn* alien, bizarre, different, eccentric,

exceptional, foreign, imported, novel, outlandish, quaint, remarkable, singular, surprising, unconventional, unusual, unwonted, variant; ▪ *Ant* customary, normal, usual.

unadvised [*adj*] *not smart; careless*
▪ *Syn* brash, hasty, heedless, ignorant, imprudent, inadvisable, incautious, indiscreet, injudicious, rash, reckless, thoughtless; ▪ *Ant* advised, cautious, wise.

unaffected [*adj1*] *honest, unsophisticated* ▪ *Syn* artless, candid, direct, forthright, frank, genuine, guileless, ingenuous, modest, naive, plain, simple, spontaneous, straightforward, true, unpretentious; ▪ *Ant* phony, refined, sophisticated, unnatural, worldly.

unaffected [*adj2*] *unchanged, unmoved* ▪ *Syn* aloof, callous, casual, cool, easygoing, impassive, steady, unconcerned, unimpressed, unresponsive, untouched; ▪ *Ant* affected, changed, disturbed, sympathetic.

unanimous [*adj*] *in agreement; uncontested* ▪ *Syn* accepted, accordant, as one, assenting, collective, combined, communal, concordant, concurrent, consistent, harmonious, homogeneous, in complete accord, like-minded, shared, solid, unified, united, universal; ▪ *Ant* inharmonious, schismatic, split.

unappetizing [*adj*] *distasteful*
▪ *Syn* flat, flavorless, insipid, savorless, tasteless, unappealing, unpalatable, unsavory, vapid; ▪ *Ant* attractive, delicious, savory, tasty.

unapproachable [*adj1*] *unfriendly*
▪ *Syn* aloof, cold, distant, frigid, hesitant, inaccessible, remote, reserved, standoffish, uncommunicative, unsociable, withdrawn; ▪ *Ant* accessible, amiable, approachable, friendly, outgoing.

unapproachable [*adj2*] *difficult to get to* ▪ *Syn* inaccessible, out of reach, out-of-the-way, remote, unattainable, unobtainable, unreachable; ▪ *Ant* accessible, approachable.

unasked [*adj*] *voluntary*
▪ *Syn* gratuitous, impudent, presumptuous, spontaneous, unbidden, uncalled-for, uninvited, unprompted, wanton; ▪ *Ant* asked, invited, solicited, welcome.

unassuming [*adj*] *shy*
▪ *Syn* bashful, diffident, humble, meek, prim, quiet, reserved, retiring, self-effacing, unambitious, unpretentious; ▪ *Ant* bold, brave, confident, presumptuous.

unauthorized [*adj*] *not sanctioned, permitted* ▪ *Syn* clandestine, furtive, illegal, illegitimate, pirated, unapproved, underhand, unsanctioned, wrongful; ▪ *Ant* allowable, certified, official, permitted.

unavoidable [*adj*] *bound to happen*
▪ *Syn* certain, compulsory, fated, impending, ineluctable, inescapable, inevasible, inevitable, necessary, obligatory, set, sure; ▪ *Ant* avoidable, escapable, optional, preventable.

unaware [*adj*] *ignorant*
▪ *Syn* blind, careless, daydreaming, forgetful, heedless, ignorant, inattentive, insensible, mooning, negligent, nescient, oblivious, unconcerned, unconscious, uninformed, unwitting; ▪ *Ant* aware, cognizant, informed, knowing.

unawares [*adv*] *without warning; suddenly* ▪ *Syn* abruptly, by accident, by surprise, carelessly, inadvertently, mistakenly, off guard, short, sudden, unconsciously, unwittingly, without warning; ▪ *Ant* consciously, knowingly, wittingly.

unbalanced [*adj1*] *not even, stable*
▪ *Syn* asymmetrical, disproportionate, irregular, lopsided, off-balance, shaky, top-heavy, treacherous, unequal, unstable, unsteady, wobbly; ▪ *Ant* balanced, even, sound, stable.

unbalanced [*adj2*] *crazy; mentally disturbed* ▪ *Syn* daft, demented, deranged, eccentric, erratic, insane, irrational, lunatic, mad, psychotic, touched, troubled, unsound, unstable; ▪ *Ant* balanced, sane, well.

unbearable [*adj*] *very bad; too much*
▪ *Syn* insufferable, insupportable, intolerable, oppressive, unsurpassable; ▪ *Ant* acceptable, tolerable.

unbecoming [*adj*] *improper, unsuitable*
▪ *Syn* awkward, clumsy, gauche, ill-suited, inappropriate, incongruous, indecent, inept, maladroit, malapropos, offensive, rough, salacious, tasteless, unattractive, unbefitting, unsightly; ▪ *Ant* acceptable, becoming, fitting, proper, seemly, suitable.

unbelievable [*adj*] *beyond the imagination* ▪ *Syn* beyond belief, doubtful, dubious, farfetched, implausible, improbable, incredible, lamebrained, outlandish, phony, questionable, reaching, staggering, suspect; ■ *Ant* credible, plausible, real.

unbending [adj] *rigid, tough*
■ *Syn* crisp, distant, firm, formal, incompliant, inelastic, inexorable, inflexible, intractable, obdurate, obstinate, relentless, resolute, severe, single-minded, stiff, strict, stubborn, uncompromising, uptight; ■ *Ant* bending, flexible, pliable, pliant, relaxed, soft.

unbiased [adj] *not prejudiced*
■ *Syn* aloof, cold, dispassionate, equitable, even-handed, fair, honest, impartial, just, neutral, nondiscriminatory, nonpartisan, open-minded; ■ *Ant* prejudiced, subjective.

unblemished [adj] *not flawed*
■ *Syn* chaste, decent, faultless, flawless, immaculate, modest, perfect, sound, spotless, stainless, unmarred, unstained, unsullied whole; ■ *Ant* blemished, flawed, imperfect.

unbreakable [adj] *strong, tough*
■ *Syn* armored, brass-bound, durable, everlasting, incorruptible, indestructible, lasting, nonbreakable, perdurable, resistant, rugged, shatterproof; ■ *Ant* delicate, fragile, weak.

unbroken [v] *continuous, whole*
■ *Syn* ceaseless, constant, deep, endless, even, fast, incessant, perfect, perpetual, profound, regular, solid, successive, total, uninterrupted; ■ *Ant* broken, discontinuous, inconstant, intermittent, partial.

unburden [adj] *get rid of*
■ *Syn* clear, confess, confide, disburden, discharge, disclose, disencumber, dispose of, divulge, ease, empty, lighten, lose, relieve, relinquish, reveal, shake, tell all, throw off; ■ *Ant* conceal, hide, repress.

uncanny [adj] *very strange, unusual*
■ *Syn* creepy, devilish, eerie, exceptional, fantastic, ghostly, incredible, inexplainable, inspired, magical, mysterious, mystifying, preternatural, prodigious, queer, scary, superhuman, supernatural, weird; ■ *Ant* common, earthly, natural, usual.

uncertain [adj] *doubtful, changeable*
■ *Syn* ambiguous, ambivalent, chancy, conjectural, dubious, erratic, fitful, hazy, hesitant, iffy, incalculable, inconstant, indefinite, indeterminate, indistinct, insecure, irregular, irresolute, precarious, questionable, risky, speculative, unpredictable, unreliable, unresolved, vacillat-

ing, vague, variable, wavering; ■ *Ant* certain, clear, definite, determined, foreseeable, secure, sure, unchanging.

unchangeable [adj] *constant, steadfast*
■ *Syn* changeless, continuing, firm, fixed, immovable, immutable, inalterable, inevitable, inflexible, invariable, irreversible, permanent, resolute, stable, strong, unalterable; ■ *Ant* changeable, changing, inconstant, intermittent, temporary.

unchanging [adj] *constant, permanent*
■ *Syn* abiding, changeless, consistent, continuing, enduring, equable, eternal, even, fixed, immutable, imperishable, invariable, lasting, perpetual, rigid, same, stabile, static; ■ *Ant* changeable, inconstant, intermittent, temporary.

uncivilized [adj] *wild, uncultured*
■ *Syn* barbarian, barbaric, barbarous, boorish, brutish, churlish, coarse, crass, crude, discourteous, disrespectful, ill-bred, illiterate, impertinent, impolite, loutish, mannerless, outrageous, philistine, primitive, rude, rugged, savage, uncouth, uncultivated, unsophisticated, vulgar, wicked; ■ *Ant* civilized, cultured, domesticated, polished, refined, sophisticated.

unclean [adj] *dirty*
■ *Syn* bedraggled, befouled, besmirched, common, contaminated, decayed, defiled, evil, feculent, fetid, foul, grimy, impure, messy, muddy, nasty, polluted, putrid, rancid, rotten, sloppy, slovenly, soiled, sordid, spotted, stained, stinking, sullied, tainted, tarnished, vile; ■ *Ant* holy, hygienic, pristine, pure, uncontaminated, unpolluted.

uncomfortable [adj1] *painful, rough*
■ *Syn* afflictive, agonizing, annoying, awkward, bitter, cramped, difficult, disagreeable, excruciating, galling, grievous, hard, ill-fitting, incommodious, thorny, torturing, troublesome, vexatious, wearisome; ■ *Ant* comfortable, easy, painless.

uncomfortable [adj2] *distressed, upset*
■ *Syn* aching, awkward, chafed, cheerless, discomfited, discomposed, embarrassed, galled, ill at ease, miserable, nervous, pained, restless, self-conscious, smarting, stiff, strained, troubled, wracked; ■ *Ant* comfortable, content, happy.

uncommitted [adj] *free; not involved*
■ *Syn* floating, free-spirited, neutral, non-

aligned, nonpartisan, unaffiliated, unattached, unpledged; ▪ Ant aligned, attached, committed, involved.

uncommon [adj1] very different
▪ Syn aberrant, abnormal, anomalous, arcane, bizarre, curious, eccentric, exotic, extraordinary, fantastic, freakish, infrequent, irregular, noteworthy, novel, odd, original, peculiar, rare, remarkable, scarce, seldom, singular, sporadic, startling, strange, surprising, weird; ▪ Ant common, familiar, normal, regular, usual.

uncommon [adj2] wonderful, exceptional ▪ Syn distinctive, extraordinary, incomparable, inimitable, notable, noteworthy, outstanding, rare, remarkable, singular, special, superior, unimaginable, unique, unparalleled; ▪ Ant blah, commonplace, ordinary.

uncommonly [adv] infrequently
▪ Syn exceptionally, extremely, hardly ever, in few instances, irregularly, now and then, occasionally, particularly, peculiarly, rarely, scarcely ever, seldom, sporadically, strangely, unusually, very; ▪ Ant commonly, frequently.

uncommunicative [adj] shy, silent
▪ Syn aloof, curt, distant, evasive, guarded, quiet, reserved, reticent, secretive, standoffish, taciturn; ▪ Ant confident, extroverted, responsive.

uncompromising [adj] stubborn
▪ Syn decided, determined, firm, inexorable, inflexible, locked, obstinate, relentless, resolute, rigid, steadfast, strict, tough; ▪ Ant compromising, cooperative, flexible, open, willing.

unconcerned [adj] carefree; apathetic
▪ Syn aloof, blind, callous, cool, detached, dispassionate, easy, feckless, forgetful, hardened, hard-hearted, inattentive, incurious, indifferent, insensible, lukewarm, negligent, neutral, nonchalant, oblivious, phlegmatic, relaxed, serene, supine; ▪ Ant caring, curious, interested.

unconditional [adj] absolute, total
▪ Syn all out, assured, categorical, decisive, definite, entire, explicit, final, flat out, genuine, outright, plenary, thorough, unequivocal, utter, whole, wide; ▪ Ant ambiguous, provisional, qualified.

unconscionable [adj] immoral, immoderate ▪ Syn barbarous, criminal, dishonest, excessive, extreme, inordinate,

knavish, outrageous, preposterous, sneaky, unscrupulous, wanton; ▪ Ant decent, good, moderate, moral, principled.

unconscious [adj1] not awake; out cold
▪ Syn benumbed, comatose, drowsy, entranced, inanimate, inert, insensible, lethargic, numb out, senseless, stunned, stupefied, swooning, torpid, tranced; ▪ Ant awake, aware, conscious.

unconscious [adj2] ignorant; automatic
▪ Syn accidental, ignorant, inadvertent, inattentive, innate, involuntary, latent, lost, reflex, repressed, subconscious, subliminal, suppressed; ▪ Ant aware, conscious, decided, intended, intentional, knowing.

uncontrollable [adj] wild; carried away
▪ Syn beside oneself, disorderly, excited, frantic, furious, insurgent, irrepressible, lawless, mad, uncontainable, ungovernable, unruly; ▪ Ant manageable, mild, moderate.

unconventional [adj] very different; odd ▪ Syn anarchistic, avant-garde, bizarre, crazy, eccentric, freakish, idiosyncratic, irregular, nonconformist, offbeat, original, out in left field, unique, unorthodox, unusual; ▪ Ant conventional, formal, normal, standard, usual.

uncouth [adj] clumsy, uncultivated
▪ Syn awkward, barbaric, boorish, clumsy, coarse, discourteous, heavy-handed, ill-bred, impertinent, impolite, loud, loud-mouthed, loutish, oafish, raunchy, raw, rustic, vulgar; ▪ Ant cultivated, polished, refined, sophisticated.

uncover [v] reveal, disclose
▪ Syn bare, betray, denude, disclose, divulge, expose, give away, hit upon, lay bare, leak, make known, open, reveal, show, strike, subject, tap; ▪ Ant conceal, cover, hide, suppress.

uncritical [adj] casual, unfussy
▪ Syn careless, cursory, easily pleased, imperceptive, imprecise, inaccurate, indiscriminate, offhand, perfunctory, shallow, slipshod, superficial; ▪ Ant critical, discriminating, formal, fussy, important.

undaunted [adj] brave, bold
▪ Syn audacious, courageous, dauntless, fearless, gallant, indomitable, intrepid, resolute, steadfast, valiant, valorous; ▪ Ant cowardly, discouraged, irresolute, shrinking.

undecided [adj] not sure, not definite
▪ Syn ambivalent, borderline, doubtful,

dubious, equivocal, hesitant, indecisive, irresolute, moot, open, pending, tentative, torn, vague, waffling, wavering; ▪ *Ant* certain, decided, determined, settled, sure definite, undoubted.

undeniable [*adj*] *definite, proven*
▪ *Syn* actual, beyond doubt, binding, certain, compulsory, evident, for sure, inarguable, incontestable, indubitable, irrefutable, manifest, necessary, obligatory, patent, real, sound, true; ▪ *Ant* contestable, disputable, doubted, dubious, indefinite, unproven.

undependable [*adj*] *irresponsible*
▪ *Syn* capricious, careless, dubious, erratic, fickle, inconsistent, inconstant, treacherous, tricky, trustless, variable; ▪ *Ant* reliable, responsible, trustworthy.

under [*adv1/prep1*] *below*
▪ *Syn* beneath, bottom, concealed by, covered by, downward, held down, inferior, lower, nether, on the bottom, on the underside, pinned, supporting, underneath; ▪ *Ant* above, higher, more, over, up, upward.

under [*adv2/prep2*] *secondary*
▪ *Syn* amenable, collateral, consequent, corollary, dependent, following, governed, included, inferior, junior, lesser, lower, obedient, reporting, subjugated, subordinate, subsidiary, subtract, subsumed; ▪ *Ant* primary, superior.

undercover [*adj*] *secret, spy*
▪ *Syn* clandestine, concealed, confidential, covert, furtive, hidden, intelligence, private, stealthy, surreptitious, underground, underhand, underneath; ▪ *Ant* known, open, overt, public.

underdog [*n*] *person who is not expected to succeed* ▪ *Syn* casualty, failure, prey, underling, victim; ▪ *Ant* favorite.

underestimate [*v*] *minimize; rate too low* ▪ *Syn* belittle, deprecate, miscalculate, slight, underrate, undervalue; ▪ *Ant* exaggerate, maximize, overestimate.

undergo [*v*] *be subjected to*
▪ *Syn* abide, bear, endure, go through, meet with, put up with, share, stand, submit to, suffer, sustain, tolerate, weather, withstand, yield; ▪ *Ant* escape, evade, shun, sidestep.

underground [*adj1*] *below the surface*
▪ *Syn* buried, covered, in the recesses, subterranean, subterrestrial, sunken, underfoot; ▪ *Ant* aboveground, exposed, on the surface, surface.

underground [*adj2*] *secret, subversive*
▪ *Syn* alternative, avant-garde, clandestine, concealed, experimental, hidden, private, radical, revolutionary, surreptitious, undercover; ▪ *Ant* authorized, legal, overt, public.

underhand [*adj*] *deceitful*
▪ *Syn* clandestine, concealed, crooked, cunning, deceptive, devious, dishonest, duplicitous, fraudulent, furtive, guileful, indirect, oblique, secret, shady, shifty, sneaky, stealthy, surreptitious, treacherous, tricky, undercover, wily; ▪ *Ant* aboveboard, forthright, frank, honest.

underlying [*adj*] *fundamental, latent*
▪ *Syn* basal, bottom, cardinal, concealed, critical, crucial, elemental, essential, hidden, intrinsic, lurking, necessary, nub, primary, radical, root, vital; ▪ *Ant* attendent, peripheral, subsidiary.

undermine [*v*] *weaken*
▪ *Syn* attenuate, corrode, cripple, debilitate, disable, enfeeble, erode, excavate, foil, frustrate, hurt, impair, mine, ruin, sabotage, sap, soften, subvert, thwart, undercut, whittle away, wreck; ▪ *Ant* aid, buttress, reinforce, strengthen.

underneath [*adv/prep*] *below*
▪ *Syn* beneath, bottom, covered, lower, neath, nether, under; ▪ *Ant* above, over, up.

underprivileged [*adj*] *poor*
▪ *Syn* depressed, deprived, destitute, disadvantaged, handicapped, hapless, ill-fated, ill-starred, impoverished, indigent, in dire straits, in need, in want, needy, unfortunate,. unlucky; ▪ *Ant* privileged, rich, wealthy.

understand [*v1*] *appreciate, comprehend* ▪ *Syn* accept, apprehend, be aware, be conscious of, catch, catch on, conceive, deduce, discern, distinguish, explain, fathom, figure out, find out, follow, grasp, infer, interpret, learn, make sense of, master, note, perceive, possess, read, realize, recognize, register, savvy, see, seize, sense, sympathize, take meaning, tolerate; ▪ *Ant* misinterpret, misunderstand.

understand [*v2*] *think, believe*
▪ *Syn* accept, assume, be informed, concede, conceive, conclude, conjecture, consider, count on, deduce, expect, fancy, gather, guess, imagine, infer, learn, presume, reckon, suppose, sur-

mise, suspect, take for granted, take it, think; ▪ *Ant* disbelieve, mistake.

understanding [*adj*] *accepting, tolerant*
▪ *Syn* compassionate, considerate, discerning, empathetic, forbearing, forgiving, generous, kind, kindly, patient, perceptive, responsive, sensitive, sympathetic; ▪ *Ant* intolerant, unaccepting, unsympathetic.

understood [*adj*] *assumed, implicit*
▪ *Syn* accepted, appreciated, axiomatic, implied, inferred, known, pat, presumed, tacit, unexpressed, unspoken, wordless; ▪ *Ant* explained, explicit, spoken, written.

undertake [*v*] *attempt, engage in*
▪ *Syn* address oneself, begin, commence, commit, contract, devote, embark, endeavor, guarantee, have a try, hazard, initiate, launch, move, offer, pitch in, pledge, shoulder, stake, stipulate, tackle, take on, take upon oneself, try, venture, volunteer; ▪ *Ant* abstain, eschew, forego, forget.

underweight [*adj*] *thin*
▪ *Syn* angular, anorexic, bony, gangly, malnourished, puny, scrawny, shadow, skinny, starved, undernourished, undersized; ▪ *Ant* chubby, fat, overweight, plump, thick.

underwrite [*v*] *endorse, insure*
▪ *Syn* accede, agree to, approve, back, bankroll, collateral, countersign, endow, finance, float, fund, guarantee, pay, provide financing, sanction, secure, sign, sponsor, stake, subsidize, support; ▪ *Ant* disapprove, invalidate, refuse, reject.

undesirable [*adj*] *offensive, unacceptable* ▪ *Syn* abominable, annoying, bothersome, disagreeable, displeasing, distasteful, dreaded, icky, incommodious, insufferable, loathed, loathsome, objectionable, obnoxious, offensive, rejected, repellent, repugnant, scorned, shunned, to be avoided, troublesome; ▪ *Ant* acceptable, appealing, pleasing, savory.

undeveloped [*adj*] *immature*
▪ *Syn* abortive, backward, behindhand, embryonic, half-baked, ignored, inchoate, incipient, inexperienced, latent, potential, primitive, primordial; ▪ *Ant* adult, developed, grown, mature.

undisputed/undisputable [*adj*] *positive, accepted* ▪ *Syn* acknowledged, arbitrary, beyond question, certain,

conclusive, decided, dogmatic, final, incontestable, incontrovertible, indisputable, indubitable, irrefutable, positive, recognized, sure, tyrannous, undeniable, unequivocal; ▪ *Ant* disputable, doubtful, dubious, uncertain, unsure.

undivided [*adj*] *whole*
▪ *Syn* collective, combined, complete, concerted, entire, exclusive, joined, scrupulous, single, solid, steady, thorough, unanimous, unbroken, united, wholehearted; ▪ *Ant* divided, partial, separate.

undo [*v1*] *open*
▪ *Syn* disengage, disentangle, free, loose, loosen, release, unbind, unblock, unbutton, unclose, unfasten, unlock; ▪ *Ant* close, fasten.

undo [*v2*] *nullify, invalidate*
▪ *Syn* abolish, abrogate, annihilate, annul, break, bring down, cancel, defeat, destroy, impoverish, injure, mar, negate, neutralize, offset, outfox, outmaneuver, outsmart, overreach, overthrow, overturn, quash, queer, raze, reverse, ruin, shatter, smash, spoil, subvert, undermine, upset, vitiate, wrack, wreck; ▪ *Ant* accomplish, approve, permit, validate.

undoubtedly [*adv*] *certainly*
▪ *Syn* assuredly, beyond question, definitely, doubtless, easily, indeed, of course, really, surely, truly, undeniably, unmistakably, unquestionably, well, without doubt; ▪ *Ant* doubtfully, indefinite, questionably.

undress [*v*] *take off clothes*
▪ *Syn* denude, disarray, disrobe, doff, get out of, husk, peel, shed, slip out of, strip; ▪ *Ant* clothe, cover, dress.

undue [*adj*] *excessive, unnecessary*
▪ *Syn* disproportionate, exorbitant, ill-timed, immoderate, improper, inapt, indecorous, intemperate, needless, overmuch, sinister; ▪ *Ant* moderate, reasonable, sensible.

unduly [*adv*] *excessively*
▪ *Syn* disproportionately, extravagantly, illegally, immensely, immoderately, improperly, indecorously, inordinately, out of proportion, overly, overmuch, too, unfairly, unjustifiably, unnecessarily, unreasonably; ▪ *Ant* moderately, reasonably, sensibly.

undying [*adj*] *never-ending*
▪ *Syn* constant, deathless, eternal, everlasting, immortal, imperishable, inextinguishable, infinite, perennial, per-

petual, persistent, unceasing, undiminished; ▪ *Ant* ending, ephemeral, impermanent, mortal, passing.

unearth [v] *dig up*
▪ *Syn* delve, discover, disinter, dredge up, excavate, exhibit, exhume, expose, ferret, find, hit upon, see, show, spark, strike, stumble on, turn up, unbury; ▪ *Ant* bury, cover.

unearthly [adj] *supernatural; very strange* ▪ *Syn* abnormal, demonic, devilish, ethereal, extraordinary, fiendish, frightening, funereal, ghostly, ghoulish, hair-raising, miraculous, not of this world, phantom, preternatural, ridiculous, sepulchral, spectral, spooky, superhuman, weird; ▪ *Ant* earthly, mundane, natural, physical.

uneasy [adj] *awkward, uncomfortable*
▪ *Syn* agitated, alarmed, apprehensive, bothered, constrained, dismayed, disturbed, edgy, fidgety, fretful, ill at ease, insecure, irascible, jumpy, nervous, on edge, palpitant, peevish, restless, shaken, strained, suspicious, tense, tormented, troubled, vexed, worried; ▪ *Ant* comfortable, composed, easygoing, laid-back.

uneducated [adj] *lacking knowledge*
▪ *Syn* benighted, empty-headed, ignorant, illiterate, uncultured, unlearned, unlettered, unrefined, unschooled, untutored; ▪ *Ant* educated, intelligent, learned, lettered, taught.

unemotional [adj] *not responsive*
▪ *Syn* apathetic, callous, deadpan, dispassionate, emotionless, flat, frigid, glacial, heartless, indifferent, listless, obdurate, phlegmatic, quiet, reserved, reticent, unresponsive; ▪ *Ant* excitable, feeling, lively, responsive, sanguine.

unemployed [adj] *without a job*
▪ *Syn* disengaged, free, idle, inactive, jobless, laid off, out of a job, out of work, resting, without gainful employment; ▪ *Ant* employed, occupied.

unending [adj] *continuing*
▪ *Syn* amaranthine, ceaseless, constant, eternal, everlasting, immortal, incessant, interminable, never-ending, perpetual, steady, unceasing; ▪ *Ant* completed, discontinuous, ending, finished, intermittent, transient.

unequal [adj1] *different*
▪ *Syn* differing, disparate, dissimilar, divergent, diverse, mismatched, not

uniform, odd, variable, various, varying; ▪ *Ant* identical, matched, same, similar.

unequal [adj2] *not balanced; lopsided*
▪ *Syn* asymmetrical, disproportionate, ill-matched, inequitable, irregular, off-balance, one-sided, overbalanced; ▪ *Ant* balanced, equal, even, level, same.

unequaled [adj] *supreme, pre-eminent*
▪ *Syn* beyond compare, incomparable, matchless, nonpareil, paramount, surpassing, towering, transcendent, ultimate, unique, without equal; ▪ *Ant* commonplace, inferior, minor, pedestrian, second-rate.

unequivocal [adj] *definite, positive*
▪ *Syn* absolute, apparent, categorical, certain, clear, decided, decisive, direct, distinct, downright, evident, explicit, indisputable, manifest, obvious, palpable, straight; ▪ *Ant* ambiguous, equivocal, indefinite, obscured, vague.

unerring [adj] *accurate*
▪ *Syn* certain, exact, faultless, impeccable, inerrable, inerrant, infallible, invariable, just, perfect, reliable, sure, true, trustworthy, unfailing; ▪ *Ant* imperfect, inaccurate, mistaken.

unethical [adj] *dishonest, immoral*
▪ *Syn* cheating, corrupt, crooked, dishonorable, disreputable, illegal, improper, mercenary, underhand, unprincipled, unscrupulous, wrong; ▪ *Ant* good, honest, moral, right, upright.

uneven [adj] *not smooth or balanced*
▪ *Syn* asperous, asymmetrical, changeable, craggy, disparate, disproportionate, fitful, fluctuating, harsh, ill-matched, intermittent, irregular, jagged, jerky, leftover, lopsided, notched, off-balance, overbalanced, patchy, remaining, scabrous, scraggy, serrate, spasmodic, spotty, variable; ▪ *Ant* balanced, continuous, level, smooth.

uneventful [adj] *monotonous, dull*
▪ *Syn* boring, commonplace, inconclusive, indecisive, ordinary, prosaic, quiet, routine, tedious, unremarkable, unvaried; ▪ *Ant* exciting, extraordinary, memorable.

unexpected [adj] *surprising*
▪ *Syn* abrupt, astonishing, chance, fortuitous, impetuous, impulsive, prodigious, startling, stunning, sudden, swift, unpredictable, wonderful; ▪ *Ant* anticipated, awaited, foreseen, planned.

unfailing [*adj*] *certain, unchanging*
▪ *Syn* absolute, boundless, consistent, continuous, delivering, dependable, diligent, endless, eternal, faithful, infallible, loyal, never-failing, persistent, reliable, staunch, steadfast, straight, sure, trustworthy; ▪ *Ant* disloyal, treacherous, undependable, wavering.

unfair [*adj*] *prejudiced, wrongful*
▪ *Syn* arbitrary, base, culpable, discriminatory, dishonest, foul, grievous, improper, iniquitous, one-sided, partial, partisan, petty, wrong; ▪ *Ant* fair, honest, just, unprejudiced.

unfaithful [*adj*] *disloyal, adulterous*
▪ *Syn* adulterine, cheating, deceitful, faithless, false, fickle, foresworn, inconstant, incontinent, not true to, perfidious, philandering, recreant, sneaking, traitorous, treacherous, treasonable; ▪ *Ant* faithful, loyal, trustworthy.

unfaltering [*adj*] *steadfast*
▪ *Syn* abiding, bound, enduring, firm, indefatigable, never-failing, persevering, resolute, set, steady, stubborn, sure, tireless, wholehearted; ▪ *Ant* faltering, vacillating.

unfamiliar [*adj1*] *different, strange*
▪ *Syn* alien, anomalous, bizarre, curious, exotic, extraordinary, foreign, little known, novel, obscure, outlandish, peculiar, recondite, remarkable; ▪ *Ant* common, familiar, known, usual.

unfamiliar [*adj2*] *inexperienced; not knowing about* ▪ *Syn* ignorant of, incognizant, inconversant, not versed in, oblivious, out of contact; ▪ *Ant* experienced, familiar, knowing, versed.

unfathomable [*adj1*] *bottomless*
▪ *Syn* abysmal, boundless, deep, eternal, immeasurable, infinite, soundless; ▪ *Ant* comprehensible, explainable, explicable.

unfathomable [*adj2*] *hard to believe; difficult to understand* ▪ *Syn* abstruse, baffling, enigmatic, esoteric, heavy, impenetrable, incognizable, incomprehensible, indecipherable, inexplicable, obscure, profound; ▪ *Ant* believable, comprehensible.

unfavorable [*adj*] *very bad*
▪ *Syn* adverse, antagonistic, calamitous, damaging, destructive, disadvantageous, hostile, ill-advised, infelicitous, inimical, inopportune, negative, objectionable, ominous, opposed, poor, regrettable, threatening, troublesome, wrong; ▪ *Ant* friendly, good, positive, well-disposed.

unfeeling [*adj*] *hard-hearted, numb*
▪ *Syn* anesthetized, apathetic, benumbed, brutal, callous, cantankerous, churlish, crotchety, cruel, deadened, hard, hardened, inhuman, insensitive, merciless, obdurate, pitiless, ruthless, senseless, severe, surly, tough; ▪ *Ant* benevolent, caring, concerned, loving, sensitive, sympathetic.

unfinished [*adj*] *not completed*
▪ *Syn* amateurish, bare, crude, deficient, formless, found wanting, fragmentary, immature, imperfect, incomplete, lacking, plain, raw, rough, roughhewn, shapeless, sketchy, tentative, under construction, wanting; ▪ *Ant* completed, polished, refined, whole.

unfit [*adj1*] *not appropriate or suited*
▪ *Syn* debilitated, decrepit, feeble, flimsy, ill-adapted, inadequate, inapplicable, inappropriate, incompatible, incongruous, ineffective, infelicitous, inharmonious, out of shape, poorly, valueless; ▪ *Ant* appropriate, suitable, useful.

unfit [*adj2*] *not ready*
▪ *Syn* amateur, awkward, blundering, bungling, clumsy, debilitated, disqualified, feeble, ill-equipped, impotent, inadequate, incapable, incapacitated, incompetent, ineffective, inefficient, inept, inexperienced, maladroit, not equal to, weak; ▪ *Ant* able, fit, qualified, ready, willing.

unflagging [*adj*] *persistent*
▪ *Syn* assiduous, constant, diligent, dynamic, fixed, indefatigable, inexhaustible, persevering, staunch, steady, tireless; ▪ *Ant* flagging, halfhearted, inconstant, variable, wavering.

unflappable [*adj*] *cool and calm*
▪ *Syn* collected, composed, deliberate, disimpassioned, impassive, imperturbable, levelheaded, nonchalant, relaxed, self-possessed; ▪ *Ant* disconcerted, nervous, upset, worried.

unfold [*v1*] *spread out*
▪ *Syn* disentangle, display, expand, extend, fan, fan out, flatten, loosen, open, outspread, outstretch, reel out, release, shake out, spread, straighten, stretch out; ▪ *Ant* crease, curl, encase, envelope, fold, wrap.

unfold [*v2*] *make known*
▪ *Syn* announce, clarify, describe, disclose, display, divulge, dope out, elucidate, explain, explicate, expose,

illustrate, present, publish, resolve, reveal, show, solve, uncover, unravel; ▪ *Ant* conceal, hide, withhold.

unfold [*v3*] *develop*
▪ *Syn* bear fruit, demonstrate, elaborate, evidence, evince, evolve, expand, grow, manifest, mature; ▪ *Ant* block, check, stagnate, stop.

unforeseen [*adj*] *surprising*
▪ *Syn* abrupt, accidental, startling, sudden, surprise, unanticipated, unexpected; ▪ *Ant* anticipated, expected, foreseen, predictable, predicted.

unfortunate [*adj*] *unlucky, bad*
▪ *Syn* adverse, afflicted, burdened, calamitous, cursed, damaging, desperate, destitute, doomed, forsaken, hapless, hopeless, ill-fated, infelicitous, inopportune, jinxed, lamentable, luckless, pained, poor, regrettable, ruined, shattered, stricken, troubled, wretched; ▪ *Ant* fortunate, good, happy, lucky, timely.

unfounded [*adj*] *not based on fact*
▪ *Syn* baseless, fabricated, fallacious, gratuitous, groundless, idle, illogical, mendacious, misleading, off-base, spurious, vain, without basis, without foundation; ▪ *Ant* justified, proven, substantiated, supported.

unfriendly [*adj*] *nasty, hostile*
▪ *Syn* acrimonious, antagonistic, censorious, chilly, contrary, disagreeable, distant, estranged, grouchy, gruff, ill-disposed, inauspicious, inhospitable, malicious, misanthropic, quarrelsome, sour, spiteful, warlike; ▪ *Ant* approachable, congenial neighborly, friendly, kind, sociable, warm.

ungodly [*adj1*] *immoral*
▪ *Syn* blasphemous, corrupt, depraved, godless, impious, improper, indecent, indecorous, indelicate, irreligious, malevolent, profane, sinful, vile, wicked; ▪ *Ant* clean, godly, moral, pious, religious.

ungodly [*adj2*] *outrageous*
▪ *Syn* atrocious, barbarous, dreadful, horrendous, horrid, intolerable, nasty; ▪ *Ant* reasonable, sensible.

ungrateful [*adj*] *not appreciative*
▪ *Syn* careless, demanding, dissatisfied, faultfinding, forgetful, grasping, grumbling, heedless, oblivious, self-centered, selfish, thankless; ▪ *Ant* appreciative, grateful, thankful.

unguarded [*adj*] *thoughtless; unwary*
▪ *Syn* artless, candid, casual, foolhardy,

frank, heedless, ill-considered, imprudent, impulsive, incautious, ingenuous, naive, offhand, rash, spontaneous, straightforward, weak; ▪ *Ant* careful, cautious, thoughtful.

unhappy [*adj1*] *sad*
▪ *Syn* bleak, crestfallen, dejected, depressed, despondent, dispirited, downcast, dreary, gloomy, heavy-hearted, long-faced, low, melancholy, mirthless, miserable, oppressive, sad, saddened, sorrowful, troubled; ▪ *Ant* cheerful, glad, happy, joyous.

unhappy [*adj2*] *unfortunate, unlucky*
▪ *Syn* afflicted, cursed, hapless, ill-fated, ill-starred, luckless, misfortunate, troubled, untoward, wretched; ▪ *Ant* fortunate, happy, lucky, timely.

unhealthy [*adj1*] *sick*
▪ *Syn* ailing, below par, debilitated, dragging, feeble, ill, infirm, in poor health, invalid, peaked, poorly, run-down, shaky, sickly, weak; ▪ *Ant* healthy, strong, well.

unhealthy [*adj2*] *very bad in effect on well-being* ▪ *Syn* baneful, chancy, corrupt, dangerous, degenerate, deleterious, demoralizing, depraved, harmful, hazardous, insalubrious, jeopardous, morbid, nefarious, negative, noxious, perilous, risky, rotten, treacherous, villainous, virulent, wicked; ▪ *Ant* good, healthy.

unheard-of [*adj*] *unique, obscure*
▪ *Syn* exceptional, inconceivable, little-known, nameless, new, novel, outlandish, preposterous, rare, shocking, singular, unbelievable; ▪ *Ant* familiar, normal, usual.

unholy [*adj1*] *sacreligious*
▪ *Syn* base, blameful, corrupt, culpable, depraved, evil, godless, guilty, heinous, immoral, irreligious, irreverent, profane, sinful, vile, wicked; ▪ *Ant* godly, holy, pious, religious.

unholy [*adj2*] *outrageous*
▪ *Syn* appalling, awful, barbarous, dreadful, horrendous, shocking, uncivilized, unearthly, unreasonable; ▪ *Ant* pleasant, reasonable, sensible.

unidentified [*adj*] *secret*
▪ *Syn* anonymous, mysterious, nameless, not known, pseudonymous, unknown, unmarked, unrevealed; ▪ *Ant* designated, known, public, recognized.

uniform [*adj1*] *consistent*
▪ *Syn* compatible, consonant, equable,

even, fixed, habitual, homogeneous, inflexible, level, methodical, ordered, plumb, regular, stable, symmetrical, true, well-balanced, well-proportioned; ▪ *Ant* changing, different, divergent, inconsistent, varied.

uniform [*adj2*] *alike*
▪ *Syn* agnate, analogous, comparable, consistent, consonant, correspondent, equal, identical, like, mated, parallel, same, self-same, similar; ▪ *Ant* deviating, different, dissimilar, divergent, unalike, unlike.

unimaginable [*adj*] *mind-boggling*
▪ *Syn* doubtful, exceptional, extraordinary, fantastic, impossible, improbable, inapprehensible, incogitable, incomprehensible, inconceivable, incredible, indescribable, ineffable, rare, singular, unique; ▪ *Ant* believable, describable, imaginable.

unimaginative [*adj*] *dull, predictable*
▪ *Syn* banal, barren, bromidic, common, derivative, dry, flat, hackneyed, lifeless, matter-of-fact, ordinary, pedestrian, prosaic, routine, tame, tedious, trite, usual, well-worn; ▪ *Ant* creative, imaginative, inspired, interesting, novel, original.

unimportant [*adj*] *of no real worth, value* ▪ *Syn* casual, frivolous, immaterial, inconsequential, inconsiderable, insignificant, irrelevant, little, low-ranking, meaningless, minor, minute, negligible, nugatory, null, paltry, petty, picayune, slight, trifling, trivial, useless, worthless; ▪ *Ant* important, relevant, serious, useful, worthwhile.

uninhibited [*adj*] *free and easy; without restraint* ▪ *Syn* audacious, candid, expansive, frank, free, informal, instinctive, liberated, natural, open, relaxed, spontaneous; ▪ *Ant* careful, inhibited, modest, shy.

uninspired [*adj*] *dull, unoriginal*
▪ *Syn* bromidic, commonplace, everyday, heavy-handed, indifferent, ordinary, prosaic, stale, stock; ▪ *Ant* creative, inspired, original.

unintelligible [*adj*] *not understandable*
▪ *Syn* ambiguous, equivocal, fathomless, Greek, illegible, impenetrable, inarticulate, incomprehensible, indecipherable, jumbled, meaningless, obscure, opaque, tenebrous, vague; ▪ *Ant* comprehensible, intelligible, meaningful, understandable.

unintentional/unintended [*adj*] *not planned* ▪ *Syn* accidental, aimless, chance, erratic, extemporaneous, fortuitous, haphazard, inadvertent, purposeless, random, unconscious, unwitting; ▪ *Ant* definite, deliberate, intended, intentional, planned.

uninterested [*adj*] *oblivious to*
▪ *Syn* aloof, apathetic, blas, casual, detached, distant, impassive, incurious, listless, remote, unconcerned, unresponsive, weary, withdrawn; ▪ *Ant* caring, concerned, enthusiastic, feeling, interested.

uninteresting [*adj*] *boring, uneventful*
▪ *Syn* arid, banal, common, commonplace, drab, dry, dull, flat, insipid, jejune, monotonous, pedestrian, prosaic, stale, tedious, tired, trite, wearisome; ▪ *Ant* eventful, exciting, interesting.

uninterrupted [*adj*] *continuing; unbroken* ▪ *Syn* ceaseless, consecutive, constant, continuous, direct, endless, interminable, nonstop, peaceful, perpetual, steady, straightforward, sustained, through; ▪ *Ant* broken, discontinuous, intermittent, interrupted.

union [*n1*] *merger, joining*
▪ *Syn* abutment, accord, amalgamation, blend, combination, coming together, compound, conciliation, concord, conjunction, consolidation, coupling, fusion, harmony, incorporation, joint, meeting, melding, merging, seam, symbiosis, synthesis, tie-in, unanimity; ▪ *Ant* division, divorce, separation.

union [*n2*] *group with shared interest, cause* ▪ *Syn* alliance, association, brotherhood, club, coalition, confederation, congress, employees, federation, guild, league, order, society, sodality, syndicate, trade union; ▪ *Ant* management.

unique [*adj*] *one-of-a-kind; without equal; singular* ▪ *Syn* anomalous, best, exceptional, exclusive, extraordinary, incomparable, inimitable, matchless, most, nonpareil, novel, only, peerless, rare, singular, solitary, solo, special, standout, strange, uncommon, unequaled, unprecedented, unrivaled, utmost; ▪ *Ant* like, similar, standard, trite.

unison [*n*] *harmony*
▪ *Syn* accord, accordance, agreement, alliance, community, concert, concord, concordance, conjunction, consent, consonance, cooperation, federation, fellowship, league, reciprocity, sympathy,

unanimity, union, unity; ▪ *Ant* discord, disharmony.

unite [v] *combine; join together*
▪ *Syn* affiliate, ally, amalgamate, associate, band, band together, become one, blend, coadjute, coalesce, commingle, concur, confederate, conjoin, connect, consolidate, cooperate, couple, embody, fuse, gather together, harden, incorporate, intertwine, join, join forces, league, link, marry, meet, merge, mix, pool, pull together, strengthen, unify, wed; ▪ *Ant* detach, divide, separate, severe, split.

universal [adj] *worldwide, entire*
▪ *Syn* all-embracing, all-inclusive, broad, catholic, common, comprehensive, extensive, general, global, international, multinational, omnipresent, prevalent, regular, sweeping, total, ubiquitous, usual, widespread, worldwide; ▪ *Ant* confined, local, partial, particular.

unjust [adj] *not fair*
▪ *Syn* biased, inequitable, one-sided, partial, partisan, prejudiced, underhand, wrong, wrongful; ▪ *Ant* equitable, fair, just, unbiased, unprejudiced.

unkempt [adj] *shabby, sloppy*
▪ *Syn* bedraggled, coarse, dirty, disarranged, disheveled, disordered, messed up, neglected, rumpled, scruffy, shaggy, slipshod, slovenly, tousled, untidy, vulgar; ▪ *Ant* kempt, neat, tidy, trim.

unkind [adj] *not nice*
▪ *Syn* barbarous, brutal, cruel, hardhearted, inconsiderate, insensitive, malevolent, malicious, mean, nasty, sadistic, savage, spiteful, thoughtless; ▪ *Ant* considerate, friendly, giving, kind, nice.

unknown [adj] *obscure, mysterious*
▪ *Syn* alien, anonymous, concealed, dark, foreign, hidden, incognito, little known, nameless, remote, secret, strange, uncharted, unexplored, unidentified; ▪ *Ant* celebrated, familiar, identified, known, renowned.

unlawful [adj] *against the law*
▪ *Syn* actionable, banned, criminal, flagitious, forbidden, illegal, illegitimate, illicit, iniquitous, lawless, nefarious, outlawed, prohibited, taboo, wrongful; ▪ *Ant* authorized, lawful, legal, right.

unlike [adj] *different*
▪ *Syn* clashing, conflicting, contradictory, contrasted, discordant, disharmonious, dissonant, distant, divergent, heterogeneous, hostile, incompatible, incongruous, mismatched, opposed, opposite, separate; ▪ *Ant* alike, like, related, same, similar.

unlikely [adj] *not probable*
▪ *Syn* absurd, contrary, dubious, faint, implausible, inconceivable, not likely, outside chance, questionable, rare, remote, slight, strange; ▪ *Ant* imaginable, likely, probably.

unlimited [adj] *extensive, complete*
▪ *Syn* absolute, all-encompassing, boundless, countless, endless, immeasurable, incalculable, infinite, interminable, limitless, numberless, total, universal, vast, wide open; ▪ *Ant* bounded, controlled, incomplete, limited, partial, restricted.

unload [v] *take off; empty*
▪ *Syn* cast, clear out, disburden, discharge, disencumber, dump, get rid of, jettison, lighten, off-load, relieve, remove, rid, slough, take a load off, void; ▪ *Ant* fill, load, put on.

unlucky [adj] *unfortunate, doomed*
▪ *Syn* afflicted, calamitous, cataclysmic, catastrophic, dire, hapless, ill-fated, inauspicious, luckless, miserable, ominous, tragic; ▪ *Ant* fortunate, happy, lucky.

unmarried [adj] *not presently wed*
▪ *Syn* bachelor, eligible, husbandless, maiden, single, spouseless, unattached, unwed, widowed, wifeless; ▪ *Ant* married, mated, wed.

unmerciful [adj] *cruel*
▪ *Syn* bestial, bloodthirsty, brutal, hard, heartless, implacable, inhumane, monstrous, pitiless, relentless, remorseless, ruthless, vengeful, vindictive; ▪ *Ant* benevolent, compassionate, generous, humane, merciful.

unmistakable [adj] *certain, definite*
▪ *Syn* apparent, clear, conspicuous, decided, distinct, evident, for certain, glaring, indisputable, manifest, obvious, palpable, pronounced, self-explanatory, sure, transparent; ▪ *Ant* doubtul, hidden, indistinct, uncertain, vague.

unmitigated [adj] *absolute, pure*
▪ *Syn* arrant, clear-cut, consummate, damned, downright, gross, intense, outright, perfect, relentless, sheer, simple, thorough, utter; ▪ *Ant* abated, lessened, mitigated, relieved.

unnatural [adj] *not regular; artificial*
▪ *Syn* abnormal, affected, assumed, bizarre, concocted, contrived, extraordi-

nary, fabricated, feigned, forced, imitation, insincere, irregular, labored, odd, outlandish, outrageous, perverse, perverted, phony, preposterous, staged, stiff, strained, studied, synthetic, theatrical; ▪ *Ant* acceptable, genuine, natural, real.

unnecessary [*adj*] *not required*
▪ *Syn* additional, avoidable, chance, dispensable, expendable, extraneous, futile, gratuitous, haphazard, irrelevant, needless, noncompulsory, optional, prodigal, profuse, redundant, superfluous, surplus, useless, wanton, worthless; ▪ *Ant* indispensable, necessary, needed, required.

unnerve [*v*] *upset, intimidate*
▪ *Syn* agitate, bewilder, confound, daunt, demoralize, disconcert, discourage, dispirit, fluster, frighten, perturb, rattle, shake, spook, throw, weaken; ▪ *Ant* encourage, steel, strengthen.

unnoticed [*adj*] *ignored*
▪ *Syn* disregarded, inconspicuous, neglected, overlooked, passed by, pushed aside; ▪ *Ant* noted, noticed, seen.

unobtrusive [*adj*] *keeping a low profile*
▪ *Syn* humble, inconspicuous, low-key, meek, modest, quiet, reserved, restrained, self-effacing, subdued, tasteful; ▪ *Ant* assertive, brazen, conspicuous, flaunting, noticeable, obtrusive.

unorthodox [*adj*] *abnormal; other than accepted* ▪ *Syn* different, dissident, eccentric, far-out, heretical, heterodox, irregular, nonconformist, schismatic, sectarian; ▪ *Ant* commonplace, conventional, normal, standard.

unpaid [*adj*] *not settled; taken without remuneration* ▪ *Syn* delinquent, due, in arrears, not discharged, outstanding, overdue, owing, past due, payable; ▪ *Ant* paid, settled.

unparalleled [*adj*] *superlative*
▪ *Syn* alone, beyond compare, champion, exceptional, greatest, incomparable, matchless, only, peerless, rare, singular, unique, unmatched, unsurpassed, winner, without equal; ▪ *Ant* inferior, lower, second-rate, surpassable.

unpleasant [*adj*] *bad*
▪ *Syn* abhorrent, disagreeable, distasteful, fierce, irksome, lousy, nasty, objectionable, poisonous, repulsive, rotten, sour, troublesome, unpalatable; ▪ *Ant* agreeable, delightful, good, great, pleasing, wonderful.

unpopular [*adj*] *not liked or sought after*
▪ *Syn* abhorred, avoided, despised, detested, disfavored, disliked, execrated, loathed, ostracized, out, rejected, scorned, shunned; ▪ *Ant* desirable, fashionable, sought-after, wanted.

unprecedented [*adj*] *exceptional, original* ▪ *Syn* anomalous, bizarre, eccentric, extraordinary, fantastic, freakish, idiosyncratic, marvelous, modern, new, novel, odd, outlandish, preternatural, prodigious, remarkable, singular, unique, unparalleled; ▪ *Ant* known, unexceptional, unremarkable, usual.

unpredictable [*adj*] *changeable*
▪ *Syn* capricious, chancy, erratic, fickle, fluctuating, inconstant, random, touchy, unstable, variable, whimsical; ▪ *Ant* constant, predictable, unchanging, unvarying.

unprejudiced [*adj*] *fair*
▪ *Syn* balanced, dispassionate, equitable, even-handed, fair-minded, impartial, just, nondiscriminatory, nonpartisan, objective, open-minded, straight; ▪ *Ant* biased, prejudiced, unfair, unjust.

unpretentious [*adj*] *simple, honest*
▪ *Syn* discreet, humble, modest, plain, prosaic, straightforward, unaffected, unassuming, unimposing, unpresumptuous, up front; ▪ *Ant* affected, dishonest, flaunting, pretending, pretentious.

unprincipled [*adj*] *corrupt*
▪ *Syn* amoral, cheating, crooked, deceitful, devious, dishonest, immoral, licentious, mercenary, praetorian, profligate, reprobate, shady, tricky, underhand, venal, wanton; ▪ *Ant* ethical, moral, principled.

unprofessional [*adj*] *not done well or skillfully* ▪ *Syn* amateurish, improper, inadequate, incompetent, inexpert, lax, negligent; ▪ *Ant* above board, experienced, expert, professional, skilled.

unqualified [*adj1*] *not prepared, competent* ▪ *Syn* amateur, bush, ill-equipped, inadequate, incapable, incompetent, ineligible, inexperienced, not equal to, unequipped, unfit, unprepared, unskilled; ▪ *Ant* competent, prepared, qualified, ready.

unqualified [*adj2*] *outright, absolute*
▪ *Syn* abiding, blessed, categorical, complete, consummate, downright, entire,

express, firm, infernal, never-failing, positive, rank, sheer, simple, steadfast, thoroughgoing, total, unconditional, unmitigated, unreserved, utter, whole-hearted, without reservation; ■ *Ant* conditional, indefinite, temporary, tentative.

unquestionable [*adj*] *definite; beyond doubt* ■ *Syn* absolute, authentic, certain, conclusive, dependable, downright, established, faultless, genuine, irrefutable, manifest, obvious, pat, patent, positive, reliable, self-evident, true, veritable, well-grounded; ■ *Ant* doubtful, indefinite, questionable, uncertain, unsure.

unreal [*adj*] *fake, make-believe; hypothetical* ■ *Syn* artificial, chimerical, dreamlike, fabled, false, fanciful, fictitious, hallucinatory, illusory, imaginary, impalpable, invented, legendary, mock, mythical, nebulous, ostensible, pretended, romantic, theoretical, visionary; ■ *Ant* authentic, genuine, real.

unrealistic [*adj*] *not believable or practical* ■ *Syn* impracticable, impractical, improbable, nonsensical, quixotic, romantic, starry-eyed, unworkable; ■ *Ant* believable, practical, pragmatic, realistic, reasonable, sensible.

unreasonable [*adj1*] *not logical or sensible* ■ *Syn* absurd, arbitrary, biased, capricious, contradictory, erratic, fallacious, foolish, headstrong, illogical, incongruous, irrational, loose, mad, nonsensical, opinionated, preposterous, quirky, silly, stupid, thoughtless, vacant; ■ *Ant* logical, practical, pragmatic, prudent, realistic, reasonable, sensible.

unreasonable [*adj2*] *extravagant; beyond normal limits* ■ *Syn* absonant, arbitrary, excessive, exorbitant, extreme, illegitimate, immoderate, inordinate, overmuch, peremptory, senseless, too great, wrongful; ■ *Ant* economical, moderate, reasonable, warranted.

unrelated [*adj*] *independent; different* ■ *Syn* dissimilar, extraneous, inapplicable, inappropriate, irrelevant, mismatched, nongermane, not kindred, separate; ■ *Ant* dependent, related, relevant, similar.

unrelenting [*adj*] *merciless* ■ *Syn* ceaseless, constant, endless, grim, implacable, incessant, inexorable, intransigent, iron-fisted, persistent, relentless, remorseless, rigid, ruthless, stern, stiff,

tenacious, tough; ■ *Ant* compassionate, flexible, merciful, relenting, sympathetic.

unreliable [*adj*] *not trustworthy, not true* ■ *Syn* capricious, deceitful, dubious, erroneous, fallible, false, furtive, hollow, implausible, inaccurate, irresponsible, makeshift, meretricious, questionable, shifty, specious, treacherous, tricky, vacillating, wavering, weak; ■ *Ant* honest, reliable, responsible, true, trustworthy.

unresolved [*adj*] *uncertain; not settled* ■ *Syn* changing, doubtful, faltering, hesitant, incomplete, indecisive, irresolute, moot, pending, problematical, vacillating, vague, waffling; ■ *Ant* certain, definite, settled, solved, sure.

unrest [*n*] *state of agitation; disturbance* ■ *Syn* anarchy, anxiety, bickering, bother, change, confusion, controversy, crisis, discontent, discord, distress, insurrection, perturbation, protest, quarrel, rebellion, sedition, sorrow, strife, tension, trouble, tumult, turmoil, uproar, upset, vexation; ■ *Ant* calm, harmony, peace, rest.

unruly [*adj*] *disobedient* ■ *Syn* bawdy, disorderly, forward, fractious, headstrong, heedless, impetuous, imprudent, incorrigible, lawless, mutinous, obstreperous, ornery, out of control, perverse, quarrelsome, rash, recalcitrant, reckless, riotous, rowdy, turbulent, wayward, wild; ■ *Ant* compliant, obedient, reserved, well-behaved, yielding.

unsafe [*adj*] *dangerous* ■ *Syn* alarming, chancy, erratic, fearsome, hazardous, insecure, perilous, precarious, risky, slippery, treacherous; ■ *Ant* harmless, protected, safe, secure.

unsatisfactory [*adj*] *insufficient, inadequate* ■ *Syn* amiss, deficient, disappointing, displeasing, lame, mediocre, not good enough, poor, regrettable, second, thin, weak, wrong; ■ *Ant* acceptable, adequate, ok, satisfactory, sufficient.

unsavory [*adj*] *revolting, sickening* ■ *Syn* acid, bitter, disagreeable, insipid, lousy, nasty, objectionable, offensive, rancid, rank, sharp, sour, stinking, tainted, tart, tough; ■ *Ant* agreeable, good, virtuous.

unscathed [*adj*] *not hurt* ■ *Syn* safe, sound, unharmed, uninjured, unmarked, unscarred, unscratched, untouched, whole; ■ *Ant* harmed, hurt, injured.

unscrupulous [adj] immoral
• Syn arrant, base, corrupt, crooked, deceitful, dishonest, exploitative, improper, knavish, mercenary, perfidious, petty, recreant, ruthless, scheming, shady, shameless, shifty, sinister, slippery, underhand, underhanded, venal, wicked, wrongful; • Ant ethical, good, moral, principled, scrupulous.

unseemly [adj] improper; in bad taste
• Syn cheap, coarse, crude, disreputable, inappropriate, indecent, indecorous, in poor taste, malapropos, out of place, poor, raffish, rude, ruffian, tawdry, unbefitting, vulgar, wrong; • Ant appropriate, due, fitting, proper, suited.

unselfish [adj] kind, giving
• Syn altruistic, benevolent, charitable, generous, helpful, humanitarian, incorruptible, indulgent, liberal, loving, magnanimous, noble, open-handed, self-effacing, self-sacrificing; • Ant greedy, selfish, uncharitable.

unsettle [v] bother, upset
• Syn agitate, confuse, dement, derange, discommode, disconcert, disturb, fluster, jumble, needle, perturb, rattle, ruffle, spook, throw, trouble, unnerve; • Ant balance, compose, order, settle.

unsettled [adj2] not decided, taken care of • Syn debatable, dubitable, due, immature, in arrears, moot, open, outstanding, payable, pending, problematic, waffling; • Ant certain, decided, definite, settled, sure.

unsightly [adj] not pretty
• Syn deformed, disagreeable, drab, dull, hideous, homely, horrid, lackluster, repulsive, revolting, ugly, unattractive, unpleasant, unprepossessing, unshapely; • Ant beautiful, nice, pleasing, pretty, sightly.

unsociable [adj] unfriendly
• Syn aloof, antagonistic, brooding, cold, distant, hostile, inaccessible, introverted, reclusive, reserved, retiring, shy, timid, withdrawn; • Ant amiable, approachable, friendly, open.

unsolicited [adj] unasked for
• Syn free, freewilled, gratuitous, offered, spontaneous, unforced, uninvited, unsought, unwelcome, voluntary, volunteered; • Ant asked, invited, requested, solicited, welcome.

unsophisticated [adj] natural, simple
• Syn artless, callow, crude, folksy, genuine, guileless, inexperienced, ingenuous, innocent, naive, pure, straightforward, unrefined, unstudied, unworldly; • Ant cultured, experienced, refined, sophisticated, worldly.

unsound [adj] not well; flimsy
• Syn ailing, dangerous, decrepit, demented, erroneous, fallacious, faulty, flawed, fragile, ill, illogical, incongruous, in poor health, insane, insecure, invalid, lunatic, mad, rickety, shaky, specious, tottering, weak, wobbly; • Ant safe, sound, stable, strong, well.

unspeakable [adj] very bad; beyond description • Syn abominable, alarming, atrocious, beastly, calamitous, detestable, dire, disgusting, dreadful, evil, execrable, fearful, frightening, frightful, heinous, horrid, indescribable, inexpressible, inhuman, loathsome, monstrous, odious, offensive, preternatural, repugnant, revolting, shocking, unutterable; • Ant good, nice.

unstable/unsteady [adj] doubtful, weak • Syn ambiguous, borderline, capricious, dubious, erratic, fickle, fluctuating, giddy, inconsistent, insecure, lubricious, mercurial, precarious, rickety, rocky, shaky, shifty, slippery, teetering, temperamental, vacillating, variable, volatile, wavering; • Ant stable, steady, strong.

unsuitable [adj] not proper, appropriate
• Syn discordant, discrepant, disproportionate, dissonant, ill-suited, improper, inappropriate, inapt, jarring, malapropos, out of character, out of keeping, out of place, senseless; • Ant appropriate, proper, suitable.

unsure [adj] doubtful, insecure
• Syn borderline, dubious, fluctuant, hesitant, indecisive, irresolute, lacking, mistrustful, open, problematic, rootless, shaky, skeptical, vacillating, wavering, weak, wobbly; • Ant certain, definite, secure, sure, undoubted.

unsuspecting [adj] gullible
• Syn confiding, credulous, easy, inexperienced, ingenuous, innocent, naive, simple, trustful, trusting; • Ant conscious, expecting, knowing, realizing, suspecting.

unsympathetic [adj] heartless
• Syn aloof, antipathetic, callous, cruel, disinterested, hard, indifferent, insensi-

tive, mean, nasty, obdurate, repellent, stony, tough; ▪ *Ant* kind, merciful, sympathetic.

untangle [v] *straighten out*
▪ *Syn* clear up, disencumber, disentangle, explain, extricate, put in order, solve, unravel; ▪ *Ant* confuse, muddle, tangle, twist.

unthinkable [adj] *incredible, unusual*
▪ *Syn* absurd, beyond belief, exceptional, extraordinary, illogical, inconceivable, insupportable, outlandish, preposterous, rare, singular, unique; ▪ *Ant* believable, conceivable, credible.

unthinking [adj] *careless*
▪ *Syn* blundering, brutish, feckless, heedless, impulsive, inadvertent, inconsiderate, negligent, oblivious, rash, rude, selfish, senseless, tactless, thoughtless, vacant, witless; ▪ *Ant* careful, cautious, thoughtful.

untimely [adj] *inappropriate*
▪ *Syn* abortive, anachronistic, awkward, disagreeable, ill-timed, inappropriate, inauspicious, inopportune, malapropos, mistimed, premature, too early, too late, wrong; ▪ *Ant* appropriate, opportune, timely.

untiring [adj] *determined, persevering*
▪ *Syn* constant, dedicated, devoted, dogged, firm, incessant, indefatigable, inexhaustible, persistent, pertinacious, plodding, resolute, staunch, steady, tenacious, tireless; ▪ *Ant* failing, irresolute, tiring, unpersevering.

untold [adj] *very many; enormous*
▪ *Syn* beyond measure, countless, hidden, incalculable, innumerable, mammoth, manifold, measureless, multitudinous, myriad, numberless, prodigious, staggering, titanic, vast; ▪ *Ant* few, limited, little, small, tiny.

untouched [adj] *whole; not spoiled*
▪ *Syn* clear, entire, flawless, good, immaculate, incorrupt, intact, perfect, pure, secure, sound, spotless, virgin, virginal, without a scratch; ▪ *Ant* affected, partial, spoiled, touched.

untoward [adj1] *troublesome; not suitable* ▪ *Syn* adverse, awkward, contrary, disturbing, fractious, hapless, ill-starred, inappropriate, indecent, inopportune, irritating, luckless, misfortunate, perverse, recalcitrant, refractory, star-crossed, vexatious, wild; ▪ *Ant* auspicious, happy, lucky.

untroubled [adj] *calm, peaceful*
▪ *Syn* composed, cool, halcyon, hushed, placid, quiet, serene, steady, still, tranquil, undisturbed; ▪ *Ant* anxious, disturbed, troubled, unnerved.

untrue [adj] *dishonest*
▪ *Syn* apocryphal, cheating, deceptive, delusive, deviant, disloyal, erroneous, faithless, fallacious, hollow, inaccurate, incorrect, lying, meretricious, misleading, mistaken, perfidious, perjured, prevaricating, recreant, specious, spurious, traitorous, treacherous, unfaithful; ▪ *Ant* faithful, honest, true.

untrustworthy [adj] *not dependable, faithful* ▪ *Syn* capricious, conniving, crooked, deceitful, devious, dishonest, false, fickle, guileful, irresponsible, questionable, shady, slippery, sneaky, treacherous, tricky; ▪ *Ant* dependable, faithful, honest, reliable, trustworthy.

unusual [adj] *different*
▪ *Syn* abnormal, amazing, astonishing, atypical, awe-inspiring, bizarre, conspicuous, different, distinguished, eminent, exceptional, incredible, memorable, noteworthy, odd, outstanding, phenomenal, prodigious, prominent, rare, refreshing, remarkable, significant, singular, surprising, unique; ▪ *Ant* common, familiar, normal, orthodox, regular, standard, typical, usual.

unusually [adv] *extremely*
▪ *Syn* almighty, awfully, curiously, especially, extraordinarily, oddly, peculiarly, plenty, powerful, rarely, real, really, remarkably, strangely, surprisingly, terribly, terrifically, too much, very; ▪ *Ant* normally, usually.

unvarnished [adj] *plain, honest*
▪ *Syn* bare, candid, clean, frank, genuine, naked, open, pure, simple, sincere, stark, straight, straightforward; ▪ *Ant* dishonest, embellished, exaggerated, falsified.

unwarranted [adj] *not reasonable or right* ▪ *Syn* baseless, bottomless, foundationless, gratuitous, groundless, indefensible, inexcusable; ▪ *Ant* called-for, justifiable, reasonable, warranted.

unwavering [adj] *consistent, unchanging* ▪ *Syn* abiding, dedicated, determined, enduring, firm, fixed, intense, never-failing, resolute, set, single-minded, solid, staunch, steadfast, steady, sure, tenacious; ▪ *Ant* changeable, changing, inconsistent, varying, wavering.

unwelcome [adj] *not wanted, desired*
▪ **Syn** disagreeable, displeasing, distasteful, exceptionable, ill-favored, inadmissible, objectionable, obnoxious, repellent, shut out, thankless; ▪ **Ant** desirable, wanted, welcome.

unwieldy [adj] *awkward, bulky*
▪ **Syn** burdensome, clumsy, cumbersome, encumbering, gross, hefty, lumbering, massive, onerous, ponderous, weighty; ▪ **Ant** convenient, handy, manageable, maneuverable.

unwilling [adj] *reluctant*
▪ **Syn** averse, begrudging, contrary, disinclined, disobliging, evasive, grudging, hesitating, indocile, laggard, loath, malcontent, recalcitrant, reluctant, remiss, shrinking, shy, slow; ▪ **Ant** accommodating, cooperative, prepared, ready, willing.

unwise [adj] *stupid, irresponsible*
▪ **Syn** childish, foolhardy, ill-advised, immature, impolitic, improvident, imprudent, inadvisable, inane, injudicious, misguided, naive, rash, reckless, senseless, short-sighted, silly, thoughtless, witless; ▪ **Ant** responsible, sagacious, thoughtful, wise.

unwitting [adj] *without fully realizing*
▪ **Syn** accidental, aimless, chance, comatose, forgetful, haphazard, ignorant, inadvertent, innocent, involuntary, numb, oblivious, senseless; ▪ **Ant** conscious, intentional, realizing, witting.

unworldly [adj2] *not sophisticated; inexperienced* ▪ **Syn** artless, clean, country, idealistic, ingenuous, innocent, naive, natural, simple, trusting; ▪ **Ant** cultured, experienced, refined, sophisticated, worldly.

unworthy [adj] *not of value*
▪ **Syn** base, beneath, blamable, contemptible, degrading, dishonorable, disreputable, good-for-nothing, ignoble, improper, inappropriate, ineligible, inexcusable, not deserving, not fit; ▪ **Ant** honorable, useful, valuable, worthwhile, worthy.

unwritten [adj] *understood*
▪ **Syn** accepted, conventional, customary, tacit, traditional, verbal, word-of-mouth; ▪ **Ant** explained, explicated, stated, written.

unyielding [adj] *steadfast, resolute*
▪ **Syn** adamant, determined, firm, fixed, hard, immalleable, implacable, impli-able, inflexible, intractable, locked in, merciless, mulish, obdurate, obstinate, pertinacious, refractory, relentless, resolute, rigid, ruthless, single-minded, solid, staunch, stiff, stubborn, tough; ▪ **Ant** flexible, irresolute, surrendering, yielding.

upbeat [adj] *cheerful*
▪ **Syn** buoyant, cheery, encouraging, favorable, fond, happy, heartening, hopeful, optimistic, positive, promising, rosy, sanguine; ▪ **Ant** depressed, down, sad.

upheaval [n] *major change*
▪ **Syn** cataclysm, catastrophe, clamor, commotion, disorder, disruption, disturbance, eruption, explosion, ferment, outbreak, outburst, revolution, shakeout, tumult, turmoil; ▪ **Ant** calm, harmony, order, serenity.

uphill [adj1] *going up*
▪ **Syn** acclivous, ascending, climbing, mounting, rising, skyward, sloping upward, toward summit, up, uprising; ▪ **Ant** downhill.

uphill [adj2] *difficult, laborious*
▪ **Syn** arduous, effortful, exhausting, grueling, hard, labored, operose, punishing, rugged, strenuous, taxing, toilsome, tough, wearisome; ▪ **Ant** easy, facile.

uphold [v] *maintain, support*
▪ **Syn** advocate, assist, back up, bolster, boost, brace, buttress, champion, defend, elevate, endorse, help, hoist, justify, promote, raise, second, side with, sustain, uplift, vindicate; ▪ **Ant** abandon, attach, belittle, denigrate, let down, weaken.

upper [adj1] *above*
▪ **Syn** high, higher, loftier, more elevated, overhead, top, topmost, uppermost, upward; ▪ **Ant** below, lower, under.

upper [adj2] *superior*
▪ **Syn** beautiful, elevated, eminent, greater, important, more important; ▪ **Ant** inferior, junior, lower.

uppermost [adj] *most important; chief*
▪ **Syn** best, big, boss, dominant, executive, foremost, greatest, leading, main, paramount, predominant, preeminent, primary, principal, supreme, winner; ▪ **Ant** humblest, lowest, trivial.

upright [adj1] *straight-up*
▪ **Syn** cocked, erect, on end, perpendicular, plumb, raised, sheer, standing, steep, straight, upended, upstanding, upward, vertical; ▪ **Ant** fallen, lying, prone.

upright [adj2] *honorable, honest*
▪ *Syn* aboveboard, blameless, circumspect, correct, equitable, exemplary, faithful, good, high-minded, incorruptible, just, moral, noble, principled, pure, righteous, square, straight, true, trustworthy, virtuous; ▪ *Ant* dishonest, dishonorable, disreputable, unrespected.

uprising [n] *disturbance*
▪ *Syn* insurgence, insurrection, mutiny, outbreak, rebellion, revolt, revolution, riot, upheaval; ▪ *Ant* calm, harmony, peace.

uproar [n] *commotion, pandemonium*
▪ *Syn* ado, bedlam, brawl, bustle, chaos, clamor, confusion, din, disorder, furor, hassle, jangle, mayhem, melee, noise, outcry, riot, row, ruction, stir, turbulence, violence; ▪ *Ant* serenity, stillness, tranquility.

uproot [v] *destroy; rip out of a place*
▪ *Syn* abolish, annihilate, demolish, displace, eliminate, eradicate, excavate, exterminate, extirpate, extract, move, overthrow, overturn, pull up, root out, tear up, weed out, wipe out; ▪ *Ant* abet, create, encourage, plant, settle, sow.

upset [adj] *disturbed, bothered*
▪ *Syn* agitated, apprehensive, chaotic, confused, disconcerted, disordered, disquieted, distressed, frantic, grieved, hurt, ill, jumpy, low, muddled, overwrought, rattled, shocked, sick, thrown, troubled, upside-down, worried; ▪ *Ant* composed, happy, pacified, undisturbed, unworried.

upset [v1] *disorder; knock over*
▪ *Syn* capsize, disarray, disorganize, invert, jumble, keel over, muddle, overturn, put out of order, reverse, rummage, spill, subvert, tilt, tip over, topple, tumble, turn, upend, upturn; ▪ *Ant* hold, order, place, straighten.

upset [v2] *bother, trouble*
▪ *Syn* afflict, agitate, bewilder, confound, craze, debilitate, discompose, disconcert, dismay, distress, disturb, flurry, grieve, incapacitate, lay up, perturb, rattle, ruffle, sicken, spook, stir up; ▪ *Ant* delight, make happy, please.

upset [v3] *defeat*
▪ *Syn* beat, be victorious, conquer, outplay, overcome, overpower, overthrow, overturn, topple, triumph over, win; ▪ *Ant* fail, lose.

upshot [n] *end result*
▪ *Syn* aftereffect, aftermath, burden, climax, conclusion, consequence, culmination, denouement, effect, finale, gist, issue, meaning, outcome, payoff, result, sequel, termination, thrust; ▪ *Ant* cause, origin, source.

upside-down [adj] *overturned, inverted*
▪ *Syn* backward, bottom-side up, confused, disordered, in chaos, in disarray, jumbled, mixed-up, on head, reversed, tangled, upended, wrong-side-up; ▪ *Ant* calm, ordinary, right-side-up.

upstanding [adj] *honorable*
▪ *Syn* ethical, good, honest, incorruptible, moral, principled, straightforward, true, trustworthy, upright; ▪ *Ant* bad, corrupted, dishonorable, disreputable.

uptight [adj] *nervous*
▪ *Syn* anxious, apprehensive, cautious, conventional, edgy, nervy, old-fashioned, restive, strict, tense, troubled, withdrawn, worried; ▪ *Ant* calm, collected, cool.

up-to-date [adj] *current, modern*
▪ *Syn* abreast, advanced, au courant, brand-new, contemporary, dashing, expedient, fashionable, in, in fashion, in vogue, modish, neoteric, new, newfangled, opportune, popular, state-of-the-art, stylish, timely, trendy, up-to-the-minute; ▪ *Ant* cliched, old, outdated, out-of-date, passé, past.

urban [adj] *city*
▪ *Syn* burghal, central, citified, civic, civil, downtown, inner-city, metropolitan, municipal; ▪ *Ant* country, rural, suburban.

urbane [adj] *civilized*
▪ *Syn* affable, balanced, civil, cosmopolitan, cultivated, cultured, debonair, elegant, genteel, gracious, mannerly, poised, refined, sophisticated, suave, well-bred, well-mannered; ▪ *Ant* provincial, tactless, uncivilized, uncouth, unrefined, unsophisticated.

urge [v] *beg, push for, encourage*
▪ *Syn* adjure, advance, advocate, beseech, champion, commend, conjure, counsel, countenance, drive, endorse, favor, further, goad, hasten, implore, incite, induce, insist on, inspire, instigate, move, plead, press, promote, propel, propose, recommend, request, sanction, solicit, stimulate, support, tempt, wheedle; ▪ *Ant* discourage, dissuade, hinder, prevent, restrain.

urgent [adj] *needing immediate attention*
▪ **Syn** called-for, clamorous, compelling, critical, crucial, driving, essential, exigent, foremost, immediate, impelling, imperative, important, importunate, indispensable, insistent, leading, momentous, necessary, paramount, persuasive, pressing, primary, principal, required, salient, serious, top-priority, vital; ▪ **Ant** trifling, trivial, unimportant, unnecessary.

use [v] *work with; consume*
▪ **Syn** accept, adopt, apply, bestow, capitalize, control, draw on, employ, exercise, exhaust, expend, exploit, find a use, govern, handle, manipulate, operate, put into action, put to work, regulate, run, set in motion, spend, turn to account, utilize, waste, wield, work; ▪ **Ant** abstain, leave alone.

useful [adj] *beneficial, valuable*
▪ **Syn** advantageous, appropriate, commodious, convenient, effective, favorable, fruitful, functional, good, handy, instrumental, meet, of service, pragmatic, profitable, propitious, salutary, suitable, utilitarian, worthwhile; ▪ **Ant** fruitless, useless, vain, worthless.

useless [adj] *not working; not valuable*
▪ **Syn** counterproductive, disadvantageous, dysfunctional, expendable, feckless, fruitless, hopeless, idle, impractical, ineffectual, inept, inoperative, pointless, purposeless, scrap, vain, valueless, waste, weak, worthless; ▪ **Ant** helpful, usable, useful, valuable, working, worthwhile.

user-friendly [adj] *easily operated*
▪ **Syn** accessible, adaptable, convenient, easy to use, feasible, fool proof, handy, manageable, practical, simple, straightforward, uncomplicated, useful, wieldy; ▪ **Ant** brutal, challenging, complex, complicated, cumbersome, difficult, grueling, hard, irksome, ponderous, rough, severe, tough, tricky, trying, unmanageable, unwieldy.

usual [adj] *common, typical*
▪ **Syn** accepted, accustomed, chronic, commonplace, customary, everyday, expected, familiar, frequent, general, habitual, mainstream, normal, ordinary, prevailing, prevalent, quotidian, regular, routine, standard, stock, typic, wonted, workaday; ▪ **Ant** abnormal, atypical, irregular, uncommon, unusual.

usually [adv] *for the most part*
▪ **Syn** as a rule, as is the custom, by and large, customarily, frequently, generally, habitually, mainly, more often than not, mostly, most often, normally, now and then, occasionally, on the whole, ordinarily, regularly, routinely; ▪ **Ant** exceptionally, unusually.

usurp [v] *take over*
▪ **Syn** accroach, annex, appropriate, arrogate, assume, commandeer, displace, infringe upon, lay hold of, preempt, seize, supplant, swipe, take, wrest; ▪ **Ant** give in, relinquish, surrender.

utilitarian [adj] *practical*
▪ **Syn** commonsensical, down-to-earth, effective, efficient, functional, hard, hardheaded, matter-of-fact, pragmatic, realistic, sensible, serviceable, unromantic, useful; ▪ **Ant** extravagant, fanciful, impractical, unnecessary.

utmost [adj] *extreme, maximum*
▪ **Syn** absolute, chief, complete, entire, exhaustive, farthest, final, full, furthermost, greatest, highest, last, maximal, most, most distant, outermost, outside, paramount, plenary, preeminent, remotest, sheer, supreme, thorough, thoroughgoing, top, topmost, total, ultimate, unmitigated; ▪ **Ant** least, minimal, poorest, smallest.

utopian [adj] *imaginary, ideal*
▪ **Syn** abstract, airy, arcadian, chimerical, fanciful, grandiose, hopeful, idealist, idealistic, illusory, impractical, lofty, otherworldly, perfect, pretentious, quixotic, romantic, transcendental, visionary; ▪ **Ant** practical, real, realistic.

utter [adj] *outright, absolute*
▪ **Syn** arrant, complete, confounded, consummate, downright, entire, infernal, perfect, pure, sheer, stark, thorough, thoroughgoing, total; ▪ **Ant** incomplete, moderate, partial, relative, uncertain.

utter [v] *say, reveal*
▪ **Syn** announce, articulate, assert, blurt, bring out, chime, declare, disclose, divulge, ejaculate, enunciate, exclaim, jaw, make known, modulate, proclaim, pronounce, recite, say, shout, speak, state, talk, verbalize, voice; ▪ **Ant** conceal, hide, remain silent.

utterly [adv] *completely*
▪ **Syn** absolutely, all in all, altogether, entirely, exactly, fully, just, perfectly, quite, thoroughly, totally, well, wholly;

▪ *Ant* incompletely, moderately, partially, uncertain.

V

vacant [adj1] *empty; unoccupied*
▪ *Syn* abandoned, bare, clear, deserted, disengaged, free, idle, not in use, stark, void, without contents; ▪ *Ant* full, occupied, overflowing.

vacant [adj2] *absentminded; expressionless* ▪ *Syn* abstracted, blank, daydreaming, deadpan, dreamy, emptyheaded, foolish, idle, inane, silly, thoughtless, vacuous, vapid, witless; ▪ *Ant* aware, cognizant, comprehending.

vacate [v] *leave empty*
▪ *Syn* abandon, abrogate, clear, depart, dissolve, empty, evacuate, leave, move out, move out of, quit, relinquish, rescind, retract, revoke, void, withdraw; ▪ *Ant* employ, move in, occupy, retain.

vacation [n] *planned time spent not working* ▪ *Syn* break, day of rest, fiesta, furlough, holiday, intermission, leave, liberty, recess, respite, sabbatical, spell, time off; ▪ *Ant* academic year, active duty, occupation, work.

vacillate [v] *go back and forth*
▪ *Syn* alternate, be irresolute, change, dither, fluctuate, hedge, hesitate, hover, oscillate, pause, reel, rock, straddle, swing, waffle, waver; ▪ *Ant* be determined, be resolute, remain, stay, steady.

vacuous [adj] *empty; unintelligent*
▪ *Syn* blank, dull, dumb, foolish, inane, shallow, stupid, superficial, vacant, void; ▪ *Ant* aware, full, intelligent.

vagabond/vagrant [n] *person who wanders from place to place* ▪ *Syn* beggar, bum, derelict, drifter, floater, gypsy, hobo, idler, migrant, nomad, outcast, rascal, rogue, stray, transient, traveler, wanderer, wayfarer; ▪ *Ant* inhabitant, resident.

vagabond [adj] *poor and homeless*
▪ *Syn* aimless, begging, destitute, drifting, errant, idle, migratory, nomadic, peripatetic, prodigal, profligate, roaming, roving, sauntering, shiftless, straggling, strolling, transient, vagrant, wandering, wayfaring, wayward; ▪ *Ant* employed, inhabiting, purposeful, rooted, settled.

vague [adj] *not definite or clear*
▪ *Syn* ambiguous, amorphous, blurred, cloudy, dark, dreamlike, dubious, enigmatic, equivocal, faint, fuzzy, generalized, hazy, ill-defined, impalpable, indeterminate, indistinct, lax, loose, muddy, nebulous, obscure, perplexing, questionable, shadowy, superficial, tenebrous; ▪ *Ant* certain, clear, definite, sure.

vain [adj1] *egotistical*
▪ *Syn* arrogant, big-headed, boastful, conceited, egocentric, egoistic, haughty, inflated, narcissistic, ostentatious, overweening, proud, self-important, vainglorious; ▪ *Ant* bashful, humble, modest, shy.

vain [adj2] *futile, useless*
▪ *Syn* abortive, barren, bootless, delusive, empty, fruitless, hollow, idle, inefficacious, misleading, nugatory, otiose, paltry, petty, pointless, senseless, sterile, time-wasting, trifling, trivial, valueless, void, worthless; ▪ *Ant* beneficial, effective, fruitful, successful, worthy.

valedictory [adj] *farewell*
▪ *Syn* departing, final, goodbye, last, parting, terminal; ▪ *Ant* welcoming.

valiant [adj] *brave*
▪ *Syn* adventurous, audacious, bold, brave, chivalrous, courageous, dauntless, fearless, gallant, heroic, intrepid, lionhearted, magnanimous, noble, powerful, stalwart, steadfast, undaunted, valorous, venturesome; ▪ *Ant* afraid, cowardly, craven, fearful, timid.

valid [adj] *right, genuine*
▪ *Syn* accurate, attested, authentic, authoritative, binding, bona fide, cogent, compelling, conclusive, confirmed, convincing, credible, determinative, efficacious, efficient, good, in force, irrefutable, just, lawful, legal, legitimate, logical, official, original, persuasive, potent, powerful, proven, pure, solid, sound, stringent, strong, substantial, telling, tested, true, trustworthy, ultimate, weighty, well-founded; ▪ *Ant* invalid, unacceptable, unreal, unsound, vague, wrong.

validate [v] *ascertain the truth, authenticity of something* ▪ *Syn* approve, authenticate, authorize, bear out, certify, confirm, constitute, corroborate, endorse, justify, legalize, legitimize, ratify, sanction, substantiate, verify; ▪ *Ant* cancel, refuse, reject, veto.

valley [n] *hollow in the land*
▪ *Syn* basin, bottom, canyon, channel,

coulee, dale, dell, depression, dingle, glen, gorge, lowland, notch, plain, swale, trough, vale; ▪ *Ant* bluff, butte, hill, hillock, knoll, mount, mountain, peak, ridge, rise, rise.

valuable [*adj*] *very important; priceless*
▪ *Syn* admired, appreciated, beneficial, cherished, collectible, costly, dear, esteemed, estimable, expensive, heirloom, held dear, helpful, high-priced, important, in demand, inestimable, precious, prized, profitable, relevant, respected, scarce, serviceable, treasured, useful, valued, worthwhile, worthy; ▪ *Ant* unimportant, useless, valueless, worthless.

vanish [*v*] *disappear*
▪ *Syn* become invisible, be lost, clear, dematerialize, die, die out, dissolve, evanesce, evaporate, exit, fade, fade away, go away, melt; ▪ *Ant* appear, arrive, come, enter, remain.

vanity [*n*] *conceit, egotism*
▪ *Syn* affected way, affection, airs, arrogance, conceitedness, display, egotism, narcissism, ostentation, pretension, pride, self-admiration, self-love, self-worship, smugness, vainglory; ▪ *Ant* diffidence, humility, masochism, modesty, self-effacement.

vanquish [*v*] *defeat soundly*
▪ *Syn* bear down, beat, conquer, crush, humble, master, overcome, overpower, overturn, overwhelm, put down, quell, reduce, repress, rout, subdue, subjugate, subvert, surmount, trample, triumph over; ▪ *Ant* capitulate, fail, lose, surrender, yield.

vapid [*adj*] *flat, dull*
▪ *Syn* bland, boring, colorless, driveling, flat, flavorless, inane, innocuous, insipid, jejune, lifeless, limp, stale, tame, tasteless, tedious, tiresome, unimaginative, uninspiring, vacuous, watery, weak; ▪ *Ant* colorful, lively, sharp, spicy, strong.

variable [*adj*] *changing, changeable*
▪ *Syn* capricious, changeful, fickle, fitful, flexible, fluctuating, fluid, inconstant, irregular, mercurial, mobile, mutable, protean, shifting, shifty, spasmodic, temperamental, ticklish, uncertain, vacillating, volatile, waffling, wavering; ▪ *Ant* invariable, unchangeable, unchanging, unvarying.

variant [*adj*] *different*
▪ *Syn* alternative, derived, differing, divergent, exceptional, modified, various, varying; ▪ *Ant* original.

varied [*adj*] *different*
▪ *Syn* assorted, conglomerate, discrete, diverse, heterogeneous, indiscriminate, miscellaneous, mixed, motley, multifarious, separate, sundry, various; ▪ *Ant* homogenous, standardized, unvaried.

various [*adj*] *miscellaneous, differing*
▪ *Syn* assorted, changing, different, discrete, disparate, distinct, distinctive, diverse, diversified, heterogeneous, individual, legion, manifold, many, many-sided, multifarious, multitudinal, multitudinous, numerous, omnifarious, peculiar, populous, separate, sundry, unlike, varied, variegated; ▪ *Ant* individual, same, similar, uniform.

varnish [*v*] *add a layer to; embellish*
▪ *Syn* adorn, coat, cover, decorate, enamel, finish, gild, glaze, gloss, japan, lacquer, luster, paint, polish, shellac, surface, veneer, wash, wax; ▪ *Ant* strip.

vary [*v*] *change*
▪ *Syn* alter, alternate, depart, deviate, digress, dissent, divaricate, diverge, diversify, fluctuate, inflect, modify, part, permutate, range, swerve, take turns, transform, turn, variegate; ▪ *Ant* regulate, standardize.

vast [*adj*] *very large; wide in range*
▪ *Syn* all-inclusive, ample, boundless, broad, colossal, comprehensive, enormous, extensive, far-reaching, gigantic, huge, illimitable, immense, limitless, mammoth, massive, monumental, prodigious, prolonged, spacious, sweeping, titanic, voluminous, widespread; ▪ *Ant* bounded, limited, little, modest, narrow, small.

vault [*v*] *jump over; span*
▪ *Syn* arch, ascend, bend, bounce, bound, bow, clear, curve, hop, hurdle, jump, mount, negotiate, over, overleap, rise, soar, spring, surmount; ▪ *Ant* crawl under, creep beneath, descend, plunge.

veer [*v*] *change direction*
▪ *Syn* angle off, avert, bear, bend, change, change course, curve, deflect, deviate, digress, dip, diverge, drift, get around, pivot, skew, skid, swerve, swing, tack, train off, twist, volte-face, wheel; ▪ *Ant* go direct, stay.

vegetate [*vl*] *be very passive*
▪ *Syn* be inert, decay, deteriorate, hiber-

nate, idle, languish, pass time, stagnate, weaken; ▪ *Ant* carry out, do, perform.

vegetate [*v2*] *grow, sprout*
▪ *Syn* bloom, blossom, bud, burgeon, germinate, shoot, spring, swell; ▪ *Ant* die, go to seed.

vehement [*adj*] *passionate, opinionated*
▪ *Syn* angry, ardent, concentrated, desperate, earnest, emphatic, enthusiastic, fervent, fervid, fierce, forceful, frantic, hearty, impassioned, impetuous, intense, lively, powerful, pronounced, rabid, strong, terrible, violent, wild, zealous; ▪ *Ant* apathetic, feeble, indifferent, lukewarm, mild, subdued, unpassionate.

veil [*v*] *hide*
▪ *Syn* blanket, camouflage, cloak, conceal, cover, dim, disguise, drape, enclose, enshroud, envelop, finesse, invest, launder, mantle, mask, obscure, shield, shroud, wrap; ▪ *Ant* denude, divulge, expose, reveal.

vendor [*n*] *person who sells wares*
▪ *Syn* businessperson, dealer, hawker, merchant, outcrier, peddler, supplier, traveler, traveling salesperson, wholesaler; ▪ *Ant* buyer, customer, purchaser.

veneer [*v*] *cover, overlay*
▪ *Syn* blanch, coat, extenuate, face, finish, gloss, palliate, plate, shellac, sugarcoat, surface, varnish, whiten, whitewash; ▪ *Ant* strip, uncover.

venerable [*adj*] *respected*
▪ *Syn* admirable, august, dignified, esteemed, estimable, experienced, grand, grave, honorable, honored, imposing, matriarchal, noble, patriarchal, philosophical, revered, sage, stately, wise, worshipful, worshiped; ▪ *Ant* callow, dishonored, ignominious, shameful, unrespected.

vengeful [*adj*] *retaliating; hating*
▪ *Syn* antagonistic, avenging, hostile, implacable, inimical, punitive, rancorous, relentless, retaliatory, revengeful, spiteful, unforgiving, vindictive; ▪ *Ant* condoning, forgiving, liking, pardoning.

venomous [*adj*] *poisonous; hateful*
▪ *Syn* baneful, cussed, deadly, destructive, dirty, evil, hostile, lethal, malefic, malevolent, malicious, malign, malignant, mean, mephitic, noxious, poisonous, rancorous, savage, spiteful, toxic, vicious, vindictive, viperish, viperous, virulent, waspish; ▪ *Ant* affectionate,

charitable, compassionate, kind, nontoxic, praising.

vent [*v*] *let out; express*
▪ *Syn* air, assert, come out with, declare, discharge, drive out, emit, empty, express, give, give off, give out, issue, loose, pour out, provide escape, put, release, state, take out on, unleash, utter, ventilate, verbalize, voice; ▪ *Ant* inhibit, repress, squelch, stifle, suppress.

ventilate [*v*] *air out; make known*
▪ *Syn* advertise, air, bring into the open, broadcast, circulate, debate, deliberate, discourse, discuss, examine, express, free, give, go into, introduce, moot, publish, put, scrutinize, sift, state, take up, talk about, thresh out, vent, verbalize; ▪ *Ant* bury, close, conceal, cover, hide.

venture [*v*] *take a chance*
▪ *Syn* advance, assay, attempt, bet, brave, challenge, chance, dare, defy, endanger, essay, experiment, expose, feel, gamble, grope, hazard, imperil, jeopardize, lay open, make bold, operate, play for, presume, risk, speculate, stake, try, try out, volunteer, wager; ▪ *Ant* assume, play it safe, protect, safeguard, secure.

venturesome [*adj*] *courageous*
▪ *Syn* adventurous, aggressive, audacious, bold, brave, daredevil, daring, enterprising, fearless, foolhardy, gutsy, intrepid, overbold, plucky, pushy, rash, reckless, resourceful, risky, spirited, spunky, stalwart, stout, sturdy, temerarious, venturous; ▪ *Ant* afraid, apprehensive, cowardly, reluctant, timid.

veracious [*adj*] *true*
▪ *Syn* accurate, credible, dependable, direct, ethical, factual, faithful, frank, genuine, high-principled, honest, just, open, reliable, right, righteous, straight arrow, straightforward, strict, trustworthy, truthful, undeceptive, valid, veridical; ▪ *Ant* false, mendacious, untrue.

verbatim [*adj*] *exactly*
▪ *Syn* accurately, direct, directly, literally, literatim, precisely; ▪ *Ant* distorted, garbled, incorrectly, unfaithfully.

verbose [*adj*] *wordy, long-winded*
▪ *Syn* bombastic, circumlocutory, diffuse, flowery, fustian, garrulous, grandiloquent, involved, loquacious, magniloquent, palaverous, periphrastic, pleonastic, prolix, redundant, repeating, repetitious, repetitive, rhetorical, talk-

ative, tautological, tedious, tortuous; ▪ *Ant* concise, curt, succinct, terse.

verdant [*adj*] *green, blooming*
▪ *Syn* flourishing, fresh, grassy, leafy, lush, verdurous; ▪ *Ant* dying, fading, waning, withering.

verge [*v*] *come near*
▪ *Syn* abut, adjoin, approach, border, brink on, edge, fringe, gravitate, incline, join, line, margin, rim, skirt, surround, tend, touch, trench; ▪ *Ant* recede, retreat, withdraw.

verify [*v*] *confirm, validate*
▪ *Syn* attest, authenticate, bear out, certify, check, confirm, corroborate, debunk, document, double-check, establish, find out, hold up, justify, make certain, prove, settle, substantiate, support, test, try; ▪ *Ant* deny, discredit, disprove, falsify, invalidate, refute.

veritable [*adj*] *authentic*
▪ *Syn* actual, bona fide, factual, for real, genuine, indubitable, positive, real, true, utter; ▪ *Ant* deceptive, fake, false, sham, spurious.

vernacular [*adj*] *native, colloquial*
▪ *Syn* common, dialectal, idiomatic, indigenous, informal, ingrained, inherent, local, mother, natural, ordinary, plebian, popular, vulgar; ▪ *Ant* formal, standard.

versatile [*adj*] *adjustable, flexible*
▪ *Syn* able, accomplished, adroit, all-purpose, conversant, dexterous, elastic, facile, functional, gifted, handy, many-sided, mobile, pliable, protean, ready, resourceful, skilled, talented, variable; ▪ *Ant* inflexible, limited, specialized, unadjustable.

versed [*adj*] *experienced, informed*
▪ *Syn* abreast, accomplished, acquainted, competent, conversant, familiar, knowledgeable, learned, practiced, proficient, qualified, savvy, seasoned, skilled, trained, versant, veteran, well-informed; ▪ *Ant* green, immature, inexperienced.

vertex [*n*] *top*
▪ *Syn* acme, apex, apogee, cap, cope, crest, crown, culmination, extremity, fastigium, height, peak, pinnacle, roof, summit, tip, upper extremity, zenith; ▪ *Ant* bottom, nadir.

vertical [*adj*] *upright*
▪ *Syn* bolt upright, cocked, erect, on end, perpendicular, plumb, sheer, steep, straight-up, up-and-down, upward; ▪ *Ant* horizontal, level, prone, supine.

very [*adj*] *real, exact*
▪ *Syn* appropriate, bona fide, correct express, genuine, ideal, indubitable, perfect, plain, precise, pure, right, sheer, simple, special, sure-enough, true, veritable; ▪ *Ant* approximate, inexact, partial.

very [*adv*] *much, really; to a high degree*
▪ *Syn* absolutely, astonishingly, awfully, certainly, decidedly, deeply, eminently, emphatically, exceedingly, extensively, extremely, greatly, highly, incredibly, largely, notably, profoundly, remarkably, substantially, superlatively, surpassingly, terribly, truly, vastly, wonderfully; ▪ *Ant* barely, hardly, little, slightly.

veteran [*adj*] *experienced, seasoned*
▪ *Syn* adept, disciplined, exercised, expert, hardened, inured, long-serving, long-time, old, old-time, practical, practiced, pro, proficient, skilled, sophisticated, steady, trained, versed, weathered, wise, worldly; ▪ *Ant* amateur, green, inexperienced.

veto [*v*] *refuse permission*
▪ *Syn* ban, burn, cut, decline, defeat, deny, disallow, disapprove, discountenance, forbid, interdict, kill, negate, pass, pass by, prohibit, refuse, reject, turn down; ▪ *Ant* allow, approve, ok, permit, ratify, sanction.

vex [*v*] *distress, bother*
▪ *Syn* abrade, aggravate, agitate, anger, annoy, chafe, displease, embarrass, exasperate, fret, harass, harry, infuriate, irk, molest, needle, offend, peeve, pester, pique, rasp, rile, tease, trouble, worry; ▪ *Ant* aid, assist, help, please, soothe.

vexatious [*adj*] *distressing, bothersome*
▪ *Syn* aggravating, annoying, burdensome, disagreeable, disturbing, exasperating, irksome, irritating, mean, nagging, pesky, provoking, teasing, tormenting, trying, upsetting, wicked, worrisome; ▪ *Ant* aiding, assisting, helpful, pleasing, soothing.

viable [*adj*] *reasonable, practicable*
▪ *Syn* applicable, doable, feasible, operable, possible, usable, within possibility, workable; ▪ *Ant* unusable, unviable, useless.

vibrant [*adj1*] *alive, colorful*
▪ *Syn* active, animated, dynamic, electrifying, energetic, lively, peppy, respon-

sive, sensitive, sparkling, spirited, vigorous, vital, vivacious, vivid; ▪ *Ant* colorless, dull, pale.

vibrant [*adj2*] *throbbing*
▪ *Syn* aquiver, consonant, oscillating, palpitating, pulsating, pulsing, quaking, quivering, resonant, resounding, reverberant, ringing, sonorant, sonorous; ▪ *Ant* shrill, thin, weak.

vibration [*n*] *shaking, quivering*
▪ *Syn* beating, fluctuation, judder, oscillation, pulsation, quake, quiver, resonance, shimmy, throbbing, trembling, tremor, vacillation, wave, wavering; ▪ *Ant* steadiness, stillness.

vicarious [*adj*] *acting in another's place*
▪ *Syn* commissioned, delegated, empathetic, indirect, pretended, secondary, substituted, substitutional, surrogate, sympathetic; ▪ *Ant* direct, firsthand.

vice [*n1*] *bad habit; sin*
▪ *Syn* carnality, corruption, debasement, debauchery, degeneracy, depravity, evil, evildoing, immorality, indecency, iniquity, lechery, lewdness, libidinousness, licentiousness, looseness, maleficence, malignance, offense, perversion, profligacy, rot, squalor, transgression, venality, wickedness, wrong; ▪ *Ant* good point, propriety, virtue.

vice [*n2*] *weakness*
▪ *Syn* blemish, defect, demerit, failing, fault, flaw, foible, frailty, imperfection, mar, shortcoming, weak point; ▪ *Ant* good point, strength, talent.

vicious [*adj1*] *corrupt, wrong, nasty*
▪ *Syn* abandoned, atrocious, bad, bloodthirsty, contaminated, dangerous, debased, degraded, demoralized, faulty, ferocious, fiendish, flagitious, heinous, immoral, impious, lewd, licentious, malevolent, monstrous, nefarious, perverse, reprehensible, reprobate, rotten, sinful, vile, villainous, violent, wicked; ▪ *Ant* gentle, good, kind.

vicissitude [*n*] *change*
▪ *Syn* alternation, diversity, fluctuation, innovation, mutability, permutation, progression, reversal, revolution, shift, switch, switchover, transposition, turnaround, variation, variety; ▪ *Ant* stability, stagnation.

victimize [*v*] *cheat, fool*
▪ *Syn* con, cozen, deceive, defraud, discriminate against, dupe, exploit, hoax, hoodwink, immolate, persecute,

pick on, prey on, swindle, take advantage of, trick, use; ▪ *Ant* aid, assist, help, protect.

victorious [*adj*] *successful, winning*
▪ *Syn* arrived, champion, conquering, mastering, on top, prizewinning, triumphant, vanquishing; ▪ *Ant* failing, losing, unsuccessful.

vie [*v*] *compete*
▪ *Syn* be rivals, buck, challenge, contend, contest, counter, match, oppose, pit, play, play off, push, rival, scramble for, strive, struggle, sweat; ▪ *Ant* cooperate, negotiate, share.

view [*v1*] *look at*
▪ *Syn* beam, behold, canvass, check out, check over, consider, discern, espy, examine, explore, gaze, inspect, lay eyes on, notice, observe, perceive, read, regard, scan, scope, scrutinize, see, set eyes on, spot, spy, stare, survey, watch, witness; ▪ *Ant* ignore, overlook.

view [*v2*] *believe*
▪ *Syn* account, consider, deem, judge, look on, reckon, regard, think over; ▪ *Ant* disbelieve, mistrust.

vigilant [*adj*] *careful, watchful*
▪ *Syn* acute, agog, alert, anxious, attentive, aware, cautious, circumspect, guarded, keen, looking for, looking to, observant, on alert, on guard, on the lookout, sharp, sleepless, wary, wideawake; ▪ *Ant* careless, impulsive, inattentive, indiscreet, negligent.

vigorous [*adj*] *energetic, powerful*
▪ *Syn* active, athletic, bouncing, brisk, dashing, driving, dynamic, effective, enterprising, exuberant, fertile, flourishing, forceful, hale, hardy, hearty, intense, lively, masterful, mettlesome, peppy, potent, robust, rugged, snappy, sound, spirited, strapping, strenuous, strong, sturdy, tough, virile, vital, zealous; ▪ *Ant* enervated, idle, impotent, inactive, lethargic, weak.

vile [*adj*] *offensive, horrible*
▪ *Syn* abject, appalling, base, coarse, contemptible, corrupt, debased, degenerate, depraved, dirty, disgraceful, disgusting, evil, foul, horrid, ignoble, immoral, impure, loathsome, mean, miserable, nasty, nauseating, nefarious, noxious, perverted, repellent, repugnant, revolting, shocking, sickening, sinful, ugly, vicious, vulgar, wicked, wretched; ▪ *Ant* appealing, appetizing, kind, pleasant.

vilify [v] *criticize very harshly*
▪ *Syn* abuse, asperse, assail, attack, berate, blister, caluminate, censure, cuss, damn, debase, decry, defame, denigrate, denounce, disparage, jinx, knock, libel, malign, mistreat, revile, run down, scorch, slander, slur, speak ill of, traduce, vituperate; ▪ *Ant* compliment, praise.

village [n] *small town*
▪ *Syn* center, crossroads, hamlet, suburb; ▪ *Ant* big city, city, metropolis, urban center.

villain [n] *evil person*
▪ *Syn* antihero, brute, caitiff, criminal, devil, evildoer, heel, knave, libertine, malefactor, miscreant, offender, profligate, rapscallion, rascal, reprobate, rogue, scoundrel, sinner, wretch; ▪ *Ant* champion, hero, heroine, worthy.

vindicate [v] *prove one's innocence*
▪ *Syn* absolve, acquit, assert, bear out, clear, corroborate, defend, disculpate, exculpate, excuse, exonerate, free, justify, plead for, refute, substantiate, support, uphold; ▪ *Ant* accuse, blame, convict, punish, sentence.

vindictive [adj] *hateful, revengeful*
▪ *Syn* avenging, cruel, grim, implacable, malicious, malignant, merciless, rancorous, relentless, resentful, retaliatory, ruthless, spiteful, vengeful, venomous, wreakful; ▪ *Ant* forgiving, generous, relenting.

vintage [adj] *superior*
▪ *Syn* best, choice, classic, classical, excellent, mature, old, prime, rare, ripe, select, selected, venerable; ▪ *Ant* awful, inferior, minor, unimportant.

violate [v1] *break a law, agreement*
▪ *Syn* breach, contaminate, defy, disobey, disregard, encroach, err, infract, infringe, meddle, offend, oppose, profane, resist, sin, trample on, transgress, trespass; ▪ *Ant* comply, honor, obey, observe.

violate [v2] *rape, defile*
▪ *Syn* abuse, assault, befoul, debauch, defile, desecrate, dishonor, force, invade, outrage, pollute, profane, ravish, spoil; ▪ *Ant* harbor, protect, shield.

violent [adj1] *destructive*
▪ *Syn* bloodthirsty, brutal, crazy, cruel, demoniac, disturbed, enraged, fierce, fiery, forceful, fuming, furious, great, headstrong, homicidal, hysterical, impassioned, inflamed, mad, maniacal, murderous, passionate, potent, raging, riotous,

savage, urgent, vehement, vicious, wild; ▪ *Ant* gentle, passive, peaceful.

violent [adj2] *severe, extreme*
▪ *Syn* acute, agonizing, biting, coercive, concentrated, excruciating, great, harsh, inordinate, intense, mighty, outrageous, potent, raging, sharp, tempestuous, terrible, turbulent, wild; ▪ *Ant* calm, gentle, mild, moderate.

virgin/virginal [adj] *brand-new, unused*
▪ *Syn* abstinent, celibate, chaste, fresh, immaculate, initial, innocent, intact, modest, natural, new, original, primeval, pristine, pure, spotless, uncorrupted, undefiled, unspoiled, unsullied, untouched, untried, vestal; ▪ *Ant* defiled, sullied, used.

virile [adj] *potent, powerful*
▪ *Syn* brave, driving, energetic, forceful, generative, lusty, male, masculine, procreative, reproductive, robust, sound, strong, vibrant, vigorous, vital; ▪ *Ant* effeminate, impotent, unmanly.

virtual [adj] *in essence*
▪ *Syn* implicit, implied, indirect, in effect, in practice, potential, tacit, unacknowledged; ▪ *Ant* actual, emphatic, explicit.

virtuoso [n] *person who is an expert*
▪ *Syn* ace, artist, artiste, authority, celebrity, champion, dilettante, genius, maestro, master, maven, past master, prodigy, star, superstar, wizard; ▪ *Ant* amateur, greenhorn, rookie.

virtuous [adj] *good, ethical; innocent*
▪ *Syn* blameless, celibate, chaste, excellent, exemplary, faithful, high-principled, honest, incorruptible, moral, noble, praiseworthy, principled, pure, righteous, right-minded, spotless, straight, virginal, wholesome, worthy; ▪ *Ant* bad, sinful, unethical, vile, wicked.

virulent [adj1] *poisonous, lethal*
▪ *Syn* baneful, deadly, fatal, harmful, injurious, malign, malignant, mephitic, pernicious, poison, septic, toxic, venomous; ▪ *Ant* harmless, healthy, nonpoisonous, nontoxic.

virulent [adj2] *hostile*
▪ *Syn* acrimonious, antagonistic, bitter, cutting, hateful, malicious, rancorous, resentful, scathing, spiteful, splenetic, stabbing, unfriendly, venomous, vicious, vindictive, vitriolic; ▪ *Ant* amiable, benign, compassionate, gentle, kind, nice.

viscous [adj] *sticky, gummy*
▪ *Syn* adhesive, clammy, gelatinous, glu-

tinous, mucilaginous, ropy, stiff, syrupy, tenacious, thick, tough, viscid; ▪ *Ant* satiny, slick, slippery, unsticky, watery.

visible [*adj*] *apparent, seeable*
▪ *Syn* bold, clear, conspicuous, detectable, discernible, evident, in sight, macroscopic, manifest, marked, noticeable, observable, obtrusive, palpable, patent, perceptible, pronounced, salient, signal; ▪ *Ant* concealed, hidden, invisible, obscured, unseeable.

visionary [*adj*] *idealized, romantic*
▪ *Syn* abstracted, ambitious, astral, chimerical, daydreaming, delusory, dreaming, exalted, fanciful, fantastic, grandiose, idealistic, illusory, imaginary, impractical, introspective, lofty, musing, noble, otherworldly, pretentious, prophetic, quixotic, speculative, starry-eyed utopian; ▪ *Ant* practical, real, realistic, unromantic.

visitor [*n*] *person temporarily in a foreign location* ▪ *Syn* caller, company, guest, habitué, invitee, out-of-towner, transient; ▪ *Ant* host.

vital [*adj1*] *essential*
▪ *Syn* basic, cardinal, constitutive, critical, crucial, decisive, fundamental, imperative, important, indispensable, integral, key, meaningful, name, necessary, needed, prerequisite, required, requisite, significant, underlined, urgent; ▪ *Ant* inessential, insignficant, trivial, unimportant.

vital [*adj2*] *lively*
▪ *Syn* animated, dynamic, energetic, forceful, lusty, red-blooded, spirited, strenuous, vibrant, vigorous, virile, vivacious, zestful; ▪ *Ant* dull, lethargic, sluggish, torpid.

vital [*adj3*] *alive*
▪ *Syn* animate, animated, breathing, generative, invigorative, life-giving, live, living, quickening; ▪ *Ant* dead, inanimate, lifeless.

vitiate [*v1*] *cancel*
▪ *Syn* abate, abolish, abrogate, annihilate, annul, delete, deny, invalidate, negate, nullify, quash, recant, revoke, undermine, undo; ▪ *Ant* buttress, reinforce, strengthen.

vitiate [*v2*] *hurt, corrupt*
▪ *Syn* blemish, brutalize, contaminate, damage, debase, debauch, defile, deprave, devalue, harm, impair, mar, pervert, pollute, prejudice, spoil, sully, taint,

tarnish, violate, warp; ▪ *Ant* elevate, exalt, purify.

vituperate [*v*] *criticize harshly*
▪ *Syn* abuse, asperse, berate, blame, castigate, censure, condemn, curse, denounce, growl, insult, lambaste, malign, rail, reproach, scold, smear, traduce, upbraid, vilify; ▪ *Ant* acclaim, compliment, praise.

vivacious [*adj*] *lively, spirited*
▪ *Syn* active, animated, bouncy, brash, breezy, cheerful, ebullient, effervescent, exuberant, frolicsome, gay, happy, jolly, keen, lighthearted, merry, playful, scintillating, sparkling, sprightly, swinging, upbeat, vibrant, vital, zesty; ▪ *Ant* boring, dispirited, dull, listless, stolid.

vivid [*adj*] *intense, powerful*
▪ *Syn* active, animated, bright, clear, distinct, dynamic, energetic, flamboyant, gay, graphic, highly colored, lifelike, lucid, meaningful, memorable, picturesque, realistic, rich, sharp, spirited, striking, strong, telling, vigorous; ▪ *Ant* average, colorless, drab, dull, run-of-the-mill, weak.

vocal [*adj1*] *spoken*
▪ *Syn* articulate, articulated, choral, expressed, intonated, lyric, modulated, operatic, oral, phonetic, pronounced, sonant, uttered, verbal, viva voce, vocalized, voiced; ▪ *Ant* mute, speechless, unsaid, unspoken, written.

vocal [*adj2*] *extroverted about opinion*
▪ *Syn* articulate, blunt, clamorous, eloquent, expressive, facile, fluent, frank, free, glib, outspoken, plainspoken, stentorian, strident, venting, vociferous; ▪ *Ant* introverted, modest, quiet, shy.

vocalize [*v*] *put into words or song*
▪ *Syn* chant, chirp, communicate, convey, croon, enunciate, express, groan, impart, moan, pronounce, say, sing, speak, talk, utter, vent, verbalize, voice, warble, yodel; ▪ *Ant* hush, keep secret, leave unsaid, suppress.

vocation [*n*] *life's work*
▪ *Syn* art, calling, career, duty, employment, field, game, job, métier, mission, occupation, office, post, profession, role, trade, undertaking; ▪ *Ant* avocation, entertainment, fun, hobby, pastime.

vociferous [*adj*] *loud, insistent*
▪ *Syn* boisterous, clamorous, distracting, loud-mouthed, noisy, obstreperous, ranting, shrill, strident, uproarious,

vehement; ▪ *Ant* quiet, reticent, silent, soft-spoken.

vogue [*adj*] *fashionable*
▪ *Syn* chic, latest, modish, now, popular, prevalent, state-of-the-art, stylish, trendy; ▪ *Ant* dowdy, out, out-dated, pass, unfashionable, unpopular, unstylish.

voice [*v*] *express opinion; put into words*
▪ *Syn* announce, articulate, assert, cry, declare, divulge, emphasize, enunciate, give expression, inflect, modulate, proclaim, recount, sound, speak, talk, tell, utter, verbalize; ▪ *Ant* be quiet.

void [*adj1*] *empty*
▪ *Syn* abandoned, bare, barren, bereft, clear, deprived, destitute, devoid, drained, empty, free, lacking, unoccupied, vacant, vacuous, without; ▪ *Ant* abounding, cluttered, filled, full, occupied, replete.

void [*adj2*] *nullified, meaningless*
▪ *Syn* dead, fruitless, ineffective, ineffectual, inoperative, invalid, negated, nugatory, null and void, sterile, useless, vain, voided, worthless; ▪ *Ant* full, meaningful, productive, valid, viable.

void [*v1*] *get rid of; empty*
▪ *Syn* clear, deplete, dispose, drain, dump, eject, eliminate, evacuate, flow, give off, go, pour, relieve, remove, throw out, vacate; ▪ *Ant* digest, fill, ingest, keep, replenish.

void [*v2*] *nullify, cancel*
▪ *Syn* abnegate, abrogate, annul, clean up, cut, discharge, dissolve, invalidate, launder, rescind, sanitize, sterilize, take out, trim, vacate; ▪ *Ant* allow, permit, sanction, validate.

volatile [*adj*] *explosive, changeable*
▪ *Syn* airy, buoyant, capricious, effervescent, ephemeral, fickle, fleeting, flippant, frivolous, gaseous, giddy, impermanent, inconstant, lubricious, mercurial, momentary, resilient, short-lived, sprightly, subtle, temperamental, ticklish, transient, transitory, up and down, variable; ▪ *Ant* calm, firm, stable, steadfast.

volition [*n*] *free will*
▪ *Syn* accord, choice, choosing, desire, determination, election, option, purpose, resolution, selection, will, willingness, wish; ▪ *Ant* coercion, compulsion, constraint, duress, force, threat.

voluminous [*adj*] *big, vast*
▪ *Syn* abundant, ample, billowing, bulky, capacious, cavernous, comprehensive, convoluted, copious, expansive, full, great, large, legion, massive, multitudinous, numerous, prolific, roomy, several, swelling, various; ▪ *Ant* little, restricted, scant, skimpy, slight, small, tiny.

voluntarily [*adv*] *of one's own free will*
▪ *Syn* at one's discretion, by preference, deliberately, freely, intentionally, on one's own, spontaneously, willingly, without prompting; ▪ *Ant* forced, involuntarily, obligatory.

voluntary [*adj*] *willing*
▪ *Syn* deliberate, discretional, elected, free, freely, free-willed, gratuitous, optional, spontaneous, volitional, willed, witting; ▪ *Ant* forced, involuntary, obligatory, unwilling.

volunteer [*v*] *offer to do something*
▪ *Syn* advance, bring forward, come forward, enlist, offer services, present, put forward, sign up, step forward, submit oneself, tender; ▪ *Ant* compel, draft, force, obligate.

voluptuous [*adj*] *well-developed, erotic*
▪ *Syn* ample, buxom, carnal, curvaceous, enticing, fleshly, full-bosomed, indulgent, luscious, provocative, seductive, sensual, shapely, wanton; ▪ *Ant* abstemious, ascetic, flat, underdeveloped.

voracious [*adj*] *very hungry, greedy*
▪ *Syn* avid, covetous, devouring, edacious, empty, gluttonous, insatiable, omnivorous, piggy, prodigious, rapacious, ravening, sating, starved, starving; ▪ *Ant* quenched, satisfied.

vote [*v*] *decide on representation*
▪ *Syn* ballot, cast ballot, cast vote, choose, confer, declare, determine, elect, enact, enfranchise, establish, grant, judge, opt, pronounce, propose, recommend, return, second, suggest; ▪ *Ant* abstain.

vouch [*v*] *give assurance*
▪ *Syn* act as a witness, affirm, answer for, asseverate, attest to, avow, back, certify, confirm, corroborate, declare, give an affidavit, guarantee, predicate, prove, sponsor, substantiate, support, swear to, testify, uphold, verify, warrant, witness; ▪ *Ant* deny, disavow, refute, reject, renounce.

vulgar [*adj1*] *rude, offensive*
▪ *Syn* base, boorish, cheap, contemptible, crude, dirty, fractious, impolite, improper, indecent, indecorous, inferior,

low, malicious, nasty, odious, profane, raw, repulsive, risqué, scatological, slippery, sneaking, suggestive, tasteless, tawdry, villainous; ▪ **Ant** decent, elegant, mannerly, polite, refined.

vulgar [adj2] *common, general*
▪ **Syn** colloquial, conversational, everyday, familiar, low, native, ordinary, plastic, plebeian, vernacular; ▪ **Ant** aesthetic, aristocratic, artistic, educated, fashionable.

vulnerable [adj] *open to attack*
▪ **Syn** accessible, assailable, defenseless, exposed, liable, naked, sensitive, susceptible, tender, weak; ▪ **Ant** closed, guarded, invincible, protected, safe, secure.

W

wacky [adj] *acting crazy*
▪ **Syn** absurd, crazed, crazy, demented, eccentric, erratic, foolish, hare-brained, irrational, lunatic, mad, odd, preposterous, silly, wild; ▪ **Ant** calm, collected, rational, sane, sober.

wage [v] *carry on*
▪ **Syn** carry out, conduct, do, engage in, fulfill, make, practice, proceed with, prosecute, pursue, undertake; ▪ **Ant** cease, halt, stop.

wail [v] *cry loudly*
▪ **Syn** bay, bemoan, complain, deplore, fuss, grieve, howl, jowl, keen, lament, moan, repine, sob, squall, ululate, weep, whimper, whine; ▪ **Ant** chuckle, grin, laugh.

wait [v] *pause, rest*
▪ **Syn** abide, anticipate, bide, delay, expect, fill time, hang, hang around, hold back, linger, remain, stall, stay, tarry; ▪ **Ant** begin, carry out, commence, continue, forge, go ahead, resume.

waive [v] *give up; let go*
▪ **Syn** abandon, allow, cede, defer, disclaim, disown, forgo, grant, hand over, postpone, reject, relinquish, remit, renounce, reserve, set aside, shelve, stay, surrender, suspend, turn over, yield; ▪ **Ant** claim, demand, exact, insist.

wake/waken [v1] *stop sleeping*
▪ **Syn** arise, awaken, be roused, bestir, call, get up, nudge, prod, rise, rouse, shake, stir, turn out, wake up; ▪ **Ant** nap, sleep.

wake/waken [v2] *excite, stimulate*
▪ **Syn** activate, animate, awaken, challenge, enliven, freshen, grasp, kindle, provoke, quicken, rally, renew, rouse, stir up, understand, whet; ▪ **Ant** appease, discourage, dissuade, quell, quiet, soothe.

wakeful [adj] *alert, restless*
▪ **Syn** alive, attentive, careful, heedful, insomniac, observant, on guard, sleepless, vigilant, waking, wary, watchful; ▪ **Ant** drowsy, inattentive, sleepy, unaware.

walk [v] *move along on foot*
▪ **Syn** amble, foot, go, hike, hoof it, locomote, lumber, pace, pad, plod, roam, rove, saunter, shamble, shuffle, stalk, step, stride, tramp, traverse, trek, trudge, wander; ▪ **Ant** run.

wallop [v2] *defeat soundly*
▪ **Syn** beat, best, rout, trounce, vanquish; ▪ **Ant** fail, lose, surrender.

wan [adj] *colorless, weak*
▪ **Syn** anemic, ashen, bilious, blanched, bloodless, cadaverous, feeble, ghastly, haggard, livid, pale, pasty, peaked, sickly, washed-out, waxen, white; ▪ **Ant** colorful, flushed, ruddy, strong.

wander [v1] *move about aimlessly*
▪ **Syn** aberrate, amble, circumlocute, cruise, deviate, divagate, diverge, drift, float, globe-trot, hike, jaunt, meander, peregrinate, ramble, roam, saunter, straggle, stray, stroll, trail, tramp, trek, vagabond; ▪ **Ant** pause, remain, settle, stay, stop.

wander [v2] *digress; get lost*
▪ **Syn** depart, deviate, divagate, diverge, err, lapse, lose one's way, ramble, rave, shift, stray, swerve, veer; ▪ **Ant** comply, conform.

wane [v] *diminish, lessen*
▪ **Syn** abate, atrophy, decline, decrease, die away, die down, die out, dim, drop, dwindle, ease off, ebb, fade, fade away, fail, fall, fall short, let up, moderate, relent, shrink, sink, slacken, slack off, subside, taper off, waste away, weaken, wind down, wither; ▪ **Ant** expand, grow, increase, raise, rise, wax.

want [v1] *desire*
▪ **Syn** ache, aspire, choose, covet, crave, desiderate, fancy, hanker, have an urge for, hunger, incline toward, itch for, long, lust, need, pine, prefer, require, thirst, wish, yearn, yen for; ▪ **Ant** be sated, be satisfied, decline, reject.

want [v2] *lack, need*
▪ *Syn* be deficient, be deprived of, be found wanting, be insufficient, be poor, be short of, be without, call for, demand, fall short in, have need of, miss, require, stand in need of, starve; ▪ *Ant* have, own, possess.

wanting [adj] *lacking, inadequate*
▪ *Syn* bereft, deficient, deprived, destitute, devoid, disappointing, empty, failing, faulty, gone, missing, needed, omitted, patchy, poor, scant, scanty, scarce, short, shy, sketchy, substandard, unfulfilled, unsound; ▪ *Ant* adequate, perfect, satisfactory, sufficient.

wanton [adj1] *extravagant, lustful*
▪ *Syn* abandoned, carnal, dissipated, fast, immoral, lax, lewd, libertine, licentious, lustful, profligate, promiscuous, rakish, shameless, wayward; ▪ *Ant* clean, decent, prudish, puritanical.

wanton [adj2] *cruel, malicious*
▪ *Syn* arbitrary, contrary, evil, gratuitous, groundless, malicious, mean, merciless, ornery, perverse, senseless, spiteful, vicious, wayward, wicked; ▪ *Ant* benevolent, circumspect, prudent, restrained.

wanton [adj3] *careless*
▪ *Syn* capricious, extravagant, fanciful, fitful, fluctuating, frivolous, heedless, immoderate, inconstant, prodigal, profuse, rash, variable, volatile, wasteful, whimsical, wild; ▪ *Ant* careful, observant, thoughtful, wise.

war [v] *fight, battle*
▪ *Syn* attack, bombard, campaign against, challenge, clash, combat, contend, contest, differ, disagree, endeavor, go to war, kill, make war, murder, oppugn, shell, shoot, struggle, take on, tug, wage war; ▪ *Ant* agree, call a truce, ceasefire, make peace.

ward/ward off [v] *defend, guard*
▪ *Syn* avert, avoid, beat off, block, check, deflect, divert, fend, foil, frustrate, hold off, interrupt, keep off, obviate, parry, prevent, rebuff, rebut, repel, repulse, rule out, stave off, thwart, turn, turn aside; ▪ *Ant* abet, conspire, embolden, encourage, submit, yield.

warlike [adj] *hostile, battling*
▪ *Syn* aggressive, bellicose, belligerent, bloodthirsty, combative, contentious, hawkish, inimical, martial, militaristic, pugnacious, quarrelsome, ructious, soldierly, truculent; ▪ *Ant* harmonizing, peaceful.

warm [adj1] *moderately hot*
▪ *Syn* balmy, clement, glowing, heated, lukewarm, mild, pleasant, snug, summery, sunny, temperate, tepid, thermal, toasty; ▪ *Ant* cold, cool.

warm [adj2] *friendly, kind*
▪ *Syn* affable, affectionate, amiable, compassionate, cordial, empathetic, fervent, genial, hospitable, kindhearted, loving, pleasant, responsive, sincere, sympathetic, tender, wholehearted; ▪ *Ant* aloof, cold, cool, uncaring, unfeeling, unfriendly, unkind.

warm [adj3] *enthusiastic*
▪ *Syn* amorous, animated, ardent, effusive, emotional, excitable, fervent, glowing, heated, intense, keen, lively, passionate, spirited, vehement, zealous; ▪ *Ant* apathetic, cool, indifferent, unenthusiastic.

warm [v] *heat up*
▪ *Syn* bake, chafe, cook, fix, heat, melt, microwave, prepare, put on the fire, thaw, toast, warm over, warm up; ▪ *Ant* chill, cool, freeze.

warp [v] *bend, distort*
▪ *Syn* brutalize, color, contort, corrupt, debase, debauch, deprave, deviate, misrepresent, misshape, pervert, swerve, torture, turn, twist, vitiate, wind; ▪ *Ant* straighten.

warrant [v] *guarantee, justify, authorize*
▪ *Syn* affirm, approve, assert, assure, attest, avouch, call for, certify, claim, commission, contend, declare, delegate, empower, endorse, ensure, entitle, guarantee, guaranty, insure, license, maintain, necessitate, permit, pledge, privilege, promise, sanction, secure, sponsor, stand behind, state, stipulate, swear, take an oath, undertake, underwrite, uphold, vindicate, vouch for, vow; ▪ *Ant* discredit, refuse, refute, undermine.

wary [adj] *careful, cautious*
▪ *Syn* alert, attentive, calculating, canny, chary, circumspect, considerate, discreet, distrustful, doubting, frugal, gingerly, guarded, heedful, leery, on guard, provident, prudent, safe, saving, sly, sparing, suspicious, thrifty, unwasteful, vigilant, watchful, watching out, wide-awake; ▪ *Ant* careless, foolish, heedless, incautious, indiscreet, rash, reckless.

wash [v] *bathe, clean*
▪ *Syn* bath, cleanse, clean up, dip, douse, drench, hose, immerse, lap, launder, lave, rinse, scour, scrub, shampoo, shine, shower, soak, soap, sponge, swab, tub, wet, wipe; ▪ *Ant* dirty, smudge, soil.

waste [v1] *spend or use without thought; dwindle* ▪ *Syn* atrophy, blow, burn up, consume, corrode, crumble, debilitate, decay, decline, decrease, deplete, disable, disappear, dissipate, divert, drain, droop, eat away, ebb, emaciate, empty, enfeeble, exhaust, fade, lavish, lose, misapply, misemploy, misuse, sap, sink, splurge, squander, thin, trifle away, wane, wear, wear out, wilt, wither; ▪ *Ant* economize, hoard, save.

waste [v2] *ruin, destroy*
▪ *Syn* depredate, desecrate, desolate, despoil, devastate, lay waste, pillage, rape, ravage, raze, sack, spoil, wreak havoc; ▪ *Ant* build, create, preserve.

wasteful [adj] *not economical*
▪ *Syn* careless, cavalier, destructive, extravagant, immoderate, improvident, lavish, liberal, profligate, profuse, reckless, spendthrift, squandering, thriftless, wanton, wild; ▪ *Ant* economical, thrifty.

watch [v1] *look at*
▪ *Syn* attend, check out, examine, focus, gaze, mark, note, observe, pay attention, regard, scan, scope, scrutinize, see, stare, take notice, view; ▪ *Ant* ignore, overlook, pass by.

watch [v2] *guard, protect*
▪ *Syn* attend, be wary, be watchful, care for, keep watch over, look after, mind, oversee, patrol, pick up on, police, superintend, take care of, tend, wait; ▪ *Ant* abandon, neglect.

watchful [adj] *on the lookout*
▪ *Syn* alert, attentive, careful, cautious, guarded, heedful, keen, observant, on guard, on the watch, prepared, ready, vigilant, wary; ▪ *Ant* heedless, inattentive, negligent.

water [v] *dampen; put water in*
▪ *Syn* bathe, dilute, douse, drench, flood, hose, irrigate, moisten, saturate, soak, sodden, souse, spatter, spray, sprinkle, steep, wash, weaken, wet; ▪ *Ant* dehydrate, dry.

watery [adj] *liquid, diluted*
▪ *Syn* adulterated, anemic, bloodless, colorless, damp, dilute, doused, flavorless, humid, insipid, marshy, moist, pale, runny, soggy, tasteless, thin, washed, water-logged, weak, wet; ▪ *Ant* concentrated, dehydrated, dry, solid.

waver [v] *shift back and forth; be indecisive* ▪ *Syn* be irresolute, change, deliberate, falter, fluctuate, hedge, oscillate, palter, quiver, reel, shake, sway, teeter, tremble, undulate, vacillate, vary, waffle, wave; ▪ *Ant* be certain, be resolute, be steadfast, be steady, stand firm.

wax [v] *become large, fuller*
▪ *Syn* augment, build, develop, dilate, enlarge, expand, fill out, get bigger, grow, grow full, heighten, increase, magnify, multiply, rise, run, swell, turn, upsurge; ▪ *Ant* contract, decrease, deflate, diminish, shrink.

wayfaring [adj] *traveling*
▪ *Syn* drifting, gadabout, globe-trotting, itinerant, journeying, nomadic, perambulant, perambulatory, peripatetic, rambling, roving, vagabond, voyaging, walking, wandering; ▪ *Ant* fixed, resident, rooted, sedentary, unmoving.

waylay [v] *intercept, ambush*
▪ *Syn* accost, ambuscade, assail, attack, catch, hold up, intercept, jump, lie in wait, lurk, pounce on, prowl, set upon, skulk, slink, surprise; ▪ *Ant* advance, propel.

wayward [adj] *contrary, unmanageable; changeable* ▪ *Syn* aberrant, arbitrary, balky, capricious, cross-grained, delinquent, disobedient, disorderly, errant, fickle, fractious, froward, headstrong, immoral, inconstant, incorrigible, mulish, obdurate, obstinate, perverse, rebellious, recalcitrant, stubborn, variable, willful; ▪ *Ant* controllable, manageable, obedient.

weak [adj1] *not strong*
▪ *Syn* anemic, debilitated, delicate, enervated, feeble, frail, hesitant, impotent, impuissant, infirm, languid, limp, makeshift, powerless, prostrate, rotten, shaky, sickly, spindly, supine, tender, torpid, wasted; ▪ *Ant* firm, potent, strong.

weak [adj2] *cowardly*
▪ *Syn* faint-hearted, frightened, hesitant, impotent, insecure, irresolute, nerveless, palsied, powerless, spineless, timorous, vacillating, wavering, wobbly; ▪ *Ant* bold, brave, confident.

weak [adj3] *faint, soft*
▪ *Syn* bated, dull, feeble, gentle, inaudi-

ble, indistinct, low, muffled, pale, quiet, reedy, slight, stifled, thin, whispered; ▪ *Ant* loud, noisy, potent, strong.

weak [*adj4*] *deficient, feeble*
▪ *Syn* faulty, flimsy, forceless, handicapped, hollow, immature, implausible, impotent, inadequate, incompetent, ineffective, inept, lacking, lame, pathetic, raw, shaky, spineless, substandard, thin, unsure; ▪ *Ant* able, capable, fit, sufficient.

weak [*adj5*] *exposed, vulnerable*
▪ *Syn* accessible, assailable, defenseless, helpless, indefensible, untenable, wide open; ▪ *Ant* guarded, protected, safe, secure.

weak [*adj6*] *watered-down*
▪ *Syn* dilute, diluted, insipid, runny, tasteless, thin, washy, waterish, watery; ▪ *Ant* concentrated, strong, thick.

weaken [*v*] *reduce the strength of*
▪ *Syn* abate, cripple, debase, debilitate, depress, diminish, dwindle, ease up, emasculate, fade, fail, flag, give way, halt, impair, impoverish, invalidate, languish, lessen, minimize, mitigate, reduce, sap, slow down, soften, temper, thin, tire, totter, tremble, vitiate, water down; ▪ *Ant* build up, energize, enhance, invigorate, strengthen.

wealthy [*adj*] *rich; having a lot of money*
▪ *Syn* affluent, booming, comfortable, independent, loaded, moneyed, of independent means, opulent, prosperous, substantial, upscale; ▪ *Ant* deprived, lacking, needy, poor, poverty-stricken, wanting.

wear [*v1*] *be clothed in*
▪ *Syn* array, attire, bear, carry, cover, display, don, draw on, exhibit, fit out, get into, get on, harness, put on, show, slip on, sport, wrap; ▪ *Ant* disrobe, take off.

wear [*v2*] *corrode, use*
▪ *Syn* abrade, chafe, decay, deteriorate, diminish, drain, erode, exhaust, fatigue, fray, grind, impair, jade, overuse, rub, scrape, scuff, shrink, tax, use up, waste, wear thin; ▪ *Ant* freshen, rebuild, refresh.

wear [*v3*] *bother, undermine*
▪ *Syn* annoy, drain, enervate, exasperate, fatigue, get the better of, harass, irk, pester, reduce, tax, vex, weaken, weary; ▪ *Ant* cheer, delight, please.

wear [*v4*] *endure*
▪ *Syn* bear up, be durable, hold up, last, remain, stand, stand up; ▪ *Ant* erode, fail.

weary [*adj*] *tired*
▪ *Syn* bored, bushed, discontented, drained, drooping, drowsy, enervated, exhausted, fagged, fatigued, fed up, flagging, impatient, jaded, sleepy, taxed, wearied, wearing; ▪ *Ant* activated, energetic, fresh, lively.

weary [*v*] *make tired*
▪ *Syn* annoy, burden, cloy, debilitate, depress, drain, enervate, exasperate, fade, fag, fail, fall off, fatigue, glut, harass, irk, jade, oppress, plague, sap, strain, tax, tire, weaken, weigh; ▪ *Ant* activate, energize, enliven.

weather [*v*] *endure*
▪ *Syn* acclimate, become toughened, brave, come through, expose, get through, harden, overcome, pull through, resist, season, stand, survive, toughen, withstand; ▪ *Ant* be defeated by, surrender to.

weave [*v*] *blend, unite; contrive*
▪ *Syn* braid, complect, compose, crisscross, crochet, entwine, fabricate, incorporate, interlace, interlink, intermingle, intertwine, knit, loop, make, manufacture, merge, net, piece together, ply, reticulate, sew, snake, splice, twine, twist, wind, wreathe, writhe, zigzag; ▪ *Ant* disentangle, divide, separate, unravel.

wed [*v1*] *marry*
▪ *Syn* become man and wife, be married, couple, espouse, get married, join, lead to the altar, receive in marriage, take in marriage, unite; ▪ *Ant* divorce, separate.

wed [*v2*] *join, unite*
▪ *Syn* ally, associate, blend, coalesce, cojoin, combine, commingle, connect, couple, dedicate, fuse, interweave, link, marry, merge, relate, unify, yoke; ▪ *Ant* disentangle, divide, separate.

wedge [*n*] *solid piece, often triangular*
▪ *Syn* block, chock, chunk, cleat, cotter, cusp, keystone, lump, prong, quoin, shim, spire, taper; ▪ *Ant* whole.

weigh [*v*] *consider, contemplate*
▪ *Syn* analyze, appraise, balance, deliberate, evaluate, examine, excogitate, give thought to, meditate, mind, mull over, perpend, ponder, rate, reflect upon, rehash, sort out, study, sweat, think over; ▪ *Ant* dismiss, ignore, neglect.

weigh down [*v*] *depress*
▪ *Syn* bear down, burden, cumber, get down, hold down, oppress, overburden,

overload, press, press down, prey on, pull down, sadden, task, trouble, weight, weigh upon, worry; ▪ *Ant* animate, cheer, delight, please.

weighty [*adj1*] *heavy*
▪ *Syn* burdensome, cumbersome, cumbrous, dense, fleshy, hefty, massive, obese, overweight, ponderous, porcine, portly, stout; ▪ *Ant* light, small, thin, unsubstantial.

weighty [*adj2*] *serious, important*
▪ *Syn* big, consequential, considerable, critical, crucial, earnest, grave, heavy, heavyweight, material, meaningful, momentous, portentous, severe, significant, sober, solemn, somber, staid, substantial, underlined; ▪ *Ant* inconsequential, trivial, unimportant, unsubstantial.

weighty [*adj3*] *troublesome, difficult*
▪ *Syn* backbreaking, burdensome, crushing, demanding, exacting, exigent, grievous, onerous, oppressive, superincumbent, taxing, tough, worrisome; ▪ *Ant* easy, facile, solvable.

weird [*adj*] *odd, bizarre*
▪ *Syn* awe-inspiring, curious, eccentric, ghastly, haunting, magical, mysterious, occult, ominous, outlandish, peculiar, secret, spooky, strange, supernal, supernatural; ▪ *Ant* normal, regular, usual.

welcome [*adj*] *gladly received*
▪ *Syn* accepted, agreeable, cherished, congenial, cordial, delightful, esteemed, favorable, genial, good, grateful, gratifying, honored, invited, nice, pleasant, refreshing, satisfying, wanted; ▪ *Ant* displeasing, excluded, unacceptable, unwelcome.

welcome [*v*] *receive gladly*
▪ *Syn* accept, accost, admit, bid welcome, embrace, entertain, greet, hail, hug, meet, receive, salute, take in, usher in; ▪ *Ant* reject, turn away.

weld [*v*] *bind, connect*
▪ *Syn* bond, braze, cement, combine, fix, fuse, join, link, solder, unite; ▪ *Ant* disconnect, separate.

well [*adj1*] *healthy*
▪ *Syn* able-bodied, blooming, fine, fit, fresh, hale, hardy, in good health, robust, strong, together, trim, vigorous, wholesome; ▪ *Ant* diseased, ill, sick, unhealthy.

well [*adj2*] *lucky, fortunate*
▪ *Syn* advisable, agreeable, bright, comfortable, fine, flourishing, good, happy, pleasing, profitable, proper, prosperous, providential, prudent, right, satisfactory, thriving; ▪ *Ant* unfortunate, unhappy, unlucky.

well [*adv1*] *happily, pleasantly; capably*
▪ *Syn* ably, accurately, adequately, attentively, carefully, commendably, competently, efficiently, expertly, famously, proficiently, skillfully, splendidly, successfully, suitably, thoroughly, with skill; ▪ *Ant* badly, incapably, unpleasantly.

well [*adv2*] *sufficiently*
▪ *Syn* abundantly, adequately, by a wide margin, completely, entirely, extremely, far, greatly, heartily, highly, plentifully, readily, substantially, suitably, thoroughly, very much, wholly; ▪ *Ant* badly, insufficiently.

well-bred [*adj*] *mannerly*
▪ *Syn* aristocratic, civil, courtly, cultured, genteel, noble, patrician, polished, refined, taught, trained, urbane, well-mannered; ▪ *Ant* coarse, ignoble, unmannered, unrefined, unsophisticated, vulgar.

well-known [*adj*] *familiar, famous*
▪ *Syn* acclaimed, big, celebrated, conspicuous, eminent, illustrious, infamous, known, leading, name, notable, notorious, outstanding, popular, public, renowned, superstar; ▪ *Ant* nameless, obscure, unfamiliar, unheard-of, unknown.

well-off [*adj*] *successful, wealthy*
▪ *Syn* affluent, comfortable, easy, flourishing, fortunate, loaded, lucky, moneyed, prosperous, rich, substantial, thriving, well, well-to-do; ▪ *Ant* destitute, failing, poor.

wet [*adj*] *damp, moist*
▪ *Syn* aqueous, clammy, dank, dewy, drenched, foggy, humid, misty, moistened, muggy, pouring, raining, saturated, showery, slushy, snowy, soaked, sodden, soggy, soused, stormy, waterlogged, watery; ▪ *Ant* dehydrated, dry, parched.

wet [*v*] *cause to become damp, moist*
▪ *Syn* bathe, dampen, deluge, dip, douse, drench, drown, hose, humidify, imbue, irrigate, moisten, rinse, saturate, soak, steep, wash, water; ▪ *Ant* dehydrate, dessicate, dry, evaporate.

wheedle [*v*] *talk into*
▪ *Syn* banter, butter up, cajole, charm, coax, con, court, draw, entice, finagle, inveigle, persuade, seduce; ▪ *Ant* bully, coerce, compel, dragoon, force, oblige.

whet [*v1*] *make sharp*
▪ *Syn* edge, file, finish, grind, hone, sharpen, strop; ▪ *Ant* blunt, dull.

whet [*v2*] *arouse, excite*
▪ *Syn* animate, awaken, challenge, enhance, incite, kindle, pique, provoke, quicken, rouse, stimulate, stir, waken; ▪ *Ant* blunt, dampen, dishearten, quench, sate, slake.

whim [*n*] *sudden idea*
▪ *Syn* caprice, conceit, disposition, dream, fad, fancy, fantasy, freak, humor, impulse, notion, passing thought, quirk, sport, thought, urge, vision, whimsy; ▪ *Ant* blueprint, plan, scheme, strategy.

whimper [*v*] *cry softly*
▪ *Syn* bleat, blubber, complain, fuss, mewl, moan, object, pule, snivel, sob, weep, whine; ▪ *Ant* howl.

whimsical [*adj*] *playful, fanciful*
▪ *Syn* amusing, arbitrary, capricious, chimerical, droll, eccentric, funny, odd, peculiar, quaint, singular, waggish, wayward; ▪ *Ant* reasonable, sensible, serious.

whine [*n*] *complaint, cry*
▪ *Syn* gripe, grouse, grumble, moan, plaintive cry, sob, wail, whimper; ▪ *Ant* compliment, eulogy, praise.

whip [*v*] *defeat soundly*
▪ *Syn* beat, best, clobber, conquer, drub, lambaste, outdo, overcome, overpower, overwhelm, rout, subdue, thrash, top, trounce, vanquish, wallop; ▪ *Ant* lose, surrender.

whip up [*v*] *incite, excite*
▪ *Syn* abet, agitate, arouse, compel, disturb, foment, goad, hound, instigate, kindle, prick, provoke, push, raise, spur, stir up, urge, work up; ▪ *Ant* abate, alleviate, discourage, dissuade.

whirlwind [*adj*] *very fast*
▪ *Syn* cyclonic, hasty, impetuous, impulsive, lightning, quick, rapid, short, speedy, swift; ▪ *Ant* careful, leisurely, lengthy, long, plodding, slow, thoughtful, well-considered.

whisk [*v*] *brush quickly; hasten*
▪ *Syn* barrel, bullet, dart, dash, flick, flutter, hurry, race, rush, speed, sweep, tear, wipe, zip; ▪ *Ant* crawl, creep, drag, inch.

whisper [*v*] *speak softly*
▪ *Syn* breathe, confide, gossip, hint, insinuate, mumble, mutter, sibilate, sigh, speak confidentially, susurrate, talk low,

tell; ▪ *Ant* bellow, roar, scream, shout, shout, whoop.

whit [*n*] *very tiny bit*
▪ *Syn* atom, crumb, dash, drop, fragment, grain, hoot, iota, jot, little, modicum, particle, piece, shred, speck, trace; ▪ *Ant* gobs, lot, slew.

white [*adj*] *extremely pale; clean*
▪ *Syn* achromatic, alabaster, blanched, bleached, bloodless, chalky, fair, ghastly, hoary, ivory, light, milky, neutral, pallid, pure, silver, snowy, spotless, transparent, unblemished, unsullied, wan; ▪ *Ant* florid, flushed, pink, ruddy.

whiten [*v*] *make or become extremely pale* ▪ *Syn* blanch, bleach, chalk, decolor, decolorize, dull, etiolate, fade, frost, lighten, pale, silver, turn pale, white, whitewash; ▪ *Ant* blacken, darken, dull.

whitewash [*v*] *cover up the truth*
▪ *Syn* camouflage, conceal, exonerate, extenuate, gloss over, launder, paint, suppress, vindicate; ▪ *Ant* expose, reveal, tell truth.

whittle [*v*] *cut away at; reduce*
▪ *Syn* carve, chip, consume, decrease, diminish, eat away, erode, fashion, form, hew, lessen, model, mold, pare, sculpt, shape, shave, trim, undermine, wear away; ▪ *Ant* bolster, build, buttress, increase.

whiz [*v*] *move quickly by*
▪ *Syn* bullet, buzz, dart, flit, fly, hiss, hum, hurry, hurtle, race, speed, swish, whir, whirl, whisk, whoosh, zip; ▪ *Ant* decelerate, slow down, slow up.

whole [*adj1*] *entire, complete*
▪ *Syn* choate, conclusive, consummate, exhaustive, full-length, gross, inclusive, in one piece, plenary, total, unexpurgated, utter; ▪ *Ant* fractional, incomplete, part, partial.

whole [*adj2*] *unbroken, perfect*
▪ *Syn* faultless, flawless, good, intact, mint, ship-shape, solid, sound, thorough, without a scratch; ▪ *Ant* broken, deficient, imperfect, insufficient, partial.

whole [*adj3*] *healthy*
▪ *Syn* able-bodied, fit, hale, hearty, in fine fettle, in good health, right, robust, sound, strong, well, wholesome; ▪ *Ant* hurt, impaired, sick, unhealthy.

wholehearted/whole-hearted [*adj*] *enthusiastic, sincere* ▪ *Syn* abiding, authentic, bona fide, candid, complete, dedicated, devoted, earnest, enduring, fervent, genuine, impassioned, never-failing, passionate, real, serious, true, warm, zealous; ▪ *Ant* disinterested, half-hearted, insincere, unenthusiastic.

wholesale [*adj*] *all-inclusive*
▪ *Syn* broad, bulk, complete, comprehensive, extensive, far-reaching, general, in bulk, large-scale, overall, sweeping, total, wide-ranging; ▪ *Ant* part, partial, retail.

wholesome [*adj*] *healthy, decent*
▪ *Syn* clean, ethical, exemplary, fit, good, hale, helpful, hygienic, innocent, moral, nice, normal, nourishing, pure, restorative, salubrious, sanitary, sound, virtuous, worthy; ▪ *Ant* bad, impure, indecent, unhealthy, unwholesome.

wholly [*adv1*] *completely, entirely*
▪ *Syn* all, comprehensively, fully, outright, perfectly, quite, roundly, thoroughly, utterly, well; ▪ *Ant* incompletely, partially, partly.

wholly [*adv2*] *exclusively*
▪ *Syn* individually, just, only, purely, solely, specifically, without exception; ▪ *Ant* inclusively.

whopping [*adj*] *enormous*
▪ *Syn* big, colossal, extraordinary, gargantuan, gigantic, huge, immense, large, mammoth, massive, mighty, prodigious, tremendous; ▪ *Ant* little, small, teeny, tiny.

wicked [*adj1*] *corrupt, bad*
▪ *Syn* abominable, amoral, atrocious, base, contemptible, debased, degenerate, depraved, evil, foul, guilty, heinous, immoral, impious, incorrigible, low-down, mean, mischievous, nasty, naughty, nefarious, profane, reprobate, scandalous, sinful, villainous, wayward; ▪ *Ant* decent, ethical, good, honest, moral, righteous.

wicked [*adj2*] *destructive, troublesome*
▪ *Syn* acute, agonizing, awful, barbarous, chancy, dangerous, distressing, fearful, fierce, galling, hazardous, intense, offensive, painful, risky, severe, terrible, treacherous, trying; ▪ *Ant* aiding, assisting, helpful, useful, worthwhile.

wide [*adj1*] *expansive, roomy*
▪ *Syn* all-inclusive, ample, broad, capacious, commodious, comprehensive, distended, encyclopedic, extensive, far-reaching, full, general, inclusive, liberal, open, outstretched, progressive, radical,

scopic, spacious, splay, squat, tolerant, universal, vast, voluminous; ▪ *Ant* cramped, narrow, restricted.

wide [*adj2*] *off-course*
▪ *Syn* astray, away, distant, far, far-off, inaccurate, off, off-target, off the mark, remote; ▪ *Ant* on-course, straight.

widen [*v*] *open up*
▪ *Syn* add to, augment, broaden, distend, enlarge, extend, grow, increase, multiply, open, ream, spread, spread out, stretch, swell; ▪ *Ant* contract, cramp, narrow, restrict.

widespread [*adj*] *extensive*
▪ *Syn* boundless, broad, comprehensive, diffuse, epidemic, far-reaching, general, overall, pandemic, prevalent, public, regnant, ruling, sweeping, universal, unlimited, unrestricted, wholesale; ▪ *Ant* confined, limited, local, narrow.

wild [*adj1*] *untamed*
▪ *Syn* barbarian, barbaric, barbarous, dense, desolate, feral, ferocious, fierce, free, indigenous, lush, luxuriant, native, natural, overgrown, overrun, primitive, rampant, rude, savage, unbroken, uncivilized, undomesticated; ▪ *Ant* civilized, controlled, gentle, manageable, tame.

wild [*adj2*] *disorderly, rowdy*
▪ *Syn* avid, berserk, boisterous, chaotic, crazed, extravagant, flighty, foolhardy, foolish, giddy, hysterical, impetuous, impracticable, imprudent, incautious, irrational, lawless, licentious, mad, madcap, noisy, nuts, outrageous, preposterous, profligate, rabid, rash, raving, reckless, riotous, rough, self-willed, turbulent, unruly, uproarious, violent, wayward; ▪ *Ant* behaved, calm, law-abiding, lawful, orderly, tranquil.

wild [*adj3*] *intense, stormy*
▪ *Syn* blustering, blustery, choppy, disturbed, furious, howling, inclement, raging, rough, storming, tempestuous, turbulent, violent; ▪ *Ant* calm, mild, moderate.

wile [*n*] *cunning*
▪ *Syn* angle, artfulness, artifice, chicane, chicanery, contrivance, craft, craftiness, deceit, deception, device, dishonesty, dissimulation, dodge, feint, fraud, gambit, game, gimmick, guile, hoax, horseplay, lure, maneuver, plot, ploy, ruse, scheming, subterfuge, switch, trick, trickery, twist; ▪ *Ant* artlessness, candor, frankness, openness.

will [v] *choose*
▪ *Syn* be inclined, crave, desire, elect, incline, like, opt, please, prefer, want, wish; ▪ *Ant* neglect, pass.

willful [adj1] *stubborn, obstinate*
▪ *Syn* adamant, bullheaded, contumacious, determined, dogged, factious, headstrong, inflexible, intractable, mulish, obdurate, persistent, perverse, refractory, resolved, self-willed; ▪ *Ant* amenable, flexible, submissive, willing, yielding.

willful [adj2] *voluntary*
▪ *Syn* conscious, contemplated, deliberate, intended, intentional, planned, purposeful, studied, volitional, willed, willing; ▪ *Ant* accidental, involuntary, unintended.

willing [adj] *agreeable, ready*
▪ *Syn* accommodating, compliant, desirous, eager, enthusiastic, fair, favorable, game, inclined, intentional, like, minded, obedient, pleased, predisposed, prepared, prompt, prone, reliable, tractable, voluntary, well-disposed, willful, witting, zealous; ▪ *Ant* disinclined, reluctant, unprepared, unwilling.

willpower [n] *personal determination*
▪ *Syn* discipline, drive, firmness, fixity, force, grit, resolution, resolve, self-control, self-discipline, self-restraint, single-mindedness, strength, will; ▪ *Ant* apathy, impotence, indecision, lack of strength, weakness.

wilt [v] *sag, fail*
▪ *Syn* become limp, break down, cave in, collapse, diminish, droop, drop, dry up, dwindle, ebb, fade, faint, flaccid, flag, give out, languish, melt, mummify, shrivel, sink, succumb, wane, waste, waste away, weaken, wither, wizen; ▪ *Ant* bloom, rise.

wily [adj] *crafty, clever*
▪ *Syn* arch, artful, astute, crooked, cunning, deceitful, deceptive, deep, designing, foxy, guileful, insidious, intriguing, knowing, sagacious, scheming, sharp, shifty, shrewd, sly, smooth, sneaky, streetwise, tricky, underhanded; ▪ *Ant* aboveboard, artless, candid, factuous, frank, guileless, innocent, naive, open, simple, sincere.

win [v1] *finish first; succeed*
▪ *Syn* achieve, beat, be first, be victorious, come in first, conquer, edge, finish in front, finish off, gain, gain victory, overcome, overwhelm, prevail, take the prize, triumph, upset; ▪ *Ant* fail, forfeit, lose.

win [v2] *achieve, obtain*
▪ *Syn* accomplish, acquire, annex, approach, attain, bring in, catch, collect, derive, earn, effect, gain, get, harvest, have, make, net, pick up, procure, reach, realize, receive, score, secure; ▪ *Ant* fail, miss.

win/win over [v3] *influence, persuade*
▪ *Syn* allure, argue into, attract, bring around, carry, charm, convert, convince, disarm, draw, get, induce, overcome, prevail upon, prompt, slay, sway, talk into, wow; ▪ *Ant* advise against, discourage, dissuade.

wind [v] *bend, turn*
▪ *Syn* coil, convolute, corkscrew, crook, curl, curve, deviate, distort, encircle, enclose, entwine, envelop, fold, furl, loop, meander, ramble, reel, roll, screw, slither, snake, spiral, swerve, twine, twist, weave, wrap, wreathe, wriggle, zigzag; ▪ *Ant* smooth out, straighten, uncurl, unfurl.

winding [adj] *bending, turning*
▪ *Syn* anfractuous, circuitous, convoluted, crooked, curving, devious, flexuous, gyrating, indirect, intricate, involved, labyrinthine, mazy, meandering, roundabout, serpentine, sinuous, snaky, spiraling, tortuous, twisting, wriggly, zigzag; ▪ *Ant* straight, unbent.

wind up [v] *finish*
▪ *Syn* be through with, bring to a close, close, close down, come to the end, complete, conclude, determine, do, end, finalize, finish up, halt, liquidate, settle, terminate; ▪ *Ant* begin, commence, open, start.

windy [adj1] *breezy*
▪ *Syn* airy, blowing, blowy, blustering, blustery, boisterous, brisk, drafty, fresh, gusty, raw, squally, stormy, tempestuous, wild, windswept; ▪ *Ant* calm, still, windless.

windy [adj2] *talkative; boastful*
▪ *Syn* bombastic, diffuse, garrulous, long-winded, loquacious, meandering, palaverous, pompous, prolix, rambling, redundant, turgid, verbose, wordy; ▪ *Ant* concise, pithy, succinct, terse.

winning/winsome [adj1] *attractive, charming* ▪ *Syn* adorable, agreeable, alluring, amiable, bewitching, captivating, cute, delectable, delightful, disarming, dulcet, enchanting, endearing, engaging, fascinating, fetching, gratifying, lovable, lovely, pleasing, prepossessing, sweet, taking; ▪ *Ant* disenchanting, ugly, unappealing, unattractive.

winning [*adj2*] *triumphant*
▪ *Syn* champion, conquering, leading, successful, victorious; ▪ *Ant* failing, forfeiting, losing.

wintry [*adj*] *cold, snowy*
▪ *Syn* biting, bleak, brumal, chilly, cutting, desolate, dismal, freezing, frigid, frosty, frozen, harsh, hibernal, hiemal, icy, raw, snappy; ▪ *Ant* balmy, bright, hot, humid, languid, summery, tropic, tropical.

wipe out [*v*] *destroy; get rid of*
▪ *Syn* abate, abolish, annihilate, black out, blot out, cancel, decimate, delete, efface, eliminate, eradicate, erase, expunge, exterminate, extinguish, extirpate, kill, massacre, obliterate, remove, root out, slaughter, slay, uproot; ▪ *Ant* build, create, establish.

wiry [*adj*] *thin and strong*
▪ *Syn* agile, athletic, bristly, fibrous, lean, light, limber, muscular, ropy, sinewy, stiff, strapping, stringy, supple, tough; ▪ *Ant* flabby, pudgy, small, tiny, weak.

wise [*adj*] *intelligent, reasonable*
▪ *Syn* astute, aware, calculating, careful, clever, cogitative, contemplative, crafty, cunning, discerning, discreet, educated, enlightened, erudite, experienced, foresighted, informed, insightful, intuitive, judicious, keen, knowing, perceptive, perspicacious, politic, prudent, rational, reflective, sagacious, sapient, scholarly, sensible, sharp, shrewd, smart, sophic, sound, thoughtful, understanding, wary, well-informed, witty; ▪ *Ant* foolish, ignorant, stupid, unintelligent, unreasonable, unwise.

wish [*n*] *desire*
▪ *Syn* ambition, aspiration, choice, disposition, hankering, hope, hunger, inclination, intention, invocation, itch, liking, longing, pleasure, prayer, preference, request, thirst, urge, want, whim, will, yearning, yen; ▪ *Ant* aversion, disinclination.

wishy-washy [*adj*] *bland, dull*
▪ *Syn* banal, cowardly, enervated, feeble, flat, flavorless, indecisive, ineffectual, irresolute, jejune, listless, mediocre, spiritless, tasteless, vacillating, vapid, watered-down, wavering, weak; ▪ *Ant*

aggressive, dynamic, effective, exciting, interesting, lively, tangy.

wistful [*adj*] *daydreaming, longing*
▪ *Syn* contemplative, disconsolate, dreaming, forlorn, hopeless, meditative, melancholy, nostalgic, pensive, reflective, sad, thoughtful, wishful, yearning; ▪ *Ant* replete, sated, satisfied.

wit [*n*] *humor*
▪ *Syn* aphorism, banter, burlesque, drollery, facetiousness, fun, gag, jest, jocularity, lark, levity, pleasantry, prank, pun, quip, raillery, sally, satire, trick, whimsicality, wisecrack, wittiness, wordplay; ▪ *Ant* gravity, seriousness, sobriety, solemnity.

withdraw [*v1*] *remove something or someone from situation* ▪ *Syn* abjure, back out, check out, depart, detach, draw back, ease out, exfiltrate, fall back, get away, leave, pull back, quail, recede, recoil, retreat, secede, shrink, switch, take leave, vacate; ▪ *Ant* appear, arrive, draw near.

withdraw [*v2*] *retract; declare void*
▪ *Syn* abjure, abolish, annul, ban, call off, disavow, disclaim, forswear, invalidate, nullify, palinode, quash, recall, repress, rescind, revoke, stamp out, suppress, take back; ▪ *Ant* advance, introduce, propose, repeat.

withdrawn [*adj1*] *unsociable*
▪ *Syn* aloof, aseptic, casual, detached, distant, introverted, quiet, reclusive, remote, reserved, restrained, silent, standoffish, taciturn, timorous; ▪ *Ant* extroverted, friendly, outgoing, sociable.

withdrawn [*adj2*] *hidden, remote*
▪ *Syn* cloistered, departed, isolated, private, recluse, removed, secluded, solitary, taken out; ▪ *Ant* known, seen, visible.

wither [*v*] *droop, decline*
▪ *Syn* atrophy, blight, decay, deflate, desiccate, deteriorate, dry up, fade, fold, languish, perish, shrivel, wane, waste away, wilt, wizen; ▪ *Ant* bloom, flourish, flower, grow.

withhold [*v*] *keep back*
▪ *Syn* abstain, bridle, check, conceal, curb, deduct, deny, disallow, hide, hold, inhibit, keep, keep secret, kill, refrain, refuse, repress, reserve, resist, restrain, retain, sit on, spike, stop oneself, suppress; ▪ *Ant* disclose, give, provide, release, reveal.

within [*adv*] *inside*
▪ *Syn* in, in a period, indoors, inner, in

reach, interior, inward, not beyond, not outside, not over; ▪ *Ant* outside.

without [*adv*] *outside*
▪ *Syn* after, beyond, externally, left out, on the outside, out, outdoors, out-of-doors, outwardly, past; ▪ *Ant* inside.

withstand [*v*] *endure, bear*
▪ *Syn* brace, brave, combat, confront, contest, defy, dispute, duel, face, fight, grapple with, oppose, put up with, remain firm, repel, resist, stand, suffer, take, thwart, tolerate, traverse, violate, weather, win out; ▪ *Ant* falter, give way, retreat, surrender, yield.

witness [*v1*] *observe*
▪ *Syn* attend, be a witness, behold, be present, look on, mark, note, notice, perceive, pick up on, read, see, sight, spot, spy, take in, view, watch; ▪ *Ant* ignore, miss, overlook.

witness [*v2*] *testify; authenticate*
▪ *Syn* affirm, attest, bear witness, bespeak, certify, confirm, depose, endorse, give testimony, say under oath, stand for, subscribe, vouch for; ▪ *Ant* deny, keep silent, refute.

witty [*adj*] *funny and clever*
▪ *Syn* amusing, bright, diverting, droll, entertaining, facetious, gay, humorous, ingenious, jocular, keen, lively, original, penetrating, piercing, piquant, quick-witted, ridiculous, sparkling, waggish; ▪ *Ant* serious, unamusing, unfunny.

wizard [*n*] *person who is highly skilled*
▪ *Syn* adept, artist, authority, expert, genius, maestro, marvel, master, past master, prodigy, professional, proficient, star, virtuoso; ▪ *Ant* amateur, rookie.

wizened [*adj*] *dried, shriveled up*
▪ *Syn* diminished, gnarled, lean, macerated, mummified, old, reduced, shrunk, shrunken, wilted, withered, worn, wrinkled; ▪ *Ant* moist, rounded, smooth, swollen, unwrinkled.

wobbly [*adj*] *shaky*
▪ *Syn* fluctuant, insecure, precarious, rattletrap, rickety, rocky, teetering, tottering, unbalanced, uneven, unsafe, unstable, unsteady, unsure, vacillating, wavering, wavy, weak, wiggling; ▪ *Ant* stable, steady, unshaky.

woebegone [*adj*] *depressed, troubled*
▪ *Syn* black, bleak, cheerless, crestfallen, dejected, despondent, disconsolate, dismal, dispirited, doleful, down, downcast, downhearted, dreary, forlorn, gloomy, grief-stricken, grim, hurting, low, lugu-

brious, melancholy, miserable, mournful, sad, sorrowful, unhappy, woeful, wretched; ▪ *Ant* enthused, excited, happy, untroubled.

woeful [*adj*] *terrible, sad*
▪ *Syn* afflicted, agonized, anguished, appalling, awful, bad, calamitous, catastrophic, cruel, deplorable, disappointing, disconsolate, disgraceful, distressing, doleful, dreadful, feeble, gloomy, grieving, grievous, grim, heartbreaking, heartrending, heartsick, hopeless, inadequate, lamentable, lousy, mean, miserable, mournful, paltry, pathetic, pitiful, plaintive, racked, sorrowful, tortured, tragic, wretched; ▪ *Ant* glad, happy, joyful.

wolf [*v*] *consume sloppily and fast*
▪ *Syn* bolt, cram, devour, gobble, gorge, gulp, guzzle, ingurgitate, pack, slop, slosh, stuff, swallow; ▪ *Ant* nibble.

wonder [*v1*] *doubt; ponder*
▪ *Syn* ask oneself, be curious, be inquisitive, conjecture, inquire, meditate, puzzle, query, question, speculate, think; ▪ *Ant* believe, comprehend, fathom, know.

wonder [*v2*] *be amazed*
▪ *Syn* be astonished, be awestruck, be confounded, be dumbstruck, be fascinated, be flabbergasted, be startled, be taken aback, boggle, gape, gawk, marvel, stare; ▪ *Ant* accept, anticipate, expect.

wonderful [*adj*] *great, extraordinary*
▪ *Syn* admirable, amazing, astonishing, astounding, awe-inspiring, awesome, brilliant, cool, divine, dynamite, enjoyable, excellent, fabulous, fantastic, fine, incredible, magnificent, marvelous, miraculous, outstanding, phenomenal, pleasant, pleasing, prime, remarkable, sensational, staggering, startling, strange, stupendous, super, superb, surprising, swell, terrific, tremendous, unheard-of, wondrous; ▪ *Ant* average, indifferent, mediocre, ordinary.

woo [*v*] *seek as romantic partner*
▪ *Syn* address, beg, caress, charm, chase, court, cultivate, date, entreat, gallant, go steady, importune, keep company, make advances, make love, propose, pursue, run after, rush, set one's cap for, solicit; ▪ *Ant* ignore, rebuff, repel, spurn.

wooden [*adj*] *stiff, inflexible*
▪ *Syn* awkward, bumbling, clumsy, gauche, gawky, graceless, heavy, heavy-handed, inelegant, inept, maladroit,

obstinate, ponderous, rigid, stilted, unbending, unyielding; ▪ *Ant* bending, flexible, pliable.

wordy [*adj*] *talkative*
▪ *Syn* bombastic, diffuse, discursive, flatulent, garrulous, inflated, lengthy, long-winded, loquacious, palaverous, pleonastic, prolix, rambling, redundant, rhetorical, tedious, turgid, verbose, voluble; ▪ *Ant* concise, pithy, terse, untalkative.

work [*v*] *be employed; exert oneself*
▪ *Syn* apply oneself, be gainfully employed, carry on, dig, do a job, do business, drive, drudge, freelance, have a job, hold a job, hustle, labor, manage, moil, ply, pursue, report, scratch, slave, specialize, strain, strive, take on, toil, try; ▪ *Ant* idle, laze, relax, rest.

workable [*adj*] *feasible*
▪ *Syn* applicable, doable, easy, exploitable, functional, possible, practicable, practical, snap, usable, useful, viable, working; ▪ *Ant* impractical, unfeasible, unworkable, useless.

working [*adj*] *active, occupied*
▪ *Syn* alive, busy, dynamic, effective, employed, engaged, functioning, going, in full swing, in gear, in process, laboring, on the job, operative, practical, running, useful, viable; ▪ *Ant* idle, inoperative, passive, unoccupied, unworking.

workout [*n*] *exercise, practice*
▪ *Syn* conditioning, constitutional, drill, rehearsal, routine, session, test, training, tryout, warm-up; ▪ *Ant* inactivity.

work up [*v*] *stimulate*
▪ *Syn* agitate, animate, arouse, breed, cause, develop, engender, excite, generate, get up, hatch, improve, incite, induce, inflame, instigate, move, occasion, produce, rouse, spur, stir up; ▪ *Ant* alleviate, discourage, dissuade.

worldly [*adj1*] *material, nonreligious*
▪ *Syn* carnal, earthly, earthy, fleshly, human, lay, mercenary, mundane, natural, physical, practical, profane, secular, sublunary, telluric, temporal, terrestrial; ▪ *Ant* celestial, holy, otherworldly, religious, spiritual.

worldly [*adj2*] *sophisticated*
▪ *Syn* blasé, callous, cosmopolitan, disenchanted, hardened, knowing, opportunistic, power-loving, practical, self-centered, urbane, worldly-wise; ▪ *Ant* low, unrefined, unsophisticated.

worldwide [*adj*] *general*
▪ *Syn* catholic, common, comprehensive, cosmic, ecumenical, extensive, global, international, multinational, omnipresent, pandemic, planetary, ubiquitous, universal; ▪ *Ant* circumscribed, limited, local.

worn/worn-out [*adj*] *used, tired*
▪ *Syn* beat, clichéd, depleted, destroyed, deteriorated, drained, drawn, effete, exhausted, fatigued, frayed, hackneyed, haggard, jaded, old, overused, overworked, ragged, ruined, shabby, shot, spent, stale, tattered, threadbare, timeworn, tired out, used up, wearied, weary, well-worn, wiped out; ▪ *Ant* energetic, fresh, new, refreshed, undamaged, unused.

worried [*adj*] *anxious, troubled*
▪ *Syn* afraid, apprehensive, beside oneself, bothered, clutched, concerned, distracted, distraught, distressed, disturbed, fearful, fretful, frightened, ill-at-ease, nervous, overwrought, perturbed, solicitous, tense, tormented, uneasy, upset, uptight; ▪ *Ant* calm, untroubled.

worry [*v*] *be or make anxious, troubled*
▪ *Syn* afflict, aggrieve, agonize, ail, annoy, attack, bedevil, beleaguer, beset, bother, brood, chafe, concern oneself, depress, despair, disquiet, distress, disturb, dun, feel uneasy, fret, gnaw at, goad, harass, harry, hassle, have qualms, hector, importune, irritate, oppress, persecute, perturb, pester, plague, take on, tantalize, tear, tease, test, torment, torture, trouble, try, unsettle, upset, vex, wince, writhe, wrong; ▪ *Ant* comfort, console, reassure, solace.

worsen [*v*] *diminish, decay*
▪ *Syn* aggravate, corrode, damage, decline, degenerate, depress, descend, deteriorate, disintegrate, exacerbate, fall off, get worse, impair, lower, retrograde, retrogress, rot, sink; ▪ *Ant* ameliorate, improve, increase.

worship [*v*] *honor, glorify*
▪ *Syn* admire, adore, adulate, bow down, canonize, celebrate, chant, deify, dote on, esteem, exalt, extol, idolize, laud, love, magnify, offer prayers to, pay homage to, praise, pray to, respect, revere, reverence, sanctify, sing, venerate; ▪ *Ant* dishonor, disrespect, hate.

worthless [*adj*] *of no use; without value*
▪ *Syn* abject, barren, base, bogus, contemptible, despicable, empty, futile, good-for-nothing, ignoble, inconsequen-

tial, ineffective, ineffectual, inferior, insignificant, inutile, meaningless, mediocre, paltry, pointless, poor, profitless, sterile, trashy, trifling, trivial, useless, valueless, waste, wretched; ▪ *Ant* valuable, worthwhile, worthy.

worthwhile [*adj*] *helpful*
▪ *Syn* advantageous, beneficial, constructive, estimable, excellent, gainful, good, important, invaluable, justifiable, lucrative, meritorious, money-making, paying, priceless, productive, profitable, remunerative, rewarding, serviceable, useful, valuable, worthy; ▪ *Ant* valueless, worthless.

worthy [*adj*] *honorable, respectable*
▪ *Syn* admirable, blameless, choice, commendable, decent, dependable, deserving, desirable, estimable, excellent, good, honest, incorrupt, invaluable, laudable, meritorious, model, moral, pleasing, precious, priceless, pure, reliable, reputable, right-minded, sterling, true, upright, valuable, virtuous, winner, worthwhile; ▪ *Ant* dishonorable, disreputable, unethical, unrespected.

wound [*v1*] *cause bodily damage*
▪ *Syn* bruise, contuse, cut, damage, gash, hit, hurt, injure, lacerate, nick, open up, pierce, scrape, scratch, slash, total; ▪ *Ant* aid, cure, heal, help.

wound [*v2*] *cause mental hurt*
▪ *Syn* bother, distress, disturb, grieve, hurt, hurt one's feelings, mortify, offend, outrage, pain, sting, traumatize, trouble, upset; ▪ *Ant* appease, bolster, calm, compliment, praise, soothe.

wrangle [*n*] *fight, argument*
▪ *Syn* altercation, bickering, branigan, brawl, clash, controversy, disagreement, dispute, exchange, fracas, hassle, quarrel, row, ruction, rumpus, scene, squabble, tiff; ▪ *Ant* agreement, harmony, peace.

wrap [*v*] *surround with a covering*
▪ *Syn* bandage, bind, bundle, camouflage, cloak, cover, drape, encase, encircle, enclose, envelop, fold, hide, immerse, invest, mask, muffle, pack, package, protect, roll up, sheathe, shroud, swaddle, twine, veil, wind; ▪ *Ant* unbind, uncover, undo, unfurl, unwrap.

wrap up [*v*] *finish*
▪ *Syn* bring to a close, close, complete, conclude, determine, end, halt, polish off, terminate, wind up; ▪ *Ant* begin, introduce, start.

wrathful [*adj*] *very angry*
▪ *Syn* beside oneself, displeased, enraged, furious, heated, incensed, indignant, infuriated, irate, mad, raging, storming; ▪ *Ant* contented, equable, happy, pleased.

wreck [*v*] *ruin, destroy*
▪ *Syn* bash, batter, beach, break, capsize, crash, cripple, dash, decimate, demolish, devastate, dilapidate, disable, efface, founder, impair, injure, mangle, mar, ravage, raze, run aground, sabotage, scuttle, shatter, shipwreck, sink, smash, smash up, spoil, strand, subvert, tear apart, take out, tear up, total, trash, undermine, vandalize; ▪ *Ant* build, create, mold, originate, repair, shape.

wretched [*adj*] *terrible, very bad*
▪ *Syn* abject, afflicted, base, bummed, calamitous, cheap, contemptible, dejected, deplorable, depressed, despicable, disconsolate, distressed, dolorous, down, downcast, faulty, flimsy, forlorn, gloomy, hapless, hopeless, hurting, inferior, low, mean, melancholy, miserable, paltry, pathetic, pitiable, pitiful, poor, shabby, shameful, sordid, sorrowful, sorry, spiritless, tragic, vile, weak, woeful, worthless; ▪ *Ant* admirable, good, noble, virtuous, worthy.

wring [*v*] *twist, contort*
▪ *Syn* choke, coerce, compress, draw out, exact, extort, extract, force, gouge, hurt, pain, pinch, pry, push, screw, shake down, squeeze, strain, strangle, throttle, turn, wrench, wrest; ▪ *Ant* expand, loosen, untwist.

wrinkle [*v*] *crinkle, fold*
▪ *Syn* compress, corrugate, crease, crimp, crisp, crumple, furrow, gather, line, prune up, pucker, purse, rimple, ruck, rumple, screw up, scrunch, seam, shrivel, twist; ▪ *Ant* iron out, smooth, straighten, unfold.

write [*v*] *put language down on paper*
▪ *Syn* author, autograph, compose, copy, draft, drop a line, ink, inscribe, jot down, knock off, knock out, letter, note, note down, pen, pencil, print, put in writing, record, rewrite, scrawl, scribble, scribe, scriven, set down, set forth, sign, take down, transcribe, typewrite, write down, write up; ▪ *Ant* listen, read, speak, tell.

write off [*v*] *devalue; forget about*
▪ *Syn* cancel, cross out, decry, depreciate, disregard, downgrade, give up, lower, mark down, shelve, take a loss on, un-

derrate, undervalue; ▪ *Ant* estimate, figure in, include.

writhe [*v*] *contort; toss back and forth*
▪ *Syn* agonize, bend, distort, jerk, recoil, squirm, struggle, suffer, thrash, thresh, twist, wiggle, wince, worm, wriggle; ▪ *Ant* be still, relax.

wrong [*adj1*] *incorrect*
▪ *Syn* amiss, askew, astray, at fault, awry, bad, defective, erratic, erroneous, fallacious, false, faulty, inaccurate, in error, inexact, miscalculated, misconstrued, misguided, mistaken, not precise, not right, not working, off-target, out, perverse, rotten, sophistical, specious, spurious, untrue, wide; ▪ *Ant* correct, right.

wrong [*adj2*] *immoral, dishonest*
▪ *Syn* amoral, bad, blamable, blasphemous, censurable, corrupt, criminal, crooked, debauched, depraved, dishonorable, evil, felonious, illegal, illicit, indecent, naughty, profane, reprobate, risqué, sacrilegious, salacious, shady, sinful, smutty, vicious, wanton, wicked, wrongful; ▪ *Ant* decent, good, honest, moral.

wrong [*adj3*] *inappropriate, not suitable*
▪ *Syn* amiss, awkward, disproportionate, gauche, ill-advised, improper, inapt, incongruous, incorrect, indecorous, infelicitous, malapropos, not done, off-balance, rotten; ▪ *Ant* acceptable, appropriate, correct, ok, suitable.

wrong [*v*] *hurt, mistreat another*
▪ *Syn* abuse, aggrieve, cheat, damage, defame, dishonor, harm, ill-treat, injure, malign, maltreat, mistreat, offend, outrage, persecute, take advantage of; ▪ *Ant* aid, assist, help, sympathize.

wrongful [*adj*] *evil, illegal*
▪ *Syn* blameworthy, criminal, dishonest, felonious, illegitimate, illicit, immoral, improper, lawless, reprehensible, wicked; ▪ *Ant* ethical, fair, good, just, legal, rightful.

wry [*adj*] *sarcastic, distorted*
▪ *Syn* askew, awry, contorted, crooked, cynical, deformed, droll, dry, ironic, mocking, sardonic, twisted, warped; ▪ *Ant* straight, straightforward.

Y

yank [*v*] *pull hard and fast*
▪ *Syn* draw, evulse, extract, hitch, jerk, lug, snap, snatch, tear, tug, twitch, vellicate, wrench; ▪ *Ant* push, shove.

yearn [*v*] *desire strongly*
▪ *Syn* ache, be desirous of, covet, crave, dream, hanker, hunger, itch, languish, long, lust, pine, thirst, want, wish for, yen; ▪ *Ant* be revolted by, dislike, hate, recoil from.

years [*n*] *old age*
▪ *Syn* age, agedness, caducity, elderliness, senescence; ▪ *Ant* greenness, youth.

yell [*n/v*] *loud communication*
▪ *Syn* bawl, bellow, call, complain, cry, holler, hoot, howl, lament, roar, scream, shout, shriek, squawk, squeal, ululate, vociferate, whoop, yap, yelp; ▪ *Ant* whisper.

yellow [*adj*] *cowardly*
▪ *Syn* craven, deceitful, gutless, low, offensive, pusillanimous, sneaking, treacherous, tricky; ▪ *Ant* bold, brave, confident, courageous.

yen [*n*] *strong want*
▪ *Syn* craving, desire, hankering, hunger, itch, longing, lust, passion, thirst, urge, yearning; ▪ *Ant* dislike, hate, hatred, revulsion.

yes [*adv*] *agreed*
▪ *Syn* affirmative, beyond a doubt, certainly, definitely, exactly, fine, gladly, good, granted, indubitably, just so, naturally, of course, positively, precisely, surely, true, very well, willingly, without fail; ▪ *Ant* inaccurately, incorrectly, nay, negative, never, no, opposed.

yesterday [*n*] *the day before today*
▪ *Syn* bygone, foretime, last day, not long ago, past, recently, the other day; ▪ *Ant* tomorrow.

yield [*v1*] *produce*
▪ *Syn* accrue, admit, afford, allow, beam, bear, blossom, bring forth, bring in, discharge, earn, furnish, generate, give, give off, hold out, net, offer, pay, proffer, provide, return, sell for, supply, tender, turn out; ▪ *Ant* disallow, fail, withhold.

yield [*v2*] *give in, surrender*
▪ *Syn* abandon, abdicate, admit defeat, back down, bend, bow, break, buy, capitulate, cave in, cede, collapse, crumple, defer, fold, fold up, give oneself over, give up, go, hand over, knuckle, leave, part with, relax, relent, relinquish, resign, sag, submit, succumb, suffer defeat, surrender; ▪ *Ant* combat, oppose, prevent, refuse, reject, repel.

yield [*v3*] *grant, allow*
▪ *Syn* accede, accept, acknowledge, acquiesce, admit, agree, assent, bow, break, comply, concede, concur, consent,

defer, fail, fit in, permit, surrender, waive; ▪ *Ant* counter, disallow, disapprove, veto.

yielding [*adj1*] *accommodating*
▪ *Syn* acquiescent, biddable, compliant, docile, easy, flexible, humble, nonresistant, obedient, passive, pliable, pliant, resigned, submissive, tractable; ▪ *Ant* inflexible. obstinate, resistant.

yielding [*adj2*] *soft, flexible*
▪ *Syn* elastic, malleable, mushy, plastic, pliable, pulpy, quaggy, resilient, spongy, springy, squishy, supple, tractable, tractile, unresisting; ▪ *Ant* hard, inflexible, rigid, solid.

yoke [*v*] *bond together; join*
▪ *Syn* associate, attach, bracket, buckle, combine, conjoin, conjugate, connect, couple, fasten, fix, harness, hitch, link, secure, splice, strap, tack, tie, unite, wed; ▪ *Ant* disconnect, disjoin, divorce, uncouple, unhitch.

yonder [*adv*] *faraway*
▪ *Syn* away, beyond, distant, farther, further, remote, yon; ▪ *Ant* close, near, nearby.

young [*adj*] *immature*
▪ *Syn* adolescent, blooming, blossoming, budding, burgeoning, callow, childish, childlike, crude, developing, fledgling, fresh, growing, half-grown, ignorant, inexperienced, infant, inferior, junior, juvenile, little, modern, new, newborn, newish, pubescent, puerile, raw, recent, tender, undeveloped, untried, unversed, vernal, youthful; ▪ *Ant* mature, old, older, ripe, seasoned.

youthful [*adj*] *new, immature*
▪ *Syn* active, adolescent, budding, buoyant, callow, childish, childlike, enthusiastic, fresh, inexperienced, juvenile, keen, pubescent, puerile, tender, vernal, vigorous, young; ▪ *Ant* experienced, mature, old.

yuppie [*n/adj*] *young upwardly mobile professional*
▪ *Syn* button-down, clone, conspicuous consumer, suit, three-piecer, urban professional, white-collar worker; ▪ *Ant* beatnik, Bohemian, castaway, castoff, derelict, hippie, nonconformist, pauper.

Z

zany [*adj*] *crazy, funny*
▪ *Syn* clownish, comical, dumb, eccentric, fool, foolish, goofy, humorous, joshing, witty; ▪ *Ant* sedate, serious, sober.

zealous [*adj*] *enthusiastic*
▪ *Syn* afire, antsy, ardent, burning, dedicated, eager, earnest, fanatic, fervent, frenetic, impassioned, keen, obsessed, passionate, possessed, rabid, spirited; ▪ *Ant* apathetic, indifferent, lethargic, unenthusiastic.

zenith [*n*] *top*
▪ *Syn* acme, apex, apogee, cap, capstone, climax, crest, culmination, elevation, height, meridian, peak, pinnacle, roof, summit, tiptop, topper, vertex; ▪ *Ant* bottom, nadir.

zero [*n*] *nothing*
▪ *Syn* aught, blank, bottom, cipher, lowest point, nadir, naught, nonentity, nought, nullity, oblivion, scratch, shutout, void; ▪ *Ant* anything, being, everything, infinity, something, thing.

zest [*n1*] *taste, flavor*
▪ *Syn* bite, body, charm, flavoring, ginger, interest, nip, piquancy, pungency, relish, salt, savor, seasoning, spice, tang; ▪ *Ant* blandness, dullness.

zest [*n2*] *energy, gusto*
▪ *Syn* appetite, bliss, bounce, cheer, delectation, eagerness, elation, enjoyment, enthusiasm, fervor, happiness, keenness, passion, pleasure, satisfaction, zeal; ▪ *Ant* apathy, indifference, laziness, lethargy.

zigzag [*adj*] *moving side to side*
▪ *Syn* askew, awry, bent, crinkled, crooked, devious, diagonal, erratic, fluctuating, inclined, indirect, irregular, jagged, meandering, oblique, oscillating, rambling, serrated, sinuous, sloping, snaking, transverse, twisted, twisting, undulating, waggling, winding; ▪ *Ant* direct, straight, unrelieved, unwavering.

zip [*v*] *move about quickly*
▪ *Syn* bustle, dash, flash, fly, hurry, run, rush, shoot, speed, tear, whisk, whiz, zoom; ▪ *Ant* crawl, creep, decelerate, inch, slow.

zoom [*v*] *move very quickly*
▪ *Syn* buzz, dart, dash, dive, flash, fly, hum, hurtle, outstrip, rip, rocket, shoot, shoot up, skyrocket, speed, streak, surge, tear, whirl, whiz; ▪ *Ant* crawl, decelerate, descend, plunge, slow.